Ben-Hur

Screening Antiquity

Series Editors: Monica S. Cyrino and Lloyd Llewellyn-Jones

Screening Antiquity is a cutting-edge and provocative series of academic monographs and edited volumes focusing on new research on the reception of the ancient world in film and television. Screening Antiquity showcases the work of the best-established and up-and-coming specialists in the field. It provides an important synergy of the latest international scholarly ideas about the conception of antiquity in popular culture and is the only series that focuses exclusively on screened representations of the ancient world.

Editorial Advisory Board

Antony Augoustakis, University of Illinois, Urbana-Champaign, USA
Alastair Blanshard, University of Queensland, Australia
Robert Burgoyne, University of St Andrews, UK
Lisa Maurice, Bar-Ilan University, Israel
Gideon Nisbet, University of Birmingham, UK
Joanna Paul, Open University, UK
Jon Solomon, University of Illinois, Urbana-Champaign, USA

Titles available in the series

Rome *Season Two: Trial and Triumph*
Edited by Monica S. Cyrino

Ben-Hur: *The Original Blockbuster*
By Jon Solomon

Cowboy Classics: The Roots of the American Western in the Epic Tradition
By Kirsten Day

Forthcoming Titles

STARZ Spartacus*: Reimagining an Icon on Screen*
Edited by Antony Augoustakis and Monica S. Cyrino

Broadcasting Ancient Greece on Television
Edited by Fiona Hobden and Amanda Wrigley

Ben-Hur
The Original Blockbuster

Jon Solomon

EDINBURGH
University Press

Edinburgh University Press is one of the leading university presses
in the UK. We publish academic books and journals in our selected
subject areas across the humanities and social sciences, combining
cutting-edge scholarship with high editorial and production
values to produce academic works of lasting importance. For more
information visit our website: www.edinburghuniversitypress.com

© Jon Solomon, 2016

Edinburgh University Press Ltd
The Tun – Holyrood Road
12(2f) Jackson's Entry
Edinburgh EH8 8PJ

Typeset in 11/13 Trump Medieval by
Servis Filmsetting Ltd, Stockport, Cheshire
and printed and bound in Great Britain by
CPI Group (UK) Ltd, Croydon CR0 4YY

A CIP record for this book is available from the British Library

ISBN 978 1 4744 0794 6 (hardback)
ISBN 978 1 4744 0796 0 (webready PDF)
ISBN 978 1 4744 0795 3 (paperback)
ISBN 978 1 4744 0797 7 (epub)

The right of Jon Solomon to be identified as the author of this work
has been asserted in accordance with the Copyright, Designs and
Patents Act 1988, and the Copyright and Related Rights Regulations
2003 (SI No. 2498).

Published with the support of the Edinburgh University Scholarly
Publishing Initiatives Fund.

Contents

List of Figures		vii
Acknowledgements		x
A Note about the Hyphen: Ben-Hur vs Ben Hur		xii
Series Editors' Preface		xiii
List of Abbreviations		xvi
1	The First Blockbuster	1
2	Lew Wallace Before *Ben-Hur*	19
3	"How I Came To Write *Ben-Hur*"	46
4	Publication and Early Reception of the Novel	102
5	The Transformations of the Novel	138
6	Reasons for Success	188
7	Early Staged Readings: *Ben-Hur, in Tableaux and Pantomime*	218
8	*Ben-Hur* in Song and Instrumental Music	269
9	"My God! Did I Set All This Into Motion?": The Klaw & Erlanger *Ben-Hur*	311
10	"Ben-Hur Flour Has The Go To Make The Dough": Early Ben-Hur Commerce	408
11	*Ben-Hur* in Moving Pictures: Stereopticon Lectures and the 1907 Kalem *Ben-Hur*	509
12	"The Greatest Motion Picture Property in the History of the Screen": The 1925 MGM *Ben-Hur*	561
13	Between the MGM Films	661
14	"The World's Most Honored Motion Picture": The 1959 MGM *Ben-Hur*	728

| 15 | The Next Half-Century: New Formats and New Versions | 824 |

Bibliography	863
General Index	884
Ben-Hur Index	897
Personal Names, Companies, Institutions, Societies, and Unions Index	900
Non-*Ben-Hur* Title Index	909

Figures

Figure 1.1	Cover of Grosset & Dunlap's "Novels of Inspiration" edition.	2
Figure 1.2	Advertisements for Ben-Hur products.	4
Figure 1.3	Ben-Hur across the landscape.	8
Figure 1.4	Christmas dedications from inscribed copies of *Ben-Hur*.	16
Figure 2.1	Major-General Lew Wallace on the cover of *Harper's Weekly*, July 12, 1862.	33
Figure 2.2	"The Stolen Stars," a poem by Wallace, set to music and sold in 1863.	36
Figure 2.3	The Ben Hur Room in Santa Fe, c. 1910.	42
Figure 3.1	The Preface to *The First Christmas* (1899).	51
Figure 3.2	Wallace in Crawfordsville and "The Ben-Hur Beech."	55
Figure 3.3	Jebel es Zubleh on an Augustus Petermann map in *The New Biblical Atlas and Scripture Gazetteer*.	85
Figure 4.1	Targeting the younger demographics in *Harper's Young People* in 1891 and Aldrich's *Progressive Course in Reading*.	114
Figure 4.2	Preface to Warne and Routledge editions of *Ben-Hur*.	132
Figure 5.1	A variety of early types of *Ben-Hur* by-products.	139
Figure 5.2	A variety of bindings for the novel.	143
Figure 5.3	An ad for the Garfield edition and a facsimile of the 1881 Garfield letter to Wallace.	153
Figure 5.4	Wallace as a celebrity author.	161
Figure 5.5	The Sears edition.	176
Figure 5.6	Sears ads.	179
Figure 7.1	The March 14, 1889, Palmer's Theatre program for "Tableaux and Readings from Ben Hur".	238
Figure 7.2	*Ben-Hur, in Tableaux and Pantomime* ads.	254
Figure 8.1	*Ben-Hur* song covers.	277
Figure 8.2	E.T. Paull cover adapting elements from both the Wagner and Checa compositions.	290
Figure 8.3	E. T. Paull recordings.	302

Figure 9.1	The chariot race treadmill and cyclorama in *St. Nicolas* and *Scientific American*.	336
Figure 9.2	The Klaw & Erlanger *Ben-Hur Souvenir Album*.	350
Figure 9.3	Harper's "Player's Edition," Williamson's Australian edition, Kelley's piano/choral reduction, and a 1901 program for the Illinois Theatre in Chicago.	365
Figure 10.1	The Tribe of Ben-Hur.	418
Figure 10.2	Ben-Hur Cigars.	426
Figure 10.3	Ben-Hur Flour ads.	433
Figure 10.4	The Ben-Hur Flour Dough Boys.	436
Figure 10.5	Ads for Ben-Hur Coffee, Teas, Spices, & Extracts products and Ben-Hur Soap.	441
Figure 10.6	Ben Hur Perfume.	446
Figure 10.7	Ben-Hur razors.	447
Figure 10.8	Ben-Hur Shoes.	449
Figure 10.9	Boats named *Ben-Hur*.	453
Figure 10.10	Ben-Hur Bicycle logo and catalog.	459
Figure 10.11	The Ben Hur Racer at Ocean Park, California, c. 1914.	463
Figure 10.12	Pasadena New Year's Day "Roman Chariot Races".	471
Figure 10.13	Elwood Rice's "A Roman Chariot Race" atop the Hotel Normandie in Herald Square.	474
Figure 10.14	1890s advertising card for the Page Fence.	479
Figure 10.15	Ben Hur clocks and watches.	481
Figure 10.16	The name Ben-Hur was given to animals, restaurants, sports teams, roadways, municipalities, businesses and people.	487
Figure 11.1	Stereopticon slides.	519
Figure 11.2	Ads for Kalem's unauthorized *Ben-Hur*, 1907.	538
Figure 12.1	Parufamet card and educational leaflet in the U.S. to promote MGM's 1925 *Ben-Hur*.	609
Figure 12.2	Different sets of trading cards extending the reach of MGM's 1925 *Ben-Hur* overseas.	612
Figure 12.3	Commercial applications of the 1925 MGM *Ben-Hur*.	641
Figure 13.1	The exploitation of the Ben-Hur name in commerce from the 1920s into the early 1950s.	687
Figure 13.2	The Ben-Hur Jiffy Camper (1940s), and the Ben-Hur Freezer (1950s).	694
Figure 13.3	Ben-Hur logo for Urich gas stations.	700
Figure 14.1	*Ben-Hur* educational guides.	770
Figure 14.2	The large-format MGM Pressbook.	771
Figure 14.3	Ben Hur toys and games.	803
Figure 14.4	Broad demographics of the 1959 MGM *Ben-Hur*.	810

Figure 15.1	The 1959 *Ben-Hur*: videos and DVDs.	837
Figure 15.2	*Ben-Hur* musical and dramatic formats.	854

Acknowledgements

This project began more than fifteen years ago when I first noticed *Ben-Hur* by-products on eBay. At first I assumed that such items as Ben-Hur Cigar boxes and unprovenienced single-page Ben-Hur Flour advertisements ripped out of century-old magazines were curious oddities, but soon their sheer number and variety made it clear that they represented a historical phenomenon that required collection and scholarly analysis. I have my wife Lois to thank for purchasing me my first copy of E. T. Paull's "Chariot Race, or Ben Hur March." To continue the study I received financial and sabbatical awards from the University of Arizona and the University of Illinois at Urbana-Champaign, and the research funds available to me through the Robert D. Novak Chair of Western Civilization and Culture allowed me to complete the task. At the business end of that I owe thanks to Deborah Ludden and Cody Mayfield.

I have had immeasurable encouragement and assistance from fellow scholars. Martin Winkler was the first to suggest expanding my research into a book-length project and has given me assistance all along. I also want to acknowledge the special assistance provided by Maria Wyke of University College London, Ivo Blom of the University of Amsterdam, Mario Musumeci of the Cineteca Nazionale in Rome, Jon Schmitz of the Chautauqua archives, Robert Dalton Harris and Diane DeBlois of the Ephemera Society of America, Robert Ketterer of the University of Iowa, Cinnamon Catlin-Legutko of the Lew Wallace Study & Museum, Henry Raine of the New York Historical Society, Patricia Hewitt and Tomas Jaehn of the New Mexico History Museum, Felicia Campbell of the University of Nevada Las Vegas, John Miller of the University of Virginia, Monica Cyrino of the University of New Mexico, Andrew Simpson of The Catholic University of America, Stephan Heilen of Osnabrück Universität, Danuta Shanzer of Universität Wien, Egert Pöhlmann, Gillian Anderson, and Ariana Traill of UIUC. Collectively they helped me find materials, test out my findings on scholarly audiences to elicit their valuable suggestions, and arrange enough time to complete the project.

I consulted numerous libraries, archives, and ephemera collections as will be evident from the citations, and there were a number of people and offices along the way that gave me knowledgeable assistance in locating and accessing materials. I owe a special gratitude to Kathryn Danner of Interlibrary Borrowing at the University of Illinois at Urbana-Champaign, who bore the brunt of my numerous and very odd requests for trade catalogs, comic books, magazine PDFs, and countless scripts. In addition I am grateful for the assistance provided me by Scott Schwartz at the Sousa Archive of UIUC; Jenny Romero at the Margaret Herrick Library; Sandra Garcia-Myers and Edward Comstock at the Cinema Arts Library at the University of Southern California; Mark Quigley at the UCLA Film & Television Library; Leeke Ripmeester and Elif Rongen at EYE; Anna Batistová of the National Film Archive in Prague; Jacqueline Johnson at Miami University; and Jennifer Ringle, Production Manager of the San Diego Symphony. I am grateful as well to the staffers at the Indiana Historical Society Library, Lilly Library at Indiana University, Indiana State Library, University of Chicago Library, Ryerson Library at the Art Institute of Chicago, Butler Library at Columbia University, Huntington Library, Albert and Shirley Small Special Collections Library at the University of Virginia, Crawfordsville Library, Cincinnati Historical Museum, Newberry Library, Museum of Modern Art, Morgan Library, New York Public Library, Library of Congress, British Film Institute, and Bibliothéque Nationale de France.

Thanks to many of these and a number of others that have assisted me in assembling an extensive collection of Ben-Hur artifacts, almost all the illustrations in this book are in the current possession of the author. The others are long since out of copyright.

A Note about the Hyphen: Ben-Hur vs Ben Hur

In 1880 Lew Wallace hyphenated the name of his novel and its eponymous protagonist. In subsequent years, however, many writers, advertisers, and companies omitted the hyphen, so much so that in 1959 MGM insisted that their advertisers and exhibitors include it on all press releases, merchandise, and theater marquees. Most of them did, but consistency has never prevailed. Over the course of more than a century, sources have employed both the *Ben-Hur* and *Ben Hur* spellings. Throughout this book I use the original hyphenated spelling unless an official name or an original quoted source specifically uses the dehyphenated form. Similarly, the name of the novel as a literary property is always italicized, but as a commercial property it is not.

Series Editors' Preface

At Cinecittà Studios in Rome, the tour buses would slow down for a look as the costly shoot ran longer than anyone expected. But on January 7, 1959, when the state-of-the-art cameras stopped rolling and Willy Wyler shouted, "Cut! That's a wrap!", one million feet of film was in the can and MGM's new widescreen spectacular *Ben-Hur* was complete. Well, almost complete: the first cut of the movie ran for over six hours. So in the months that followed, Wyler's sound and color extravaganza was trimmed to a more agreeable four hours . . . a manageable length for the audience in the movie theater, given that an intermission was built into the edit, and yet *Ben-Hur* would retain an appropriate size and scale that assured the sobriquet 'epic' still meant something.

It was during these initial post-production months that *Ben-Hur* fever erupted. Hollywood went into overdrive as the MGM marketing machine sprang into action: the studio mass-produced glossy stills from the movie's most elaborate scenes and dramatic portrait shots of leading man Charlton Heston in Roman costume, while giant billboards dotted the California landscape announcing *Ben-Hur* as the "Greatest Movie Ever Made!" Soon fans could purchase *Ben-Hur* toy armor, swords, and helmets; there was a miniature arena complete with plastic horses and chariots; *Ben-Hur* candy bars and T-shirts were on sale everywhere; and *Ben-His* and *Ben-Hers* bathrobe and towel sets were readily available for all those moms and pops out there in a heartland that had gone certifiably movie-mad. By the time the film finally premiered on November 18, 1959, America was saturated with *Ben-Hur* mania.

The reviews of *Ben-Hur* (more so than the bathrobes) were universally flattering:

> "William Wyler has proved with *Ben-Hur* that taste and spectacle need not be lacking in a film spectacle." ~ *Saturday Review*
>
> "Spectacular . . . Tasteful . . . Intelligent." ~ *The New York Herald Tribune*
>
> "The . . . most visually exciting film spectacle yet produced!" ~ *Film Quarterly*

No doubt about it: *Ben-Hur* was a massive popular hit. And the fans spared no expense to show their boundless enthusiasm for the film, buying $80 million worth of movie tickets, and spending millions more on commercial product tie-ins.

The legacy of the 1959 *Ben-Hur*, considered by many the zenith of the Hollywood epic cycle and still one of the most successful box-office grossers ever, remains with us today. *Ben-Hur* received an unprecedented twelve Academy Award nominations, and won eleven statuettes – including Best Picture, Best Director for Wyler, and Best Actor for Heston – a longstanding record that has only recently been matched but never surpassed. *Ben-Hur* continues to be enormously influential on modern film-makers: famously, when making his own Oscar-winning film *Gladiator* (2000), director Ridley Scott consciously turned to Wyler's movie for inspiration, and *Ben-Hur* was one of several 1950s epics Oliver Stone screened for his production team during the making of his *Alexander* (2004). The American Film Institute ranks *Ben-Hur* on its list of the 100 greatest films of all time.

So that is why *Ben-Hur* justifiably takes center stage in the popular conception of the cinematic epic. With its thunderingly good (if melodramatic) storyline, its measured dose of Christian ethics, its weighty script, powerful musical score, and refined art direction, and of course its overwhelming sense of visual spectacle – that thrilling sea battle! the chariot race to end all chariot races! – Wyler's *Ben-Hur* is a masterpiece of mid-century Hollywood film-making.

Yet the 1959 *Ben-Hur*, for all its fame, hype, and notoriety, is only one part of a much longer, broader, and deeper history. Jon Solomon's Ben-Hur: *The Original Blockbuster* tells that awe-inspiring story, delving into many of its previously unexplored aspects and finding countless nuances that have never before been exposed. In this book, Solomon investigates the *Ben-Hur* phenomenon as a bestselling novel, spectacular drama, and inspiration for three landmark movies, as he proves definitively that *Ben-Hur* was the first popular artistic mega-property to generate dozens of business synergies. Now for the first time ever, the entire *Ben-Hur* story – so far – can be told. And who wouldn't agree with the movie's Sheik Ilderim when he says, "I hope to see you again, Judah Ben-Hur."

ABOUT THIS SERIES

Screening Antiquity is a new series of cutting-edge academic monographs and edited volumes that present exciting and original research on the reception of the ancient world in film and television. It provides an important synergy of the latest international scholarly ideas about the onscreen conception of antiquity in popular culture and is the only book series to focus exclusively on screened representations of the ancient world.

The interactions between cinema, television, and historical representation is a growing field of scholarship and student engagement; many

Series Editors' Preface

Classics and Ancient History departments in universities worldwide teach cinematic representations of the past as part of their programs in Reception Studies. Scholars are now questioning how historical films and television series reflect the societies in which they were made, and speculate on how attitudes towards the past have been moulded in the popular imagination by their depiction in the movies. *Screening Antiquity* explores how these constructions came about and offers scope to analyse how and why the ancient past is filtered through onscreen representations in specific ways. The series highlights exciting and original publications that explore the representation of antiquity onscreen, and that employ modern theoretical and cultural perspectives to examine screened antiquity, including: stars and star text, directors and *auteurs*, cinematography, design and art direction, marketing, fans, and the online presence of the ancient world.

The series aims to present original research focused exclusively on the reception of the ancient world in film and television. In itself this is an exciting and original approach. There is no other book series that engages head-on with both big screen and small screen recreations of the past, yet their integral interactivity is clear to see: film popularity has a major impact on television productions and for its part, television regularly influences cinema (including film spin-offs of popular television series). This is the first academic series to identify and encourage the holistic interactivity of these two major media institutions, and the first to promote interdisciplinary research in all the fields of Cinema Studies, Media Studies, Classics, and Ancient History.

Screening Antiquity explores the various facets of onscreen creations of the past, exploring the theme from multiple angles. Some volumes will foreground a Classics 'reading' of the subject, analysing the nuances of film and television productions against a background of ancient literature, art, history, or culture; others will focus more on Media 'readings' by privileging the onscreen creation of the past or positioning the film or television representation within the context of modern popular culture. A third 'reading' will allow for a more fluid interaction between both the Classics and Media approaches. All three methods are valuable, since Reception Studies demands a flexible approach whereby individual scholars, or groups of researchers, foster a reading of an onscreen 'text' particular to their angle of viewing.

Screening Antiquity represents a major turning point in that it signals a better appreciation and understanding of the rich and complex interaction between the past and contemporary culture, and also of the lasting significance of antiquity in today's world.

Monica S. Cyrino and Lloyd Llewellyn-Jones
Series Editors

Abbreviations

FREQUENTLY CITED NEWSPAPERS AND MAGAZINES

AC	The Atlanta Constitution
BE	Brooklyn Eagle
BG	Boston Globe
BH	Boston Herald
CE	Cincinnati Enquirer
CJ	The Crawfordsville Journal
CPD	Cleveland Plain Dealer
CT	Chicago Tribune
DFP	Detroit Free Press
HW	Harper's Weekly
LAT	Los Angeles Times
MS	Milwaukee Sentinel
NYHT	New York Herald Tribune
NYT	New York Times
NYTr	New York Tribune
PI	Philadelphia Inquirer
PW	The Publishers' Weekly
StLPD	St. Louis Post-Dispatch
SFC	San Francisco Chronicle
TBS	The [Baltimore] Sun
TCSM	The Christian Science Monitor
TFD	The Film Daily
ToI	The Times of India
WP	The Washington Post
WSJ	Wall Street Journal

FREQUENTLY CITED ARCHIVES

BL	*Butler Library, Columbia University*
HL	*Herrick Library of the Academy of Motion Picture Arts and Sciences*
IHS	*Indiana Historical Society*
LL	*Lilly Library, Indiana University*
LoC	*Library of Congress*
NMHM	*Fray Angélico Chávez History Library, New Mexico History Museum*
NYPL	*New York Public Library*
UVA	*Albert and Shirley Small Special Collections Library, University of Virginia*

FREQUENTLY CITED BOOKS

An Autobiography	Lew Wallace, *Lew Wallace: An Autobiography* (New York: Harper & Brothers, 1906).
M&M	Robert E. Morsberger and Katharine E. Morsberger, *Lew Wallace: Militant Romantic: The Colorful Life of America's Foremost Literary Adventurer, the Author of Ben-Hur* (New York: McGraw Hill, 1980).
McKee	Irving McKee, *"Ben-Hur" Wallace* (Berkeley: University of California Press, 1947).
Russo & Sullivan	Dorothy Ritter Russo and Thelma Lois Sullivan, *Bibliographical Studies of Seven Authors of Crawfordsville, Indiana* (Indianapolis: Indiana Historical Society, 1952).

1 *The First Blockbuster*

Consider for a moment some of the greatest blockbuster literary properties: *The Hunger Games, Harry Potter, Star Wars, Lord of the Rings, Gone With the Wind, The Wizard of Oz*. They sold an enormous amount of books, generated highly anticipated or even beloved films, and, especially *Star Wars*, developed lucrative commercial tie-ins.

Now let's work backwards in time to consider *Ben-Hur: A Tale of the Christ*, the most commercially successful literary property of the late nineteenth century. In 1959 MGM's colossal *Ben-Hur* was the most expensive movie ever made, one of the most profitable, the most heavily merchandised, and earned a record eleven Academy Awards.[1] When it premiered on network television in 1971, a record sixty million people watched, fourteen million more than watched the Super Bowl that year. The 1925 MGM *Ben-Hur* cost more to produce and earned more internationally than any film in the silent era. In 1913 a record one million volumes of the novel was sold to Sears, Roebuck in a single transaction. In 1903 color ads for Ben-Hur Flour reached over two million national magazine subscribers every month. Beginning in 1899 the Broadway production of *Ben-Hur* set attendance records in every major American city, not to mention London, and continued on for some 6000 performances over twenty-one years and was seen by over ten million people, approximately 10 percent of the population of the U.S. at the time. In 1891 alone, 6,983,207 Ben-Hur Cigars were sold across the Midwest and East Coast. From 1889 the *Ben-Hur, in Tableaux and Pantomime* toured the country for over ten years. And in 1880 General Lew Wallace and Harper & Brothers published the original novel, *Ben-Hur: A Tale of the Christ*, that would sell over one million volumes even before the Sears transaction. Attracting tens of millions of customers over a period of 135 years and with another big-budget film scheduled for release in 2016, *Ben-Hur: A Tale of the Christ* remains one of the most successful creations of commercialized American popular literature.

While these numbers certainly confirm the status of *Ben-Hur* as an

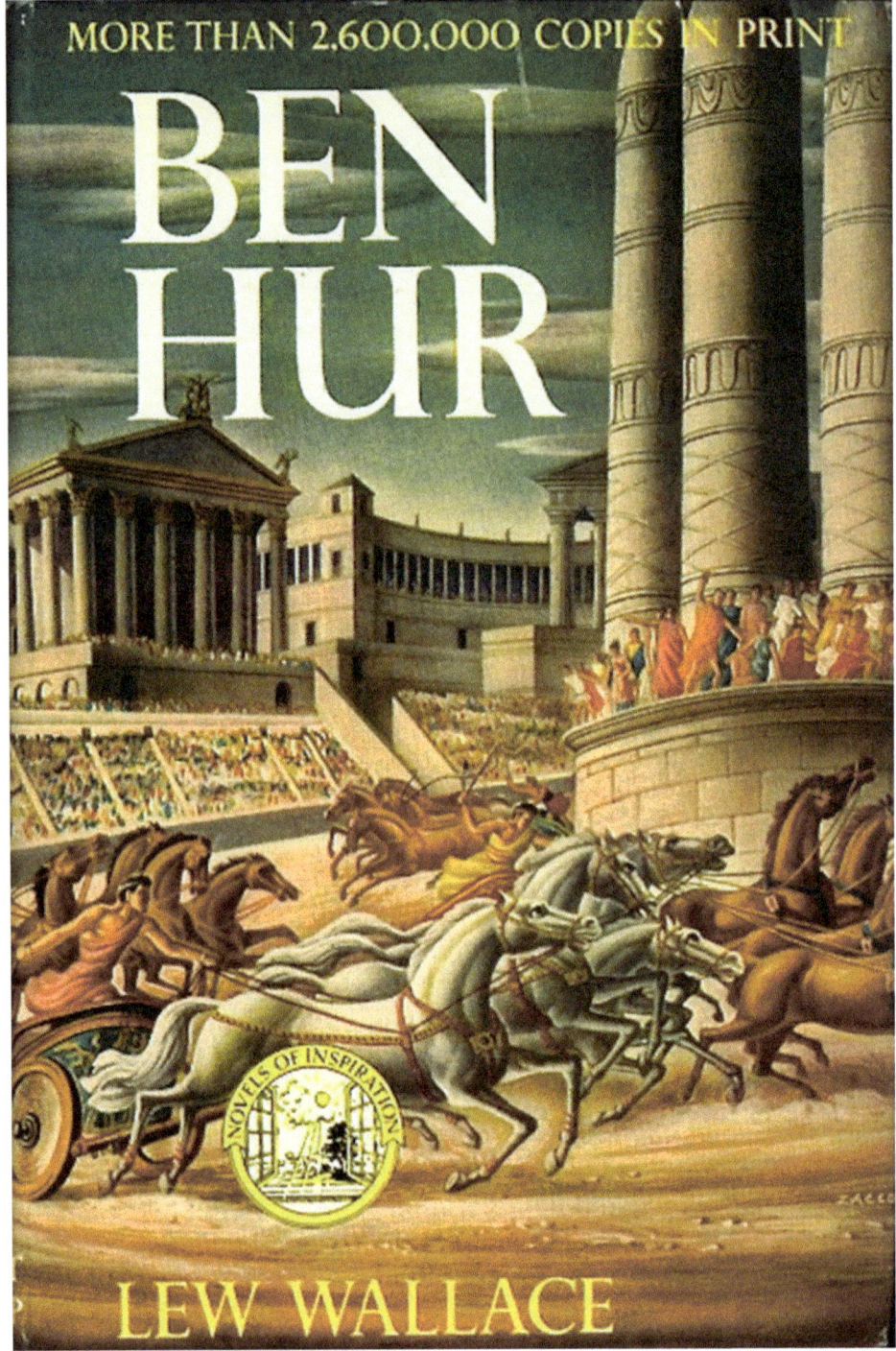

Figure 1.1 Huge production and sales numbers and dynamic chariot race imagery helped perpetuate the *Ben-Hur* phenomenon for more than a century, as represented in the late 1940s on the cover of Grosset & Dunlap's "Novels of Inspiration" edition.

exceptional artistic property, the reader – Wallace frequently addresses "the reader" in his novel – may think that Ben-Hur Cigars and Ben-Hur Flour were anomalies. They were not. Beginning in the late 1880s, business enterprises named Ben-Hur as well as individual Ben-Hur brands and a wide array of Ben-Hur retail products proliferated and were marketed locally, regionally, or nationally for many decades. The Tribe of Ben-Hur and Ben Hur Construction Company provide two illustrative but different models. The founders of The Tribe of Ben-Hur directly approached Wallace in 1893 to seek his approval and advice before inaugurating their fraternal organization and developing it into one of the country's larger insurance companies with over 100,000 subscribers in twenty-nine states. In contrast, the founder of the Ben Hur Construction Company had no connection to *Ben-Hur* at all until he reluctantly accompanied his wife to a performance of the Klaw & Erlanger production at St. Louis' Olympic Theatre in 1908. But he was so impressed with the character of the protagonist that he decided to name his new business Ben Hur Construction. Now the oldest surviving steel construction company in the United States, Ben Hur Construction operates out of four different cities and displays on its website an impressive portfolio of more than a century's worth of large municipal construction projects, not to mention a stylized chariot logo.

Similarly, Shrine chapters like Ben Hur Lodge No. 322 A. F. & A. M. in Kansas City and the Ben Hur Temple of the Nobles of the Mystic Shrine in Austin, Texas, were formed within a decade of the publication of the novel, and their active websites and Facebook pages demonstrate continued communal activity and charity fundraising. In manufacturing and retail, the chariots on the red cans of Ben-Hur Coffee, Teas, & Spices remained a recognizable logo in California and the West for a half century, Cincinnati's Jergens sold Ben Hur Perfume nationwide for several decades, and Milwaukee's Ben Hur Manufacturing Company supplied the U.S. Army with Ben Hur trailers during World War II. From the 1880s into the 1950s consumers bought Ben-Hur brands of oranges, tomatoes, whiskey, bitters, chewing tobacco, shoes, shoe polish, Bakelite, china, clocks, watches, perfumes, sewing machines, tools, harnesses, freezers, and many additional items. They could ride on Ben-Hur trains, trolleys, bicycles, and a Ben-Hur automobile. Prize horses, bulls, pigs, and dogs were named Ben-Hur, and there were a few famous people named Ben Hur. The Ben-Hur name was also given to roads, streets, bridges, and even whole towns.

The chariot imagery as well as the *Ben-Hur* story and name continued to be marketable into the 1950s. At that point, the highly anticipated 1959 MGM film generated a renascence that lasted into the 1970s, when new media technologies began to transfer *Ben-Hur* into additional formats, a process that continued into the new millennium. And now the *Ben-Hur* phenomenon is seeing yet another renascence, as evidenced by fresh evangelical interpretations, by two European stadium spectaculars

Figure 1.2 The many dozens of Ben-Hur companies, brands, and products helped transform a literary bestseller into a unique kind of blockbuster: Clockwise: Ben-Hur oranges, Ben Hur Touring Car, Ben-Hur Cigars, Ben Hur Harness and Whips, Ben Hur Whiskies, Ben Hur Sewing Machines, Ben Hur Shoe Polish.

that attracted several hundred thousand spectators, and by newly written radio, stage, and television versions. MGM's newest film adaptation of *Ben-Hur* will provide yet another version for a new generation of viewers. Since the 1880s the novel has never been out of print, and there has never been a decade in which various Ben-Hur items were not available commercially. Today's author could only dream of creating a novel that would still be in print and spun-off into numerous media and live presentations 136 years after its initial publication, and a character whose name and imagery would have dozens of commercial and even municipal applications for over a century. By several standards of measurement, the size of its profits, the number of artistic genres and commercial fields it has impacted, and its endurance for more than a century, *Ben-Hur* should be recognized as one of the most successful popular artistic properties ever created, and, considering that it was originally published in 1880, the first of its kind as a blockbuster.

LEW WALLACE AND THE *BEN-HUR* PHENOMENON

This was not accidental. *Ben-Hur* was the prototype for the business synergies that today form the quintessential relationships between marketable artistic properties and consumer commerce. As soon as sales receipts demonstrated that *Ben-Hur: A Tale of the Christ* was a top seller, Harper commissioned Wallace to write a prequel, *The Boyhood of Christ*, for *Harper's Monthly* in 1885 and then published an expanded and illustrated version with gilt-edged pages for the gift-book market in 1889. As soon as Wallace returned from Turkey, where he had been President Garfield's appointee to serve as United States Minister Plenipotentiary to the Ottoman Empire, he embarked on an ambitious series of lecture tours that helped popularize the novel as it was rapidly becoming institutionalized. One of his first stops was at Chautauqua, where he himself realized for the first time the enormous popular potential of *Ben-Hur* and its chariot race. To increase sales in the 1890s, Harper – at Wallace's instigation – issued its Garfield edition memorializing the assassinated U.S. president. This was a two-volume set bound in orange silk, packaged in a Gladstone box, profusely illustrated on every page, and featuring a facsimile of the letter of endorsement Garfield had written Wallace in 1881. As late as 1908 Harper was still issuing gift-book publications excerpted from the novel, like *The First Christmas* and *The Chariot Race*.

Those were all proactive literary publications written by Wallace and published by Harper. Because U.S. law did not allow trademarking or brand-naming intellectual property in the 1880s, Wallace and Harper had to navigate carefully between vigorously defending their literary property against copyright infringement in a hostile environment and granting licenses to a select number of trustworthy businessmen, producers, or individual artists who in turn could spread the Ben-Hur name into non-literary markets. Trained in the law, Wallace understood from the outset many of the legal implications of authoring a popular novel. His extant correspondence contains several important exchanges regarding copyright issues, and in the early 1890s, when modernized international copyright laws and guidelines were still being forged, Wallace and Harper were at the forefront. By the end of that decade Wallace, now the resident *literatus* in his self-designed study in Crawfordsville, Indiana, had fully transformed himself from a high-level government administrator and part-time author to a wealthy literary businessman capitalizing on his unique property and his own celebrity.

In the late 1880s and early 1890s Wallace and Harper carefully monitored Ellen Knight Bradford's independent and unauthorized touring production of "An Evening With Ben Hur" and public lectures illustrated with equally unauthorized Riley Brothers stereopticon slides and *Ben-Hur* texts, and they used every legal means against them. Meanwhile Wallace rejected written requests to dramatize his novel lest any of these productions interfere with book sales and disrespect the reverent portions of the book. They did, however, grant local Crawfordsville businessmen a license to form the *Ben-Hur, in Tableaux and Pantomime* in 1889. Wallace himself wrote and copyrighted the script and received a royalty for the entire ten-year run. A few years later Wallace gave the founders of The Tribe of Ben-Hur, also local Crawfordsvilleans, invaluable advice and called upon his artistic talent to draw their Roman galley logo. Finally in 1899, having developed his business acumen, Wallace negotiated a huge percentage from Marc Klaw and Abraham Erlanger. The Klaw & Erlanger *Ben-Hur* ultimately earned Wallace and his estate nearly $1 million. Unlike any other popular literary property of the nineteenth century, most notably *Uncle Tom's Cabin*, almost all of these *Ben-Hur* by-products were not only huge financial successes created, written, authorized, or at least approved by Wallace, his estate, Harper, or the parties who purchased the rights directly from them, but also paid significant royalties.

After Wallace's death in 1905, Henry Wallace, his son and heir, encouraged the mass-production of the "Wallace Memorial Edition" to help reach readers from a broader spectrum of economic levels. This was the edition sold to Sears, Roebuck. Again, this was only the literary property. Clearly inheriting some of his father's negotiating skills, Henry sold the *Ben-Hur* film rights to Abraham Erlanger for an astounding $600,000, and Erlanger in turn negotiated with the Samuel Goldwyn Company to receive 50 percent of the gross from a film that would bring in over $9 million in receipts from its initial release.

THE CULTURAL AND COMMERCIAL IMPACT OF *BEN-HUR*

Between 1880 and 1920, the popularity of the novel, tableaux performances, and Klaw & Erlanger production not only continued to draw millions of readers and spectators but also attracted new consumers to the commercialized popular arts. The traditionally puritanical rural population generally shunned reading popular novels as an immoral and idle activity and attending live plays as an improper indulgence. But *Ben-Hur* as a "tale of the Christ," beginning with a reverent representation of the Nativity and culminating with Christ's miraculous curing of Judah Ben-Hur's leprous mother and sister, provided these potential patrons with a wholesome, uplifting experience. Balthasar, one of the three Wise Men, is an essential character in the narrative, and by the end of the novel Judah Ben-Hur, a Jewish aristocrat, has witnessed the mission of Christ. By design the romantic mores of the main characters are clearly defined. Judah has a slowly developing romance with Esther, a modest, selfless woman, and the Egyptian seductress Iras, along with her unrelentingly villainous Roman lover Messala, is punished. Thrilling cultural neophytes with their naval battle and chariot race, the various incarnations of *Ben-Hur* expanded the consumer market, "battering down the last vestiges of prejudice against fiction."[2] Carl Van Doren estimated that *Ben-Hur* was a novel "which thousands have read who have read no other novel except perhaps *Uncle Tom's Cabin*."[3]

As *Ben-Hur* developed into such a conspicuous presence in the popular literary and dramatic worlds and many of its reiterations became gigantic successes, it was identified as a work of popular art that could generate a universe of synergistic business activity and developed into the most widely used and longest-enduring, unofficial "brand name" ever created. Along with the financial success and high visibility of Ben-Hur Flour, Ben-Hur Coffee, and The Tribe of Ben-Hur, the commercial spillover ranged from coast to coast. There were Ben Hur roller coasters from Coney Island to Ocean Park, Ben-Hur paddle-wheel steamers operated on the Ohio and Mississippi as well as in Minnesota and Texas, Ben-Hur mines operated from Washington and Nevada to West Virginia, there were Ben-Hur apartment buildings in New York and San Francisco, and six months after thousands of New Yorkers began gazing at the huge electric-light "Ben-Hur" chariot race display above the Hotel Normandie in June 1910, Pasadena held its annual, *Ben-Hur*-inspired New Year's Day chariot races in front of as many as 20,000 spectators. The novel also inspired a number of musical compositions ranging in levels of sophistication from a classical cantata to E. T. Paull's ragtime "The Chariot Race or Ben Hur March," which not only sold hundreds of thousands of copies as sheet music in 1894 but was also widely recorded on the newly invented mechanical media at the turn of the century.

Climbing on the *Ben-Hur* juggernaut in the fall of 1907, Kalem, then a newly formed film company, produced the first cinematic version of *Ben-Hur* without obtaining copyright clearance. Those who held the dramatic rights to *Ben-Hur* – Henry Wallace, Klaw & Erlanger, and Harper – sued Kalem, and the case worked its way to the U.S. Supreme Court. In 1911 Justice Oliver Wendell Holmes crafted a landmark decision, determining that a moving picture was different from a series of still photographs and, as a unique dramatic narrative, any film produced or manufactured in the United States was now eligible for copyright protection.

Other nineteenth-century bestsellers like *Uncle Tom's Cabin* (1852) which preceded *Ben-Hur: A Tale of the Christ*, and Charles Sheldon's *In His Steps* (1896), which followed it, did not generate any significant

Figure 1.3 A century ago the name Ben-Hur was so ubiquitous that it was unintentionally captured on these postcards of a Wisconsin riverscape (Ben-Hur Flour), an unidentified rural general store (Ben-Hur Flour), the Crawfordsville Terminal Station, and downtown Detroit (Ben-Hur Cigars).

business interest outside of the publishing industry and dramatic productions, let alone a well-populated spectrum of brands and products. Even later nineteenth and early twentieth-century works that became extremely popular among juvenile and family demographics, e.g. *Alice's Adventures in Wonderland, Peter Pan,* and *The Wonderful Wizard of Oz,* did not generate significant and enduring commercial activity until decades later. Although *The Last Days of Pompeii* (1834), the first modern novel to be set in classical antiquity, and *Quo Vadis?* (1896), which helped its author Henryk Sienkiewicz win the Nobel Prize for Literature in 1905, both sold very well and were turned into popular and commercially successful entertainments of various sorts, *Ben-Hur* proved and continues to prove itself to be the most successful exemplar of popular classical reception in the modern era. Since the publication of the novel thirteen decades ago, millions of readers, lecturers, spectators, customers, manufacturers, retailers, and collectors as well as antique and ephemera dealers have consumed, bought, and sold Ben-Hur-related merchandise and items, and the process continues. In sum, even when the Ben-Hur gold and silver mines and heavy industry are not included, the novel, plays, films, and merchandising have grossed or generated several hundred million dollars. The 1959 film alone is estimated to have generated over $1 billion when adjusted for inflation, and much of the rest accrued before 1930, and even more of it before 1910. This many millions, if adjusted for a century's worth of inflation, amounts to several billion, making *Ben-Hur* the first spectacularly lucrative popular artistic product in the emerging culture of American consumerism and among the most lucrative ever created.[4]

PREVIOUS SCHOLARSHIP

A disproportionate number of published works have recognized the *Ben-Hur* phenomenon as such or provided a representative compilation and evaluation of the unique impact of the novel and its variegated scions. Previously there had been one per generation, Glenmore Davis's 1914 article in *Green Book*, the chapter "Ben-Hur" in Irving McKee's 1947 biography of "'Ben-Hur' Wallace," and several chapters in the Morsbergers' *Lew Wallace: Militant Romantic* of 1980.[5] Now at least there are a number of relatively brief ones.[6] *Ben-Hur* has also been disproportionately under-represented in literary, theatrical, cinematic, and historical scholarship and legal literature as well as merchandise summaries and histories of business. Many widely disseminated academic studies of American novels regularly omitted even a simple mention of *Ben-Hur: A Tale of the Christ*, be it John Erskine's *Leading American Novelists* of 1910, or D. H. Lawrence's *Studies in Classic American Literature* of 1923.[7] Alan Trachtenberg in *The Incorporation of America; Culture and Society in the Gilded Age* categorized *Ben-Hur* as simply a "sentimental romance" along with *Little Lord Fauntleroy* (1885/6) and *Trilby* (1894).[8]

More recent critics have addressed the novel's great success but derided Wallace's motivations for writing it. Paul Carter in *The Spiritual Crisis of the Gilded Age* assumed that "the novelist seems to have chosen the birth and death of Jesus as thematic material for the most crassly commercial of reasons."[9] In 1999, Paul Gutjahr in *An American Bible: A History of the Good Book in the United States, 1777–1880*, accused Wallace of calculating that "any book associating itself with the Bible had a good chance of riding its coattails."[10] As carefully delineated in the following chapters, *Ben-Hur: A Tale of the Christ* was not the result of a calculated plan by Lew Wallace to write a commercially successful novel exploiting a Christological theme. In contrast, what makes Wallace's success so particularly unique was not only his metamorphosis from a lawyer, government administrator, and part-time author to one of the most successful literary businessmen of his era, but the dispassionate manner in which he spoke publicly of the Christian revelation and the rarity with which he referred to it in his private correspondence.

As for older surveys of drama and film, Fred Eastman's *Christ in the Drama* failed to mention the drama at all while listing hundreds of toga plays connected with Christ and early Christianity.[11] David Mayer's introduction to *Playing Out the Empire* discusses the relatively short-lived dramatic productions of *Quo Vadis?*, *The Sign of the Cross*, and *The Last Days of Pompeii* to a much greater extent than he does the long-running *Ben-Hur*.[12] Moreover, his explanation for why toga plays tended to fail on stage compared to their success in book form and on film is that staged productions could not generate credible physical excitement, but this certainly does not apply to the great success of the Klaw & Erlanger *Ben-Hur* and its astounding stage effects created by Claude Hagen. Robert Klepper's *Silent Films, 1877–1996*, in examining 646 silent films fails to make mention of Kalem's film and erroneously names the protagonist of the 1925 MGM film "Judas Ben-Hur" and confuses the copyright date (1927) for the release date (1925).[13] In their lengthy study of novels rendered into film, John Tibbetts and James Welsh mentioned only the two silent film versions of *Ben-Hur*, and they did this only in the introduction, and only because the two films both had women scenarists, Gene Gauntier and Bess Meredyth.[14] In his 1979 study of previously overlooked popular literature warranting more sophisticated analysis by literary scholars, Leslie Fiedler in *The Inadvertent Epic: From Uncle Tom's Cabin to Roots* examined *Uncle Tom's Cabin* and then listed popular books "even more despised by established critics": Thomas Dixon's *The Clansman*, Margaret Mitchell's *Gone With the Wind*, and Alex Haley's *Roots*.[15] All of these, he points out, were turned into films, but he fails even to mention *Ben-Hur*, which had already been turned into three high-profile films. Similarly, Wallace's novel is not mentioned in either Gordon Weil's *Sears, Roebuck, U.S.A.* or James Worthy's *Shaping an American Institution: Robert E. Wood and Sears, Roebuck.*[16] In his history of Sears, David L. Cohn does mention the sale of *Ben-Hur* but only within the context of the volume book sale of many titles.[17] It was not until 1956 that Robert Ernest Spiller's *Literary History of the United States* pointed out its importance but did so in only a single sentence:

> In 1913 new horizons opened in the reprint field when Sears Roebuck printed from Harper's plates of Lew Wallace's *Ben-Hur* an edition of one million at a royalty of twelve cents.[18]

There are several reasons why the tremendous presence *Ben-Hur: A Tale of the Christ* had during the formative period of our popular consumer culture has not been widely acknowledged or thoroughly studied. An integral part of the explanation is that the phenomenon of *Ben-Hur*, particularly the initial popularity of the novel and its early by-products, typified popular culture long before popular culture was deemed worthy of scholarly analysis. *Ben-Hur* had flourished when popular culture was for the most part produced and experienced, not studied, and while it achieved a level of success and recognition far above the multitudes of contemporary popular artistic products, it failed to achieve the level of sophistication that would warrant recognition by contemporary critics and subsequent scholars. The more it warranted attention as a work of popular culture, the less attention it received.

The scholarly community began focusing its attention on popular culture almost an entire century after the publication of the *Ben-Hur: A Tale of the Christ*. At that point, just after the 1969 theatrical rerelease and the 1971 network television premiere of the 1959 film, the *Ben-Hur* phenomenon would step out of the limelight as entirely new modern blockbuster synergies of popular art and consumerism emerged, most notably in the *Star Wars* universe and the simultaneous releases of films, action figures, and fast food co-promotions. In other words, because *Ben-Hur* was a popular phenomenon, it had been ignored, demeaned, or dismissed by those who evaluated the finer arts and culture for the first century or so since the novel's publication in 1880 to the beginning of the 1970s, and because popular culture became a subject for academic study only in the 1970s, the *Ben-Hur* phenomenon was generally ignored or dismissed as an archaic relic by scholars who were interested in investigating contemporary popular culture and not the history of popular culture. The proliferation of *Ben-Hur* by-products into so many facets of American life and culture was unlikely to interest the previous generations of scholars who worked almost entirely in discrete genres and academic disciplines. Interdisciplinary studies, not to mention film studies programs, were relatively rare before the 1970s, and at the time humanists were not generally interested in commercial applications, nor economics or business faculty in the distant monuments of popular culture.

Furthermore, fundamental to the *Ben-Hur* concept are two specialized areas – the New Testament and classical, i.e. Greco-Roman, traditions. Despite their long-established presence in popular arts, neither tradition lends itself naturally or easily to analysis.[19] Formal theologians rarely considered biblical film adaptations worthy of interpretation, and despite the fact that hundreds of films have been produced in the ancient genre, it has never warranted status as a stand-alone genre with a separate rubric. Even today the books that examine these films have such periphrastic titles as *The Ancient World in the Cinema* and *Jesus of Hollywood*. Unlike "Westerns," there is no genre widely recognized as "Ancients."

In his 1993 book, *Land of Desire: Merchants, Power, and the Rise of a New American Culture*, William Leach traced the history of the popular commercial tie-in.[20] There he discussed the orientalism trope that was so successful in the period before the 1920s. After citing (now mostly forgotten) novels like Robert Hichens's *The Garden of Allah* (1904), L. Frank Baum's *The Last Egyptian: A Romance of the Nile* (1908), and Edward Sheldon's *Garden of Paradise* (1914), he defines the tie-in as "a concept unique to twentieth-century business." He explains:

> In the most highly charged form of linkage, superficially dissimilar commercial institutions – theaters, retail stores, restaurants, hotels, and movie houses – embraced similar themes. Unlike the more sophisticated concoctions of the 1920s, these prewar tie-ins were largely informal, even slightly naïve, and based on a mutual recognition by merchants that certain themes had obvious marketing appeal.[21]

Of course from 1880 to 1925 there was nothing that even closely resembled the complex tie-in process that mushroomed in the last quarter of the twentieth century. Today mass-marketed popular artistic projects require authors, agents, publishers, attorneys, and accountants to negotiate with film producers, manufacturers, retailers, restaurant chains, and advertisers to construct legally licensed and meticulously choreographed commercial campaigns. Leach's summary applies very well to the commercial applications of almost every popular artistic product available to the American marketplace in that period more than a century ago. For two notorious examples of bestselling literary properties that failed to generate commercial synergies we return to *Uncle Tom's Cabin* and *In His Steps*. Of course Harriet Beecher Stowe's novel had an incalculably powerful non-commercial importance, and George Aiken and many others created "Tom shows" that played for many decades leading up to two filmizations in 1903. But as an author Stowe lost control already in 1853 after F. W. Thomas printed an unauthorized German translation of her novel. Stowe sued but lost the case.[22] Then she failed to authorize any dramatized version of her novel.[23] Sheldon's copyright for *In His Steps* was flawed. He immediately lost control of his property and seems to have compensated by wildly inflating claims of having sold thirty million copies, far more than the approximately two million assumed to have been sold in the United States,[24] and the religious essence of the book made it unsuitable for turn of the century dramatization. And even Lew Wallace was limited because literary properties in the 1880s could not be trademarked or registered as a brand name, and this limitation continued long after the novel's original twenty-eight year copyright and two fourteen-year extensions had expired in 1936.

Leach's summary applies to these kinds of arrangements, but it does not accurately describe what happened with *Ben-Hur: A Tale of the Christ*. This was a bestseller for decades that the author, his estate, and publisher effectively advertised and marketed in a variety of editions and bindings, and exploited to increase magazine subscriptions (*Harper's*) and sales of the author's previous novel (*The Fair God*) and his subsequent one (*The Prince of India*), and they published a spin-off (*The Boyhood of Christ*) and excerpted sequences of the novel for gift items in separate volumes (*The First Christmas*; *The Chariot Race*), school readers (e.g. George Aldrich's *Progressive Course in Reading* 5.1), and declamation manuals (e.g. *The Tuxedo Reciter*), licensed an independent publishing project designed specifically for the Christmas and Easter markets (*Seekers After "The Light" From "Ben-Hur"*), signed binding contracts with several dramatic producers (Clark & Cox; Klaw & Erlanger) who generated approximately $1 million in royalties from their stage productions and acknowledged the copyright of the original novel in every printed program, and elsewhere vigorously guarded their copyright, pressing for international copyright protection, writing stern admonitions (Bradford) or even cease-and-desist letters (Riley) to would-be independent and incorporated producers, and suing the first film company (Kalem) that infringed upon it, ultimately receiving $25,000. Wallace himself became somewhat of a commercial entity by writing the introductions to several non-*Ben-Hur* publications and endorsing Holland Pens in magazine ads that included a photograph of him and an image of a chariot race representing his novel.

It is also important to emphasize, since the predicate of the *Ben-Hur* equation is commercial success, that most of these associations that were officially and legally licensed were developed on an enormous scale. The original novel, the Garfield edition, the Sears adoption, the Klaw & Erlanger stage production, and the 1925 MGM film were some of the most ambitious and successful popular artistic commercial projects in the fifty-year period from the mid-1880s to the mid-1930s. They sold coast-to-coast and internationally, and for decades. As for the non-synergistic, unauthorized Ben-Hur companies and products, in addition to the few that grew into large regional corporations, those that were small and independent concerns were, as Leech suggests, connected by a less well integrated nexus of manufacturers, retailers, and advertisers. But unlike any other unofficial brand name associated with a literary property, this one proliferated by the dozens and represented almost every major category of American retail business.

Ben-Hur: A Tale of the Christ was published in 1880 just as an inchoate popular consumer mentality was beginning its voracious sweep of the late nineteenth-century American landscape, and the first major popular artistic object for which this popular consumer mentality developed a broad, keen, and continuous yearning was anything having to do with *Ben-Hur*. Over the next few decades, as the confluence of commercial ingenuity, determined entrepreneurs, and expanding industries provided the American public with the tools they needed to consume and enjoy an increasing variety of popular merchandise, *Ben-Hur* was ready for consumption, already well established as a veritable artistic and commercial brand name. As the consumer element of the American economy continued to expand, *Ben-Hur* would repeatedly provide a respected, alluring, and memorable name and, insofar as the chariot race was concerned, a recognizable visual icon ripe for exploitation through persuasive advertising and mass marketing.

For well more than a century, *Ben-Hur* has entertained and inspired millions of people, and for more than a century *Ben-Hur* has made lots of people lots of money. From the outset, entrepreneurs in a wide variety of artistic and commercial sectors exploited the popularity and imagery of Lew Wallace's novel to forge what would turn out to be a prototype for the marketing of a high-profile artistic product. In that this merger was so successful in many respects, and in that the cachet of *Ben-Hur* as an artistic product has lasted for well over a century, the *Ben-Hur* property should be recognized as an avatar of American popular artistic commercialism.

THE RE-EMERGENCE OF *BEN-HUR*

For those twenty-one years that *Ben-Hur* played on stage to millions of audience members and was then transformed into cinematic blockbusters twice in four decades, it has been called a "warhorse."[25] That is a label that fit well the concept of its reliability for the eight decades between the publication of the book in 1880 and the release of the MGM film in 1959. But now more than fifty years later, the story is still displaying its adaptability to new and young audiences, innovative entrepreneurs, and contemporary media. Combining Christian values, popular entertainment, and merchandising, this movement is the fitting modern equivalent of the environment into which Wallace introduced the novel over a century earlier. That was when this artistic property was developed into the exemplar of American consumer popular culture, and the race carries on into the third millennium as *Ben-Hur* continues to prove its venerable tradition.

Nonetheless, by the 1970s the vast majority of *Ben-Hur* by-products had been discontinued, and many Ben-Hur commercial relics were relegated to dusty shelves or boxes stored in basements and attics. But the dormancy of the 1970s and 1980s helped preserve this legacy. Safely stowed away until the 1990s, *Ben-Hur* items began to reappear as a means of earning cash (once again) in antique shops, and many moved from there to the cybermarket of eBay soon after its inception in 1995. Ben Hur Bakelite, Ben-Hur Perfume, and many other forgotten Ben-Hur products were once again for sale. Meanwhile, as historical newspaper, magazine, and trade journal archives were scanned and readied for digital searches over the past decade or so, appropriate tools were developed by research libraries and related businesses. Now after years of development, an entire nationful of once inaccessible *Ben-Hur* items has been made available for identification, categorization, and study. Understanding the scope of the commercial impact of the *Ben-Hur* phenomenon would not have been practicable before this. Online newspaper resources now make available previously confined local and regional information, and electronic, untraditional, and "fugitive" sources have made it possible after all these years finally to collect the disparate ephemeral elements of the *Ben-Hur* phenomenon.

One copy of *Ben-Hur: A Tale of the Christ* inscribed by a caring relative and given as a Christmas gift in the late nineteenth century begins as a personal gift and then becomes a family heirloom, but a century later hundreds of copies of *Ben-Hur: A Tale of the Christ* found in online bookstores, many of them with an endearing personal inscription celebrating Christmas or serving as a graduation gift, or others with newspaper clippings of General Wallace's death or announcements of the performance of the Klaw & Erlanger production the owner attended, provide ample evidence that this was a cultural phenomenon. A Google search for something as seemingly unlikely as "Ben Hur boat" turns up some 500,000 hits ranging chronologically from the Ohio River packet built in 1887 to Hal Kelly's hydroplane design of the late 1950s. An eBay search for "Ben-Hur" has been turning up nearly 2000 hits per day for over a decade. There bits and fragments of the history of the *Ben-Hur* phenomenon accumulated as a Ben-Hur Cigar box or a razored-out magazine page with an ad for Ben-Hur Flour or a postcard from Coney Island depicting the Ben Hur Race surfaced for or a week or so and then disappeared again. But this was enough to build a database that could be supplemented with background information from the aforementioned research resources and then in turn pieced together to provide a comprehensive chronological narrative.

This material can now be organized and analyzed in a scholarly context, and this has allowed us to investigate the historical, theological, intellectual, artistic, and commercial contexts into which Lew Wallace and Harper & Brothers introduced *Ben-Hur: A Tale of the Christ* in 1880 and then connect the threads of evidence left behind in a variety of archival, ephemeral, material, and traditional sources. The result is a broad-ranging

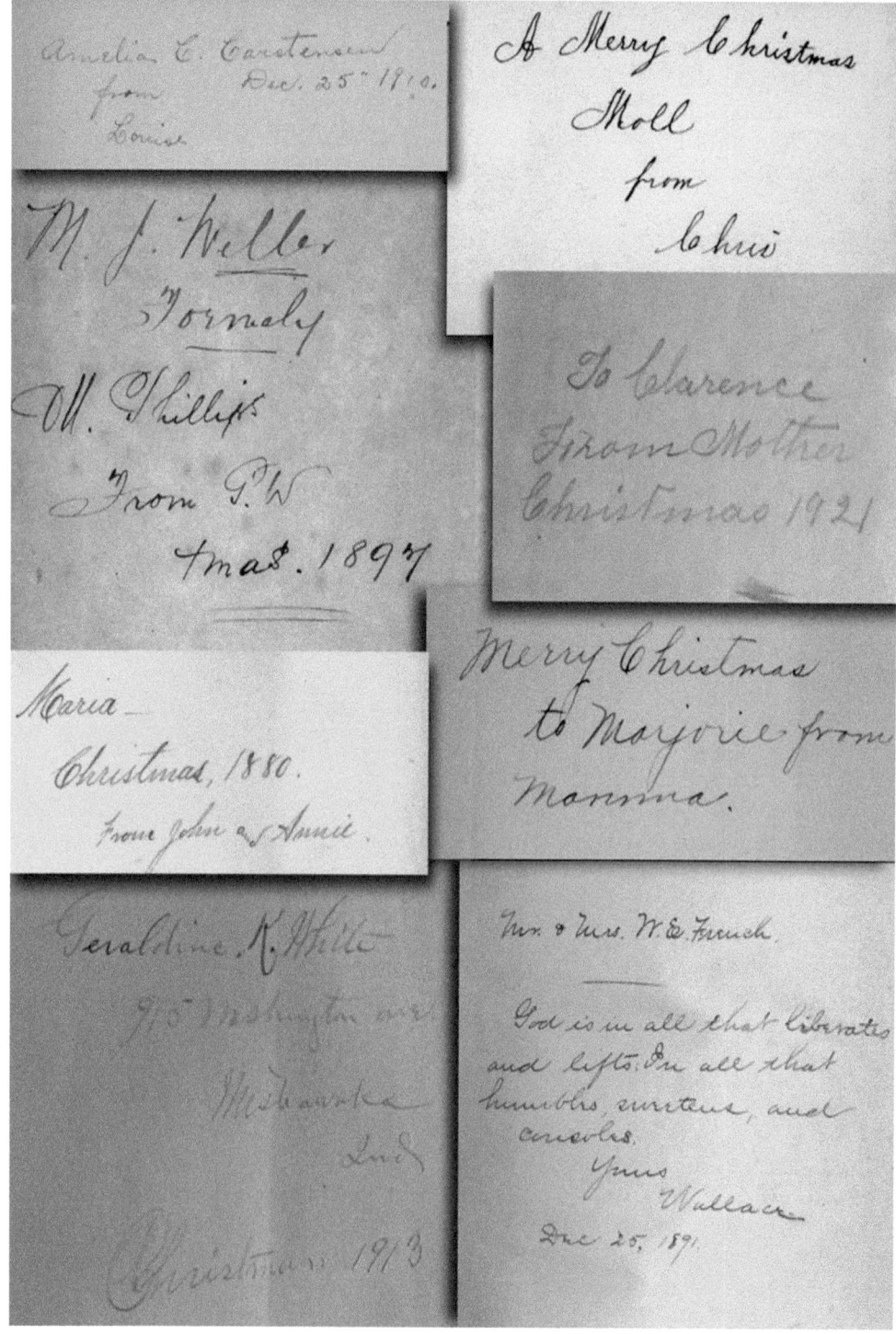

Figure 1.4 A sampling of Christmas dedications from inscribed copies of *Ben-Hur: A Tale of the Christ*, covering a span of over forty years.

history of this multifaceted, multi-generational mega-hit, a unique commercial prototype of popular consumerism and the signature example of the modern continuance of the classical tradition. There are drawbacks. There is so much information about *Ben-Hur* that it renders a few of the passages in this book as a walking reference narrative, and despite the amount of information uncovered, the nature of research in popular culture inevitably suffers from sporadic and inaccurate records and the lack of a standardized, cumulative inventory. I have done my best to balance the two to make sure this book contains a comprehensive but interesting story quite sufficient for identifying *Ben-Hur: A Tale of the Christ* as a prototype of the commercially successful popular artistic product.

NOTES

1 Specific details and citations will be provided in the subsequent chapters.
2 Kelly, "Historical Fiction," 177–8.
3 Van Doren, *The American Novel*, 123–4.
4 Cf. Theisen, "'My God, Did I Set All This in Motion?'" 37.
5 Davis, "The Most Successful Play Ever Produced," 36–45; McKee 164–88; M&M 447–96.
6 M&M 447–96; Malamud, *Ancient Rome and Modern America*, 122–49; Miller, "The Charioteer and the Christ, 153–75; Russo and Sullivan 305–416; Hovet, "The Case of Kalem's Ben-Hur (1907), 283–94; Hovet, *Realism and Spectacle*, 1–35; Theisen, "'My God, Did I set all of this in Motion?'" 33–41; Smiley, "Epics of Christianity," 31–51; Lifson, "Ben-Hur, 14–20 <http://www.neh.gov/humanities/2009/novemberdecember/feature/ben-hur>. Cf. Hanson, *Ripples of Battle*, 139–43.
7 Erskine, *Leading American Novelists*; Lawrence, *Studies in Classic American Literature*.
8 Trachtenberg, *The Incorporation of America*, 197. In 1888 the "Little Lord Fauntleroy case" established an author's right to forbid unauthorized dramatizations in England.
9 Carter, *The Spiritual Crisis of the Gilded Age*, 65–74.
10 Gutjahr, *An American Bible*, 166.
11 Eastman, *Christ in the Drama*. Cf. BG (January 4, 1915) 12; *Trenton Evening Times* (March 24, 1907) 15.
12 Preston and Mayer, *Playing Out the Empire*, 1–29.
13 Klepper, *Silent Films*, 394–5; cf. Bowser, *The Transformation of Cinema*, 21–36.
14 Tibbetts and Welsh, *The Encyclopedia of Novels Into Film*, xvi.
15 Fiedler, *The Inadvertent Epic*, 13–16.
16 Weil, *Sears, Roebuck, U.S.A.*; Worthy, *Shaping an American Institution*.
17 Cohn, *The Good Old Days*, 118.
18 Spiller, et al., *Literary History of the United States*, 1:966.
19 Solomon, *The Ancient World in the Cinema*; May and Bird, *Religion in Film* were the first books of their kind in these disciplines.

20 Leach, *Land of Desire*, 104–11.
21 Leach, *Land of Desire*, 107–8.
22 Homestead, *American Women Authors*, 105–49.
23 Lott, *Love and Theft*, 211–33.
24 Mott, *Golden Multitudes*, 197.
25 E.g. Eyman, *Lion of Hollywood*, 110.

2 *Lew Wallace Before* Ben-Hur

Unlike many of the best-known nineteenth-century American writers, Lew Wallace did not have an extensive formal or higher education, spend his formative years training as a journalist or magazine editor, or travel in Europe, all or any of which might have provided foundational training to a future novelist, playwright, artist, statesman, and diplomat. Wallace was quite different. Unlike Edgar Allen Poe and Henry David Thoreau, the author of one of the most successful novels about ancient Eastern Mediterranean religions had very little knowledge of Latin, let alone any of Greek, Hebrew, or Aramaic, languages generally considered essential for the study of ancient Roman civilization, the paleo-Christian era, and ancient Judaism. Unlike Stowe, Ralph Waldo Emerson, Steven Crane, and Henry James, the author of "a tale of the Christ" was not the child of a clergyman, theologian, or philosopher. And unlike Edgar Allen Poe, the youngest major-general in the Civil War and the author often referred to as "General" never attended West Point. Born eight years before Samuel Clemens, he became one of the first successful American authors not born or raised on the East Coast, which isolated him from its literary circles and cultural elite. And unlike Clemens, Wallace did not travel to the Holy Land until he was over fifty years old and had already published *Ben-Hur: A Tale of the Christ*.

As we will see, this brief profile of what Lew Wallace was not says much about what he was to become and why he became the author of *Ben-Hur: A Tale of the Christ*. His father, David Wallace, was appointed to West Point by the "Indian Fighter Old Tippecanoe," William Henry Harrison, as a favor to Lew's grandfather, Andrew Wallace. Although David Wallace graduated and briefly taught mathematics at the Academy, he resigned from the army and returned to the Indiana frontier before Lew was born in Brookville in 1827.[1] Lew's earliest memories were of contracting scarlet fever during the 1831 trek from Brookville to Covington, which claimed the life of his younger brother John. When his father became lieutenant governor in 1831, he moved the family into a one-story, two-room wood structure in Covington. The school Lew first attended was the proverbial one-room school house, where he did not at all excel. He rarely attended, and when he did he was frequently beaten. More Huck Finn than Tom Sawyer, he was a free spirit from an unstable environment. That was Wallace's recollection, and there is nothing to disprove it.

Lew's mother died when he was still quite young, and his father was often in Indianapolis, leaving Lew separated from even his two remaining brothers during years of fostering by two different sets of unrelated adults.[2] But his youthful exposure to frontier life fed his natural inclinations, freeing him from the fetters of the sophisticated East Coast and European traditions, and filling his mind with imaginings of warfare and heroic adventure. Never apologetic for his uncontrollable wanderlust or his lack of formal education, Wallace would eventually soldier and travel to exotic locations while both performing some extraordinarily diverse and demanding governmental duties and also writing his novels. Thereafter he would carve out a unique path through the world of letters and literature into popular success and celebrity, developing into one of the first successful authors to control the legal and synergistic applications of a popular literary property.

WALLACE'S EDUCATION

In *An Autobiography*, an unfinished memoir posthumously edited by his widow Susan and her friend Mary Hannah Krout in 1906, Wallace recalls realizing for the first time his natural ability to sketch portraits of his young classmates and then drawing his father dressed in uniform while drilling local Covington militia armed with swords, muskets, corn stalks, hickory staves, and umbrellas to fight in the Black Hawk War. Always confident in his talents, Wallace preserved the sketches he made at the time and inserted two into these pages of his autobiography (1:13–20). His quest for military adventure was also born on that day, as he writes in the vivid conclusion of this passage.

> When night came, and my mother tucked me in the little trundle-bed with my elder brother, I had gained such store of wisdom pertaining to war that it passed into my dreams, and from them into my life; so I promised myself, saying many times, "Wait until I am a man."

Wallace never claims to have done well at school, but during the winter months, when severe weather forced him indoors, he spent considerable time reading books of his own choosing and quickly developed an insatiable passion for it. He describes the first book he ever read as "one of Peter Parley's," i.e. the series of juvenile books written by Samuel Goodrich (a son of a minister, from the East Coast, who worked as a publisher). (1:20–1) Wallace does not record the title, but his ensuing description bears many resemblances to *The Tales of Peter Parley About Africa*. Wallace's recollection of a young lad who was captured by pirates, nearly sold into slavery, escaped to a small boat, and, nearly exhausted by hunger and thirst, finally rescued by Christians, somewhat foreshadows the adventures of Judah Ben-Hur. Although it is not ultimately the source of his *Ben-Hur* story, it shows that at a very young age the boy found this type of story to have considerable allure. The second book he recalls, Jane Porter's *The Scottish Chief*, continued to inflame his imagination and expand his artistic expression, as did Jesse Olney's geography textbook, which he says inspired in him additional fantasies of foreign lands. Lew and his older brother William not only shared the excitement of reading the exploits of the latter's famed namesake, William Wallace, they also regularly engaged a few friends to turn the Scottish chronicles into an imaginary war against the British. In short order they took to the boundless farmland, woods, and wilderness that bordered the banks of the Wabash River and imagined that they were in Spain fighting a noble battle against the Moors.

After the death of his mother, Esther Wallace, whose first name he would memorialize as the faultless and devoted daughter of Simonides in *Ben-Hur: A Tale of the Christ*, Wallace at the age of nine stole away from his temporary caregivers to join his brother at the Presbyterian preparatory school in Crawfordsville, the future Wabash College. Characteristically, the wild youth showed up barefoot and filthy. Wallace (1:41–2) describes his brief educational experience there:

> The faculty, out of respect for my father, doubtless, admitted me to the preparatory department, and set me at grammar, arithmetic, and Latin, with weekly compositions and recitations. A man named Barlow was the tutor. He also was of the army of indiscriminates who think they are doing their duty in giving impossible tasks to helpless incapables, and, if they are small, punishing them. I, a boy of nine, was expected to be ready with lessons which tried the grown men of my class. I strove hard, but gave up in a few weeks.
>
> The building was in the woods west of Crawfordsville. North of it, under a hill, there was a stream, half river, half creek. And they, the woods and the little river, invited me, and I accepted and took to them. Returning once, the tutor caught me, and, in full session of the class, stood me on a stove through the afternoon. At the letting-out I escaped for good. There are people who think me a graduate with a diploma to fatten my pride. In fact, I was a "prep" of Wabash College less than two months. Further it is not mine to boast. The faculty did not expel me. Most likely they were glad when I took myself off.

He next spent at least the better part of one year at "a county seminary in Crawfordsville conducted by an Episcopalian divine of recent emigration from the state of New York ... a person of education." Wallace was beaten so often that he distinguishes between his master's different tools – the ferule and the gad. His description (1:42–3) of the experience contains this romantic juxtaposition of his attraction for the outdoors and his struggles with a formal education:

> The river was a siren with a song everlasting in my ears. I could hear it the day long. It seemed specially addressed to me, and was at no time so sweet and irresistible as when I was struggling with the multiplication table or some abstruse rule of grammar.

It is impossible from this description to determine if the "abstruse rule of grammar" refers to English or Latin. Presumably if it had been Latin, Wallace would have said so, and certainly he would eventually master English grammar but never Latin (1:88).

Plutarch

Wallace's father, "by no means indifferent to my habits, especially the indisposition to study," moved him next six miles north of Crawfordsville to the Kerr family farm where he was given his first rifle and ammunition ample enough to keep the family dinner table supplied with game. Wallace (1:44–5) remembers these years with fondness:

> Whether profitable or unprofitable, they were certainly among the very happiest of my early life. Withal, moreover, I persisted in reading, and, returning to town, was richer of a thorough knowledge of *Plutarch's Lives* and *The Life of Daniel Boone*, which, by happy chance, constituted Mr. Kerr's entire library, unless his family Bible be catalogued a part of it. The heroes of the latter, however, were not nearly so engaging to my boyish fancy as those of the immortal Boeotian.

In a newspaper interview in the early 1890s, Wallace recollected, "The book which had most influence over me was and is yet, 'Plutarch's Lives.'"[3] Wallace offers a similar adoration for Plutarch in his 1884 letter to the Rev. George Baintow:

> Even now at the age of 66, when my will grows drowsy and begins to halt, I take up that old book, and it acts with the old charm. I am well again directly.[4]

Plutarch's Lives would provide Wallace with a propitious entry into the world of ancient Greece and Rome. The forty-eight biographies of Plutarch, the encyclopedic Greek (Boeotian) author who lived during the Roman Empire, contain hundreds of stories involving military prowess and magnanimity as well as political intrigue and corruption. It is difficult to pinpoint all of those that may have influenced Wallace in writing *Ben-Hur: A Tale of the Christ*, but Plutarch's description of the street battle that caused the death of Pyrrhus in 272 BC almost certainly provided a model for the critical tile incident that begins the demise of the House of Hur in Book Second of the novel.

We join the fatal urban battle in the Greek city of Argos as Plutarch (*Pyrrhus* 34.2–4), in the early nineteenth-century Langhorne & Langhorne translation, vividly describes the actions of the mother of a local freedom fighter:

> This woman, among others, looking upon the fight from the roof of a house, beheld her son thus engaged. Seized with terror at the sight, she took up a large tile with

both hands, and threw it at Pyrrhus. The tile fell upon his head, and notwithstanding his helmet, crushed the lower *vertebrae* of his neck. Darkness, in a moment, covered his eyes, his hands let go the reins, and he fell from his horse.[5]

This scene, featuring an urban battle of resistance, a tile thrown from a rooftop onto the head of the enemy leader below, knocking him to the ground, unconscious, not to mention the heroism of a local patriot and his mother's undying love for him, are all specified in Wallace's adaptation (2.6):

> While the [Roman procurator] was yet in the distance, Judah observed that his presence was sufficient to throw the people looking at him into angry excitement. They would lean over the parapets or stand boldly out, and shake their fists at him; they followed him with loud cries, and spit at him as he passed under the bridges; the women even flung their sandals, sometimes with such good effect as to hit him.
> . . .
> To say truth now, the Roman under the unprovoked storm had the young Jew's sympathy; so that when he reached the corner of the house, the latter leaned yet farther over the parapet to see him go by, and in the act rested a hand upon a tile which had been a long time cracked and allowed to go unnoticed. The pressure was strong enough to displace the outer piece, which started to fall. A thrill of horror shot through the youth. He reached out to catch the missile. In appearance the motion was exactly that of one pitching something from him. The effort failed – nay, it served to push the descending fragment farther out over the wall. He shouted with all his might. The soldiers of the guard looked up; so did the great man, and that moment the missile struck him, and he fell from his seat as dead.

This is also true of Wallace's description (2.6) of the melee that followed Judah Ben-Hur's apparent attack on the Roman procurator:

> A mischievous spirit flew with incredible speed from roof to roof along the line of march, seizing the people, and urging them all alike. They laid hands upon the parapets and tore up the tiling and the sunburnt mud of which the house-tops were for the most part made, and with blind fury began to fling them upon the legionaries halted below. A battle then ensued.

English translations of Plutarch had circulated since Thomas North translated Jacques Amyot's French translation of the Greek text in 1579. While it is impossible to identify precisely which edition of Plutarch the Kerrs owned, only so many English translations would in all likelihood have been available in Indiana in the 1830s. The most widely distributed by far was the translation by the poet John Langhorne and his brother William, first published in England in 1770.[6] By 1804 this translation was being published in Philadelphia and Worcester, Massachusetts, and David Huntington published a New York edition in 1816, and then a burst of new editions appeared in the 1820s and 1830s.[7] The original London edition consisted of six volumes, but the 1822 New York version published by Samuel Campbell had been extended to eight volumes revised and corrected by the prolific British clergyman Francis Wrangham. This edition began with a 44-page life of Plutarch and an impressively formatted series of informative tables listing Greco-Roman months, calendars, coins, weights, and measures, followed by an eighteen-page table putting the fifty names Plutarch treats in historical context. This table moves in chronological order, using both Christian and World Year dating systems, from the creation of the world and the deluge to the death of the emperor Otho in the year 69. Wallace later tells us that he did extensive historical research in preparation for writing *Ben-Hur: A Tale of the Christ*, and this is precisely the sort of information that might have attracted the young author to appreciate the detailed elements of daily life in the ancient world. Similarly, Wallace (1:88) says that at the age of sixteen he read Prescott's *Conquest of Mexico*, "a book of such wonderful brilliance that I devoured it, preface, text, notes, and appendix." This research would lead directly to the writing of his first novel, *The Fair God*.

Again, we do not know if the young Wallace perused these pages, but his novel would certainly bear the imprint of his fascination for such technical and pragmatic details of ancient life. For instance, his description (1.6) of the date of the Nativity glories in the various Hebrew and Greco-Roman dating systems:

> Following the Hebrew system, the meeting of the wise men described in the preceding chapters took place in the afternoon of the twenty-fifth day of the third month of the year; that is say, on the twenty-fifth day of December. The year was the second of the 193d Olympiad, or the 747th of Rome; the sixty-seventh of Herod the Great, and the thirty-fifth of his reign; the fourth before the beginning of the Christian era. The hours of the day, by Judean custom, begin with the sun, the first hour being the first after sunrise.

Lastly, the reader may now muse upon the fact that in Plutarch's *Life of Brutus* (40–2, 53), Wallace for the first time could have encountered the name Messalla.

THE END OF THE PAINTER AND THE POET

Although Wallace spent his first ten years living in four different households and family structures and was often separated from one or more or all of the members of his biological family, the reader should not think of him as some Dickensian wretch devoid of proper care or surrounded by juvenile delinquents. He does not celebrate it in his autobiography, but his father was very well connected, and young Lew shared his foster-family situations with several children who as adults would make notable achievements. Elizabeth [Waller] Hawkins at the time was in the process of raising her daughter Louisa, who would marry General Edward R. S. Canby, a graduate of West Point, and her son, (General) John Hawkins, would have a lengthy military career.[8] Mrs. Kerr was the mother of Joseph Ewing McDonald, another graduate of Wabash College and a Crawfordsville attorney who would be elected United States Senator during the years Wallace was writing *Ben-Hur: A Tale of the Christ*. Subsequently he was Democratic candidate for President.[9] Several more notables with whom Lew grew up will be discussed later.

David Wallace reunited the family at the end of 1836 when he married Zerelda Sanders, who many decades later would organize the Indiana branch of the Women's Christian Temperance Union, serve as its first president, and also become a leading spokesperson for the suffrage movement.[10] He moved the entire family to Indianapolis the next year when he was elected governor. This and the influence of his stepmother still did not fully temper the wildness in young Wallace's spirit, but she kept him washed and well dressed and took him to her father's Church of Christ every Sunday. Though he loved her and respected her, and although she was already a prominent member of the church, the future author of *Ben-Hur: A Tale of the Christ* recalled (1:47–8) that their regular attendance at religious services "failed to impress me as she desired." Far from accepting the miracle of the Christian Revelation, Wallace spent his time in church sketching the likenesses of anyone who had a "peculiarity of face or manner."

It was at this time that he met Jacob Cox, the artist commissioned to paint his father's gubernatorial portrait. Originally from Philadelphia, Cox supported himself in Indianapolis by running a shop dealing in tin and copper. Young Wallace volunteered to help Cox grind his colors and, neither his unruliness nor romantic leanings yet fully under control, promptly stole some samples, took them home, mixed them with castor oil, made a brush by plucking hairs from a dog and tying them to a stick, and created his first painting – a portrait of Black Hawk.

The importance of this incident was not so much that it further demonstrates Wallace's natural penchant for pursuing the arts or creating his own universe despite what was expected of him. It was his father's stern instructions to repress any impractical desire to become an artist:

> I will not have it. If you are thinking of being an artist, listen to me. In our country art is to have its day, and the day may not come in your time. There is no demand for pictures. Rich men are too few, and the poor cannot afford to indulge a taste of the kind. To give yourself up to the pursuit means starvation. Do you understand me? . . . Mr. Cox is a good man; but he has a trade to fall back upon – a shop to help him make the ends meet.[11]

In recalling this conversation, Wallace does not comment except to say that he was too young to appreciate his father's warning at the time. But the reader will wonder what these words, or something like them, allowing for Wallace's literary embellishment, may have ultimately meant to the adult Lew Wallace who had made a fortune as a popular writer by the time he wrote this into his autobiography. Wallace rarely took his father's advice, let alone anyone else's, but in this instance he did listen to his father, and the world of popular literature would not be the same if he had not soon heeded it and become a painter instead of everything else he became. The reader also gets a glimpse of David Wallace's perspicacity in predicting that America would some day have the wealth to support its artists. This was a reasonable prophecy from a West Point mathematician turned lawyer and politician. However, he seems to have envisioned more of the traditional European model supported by wealthy patrons. America's Gilded Age would indeed produce some of that patronage decades later, but by far the greatest support for an artist like his son would come from the middle class, whose rise he would have been unable in 1837 to predict.

Wallace's dream of becoming a painter had received an imperceptibly mortal wound but was not dead. His next effort was to draw an image of a rabbit on his school blackboard with the face of his teacher, "Mr. K—r." The caricature with an uncanny likeness generated the usual flogging, but when the teacher then instructed Wallace to erase the drawing, he refused. As the teacher approached with "fury in his face," Wallace leapt out the window and ran three miles to a nearby farm. Wallace's conclusion (1:51–4) is very telling in its prescription for success in pursuing an artistic career:

> My father's peremptory lecture against the allurements of art had failed its purpose. Now, however, one point in it had landed home. After the affair with Mr. K—r, I could no longer deny the non-existence of the appreciation urged as a prime essential to success in the life. To starvation there was superadded a likelihood of being done to death by sticks and stones. I resolved to give up the dream. It still haunts me.

Wallace learned early on in life from two male authority figures not to pursue a career in art for art's sake. Ultimately he would not, but instead he would blaze a new path in popular art.

SAMUEL K. HOSHOUR

In his thirteenth year young Wallace finally encountered a teacher who recognized his budding talents. This was Samuel K. Hoshour. Wallace writes about him with respect and gratitude, but he does not mention his accomplishments or positions. Samuel Klinefelter Hoshour was born into a German-speaking Pennsylvania family in 1803.[12] A Lutheran minister with a formal education, he was excommunicated in 1835 because of his conversion to Baptism. Ousted from Maryland but welcomed in Indiana, he became the principal of the Wayne County Seminary, which is where he counted among his pupils not only Lew and William Wallace but also Oliver P. Morton, who as Governor of Indiana in 1862 would appoint Hoshour to the post of Superintendent of Public Instruction.[13] Hoshour would also teach at Indiana University and serve as president of Northwestern Christian University (now Butler University), where he taught French, German, Latin, and Greek.

At this time Hoshour had just recently relocated in Centreville (Centerville), and David Wallace shipped off Lew and William to live with their Aunt Rebecca (their biological mother's sister) for the year. He must have been hoping that this double supervision might help control Lew's animal spirits. As it turned out, Hoshour was more than sufficient (1:55–6):

> Professor Hoshour was the first to observe a glimmer of writing capacity in me. An indifferent teacher would have allowed the discovery to pass without account; but he set about making the most of it, and in his method there was so much wisdom that it were wrong not to give it with particularity.

Wallace explains that Hoshour would invite him to his house in the evening and tutor him in literature, emphasizing "clearness of expression." In addition to a number of authors and books, e.g. Byron and Shakespeare, he says Hoshour introduced him to the New Testament.

> This was entirely new to me, and I recall the impression made by the small part given to the three wise men.[14] Little did I dream then what those few verses were to bring me – that out of them *Ben-Hur* was one day to be evoked.

There is a contradiction here, as we will see in the next chapter, for earlier (e.g. *The First Christmas*) Wallace had recalled that the story of the Wise Men was read to him first by his mother.

Despite his knowledge of the classical languages, Hoshour did not teach Wallace any Latin. But Wallace comments further on (1:88) that Hoshour taught him that education was a continuing process, and accordingly Wallace would re-educate himself as part of his preparation for writing *Ben-Hur: A Tale of the Christ*.

ALLUSIONS TO CLASSICAL LITERATURE

The next year, 1841, Wallace returned to Indianapolis, where he joined a literary activity group, the Union Literary Society. On Friday evenings they read aloud and criticized each other's writing. Wallace composed an epic poem, "Marmion," the name derived from Sir Walter Scott. He also composed poetic satire. One example of the latter, "Travels of a Bed-bug," was distributed locally and incurred the wrath of the lampoon's target to the extent that Wallace was once again threatened with a beating. He "went hunting" until the matter blew over (1:62).

> Thereupon, finding that, like painting, poetry did not succeed best in the shadow of cudgels, I wisely quit it. I say wisely, for it is my mature judgment that under similar circumstances Homer had not persisted in supplying the world with masterpieces.

As the author of a novel set during classical antiquity, Wallace's allusion to Homer here is noteworthy. How often does he allude to classical antiquity in his other writings? Supplementing the list in the first paragraph of this chapter, we could point out that such nineteenth-century American authors as Edgar Allen Poe and Nathaniel Hawthorne filled many pages with material derived from the classical tradition. Wallace lacked that type of formal education. Up to this point in his autobiography, Wallace has evoked the names of only Alexander and Caesar – two of Plutarch's paired figures – saying that their conquests were no match for the number of men he literally wiped out when erasing most of his early military drawings. This is the only mention of Homer in either volume of his autobiography, and it appears merely ten pages before his confession that in those years "there was a copy of *Ossian* in my father's library to which I was addicted." During the first half of the nineteenth century, Ossian was reputed to be an "ancient author," and for those without a classical education the Ossian corpus served as a satisfactory Homeric substitute.

Nonetheless, Wallace does evoke Homer in *Ben-Hur: A Tale of the Christ* in six different passages, five referring to the *Iliad*. Three of them (1.5; 2.5; 4.15) are not direct quotations, and the fourth (5.6) occurs where he compares Greek chariots to Roman. It refers obliquely to "the chariot of Achilles," although not in an Iliadic context.

> Speaking generally, the carriage-makers of Rome built for the games almost solely, sacrificing safety to beauty, and durability to grace; while the chariots of Achilles and "the king of men," designed for war and all its extreme tests, still ruled the tastes of those who met and struggled for the crowns Isthmian and Olympic.

The phrase "crowns Isthmian and Olympic" was probably inspired ultimately by Pindar, albeit perhaps digested through a reference work on Greek chariots.

The fifth (5.14) occurs during the chariot race, where Wallace inserts six relevant lines from Alexander Pope's much circulated translation of the *Iliad* in rhyming couplets:

> First flew Eumelus on Pheretian steeds;
> With those of Tros bold Diomed succeeds;
> Close on Eumelus' back they puff the wind,
> And seem just mounting on his car behind;
> Full on his neck he feels the sultry breeze,
> And, hovering o'er, their stretching shadow sees.

A note that was included in many contemporary editions of Pope's translation says: "The poet makes us spectators of the race, we see Diomed pressing upon Eumelus so closely, that his chariot seems to climb the chariot of Eumelus," so perhaps Wallace inserts this quotation here to foreshadow the end of the race when Judah drives his chariot into Messala's.

Where Wallace describes how his satirical bedbug died, "like Alexander, it succumbed to overdrink," (1:62) it may be an example of an early plot device taken from Plutarch, in this instance Plutarch's *Life of Alexander* (75.2–4). Similarly, a few pages later in *An Autobiography* (1:76), when describing how at the age of fifteen or sixteen he tried to make his way down river to join in the Battle of the Alamo, Wallace recounts how he tried to steal a goose for dinner:

> We flung the bird aboard, thinking it dead; but just as we swung past a field lively with harvesters the goose revived and uttered a "honk" so loud, so long, made doubly embarrassing by a fight for life with its great wings, that I have ever since been able to understand how its possible ancestors on the Capitoline Hill could have saved Rome.

Although the account of Rome being saved by the Capitoline geese could be found in a variety of sources, Wallace may be alluding to the account in Plutarch, *Life of Camillus* (27.2).

There is one particularly important example of the influence the classical tradition had on Wallace at this point in his life, despite his ignorance of Latin and Greek. Lew and his brother William spent many hours reading with their father, benefitting from the latter's considerable library. In *An Autobiography* (1.5) Lew later described it as if it were a Greco-Roman literary paradise:

> There were fewer books then, and they were of the best, and constant familiarity with them gave a stateliness of speech and a certain dignity that comes of keeping good company. They dined with Horace and supped with Plutarch, and were scholars without knowing it.

In an effort to give his older sons the benefit of his education, David Wallace scheduled these frequent sessions that involved not just reading but declamation, critiques, and, when needed, repetition and "laborious drilling." His father's education and love for literature made a strong impression on Lew. Macaulay was his father's favorite author, along with Shakespeare, Milton, and others. Wallace does not mention it here, but his father's library included Gibbon's *The History of the Decline and Fall of the Roman Empire*.[15] The memoirs of John Hazlehurst Boneval Latrobe, a fellow cadet at West Point, describe the literary and debating association, The Amosophic Society, to which he and David Wallace belonged at the Academy.[16] He says that one of their goals was to expand the library, and that Gibbon's work was one of the books they purchased. As we will see in the next chapter, Gibbon seems to have played an important role in the shaping of the character Judah Ben-Hur.

Wallace's account (1:82) here focuses on one particular ancient author, the Greek historian Thucydides:

> Once he gave an evening to Thucydides, and so powerful was his rendition of the retreat of the Athenians from Syracuse that it has since been one of my exemplars in historical writing.

This passage in Thucydides (5.75–87) describes in vivid detail the cries and pleas of the Athenian sick and wounded as their defeated comrades had to abandon them in the hope of escaping alive, the Syracusan ruse that trapped thousands of others, and the defeat, death, or enslavement of the few thousand survivors. As Wallace suggests, it would have supplied the young writer with an array of historical events, military stratagems, treaty negotiations, tragic situations, and literary techniques.

At the time there were only two published English translations of Thucydides, those by Thomas Hobbes (1628) and William Smith (1753). The latter was published in the United States at least a half-dozen times before 1844 and is therefore most likely the one David Wallace possessed in Indiana.[17] What is intriguing about this is the brief editorial note that brings the description of the terrible defeat of the Athenian forces to a close: "Some Iambic verses of an unknown author are found at the end of this book in the later Greek editions; and I beg the reader to accept the following translation of them . . ." We can only bookmark this note as a possible exemplar for an ubiquitous feature of Wallace's "historical writing" – apostrophizing "the reader."[18] Interestingly, Hobbes uses the same technique in his introduction, where he frequently addresses "the reader."[19]

FORCED INDEPENDENCE

At the age of sixteen, Wallace wrote his most ambitious piece yet, *The Man-at-Arms* – a 250-page heroic novel set in Europe and Jerusalem during the time of the Crusades. Inspired by the popular historical novel of the same name by George Payne Rainsford James, Wallace's penchant for historical novels was now forming its own authorial voice. In *An Autobiography* Wallace makes it very clear that his goal was to please an audience. The teenager already sensed that an author should first select a subject that will garner a large audience and entertain them (1:63):

> After a great deal of casting about for a plot, I finally decided on one likely to be agreeable to my auditors. Even then the importance to a writer of first discerning a body of readers possible of capture and then addressing himself to their tastes was a matter of instinct with me.

His autobiography makes it clear that Wallace's friends and classmates enjoyed his satirical drawings and poems as well as this first historical novel. What Wallace could not have predicted at this young age was that some day he would write a historical novel that was agreeable to a huge swath of the American (and European) public, let alone that this formula would bring him greater fame and fortune than any other of his endeavors. As we will see, Wallace will claim that he had an entirely different reason for writing *Ben-Hur: A Tale of the Christ*, but as he suggests here, his ability to please the public was innate.

Wallace's aborted attempt at making his way to Texas ended in arrest by the local constable. This was the last straw. David Wallace, his political career at an end and his economic future in question, sat Lew down for a conversation and told his son that he should set out on his own. Lew accepted his father's decision and did so, albeit with his typical apparent lack of concern for what difficulties might lie ahead: "I very much fear there was lacking in me the proper appreciation of the solemnity and uncertainties of the crises." (1:84)

Despite his failures in school, Wallace had developed into a voracious reader and a practiced writer. He had found his passion for communing with other historical periods and a technique with which to pursue it. And Hoshour had inspired him to continue his learning into adulthood. His father's sophisticated manner and early military and political achievements provided some of the goals to which the directionless youth would ultimately aspire. Not among them was to earn a living as an artist, visual or literary, even though he periodically over the course of thirty years worked on his historical novel set in the age of the Mexican conquistadors.

WALLACE AS A SOLDIER, LAWYER, AND PUBLIC SERVANT

During the following three decades Wallace won and lost civic elections, held rewarding and problematic military and governmental positions, rose through the army ranks and was removed from the war, commanded important successes and defeats in battle, and married happily but faced mounting personal debt. It was a fascinating and varied period, for the details of which the reader is encouraged to turn to the Morsbergers' *Lew Wallace: Militant Romantic*. Our concern here is the development of the Wallace who would author and then market *Ben-Hur: A Tale of the Christ*, and so we will move through the rest of the 1840s, 1850s, and 1860s with a focus on Wallace's development as an author.

Once he had set out on his own, Wallace found work in the county clerk's office, joined a local teenage militia, began to study law with his brother William under the tutelage of their father, worked briefly for the *Indianapolis Journal*, and planned out *The Fair God*.[20] When the United States went to war with Mexico in 1846, Wallace, now nineteen, organized a company and as their second lieutenant led them south to the Texas border near the mouth of the Rio Grande. He seems to have had a particular genius for marshaling and parading forces.[21] Judah Ben-Hur will be equally effective in raising three anti-Roman legions in Galilee. This would only be Wallace's first visit to Mexico, and while he was eager to fight and thereby extend the arm of American empire, the experience would also introduce him to the injustices of Spanish colonialism at the expense of the indigenous Mexicans. His first two published novels, *The Fair God* and *Ben-Hur: A Tale of the Christ*, would both feature the plight of indigenous peoples under imperial rule.

His Mexican war experience provides us an early example of how Wallace responded to grave insult, in this instance the disparaging report General Zachary Taylor filed about an Indiana regiment – not even Wallace's own – that Taylor never entrusted with an engagement. When the war was over and Taylor a presidential candidate, Wallace attacked him in a stump speech modeled after the *Philippics* of Demosthenes, and he borrowed additional money so he could co-publish on a weekly basis *The Free-Soil Banner*, with incessant assaults on Taylor (1:203). Although Taylor won the presidency, he did not win Indiana.

After the war Wallace hastened his resolve to succeed in the legal and political arenas, so he spent 1849 studying law with his father and finally acquired his license to practice. His training as a lawyer would later differentiate him from most other popular authors. It would prove to be invaluable when defending the copyright of *Ben-Hur: A Tale of the Christ* and negotiating contracts with Harper, Klaw & Erlanger, and others. However, he did not enjoy law as a career, and, after being elected in the early 1850s to only minor offices (prosecuting attorney of his congressional district and state senator), he realized he would not be following in his father's footsteps as a politician. Nonetheless, he remained a political operative, and this would ultimately lead him to his post in New Mexico, where he would write the final portion of *Ben-Hur: A Tale of the Christ*. Meanwhile, he says he despised lawyering and often took refuge from the tedium by writing.

In 1852 he married Susan Arnold Elston, the daughter of a wealthy Crawfordsville banker. She had studied Latin at William Gibbons' Quaker boarding school in Poughkeepsie, and, like Wallace, became a poet and prose author. With her critical eye, Susan vetted all the completed chapters of *Ben-Hur: A Tale of the Christ*, and she would be the dedicatee of the novel. She appears to have been instrumental in expediting the success of the novel's sales in the mid-1880s, and in 1902 she gave her personal endorsement for Ben-Hur Flour's national advertising campaign. After her husband's death in 1905, she helped prepare his autobiography for publication.

His marriage to Susan also helped him gain entrance to the Civil War, as did the prominent network to which he had belonged most of his life. Susan's sister Joanna married Henry Smith Lane, another Crawfordsville attorney, who in January, 1860, vacated the governorship of Indiana after serving for only two days so he could accept an appointment to the U.S. Senate. This opened the office to his lieutenant governor, Oliver Morton, Wallace's former classmate. It was Morton who appointed Wallace adjutant general shortly after receiving news of the firing on Fort Sumter. Wallace's rapid rise to military prominence culminated with the capture of the Confederate stronghold of Fort Donelson on the Cumberland River in February, 1862.[22] This brought Wallace a promotion to the high-

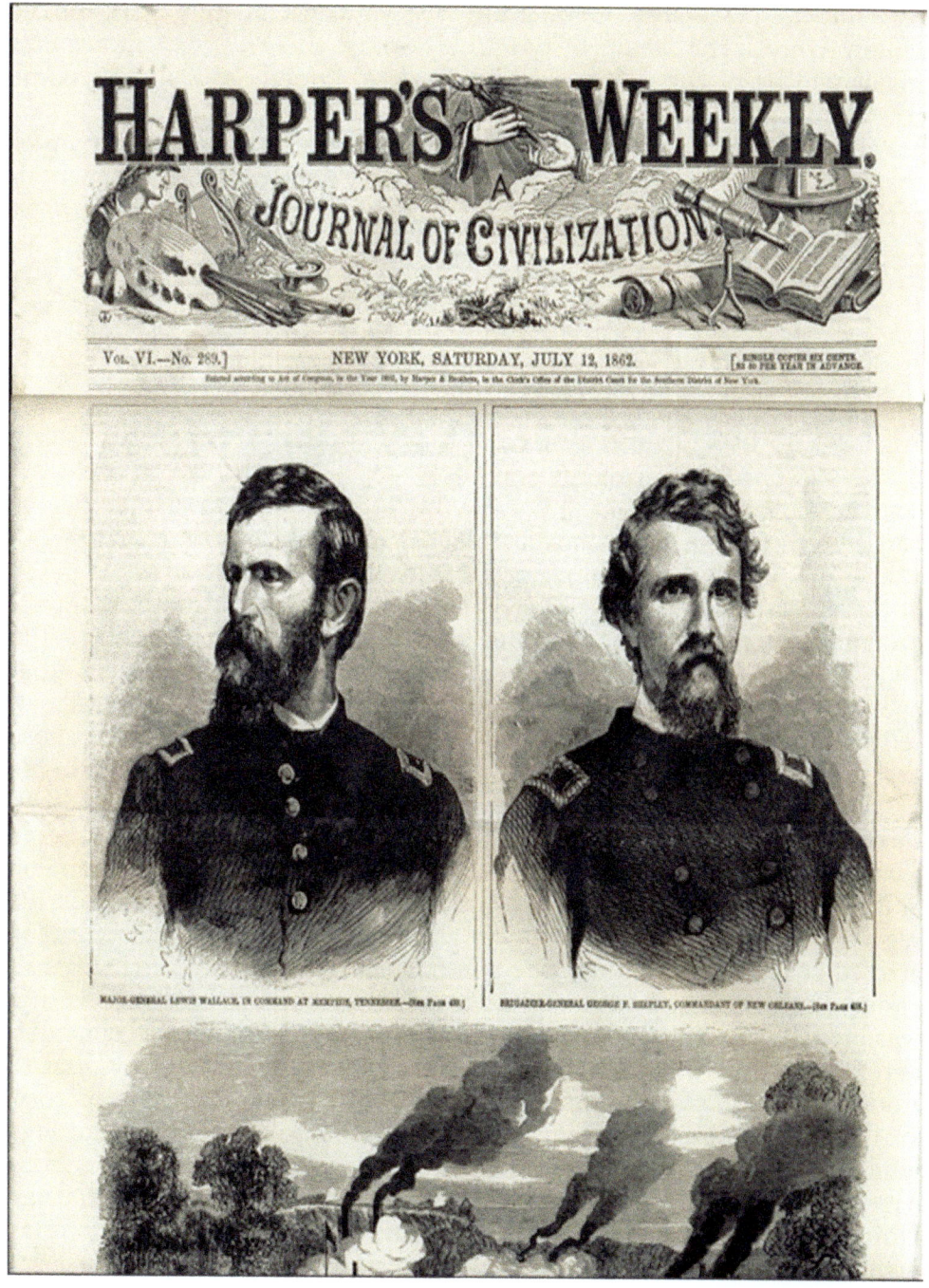

Figure 2.1 Major-General Lew Wallace on the cover of *Harper's Weekly*, July 12, 1862.

est rank then available, making him the youngest major general in the Union Army at the age of thirty-four.[23] Because this was the Union's first major victory of the war, celebrations were numerous. Wallace's name was memorialized in Herman Melville's *Civil War Poems*.[24]

Wallace had now achieved a level of self-confidence that would support the author frequently referred to as "General Lew Wallace" throughout the next four and one-half decades. He wrote later in his autobiography (1:437–8):

> Yet, as I am making confessions, it might as well be thorough – my greatest personal satisfaction was due to discovery of the fact that in the confusion and feverish excitement of real battle I could think. I do not expect this discovery at first to make the impression on the reader it did on me; but if he will reflect a moment, the fullness of my meaning will probably dawn upon him.

The Western theater of the war soon focused about 100 miles to the south of Fort Donelson, at Shiloh by the Tennessee River. The ferocious battle fought there began just before dawn on the morning of April 6, 1862, with an attack by a large force of Confederates that had taken much of Grant's army by surprise. The events that followed in the next hours produced a controversy that would follow Wallace for the rest of his life and to the present day. He had heard the gunfire in the distance, and at approximately 8:00 a.m. Grant met with him on the deck of his gunboat, telling him to await orders. We have conflicting accounts of what those orders were once they arrived less than one hour before noon. Grant in his memoirs claims that he ordered Wallace via messenger to march down the river road to Pittsburg Landing. Wallace in *An Autobiography* claims that the orders were ambiguous. He marched down the inland shunpike, and when he realized he was behind the battle, he countermarched his regiment and proceeded very slowly along a muddy path. By the time he arrived at Pittsburg Landing, the sun had set and that day's fighting had ended. Both sides had suffered heavy casualties, and the Union position was precarious. Nonetheless, the next day the Union, reinforced considerably overnight by Major General Buell's Army of the Ohio and Wallace's troops, turned the tide and emerged victorious. In the wake of this victory, Wallace was ordered to occupy nearby Memphis, imposing martial law, which earned him still additional celebrity and his image on the front page of the July 12 *Harper's Weekly*.[25] That same week he addressed the United States Senate, urging them to recruit and train "negro" soldiers, as he himself would do two years later in Baltimore.[26]

The tactical victory was not lasting, however. The Confederate army survivors escaped into Mississippi, and once the shocking number of Union casualties – over 10,000 – became public knowledge, President Lincoln and the War Department had to demand an accounting. It is an oversimplification to say that Major General Halleck blamed his subordinate Grant for being unprepared for the Confederate surprise attack, Grant blamed his subordinate Wallace for not arriving promptly, and Wallace in turn blamed his superiors Grant (for giving him unclear orders) and Halleck (for his inept pursuit of the defeated Confederate army). But that is all the reader needs to understand the situation. Grant was reassigned to a command of less importance, and Wallace was relieved of field command altogether and returned to Crawfordsville. He attempted for years to set the record straight. The hypothesis that this disgrace motivated Wallace to write *Ben-Hur: A Tale of the Christ* will be addressed in a later chapter.

Despite disciplinary action, the Civil War was hardly finished with Wallace. Twice he helped in the defense of northern cities from surprise attacks. Already in September, 1862, Morton called upon him to prevent the Confederates from invading and occupying Cincinnati. Wallace declared martial law and quickly organized its 200,000 citizens to build defenses, including Fort Wallace, and man their rifles.[27] Ever the artist, while awaiting the attack he entertained many of the leading artists of the city with the poem, "The Stolen Stars: An Hysterical Ballad."[28] Meanwhile, Wallace's defenses appeared to be so indomitable that the Confederates never launched an attack. For defending the city he received official commendation from the Ohio General Assembly.[29] Still frustrated in his attempts to have Halleck reinstate him with a field command, he remarked to Susan in a letter, "I will go at my books and paints again."[30]

Finally, in 1864, Lincoln himself insisted on assigning Wallace to the command of the Middle Department, headquartered in Baltimore. There Wallace boasted of rigging the election to ensure passage of an amendment to abolish slavery in Maryland and committed "several instances of tyranny," including the arrest of the owner of Margaret Toogood, the last slave in Maryland, and putting him to hard labor in prison until he produced $500 for her welfare.[31] The reader will have observed already that Wallace, through this action and declaring martial law elsewhere, was by his own admission a tyrant when charged with protecting the union and helping to abolish slavery. His commitment to abolitionism would reverberate throughout *Ben-Hur: A Tale of the Christ* in theological, sociological, and practical applications. Already in Book First (1.4) he has the Egyptian Balthasar make clear that Moses' demand to free the Hebrew slaves "was in the name of the Lord God." Making Judah Ben-Hur himself serve as a Roman galley slave for three years, Wallace describes (3.2) "the wretchedness of the slaves upon the benches," and he encapsulates their hopeless anonymity by assigning them numbers instead of names. And although Judah has inherited slaves from his father, he builds benign and even loving personal relationships with such slaves as Simonides and Esther.

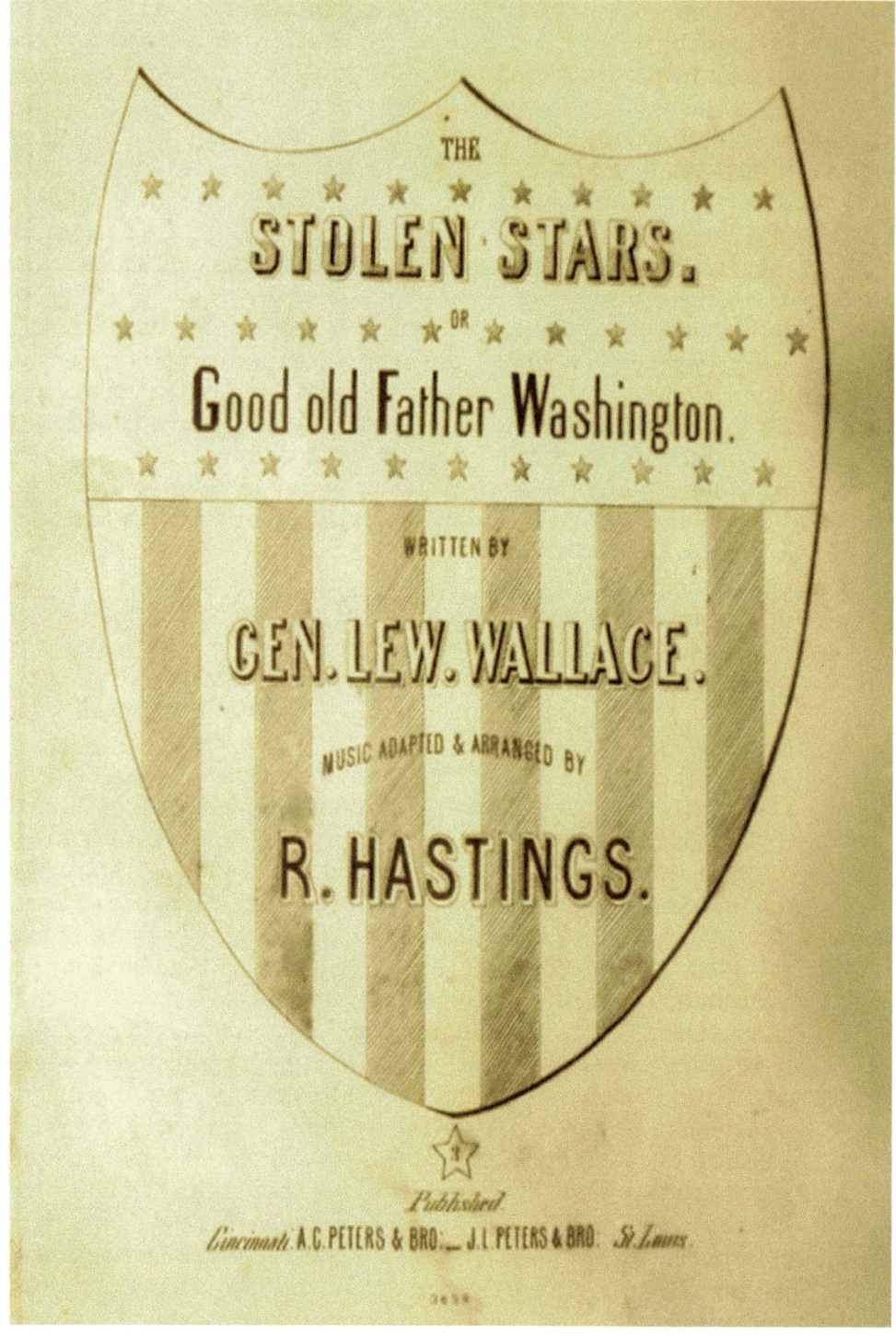

Figure 2.2 The versatile Wallace wrote this poem while defending Cincinnati from a Confederate attack in 1862. It was set to music and sold in 1863.

Wallace and most independent commentators believed that his most significant tactical accomplishment in the Middle Department was his performance in July, 1864 at the Battle of Monocacy.[32] Severely outnumbered, he lost the day but ultimately received high praise for delaying the Confederates sufficiently that they were unable to occupy Washington. This restored his prestige and brought him back into the limelight, and his command in the Middle Department and his legal training positioned him to take part in two of the most publicized inquests during the aftermath of the war. First was the military commission convened by President Johnson to try the eight defendants accused of conspiring with the Lincoln assassins. By many accounts, several of the eight, including Mary Surratt, the first white woman executed by the United States government, were innocent, but Wallace did not hesitate to convict them, while making pencil sketches of them as well. As usual, and like Judah Ben-Hur, he was unapologetic for the outcome of the trial despite the suppression of evidence and prejudice towards anyone from the Confederacy. The same is true for the trial of Henry Wirz, the commander of Confederate prison in Andersonville, Georgia. Even Wallace's chief biographers, the Morsbergers, recognized that as the President of the Commission, again appointed by Johnson, Wallace's "zeal to be a good soldier seems to have made him act as a member of the prosecution rather than as an impartial judge."[33]

Wallace resigned his military commission in November, 1865, but he immediately involved himself in international military diplomacy. Many months earlier, the veteran of the Mexican War and the author interested in Mexican culture and history had alerted Lincoln and Grant about the possibility of Confederate soldiers regrouping in Mexico to coordinate a continuation of the war against the United States with assistance from the French and Spanish colonial powers. Now Grant authorized him to negotiate, float bonds, and recruit volunteers, but the entire project was undersubscribed. Accruing considerable financial debt, Wallace hoped to raise money by offering a book manuscript, the first of four he would write between the 1840s and 1890s, for sale to Secretary of War Stanton. This was a book on military tactics, *Light Infantry Tactics*, written and revised over the past three years. Stanton appointed a commission to evaluate the work, but the commission rejected it, and Wallace, characteristically, lashed out, so angry at the military establishment that he wrote a letter to John Bingham, a fellow judge at the trial of the Lincoln assassination conspirators and a member of the House Military Committee, demanding that he abolish West Point.[34] His mission took him to New York, Washington, and then to Mexico, where, despite being briefly incarcerated and ultimately duped by Juarez, he contributed to the ultimate expulsion of the French.[35] Wallace also managed some exploratory travel, including a visit to the Santa Eulalia mines which the following year he would describe in an article, along with sixteen of his own sketches, in *Harper's New Monthly Magazine*.[36] He also collected material for a lecture, "Mexico and the Mexicans," that he would present back in the U.S., sometimes in conjunction with a reading from *Ben-Hur: A Tale of the Christ*, and for an article on buffalo hunting that he would publish in *Scribner's* in 1879.[37]

His return home to Crawfordsville in February, 1867, brought to an end his military career. He ran unsuccessfully for Congress in 1868 and 1870. He campaigned for Grant during the general elections of 1868 and 1872 in a futile attempt at obtaining an appointment to an overseas ministry in return. The decade after the war seems to have been a decade of frustration for Wallace. By necessity Wallace made a decent living as a lawyer, but he amassed an uncomfortable amount of debt when he built his two-story house on the two acres Susan inherited from her father. But those two acres featured a particularly gorgeous beech tree the shade of which would create a pleasant ambience for Wallace when writing much of the first five books of *Ben-Hur: A Tale of the Christ*. The tree would become an early part of the *Ben-Hur* mystique.[38]

THE FAIR GOD

There are those who would like to assume that after his return home in 1867 and subsequent frustrations, Wallace purposefully called upon his natural artistic inclinations and made the conscious decision to achieve fame and fortune by writing a bestselling novel based on the calculation that Christ was the most lucrative subject, and, consequently, win the final Shiloh battle after all. We will address these assumptions more broadly in the next chapter, but this is not at all the sequence that unfolded. In his spare time Wallace first wrote two dramas, *Our English Cousin* and *Commodus*. The alternate titles of *Our English Cousin*, *The Blue and the Gray* and *Conciliated*, accurately reflect its theme of peace, which of course would also be the ultimate message of *Ben-Hur: A Tale of the Christ*, also after much suffering, struggle, and death. *Commodus*, modeled on Shakespeare's history plays, was his first effort at a story set in the Roman Empire. Neither play was ever produced, although after *Ben-Hur: A Tale of the Christ* had become a success, Harper generated additional interest and revenue by publishing *Commodus* in its monthly magazine in 1889 and, in book form, in 1897.[39]

Wallace revised *Commodus* several times, but for his next focused project he returned to the manuscript he had begun in the 1840s, which would be published as *The Fair God: or, The Last of the 'Tzins. A Tale of the Conquest of Mexico*.[40] In his autobiography the author recalls that he wrote its final four books (of seven) after the Civil War, and the

Morsbergers reckoned that Wallace completed a version of *Commodus* early in 1871 and then returned to finish the novel.[41] This would mean that he wrote two plays and more than half a novel over the course of some seven years between his return to the U.S. early in 1867 and his submission of the manuscript to Osgood & Company in early 1873. This approximately matches his production rate for writing *Ben-Hur: A Tale of the Christ*, which consists of eight books and also took seven years. However, during the former period Wallace remained in Crawfordsville for the most part and, much to his disappointment, held no public position.

In addition to the necessity of stealing hours to write, Wallace spent considerable time and energy designing, planning, and researching his projects. His contributions to his autobiography ended before he could explain in detail this part of the process of writing *Ben-Hur: A Tale of the Christ*, but we learn much from the descriptions of his relatively elaborate preparations for *The Fair God*. Beginning with Prescott's *Conquest of Mexico*, which he had read years earlier in his father's library, he studied the preface, notes, and appendix, as he explains in *An Autobiography* (1:88–9):

> As a history, how delightful it was! As a tale, how rich in attractive elements! – adventure, exploration, combat, heroisms, oppositions of fate and fortune, characters for sympathy, characters for detestation, civilization and religion in mortal issue. Who, intent upon it, could relax his inthralment [sic] long enough to splatter the narrative with doubts respecting its truthfulness? Small invention was required to develop the possibilities of the theme – tears for Montezuma, and for Cortés admiration overriding maledictions. The progression, in my hand necessarily slow, would require years and years. What matter? The subject could not tire me, neither would it leaden with monotony.

There is nothing here at the outset about coldly calculating demographic targets. At most there is only an implied concern for marketability. Wallace was at this point a commercially naïve author who, once again allowing for anachronistic embellishment, inadvertently came upon a concept for a historical novel that excited his own interest. He immediate pinpoints the elements of a narrative he considers integral to a successful story, many of the same elements he used in the novel he wrote when he was a teenager, and many of the same elements he would use in his next novel. There the adventure (the battle against the pirates, organizing rebellion against the Roman Empire), exploration (the descriptions of the desert and the pagan sanctuary of Daphne), combat (Judah vs Thord), heroisms (Judah killing one of Pontius Pilate's soldiers), oppositions of fate and fortune (of Judah, the Christ, the Sheik, Simonides, Esther, Balthasar, and Iras), characters for sympathy (mother, Tirzah, Esther), characters for detestation (Messala, Gratus, Iras), and civilization and religion in mortal issue (the advent of the Christ and Christianity) would drive the narrative and lead, to a certain extent, to the novel's acceptance as popular literature.

Then Wallace confesses that this was the methodology he learned earlier when writing *The Man-at-Arms*, adding at the end that he again knew these things instinctively despite his youth and inexperience. Now he applies his imagination to flesh out the story (1:89–90):

> It taught me that there was a deal to be done preliminarily. There was a plot to be invented for skeleton, a mass of successive incidents had to be devised and applied as flesh to the skeleton. Then there were characters to be chosen. Of the Aztecs, whom should I use? Of the Spaniards, whom? Next, how can one depict a dead people with so much as an approach to realism unless he first make himself thoroughly acquainted with them – their customs, costumes, sociology, and their political and religious systems? Of the races to figure in the plot he must have all the knowledge obtainable; so of the geography, topography, and vegetation of their country. Here, an especial need, I had to familiarize myself with a great capital city, its palaces and temples, its thoroughfares, all *à la* Venitia; otherwise how could I take a stranger in and out? In such points lie the colors, without which a historical story shall be lifeless as a cosmograph. At that time, perhaps, I could not have stated these things as they are given here; yet I saw them and felt their significance.

Finally Wallace turns from imaginative and descriptive storyteller to technical researcher and historical advisor to himself:

> Prescott is generous in the citation of his authorities. From his notes, one and another, a student can make a list of all the books upon the conquest, with the names and, in instances, biographies of their authors. I made such a list very early, and was particularly drawn to an account purporting to have been by Bernal Diaz del Castillo, one of the *conquistadores*; and it struck me that what he had to say must have a sanction by virtue of his opportunities as an eye-witness. To get his book took time; at last I had it; and then the two, Prescott and Diaz, were always within touch when needed. Later on, during sojourns in Washington, I annotated the authorities in the Congressional Library, Hervara, Sahagún, and Torquemada.[42]

He even adds a footnote to describe how he filled the flyleaves, margins, and empty spaces of his copy of Prescott with notes, including many in Spanish, which he had learned along the way.

There are many narrative and structural similarities between *The Fair God* and *Ben-Hur: A Tale of the Christ*. Both feature Wallace's solemn and authoritative third person narrative, the periodic use of the apostrophic device of addressing and guiding "the reader," and romanticizing his variegated ethnic subjects. In both novels Wallace shows considerable understanding and sympathy towards the indigenous religious beliefs he had studied and incorporates them into "a sort of religious universalism."[43] There are some parallel set pieces as well. Mualox's idyllic grotto, for instance, recalls Antioch's Daphne, and there is spectatorial combat in an arena, although these are used for very different purposes in the two novels.

Selling 7000 copies initially, *The Fair God* was sufficiently successful to encourage Wallace to begin another novel by the end of 1873.[44] However, the book created a backlash at home that provides us with a useful snapshot of Wallace's progress as a popular author and commercial innovator. This is how he recalled the period to fellow Indianan author Booth Tarkington years later:

> The publication of my first novel was almost enough to ruin my law practice. Whenever I took a case into court for a jury trial, the opposing lawyer knew that all he had to do was to mention my authorship and I was demolished... As soon as the jury of farmers and village merchants heard the word "novel" they uttered hearty guffaws... I might as well have appeared in court dressed as a circus clown.[45]

This comment demonstrates that despite the extra income his 10 percent royalty from *The Fair God* provided, it did not permanently free him from his detested legal practice. More importantly, it argues against the idea that Wallace set about writing *Ben-Hur: A Tale of the Christ* thinking that it would re-establish the honor and respect he lost at Shiloh. Similarly, his subsequent attempt at profiting from a lecture tour in New England, featuring his lecture on "Mexico and the Mexicans" followed by readings from *The Fair God*, left him quite dissatisfied, despite positive reviews and earning hundreds of dollars per appearance. Wallace told Tarkington that "a lecturer was more like a freak in the circus than a hero on the stage."[46] At least, this is the portrait his biographer McKee paints, and he suggests that Wallace's next literary project was *Commodus*, not *Ben-Hur*. He points out that *Commodus* was published in Crawfordsville at Wallace's own expense in 1876 and then reprinted the following year.[47] But Wallace's sequence of projects as described by McKee seems confused. Wallace was already working on his next novel by December, 1873. We will detail that process in the next chapter, although we first need to establish briefly Wallace's public career status during this period.

While writing *Ben-Hur: A Tale of the Christ*, Wallace would continue to busy himself with non-literary projects and take on important and time-consuming responsibilities. The former included five (extant) oil paintings as well as sketches and sculptures, and the aforementioned lecture tour to New York, Boston, and Chicago. The latter includes his service as one of the "visiting statesmen" sent to Louisiana and Florida to gain control of the White House in the wake of the disputed 1876 election. Here on the one hand Wallace demonstrated great integrity and maintained the high ground by observing that fraud had been committed by both parties, but on the other he acted as a Republican operative in making sure the initial results were reversed, thereby succeeding in advancing Rutherford Hayes towards victory.

Once Hayes took office in March, 1877, Wallace requested and expected an appointment to a foreign ministry, the reward handed out to other loyal Republican operatives who were heading off to represent the United

Figure 2.3 A postcard depicting the "venerable walls" of The Ben Hur Room in Santa Fe, then under the auspices of the American Institute of Archaeology, c. 1910.

States in such countries as France, Austria, and Russia, but none was forthcoming until 1878, when the Hayes administration offered him the position of serving as minister and Consul General to Bolivia with a salary of $5000. Not so easily dismissed, Wallace refused. He had originally hoped for Italy or Brazil. However, a few weeks later he was offered the position of serving as Governor of the Territory of New Mexico for just $2,600, and he readily accepted. Susan reluctantly agreed to follow him, although she would detest living in the desert and returned to Indiana long before his term had finished. One of Wallace's friends, the novelist Maurice Thompson, also living in Crawfordsville, worried that accepting this demanding position would prevent him from finishing his novel.[48] But the reader will understand Wallace's eagerness in accepting a domestic appointment at half the salary because, in his own words, "I had traveled in Mexico and had a desire to see the country to which I am going."[49] This meant he was returning to the frontier that during his lifetime had shifted from his back door to the Southwest, where the legendary "Wild West" was breathing its final breaths in the exploits of the Lincoln County range war, Billy the Kid, and renegade Apaches. As the Governor of the New Mexico Territory Wallace would assume a level of civil governmental authority commensurate to his age, achievements, and years of service while also indirectly controlling a significant military presence. To remain home, the only option would be "the intolerable old rut":

> The routine was simply abominable – horrible. The conduct of cases in court was all that relieved the practice. When you came in contact with good lawyers and superior minds, the collision was always full of interest and excitement. But for that I think I would just as lieve have spent so many years in the penitentiary.[50]

In early October, 1878, Lew Wallace arrived in Santa Fe, his incomplete book manuscript in hand.

NOTES

1. *An Autobiography* 1:3; M&M, 3; <http://www.math.usma.edu/people/rickey/dms/USMA-cadet-faculty.html>
2. *The Chariot* 1 (November, 1895) 1.
3. *LAT* (July 2, 1893) 23.
4. Letter from Wallace to Reverend George Baintow (November 22, 1884). *LL*
5. Mavor (trans.), *Select Lives of Plutarch*, 239; the title page heralds this as the "First American Edition."
6. Langhorne and Langhorne (trans.), *Plutarch's Lives*.
7. Philadelphia editions: J. Hoff and W. F. M'Laughlin (1803/4), Brannan and Morford (1811), Hickman and Hazzard (1822), and J. Crissy (1825). New York editions: David Huntington (1816), Samuel Campbell (1822), W. C. Borradaile (1832), Robinson, Pratt, & Co. (1835), Harper & Brothers (1836). Worcester edition: Isaiah Thomas (1804). Baltimore edition: William and Joseph Neal (1831).
8. Wallace, *An Autobiography*, 1:34; *CJ* (December 17, 1888) 4.
9. According to Monks, ed., *Courts and Lawyers of Indiana*, 393, McDonald's father died shortly after his birth in 1819; his mother remarried John Kerr and moved to Indiana in 1826.
10. Boyer, "Wallace, Zerelda Gray Sanders," 3:535–6.
11. *An Autobiography* 1:50.
12. *Indiana Magazine of History* 27.4 (December, 1931) 288–90; Hoshour, *Autobiography*.

13 Hoshour, *Autobiography*, 61–2. Cf. Foulke, *Life of Oliver P. Morton*, 1:8–9.
14 *Washington Post* (February 23, 1902) 20: "I learned Christianity at my mother's knee."
15 Rabb, *A Tour Through Indiana in 1840*, 169.
16 Latrobe, *Reminiscences of West Point*, 23–5.
17 Edward Earle (Philadelphia, 1818), T. Wardle (Philadelphia, 1835, 1840, 1845), Hogan & Thompson (Philadelphia, 1836), Harper & Brothers (New York, 1836, 1839, 1844).
18 Smith (trans.), *Thucydides*, 390.
19 Hobbes (trans.), *The History of the Grecian War*, vi–vii, xvi–xxvii, xx, xxiii, et alibi.
20 M&M 21; cf. *BG* (October 18, 1959) A24.
21 *MS* (June 16, 1863) 2; *HW* (February 25, 1905) 289.
22 *HW* (March 1, 1862) 130; (March 15, 1862) 166.
23 *New Hampshire Statesman* (May 17, 1862) 4.
24 Melville, *Battle-Pieces and Aspects of the War*, 49.
25 *HW* 6 (July 12, 1862) cover and 439.
26 *Daily Cleveland Herald* (July 11, 1862) 2; *Wisconsin State Register* (July 19, 1862) 2; *The Liberator* (July 25, 1862) 1; *Daily National Intelligencer* (July 30, 1864) 2.
27 *The Daily Cleveland Herald* (September 12, 1862) 1; *HW* (September 23, 1862) 603; *Atlantic Monthly* (February, 1863) 229–34; *Civil War History* 33 (September, 1987) 242–55.
28 Reprinted in Moore, *Rebellion Record*, 8.III.32–3.
29 Mortenson, *Lew Wallace and the Civil War*, 201–2.
30 Mckee 65.
31 Lossing, *Pictorial History*, III, 347.
32 *NYT* (July 11, 1864) 1; M&M 154.
33 M&M 193.
34 M&M 201.
35 *MS* (May 4, 1865) 2; *Daily Cleveland Herald* (July 17, 1865) 2.
36 *Harper's New Monthly Magazine* 35 (November, 1867) 681–702.
37 "A Buffalo Hunt in North Mexico," *Scribner's Monthly* 17 (March, 1879) 713–24. Rutherford, *American Authors*, 540, reports that "his brother said, 'I picked up "Scribner" and saw *A Buffalo Hunt by Lew Wallace*, and I knew that the only buffalo he had ever seen or hunted was done to death with a crayon at that County Fair in Rockville.'"
38 *Omaha World Herald* (August 15, 1902) 2.
39 *The Literary World* 7 (1876) 46–7.
40 McKee 129.
41 M&M 223, suggests that Wallace completed his two dramas after the publication of *The Fair God*.
42 *An Autobiography* 1:90.
43 M&M 226.
44 M&M 239.
45 McKee 127.
46 McKee 132.

47 McKee 130, 280.
48 Letter from Maurice Thompson to Lew Wallace (September 4, 1878), IHS; cf. M&M 256.
49 McKee 138.
50 M&M 256, n. 32.

3 "How I Came To Write Ben-Hur"

CHRONOLOGICAL CONFUSION

In 1893 Wallace published an article in *Youth's Companion*, a long-running Boston publication focusing originally on religion and juvenile issues and now expanding into the entertainment field. Titled "How I Came to Write *Ben-Hur*," this brief article of some 3,300 words offered the public Wallace's own account of the writing of *Ben-Hur: A Tale of the Christ*. A version slightly edited by his widow Susan was published in 1906 in *An Autobiography*, and a much abbreviated account served as the preface to *The First Christmas*, a small gift volume extracted from the novel and published in 1899.[1] All of these derive from the lecture Wallace gave frequently when on tour.[2] An earlier but much shorter and less specific "Gossip From Indianapolis" account by an "intimate friend" circulated in newspapers in 1883, and Wallace spoke about it briefly in a *Harper's Weekly* interview in 1886.[3] This story circulated again in 1912,[4] and Wallace gave a personal explanation with very much the same outline but not the same details in a private letter to the poet Paul H. Hayne in 1881.[5] Collectively these have served as the basis for general biographical sketches of Lew Wallace.[6] The commonality between these accounts is that in approximately 1875, Wallace wrote a short story about the three Wise Men and set it aside. At that point in his life he had "no convictions about God or Christ." Some time later, most probably in 1876, he had a disturbing encounter with Robert Ingersoll, who made such a powerful argument against the Christian faith that Wallace determined to write the novel to examine and confirm his own belief in the Christ.

Actually, Wallace worked on the novel from 1873 to 1880, but he never made this clear in any publication. In the *Youth's Companion* version of "How I Came to Write *Ben-Hur*," he stated that he worked on the novel for "more than five years."[7] The "intimate friend" in the 1883 version recalls that Wallace told him he had spent six years on the novel, apparently after the Ingersoll encounter. In *An Autobiography* (2:934) Susan corrected the amount of time spent writing the book to "more than seven years."[8] Most of these sources also variously recollect the origin, chronology, and scope of the Wise Men component of the subsequent novel and then assert that the meeting with Ingersoll was the reason Wallace wrote the novel. In doing so they fail to put the Jewish youth component into a comprehensive chronology and tacitly suggest that there was no work done on the novel prior to 1875 or even 1876. Because these accounts so emphasize the Wise Men and Ingersoll components, and because they have an autobiographical imprimatur along with a bit of self-mythologizing, they have created considerable confusion as to when Wallace began the novel and how he integrated its three separate components – the elaboration of Matthew's account of the Wise Men, the fictional narrative about a Jewish youth named Judah Ben-Hur, and the reverent retelling of the Passion of the Christ – into such a successful novel.

The Wise Men
The account included in the two longer versions of "How I Came to Write *Ben-Hur*" begins by saying that as "far back as my memory goes of things read by or to me," the brief mention of the Magi from the Book of Matthew "took a hold on my imagination."[9] Matthew 2: 1–2 is quite brief:

> Now when Jesus was born in Bethlehem of Judea, in the days of Herod the king, behold, there came wise men from the east to Jerusalem, saying, Where is He that is born King of the Jews? For we have seen His star in the east, and are come to worship Him.

Wallace's "as far back as my memory goes" may refer to a retelling he heard as a young child, but otherwise it will disagree with the later recollections in *The First Christmas* that his mother read it to him and in his autobiography (1:55–6) that Hoshour introduced him to the New Testament in his thirteenth year.

Wallace continues:

> In 1875 – the date is given from best recollection – when I was getting over the restlessness due to years of service in the War of the Rebellion, it occurred to me to write the conceptions which I had long carried in my mind of the Wise Men.

He makes clear that it was Matthew's very vagueness that inspired him many years later to specify and elaborate on their number, origins, appearance, mode of transportation, and much else, especially their pre-Christian religious tenets, the purpose of this new mission, and the divine power represented by the star they followed. In the *Youth's Companion* version of "How I Came to Write *Ben-Hur*," he explains that it was because he had no religious commitment at the time that he was capable of generating his characters' words and thoughts as if he had himself created living persons:

This was purely natural; for it is with me, presumably, as with every writer who creates as he goes. My characters are essentially living persons. They arise and sit, look, talk, and behave like themselves.

In dealing with them I see them; when they speak I hear them. I know them by their features. They answer my call. Some of them I detest. Such as I most affect become my familiars. In turn they call me, and I recognize their voices. Such being the case, I think of the society to which the serial directly admitted me!

Lastly, he tells us that he conceived the piece as a magazine submission complete with illustrations, but it was not to be part of a novel:

Well, I finished the proposed serial and deposited it in my desk, waiting for a season of courage in which to open communication with the Harpers.

In the time of writing, down to the hour I laid the manuscript by, as said, never once did the possibility of a formal book occur to me.[10]

"The Jewish Story"

The posthumous section of Wallace's autobiography (2:890–1) includes a December 21, 1873, letter written to his sister-in-law, Joanna. It was written in Washington, DC:

I spend most of my time in the library. Mr. Spofford and I are on excellent terms. He thinks I have a book in mind – not a very remarkable case of shrewdness, seeing that I have gone through everything on the shelves relating to the Jews. From the mass I selected two works indispensable to my plot. One I can duplicate in New York, the other I will have to steal, as I can get it nowhere else.

The library, he makes clear elsewhere in the letter, is the Library of Congress, which was under the directorship of Ainsworth Rand Spofford at the time. This letter confirms that Wallace was working on his new novel during a visit to the Library of Congress late in 1873. Susan (2:895) thereby clarifies the chronology, adding that "as soon as the success of *The Fair God* was assured, the author began to shape the Jewish story." *The Fair God* was published in 1873.

Wallace's arrival at the Library of Congress was particularly timely in that just three years earlier the library under Spofford's skillful guidance had embarked upon its ambitious trajectory to model itself after the great European national libraries and become the most complete library in the United States. That Spofford was director was equally fortunate for Wallace. Besides sharing a love of books and literature, Wallace and Spofford shared war experiences in Cincinnati and their zeal for the Republican Party, and both of them were Lincoln appointees. Apparently Spofford was of great assistance to Wallace's research, and although Wallace never names the "two works indispensable to my plot," it is beyond question that one of them must have been a translation of Josephus or a book heavily dependent upon Josephus, perhaps William Hepworth Dixon's *The Holy Land*, a two-volume description of various sites and traditions originally published in 1865,[11] or a map of the Holy Land, as in in *The New Biblical*

Atlas and Scripture Gazetteer published earlier in Philadelphia.[12] If we take Wallace at his word, that the focus of his research and the plot of the new book involved ancient Judaism, then these are the types of works that would have best informed and inspired him, as we shall see.

Eleven months after the letter about his work at the Library of Congress, Wallace confirms his work on a new novel, beginning a November 27, 1874, letter to his half-sister Agnes with the following:

> I have just come out of the court room, and business is over for the day. Now, for home, and a Jewish boy whom I have got into terrible trouble, and must get out of it as best I can – all in my book. In that there is a deal more pleasure than in the court room, where I am so everlastingly antagonized.
>
> As I slipped on my rubbers to come away, thinking what remained undone of the day's work, I suddenly recollected that you had sent me "Thucydides" and with it [a] letter full of pleasantries. Bless your little soul! Men love compliments better than women. The difference is, the women show their happiness, and the men keep mum – that's all.
>
> So, I acknowledge the book, the letter, and the satisfaction they gave me, honestly, and without hiding. And I give you a thousand thanks. The book I hadn't seen for twenty years, but how well I described it![13]

In addition to reconfirming and updating that he had begun work on "the Jewish story" by late 1873, this 1874 letter identifies a specific protagonist, who must be Judah Ben-Hur, and reveals that he is in "terrible trouble." That would suggest that he had already conceived of the tile incident (2.6). Perhaps he had already committed Judah to the galleys as well (3.1–3), for that happens immediately afterwards. Wallace would eventually insert the Nazareth encounter with Jesus at the well (2.7) between the tile and galley episodes, but the various accounts of "How I Came to Write *Ben-Hur*" suggest that the Christ figure had not yet been inserted into the novel in 1873–4, let alone fully integrated. We will therefore mark this as a critical insertion point and return to it later.

We will return also to the tile incident, but the reader will want to know at this point that the victim of the fallen tile was the Roman procurator Valerius Gratus, and that Josephus (*Jewish Antiquities* 18.2) is our only ancient source for the historical procuratorship of Valerius Gratus, who served between the years 15 and 26.[14] Gratus is integral to the story of the Jewish boy and the "terrible trouble" that Wallace put him into already by 1874. The historical Gratus, as well as Wallace's Gratus, replaced the Jewish high priest, and in the novel this is the catalyst that creates the quarrel between Judah Ben-Hur and Messala. Gratus' march through Jerusalem puts him in position to be hit with the tile from the Hur palace. And it is Gratus who imprisons Judah's mother and sister and confiscates the Hur property. Without Gratus there is no "terrible trouble." Without Gratus there is no plot, and Gratus is in Josephus.

The Passion of the Christ

In "How I Came to Write *Ben-Hur*," after Wallace discusses how he fleshed out the Magi story, designed it as a serial publication, and put it away indefinitely, he then comes to the Ingersoll encounter:

> If any reader before whom this confession may chance to fall will return to the volume now known as "Ben-Hur: A Tale of the Christ," and examine critically the commencement of the part designated Book Second, he cannot fail to be struck with its similitudes to the opening of a novel. Such, in fact, it was.
>
> It is possible to fix the hour and place of the first thought of a book precisely enough; that was a night in 1876. I had been listening to a discussion which involved such elemental points as God, heaven, life hereafter, Jesus Christ, and His divinity.

Here he does not specify the precise date or the central figures of the discussion, but the 1883 newspaper accounts make clear that the discussion took place between Robert Ingersoll and Wallace as they rode together on a train to Indianapolis.[15] The preface to *The First Christmas* (vi) identified the reason they were riding on the same train. They were both traveling to attend "a great mass Convention of Republicans." The same passage specifies that this was "the evening before the meeting." A simple Google search identifies the meeting as the third convention of Republican veteran soldiers – both (Major General) Wallace and (Colonel) Ingersoll had fought at Shiloh. Ingersoll was to deliver his address, "A Vision of the War," on the second day of the convention, September 21.[16] This means that their meeting took place on the evening of September 19, 1876.[17] In the preface to *The First Christmas* Wallace adds the additional detail that as he was passing by a stateroom, Ingersoll knocked from the inside to invite Wallace in for a conversation.

Robert Ingersoll, "the great Agnostic," was known for his eloquence in the service of his commitment to rational thought and opposition to the most basic concepts of Christianity. Wallace wrote of the profound impression Ingersoll made on him that evening:

> His manner of putting things was marvelous; ... I sat spellbound, listening to a medley of argument, eloquence, wit, satire, audacity, irreverence, poetry, brilliant antitheses, and pungent excoriation of believers in God, Christ, and Heaven, the like of which I had never heard.[18]

That the most adamant and persuasive proponent of agnosticism had been invited to speak to a group of Republican veterans in Indianapolis and happened to board the same train and engage Lew Wallace in conversation was no doubt serendipitous but turned out to be a profound moment in the life of the latter and for the future of American popular literature and culture.

The preface to *The First Christmas* (viii–ix) contains the most specific account of the immediate result:

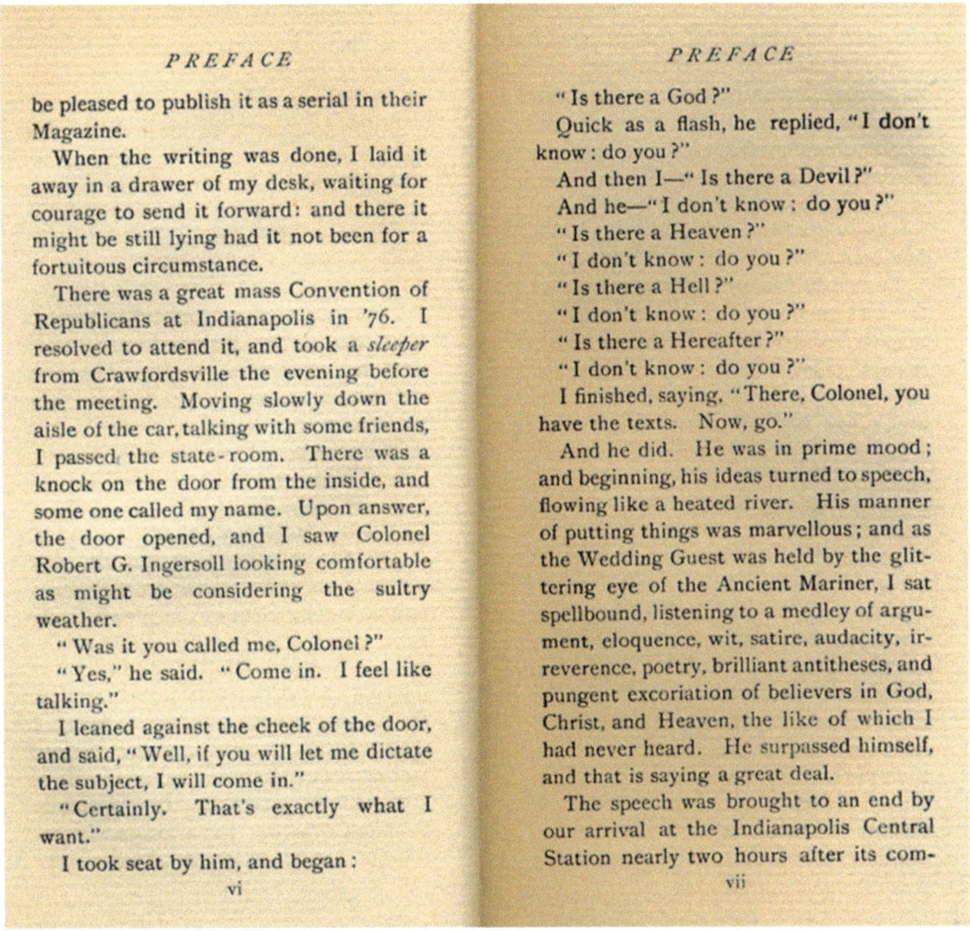

> PREFACE
>
> be pleased to publish it as a serial in their Magazine.
>
> When the writing was done, I laid it away in a drawer of my desk, waiting for courage to send it forward: and there it might be still lying had it not been for a fortuitous circumstance.
>
> There was a great mass Convention of Republicans at Indianapolis in '76. I resolved to attend it, and took a *sleeper* from Crawfordsville the evening before the meeting. Moving slowly down the aisle of the car, talking with some friends, I passed the state-room. There was a knock on the door from the inside, and some one called my name. Upon answer, the door opened, and I saw Colonel Robert G. Ingersoll looking comfortable as might be considering the sultry weather.
>
> "Was it you called me, Colonel?"
>
> "Yes," he said. "Come in. I feel like talking."
>
> I leaned against the cheek of the door, and said, "Well, if you will let me dictate the subject, I will come in."
>
> "Certainly. That's exactly what I want."
>
> I took seat by him, and began:
>
> PREFACE
>
> "Is there a God?"
>
> Quick as a flash, he replied, "I don't know: do you?"
>
> And then I— "Is there a Devil?"
>
> And he— "I don't know: do you?"
>
> "Is there a Heaven?"
>
> "I don't know: do you?"
>
> "Is there a Hell?"
>
> "I don't know: do you?"
>
> "Is there a Hereafter?"
>
> "I don't know: do you?"
>
> I finished, saying, "There, Colonel, you have the texts. Now, go."
>
> And he did. He was in prime mood; and beginning, his ideas turned to speech, flowing like a heated river. His manner of putting things was marvellous; and as the Wedding Guest was held by the glittering eye of the Ancient Mariner, I sat spellbound, listening to a medley of argument, eloquence, wit, satire, audacity, irreverence, poetry, brilliant antitheses, and pungent excoriation of believers in God, Christ, and Heaven, the like of which I had never heard. He surpassed himself, and that is saying a great deal.
>
> The speech was brought to an end by our arrival at the Indianapolis Central Station nearly two hours after its com-

Figure 3.1 The Preface to *The First Christmas* (1899) contains one of many accounts of Wallace's Ingersoll encounter.

The speech was brought to an end by our arrival at the Indianapolis Central Station nearly two hours after its commencement. Upon alighting from the car, we separated: he to go to a hotel, and I to my brother's a long way up northeast of town. The street-cars were at my service, but I preferred to walk, for I was in confusion of mind not unlike dazement.

To explain this, it is necessary now to confess that my attitude with respect to religion had been one of absolute indifference.... I had read the sermons of great preachers – Bossuet, Chalmers, Robert Hall, and Henry Ward Beecher – but always for the surpassing charm of their rhetoric. But – how strange! To lift me out of my indifference, one would think only strong affirmations of things regarded holiest would do. Yet here was I now moved as never before, and by what? The most outright denials of all human knowledge of God, Christ, Heaven, and the Hereafter which figures so in the hope and faith of the believing everywhere. Was the Colonel right? What had I on which to answer yes or no? He had made me ashamed of my ignorance: and then – here is the unexpected of the affair – as I walked on in the cool darkness, I was aroused for the first time in my life to the importance of religion. To write all my reflections would require many pages. I pass them to say simply that I resolved to study the subject. And while casting round how to set about the study to the best advantage, I thought of the manuscript in my desk. Its closing scene was the child Christ in the cave by Bethlehem: why not go on with the story down to the crucifixion? That would make a book, and compel me to study everything of pertinency; after which, possibly, I would be possessed of opinions of real value.

It only remains to say that I did as resolved, with results – *first*, the book "Ben-Hur," and, *second*, a conviction amounting to absolute belief in God and the divinity of Christ.

Neither Wallace's skill as a storyteller nor the conflicting chronological timelines puts the basic veracity of this account into question. Wallace's admission that he was never religious before the encounter, the unlikelihood of an uncommitted Christian being converted by a persuasive agnostic, and Wallace's subsequent lack of interest in Christianity other than periodically reaffirming publicly his fundamental belief in the Revelation and refusing to allow the representation of Jesus in dramatizations of his novel, not to mention the "dazement" that perhaps even the reader has encountered after a provocative conversation while in the limbo of long-distance travel, all contribute to a considerable degree of plausibility. Of equal importance for consideration by those who would question the veracity of Wallace's account, is that if Wallace were fabricating this or even exaggerating, Ingersoll, who lived until 1899, would hardly have tolerated a widely published story that his lifelong commitment to rational agnosticism had inspired the creation of one of the most popular literary icons of Christian affirmation.

ORDERING THE NARRATIVE OF *BEN-HUR*

Wallace's Account

In "How I Came to Write *Ben-Hur*" Wallace recounts the sequence of decisions he made as an author composing his novel. He says that after the Ingersoll encounter he decided to revive his short story about the Wise Men and the Nativity and employ it as the opening of his novel. For the ending, he asks rhetorically, "What could be more stupendous than the Crucifixion?"[19] Easily assigning the beginning and the ending, he then says he had difficulty filling out the period after the Nativity, lamenting the dearth of information about the childhood, adolescence, and early adult ages of Jesus.

> And here in this story there was a lapse of eighteen or twenty years – being the interval between the remarkable appearance of the Holy Child in the Temple, what time He came up to the Passover, and His reappearance a man [sic] with a mission.[20] . . . I scarcely dare tell of my travail; but after weeks of reflection, at last I decided to use the blank to show the religious and political condition of the world at the time of the coming. Perhaps those conditions would demonstrate a necessity for a Saviour.

This is one of the statements that give the impression that Wallace began his novel only after the Ingersoll encounter in 1876. It is impossible to determine whether in making this statement Wallace was being earnest, disingenuous, or simply mistaken. It may be that in Wallace's mind the inspiration for the novel actually took place only after he "became a believer in God and Christ," as he says at the end of the essay.[21] Taking him at his word then, the historical novel about the Jewish boy he had begun in 1873 provided the material that fit chronologically between the Nativity and Passion. A more cynical assessment would be that Wallace realized that his potential audience was not nearly so interested in the researched historical passages that preceded the religious inspiration that drove the later narrative portions of the novel and moved its readership as well. Whatever Wallace's thinking was in the weeks that followed the Ingersoll encounter in 1876, the interval between the birth of Jesus and his entry into Jerusalem is one of the periods Wallace would have read about in 1873 at the Library of Congress.

Next Wallace is ready to address the "constituents of the tale," and although at this point the reader might want him to clarify the chronological timeline, he says merely:

> There was no lack of incident, none of persons; only, I was hampered in the selection by the requirement to discard all which did not serve the conditions mentioned.

For the average reader this could mean that his next step was to invent the plot and its characters, but our reader knows that at least the initial stages of the plot – enough for the "Jewish boy" to be in "terrible trouble" – were already established. Wallace's language allows for this. In fact, it specifies that his task was to discard what did not belong to the newly configured design and purpose of the book.

When describing his design for *The Fair God*, Wallace had made clear that what he considered to be essential elements were "oppositions of fate and fortune, characters for sympathy, characters for detestation."[22] "How I Came to Write *Ben-Hur*" now addresses these elements in three revealing paragraphs. Here are the first two:

> Rome furnished the politics, and made the evolution of Messala easy. Save the few pearls of faith glistening on the marble steps of the Gate Beautiful in the Herodian Temple at Jerusalem, there was nowhere a suggestion of religion; out of that circumstance I wrought Ben-Hur, his mother and sister, Simonides and Esther – naming the latter after my own dear mother, departed long ago in the fairness of her youth.
>
> The commitment to the galley, the sea-fight, the chariot-race and its preceding orgies were Roman phases; just as the love marking the Hur family, the steady pursuit of vengeance by the son, and his easy conversion by Simonides to the alluring idea of the Messiah a ruler like Caesar, were Jewish.[23]

They exclusively address the original story about the Jewish boy and his Roman enemy. Wallace specifies that in this aspect of the story "there was nowhere a suggestion of religion," i.e. that the old Hebrew faith had become ineffective during the Roman occupation. The mention of the Messiah does not refer to the Christ as the Redeemer but to the concept, embraced by Judah in the final third of the novel, that the Messiah was to be a new king of the Jews whose purpose was to oust the Romans. In this sense the protagonist of *Ben-Hur: A Tale of the Christ* was very much the structural cousin of Guatamozin, the heroic warrior in *The Fair God*, who aspires to replace the ineffective Montezuma in order to drive out the Spanish invaders, making the novel Wallace began in 1873 a Judaic counterpart to *The Fair God*.[24] Guatamozin even believed in "Nature, the God Supreme," a pagan divinity parallel in cosmic scope to Judah's Old Testament god.[25]

The third paragraph then turns to the Christian aspects of the narrative:

> The derivation of what may be termed the Christian incidents is apparent. Wanting to convey a commensurate conception of the awful power underlying a miracle, I struck the mother and sister of my hero with leprosy. It was cruel, but essential. Finally, wanting a connecting thread for the whole story, but more particularly for the two periods so wide apart, that given to Christ the Child and that given to Christ the Saviour, I kept Balthasar alive to the end.

There are actually three periods. He had made clear that the Magi and Nativity material that comprise the entire Book First was originally a discrete composition, and now he identifies Balthasar as the character that connects the beginning and the end of the novel. But in doing so he discounts the entire middle – Judah, Messala, the tile incident, the galley, and the chariot race. Considering the widely promulgated presence of this account and that it appeared in print in 1883, 1893, 1899, 1906, and 1912, the reader may follow here one of the subsidiary reasons for the novel's continuing popularity. Wallace's revisionist account of the Ingersoll encounter helped to shape the collective mind of the public, molding the genesis of the novel under an aura of religious inspiration, layered upon its procreator's preliminary historical and geographical research in the Library of Congress. This is not the same as writing the book for the express purpose of profiting from the exploitation of Christ. It was a means of selling it long after publication.

Wallace's Method of Composition

Wallace's correspondence and publications as well as some anecdotal information tell us four important details about how Wallace composed his novels: (1) he wrote in sequence, (2) he could write during periods in which he was otherwise occupied with professional matters, (3) he often interrupted his major writing projects with lesser ones, and (4) he often revised extensively. All four were integral in producing the novel we know as *Ben-Hur: A Tale of the Christ*.

(1) There is no question that Wallace began the novel in Indiana in 1873

Figure 3.2 Two postcards celebrating Wallace writing on his slate board at home in Crawfordsville and "The Ben-Hur Beech," venerated as the birthplace of his famous novel.

and finished it in Santa Fe in 1880. In "How I Came to Write *Ben-Hur*" he makes this clear in his fond remembrances of writing beneath the beech tree at home in Crawfordsville and compares its allure – which he enjoys while writing this article – to that of Daphne in the novel. External sources claim that he composed the earliest parts of his novel in Indiana along the shores of Lake Maxinkuckee in Culver.[26] The *Crawfordsville Evening Journal* of June 13, 1874, provides still additional albeit indirect evidence that Wallace began writing his novel earlier than he claims in "How I Came to Write *Ben-Hur*" by reporting that Wallace was fishing on the lake on June 7 and local legend has it that he was writing "the opening chapters" at the time while staying in the southeast corner bedroom of the Allegheny House.[27] At the other end of the chronological spectrum, a letter from Wallace to A. J. Wissler in Crawfordsville, dated May 6, 1890, states specifically that the final three books were written in Santa Fe:

> Touching your inquiry whether *Ben-Hur* was written in the Old Palace of Santa Fe, I beg to say it was finished there. That is, the MS was completed at the time of the appointment to the governorship of New Mexico (1877) down to the Sixth book of the volume and I carried it with me.... When in the city, my habit was to shut myself after night in the bedroom back of the executive office proper, and write 'till after 12 o'clock. The sixth, seventh, and eighth books were the results, and the room has ever since been associated in my mind with the Crucifixion.[28]

Unfortunately Wallace does not correctly identify the year he was appointed to the governorship of New Mexico, which was in late summer, 1878.[29] This makes the rest of his recollection a bit suspect but not enough to discount the point that he began the novel in Indiana and finished it in Santa Fe. A story circulated later that Wallace at the time told

Crawfordsville reporter Frank W. Gregory that he had written the final quarter of the book while in New Mexico, probably the source for McKee (168), who wrote that three-fourths of the book had been completed before arriving in Santa Fe.[30] A vivid and romantic description of finishing the eighth and final book in the extensive conference room behind the executive office of the old adobe Governor's Palace appears near the conclusion of "How I Came to Write *Ben-Hur*":[31]

> The walls were grimy, the undressed boards of the floor rested flat upon the ground; the cedar rafters, rain-stained as those in the dining-hall of Cedric the Saxon, and overweighted by tons and tons of mud composing the roof, had the threatening downward curvature of a shipmate's cutless. Nevertheless, in that cavernous chamber I wrote the eighth and last book of *Ben-Hur*.
>
> My custom when night came was to lock the doors and bolt the windows of the office proper, and with a student's lamp, bury myself in the four soundless walls of the forbidding annex. Once there, at my rough pine table, the Count of Monte Cristo in his dungeon of stone was not more lost to the world.
>
> The ghosts, if they were ever about, did not disturb me; yet in the hush of that gloomy harborage I beheld the Crucifixion, and strove to write what I beheld.

(2) The last portion of "How I Came to Write *Ben-Hur*" focuses on Wallace's routine and making time to write despite the other demands on his schedule:

> Sometimes Ben-Hur or Simonides or Balthasar or Sheik Ilderim the Generous would call me imperiously; and there being no other means of pacifying them, I would play truant from court and clients.[32]

Then he would "block out" passages, the introductory song sung by Tirzah (2.6) providing the best example, which was "the resultant of a delayed passage from Indianapolis home."[33]

The quaint image we have of the elderly gentleman sitting underneath the beech tree in Crawfordsville with the signature chalk slate on his lap, described in *An Autobiography* and captured in an extant photograph taken by Thomas Nicholson, is an idyllic snippet that ignores the fact that the bulk of Wallace's writing was executed at night after work, stolen from time spent "blocked out on the cars 'between cities' or in the waits at lonesome stations," or tucked away next to a single lamp in the governor's palace in Santa Fe even though, as Susan wrote their son Henry, Billy the Kid had boasted, "I mean to ride into the plaza at Santa Fé, hitch my horse in front of the palace, and put a bullet through Lew Wallace."[34]

(3) In *An Autobiography* (2:895), Susan asserts:

> As with the first book, the work did not progress without frequent interruptions. He was called upon to perform many public duties, and occasionally turned aside to take up something that offered change and diversion for the time, then returning to the romance with renewed interest and energy.

This is evidenced by the many other projects he undertook during the three decades he worked on *The Fair God*. Susan writes in *An Autobiography* that Lew finished [a revision of] *Commodus* in 1876.[35] In fact, the Indiana Historical Society possesses a copy of the version he self-published in Crawfordsville that same year, which of course was also the year he encountered Ingersoll and completely redesigned his novel. A few months later he revised the play yet again.[36]

(4) There is no shortage of evidence that Wallace revised his writings extensively. *An Autobiography* tells us that during the Wirz trial he employed his leisure hours revising his book on military tactics, and *Commodus* was revised several different times over a period of twenty years.[37] A letter to Susan dated December 4, 1879, thanks her for her critique and suggestions regarding his descriptions of the Crucifixion and march to Golgotha in Book Eighth.[38]

THE COMPOSITION OF *BEN-HUR:* A TALE OF THE CHRIST

We have accumulated enough information to piece the three components together. Lew Wallace originally embarked upon a novel about a "Jewish boy," more precisely a teenager of seventeen, in 1873 shortly after he published *The Fair God*. In December, 1873, he was doing preliminary research on ancient Judaism at the Library of Congress. By November, 1874, he had written at least Book Second. This part of the story begins with a historical summary accounting for the state of political tension between the people of Judea and the Roman provincial government (2.1), and this leads directly to the quarrel between Judah and Messala (2.2), his return home to the House of Hur and the servant Amrah (2.3), and an lengthy conversation with his (nameless) mother (2.4). Before he can finish his conversation with his sister Tirzah the next day, the tile falls onto Gratus' head, so the Romans imprison the immediate family and confiscate their property (2.5–6). The third book, which involves Judah's servitude on the Roman galley, keeps him in "terrible trouble" until its sixth and final chapter, when Quintus Arrius frees Judah and adopts him as son and heir (3.1–6).

If Wallace (and/or Susan) was correct in the recollection that the Wise Men piece was written in 1875, a non-election year that would have availed Wallace of more leisure time, this would suggest that this particular "something that offered change and diversion" was set aside until an unspecified number of weeks after the encounter with Ingersoll, which took place in September, 1876. At that point, when Wallace determined to incorporate the Wise Men piece and conclude the novel with the Crucifixion, he would have begun to make some essential and distinctive revisions. The Wise Men piece now became the prequel to the rest of the novel as the entirety of Book First, in which Judah is not even mentioned. Wallace made no detectable changes to Book Second. The description of politics, the quarrel, the family of Hur, the tile incident, the imprisonment, and confiscation of the House of Hur all remained exactly the same but now the author inserted a chapter in which Jesus helps Judah by giving him water at the well in Nazareth. This is the aforementioned critical insertion point, and it is the only completely non-New Testament event in the entire novel in which Jesus participates (2.7). Similarly, Wallace kept Book Third the same but into its final chapter he inserted a brief passage to echo the Jesus passage inserted at the end of Book Second. Here it is the Roman Quintus Arrius who helps Judah, and Judah remarks (3.6):

> "In the three years of my servitude, O tribune, thou wert the first to look upon me kindly. No, no! There was another." The voice dropped, the eyes became humid, and he saw plainly as if it were then before him the face of the boy who helped him to drink by the old well at Nazareth. "At least," he proceeded, "thou wert the first to ask me who I was."

It would be interesting to know for certain whether this parallel between Jesus and Arrius was the result of the retrofit after 1876. Elsewhere Arrius does not bear any Christ-like imagery or perform other appropriate charitable actions. His adoption of Judah is a Roman act, not a Christian one.

Book Fourth brings Judah back to the East, where he meets Simonides and Esther, hears that his mother and sister are "lost," and tries to lose himself in the Grove of Daphne (4.1–6). All this could have been written before the Ingersoll encounter, as could the following chapter reintroducing Messala and introducing the anti-Roman Sheik Ilderim (4.7). But much of the rest of Book Fourth must have been heavily revised after the Ingersoll encounter, and it may be that this is the point in the "Jewish story" Wallace had reached by late 1876, three years after he had commenced the project. It is here that Wallace, working in sequence, not only appends to the original story but begins to integrate the various components more extensively than mere attachments and insertions would accomplish. He reintroduces Balthasar and connects his message about the new king, not to mention his alluring daughter Iras, to the rest of the narrative, working them into the chariot race as well as the anti-Roman actions planned by Simonides, the Sheik, and Judah. Wallace makes this connection by inventing the detail that Balthasar had been the guest of Ilderim at the time of the Nativity to escape from the wrath of Herod (4.10), and this enables Wallace to have Balthasar serve as the conduit to announce to all three of them that the new king is arriving. Like the insertions into the end of the second and third books, the fourth book ends with a series of three chapters devoted to Balthasar introducing Judah to the story of the Nativity (4.15), Balthasar's belief that the child of the Nativity should now be ready to embark upon his mission as the new King of the Jews (4.16), and Judah's commitment to follow this new king (4.17). In fact, in 4.15 Wallace advises the reader that Christ will now become increasingly integral to the story.

And now there is wanting an explanation which the very discerning may have heretofore demanded; certainly it can be no longer delayed. Our tale begins, in point of date not less than fact, to trench close upon the opening of the ministry of the Son of Mary, whom we have seen but once since this same Balthasar left him worshipfully in his mother's lap in the cave by Bethlehem. Henceforth to the end the mysterious Child will be a subject of continual reference; and slowly though surely the current of events with which we are dealing will bring us nearer and nearer to him, until finally we see him a man – we would like, if armed contrariety of opinion would permit it, to add – A MAN WHOM THE WORLD COULD NOT DO WITHOUT.

Book Fifth is similar in that it focuses on Messala, the chariot race, the anti-Roman rebellion, and all the various strands of the "Jewish boy" story in fourteen of its sixteen chapters but integrates chapters showcasing Iras's "Song of Egypt" (5.3) and Simonides' numerous citations of Old Testament prophecies of the coming of the new king (5.8).

If the sixth, seventh, and eighth books were written in Santa Fe from the fall of 1878 to early in 1880 at the latest, which was two to three-plus years after the Ingersoll encounter, they demonstrate a renewed Christian vigor thoroughly integrated with all three components of the narrative. Five of the eighteen chapters belong to the original "Jewish story" in that they derive from Josephus and place Judah within the anti-Roman rebellion in the third decade described by Josephus (6.1, 6.6, 7.1, 8.5, 8.7). Even some of these chapters integrate the story of Judah with the story of the Christ by tempering Judah's anti-Roman hatred with the Christ's message of peace. Four of the chapters focus on Balthasar and his daughter Iras, connecting the final books with the first (7.2–4, 8.6). Six focus on the leprosy afflicted by the Romans upon Judah's mother and sister (6.2–5, 8.3–4), although they are cured by the Christ. And six focus directly on the passion of the Christ (6.3, 7.5, 8.2, 8.8–10), to most of which the "Jewish boy" is an eyewitness and even participant. Wallace concluded by integrating aspects of the three major narrative components in the final two chapters. In the penultimate chapter, Iras mocks Jesus and threatens Judah, on behalf of Messala, to report his murder of Pilate's centurion to Sejanus. In the final chapter, the Christ is crucified, Balthasar dies, and Judah learns of Messala's death and reunites with his family, ultimately leaving his entire estate for Christianity to "supersede the Caesars."

WALLACE AND HIS SOURCES

Josephus

Josephus would have provided Wallace with an abundance of material about ancient Judaism, much of which colors the novel. Wallace's identifications of Jews as belonging to the Pharisee, Sadducee, or Essene sects, for instance, stem directly from Josephus.[39] As we will see, the relevant passage in *The Jewish War* (2.119) was particularly important for Wallace because it also introduced him to the Essene Zealot, Judas of Galilee.[40] Judah Ben-Hur himself was one of the aristocratic Sadducees, as Messala tells us (2.2). This made him one of those who believed in human free will and the mortality of the soul, which made Judah's ultimate conversion all the more challenging. Its impact on the core plot of the novel and characterization of Judah is incalculable. The Sadducees maintained that the "eye for an eye" passages in the Old Testament justified physical retaliation for personal injury.[41] Wallace would have read this in William Whiston's 1737 English translation of *The Works of Flavius Josephus*, which warranted multiple editions and printings in the United States in the nineteenth century (*The Jewish War* 2.163–6):

> But the Sadducees ... take away fate entirely, and suppose that God is not concerned in our doing or not doing what is evil; and they say, that to act what is good, or what is evil, is at men's own choice, and that the one or the other belongs so to every one, that they may act as they please.[42]

Indeed, the premeditated, planned, and unapologetic vengeance Judah unleashes on Messala in the chariot race might have become one of the most iconic passages in American popular culture, except that it is so powerful that subsequent versions of the race usually modify it extensively by eliminating it or making Messala the aggressor. Wallace encapsulates this concept in one of Judah's most memorable lines, preserved intact or adapted in all the major versions of *Ben-Hur* that would follow on stage and on the screen: "O Lord, in the hour of thy vengeance, *mine* be the hand to put it upon him!"

The Sadducee tradition embraced what would otherwise be viewed as an illegal and villainous act by Judah. Simonides, the servant to the wealthy House of Hur, gives the justification (4.4):

> Tell me not, as the preachers sometimes do – tell me not that vengeance is the Lord's. Does he not work his will harmfully as well as in love by agencies? Has he not his men of war more numerous than his prophets? Is not his the law, Eye for eye, hand for hand, foot for foot? Oh, in all these years I have dreamed of vengeance, and prayed and provided for it, and gathered patience from the growing of my store, thinking and promising, as the Lord liveth, it will one day buy me punishment of the wrong-doers? And when, speaking of his practise with arms, the young man said it was for a nameless purpose, I named the purpose even as he spoke – vengeance!

After the race Wallace has Judah make a personal declaration of vengeance, specifying that it is a non-Christian, particularly Jewish concept (5.16):

> Whereas, in that, he had been the victim of violences done to him, henceforth he was to be the aggressor. Only yesterday he had found his first victim! To the purely Christian nature the presentation would have brought the weakness of remorse. Not so with Ben-Hur; his spirit had its emotions from the teachings of the first lawgiver, not the last and greatest one. He had dealt punishment, not wrong, to Messala. By permission of the Lord, he had triumphed.

Josephus wrote an autobiography (*Life*), which was also available in Whiston's translation. There Josephus recounts how he served as a military commander in the great anti-Roman rebellion of 66–71, became a Roman prisoner, was released, and ultimately became a Roman citizen. He describes as well his own teenage search for religious and political affiliation (he became a Pharisee), the great shipwreck he survived on his way to Rome, and the indirect influence he had at the imperial court of Caesar through Nero's wife, Poppaea. Sources of inspiration and chains of influence are always difficult to confirm, but the reader should at least consider that Wallace would have read all this with great interest and that it is not mere coincidence that Judah Ben-Hur would have many of these same experiences. If it should seem implausible that Judah could be arrested for committing an anti-Roman act of violence and then not only be set free but made a Roman citizen, not to mention put in a position of influence, then Josephus's own life provides the historical model.

Josephus was a product of Hellenistic Judaism, which meant that he introduced Wallace to his particular synthesis of Greek philosophy and Jewish theology as well as his comparisons between Jewish, Hellenic, and Roman culture. The latter will be the central topic of the extended discussion Judah has with his mother over the course of two consecutive chapters before their arrest by the Romans (2.4–5):

> But was the Hellene the first to deny the old barbaric faith? No. My son, that glory is ours; against brutalism our fathers erected God; in our worship, the wail of fear gave place to the Hosanna and the Psalm. So the Hebrew and the Greek would have carried all humanity forward and upward.

Ultimately Josephus argued as the thesis of his lesser-known treatise *Against Apion* that Jewish philosophy and culture was older and superior to the Hellenic, and far older and superior to the Roman. This is the same argument Judah and his mother will make by the end of their discussion early in the novel and will lead, of course, to the triumph of Christianity at the conclusion of the novel.

As the author of *The Jewish War*, Josephus would have provided Wallace with accounts of a number of actual historical events as well as descriptions of religious concepts, political movements, and diplomatic relations between the ancient Romans and Hebrews. Josephus (*The Jewish War* 2.9.2) described the historical event in which the Jerusalemites wake up one morning in the year 26 to find that the newly installed Roman procurator, Pontius Pilate, had ordered troops to bring into the city by stealth of night a number of ensigns – imperial images which represented a sacrilege to the Jewish population. After a five-day protest in which the Jerusalemites offered their lives instead of compromise, Pilate ultimately relented and removed the ensigns. Wallace involves Judah in this very incident (6.1). Later in the novel and at the very end of Book Sixth (6.6), just after Judah learns the sad fate of his mother and sister and thinks all is lost, he learns that Pilate has appropriated sacred monies from the temple treasuries to build an aqueduct. This, too, comes from Josephus (*The Jewish War* 2.9.4), who says that when the Jews protested this particular outrage, Pilate ordered Roman soldiers to disguise themselves as locals, infiltrate the crowd, and create a riot. Wallace recreates this part of Josephus's account, too, and then he brings it to a climax by having his protagonist hero Judah fight a victorious and impressive duel against one of the Romans. The crowd of Galileans who watch this duel are impressed and find Judah worthy of being the leader of their anti-Roman rebellion. Bringing Book Sixth to a close, Wallace has the victorious Judah exhort these Galileans to gather with him that night at Bethany and then concludes in his typical third person narrative style: "In such manner Ben-Hur obtained hold on Galilee, and paved the way to greater services in the cause of the King Who Was Coming." Wallace then immediately begins the Book Seventh (7.1) with Judah raising three legions among the Galileans.

Of course, Lew Wallace had several times in his military career "raised legions," that is, recruited Indianans to fight at the onset of both the Mexican and Civil Wars and mustered the riflemen of Ohio to the defense of Cincinnati in 1862. But for Judah Ben-Hur to raise legions of Galileans revisits what Wallace could have read in Josephus's account of an earlier but significant episode in the history of Roman Judea. There (*Jewish Antiquities* 18.4) around the year 6 or 7, after the Emperor Augustus terminated the local rule of Herod's son Archelaus, he entered Judea [Iudaea] into the Roman provincial system for the first time and had his legate (governor) Cyrenius hold a census for tax purposes. Decrying this as a political, religious, and financial affront, the Zealot Judas of Galilee – known also as Judas of Gamala, or Judas the Galonite – led a massive revolt against the Romans, proclaiming messages of freedom and making, as Josephus says, "continuous wars." This armed anti-Roman rebellion described by Josephus might otherwise have gone unnoticed by Wallace, and it therefore would not have made any impact on the plot formulation of *Ben-Hur: A Tale of the Christ* were it not for its presence in the Gospel of Luke and Gibbon's lengthy and pointed discussion of it.

Luke (2: 1–2) says:

> It happened that in those days a decree was issued by the Emperor Augustus that the whole world should be enrolled. This was the first enrollment made when Cyrenius [Quirinius] was governor of Syria.

None of the other evangelists mention this census. On the contrary, Matthew (2: 1) dates the birth of Christ during the reign of Herod, who died probably in 4 BC – some nine or ten years earlier. For an author who commences his novel with the Nativity and concerns himself with historical accuracy, this is a critical problem, as it continues to be for many scholars of the New Testament. The Matthew passage immediately precedes the Wise Men passage Wallace cites in "How I Came to Write *Ben-Hur*," and yet three times in his novel he also refers to the rebellion of Judas of Galilee against Cyrenius.[43] The first two passages in which Judas is mentioned are in connection with Joseph and Mary as they pass through Jerusalem on their way to Bethlehem "to be counted for taxation, as ordered by Caesar" (1.8). Rabbi Samuel, a fictitious acquaintance, asks Joseph, "What are the Zealots doing down in Galilee?" Joseph declines to engage in a political conversation, but then after Samuel asks Joseph if he is comfortable with paying tax to anyone but Jehovah and equates paying it to the Romans with "submission to tyranny," he asks: "Tell me, is it true that Judas claims to be the Messiah? You live in the midst of his followers." Joseph does respond to this with, "I have heard his followers say he was the Messiah." Once Samuel breaks off, a nameless stranger says to Joseph: "Rabbi Samuel is a zealot. Judas himself is not more fierce." Later in the novel, at the aforementioned critical insertion point where Judah will meet Jesus in Nazareth for the first time (2.7), Wallace describes the locals as less than friendly towards the Romans because of their regional association with Judas:

> Nazareth, it must be remembered, was not only aside from any great highway, but within the sway of Judas of Gamala; wherefore it should not be hard to imagine the feelings with which the legionaries were received.

At some point in his preliminary research Wallace no doubt came across Gibbon's discussion of this same passage in Josephus, particularly in that it is found in Gibbon's initial chapter on Christianity (1.16), "The Conduct of the Roman Government Towards the Christians, from the Reign of Nero to that of Constantine." Here Gibbon discusses the earliest non-biblical passage to mention the Christ, an essential source for identifying the historicity of Jesus and his crucifixion. The author of this passage is Tacitus, and the passage (*Annals* 15.44) includes the Christians because it is they that the Emperor Nero blamed for the great fire in Rome in the year 64. Gibbon argues that the Christians were relatively unknown in Rome at the time and that it was therefore unlikely that Nero would have originally pinpointed them as the culprits. Much better known and blameworthy, Gibbon argues, were the Jews, who were omnipresent in Rome and politically troublesome in their homeland. But Jews had influence over some of the most important people in Rome, not the least of which was Poppaea Sabina, the wife of Nero. Gibbon derived this bit of imperial gossip from the aforementioned autobiography of Josephus (13), who adds that he had himself received gifts from the empress. Gibbon continues:

> In their room it was necessary to offer some other victims, and it might easily be suggested that, although the genuine followers of Moses were innocent of the fire

of Rome, there had arisen among them a new and pernicious sect of Galilaeans, which was capable of the most horrid crimes. Under the appellation of Galilaeans, two distinctions of men were confounded, the most opposite to each other in their manners and principles; the disciples who had embraced the faith of Jesus of Nazareth, and the zealots who had followed the standard of Judas the Gaulonite. The former were the friends, the latter were the enemies, of human kind; and the only resemblance between them consisted in the same inflexible constancy, which, in the defense of their cause, rendered them insensible of death and tortures.

In other words, in their desire to be free of Roman rule, Galileans chose either to follow Jesus of Galilee and the path of peace, or Judas of Galilee and the path of war. Wallace seems to have incorporated Gibbon's insightful demarcation into his novel as its fundamental political division, that between those whose opposition to Rome will lead them to the Christ (Balthasar, Amrah, mother, Tirzah) and those whose opposition to Rome will lead them to war (Judah, Simonides, Sheik Ilderim). Above all, this is Judah's most critical dilemma and drives the plot of the finished novel from beginning to end. Of course if we are to take Wallace at his word in "How I Came to Write *Ben-Hur*," it would have been primarily the latter sect of Galileans that interested him initially in 1873. But this passage in Gibbon speaks directly to the same character and events addressed by Josephus, one of the two books "indispensable to my plot." And even without embracing Christ, the author has here an important historical opposition setting the individual adventures of the "Jewish boy" into a larger political construct much like the opposition in *The Fair God* between the Aztecs and Conquistadors.

To establish this fundamental division, Wallace begins the second book, which he describes as similar to "the opening of a novel," with a chapter (2.1) describing the political situation in Judea. It begins twenty-one years after the Nativity, and recounts the intervening period – the death of Herod, the dismissal of Archelaus, the annexation of Judea into the province of Syria, and the appointment of an imperial legate, who resides in the provincial capital Antioch, and a procurator, who resides in Caesarea. In this "rain of sorrows," the only consolation for the Jews was that their high priest still occupied the Herodian palace in Jerusalem. But the first act of the new procurator was to replace the favored high priest Hannas. This new procurator was Valerius Gratus.

(Inevitably Wallace confronted chronological problems here, but his solutions were all within the parameters of poetic license that allow for the conflation of events and the compression of time. Valerius Gratus served as procurator from 15 to 26, and he appointed Ishmael to replace Ananus in 15/16, and then Eleazar one year later. Ishmael's appointment is the subject of disagreement in Judah's argument with Messala, and Judah is arrested that same day, which, if he were to place him in recorded history, could not have been later than the year 16. According to Wallace's novel, Judah, age seventeen, was sent to the galleys immediately and returned to the East eight years later. That would move the story forward to the year 24, but the historical Tiberius replaced Gratus with Pontius Pilate in 26, and there is no two-year gap between Judah's return to the province of Syria and his victory over Messala in the chariot race. That takes just over one week, and the chariot race takes place thirty days before Pilate's arrival, as Wallace makes clear at the outset of Book Sixth. Nonetheless, Wallace says that the date of the opening of Book Fourth, which brings Judah back to Antioch, was July, 29. But this creates another discrepancy, for Josephus suggests that Pilate brought the imperial ensigns into Jerusalem shortly after his arrival in 26.)

Our only ancient source for Gratus, who, appointed by Tiberius as procurator in the year 15, ruled for eleven years before Tiberius replaced him with Pontius Pilate, is Josephus. Josephus (*Jewish Antiquities* 18.2, 6) records that Gratus deposed Ananus [Wallace's Hannas], replaced him soon after with Ishmael, then Eleazar, then Simon, and finally Ananus's son-in-law Joseph Caiaphas, well known for the role he played, along with Ananus (e.g. John 18: 19–23), in the trial and interrogation of Jesus. This was sufficient information for Wallace's narrative imagination; he finishes this first chapter by saying that one month after Ishmael took office, Gratus found it necessary to visit him in Jerusalem, bringing with him a new cohort of legionaries (as did Wallace in Memphis, Cincinnati, and Baltimore.) The angry mob in Jerusalem shouts in protest (2.6):

"Robber, tyrant, dog of a Roman! Away with Ishmael! Give us back our Hannas!"

The ensuing tile incident and wounding of Gratus, Judah's imprisonment, the leprosy contracted by his mother and sister, and even the chariot race would eventuate because of this visit, and it might be the rebellions quelled by the historical Gratus (Josephus *The Jewish War* 2.5.3) that reappear in the novel as the rebellion prepared by the Sheik, Simonides, and Judah in Book Seventh.

For almost the entirety of the novel Judah, like Judas of Galilee, determines to become a soldier and make war on Rome. (Wallace's first two novels had featured soldiers as well.) The reader sees this right from the introduction of the teenage Judah and Messala (2.2). Seeing each other for the first time in five years, they almost immediately begin to quarrel about Roman rule in Judea. The first sentence out of Judah's mouth is political: "Did you not say the new procurator is to arrive tomorrow?" Messala, who is purportedly the grandson of the historical Messala mentioned by Josephus (*Jewish Antiquities* 14.324), responds that just the previous night he heard his father confirm that fact to the new high priest Ishmael. The discussion rapidly moves to Judah's objections to Ishmael's appointment and Roman superiority and oppression. Messala recalls the Luke and Josephus passages mentioning Judas when he boasts, "I will succeed Cyrenius, and you – shall share my fortune . . . When I am prefect, with Judea to enrich me, I – will make you high-priest."[44] Now angry, Judah, warns Messala that Judea has had masters before the Romans and has outlived them all. Parrying with a different offer, Messala professes his fondness for Judah by suggesting that he become a soldier, adding, ironically, that Rome is "ready to help you." As the chapter comes to an end, Judah bids a tearful yet angry farewell, refusing Messala's hand, eliciting Messala's declaration of war: "Be it so. Eros is dead, Mars reigns!" Judah seeks consolation at home with the faithful servant Amrah (2.3) and his mother (2.4–5), who agree that that unlike the Greeks and Hebrews, the Romans exceed all other cultures only in obtaining power through warfare, leading to his mother's final advice, to "serve the Lord, the Lord God of Israel, not Rome." Beginning their conversation Judah asks (2.4), "What am I to be?" And bringing these chapters to an end (2.5), the conversation concludes with:

> "I may be a soldier then?" Judah asked.
> "Why not? Did not Moses call God a man of war?"
> There was then a long silence in the summer chamber.
> "You have my permission," she said, finally; "if only you serve the Lord instead of Caesar."

After we are introduced to Tirzah in the next chapter (2.6), Judah announces to her that he will become a soldier trained by the Romans. He will even fight for Rome "if, in return, she will teach me how one day to fight against her." Judah is only seventeen, and this is the only goal he has ever professed.

Just as he says this, the procession bringing Gratus through the city has begun, and by the end of the hour Judah and his family will all be in a Roman prison. If we fast-forward through the desert to the galley sequences (where Judah tells Arrius he wants to train as a Roman soldier [3.3]) to the chariot race, we arrive at the point in the story where Judah finds out that his mother and sister are lepers and he engages in armed combat against Pilate's disguised troops and raises three legions. Despite the relatively reserved and genteel impression the character of Judah may leave on millions of playgoers and moviegoers, in the novel he is a rebel involved in a conspiracy, and, so far as the Roman provincial government is concerned, an assassin. Fortunately Wallace inserted all the intervening material into his novel – the galley sequence and adoption by Arrius, the love interests Esther and Iras, and, of course, the antagonism with Messala and the chariot race. But it is clear that in structuring his novel Wallace created in Judah Ben-Hur a Jewish militant who, until he finally comes to understand the purpose of Christ's mission on earth, develops as an anti-Roman patriot. Judah Ben-Hur is not entirely modeled after Judas of Galilee, nor is he simply a conflation of Judas and the historical Josephus. Wallace fills Judah's life with much more than Josephus tells us about the life of Judas, and, unlike Josephus, Judah is a wealthy Jerusalem aristocrat, son of a prince, who becomes a Roman heir of consular rank. But Gibbon's discussion of Josephus and his sharp division between the peaceful and militarized anti-Roman parties seems to have led Wallace in this direction and provided a remarkable template for the imaginative author.

Edward Gibbon

Edward Gibbon's *The History of the Decline and Fall of the Roman Empire* was published in several volumes in the 1770s and 1780s, and a century later during Wallace's lifetime it still provided the standard account of the fall of the Roman Empire. As the reader knows, Wallace's father had instilled in his son an interest in this historiographical monument. Gibbon's controversial claim that the promise of a Christian paradise in the hereafter enervated the Roman Empire's civic and military spirit would have provided Wallace with an authoritative historical rationale for his own argument that Christianity replaced the spiritual bankruptcy of the ancient Romans. In the novel Balthasar several times explains this concept to Judah Ben-Hur (6.3):

> "Let me try, O son of Hur," he said, directly, "and help you to a clear understanding of my belief; then it may be, seeing how the spiritual kingdom I expect him to set up can be more excellent in every sense than anything of mere Caesarean splendor, you will better understand the reason of the interest I take in the mysterious person we are going to welcome."

and it inspired the final sentence of the finished novel:

> Out of that vast tomb Christianity issued to supersede the Caesars.

Messala, of course, who drinks, gambles, steals, and displays a profound disregard for both the law and common decency (and whose ancestor is mentioned in Gibbon's first volume [I.17]), represents the heartless imperialism of the Roman Empire. More will be said about Wallace's Messala below, but this sentence, the last of Chapter 7 of Book Fourth, demonstrates the point, particularly in the use of the word "imperialized":

> ... above all, by the expression of the cold, sharp, eagle features, imperialized in his countrymen by sway of the world through so many generations, Ben-Hur knew Messala unchanged, as haughty, confident, and audacious as ever, the same in ambition, cynicism, and mocking insouciance.

Bede and the Wise Men

Wallace recollected that he wrote the Wise Men piece in 1875, that is, after visiting the Library of Congress and well after he had commenced work on his novel about the Jewish boy. The detailed descriptions of the desert geography and the information he gives about the Greek, Hindu, and Egyptian belief systems probably resulted from his research, as did Joseph's conversation about the Zealots as the political leanings of his novel's Jewish protagonist began to take shape. It is apparent that by 1875 Wallace had exchanged his keen and long-standing interest in Mexico for another in the religions and cultural clashes in the ancient Levant.

In "How I Came to Write *Ben-Hur*" Wallace tells us that he used an additional pre-modern source, the medieval English scholarly monk often referred to as the Venerable Bede:

> So I wrote, commencing with the meeting in the desert, numbering and naming the three upon the authority of the dear old tradition-monger, Father Bede, and ending with the birth of the Child in the cave by Bethlehem.[45]

None of Bede's extant works contains the names of the three Magi Balthasar, Gaspar, and Melchior, but the names can be found in an anonymous treatise included in the Bede corpus, which employs the spelling Balthasar, not the more common "Balthazar."[46] This relatively obscure work might have been difficult for Wallace to access as a primary source, but nineteenth-century reference works contained the information and attributed it to Bede.[47] Bede himself does briefly mention the Nativity in his *Ecclesiastical History of the English Nation* (5.16), where he continues the earlier medieval tradition that the Nativity took place in a cave in or near Bethlehem.

In writing his novel, Wallace delved more deeply than the popular tradition would have demanded. In following Bede here, Wallace rejected the most familiar and easily accessible source – the New Testament, namely, Luke 2:7, which says simply that Mary "laid him in a manger because there was no room in the inn." Similarly, Wallace seems to have been inspired by the substantial body of scholarship that has supplemented Matthew's lack of specificity about the geographical and ethnic origins of the Wise Men who came "from the east." In antiquity, for instance, Tertullian determined that these "magician astronomers" were kings, perhaps from Arabia, while John Chrysostom placed them in Persia.[48] In the fourteenth century John of Hildesheim assigns them to India, Chaldea, and Persia.[49] By the nineteenth century in some accounts they represented the three races of the three continents – Europe, Asia, and Africa.[50] This was often the tradition followed by classic European painters, which would have interested the artist in Wallace, but he develops this tradition in a unique way. He never refers to them as kings, they bear no physical resemblance to the tradition passed down in the pseudo-Bede passage, and, unlike any other author, he assigns Melchior to India, Gaspar to Greece, and Balthasar to Egypt. Much of the novel is filled with ancient names, events, and concepts as well as specific details about objects, materials, and geography, all the result of his dedicated research. Compared to that, however, his lengthy and detailed description of the Wise Men in Book First (1.2–5) was not confined to the results of his research but the product of an author wishing to develop Matthew's sketchy sentences into a broader statement on ethnic characteristics, philosophy, and religion. Because we know that Wallace originally wrote this portion of the novel separately, it is no surprise to find a different authorial purpose here. Of course the style of proto-Christian sentiment espoused by Balthasar later in the novel was no doubt later adjusted into a revised version of Book First to make the novel more uniform in its theology. But the religious thought in Book First depends predominantly on the underlying concept of universalism, very much the same theology Wallace espoused in *The Fair God*.[51]

Wallace prepared himself to describe accurately the ethnic heritage of his three Wise Men. Wallace's Greek Caspar speaks of – without naming Plato – the Platonic concept of the immortality of the soul and a single God, no doubt Aristotle's Supreme or Unmoved Mover, a physical concept that over the next two millennia took on theological applications. In an effort to incorporate the ancient Greek religion best known through its attendant myths, he cites a god named Theus who lives on Olympus. The name Theus is a rarity, perhaps even a hapax, that suggests that Wallace may have tried to transliterate the Greek word for god (*theos*) by replacing the Greek masculine suffix -*os* with the Latin noun suffix -*us*. Normally the Latin word "deus" is used. Whatever his methodology, his use of the word *theos* in any form suggests that he had read about the Stoic concept of god (*theos*). Indeed, there is little doubt about this since he invents a lineage for Gaspar, naming his father Cleanthes. Cleanthes was the Stoic philosopher who believed, appropriately for Wallace's Gaspar, in the immortality of the soul. His extant "Hymn to Zeus" addresses a pantheistic Zeus who represents the greatest power in a rational universe, and this kind of Hellenic divinity is that which Wallace describes in his description of Gaspar's understanding of the nature of god.[52] Also, when listing examples of Greek philosophers, Josephus (*Against Apion* 2.135) lists three – Socrates, Zeno, and Cleanthes. That Wallace used the name Cleanthes again as the name of the Athenian charioteer is curious, perhaps even an oversight.

Melchior the Hindu cites such major works of Sanskrit literature as the Vedas and Mahabarata, briefly mentions the gods Brahma, Vishnu, and Shiva, and then describes the caste system. Balthasar the Egyptian refers to the pure natural religion of Mizraim (the Hebrew name for Egypt) and laments its corruption by a series of foreign influences, first dividing the Supreme One into the familiar divinities (Amon-Re, Isis, Osiris), then into animistic spirits (water, fire, air), and abstract concepts (strength, knowledge, love). This degradation was halted by the god of the Hebrew slaves, who revealed himself to the Egyptians with the well-known plagues. To collect these ancient names and theological concepts under the umbrella of religious universalism, Wallace invents the story that Gaspar rescued a Jew thrown overboard from a ship and learned of the true god and second coming from him. He portrays all three as outcasts or hermits, Gaspar living on the slopes of Olympus, Melchior in the Himalayas, and Balthasar abandoning Alexandria for the villages up the Nile "preaching One God, a righteous life, and reward in Heaven." But at the end of the chapters describing the initial meeting of the Wise Men, Wallace shifts from pantheism to Christian prophecy by attributing, or more probably inserting in 1876, a statement by Balthasar to proclaim that the new god may have been announced as King of the Jews, but he is to be the Redeemer of all nations (1.5):

> "I said there was a purpose in the particularity with which we described our people and their histories," so the Egyptian proceeded. "He we go to find was called 'King of the Jews'; by that name we are bidden to ask for him. But, now that we have met, and heard from each other, we may know him to be the Redeemer, not of the Jews alone, but of all the nations of the earth."[53]

Thucydides

In his November, 1874, letter to Agnes, immediately after telling her about the "Jewish boy," Wallace thanks her for sending him the copy of Thucydides which he has not seen in twenty years but "described" well. This must have been the aforementioned copy his father had owned and, as recollected in *An Autobiography*, made such an impression on young Wallace. Even though Thucydides wrote about an era (the fifth century BC) and area (Greece) not immediately relevant to Wallace's plot, in the finished novel the fulsome praise for the Hellenic genius that Judah and his mother discuss in the aforementioned passage comparing the glories of the Greeks, Romans, and Jews certainly could have been inspired by Thucydides, particularly where his mother praises Greek liberty, thought, rhetoric, and the pursuit of excellence (2.5):

> The sway of the Greek was a flowering time for genius. In return for the liberty it then enjoyed, what a company of thinkers the Mind led forth? There was a glory for every excellence, and a perfection so absolute that in everything but war even the Roman has stooped to imitation. A Greek is now the model of the orators in the Forum; ... So it happens, O my son, that of the whole world our Israel alone can dispute the superiority of the Greek, and with him contest the palm of original genius.

The last sentence again expresses Josephus's thesis of Jewish superiority represented in *Against Apion*, but the praise of Greece seems to be Wallace's condensation of the best-known passage in Thucydides, Pericles' funeral oration (2.34–46). This was the same passage cited and echoed at the dedication of the National Cemetery at Gettysburg on November 19, 1863, by Edward Everett (former Professor of Greek at Harvard) and Abraham Lincoln. Even when discussing the Jewish god or the Christ, Wallace never uses such a concentration of words like "genius ... glory ... excellence ... perfection ... model ... superiority," and this reflects the essence of Pericles' famed speech in which he praises

Athens as a superior and free city, a model of excellence to be admired and imitated.[54]

THE MAIN CHARACTERS

The House of Hur

Very near the end of "How I Came to Write *Ben-Hur*," Wallace adds as a penultimate afterthought:

> The name Ben-Hur was chosen because it is Biblical, and easily spelled, printed, and pronounced.[55]

This means that he was searching simply for a personal name, preferably from the Old Testament, that was not excessively polysyllabic, or filled with unfamiliar phonemes, consonantal clusters, or vowel combinations. It suggests that Wallace's criteria for the selection of names, even the name of his protagonist, was dictated by not specific chronological historicity but general appropriateness, euphony, and accommodation to the popular culture.

Hur is an appropriate monosyllabic Old Testament name, of which there are not very many. But Hur was also appropriate in that in Exodus (17: 10–12) Hur was one of the prominent leaders among the Hebrews, named third after Moses and his brother Aaron. Before Moses left to climb Mt. Sinai (Exodus 24: 14), he told the elders to refer to Aaron and Hur in his absence. Josephus (*Jewish Antiquities* 3.53) could have taken Wallace one step further, for he adds that Hur was the brother-in-law of Moses and Aaron, that is, married to their sister Miriam – whose name Wallace invokes in a speech by Judah's mother (2.4). Where Wallace provides his reader with much of his back story in the soothing words his (nameless) mother speaks to Judah in their initial conversation (2.4), she is recalling the day she presented Judah to the Temple – a procedure well known from Luke (2: 22) – and says his given name is "Judah, son of Ithamar, of the House of Hur." The Old Testament Ithamar is also related to Moses and Aaron: he is the youngest of Aaron's four sons and therefore a nephew of Hur, as Wallace could have found in either Exodus (6: 23) or Josephus (*Jewish Antiquities* 3.188). The use of the prefix "Ben" is found in connection with a different Hur mentioned elsewhere in the Old Testament, but only in selected, usually older, translations. In First Kings (4: 8) there is a list of King Solomon's twelve provincial governors, among whom is the "Son of Hur," as the translation is rendered in modern English translations. The King James translation, however, renders the name by transliterating the Hebrew patronymic *Ben* and attaching it to the name with a hyphen.[56]

Any significance Wallace may have attached to the protagonist's first name is not so easily identified. The Hebrew name Yehudah can be transliterated into English as either Judas or Judah, so it may be that Wallace used Judah as a simple substitute for Judas, Wallace's historical Galilean model from Josephus and Gibbon, whose name would have been entirely inappropriate and confusing for a tale of the Christ. Naming him Judah instead of Judas would have been an easy fix of a single letter and still fit the same criteria he applied to the name "Hur." If not, the name Judah is important and omnipresent in the Old Testament. It is variously assigned but primarily to the son of the patriarch Jacob, the eponymous ancestor of the kingdom of Judah and the tribe of Judah. Following this line of thinking Wallace could have been using the name as a synecdoche representing the entirety of the Jewish antiquity. But this would imply a larger statement about Judaism than Wallace ever admits to, and at most only one of Wallace's other characters is named after a larger geographical or political construct. In contrast, the process may have been as simple as reading the following in Dixon's *The Holy Land*:

> The Son of Joseph and Marian, born in the grotto, near the great khan of Bethlehem, was called JESUS; a name now sacred and set apart from use; then common among Jews as either Simon or Judah, and as William and Henry among ourselves.[57]

The character named after a larger geographical or political construct is Tirzah, Judah's sister. Like the name Judah, the name Tirzah in the Old Testament is used as both a personal and geographical name. Tirzah is the name of the youngest of five daughters of an otherwise unremarkable Zelophehad (Numbers 26: 33). Like Hur, Miriam, and Ithamar, she lives in the days of Moses and makes a personal appeal to him regarding her right to inherit property. The geographical Tirzah is an Israelite city that appears in several locations in the Old Testament and also in Josephus's *Jewish Antiquities* (8.298). In First Kings (15: 33; =*Jewish Antiquities* 8.298) it serves as the capital of Israel, and in Second Kings (15: 14; =*Jewish Antiquities* 8.228) Menahem set out from Tirzah to become king in Samaria. Known for its beauty, in the Old Testament's lyrical Song of Songs (6: 4) the city is compared by the lover to his beloved:

> You are as beautiful as Tirzah, my darling,
> As lovely as Jerusalem . . .

Perhaps it was this particular poetic application of Tirzah which caught the attention of William Blake, who expanded the symbolic significance of the name in several dozen passages, including his brief poem "To Tirzah" and its penultimate allusion to the death of Jesus.[58] There is reason to suggest that the poetic connection in particular may have inspired Wallace. When we first meet Tirzah she is singing a song (2.6), "Wake not, but hear me, love!" Again, in "How I Came to Write *Ben-Hur*" Wallace recalls with some pride that the composition of this lyric was "the resultant of a delayed passage from Indianapolis home," but the reader will recall that Wallace composed a considerable amount of poetry as a youth.[59] It is the first lyrical passage in the novel and would inspire several published musical compositions.

There may also be a political connection, albeit tangential in nature. Although modern historians have doubted the accuracy of his genealogy, Josephus (*The Jewish War* 2.443) says that the anti-Roman rebel leader Menahem, who has the same name as the Menahem who departed from the city of Tirzah centuries earlier, was the son of Judas of Galilee.

Esther and Simonides
The other two names Wallace mentions in this section of "How I Came to Write *Ben-Hur*" are Simonides and Esther. The characterization of Esther, at least in familial position and religious persuasion, derives from Rebecca in Sir Walter Scott's *Ivanhoe*, but unlike Scott's Rebecca, Wallace's Esther plays a relatively minor role and has no objectionable qualities.[60] The name Esther, familiar from the Old Testament, Wallace says in *An Autobiography* was chosen to honor his mother.[61]

Wallace in all likelihood chose the name "Simonides" in homage to Josephus, for Simonides was the cognomen of Josephus's youngest son, Flavius Simonides Agrippa.[62] Josephus himself used the name "Flavius" because he acquired his Roman citizenship under the Flavian dynasty, whose conquest of Jerusalem he documents in *The Jewish War*. The most influential Agrippa was Augustus' military strategist and son-in-law, whose name was given to the last of the Herodian princes in Judea, Agrippa II, not only a contemporary and friend of Josephus, but one of his sources. The cognomen Simonides is not a common name. It is constructed as a Greco-Jewish patronymic, i.e. "son of Simon," but the name Simon, as differentiated from Simeon (son of Jacob), seems to have proliferated in first century Judea in such New Testament figures as Simon Peter (Matthew 4: 18), Simon the Canaanite (Matthew 10: 4), and Simon the leper (Matthew 26: 6).[63]

Iras
Wallace no doubt derived the name of Iras from either Shakespeare's *Antony and Cleopatra*, where she is a loyal attendant to Cleopatra who commits suicide at the same time as her mistress, or from Shakespeare's source, Plutarch's *Life of Antony* 60.1, where Iras along with Charmion and others actually manages the principal affairs of Antony's government near the end of his life. Wallace found in this presumably historical character an exotic Egyptian woman, whose sensuality could be assumed and whose loyalty to a defeated villain was not nearly so admirable as it was despicable. The author used her sensuality to make her a foil to the demure, reserved Esther. Both of the women were attracted to Judah, and Wallace spends whole chapters and numerous paragraphs in others to explore both relationships.[64] But Iras merely toys with Judah while she is

wholly devoted to Messala – until the last chapter of the book where we learn that she has finally murdered him.

Esther as the daughter of Simonides was clearly part of the original design of the novel as the protagonist's love interest, and Iras may have been part of Wallace's original design as a foil to Esther, an exotic temptress to Judah, and a fitting companion to Messala. But because she does not appear until after Judah returns to the East and meets her father Balthasar (4.8), it is possible that Wallace did not create her until then. Balthasar and Iras make for an unnatural duo. Although in the real world parents often produce dissimilar progeny and Wallace may have conceived of Iras as a bad seed, Balthasar never attempts to reign her in, reprimand her, or even give her fatherly advice. Their lone commonality is that they are both from Egypt. In either case, near the end of the novel Wallace fully integrates Iras into the plot in that she serves to ridicule Judah's belief in the Christ as the Messiah and threatens to report Judah's murder of Pilate's centurion to Sejanus (8.6).

Sheik Ilderim
Wallace will make his Sheik Ilderim the man who hosts Balthasar and allows Judah to ride his four bays in the chariot race.[65] In this way he becomes a central character who assists Judah in his quest to humiliate Messala and together they develop an anti-Roman conspiracy. His creation seems to have been the result of patching together several different contemporary influences. The name Ilderim by itself was well known from H. G. Knight's poetic cantos, *Ilderim: A Syrian Tale* (1816). Dixon's *The Holy Land* has dozens of references to various "sheikhs," and almost as many to the desert dotted with their "black tents," the color of the tent in which Ilderim keeps his horses. On the other hand, Dixon discusses the Arab dislike for riding on horses, while other sources insist to the contrary upon a strong relationship between Arabs and horses.[66] Elizabeth Rundle Charles in her *Wanderings Over Bible Lands and Seas* of 1862 mentions an "orchard of palms" in Galilee, the name Wallace used for the Sheik's encampment.

Messala and Gratus
As the chief personification of Rome, Messala is one of Wallace's most important and effective fabrications. Unlike his partner in evil, Gratus, Messala is not a historical personage, even though many Romans named Messala appear in extant sources. The name originated in 262 BC during the First Punic War, when the consul Marcus Valerius defeated the Carthaginians and Sicilians at Messana, thereby earning the triumphal surname, Messala.[67] From that point one can trace a series of Messalas and Messallas for more than seven centuries into the final years of paganism and even into the Byzantine era.[68] Twenty-five of them served as

consul. As for Wallace's fictitious Messala, the author identifies him as the grandson of the Messala who "had been the friend of Brutus" (2.2). This would have been Marcus Valerius Messalla Corvinus. Schooled in Athens with Horace, this historical Messala served as a consul in 31 BC, was an accomplished orator, and became a generous patron of the arts.[69] He was even an author himself: Plutarch preserves part of his account of the civil wars in his *Life of Brutus* (40.1–2). Wallace could have come across his name there, or in other primary sources like Josephus or Tacitus, or even Shakespeare, or, most likely, such later sources as Gibbon or Smith's *Dictionary of Greek and Roman Biography, Mythology and Geography*.[70] The latter, which Wallace employed more than once, repeatedly used the spelling Wallace uses exclusively. It also listed several Romans named Messala who were stationed in Asia. Smith reports that one of these, Valerius Messala Volesus, served during the first decade of the new millennium as proconsul of Asia, "where his cruelties drew on him the anger of Augustus and a condemnatory decree from the senate."[71]

Neither Smith nor Wallace mention the historical connection between Messala Corvinus and Herod. It was Messala in his capacity as a praetor who introduced Herod to the Roman Senate in 40 BC.[72] The Senate reacted favorably and unanimously decreed Herod to be King of Judea. This information is found in relatively obscure ancient sources to which Wallace probably had no access.[73] Alternatively Wallace might have found a derivative account in Edward Berwick's *Lives of Marcus Valerius Messala, and Titus Pomponius Atticus*.[74] But Berwick speaks well of the association between Messala, Herod, and Mark Antony, while Wallace has nothing complimentary at all to say about Herod. In Wallace's story Herod is the New Testament's terrestrial King of the Jews who tries to kill his innocent successor in his infancy. In Book First (1.13) Wallace describes Herod this way:

> Such was Herod the Great – a body broken by diseases, a conscience seared with crimes, a mind magnificently capable, a soul fit for brotherhood with the Caesars; now seven-and-sixty years old, but guarding his throne with a jealousy never so vigilant, a power never so despotic, and a cruelty never so inexorable.

In both his major works Josephus (*The Jewish War*, 1.243; *Jewish Antiquities* 14.324) places this historical Messala by the side of Mark Antony not only in the Eastern province of Syria but in Antioch and in fact in Daphne – precisely where Judah will reconnect with Messala after his eight-year absence from the East (3.8). Dio Cassius (51.7–8) even discusses Messala in conjunction with the gladiators of Syrian Daphne. Wallace might have found this intersection of Messala, Herod, and Antony at Daphne particularly alluring because that was the first important event following Antony's first romantic encounter with the infamous Egyptian Queen Cleopatra. Wallace would not only make reference to her in three different passages of his novel, he would use her as a model for his

Egyptian femme fatale Iras, who would ultimately cause the downfall of not Antony but Messala. The first of these passages introduces Cleopatra to the novel in the same, much-quoted paragraph in which the young Messala distinguishes Eros and Mars for the younger Judah (2.2):

> "Go," said my teacher, in his last lecture – "Go, and, to make your lives great, remember Mars reigns and Eros has found his eyes." He meant love is nothing, war everything. It is so in Rome. Marriage is the first step to divorce. Virtue is a tradesman's jewel. Cleopatra, dying, bequeathed her arts, and is avenged; she has a successor in every Roman's house. The world is going the same way; so, as to our future, down Eros, up Mars!

In the treacherous world of the divisive decades of the Roman Republic, political allegiance meant the difference between life and death—as Wallace's Messala warns the young Judah in the novel (2.2). Like Horace, who had fought for the anti-Caesarian conspirator Brutus at Philippi but then changed allegiance and composed poetic praises of Augustus that would echo for centuries, the historical Messala wisely and, as Wallace writes, "without sacrifice of his honor" shifted his allegiance from Brutus to Octavius, the future Augustus.

> The Emperor Augustus, remembered the service, and showered the family with honors. Among other things, Judea being reduced to a province, he sent the son of his old client or retainer to Jerusalem, charged with the receipt and management of the taxes levied in that region; and in that service the son had since remained, sharing the palace with the high-priest. The youth just described was his son, whose habit it was to carry about with him all too faithfully a remembrance of the relation between his grandfather and the great Romans of his day.

The historical Messalla Corvinus did have a son, Marcus Valerius Messalla Messallinus, who was consul in the year 3, which was within a year or so of the birth of Wallace's Messala. But he served his military governorship in Illyria, not Syria. Still well regarded by the emperor, he married Augustus' niece. Their son, Marcus Valerius Messala Barbatus was born in 11 BC, some thirteen years before Wallace's Messala. Wallace may have been familiar with the name of his daughter, Valeria Messalina, who married the Emperor Claudius and inspired her own rather infamous tradition as the lascivious "Empress Messalina." While neither of these two generations of Messala seem to have been stationed in the province of Syria, it may be that Josephus' report of Corvinus' appearance at Daphne sufficed for Wallace to make the fictitious connection. However, the reader will note in passing that Wallace could also have read about the Messala in the generation of the father of Wallace's Messala, Marcus Valerius Messalla Barbatus Appianus. He shared the consulship of 12 BC with Quirinius, that is, the Cyrenius of Luke 2: 1–2, and his half-sister Claudia Pulchra married Publius Quinctilius Varus, famous for his defeat in the Teutoburg Forest, who quashed the Jewish anti-Roman rebellion in 4 BC after the death of Herod by crucifying 2000 victims.

Wallace did not assign a rank or position to his Messala. In their earliest encounter Messala tells Judah he would like to campaign in Africa and Scythia, and then move on to become a prefect like Cyrenius, but these are just a teenager's dreams. Eight years later in the palace at Antioch, Messala is described simply as one of the many Roman "military attaches of the consul" (4.12). It may well be intentional that we see Messala only at times of leisure – playing at dice, wagering, spending the night at an orgy, or riding his chariot.[75] He seems to be a Roman aristocratic playboy, and as such he represents (4.1) "the extravagance and dissoluteness of the age [which] had their origin in Rome."

The reader already knows that Wallace derived from Josephus the character of Valerius Gratus and his controversial act of replacing the high priest, which sparked Judah's anger, igniting the initial quarrel with Messala and thereby establishing the fundamental plot of their story. The reader also knows that the tile incident and ensuing urban riot was probably derived from Plutarch's account of the death of the historical Pyrrhus. Ancient literature and an account of actual historical events may also have served as a model for Gratus' and Messala's confiscation of the Hur property. Cicero was known to Wallace; he mentions him in two different passages in *Ben-Hur: A Tale of the Christ* (5.1; 5.16). In the latter of these passages Wallace specifically mentions the two houses Cicero's enemies confiscated from him when he was forced into exile in 58 BC. In his oration "On His House," Cicero (62) recounts how both his house on the Palatine Hill in Rome and his Tusculan villa were transferred to the two consuls, Lucius Calpurnius Piso and Aulus Gabinius, who were associated with the infamous Clodius in engineering Cicero's exile and attempted ruination of his name. In addition, the main charge against Cicero was that he had not given Catiline a trial before invoking the death sentence, just as Wallace's Judah was condemned to the galleys without a trial, and, in turn, he punished Messala without a trial as well. As a former judge, Wallace was certainly aware of the illegality of such extra-judicial condemnations, and even though he was not a classical scholar he could have found a detailed account of Cicero's consulship and the subsequent confiscation of Cicero's properties in Conyers Middleton's *The Life and Letters of Marcus Tullius Cicero* (1840).[76]

Arrius

Wallace does not even mention Quintus Arrius in "How I Came to Write *Ben-Hur*," but his fictitious Roman tribune serves as an important plot device. Arrius provides the means for releasing Judah from his imprisonment, giving him wealth and "the ease and grace of a patrician" (4.1), and introducing him to some of Rome's most influential people as well as its games and martial arts – including chariot racing and hand-to-hand combat. Judah's mastery of these skills will empower him not only to defeat Messala, the hired assassin Thord, and one of Pontius Pilate's centurions, but also fulfill his lifelong dream of becoming a soldier and the leader of Galilee's three anti-Roman legions. Wallace rendered Arrius as the one compassionate Roman in the story, providing a foil to Messala, Gratus, and Pilate, and as a Roman parallel to the Christ. Wallace connects Arrius and Judah further by suggesting that Arrius knew Judah's father Ithamar, who, unlike Arrius (and Josephus), drowned at sea. As for Arrius' adoption of Judah, Wallace, like anyone who reads about Roman history, must have come across countless adoptions among the aristocratic Roman families, especially during the historical period in which the book is set. Julius Caesar's adoption of his grand-nephew Octavius, the future emperor Augustus, and Augustus' adoption of his stepson Tiberius Claudius Nero, the future emperor Tiberius, provide two prime examples.

Like the name Messala, Arrius is another consular family name. Seven different historical men named Arrius served as consul, but none before the second half of the first century, too late to have encountered Judah Ben-Hur in a galley during the late 20s. Wallace's original inspiration for naming his one noble Roman may derive from a unique intersection of Plutarch and Cicero. Plutarch in his *Life of Cicero* (15.3) refers to Quintus Arrius as "a man of praetorian dignity," implying military prowess as well.[77]

Wallace makes it very clear at the beginning of Book Third (3.1) that his fictional Arrius has received signed orders from the historical Sejanus and Caecilius Rufus. They order Arrius to engage the pirates who originally inhabited the Thracian Chersonese (Gallipoli) but have now swept through the Bosphorus into the Aegean. During the naval battle (3.4), Judah below deck realizes the *Astroea* has been boarded when he sees "the half-naked carcass, a mass of hair blackening the face, and under it a shield of bull-hide and wicker-work – a barbarian from the white-skinned nations of the North." Historically the Romans had no major naval engagements in the Aegean in the first century, let alone any against pirates from, as he says, the Propontis and the mouth of the Black Sea. But several ancient accounts particularly notable for both the fame of their victorious generals and Wallace's familiarity with the authors, might have informed him and provided the inspiration here. His beloved Plutarch (*Life of Pericles* 19.1–2) singles out Pericles' victory over the Chersonesan pirates in 447 BC as his most cherished military expedition, and Demosthenes, whom we have seen as a source of inspiration for Wallace's political rhetoric in the 1840s, addressed the encounters between Phillip II, the father of Alexander the Great, and Chersonesan pirates in 342 BC (*On the Halonnesus* 7.2). And no doubt Wallace was familiar with the most famous triumph over pirates in all of ancient Roman history – the remarkably efficient victory the 39-year-old Pompey won over the Cilician pirates in the Aegean in 67 BC. Pompey's supreme and extraordinary command had been supported by Julius Caesar, who, Plutarch (*Life of Caesar* 1.4–2.4) records had been kidnapped by pirates for ransom a decade earlier. Armed with hundreds of ships and having designed an innovative network strategy of legates, Pompey cleared the Eastern Mediterranean of more than 1000 ships and the entire pirate menace in less than two months.[78]

If Wallace had read just a few paragraphs beyond Plutarch's fairly detailed account of this illustrious triumph (*Life of Pompey* 24–9), he would have learned that as a result of his success Pompey was commissioned to pacify lands yet further east, and that this was the expedition that in just three years would place Judea for the first time under Roman rule (*Life of Pompey* 39.2). Wallace refers to Pompey's conquest of Jerusalem, an event that would bring the Jewish and Christian religions within the orbit of the Roman world once and for all, in the first book of his novel just as he is concluding all his introductory material (1.1–7). The last paragraph there describes the absence of the true god in Jerusalem by focusing on Pompey's entrance into the great Temple (1.7):

> In other words, Jerusalem, rich in sacred history, richer in connection with sacred prophecies – the Jerusalem of Solomon, in which silver was as stones, and cedars as the sycamores of the vale – had come to be but a copy of Rome, a center of unholy practises, a seat of pagan power. A Jewish king one day put on priestly garments, and went into the Holy of Holies of the first temple to offer incense, and he came out a leper; but in the time of which we are reading, Pompey entered Herod's temple and the same Holy of Holies, and came out without harm, finding but an empty chamber, and of God not a sign.

Wallace no doubt read about Pompey's Judean expedition in Josephus (*Jewish Antiquities* 14.71–6), for it was Josephus who fully understood the significance of both Pompey's entrance into the temple and his policy of non-violation.[79] Wallace then took this event to signify that the Hebrew god was no longer present and that the Holy Land was devoid of spirituality, or, as he wrote in "How I Came to Write *Ben-Hur*," "there was nowhere a suggestion of religion." Therefore in the very next paragraphs, Wallace describes the advent of Joseph and Mary in Jerusalem, and so he begins his tale of the Christ as the historical and theological consequence of Pompey's Judean conquest in 63 BC.

As a result of his military expedition against the pirates, Pompey succeeded in restoring maritime supply lines and the essential trans-Mediterranean grain shipments to Rome. So says Plutarch (*Life of Pompey* 25.1), and Wallace echoes this in *Ben-Hur: A Tale of the Christ* (3.1), where Arrius says:

> "The corn-merchants who have ships in the East Mediterranean are frightened. They had audience with the Emperor himself, and from Ravenna there go to-day a hundred galleys, and from Misenum" – he paused as if to pique the curiosity of his friends, and ended with an emphatic – "one."

Wallace's choice of locating Arrius at the ancient Roman naval base at Misenum may be traced to the well-known fact that Pliny the Elder was stationed there in August, 79, where he witnessed – and then perished from – the catastrophic eruption of Mt. Vesuvius that destroyed Pompeii and Herculaneum. This was later famously described by his nephew (and adopted son), Pliny the Younger in a letter (6.16) which begins, "He was there at Misenum because he was commander of the fleet."

The reader will also want to know that there are two notable passages in Josephus which feature Jewish pirates. Of course Wallace would hardly have exposed Arrius and his protagonist Judean galley slave to an attack by renegade Judean pirates. But these passages certainly would have reinforced his impression that piracy was a significant problem in the Eastern Mediterranean in the first century and was worthy of inclusion in his novel. In the *Jewish War* (3.414–18) Josephus tells us that during the summer campaign of AD 67 a number of Judeans who escaped the Roman demolition of their cities built ships and turned to piracy along the Syrian, Phoenician, and Egyptian coasts. A few pages later (3.522–32), he describes the naval massacre at Lake Galilee at the hands of Vespasian. Thousands of fugitive Judeans boarded small ships "fitted only for piracy," and over 6000 of the Judeans were killed by Romans pursuing them with pikes and swords, or by drowning. This horrific account would have had a particular fascination for Wallace because Josephus himself was in command and was largely responsible for the loss of not only the lives of thousands of Judeans but his own freedom. Similar to Wallace's fictitious Judah, the historical Josephus survived by extraordinary luck as the sole survivor of a round-robin suicide pact and because of the gratitude of the commander, Vespasian. In this instance, by prophesying Vespasian's impending reign as emperor, Josephus earned the respect and admiration of his Roman overlord, a position in Rome, and Vespasian's family name, Flavius.

In addition, this passage may have helped to inspire Judah's cruel punishment at the hands of the Romans. Purists are not completely correct in arguing that the Romans never used slaves to row in their galleys. Scipio used thousands of slaves as rowers in the Second Punic War.[80] Nonetheless, the Romans did not often power their ships with slave labor. But in the aftermath of the Lake Galilee massacre Vespasian ushered thousands of Judean prisoners into the nearby stadium at Tiberias, ordered 1200 elderly to be executed, and condemned another 6000 strong young men to hard labor, sending them to the Corinthian isthmus to dig a canal. Nineteenth-century editions of Whiston's translation of Josephus add the comment that, "This is the most cruel and barbarous action that Vespasian ever did in this whole war . . . when all knew and confessed that these prisoners were no way guilty of any sedition against the Romans."[81] Judah, too, was innocent of sedition, and his punishment at the hands of the Romans was cruel. In the novel Wallace usually applies the words "cruel" and "cruelty" to Messala, Gratus, and Herod.

THE CHARIOT RACE

As an author of historical adventure fiction who already as a youth had conjured up thrilling physical events and rendered them in fictional prose and poetry, Wallace did not necessarily have to employ a historical or literary source to inspire the famed chariot race between Messala and Judah Ben-Hur. But seeing how so much of his Roman world seems to have derived from literary exempla and secondary reference works, we can at least point out a few compelling parallels and possible inspirations. The best-known examples of chariot rides and races in ancient literature end in catastrophic crashes. Of the Greek myths, Oenomaus rides in a chariot race against Pelops and ultimately crashes and is killed, as described in Pindar *Olympian* 1, and the horses pulling the chariot of Theseus' stepson Hippolytus are frightened by a monster rising from the sea and cause his death in a horrific chariot crash, as described by Euripides in his *Hippolytus* (1151–1254) and Seneca in his *Phaedra* (1000–14). Wallace could have read of either in secondary sources, and we have already seen some indirect connection to Pindar.

The most detailed account of a chariot crash in ancient literature is found in the messenger speech in Sophocles' *Electra* (699–763).[82] Edward H. Plumptre's translation of Sophocles' *Electra* was published in the United States already in 1867. The Sophoclean account in particular bears several significant similarities to the *Ben-Hur* race. Both authors focus on the hubs of the axles, the danger of the turning posts, and a disastrous crash. They both list the drivers individually and identify them by the city or area they represent, although Sophocles lists ten from the Greek world of the fifth century BC, Wallace six representing the Roman Empire of the first century AD. The only overlap was a driver representing Athens, and he is featured and connected with a crash in both.

As an author living and working in an era still dependent upon horses and horse-drawn vehicles, and as a former general, Wallace would have been sufficiently knowledgeable about horses, tack, and hitches to describe many details related to a chariot race without recourse to further research. But in his desire to flesh out his account and be accurate, he almost certainly looked at the entry on "Currus" in Smith's dictionary. Where early on in the entry Smith describes the chariot axle and cites Homer (*Iliad* 5.723; 13.30) in describing Jupiter's and Juno's metal axles, Wallace features the "iron-shod hub" of Messala's axle. Where Smith says that "one method of making a chariot less liable to be overturned was to lengthen its axle, and thus to widen the base on which it stood," Wallace described Ben-Hur's Greek chariot as "wider between the wheels ... lower and stronger." And where Smith describes Roman triumphal chariots as decorated in gold and ivory, Messala's chariot "is all of ivory and gold."

LAPSES IN HISTORICAL SPECIFICITY

Wallace never specifies Messala's rank, nor does he differentiate Judah, acting as the Roman son of Arrius, from the rest of Maxentius' attachés. Judah says only, "The consul has admitted me one of his military family" (4.12). In fact, there was no historical consul Maxentius until the early fourth century. Wallace gives Judah no position as a Judean either. He does describe Judah's father Ithamar as a "prince of Jerusalem," a term which would have carried much currency during the reigns of Herod and his immediate progeny. But he never labels Judah himself as a prince (as would several later adaptations of the novel). Several dozen times throughout the galley episode of Book Third and subsequently Wallace refers to Quintus Arrius as simply a "tribune." This is not to be confused with the more familiar elected political office of tribune but is a less well understood appointed military position below the rank of consul. Similarly, at the outset of Book Third Arrius receives his orders to command the expedition against the pirates in the Aegean in a letter from "Sejanus to C. Coecilius Rufus, duumvir."[83] Before Arrius disembarks he and his friends several times mention that Arrius may warrant promotion to that rank, and indeed the last words of Book Third describe a victory inscription celebrating "Quintus Arrius, Duumvir." Nonetheless, this term is also relatively obscure. Referring to a post held by two men, the term historically only rarely applied to the two consuls of Rome but usually applied instead to short-term magisterial offices of lesser importance. Moreover the reader will learn that Charlton Lewis, the Latin authority who read the manuscript Wallace originally submitted to Harper in 1880, pointed out that Wallace repeatedly used the term incorrectly in the plural form "duumviri."[84]

Such lapses in historical specificity and accuracy would not be extraordinary or even undesirable for a historical novelist, but it is hard to account for the rarity and vagueness with which Wallace assigns military ranks and civilian titles considering his own extensive military experience and numerous governmental appointments and elected offices in a gamut of ranks and levels. Indeed, during the years Wallace was writing *Ben-Hur: A Tale of the Christ*, he would apply for positions as a modern-day presidential legate in Italy and Brazil and then serve as the Territorial Governor of New Mexico. Specificity as to military rank would seem to have been of particular importance to Wallace, who was throughout his life often addressed in person or listed in print as "General." And specificity as to administrative position represented the quintessence of achievement and identification for an ancient Roman patrician, not to mention that it was and remains the most effective means by which moderns differentiate the thousands of Romans emperors, consuls, senators, proconsuls, governors, legates, procurators, prefects, tribunes, praetors, aediles, and quaestors whose titles were recorded for posterity in books, inscriptions, and coins.

THE CHRIST AND THE NEW TESTAMENT

Wallace next addresses his treatment of Jesus:

> The Christian world would not tolerate a novel with Jesus Christ its hero, and I knew it. Nevertheless, writing of Him was imperative, and He must appear, speak, and act. Further, and worse as a tribulation, I was required to keep Him before the reader, the object of superior interest throughout.
> And there was to be no sermonizing. How could this be done without giving mortal offence? How, and leave the book a shred of popularity?[85]

To accomplish this he writes that he prescribed himself three rules: (1) to withhold Christ's appearance until the end of the novel, (2) to avoid creating fictional events for him, the lone exception to both of these rules being the episode in which young Jesus gives Ben-Hur water at the well in Nazareth, and (3) that every word Christ uttered in the novel should be from "one of His sainted biographers." Throughout the life of the *Ben-Hur* phenomenon, reverence for and propriety in treating Jesus as a character will continue to be a concern.

In the process of integrating the original story with his post-Ingersoll conception, Wallace in several passages substituted Hur family members for anonymous characters in the New Testament account. At 8.8, for instance, where Judah is stripped naked and flees from Gethsemane, Wallace is supplying him as the "certain young man" in Mark 14: 51:

> And there followed him a certain young man, having a linen cloth cast about his naked body; and the young men laid hold on him. And he left the linen cloth, and fled from them naked.

Judah had the presence of mind to leave his outer garment on the orchard wall. At 8.10 Wallace substitutes Judah for the anonymous man who gives Jesus a drink from a sponge dipped in vinegar (Matthew 27: 48). At 8.4 Wallace has Jesus heal Judah's mother and sister of leprosy, complying with his third rule by having Jesus say, "Woman, great is thy faith; be it unto thee even as thou wilt" (Matthew 15: 28), although this is not what Jesus says when he cures the leper (Matthew 8: 3). Wallace expands his integration technique by using the Old Testament (Leviticus 13: 45) expression "Unclean, unclean!" in reference to Judah's mother and sister sixteen times in Book Sixth, Book Seventh, and Book Eighth.

GEOGRAPHICAL AND TECHNICAL DETAILS

The literary license Wallace employed in establishing some of his most prominent Roman characters was balanced by the effort he expended in researching the geography of the Roman Empire, particularly ancient Judea, as well as some of its well-known physical trappings. In "How I Came to write *Ben-Hur*" he writes:

> In the next place, I had never been to the Holy Land. In making it the location of my story, it was needful not merely to be familiar with its history and geography, I must be able to paint it, water, land, and sky, in actual colors. Nor would the critics excuse me for mistakes in the costumes or customs of any of the peoples representatively introduced, Greek, Roman, Egyptian, especially the children of Israel.
>
> Ponder the task! There was but one method open to me. I examined catalogues of books and maps, and sent for everything likely to be useful. I wrote with a chart always before my eyes – a German publication, showing the towns and villages, all sacred places, the heights, the depressions, the passes, trails, and distances.
>
> Travellers told me of the birds, animals, vegetation, and seasons. Indeed, I think the necessity for constant reference to authorities saved me mistakes which certainly would have occurred had I trusted to a tourist's memory.

The German publication he refers to would seem to be the *Bibel-Atlas* by Heinrich Keipert, published first in 1851 and in a second edition until 1870,[86] although the rarely mapped Jebel es Zubleh, the mountain chain Wallace identifies in the first sentence of the novel, could be found in *The New Biblical Atlas and Scripture Gazetteer*.[87] Either may have been supplemented with Van de Velde's *Map of the Holy Land*, published in 1858, which specifies "itineraries, elevations, routes, and distances."[88]

Some of the initial attractions of the novel were Wallace's detailed description of the desert rendezvous of the three Wise Men (1.1–5) and the variegated ethnic groups that populated the streets of Jerusalem (1.6–7). Wallace's prose gives the effect of a learned and reverent narrator, supporting and surrounding both Judah and Jesus with a wealth of historical depth.

Here, for instance, is how Wallace renders Joseph's quest for lodging at the khan of Bethlehem (1.9):

> To say, as Joseph said, "This is the house of my fathers," was to say the truth most simply and literally; for it was the very house Ruth ruled as the wife of Boaz, the very house in which Jesse and his ten sons, David the youngest, were born, the very house in which Samuel came seeking a king, and found him; the very house which David gave to the son of Barzillai, the friendly Gileadite; the very house in which Jeremiah, by prayer, rescued the remnant of his race flying before the Babylonians.

Wallace, as the reader knows, was not steeped in a biblical education, but this kind of detailed information was available in a reference work like William Hepworth Dixon's *The Holy Land*, which devotes a chapter each to the many historical and geographical sites familiar from the Old and New Testaments, including two consecutive chapters, "Syrian

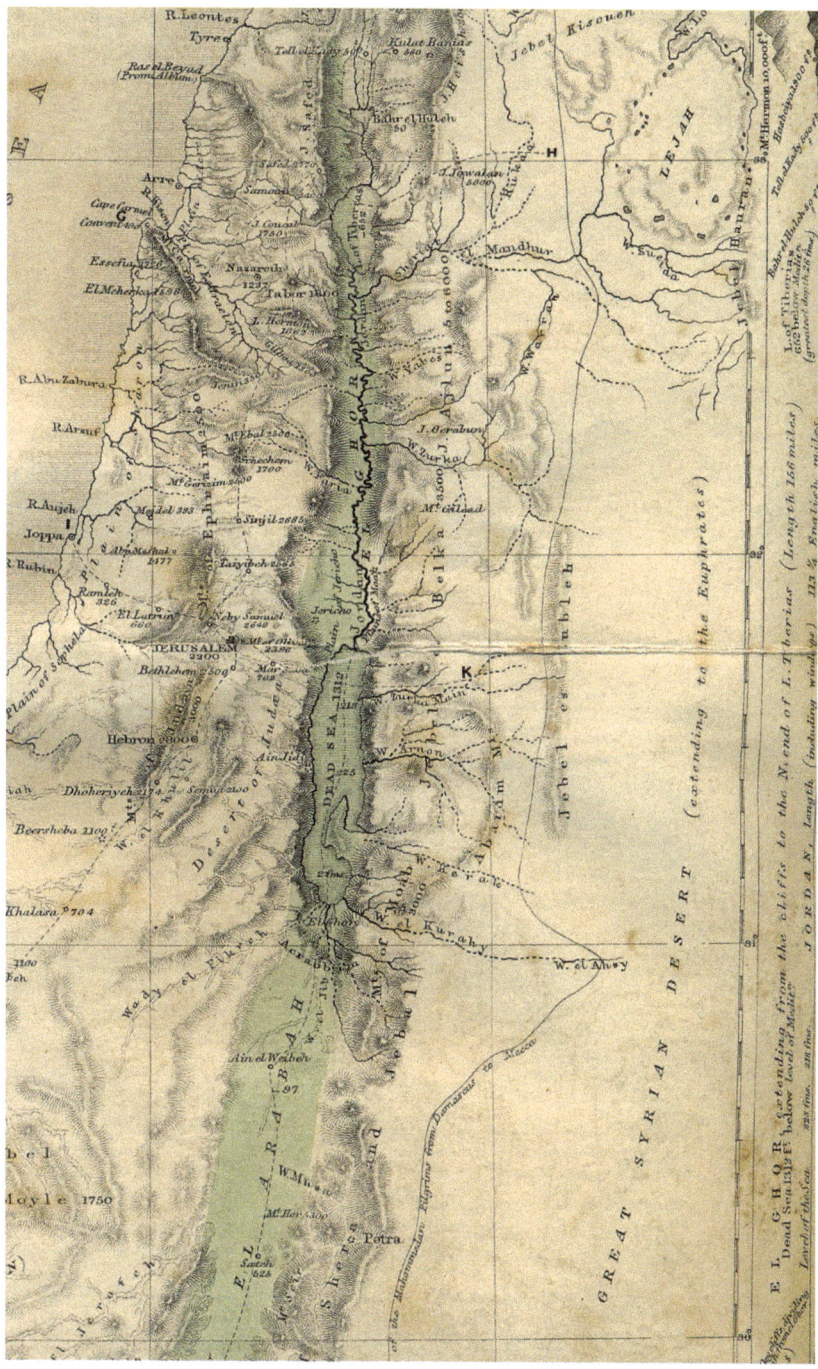

Figure 3.3 Wallace claims he used a German map of the Holy Land. Here the Jebel es Zubleh, compared in the first sentence of *Ben-Hur: A Tale of the Christ* to a "caterpillar crawling from the south to the north" appears on an Augustus Petermann map in *The New Biblical Atlas and Scripture Gazetteer*, published in Philadelphia no later than the 1850s.

Khans" and "The Inn at Bethlehem."[89] Years later, in 1885, after serving in Constantinople, Wallace had a chance to visit Jerusalem and the Holy Land in person. He felt comfortable in writing that he found "no reason for making a single change in the text of the book."[90]

Wallace soon addresses the research he did for the physical and mechanical details of ancient Roman life:

> After comparing authorities, I had frequently to reconcile them; failing in that, it remained to choose between them. There is nothing, not even a will-o'-the-wisp, so elusive as a disputed date. Once I went to Washington, thence to Boston, for no purpose but to exhaust their libraries in an effort to satisfy myself of the mechanical arrangement of the oars in the interior of a trireme.

These kinds of physical descriptions are an integral part of the book and one of the reasons for its success. Despite his efforts, there are two problematic passages in one of the most famous and influential passages in the novel – the chariot race. Wallace actually describes two chariot-racing venues, the great circus in Antioch (5.12), and the lesser one in neighboring Daphne (4.7). Our ancient sources give very limited information about this other venue, but modern scholars are quite certain that it never amounted to more than a dirt track.[91] Wallace describes it accordingly as the practice track where Judah first evaluates the Sheik's team of four bays and sees Messala's team of two blacks and two whites for the first time.

Wallace spends over a thousand words introducing the reader to the Antioch Circus, its location on the south bank of the Orontes River, the arrangement of seats for over 100,000 persons, the elevated tribunal, and the "sanded arena." This is where he writes (5.12):

> Looking across this sanded arena westwardly still, there is a pedestal of marble supporting three low conical pillars of gray stone, much carven. Many an eye will hunt for those pillars before the day is done, for they are the first goal, and mark the beginning and end of the race-course. Behind the pedestal, leaving a passage-way and space for an altar, commences a wall ten or twelve feet in breadth and five or six in height, extending thence exactly two hundred yards, or one Olympic stadium.

The wall that extends for exactly two hundred yards is the *spina*, the "backbone" of the racing course that divides it into two. Characteristically Wallace prefers not to use the Latin term. Without rigorous childhood training in Latin, his preference was usually for explaining such architectural or technical details in English. His readers expected no different, and this formula proved to be very successful.

He does employ the Latin terms *porta pompae* for the center entrance and *carceres* for the stalls. The use of these few Latin terms confirms that he used a secondary source to research the shape, size, construction, and capacity of the ancient circus (hippodrome), just as he did to research Roman ships – "to satisfy myself of the mechanical arrangement of the oars in the interior of a trireme." His description of the Antioch Circus derives in no small part from Smith's *Dictionary of Greek and Roman*

Antiquities, first published in 1842, the first of Smith's three dictionaries of ancient antiquities, biography, mythology, and geography. Smith's entry on "Circus" includes the following description:

> It will not fail to be observed that the line of the *carceres* is not at a right angle with the *spina*, but forms the segment of a circle, the centre of which is a point on the right hand of the arena; the reason for which is obviously that all the chariots might have, as nearly as possible, an equal distance to pass over between the *carceres* and mouth of the course.

Some of Wallace's wording is quite similar (2.13):

> The structure containing the stalls, it should be observed, was in form of the segment of a circle, retired on the right so that its central point was projected forward, and midway the course, on the starting side of the first goal. Every stall, consequently, was equally distant from the starting-line or chalked rope above mentioned.

He lifts one of Smith's phrases ("forms the segment of a circle") and follows the progression of details from the stalls (*carceres*) to the circle segment and right section of the arena to the purpose of making sure all the chariots were "an equal distance" ("equally distant") from the chalked rope, which he, following Smith again, explains in some detail, adding later that Messala probably had made a prearrangement to have it released just as his horses reached it (5.14).

The problem here is in measuring the length of the *spina* which Wallace says was one Olympic stadium (*stadion*), 600 feet. Of course the racing circuit extends beyond the *spina* to provide the chariots ample space for turning, and these turns Wallace uses to heighten the excitement of his narrative. The final turn, in fact, is where Judah shouts to his horses in Aramaic and then daringly but deftly guides them forward and to the left, using the iron cap of his axle to crush Messala's wheel and finally exact the vengeance he sought. As the chariots approached this final turn, Wallace writes (5.14):

> And now, to make the turn, Messala began to draw in his left hand steeds, an act which necessarily slacked their speed. His spirit was high; more than one altar was richer of his vows; the Roman genius was still president. On the three pillars only six hundred feet away were fame, increase of fortune, promotions, and a triumph ineffably sweetened by hate, all in store for him!

Again Wallace makes clear that the length of the final straightaway was 600 feet. This is too short. Wallace says that in the entire Roman Empire the Antioch Circus was second only to the Roman Circus Maximus in size and capacity, and Smith says the length of the Circus Maximus in Rome was three stadia in length. If Wallace had researched the Antioch Circus itself, the nineteenth-century predecessor to the extensive 1930s Princeton excavations was the 1839 publication, *Antiquitates Antiochenae*, by Karl Otfried Müller. This German opus may have been beyond Wallace's ability to access, but it included a printed map of ancient Antioch, including the Circus drawn to scale. The map's legend included the length of a stade, and by that measure the drawing of the Circus reaches over three stades. Müller's map was widely reproduced in reference works easily accessed by Wallace, and his placement of the Antioch Circus "on the south bank of the [Orontes] river, nearly opposite the island, differing in no respect from the plan of such buildings," probably derives from the map, where the Circus is south[west] of the palace, across from the island.[92] (In contrast, the Princeton excavation located the Antioch Circus on the island next to the palace, north of the river.[93])

In ancient Greece, and later in the Roman Empire, it was the Olympic-style "stadium" venues that were one stade [*stadion*] in length. The race courses at Olympia itself, as well as those in Epidaurus, Delphi, and Nemea in Greece and many Eastern Roman cities and sanctuaries are all one stade long. Wallace confuses here the length of the Olympic-style stadium designed for human foot races with that of the ancient circus (hippodrome) which was designed for horse races.[94] Wallace himself, albeit unintentionally, gives us the necessary clues to discover the probable source of his confusion. His statement in "How I Came to Write *Ben-Hur*" that he went "to Washington, thence to Boston, for no purpose but to exhaust their libraries," accords with an anecdote that circulated that same year (1893) and was attributed to the First Assistant Postmaster, General H. Clay Evans, representing the *Washington Star*.

> "Gen. Lew Wallace, while dining with me some time ago," said Gen. Evans, "told me how he got some of the material for the chapter which deals with the chariot race between Hur and Messala. He doubted if there existed a book in the United States that contained what he wanted and referred to his particular matter and at the period – 29 BC – but concluded that if it was not in the Congressional Library Mr. Spofford could aid him. He came to Washington and saw Mr. Spofford, explaining what he wanted." ... "You will find it," said Mr. Spofford, "in the Athenaeum Library in Boston. I don't remember its title; in fact, it has none. It is an old, plainly bound volume."[95]

The anecdote goes on to explain how Spofford drew Wallace a diagram of the Athenaeum that enabled him to find the book even though the Athenaeum librarians were unable to find it for him. The Athenaeum Library still owns a copy of Robert Berenger's *The History and Art of Horsemanship*, which contains several dozen pages on chariots, in which on page 53 Berenger writes:

> The piece of ground on which the chariot and horse-races were performed (for the same spot served for both) was called the *Hippodrome*. The Olympian Hippodrome, or horse-course, was a space of ground of six hundred paces long...[96]

If this is indeed the source Wallace used, then in his excitement at locating the book or haste in reading through the passage he seems to have confused 600 "paces" with 600 "feet." Even though Berenger's 1771 publication predated the German excavations of the site of Olympia by a century, it was already known that Olympia had two different racing venues, one the extant stadium for human racing, the other the destroyed hippodrome which would have been considerably longer than a "stadium." Smith's *Dictionary of Greek and Roman Antiquities*, s.v. "Stadium," asserts that the stadium was "600 feet . . . the Olympic racecourse was the longest in Greece."

The other, related problem involves seating capacity. During the race itself Wallace writes of "the gaze of over a hundred thousand persons." When Malluch, Simonides' assistant, is in the process of convincing Judah to race the Sheik's team of four at the Antioch Circus, he says (4.9), "ours seats two hundred thousand people, yours seats seventy-five thousand more; . . . in arrangement they are exactly the same." "Ours" is the Antioch Circus, "yours" the Circus Maximus. Yet a bit later Wallace mentions that Judah must have been influenced by his five years in Rome, "[sitting] under the purple velaria of the Circus Maximus one of three hundred and fifty thousand spectators . . ." Considering the concern for accuracy Wallace acted upon by engaging in repeated library research, such basic and large discrepancies are unexpected. In addition, the seating capacity numbers do not coordinate with the ancient sources or the most widely available nineteenth-century encyclopedias. Smith's entry on "Circus" often cites as a primary reference Dionysius, the first-century Dionysius of Halicarnassus who wrote an eyewitness description of the Circus Maximus in his *Roman Antiquities*. Dionysius (3.69 – in Edward Spelman's eighteenth-century translation that would no doubt have also been available to Wallace in Washington or Boston) specifies 150,000."[97] One century later, Pliny in his *Natural History* (36.102) seems to exaggerate in saying that the seating capacity was 250,000. Later sources, e.g. Publius Victor, confuse the issue further with estimates of 385,000.[98] None of the sources report or estimate Wallace's 275,000, so perhaps he felt free to make up a number. But this still does not account for his inconsistencies.[99]

These problematic passages give us some insight into Wallace research methodology. We see that in at least several instances he seems to have cherry-picked a variety of secondary sources without checking their references. If he had read one source that Smith cites prominently and frequently, Dionysius of Halicarnassus, he would have read there about the size of the Circus Maximus, "The circus is three stadia and a half in length, and four hundred feet in breadth."[100] The reader should understand that this observation is not so much a criticism of Wallace as a scholar, which he never claimed to be, but an insight into Wallace as a popular author and the creation of a late nineteenth-century popular historical novel. Despite Wallace's time-consuming library visits and claims of accuracy, the results of these turn out to be much less important than the creative action, atmospheric description, and reverent subject matter that would make the novel such a success. Of the millions of readers and critics of the novel over the past 130 years. Few have found the need to point out, let alone criticize, these historical imprecisions, and they have hardly affected the sales of the book, its powerful influence, or the fame of its chariot race.

On the other hand, elsewhere Wallace's research resulted in some valuable plot elements and descriptive passages. Smith (*Antiquities* 286), for instance, cites Dionysius (3.68) to point out that "the exterior of the Circus Maximus was surrounded by a portico one story high, above which were shops for those who sold refreshments." Wallace uses this to foil the assassination plot Messala plans after losing the chariot race. Judah promises Messala's paid assassin, Thord the Northman, both the one thousand sesterces Messala promised him to kill Judah plus another four, and this sum along with the five he won the previous day in the arena will enable Thord to "return to Rome and open a wine-shop near the Great Circus." Gibbon (3:23), to cite another example, spends several pages discussing the period of Julian the Apostate in the mid-fourth century, and in particular the pagan sanctuary of Daphne a few miles south of Antioch. Even Smith (*Geography* 751) says that Gibbon described Daphne "with zeal," and Smith's descriptions of the "frivolous amusements" amidst the gardens, fountains, and "gay processions that thronged from the city gate to the scene of consecrated pleasure" were further enlivened by Wallace (4.5–6), where he leads Judah to Greco-Roman temptation but thoughts of his family lead him through unscathed. Wallace concludes Book Fourth with Judah's exit: "He could not so soon forget how nearly he himself had been imposed upon."

One last example is the nebel, the stringed instrument Tirzah plays while singing what Wallace names as "THE SONG" (2.6). First, the passage in which Wallace uses the word.

> When Judah awoke, the sun was up over the mountains; the pigeons were abroad in flocks, filling the air with the gleams of their white wings; and off southeast he beheld the Temple, an apparition of gold in the blue of the sky. These, however, were familiar objects, and they received but a glance; upon the edge of the divan, close by him, a girl scarcely fifteen sat singing to the accompaniment of a nebel, which she rested upon her knee, and touched gracefully. To her he turned listening; and this was what she sang . . .

A rare word, "nebel" appears only this once in the novel, the more familiar English word "harp" being used elsewhere. "Nebel" is a direct transliteration of the Hebrew name for a musical instrument, but the King James translation renders this word as "harp" or "lyre," and Whiston in his translation of Josephus (*AJ* 7.306) renders the Greek version of the word (*nabla*) as "psaltery." This suggests that Wallace would have probably come across the term only in secondary literature, most likely in a reference work like Smith's *Dictionary of the Bible*, published in 1863. Smith writes that the nebel was "an ancient viol ... a six-stringed guitar."[101] Such attention to historical detail, albeit from a popular dictionary, tells us much about Wallace's methodology for writing a historical novel. By inserting this rarity into the midst of a passage describing Judah's dream-state and preceding the lovely lyrical passage recited by Tirzah – so lovely that the lyrics were later set by several classical composers as art-songs – he reveals his periodic preference for adding colorful, fairly arcane, non-English terms into his text, whether those terms are Greek, Latin, Arabic, or Hebrew. This passage is particularly insightful in that it develops as a progression from poetic prose to arcane color-word to poetry.

FINAL PREPARATION

Accessing a number of unidentified sources now lost, McKee in his biography of Wallace says that there were three drafts of the novel, and that the second draft still held the title *Judah: A Tale of the Christ*.[102] By employing exclusively and emphatically the first name of the protagonist and appending an expanded secondary title, Wallace employs the traditional type of title used successfully and repeatedly by William Ware, Wallace's most prominent American predecessor, for books like *Probus: or, Rome in the Third Century ...* (1838) and *Julian: or, Scenes in Judea* (1841). Artists in a variety of genres as well as producers of commercial items select their titles and names of their companies and products very carefully. Today it has become a science. Names are tested in statistical surveys and experimental unveilings. In 1880, advertising as well as name, logo, and motto selection were just about to develop as critical components of a successful company or product launch. Unfortunately we do not know when "Judah" was replaced by "Ben-Hur," or if it was Wallace's idea or a suggestion from someone at Harper & Brothers.[103] At this point the reader can only speculate as to whether without its signature name the *Ben-Hur* phenomenon could have gained such a hold on America's artistic and commercial psyche.

Wallace wrote Susan from Santa Fe on December 4, 1879, discussing the final chapters on Golgotha and the Crucifixion:

> I found a letter awaiting me here – evidently the letter written upon receipt of the MS of the Chapter upon the march to Golgotha, since which I have had and answered your letter written upon receipt of the Chapter given to the Crucifixion. I notice your criticisms upon the march to G and am of opinion that they are all just. Some of them I had in mind myself, with intention of correcting them.[104]

Although it is impossible to be certain, these chapters were in all likelihood recently written rather than recently revised in a second draft. Wallace arrived in Santa Fe in early October, 1878, with the sixth, seventh, and eighth books yet to be composed, and if he wrote the Golgotha and Crucifixion in November, 1879, then he had only fourteen months to compose three books. It took him from 1873 to 1878 to write the first five books. And now he was a governor with a small war being fought in Lincoln County. The letter seems to be referring to the original composition of those chapters. This suggests that McKee's second draft, particularly with the title "Judah," was simply the post-Ingersoll revision of the "Jewish story," which in turn would have to be counted as the first draft. However we are supposed to understand McKee's statement, Wallace was still revising the earlier sections of the book in New Mexico: at the close of a heavily edited manuscript of the ninth chapter of Book Fourth, written in pencil, Wallace wrote, "Finished in the Old Palace of the Pueblos, December, 1879, New Mexico."[105]

By January 9, 1880, Wallace was writing Susan to tell her that he was making a final copy for submission for publication, and by April 1880 he had finished that copy.[106] He took a leave of absence from his position as governor of the New Mexico Territory and hand-delivered his manuscript, which he had "written in purple ink with fastidious care," to Harper & Brothers.[107] When Joseph Harper saw it, he exclaimed, according to *An Autobiography* (2.938), "This is the most beautiful manuscript that has ever come into this house."[108] As yet he had little idea of its commercial potential.

OTHER HYPOTHESES AS TO WHY WALLACE WROTE *BEN-HUR: A TALE OF THE CHRIST*

Before proceeding to the next chapter to follow up on the actual publication and initial sales of Wallace's novel, the reader will now want to consider the accusations made against Wallace by Victor Davis Hanson and Paul Carter regarding his motives for writing *Ben-Hur: A Tale of the Christ*.

Hanson devotes one third of his 2003 book, *Ripples of Battle*, to discussing the profound effect the events at Shiloh had on Wallace.[109] After examining the various accounts, he discusses Wallace's subsequent obsession with Shiloh:

> Lew Wallace would live for another forty-three years after Shiloh. He became heavily involved in Mexican politics, served as a territorial governor of New Mexico, and was appointed by President Garfield, another Shiloh veteran, as United States minister to the Ottoman court at Constantinople. Yet throughout his long and near storybook career – he dealt on numerous occasions with Billy the Kid, the Apache renegade Victorio, and Abdul-Hamid II, the sultan of the Ottoman Empire – Wallace continued his obsession with Shiloh, all the more desperately so as his chief nemesis, Ulysses S. Grant, grew in stature from General of the Army to President of the United States. In some sense, Lew Wallace's entire life between 1862 and 1906 [*sic*] is a chronicle of all his efforts to pursue the ghost of the Shunpike.

Hanson concludes that "in some sense" Wallace's distinguished career as well as the writing of *Ben-Hur: A Tale of the Christ* were the result of Wallace's disgrace at Shiloh. In fact, to apply this to his overall thesis that an individual's experience in one particular battle can change history, Hanson seems to want to suggest that the plot of *Ben-Hur: A Tale of the Christ* derived from Wallace's obsession with setting the Shiloh record straight. Hanson describes the plot as "mostly the saga of a young, brilliant Jewish hero whose adult life is devoted to seeking revenge for an injustice done him and his family."[110] In doing so, Hanson describes only a portion of the plot of Wallace's novel. Once Judah gets his revenge on Messala (before the end of the fifth of eight books), the rest of his adult life is devoted to finding and caring for his mother and sister, committing himself to fighting for the independence of Judea and the kingdom of Christ, living happily ever after with his wife and children, and donating his money to the foundation of the Christian church.

Meanwhile behind the scenes during the last third or so of the novel, Messala and his femme fatale associate Iras seek revenge against Judah, and Iras ultimately murders Messala. Wallace's reader does not see this event unfolding, however, nor is it highlighted. It is told in an understated way and in retrospect as a denouement to the story of Messala's attempt to seek vengeance against Judah. If it was vengeance from Grant Wallace sought, he hardly would have received satisfaction by what transpired between Judah and Messala in the novel. After being defeated in the chariot race, the Roman refuses to pay the wager money he owes Judah, the very next day he tries to assassinate Judah, he later attempts to bribe Judah when Iras threatens to reveal his Jewish identity to Sejanus, and then he is ultimately murdered by his lover. Unless we are to assume Iras is Dantesque allegorical representation, this would hardly be the death Wallace would have wished for Grant. From a political perspective, it is difficult to see how Wallace, a 40-year-old Christian war veteran and a dedicated servant of the United States government, could conceive of representing himself as the teenage son of a wealthy Jewish merchant who obtains Roman military training for the sole purpose of overthrowing the Roman military establishment, i.e. in a war of rebellion.

Hanson also suggests that Wallace's "service on the board" [actually, President of the Commission] of inquiry into the horrors of Andersonville may have suggested the leper colonies in the novel, but in several aforementioned accounts Wallace makes it very clear that it was because he wanted "to convey a commensurate conception of the awful power underlying a miracle" that he struck Judah's mother and sister with leprosy. Wallace's purpose was not to describe the horrors of the disease but to allow Jesus to cure it. The leprosy in the novel is ultimately derived from Matthew 8:3, not medical reports from Andersonville.[111]

Hanson even goes so far as to suggest that Shiloh was responsible for Wallace's compulsion to write:

> Far more important, however, *Ben-Hur* was not just an allegory of Shiloh and its principal characters; Wallace's own sense of injustice following the battle may well also have been the larger catalyst for his writing career.[112]

Chapter 2 of this book offers ample testimony to the importance of reading and writing in Wallace's life long before Shiloh. He wrote an epic romance as a teenager even before his Mexican War experience, and the first book he wrote after the Shiloh debacle was a book on military tactics. Continuing on chronologically, if *Ben-Hur: A Tale of the Christ* was to be Wallace's allegory of Shiloh, then why did he spend the seven years following Shiloh writing a manual of military tactics, a novel about the Aztec conquest by the conquistadors, and a play about an ancient Roman "imperial madman"?[113] Indeed, upon publication of *The Fair God*, Wallace sent a copy to the White House accompanied by a letter asking Grant "as a reader of military experience" to comment specifically on Cortes's mistake in retreating from the city.[114] Only the most cynical of readers would claim that Wallace intended to taunt the president rather than share with him his own military knowledge and literary talent.

Hanson also failed to identify how Wallace reacted to the many incidents in his life in which he thought he had been snubbed, opposed, or frustrated. Wallace's modus operandi was to attack immediately. By July, 1863, he had already called for an official Court of Inquiry into his conduct at Pittsburg Landing.[115] When Stanton rejected his book on *Light Infantry Tactics*, he lobbied a congressman to abolish West Point. When he felt that Zachary Taylor had dishonored Indiana by not marshaling her troops for the battle at Buena Vista, he went on the offensive with personal attacks to defend his state's honor. On the campaign trail he likened himself to Demosthenes haranguing Philip. As a general Wallace declared martial law in Memphis, Cincinnati, and Baltimore.[116] As a judge he condemned Mary Surratt. And as a governor he felt no compunction to treat Billy the Kid, Victorio, or the perpetrators of the Lincoln County War with any mercy.[117] His actions of retribution were swift, severe, and real. He was not the sort of man to resort to allegorical subterfuge eleven years later in a novel disguising his innermost doppelgänger as an ancient Jewish teenager run afoul of the Roman Empire.

Indeed, when it comes down to it, the problem at Shiloh, as Grant would ultimately admit, was that Wallace had no clear written orders to follow, and there are two examples of this related to *Ben-Hur: A Tale of the Christ*, and neither produces the results Hanson's hypothesis would expect. In Plutarch's *Life of Pyrrhus* (33.2–3), very near the same episode Wallace used as his model for the tile incident in the streets of Jerusalem, one of the reasons Pyrrhus was caught in the urban fray that ultimately caused his death was that one of his soldiers misheard Pyrrhus' order to leave the city of Argos. Moreover, at the outset of Book Third, Arrius receives written orders from Sejanus to fight the pirates. Wallace makes no mention of improperly signed orders, or unclear orders, or anything of the sort. This is not vengeance: it is protocol.

Although he never received public exoneration, Wallace had for the most part processed the disgrace he had suffered at Shiloh. More importantly for him perhaps, he tells us that Grant twice told him in person that the fault was not Wallace's. In a letter Wallace wrote from Constantinople to W. R. Holloway the year after his novel was published, he says:

> I drop everything to tell you that I have just read the defense of my movements and conduct the first day of the battle of Shiloh which appears in your paper of the 25 January. Thank you a thousand times a thousand! I don't know who wrote the paper; but it is admirably done, and I charge you to give the author my best acknowledgement. If you are the man, so much the better. At last – at last one has appeared with a few, and he has studied my case, and understands it perfectly ...
>
> As to what I will do, you may announce that I will prepare an article for the magazine, and give a full and perfect history of the movements of my division throughout the two days of battle. This unmistakably upon my return home. The article shall be thorough and exhaustive. Grant seems to have utterly forgotten that he ever gave me an exoneration which covers the points he now makes against me as a glove covers a hand.
>
> He forgets another peculiarly interesting and pertinent incident. After the battle of Monocacy, he was full of gratitude. In saving Washington, I had saved his military reputation, and, in tacit acknowledgment, he invited me to spend a couple of weeks with him at City Point. I accepted the invitation. At the dinner table one day some officers were discussing the battle of Shiloh. The General and I both listened with interest. At length he turned to me, sitting at his right, and said in a low voice: "If I had known then what I know now, I would have ordered you to move as you started for the field." I never mentioned this circumstance before, because it was table-talk, and might have been considered confidential ...
>
> This is not for publication.[118]

Wallace makes no mention here of the fact that he had already absolved himself in his novel, or that he had the opportunity in 1873, just as he was beginning work on the novel, to write an account of what had happened at Shiloh but did not.[119]

Going further, Kevin Getchell, while vindicating Wallace, contends that the name Gratus was an obvious play on the name Grant.[120] Of course Gratus is a historical name that is chronologically appropriate. He also inaccurately contends that Wallace's defense of Cincinnati inspired Judah's rescue of "the Roman Senator" Arrius because Cincinnatus was also a Roman senator.

Paul Carter in *The Spiritual Crisis of the Gilded Age*, claims that Wallace "seems to have chosen the birth and death of Jesus as thematic material for the most crassly commercial of reasons."[121] Again, the reader knows that there is no evidence for this. Designing a novel to please popular taste is not at all the same as writing a novel for the most crassly commercial of reasons. Eventually many producers of American popular culture would "cash in" on successful prototypes, if that is what is meant by "crass commercialism." In fact, as this book intends to prove, Ben-Hur was at the forefront of this development in American consumerism. Surely Wallace was hoping the sales of his novel would pay off his debts and free him from working as a lawyer, which he detested, and as a public servant, for which he had not been adequately compensated until the Constantinople post, at which point he was over fifty years old. But even if Wallace could have conceived of writing a novel for purely commercial reasons in the 1870s, nothing else in his career or writings suggests that he did so.

His extant correspondence to family members preserves what we must assume are honest statements about his financial past, present, and expectations and in some instances reveals his attitude towards money. Most telling is the March 11, 1884, letter written to his son Henry from Constantinople.[122] Henry has written him about investing in a purchase of some Illinois swampland, but Lew is not at all eager to invest. In offering an explanation, he first replies says he has $5,800 in the bank and will "probably" earn $1,000 or so in *Ben-Hur* royalties, so with his government salary he has a total of $12,566. It is at this point that he reveals his innermost feelings about debt, money, and his financial future:

> I have just got out of debt, and have not forgotten the happiness of the breath of freedom. If I take the plunge, however, what can I promise myself? You say, $50,000, possibly $100,000. Whew! After years of harassment. Saying I have few years of life left me, shall it all be given up to creditors? God forbid! Money may gild tombs of dead men; it adds nothing to the reputation of the living. I have lived caring nothing for money, and it is now too late to acquire a new passion. Your mother and I together have just enough to support us comfortably the remainder of our days. It is best that we keep it.

As we will see, Wallace did not fully comprehend the lucrative possibilities of the *Ben-Hur* property until well after his return from Constantinople, and even then he maintained his taboo against dramatizing the novel for an additional dozen years. Successful popular art can always be criticized for producing a commercially viable but poorer imitation of a purer form of art, but Carter's accusation blurs the clear distinction between crass, profit-only focused commercialization and a work that aims to be successful and well received by its audience. Moreover, the road to commercial success in the 1870s did not include performing months of library research on ancient Judaism, writing a novel for seven years in Crawfordsville and the New Mexico Territory, and then painstakingly preparing the submission copy "written in purple ink with fastidious care."

NOTES

1. "How I Came to Write *Ben-Hur*," *Youth's Companion* 66 (February 2, 1893) 57; *An Autobiography*, 2:926–36, and *The First Christmas*, v–ix; cf. *The Chariot* 1 (November, 1895) 3. Cf. Harper, *The House of Harper*, 269–70; *NYT* (December 13, 1902) Suppl., 894.
2. *BE* (January 4, 1895) 7;
3. E.g. *NYT* (September 16, 1883) 1; *TBS* (September 17, 1883) 1; *HW* (March 6, 1886) 151.
4. *NYT* (February 18, 1912) SM10.
5. Letter from Wallace to Paul H. Hayne (January 19, 1881), IHS.
6. E.g. Smiley, "Epics of Christianity," 32–6; Dans, *Christians in the Movies*, 27; Lew Wallace, *Ben-Hur: A Tale of the Christ* (Barnes & Noble, 2004) xii.
7. Cf. *The [Colorado Springs] Daily Gazette* (December 19, 1880) 2. *The Chariot* 1 (November, 1895) 3, claims that Harper commissioned Wallace to write a magazine story called "Ben-Hur, a Tale of the Christ" in 1875.
8. Cf. *NYT* (April 5, 1886) 5; *Cleveland Leader* (April 28, 1886) 1.
9. *An Autobiography* 2:926–7.
10. *An Autobiography* 2:929.
11. Dixon, *The Holy Land*[3]. Letter from Lew to Susan Wallace (July 29, 1880), IHS, mentions Geikie's *Life of Christ* while proofing the manuscript of *Ben-Hur*.
12. *The New Biblical Atlas and Scripture Gazetteer*, 56–7.
13. Letter from Lew Wallace to Agnes Wallace (November 27, 1874), IHS.
14. E. Smallwood, *The Jews Under Roman Rule*, 156–60.
15. *WP* (February 9, 1902) 14, reports that Wallace and Ingersoll were on a train to Chicago; cf. *HW* (March 6, 1886) 151.
16. De Puy, *The University of Literature*, q.v. "Ingersoll, Robert Green."
17. Cf. McKee 166–7; M&M 300.
18. Wallace, *The First Christmas*, vii.
19. *An Autobiography* 2:931.
20. Cf. McKee 167–8.
21. *An Autobiography* 2:936.
22. *An Autobiography* 1:88–9.
23. *An Autobiography* 2:931–2.
24. Murphy, *Hemispheric Imaginings*, 97–118.
25. Wallace, *The Fair God*, 105.
26. Roeder, *A History of Culver*, 43 and 72; Karst, "Maxinkuckee Magic," 14.
27. <http://www.culver.lib.in.us/assorted_hotels.htm>
28. Quoted in Jones, "Lew Wallace," 130.
29. Chronology compiled from the *Santa Fe New Mexican* in the "Lew Wallace clippings" folder, NMHM.
30. E.g. *AC* (February 4, 1927) 8.
31. *An Autobiography* 2:936. M&M 291, point out that Wallace compares the Rio Grande Valley with "the region of the Nile."
32. *An Autobiography* 2:934.
33. *An Autobiography* 2:934.

34 *An Autobiography* 2:921, 934–5; Photo M0292, IHS. <http://images.indianahistory.org/cdm4/item_viewer.php?CISOROOT=/V0002&CISOPTR=749&CISOBOX=1&REC=1>
35 He sent a copy to Lawrence Barrett in 1871, published a version in Crawfordsville in 1876, returned to it again in April, 1881, shortly after the publication of *Ben-Hur: A Tale of the Christ* [Letter from Lew to Susan Wallace (April 4, 1881), IHS], and ultimately published it with Harper in 1898.
36 Cf. Russo & Sullivan 314–5.
37 *An Autobiography* 2:857; M&M 220.
38 Letter from Lew to Susan Wallace (December 4, 1879; July 29, 1880) IHS.
39 Josephus, *Life of Flavius Josephus* 7; *The Jewish War* 2.119; and *Jewish Antiquities* 18.11.
40 Collins, "Josephus on the Essenes." 56–7.
41 Leviticus 24: 20, Exodus 21: 24, and Deuteronomy 19: 21.
42 Whiston (trans.), *The Works of Flavius Josephus*, 557.
43 Cf. Acts 5: 37.
44 Because Dixon, *The Holy Land*, 90, says "St. Luke ... is thought to have heard the story which he tells of his Master's birth from the lips of Mary in her old age," Wallace could not easily dismiss his account of the Cyrenius census and taxation.
45 *An Autobiography* 2:927.
46 Pseudo-Bede, *Excerptiones partum, collectanea, flores ex diversis, quaestiones, et parabola* [=Migne, P.L. 94.541C-D].
47 E.g. Trench, *The Star of the Wise Men*, 15; Smith, *A Dictionary of the Bible*, 2:192.
48 Tertullian *Against the Jews* 9.12; *Against Marcion* 3.13.8; cf. Psalm 72: 10; John Chrysostom, *Homilies on Matthew* 6.2.
49 History of the Three Kings 1.10–12 [Horstmann].
50 King, *The Gnostics and Their Remains*, 133–4; cf. Jameson, *Legends of the Madonna*, 227.
51 Cf. M&M 226.
52 E.g. Cocker, *Christianity and Greek Philosophy*, 452–3. Cocker (144–5, n. 1), following the tradition that assigns this quotation to Cleanthes rather than Aratus, equates Zeus with *theos* and "God," e.g. Acts 17: 28. Cf. Lightfoot, *Saint Paul's Epistle to the Philippians*[2], 318.
53 McKee 164–5, cites Wallace's three Wise Men as allegories for Faith (Gaspar the Greek), Love (Melchior the Hindoo), and Good Works (Balthasar the Egyptian).
54 Wills, *Lincoln at Gettysburg*, 41–57.
55 *An Autobiography* 2:936.
56 *The Logansport Pharos* (August 26, 1897) 6.
57 Dixon, *The Holy Land*, 224. Any similarity between the name and the title of the Breton book, *Buhé hur Salvér Jesus-Chrouist* (Guénèd: Y.-M. Galles, 1861) is coincidental.
58 Frye, *Fearful Symmetry*, 228, 327–9; cf. Stallard, *Paradise Lost*, 326.
59 *An Autobiography* 2:934.

60 McKee 165.
61 Cf. *History of Montgomery County*, 561, where Wallace attributes Esther's character to that of his stepmother Zerelda Sanders.
62 Whiston, *The Works of Flavius Josephus*, 1.71 [=#422].
63 An alternative is offered in the recent Josephus translation by Mason, *Flavius Josephus*, 10, n. 39, who points out that Josephus' contemporaries in the late first century included Plutarch and Quintilian, both of whom had written about the late sixth-century Greek lyric poet, Simonides of Ceos. He implies that is possible that Josephus and Quintilian crossed paths in the court of Vespasian, but it is doubtful that either Quintilian or Plutarch began their works at the time of Simonides' birth in 79. Then again, the name Simonides may have been bestowed after his birth.
64 E.g. 4.3–4, 4.8, 4.10–11, 5.3, 5.6–9, 5.13–15, 7.4, 8.1–2, 8.6–7, 8.9–10.
65 Charles, *Wanderings*, 349.
66 Dixon, *The Holy Land*, 29; David Morgan, *Visual Piety*, 84.
67 Pliny, *Natural History* 7.214; Polybius, *Histories*, 1.16.
68 Macrobius *Saturnalia* 1.6.26; Martindale, *The Prosopography of the Later Roman Empire*, 2:760–1; Cameron, *The Last Pagans of Rome*, 241–2.
69 Cicero, *Ad Att.* 12.32.2; Horace, *Odes* 3.21.7; Shuckburgh, *The Epistles of Horace, Book I*, x.
70 Smith, *Dictionary of Greek and Roman Biography and Mythology*, 505. Messala appears briefly in *Julius Caesar* 4.3, 5.2–3, 5.5. Wallace's study in Crawfordsville included a copy of Arthur Murphy's *Tacitus*, as well as copies of [George] Baker's *Livy* and [Charles] Rollin's *Ancient History*.
71 Smith, *Dictionary*, 506; Tacitus, *Annals* 3.68; Seneca, *De ira* 2.5.5.
72 Roller, *The Building Program of Herod the Great*, 13–16.
73 E.g. Polybius 6.13; Cicero *Ad Quintum fratrem* 2.12.3.
74 Berwick, *Lives*, 22–6.
75 Schwartz, "Gambling in Ancient Jewish Society and in the Graeco-Roman World," 145–65.
76 Middleton, *The Life and Letters of Marcus Tullius Cicero*, 92–4.
77 Cf. Skeat, *Shakespeare's Plutarch*, 223–4.
78 Wallace employs none of the now familiar pirate iconography established by *Treasure Island* (1881/3), e.g. the peg-leg, the parrot on the shoulder, the "dead man's chest," and "X marks the spot."
79 Cicero (*Pro Flacco* 67) notes only that Pompey violated nothing in the temple.
80 Libourel, "Galley Slaves in the Second Punic War," 116–19.
81 Whiston (trans.), *The Works of Flavius Josephus*, 674.
82 I am grateful to Egert Pöhlmann for these and other suggestions.
83 Cf. Smith's *Dictionary of Greek and Roman Antiquities*, 1088, where the name is printed as C. Caecilius Rufus, his position was officially designated as consul, not duumvir, and in the year 17, not 24. Here Wallace substitutes the diphthong "oe" for "ae," as he does in the name of Arrius' flagship "Astroea" instead of the more common name "Astraea."
84 *British Musician and Musical News* 6 (February, 1930) 38–41.
85 *An Autobiography* 2:933–4.

86 Keipert, *Bibel-Atlas*, n.p.
87 *The New Bible Atlas and Scripture Gazetteer*, 56–7.
88 Van de Velde, *Map of the Holy Land*; and *Memoir* Table of Contents.
89 Dixon, *The Holy Land*, 92–103.
90 *An Autobiography* 2:936–7; *LAT* (July 18, 1887) 9; cf. *DFP* (July 1, 1894) 12.
91 Norman (trans.), *Antioch as a Centre of Hellenic Culture*, 64, n. 151; Humphrey, *Roman Circuses*, 456–7.
92 Smith's *Dictionary of Greek and Roman Geography*, q.v. Antioch; McLintock and Strong, *Cyclopaedia*, 267; Conybeare and Howson, *The Life and Epistles of St. Paul*, 1.150.
93 Downey, *Ancient Antioch*, fig. 5; Leblanc and Poccardi, "Étude," 91–126.
94 A few small venues with a center "wall" measuring approximately one stade have been identified, e.g. at Caesarea by Anazarbus, but such combination stadium-hippodrome constructions were built in lesser municipalities, not in large capital cities like Antioch; Humphrey, *Roman Circuses*, 527.
95 *Current Opinion* 13 (May–August, 1893) 130; *LAT* (16 April 1893) 23.
96 Berenger, *The History and Art of Horsemanship*, 53.
97 Spelman (trans.), *The Roman Antiquities*, 3.69 [132].
98 Richardson, *A New Topographical Dictionary*, 86–7.
99 In *LAT* (April 17, 1899) 2, Wallace makes clear that Gerome's painting, *The Chariot Race*, had some influence on him, but the *spina* in the painting is not measurable.
100 Spelman, *The Roman Antiquities*, 131 [3.68].
101 Smith, *A Dictionary of the Bible*, 2.960.
102 McKee 168; *The Writer* 17 (May, 1905) 107–8: seven drafts.
103 McKee 169, implies that it was Harper who changed the title.
104 Letter from Lew to Susan Wallace (December 4, 1879), IHS.
105 *Ben Hur – Chapter IX – Book IV*, UVA.
106 Letter from Lew to Susan Wallace (January 9, 1880), IHS.
107 Cf. M&M 292; *The Christian Advocate* 80 (April 27, 1905) 653.
108 Rutherford, *American Authors*, 543–4: "writes on a slate, so that he can easily erase what is wrong; then he writes on soft paper with a pencil. He patiently goes over the same ground until he has brought the expression of his thoughts up to his standard of excellence. The final copy is on large unruled paper in violet ink."
109 Hanson, *Ripples of Battle*, 132–3; cf. Hanson, "Lew Wallace," 67–86.
110 Hanson, *Ripples of Battle*, 137.
111 *An Autobiography* 2:932; Matthew 8: 2–3, Mark 1: 40–2, Luke 5: 12–13.
112 Hanson, *Ripples of Battle*, 138.
113 Letter from Lew Wallace to Mr. Conway (September 25, 1886), UVA.
114 Letter from Lew Wallace to President U. S. Grant (August 13, 1873), UVA.
115 *Boston Daily Advertiser* (July 30, 1863) 2.
116 In Maryland he issued General Order No. 112 providing "special military protection" to protect freedmen. Cf. Escott, "What Shall We Do with the Negro?"; Vorenberg, *Final Freedom*, 173–4.
117 E.g. *Weekly New Mexican* (November 23, 1878) n.p., NMHM.
118 Letter from Lew Wallace to W. R. Holloway (February 17, 1881), IHS.

119 Wallace published his *Shiloh Address* (Crawfordsville, IN: New Review Print, 1903) after the April 6, 1903, dedication ceremony of Indiana's monuments on the battlefield.
120 Getchell, *La Crónica*, 1–2; cf. Getchell, *Scapegoat of Shiloh*.
121 Carter, *The Spiritual Crisis of the Gilded Age*, 65–74.
122 Letter from Lew to Henry Wallace (March 11, 1884), IHS.

4 Publication and Early Reception of the Novel

As the fortune of *Ben-Hur: A Tale of the Christ* develops through Harper's internal readers' evaluations, publication, external reviews, publicity, and sales reports, the reader will have the opportunity to observe many of the processes that are requisite to and the consequence of popular success, keeping in mind that while *Ben-Hur: A Tale of the Christ* was not the only extremely popular book of its era nor the first commercially viable artistic property, it would surpass every other book of its era by maintaining its popularity for decades and expand considerably the breadth of popular demographics as well as the boundaries of artistic and literary commercial success. The expansion into formal and for-profit types of public presentations, drama, cinema, and industrial and retail commerce will be discussed in detail in subsequent chapters. Here the focus is on the publication of the novel, some of the most notable critiques and reviews the book received, its gradual trajectory towards becoming a bestseller in the book trade, and the impact this had on the celebrity of Lew Wallace.

THE HOUSE OF HUR IN THE HOUSE OF HARPER

Henry Harper passed Wallace's beautiful manuscript over to George Ripley, Harper & Brothers' principal reader. Ripley would not seem to have represented Wallace's immediate demographic in that he had been a Unitarian and Transcendentalist – a religious liberal, hardly a simplistic believer in the Christ – and was now a highly respected literary critic. Indeed, Ripley would not categorize Wallace's manuscript as "legitimate literature," but he had considerable publishing experience and an appreciation for the components of popular literature. In his autobiography Henry Harper reprinted part of Ripley's reader's report:

> The author of this sacred romance has acquired considerable reputation by his imaginative pictures from the Mexican mythology which he interwove with a gorgeous narrative of love and passion. He is an original and powerful writer, without precedent or prototype. He belongs to an exceptional sphere of literature, and

soars on too daring wings into a too radiant atmosphere, to be reckoned among the classics. He flashes like a glittering meteor through the sky, but never shines like one of the serene and eternal lights of the firmament. The present work is a bold imaginative experiment. The plot is founded partly on the Greek and Roman antiquities of the period, which furnish the principal figures, and partly on scenes in the history of Christ, whose person occupies a conspicuous place in the foreground of the picture. The story may be described as a collection of scenes from the evangelical narrative presented in the form of high-colored melodrama, with episodes from the traditions and poetry of the day. It is a work of superior order to the fantastic inventions of Ingraham, Headley, and others of the inflated religious school, and may rather be compared to a sacred epic in the style of Klopstock, a sublime prose poem, in which the facts of the Christian history are clothed in the gorgeous splendors of fancy. I do not regard it, either in the selection of theme or the style of execution, as belonging to classical or even legitimate literature, and if it were the production of a new and unknown writer I could not bring myself to recommend its publication. But with the prestige of the author and his really uncommon gifts of invention and illustration, together with the features of popular interest that would give it a wonderful fascination among a multitude of readers, I think it might be well to accept the manuscript.[1]

Despite its illegitimacy as literature, Ripley recommended the manuscript in part because Wallace was inventive and had a unique talent for literary description, and in part because the manuscript had a "fascination" and offered "features of popular interest," no doubt including the chariot race, gladiatorial challenge, and the pirate attack and subsequent shipwreck. Another reason for his recommendation was "the prestige of the author." Wallace's current position as governor of a Western territory may have been of some importance to the Eastern literary and publishing establishment, but Wallace's name also carried the gravitas of his military, legislative, and political careers, including his Civil War credibility. Ripley had worked for many years with Horace Greeley at the *New York Tribune*, and Greeley had been one of the staunchest defenders of Wallace's actions on the first day of the battle at Shiloh.[2]

That Ripley included Greek antiquity in his description of what was primarily a book about Rome and Judea suggests either that Ripley's education at Harvard made him automatically think of Greco-Roman antiquity as a unity, or that Wallace's application of the Greek names Simonides and Cleanthes, not to mention making the magus Gaspar spout some Greek philosophy, struck a special chord with him. In addition, Ripley's observation that Wallace created "episodes from the traditions and poetry of the day," may refer to the two quotations Wallace includes from Homer for the chariot race (5.13–14),[3] and the four lines he assigns to Anacreon for his description of Daphne (4.6). Depending on the extent of his Latin education, Ripley may also have picked up on the fact that a Messala was a Roman patron of the arts and a friend of Ovid and Horace.[4]

Remarkably, another of Harper's readers at the time was Charlton T. Lewis, a particularly versatile scholar who, although at the time was an attorney with a specialty in the insurance field, had been a professor of both Greek and mathematics and the primary compiler of the "Lewis & Short" Latin dictionary.[5] Lewis had published *A Latin Dictionary* just one year earlier in 1879, and for students and scholars it would remain the standard Latin-English dictionary for a century. Lewis also recommended publication but pointed out, appropriately, the errors Wallace made in his use of the Latin term *duumvir*.

> I think the story may be published with some confidence that it will have a fair sale, and with the chance of a great success. It is one of the boldest attempts ever made to represent before the imagination the scenes and life of the time of Christ; to link together profane history and the story of the New Testament. Its boldness is its characteristic; there is ingenuity in the plan and life in some of the characters; but not enough of incident or of human nature to furnish a modern novel of this length, while the disquisitions and reflections are often tedious, and there are some errors which ought to be corrected – for example, the constant use of the plural for *duumviri*, when a single man is spoken of. Yet the book has a species of fascination in the realism with which it clothes the infancy of Christianity, and in the reverent spirit with which the subject is treated; and it will find eager readers and lenient critics.

Including his observation of Wallace's Latin errors, which were corrected in the printed volume, Lewis was the first to put into writing that the novel would find "eager readers" and had "the chance of a great success." Like Ripley, Lewis uses the word "fascination," probably attributable in no small way to the description of the desert, the Wise Men, and the Nativity which the readers encounter immediately in Book First. Of interest, too, is the phrase "reverent spirit," a concept that would apply to not just the novel but its dramatic by-products for several decades.

The manuscript's daring synthesis of history, the New Testament, and a fictional tale satisfied Lewis as a scholar of antiquity, but as a reader, in contrast to Ripley, he found fault with the manuscript's dearth of incident and tedious disquisitions and reflections. The tedium would be the subject of criticism after publication as well, but many would be won over by Wallace's ability to write descriptions so filled with physical detail that they found themselves convinced of the story's realism. As for the dearth of incident, compared with the page-turning incidents of his first unpublished novel, this one has relatively few, but they are large in scope. Book First contains the Nativity, Book Second the tile incident and Judah's imprisonment, Book Third the naval battle and Judah's liberation, Book Fifth the chariot race and single combat against the hired assassin, Book Sixth the freeing of the lepers, the rebellions against Pilate, and Judah's victory in single combat against one of Pilate's infiltrators, and Book Eighth the Crucifixion. Lewis did not think this was an adequate amount for a 552-page book. As it would turn out, the "fascination" and "reverent spirit" the book features would captivate thousands upon thousands of readers, while its major "incidents," namely, the galley sequences and chariot race, would become central to the story's marketability on stage, on screen, and in the world of commerce. Like any property that is to achieve huge and lasting popular success, Wallace's novel would satisfy or entertain a variety of demographic sectors for a variety of reasons.

Not just these two readers appreciated the feasibility of publishing Wallace's manuscript. McKee records that "Mrs. Harper predicted that the firm would publish the work if it should never publish another."[6] Henry Harper himself was concerned about making Christ a central figure in the novel. Although Harper did not say so, sectarian differences between Catholics and Protestants would add to the potential hazard in making Christ a central figure in the novel. This issue alone helps to demonstrate that *Ben-Hur* was not written specifically to profit from an already well-established retail market in fictionalized embellishments of the life of Jesus. That easy road to riches was not yet paved. To the contrary, Wallace's *Ben-Hur* was the novel that reinvented the genre in popular literature and enabled the successes more than a decade later of such popular works as *Quo Vadis?* and *In His Steps*.

Having followed his own three rules, Wallace assured Harper that there was nothing excessive about his treatment of Jesus.[7] Harper accepted the manuscript in early May, offered Wallace a contract, and put the book into production without delay.[8] The contract offered the typical 10 percent royalty and was otherwise standard, revealing no hint of future success or extraordinary legal challenges. Of note here is the standard clause (3) that confirms that "the compensation for translations and dramatizations shall be subject to agreement between the parties [Wallace and Harper & Brothers] hereto." Future agreements relying on this legal partnership in matters of dramatization would generate millions of dollars, and copyright infringements would land both parties, albeit after Wallace's death, before the United States Supreme Court.

On May 26, Harper issued a press release in the *New York Herald Tribune*.[9] The reader might take note that this was the first of tens of thousands of press releases that would promote *Ben-Hur* products over the next century. This one noticeably accents the author's military and political prestige. Indeed, although the contract with Harper is signed by "Lewis Wallace," Harper's ledger books would nonetheless list him as "Gen'l Lew Wallace." The release specifies the setting of the story but does not mention its eyewitness account of the passion of Christ, using it simply as a chronological marker.

> General Lew Wallace, Governor of New Mexico, has written a new novel called "Ben-Hur." The scene is laid in Antioch and Jerusalem, and the time is during the life of Christ.

In contrast, an editor in *The Washington Post* made sure to demean the project by appending, "Gen. Wallace, it will be remembered, once wrote something or other called "The Fair God."[10]

On July 29 Wallace wrote to Susan that he was on page 448 of the proofs,[11] and on September 2 he sent off the last page, adding that it had been a "long, long job."[12] On October 9 Harper sent Wallace a letter along with a copy of the novel "in sheets" and a copy of the cover, saying they could publish the novel around October 22 and were securing a sale in England but suggesting a delay:

> It has occurred to us, however, that the interests of the book would be hazarded if published before the holidays. The pressure of books intended for the holiday season absorbs the attention of the trade and drives from their counters books not specially suited for gifts. In addition, the newspapers are apt to pay less attention at that time to books of a general character. We think that it would be better for the book, if its publication were deferred until after New Year's.[13]

To be sure, there was a vibrant market for books during the Christmas season. The October 23, 1880, issue of *The Publisher's Weekly*, for instance, features a full page ad for Appleton's edition of a work of similar interest and known to Wallace, Geikie's *Life and Words of Christ*, which had already been issued in some twenty-five editions.[14] This letter illustrates that Harper did not at all foresee how well Wallace's novel, and later such published extracts as *Seekers After the Light* and *The First Christmas*, would perform for the Christmas gift market in the years to come. Later, however, in 1886, it was Henry Alden at Harper & Brothers who would ask Wallace to write "The Boyhood of Christ" for the December Christmas issue of their magazine, and from that year "Ben-Hur" and Christmas would be a frequent tandem in a variety of ways. Even four decades in the future, for instance, MGM would schedule the premiere of its first version of *Ben-Hur* for late December, 1925. Ultimately Harper did not delay publication after all and published the novel on November 12, 1880, and one of its early reviewers judged the new novel "an appropriate Christmas gift-book."[15]

REVIEWS

Secular Reviews

The initial daily newspaper reviews that appeared in the next weeks were generally favorable. *The New York Times* devoted almost two columns to their review, providing ample phrases for Harper to extract for their advertising:

> The spirit in which Mr. Wallace writes is at once picturesque and eloquent, and yet thoroughly devotional ... Some of Mr. Wallace's writing is remarkable for its pathetic eloquence ... It is written not only with considerable power, but with a rare and delicate appreciation of the majesty of the subject with which it presumes to deal.[16]

Harper would quote some of these phrases in their advertising even in the next decade.[17]

The *Times* review contains a long plot summary and two sizable quotations of reverent passages, and in the former the anonymous author lays out the importance of the Judean political situation that underlies the events of the novel and focuses on the various incidents. It is a bit disconcerting that there are several blatant errors, e.g. that the novel is divided into seven books, that Ben-Hur is a boy "playing on the roof" when the tile falls, and that Judah used Maxentius' Roman legions to fight for the new king. The review devotes a few inches to the hand-to-hand combat against Messala's would-be assassins at the palace in Idernee (5.16). This passage will lose its popularity in future renditions of the Ben-Hur story, but in the early years it was often a highlight. In contrast, the review found this incident preferable to the chariot race, for it describes Judah's method of critically injuring Messala at the end of the race as "scarcely worthy of a hero."

The final evaluation in the *Times* review wrestles with matters of propriety and faith, as would most subsequent reviewers, for it is the most important judgment to make. A negative determination here might condemn the book as tasteless and irreverent; a positive one would at least allow the book to circulate. The *Times* reviewer is satisfied that Wallace was sincere in his reverence but adds that it will depend on different readers as to "whether propriety is not offended and the sentiment of reverence shocked by the intermingling of so many chapters of fiction with the sacred history." The reviewer points out also that there "can be no question that Mr. Wallace has laid himself open to attack," adding that previous attempts at paraphrasing the Gospel story are usually "those chiefly in circulation among the adherents of the Roman Church." The Catholic reaction to the book, as well as the Protestant, we will examine shortly.

The *Chicago Tribune* reviewer begins by focusing on historical authenticity, a standard by which many high-profile works of popular art set in antiquity will continue to be judged.[18] The reviewer in *The Californian*, for instance, writes about "the improbability of many of the incidents of the story."[19] Our reader knows that some of the "improbable incidents" were taken directly from historical events not only described but actually experienced by Josephus. Antiquity has long been the object of student and scholarly pursuit, so it presents an easy target for those who would find fault in technical and background details while ignoring the fact that most of the audience does not know or does not concern itself with such details. What matters in such popular works is not the accuracy but the presumption and appearance of accuracy that allows the audience to accept an ancient setting as a plausible background before they proceed into the story. One will always find inaccuracies or educated guesses that will not be considered plausible, and often questions of historical authenticity are not so easily answered. In this instance, the *Tribune* reviewer says "surely the invalid's wheelchair is a *modern* invention."

While unattested in ancient literature and material remains, Simonides' anachronistic "wheelchair" is not entirely implausible. Wallace says only that Simonides has a set of "little wheels for the purpose" of giving him access to an exterior patio. Otherwise he is immobile unless he is carried in the chair or on a litter. The Greeks were using wheels to move stage interiors six hundred years earlier, and, after all, Simonides was one of the richest men in the world. Caught in his own historical authenticity "gotcha" trap, the reviewer himself erred in stating that the commencement of Book Fourth was in the year 27; Wallace writes that it was 29, fifteen years after the accession of Tiberius, as it says in Luke 3: 1.

The review then launches into its discussion of propriety and faith, positing that:

> To introduce the Christ Himself will, to many, seem little less than blasphemy, while others, less rigid possibly in their religious tenets, will still consider it a matter of very questionable taste. The entire question seems to resolve itself into one of good or bad judgment.

This reviewer defends Wallace by arguing that the more the New Testament story is told, "the better it will be for mankind," thereby rendering *Ben-Hur: A Tale of the Christ* as a vehicle of Christian instruction, not far from Wallace's publically announced intention. However, although admitting that it is a matter of taste, the reviewer adds that "we do object to the manner in which the personality of the Christ is introduced into the different chapters to work up a climactic effect." If the reviewer found objectionable the synthesis of a fictional story and the story of the New Testament, nonetheless the plot summary includes without comment the critical insertion point where Jesus gives Judah a drink of water by the well in Nazareth. The reader knows that this is the only completely fictional passage involving Jesus in the entire novel.

In the final paragraph the Chicago reviewer points out that the female characters are not as well drawn as the male. Indeed, Judah's mother and Tirzah spend most of the novel hidden away in prison and presumed dead. Esther is by design demure and obedient, as is Amrah. Iras is much more colorful, of course, but as we will see, the reviewer in the *Baptist Review* will find her presence objectionable. The dearth and limited roles played by women in the novel will continue to be a problem for those faced with adapting *Ben-Hur* for the stage and cinema. Various adjustments will have to be made to address the issue. The *Ben-Hur, in Tableaux and Pantomime* will add multiple choruses of dancers, the 1925 film will have Erté design the fashions for Iras, and the 1959 film will cast a much-hyped Israeli starlet to play Esther while eliminating the character of Iras.

Several additional reviewers, even in generally favorable reviews, questioned the "Tale of the Christ" subtitle and the role Jesus plays in the narrative. *The Literary World*, for instance, describes the title as "misleading and inaccurate," complaining that "the author does not attempt so much as to give us a full-faced picture of the Nazarene."[20] In this instance Wallace did not have the opportunity to respond that this was directly by design, but in the popular arts in general, particularly regarding works relatively easy to assimilate by the public, an inherent problem for the artist is that members of the audience digest the work in a quick perusal and then immediately make positive or negative judgments about matters the artist has pondered, labored over, and reconsidered for days, weeks, months, or years. Another constant, found in *The Independent*, *The Advance*, and *The Californian*, is in making incompatible criticisms, with one reviewer praising Wallace's descriptive detail and another finding this detail tedious.[21] In addition to this and the issue of plausibility, still another constant Wallace would encounter was the smarmy abuse of his celebrity. In this instance even in a congregational weekly like *The Advance*, the reviewer's knowledge of the celebrity contaminated the review by asserting:

> If he will pardon us for saying it, there are many parts of the story which we suspect his wife would have told better, interweaving with a more deft skill information and story.

Sectarian Reviews

The reviews in *Christian Union* and *Western Christian Advocate* were quite favorable.[22] Both compliment Wallace's good taste, the latter remarking:

> We hazard nothing, we believe, in saying that no one has ever so well succeeded, as has General Wallace, in writing a book with these materials which is neither grotesque, irreverent, nor repulsive. He has produced a book which is full of dramatic power, elevated thought, profound insight into Jewish characters. It is a book which can not fail to move the heart and command the intellect.

Also positive was *Baptist Review*, although this is the aforementioned review that took issue with Iras. The objection was that Wallace had created and inserted this beautiful Egyptian temptress in a story involving the resurrection of Christ. In doing so the reviewer is ignoring her narrative purpose as a foil. She ridicules Jesus to Judah, she tests Judah's loyalty to Esther and his commitment to the new king, and as a consequence of her actions, she suffers bitterly.

Some of the reviewers in religious monthlies found quite offensive the material the secular reviewers found to be so tastefully and respectfully treated. E. H. L., the reviewer for *American Church Review*, formed a two-pronged attack, the first expressing outrage at novels depending upon Jesus as a character:

> It is high time for the Christian Church to set some seal of rebuke upon such audacious profanation of things sacred. Some of our older readers will remember "The

Prince of the House of David" by Professor Ingraham ... the very recollection of whose ephemeral popularity is enough to call a blush to the cheek of the thoughtful Christian.[23]

Ripley had compared Wallace's manuscript favorably to "the fantastic inventions of Ingraham," but E. H. L. condemns them both along with the latter's "ephemeral popularity." This sets up the secondary attack on Wallace's presumption in creating a story dependent upon "religious fancies and sentimentality." This review reduces Wallace to a "mere literary apprentice" and a "fledgling author," and claims that the only reason *The Fair God* received positive reviews was "probably in consideration of the General's noble war record." This turns the personal prestige Harper considered a positive reason for warranting publication into a negative.

Just as the review calls for a rebuke by the Christian Church of the literary subgenre, it also includes a corollary execration of its commercial viability:

> The best we can bring ourselves to wish for the General's venture is that a copy may never be sold. Alas! we much fear there is still enough pious sentimentalism in the land, after the success of the "Prince of the House of David," to water with its maudlin tears the book into at least a temporary popularity. Toward one congenial spot, we know, it will inevitably gravitate – the Sunday-school Library, which orders books wholesale by the catalogue, and makes a pious title a free ticket of admission.

E. H. L.'s wish that not a single copy would ever be sold was not to be granted, but the assumption that the Sunday school movement would embrace the novel would turn out to be correct. Within a few years, *Ben-Hur: A Tale of the Christ* would become not only a bestselling popular novel and a Christmas gift but also a Sunday school staple. The charge of sentimentality yielded to praise for its reverence.

The January, 1884 review in *Catholic World* provides an example.[24] According to the review, Harper failed to send them a review copy in 1880, but the editorial staff thought they would now be doing a service to their readers by "recommending it to them as a genuine and rare gem of literature." The intervening years had convinced them that the novel provided a positive influence and a powerful argument for the divinity of Christ. Instead of objecting to the critical insertion point at the end of Book Second, *Catholic World* describes the teenage encounter between Judah and Jesus as "simply exquisite, and worthy to be compared to a picture by one of the great masters."

Reviewers often disagreed as to how to characterize Judah Ben-Hur, uncertain whether he was "natural," the type literati and literary critics of the late nineteenth century generally preferred, or the old-fashioned heroic type. In 1880 the *Chicago Tribune* identified him as the former, while the *New York Times* found that by attacking Messala's chariot in the great race Judah was "scarcely worthy a hero." Three years later the otherwise positive *Catholic World* reviewer would find fault in the young Judah's excessive heroism:

> We will not call it faultless, and in our opinion, although in parts it reaches the excellence of the highest form of art, the author's exuberant imagination generally inclines him to overdraw and to color too highly. The young Prince Ben-Hur is too heroic and too much resembling a mythical demi-god, and the scene of the sixteenth chapter in the palace of Idernee borders too closely on the marvelous. These defects do not, however, detract from the fascinating charm of the story, and for young readers they doubtless add to it.

Again a review focuses on the gladiatorial incident at the palace of Idernee in 5.16. In doing so it becomes the first to identify young readers as a target demographic, and young readers would eventually help to proliferate the *Ben-Hur* phenomenon in many ways from generation to generation.

The review also includes a lengthy quotation describing Wallace's meeting with Robert Ingersoll, which the reader would know immediately to derive from the "Gossip from Indianapolis" article that had circulated in September, 1883. Armed with the confession of the author himself, *Catholic World* attacks earlier reviewers, albeit without citing them, charging that either they preferred straightforward historical accounts or recoiled at religious inspiration:

> Perhaps it is because of the genuine and clear Christian ideas and the deep religious sentiments embodied in *Ben-Hur* that its merits as a work of literary art have not been more distinctly recognized. Had it been written after the manner of Renan it would have won for itself and its author the highest praises of the literary critics, and would have become famous at once. But having been written in accordance with the truth of the Gospel, it could only await a reception of cold indifference from all except those who believe in that truth or at least feel no positive dislike of it. Even with these it is very likely that the deeply religious impressions which it conveys to their minds and hearts have caused them to forget the consideration of its literary excellence.[25]

Two Opposing Views: Horace Scudder and President Garfield

Horace Scudder wrote the review for the *Atlantic Monthly*.[26] A lifelong man of letters, he was the living embodiment of what Wallace was not. Educated in New England, a college graduate, an influential magazine editor, and a successful author of fiction and non-fiction, including the popular Bodley Books, Scudder would hardly be well disposed towards either an amateur author of fiction or non-clerical purveyor of sentimental reverence, let alone a synthesis of the two. In this well-crafted critique, Scudder initially warns readers about taking up another historical romance, especially one about Jesus. If they do, they should be "conscious of a repulsion." This actually introduces a tempered compliment when he concludes that readers will be "agreeably disappointed." But what he means is not that Wallace handles the material well but that he "endeavored to avoid the intellectual and speculative anachronisms inherent in such a project by merely disguising them in archaic forms." Scudder continues with a series of laudatory phrases worthy of a Harper ad – "singularly picturesque and romantic . . . powerful scenes . . . ingenious devices" – but immediately adds:

> It is to be regretted that the book, with all its irregular power, should fall so frequently into sloughs which intimate an untrained hand in the writer.

He laments that readers will become entangled and confused in the story, and he even suggests that "the book is always in danger of dropping into the habits of the dime novel."[27] In addressing the question of propriety and faith, he clearly despises Wallace's "reverent timidity" in describing the Crucifixion and juxtaposing that with the joyful outcome for the Hur family. Scudder concludes, ". . . in spite of its merits, – and these are by no means inconsiderable, – the book must be pronounced a failure, artistically."

Interestingly, Scudder published his Bodley Books series with Houghton, Osgood and Company and their successors, Houghton Mifflin and Company, the company which still held the copyright to Wallace's *The Fair God*. One month after Scudder's review was published, Benjamin H. Ticknor of Osgood wrote a letter to Wallace lamenting that the latter had switched to Harper and suggesting there had been some misinformation that prompted him to do so:

> I am sorry that you were misinformed about the business, so that Harper got Ben-Hur, for I should feel it an honor to have had our name on that book. I have read and reread it, and if other people are only of my view about it, I doubt not you have had substantial proof in the sales how good it is.

Many of Scudder's criticisms are worthy of consideration, but his review was aimed at his knowledgeable and literate readers, not the hundreds of thousands of consumers who would purchase and embrace the novel in the next few years. In fact, just one particular reader, not a critic, was needed to counter its impact on Wallace and ultimately the continuing sales of *Ben-Hur: A Tale of the Christ*. This was President James Garfield. The Ohioan Garfield and Wallace had campaigned together during the Civil War, and Garfield had a special interest in the setting of the novel because just before the war he had been hired as a professor of classical languages at Hiram College.[28]

On April 29, 1881, Wallace, still in Santa Fe, wrote to Susan inquiring about the *Atlantic* review, and on the very same day he had received the soon-to-be-famous letter from President James A. Garfield:

> Dear Sue.
>   . . .
>   You say the *Atlantic* contains a review; but you don't say of what. I infer it is of Ben-Hur. Is it favorable or unfavorable? You don't say: wherefore, I opine it is <u>contra</u>. I can stand it, and for a number of reasons, the following amongst them:

> I received, not a letter to my surprise, a letter from Pres. Garfield, which I copy, having sent the original to the Harper's, to be returned to you when they have made such use of it as they think appropriate.[29]

Wallace's initial comments and question make it clear that he might have been anxious about the negative *Atlantic* review, but the coincidental arrival of the Garfield letter would turn out to be much more influential. Actually, the coincidence was not entirely an accident. In late 1880, as Harper sent out its review copies, Wallace had sent copies of the novel to both outgoing President Hayes and President-Elect Garfield.[30] Hayes acknowledged receipt only, but Garfield immediately responded positively and "hopes to find the leisure time to read it before long." He did find the time to read it between April 13 and 19, 1881.

Then Wallace quotes Garfield's brief but laudatory letter, dated April 19.

> Dear General,
> I have this morning, finished reading "Ben-Hur"- and I must thank you for the pleasure it has given me.
> The theme was difficult, but you have handled it with great delicacy and power.
> Several of the scenes such as the wise men in the desert, the sea fight, the chariot race – will I am sure take a permanent and high place in literature.
> With this beautiful but reverent book you have lightened the burden of my daily life and renewed our acquaintance which began at Shiloh.[31]

Wallace continues in his letter to Susan:

> There now, my dear, what do you think of that! I think a great deal of it. Partly because he ... is a man of literary taste, partly because it must be honest, judging from the fact that he could have no notion to deceive or even be polite. The Harper's, I have no doubt, will know how to make the letter most profitable.

Harper immediately introduced it into their advertising. A press release placed in the very first volume of *The Critic*, a twice-monthly literary journal edited by Jeannette Leonard and Richard Watson Gilder, quotes the letter in its entirety.[32] More importantly, Harper also printed the entire text on in a full-page ad on the cover of *Harper's Young People*, their illustrated weekly aimed at a separate demographic.[33]

In the end, Wallace's important positions in the government as well as his military reputation and acquaintance with a number of leading members of the government became an important element in the initial success of the *Ben-Hur* phenomenon. Even a decade before the Garfield edition was published in 1891, while Wallace's senior position in the Union army made him well remembered to Garfield, his governorship in New Mexico made him one of Garfield's employees, as it were, and the quality of *Ben-Hur: A Tale of the Christ* made him seem underemployed. Grant had been targeting Wallace for the post in Paraguay, but the novel made the obvious choice Constantinople, which, as Garfield is reported

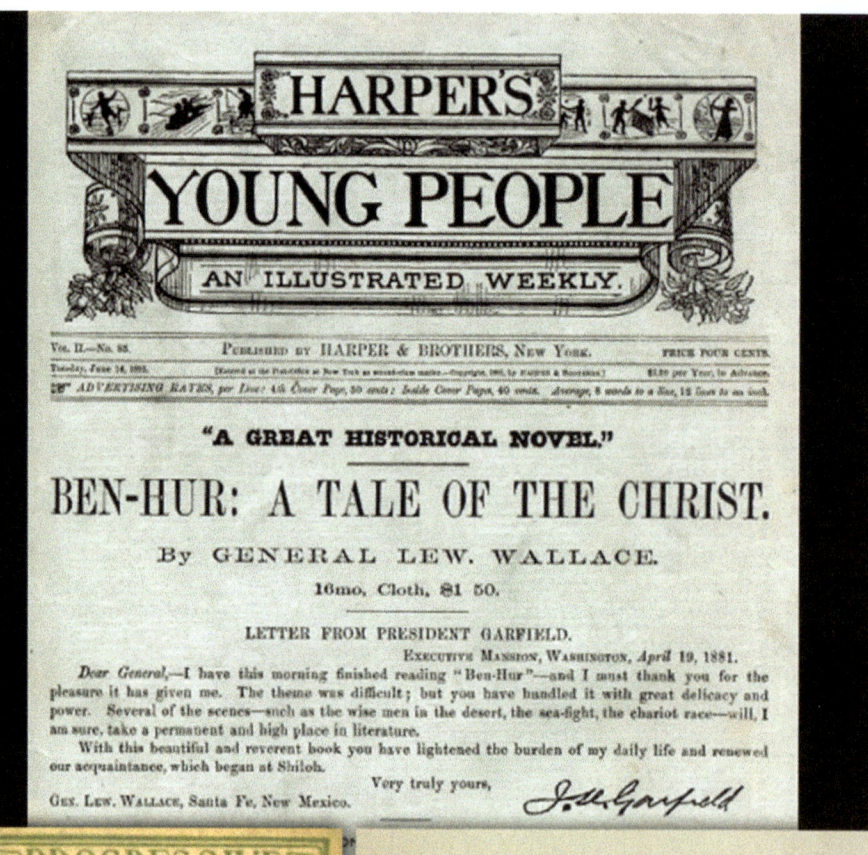

Figure 4.1 Targeting the younger demographics, Harper advertised the Garfield edition in *Harper's Young People* in 1891 and excerpted "The Star of Bethlehem" in Aldrich's *Progressive Course in Reading* in 1900.

to have said, "would give him opportunities for still greater success" in the East.[34] Wallace resigned his New Mexico post around this time, and on May 31 he departed for Turkey.[35] Thereafter, while sales of the novel were increasing in the early 1880s, an added cachet was that the author was currently serving as the "Envoy Extraordinary and Minister Plenipotentiary of the United States of America to Turkey."[36] When he returned home five years later, he would earn additional thousands of dollars and increase his celebrity by giving lectures based on his experiences in and knowledge of Turkey along with readings from *Ben-Hur: A Tale of the Christ*. In addition, as Garfield had hoped, Wallace's time in Turkey gave him the inspiration to write *The Prince of India*, his next and last novel. The publication of this novel in turn increased Wallace's fame and fortune and laid open the path towards the even more lucrative Klaw & Erlanger production.

INITIAL SALES AND GROWTH (1880–6)

A lack of internal Harper records obscures their marketing strategy, but accounting ledgers at Columbia University's Butler Library, external correspondence, and such extant ephemera as advertisements and published press releases paint a fairly clear picture. The growth of the novel's popularity was a relatively slow process that responded moderately well to Harper's initial efforts. Then sales doubled in 1883, and doubled again in 1885, tripled in 1886, and doubled yet again in 1887. In a subsequent chapter we will examine how several aspects of the cultural conditions of the late nineteenth century provided such a welcoming and fertile environment for *Ben-Hur*, especially after 1885. Here we will rely more upon statistical and anecdotal information to reconstruct the all-important first few years after publication.

As we have seen, Harper did not present the novel to the public as a Christmas item in late 1880, nor did they design or implement immediately after the Christmas season any extraordinary publicity campaign of the sort that often accompanies modern popular artistic releases thought to have bestseller potential. But they did give it preferred status. Highlighting the "new" book from "General" Lew Wallace, they often placed it near the top of their ads in literary sections of various publications. Telling is that Harper sometimes listed *Ben-Hur: A Tale of the Christ* first on its list of "The New Novels" even before Henry James's *Washington Square*, e.g. in the November 25, 1880, edition of *The Independent*.[37] In the Harper announcements in *the American Bookseller*, *Ben-Hur: A Tale of the Christ* is listed second only to John Green's *History of the English People* (Volume IV), and it is second in the "Literary Notes" section of the November 24, 1880, issue of *Christian Union*.[38]

The announced retail price of the book seems to have changed after publication. In the September 1, 1880, issue of *American Bookseller* and then the November 13 and December 4, 1880, issues of *The Publishers' Weekly*, Harper first listed it at the price of $1.00.[39] The price is listed at $1.50 in the December 11 issue, and it would remain unwaveringly at $1.50 until a number of years into the next century, although by the 1890s one could pay much more for the novel in deluxe bindings and editions.

According to Wallace's autobiography (2:941), "for the first year of its existence the book showed no signs of its future popularity," and McKee (173) reports that by June, 1881, sales had reached about 2,800 copies. This number is not corroborated by an accounting sent on letterhead by Harper & Brothers to Susan Wallace in response to her demand (while Lew was in Constantinople) for an annual accounting of sales.[40] The Harper letter to Susan lists 4,187 books sold from November 12, 1880, to June 24, 1881.[41] Nonetheless, for comparison, *Uncle Tom's Cabin* was said to have sold as many as 300,000 copies in its first year alone.[42]

In *An Autobiography* (2:941) Wallace continues by saying, "nor did its sale improve much in the second year," while McKee says, "then came a sharp decline, and it looked as if the book's little fame had evaporated; at the end of 1881 the demand was practically nonexistent." By Harper's accounting the novel had sold an additional 9,085 copies during the twenty-one month period between June 24, 1881, and March 3, 1883. These accounts need not be entirely contradictory, for the bulk of those sales may have been transacted after the conclusion of 1881. This rate of approximately 430 sales per month is almost one-third lower than that of the initial period in which approximately 600 books were sold per month, so clearly there was a decline but not necessarily a drastic one. Throughout this first two and one-half years, although there was as yet no evidence that the novel would become a market phenomenon, many of the required building blocks for commercial success were in place. The novel itself appealed to a variety of readership types, and Harper was designing its ads to emphasize the unique reputation of the author and the work's integral but respectful Christian element. In addition, on November 27, 1880, Harper had already notified Wallace that they had secured an English counterpart.[43] By March 28, 1881, the British publisher Sampson Low was announcing in the *New York Times* that "Gen. L. Wallace's religious novel" had been added to their list of standard six-shilling novels.[44]

Interest picked up considerably in January, 1882, when the *Chautauqua Hand-Book* (No. 2) added *Ben Hur* to the list of the novels included in the reading list for courses offered by the Chautauqua Literary and Scientific Circle [C.L.S.C.].[45] On August 31, Lawrence Barrett sent Wallace a letter from New York asking permission to dramatize the novel – the first hint of the *Ben-Hur* phenomenon that would begin to take shape much later in the decade. In September Harper demonstrated their continued support for the property by announcing a new edition in a press release, and they prominently displayed this announcement before listing their new books.[46] In October the "Washington *Critic*" circulated a rumor that Wallace was "preparing a Turkish novel to rival 'Ben-Hur.'"[47] In February, 1883, the gossip column in *Frank Leslie's Illustrated Newspaper* stated that "General Lewis Wallace, our Minister to Turkey, is said to be the most successful writer of fiction among Americans."[48] Nonetheless, just one month earlier Wallace had written to his son Henry that he expected to earn only $100 per year in royalties from his two novels.[49] The next year his royalty would amount to $3,200.[50]

The 13,491 copies sold during that twelve-month period from March, 1883, to March, 1884, matched the total of 13,272 sold in the preceding twenty-eight months. Several different developments may account for this. Cashing in on Wallace's appointment in Turkey, Harper adjusted their marketing angle slightly and was now advertising the new edition by identifying the author as "Gen. Lew Wallace, United States Minister to Turkey."[51] Clearly Wallace's reputation provided good publicity, as did his current exotic location overseas. Even the *New York Times* would follow Wallace's progress as he prepared to return to the United States.[52] There was also a negative factor. British editions had been filtering into the United States through the Canadian border and were being sold for 50¢ less than the Harper price. On the one hand, such illegal sales may have helped to spread the reputation and popularity of the novel, but they would not have accrued to either Harper's account or Wallace's royalties. By January, 1884, Harper was already taking action and circulating a warning in print. We will return to this and other copyright infringement problems below.

The most important new external factor may have been the "Gossip From Indianapolis" newspaper article that circulated in September, informing the public at large about Wallace's Ingersoll encounter and quoting Wallace's Christian mantra in its final line:

> The result of my long study was the absolute conviction that Jesus of Nazareth was not only a Christ and the Christ, but that he was also my Christ, my Saviour, and my Redeemer. That fact settled in my own mind, I wrote "Ben Hur."

That the esteemed "Gen. Wallace" had embraced Jesus as his personal Savior and Redeemer as a direct result of his thought-provoking encounter with "Col. Ingersoll, the infidel," as the article described him, no doubt provided some very positive inspiration to potential readers.

As this might have inspired additional devout Christian readers, there is contemporary evidence for how the novel's literary qualities attracted a secular element.[53] An essay in the *Fort Wayne Gazette* in July, 1883, commends Wallace's direct style of narrative, perhaps even his frequent apostrophes to "the reader":

Lew Wallace's Ben Hur has been most widely read in Fort Wayne not because the author is an Indiana man, for if there ever was a place where the proverb, "no man is a prophet in his own country" applies, it is in Indiana and Fort Wayne in particular. It is the power of the author that commands respect and makes of every reader a friend.[54]

Similarly, a letter to the editor of *The Literary World* (a few months after our period) awards the novel very high praise as a work of American fiction, comparing it favorably to *Ivanhoe*:

> One of your correspondents asks your opinion respecting the best work of fiction that was ever written in any language. If by "fiction" he means *The Novel*, then surely we have a book, written by an American, on the very loftiest possible theme, that meets the requirements of his question. No book since *Ivanhoe* is at all worthy to be placed by its side. Its pure and elevated tone is sustained throughout, and its power over the imagination and the heart has never been excelled. Its author is Lew Wallace, and its name is *Ben-Hur*.[55]

In addition, the reputation of the book's accuracy in representing the ancient world continued to be a selling point. Local literary clubs were beginning to employ *Ben-Hur: A Tale of the Christ* as a handbook for the study of Roman history, and *The Century* declared that it was filled with "useful knowledge":

> There is so much "information" in it. It must have taken so much labor to write it that one is willing to bestow a great deal in reading it; and when one has come to the last of its five hundred and fifty-two pages he feels that he has not been merely trifling with society nonsense, but has stored his mind by the way with useful knowledge.[56]

By the end of 1884 sales were mushrooming. Harper sold over 13,000 more copies by the end of the year, another 32,000 before the end of 1885, another 57,000 in 1886. This phenomenal growth in sales over just two years was due in no small part to the religious, literary, and reputational factors just discussed, but both the Wallaces and Harper continued to be dynamic participants in perpetuating the momentum. Harper issued a syndicated press release when sales reached the 80,000 mark. A syndicated comment in the *Detroit Free Press* mused about Wallace that "many authors would like to have 'Ben Him.'"[57] Then Susan wrote a brief but important letter to Harper on November 24, 1884.

> Dear Sir,
> Because of inquires of correspondents as to the *number* of *wives* Gen. Wallace has had, I have thought best to instruct you to add the dedication of Ben-Hur, making it:
>
> To
> The Wife of My Youth
> who still abides with me
>   This with Gen. Wallace's consent.

Several literary clubs have made it a handbook for study in connection with Roman History. If by some means you could have it adopted by the Chautauqua Club, which numbers twenty thousand members, it might be worth while to try. Pardon the suggestion.
May I ask you to furnish me a report of the sales of Ben-Hur, year by year, from the beginning?
With high regard,
   Very truly yours,
      Susan E. Wallace[58]

The many correspondents inquiring about the dedication (that Wallace had adapted from Tupper's "Marriage"), demonstrate once again the personal element that seems to have had the effect of making Lew Wallace a "friend" to his readers.[59] Changing the dedication would of course affect first-edition book resale in the distant future and also help antiquarians to price otherwise undated editions.[60] And in response to Susan's request, Harper began to send annual statements, which she preserved, making available some of the sales statistics quoted in this chapter.

Harper contacted Lew Wallace at his offices in the Hotel Luxemburg in Constantinople in early 1885, as he relates in his letter of February 8 to Susan, "reminding me that I am to write its Christmas article for the magazine for next year."[61] Now that Wallace had written a very successful novel for them and would be free of his duties in Constantinople, Henry Alden at Harper commissioned him to write an article to help sell their signature magazine, and because his novel was so identified with the Christ, the popular December issue was an obvious fit. In turn Harper would use the magazine article to publicize Wallace, his novel, and his association with Harper. By April Wallace writes Susan that he has selected the boyhood of Christ as his topic.[62] Because it was a story involving children, it was hoped to attract a broader family demographic, and he made it clear that he designed the narrator of the story, Uncle Midas, as a transparent version of himself, for "Uncle Midas had led a busy life; he had been a lawyer, a soldier, an author, and a traveller; he had dabbled in art, diplomacy, and politics."[63] The sixteen-page story, which takes place on Christmas Eve, was amply illustrated and published the following year in the December, 1886, issue of *Harper's New Monthly Magazine*, the author being listed not as Lew Wallace but as "The Author of 'Ben Hur.'" Promoting it widely, they placed ads for the story in other periodicals, e.g. the November 15 issue of *The Nation*.[64] Reader comments to Harper were so positive that they almost immediately asked Wallace if he would be interested in developing the story into book form.[65] That would be published in 1888, adding additional fuel to the fire and cementing the public's association between Lew Wallace, tales of the Christ, and Christmas gifts.

PROMOTING *BEN-HUR*

Marking Time in Indiana and New Mexico

The *New York Times* reported in an otherwise political column in 1884 that Wallace had no plans to run for governor of Indiana and would instead continue gathering material for his next novel, "which the readers of 'Fair God' and 'Ben Hur' will welcome."[66] In New York on July 4, 1885, as he stepped off the steamship bringing him home from his Constantinople appointment, he told a *Chicago Tribune* reporter that he was traveling the next week to New Mexico to give his extensive mining interests "his undivided attention."[67] An additional winter trip to New Mexico to inspect these non-producing mine investments makes it clear, as does his earlier trip in the summer of 1884 (while on leave) as well as his frequent correspondence with Henry on financial matters, that although he had finally retired from government service and his legal practice, he intended to stay active and earn extra income, but there was no mention of promoting *Ben-Hur: A Tale of the Christ* or developing his celebrity status as a lecturer and author.[68]

The following year the *Times* printed Harper's press release that Notre Dame University, no doubt encouraged by the belated but laudatory *Catholic World* review, had placed "*Ben Hur* . . . first on the list of books to be read to the students in the refectory."[69] The March 6, 1886, edition of *Harper's Weekly* featured an engraving of Wallace on the cover and a biographical interview by Eugene Lawrence.[70] The articles, however, said nothing about his future plans except the possibility of taking up a position in Constantinople offered by the Sultan. There were many additional press reports quoting Wallace's opinions about Turkey and his criticisms of Civil War figures, particularly General Halleck.[71] This kind of national publicity reinforced Wallace's local Indiana stature, where he was much in demand by church and civic organizations, but recalling the unpleasant lecture tour he experienced after the Mexican War, he refused most of these invitations. However, for an April 7 engagement at the Plymouth Church in Indianapolis, the promise of satisfactory payment for himself and raising money for the church, plus the size of the venue, seem to have provided enough reasons for him to acquiesce. A thank-you letter from E. B. Martindale reports that "after paying all expenses," the church netted $351, "so you see there were really more than 1000 people in the house. Mr. McCulloch says it was "the largest audience ever assembled in this city to hear a paid lecture."[72]

It is important to observe that Wallace's standard lecture at this time was on "Turkey and the Turks," not *Ben-Hur: A Tale of the Christ*. He would develop two additional public lectures, one on "Mexico and the Mexicans" and another on the Civil War, titled "The Third Division of the Army of the Tennessee at Shiloh." He had published the novel six years earlier and had moved on to many other projects, literary and otherwise. According to his personal correspondence and public interviews in this period, he was pleased that the *Ben-Hur* project had achieved popularity as a novel. It had earned him a commission to write the *Harper's Weekly* Christmas article, brought him enough royalty income to retire from the government but not enough to relieve him of the stalled investments in New Mexico, and increased his celebrity by giving him a popular byline most could recognize. But Wallace had not yet realized that he had not nearly exhausted the money-making capability of his *Ben-Hur* property, nor had he as a literary businessman reached the level that his unique property would afford him.

Chautauqua

We do not know what Harper's response was to Susan Wallace about contacting "the Chautauqua Club." Since their responses to her requests to send her a regular accounting and change the dedication of the book were positive, chances are good that they did contact Chautauqua. Although we do not know precisely when Harper was in contact with Chautauqua about sales, or which party made the first contact, we do have vital and particularly interesting information about Wallace's promotional visit to Chautauqua on the second weekend of August, 1886. This would prove to be a significant turning point in the process of turning Wallace's book into a super-bestseller and its author into a celebrity, reinforcing the importance of making appearances in public and establishing a personal rapport with potential promoters. This was the first time Wallace gave a public reading of the chariot race passage from his novel, and it would provide an extra degree of intensity to the burgeoning *Ben-Hur* mania.[73]

The novel had been on the Chautauqua course list at least since January, 1882, and now Wallace himself was scheduled to give his lecture on "Turkey and the Turks" on Saturday, August 7, following Willis Beecher's lecture on "Nehemiah and His Bible" and George Sherman Batcheller's on "Egypt: Ancient and Modern."[74] This was an impressive program. Beecher was a professor of the Hebrew Language and Literature in New York, while Batcheller, another New Yorker, had served as an American judge on the International Tribunal in Egypt for eleven years. Wallace, of course, had just finished serving as the U.S. minister to the Sublime Porte, and "Turkey and the Turks" was Wallace's standard lecture at the time. The following Monday he was also scheduled to read from his novel, *Ben-Hur*. This was featured on the front page of the Chautauqua *Assembly Herald*:

> Monday, General Lew. Wallace, ex-United States Minister to Turkey, and author of "Ben Hur," will read from that novel, for the first time in public.

[Wallace's first name in print occasionally reflects the way he signed autographs, that is, with a dot after Lew.]

Someone along the way in the past 129 years placed six asterisks around the announcement, suggesting that Lew Wallace warranted a lecture on Turkey because of his diplomatic experience and its political timeliness, but what really interested the public was *Ben-Hur*. This was reaffirmed in 1966 when an entry in *The Chautauquan* recalled the reading from *Ben-Hur* but not the earlier lecture on Turkey, but in contrast the contemporary *New York Times* article spent the bulk of the article on Chautauqua events reporting on Wallace's detailed account of the Turkish people and their culture, habits, and reputation as well as the Sultan himself and Turkey's future in international relations.[75] But it was the chariot race that made the deepest impression on the thousands of auditors.

Press reports confirmed that Wallace read the passage "magnificently" and that "the intensely dramatic description lost nothing of its force in his reading."[76] The first column of the first page of the August 10 *Assembly Herald* included this poetic-like description of the event in the "History of a Day" column:

> Wallace and the audience join in the chariot race with "Ben-Hur." Faster and faster audience and reader fly around the track – the race is won. Breathless speed. Great victory. Laurels for the conductor.[77]

In contrast, the anecdotal report in Jesse Lyman Hurlbut's 1921 history, *The Story of Chautauqua*, is quite negative.[78] Hurlbut admits:

> an immense crowd packed the Amphitheater to hear General Wallace read from his *Ben Hur* the story of the Chariot Race.

But immediately thereafter Hurlbut continues:

> But candor compels us to say that it was not very thrillingly rendered. One who listened said, "He never got his horses off on a walk."

It is impossible to recover Hurlbut's motivation here, whether the goal was to demean the popular novel in order to preserve the educational and more sophisticated reputation of Chautauqua's lectures and public programs, or professional jealousy from one author against another who was a self-educated Midwestern military man but author of one of the most popular books ever written, or simply the desire to insert an amusingly sarcastic statement into an otherwise fairly somber book. But the many positive accounts and the ultimate positive outcome probably more accurately portray the general reaction.

Historically the most important reaction was that Wallace himself described in an extraordinary letter to Susan written on Chautauqua letterhead the evening after his reading.[79] The letter is written in a lax cursive, with a number of incomplete sentences, a few odd turns of phrase, and a personal note appended in a postscript written vertically and filling the left margin entirely. No other piece of personal correspondence Wallace wrote was so disorderly. Whatever exhausted or ecstatic condition may have caused these irregularities, this important piece of ephemera captures the moment an artist in amazement discovers the popular and commercial value of their creation, realizes its tremendous prospects, and recalculates expectations. That the creation was *Ben-Hur* and the moment was in 1886 makes it a foundational monument of American popular culture. That the artist was a 59-year-old former major general, governor, and ambassador who almost always projected a controlled, professional, or authoritarian persona makes it all the more revealing.

> It's all right. Delivered the lecture; got thro' to the general satisfaction; had audience said to be 8000. Spoke in the amphitheatre which seats fully that many. Delivered the reading at 11 o'clock today. Every seat was occupied. Vincent pronounced it a great success, and was proud that he was the suggestor of the idea. He says I need not be afraid to read it anywhere. Got my money, and will leave tomorrow morning via the Lake Shore road to Cleveland; thence to Indianapolis.
>
> "Ben-Hur" is my card. My time goes autographing. Books fill my office book; books cover my table; they way lay me on the road. Signing my name has been my principle occupation. Next best thing of all 75 copies of Ben-Hur sold within an hour after the Chariot Race was finished – the best thing is that the managers have decided to put Ben-Hur on the Chautauqua list of books for next year, which Mr. Miller, the president says, will be equivalent to a sale of 30,000 volumes. It would be 40,000 he says, but at least 10,000 of the circles have the book already.

The two men he mentions were the Chancellor John Heyl Vincent and President Lewis Miller, the co-founders of the Chautauqua Assembly and University. The former, although a Methodist minister, crafted his movement as Christian but nondenominational, making *Ben-Hur: A Tale of the Christ* a perfect fit. A few weeks later, a more businesslike Wallace informed Harper:

> While at Chautauqua, I spoke to Mr. Miller, President, and he told me it had been already resolved to put B.-H. upon their book list for the next year, meaning, as I supposed, the season of 1887.[80]

If Miller, a businessman, was correct about Chautauqua members buying so many copies of Wallace's book, it would account for many thousands of the almost 79,841 copies that were sold between July 15, 1886 and June 22, 1887, although there were many factors at work.

A Celebrity on the Lecture Circuit, 1886–7

Building on these two great successes, he soon embarked on three extensive tours of the Midwest and East from the fall of 1886 into the spring of 1887. The extant log of the spring tour meticulously records the city and state of the lecture, the hosting organization, the name of the correspondent, and the fee charged.[81] He scheduled lectures six evenings a week, Monday through Saturday, although there were a few open dates. He never spent more than one night in any town. This meant a considerable amount of time spent each day traveling from venue to venue, some of them over 200 miles apart. On April 27, for instance, he lectured in Richmond, Indiana. The next day he took a train to Chicago to reach Evanston, Illinois, some 250 miles north-west. May 6 he lectured in Ottumwa, Iowa, the next day he was in Lincoln, Nebraska, approximately 250 miles west. Regularly venues in smaller cities were 50–100 miles apart. Along the way he refers to this as "a grind."[82] Nonetheless, in this tour alone Wallace collected fees of $100–200 per night on twenty-eight nights, earning a total of $3,470 in thirty-eight days. According to his log, almost all of these appearances were sponsored by organizations, many of them churches and colleges, ironically, in Indiana where he had failed as a student.[83] Including the aforementioned Notre Dame, colleges constituted still another favorable audience demographic and corroborated the educational nature of the featured lecture on Turkey and the Turks.

The presence of General Wallace, and with him the spirit of *Ben-Hur*, was often a cause for a local news notice or advertising. The day of his first lecture at the Detroit Opera House on October 6, 1886, the Macauley Bros. bookshop placed an ad on page one of the *Detroit Free Press* for a "new edition" of *Ben Hur*.[84] Local newspapers advertised not only the lecture itself but sometimes Wallace's arrival in town as well. The Decatur *Daily Republican* of May 2, 1887, for instance, announced in the "Personal Mention" column that "Gen. Lew Wallace, who is to lecture tonight, will arrive from Chicago this afternoon."[85] In the "Local News" column the lecture is listed twice, first as "HEAR the Gen. Lew Wallace lecture this evening at the opera house," then ten items lower: "DON'T miss the rare opportunity of hearing the greatest American author, Gen. Lew Wallace, lecture Monday evening."[86] For his April 30 lecture in Chicago, the *Tribune* first put in a notice on April 21 in the "Voice of the People" column, which suggested that Wallace should run for president in 1888: "I think his military, diplomatic, and literary record entitles him to consideration. Any man who could write 'Ben-Hur' would make a good president."[87] On April 29, the *Tribune* ran the ad for the lecture that evening at the Union Park Congregational Church:

GEN'L LEW WALLACE
Author of "Ben Hur," will deliver his new lecture,
"TURKEY AND THE TURKS,"
Tickets, Fifty Cents

The following day the *Tribune* filled much of the second column on the first page with its account of the lecture, which "all heartily enjoyed."[88] His lecture on Saturday, January 15, 1887, at Entertainment Hall in St. Louis was advertised twice in the *St. Louis Globe-Democrat*, the first with the variant title "Life in the Palace and Harem," the second sponsored by Balmer & Weber Music House, offering tickets for 50¢, reserved 25¢ extra.[89] The paper reported the success of his presentation, given to "a large and intellectual audience."[90] Very few of the accounts report the attendance, but in Milwaukee we know that he brought in 1,500 people, each paying at least 50¢, making his presentation quite profitable for the hosts, and a solid payday for himself.

Audiences or hosts also sometimes requested readings from the novel. On August 17, 1886, Wallace writes to Susan that he read the Chariot Race gratis for the audience in Bethany, Kansas.[91] While in Michigan on October 31, 1886, he wrote to Susan:

> Yesterday afternoon (being Sunday), I read at Dr. Fiske's insistence the Crucifixion, from all I hear, and the many congratulations received, I think it may be set down as a success.[92]

As at Chautauqua, after the Turkey lecture he spent the Sunday at the Union Methodist Church reading a chapter from the novel, in this instance on the Crucifixion.[93] On at least one occasion the booking was for the novel specifically. The *New York Times* of December 9, 1886, advertised that "Gen. Lew Wallace will read 'The Chariot Race' from 'Ben Hur' in Association Hall tomorrow evening."[94]

The underlying importance and influence of *Ben-Hur: A Tale of the Christ* becomes clearer in the most complete piece of ephemera that survives from this decade: a four-page program from 1887 now in the Indiana Historical Society. The cover page announces:

> Gen. Lew. Wallace. Author of Ben-Hur: A Tale of the Christ, and late U.S. Minister to Turkey, will deliver his new lecture, Turkey and the Turks, with glimpses of life in the palace and harem, at Buck's Opera House, Lansing, Mich., Wednesday Evening, March 2d, 1887, under the auspices of the Y.M.C.A. – Reserved Seats – 50 cents.

The bottom of the page contains an ad for the novel *Ben-Hur: A Tale of the Christ*, adding "152d Thousand Now Ready." The second page contains a full-page portrait engraving of Wallace, signed "Always Yours, Lew. Wallace." The third page contains excerpts from *Ben-Hur: A Tale of the Christ* that continue onto the fourth. The extracts are four in number: "Description of the Mother of Christ" (1.9); "Description of the Person of Christ" (7.5); "Christ's Spiritual Kingdom" (4.16); "Iras, Daughter of the Egyptian" (4.8). Three of them are descriptive passages showcasing Wallace's ability as a literary artist. The juxtaposition between the description of Iras and Mary is sharp, no doubt intended to demonstrate the kind of tension Wallace had built into the book. The passage on "Christ's Spiritual Kingdom" serves a similar purpose, contrasting Judah's understanding of Christ as a new Caesar and Balthasar's as the Redeemer. After the Iras passage, the program appends "Press Notices" about the novel, including excerpts of reviews from the *New York Tribune, Christian Union, Christian Advocate,* Boston's *Saturday Evening Gazette* and *Courier, Indianapolis Journal,* and *Chicago Inter-Ocean.* Clearly the purpose of the program is to sell more copies of *Ben-Hur: A Tale of the Christ,* not to introduce or provide historical or cultural background to the lecture on "Turkey and the Turks."

Audiences generally enjoyed his vivid presentation and eloquent style of performance art, and Wallace himself was treated like a visiting dignitary. His lecture at the Brooklyn Academy of Music on February 10, under the auspices of the Long Island Historical Society, was attended by two ex-mayors, a number of additional distinguished guests, and a standing-room-only crowd. According to the *Brooklyn Eagle,* his lecture "held the attention of the audience from the beginning to the end and drew much applause."[95] The *New York Times* reports that "for two hours [he] interested his auditors with amusing incidents of life in Constantinople."[96] The *Milwaukee Sentinel* reported that before his lecture at Immanuel Church on Thursday, January 13, the Rev. Judson Titsworth of the Plymouth Church introduced him as "a man of extraordinary ability – at once a student of war, diplomacy and religion," and that after the lecture he was received by a committee from the E. B. Walcott Post, G[rand] A[rmy of the] R[epublic] and escorted to a reception at the Armory.[97] Although the headliner was General Lew Wallace and the subject was always Turkey and the Turks, the tour by design contributed to the proliferation of sales of *Ben-Hur: A Tale of the Christ.* As Wallace toured from the fall of 1886 to the spring of 1887, the novel sold some 60,000–70,000 copies, and the following year it would sell 100,000 more.

PROBLEMS INHERENT IN POPULAR SUCCESS

Fatigue, Tedium, and Rejection

There are negatives that inevitably accompany a celebrity book tour, as Wallace soon discovered. It took him a few months to become fatigued by the drudgery he had complained about in the past. Understandably, he hit a low point around Christmas, but fortunately for us Wallace documented both his emotional dislike for the grind and his financial calculations in frequent letters to Susan.

Part of the reason for the Christmas crisis was a great disappointment in Boston, despite being treated warmly by two of the luminaries of the publishing industry establishment there. Both Benjamin Ticknor and Henry O. Houghton hosted receptions in Wallace's honor. He was introduced to a number of important people and a host of appreciative readers, and he received very high compliments. But of the four great contemporary Boston literati invited to the receptions – William Dean Howells, Oliver Wendell Holmes, James Russell Lowell, Thomas Bailey Aldrich – not one of them deigned to show up. We do not know if this was intentional, let alone a concerted effort by the literary Brahmins of Boston to snub the otherwise acclaimed author of a commercially successful novel, but Wallace understood it to be just that:

> The literati were all present except Mr. Lowell, Mr. Holmes, Mrs. Aldrich and the Howells. All these latter were special invitees. Why did they not come? Or rather why were they *all* absent? Would their presence been [sic] too much of a sanction or endorsement for the wild westerner? Think of it.[98]

Wallace admired Aldrich to the extent that he employed six lines of his "Pampina" for the epigraph preceding Book Seventh of *Ben-Hur; A Tale of the Christ*. Ironically, it would be Holmes's son who would rule in the favor of Wallace's son in the Kalem case in 1911, and noted New England composer G. W. Chadwick would compose art-songs from lyrics written by both Aldrich and Wallace in 1887.

In the same letter he complains about the tedium:

> Getting up at all beastly hours to take trains, under penalty of losing an appointment and the $100 at its end – tired of audiences who listen in deadly silence and applause always at exactly the same place. Taking it all in all, this has been the longest month I can recall in years. Will it never be done? I keep asking.

However, at the end of the letter he says he will stop the tour and come home after he has made a total of $15,000, and that "the thought of this sum as it now is makes me feel quite comfortable."

From Rochester, Minnesota, on January 28 he expressed to Susan a sense of purposelessness that only she and *Ben-Hur* might undo:

> Here I am ready for tonight's grind – a long journey from Sioux Falls, Dakota, to this city in the east of Minnesota. Talk about Hegiras! That of Mahomet was a mere snails journey – a nothing in comparison. Yet nobody will ever take account of my performances, much less write it in history books, unless you do it. I am looking to you and Ben-Hur to keep me unforgotten after the end of life.[99]

In March he says he rationalizes by comparing his tour to his service in Turkey:

> This makes my total earnings by lecture this season $11,480.61; my net earnings $9125.16. This latter is the total after deduction of traveling expenses and the %15 due the Bureau. The remaining appointments for two months should make the net earning about $10,000, good compensation for six months of genuine hard work. Better than being Minister to Turkey.[100]

The Mahan Affair

Celebrity exposed Wallace to another set of liabilities – plagiarism and claims of fraud. Popular works of art by the very nature of their success sometimes reach those who then plagiarize the material in their own works, or claim that the original artist has plagiarized it from them. As Wallace's fame and his book continued to reach into every corner of the country, he encountered instances of both. The most notable instance was brought to Wallace's attention in January, 1885, by the Rev. James A. Quarles of the Elizabeth Aull Female Seminary in Lexington, Missouri.[101] He wrote to Wallace to ask if he had copied the Wise Men passage of *Ben-Hur: A Tale of the Christ* from an obscure manuscript in the library of St. Sophia in Constantinople.[102] The reader will recognize immediately that this is impossible, for Wallace published the novel long before he ever reached Constantinople. Indeed he was assigned to Constantinople because his novel had prompted such a positive response from President Garfield. But Wallace considered this matter serious enough to verify his accuser and investigate the charges, thereby preserving the details for posterity.[103]

Relying on his reputation and calling upon some of his administrative contacts, Wallace first received a return letter from Senator Francis Cockrell of Missouri, confirming that Quarles was bona fide, and then in February he received reply letters from officials at both St. Sophia and Robert College confirming that no such manuscript was in the library in Constantinople and that no American had been there looking for one like it. Soon after, Quarles wrote an apology to Wallace for the accusation because it had become evident that the original accuser, the soon-to-be infamous Rev. W[illiam] D[ennes] Mahan, had been the one engaging in fraud from the beginning. The letters Mahan sent home during the period he claimed to be in Constantinople turned out to be postmarked in Illinois, and although his forgery of the *Acta Pilati* convinced a number of people and is still widely distributed today, Vatican, Constantinopolitan, and local officials exposed him as a fraud. Although Mahan claimed that Wallace copied Book First of *Ben-Hur: A Tale of the Christ* from the same St. Sophia manuscript he had used for his 1884 publication, *Archaeological Writings of the Sanhedrin and Talmuds of the Jews*, the opposite is clearly true. Mahan lists along with the Jewish sages Hillel and Shammai another who bears an otherwise unattested Jewish name – Hilderium.[104] The reader will immediately recognize that unique name as a crude imitation of the name of Wallace's Sheik Ilderim. Mahan's eighth chapter in that book, "Eli's Story of the Magi," often paraphrases Wallace's account of the Egyptian, Greek, and "Hindoo" wise men, and it is sometimes verbatim, although Mahan tries to mask the similarities by omitting the names Balthasar, Gaspar, and Melchior. Mahan even includes the brief political questioning the fictional Rabbi Samuel asks of Joseph, including the question about Judas of Galilee!

On June 30, Harper & Brothers sent Mahan an order to "remove from your book the chapter in question and any other portion of its contents which may be an infringement of our copyright in *Ben Hur* or of any other copyright belonging to us."[105] In late September Mahan was tried by his church, found guilty of unchristian conduct and falsehood by the Presbytery, and suspended from the ministry for twelve months.[106] Because Wallace had been living in Constantinople during the very period Mahan claimed to have visited the library at St. Sophia, Wallace could fully expose the falsehoods that ultimately condemned Mahan and consequently alerted Harper to the copyright infringement. One might also consider that Mahan might have thought he had a better chance of getting away with plagiarizing *Ben-Hur: A Tale of the Christ* in 1882 or 1883. Once it became a bestseller, he was bound to be discovered.

This would not be the end of it. In the summer of 1889, an otherwise unknown J. W. Graybill of Kentucky wrote to Wallace claiming that he had in his possession "translations of some ancient parchments and scrolls which are found in the Vatican at Rome and at Constantinopile [sic], of which page after page is indentical [sic] with some parts of Ben-Hur verbatim et literalim [sic]."[107] In a return letter, Wallace dismissed him by recounting what had happened to Mahan. Two years later, in 1891, Wallace received a letter from Charles H. Bradley of the Denver High School, informing him that a friend claimed to be an "intimate friend of yours and that he wrote the story of 'The Roman Chariot Race' in Ben Hur, and gave it to you."[108] In 1893 the charge that he plagiarized *The Prince of India*, published that same year, appeared even in the *New York Times*.[109] Wallace responded in print that Mahan had been "tried by his congregation on a charge of lying and expelled from his pulpit." The brief article ends with the following:

> Wallace said further that he is engaged in writing a new work, but declined to discuss its nature, remarking that if the plot were known some other author would seize upon it, write a book, and afterward accuse him of plagiarism.

Foreign Copyright Issues

The Mahan affair had already begun to acquaint Wallace with the negative realities of popular artistic celebrity by attracting a reader who then turned on his work by plagiarizing it and infringing upon his copyright. A much more extensive problem was already developing beyond the borders of the United States, and in this case Harper's and Lew Wallace's international presence as well as another action-alert letter from Susan Wallace played an integral role in the process of discovery and reaction, although the laws protecting American authors from abuse beyond U.S. borders (and vice versa) were as yet to be adequately codified.

Because Canada was part of the British Empire and not subject to our copyright laws, it was not uncommon at the time for booksellers working in Canada to reprint illegally American copyrighted books and then sell them, again illegally, in the United States. Harper issued the following warning in the press:

> Lew Wallace's Ben-Hur [is] among the most popular novels recently produced in this country. The edition issued by the Messrs Harper is the only edition which can be legally printed on the American continent, the story having been copyrighted in the United States and in England. The English copyright, while admitting the importation of the United States edition into Canada, prevents reprinting of the book in that portion of the British empire, and the legal proprietor of the English copyright has taken steps to enforce the law in the interest of the author. Should an attempt be made therefore to issue a Canadian edition of this brilliant work, it would have to run the gauntlet between two prohibitory laws ... if put on sale, it would be liable to confiscation in the United States under the copyright law of this country, and in Canada under the copyright law of the British empire.[110]

Others imported books printed in England through the Canadian border. Susan Wallace, having just published *The Storied Sea* with Harper in 1883, alerted them to one of these illegal importations on a large scale. It was from a friend in Chicago, apparently someone somewhat familiar with the publishing business, that she heard about a large volume of non-Harper editions of her husband's novel being sold at a discounted rate. The day before Christmas, 1884, just one month after she asked Harper to change the dedication, suggested that they sell directly to Chautauqua, and requested an annual accounting, she advances this additional information to Harper:

> After some hesitation I mention to you that a friend of mine recently in Chicago says he saw *Ben-Hur* there, offered for $1.00. The seller affirming it was being sold at the rate of 500 volumes a month.
> My informant could not remember the name of the house, but remembers the books were in *gay binding*, which inclines me to think the English edition may have come back.
> Pardon this very indefinite information.[111]

The 500 volumes per month, if accurate, should be compared to the 8479 volumes Harper recorded as sold between November, 1884, and March, 1885, at a rate of approximately 2120 per month, meaning a loss of some 20 percent of sales and royalty. The "gay binding" cannot be specified. As it was, the Wallaces had objected to Harper's cover on the first edition that depicted a flowering herb design on a light blue-green base.[112] The next few binding states of Harper's first edition were plain boards. By comparison, most of the British and Canadian editions had colorful bindings. In addition, many are hard to specify because they do not include a publication date.

In England, the Sampson Low edition licensed by Harper for sale in that country shortly after the publication of *Ben-Hur: A Tale of the Christ* in the United States had been joined by editions from Murdoch and Ward, Lock, Bowden. Now they were all being challenged by Frederick Warne & Co.'s "Warne's Star Series edition," which seems to have appeared as early as 1882.[113] Not surprisingly, this did not become an issue until sales began to proliferate and Warne began to advertise another printing in 1884. Their advertisement in *The Guardian* is tailored to the English market, comparing the sales prospects for Wallace's novel to those of established neo-biblical novels like the works of Ingraham:

> "Ben-Hur" is expected to have as large a sale as the Rev. J. H. Ingraham's "The Prince of the House of David," "The Pillar of Fire," and "The Throne of David," and, we believe, will be found on perusal to be even more interesting than those very popular works.[114]

Perhaps reacting to this subject categorization and market projection, the review in *Lloyd's Weekly London Newspaper* echoed the sentiments of some of the sectarian American reviews of several years earlier:

> Although not open to any charge of want of reverence, so far as the writing is concerned, he deals with scenes and events that are too sacred in their significance to be brought within the scope of imaginative romance ... [an] unfortunate choice of a subject."[115]

The Guardian agreed, although allowing for the popularity of "that strange book" originally published a few years earlier:

> We do not wonder at its popularity with many readers, for it is a most sensational life of a Jew in the Gospel times; jarring indeed on reverence, and not bearing the test of close criticism as to possibilities, but certainly arresting the attention in no slight degree.[116]

Wallace himself traveled to London in the winter of 1884/5 while returning to Constantinople from his leave of absence. There he read an ad for the Warne edition and followed the printed address to their offices, eager to look at the edition, get a sense of the quality of the publishing firm, and inquire as to the number of sales abroad. When he visited them and inspected the book, much to his horror he saw that it had been retitled *Ben-Hur, or, the Days of the Messiah*, and that a "publisher's preface" had been added:

> IN the following pages an attempt is made to portray the people and the land of Judea in the days of the Messiah.
> The tyranny of Rome – the turbulence and discontent of the Jewish people – and their vain expectations of a conquering king, who should exalt them to the sovereignty of the world, are here depicted in connection with the fortunes of a Prince of Judah, who learned, through much suffering and many mistakes, what the true kingdom of the Messiah is.
> It is hoped that his story will present features of interest, apart even from the mighty national events amongst which he moved; and that the record of his troubled career may win from the reader of today, interest in and sympathy for Ben-Hur.[117]

Wallace admitted, "Of course I know I have no legal rights in England," but he insisted on talking to members of the firm about his "stolen book" and asked who had authorized the change of title:

> The reply was that the publishers had done it to avoid hurting the sensibilities of religious readers in England. In other words, they had appropriated my property and had changed it to suit their own views of what its language and tone should be.

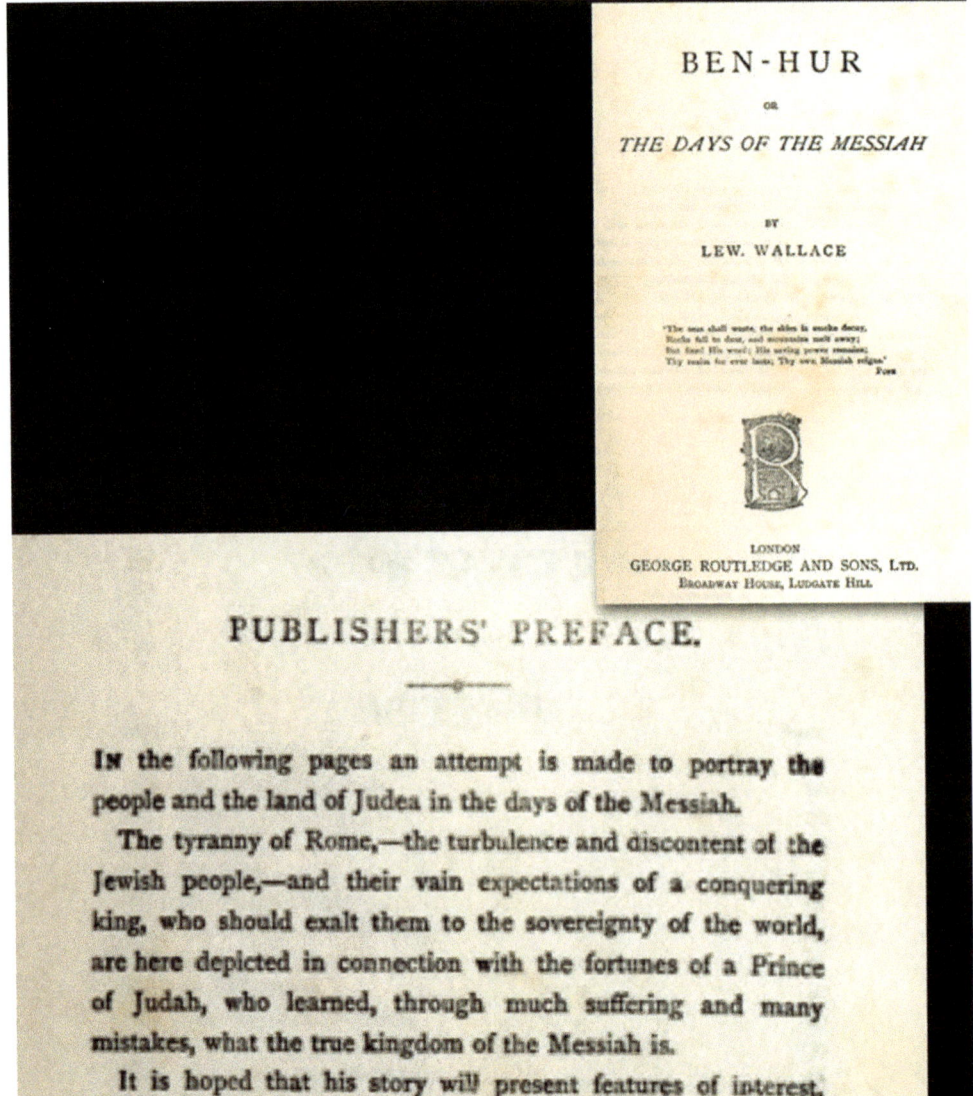

Figure 4.2 In London Wallace was displeased to see this preface added to the Warne and Routledge editions of his novel but had to protest without legal recourse.

Wallace said that he demanded some remuneration for altering his book, which was selling as many as 2000 copies per week.[118] Although "the scoundrel" promised him some consideration for the thousands of copies already sold, no royalty was ever paid.

This same version with the Publisher's Preface would appear again in 1887 and in subsequent Routledge editions. The relevant correspondence with Harper demonstrates how the publisher maintained that Wallace was an integral part of decisions about copyright:

> "We observe that Messrs. Warne & Co. intimate that they are considering the preparation of a cheap edition of *Ben Hur* for the Canadian market. We trust General Wallace will take prompt and vigorous exception to such a course, as – in view of our experience in similar cases – we apprehend that it would not only practically close the Canadian market to our own edition, but might also seriously interfere with the market in the United States. It is doubtful if, even with the utmost vigilance, a cheap Canadian edition could be kept out of this country. This is very important.[119]

Constantly reminded of this and similar arrangements, Harper and Wallace strongly supported the growing movement to create a binding international copyright agreement to prevent such "international petty larceny."[120] This would not happen until 1891, when the Chace Act was signed into law, but in the interim Wallace joined the American Copyright League.[121] In 1889 he was elected one of the vice-presidents to serve with President James Russell Lowell, no doubt a sign that Eastern and Western writers were united in this movement.[122] Even after the passage of the Chace Act, agreements with individual countries could still be problematic, as Wallace discovered with his next novel, *The Prince of India*.[123]

These copyright incidents and a number of others of even greater importance will become an integral part of the *Ben-Hur* phenomenon. This is in part because the novel *Ben-Hur: A Tale of the Christ* became so popular and sold so many copies that it was bound to attract schemers. It was also in part because Harper had a competent administrative and legal staff working through a period in which copyright issues were undergoing modern renovation, with the American Copyright League and the resulting Chace Act providing contemporary examples. In addition, the author was quite experienced in legal and international matters, and his wife was a published author. As we saw with the Mahan case, the religious aura surrounding the novel would not shelter it from a complicated scheme of copyright violations. And yet it was particularly because Wallace wanted to protect not just the novel's copyright but also its "reverent spirit" that he would continue to be so careful about choosing to whom he, and Harper, would issue a license.

NOTES

1. Harper, *The House of Harper*, 267–8.
2. Greeley, *The American Conflict*, 2:64–5.
3. Wallace uses Pope's translation of Homer's *Iliad* (23.383–4; 23.455–60).
4. Ripley also alludes to three authors who wrote novels or epics involving or alluding to antiquity and religion: Joseph Holt Ingraham, *The Prince of the House of David; or, Three Years in the Holy City* (1855) and *Pillar of Fire; or Israel in Bondage* (1859); Phineas Camp Headley, *Historical and Descriptive Sketches of the Women of the Bible, from Eve of the Old to the Marys of the New Testament* (1850); and Friedrich Gottlieb Klopstock, *The Messiah* (1750).
5. Ferree, *Yearbook of the Pennsylvania Society*, 69–70.
6. McKee, 169.
7. Harper, *The House of Harper*, 269.
8. Contract (May 7, 1880), BL.
9. *NYHT* (May 26, 1880) 4; *The Advance* (June 17, 1880) 666.
10. *WP* (May 29, 1880) 2.
11. Letter from Lew to Susan Wallace (July 29, 1880), IHS.
12. Letter from Lew to Susan Wallace (September 6, 1880), IHS.
13. Letter from Harper to Wallace (October 9, 1880), LL.
14. *The Publishers' Weekly* 458 (October 23, 1880) 524.
15. The reviewer for *The American Bookseller* (December 1, 1880) 537.
16. *NYT* (November 14, 1880) 4.
17. E.g. *HW* (November 27, 1880) 767; the penultimate end advertisement in the 1895 reissue of James De Mille, *The Dodge Club, or, Italy in MDCCCLIX* (New York, Harper & Brothers, 1869).
18. *CT* (November 27, 1880) 9.
19. *The Californian* 3 (April, 1881) 377–8.
20. *The Literary World* 23 (June 17, 1881) 381, the London publication being slightly different from the Boston version: *The Literary World* 12 (March 26, 1881) 114.
21. *The Independent* 32 (December 30, 1880) 11; *The Advance* (December 23, 1880) 692; *The Californian* 3 (April, 1881) 377–8.
22. *Christian Union* 22 (December 8, 1880) 500; *Western Christian Advocate* 47 (December 1, 1880) 382.
23. *American Church Review* 33 (January, 1881) 253–4.
24. *Catholic World* 38 (January, 1884) 572–4.
25. Cf. *NYHT* (January 7, 1934) 20.
26. *Atlantic Monthly* 47 (May, 1881) 710–11.
27. Cf. Malamud, *Ancient Rome and Modern America*, 134.
28. Wiltshire, "The Classicist President," 1–3.
29. Letter from Lew to Susan Wallace (April 29, 1881), IHS.
30. M&M 294
31. Letter from James A. Garfield to Lew Wallace (April 19, 1881), IHS.
32. *The Critic* 1 (May 21, 1891) 137; *An Autobiography* 2:939–40.
33. *Harper's Young People* (June 14, 1891) 1.

34 *Wisconsin State Journal* (September 6, 1881) 1.
35 Cf. reports in the *Santa Fe New Mexican* summarized in the "Lew Wallace clippings" folder [M72–5/14], NMHM.
36 Letter from Lew to Susan Wallace (May 15, 1886), IHS.
37 *The Independent* (November 2, 1880) ad #115. The opposite is true in *PW* (December 4, 1880) 797.
38 *American Bookseller* 10 (September 1, 1880) 183; *Christian Union* 22 (November 24, 1880) 449.
39 *American Bookseller* 10 (September 1, 1880) 183; *PW* (December 11, 1880) 811 and 812.
40 Letter from Susan Wallace to Harper (November 24, 1884), IHS.
41 Letter from Harper to Susan Wallace (January 24, 1890), IHS.
42 Homestead, *American Women Authors and Literary Property*, 108.
43 Letter from Harper to Wallace (November 27, 1880), IHS.
44 *NYT* (March 28, 1881) 3; *The Academy* (April 16, 1881) 276.
45 *The Chautauquan* 2 (January, 1882) 245; (June, 1882) 565; *Christian Advocate* 57 (March 30, 1882) 16.
46 E.g. *The Churchman* 42 (September 16, 1882) 322, where the new edition of *Ben-Hur* is announced along with a new edition of Ignatius Donnelly's popular *Atlantis*.
47 *Syracuse Herald* (October 1, 1882) 4.
48 *Frank Leslie's Illustrated Newspaper* (February 17, 1883) 435.
49 Letter from Lew to Henry Wallace (January 16, 1883), IHS; McKee 173.
50 *Frank Leslie's Illustrated Newspaper* (August 29, 1885) 27.
51 *NYT* (December 18, 1883) 5; (March 11, 1884) 5.
52 *NYT* (April 14, 1884) 2.
53 Cf. Jackson, "A Game Theory of Evangelical Films," 458.
54 *Fort Wayne Gazette* (July 29, 1883) 5.
55 *The Literary World* 14 (August 25, 1883) 274.
56 *The Century* 28 (November, 1884) 155.
57 *Shenango [Greenville, PA] Valley News* (May 14, 1886) 2; *Spirit Lake [IA] Beacon* (May 14, 1886) 3.
58 Letter from Susan Wallace to Harper (November 24, 1884), IHS. This letter can be traced to the private collection of Marjorie Wiggin Prescott via Tarbell, *All in the Day's Work*, 71.
59 Tupper, *Tupper's Proverbial Philosophy*, 104; lines 5–8:

> "If thou art to have a wife of thy youth, she is now living on the earth;
> Therefore think of her, and pray for hear weal; yea, though thou has not seen her.
> They that love early become like-minded, and the tempter touches them not:
> They grow up leaning on each other, as the olive and vine."

60 *Duluth News-Tribune* (April 3, 1899) 4.
61 Letter from Lew to Susan Wallace (February 8, 1885), IHS.
62 Letter from Lew to Susan Wallace (April 21, 1885), IHS. M&M 355, trace the inspiration for Wallace's story to *The Innocents Abroad*.
63 Wallace, "The Boyhood of Christ," 4.
64 *The Nation* 43 (November 15, 1886) I (Christmas ad).
65 Letter from Kirk Hanrahan to Harper and Wallace (December 7, 1886), LL.

66 *NYT* (April 14, 1884) 2.
67 *CT* (July 5, 1885) 5.
68 Letters from Lew to Henry Wallace (April 28, 1882; August 24, 1882; January 16, 1883; May 17, 1883; October 13, 1883; March 11, 1884; March 28, 1885; March 31, 1885), IHS.
69 *NYT* (December 28, 1885) 3.
70 *HW* 30 (March 6, 1886) 151.
71 E.g. *CT* (January 22, 1886) 6; (January 25, 1886) 6.
72 Letter from E. B. Martindale to Wallace (April 11, 1886), IHS.
73 Cf. McKee 225.
74 *[Chautauqua] Assembly Herald* 11 (August 7, 1886) 1.
75 *NYT* (August 8, 1886) 7.
76 *StLPD* (August 27, 1886) 4; *Biddeford [ME] Journal* (August 13, 1886) 1.
77 *Assembly Herald* (August 10, 1886) 1.
78 Hurlbut, *The Story of Chautauqua*, 230-1.
79 Letter from Lew to Susan Wallace (August 9, 1886), IHS.
80 Letter from Wallace to Harper (September 6, 1886), Rudy L. Ruggles Collection, Newberry Library, Chicago.
81 Wallace Collections II, LL.
82 Letter from Wallace to Harper (March 11, 1887), UVA.
83 *The Fort Wayne Daily Gazette* (September 3, 1886) 6; *The Daily Inter Ocean* (January 8, 1887) 1.
84 *DFP* (October 6, 1886) 1.
85 *[Decatur] Daily Republican* (May 2, 1887) 3.
86 *Cedar Rapids Evening Gazette* (November 3, 1886) 3.
87 *CT* (April 21, 1887) 10.
88 *CT* (April 30, 1887) 1.
89 *St. Louis Globe-Democrat* (January 15, 1887) 7.
90 Ibid., 8.
91 Letter from Lew to Susan Wallace (August 17, 1886), IHS.
92 Letter from Lew to Susan Wallace (October 31, 1886), IHS.
93 *St. Louis Globe-Democrat* (January 15, 1887) 8.
94 *NYT* (December 9, 1886) 8.
95 *BE* (February 11, 1887) 4.
96 *NYT* (February 11, 1887) 4.
97 *MS* (January 14, 1887) 2.
98 Letter from Lew to Susan Wallace (December 25, 1886), IHS.
99 Letter from Lew to Susan Wallace (January 28, 1887), IHS.
100 Letter from Lew to Susan Wallace (March 23, 1887), IHS.
101 Goodspeed, *Strange New Gospels*, 54-5; Tyler, *Men of Mark in Virginia*, 3:328-33.
102 Letters (January 20, and 26, February 21, 23, and 24, and March 4 and 28, 1885), IHS.
103 *An Autobiography* 2:942-4; cf. MacDougall, *Hoaxes*, 95-6.
104 Mahan, *Archaeological Writings*, 243.
105 Letter from Harper to the Rev. W. D. Mahan (June 30, 1885), LL.
106 Letter from James Martin to Wallace (October 3, 1885), IHS.

107 Letter from J. W. Graybill to Wallace (July 17, 1889), IHS.
108 Letter from Charles A. Bradley to Wallace (February 2, 1891), LL.
109 *NYT* (December 24, 1893) 5.
110 E.g. *[Colorado Springs] Daily Gazette* (January 4, 1884) 2.
111 Letter from Susan Wallace to Harper (December 24, 1884), IHS.
112 Cf. Russo & Sullivan 318–9.
113 The date is estimated from its place in the sequence of Star Series books advertised at the beginning and end of the edition.
114 *The Guardian* (May 7, 1884) 683.
115 *Lloyd's Weekly London Newspaper* (June 1, 1884) 5.
116 *The Guardian* (September 17, 1884) 1393.
117 *The Critic* 9 (September 26, 1885) 152; *The American Bookseller* 18 (July 15, 1885) 34; *Public Opinion* 3 (September 3, 1887) 451.
118 Letter from Wallace to John A. Kasson (February 22, 1885), UVA.
119 Letter from Harper to Warne & Co. (March 4, 1887), LL; Letter from Wallace to Mr. Johnson (November 11, 1887), UVA.
120 *Christian Union* (November 12, 1885) 8; cf. *NYT* (January 20, 1884) 7.
121 *NYT* (December 23, 1899) BR896.
122 *The Critic* 11 (November 16, 1889) 246.
123 *The Albany Law Journal* 57 (January 28, 1898) 66–7.

5 The Transformations of the Novel

The years 1886–9 were the formative years of what was to become the *Ben-Hur* phenomenon. Even with 57,112 copies sold between December 1885 and 1886, sales of *Ben-Hur: A Tale of the Christ* were yet to hit their initial peak. A contemporary note in *The Critic* estimated that an author could earn $500 a year from a book that sold reasonably well. Wallace received a $4691 royalty check on December 4, 1886, that covered just the previous six-month period.[1] Book sales kept gathering with rarified momentum, aided by Harper's marketing strategy of maintaining a high profile for Wallace, commissioning him to write periodic contributions to their publications, Wallace's own willingness to embark upon a grueling lecture tour, and the high esteem in which he was held by the public and the press, not to mention immeasurable circulation by word of mouth. As a result, in the two years between December, 1886, and December, 1888, 198,057 copies were sold. The first spin-off, the expanded hardcover edition of *The Boyhood of Christ*, was published, and, mostly with legal permission from Harper and Wallace, the novel was for the first time also translated into several different languages, rendered and copyrighted in dramatic form as the *Ben-Hur, in Tableaux and Pantomime*, and provided the lyrics and inspiration for several different types of classical art-songs and parlor-type songs.

By the mid-1890s, several Ben-Hur by-products licensed, authorized, or sanctioned by Wallace were already proliferating. *Seekers After "The Light" from "Ben-Hur"* was licensed by Harpers, The Ben-Hur Tribe had tens of thousands of subscribers, E. T. Paull's "Ben-Hur, or the Chariot Race March" had a popular following developed by an aggressive seller, and the *Ben-Hur, in Tableaux and Pantomime* had already been playing across the country for six years and bringing in additional royalties for Wallace. This period also saw the introduction of stereopticon presentations illustrating the novel, a constant thorn in the side to Wallace and Harper, particularly since the main perpetrator was the Riley Brothers, who were English and therefore protected somewhat by international

Figure 5.1 A variety of early types of *Ben-Hur* by-products: Harper licensed *Seekers After "The Light"*, excerpted *The First Christmas* and *The Chariot Race*, and paid Wallace to write *The Boyhood of Christ* as a prequel. Independently The New Lindell Mills of Ft. Collins was selling a Ben-Hur Flour already in 1888.

restrictions but representing a revolutionary technology that would bring the *Ben-Hur* phenomenon to new audiences. This meant that a number of different lecturers, speakers, and performers had begun snipping away at the Ben-Hur bastion. Independently, chapters of Ben-Hur shrines were being formed, and Ben-Hur Flour and Ben-Hur Cigars were already selling in Minnesota and Michigan. Ben-Hur ships as well as pedigreed or much beloved horses, pigs, and dogs were popping up nationwide. In Indianapolis almost every page of Ben-Hur Bicycle's 24-page catalog for 1896 reflected the ancient themes inspired by Wallace's novel.

Again, all the literary performance, dramatic, musical, and commercial aspects of the *Ben-Hur* phenomenon will be discussed in subsequent chapters dedicated to like products. For now the focus will remain on the novel itself, its initial proliferation into new editions and extracts, and Wallace's continued celebrity.

NEW EDITIONS, NEW ARTISTS, NEW LANGUAGES, 1886–90

Books in English

Since the emergence of *Ben-Hur: A Tale of the Christ* as a top-seller, Harper & Brothers had been actively searching for additional opportunities to profit from both *Ben-Hur: A Tale of the Christ* and Wallace's popular reputation and versatile talents. This begins in earnest with the March 6, 1886, issue of *Harper's Weekly* featuring Wallace on the cover and Eugene Lawrence's feature inside and then the publication of Wallace's short story, "The Boyhood of Christ," in the 1886 Christmas issue of *Harper's New Monthly Magazine.* In the same month Harper carried on negotiations with Houghton Mifflin to purchase the plates of *The Fair God* to make a "companion volume" to *Ben-Hur: A Tale of the Christ.* A letter from Harper to Wallace, informing him that negotiations had failed, suggests that Wallace had been the driving force behind this:

> "This closes the negotiations on this subject, unless you wish to take a hand in it. You will observe that we have been careful to conduct the negotiations in such a way that Messrs. Houghton Mifflin Co. know nothing of the desire which you expressed to us."[2]

Both parties seem to have foreseen the probability of such coat-tail success for Wallace's early novel. Part of the correspondence with Houghton Mifflin included a plan for tandem advertising in connection with "The Boyhood of Christ":

> But, as we explained, we had the impression that if the two books were associated together under our imprint, The Fair God would be likely to benefit more largely by the extraordinary popularity of Ben Hur – especially as we expect soon to publish in book-form a contribution to our Magazine from General Wallace's pen, which will afford an opportunity for special advertising of an effective kind.[3]

Bundling two discrete products and developing "special advertising" were innovative and aggressive business practices in the 1880s.

Meanwhile Houghton Mifflin would continue to issue new editions and printings in almost every year between 1886 and 1899 and beyond into the next century when the 1905 edition illustrated by Eric Pape was issued by the Riverside Press of Cambridge.[4] Clearly the impetus to purchase a copy of *The Fair God* was that it was written by Lew Wallace, the author of *Ben-Hur: A Tale of the Christ*. In the calendar year 1880, at the very end of which *Ben-Hur: A Tale of the Christ* went on the market, *The Fair God* sold just thirty-five copies. In 1884 it sold 1,263.[5] Harper's final offer in 1887 was to pay Houghton Mifflin $3000 plus the cost of the plates, figuring that would be roughly equivalent to the profits on no more than 20,000 volumes sold in the next five years.[6] In that year alone 14,098 copies were sold.[7] In a letter to Susan dated November 14, 1890, Houghton Mifflin estimated that total sales for the novel had reached over 80,000.[8] In *An Autobiography* Susan updated the statistics, recording that 145,750 copies had been sold between 1873 and 1905.[9] Sales would eventually reach over 200,000.[10] An additional by-product of the novel's success was Susan Wallace's "Oriental Splendors," an article on the three Wise Men solicited by the *Louisville Courier Journal* and then syndicated.[11]

1886 was also the year in which the first license to the *Ben-Hur* property was granted to another company and to an artist other than Lew Wallace. The details of the agreement are little known today, but George R. Lockwood & Son of New York took a license to publish *Seekers After "The Light" From "Ben-Hur."* The only information we have is from a September 6, 1886, letter Wallace wrote to Harper, in which he acknowledges receiving the "Lockwood Ben Hur brochure" and concludes with the abbreviated sentence: "Opinion reserved."[12] Lockwood was a small Manhattan publisher that specialized in Christmas items. Their first production in 1884 was *Their Christmas Dinner*, a thirteen-page extraction from Dickens' *Christmas Carol* bound in printed paper wrappers and tied with violet cloth ribbon. The next year they produced the fifteen-page *Saint Nicholas and Christmas Eve* derived from "A Visit From St. Nicholas," better known as "Twas the Night Before Christmas." As a harbinger of the growth potential of the *Ben-Hur* property, this small but aggressive commercial publishing house next turned to Wallace's novel as an icon of the Christmas market even though it had not had a chance to develop the patina of nostalgia associated with their previous two publications.

Seekers After "The Light" From "Ben-Hur" is a precious 5in. × 7in. booklet bound between two pieces of green-tinted cardstock, the cover of which is decorated with an embossed silver star and stellar rays.[13] A satin ribbon, in either green or deep red, is interwoven through the binding ("tape tied"), and the ribbon displays the word "Christmas" embossed in metallic silver cursive and elegantly underscored with a looped flourish. Inside there are ten pages consisting of four etchings by the artist known as F. M. on parchment-backed cloth.[14] The four etchings are tinted in sepia, green, red, and gray, and paired on the opposing pages with quotations from the novel: Book First, Balthasar awaiting the others, "They will come." (1.2), Balthasar and Melchior awaiting Gaspar, "Let us wait." (1.2), Melchior exclaiming "What glory is ours, O brethren! We are to see the Redeemer – to speak to him – to worship him; I am done." (1.4), and all three Wise Men exclaiming, "The Star! The Star! God is with us!" (1.5).[15] *Seekers After "The Light" in "Ben-Hur"* seems to have hit the market at a propitious moment. At least it warranted a second printing in 1887, although the tints were eliminated in favor of black ink. An announcement in the "Birthday-Books, Bible Text-Books, Booklets, Calendars, Almanacs, Etc." section of *Publishers' Weekly* in the fall of 1887 boasts of "greatly improved etchings in black, revised text."[16]

An acknowledgment page dispels any doubt that this was licensed by Harper and Wallace and designed to be a Christmas gift.

> ACKNOWLEDGMENT
> Is due to Messrs. Harper & Bros. publishers of "BEN HUR," and Gen. Lew Wallace, its author, for their kind permission to issue this little token, so appropriate for Christmas Tide, illustrating the meeting of the three wise men as SEEKERS AFTER THE LIGHT, and the appearance of the Star announcing the birthplace of the Redeemer.

The price was $1.25, nearly the price of the novel itself. In fact, when purchased in a box, the cost was $1.50.

The advertising focuses more on the association with the novel *"Ben-Hur"* than with Christmas. The description in *Publishers' Weekly* mentions the name of the novel in three of its five sentences, again asserting their legal propriety, probably repeating a required statement given them by Harper:

> This souvenir is issued with the kind permission of Messrs. Harper & Bros., publishers of "Ben Hur," and Gen. Lew Wallace, its author ... The etchings are accompanied by text explanations selected from "Ben Hur." ... The unprecedented and continued sale of "Ben Hur" needs no comment, and we therefore feel confident that the many thousand readers of that interesting book will be gratified also to possess this little token, so appropriate for a Christmas gift.[17]

In attempt to expand the market for this gift book, the second edition in 1887 was advertised also as an Easter novelty.[18] A brief review in *The Literary News* connected *Seekers After "The Light" From "Ben Hur"* with the recent publication of "The Boyhood of Christ."[19]

The February, 1887, issue of *The Literary News* began with a five-page feature on Lew Wallace. Included as illustrations were a facsimile of one page of Wallace's original manuscript and one of Wallace's illustrations for Susan's *Ginevra, or, The Old Oak Chest: A Christmas Story*, published

The Transformations of the Novel

Figure 5.2 The 1887 second edition made permanent the Christmas imagery. Harper also sold the novel in varieties of Moroccan leather bindings.

in 1886. The secondary title of the latter speaks for itself. To help fuel the *Ben-Hur* mania among the book-reading public, Harper issued a second edition of *Ben-Hur: A Tale of the Christ* in 1887. They had long since abandoned the gray-blue cover with the floral design and replaced it with a plain brown (or olive) cloth or mesh. Now they made the Christmas imagery permanent by producing an edition with a dark-blue cover decorated with a small, gold-embossed six-pointed star that emits forty-one gold-embossed rays. The rays cover almost the entire upper right-hand quadrant of the cover, and the rays are focused on the centered title "*Ben-Hur*" – also embossed with gold highlights. This edition is the first to use the full dedication requested by Susan, and the text ran a little longer than the first, ending on page 560. This would remain the standard edition of the novel until 1899.

In 1887 the American Printing-House for the Blind issued twenty-five copies of *Ben-Hur: A Tale of the Christ* in embossed Boston line type for the American Association of Instructors for the Blind. This special edition was published in large format (35 centimeters) and comprised four volumes.[20] In July, 1890, D. B. Gray, the Superintendent of the Oregon Institution for the Blind, delivered a paper to the Biennial Meeting of the American Association of Instructors of the Blind in Jacksonville, Illinois. Here he addressed the need to make contemporary literature available, and the only two contemporary works he proposes are Wallace's *Ben-Hur* and Henry Drummond's *Natural Law in the Spiritual World*, to a certain extent the scientific counterpart to the former.[21]

The novel found increased activity abroad as well. Before the 1891 agreement, a number of British publishers found it particularly profitable to sell inexpensive but attractively packaged and amply advertised books by American authors, often in numbered series with a memorable title.[22] In London three different publishing houses issued versions of Wallace's novel in 1887. Ward, Lock & Bowden produced *Ben-Hur: A Tale of the Christ* as part of their Lily Series, a series designed "to include no books except such as are peculiarly adapted, by their high tone, pure taste, and thorough principle, to be read by those persons, young and old, who look upon books as upon good qualities and excellent characters."[23] Warne reissued *Ben-Hur, or The Days of the Messiah* in their Star Series. James Nisbet & Company published their edition of *Ben-Hur: A Tale of the Time of Our Lord* as an individual product and inserted six leaves of plates. In addition, the Walter Scott Publishing Company reprinted Harper's first edition with its shorter dedication. Roger Adams lists additional editions by British publishers, but without a copyright date and with multiple printings and editions, it is difficult to determine when they were issued.[24] A syndicated newspaper report from 1902 reported that there were then currently twenty-seven British editions of the novel.[25]

1887 was also the year in which the Rose Publishing Company of

Toronto issued the Canadian version of the Warne edition mentioned above in connection with copyright issues. On May 4 Harper notified Wallace that they were incapable of putting a stop to the Canadian publication of the Warne edition, but they did promise "to put ourselves in communication with the Customs Offices at all the ports of entry on the frontier, with a view to the protection of your interest, and ours." An August article in *The Critic* demonstrates that they delivered on this promise on his behalf:

> Messrs. Harper have notified Collector Seeberger, of Chicago, of their ownership of the copyright of Gen. Lew Wallace's "Ben Hur." The book is being published in Canada with a view to its importation into the United States, and the Government authorities are requested to detain all copies of the Canadian publication.[26]

Anthony Seeberger had been appointed by President Cleveland in 1885 to be Collector of Customs in Chicago. There is no record as to whether Harper's notification had any effect.[27]

The following year, 1888, the German publisher Bernhard Tauchnitz published an English-language version of the novel. The title page states that it is an "Authorized Edition," and the previous page does indeed carry the Harper & Brothers 1880 copyright. This edition, too, was part of a reprint series, Tauchnitz's *Collection of British and American Authors*, a series they launched in 1841 to provide inexpensive, paperbound English-language works for the most part to English-speaking travellers on the Continent. Volume 2501 was *Ben-Hur: A Tale of the Christ*, published in two volumes bound as one, dividing the work in half at the end of Book Fourth.

In the 1890s Harper began allowing other publishers to excerpt the novel. In addition to collecting additional fees, this had the effect of introducing *Ben-Hur: A Tale of the Christ* to school students as a work ranked among the classics of English literature. In 1891, of the fifty works excerpted in Benjamin Davenport's *The Fifty Best Books of the Greatest Authors Condensed for Busy People*, three were American – Cooper's *The Last of the Mohicans*, Hawthorne's *The Scarlet Letter*, and Wallace's *Ben-Hur: A Tale of the Christ*.[28] There would be many subsequent deals. In 1896 Charles Dudley Warner's huge volume, *The World's Best Literature*, included excerpts from the "Galley Fight" and "The Chariot Race," tailor-made for young boys.[29] These excerpts were still being used in the 1917 version of *The Warner Library*. In 1897 two paragraphs from the description of Christ (7.5) were excerpted in *Famous Authors and the Literature of England and America*.[30] And in 1900 "The 'Ben-Hur' Chariot Race" was adapted by Benjamin E. Smith and illustrated by I. W. Taber in the "Young Folks" magazine *St. Nicholas*, and "The Star of Bethlehem" was excerpted in George Aldrich's *Progressive Course in Reading*, introducing the new generation to the favorite novel of their parents.[31]

Books in Translation

Of course the number of Anglophones in Continental Europe represented only a fraction of potential customers, but because of the lack of international copyright protection Harper generally had little interest in paying for the labor of translators or all the other costs associated with printing and selling a book in a foreign language in a foreign country. However, an exception was made at least for an authorized German version. Late in 1886 Wallace and Harper authorized a translation by [Johannes] Bonaventure Hammer, and Harper issued this press release:

> General Lew Wallace's "Ben Hur" is soon to be published in German, having been translated by a Catholic priest living at Lafayette, Ind., General Wallace's home.[32]

It may be that Wallace referred to Hammer, although not by name, in a letter to Susan dated March 31, 1885, where he mentions "a note from a German Catholic priest, apparently from Ohio."[33] Hammer had been ordained in Cincinnati in 1865. That we have little or no correspondence between Wallace and Hammer may be because their discussions were in person. Hammer was born in Germany in 1842, and after his family moved to Pittsburg in 1846, he lived the rest of his life in the United States. In 1882 he was sent to Lafayette, which is only thirty miles from Crawfordsville, specifically to write, not to engage in parish work. He wrote several dozen books and made frequent contributions to both German and English periodicals, thereby contributing, as would James Whitcomb Riley and Booth Tarkington, to Indiana's budding identity as a productive haven for writers. Wallace would likely have been impressed with his literary experience, his special status in the church, and his presence in Indiana. Hammer's German background and bilingual ability might have also reminded Wallace of Hoshour. Whatever the reason, this arrangement for a foreign translation was unique. Two years later Wallace even offered to suggest passages to be illustrated, but he specifies that "the arrangement was limited to Europe."[34]

His German translation, *Ben Hur: eine Erzählung aus der Zeit Christi*, was published in Stuttgart and Leipzig by Deutsche Verlags-Anstalt in 1887. It sold very well. The publisher issued a two-volume edition the next year illustrated by Antonio C. Baworowski.[35] And in 1890 they contacted Wallace directly, as Harper often did, asking his permission to serialize the translation:

> You know undoubtedly that we are the publisher of the authorized German translation by Father Hammer of your admirable "Ben Hur." Now, we beg leave to inform you that we are about to start a new periodical wherein only novels and by the most renowned foreign authors in first-class translations shall be published.[36]

In 1902 Hammer's translation of *Ben-Hur* was in its 91st printing, and in 1913 its 133rd.[37] Not surprisingly, its success inspired an unauthorized competitor in 1890. This was Paul Heichen's translation, *Ben Hur; oder die Tage des Messias*, which begins with a two-page preface featuring a biography of Wallace.[38] This was an important beginning to a widespread popularity of the *Ben-Hur* property throughout Europe that would culminate in the extraordinary reception of the 1925 MGM film adaptation, to be discussed later.

Meanwhile, several enthusiastic readers had been contacting Wallace to ask permission to translate his novel into another language. The first had come in 1882 from the Ottoman Sultan, who had his imperial scribe translate the work into Turkish.[39] Already before Wallace returned to the United States, a request came in March, 1885, from a Mrs. Daniels, "a German woman, living in Washington," to render the novel into German.[40] In the letter she claimed an endorsement from Brigadier General William B. Hazen of the U.S. Army's Chief Signal Office.[41] Wallace deferred to Harper for a decision. This was the same month in which he received word from the German Catholic priest, who had written a review of Wallace's novel in German "much past my reading." Although the simultaneity of the two communications was coincidental, it represented the large German population in the United States, particularly in the Midwest, that would eventually develop into a sizable audience.

Similarly, in 1887 Wallace received a note from a Mrs. N. S. Moore of Winsted, Connecticut, who was preparing a Swedish translation. She wrote first to Harper and, not pleased or understanding the prohibition against marketing her translation in the United States, she then appealed to the author:

> The latter condition did not seem just to me, but I wanted to do the work so I consented. I wish Gen. Wallace would assist me in having that modified so as to have the condition cover both Sweden and America. The Scandinavian population is so large in this country it would double the sale of the translation.[42]

Moore reportedly completed her translation in 1889, but there is no record of a publication.[43] The National Library of Sweden catalog lists only A. Boggiano's Swedish translation published in 1888.[44] In June, 1888, Wallace wrote Harper that "he ought to pay at least 5% royalty on sales in this country."[45]

On April 6, 1887, Harper consulted Wallace about a proposal from the Rev. W. Monti to translate the novel into Italian. The following paragraphs from this letter illustrate the concerns of all the major parties – Wallace, Harper, and the translator – involved in these types of negotiations:

> We enclose herewith the replies which we have received from Archbishop Elder, of Cincinnati, and Bishop Janssons of Natchez, to our inquiries regarding the Rev. Dependent Monti. In view of the confidence expressed by these gentlemen as to the ability of the Rev. W. Monti to translate Ben Hur into the Italian language, as he proposes, we think the permission for which he has applied might be presented to him. As we understand his proposition, which you have seen, the enterprise will not be of any pecuniary advantage to you, on account of the very limited extent of

the payment which the Italian publishers would make for the translation. But so far as we know, the Rev W. Monti could not be prevented from translating the book for publication in Italy if he were disposed to do so without permission.

If you have no objection, therefore, we propose to write to him granting him, in your behalf, permission to proceed with the understanding and stipulating that the Italian translation shall neither be published here nor imported into this country. Kindly let us hear from you on the subject.[46]

First Harper addresses quality control, namely, personal recommendations to verify the character and the ability of the translator. They seem to be satisfied. Then they make clear that this is not a matter of sales, profit, and royalty since neither Harper nor Wallace could demand payment from Italian publishers, nor could they prevent Monti from publishing his translation in Italy. Lastly, Harper demonstrates that they considered Wallace to be the ultimate judge of how to proceed, presumably following their executive, marketing, and legal advice.

On April 25 Harper had written Wallace again, and it is apparent from this letter that Wallace had approved the Italian translation.[47] There seems to be no bibliographical record that it was ever completed or published, but a review of the Hammer translation suggests that by late 1887 Turkish, Swedish, French, and Italian translations had been published.[48] The first authorized Italian translation to appear was that by Alfonso Maria Galea in 1895, but Russo & Sullivan (325) inform us that Galea rendered his Italian translation from Hammer's German translation.[49] The first French translation was also derived from Hammer's translation.[50] In 1900 H. Mildmay and Gastone Cavalieri produced the "First Italian Translation" as *Ben Hur: una storia di Cristo*.[51] Interestingly, their translators' preface confesses that the success of Henryk Sienkiewicz's *Quo Vadis?* provided their inspiration, as *Quo Vadis?*, along with *Ben-Hur*, would have continuing popular success in Italy for decades. Just two years later, the publishers to the Holy See, Desclée, Lefebvre & Company, issued Professor Enrico Salvadori's 850-page, two-volume Italian translation of Wallace's novel, illustrated by Antonio C. Baworowski.[52] Salvadori was one of the Pope's "secret honorary chaplains," and he presented his translation to the nonagenarian Pope Leo XIII, thereby generating the commonly circulated statement that *Ben-Hur* was the first work of fiction to be blessed by a pope.[53] But that is a bit imprecise. Wallace's basic premise that Christ was human sharply contradicted church doctrine. Cardinal Rampolla, the Papal Secretary of State, conveyed the Apostolic Blessing specifically on Salvadori's rendering because of the "various modification of ideas which the translator has taken the liberty to introduce into the work in the interest of piety."[54] In contrast, as we will see, *The Boyhood of Christ* and *The Prince of India* would be censured for doctrinal and historical errors.[55]

Harper's letter continues by introducing the request by Rev. Earl Cranston and William P. Stowe, agents for the Western Methodist Book

Concern, for permission to prepare a German translation for sale in the United States. Established in Cincinnati already in 1820, this company had offices in Chicago and St. Louis as well, published Methodist magazines and a Sunday school weekly, served as the Western Agency for the Chautauqua Literary and Scientific Circle, and had separate Swedish and German departments.[56] The letter makes clear that Wallace supported this idea, and that Harper did as well to such an extent that while they had originally expected Wallace to pay for half the cost of a translator, they now were waiving that request and would be willing to purchase a set of plates from "the German publishers," presumably Deutsche Verlags-Anstalt. Here however the trail goes cold. The first German edition published in the United States was the 1895 edition with the title *Ben-Hur: Eine Geschichte aus der Zeit des herrn Jesu*, translated by H. W. S. [Henry W. Seibert]. This was published by Harper & Brothers, whose imprint appears in Fraktur, and who paid $300 for the translation.[57] It was marketed for several more decades. Nonetheless, by September, 1891, the Chicago Public Library had already added the Hammer German edition of Wallace's novel to its German Literature catalog.[58]

It is not known what happened to the plan to publish the American German edition between 1887 and 1995, but there is no evidence that Harper made another attempt at translating the novel for some of the vast numbers of immigrants who had been arriving in the United States in the last two decades of the nineteenth century. To the contrary, in late October, 1890, Harper notified Wallace that their counsel in Chicago had taken steps to force August Zimmerman of Minneapolis to cease publishing a serialization of *Ben-Hur* in his Norwegian newspaper, *Foedrelandet og Emigranten* [*The Fatherland and the Emigrant*].[59] The mutual agreement was that publication would stop immediately and that no damages were owed, except that for six weeks they would have to advertise Harper books as compensation.[60] In 1888, in addition to Skoglund's aforementioned Swedish translation in Stockholm, native-language translations appeared in Denmark and Russia.[61]

THE BOYHOOD OF CHRIST AND *COMMODUS*

Wallace was still trying to capitalize on the success of his novel not so much as a creator repackaging his celebrated popular work as an artist building on that success.[62] In the January, 1888, *Harper's New Monthly Magazine*, he published an "Early Poem By the Author of 'Ben-Hur.'"[63] Later that same year Harper & Brothers released the expanded, book-length version of *The Boyhood of Christ*, adding into its central part a "reading" by Uncle Midas of "The First Gospel of the Infancy of Jesus Christ," consuming 39 of its 101 pages, doubling the length of the initial *Harper's* article. The rest of its gilt-edge pages were filled with fourteen full-page engravings, each printed on plate paper and surrounded by blank pages and a separate caption page. The book was bound in ornamental leather. Harper promoted the book mostly by inserting ads and positive reviews in their other new publications.[64] It very quickly sold 9,439 copies at $3.50 each during the first year.[65] But because *The Boyhood of Christ* featured disquieting stories about Jesus casting out Satans, metamorphosing a mule into a human, disposing of another, inserted a hodgepodge of stories like that of Titus and Dumachus (known via Longfellow), and connected the Holy Family with unfamiliar Orthodox, Muslim, and Persian traditions, the initial audience dissipated after several years.

Adding to the cool reception was that the Catholic Church censured the book for its non-doctrinal beliefs.[66] As in *Ben-Hur: A Tale of the Christ*, Jesus is said to suffer on the cross, and now an additional element was Wallace's emphasis on the human nature of Jesus's fictional childhood. Indeed, he begins the book with a preface – following the example of the Warne edition? – stating this clearly as his personal belief:

> Should one ask of another, or wonder to himself, why I, who am neither minister of the Gospel, nor theologian, nor churchman, have presumed to write this book, it pleases me to answer him respectfully – I wrote it to fix an impression distinctly in my mind.
>
> Asks he for the impression thus sought to be fixed in my mind, then I would be twice happy did he content himself with this other answer – the Jesus Christ in whom I believe was, in all the stages of his life, a human being. His divinity was the Spirit within him, and the Spirit was God.

Wallace followed with the national publication of his play *Commodus*. It appeared as the lead article in *Harper's New Monthly Magazine* in January, 1889, and was accompanied by five engravings.[67] As often, the author line read: "By General Lew. Wallace, Author of 'Ben-Hur.'" Of course the play had been written almost two decades earlier, but the negotiations with Harper that took place early in 1888 are interesting in that they laid the foundations for the next step in Wallace's growth as a literary businessman. On January 25, 1888, Harper offered Wallace $1000 to publish *Commodus* in their magazine and an additional 10 percent on its subsequent publication as a book. Wallace demanded $2000.[68] By April 5, Henry M. Alden at Harper's had agreed to this amount, anticipating the contract they would offer for Wallace's next novel, for which, of course, the stakes were much higher. One of Wallace's negotiating points was that he was considering establishing residence in England in order to comply with British copyright law and thereby not lose again the substantial royalties he had lost from the tens of thousands of copies *Ben-Hur* with its various subtitles had sold in England. Harper responded that they could offer whatever an English publisher could, and suggested instead that he serialize the book, thereby establishing copyright protection "so far as it is possible for an American in England."[69] We will return to these negotiations below, for at this point Wallace ends this series of letters by telling Alden, "The new book grows, but – Oh, so slowly!" But the reader can already see in Wallace's development an increasing confidence which would enable him to act more aggressively toward Harper and, ultimately, Klaw & Erlanger. The reader may also observe at this point that the name of the novel has now commonly been reduced to *"Ben-Hur"* without the subtitle.

THE GARFIELD EDITION

Eventually even popular items saturate their target audience, and sales of *Ben-Hur: A Tale of the Christ* now peaked, with the record (December to December) 103,893 copies sold in 1887, 94,164 in 1888, and then 63,759 in 1889. Harper responded with the Garfield edition.[70] Designed as a deluxe edition in a variety of bindings, it sold for much more than the $1.50 original novel and for twice as much as the *The Boyhood of Christ*.

We have already seen that Wallace had taken the initiative in late 1880 by sending copies of his newly published novel to President Hayes and President-elect Garfield, and that Wallace received and forwarded the latter's complimentary response to Harper in April, 1881. Although Harper immediately introduced the letter into its advertising for the novel, propriety postponed any further implementation of an advertising campaign after Garfield was severely wounded by an assassin's bullet on July 2 and then died of complications two months later. The shock of Garfield's assassination gradually receded, but it was not until the dedication of his monument and final resting place in Cleveland in May, 1890, that Harper felt comfortable in using the letter for publicity again.

Harper now targeted this new edition to the art-gift market. To design it they called upon Arthur B. Turnure, their in-house art director.[71] Turnure was both a designer and an influential book enthusiastic. He had been a co-founder of the Grolier Club in New York in 1884, and the year after the Garfield edition was published he left Harper to become the founding editor of *Vogue*. For the Garfield edition he divided the novel's text into two halves, the first volume ending after the end of Book Fourth. The pages of the first volume unfold with elegance in that they begin with three blank leaves, a page with the half title, and then a halftone, full-page photograph of Lew Wallace backed by a tissue page with "General Lew. Wallace" printed in red ink. The title page used both red and black inks – red for the title and epigraph from Count de Gabalis ("Learn of the philosophers always to look for natural causes for extraordinary events; and when such natural causes are wanting recur to God"), and black for the author line and the name of the illustrator. After the copyright page, there is a caption page ("From General Garfield to General Wallace, April 19, 1881"), and this is followed by a two-page facsimile of Garfield's letter to Wallace, complete with the letter head "Executive Mansion, Washington." Next comes the dedication page, a page containing the two original epigraphs from Jean Paul F[riedrich] Richter and John Milton, the Table of Contents listing the chapter headings for the first volume, and a list of its ten full-page photogravures. The latter provide contemporary views of the Holy Land, many of them illustrating locations found in the novel, e.g. the Jaffa Gate, the Tower of Antonia, and the Pool of Bethesda. There follows an illustrated title page for "Book First," and then the beginning of the novel itself. The frontispiece of the second volume begins with a unique depiction of the protagonist, devised by H[enry] Siddons Mowbray, who this same year was made a member of the National Academy of Design and would in the next decade paint the ceiling of the Morgan Library in New York. The drawing depicts a young man with closely cropped hair, wearing a white tunic and high-boot sandals.[72] At waist level his right hand holds a horse goad, and his left hand is raised to hold the harness of one of a four-horse team. Early in the next decade this same image would be used in an advertisement for Ben-Hur Flour.

Every page of the edition was illustrated. Harper did not hire an established, let alone famous, illustrator but the young William Martin Johnson. Johnson had trained at the Boston Museum of Fine Arts before moving to New York and studying at the Art Students' League. The Garfield edition was Johnson's first prominent achievement. As a result of this and his subsequent works at Harper's, particularly his deluxe edition of one of Wallace's predecessors, Charles Kingsley's *Hypatia* (1853), in 1895 he would be named the Art Editor of the *The Ladies' Home Journal*, one of the leading home magazines in the heyday of home magazines, and, it should be pointed out here, one of those that carried ads for Ben-Hur Flour.[73]

Johnson was a precise and prolific illustrator. His illustrations in the Garfield edition shift to various places in and about the margins. On some pages festoons, vines, or scrolls wrap around one or more corners of the text box, which covers just more than half the surface of the page.[74] Some illustrations are figured drawings, whether of street scenes or anonymous profiles, and many illustrate rooms, buildings, or architectural landscapes. Others represent a single object like a flagellum or candelabrum, or gladiatorial armor and weapons. Although none illustrate the events of the novel and none of the characters of the novel are depicted, many of the illustrations are appropriate to the text. Passages in which Iras appears often have Egyptian artifacts or vignettes. The first page (1:209) of Book Third, set at Misenum, contains a romantic landscape of the Bay of Naples. The page (2:551) that introduces the Antioch Circus contains a reconstructive drawing of the *carcares* of the Circus of Caracalla in Rome. The page (1:192) on which Judah sees Gratus contains an illustration of a generic Roman commander on horseback. There follow representations of the

The Transformations of the Novel 153

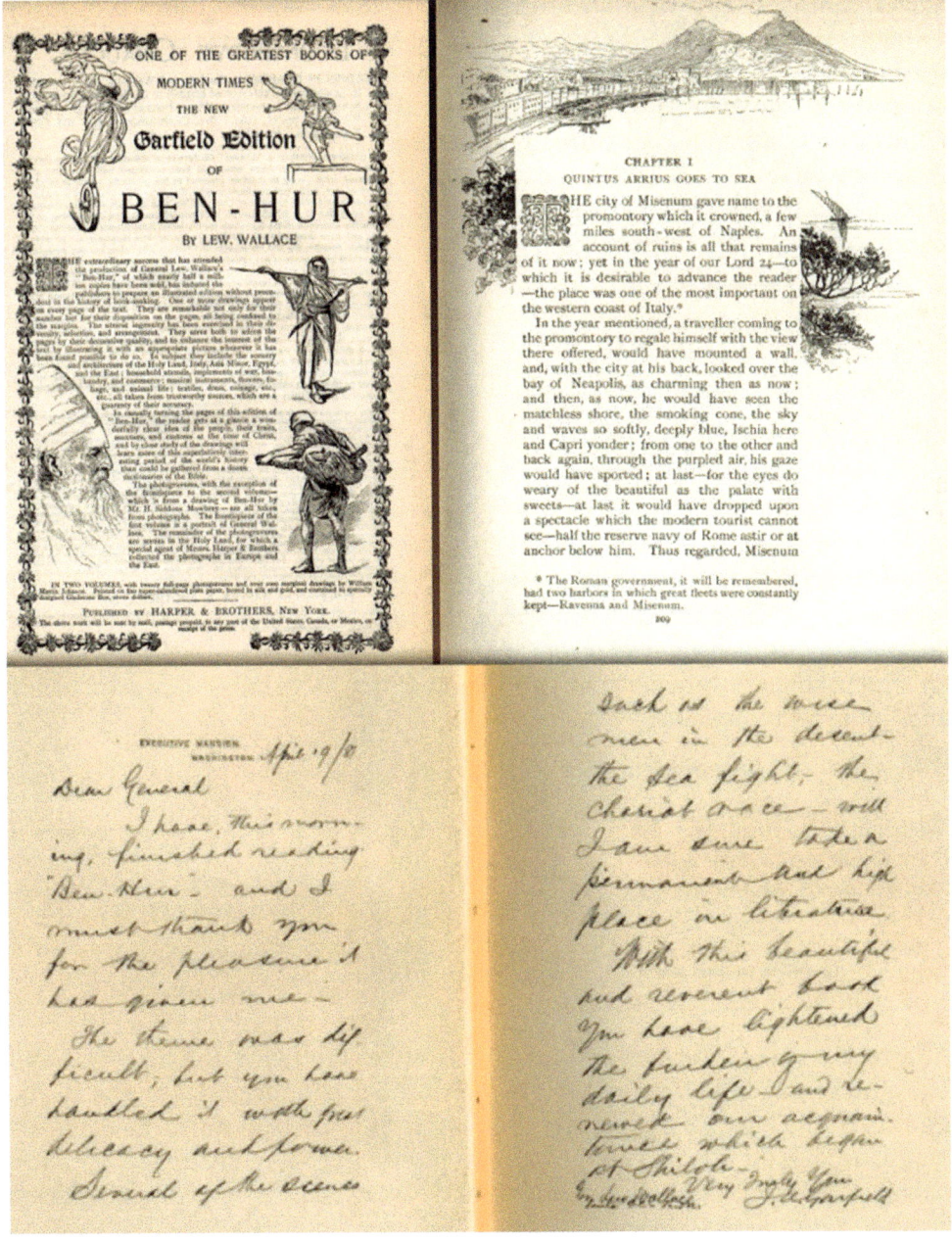

Figure 5.3 An ad for the Garfield edition, the page introducing Arrius at Misenum accompanied by Johnson's illustrations, and a facsimile of the 1881 Garfield letter to Wallace sent from the "Executive Mansion," as the White House was called in the nineteenth century.

entrance stairway of an oriental house (1:194), a Roman soldier mounting a stairway (1:195), and a 5-inch allegorical illustration of a serpent coiling itself around a sword on the page (1:196) where Judah declares, "In the hour of thy vengeance, O Lord ... be mine the hand to put it upon him!" A few of Johnson's illustrations recreate ancient sculpture. The Borghese Boxer, for instance, is drawn for the page (2:598) in which Judah slays one of Messala's two hired assassins with one blow. The head of the Apollo Belvedere is used for the page (1:142) on which Messala refers to Apollo as the god of Delphi. The illustrations for some of the pages (836–41) in the final chapter witnessing the Crucifixion are reduced to simple floral borders around all four sides of the text box.

Harper initially printed the book on gilt-edged, supercalendered paper, bound it in orange silk with a gold border, and then inserted the two volumes in a specially designed Gladstone, or hinged leatherette, box. They matched their publicity with the scope of the edition itself. They printed a full-page ad, for instance, in 1891's *The Christmas Book Shelf*, the Christmas number of *The Publishers' Weekly*. The uppermost banner claims that this is "The Gift-Book of the Year," and that "*Ben-Hur*" – the subtitle is omitted throughout the ad – is "one of the greatest books of modern times." Much of the text describes the variety, arrangement, and purpose of the illustrations, stressing their accuracy and appropriateness:

> An illustrated edition without precedent in the history of book-making. The [illustrations] serve both to adorn the pages by their decorative quality and to enhance the interest of the text by illustrating it with an appropriate picture whenever it has been found possible to do so ... all taken from trustworthy sources, which are a guaranty of their accuracy ... In casually turning the pages of this edition of "Ben-Hur," the reader gets at a glance a wonderfully clear idea of the people, their traits, manners, and customs at the time of Christ, and by close study of the drawings will learn more of this superlatively interesting period of the world's history than could be gathered from a dozen dictionaries of the Bible.[75]

Additional press releases tell us that the research for the illustrations reproducing ancient artifacts and sculptures was conducted at the Astor Library in the East Village, under the direction of Charles Parsons, Harper's long-time art director. It may not be coincidence that in the fall of 1891 newspapers circulated the rumor that Wallace was to be made Secretary of War.[76]

Although Johnson himself later stated that he thought his youth evidenced itself in the Garfield edition, the edition itself was generally well reviewed.[77] Brander Matthews concluded:

> Illustrative or decorative, explanatory or pictorial, the pictures of Mr. Johnson accompany the words of General Wallace from the first page to the last; and we have here probably the most elaborately and abundantly adorned edition of any novel ever published.[78]

Over the next few years, Harper would offer the Garfield edition in a number superior leather bindings to attract buyers in the luxury and art-gift markets. One of their 1895 advertisements lists the price of the Garfield edition bound with the regular orange silk at $7.00, three-quarter calf at $12.00, and three-quarter Levant at $14.00.[79] And now Harper also offers "the popular edition" in a variety of bindings as well. In addition to the standard cloth binding, still at $1.50, the novel is available in half leather ($2.00), three-quarter leather ($2.50), three-quarter calf ($3.00), full leather ($3.50), and three-quarter crushed Levant ($4.00). Although not widely advertised, Harper also offered an "Edition de Luxe" for $30. They issued only 350 copies of this edition, individually numbered. Eager to capture the 1891 Christmas market, although the second of two volumes would not be ready until January 15, 1892, they issued the first volume on December 18. The publisher's preface describes the unique qualities of this collector's item:

> The sheets of paper used in this edition are hand-made, each sheet having been made separately in a mould and not by a machine. It is a smaller sheet than the regular edition but a large page, and the actual number of times the sheets have been fed into the press are eight, as against two in the large edition. As the paper is made by hand it has a rough edge, and therefore the sheets have had to be fastened before each impression upon points of needles; a slow and laborious process. If this had not been done the illustrations would not fit perfectly to the letter-press.
>
> The tint used for the illustrations is a specially made ink and is unique. The volume is bound in vellum and stamped with two colors of gold. The illustrations are all printed from the original engravings. By actual experience it has been found impossible to finish more than 140 sheets of this edition in a day, and we publish this work in the confident belief that it will be appreciated at its full value.

In 1893 Harper even published a supplement to the Garfield edition, the *Referendum for the Illustrations in the Garfield Edition of General Lew. Wallace's Novel "Ben-Hur."* Prepared by Paul Van Dyke, an academic historian of the church, this fifty-page catalog identifies almost every illustration, listing them by page number. He offers archaeological, historical, geographical, mythological, and scriptural detail in a few sentences each, many of them concluding with references to one of Smith's dictionaries or the *Encyclopedia Britannica*. On page 267, for instance, Arrius announces that Judah is his son and heir. Johnson illustrates this with a partial view of what seems to be the ruins of a Roman theater. Van Dyke explains:

> 267. Ruins of an amphitheatre, like the amphitheatre of Scaurus, in which Arrius' triumphal pillar was shown. It was a circus-ring built of stone and open to the sky. The Coliseum (p. 239) was not yet built. – Dict. Ant., "Amphitheatrum."[80]

The result is a learning guide to supplement the novel. Harper listed the price of the *Referendum* at 50¢.

The Garfield edition sold well. 18,288 copies – plus 247 of the de Luxe editions – were sold already in the second half of 1891. By January, 1893 another 10,030 copies had been sold, and the de Luxe edition was sold out. The reports do not specify the price of the bindings for these sold copies. In 1899 the luxury market seems to have been satisfied. At least Harper began issuing a clothbound edition for a lower cost, and Wallace was very supportive of the change.[81]

Now over a dozen years beyond its initial publication, *Ben-Hur: A Tale of the Christ*, was about to more than double Wallace's wealth, indirectly. Bolstered by his novel's tremendous success, Wallace was now in a condition to negotiate from strength and set a standard of compensation that previous authors could not have thought possible. Unlike most authors, Wallace did not produce novels at frequent intervals. Occupied with minor writing projects throughout the next few years, he did not have a track record of an author who produced a succession of well-received novels. Nonetheless, like other noted authors of his day, he was developing a business acumen that would become widely acknowledged. In October, 1893, William Dean Howells had published an article describing "The Man of Letters as a Man of Business," which had become a noted phenomenon in the early 1890s.[82] The following month newspapers circulated a more general article about authors as businessmen, including Wallace:

> General Lew Wallace, who has written a book which has probably had a larger sale than any other story written by an American, excepting "Uncle Tom's Cabin," is one of the most careful, shrewd and prompt of business men, and his manner in business circles is that of a person whose entire experience has been in business life. Mr. Howells himself is earning a repute for business shrewdness and insistence upon his rights which is almost equal to that which Mark Twain has obtained.

A NEW NOVEL AND THE LECTURE CIRCUIT

As of 1893, Wallace had written one enormously profitable novel, and this had increased the sales of his first novel forty-fold, so now his third novel was eagerly anticipated. On January 21 Wallace notified Harper that he had finally finished *The Prince of India*. As we left it, Harper had encouraged Wallace to serialize his next novel, and Wallace had even flirted with English publishers to change its international copyright status, but revised international copyright laws now protected American properties. On January 26 Harper immediately – before even reading the manuscript – offered Wallace 15 percent royalty on retail sales of the novel and an additional $15,000 payment for the right to serialize it in *Harper's Weekly*, which would establish copyright in Canada as well. Wallace responded three days later, declining serial publication at any price and demanding a royalty of twice the offered amount, an incredible 30 percent. The extant copy of that letter in the Indiana Historical Society reveals the initialed responses of the Harpers: "Of course accept –" and "I would promptly accept."[83] Wallace also asked Harper to sell the copyrights in Canada and

Great Britain along with Germany, France, Austria, and Italy. Focusing on the continuing importance of *Ben-Hur* in this process, he adds:

> It is to our mutual advantage that your house have the control of this next venture, since, in my view, it will help *Ben-Hur* even as *Ben-Hur* will help it.

Wallace wrote an exuberant letter to Susan from Gilsey House in New York, claiming that "for the first time in the history of American literature the author of the 'Prince of India' gets his publisher's share . . . the largest royalty ever conceded to an author."[84]

The Prince of India was neither a critical nor popular success, at least when compared to *Ben-Hur: A Tale of the Christ*. Readers were generally disappointed. But Wallace's estimation of its relationship to *Ben-Hur* proved to be prophetic. The novel immediately attracted 200,000 buyers, eager to buy Wallace's next book.[85] On March 6, 1894, Wallace received word from Harper that since July 18, 1893, *The Prince of India* had sold 278,418 copies, the standard *Ben-Hur* an additional 26,068, the Garfield edition 2,470, *The Boyhood of Christ* 533, and the *Ben-Hur, in Tableaux and Pantomime* 9, and that they would send him a check for $83,982.22.[86]

The publication of the new novel returned Wallace to the lecture circuit. For several years Major James B. Pond had been trying to schedule Wallace for his Lyceum Theatre Lecture Bureau. In the 1890s Pond was the most important impresario in the country, producing lecture tours for the likes of Samuel Clemens, P. T. Barnum, and Susan B. Anthony. According to Pond's memoirs, Wallace was already in great demand, particularly by Y.M.C.A. groups.[87] By July, 1894, Wallace had signed on with Pond to arrange for 100 lectures to be given across the country, and then in the fall he set out for his first tour of the West Coast. Now his standard performance fee was $300. Pond remarked that Wallace was very kind in suggesting to Pond that he keep 25 percent as his booking fee rather than the usual 15 percent. The reader will remember here that Wallace had recently received his royalty check for nearly $84,000. Pond speaks well of Wallace. He kept his engagements, the tours were profitable, and Wallace "had kind words for every person he met; they were genuine, too."

The programs for many of these were more ambitious than the 1886–7 one-night stands, and they included *Ben-Hur* to a much greater extent. Many of Wallace's appearances included only one lecture, the aforementioned "How I Came to Write '*Ben-Hur*.'" The Indiana Historical Society preserves the "Special Announcement" Pond issued for Wallace's tour of the East and Midwest during the months of January, February, and early March, 1895. The first of four pages featured the large portrait photo of Wallace copyrighted by Harper & Brothers in 1893, along with the practical information regarding the tour. The second page listed the schedule for "Five Enjoyable Evenings." The first was "Turkey and the Turks (with glimpses of the Harem)." The second had the generic title "Miscellaneous," which consisted of readings from *Ben-Hur* ("How the Beautiful Came to Earth" [7.4]); *The Fair God* ("The Death of Teceti" [6.10]); and *The Prince of Persia* ("Sergius to the Lion" [5.10]), finishing with "The Chariot Race." (5.14). The third was "Mexico and the Mexicans." Fourth was "The Third Division of the Army of the Tennessee at Shiloh." And fifth was "How I Came to Write 'Ben-Hur.'" The rest of this page and the next contain a laudatory biographical sketch of Wallace, for example:

> He was very fond of reading, and spent much of his time in his father's fine library, which was always open to him. He was seldom seen without a book in his pocket. It is said that he used to disappear from the house immediately after breakfast and come back only when hunger or the approach of night drove him home. He would spend the whole day in solitary wanderings, reading, or studying the wonders of plant and insect life.[88]

The third page finished with some selected reviews of *Ben-Hur: A Tale of the Christ* and *The Prince of India*. The last page contains Harper's advertisements for *The Prince of India*, the Garfield edition of *Ben-Hur* with the choice of leather bindings, and *The Boyhood of Christ*.

The only lecture given at Oakland's First Presbyterian Church on October 29, 1894 and Brooklyn's Academy of Music and Manhattan's Calvary Baptist Church in January, 1895, was "How I Came to Write *Ben-Hur*."[89] Many of these venues were capacious and grandiose. Brooklyn's Academy of Music speaks for itself, while the Calvary Baptist Church featured a 229-foot spire and a 1,500-seat auditorium, not to mention a congregation that included John D. Rockefeller.[90] Often the prominence of these lectures was enhanced by a local celebrity who introduced Wallace. The Manhattan presentation, for instance, was introduced by Egbert Viele, former Union brigadier general, U.S. congressman, New York City commissioner of parks, and the engineer who had compiled what is still known as the Viele Map of New York. The *Oakland Tribune* reported that despite the various political activities taking place outside in the streets, the audience was "large and appreciative."[91] In anticipation of the arrival of Lew Wallace, the *Tribune* connected Wallace's personal appearance with its advertising for the *Ben-Hur, in Tableaux and Pantomime*, which was to be performed the same month.[92] At the end of a 10-inch description of the venue, cast, and program of the performance given for the benefit of the Young Women's Christian Association Home, the running ad concludes:

> As General Lew Wallace is expected on the coast this winter the entertainment on Friday night will have an added interest.

By the time Wallace had fulfilled his contract, he had once again found the travel regimen dissatisfying. It was not the rigors or nostalgia of travel: he had arranged in advance to be home for Christmas. Nor was it the incident at Chicago, where a number of Armenians in attendance at his lecture hissed several times when his comments about the Sultan and the Turks proved to be excessively complimentary. According to the newspaper account, "General Wallace paid no attention to the interruption and continued his address as though nothing had happened."[93] Wallace was adamant that the reports of the Armenian massacre seemed exaggerated and was awaiting the assessment of the international commission before making final judgment. He expressed his reason for permanently discontinuing lecture tours in his July 8, 1895, letter to Pond, who had advanced him an offer to arrange another tour for 1896.

> I have a big lot of writing to do, and, to say truth, writing is both easier and more profitable.[94]

Indeed, it became a practical matter. Two memos from Harper's illustrate his point. Between March and December, 1895, the standard *Ben-Hur: A Tale of the Christ* sold 16,575 copies and the Garfield edition 10,452, along with 2,400 German sales. In 1897 his financial position had become even more comfortable. He told Pond on May 21, 1897, that he had been offered $4000 for twenty lectures, and declined. Just the month before he had received a telegram from the noted millionaire journalist William Randolph Hearst, asking Wallace if he would travel to Greece to work as a correspondent for the Greco-Turkish War which had broken out in April:

> Are there not terms under which you will go to Greece to represent the [New York] Journal during the campaign in this war between Christians and moslems, we are most anxious to secure authoritative utterance as yourself, a general and a great Christian writer, would supply. Please consider favorably and name any terms. W R Hearst.[95]

Wallace's response is telling:[96]

> It is for Mr. Hearst to decide whether my services in Greece at this present juncture are worth to him, and papers:
> For thirty days, $25,000, and expenses, including hire of assistants, and fees for information (secret service).
> For six months, $50,000, and expenses, including hire of assistants, and fees for information (secret service).
> For thirty days not to include time going and coming.
> As my affairs now stand, it is worth $50,000 to me to break off the work in which I am now engaged for six months; to that, in the next place, I add risk of life, and the loan of my reputation.
> Lawyers receive the amount stated for their services every day.[97]

The Publishers' Circular of late October, 1897, reports that Wallace's novel had now sold some 600,000 copies in the United States.[98]

CELEBRITY ENDORSEMENTS

Wallace and his novel had reached heights and breadths and depths of the popular culture hitherto unexplored, particularly by just one product. *Ben-Hur* was the champion par excellence. And Wallace was the proud, protective but then increasingly aggressive creator who oversaw the process, with Harper supporting him whenever legal, professional, and institutional support was required. Over the next few years, Wallace increased his professional standing as an author through additional publications like *The Wooing of Malkatoon*, an epyllion, which was bound with another issuance of his historical drama *Commodus*, and illustrated by the Impressionist Frank Du Mond and neoclassical painter John Reinhard Weguelin.[99]

He called upon his political influence to propose a bill establishing a national academy for writers, artists, and inventors:

> There is all outdoors for our soldiers and sailors, a hall in the capitol for our statesmen, but not place for the heroes of study and patient essay, whose battles are fought in silence and out of the world's ken.[100]

Because of his success as an author and respected celebrity status he was asked to write the forewords for a number of publications. Some of these were collections, for example, *Famous Paintings of the World* which was produced in connection with the World's Columbia Exposition in Chicago in 1893.[101] The impressive title page of this large format book contains the work's lengthy seventy-two word title and subtitle as well as the full names and titles of six additional judges and editors, but the only seven of its 155 words that are printed in large seventy-two point type are "FAMOUS PAINTINGS OF THE WORLD" and "LEW. WALLACE," the latter followed by "author of 'Ben Hur' and 'The Prince of India.'" This was reissued as *Scenes and Gems of Art From Every Land* and *Gems of Modern Art* and used as a loss-leader for potential subscribers to local newspapers.[102] In Funk & Wagnalls' reissue of George Croly's 1828 novel, *Salathiel, the Wandering Jew*, not only does Wallace's introductory letter conclude with his signature reproduced in facsimile but his letter is preceded by the publishers' note which remarks:

> We are glad in the belief that we have carried out successfully General Lewis Wallace's wish, that the story be worthily illustrated. We were fortunate in securing a masterful artist who shared the great enthusiasm of the author of "Ben Hur" for this story of Croly's.[103]

Still another was *Constantinople*, a two-volume scholarly work by Edwin Grosvenor, Professor of European History at Amherst.[104]

The national press paid attention when Wallace was asked to judge an angling tournament in Indianapolis and even when he attended a baseball game.[105] The press also ridiculed his thoughts about running for the U.S. Senate:

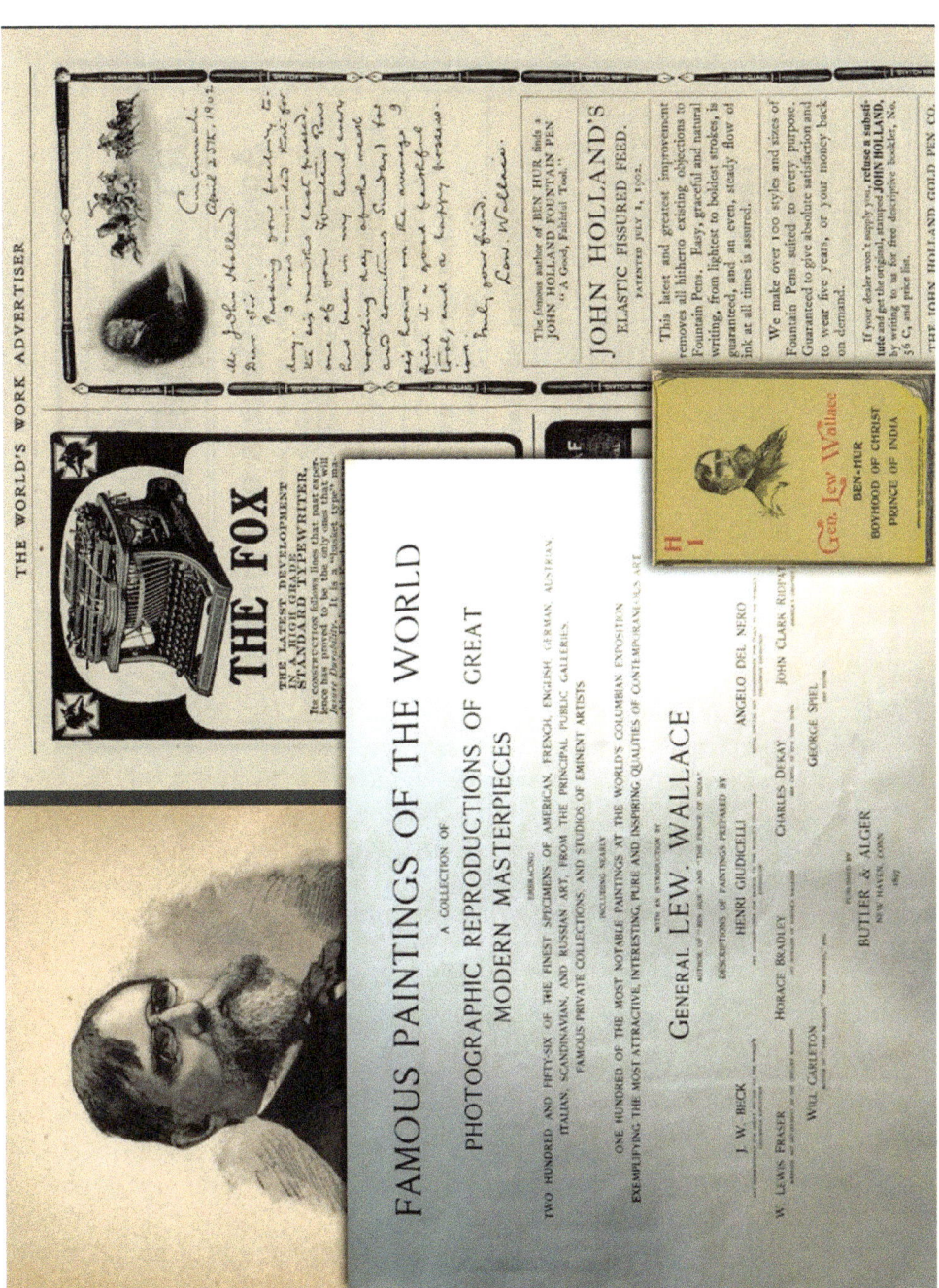

Figure 5.4 Wallace as a celebrity author, endorsing books and John Holland's Pens, his image reinforcing his authoritative reputation.

> Gen. Lew Wallace intends to make himself a United States Senator; but Ben Hur in a chariot race and Ben Hur in a political race may be two quite different persons.[106]

He was particularly admired in his native Indiana, of course, but Santa Fe also laid its claim to his celebrity. Already by 1890, A. J. Wissler, the curator of the New Mexico Historical Society, responding to numerous questions from visitors and tourists, wrote a letter to Wallace. His purpose was to inquire whether *Ben-Hur: A Tale of the Christ* was written in the Old Palace of Santa Fe. Wallace responded with the letter quoted in Chapter 3, confirming that he had written the final three books in Santa Fe.[107] The "Ben Hur Room" became a tourist attraction, and both official photographs and postcards were issued.[108] In 1908 the School of American Archaeology was established in the Old Palace, and by then the "Ben Hur Room" was considered "a veritable shrine":

> It simply would not do to tell the visitors that *Ben Hur* was composed in this building.... The fact was that the room had become a veritable shrine, a rival to any relics described in Mark Twin's *Innocents Abroad*. If there were no Ben Hur room, these visitors would demand that one be at once created. All the beautiful things of the museum are passed by with hardly a glance by these shrine pilgrims.[109]

In 1915 Henry Wallace shipped his father's Morris chair and lapboard, along with a bronze bust sculpted by Randolph Rogers, to house in the room.[110] But as it turned out, a long-brewing controversy was developing as to precisely which room served as the author's study. Edgar L. Hewett, long-serving director of the museum and the school, later published a pamphlet that presented all the available evidence but concluded that the precise location could "never be conclusively established."[111]

Wallace also agreed to endorse a commercial product for the John Holland Golden Pen Company. Based in Cincinnati, they were the largest manufacturer of pens in the West. Wallace endorsed in particular the John Holland Elastic Fissured Feed Fountain Pen, patented July 1, 1902. The April, 1903, issue of *The World's Work*, published by Doubleday, Page, and Company in New York, has an insert box saying, "General Lew Wallace, the famous author of *Ben Hur* writes: 'I find it a good, faithful tool.'"[112] Another fills half a column with an endorsement letter from Wallace to "Mr. John Holland, dated April 25, 1902." Above it is a small photograph of Wallace writing on his slate board and an engraving of a chariot race derived from Alexander von Wagner's sizable oil painting, *The Chariot Race*. Wagner's painting which will be used to advertise many Ben-Hur products, was painted by the Munich-school academic in the mid-1870s, almost immediately popularized in the United States through engravings, photographs, and exhibition at the 1876 Philadelphia World's Fair, and bequeathed to the Manchester City Art Gallery in 1898.

The letter from Cincinnati is reproduced in Wallace's handwriting in facsimile:

Passing your factory today, I was reminded that for the six months last passed, one of your Fountain Pens has been in my hand every working day of the week and sometimes Sunday, for six hours on the average. I find it a good faithful tool, and a happy possession. – Truly your friend, Lew. Wallace[113]

Similar ads appeared in *New Outlook*, *Public Opinion*, and *The Book-Keeper*.[114] He also wrote a letter of endorsement for the Chicago, Milwaukee, & St. Paul Railway that appeared in regional newspapers under the title, "A Celebrated Man on a Celebrated Railroad."[115] And he signed on to the list of dignitaries endorsing *The Century Dictionary and Cyclopedia and Atlas*, along with President William McKinley, ex-president Grover Cleveland, Rudyard Kipling, and William Rainey Harper.[116]

IMPACT ON POPULAR LITERATURE

Once *Ben-Hur: A Tale of the Christ* had become well established in the mid-1880s and continued to sell well for years and even decades, a number of authors created imitations and derivative stories about Jesus or early Christianity, whether set during the same period, the subsequent generation, or even in modernity. For the most part, these were written by the authors who could rightly be accused of seeking popular success and profitability in novels about Christ and paleo-Christianity, much more so than Lew Wallace who trailblazed a full decade or two before them and established a niche in the literary market. Some were self-aware, for instance, Hermann Milton Bien's like-named *Ben-Beor: A Story of the Anti-Messiah* (1891) and Carlisle B. Holding's *Her Ben: A Tale of Royal Resolves* (1889).[117] One presented itself not only as a sequel but included *Ben Hur* in the title. That was J. O. A. Clark, *Esther: A Sequel to Ben Hur; or, The Lost Epistles of the First and Second Centuries and the Lost Records of the Great International Camp Meeting, Held at Alexandrea Troas, in Asia Minor, A.D. 80, in the Reign of the Emperor Titus* (1892).[118] Other contemporary titles adapted either the concept of the young Jewish protagonist, e.g. Eldridge S. Brooks' *A Son of Issachar* (1890), or the format of the title, e.g. Ellis John Breckenridge's *Adnah: A Tale of the Time of Christ* (1902).[119]

Many of these derivative works were advertised by being compared to *Ben-Hur*. The publisher claims Annie Fellows Johnston's *Joel: A Boy of Galilee* (1904) to be: "as accurate a picture of the times of the Christ as has been given to older readers through 'Ben Hur.'"[120] Miles Gerald Keon's *Dion and the Sibyls* was first published in 1871 but reissued in 1890 with a preface that begins, "*Dion and the Sibyls* comes into direct comparison with *Ben-Hur*."[121] Similarly, in 1897 J. B. Lippincott advertised a new version of Wilson Barrett's venerable *The Sign of the Cross*, which was set during the reign of Nero, by boasting that it "deserves to be classed with Lew Wallace's religious masterpiece":

Suffice it to say that the infamous slaughter of the Christians in the arena is depicted, that the life of imperial Rome is brought into vital touch with our own daily life by the naturalness of the characters and incidents, and that the same literary methods which made *Ben-Hur* one of the most widely read of contemporary books have here been employed with singular felicity and effectiveness.[122]

The Publishers' Weekly headlines its full-page ad for Elizabeth Miller's *Saul of Tarsus: A Tale of the Early Christians* (1906) as "The Greatest Religious Romance Since Ben-Hur."[123]

Even reviewers make comparisons to *Ben-Hur*. The race in Arthur Conan Doyle's *Rodney Stone: A Novel* is compared to the *Ben-Hur* chariot race.[124] F. M. Kingsley's *Paul, A Herald of the Cross* (1897) prompted a reviewer, who does not understand the attraction of novels retelling New Testament tales, to admit that "the people like it ... but then, it may be remembered, they like *Ben Hur*, even to the extent of naming a secret society and a brand of bicycles from it."[125] As the reviewer implies, the commercial applications of *Ben-Hur* were not the norm.

The most successful by far were Charles Sheldon's *In His Steps: What Would Jesus Do?* (1897) and Henryk Sienkiewicz's *Quo Vadis?* (1896) originally written in Polish but translated into English by Jeremiah Curtin in 1897. It is important to digress for the moment to make a comparison between the ultimate successes of these two works and *Ben-Hur*. According to a study done by *The Atlantic Monthly* in 1934, by which time *Ben-Hur: A Tale of the Christ* had sold 1.9 million copies, *In His Steps* had already sold eight million.[126] The latter number would soon be deflated when Frank Luther Mott's 1947 study, *Golden Multitudes: The Story of Bestsellers in the United States*, ranked *Ben-Hur* along with six other titles in the 2.5 million category, but *In His Steps* in the second ranking of two million, and *In His Steps* would be adapted as only a minor film in 1964.[127] But *Quo Vadis?* would inspire one of the first cinematic mega hits (1913), another high-profile Italian film in 1925, MGM's 1951 successful predecessor to the 1959 *Ben-Hur*, a European television miniseries (1985), and a highly regarded Polish film (2001).[128] As a play Stanislaus Stange's adaptation played across the country in 1900/1, was even more successful in Italy, and the Jean Nouguès/Henri Cain operatic rendition premiered in 1909.[129] Jan Styka's *Quo Vadis* paintings created a sensation in 1902.[130] Like the 1916/17 Ben Hur, there was a French automobile named Quo Vadis manufactured for a few years in the 1920s, a Quo Vadis whist club in Boston,[131] and the Quo Vadis restaurant in London is still operating, having opened its doors in 1926. And there have been still other commercial applications of *Quo Vadis?*[132] Nonetheless, as the remainder of this book will overwhelmingly demonstrate, the sum of all its parts pale in comparison to the popular success and commercial applications of *Ben-Hur*, which had already established the precedent and developed in numerous directions before either of these other two novels went to press.

Moreover, of prime importance here are the methods Wallace and Harper used to protect their copyright and merchandise the *Ben-Hur* product. Because of a defect in Sheldon's copyright, of the seventeen houses that published *In His Steps*, only Grosset & Dunlap paid him substantial royalties.[133] As we have seen and will continue to see, Wallace himself was instrumental in developing and shaping the *Ben-Hur* property. Sheldon and Sienkiewicz, like Stowe, were not able to do the same with their novels, which meant that in the coming years and decades they would not be able to profit from, let alone have any artistic or strategic control over, any of these artistic or commercial applications.

THE CONTINUED SUCCESS OF *BEN-HUR*

As Wallace continued to achieve greater fame, fortune, and celebrity, the name *Ben Hur* was ever present, whether in connection with Wallace himself, his lectures, his political opinions, or his novel and its dramatic ramifications. Just to quantify this, a ProQuest search reveals that the *New York Times* alone found reason to print that title 512 times between 1890 and 1905, an average of almost three times per month for fifteen years, in a paper and city that were far removed from the American heartland. As Harper was suffering in the 1890s through the process of receivership and reorganization, they developed a new strategy, and that was to excerpt sections from well-known novels and bind them as small Christmas gifts. They advertised these "Little Books by Famous Writers" as "the Best Stories, Sketches and Verse by Best Authors, Bound in a dainty and convenient form."[134] They were printed on heavy, cream-tinted laid paper with rough pages, bound in blue cloth covers decorated with silver – an outer border, a frame of two Ionic columns, and the names of the title and author. The format was small so "that makes them an excellent substitute for the old-fashioned Christmas card."[135] The first on their list was *The First Christmas (From "Ben-Hur")*, published in 1899, the same year in which the University of Chicago economist Thorstein Veblen published *The Theory of the Leisure Class* with its memorable chapter title "Conspicuous Consumption." This particular consumer item consisted of the entirety of Book First from *Ben-Hur: A Tale of the Christ*. Wallace added a preface, which was a shortened version of "How I Came to Write 'Ben-Hur,'" and it was here that Wallace recalled that the story of the Wise Men was read to him first by his mother, not Samuel Hoshour. The 140-page book included a photogravure of the Jaffa Gate in Jerusalem as its frontispiece and was priced at 50¢. Although the book does not seem to have been heavily advertised, new issues were warranted in 1902, 1903 (in a red cover), and 1906 (in purple). The latter two replaced the silver on the cover with gold, and the Ionic columns were eliminated. Around the same time the company was distributing "Harper's Portrait Catalogue," a set of alphabetized cards displaying pictures of "distinguished and popular" Harper authors and the names of three of their books. Lew Wallace's *Ben-Hur*, *The Boyhood of Christ*, and *Prince of India* were placed at letter 'H.'[136]

By 1899 the successful *Ben-Hur, in Tableaux and Pantomime* had been replaced by the even more successful Klaw & Erlanger production. This in turn inspired Harper to release still another edition of the novel, "The Player's Edition," in 1901, "illustrated with scenes and characters from the play." The Harper advertisements announced that the book was made from new plates, contained forty-eight illustrations, and, to enhance the detail visible in the photographs, "printed with an India tint on specially selected paper." The cover included a photograph of William Farnum in costume as Judah Ben-Hur, raised over an art-nouveau image featuring classical tragic and comic masks. Replacing the name of the author is the label, "The Player's Edition." The photos inside are all full-page production stills, and they are distributed throughout the book. The frontispiece is a full-page version of the Farnum cover photo. The characters, setting, and place in the play are revealed in the captions, which are also summarized after the Table of Contents. As in *The First Christmas*, the novel is printed on rough cut, gilt-topped pages, and a gold border surrounds the text box on every page, the full title of the book – also in gold – spread across the top of each two leaves. The Player's Edition was not the only publication by-product of the Klaw & Erlanger production. Others contained William Young's drama, Edgar Stillman Kelley's music, or the souvenir program, all of them available for purchase. It was at this point that the account books at Harper listed a section for the "Ben Hur Copyright" by itself, separate from the Wallace books.

Harper advertised the Klaw & Erlanger production by featuring a magazine article on the specially designed treadmill Claude Hagen had designed for the chariot race, and then they advertised the new edition of the novel in *Harper's* as early as May, 1901.[137] They often sold copies at the theater where the play was being performed.[138] In addition to the synergy of selling additional copies of the novel by publicizing and merchandizing the play, and publicizing the play through additional publicity of the novel, the various editions of the novel include ads for not just Harper releases in the endpapers but specifically "Other Books by Lew. Wallace." Opposite the dedication page in the 1901, 1903, and 1904 editions, Harper offers *The Prince of India* in ornamental cloth for $3.00, *The Boyhood of Christ* in full leather for $3.50, and *The Wooing of Malkatoon; Commodus* in cloth for $2.50.

Overseas translations still proliferated as well, with new translations, versions, or editions in Spanish, Russian, French, Czech, Dutch, Danish, Icelandic, Finnish, Polish, and Slovenian. The 1897 Arabic translation by Cornelius van Dyke, a missionary in Syria, was accused of fomenting Arab anti-Semitism in Palestine.[139] Nonetheless, this was later reputed to be the first "Aryan" work translated into Arabic.[140] Additional German versions appeared almost every year. Although most of these publications and sales did not have any effect on the American market, some did. In addition to the aforementioned American German edition, Wladyslawa Dyniewicza published a Polish edition in Chicago in 1904, and in 1907 it was published again in Pittsburgh by Drukarnia "Wielkopolanina."

These were not the only copies of the novel which served to spread the name of *Ben-Hur* without bringing profits to Harper or royalties to Wallace. Those owned by public libraries in the United States would do the same. *Ben-Hur: A Tale of the Christ* became popular along with the expansion of public libraries in the United States at the end of the nineteenth century. Contemporary documents demonstrate just how popular it was. Already in 1885, Klas Linderfelt, the prominent librarian at The Milwaukee Public Library, observed the sudden explosion of interest in the novel:

> For over a year I had a copy of Gen. Lew Wallace's "Ben-Hur" on the shelf, and no one ever called for it, but suddenly it was asked for, and now it hardly ever finds its way back to the shelf. Everyone wants it, but why I cannot tell. It is just so about many other works, but I never saw anything like this rage for a book, and other librarians tell me that their experience with the same novel has been identically the same.[141]

In 1893 J. Selwin Tait and Sons did a study, and they found that Wallace's novel was the fifth most requested novel in all the public libraries they surveyed, ranking behind *David Copperfield*, *Ivanhoe*, *The Scarlet Letter*, and *Uncle Tom's Cabin*, with *The Last Days of Pompeii* ranked as ninth.[142] Local corroboration is found the same year from the Chairman of the Massachusetts Public Library Commission and one year later in the *Galveston Daily News*, where Mary Felton of the municipal library had the opportunity to compliment the people:

> Her reasons for believing the taste of the Galveston reading public is above par is that they like Scott, Dickens, Bulwer, E. P. Roe, Lew Wallace and other writers of fiction upon whom time and a reading people have set the stamp of approval.[143]

BEN-HUR IN READINGS, RECITATIONS, AND DECLAMATIONS

Wallace's description of the chariot race was frequently excerpted in instructional and performance guides. In 1887 Henry M. Soper, who ran his own School of Oratory in Chicago, included a shortened adaptation of the chariot race in his *Scrap-Book Recitation Series* "by special permission of the author."[144] An 1894 ad for *The Tuxedo Reciter* claimed to contain recitations that have "received the sanctions of the most prominent elocutionists in this country and Europe," and the first selection listed in the ad as "popular" is "'The Chariot Race' from 'Ben Hur.'"[145] The 1895 *World Almanac* contains an advertisement for the next year's edition of *The Tuxedo Reciter*, an elegant, gilt-topped volume in a box. The contents consisted of "popular recitations," of which "'The Chariot Race' from *Ben Hur*" is the second listed.[146] In 1904 Richard Linthicum included an excerpt from "Ben Hur's Chariot Race" in *The Ideal Orator*, an elocution handbook, to provide students with an opportunity for "the full and varied display of dramatic and oratorical powers."[147] He uses it to introduce the section Binney Gunnison of Boston's School of Expression adapted as a scene between Ben-Hur and Iras for "the higher grades of school work."[148] And in 1901, Wilmot Brookings Mitchell, Professor of Rhetoric and Oratory at Bowdoin College, edited "The Chariot Race" as "a declamation adapted to school and college boys and girls ... instruction in the essentials of Elocution."[149]

Year after year from coast to coast, Wallace's novel served for school instruction, formal recitations, and school graduations. According to the *New York Times'* description of the 1893 commencement exercises of the New York Evening High Schools, for instance, Music Hall was filled to capacity, and after remarks by the Chairman of the Board of Education Miles O'Brien and ex-Mayor Abram Hewitt:

> Music, recitations, declamations, and essays by the students followed. A declamation – the race scene from "Ben Hur" – by Charles R. Charlton of the Harlem School, caused prolonged applause.[150]

Just a few months later Uriel M. Lowenbaum "won a great deal of applause" for his recitation of "The Chariot Race" among the younger age students of Grammar School No. 77.[151] Marguerite Moston donned a Roman costume of white and gold to recite the chariot race passage for a presentation at Association Hall in St. Paul, Minnesota.[152] An otherwise minor occasion, the awarding of second prize in Declamation for reading the "Chariot Race, from Ben Hur" to young Sewell Avery at the Michigan Military Academy, might have gone unnoticed had Avery not gone on to become the Chairman of the Board and President of Montgomery Ward.[153] In the same year an essay written about public libraries and education in Worcester, Massachusetts, proposed that students should read novels at home and then discuss them in school. Of course *Ben-Hur: A Tale of the Christ* was among those discussed. Representing the younger generation, one student wrote:

> I liked "Ben Hur" because the life of Christ, and the habits, ways, and customs of the people are so graphically described. I felt as if I had found a friend in Ben-Hur. I liked him because if he did have a great many obstacles in his way he overcame them, and at last triumphed over his enemies. One scene which I particularly fancied was the chariot race. One could almost hear the shouts of the multitude and the sound of the chariot wheels.[154]

The Silent Educator reports that the Ben-Hur exhibition given in Omaha in 1892 by the Nebraska School for the Deaf was "a great success and there is a great demand for its reproduction."[155] *The Chautauquan* of February, 1897, reports that a group in the New Mexico circle of Santa Fe call themselves the "Ben Hur Club."[156] The same month in Los Angeles, a Concordia Club recitation of "Chariot Race" was given by "Master Both, the boy orator, rival of William Jennings Bryan."[157]

Churches also made use of the novel, whether in services or in crossover presentations. The June 3, 1888, "Church Notices" section of *The Morning Oregonian* announced that Wallace's account of the Crucifixion would be substituted for a church sermon.[158] Included in an 1895 *New York Times* "Church Entertainments" section was the Progress Club program to be held at the Congregational Church in Upper Montclair.[159] Here the Rev. F. B. Carter was to speak on his "Visit to Minneapolis," Paul Wilcox on "Some Problems of City Growth," and F. B. Littlejohn read "The Chariot Race" from *Ben-Hur*. A number of churches, as well as schools, gave copies of the novel to meritorious youth and prize-winning students. Most of these are identifiable from plates inserted on the flyleaf, as in a 1906 British Wesleyan Methodist Juvenile Home & Foreign Missionary Society gift to a young woman "in recognition for her services as a Collector for this Society."[160] Beyond church grounds the novel also inspired the syndication of the 1889 Will Davis poem, "The Leper's Prayer,"[161] and the members of the Tourist Club of Trinidad, Colorado, were reported to have responded to roll call at their Christmas meeting in with quotations from *Ben-Hur*.[162]

Recitations were not limited to institutional groups, and enthusiastic receptions were not elicited from youths alone. The reviewer's praise for Jessie Eldridge's public rendition of the chariot race portion of the novel in late November, 1890, was typically effusive:

> Miss Jessie Eldridge gave in a marvelous manner "The Chariot Race," from Ben Hur. As read by her in sharp, clear tones, the active, speaking gestures full of meaning, is most superb. [sic] Each scene was so vivid in descriptive power, and so perfect was the reading of the lines that her own personal interest, stimulated by the brilliancy of the text, had peculiar power in holding her audience as few have ever done in Boston.[163]

The reader will find many visual, musical, dramatic, and cinematic adaptations of the chariot race in the following pages and chapters, so it is important to understand the impact that Wallace's literary description often had on his contemporaries, particularly when read by an expert. Before those dramatic applications of Wallace's novel were fully realized, an afternoon's or evening's program often included a reading of the chariot race segment along with other forms and subjects of entertainment. The declamation by Ednorah Nahar, a Bostonian invited to perform in Cincinnati in May, 1890, demonstrates the thrill Wallace's passage could instill in a large audience, as described in the *Cincinnati Enquirer*:

> The treat of the evening was her reading of the "Chariot Race" from General Lew Wallace's famous novel "Ben Hur." As she described during the course of the race the different positions of the contestants and the herculean struggle for mastery between the Roman and the Jew she carried her audience with her, leading them step by step to the highest point in the scale of enthusiasm until, as the panting Arabian horses driven by Ben Hur carry him to victory, there was a unanimous burst of applause coming from all parts of the house that was a well-deserved tribute to the talent of the young artiste.[164]

The *Bangor Daily Whig & Courier* announced a May 21, 1889, entertainment at the City Hall featuring Adelaide Drew's reading of the "Chariot Race," specifying that it had been "repeated by request."[165] Although the elements of reverence in Wallace's novel lend themselves more naturally to charity and benefit performances, in 1893 even a recitation of the chariot race passage served for the eighth annual benefit concert in aid of the Sick relief Fund of United Council No. 1035, American Legion of Honor.[166]

These presentations were hardly limited to young men. A Milwaukee Athenaeum rendition of the chariot race makes it clear that an evening's entertainment designed by women in honor of another woman could still feature a reading of "the chariot race." The *Milwaukee Daily Journal* in 1890 describes this kind of environment, in this instance, at a reception arranged at the local Athenaeum.

> A reception was tendered to Mrs. S. L. Sheldon, of Madison, at the Athenaeum last night by a large number of her Milwaukee friends. For the past two years Mrs. Sheldon has been conducting classes of history in the city, which have been attended by a large number of ladies, who, as an evidence of their esteem, planned the entertainment of last evening. A pleasing feature was the presentation of a series of tableaux. Miss Burpee, the elocutionist, delighted the audience with a realistic rendition of the chariot race in "Ben Hur." Special singing was rendered by Miss Hearding.[167]

Another took place in Warren, Pennsylvania, on October 27, 1893, where an evening of various charitable entertainments concluded with Fannie Smith's rendition of the "'The Chariot Race' from Ben Hur."[168]

The chariot race would have its own spiritual attraction as a popular didactic metaphor. In 1888, for instance, C. L. Colby's address on "The Elements of Success" in a crowded room of the Y.M.C.A. in Milwaukee featured "a large picture of a Roman chariot race" and compared it to the "race of life."[169] After renaming the four Arabs Thought, Taste, Temper, and Habit, and identifying Messala's team as the devil's Rage, Despair, Desperation, and Ruin, he finishes by saying, "We are driving the King's horses and must win or die." The reader may also have noticed that many of these presentations were given in the early 1890s. This was the same period, in the winter of 1891, that Wallace received a letter from a former military subordinate whose friend overheard a man from Montana claim that he had written "the story of the Roman Chariot Race" and given it to Wallace.[170]

Recitations were not necessarily limited to the chariot race. Carrie McIntire entertained her fellow members of the Ohio Association of Elocutionists with "The Angel and the Shepherds," which she arranged from the novel.[171] Maude Burt McCall gave a "very vivid and graphic recitation of 'The Miracle of the Lepers,' from 'Ben Hur,'" in Philadelphia at the Minnie M. Jones School of Elocution in May, 1893.[172] A performance at Bangor's Old Town Congregational Fair at the end of the year warranted an encore after "the reading of 'Ben Hur.'"[173] In 1890 *The New York Age* cited Ednorah Nahar for her dramatic readings, including "her rendition of 'Ben Hur.'"[174] And in 1897 the Knapp mansion in Brooklyn was "filled with an audience that enjoyed for nearly two hours the recital of a number of selections from 'Ben Hur' by Mrs. Henry A. Powell."[175] The purpose of this society gathering was to raise money for a free kindergarten (a popular charitable cause at the time), but the six "scenes selected for interpretation" featured Messala's "insult" to Judah and "cruelty," "the galley slave," Judah's visit to the grove of Daphne, and Messala's "midnight revel" – hardly material for children – as well as the chariot race.

The intersection of Wallace's novel and the late nineteenth-century delight in public entertainments by readers, reciters, and elocutionists filled large venues and titillated audiences with enlightened entertainment. The reader will find more about leading exponents like Minnie Jones and Lida Hood Talbot in the chapter on the *Ben-Hur, in Tableaux and Pantomime*, but for this discussion on the popularity of the book itself, the scant information that survives regarding Virginia Saffel Mercer provides an illustrative example.

Not at all a major figure, she enters the historical record as the wife of the Mayor of Salem, Ohio, in 1892, when she hosted the elocutionist known as Miss McCrae.[176] McCrae gave an entertainment at the local Disciple church which included a reading of "The Chariot Race" which "was especially fine, showing rare grace combined with great power, and was a succession of classical pictures, both by word and attitude." It was so successful that the following night she read it again for a private party.[177] Two years later Virginia Saffel Mercer was inspired to develop an entire evening's entertainment derived entirely from *Ben-Hur: A Tale of the Christ* and began to advertise nationally.[178] Late in 1896 she wrote Lew Wallace.[179] She tells him that she called it "The Healing of the Lepers," and (like Bradford) she "embraces the quieter scenes, especially showing the depths of misery to which the mother and daughter have sunken, their great love for Ben-Hur, their faith, their struggle to reach Christ and the wonderful healing which follows." She then offers to read it for Wallace, whether in public, for a charitable cause, or in his well-publicized private study.[180] Finally, she informs Wallace that she will read "The Angel and the Shepherds" and "The Hidden Cell" in Sharon, Pennsylvania, on Christmas Day. Wasting no time, the day after Christmas Wallace asked

Susan to forward the letter to Harper, suggesting that her readings constituted a copyright infringement.[181] This did not put an end to her endeavors, however. The *Salem Daily News* of April 21, 1897, carried a large ad listing the program for the "Entertainment" to be offered by Virginia Saffel Mercer at the Grand Opera House in two nights.[182] Not only is "The Chariot Race" the climactic piece on the program, but at the bottom of the ad a reference from a previous Iowa recital claims that she read the Chariot Race "so vividly before her hearers that the turn of the wheels and charge of the steeds became a part of their consciousness." Ironically, two years after Wallace had passed away, Mercer's name surfaces once again when she presented "The Healing of the Lepers" in Steubenville, Ohio. According to the local newspaper ad, the *Record* of St. Augustine, Florida, praised her work as "excellent, winning enthusiastic applause."[183]

Fast forwarding to 1917, we find Ralph Albert Pariette using the ultimate triumph of Judah Ben-Hur as an exemplar for the rest of humanity in his very popular motivational book, *The University of Hard Knocks: The School That Completes Our Education*:

> Ben Hur wins the race! Where got the Jew those huge forearms? From the galleys! Had Ben Hur never pulled on the oar, he never could have won the chariot race.
> Sooner or later you and I are to learn that Providence makes no mistakes in the book-keeping. As we pull on the oar, so often lashed by grim necessity every honest effort is laid up at compound interest in the bank account of strength. Sooner or later the time comes when we need every ounce. Sooner or later our chariot race is on – when we win the victory, strike the deciding blow, stand while those around us fall – and it is won with the forearms earned in the galleys of life by pulling on the oar.[184]

REFORMULATING THE CALCULUS: THE WALLACE MEMORIAL EDITION

Lew Wallace died on February 15, 1905. His death served to further the progress of the phenomenon he had long since set into motion. Susan oversaw the Harper & Brothers publication of her husband's autobiography in 1906, for which she received a royalty of 30 percent.[185] Like his father, Henry Wallace as executor was vigilant in regard to copyright matters. He had been signatory as witness to the original contract drawn between his father and Harper outlining the arrangement with Klaw & Erlanger,[186] and now his first battle would be the most important and visible of all – joining Harper and Klaw & Erlanger in the suit against Kalem for producing, distributing, and exhibiting the first film version of *Ben-Hur* in late 1907 and early 1908. During these months Henry again stepped into the breach when the novel's original copyright was due to expire after twenty-eight years, as prescribed by the Copyright Act of 1831. Henry assigned his name to the United States copyright renewal, valid for another fourteen years, and so it was that same year that Harper issued the "Wallace Memorial Edition" of *Ben-Hur: A Tale of the Christ*.[187]

This was a standard edition, simple, although it was often sold in a paper jacket reproducing a painting of a chariot race in color.[188] The painting was the watercolor *Carrera de cuádrigas en el Circo Máximo de Roma*. Ulpiano Fernández-Checa y Sanz, known more widely as Ulpiano Checa, had entered it in the 1890 Paris Salon as *Course de chars romains* and won third prize. The following spring Léon Henri Lefèbre commissioned a reduced version, and by the end of 1891 the print version by M. Maurice Deville was being reviewed in the British press as being "extremely spirited and vigorous" and maintaining the "striking energy" of the original.[189] Soon after prints, etchings, and color facsimiles began to circulate in the United States, and despite the lack of the name Ben-Hur in the title, the scene depicted by Checa seems to be taken from the novel, specifically in that a chariot and four bays pass a crashed chariot with two fallen whites and blacks. The low-priced Wallace Memorial edition was not widely advertised. No advertisements appear in the various ephemera databases. Nonetheless, it would ultimately sell more than a million copies because this would be the edition sold to Sears, Roebuck, and Company in 1913, and many of these copies would then be distributed through Grosset & Dunlap. Although the strategy is not documented, it may be that Henry thought that sales of the relatively inexpensive edition of the novel were necessary but not nearly as lucrative as the major component of the *Ben-Hur* empire he had recently inherited, the Klaw & Erlanger production. Though beyond Henry's control, as it turned out the release of the 1907 Kalem film adaptation also helped increase sales.[190]

Whatever his reason, he seems to have been following his father's initiative and clearly put much of his energy into producing profitable publications of *Ben-Hur: A Tale of the Christ* and its scions. For many years at the outset Harper had been quite proud that they had never sold a cheap edition of Wallace's novel, and they frequently expressed their concern about those cheaper British and Canadian imports.[191] But when configuring the size and price of *The Prince of India* in 1893, Lew Wallace himself indicated in a letter to Harper that he would be comfortable with both cheaper and more expensive editions:

> Let the cheap form go together with the dear. People love to have a choice in everything, and in nothing so much as the books they buy.[192]

And in 1899 he would wholeheartedly embrace the idea of selling the Garfield edition at a lower cost.[193]

Another example of the new strategy seems to be in allowing the Frank A. Munsey Company to print excerpts from *Ben-Hur: A Tale of the Christ* in their monthly magazine, *The Scrap Book*. Mr. Munsey had his assistant contact Colonel George B. Harvey directly in February, 1907.[194] Two years after falling into receivership in 1899, Harvey had bought the Harper weekly magazine and was now serving as president of the company.

Harvey agreed to Munsey's proposal, stipulating that they include their copyright line. The April, 1907, issue contains two short excerpts from the chariot race episode of the novel (5.13 and 5.14, labeled as "I – The Start" and "II – The Race"), preceded by a paragraph each summarizing Wallace's career and the plot of the novel.[195] At the end of the brief preface it says that the excerpts are printed "by special permission of the Messrs. Harper & Bros., through the courtesy of Colonel George B. Harvey." This was not adequate for Harper, however. A subsequent letter to Munsey politely reprimands them for not including the statement that every other authorized edition and adaptation of Wallace's novel had always contained: "Copyright 1880 by Harper & Brothers."[196]

A very successful entrepreneur and publisher, Colonel Harvey along with Henry Wallace in 1908 had Harper issue another extracted volume designed for the gift market, *The Chariot-Race From Ben-Hur*. The text included a brief extract from 4.1 ["The Month is July . . . the place Antioch . . ."], and then includes the pre-race and race account from Judah's visit to the Daphne circus to the end of the race (4.7–10, 4.13, 5.2, 5.6, 5.10–14), excluding the intervening, unrelated chapters. Each of its ten chapters is headed by a title printed in a gothic-style font, and the text of each chapter begins with an enlarged capital letter printed with an elaborately foliated block design. The rest of the text is printed in large font placed comfortably within unbordered text boxes. Harper commissioned Sigismond Ivanowski, recently featured in the *New York Times*, to prepare four color paintings printed on glossy paper and arranged as the frontispiece and three full-page inserts.[197] Harper's ad in the December 17, 1908, *Life* placed the book first among its "Beautiful Holiday Books."[198] Similarly, Harper issued a 1908 edition of "The Player's Edition," with copyright also now assigned to Henry Wallace. Opposite the dedication page they advertised various editions and bindings of *Ben-Hur*, nine of them, ranging from the standard edition and various leather bindings to the Garfield (in its own various bindings) and the German edition. There was also the aforementioned attempt in early spring of 1908 at reprinting *Ben-Hur: A Tale of the Christ* with *The Fair God* in a "Library Edition" set, to be sold by subscription only. The exchange of letters between Harper and Houghton Mifflin reveals that the latter agreed to have Harper publish this set and pay them a 5 percent royalty, but there is no evidence of such a set ever being printed.[199]

THE SEARS, ROEBUCK EDITION

At the end of the decade, distribution remained a considerable problem in the book trade. More than half the population of the United States still lived in rural areas, potential consumers with increasing amounts of leisure time and disposable cash. By this time Sears, Roebuck & Company, followed by Montgomery Ward, had emerged as the largest mail-order retailer in the United States, and both searched for cheaper and more efficient ways of reaching these non-urban areas. Retailer John Wanamaker, after becoming Postmaster General in 1889, had established Rural Free Delivery. However, many rural retailers vehemently opposed these kinds of urban incursions and even accused "the Chicago capitalists and New York financiers" of encouraging personal indulgence.[200] After numerous hearings, Congress ultimately created the Parcel Post system in 1912, and it went into operation on the first day of 1913. Sears, Roebuck had been listing books in its huge catalog every year since 1897, and since biblical and historical material had always sold well, the company would undoubtedly find Lew Wallace's novel to be appropriately marketable, particularly as part of their still relatively new strategy of targeting mass-marketed cheap editions at this new consumer demographic. Very often the retailers lost money on the sale of books, but they knew well in the mid-1890s that making them available at low cost attracted buyers for other, more profitable items.[201]

As January, 1913, approached, Harper and Sears, Roebuck brokered a new kind of publishing arrangement, revolutionary, like the most visible scions of the *Ben-Hur* phenomenon, for its sheer size.[202] The deal was negotiated by Henry Hoyns, P. A. Murkland, and R. P. Sniffen. Hoyns had started with Harper in 1883 as a clerk at the age of sixteen, and in 1900 he became Sales Manager under Colonel Harvey, and would become chairman in 1929.[203] Similarly, Murkland in 1911 had been the crockery and glass buyer for Sears, Roebuck & Company, but by 1913 he had become Manager of the Book Department.[204] Sniffen was the Eastern Representative for Sears, Roebuck & Company, the headquarters of which were based in Chicago. Negotiations were concluded in February, 1913. The terms of the agreement were not revolutionary: Harper had granted rights to issue what were then known as "cheap editions" to other publishing houses for other books. But this one, of course, involved an extremely large number of copies. The agreement stipulated that Harper would provide the plates, that Sears, Roebuck would publish the first 750,000 copies by July 1, 1913, and that Sears, Roebuck in return would send two payments of $45,000 based on a fee of 12¢ per copy. The arrangement for the remaining 250,000 copies would be the same, with a publication date of no later than January 1, 1915. Near the end of the agreement is a paragraph that reads:

> We also agree that while this sale is limited to one million (1,000,000) copies, if at any time we should decide to permit anyone to have another edition of the book for this purpose, you would be given the first opportunity to decline to take such an edition.

On the copyright page of the Sears, Roebuck edition, therefore, Harper placed a thin black border around the following statement, which

Figure 5.5 The Sears edition came in a cardboard box and paper cover depicting Checa's chariot race, with an ad to purchase a larger version ready for framing. Harper "limited" the one million volumes sold to Sears.

accounts for the word "limited," which might seem ludicrous out of context:

THE WALLACE MEMORIAL EDITION LIMITED TO 1,000,000 COPIES SOLD TO SEARS, ROEBUCK AND COMPANY BY HARPER & BROTHERS

The Sears, Roebuck edition dressed up the standard "Wallace Memorial Edition" nicely. It was slipped into a cardboard box decorated with a blue-ink engraving of Checa's painting. A caption is printed on this engraving, "Ben-Hur drives Sheik Ilderim's Stars of the Desert to victory in the Antioch Circus defeating his arch enemy, Messala," and the entire side contains a Greek meander-design border. The other three sides of the box are also printed, each labeling its contents: "This box contains one copy of Ben-Hur – Wallace Memorial Edition – published by Sears, Roebuck and Co., Chicago." The book itself came in a color paper jacket depicting Checa's image, and the front flap of the jacket had an offer for a 17½in. × 28in. reproduction of Checa's painting on extra heavy white art stock, shipped rolled in a tube, for 25¢. On both the front and the spine of the cloth cover, which came in blue (later red), the name "Ben" was stamped above the name "Hur" – without either the hyphen or the subtitle. The front endpaper contains a two-tone illustration of the three Wise Men gazing at the star radiating over the city of Bethlehem, balanced on the endpapers with an illustration of Christ healing Judah's mother and sister. Opposite the title page is the same full-page photograph of Lew Wallace used for the Garfield edition, but now with a facsimile of the author's signature.

Advertising for this edition did not follow the typical procedures used by publishers. A press release was issued to trade journals and the *New York Times*.[205] Murkland reportedly told the *Chicago Tribune* that if piled atop one another the one million volumes "would reach more than sixteen miles into space."[206] But rather than advertise to the trade, Sears, Roebuck featured the book in a full-page, color ad in their next book catalog. The ad for *Ben-Hur* is the only color ad in the entire catalog. On the first page is Checa's watercolor and a description of the book offered for "the new reduced price" of 39¢; on the second is a synopsis of the novel. It concludes with some telling advertising copy appealing to a variety of potential purchaser demographics: "Why Should You Own a Copy of 'Ben-Hur'":

If you love books and have not read "Ben-Hur" you have missed a wonderful treat. If you have a library "Ben-Hur" should have a place in it. If you have children you should see that this marvelous book with its enlightening and inspiring story is read by them. If you intend to make a gift, what could be more acceptable than a copy of "Ben-Hur"? It is a book for parents to give to children, a book for children to give to parents, a book for friends to give to friends. A book for everybody in America. A book that men, women and children of every nationality, creed or religion can read with unalloyed pleasure. Do not fail to obtain not only a copy for yourself and your family, but also copies to be given to your friends as gifts at Christmas and other appropriate occasions.

The most prevalent vehicle for Sears, Roebuck's advertising campaign was a postcard.[207] The entire face of the postcard was filled with a color reprint of the Checa painting, with "Wallace Memorial Edition – Sears, Roebuck & Co." in two lines in the lower left-hand corner, and "BEN-HUR" in the lower right. The back of the card – the era of the divided card had begun in 1907 – contained the full title, name of the edition, and an alluring description of the edition, ending with: "It is a thrilling story and the handsomest book of the year." The use of advertising postcards became prevalent a few years after the turn of the century. These were not mailed to potential customers but distributed in stores. They were usually designed so that customers could order the item by filling out the postcard and returning it to the store via the stamped address. The Sears, Roebuck Ben-Hur card, however, was intended for general postal use, with "This space for correspondence" marked on the left of the division and three lines for the address on the right. In general these kinds of postcards rarely survived, but many extant examples of the Sears, Roebuck *Ben-Hur* cards, even though they were not postally used, were kept for their free, colorful copy of Checa's dynamic painting.[208]

Russo & Sullivan (320) report that by July, 1926, 611,511 copies had been sold. In his history of Sears and Wards, Cecil Hoge reports that it took "several years" to sell the million copies.[209] On the advertising postcard the cost of the book is listed as 48¢, plus another 12¢ for postage if the product was to be shipped. Other ads list the book for as little as 39¢ and as much as 63¢.[210] The variations in price depend to a certain extent on the issuer. There are copies of the Wallace Memorial Edition issued by Harper that are identical to the Sears, Roebuck release except that the ad on the front jacket flap is replaced by a tease for the novel, and inside the paper jacket are lists of Grosset & Dunlap publications. Murkland had written Hoyns in September, 1913, informing him that Sears, Roebuck had decided to allow Grosset & Dunlap to issue a trade edition of the novel but requested that they remove the reference to the "Wallace Memorial Edition." In 1922, when the fourteen-year extension on the 1908 copyright had to be renewed, Grosset & Dunlap continued their sales with some minor formatting changes, especially after 1926 when they inserted a photograph of the three Wise Men standing before Mary from the MGM film. One extant copy of this issue contains a wrapper which boasts: "Originally Published at $2.00 – Now 75¢ in the Grosset & Dunlap Edition." Grosset & Dunlap would also issue an edition in a larger format, the paper jacket of which contained a chariot race illustration by [Fabian] Zaccone, and the statement that there are "more than 2,600,000 copies in print," suggesting that the balance of the one million copies sold

The Transformations of the Novel

Figure 5.6 Sears advertised the Wallace Memorial Edition in their catalog and on in-store postcards, many of which were preserved as keepsakes.

to Sears, Roebuck had at least all been printed, and ranking it among the top ten sellers of American novels in mid-century.[211]

The Grosset & Dunlap issuance had another large organizational audience – the Boy Scouts of America. Sniffen had been connected with Boy Scouts when the Harper contract was signed. That was in 1913, when he was a member of the Committee on Scout Supplies. The edition used was again the 1908 Wallace Memorial Edition distributed through Grosset & Dunlap, but preceding the title and copyright pages the Scouts inserted a two-page endorsement – a facsimile of a letter from James E. West, Chief Scout Executive, on letterhead from the Boy Scouts of America, the emblem of which was displayed on the dust jacket as well as the cloth cover. West specifically endorses "Every Boy's Library," the titles of which are printed on the back of the dust jacket, to meet the peril of "the great mass of cheap juvenile literature."

The Sears, Roebuck adoption of the Wallace Memorial Edition was another monument in the history of the *Ben-Hur* phenomenon. Before Sears, Roebuck agreed to the arrangement to purchase and then sell one million copies, the novel had already sold approximately one million copies, the total population of the United States at the time not yet having reached 100 million, many of whom were either illiterate or did not speak English as their mother tongue.[212] For thirty-three years Harper had sold the novel at full price, ranging from the $1.50 it first charged in 1880 to the $4.00–$30.00 it charged for the various versions of the Garfield edition. Now the publisher had turned the property over to mass marketing, making the book even more "popular" in the commercial sense, and in that sense also making it more apt for commercial synergy, association, and exploitation. In addition, we must consider that in 1913, those who had memories of their parents reading *Ben-Hur: A Tale of the Christ* to them, as did Lloyd C. Douglas, represented a new generation which would comprise a large percentage of the audience that flocked to see the MGM film in the 1920s, just after Harper reissued its 1922 edition – the date of the final available copyright renewal.[213] That edition, too, was wrapped in the illustrated dust jacket from the Sears, Roebuck release.

NOTES

1 *The Critic* 21 (March 4, 1886) 135.
2 Letter from Harper to Wallace (March 30, 1887), LL.
3 Letter from Harper to Houghton Mifflin (December 14, 1886), LL.
4 *Current Literature* 26 (December, 1899) 566.
5 Note from Houghton Mifflin to Susan Wallace (January 30, 1885), LL.
6 Letter from Harper to Houghton Mifflin (March 25, 1887), LL.
7 Letter from Houghton Mifflin to Susan Wallace (November 1, 1887), LL.

8 Letter from Houghton Mifflin to Susan (November 14, 1890), LL.
9 *An Autobiography* 893.
10 Mckee 28 and 126.
11 Wallace, "Oriental Splendors," 9.
12 Letter from Wallace to Harper (September 6, 1886), Newberry Library, The Rudy L. Ruggles Collection.
13 *Seekers After "The Light" From "Ben-Hur"* (New York: Geo. R. Lockwood & Son, 1886).
14 F. M. seems to have published previously in London, e.g. *The Young Archer's Assistant* (London: n.p., 1854), and *The Divine Sequence: A Treatise on Creation and Redemption* (London: n.p., 1873).
15 The book cites pages 10, 11, 12, 13, and 30.
16 *PW* (September 24, 1887) 298.
17 *PW* (August 14, 1886) 198; cf. *The American Bookseller* 22 (August 15, 1887) 106.
18 *The Literary News* 8 (March, 1887) 96.
19 *The Literary News* 8 (February, 1887) 37.
20 Lew Wallace, *Ben-Hur* (Louisville KY: American Printing-House for the Blind, 1887).
21 *Proceedings of the Eleventh Biennial Meeting of the American Association of Instructors of the Blind*, 43 <http://www.archive.org/stream/proceedingsof18861908unse/proceedingsof18861908unse_djvu.txt>
22 Matthews, "American Authors and British Pirates," 201–13; excerpted in *The Critic* 8 (October 1, 1887) 168–70.
23 Horder, *The Poet's Bible*[3], 517.
24 <http://www-personal.ksu.edu/~rcadams/gallery.html>
25 *[Coshocton OH] Democratic Standard* (March 14, 1902) 6.
26 *The Critic* 8 (August 20, 1887) 97; *Good Housekeeping* 5 (September 17, 1887) 246.
27 *NYT* (September 5, 1887) 2.
28 Davenport, *The Fifty Best Books*, 761–71.
29 Warner, et al., *Library of the World's Best Literature*, 15531–54.
30 Birdsall and Jones, *Famous Authors*, 392–4.
31 Aldrich and Forbes, *The Progressive Course in Reading*, 92–8; *St. Nicholas* 28 (November, 1900) 45–8.
32 *PW* 30 (December 25, 1886) 975.
33 Letter from Lew to Susan Wallace (March 31, 1885), IHS.
34 Letters from Wallace to Harper & Brothers (October 3 and December 23, 1887), UVA.
35 *Blätter für literarische Unterhaltung* (November 17, 1887) 732.
36 Letter from Deutsche Verlags-Anstalt to Wallace (November 6, 1890), LL.
37 *Donohoe's Magazine* 53 (April, 1905) 408; Vollmer, *The American Novel in Germany*, 92.
38 Lew Wallace (Paul Heichen, trans.), *Ben Hur; oder die Tage des Messias* (Halle: O. Hendel, 1890); cf. *Halbjahrsverzeichnis der neuerscheinungen des deutschen Buchhandels* (Leipzig: Verlag des Börsenvereins der Deutschen Buchhändler, 1890) 2:54.

39 *The Phi Gamma Delta* 5 (May, 1883) 121.
40 Letter from Lew to Susan Wallace (March 31, 1885), IHS.
41 *NYT* (January 17, 1887) 5.
42 Letter from Mrs. N. S. Moore to Wallace (May 2, 1887), LL.
43 *Home Missionary* 61 (July, 1888) 168.
44 A. Boggiano (trans.), *Ben-Hur: en berättelse från Kristi tid* (Stockholm: Fr. Skoglund, 1888).
45 Letter from Wallace to Harper (June 27, 1888), UVA.
46 Letter from Harper to Wallace (April 6, 1887), LL.
47 Letter from Harper to Wallace (April 25, 1887), LL.
48 *Blätter für literarische Unterhaltung* (November 17, 1887) 732.
49 Lew Wallace (Alfonso Maria Galea, trans.), *Ben-Hur: ossia I giorni del messia* (Modena: Tipografica Pontificia ed Archivescovile, 1895). Cf. Russo & Sullivan, 325. Agreement (June 16, 1893), BL, sent from Malta, stipulates that Galea should pay Wallace "an honorarium of ten pounds sterling (in place of a royalty)."
50 The French translator was Joseph Autier, which is a pseudonym for Louise Cornaz. WorldCat lists an 1885 printing of this edition. But this would predate the Hammer translation, and the date of the only extant copy is uncertain. It is located at Assumption College, and their online catalog lists the date as "[1885?]". The first verifiable French translation: Joseph Autier (trans.), *Ben-Hur* (Lausanne: H. Mignot, 1890). The second edition is described in *Bibliographie und litterarische Chronik der Schweiz* 24 (October, 1894) 238; cf. the claim that "J. Autin" translated the English text in 22 (December, 1892) 190. The same edition was also published by Grassart in Paris.
51 H. Mildmay and Gastone Cavalieri (trans.), *Ben Hur: una storia di Cristo* (Milan: Baldini, Castoldi & Co., 1900). The title page boasts it as the "*Prima Traduzione Italiana.*"
52 Lewis Wallace, *Ben-Hur: Racconto storico dei tempi di Cristo* (Rome: Desclée, Lefebvre e Cia editori pontifici, 1902), as advertised in *La Civiltà cattolica* 10 (1903) 128.
53 E.g. Brownlow, *The Parade's Gone By ...*, 386.
54 *The Christian Work and the Evangelist* 74 (June 20, 1903) 895. Cf. *An Autobiography* 2:841–2.
55 *New Catholic World* 81 (April, 1905) 138.
56 *PW* 26 (August 2, 1884) 169.
57 *Book News* 14 (October, 1895) 59; Note, June 25, 1895, BL.
58 *Books in Foreign Languages Added to the Chicago Public Library From May, 1890 to September, 1891*, (Bulletin No. 15) 16.
59 Lovoll, *Norwegian Newspapers in America*, 369.
60 Letter from Harper to Wallace, (October 30, 1890), LL.
61 Danish: Vilh. Møller (trans.), *Ben Hur: En Fortaeling fra Kristi Tid*. (Copenhagen: n.p., 1888). Russian: *Vo vremja ono* (St. Petersburg: Lebedev, 1888). Russian: E. Beketovoi (trans.), *Vo dni ony, Ben Gur: poviest' iz pervykh liet kristianstva* (St. Petersburg: A. S. Suvorina, 1890).
62 Lighty, *The Fall and Rise of Lew Wallace*, 81–6.
63 *Harper's New Monthly Magazine* 76 (January, 1888) 325.

64 E.g. Charles King, *Between the Lines* (1888), Sergei Stepniak, *The Career of a Nihilist* (1889), and James Meeker Ludlow, *The Captain of the Janizaries* (1890).
65 The statistics are compiled in LMC-2060, Lilly Library, Indiana University.
66 *New Catholic World* 81 (April, 1905) 138.
67 *Harper's New Monthly Magazine* 78 (January, 1889) 169–93.
68 Letter from Harper to Wallace (January 25, 1888), LL.
69 Letter from Harper to Wallace (April 5, 1888), LL.
70 Lew Wallace, *Ben-Hur: A Tale of the Christ* (New York: Harper & Brothers, 1891).
71 *PW* 40 (December, 1891) 30.
72 *PW* 40 (December, 1891) 19.
73 *The Book Buyer* 13 (February, 1896) 17–19; cf. *The Literary World* 51 (June 21, 1895) 583.
74 *The Critic* 16 (December 5, 1891) 313.
75 *PW* 40 (December, 1891) 19.
76 *LAT* (September 16, 1891) 4.
77 *The Book Buyer* 13 (February, 1896) 18; 8 (Christmas Issue, 1891) 478–80.
78 *The Cosmopolitan* 12 (January, 1882) 384.
79 Lawrence, *Modern Missions in the East*, 333.
80 Van Dyke, *Referendum*, 17.
81 Letter from Wallace to Harper (July 7, 1899), BL.
82 *Scribner's* 14 (October, 1893) 429–46.
83 Letter from Wallace to Harper (January 29, 1893), IHS.
84 Letter from Lew to Susan Wallace (1893 [year only]), IHS.
85 *The Waukesha* [WI] *Freeman* (August 31, 1893) 8.
86 Memo from Harper to Wallace, March 6, 1893, LL; cf. *The Washington Post* (March 3, 1907) A12.
87 Pond, *Eccentricities of Genius*, 465–7.
88 Special Announcement, IHS.
89 *Oakland Daily Evening Tribune* (October 30, 1894) 7; *Brooklyn Eagle* (January 5, 1895) 3; *NYT* (January 18, 1895) 6.
90 Redmond, *Welcome to America*, 44.
91 *Oakland Daily Evening Tribune* (October 30, 1894) 7.
92 Ibid., 5.
93 *CT* (February 22, 1895) 11.
94 Letter from Wallace to Pond (July 8, 1895), IHS.
95 Telegram from Hearst to Wallace (April 21, 1897), IHS.
96 Letter from Wallace to Chambers (April 27, 1897), IHS.
97 *PW* 40 (December, 1891) 19.
98 *The Publishers' Circular* (October 30, 1897) 517.
99 Lew Wallace, *The Wooing of Malkatoon; Commodus* (New York: Harper & Brothers, 1897 and 1898).
100 Draft (March 8, 1894), LL.
101 John Clark Ridpath, George J. Bryan, and George Spiel, *Famous Paintings of the World: A Collection of Photographic Reproductions of Great Modern Masterpieces . . .* (New York: Fine Art Pub. Co, 1894).

102 *Albuquerque Morning Democrat* (August 7, 1894) 3; *Gems of Modern Art, A Collection of Photographic Reproductions of Great Modern Paintings* (New York: Knight and Brown, 1900).
103 Croly, *Tarry Thou Till I Come*.
104 *NYT* (December 25, 1895) 14, details the extent to which Wallace gave Grosvenor advice and the benefit of his experience; cf. the Rev. Alfred Kummer, *The Sling of David, and Other Poems* (New York: Hurst & Co., 1896), for which Wallace wrote two pages introducing "the author . . . my good friend."
105 *The Outing* 12 (July, 1888) 312; Zach, *Crawfordsville, Athens of Indiana*, 43.
106 *StLPD* (October 1, 1897) 4.
107 Letter from Lew Wallace to A. J. Wissler (May 6, 1890), NMHM.
108 <http://econtent.unm.edu/cdm/singleitem/collection/acpa/id/5144/rec/8>
109 *Old Santa Fe* 1 (1913–14) 441.
110 Letter from Henry Wallace to Paul Walter (October 30, 1915), NMHM.
111 Hewett, *Lew Wallace and the Ben Hur Room*, 6.
112 *The World's work Advertiser* 5 (April, 1903) 3494.
113 Pythian, *City of Manchester Art Gallery*, 53 [#141]; *New York Tribune* (May 10, 1876) 1.
114 *New Outlook* 74 (August 29, 1903) 1164; *Public Opinion* 33 (December 4, 1902) 729; (December 11, 1902) 764; *The Book-Keeper* 15 (April, 1903) 89.
115 *Morning [WA] Olympian* (May 6, 1895) 4; *Grand Forks [ND] Herald* (May 30, 1895) 2.
116 *Dallas Morning News* (September 16, 1900) 10.
117 Hermann Milton Bien, *Ben-Beor: A Story of the Anti-Messiah* (Baltimore: I. Friedenwald, 1891); Carlisle B. Holding, *Her Ben: A Tale of Royal Resolves* (Cincinnati: Cranston & Stowe, 1889).
118 J. O. A. Clark, *Esther: A Sequel to Ben Hur; or, The Lost Epistles . . .* (Nashville: Pub. House of the M. E. Church, South, 1892).
119 Eldridge S. Brooks, *A Son of Issachar* (New York: Putnam, 1890); Ellis John Breckenridge, *Adnah: A Tale of the Time of Christ* (Philadelphia: George W. Jacobs & Co., 1902).
120 Annie Fellows Johnston, *Joel: A Boy of Galilee* (Boston: L. C. Page & Co., 1904).
121 Miles Gerald Keon, *Dion and the Sibyls* (New York: Benziger Brothers, 1890).
122 *Lippincott's Monthly Magazine* 59 (January, 1897) 145.
123 *PW* (November 10, 1906) 1283.
124 *The Critic* 27 (April 10, 1897) 246.
125 *The Chap-Book* 7 (May 15, 1897) 29.
126 *WSJ* (April 18, 1934) 6.
127 Mott, *Golden Multitudes*, 197; *NYT* (October 29, 1947) 25; *American Quarterly* 23 (1971) 61.
128 Scodel and Bettenworth, *Whither Quo Vadis*; Wyke, *Projecting the Past*, 110–46; Blom, "*Quo Vadis?*" 284–5.
129 *NYT* (December 13, 1899) 6; *DFP* (August 15, 1900) 4; *CT* (March 26, 1911) 8.

130 *St. Louis Post-Dispatch* (December 14, 1902) B22B.
131 *BG* (January 28, 1899) 5.
132 E.g. Wyke, *Projecting the Past*, 110.
133 Petaja, *Photoplay Edition*, 5.
134 *Public Opinion* 27 (December 1, 1899) 736.
135 *Harper's New Monthly Magazine* (November, 1899) 36.
136 *Harper's New Monthly Magazine* (November, 1899) 41.
137 *HW* 43 (November 18, 1899) 1167–8; *Harper's New Monthly Magazine* (May, 1901) 18.
138 Loney, "The Heyday of the Dramatized Novel," 198, citing Mott, *Golden Multitude*, 174.
139 Mandel, *The Arabs and Zionism Before World War I*, 53.
140 *NYHT* (December 27, 1925) D3.
141 *MS* (March 29, 1885) 6.
142 Mabie, "The Most Popular Novels in America," 508.
143 *Review of Reviews* 8 (October, 1893) 472; *The Galveston Daily News* (November 10, 1894) 10.
144 Henry M. Soper, ed., *Scrap-Book Recitation Series*, Number 5 (Chicago: T. S. Denison & Company, 1887) 24–9.
145 *Werner's Magazine* 16 (December, 1894) 472.
146 *The World Almanac and Encyclopedia 1895* (New York: The Press Publishing Co., 1895) 498.
147 Lithicum, *The Ideal Orator*, 221–4.
148 Gunnison, *New Dialogues and Plays for Young People*, 149–56.
149 Mitchell, *School and College Speaker*, 251–4.
150 *NYT* (March 31, 1894) 2.
151 *NYT* (June 28, 1894) 9.
152 *St. Paul Daily News* (February 19, 1892) 2.
153 *The Long Roll* 1 (1892) 71 <http://www.gwbhs.com/research/michigan-military-academy-people>
154 *The Christian Union* 46 (December 10, 1892) 1113.
155 *The Silent Educator* (June, 1892) 198.
156 *The Chautauquan* 24 (February, 1897) 627.
157 *LAT* (February 7, 1897) 10.
158 *Morning Oregonian* (June 3, 1888) 3.
159 *NYT* (November 3, 1895) 11.
160 eBay #360599447158, ended January 25, 2014.
161 *The [Forth Worth] Gazette* (January 20, 1889) 4; Davis, *The Trial of Jesus*, 75.
162 *Rocky Mountain News* (December 26, 1897) 21.
163 *The Fitchburg Sentinel* (November 26, 1890) 3.
164 *CE* (May 31, 1890) 16.
165 *Bangor Daily Whig & Courier* (May 14, 1889) 1.
166 *NYT* (May 22, 1893) 7.
167 *Milwaukee Daily Journal* (April 17, 1890) 1.
168 *Warren [PA] Evening Democrat* (October 28, 1893) 2.
169 *MS* (May 28, 1888) 3.
170 Letter from Charles A. Bradley to Wallace (February 20, 1891), LL.

171 *Werner's Magazine* (July, 1900) 505.
172 *PI* (January 24, 1891) 3.
173 *Bangor Daily Whig & Courier* (December 14, 1889) 1.
174 *New York Age* (January 18, 1890) 1.
175 *BE* (January 20, 1897) 2; cf. *Keota [Iowa] Eagle* (January 5, 1899) 4.
176 *Salem Daily News* (March 24, 1892) 3.
177 *Salem Daily News* (March 24, 1892) 3.
178 *Werner's Magazine* 18 (May, 1896) 486.
179 Letter from Virginia Mercer to Wallace (December 20, 1896), LL.
180 *Ladies Home Journal* 16 (December, 1898) 5.
181 Letter from Susan Wallace to Harper (December 26, 1896), LL.
182 *Salem Daily News* (April 21, 1897) 5.
183 *Steubenville Herald Star* (April 6, 1907) 4.
184 Pariette, *The University of Hard Knocks*, 126.
185 Contract (November, 1906), BL.
186 Contract (April 7, 1899), BL.
187 Letter from Henry Wallace to Frederick A. Duneka of Harper & Brothers (May 19, 1908), Morgan Library, says he initiated the application only after the Tax Commissioner cleared him of any inheritance tax from the *Ben-Hur* copyright. For the announcement, see *HW* 52 (August 22, 1908) 31.
188 The edition was ultimately printed in at least two slightly different format sizes.
189 *Athenaeum* (December 26, 1891) 872.
190 Tebbel, *A History of Book Publishing in the United States*, 3:20.
191 Harper, *House of Harper*, 268–9.
192 Letter from Wallace to Harper (March 20, 1893), LL.
193 Letter from Wallace to Harper (July 7, 1899), BL.
194 Letter from R. H. Titherington to Colonel George B. Harvey (February 8, 1907), BL.
195 *The Scrap Book* 3 (April, 1907) 237–43.
196 Letter from Harper to Munsey (April 17, 1907), BL.
197 *NYT* (February 9, 1907) BR78.
198 *Life* 52 (December 17, 1908) 688.
199 Letters between Harper & Brothers and Houghton Mifflin (May 7, 8, and 9, 1908), BL.
200 Werner, *Julius Rosenwald*, 60.
201 Loney, "The Heyday of the Dramatized Novel," 198; cf. Emmet and Jeuck, *Catalogues and Counters*, 38.
202 *PW* 83 (March 1, 1913) 760.
203 *NYT* (January 24, 1945) 21.
204 Blaszczyk, *Imagining Consumers*, 100.
205 *PW* 83 (March 1, 1913) 760.
206 *The Phi Beta Gamma* 35 (April, 1913) 674.
207 *The Paper & Advertising Collectors' Marketplace* 29 (April, 2007) 10, 14.
208 Miller and Miller, *Picture Postcards in the United States*, 73–4 and 87.
209 Hoge, *The First Hundred Years Are the Toughest*, 68; cf. *The Sun* (February 14, 1937) SC7.

210 Cohn, *The Good Old Days*, 117–21.
211 Korda, *Making the List*, xvi–xvii.
212 *The Westminster* 30 (March 11, 1905) 24.
213 *LAT* (October 7, 1951) D6.

6 Reasons for Success

The reader may reflect upon George Ripley's opinion that the manuscript Wallace submitted to Harper & Brothers had "features of popular interest that would give it a wonderful fascination among a multitude of readers," and Charlton Lewis's conclusion that, "the story may be published with some confidence that it will have a fair sale, and with the chance of a great success." While not exuberant about the literary quality of Wallace's manuscript, both readers suggested that the story and its popularizing features could bring it considerable success. Despite their prophetic skills, they did not and could not have predicted that *Ben-Hur: A Tale of the Christ* would become one of the most successful novels of the nineteenth century and one of the most marketable artistic properties in the history of American popular culture. Popularity, especially the extraordinary popularity of a mega-hit, is very difficult to predict. Even repeatedly successful modern publishers and producers with keen instincts, many years of experience, with access to scientific testing and demographic studies can fail at predicting the next "sleeper" hit, as *Ben-Hur: A Tale of the Christ* would prove to be. But we have the advantage of hindsight. Not only do we know that the novel would achieve unparalleled success in a number of ways for many years, but decades of accumulated cultural-historical scholarship have clarified within the milieu of the period several factors that prepared so many readers of Wallace's and the subsequent generation to embrace his novel and support its continued influence in the arts and commerce.

As often with a property that becomes a popular phenomenon, timing was critical. The period in which *Ben-Hur: A Tale of the Christ* was written, marketed, and flourished transitioned from the Reconstruction era and the closing of the Western frontier to the modern industrialized, mechanized, and electrified advent of the twentieth century, as different segments of the American population and many waves of first- and second-generation immigrants redistributed themselves among self-sufficient farms and small, rural communities, larger municipalities dependent on thriving commercial activity, and expanding industrial cities.[1] The rapid growth brought boom and bust. The Panic of 1873 occurred less than two months before Wallace's visit to the Library of Congress to research his "Jewish story." As fate would have it, Wallace continued writing his novel until the end of the decade, when the "Long Depression" that followed upon the Panic of 1873 ended. The novel was therefore released into an accelerating upturn in the economy that would last until the next economic downturn in 1893, the year in which Wallace published his next novel that was accordingly, if one follows socionomic principles, not nearly so successful.

Despite several disruptive downturns along the way, the long-term economic cycle was in a tremendous uptrend, and the last decades of the nineteenth century would be characterized by powerful wealth creation that greatly expanded the number of middle-class consumers. Throughout the Gilded Age and beyond, proliferating retail businesses and expanding corporations integrated a new trend towards commercial secularism and challenged cherished values of family, church, and community. *Ben-Hur: A Tale of the Christ* spoke to many different facets of these developments. The novel – by design – is about poor and rich, lowly and powerful, and secularism, sectarianism, and revelation. Churchgoers reveled in its triumphant message of Christian redemption. Modest rural populations as well as a spectrum of urbanite consumers, retailers, and businessmen found reassuring moral value and triumphant heroism in its pages. And teachers and students alike admired its historical sweep and action sequences, particularly the chariot race, the latter for its thrilling description, the former for its value as a declamatory exercise.

While Wallace may not have rivaled the critically valued authors of his day in literary skill and artistry, his confident narrative voice, reinforced by the respect his personal reputation commanded, spoke with convincing authority. His perceptive and studied descriptions of individual characters, ethnic groups, physical artifacts, and historical events, along with the celebrated action sequences and an eye-witness account of the Crucifixion were more than sufficient to allow his presentation to achieve a modicum of popular success. The reader is already sufficiently familiar with the institutional success Wallace's novel achieved within the Chautauqua movement and at churches and Sunday schools, multiplying sales considerably, and how popular it was when introduced at not just the Notre Dame refectory but a variety of secondary schools, whether for graduations, charity events, or entertainments. But still larger forces were directly in sync with economic and cultural developments in the 1870s, 1880s, and 1890s, and these seem to have had a profound effect on the public and established the environment in which Wallace's novel could achieve its extraordinary success. While it would be impracticable to offer a comprehensive description of the entire period or even to attempt to identify all the factors that contributed to the novel's reception, the following discussion of four elements, environments, and movements of the period – theological, ethnographic, political, and economic – will make clear that some of the areas of research that fascinated Wallace equally fascinated some of his readers and lured many others into contemplative states of reverence, chauvinism, or emotional glimpses of glory.

THE THEOLOGICAL ENVIRONMENT

Wallace, the Stone-Campbell Movement, and Liberal Protestantism in the 1870s

In "How I Came to Write *Ben-Hur*," Wallace states that until 1876 his "attitude with respect to religion had been one of absolute indifference," and, as we have seen, after his encounter with Robert Ingersoll, Wallace would repeatedly make clear that this attitude of absolute indifference would be replaced by one of "absolute belief in God and the Divinity of Christ." At the very beginning of *An Autobiography*, Wallace declares that "I believe absolutely in the Christian conception of god." He hastens to add that he is "not a member of any church or denomination," and he concludes the paragraph with the statement he made in the preface to his novelette, *The Boyhood of Christ*:

> The Jesus Christ in whom I believe was, in all the stages of his life, a human being. His divinity was the Spirit within him, "and the Spirit was God."[2]

In parsing the divinity of Christ in this way, Wallace reveals his own particular Christian perspective. Eloquent permutations of this appear frequently in *Ben-Hur: A Tale of the Christ*, wherein Balthasar is often employed as the most articulate mouthpiece for Wallace's basic theology (4.16):

> "The Savior I saw was born of woman, in nature like us, and subject to all our ills – even death. Let that stand as the first proposition. Consider next the work set apart to him. Was it not a performance for which only a man is fitted? – a man wise, firm, discreet – a man, not a child? To become such he had to grow as we grow. Bethink you now of the dangers his life was subject to in the interval – the long interval between childhood and maturity.

Wallace's formulation in a novel subtitled *A Tale of the Christ* carefully details a human being within whom the spirit of god was ever present. He cloaks his powers in mystery but describes his presence vividly and thereby seems to verify his earthly presence, then follows him closely during his last days leading to divine revelation. As narrator and through the prophetic speeches he gives to Balthasar, Wallace prepares the reader for the coming of the Christ and skillfully animates him through the eyes and experience of Judah Ben-Hur, at first a detached sufferer whom Jesus assists at the Nazareth well, but then a sympathetic and admiring observer after he cures his mother and sister of leprosy, and finally a fully resolved devotee of nearly apostolic proportion by giving tremendous financial support to his church. By placing the Christ in physical proximity to his dynamic protagonist, Wallace gives Jesus tangential participation in human adventures while Judah takes on a uniquely privileged perspective. He gave Jesus this same type of anthropomorphic characterization in *The Boyhood of Christ*.

This is a key to understanding both Wallace's theological perspective and the attraction and plausibility it offered his readership. As Charles Lippy wrote in *Being Religious, American Style*:

> The Jesus of fiction cannot be identified as a Baptist or a Methodist or a Catholic; such labels are irrelevant. The Jesus of fiction, as in Ben-Hur, is one whose power common folk can grasp, understand, and use. That is precisely the appeal of Ben-Hur and the reason it promotes popular religiosity. Ben-Hur's Jesus is one who comes alive in the mind and imagination of the reader or viewer, one who can be fashioned into the kind of Christ that one wants or needs in the continuing pilgrimage to give meaning to life.[3]

Similarly, in *A History of Christianity in the United States and Canada* Mark Noll discussed Wallace's rejection of sectarian doctrine and traditional Christological idolatry in favoring Christ's human qualities.[4]

Over the course of the past two millennia there have been many opinions about the nature of Christ. Advocates of differing formulations, many of them dependent on complicated and sometimes obscure theological argument, have perpetuated multiple and enduring schisms in the Christian world. The origins of Wallace's theology and literary formulation for Jesus lie in one specific branch of nineteenth-century American theology, the Stone-Campbell Movement. Wallace himself does not make this clear, and he left behind no detailed account of any formal religious training. We have little more than discrepancies and incomplete details about his childhood religious experiences. In recalling his earliest encounter with the New Testament, as mentioned, he writes in the preface to *The First Christmas*, published in 1899, that it was his mother who first introduced him to it, while in *An Autobiography* (58), written a few years later, he says it was Samuel Hoshour. But in *The First Christmas* he does not specify whether it was his natural mother (Esther Test Wallace) or stepmother (Zerelda Sanders Wallace), and he does not say in either account to what extent he was familiarized with the New Testament, nor does he say much about worship or further religious training or experience. In *An Autobiography* (48) he tells us only that his stepmother "was a member of the Christian Church, and insisted upon my attendance once every Sunday," and that these services failed to impress him.

As we have seen, Wallace often understates the importance of the people with whom he and his parents were associated when he was a youth. He usually gives us simply a name and little else. But because his father was Governor of Indiana, many of these people were of importance and can therefore be easily identified. External sources then provide us with some more information about his mother's "Christian Church." It is now the Central Christian Church.[5] On its website one can read that it was initially chartered in 1833 as the Church of Christ of Indianapolis. Its charter membership, which met in a simple log cabin, consisted of just twenty local residents, two of whom were, notably, the bishop, John H. Sanders, and his 15-year-old daughter, Zerelda. The church maintained strict rules, one of which was that men and women were segregated during services, a policy increasingly unjustifiable to the young Sanders, who would become a leading advocate of woman's suffrage. Similarly, they used wine in the service, and she would ultimately lead the way to substituting grape juice in the Disciples of Christ group of churches.[6] Zerelda married David Wallace on Christmas day, 1836, so it was probably in 1837 that she took the 10-year-old Lew to the aforementioned Sunday services.[7] Even though he writes in *An Autobiography* that the services did not impress him and that he spent these Sunday visits sketching the interesting characters of the congregation, it is likely that the church's conception of Christ and uncomplicated theology did establish a fundamentally anthropomorphic paradigm of Jesus in the young boy's impressionable artistic palette.

As Christian worship along the frontier in the first half of the nineteenth century expanded from revivalist tents to log cabin meeting houses, many if not most of the small, local congregations depended directly upon the New Testament for their spiritual instruction. They rejected the influence of centuries-old European theology, biblical hermeneutics, and especially papal dogma. Aspiring instead to a pragmatic primitivism, their relatively simple life along the frontier emulated the life of the first-century Christians.[8] The reader can see this reflected in Wallace's dependence on words and events of the New Testament, concentration on the first Christian century, and unapologetic non-denominationalism. The focus of the Church of Christ was Christ himself, and the Christ of the New Testament would be the focus of Wallace's "Tale of the Christ."

Although there were local variations and regional factors, what is generally referred to as the (American) Restoration Movement began at the beginning of the nineteenth century with the Second Great Awakening. The proliferation of revival meetings, particularly under the influence of three prominent men, would change the face of American Christianity in the Midwest and South for almost the entire next century. The three worked at what were then opposite ends of the country – Thomas and Alexander Campbell in Pennsylvania, and Barton W. Stone in Kentucky – and then united to influence much of the territory in between. The Campbells, abhorring sectarianism, blamed church policy for the many divisions in Christendom, so they attempted to reunite Christians by limiting their creed to the Bible itself.[9] Their followers were known generally as "Disciples of Christ." Stone established his reputation at Cane Ridge, the center of the Great Revival, where he argued against the concepts of the Trinity and Original Sin, stressing instead the importance of faith as a key towards achieving salvation. Stone called his disciples simply, but pointedly, "Christians." The legacy of these men was to unite the multitudes outside the embrace of the Presbyterian and Protestant labels, joining together in 1832 and forming a small network of the "Christian Churches" or "Churches of Christ." One of these was the Sanders' Church of Christ in Indianapolis.

The Stone-Campbell Movement also fostered Christian education and established, through local congregational support, fourteen institutions of higher education in the 1830s, including seven in Kentucky, where Zerelda Sanders was born, and another four in Indiana. Their academies, institutes, and seminaries offered education through the high-school level. One of the latter was the Wayne County Seminary in Centerville, Indiana. It was here that the Campbellite Samuel Hoshour found refuge in 1835 after being ousted by the more traditional Baptists of Maryland, and so it was here as well that David Wallace placed young Lew when he heard, perhaps from Zerelda, that a teacher as capable as Hoshour had taken up a position there. The reader will recall that among other things, Wallace credited Hoshour with teaching him to educate himself. To the point, in bringing that chapter of *An Autobiography* to a close, Wallace emphatically says so by thanking his "Gentle master" in a touching apostrophe "across his grave."[10] Demonstrating the same pedagogical approach, Alexander Campbell in 1841 addressed the students for the dedication of Bethany College and concluded the day's festivities by saying, "the chief object of education is not the acquisition of knowledge ... [but] the formation of habits."[11]

Although *An Autobiography* recollects mostly Lew's secular education at the hands of the German-American and mentions the reading of the New Testament in only four brief sentences, it is clear that Hoshour's approach to biblical education developed in accord with Campbellite doctrine, specifically the non-sectarian, literal reading of the New Testament. In his own autobiography, Hoshour refers to it as "simple primitive gospel."[12] Alexander Campbell himself declared in his "Address on Colleges":

> Let no sectarian dogmata, no ready-made and finished creed or formula of faith, be introduced into any school or into any literary or philosophic institution. Let the Lord himself teach in all our seminaries in his own words and in his own arguments.[13]

That is precisely the guideline Wallace avowed to follow when inserting Jesus into his novel:

> I would be religiously careful that every word He uttered should be a literal quotation from one of His sainted biographers.[14]

Hoshour and Campbell demanded literal interpretations of the New Testament. One of the principle reasons the polyglot Hoshour left his Lutheran Church in the East was that, unlike the Campbellites, they refused to practice baptism in accordance with the literal interpretation of the Greek word *baptismos* ("immersion").[15]

Wallace's literary approach to Jesus derives from this tradition of literal interpretation. Accordingly, he aggressively combats traditional dogma. In the preface to *The First Christmas* he tells us that he had read works by "Bossuet, Chalmers, Robert Hall, and Henry Ward Beecher." He dismisses any influence they might have had on his religious thinking by claiming that he read them "always for the surpassing charm of their rhetoric." Although he writes nothing else about it, their theology must have been problematic for him. The first three represented different stages of European development and modifications of traditional thought. The late seventeenth-century Jacques-Bénigne Bossuet attempted to justify the divine right of kings, arguing that it is God who appoints them and then guides them through his precepts. In the fourth book of his *Politics Derived from the Words of Holy Scripture*, he claimed to justify these concepts from biblical passages.[16] Wallace would have seen immediately that these passages derive almost entirely from the Old Testament and apply for the most part to patriarchs and judges, not earthly kings. God may have guided their judgments, but he did not appoint them.[17] Furthermore, as a pre-revolutionary Frenchman and member of the court of Louis XIV, Bossuet would have warranted little enthusiasm from Wallace and his American readership for his royal prescriptions. The early nineteenth-century Scotsman Thomas Chalmers never rejected the Calvinist reliance on the concept of Original Sin. His slightly earlier English Baptist contemporary Robert Hall did reject it, but his vague profile of Christ could not possibly have been satisfactory to a visual and literary portrait artist like Wallace.

This is evident in the text of the novel itself. Reflecting contemporary revivalist preachers like Charles G. Finney and Dwight L. Moody who were similarly de-emphasizing the doctrine of Original Sin, Wallace never mentions it.[18] A word search reveals that Wallace used the word "sin" only twice in the entire novel, both instances harmlessly generalized in the biblical quotation from John 1: 29: "Behold the Lamb of God, which taketh away the sin of the world!" Similarly, he refers to the Holy Ghost only once, and that is ensconced in a quotation from John 1: 33. By comparison, the words "redeem," "Redeemer," and "redemption" occur thirty-four times, and "salvation" and "Saviour" another twenty-four times. As for Campbell's stressing the importance of faith as a key towards achieving salvation, Wallace describes (1.13) the path to salvation as an uncomplicated process in this brief conversation between Herod and Gaspar, the Greek Wise Man:

"What is to follow the coming of the new king?"
"The salvation of men."
"From what?"
"Their wickedness."
"How?"
"By the divine agencies – Faith, Love, and Good Works."

One of the reasons Wallace rejected the more recent American theological tradition circulated in the published sermons of Henry Ward Beecher, the highly visible and unabashedly popular Congregationalist lecturer, was that by the 1870s Beecher's sermons had come to represent the contemporary Liberal Protestant school of free interpretation of the scriptures.[19] In addition, though he had been born and educated in New England in the 1810s and 1820s and would move on to head the Plymouth Congregational Church in Brooklyn from the 1847 until his death in 1887, Beecher spent the late 1830s and most of the 1840s in Indianapolis as the founder and pastor of the Second Presbyterian Church. This of course encompassed the years Lew Wallace was a teenager living in Indianapolis with Zerelda Sanders while his father was serving as governor. There is no reason why Wallace should have had any problem with Beecher's forceful advocacy of abolition and broader social reform, but in 1871 Beecher published *The Life of Jesus Christ*.[20] Wallace may well have had theological and procedural objections to this book, for although Beecher quotes a large number of passages from the New Testament, he contaminates almost all of them with extensive sermonizing.[21] On a more personal level, after Elizabeth Tilton accused him of adultery, Beecher was tried first in the press in 1872 and then in court in 1875 in one of the most scandalous trials of the decade. The trial ended in a hung jury, and Beecher maintained his post in Brooklyn, but two of his public accusers were the prominent suffragettes Victoria Woodhull and Isabella Beecher Hooker, one of Beecher's sisters. At this point in the 1870s, Zerelda Sanders Wallace had also become a prominent suffragette, so the Beecher scandal may have provided an additional incentive for Lew Wallace to dismiss Beecher's extensive writings and design his own tale of the Christ quite differently.[22]

The Beecher scandal was not the only highly publicized church trial of the 1870s. The trial of the Presbyterian clergyman David Swing, who was accused of heresy by the conservative Princeton establishment, began in Chicago in April, 1874. Swing represented Midwestern liberalism, and his acquittal reaffirmed the rejection of Calvinist dogma that had been signaled four decades earlier in another heresy trial, that of Lyman Beecher, the progenitor of both Harriet Beecher Stowe and Henry Ward Beecher.[23] Wallace's theological discussion with Ingersoll took place the year following the latter's trial, and all three episodes in different ways demonstrate the extent to which the subjects of belief, morality, and the nature of Christ were being discussed and debated on a national level during the very years Wallace was composing his novel. This is not to say that Wallace was a qualified participant or an important theologian. Quite the opposite is true, and this would turn out to be much to his benefit in the cultural and spiritual climate that allowed readers to identify with and find comfort in his novel.

Though rates of change differed between the liberal Midwest and the traditional East Coast institutions, this decade saw the popular theological pendulum swing decidedly from the conservative to the liberal.[24] William Hutchinson places the pivotal year in 1874, the year that Swing was acquitted in his heresy trial.[25] Frank Hugh Foster, who lived and worked through the period, identified the turning point to the "New Theology" as 1877, the year in which his Congregationalist church began to abandon the concept of Calvinist future punishment.[26] Foster graduated from a conservative Andover Theological Seminary in 1877, but already by 1882 three of the traditionalist faculty had retired and been replaced by more forward-thinking theologians. The conservative East Coast Congregationalist Horace Bushnell died in 1876. Clearly the American Protestant movements that had taken root in the 1830s had finally achieved consensus support by 1880, the year of the publication of *Ben-Hur: A Tale of the Christ*. During the same period Americans were finally freed, as it were, from the seventeenth-century European text of the King James Version and rushed in eagerness to purchase their own modern version of the Bible in the *Revised New Testament*. The *Chicago Tribune* sold 100,000 copies in just four days after its release in May, 1881.

Because Wallace's New Testament theology in *Ben-Hur* is not "sermonized," to the casual reader it may play a minor role in comparison to the action in the circus and adventure on the seas as well as the pervasive effects of the desire for vengeance, hate and love.[27] The novel takes us through the origins and effects of these human endeavors and emotions in order to lead Judah Ben-Hur and the reader to the Crucifixion and ultimate understanding that Christ is the Prince of Peace.[28] The message was simple yet meaningful for American readers of the early 1880s, an enjoyable, inspirational antidote to the perplexity and confusion associated with Christian worship during the late 1870s and early 1880s.[29] And as so many works of popular art would prove in the coming century, along with their drama, romance, and action climaxes, consumers wanted a clear and uplifting message with a happy ending.

Anecdotal statements made by unassuming members of the public can be telling. In March, 1895, the response by "E.P." of Lawrence, Kansas, to the survey "The Story That Most Influenced Me" in the magazine *The Golden Rule*, demonstrates the kind of influence "*Ben-Hur*" had on readers:

> "Ben Hur" reigns supreme in its influence over my life. In the healing of Tirzah, I first realized what Christ offers, and with a longing desire I myself found the

Christ. The sad life of the beautiful Iris [sic] taught me that what personality I may have must be used to make men whom I may meet nobler and better.[30]

The results of the survey: more readers chose the story of *Ben-Hur: A Tale of the Christ* than any other.

An Appropriate Literary Iconography of Jesus

Drastically moderating the Calvinist image of the Christian god as the stern heavenly father established during the formative decades of the American colonies and substituting a new intimacy with the more forgiving and terrestrial conception of Jesus, two parallel strands, one academic, the other popular, attempted to create suitable means for describing Christ's earthly experience.[31] However, as we have just seen, acceptance of this untraditional conception of Jesus took several generations. During the first two decades of the nineteenth century, Thomas Jefferson, in his capacity as a prominent and eloquent Deist, transformed the New Testament by stripping out all its passages referring to miracles and supernatural elements and thereby rendering Jesus as a moral philosopher. Jefferson never published the work, and in the next generation David Friedrich Strauss's *Das Leben Jesu* (1835/6), a German rationalist study of the *New Testament* that also de-mythified the supernatural elements in the life of Jesus, enveloped its author in years of controversy. One generation later, as the first volume of his eight volume *Histoire des origines du christianisme*, the French historian Ernest Renan published *La vie de Jésus* (1864), a thoroughly unembellished biography of Jesus. Renan also removed the legends, miracles, and dogma that had been attached through the centuries to the life of Jesus while extracting from ancient sources the more mundane details of his life. In so thoroughly historicizing and humanizing Jesus, he succeeded in horrifying his Catholic contemporaries in Europe and found a ready audience only among French intellectuals.[32] Renan's book was no better received by American clergymen, who had almost immediate access to it that same year in the English translation published by Charles Wilbour.[33] The attack in *The American Quarterly Church Review* began by labeling Renan an "infidel" and the book as "the culmination of Unbelief."[34] The review in the *American Presbyterian Review* expanded the broadside by attacking French culture in general.[35]

While the more traditional Catholic and Presbyterian establishment failed to recognize the popular appeal of the humanized Jesus, neither did Liberal Protestantism, rapidly becoming the most dynamic force in the popular religious landscape, inspire an appropriate product to satisfy the increasing demand for a representation of its sympathetic, gentle, and "feminized Jesus."[36] The appropriate business model was already established: the American Tract Society's *Family Christian Almanac*, which sold 300,000 copies annually, and Harper & Brothers' 1846 illustrated

Bible, with its 1,600 "historical" engravings by John Adams and J. G. Chapman, were so popular that, according to Paul Gutjahr's *An American Bible: A History of the Good Book in the United States, 1777–1880*, by the 1870s nearly two thirds of American Bibles were of the illustrated variety.[37] But neither widely distributed Bible specifically addressed the kind of iconographical demand Warner Sallman's "The Head of Christ," for instance, would generate in the next century, with some 500 million reproductions.[38]

Appropriately, the transformation was much more ably expressed in the realm of popularizing literature. In 1837 the Unitarian clergyman William Ware began to serialize his *Letters of Lucius M. Piso, from Palmyra, to His Friend Marcus Curtius, at Rome* in *Knickerbocker Magazine*, expanded and collected the following year as the novel *Zenobia* set during the late third century in the final days of Roman persecution of the Christians.[39] Following the American issue of Edward Bulwer-Lytton's *The Last Days of Pompeii* (1834) by just a few years, Ware's book helped establish the subgenre of historical novels set in Greco-Roman antiquity.[40] It would not take many years before the subgenre would include events that took place in the Roman province of Judea in the first century. This is what Ware did in 1841 for *Julian; or, Scenes in Judea*.[41] Very much like *Ben-Hur* of four decades hence, its narrative contained a geographical array towards the beginning of the book, and it focused on a Roman Jew who travels to Judea and participates in a rebellion against Roman imperial rule.[42] Near the end of the second of two volumes, Julian encounters Jesus, albeit briefly, and Ware concludes that Jesus is much more a human than a god:

> I first beheld him as he sat teaching in the Beautiful Gate of the Temple, and sure I am my eyes never fell upon a human form of such majesty yet also of such graciousness. What was great and manly prevailed by a large excess over what was only fair in both the shape and the features of the countenance, yet upon these the eye rested with delight for their exceeding comeliness, but much more for the expressions of love toward all, which shot forth in every look and every motion.[43]

In her highly impactful abolitionist novel, *Uncle Tom's Cabin* (1851), Harriet Beecher Stowe shapes her Uncle Tom character as an endearing, feminized Christ-like victim.[44] Three years later Joseph Holt Ingraham wrote *The Prince of the House of David; or, Three Years in Jerusalem in the Days of Pontius Pilate* (1855), a series of letters in which Jesus is softened and supplied with fictionalized dialogue. Not surprisingly, Ingraham, whom Harper editor George Ripley cited as a precedent when evaluating Wallace's manuscript, was denigrated in the clerical reviews but achieved popular success.[45] Henry Ward Beecher's *The Life of Jesus, the Christ* (1871) offered a "living portrait" illustrated with tissue-protected etchings and printed in large format on gold-edged pages, the whole package being designed to "produce conviction" among "plain people."[46] Beecher describes Jesus as he proceeds through his labors and ministry interacting with humans, demonstrating sympathy and compassion, bearing a cheerful demeanor, and offering a familiar and natural love. Beecher's sister followed with her own *Footsteps of the Master* (1877), a reverent historical description of the advent, passion, and resurrection of Jesus.[47] Very much like Wallace's *Ben-Hur*, *Footsteps of the Master* portrays Jesus during his time on earth as quintessentially human:

> If ever there was a human being who could be supposed able to meet the trials of life and overcome its temptations in his own strength, it must have been Jesus Christ.[48]

By the time *Ben-Hur: A Tale of the Christ* was published just three years later, the transformation from menacing to loving god was complete, and the reading public was now prepared to accept the eyewitness account as represented by the narrator and protagonist, particularly in that the Jesus they encountered in the novel was with a single, inoffensive, and silent exception, the Jesus of the New Testament. That non-scriptural scene at the well between Judah and Jesus therefore becomes that much more important as the nexus between the protagonist, now brought low by Roman villainy, and the sympathetic, earthly Jesus.

Wallace paired his version of the feminized Jesus with a relatively innovative kind of masculine hero.[49] In his examination of "muscular Christianity," Clifford Putney pinpoints 1880 as the year in which the concept of physical exercise and activity as prerequisites for performing good works and energizing the church began to find wide acceptance in the United States.[50] Charles Kingsley and Thomas Hughes had developed the first prominent literary heroes of the muscular movement in the 1850s in England. Kingsley, who was fascinated by the heroes of Greek mythology, developed his idea of the physically powerful Anglo-Saxon peoples overrunning Gibbon's decadent, emasculated, overly civilized Romans in *The Roman and the Teuton* (1864).[51] Hughes then published his *Life of Alfred the Great* in 1869. Although the spiritual aspects of the movement quickly spread to the United States, where the Y.M.C.A. movement had first taken hold fairly recently in 1851, its literary development did not effectively take hold until Wallace created the martially skilled, physically courageous, and chariot race winning hero of *Ben-Hur*.[52] Two decades later, novels like Sheldon's *In His Steps* would achieve great popular success as part of the Social Gospel movement, but Wallace's novel precedes this era of social reform and delivers simply a powerful theological message of Christian redemption supported by eyewitness accounts of Jesus as a miracle worker.

Anti-Christian Romans in Literature

During those same decades, as the tender human image of Christ was emerging in successive biographical narratives, the image of the Christ-torturing ancient Romans was suffering greatly. For centuries European writers and painters had for the most part satisfied their patrons with representations of Roman nobility inspired from the pages of Livy, Cicero, and Plutarch, although by the seventeenth century such emperors as Caligula, Nero, and Domitian, described by Suetonius and Tacitus, warranted images as crazed, detested, and cruel despots. The historical revisionist spirit of the French Revolution had converted the once detested tyrannicide Brutus – condemned by Dante to the lowest circle of the *Inferno* – and the anti-Roman rebel Spartacus into heroic icons as champions of liberty, and now in the mid-nineteenth century ancient Christian prisoners who were martyred in the Roman Colosseum were being lionized as well.[53] The acclaimed American actor Edwin Forrest starred as Spartacus on stage in *The Gladiator* in 1831, and this was followed by Nicholas Cardinal Wiseman's very popular novel *Fabiola* (1854), which told a pathos engendering tale of paleo-Christian torture and martyrdom at the hands of cruel Romans. The aforementioned *Family Christian Almanac* included in the preceding year, 1853, an engraving of "A Christian Family Exposed to Wild Beasts in the Arena," the father standing defiantly, his wife and daughters fearfully clutching at his toga as the well-dressed Roman crowd seated safely above a retaining wall looks upon the growling felines and the unjustly condemned (but soon to be saved) family. This, too, would resonate with the general public. This same process of criminalizing the ancient Romans had its effect on Lew Wallace as well. He had been introduced to Plutarch's *Lives* as a youth in the 1830s, but the 1870s, following his years of military service, seem to have inverted his admiration for the Romans and rendered them, or more precisely, their brutal, anti-Christian penal system and their imperialistic armies of occupation, as the villains of his novel.

THE ETHNOGRAPHIC ENVIRONMENT

Replacing the Wild West with the Middle East

Of all the major novelists of late nineteenth-century America, Wallace was the only one who directly confronted in an official capacity a notorious outlaw. The cultural environment of the 1870s and 1880s, the period which saw the closing of the "Wild West," compensated by celebrating such popular Western icons as not just Billy the Kid but Wild Bill Hickok, Buffalo Bill Cody, Belle Starr, Jesse James, Sitting Bull, and General George Custer.[54] In contrast to these widely recognized but hardly exemplary icons, Wallace's novel offered a protagonist hero who not only excelled in the use of weapons and physical prowess but was also a devoted son, a leader of men, and an indefatigable champion against an evil empire who was advised by a biblical prophet and an eyewitness to the Crucifixion.[55] In this sense, Wallace replaced and improved upon the "wild" West with a pacified and Christianized East.[56]

The reception of Wallace's novel derived considerable attention for its vivid and convincingly accurate descriptions of exotic ancient lands, much as had happened with Gustave Flaubert's *Salâmmbo*, a very popular novel about ancient Carthage.[57] Wallace made clear in his later recollections that the most compelling reason he had for describing ancient lands and people in great detail was that he feared there would be many critics who would focus on any mistakes he made. He says in *An Autobiography* (2:932–3):

> It was needful not merely to be familiar with [the Holy Land's] history and geography, I must be able to paint it, water, land, and sky, in actual colors. Nor would the critics excuse me for mistakes in the costumes or customs of any of the peoples representatively introduced, Greek, Roman, Egyptian, especially the children of Israel.

As we have seen, Wallace was proud that he had devoted so much time and energy in preparing himself to describe the geography and topography of the Holy Land, the raiment and trappings of ancient people, the buildings in which they lived and worked, and the ships and vehicles in which they were conveyed. His attention to detail and ability to create descriptions of a foreign and ancient world provided quite a contrast to the contemporary standard of literary realism espoused in the novels of William Dean Howells and Henry James. In particular, like the protagonist of James's novella *Daisy Miller*, which Harper & Brothers published in book form in – we note with emphasis – 1880, Wallace's Judah is a youthful victim. But James sets Daisy amidst contemporary European culture, and her lone encounter with a venue of ancient Roman spectacle was to contract a fatal case of malaria ("Roman Fever") in the Colosseum.

Instead, Wallace's literary archaeology transports his reader to a provocative setting amidst the sights and airs of the Levant, as demonstrated in the first paragraph of the novel (1.1):

> THE JEBEL ES ZUBLEH is a mountain fifty miles and more in length, and so narrow that its tracery on the map gives it a likeness to a caterpillar crawling from the south to the north. Standing on its red-and-white cliffs, and looking off under the path of the rising sun, one sees only the Desert of Arabia, where the east winds, so hateful to the vine-growers of Jericho, have kept their playgrounds since the beginning. Its feet are well covered by sands tossed from the Euphrates, there to lie; for the mountain is a wall to the pasture-lands of Moab and Ammon on the west – lands which else had been of the desert a part.

The rest of the first chapter and the entire second chapter describe the desert landscape and the meeting of the three Wise Men. This was indeed an ancient and exotic setting, but it was not one that was entirely unfamiliar to the reading public, nor one which they found to be excessively foreign, strange, or lascivious. Quite the contrary, Wallace's descriptions appealed to an American audience hungering for compelling ecphrases of the Holy Land. An 1891 evaluation by Henry Field makes this clear:

> In "Ben-Hur" everything is Oriental – the country, the scenery, the manners and customs of the people, and the characters that come and go upon the stage ... Whenever we open the book, we seem to be in an Oriental picture gallery, or, better still, to be literally transported to the streets and bazaars of Damascus, to the shores of the Sea of Galilee, or the courts of the Temple in Jerusalem.[58]

Several decades before Wallace began working on his novel, some of the first photographers, e.g. Maxime Du Camp (1850), Ernest Benecke (1852), Auguste Salzmann (1854), Francis Frith (1858), and Louis De Clerq (1859–60), created a surge in popularity of Palestinian images in Europe.[59] But this photographic trend developed considerably later in the United States. It was only literary and travelers' descriptions of the Holy Land that had first captured and continued to fascinate the imagination of Americans.[60] The Rev. William M. Thomson's *The Land and the Book* (1859) sold 200,000 copies. Thomson was followed by Mark Twain's satirical *Innocents Abroad* (1869) – Twain's greatest commercial success, even though it was sold by subscription only.[61] In 1875 Selah Merrill, sponsored by the American Palestine Exploration Society, founded in 1870, led the first fully American archaeological expedition to the Holy Land. The official photographer for Merrill's expedition was Tancrède Dumas, another European. The first American photographer in the Holy Land was John Bulkley Greene, but he worked in Paris. When D. Appleton published Merrill's *Picturesque Palestine, Sinai, and Egypt* in 1881, it still contained no photographs, only engravings by Harry Fenn and J. D. Woodward.[62] What photographs were taken by American professionals, e.g. A. F. Dotterer and James Strong, were sold in the 1870s for as much as 30¢ each, but these were sold as individual stills and not published in book form.[63] After Merrill's publication in 1881, Harper & Brothers responded with Knox's *The Boy Travellers in the Far East; Part Fourth, Adventures of Two Youth in a Journey to Egypt and the Holy Land* in 1882/3.[64] Even the 1888 edition of Thomson's *The Land and the Book* still lacked photographs. Instead of photographs, Wallace's descriptive opening pages offered readers oriental mystery and fascinating landscapes in a contemporary and popular literary format. Fittingly, a limited 1887 edition of *Ben-Hur* included one dozen photographs of the Holy Land and Egypt, and then the Garfield edition of 1892 included nine in each of its two volumes.

Wallace's next three chapters (3–5) offer equally seductive, historical theologies ascribed to the Greek, Hindu, and Egyptian wise men, and then Chapter 7 sketches literary portraits of the ethnic groups that populate Jerusalem, including Roman soldiers, a Jew, a Nazarite, a Samaritan, a Greek, a Cypriote, an Arab, and a Pharisee. Contemporary European Orientalist painters like Jean-Léon Gérôme and John Frederick Lewis were capturing these same kinds of images visually.[65] Wallace's literary sketches create the impression that the Joppa Gate and the streets of the market are filled with fascinating variations of ethnic types, and that he is presenting them to "the reader" through this unique window. Today Wallace's descriptions, in part inspired by Josephus, read as ethnic stereotypes, but in the early 1880s this would have been perceived as insightful and *au courant* ethnography.[66] Wallace's novel, in fact, emerged into the popular culture just one year after the U.S. Congress appropriated funds for a Bureau of Ethnology, led by its first director John Wesley Powell, to engage in what would soon be recognized as anthropological research.[67] *Ben-Hur* provided a literary predecessor to the tour of nine Australian aborigines R. A. Cunningham marketed in 1883, and to the Kwakiutl, the "Eskimo," and the rest of the spectacular so-called "anthropological zoo" Franz Boas would display a decade later at Chicago's Columbian Exposition of 1893.[68]

Popular literature of the period reflected this proto-anthropological interest in other cultures, particularly in G. A. Henty's numerous ethnographic novels of the 1870s.[69] But Henty wrote for children, and his tone was often xenophobic. H. Rider Haggard's *King Solomon's Mines* was an immediate success upon its publication in 1885, but its protagonist, Allen Quatermain, was the quintessential "great white hunter."[70] In stark contrast, Wallace was not writing about contemporary foreigners and his tone was that of an interested observer, an artist (as he was) describing what he saw. What he saw, as the result of his research, was representative members of ancient ethnic groups that were already known, at least by name, to his readers. And because they were all subject to or threatened by the Roman Empire, they were not like the hostile tribes that Henty's and Haggard's novel portrayed. Wallace's attitude towards his non-Roman characters was relatively open-minded, enlightened if not sympathetic. In approaching with this attitude the types that populate *Ben-Hur: A Tale of the Christ*, Wallace made them all welcome subjects in the new kingdom of the Christ. Particularly in his descriptions of the universal theologies of the three Wise Men, Wallace was in his own private and non-denominational way anticipating the movement that would result in the World's Parliament of Religions assembled at the 1893 Columbian Exposition.[71]

THE POLITICAL ENVIRONMENT

Manifest Destiny and Social Darwinism

Wallace's interest in foreign as well as ancient people and his care in researching the peoples and places of his story helps account for the realistic background onto which he superimposed his story, and recent and contemporary Christological portrayals, not to mention his own newly inspired theological revelation, help account for the concluding books of the novel. But Wallace also infused his novel with a vision of a righteous rebellion against Roman imperialism, barely masking the paradoxical conception of the American empire then being promulgated by prominent spokespersons and gaining the support of a significant popular following.

The movement that culminated in the United States' taking possession of Guam, Cuba, Puerto Rico, and the Philippines in 1898 grew from deep within the nineteenth-century American psyche, building upon the westward expansion of the previous forty years and concepts embedded in the Monroe Doctrine of the 1820s, de Tocqueville's "American Exceptionalism" of the 1830s, John L. O'Sullivan's "manifest destiny" of the 1840s, William Graham Sumner's "social Darwinism" and Herbert Spencer's "survival of the fittest" of the 1860s, and William Gilpin's "untransacted destiny of the American people," which he described in *The Mission of the North American People* in 1873.[72] Because these concepts, both popular and political in nature, were pertinent for the most part to American expansion to the west, they prepared the way for the subsequent expansion abroad by offering many of the same assumptions and rationales. As a young man Wallace twice volunteered to fight in Mexico, the second time declaring in reference to the recent ethnocentric reinterpretation of the Monroe Doctrine: "Already Louis Napoleon disputes our mastery of the continent!"[73] And years later as he was composing and editing the final chapter of his novel in the New Mexico Territory, he was quelling Apache raids. Significantly, *Ben-Hur* appeared during the transition between American continental expansion and expansion abroad.

Inherent in Wallace's most basic assumptions and American political ethnocentrism in general during the late nineteenth century were the parallel assertions of Anglo-Saxon and Christian superiority. The writings of the contemporary historian John Fiske record the development of this line of thought, beginning in 1872, just as Wallace was finishing *The Fair God*:

> "No previous century ever saw anything approaching to the increase in social complexity which has been wrought in America and Europe since 1789. In science and in the industrial arts the change has been greater than in the ten preceding centuries taken together."[74]

Fiske here seems to have been referring only to the rapidity of developments in the modern world compared with the ancient and medieval. Eight years later, the year *Ben-Hur* was published, Fiske, moving from the quantitative to the qualitative, offered this analysis:

> After the survey of universal history which we have now taken, however, I am fully prepared to show that the conquest of the North American continent by men of English race was unquestionably the most prodigious event in the political annals of mankind.[75]

Moving forward another two years, now a full-fledged social Darwinist, Fiske writes *The Destiny of Man* (1882), in which he concludes that Darwin's theory of evolution, as applied by Herbert Spencer, suggests that human spirituality is the goal of natural selection:

> I believe it has been fully shown that so far from degrading Humanity, or putting it on a level with the animal world in general, the doctrine of evolution shows us distinctly for the first time how the creation and the perfecting of Man is the goal toward which Nature's work has been tending from the first. We can now see clearly that our new knowledge enlarges tenfold the significance of human life, and makes it seem more than ever the chief object of Divine care, the consummate fruition of that creative energy which is manifested throughout the knowable universe.[76]

His ultimate conclusion is that human spirituality has survived the Copernican and Darwinian revolutions:

> Nay, if the foregoing exposition be sound, it is Darwinism which has placed Humanity upon a higher pinnacle than ever. The future is lighted for us with the radiant colours of hope. Strife and sorrow shall disappear. Peace and love shall reign supreme. The dream of poets, the lesson of priest and prophet, the inspiration of the great musician, is confirmed in the light of modern knowledge; and as we gird ourselves up for the work of life, we may look forward to the time when in the truest sense the kingdoms of this world shall become the kingdom of Christ, and he shall reign for ever and ever, king of kings and lord of lords.[77]

By 1886 these concepts of cultural and theological immanentism had become fully merged with the parallel assumption of Christian superiority.[78] One of the founders of the Social Gospel movement, Josiah Strong, delivered one of his most eloquent pronouncements of "Anglo-Saxonism" in *Our Country* (1886):

> The world's scepter passed from Persia to Greece, from Greece to Italy, from Italy to Great Britain, and from Great Britain the scepter is today departing. It is passing on to "Greater Britain," to our mighty West, there to remain, for there is no further West; beyond is the Orient. Like the star in the East which guided the three kings with their treasures westward until at length it stood still over the cradle of the young Christ, so the star of empire, rising in the East, has ever beckoned the wealth and power of the nations westward, until today it stands still over the cradle of the young empire of the West, to which the nations are bringing their offerings.
>
> The West is today an infant, but shall one day be a giant, in each of whose limbs shall unite the strength of many nations.[79]

The similarity in imagery to the opening chapter of *Ben-Hur* is notable. Further along in *Our Country*, Strong admonished:

> Notwithstanding the great perils which threaten it, I cannot think our civilization will perish; but I believe it is fully in the hand of the Christians of the United States, during the next fifteen or twenty years, to hasten or retard the coming of Christ's kingdom in the world by hundreds, and perhaps thousands, of years. We of this generation and nation occupy the Gibraltar of the ages which commands the world's future.[80]

This spiritual belief in the "imperialism of righteousness" percolated up to the White House during the presidency of William McKinley, who sought to "civilize and Christianize":

> Territory sometimes comes to us when we go to war in a holy cause, and whenever it does the banner of liberty will float over it and bring, I trust, the blessings and benefits to all people.[81]

In that Judah defeats Messala in the chariot race, acquires the wealth of Messala and Quintus Arrius, i.e. two consular families, and helps fill the world's spiritual void with the message of the Christ, *Ben-Hur: A Tale of the Christ* symbolically overthrows the might of the Roman Empire. This, too, would have resonated with contemporary American political thought, as the inevitable, correct, and positive outcome of ancient secular and biblical history. It played into the inherent paradox within the American psyche that detested empire while simultaneously building one.[82] But this paradox was enabled by the assumption that benign empires fulfill the demands of natural destiny. Citizens of the democratic nation of the United States in the late nineteenth century embraced the anti-Roman sentiments of Wallace's novel, but no doubt some of them had difficulties accepting the expansion of American sovereignty. Chief among these would turn out to be Wallace himself, who had volunteered to serve in the invasion of Mexico as a young man and then offered his services again at the outbreak of the Spanish-American War. However, horrified by the imperialistic results of the war, in February, 1900, Wallace drafted an amendment to the U.S. Constitution that purported to prevent future imperialistic ventures without voter approval.[83]

The aforementioned theological, anthropological, and political movements that were beginning, developing or culminating from the late 1870s through the 1880s helped to create a unique window of opportunity that would enable the novel to flourish for years, and not just as a popular commercial item but as a spiritual and political monument. The story of the novel took place in ancient Judea when it belonged to the Roman Empire, but its underlying theology and politics were patently American, conveying the spirit of the era. From manifest destiny and the conquest of the West to "civilize and Christianize" and the acquisition of portions of the former Spanish Empire, the themes of *Ben-Hur*, that is, rebellion against an oppressive empire, universal freedom for ethnically variegated, non-Christian peoples, and the establishment of peace and ultimate salvation in the Christ, stirred in the hearts of hundreds of thousands of Americans during the 1880s the inherent Christian patriotism and chauvinistic spirituality that was rapidly transforming the United States from a colonial and pioneer refuge into an international power.[84]

Anecdotal evidence helps to demonstrate that *Ben-Hur* and American patriotism were interlinked. The 1904 Fourth of July celebration held in Eau Claire, Wisconsin, was held under the auspices of the local Congregational, Presbyterian, and Baptist churches.[85] The feature presentation was a showing of "Ben Hur" stereopticon views projected upon a 15-foot square screen, preceding such patriotic songs as "The Star-Spangled Banner", "America the Beautiful," and "The Red, White, and Blue," sung by the combined church choirs. The next chapter will find Evelyn Gurley-Kane inviting President Wilson to her performance readings from *Ben-Hur* in Washington, DC and associating the American government with the "principles taught by the beautiful Child born in Bethlehem."[86]

Representing a similarly unifying concept of uniformed armies for Christ in the real world was The Christian Mission in London, which was renamed The Salvation Army and adopted its quasi-military trappings in 1878, and which George Scott Railton then brought to the United States in 1880, the year *Ben-Hur: A Tale of the Christ* was published.[87] The same decade produced the institutionalization of Mary Baker Eddy's Christian Science movement, just one of a number of contemporary movements that sought to give voice to the inner power of Christian spirituality.[88] Early in the novel Jesus had assisted Judah by giving him a drink of water in the midst of his forced trek across the desert, thereby providing him simple physical aid and incipient spiritual comfort. But at the end of the novel (8.5), the work of Jesus, including the cure of Judah's mother and sister, suggests the presence of a powerful divinity who will overthrow the Romans and establish a better world:

> In the miracle of which Tirzah and his mother were the witnesses even more nearly than himself, he saw and set apart and dwelt upon a power ample enough to raise and support a Jewish crown over the wrecks of the Italian, and more than ample to remodel society, and convert mankind into one purified happy family; and when that work was done, could any one say the peace which might then be ordered without hindrance was not a mission worthy a son of God? Could any one then deny the Redeemership of the Christ?

Although the mental vagaries of individuals and their responses not only to contemporary developments in spirituality but to a particular book about spirituality are very difficult to specify, especially when the spiritual movements in question were developing well over a century ago and were themselves the result of and inspiration for other eclectic and syncretized modes of spirituality, it is certainly plausible in retrospect to posit that the metaphysical aspect of contemporary spirituality in the 1880s was part of the same popular intellectualizing process that accompanied the willingness to read a popular adventure novel that included the historical Jesus.

In a summary chapter leading up to a discussion of the novels of "Henry James and the American Rush of Experience," Charles L. Sanford describes Americans as:

> ... a nation of energetic, moralizing reformers, passionately and actively engaged, dizzily, exhaustingly involved, in the serious business of realizing the delights of heaven on earth. This picture conflicts with one frequently encountered in the literature of the social scene which depicts a national scene of political indifference and apathy, evasive compromise, smug complacency, and stifling conformity. Yet the two pictures are not as dissimilar as they might at first appear. Conformity is a matter of the voluntary association of free persons united under the banner of the same individualistic goals. Free individuals are likely to be politically indifferent and apathetic, for they distrust the machinery of government and the semblance of authority. They prefer ... the fulfillment of the promise of American life, whose chief instrumentality is individual effort. Optimistic fatalism, born of the illusion of being a favored people, has been chiefly responsible for complacency.[89]

Sanford articulates a number of key ingredients that helped make *Ben-Hur: A Tale of the Christ* such a popular success, for it offered late nineteenth-century readers a moralizing narrative about a struggling individual who distrusted and then trampled Roman authority in leading his once chosen people to a veritable heaven on earth, thereby feeding the conformity of the consuming public by giving, or rather, selling, to them a thrilling and inspiring story that funneled the visions of many less popular and less timely prophets, philosophers, sermonizers, and authors. In searching for the quintessential American epic, Sanford as well as John P. McWilliams, Jr. discounted *Ben-Hur: A Tale of the Christ* because it failed to meet the poetic requirements. Neither the subject nor the setting is American, nor are Wallace's prose descriptions of scenic and military passages or such characters as the haughty Messala and the vampish Iras, developed or disposed of according to the traditional epic technique.[90] But McWilliams, before refitting the romantic prose of Cooper and Melville and the verse of Whitman into a transformed American epic genre, said in the very first sentence of his book: "The last act of poetry, Americans have long suspected, must create the future, not memorialize the past."[91] Nothing could better describe the hope of the future inspired in the devoted late nineteenth-century reader of *Ben-Hur: A Tale of the Christ*.[92] The future was now the result of what had transpired almost nineteen centuries earlier so carefully delineated by General Wallace.

THE ECONOMIC ENVIRONMENT

The Wealthiest Roman of the Gilded Age
Although the rapidly increasing international influence and territorial expansion of the United States would be justified in popular slogans, legalized by the government, and enforced by its marines, the quintessential power behind it was American economic muscle and its need for new markets. Looking again to the years immediately surrounding the publication of *Ben-Hur: A Tale of the Christ*, we find that the forces that were in the process of creating the great American leviathan were

accumulating and gathering strength for the approaching industrial and commercial explosions. Preparing the way for the continued growth of once small companies into gigantic corporations was the establishment of the comprehensive Trademark Act of 1881, as retail brand names were beginning to increase rapidly. In 1871 there were 121 registered with the United States Patent Office. In 1875 there were already 1,138. The transformative decades immediately preceding and following the publication of *Ben-Hur: A Tale of the Christ* engendered some of the nation's most enduring household consumer product names, like Vaseline (1870) and Colgate (1873), and numerous companies that would rapidly become iconic images across the American landscape along with *Ben-Hur*, notably American Telephone and Telegraph Company (1885), Coca-Cola (1886), and Sears, Roebuck & Company (1886), the latter of course being the same company that would years hence offer for resale one million volumes of *Ben-Hur: A Tale of the Christ*.

The 1876 United States Centennial Exposition in Philadelphia offered a vast conglomeration of showrooms for American technology that included the first typewriter and telephone on public display. This grand celebration of the United States, its ample resources, and its burgeoning industries was witnessed by some ten million visitors. Following the premier of Richard Wagner's "Centennial March," the Centennial's convocation by Methodist Bishop Matthew Simpson connected the Christian divinity to the nation's newfound, technology-driven prosperity: "We thank Thee for national prosperity and progress, for valuable discoveries and multiplied inventions, for labor saving machinery relieving the toiling masses."[93] Ironically, the 1876 Centennial celebration came as the economic depression that followed the Panic of 1873 had hit bottom. The huge expansion of the economy in 1880 would be fueled and serviced in no small part by the infusion of millions of immigrants.[94] As *Ben-Hur: A Tale of the Christ* was being published, the world of consumers was undergoing a radical and permanent transformation.[95]

One of the most significant preconditions for the rapid growth of consumerism during this period was the discovery of the effectiveness of advertising.[96] In 1880, a year which the reader surely by now regards as a landmark, John Wanamaker hired John E. Powers, the first full-time advertising copywriter, and Wanamaker's sale volume almost immediately doubled. In 1882 Proctor & Gamble began to hail Ivory Soap as the "soap that floats" and budgeted an unprecedented $11,000 for advertising, creating the first national ad campaign. By 1889 James Duke is already spending one of every five dollars on advertising, and at the end of the century, America's advertising budget was $500 million, 3.2 percent of GNP.[97] Along the way such developments in printing and graphic design as full-page ads (1878) and half tones (1880) in newspapers as well as the invention of the Linotype machine (1884) revolutionized mass marketing.

At first there was a relatively limited amount of products and a relatively limited number of ways to advertise them, but the 1880s transformed the consumer palette from a sprinkling of simple trading cards and text-only newspaper ads to a saturation of colorful, glossy ads on the back covers of nationally circulated home magazines and brightly colored packages displaying thoroughly recognizable trademarks and brand names.[98]

It was the period after the Civil War that produced the mechanical production and literate populace that would allow *Ben-Hur: A Tale of the Christ* to become a bestseller. It was largely linotyping that helped usher in the era of mass communications.[99] And now chromolithography, invented by Godefroy Engelmann in 1837, began to be used for advertising cards in 1873, and the use of this process grew tenfold between 1860 and 1890.[100] Distribution of printed material was expedited along the tens of thousands of miles of railroad tracks that had been laid down coast to coast in the previous decades. As for literacy, in 1852 Massachusetts became the first state to pass a compulsory school attendance law, followed by most of the other states in succeeding decades, not to mention the Morrill Act of 1862 that established land-grant institutions of higher learning in a number of non-rebel states.[101] The end result of the inventions, developments, and processes outlined here was that by the 1880s an increasing number of literate Americans were regularly and aggressively encouraged to spend their leisure time and increasing amounts of disposable income by purchasing and reading inexpensively produced books that they were able and eager to read and, if necessary or desirable, could be delivered to their door.[102]

After Thomas Edison's invention of the cylinder phonograph in 1877 and the Kinetoscope of 1888 and their subsequent transformations, not to mention Edison's first successful public display of an incandescent lighting system in Menlo Park in December of 1879, popular culture would be broadly expanded in the near and distant future by means of a flood of new inventions, machines, gadgets, and techniques. Other inventors flourished and additional inventions were patented in the 1880s, including George Eastman's roll film (1880) and portable, hand-held camera (1888), L. N. Thompson's roller coaster (1884), J. K. Stanley's safety bicycle (1885), and Emile Berliner's gramophone (1887), not to mention numerous essential components and early versions of batteries, printing machines, and much more. All of these inventions would soon be used to capture, record, project, play, or imitate adaptations of or images from *Ben-Hur: A Tale of the Christ*.

As Judah wends his way through injustice, vengeance, good fortune, a miracle, and salvation, he inherits Arrius' estate, wrestles away Messala's in the chariot race wager, recovers his own from Simonides, who has increased it fivefold to 673 talents, and inherits the Sheik's Orchard of Palms as well. Simonides says that this is "all thine – making thee,

O son of Hur, the richest subject in the world." Such accumulation of great wealth would certainly have resonated among readers of the Gilded Age. The final third of the nineteenth century was creating a whole new class of industrial and retailing millionaires, and already by the 1880s the likes of John Wanamaker, Marshall Field, and Cornelius Vanderbilt had become celebrated tycoons. Of course unfair labor practices, high prices, periodic depressions, and Vanderbilt's infamous sound bite, "the public be damned," periodically tarnished the reputations of some of these economic titans. But that would not mean that hundreds of thousands of Wallace's readers would not embrace the "Gospel of Wealth" and take vicarious pleasure in Judah's ultimate financial success as a fitting and honorable outcome of familial devotion, triumphant action, and religious conversion.[103] Without a European-style class structure, the American "land of opportunity" would often recognize its new millionaires as celebrities and modern-day heroes.[104]

In the 1880s a wealthy man or family would be expected to share their wealth for the betterment of humankind. It was as recently as 1877 that Cornelius Vanderbilt had bequeathed $1 million to establish Vanderbilt University in Nashville. John D. Rockefeller would fund the future Spelman College in 1884, and Andrew Carnegie, who had already begun funding the first of several thousand public libraries, codified contemporary philanthropy with his treatises on wealth, *Triumphant Democracy* (1886) and *Gospel of Wealth* (1889). Judah Ben-Hur's bequest bested those of even the most prominent contemporary industrialists of the Gilded Age: he funded the establishment of the Christian church in Rome. Wallace's novel ends with an afterword that professes this grand philanthropy:

> If any of my readers, visiting Rome, will make the short journey to the Catacomb of San Calixto, which is more ancient than that of San Sebastiano, he will see what became of the fortune of Ben-Hur, and give him thanks. Out of that vast tomb Christianity issued to supersede the Caesars.

Even so, the pervasive industrialization and burgeoning consumerism of the Gilded Age represented only one side of the picture. The relatively simplistic tenets expressed by Emersonian Transcendentalism that had been receding to the background since the Civil War period were not so easily dismissed. William Dean Howells concluded his 1878 essay on "Certain Dangerous Tendencies in American Life" with the observation that "The character of our nation is highly complex," that is, the simple life unaffected by greed and not obsessed by wealth was still valued by many.[105] Walt Whitman represented this aspect of the American spirit in poetry. E. L. Godkin, editor of the *Nation*, maintained that the United States was committed to "the virtues of frugality and simplicity."[106] In popular literature there was *Ben-Hur: A Tale of the Christ*. The novel opens with the simplistic beauty of the three Wise Men in the desert and the somber, silent nativity scene, and its penultimate setting, just before the afterword, depicts an idyllic family scene represented by Judah, Esther, and their three children. Such a portrait of simplicity representing a hard-won, divinely blessed familial tranquility may have been equally satisfying to a segment of Wallace's readership.

The first six chapters of this book have explored the education and development of Lew Wallace and the writing, publication, marketing, and reception of *Ben-Hur: A Tale of the Christ*. By the 1890s the novel was already an unparalleled success. *Uncle Tom's Cabin* undoubtedly sold more copies as a novel, and Sheldon's *In His Steps* was more or less comparable. But the distinction for Lew Wallace and Harper lies in their paying such careful attention to the novel's copyright before and after it became such a major success. Then, once they realized they had such a juggernaut within their grasp, they approached sales and marketing capably and energetically. They issued new editions with illustrations or photographs. They targeted a spectrum of consumer sectors by making direct sales to literary groups, offering the novel in elegant, expensive bindings to collectors and well-healed gift givers, and then selling discount copies to Sears, Roebuck. They extended the life of the *Ben-Hur* property further by publishing related and excerpted books for the Christmas and gift markets. Wallace himself made personal appearances, and Harper published his work in their magazines. Together they aggressively attacked copyright infringements. *Ben-Hur* had become a bestseller, but they turned it into a historic icon of popular literary success. Wallace metamorphosed from a high-level government administrator and diplomat into a professional author, much admired celebrity, and literary businessman. As this metamorphosis was taking place, Wallace, never lacking for confidence in his abilities, learned to apply his commanding presence in negotiations that would create new artistic genres and venues for his novel and also make him very wealthy. And these successes in turn opened up opportunities for those who wanted to make their own profits from his artistic property by propagating its story and admired protagonist.[107]

There would be many more editions and versions of Lew Wallace's novel published over the next century or so, but we now shift our focus to examine the novel's incredibly successful proliferation into the worlds of staged readings, stereopticon lectures, music, drama, and film as well as commercial ventures, broader cultural impacts, and even more exceptional applications of the *Ben-Hur* phenomenon outside the artistic realm.

NOTES

1 Cf. Malamud, *Ancient Rome and Modern America*, 122: "In Lew Wallace's novel *Ben-Hur*, the conflicts between Romans, Jews, and Christians pro-

vided a metaphorical narrative from the Roman world of the New Testament for articulating and assuaging the anxieties of America's middle classes after the Civil War, an era of tumultuous social and economic change, matched by political unrest and a growing fissure between science and religion."
2 *The Chariot* 1 (November, 1895) 5; *Homiletic Review* 33 (June, 1897) 568. Wallace's family belonged to Rev. S. V. Leech's First Methodist Church.
3 Lippy, *Being Religious, American Style*, 150–1.
4 Noll, *A History of Christianity*, 41.
5 <http://www.indyccc.org/ccchistory.html>; <http://www.in.gov/history/3636.htm>
6 Hull, *Christian Church Women*, 52–6.
7 *The [Los Angeles] Herald* (January 29, 1894) 2, describes her as "the mother of Ben Hur."
8 Hughes, *Reviving the Ancient Faith*, 1–3.
9 Campbell, *Declaration and Address*, 17–18, calls sectarianism "a horrid evil, fraught with many evils. It is anti-christian, as it destroys the visible unity of the body of Christ; as if he were divided against himself, excluding and excommunication a part of himself. It is anti-scriptural, as being strictly prohibited by his sovereign authority; a direct violation of his express command."
10 *An Autobiography* 1:59.
11 Gresham, *Campbell and the Colleges*, v–vi.
12 Hoshour, *Autobiography*, 65.
13 Campbell, *Popular Lectures and Addresses*, 309.
14 *An Autobiography* 2:933–4.
15 Hoshour, *Autobiography*, 42–50; Evans, *Biographical Sketches*, 230–4.
16 Bossuet, *Politique tirée des propres paroles de L'Escriture sainte*.
17 2 Chron. 19: 6; Riley (trans.), *Politics Drawn from the Very Words of Holy Scripture*, 82.
18 Cooper, *The Great Revivalists in American Religion*, 54–127.
19 McLoughlin, *The Meaning of Henry Ward Beecher*, 11.
20 Beecher, *The Life of Jesus Christ*.
21 Marsden, *Fundamentalism and American Culture*, 22–6, addresses the transition to the "New Theology" within the parameters of Henry Ward Beecher's career during the 1870s.
22 Clark, *Henry Ward Beecher*, 197–232, connects Beecher's adultery trial with contemporary movements for suffrage and women's rights.
23 Dorrien, *The Making of American Liberal Theology*, 1:275–9.
24 Dorrien, *The Making of American Liberal Theology*, 1:279.
25 Hutchison, *The Modernist Impulse*, 41, cites Buckham, *Progressive Religious Thought in America*.
26 Foster, *The Modern Movement in American Theology*, 14–15. Cf. Fox, *Jesus in America*, 274–6.
27 For an analysis of the intellectual contrasts within the antimodernist movement, see Lears, *No Place of Grace*, 103–7.
28 Although it can be implied, anti-Semitism was almost certainly not integral to Judah's acceptance of Jesus. American anti-Semitism was relatively

limited in scope and intensity during this period of "inclusionary pluralism." As of 1885, the year of the "Pittsburgh Platform," both reformed Jews and Americanist Catholics were enthusiastic about making concessions and urging Europeans to do the same, leading to 1893's World Parliament of Religions. See Hutchison, *Religious Pluralism in America*, 122–32.
29. For the nature of the confusion, see Fox, *Jesus in America*, 277. For the similar effects of Darwinism and "modern doubt," see Lighty, *The Fall and Rise of Lew Wallace*, 38 and 40–2 <=http://www.ohiolink.edu/etd/send-pdf.cgi?miami1130790468>. Cf. Godkin, "The New and Old Version," 401–2.
30. *The Golden Rule* 9 (March 14, 1895) 537.
31. For comparison, see the English biography by Wright, *The New and Complete Life*, which was illustrated with engravings but traditional in its dogma and presentation.
32. Renan used primarily Philo, Josephus, the *Apocrypha*, and the *Talmud* in addition to the *New Testament*.
33. Ernest Renan (Charles E. Wilbour, trans.), *The Life of Jesus*.
34. Leavitt, "Renan, and the Supernatural," 489–507.
35. Smith, "Renan's Life of Jesus," 136-69.
36. Prothero, *American Jesus*, 56–61 and 85–6. Similar terminology is used by Morgan, *Visual Piety*, 97–111. Gutjahr, *An American Bible*, 162, in describing the "womanly redeemer," cites Douglas [*The Feminization of American Culture*, 110] for a clergyman's discussion of "The Woman Question" already in 1854. In *Ben-Hur* (8.6) Wallace will describe Jesus as having "a woman's face and hair," although that description is offered by Iras in ridicule.
37. Gutjahr, *An American Bible*, 37; cf. Nord, "The Evangelical Origins of Mass Media in America, 1815–1835"; cf. Morgan, *Visual Piety*, 78–93.
38. Morgan, *Icons of American Protestantism*, 26.
39. Volume I of the early edition [Ware, *Letters of Lucius M. Piso*] concludes with a "Note" [317–20] containing the relevant Latin texts from the *Historiae Augustae* [*Zenobia* 30.2-3, 5–8 and 13–27; *Odenatus* 15.7-8.] derived from Casaubon's 1661 Leiden edition. Volume II concludes with a seven-page "Note" [333–9] in Latin and English discussing some of his ancient sources – Pollio, the biographer of Zosimus, Vopiscus, the biographer of Aurelian, and Zonaras.
40. Cf. Smith, *Zerah*.
41. The book was originally serialized in *Christian Examiner* in 1839–40.
42. The second paragraph [5] contains the following description of Antioch, a city also very central to the narrative of *Ben-Hur*: "After the dulness [sic] of Athens, and the worse than dulness of Smyrna, Ephesus, and Rhodes, it was refreshing to witness the noise and stir of the mistress of the East. So frequent were the theatres, baths, and porticos, the shows, the games, the combats of wild beasts, that I felt myself almost in the Elysium of my own Rome." While comprehensive, it lacks the descriptive detail which Wallace was able to offer after several months of concentrated research at the Library of Congress and Boston, followed by months of study back in Crawfordsville.
43. Ware, *Julian*, 2:44; cf. Hutchison, *The Modernist Impulse*, 12–40, on the influence of the Unitarians.

44 Williams, *Playing the Race Card*, 61–4.
45 *The London Quarterly Review* 58 (April, 1882) 349–50.
46 Fox, *Jesus in America*, 295–6.
47 O'Connor, *Religion in the American Novel*, 36–46, describes her journey away from traditional Calvinism.
48 Stowe, *Footsteps of the Master*, 106.
49 Cf. the analysis in Miller, "The Charioteer and the Christ, 157–8.
50 Putney, *Muscular Christianity*, 1–5; Prothero, *American Jesus*, 87–94.
51 Turner, "Christians and Pagans in Victorian Novels," 173–87.
52 McKee 165, lists *The Last Days of Pompeii* and Kingsley's *Hypatia* as two of Wallace's favorite books.
53 Wyke, *Projecting the Past*, 34–7.
54 Tuska, *Billy the Kid: A Handbook*, 94–5, points out that in April, 1881, just as Billy the Kid was being sentenced to death by courts under Wallace's jurisdiction, the governor was in the process of receiving his appointment to the Sublime Porte from President Garfield.
55 Cf. Malamud, *Ancient Rome and Modern America*, 136–9; Brown, *The Year of the Century: 1876*, 196; Jones, "Lew Wallace," 129–58.
56 Wiebe, *The Search for Order*, 66; Lighty, *The Fall and Rise of Lew Wallace*, 10–40; Hanson, *Ripples of Battle*, 137–43.
57 Green, *Flaubert and the Historical Novel*, 3: "When Flaubert came to write *Salammbô* he was worried that his novel would meet with hostile reaction because it could not possibly give an accurate representation of life in ancient Carthage."
58 *Book Buyer* 8 (Christmas Issue, 1891) 478–80.
59 Howe, *Revealing the Holy Land*, 132.
60 Vogel, *To See a Promised Land*, 28–60.
61 Steinbrink, "Why the Innocents Went Abroad," 278–86; cf. Samuel L. Clemens, "To Charles L. Webster & Co., 18 September, 1887," in Hamlin Hill, ed., *Mark Twain's Letters to His Publishers, 1867–1894*, 234.
62 Edward Robinson's *Physical Geography of the Holy Land* (1865) and Henry J. Van-Lennep's *Bible Lands, their Modern Customs and Manners Illustrative of Scripture* (1875) also lacked photographs.
63 For the stereo views of Egypt, Sinai, and Palestine by the Dotterer and Strong, see Perez, *Focus East*, 159 and 224–5.
64 Knox, *The Boy Travellers in the Far East*.
65 Gérôme's painting of a chariot race, *La course de chars* [*The Chariot Race*], part of the George F. Harding Collection now housed in the Chicago Art Institute, dates from 1876. See Marc Gottlieb, "Gérôme's Cinematic Imagination," in Allan and Morton, *Reconsidering Gérôme*, 54–64; cf. Edwards, *Noble Dreams, Wicked Pleasures*.
66 Riesman, "Psychological Types and National Character," 330.
67 Wallace would purchase copies of Powell's annual reports (for 1880–1, 1881–2, and 1882–3) for his personal library; cf. Stocking, *Victorian Anthropology*, 139–72 and 257–73.
68 Stocking, *Race, Culture, and Evolution*, 133–8. For Wallace's detail about the Aztecs in *The Fair God*, see Murphy, *Hemispheric Imaginings*, 97–118.

69 Street, *The Savage in Literature*, 6.
70 Street, *The Savage in Literature*, 13.
71 Seager, *The World's Parliament of Religions*, 64; Smith, *Popular Culture and Industrialism*, xv-xviii.
72 Smith, *Virgin Land*. Sampson, *John L. O'Sullivan and His Times*, 192–3, discusses O'Sullivan's original use of the phrase "manifest destiny" in a peaceful context; cf. 244–5, for the attribution to Jane McManus Storm Cazneau.
73 M&M 158; cf. Murphy, *Hemispheric Imaginings*, 26–8.
74 Fiske, "The Progress From Brute to Man," 256.
75 Fiske, *American Political Ideas*, 125.
76 Fiske, *The Destiny of Man*, 20. Cf. McLoughlin, *The Meaning of Henry Ward Beecher*, 221–42.
77 Fiske, *The Destiny of Man*, 22.
78 Hutchison, *The Modernist Impulse*, 2–11.
79 Strong, *Our Country*, 29.
80 Strong, *Our Country*, 180.
81 Judis, *The Folly of Empire*, 4.
82 Solomon, "*Ben-Hur* and *Gladiator*, 17–39.
83 Draft, IHS: "The United States shall not in any manner acquire, hold, maintain, provide for, or exercise sovereignty or jurisdiction over any land, territory, or country now foreign, except a majority of the voters of the United States shall have first consented thereto . . .
84 Overthrowing the Roman state was also the narrative thrust of Wallace's 1876 drama, *Commodus*, but there instead of Christian salvation the heroic protagonist met with a femme fatale and tragedy. Putney, *Muscular Christianity*, 200–1, contrasts Wallace's glorious hero with Hemingway's soldier-narrator in *A Farewell to Arms*.
85 *The [Eau Claire WI] Daily Telegram* (July 1, 1904) 7.
86 Program for *Ben Hur: The Noted Gurley-Kane Arrangement*, February 11, 1919, LoC.
87 Winston, "Living in the Material World, 13–26.
88 Lippy, *Being Religious, American Style*, 140–3.
89 Sanford, *The Quest for Paradise*, 202.
90 Ibid., 155; McWilliams, *The American Epic*.
91 Ibid., 15; Phy, "Retelling the Greatest Story Ever Told," in Phy, ed., *The Bible and Popular Culture in America*, 48, credits Wallace with achieving "a minor epic tone" worthy of the sobriquet, "the Homer of Sears-Roebuck fiction."
92 Gutjahr, *An American Bible*, 166, credits *Ben-Hur* for finally toppling the remaining Protestant resistance to mixing fiction with the gospels. Murphy, *Hemispheric Imaginings*, 112, says *The Fair God* "identifies Aztecs as the true Americans, authorizing their demise as an originary site of New World democracy."
93 Jacobson, *Barbarian Virtues*, 15.
94 LaFeber, *The New Empire*, discusses how the periodic economic booms and ensuing depressions of the late nineteenth century led to the American imperialism that then restored the economy – the same scope and pattern, albeit ancient and fictional, described in the narrative arc of *Ben-Hur*.

95 Munslow, *Discourse and Culture*, 11–13, identifies the relationship between monopoly capitalism and cultural pluralism in the period following the 1870s.
96 Potter, *People of Plenty*, 166–88, argues that advertising was the quintessential institution developed for the unique society of abundance created in late nineteenth-century America.
97 Fox, *The Mirror Makers*, 27 and 39; and Pope, *The Making of Modern Advertising*, 23.
98 Strasser, *Satisfaction Guaranteed*, 30–2, briefly discusses the development of branding, packaging, and advertising and how they reinforced each other.
99 Meggs, *A History of Graphic Design*^{2}, 137–41.
100 Meggs, *A History of Graphic Design*^{2}, 154–65. In general, see Last, *The Color Explosion*, 1–4.
101 The first volume of the periodical *Practical Education* was published in 1860; the Chautauqua movement, sponsoring uplifting lectures (and, later, dramatic presentations of *Ben-Hur*), dates to 1874.
102 Cf. Oberdeck, *The Evangelist and the Impresario*.
103 For Russell Conwell, the Baptist minister who delivered his "Acres of Diamonds" lecture over 6000 times, encouraging his listeners to create wealth for the cause of Christ, see Kyle, *Evangelicalism*, 65.
104 Carnes, *Secret Ritual and Manhood in Victorian America*, 124, makes an interesting comparison between the narrative arc of Wallace's novel and the typical (contemporary) Horatio Alger dime novel, in which a youth comes of age, faces desperate circumstances, is taken in by a paternally splendid patron, and then by good fortune becomes wealthy – in one sense or another. At the end of *Ben-Hur*, of course, Judah has become fabulously wealthy both financially and spiritually. For the contemporary equation of wealth and virtue, see M&M 306–7. Gutjahr, "To the Heart of Solid Puritans, 53–67, esp. 56, avers that "the novel's basic . . . outcome consists in the restoration of material wealth."
105 Howells, "Certain Dangerous Tendencies in American Life," 385, 387.
106 On Godkin and a more comprehensive discussion of the movement, see Shi, *The Simple Life*, 154–74.
107 Cf. Solomon, "Lew Wallace and the Dramatization of *Ben-Hur*," 423–36.

7 *Early Staged Readings:* Ben-Hur, in Tableaux and Pantomime

WALLACE AND HIS PETITIONERS

In a scribbled but succinct letter sent from New York's luxurious Fifth Avenue Hotel in 1882, Lawrence Barrett asked Lew Wallace's permission to produce a dramatic play derived from *Ben-Hur*.[1] Wallace knew very well that Barrett was one of the most prominent American actors of the period, known for his roles in Edward Bulwer-Lytton's popular play, *Richelieu: On the Conspiracy*, and several of Shakespeare's plays, on occasion playing opposite Edwin Booth. In 1876, Wallace had sent Barrett a copy of his own play *Commodus*, and although *Commodus* was never produced, Barrett sent a very positive reply, saying that Wallace had "written the best play since 'Richelieu.' ... Both as a poem and acting play, 'Commodus' is the best English drama."[2] This was high praise from the prominent thespian, but even though Wallace in his autobiography reports that he spent an entire evening listening to Barrett's proposal, including an assurance that there would be no "appearance of the Saviour," Wallace refused.[3] More than a decade later, in May, 1895, Alexander Salvini, the son of Tommaso Salvini, another established Shakespearean, wrote Wallace twice about producing a Ben-Hur play, and then his manager wrote in August, to say that they were still hoping Wallace would honor their request.[4]

In his autobiography Wallace refers to both Barrett and Salvini as "persistent," and he would receive many additional proposals between the late 1880s and 1899.[5] One of them was from the Hungarian-born Kiralfy Brothers. Imre, Arnold, and Bolossy Kiralfy produced thrilling spectaculars, and the *Ben-Hur* property with its action scenes and displays of early Christian reverence would have been an attractive addition to their list. Imre's "Nero, or, The Destruction of Rome" featured the "Sports of the Circus Maximus" and "Scenes of Christian Martyrdom," and four of their popular productions were based on works by Jules Vernes, the author of some of the most commercially applicable literary predecessors to Wallace's novel. This Kiralfy proposal was to recreate *Ben-Hur*-

inspired chariot races in an outdoor spectacular on a two-acre parcel on Staten Island, much like "The Last Days of Pompeii" spectaculars Pain's Fireworks first produced in 1879 at Manhattan Beach. In fact, the Lilly Library at Indiana University preserves a copy of an unproduced and undated scenario for a "Pyro-Spectacular Dramatization of General Lew Wallace's Great Work" by Frank Oakes Rose, Pain's stage director.[6] In 1895 Josef J. Reinisch of Cologne wrote a letter to Wallace in German, proposing a production modeled upon the German opera *Christus*, written by Heinrich Bulthaupt, set by Anton Rubinstein, and premiering the previous year.[7] The most detailed proposal Wallace received was from the Englishman W. W. Allen.[8] He appended to his letter of October 26, 1898, sent from the Eastville area of Bristol, a six-page written scenario designed by his wife Elizabeth, which he said was inspired by Wilson Barrett's *Sign of the Cross*. Her scenario of "Ben Hur, or, The Fallen Tile," consisted of five acts and included a list of Wallace's most important twenty-one characters, with "Hamutal" supplied as the name of Judah's mother. Act II included a Bethlehem scene ("a straggling village") with a character identified as "A Youth," the son of "the Carpenter, Rabbi Joseph."

Wallace refused them all. There were two notable exceptions. He and Harper did allow Helen McGregor Morse to perform a matinee performance of "Tableaux and Readings from Ben-Hur" on Thursday, March 14, 1889, at Palmer's Theatre in New York City.[9] Morse was a respected writer descended from Puritan New England ancestry who founded the Society of New England Women. Her husband, Albert W. Berg, was a New York classical composer of some distinction.[10] Harper's letter to "Mrs. Berg" specified that General Wallace had granted permission for one performance only with the stipulations the she not print any selections from the novel, that her printed program contain full copyright acknowledgment "in conspicuous type," and that she send Harper a certified check for $50 made out to General Wallace. Also, their permission was granted under the assumption that the performance was for the benefit of the Society for the Aid of Self-Supporting Women. As we will see, Harper and Wallace at this point will limit licensing their property primarily for theatrical presentations associated with charitable causes.[11]

The other exception was for a musical dramatization by Ruford Brauer of Vienna. In a letter written in April, 1896, Wallace granted permission so long as performances were restricted to Europe, adding that Brauer should send him a copy of the finished composition.[12] Considering the futility of maintaining his copyright overseas in that era, it is not difficult to understand why he made this exception. In any case, there seems to have been no finished product. At least bibliographical, newspaper, and online searches have turned up no further accounting of Brauer's work.

Wallace attended the Palmer's Theatre performance, and an interview he gave to *The New York Times* made clear his current opinion about a theatrical adaptation of *Ben-Hur*: "I have not given any one the right to present a stage version of it. I have never entertained the idea, and it is not likely that I will ever sell such a privilege."[13] He reaffirmed this nine years later. In responding to Allen he wrote:

> My dear sir, the number of persons who have asked the same sanction would surprise you, yet I have steadily set my face against every scheme of this kind, although, in instances, the concession would have been very profitable to me. In my view, the subject ought not to be put on the stage; that would be profanation, not of the book, but the most sacred of characters to which it must be considered dedicated; especially would that be the case if given in ordinary dramatic or spectacular form.[14]

ELLEN KNIGHT BRADFORD'S "AN EVENING WITH BEN HUR"

Meanwhile, several private individuals proceeded without requesting, let alone obtaining, the proper permission. Ellen Knight Bradford seems to have been the first and was by far the most successful. In the spring of 1887, the Ladies Aid Society of the First Congregational Church in Washington, DC proposed giving an entertainment "selecting some of the most striking points in *Ben-Hur* and illustrating the same by tableaux, each tableau to be accompanied by a short descriptive reading."[15] According to a subsequent account in *The Washington Post*:

> To Mrs. E. K. Bradford, a member of this church, was assigned the task of selecting the readings, and, in company with two others, of selecting the pictures or tableaux. The great possibilities of the book came to Mrs. Bradford like an inspiration, and she conceived the idea of condensing the entire story of "Ben-Hur" into an evening's reading and illustrating by the tableaux wherever it was possible, thus necessarily arranging the entire programme.

Bradford, like Morse, was neither unaccomplished nor insignificant. Born in Ypsilanti, Michigan, Ellen ["Nellie"] Jane Knight grew up in the house of her uncle Horatio Gates Knight, who held many important political appointments and elected positions in Massachusetts. She graduated from Williston Seminary, taught music, and then became a correspondent of *The Congregationalist*.[16] She published several poems and hymns.[17] In 1868, together with her husband, Chaplain James Henry Bradford, she founded the Industrial School for Girls in Middletown, Connecticut, before moving to the Washington area.

Bradford spent five weeks condensing Wallace's novel, arranging the tableaux, and designing the costumes, for which she said she "followed minutely the descriptions in the book."[18] By the time she presented her finished adaptation, however, the women of the society were daunted by its size and length. She assured them the performance would last only two hours, and the premiere was so well received that a repeat performance was then followed by another at the National Rifles' Armory in Springfield, Massachusetts.[19] On September 29, 1887, as offers began to pour in from around the country, Bradford deposited in the U.S. Copyright Office of the Library of Congress her "dramatic composition" with the title, *Selections From Ben Hur Adapted for Readings with Tableaux*. The copyright submission, signed by none other than A. R. Spofford, describes Bradford as "Author and Proprietor." There is no mention of Lew Wallace or Harper & Brothers.

Bradford decided to devote herself full time to the "Ben Hur Tableaux" and "An Evening With Ben Hur," as these performances were variously called. In no apparent pattern the show toured the eastern half of the country. The reader can continue the narrative from the pre-show interview she gave *The Detroit Free Press* in 1891. It provides a rare glimpse into the intent, methods, and performance practices of this long lost theatrical art-form:

> While in Springfield I received so many calls from various points that I made arrangements to devote my entire time, for a while at least, to giving the tableaux. They have been shown all through the East, as far south as Savannah and in the far West, but this will be their first production in Michigan. As the people here seem to be ignorant of the nature of the entertainment, perhaps a few words of explanation will be in order. In the first place I condensed the story of "Ben Hur" so that anyone who has never read the novel can form a clear and comprehensive idea of the life of "Ben Hur" from it. Thirty tableaux are shown, careful attention being observed as to the posing of the different characters represented, and the costumes worn, which are all historically correct. There are no tedious waits between the tableaux, and throughout the course of the entertainment a very fine elocutionist, who accompanies me, reads from the condensed version of the novel that I prepared. While the curtain is up this lady reads the lines of the dialogue and between tableaux reads the lines leading up to the scene, and also some descriptive paragraphs. There are seventeen characters represented in the tableaux, and as I have to choose a different cast in every city, the entertainment is necessarily of a more or less amateur nature. I may say that it is an entertainment that appeals to both classes – theater-goers and church people, and wherever the tableaux have been shown crowds have flocked to see them. They were shown to an audience of 3,000 people in Philadelphia about two years ago, the entertainment there being given in the Academy of Music, and when I returned to that city less than a year afterward, the house was again packed.
>
> The first picture shown is that of the wise men before Herod, the others all pertain to the life of "Ben Hur."[20]

We know from numerous newspaper accounts that Bradford assigned the cast selection to local organizers, many of whom were often chosen from the sponsoring organization.[21] Closer to the performance date, Bradford arrived on the scene, brought the stage properties, and directed the rehearsals.[22] The record shows that she spent considerable effort on newspaper publicity as well, often beginning three or four weeks before the performance.

The Academy of Music in Philadelphia was not the only major metropolitan venue to host the Bradford *tableaux vivant*.[23] Among the one hundred or so productions performed between 1887 and 1892, newspaper accounts advertise or review performances at the Boston Music Hall,[24] Brooklyn's Academy of Music,[25] Baltimore's Lyceum Theatre,[26] St. Louis' Exhibition Hall,[27] DeGive's Opera House in Atlanta, English's Opera House in Indianapolis, and Detroit's Opera House.[28] *The Washington Post* lists the important attendees at the April, 1890, Lincoln Hall performance – President Harrison, the entire cabinet, and a number of senators, many of them having procured their own private box.[29]

This Washington performance is documented better than most. A copy of the program, held in the Performing Arts Library of the New York Public Library, is quite unadorned. The cover is a simple title page listing Bradford, the reader (Philadelphia's Estelle H. Schively), the schedule of performances, and the beneficiary (the National Homeopathic Hospital).[30] The second page lists the thirty scenes, and the third includes the cast list, assigning more than seventeen roles in the following order: Wise Men, Herod, Ben Hur, Messala, Amrah, Mother, Tirzah, Simonides, Ilderim, Esther, Balthazar, Iras, Malluch, Guards, and Children. Also listed are two soloists and a musical quartet as well as the name of the orchestra director (R. C. Bernays). According to a newspaper account, the vocal music seems to have been concentrated in three numbers, "a boat song, a slumber song, and a chant," the former two referring to Wallace's lyric passages written for Iras and Tirzah.[31] The fourth page of the program contains information about the hospital and an ad for Hardman pianos.

There is also a fifty-page libretto, "Selections from 'Ben-Hur' – Adapted for Readings with Tableaux," preserved in the Library of Congress.[32] It is dated February 12, 1892, representing one of her final performances. This version was divided into two Parts. [The terms "tableaux," "pictures," and "scenes" seem to be interchangeable.]

Part I:

1: "The Wise Men before Herod," "Herod and The Wise Men" (2 tableaux)

2: "Judah (Ben-Hur) and Messala (2 tableaux)

3–5: "Judah and Amrah", "Judah and His Mother," "Judah and Tirzah." (4 tableaux)

After Tirzah's song follows a one and one-half page narrated summary of the years covering from the tile incident and Judah's assignment to the galleys until his adoption by Arrius and return to Antioch five years later.

6–10: Simonides and Esther, Ilderim, Servant, and Balthasar, and "Ben Hur and Iras on the Lake," providing the second song. (7 tableaux)

11–13: "The Chariot Race – Box of Simonides at Circus" frames a "Recitation of the Chariot Race," for which the reciter stood up and read in front of the curtain.[33] Normally she sat at a desk near the footlights, but this was an extensive reading comprising more than a chapter of the novel (5.13–14).[34] The novel's text of the chariot race is not included in the libretto, which prints simply "The competitors, etc. Race." (3 tableaux)

Intermission.

Part II:

14–18: Care and healing of the Lepers, in the midst of which (16) "Ben Hur Tells the Story of the Nazarine." (7 tableaux)

There are very brief narrations, without tableaux, of the Thord encounter and Judah's combat against the Roman centurion. Christ is not given a stage presence, "and yet His relation to all the latter part of the story being felt in the pictures as it is in the book," when Judah's mother and sister are healed and restored to him.[35]

The narration refers to the Crucifixion as follows:

"We would not if we might, raise the curtain upon the picture that presented itself to their sorrowing eyes, from the time of the first stroke of the hammer upon Calvary, to the utterance of the words, 'It is finished.'"

19–21: Domestic scenes featuring Ben Hur, Esther, their children, and Tirzah, as well as Iras's final appearance. (3 tableaux)

22: Curtain calls. (1 tableau)

The design of the narrative arc consigned the anti-Roman struggles and especially the chariot race to Part I and then focused in Part II on the healing of the Lepers.[36] One of the newspaper descriptions, probably suggested by Bradford herself, confirms this:

> A thousand people in tears at the sad fate of the mother and sister of Ben Hur are still in tears of joy when the miraculous healing of the lepers takes place.[37]

The audience seems to have embraced this conception of the story. The reviewer in the *Brooklyn Daily Eagle*, after remarking that the picturesque tableaux poses were steady, mostly free of any trembling or involuntary movement, concludes:

> One of the most effective tableaux was that of the white robed lepers with outstretched arms praying for cleansing.[38]

Pity for the Hur lepers would move as well audiences attending the future stage and 1925 film adaptations.

Bradford employed a variety of readers with superior elocution skills. Many of them were cited in particular for their reading of the chariot race passages, as was Estelle Shively.[39] In Boston Bradford used Marion Stearns, whose "rendering of the 'Chariot Race' was highly dramatic and exciting and placed her high in the favor of the audience."[40] A year earlier, *The Hartford Courant* reported that "Miss Stearns rose, stood before the curtain and gave a dramatic recital of the story of the race. It was very artistically done and quite carried the audience away with enthusiasm."[41] In Detroit Gertrude Marchand of Pittsburg was labeled "a recitationist of power and rare discernment."[42] Her rendering of the chariot race caused the audience to demand an encore. In Philadelphia Bradford employed Minnie Jones, described as "a reader of great power and charming manners," whom we have met before and ran her own school of elocution.[43] *The Atlanta Constitution*'s account of her rendering of the chariot race expresses the excitement such a unique dramatic ecphrasis caused among the auditors:

> The audience might have read General Lew Wallace's "Chariot Race," from "Ben Hur," but by their enthusiasm showed that they never were so interested in a chariot race before. From the start of the race, and all through the circuit, they were like the spectators around the arena, gazing on the great race between "Ben Hur" and the "Jew." [sic] The description of the neck-and-neck race was so real that the hearer's imagination of the close finish was only discarded by her declaration that "Ben Hur" had turned the first goal and won the race.

Other reviews describe the beauty of the costumes, the unique ambience, the blend of artistic genres, and the overall effect of the elegant tableaux positions. Even though the players were local amateurs, one account pointed out that "the posing of the living figures [was] so graceful and artistic that there was nothing amateurish in the effect."[44] In addition, because the local managers selected as cast members "well known society people" and "some of our most beautiful ladies and prominent gentlemen," the audience as well as the press were that much more inclined to eagerly anticipate and fully appreciate the performance.[45] Indeed, a pre-publicity announcement in the *Brooklyn Daily Eagle* summarized, "Ben Hur entertainments ... have been leading social events of the winter in Philadelphia and Washington."[46] This also stimulated the male gaze, as the *Boston Globe* describes: "tableaux vivant, in which, of course, pretty girls, in all the gorgeousness of oriental costumes and finery, took prominent parts."[47]

Equally important for us was that each high-profile performance expanded the horizons of the *Ben-Hur* phenomenon. The review in *The Washington Post* after the Lincoln Hall performance in April, 1890, begins by saying:

> Probably many persons in this city are better acquainted with Gen. Lew Wallace's great book, "Ben-Hur," today than they were twenty-four hours ago, and they are indebted for that knowledge to the representations taken from it and produced last evening at Lincoln Music Hall, under the auspices of the ladies of the National Homeopathic Hospital, and arranged and conducted by Mrs. Ellen Knight Bradford.[48]

The review after the April 30, 1890, performance at the Brooklyn Academy of Music went further, analyzing the applicability of *Ben-Hur: A Tale of the Christ* to the tableaux genre:

> "Ben Hur" is an excellent book for this sort of treatment, because its Oriental color lends itself readily to the composition of gorgeous stage pictures and because it contains so many scenes in which the appearance and attitude of the characters tell the story.

The growth of the *Ben-Hur* phenomenon would gradually encompass a number of artistic genres and commercial spheres, and this kind of secondary exposure to the novel would attract millions of customers over many decades, even if they had not read the novel. This would be true particularly in the theatrical arts.

What little evidence remains for the cost of admission is fairly consistent in reporting that the cost was 75¢ to $1.00 in larger cities, 25¢ to 50¢ in smaller ones, with an additional 25¢ for a reserved seat.[49] These prices can be compared to the cost of the novel, still $1.50. Child admission policies varied. A June, 1890, pre-performance announcement in *The Atlanta Constitution*, for instance, says that, "The price of admission has been fixed at 75¢ for adults and 25¢ for children, no extra charge being made for reserved seats, except in the case of children, who will be required to pay full price when seats are reserved for them."[50] Nonetheless, the educational, artistic, and moral value of Bradford's "Evening With Ben-Hur" for children was made clear in *The Washington Post*:

> The wish has been expressed that the older children of the public schools might witness and enjoy this entertainment, and arrangements for the matinee on Saturday at 4:15 p.m. have been undertaken to that end.[51]

All of the performances on record raised money for designated charities, some for very specific purposes. Besides the 1890 Lincoln Hall performance for the benefit of the National Homeopathic Hospital, the March, 1889, Baltimore performance was on behalf of the Baltimore Street Free Kindergarten, the Detroit premiere was presented under the auspices of the "ladies of Westminster Church," and the December, 1890, Washington "Evening With Ben-Hur" was offered to the public by the "Ladies of the Non-Partisan Woman's Christian Temperance Union." The late-February performances in Boston's Music Hall raised money for expanding the accommodations for the Dorcastry reading room in the Berkeley Temple, and the June, 1890, performance at DeGive's Opera House was designed to raise money for a new building to house Atlanta's Home for the Friendless. The April 30, 1890, performance in Brooklyn was given in aid of the Brooklyn Indian Association.[52]

Because Bradford used local amateurs, costs were kept to a minimum and more money could be raised for charity. The last line of the *Chicago Daily Tribune* review of an 1887 church performance sums up by saying, "From a financial standpoint, the entertainment was a great success."[53] Even more, despite the size of the venues and audiences, a community feeling pervaded the audience. In Milwaukee the *Sentinel* printed the names of various locals who performed in the Grand Opera house a few days before.[54] And after an 1888 performance in Richmond, the local paper shared the good feeling:

> The ladies who had the management of the Ben Hur Tableaux desire to return thanks to all who assisted in the entertainment. Especially would they mention Mr. Ramos, who loaned the pianos and other musical instruments; Mr. Harvey, who furnished the palms and tropical plants, and Messrs. Campbell & Co., who kindly lent the balcony used in the chariot scene.[55]

The use of the *Ben-Hur* property for community and charitable causes was of course a natural by-product of a popular literary property that paralleled many of the most dynamic and memorable passages in the New Testament and concludes with the wealthy protagonist assigning substantial sums of money to Christian charity. It took Lew Wallace twenty years or so after the publication of *Ben-Hur: A Tale of the Christ* to accept fully the concept of synergy and perfect his businesslike approach. During these early years, civic and charitable causes, as well as the Tribe of Ben-Hur fraternal organization, were suitable outlets for the commercial power that the story of the novel would prove to be capable of generating – even before Wallace, Harper & Brothers, Klaw & Erlanger, and many other business concerns marketed Ben-Hur for additional profits.

That Bradford organized her first performances and then copyrighted her work without seeking permission from Wallace or Harper and without acknowledging in print that *Ben-Hur* was written by Wallace or consisted of copyrighted material did not long escape Wallace's attention. The publicity before the Montpelier performance reported in the October 3, 1888, *Vermont Watchman* inaccurately claims that "her production has been shown in the cities of Maryland and Virginia, and has been seen and highly approved by General Wallace himself."[56] There is no evidence for that. To the contrary, Wallace went to Indianapolis in May, 1888, and harshly critiqued the performance at English's Opera House in a report to Harper & Brothers:

> The readings, by a Miss Sears, saved the rendition from overwhelming ridicule. The costuming was both absurd and beggarly cheap. Through the night years lapse B – H appeared in the same white muslin tunic 3 cents per yard. That for sample of the rest. The lady moreover thinks she had a perfected copyright covering her show. I laughed – then I swore – consol[e]d only by the indignation of the hubbie. ... I think it well enough to notify her that she is infringing the copyright – unless, of course, you have committed yourselves.[57]

Despite his contempt for the performance and its alleged infringement, Wallace admits in the same letter that "the possibilities of such a performance were made plain," marking the first time he openly entertained such a notion. The entrepreneurial activity of an East Coast society woman seems to have ignited the spark that would eventually lead to a much more lucrative and international exposure for the *Ben-Hur* phenomenon.

This Indianapolis performance also marks the first genuine synergy between an artistic Ben-Hur by-product and a commercial outlet. In this instance, Indianapolis's When Clothing Store ran a newspaper ad:

> Ben-Hur,
> Messala, nor Simonides
> Did not buy their costumes at the
> WHEN
>
> Because they lived a little too previous, but if they had lived in the nineteenth century it is altogether probable that their orders would be given us. Fine suits told with Messala; in fact, nobby attire goes a long way toward making the good-looking man. Come and buy before going to see the above-named characters at the Ben-Hur entertainment at English's opera house, May 29 and 30.[58]

This kind of advertising linkage will continue for many years of *Ben-Hur* tableaux performances.

Harper did not respond until January 29, 1889. The apparent lack of urgency no doubt reflects economic, pragmatic, and legal realities. There was no evidence that Bradford was interfering significantly with the sale of the novel. An astounding 94,164 copies were sold in 1888. As we have seen, of greater concern to Wallace and Harper between late 1887 and 1889 was the completion and marketing of a number of Wallace's publications – the second edition of *Ben-Hur: A Tale of the Christ*, *The Boyhood of Christ*, *Commodus* – as well as licensing the small literary venture *Seekers After the Light*, and dealing with foreign translations and British and Canadian copyright violations. Also, Wallace was occupied with a lecture tour when Bradford began her series of performances, and, as we saw at the outset of this chapter, he was generally dismissive and relatively uninterested in dramatic adaptations of his story. Simply put, Wallace was an author and Harper his publisher, and their primary concern was their novel and its literary scions.

Harper did not ignore the issue entirely. Their agreement with Wallace stipulated that they would not act on matters of copyright violation without his authorial approval, and because their most successful author had brought this to their attention, they had to respond appropriately. Their January 29, 1889, letter assured Wallace that they had consulted their legal counsel and confirmed that the copyright infringement in the matter was in violating the right to dramatize the work "which the law declares to be one of the rights which the author 'may reserve.'"[59] They instigated a search in Washington and learned about Bradford's September, 1887, copyright, and confirmed to their own satisfaction that she had presented her "Selections from Ben Hur" in public and was, as Wallace had reported to them, "making something of a business of it." They next determined that there were two questions involved: the interpretation of the clause "authors may reserve the right to dramatize" as stated in the Copyright Act of 1870, and whether reading from a book while publicly representing tableaux that recreated images from the book was a dramatization covered by the previous clause. Similar issues would resurface almost two decades later, in 1911 in the court case involving Kalem's unlicensed film version of Wallace's novel.

At this point Harper was not interested in pursuing a legal confrontation, which they suspected Bradford was willing to risk, and so they contacted her Washington attorney, Reuben D. Mussey, in an attempt to have Bradford acknowledge their copyright by taking a license and agree by contract to pay a royalty. They sent a letter on October 5, 1888, but did not receive Mussey's response until the following January 8, at which point Wallace wrote Harper two letters regarding the tableaux production company he was in the process of forming in Indiana. None of these letters seem to be extant, but it is clear enough from the next passage in the letter of January 19, which followed upon all of them, that Harper was urging Wallace to consider granting Bradford a license along these same terms, with the added provision that performances be allowed "only in aid of a Christian church or congregation thereof and when the representation is by members of such church or congregation and in the town or city in which such church congregation is located."

Even though Wallace and Harper did not pursue legal recourse, which Harper's attorneys assured them would not have been worth the effort, they clearly put Bradford on the defensive, as is evident in her pre-performance publicity interview recorded in *The Baltimore Sun* some six weeks later.[60] In addition to the statements Bradford typically made elsewhere about how interesting the tableaux would be for those who have not read the book, how there would be no tedious waits between tableaux because readings would continue during scene changes, how talented the reader was, and so on, she made statements that had not appeared in any of the previous interviews, emphasizing that the music "will be by some of the best amateur talent of the city," pointing out that "no representation of Christ is attempted in any manner," and even suggesting that "the sale of 'Ben-Hur' has largely increased, it is said, through these tableaux." More significantly, there are few surviving records of any performances after 1890, and apparently none after the February, 1892, performance at Raleigh's Metropolitan Hall.[61]

Harper did pursue the matter further but as a matter of inquiry, not as a legal challenge. Shortly before they wrote Wallace again about the Bradford matter in August, 1889, they contacted the Library of Congress for an explanation of why Bradford was granted her copyright of material that they had already copyrighted.[62] The response apparently focused on the clause "all rights reserved." Failure to include or abide by that could cause the copyright holder to lose "rights they might otherwise acquire, or possess." This clause will be important again in 1907 as part of the Kalem film dispute. By that time, however, there was no question that the rights to dramatize the story of Ben-Hur were held by Henry Wallace, Harper, and Abraham Erlanger.

INDEPENDENT TABLEAUX, RECITATIONS, AND PAGEANTS

Still other independent presentations demonstrate how the novel was rapidly becoming part of the popular dramatic repertoire even without the author's or publisher's consent. As part of its 1887 Christmas entertainment, the Baptist Sunday School of Austin, Illinois, presented eight tableaux representing scenes from the meeting of the Wise Men to their arrival at Bethlehem.[63] The second evening of the November, 1888, Baptist Fair held at the Broadway Rink in Logansport, Indiana, featured "selections from Ben Hur read by Mrs. Julia Tucker, illustrated by tableaux."[64] The program offered twelve tableaux, including "The Wager" [#7], "The Duel" [#8], and a two-part "Pantomime" [#9] with the subtitles "Found by the Lepers at His Father's Gate" and "Ben Hur and Amrah."[65] Fifteen tableaux entertained an audience at the recently completed city hall in Velasco, Texas, in April, 1892.[66] A single "Ben Hur" tableau was one of many musical, dance, and physical entertainments presented at St. Ramsey's in St. Paul in July, 1896.[67] The headline of an extant program from a performance at Oakland's Hamilton Hall on Friday evening, March 2, 1894, reads "Tableaux from Ben Hur."[68] The first page of the program describes this as a "Dramatization of the Story," terminology Wallace would certainly not have condoned. This version consisted of eleven tableaux, including "The Annunciation to the Shepherds," a song celebrating the reunification of the Hur family ("The Lost Found"), and a final tableaux listed as "Consecration." The same program was repeated on behalf of the Y.W.C.A. in an October, 1894, performance held in the same venue, which belonged to the First Unitarian church of Oakland.[69] Despite the similarity of the titles and sequence of the eleven tableaux and the inclusion of the reunification song, the names of the vocalist and reader on the March program are not the same as those listed in the October newspaper account, which also specifies that the evening's entertainment was "dramatized by Grace Dothea Fisher, read by Miss Helen Kelleher, and under the direction of Mrs. H. C. Mygatt."[70] One month later an advertisement in the *Oakland Tribune* for a church entertainment highlighted the participation of Kelleher, "who so charmed the audience when the 'Living Pictures from Ben-Hur' were presented."[71] Highlighting this convergence of *Ben-Hur* performances in Oakland was that one of them was cross-advertised with a personal appearance by Wallace in San Francisco the following winter. According to the October 12, 1894, *Oakland Daily Evening Tribune*, Wallace would visit the Bay area to lecture on "How I Came to Write 'Ben-Hur'" on November 31.[72]

Although most of these tableaux presentations were single events, and although Bradford seems to have slowed her schedule considerably in 1891 and retired her tableaux after 1892, there was no lull in theatrical performances inspired by *Ben-Hur: A Tale of the Christ*. Indeed, between the last two months of 1888 and the summer of 1890, representations of *Ben-Hur* were criss-crossing the country, for by this time the authorized Clark & Cox *Ben-Hur, in Tableau and Pantomime* had begun touring the country, and we know of an independent performance by Lida Hood Talbot in Fort Wayne on May 13–14, 1889, and another by Adelaide Drew in Bangor just one week later.[73]

Of course *Ben-Hur* was not the only artistic property being rendered in tableaux. For example, two of the public readings mentioned in Chapter 5, those at the Chicago Art Institute in 1889 and the 1890 reception at the Milwaukee Athenaeum, were indeed just public readings, but they were accompanied by a selection of tableaux depicting non-*Ben-Hur* stories, as was that in Chelten Hills, Pennsylvania, in 1888.[74]

Two other non-dramatic representations deserve separate mention because they were visual, contemporary, and public in nature. In 1887 the city of Louisville, Kentucky, established the Satellites of Mercury, a series of "moving tableaux" modeled after the New Orleans Mardi Gras pageants, followed by a society ball. The Satellites were an ambitious undertaking involving as many as 850 men and 250 animals.[75] The 1890 Satellites featured "Ben Hur" in nineteen tableaux, intentionally avoiding references to the Christ:

> This story, being full of tragic situations and beautiful imagery, appeals with a special emphasis to the finer instincts of an enlightened community. Great care was taken to select only such parts of the story as would afford pleasure to the beholders.[76]

Harper, seizing upon this opportunity to promote visual images that illustrated their bestselling book, placed a color drawing of the three Wise Men tableau on the cover of the October 11 *Harper's Weekly*.[77] The three sit under a half-tent, with three camels sitting and standing next to the tent amidst two palm trees and desert-like shrubbery. Horses pull the float, and on both sides march several dozen men wearing oriental garb. Some hold torches, for the pageant was held after sunset. Inside the issue, *Harper's* lists the names of the other eighteen tableaux, including brief descriptions of the scenes quoted from the novel itself. These literary snippets describe such tableaux as the Joppa Gate [#3], the tile incident [#6], the shipwreck [#8], the Palace of Idernee [#16], the Tombs [#18], and the Misenum Villa [#20]. The lone exception was the chariot race [#15], for which *Harper's* prints:

> No summary of this bit of magnificent color-painting, which has gained for its author the plaudits of the world as a description beyond parallel, can be made of the chariot-race in *Ben-Hur*.

Similarly, the annual Veiled Prophet pageant in St. Louis in 1891 included a parade celebrating "The Ten Most Popular Authors." Numbers 18–20 represented two of Wallace's novels – the meeting of Cortez and Montezuma and the death of Montezuma from *The Fair God*, and the "Ben Hur" chariot race.[78]

THE AUTHORIZED *BEN-HUR, IN TABLEAUX AND PANTOMIME*

The reader may pause here to consider this very important step that is about to unfold. Lew Wallace, as a bestselling American author, was going to license his literary property to business managers and form a company for the purpose of presenting an adaptation of his artistic creation for commercial purposes, thereby generating a significant new but authorized market for the *Ben-Hur* phenomenon. The licensing aspect of this step is essential, as are the participation of the author himself and his insistence on maintaining ultimate control. They are what differentiated the commercial legacy of *Ben-Hur: A Tale of the Christ* from the commercial legacies of such earlier popular and widely marketable properties as *The Last Days of Pompeii, Alice's Adventures in Wonderland, Uncle Tom's Cabin*, and *20,000 Leagues Under the Sea*. As we are seeing, tableaux were so popular in the late 1880s, as was Wallace's novel, that this ramification of the latter was perhaps inevitable. But unlike the vast majority of *tableaux vivant* productions of the 1880s and 1890s, this one had an unusually large and ambitious scope, achieved great success, and enjoyed considerable longevity while maintaining authorization from the original artist. The inception of this version of a *Ben-Hur* tableaux did not lead immediately to full commercial exploitation instead of exclusively charitable causes, nor was it designed as or did it ever become an actual dramatization of his novel. But, as we will see, Wallace's *Ben-Hur, in Tableaux and Pantomime* would continue to produce additional business synergies that were unprecedented for a licensed literary property in the 1890s, and they would not be terminated until the even more commercialized and lucrative Klaw & Erlanger production became available more than ten years later.

The Crawfordsville Church Production

As with most Ben-Hur by-products of the late 1880s, there is no single source that describes the formation of the authorized *Ben-Hur, in Tableaux and Pantomime*. Although Wallace would in several ways forge new standards for making a novel more profitable, forming his own tableaux production company would have been inconsistent with the way he became involved in all his other non-literary artistic commercial ventures. Wallace was an author and artist, but not an impresario, and yet he was clearly involved in the process. A nearly contemporary model would be the formation of the Tribe of Ben-Hur in 1894, when local businessmen approached Wallace with their business concept and asked for his advice and consent. The principals associated with the early formation of the *Ben-Hur, in Tableaux and Pantomime* also lived in Crawfordsville, and they would certainly have known Wallace both as a local celebrity and in some more familiar type of association.[79] And we know that Wallace was in residence in Crawfordsville during the second half of 1888. Shortly after Benjamin Harrison received the Republican nomination for president in late June, 1888, he asked the famed Indianan Republican author to write his campaign biography. Wallace worked quickly and dated his Preface on August 6.[80] He then campaigned for Harrison through October exclusively in Montgomery County, so this places him in the proximity of Crawfordsville.[81] For sure, when the votes were tallied in the second week of November, a triumphant Wallace sent out a victory announcement from Crawfordsville.[82]

As we have seen, the initial inspiration for creating the tableaux company came after seeing one of the two Bradford performances in nearby Indianapolis in May, 1888. Indiana provided fertile soil for additional productions. Adaptations of *Ben-Hur* were prepared in Winchester that summer and the following autumn in both Logansport and Crawfordsville.[83] Daily reports of the Logansport production began to appear in the *Logansport Journal* by November 14, and three days later the first report of a Crawfordsville production appeared in *The Daily Journal*,[84] and the Logansport performance on November 21, 1888, preceded the Crawfordsville version by four weeks.[85]

When David W. Cox, one of the original producers, died at the age of ninety-four in 1942 in St. Joseph, Michigan, the *New York Times* obituary reported that he had been a semi-invalid as a youth and turned to writing poetry, ably assisted by his "neighbor and intimate friend," General Lew Wallace.[86] A considerably more detailed obituary in the Benton Harbor *News-Palladium* reports that during the 1880s, Cox was a "friend and neighbor" of the late Rev. George Washington Switzer, also of St. Joseph, who lived at that time in Crawfordsville.[87] Like Cox and Wallace, Switzer was born in rural Indiana.[88] His biography in *Indiana and Indianans* records that his education was extensive, earning him a number of important positions in the Northwest Indiana Conference of the Methodist Episcopal Church and an honorary Doctorate of Divinity in 1900. Between 1887 and 1892 he served at Crawfordsville's First Methodist Church, to which the Wallace family belonged.[89] In addition to his regular duties, Switzer became "a highly successful businessman, and his abilities as an executive and administrator ... in the field of religious organization" are noted as well.[90] It would not have been out of character, therefore, for Switzer to have taken the initiative to produce a series of tableaux derived from Wallace's novel to assist the women's benefit for the organ fund of his church. However, the *News-Palladium* obituary inaccurately claimed that Cox had built the scenery and properties and drafted the scenario and then toured the United States and Canada with the show for the next nine years, but Cox sold out to Walter C. Clark in 1894, and it was Wallace that wrote and published the libretto used for the touring production.[91]

Several items in Crawfordsville's *Daily Journal* confirm and expand upon this information. Cox was not only a poet but an expert floral designer. In early November, "our florist" was winning awards for his Indianapolis Floral Exhibition exhibit of a Japanese house built out of chrysanthemums.[92] This was particularly newsworthy because he presented one of these awards to President-Elect Harrison. After this he returned to Crawfordsville to design and oversee the construction of the scenery, "working like beavers" along with Neal Watson, whose regular activities involved porcelain window signs.[93] According to the *Indianapolis Journal*, "special scenery and costumes had been prepared under the direction of General Wallace."[94] Meanwhile, the actors were being organized and trained by members of the Ladies' Aid Society committee, chaired by Mrs. J. W. Ramsay, who placed several notices into the *Daily Journal* urging participants to attend rehearsals.[95] From early December it becomes clear that these "ladies of the Methodist church" were in charge of the program, much as Bradford's initial production which developed within the Ladies Aid Society of Washington's First Congregational Church. Corroborating the participation of all these parties, the *Daily Journal* published this summary the Saturday before the first performance:

> In the first place the ladies of the Methodist church are back of the whole thing and their well known reputation for hustling alone would assure success. But they have also secured the services of Stanley Simpson, Neal Watson, and D. W. Cox and they also have had the benefit of Gen. Wallace's suggestions.[96]

The December 17 debut of the Crawfordsville performance was clearly a success. Receipts amounted to $516, less expenses of approximately $150.[97] The day after the premiere, the review in *The Daily Journal* praises the Garden of Daphne set as the most elaborate, and the chariot race as climactic.[98] The reader will not be surprised to learn that the success echoed all the way to the West Coast. After all, this was a *Ben-Hur* project radiating from its veritable birthplace, Crawfordsville. Portland's *Oregonian* carried the full report.[99] After stating that "special" scenery and costumes had been prepared under the direction of Wallace, the article describes fourteen tableaux, proceeding in order from the Wise Men and Herod to the quarrel between Judah and Messala; the domestic scenes with Amrah and Tirzah, the latter including a song; the meeting of Judah, Simonides, and Esther; the Grove of Daphne and surrounding Statuary[100] (which evoked a second round of applause); the Orchard of

Palms; Iras's song; Judah sleeping upon the doorstep of his condemned palace; the meeting of Iras, Esther, Judah, Balthasar, and Simonides; the reunification of the Hur family; Judah and Esther; and Iras's farewell. The performance concluded with a tableau of the chariot race that included live horses:

> It represented Ben-Hur and his fiery steeds dashing in to the winning goal. One of the front horses had partly fallen down, and the horse behind was running up with the mane floating in the breeze. The other two horses were seeming to be coming as under a check. Ben-Hur was standing in his chariot, with the lines firmly grasped in both hands, and slightly drawn back upon the walls were people who had witnessed the great race. This last tableau alone was worth a long journey to see.[101]

As in the Bradford productions, we again see the synthesis of readings and recitations by costumed characters positioned in postured arrangements and selected from local talent. But the use of live horses created a more dynamic adaptation of the novel and highlighted the concept that most people would associate with the subsequent dramatic and filmed versions of *Ben-Hur*. Of equal importance is that the Crawfordsville production inspired the second genuine synergy between an artistic Ben-Hur by-product and a commercial outlet. On the day of the second performance, a local clothier, Eph Joel, changed the layout of his large, daily display ad in *The Daily Journal*.[102] The 6-inch ad now for the first time includes "Ben Hur – Suits, Overcoats, – And Hats and Caps." The name "Ben Hur" is printed in a larger font than any other in the ad. The ad ran daily through Christmas.[103]

The final quarter of 1888 was a productive period for Lew Wallace and an expansive one for the *Ben-Hur* phenomenon. As of November 8, "his work" had resulted in Benjamin Harrison's election to the presidency,[104] soon after which Wallace was rumored to be a prime candidate for nomination as his Secretary of War,[105] and just before Christmas the book version of *The Boyhood of Christ* was advertised and released.[106] And then the first Crawfordsville performances were held on Monday and Tuesday, December 17 and 18, 1888. This confluence of Ben-Hur producer success and product release was not lost on a writer for the *Elkhart Daily Review*, who put this into perspective and included a brief statement about the origins of the authorized tableaux:

> The world is awake to the absorbing and really wonderful book by General Wallace, known as "Ben Hur." This story of the Christ came in good time, for the thought of the world has been for years, and is now, centered on the Nazarene, as never before. General Wallace, by his article on the childhood of Christ and the marvelous book, "Ben Hur," has greatly stimulated this thinking and study. The well wrought story and characters of this book have attracted the study and attention of the thoughtful student of the beautiful, and the lovers of art. This movement led some of the friends and neighbors of Gen. Wallace to have the scenes of the story pictured in dramatic scenery of rare merit.[107]

Like Bradford, the "management" (the church committee) of the initial Crawfordsville production, was not only successful but ambitious. A brief notice on December 8, 1888:

> Already parties are negotiating to have the same troupe with their brilliant and costly scenery exhibit at other cities in the State,[108]

was followed by another on December 19:

> The management are now in communication with Danville, Ill., Lafayette, Greencastle, and Terre Haute parties with a view to taking the entertainment to one or all of these places.[109]

These notices suggest the opportunity for the future development of the project. Russo and Sullivan add that "its success encouraged Cox to organize a company which gave other performances in Crawfordsville, on March 7, 1889, and November 3, 1890."[110] The March 7, 1889, performance and the subsequent Palmer's Theatre performance on March 14 preceded by just a few weeks the letter Wallace would write granting his official authorization to Cox and his partners. In addition, in late January, 1889, the *Logansport Pharos Tribune* reported a Lafayette, Indiana, version involving sixty participants.[111] Later the following year, another Crawfordsville production would be said to be "under new management," and that must have been the Wallace-authorized production company that would tour for the next decade. It was on November 4, 1890, that *The Daily Journal* reported:

> The first presentation in Crawfordsville of the Ben Hur tableaux under the new management occurred last evening at Music Hall before a large and select audience. Gen. Lew Wallace, under whose supervision the scenery and costumes have been prepared, together with his wife occupied prominent seats in the parquette. The scenery is indeed grand, and it is a pleasure to know that it is correct.... The drills and dances were all entirely new and brought down the house on several occasions.[112]

In addition to supervising the scenery and costumes, not to mention writing the libretto, Wallace may have also lent his considerable military expertise to the drills.

Wallace and the Formation of the Company
The first evidence for Wallace's participation in the legal establishment of a tableaux company is found within the libretto he wrote and originally self-published with the title *Ben-Hur, in Tableaux and Pantomime*.[113] The title page is divided into two parts by a central etching, which is executed in a style reminiscent of that F. M. employed to illustrate 1886's *Seekers After the Light* and features the three Wise Men riding their camels towards the Light – equally reminiscent of the radiant gold star on the upper right-hand corner of the blue cover of Harper's recently released 1887 edition of *Ben-Hur: A Tale of the Christ*. Although the publication date of the

libretto was 1890, below the etching Wallace placed a printed version of a letter dated April 2, 1889, which he had written to Messrs. Clark & Cox:

> Gentlemen: this is to certify that you are the only persons authorized by the Messrs. Harper & Brothers and myself, to give exhibitions from my book, "Ben-Hur." All other entertainments of this kind, no matter by whom offered, are absolutely without license.
> Very respectfully,
>
> LEW WALLACE[114]

The wording makes clear that Wallace, along with Harper, has protected the original copyright, and all else depends upon and develops from that. Curiously, however, Clark's name does not appear on any of the memoranda of agreements or contracts until March 19, 1891.

This is not the only important inconsistency in the record. Despite the fact that Wallace's published title was *Ben-Hur, in Tableaux and Pantomime*, the traveling show never maintained a consistent title in advertisements or on programs. The term "Pantomime" does not always appear, the hyphen rarely does in advertisements, and there seem to be as many instances of "Ben Hur Tableaux" as there are of "the Ben Hur Company." Although Clark bought out Cox entirely in 1894, the designation of "Clark & Cox" persists for several more years. And the subtitle on programs describes the presentation irregularly as "Romantic Pantomime," "Spectacular Pantomime," or "Grand Oriental Spectacle." To distinguish the authorized tableaux from Bradford's and the many others, this book by default uses the published designation *Ben-Hur, in Tableaux and Pantomime* unless the specific item under discussion uses a different title.

The amount of control Wallace would command is evident already in the January 15, 1889, memorandum of agreement he signed with David W. Cox, William S. Brown, and Albert S. Miller.[115] He insisted on writing his own adaptation of the novel, and in exchange for delivering the libretto he was to receive a 5 percent royalty for all charity benefit performances, 6 percent for non-charity performances. To monitor the progress of the venture, Wallace demanded a written accounting after every performance. The agreement also spelled out in detail exactly how Wallace's authorship and the copyright held by Harper were to be printed on every program. For the security of Cox and the others, he made the agreement exclusive, disallowing any other party "the right to produce tableaux for public exhibition." This clause would be tested in 1896 when Riley Brothers introduced their stereopticon lectures. On the other hand, Wallace reserved the right to void the agreement if the performances seemed to be interfering with book sales, a right he and Harper would ultimately exercise in 1899, albeit without merit. And of course there was his restriction against "introducing the Lord Jesus Christ as a character or person or make any personal representation of Him in any manner."

The memorandum of agreement he had signed with Cox, Brown, and Miller was approved by Harper one month later on February 14. Harper, however, distanced their publishing firm from further involvement in the matter by saying, "In the matter of the tableaux from 'Ben-Hur' we prefer to deal directly with you, and have had a formal approval prepared."[116] Harper would not become further involved in the theatrical adaptation until it was time to negotiate with Klaw & Erlanger at the end of the next decade, by which time Harper had seen its nadir of financial distress.

Final Preparations and the Palmer's Theater Performance
With all the legal arrangements settled by late winter of 1889, the *Ben-Hur, in Tableaux and Pantomime* was ready to go on the road. Although as many as 150 people participated in the tableaux, the company traveled with only ten, the balance being recruited, as in the Bradford productions, from local society people. The managers secured the services of Lafayette W. Seavey to prepare the several dozen sets, to be approved by Wallace. Just three years earlier, Seavey had revolutionized theatrical arts by inventing and patenting a light and transportable system for traveling shows, and his large designs, some 20ft × 30ft, painted with aniline dyes on flexible white cotton cloth, would endure the rigors of the ever-moving company, which required a carload of equipment.[117] This consisted mostly of approximately forty types of costumes designed and created by another resident of Crawfordsville, Nell Brown (also approved by Wallace), and a powerful calcium lighting, i.e. limelight, system used to highlight the tableaux with special effects.[118] An 1896 newspaper announcement emphasizes the importance of the lighting:

> The absence of spoken language from first to last in this production serves to concentrate the attention on the artistic and gorgeous spectacle. Form and color and light harmony are so presented that in the minds of many the efforts of the Hanlons and Kiralfys are outdone. Under the multi-colored calcium lights the scene is dazzling.[119]

Meanwhile, the authorized, single-performance Palmer's Theatre production took place on March 14, with Wallace himself and the wife of Grover Cleveland in the audience.[120] The printed program, twice stating "Special Permission of Harper & Brothers," begins with a listing of "Part I," but omits "Part II." It lists twenty-one tableaux plus a "Farewell." Many of the numbers have subtitles, making fifty-four tableaux in all – by far the greatest number in any of the Ben-Hur productions – including #14: The Prison, which includes:

1. Mother and Daughter
2. Listening at the Opening
3. Breaking into the Prison
4. Women Telling Their Story

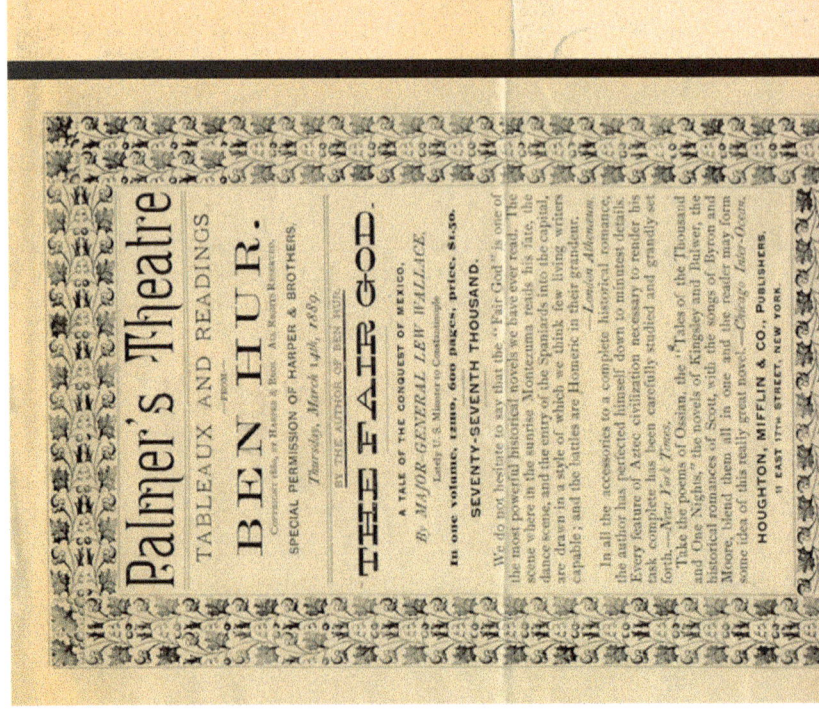

Figure 7.1 The March 14, 1889, Palmer's Theatre program for "Tableaux and Readings from Ben Hur" included transmedia advertisements for both Harper & Brothers' *Ben-Hur* and Houghton Mifflin's *The Fair God*.

Curiously, the penultimate tableau is "Ben Hur in the Galley," placed after the final departure of Iras. The program lists Clinton Burling, director of The Burling School of Acting, as the reader. The scenery was again painted by Lafayette W. Seavey, with music provided by a male chorus and Palmer's Theatre Orchestra.

The program does not list the director, but newspaper accounts make it clear that it was Robert Frazer, the manager of the Broadway Theatre.[121] Six weeks later, in early May, Frazer let it be known that he was producing another *Ben-Hur* presentation at his own theater.[122] Suddenly, just before the May 16 matinee premier, Frazer announced a postponement. He publicly cited his wife's illness and the excessively warm weather as reasons. Behind the scenes, however, despite his claim that he had the permission of Wallace and Harper, David W. Cox & Company were threatening an injunction.[123] Frazer then promised a production in the fall, but that did not take place either. Even though legal action was not necessary, the threat of injunction demonstrates how the *Ben-Hur* phenomenon was one of the first artistic properties to extend its legal arm into assigned rights for a related but separate artistic property. In this instance, Harper had agreed to assign dramatic infringements to Wallace, and Wallace had granted "exclusive right of production" to Clark and Cox. And now in May, 1889, they were protecting that right. It was just four months later that Harper and Wallace effectively cast a legal pall over Bradford's production, and in the same month, January, 1889, Wallace personally responded to a request by Zara McCosh of Salem, Ohio, to produce her own prepared readings, tableaux, and songs by citing these same contractual agreements:

> Candor requires me to add that I cannot give you the approval asked, for the reason that I have, by formal contract, conferred upon Messrs. D. W. Cox & Co., of Crawfordsville, Indiana, the sole privilege of exhibiting such tableaux. . . . I am thus specific [in] thinking it but fair to warn you, lest Messrs. Cox & Co. should, by virtue of their superior legal rights, enjoin you from making exhibition of your tableaux outside your own town, and thus subject you to expense.
> Let me hope, my dear madam, that you will believe me.[124]

Wallace would maintain this stance in a letter of July 8, 1895, to Major Pond. He declines Pond's proposal to stage a version of the novel "on account of an existing contract with a Mr. Clark, who is making season with tableaux in pantomime, and doing well with them."[125]

According to the urbane reviewer in the *New York Times*, the Palmer's Theatre performance suffered from the "futile efforts of the gentleman employed to read explanatory selections from the book to keep up with the procession," "some awkward posturing," and the lack of "personal beauty" except for Iras, who was "a comely and graceful girl."[126] But the reviewer's disparaging remarks clearly stem from his metropolitan attitude towards the provincial popularity of the novel itself:

The pictures were intended to represent scenes in Lew Wallace's florid romance called "Ben Hur," which is regarded in some rural districts as a great imaginative work. In the same rural neighborhoods the exhibition of yesterday might reasonably be considered a triumph of stage art. . . . The exhibition is not likely to be repeated within the city limits. It would make a great hit in St. Louis.

Ben-Hur, in Tableaux and Pantomime Performances and Touring

In fact, Bradford would exhibit her tableaux at Entertainment Hall in St. Louis (with much approval) on April 4–5, 1889, while David Cox began touring with the authorized tableaux in other eastern Indiana and central Ohio cities, beginning March 22–3 at the Globe Opera House in Hamilton, Ohio.[127] He hired Clara Louise Thompson as the reader for April performances in Cedar Rapids and Waterloo, Iowa, and St. Paul, Minnesota. One review describes in addition to her "intelligent reading" the two elaborate costumes she wore during the performance, the second featuring an oriental-jeweled headdress, pearl and gold beads, a jeweled belt, and white silver-embroidered Persian slippers.[128] Lida Hood Talbot was used in Cincinnati (for an extended five nights), Miami, Hamilton, Piqua, Dayton, and Lima as well as Fort Wayne, Indiana, into May, when Cox took the show to St. Paul, Minnesota.[129]

Talbot, a native of Evanston, Illinois, became a favorite. She established a reputation as an elocutionist, but she suggested instead that she was "a student of the meanings of things, and my readings are careful studies."[130] Also a suffragette, she would soon co-author a novel with the influential Alice B. Stockham, and she appeared in public programs along with another leading suffragette, Zerelda Wallace.[131] It cannot be confirmed that it was through Wallace that Talbot was hired for the tour, but when asked how she secured her engagement, she stated in an interview, "I knew the people and they sent for me. It was given in Crawfordsville just for two evenings, and I had General Wallace in my audience."[132] Although all the participants in the tableaux themselves were local amateurs, she was paid $150 per week.[133]

In describing the effect she had on audiences the reviewer for the *Cincinnati Enquirer* remarked:

> Last evening the exhibition was superb in all its appointments, and the descriptive text, recited with rare dramatic power, and particularly that preceding the splendid chariot race, by Miss Talbot, wrought the audience to a high pitch of rapture, which was expressed by round after round of applause.[134]

In Cincinnati she so impressed the directors of the College of Music that she was then asked to repeat her readings at the Trinity Methodist Church on the Sunday evening following the close of the engagement. She wore a costume "which heightened the favorable impression produced by a naturally striking stage presence."[135]

Unlike the Bradford and independent productions, which at best referred to General Wallace's famous book in newspaper pre-publicity, the ad placed in the March 21, 1889, *Hamilton Daily Democrat* begins with "Ben Hur! A Tale of the Christ by LEW WALLACE, Copyright 1880 by Harper & Bros, and by their permission, will be given at the Globe Opera House."[136] For the public at large this statement may have served more as an advertisement and a claim of exclusivity than a warning aimed at answering specifically the demands made by Wallace and Harper. But a *Miami Helmet* article echoed the stipulations outlined in the January 29, 1889, letter from Harper to Wallace:

> The first exhibition of the Ben Hur Tableaux was given Monday night to a large and appreciative audience. The company that owns the scenes and costumes was brought here by the Presbyterian ladies of the first section. The conditions of Gen. Lew Wallace and the Harper Brothers, publishers, are that no attempts shall be made to impersonate Christ and that no presentation shall be made for other than church or benevolent purposes by non-professional dramatis personae without compensation in whatever locality it is portrayed.[137]

Copyright and contractual issues may have provided the underlying legal necessity for such statements, but for the public they would only add to the awe, mystique, and reverence already associated with the name *Ben-Hur* and rapidly propelling it into new segments of society.

Following Wallace's caveats, Cox made an effort to educate the public as to the accuracy of the tableaux themselves and the secular but reverential substratum of the program. The newspaper ad for the Hamilton, Ohio, debut described the tableaux as "reproduced from BEN HUR with Scenery, Historically and Literally True; Elegant Costumes and Mechanical Effects."[138] Targeting the more sophisticated Cincinnati audiences, the *Enquirer* ran a piece in which he asserted that Wallace had made a careful study of how to most properly stage a representation of his novel. Differentiating these tableaux from a Passion Play, Cox also cited the Oberammergau tradition and distanced himself from Salmi Morse, who in 1879 produced a Passion Play in San Francisco which "so offended the public conscience that it was suppressed by the municipal authorities to prevent an impending riot," ultimately ending in Morse's bankruptcy and subsequent suicide.[139] For smaller venues Cox placed personal testimonials of approval from clergy, beginning with his Crawfordsville supporters. The *Piqua Miami Herald* ran the following notices four days before the first of two performances:

> The following is from a minister, who is well-known in Piqua, concerning the Ben Hur Tableaux to be given May 6th and 7th by the Presbyterian ladies.
>
> WABASH COLLEGE, CRAWFORDSVILLE, IND., APRIL 1
> It gives me special pleasure after having witnessed the splendid spectacular presentation of "Ben Hur" by the "Ben Hur Company" of this city to commend it to churches and communities as a very enjoyable and instructive entertainment. I write this after having witnessed it two evenings.
> JOSEPH F. TUTTLE, PRESIDENT[140]

The next column includes support from "Mrs. E. B. Thomson, wife of the former pastor of the Presbyterian Church of Piqua," who had moved to Crawfordsville and seen the performance:

> This expression of opinion has much weight coming from the home of the author of "Ben Hur," and from a lady so highly respected, and well known in Piqua.[141]

The Hamilton premier was prefaced by this statement from the Rev. Vance of Middletown:

> I understand D. W. Cox & Co. are to give readings from Ben Hur illustrated by tableaux for the benefit of your church Friday and Saturday evening. I was out at the entertainment last night and expect to go tonight. It is one of the finest things I ever saw and free from any objectionable features. Rally your people to attend it.[142]

This approach is entirely consistent with Wallace's reverence for Christ and the public perception of both of them. Indeed, the publicity emphasized the accuracy of the tableaux and costumes that were "Historically and Literally True" by reminding readers that Wallace:

> ... while a minister in the United States service in the Asiatic East studied the traditions, scenery, costumes and characteristics of oriental people with a view to historical accuracy.[143]

Of course this fed on the common misperception that Wallace wrote *Ben-Hur: A Tale of the Christ* after he had visited the Holy Land, but this was for useful for publicity.[144]

Moreover, a clear statement of Wallace's non-denominationalism seemed to be required where audiences represented warring sects. In her July interview in Chicago's *Daily Inter Ocean*, Talbot commented that even Catholic priests personally expressed their appreciation to her:

> I am sorry to say that there was not equal generosity manifested on the part of the Protestant churches. Frequently, if we gave the entertainment for the benefit of the Methodist Church the Presbyterians would not come, and the Methodists or Baptists stayed away when the case was reversed. They seemed to be always in a broil with each other. We had to have a letter from General Wallace to keep the peace and to show that we were really authorized by him.[145]

To encourage repeat attendees, Cox for at least the next two years often advertised that the second night's program might be different. The Monday, May 6, 1889, performance in Miami included ten tableaux:[146]

The Three Wise Men in the Desert
The Joppa Gate
The Three Wise Men Before Herod
On the House Top
On Board the Galley
House of Simonides
Grove of Daphne
Desolate Home of the Hurs

Cleansing of the Lepers
The Chariot Race

The following night repeated "The Chariot Race" but also introduced:

The Parting of Ben Hur and Messala
The Arrest
The Orchard of Palms
The Lake of Palms
The Palace of Idernee
The Home of Ben Hur

Nonetheless, attendance the second night was "surprisingly rather meager."

Chautauqua Venues
Considering his previous success and personal contacts, Wallace himself may have been the person who suggested performing the *Ben-Hur, in Tableaux and Pantomime* at Chautauqua venues in the summer of 1890. An announcement appeared in *The Chautauquan* already in March, 1890, where the "Ben Hur Tableaux" are described as a "decided innovation" and "one that will give great pleasure to Chautauquan audiences."[147] Specific mention is made that the presentation will be under "the management of a company which has the recommendation of Gen. Lew Wallace himself."

The first was held on the West Coast, where the city of Redondo Beach had recently established Vincent Park, named after the Chautauqua Chancellor John Heyl Vincent, whom the reader will recall had been instrumental in promoting Wallace's novel in 1886.[148] Led by the Rev. S. J. Fleming, the California city constructed its oval park specifically to attract a Chautauqua venue, which it did for the first and only time in the summer of 1890. The version of the *Ben-Hur, in Tableaux and Pantomime* that was presented on August 2, at a reported cost of $2000–3000, drew the largest crowd the new amphitheater had yet seen.[149] It consisted of twelve tableaux and the songs by Tirzah and Iras similar to the usual Cox numbers, but for this production Professor Henry Ludlam of Ellis College, a girls' boarding school, added dialogue between Judah and Arrius "in which the Jewish boy told the story of his life, and pitifully besought the haughty Roman for news of his mother and sister."[150] Ludlam also added a recitation of "The Fallen Tile" (by Gertrude Foster), played the role of Arrius, and rendered the reading of the chariot race. His final tableau was called "The Happy Hearth Stone." The August 2 performance was such a success, and perhaps ran so long, the final three events of the evening were cancelled so patrons could make their way back to the city on the "Moonlight Excursion," a special train scheduled by the Southern California Railway to depart at 10:30 p.m.[151]

Attendance at the New York "mother" Chautauqua, held just a few days later, was at a premium, made even more so by the presence of Amos Alonzo Stagg, the All-American football player from Yale, who reportedly played the role of Judah Ben-Hur.[152] The *Pittsburgh Dispatch* reported that Chautauquans scrambled for seats to see the celebrated tableaux rather than attend prayer meetings or even eat their evening meal:

> "Well, you see, the people like the show a little better than the prayer meeting," said Dr. Flood, editor of *The Chautauquan*, as he tried to contemplate the vast sea of humanity gathered in the Amphitheater. It was not yet 7 o'clock, and all the people on the grounds, regardless of the dozen denominal prayer meetings, had flocked to the great auditorium in order to get a seat for the "Ben Hur" tableaux that took place at 8. Before this hour all the available sitting and standing room was taken. Some of the old timers even went without supper to get there in time.[153]

This was more like an official report. The real demand for seating among the throng was brought out in the next paragraph:

> Every imaginable means was taken by the people to see the realistic scenes of General Wallace's romance. You would have thought their lives depended on it. They fought, scrambled, pushed and pulled to get standing room. One poor fellow, with arms extended, was endeavoring to hold four young ladies on a single chair, while another part was quarreling over the space on a rickety stepladder, and the crowd up in the trees was trying to persuade the unfortunates below that there was room for no more. One fellow, a Pittsburger, with the activity characteristic of his city, sat upon a chair suspended in mid-air by means of straps hitched to the Amphitheater ceiling.

Another article said that the ancient crowd of "barbarian spectators" who witnessed the chariot race between Ben-Hur and Messala "could not have been wilder than . . . these pious ministers, dignified professors, and modest girls."[154]

The next day the Chautauqua management decided to clear the Amphitheater at the end of the first half of the presentation to allow others their seats, but the "old-timers" who sacrificed their supper to grab seats at 4:00 p.m. objected. And at least one commentator disparaged the Chautauqua population for undermining the purpose of the Chautauqua movement by favoring the tableaux over a learned lecture by Thomas Wentworth Higginson, who attracted only one fifth of Ben-Hur's 10,000 spectators. The reader should keep this kind of *Ben-Hur* mania in mind when contemplating the extraordinary ticket sales for the Klaw & Erlanger production later in the decade and the next, especially when contemplating that the 1890 Chautauqua performances took place already a few years after sales of the novel had peaked.

In the summer of 1891, *Ben-Hur, in Tableaux and Pantomime* was presented at the Kentucky Chautauqua at Lexington and the Piedmont Chautauqua near Atlanta, the first appearance of the *Ben-Hur, in Tableaux and Pantomime* in the Deep South. Perhaps because Clark was now acting as the spokesperson for the company, the pre-publicity seems to have a new energy.[155] A lengthy article in the *Atlanta Constitution* praised Wallace's novel as one that "no one can read without being made better," and there Clark boasts that the Lexington Chautauqua attracted 3000 spectators per night and that the production included 11,000 square feet of scenery and more than 100 persons in elegant costumes. The articles conclude with a half-dozen testimonials, finishing with the remarks of two reverends who concur in recommending the work "to all who love the chaste and beautiful."[156] Of particular interest to us is the developing, quasi-legendary status of the origins of *Ben-Hur: A Tale of the Christ*. According to the article, Wallace made a wager with Ingersoll that when he took up his appointment in Turkey and visited the Holy Land he would become an infidel:

> The story goes that he was so impressed with the scenes of his visit as to become a confirmed Christian, and "A Tale of the Christ" was the expression of his devotion.

Although this is a revisionist history of the chronology, it surely helped. The specially arranged trains from Atlanta to the Chautauqua venue "were filled to the guards."[157]

Having heard of the great early successes, Philadelphia's Mary Bonsall in September wrote the vice-principal of Chautauqua, George Vincent, to ask them to sponsor a performance of the *Ben-Hur, in Tableaux and Pantomime* for a Philadelphia orphanage.[158] Perhaps not wanting more crowd control issues, Vincent refused. Bonsall pleaded with Wallace the following September, but scheduling was not under his control, and there is no record of a subsequent Philadelphia performance. Nonetheless, Michigan's Methodist Bay View Association did schedule a performance that season, and there was a return Cincinnati engagement in November.[159] Additionally, the University of Iowa Libraries possess a six-page brochure for the "Ben Hur Singers & Players" in their Redpath Chautauqua Collection.[160] Remarkably, the brochure is said to date from the 1910s.

Changes in the Libretto and Management

The same month that Bonsall appealed to Wallace, the latter was signing a contract with Harper & Brothers for the formal publication of his libretto for *Ben-Hur, in Tableaux and Pantomime* and securing a copyright.[161] Of interest is that within the printed text of the September 25, 1890, agreement there are several handwritten insertions and deletions, all making reference to matters of potential copyright infringement. Here Harper stipulates again in writing that they shall not be expected to seek redress in the event of any copyright infringement, whether by copying, printing, reprinting, or publishing, and they specifically delete the word "dramatization" from their rights, carefully distinguishing between their responsibilities and interest as a publisher and Wallace's claim as author to the dramatic rights of the work. Wallace self-published the libretto in 1890. The thirty-four pages of this version of the libretto contain much more narrative detail and dialogue than the tableaux require, and the printing is marred by organizational errors and inconsistencies. It was arranged in several "Parts" consisting of six pantomimes, numerous scenes, and an occasional "Explanatory" with background detail, but it lacks a label for "Part First," mislabels Pantomime III as "I," and inserts "Act II" although no other acts are indicated. At least one tableau, that of Joseph, Mary, and Rabbi Samuel at the Joppa Gate, does not appear. Harper published a revised version in 1891, inserting the missing tableau as Scene II and then changing the numbering of the subsequent scenes. Affixed to the title page of this edition is an addendum citing Section 4966 of the Revised Statutes, warning that any copyright infringement by law carries a penalty of $100 for the first infraction and $50 for each additional infraction.[162] Inside, the libretto is divided into two acts consisting of fifteen and eight scenes, respectively, with an independent scene for the chariot race inserted in between. After the end of Act Second there is a "Transformation: Iras's Story of the Nile," divided into five scene titles with no descriptions. The designation of "Pantomime" appears three times, at the start of each act and the end of I.14 with Simonides, Esther, and Judah, but without any description of the staging.

In March, 1891, six months after the libretto agreement was negotiated, the original agreement establishing the management was revised. The new agreement, signed April 16, 1891, was between Wallace, Cox, and Clark, with Miller and Brown now being omitted.[163] Although Clark, that is Walter C. Clark of Pewaukee, Wisconsin, had previously been listed only in the advisory placed on the title page of the 1890 printed libretto, from this point he begins to overshadow "Clark & Cox" and would eventually take over from the original Crawfordsville syndicate completely. A program from a January, 1892, Bleecker Hall performance of "Clark & Cox's Spectacular Pantomime BEN-HUR" in Albany, New York, lists Clark as "General Manager" and Cox as "Stage and General Director." Moreover, the new agreement between Harper, Clark, and Cox stipulates that the copyrights of both the original 1880 novel and the 1890 libretto must be printed separately on each program or "other circulated notice advertising the Tableaux or the Pantomime, both or either." Preferring to protect their own rights, however, they printed only the copyright notice of the 1880 novel and then added:

> NOTICE: Messrs. Clark & Cox state that, by special arrangement with Gen. Lew Wallace and Harper Bros., they have secured the exclusive right of production from the copyrighted libretto, "Ben-Hur in Tableau [sic] and Pantomime," and will prosecute any infringement thereon, public or private. For dates, terms, etc., address CLARK & COX, Crawfordsville, Ind.[164]

By October, 1894, Clark wrote Wallace from Pewaukee that "the differences between Clark & Cox have been settled by purchase, I being the buyer."[165] His explanation refers to "differences" between him and Cox, which seem to have been about the size of the venues. Clark preferred to make "bookings for first class cities," whereas Cox had made most of his in "smaller towns." He complains that the number of bookings thus far engaged for the next season was limited to two – Defiance, Ohio, and Richmond, Indiana. After the buyout, the legal statements printed on the programs changed only slightly, maintaining the ownership name as "Clark & Cox" but now including the internal title phrases:

> Walter C. Clark's
> (Successor to Clark & Cox)
> ROMANTIC PANTOMIME
> BEN-HUR
> Arranged from Lew Wallace's great novel.[166]

Clark used this same nomenclature on his "Sharing Contract" form for bookings.[167] In the final months of its run, Clark printed the title *Spectacular Ben-Hur Pantomime* on the cover of the program.[168]

The aforementioned obituary in the *News-Palladium* reported that Cox became a landscaper for the Vandalia Railroad in St. Joseph, Michigan, where he lived out his years until 1942: "One of his most prized possessions was an autographed copy of Ben Hur presented to him by Gen. Wallace."

Beyond *Ben-Hur*

A few extant programs from 1892–4 preserve the most detailed descriptions of the performances that were longer and much more elaborate than the 1889 versions, and they diverged increasingly from the original story and Wallace's libretto. They begin with fifteen scenes in Act I but then have only six scenes in Act II, eliminating scene 5 that takes place on the roof of the Restored House of the Hurs and scene 7 ("The Shadow of the Cross"), thereby eliminating even Wallace's oblique description of the Crucifixion. More noticeably, they minimize the narrative and textual elements, which had been so important to the Bradford tableaux, and liven up the proceedings with a variety of visual entertainments. Accordingly the name of the reader is no longer prominently displayed in the programs, and it rarely appears in press releases.

Wallace's libretto does not include Tirzah's song but instead introduces the "Beautiful entertainment of Ben Hur by Arab maidens" (I.12) and "Dance, Candida-Pax" (II.5). The "Lament" of Iras that had been integral in both the Bradford and 1889 Wallace versions and is included in the published libretto is now not only moved to the end of the performance but also renamed. The 1892 Albany program includes the note:

> The audience will please remain seated a few moments for the last Scene. Grand Closing Allegory: "Iras' Story of the Nile."

The extant programs include now the "Statuary" dance section featuring the Three Fates, Diana, and Minerva, and also the relatively large number of cast members in the many other numbers, including Drill of the Naiads (26), Dance of Blackbirds (16), Gondoliers (15), Butterfly Dance (12), Priestess or Hindo [sic] Scarf Dance (12), Tambourine Dance with Arab Naiads (12), as well as "Statues" (4) and Dance of the Graces (3), not to mention the drilling Roman soldiers (15). At various points different names or additional numbers appear such as a "Sprites Fantasie," "Arabian Girls Frolic," an "Egyptian Fandango," a "balletic interlude in the Imperial Gardens," and "Sylvides [Queen of Butterflies] in dance Gracieux." The arrangement of such numbers seems to have been quite consistent for the next years, although spellings ("Iris" for Iras) and names ("Dream of the Nile" for "Story of the Nile") are not always so.[169]

A report in the January 12, 1893, *Wichita Eagle* says that from the rise of the curtain to its final fall, the house orchestra played continuous music along with the "rapid change of scenes."[170] Incorporating a hand-to-hand combat scene (II.1) as well, the production consisted of a pantomime drama interspersed with a series of production numbers performed by local talent – a popularized, American variation on a traditional French drama interspersed with entr'acte numbers embellished by an abundance of ballet.

The reaction from the reviewer in *The Wichita Eagle*, who found numerous flaws, was effusive, but not about the drama:

> But the dances more than made amends for the shortcomings of the drills. It is safe to say that a prettier set of girls could not be found in the length and breadth of the land. They were grace and modesty embodied. With their flowing locks, their bright eyes, graceful figures, and dainty feet with their variegated costumes, tambourines, castanets, and gay scarves. They were symbolic of all that is pure and lovely, joyous and light-hearted. Many were the murmurs of approbation heard on all sides.[171]

This kind of fascination with the young women in costume, whether posed or dancing, was certainly much more prevalent than the historical record implies. But a Milwaukee report confirms that one of the main attractions of the performances was the display of young society women, as it had been in the Bradford productions. It lists three reasons the performances should appeal to the public but promotes the appeal of seeing young society women dance before the appeal of raising money for charity and experiencing a "very gorgeous spectacle":

> The entertainment called "Ben Hur," to be given at the Academy of Music on Thursday, Friday and Saturday of this week, seeks to woo and win ticket-buyers with a triple appeal. In the first place, it is a society affair. Young women who do most of their dancing within the sacred precincts of the Athenaeum or in houses

not many blocks away; who take up or let alone, make or mar, create or destroy the young men who come to Milwaukee from other cities; who seldom emerge from the social holy of holies to the court of the Gentiles – these will appear before the public in several sinuous and delectable dances.[172]

As we are seeing, the mature Clark & Cox Tableaux surrendered its narrative continuity to feature a series of diversions. Audiences first saw "A Lonely Desert" with the Wise Men, then these reverent scenes moved to within Herod's Palace via the Joppa and Damascus Gates (2–4). As in the novel, the setting now leaps ahead twenty-one years and the quarrel between Judah and Messala establishes the narrative argument (5). After a scene with Judah and his mother (6), the mood that would have been established by the song of Tirzah alone is fully transformed by the "Parade and Grand Drill of Roman Soldiers" (7).[173] The Butterfly Dance is inserted between the arrest and galley scenes (8–10). In the novel Wallace used both the Grove of Daphne and the character Iras as pagan temptations for Judah to reject. In his libretto he does include a notation for the "Dance of the Dervassi or Priestesses of Apollo," but in the programs these pagan moments are used more to seduce the audience, so Act I now proceeds through a dazzling series of production numbers, dances, drills, the Arab Naiad entertainment, and Iras's song by moonlight at the Grove of Daphne and the Orchard of Palms with its moonlit lake (11–13).[174] The first act comes to a conclusion with the satisfaction of seeing Judah receive all his money from Simonides, whom he then – contrary to the novel – frees, and the reading of the chariot race, followed by "The Blackbirds–Statuary" (14–15).

Act II lightens the mood of the attempted assassination at Idernee with the initial "Gondolier, or Arabian Dance" and the closing "The Three Graces," and of course Judah's triumph and agreement with Thord (1). The scenes at the "Desolate Home of the Hurs," the well En-Rogel, and the "House Top in Jerusalem" brought the mood to its darkest reaches (2–4). But these were counterbalanced by the cleansing of the lepers and the reunion of the Hur family celebrated in the "Candida-Pax Dance" and Statuary scenes (5). The final tableaux takes place in the Misenum villa (6), and after the farewell of Iras comes the Grand Closing Allegory. The duration of the performance was typically two hours, forty-five minutes.

Advertising Synergies
Clark introduced a number of additional advertising innovations. Although there had been many newspaper descriptions to this point, they were not accompanied by sketches, let alone photographs. But Clark released a few sketches of the sets and costumes to *The Milwaukee Journal* in November, 1893.[175] It is not known if he was giving a special dispensation to his native home, or feared that the number of engagements were trailing off and wanted to enhance ticket sales, or if the previous absence of images was

due to the printing expense or even fears that illustrations would actually discourage ticket sales (as Wallace and Harper had feared that Bradford's tableaux and the Riley stereopticon lectures would interfere with book sales). Possibly Seavey had forbidden the release of his sketches to the press. In 1892 Harry Temple, who would also be involved with the 1907 Kalem film, was credited with the scenery designs, and now Clark was using fifty-six drop designs created by Thomas Gibbs Moses, known for his Greco-Roman work on Scottish Rite temples and Shrine mosques.[176] Whatever the reason, the paper ran sketches of "Ben Hur in costume," one of the priestesses, "The Lonely Desert," and the Desolate "Home of the Hurs." On the program covers Clark boasted of "50,000 Square Feet of New Scenery" and "$2,000.00 of new and Historical Costumes."[177] In large type appeared the list of enticements: "STATUARY, TABLEAUX, PANTOMIME, DRILLS AND DANCES."

The newspaper ads for the performances at the Oshkosh Grand Opera House in November, 1893, used large font to impress upon potential customers that the performances are "Chaste, Magnificent, Historical" and "Endorsed by Pulpit and Press."[178] Clark added that this was a "story of eastern life at the time of Christ's appearance on earth."[179] In addition, before the Decatur performances of April, 1893, he inserted an announcement that sales of Wallace's novel had just reached 400,000 copies on the same page as both a review of the previous night's performance and an announcement for the coming evening's performance.[180] In the earlier years, newspaper promotions sometimes carried the main cast members and a sample list of tableaux titles. But for the 1894 Amsterdam, New York, performances at the Neff Opera House, Clark included such detailed program material as a summary of the story, a synopsis of every tableau, a cast list, and the crowded lists of local people playing the Priestess, Arab Maids, Butterflies, and the like, filling an entire column and most of a second.[181] The programs of this period list a staff for the company, i.e. Clark as "Proprietor and Manager," Representative, two Drill Masters, Costumer (Monsieur Burke), Stage Carpenter, Electrician, Calcium Light Operator, and Press Agent. The latter, W. L. Anderson, no doubt devised and implemented some of these new publicity tactics.

One of the most innovative ramifications of the extensive reach of the authorized tableaux was in advertising. Because the early independent *Ben-Hur* tableaux were local charitable or society affairs, there was little thought of advertising other than announcing the performances and some of the players in local newspapers. The new concept of secondary advertising played little role since the purpose of the entire enterprise was to raise money for the charity by selling tickets, not advertising space. As reflected throughout this book, the 1880s were witnessing the emergence of the American consumer culture, so manufacturers and retailers were just beginning to understand the powerful effect of advertising, let alone creating and developing new synergies. The Eph Joel advertisement in *The Daily Journal* was a rare and early exception, perhaps inspired by the local Crawfordsville connection. The Bradford productions were much larger and played in many sizable metropolitan venues, but Bradford herself was not interested in expanding her business or selling it to others so much as she was committed to repeating her original concept in a variety of cities for worthy charities. But when businessmen like Cox and Clark were developing their theatrical product in the early 1890s, a spectrum of new possibilities awaited them.

At the time the most common medium for advertising had always been newspapers, which were inexpensive to produce, widely distributed, and often reissued on a daily basis. Because of the nature of newspapers in the late nineteenth century, advertising for the most part remained local, not yet dominated by large corporations, their franchises, and their trademarked names and products. But book publishers, who understood the power of advertising and the effect of the print medium already, were different. They had long since learned that one of the best places to advertise their book lists was in another one of their books. As a result, the association between literary and tableaux versions of *Ben-Hur* provided obvious angles for the two national publishers associated with Wallace's works, Harper's and Houghton Mifflin. The four-page, octavo-size program printed for the 1889 Palmer's Theatre production provides an excellent example. Only the upper third of the cover fold contains the performance information, crowded together in variously sized fonts (Palmer's Theatre – Tableaux and Readings – From – Ben Hur – Copyright 1880, by Harper & Bros – All Rights Reserved – Special Permission of Harper & Brothers – Thursday, March 14th, 1889). The lower two thirds contain Houghton Mifflin & Company's half-page ad for Wallace's newly reissued novel, *The Fair God*. As we have seen, sales of *The Fair God* swelled after the issue of *Ben-Hur: A Tale of the Christ*. Houghton Mifflin was capitalizing on Harper's success with *Ben-Hur*, representing a different type of synergy in which two different companies profited by sharing in the same literary phenomenon. The Houghton Mifflin ad contained three different 40-word review quotations supplemented by the information that over 77,000 had been sold thus far, all enclosed within a 1-inch leaf border. The back page contains a full-page advertisement for Harper's new, second edition of *Ben-Hur: A Tale of the Christ* that employs a half-dozen different fonts and alternating bold and capitalized lines of different sizes. It lists from top to bottom excerpts from six reviews ranging from the secular Louisville *Courier-Journal* ("As an historical romance 'Ben-Hur' surpasses the glory of 'Ivanhoe'"), to New York's *Christian Advocate* ("Eminently calculated to add largely to the popular conception of the real historical setting of the time of the incarnation"), to President Garfield ("With this beautiful and reverend book you have lightened the bur-[den] of my daily life"). As was typical for the period, there is no advertising on the inner folds where the program information is printed along with the usual theater seating chart and fire-exit information. At most a company might pay for the printed program and claim space to say that in print.[182]

In just a few years the world of print advertising had changed considerably, both in technological improvements and in the desire of manufacturers and retailers to use it as well as the eagerness of impresarios to sell it. The Schenectady program for May 2–4, 1894, provides a superb example of how the name of *Ben-Hur* was so well known to the audience and with such a positive resonance that a number of local merchants paid to place custom-designed ads reusing and playing upon the famous name as psychological hooks. In comparison to the simple folios of the previous decade, this program – and many like it – were thick, containing twenty printed pages, with sixty-eight advertisements, not including the notice on the cover that this presentation of the "Ben-Hur Spectacular Pantomime" was being given under the auspices of St. Mary's Guild of St. George's Church. Most of the pages are divided into three columns, the text being confined to the narrower center column and the ads to the wider outer two. On page 7, Hammond's of 273 State Street claims that "Our ribbon stock is as far ahead of the assortments you find in most stores as *Ben-Hur* is above the ordinary words of fiction." The penultimate page displays an advertisement for S. R. James, purveyor of housewares and home furnishings. The wording begins with "B. H. Stands for Ben-Hur, Also for Best House." The last page ad for the H. S. Barney & Company department store begins with:

> Lew Wallace's 'Ben-Hur' has become famous the world over.
>
> H. S. Barney Co. have also become famous for their low prices and large assortment of Dry Goods, Carpets, Curtains and House Furnishing Goods.

The inside of the paper cover repeats the revised dedication of Wallace's book:

> To the Wife of My Youth ... Who still abides with me" and continues with a quasi-biblical archaisms: "Go Thou To Quiri's Shoe Store for the sake of Economy, for Extravagance is sin."

Such use of the name "Ben-Hur" was not unique to the Schenectady program. The Corry, Pennsylvania, program, from a different state and the following year, features an ad that puns, "BEN-HERE: Havn't much room, but here's some of 'em: Best Flour 90c."

Further on in the program the ad for City Planing Mill again uses the same pun substituting "Ben Hur" for "Been Here":

> Had We Ben Hur – We might have driven chariots and gotten glory. As it is we are running a Planing Mill and getting oceans of work. We have no chariots except our

dray, but we have all kinds of Lumber from black walnut to hemlock sash, doors and blinds, custom work, etc. If you don't see what you want, ask us and we will get it.[183]

Still further along the Ajax Iron Works, a company named after the strong ancient Greek mythological warrior, placed this ad:

THE
AJAX IRON WORKS
    Did not build the famous
    Chariot driven by Ben Hur,
    But they do build a . . .

    STEAM ENGINE
    That would have driven all
    the wheels in Rome, had
    they received the order in
    time.

Even in its tenth year of existence the *Spectacular Ben-Hur Pantomime* program for the March 16–17, 1899, Pottstown, Pennsylvania, performances contained an ad that begins, "'The Race Was On' for Shuler's Drug Store."

In one instance, this kind of advertising seems to have provided the impetus to create an additional commercial tie-in. On the first page of the Schenectady program the Gibson Brothers offer "Ben-Hur Suits" for sale. Although advertisers often exaggerate and mislead, the Gibson Brothers here are advertising that they have custom-designed a type of suit in the "Ben Hur" style, hoping to attract *Ben-Hur* aficionados or at least audience members who enjoy the Ben-Hur performance and wish to continue the experience in some psychological pleasant way. A different kind of spin-off was to be found in highlighting an association with the *Ben-Hur, in Tableaux and Pantomime*. In 1891, for instance, two years after the tableaux production had barnstormed Ohio in its initial foray, a certain Charles Stricker, Jr. advertised his services as a dance instructor entirely through his association with the Ben-Hur "company":

Having received a thorough course of instruction from Prof. W. B. Melville of the Ben-Hur company, I am now prepared to instruct in the latest and popular dances. For particulars and terms enquire at 487 Hazel St.[184]

Although the name and title of Professor Melville mean little to us today, at that time in northern Ohio Stricker was attempting to add benefit to his name by advertising his association with the high quality of the *Ben-Hur* company.

The last page of the program printed for the February, 1895, performances at the Grand Opera House in Wilmington, Delaware, is solely devoted to an advertisement for the photographer, J. Paul Brown. There Brown not only wants audience members to fondly recollect the

Figure 7.2 Local retailers frequently placed synergistic advertisements in programs for the *Ben-Hur*, in *Tableaux and Pantomime*.

performance and continue associating *Ben-Hur* with commercial enterprise, he also makes them a special offer:

> Everybody connected with Ben-Hur can have their photographs made at greatly reduced sales by J. Paul Brown [cursive logo], Leading Photographer.

Although this technique ran its course in the mid-1890s and would appear only sporadically in subsequent years and decades, it demonstrates the intensity and frequency with which the general public was being introduced to the *Ben-Hur* phenomenon from the late 1880s well into the 1890s. Approximately one half-million copies of the novel had been sold in the United States, and now on average every week or month a few thousand people were enjoying the same popular property in different art forms and venues. In addition to the public readings sampled in an earlier chapter and hundreds more like it, for more than a decade the Bradford and then Clark & Cox productions as well as the independent tableaux performances and pageants continued to spread the name of *Ben-Hur* to church and school groups as well as community gatherings and public venues in both medium-sized cities and large metropolitan centers like Atlanta where as late as 1898 an *Atlanta Constitution* headline could read, "'Ben Hur' Was a Great Success."[185] The popularity of *Ben-Hur* permeated a variety of demographic strata from the urban and municipal social, political, and economic elites to the rural farmer's church group, from Philadelphia's Academy of Music to the street throngs in Louisville, from charity organizers to kids sitting in the balcony. As we will soon see in the next chapters, John Philip Sousa and E. T. Paull were redistributing the Ben-Hur chariot race in major national expositions, local fairs, concert halls, and parlors all over the country, and at this same time other segments of the population were reading ads or consuming Ben-Hur Cigars, Ben-Hur Flour, or Ben-Hur Bicycles, or enrolling in the Tribe of Ben-Hur by the tens of thousands. In understanding the incessant proliferation of the *Ben-Hur* name in this period following the peak of book sales, the reader should also consider that family units were typically larger and more cohesive than they are now, so one copy of the novel, or one family's visit to one of the tableaux, would quickly and efficiently spread the word to the rest of the family and other families as well. By the time the Klaw & Erlanger dramatic adaptation was put into production in 1899, there would have been few people in the United States who did not have some familiarity or association with, or at least name recognition of, *Ben-Hur*. As we have just seen, this included business owners and retailers and helped inspire their fledgling attempts at coordinated advertising.

The End of *Ben-Hur, in Tableaux and Pantomime*
It is not known if Wallace thought the current presentations of the *Ben-Hur, in Tableaux and Pantomime* strayed too far from the original concept, but

Wallace did, at least for the Milwaukee performances in November, 1893, demand that a $25,000 bond be put up to ensure that "a certain standard" would be maintained and "not descend to ordinary drama."[186] One week before the performances began, Clark included in his newspaper pre-publicity an uncharacteristic statement in affirming Wallace's original concept:

> This famous production, which is under the management of W. C. Clark, was prepared specifically for Messrs. Clark & Cox by Gen. Lew Wallace, and is an adequate expression on this stage of the author's famous story, which is portrayed in a most picturesque manner, not a line of dialogue being spoken, pantomime being the only vehicle of expression used.[187]

In another diversion from the original concept, Clark did not always book with charitable organizations, as the newspaper and ephemeral records suggest. This may have provided for Wallace the 6 percent royalty instead of the usual 5 percent, but it is very doubtful that this had a significant influence on him. He did not need the money any longer. He was probably more interested in protecting himself from damages.

Consider the following. Clark informed *The Milwaukee Journal* in the fall of 1893 that there had been performances in seventy-five cities previously, and a February, 1897, letter from Clark to Wallace tallies up Wallace's royalty earnings of $38.50 for just one city, that is, the four performances at Buffalo's Star Theatre on February 18–20, including a matinee.[188] But this kind of royalty income, even if this payment for a few days is extrapolated into months and years, paled in comparison to the royalties Harper was obligated to pay for the initial sales of *The Prince of India*. As the reader knows, that extraordinary contract, negotiated in January, 1893, months before the Milwaukee performances, entitled Wallace to the unheard of royalty of 30 percent. Simply put, Clark's operation was now only a small source of income for Lew Wallace.

In addition, Wallace had in retrospect grown increasingly dissatisfied with the production, although he expressed this only after he determined to shut it down. At that point he wrote to Harper & Brothers:

> My own opinion is that Mr. Clark's shows are so shorn of effect and interlarded with inconsistencies with the book, such as dancing and feminine drills and butterfly performances generally, intermixed with inferior scenery and untrained characterizations, that the book must suffer.[189]

As we will detail in a subsequent chapter, on April 11, 1899, Wallace and Harper signed an agreement with the firm of Klaw & Erlanger to produce a Broadway-sized dramatization of *Ben-Hur: A Tale of the Christ*.[190] The producers issued a public statement from Crawfordsville on April 16, and the dispatch was published from coast to coast over the next two days.[191] In Washington, Chicago and elsewhere, this was front-page news.

> "Ben-Hur" is to be dramatized under the supervision of Klaw and Erlanger, with the consent of Gen. Lew Wallace. The author made this statement here tonight,

with the accompanying assertion that the religious features of his famous book will be carefully safeguarded when it is rendered on the stage.[192]

In some versions Wallace was quoted as saying:

> Yes, I have acceded to the request of Klaw & Erlanger. Their design of production was altogether new and attracted me at once. The dignity of the story, as I conceive it, was carefully preserved and due regard shown to religious opinion of all who might attend the performance.[193]

Clark had recently finished a four-performance appearance in Wilkes-Barre, Pennsylvania.[194] Saying he had read the press release in the *New York Herald*, he wrote Wallace the next day to ask if this would abrogate the contract for the "Tableaux and Pantomime," pointing out that he had already signed two contracts for the following fall.[195] Wallace replied on April 20, confirming the arrangement with Klaw & Erlanger, prohibiting any additional contracts, and disallowing any performances after June 1, the traditional end of the theater season. He also reminded Clark of his "repeated declarations in letters of an intention to go out of the Ben-Hur business."[196] Clark did not protest the decision, admitting in his return letter that "the territory for the production of the Pantomime of 'Ben-Hur' is about worked out, although I could have worked it one more season with profit."[197] Just two months earlier, the *Elmira Advertiser* had printed this notice:

> If the managers of "Ben Hur" continued the entertainment for another week, a couple of more opera houses would have to be obtained and thrown into one to hold the crowd.[198]

We cannot determine, however, if this might have been fabricated simply to sell tickets.

In the letter, Clark also expresses his hope and expectations that the dramatization will succeed, and he adds some advice:

> I hope you will pardon me for saying that all references to "The Christ" must be omitted. I have been among the people and know what they feel and think about it.

This is the only advice Clark gives Wallace after so many years in "the Ben-Hur business." Such a statement from a theatrical manager who had traveled to so many municipalities in a number of states and worked with a variety of theater managers, newspaper representatives, and community members should remind the reader that the environment in which Wallace's novel and now its artistic scions flourished had not changed in this regard. And it would not change until the next decade, when first in Europe and then in the United States Jesus began to appear in popular films. But before that barrier was overcome, the Klaw & Erlanger *Ben-Hur* had already become a very successful enterprise without portraying Jesus on stage.

Just after sending Clark his response on April 20, Wallace also wrote

Harper, forwarding them both letters, and putting the matter of closing down the *Ben-Hur, in Tableaux and Pantomime* under their control. Even though he said that "I do not think Mr. Clark will make trouble," he suggested that Harper write to Clark and exercise the aforementioned clause in the initial contract:

> You can write him that having become satisfied that the Tableaux as given by him is hurtful to the book you have decided to terminate his contract.[199]

Harper did just this on April 24, and at least one report said "it is likely that action will be taken by Klaw & Erlanger" because of the "copyright question involved."[200] But further legal action was not necessary. After performances in Newburgh, New York, in late April and Middletown, Danbury, and Hartford in mid-May, *Ben-Hur, in Tableaux and Pantomime* went dark forever.[201]

EVELYN GURLEY-KANE'S *BEN HUR*

Ben-Hur mania was far from spent. The steady stream of lectures and readings, church sermons, tableaux entertainments, Christmas pageants, monologues, and the like continued on into the new century, as in the "very talented" Miss Blegart's 1899 "dramatization of . . . Ben Hur given by herself in monologue" in Des Moines.[202] These included the New York and New Jersey presentations of "An Evening With Ben Hur" by Saidee Vere Milne, who wore a "Greek gown" during her presentations.[203] She gave one or two at Mohonk Mountain House between October, 1900, and November, 1901, and another at the Waldorf in January, 1901.[204] A decade later in 1911, she performed her monologue at a smaller venue – the Carroll Robbins School in Trenton, and this included an excerpt called "A Mother's Inspiration."[205] The "illustrated recital" given by the Rudisill Concert Company in Dallas employed "its own electrical devices and stage setting" representing Sheik Ilderim's tent.[206] Otherwise they focused on the Wise Men episode, the song of Iras, and then the chariot race. After the race was won, a violinist then "picks up the story."

The most prominent of the later *Ben-Hur* adaptations were Evelyn Gurley-Kane's recitals at Washington's New Willard Hotel beginning with the May 9, 1912, benefit for "the nation's memorial monument to the Titanic dead," and again on February 17, 1914.[207] Even more so than Bradford, Gurley-Kane was at home in the nation's capital as the niece of the former chaplain of the U. S. Senate, whose Presbyterian church had been regularly attended by Abraham Lincoln.[208] Both performances were well attended by Washington society and military brass, and for the second performance she extended special invitations to President Wilson and family, members of the diplomatic corps, and members of the cabinet with their wives and daughters.[209] Her program synthesized American and Christian values:

Down the ages America became the home for those seeking freedom for religious worship. People from many lands have come to the homeland of America. Our Government is based upon the great principles taught by the beautiful Child born in Bethlehem of Judea.[210]

Gurley-Kane had premiered her *Ben-Hur* adaptation four years earlier. She begins to appear on the record in 1902, when she alternated with Samuel Siegel, a mandolin specialist, in reading several passages from *Quo Vadis* just after – we take notice – Siegel's performance of the "Ben Hur Chariot Race March," arranged by J. W. Allen.[211] By 1908 she was being managed by W. L. Bush of Chicago's Bush Temple of Music Lyceum and had introduced her *Ben Hur*, accompanied by orchestra, in Iowa.[212] Between her Washington performances she repeated the program at Wilson College during the presidency of Anna J. McKeag and then moved on to New York and Boston, and she opened the "brilliant social season" in Fall River, with the governor as the invited guest of honor.[213] She also made a notable appearance in Gettysburg in July 12, 1913, with a number of military present as well as Washington "motor parties" who drove over for the performance, reported to be "one of the best monologue entertainments ever attended."[214] She reprised her performance, enhanced by lighting effects and accompanied by small orchestra and organ, for the San Francisco Panama-Pacific Exposition in 1915.[215]

The program for the August 20, 1909, Iowa performance prints in quotations:

> Evelyn Gurley-Kane is a master of the Dramatic Art on the platform and thrills her hearers by her magnetic voice and her gift of portrayal of this matchless story by General Wallace.

She created her own style of recitation. The *Cedar Rapids Evening Gazette* wrote that she adapted the story "into a little play in which she herself takes all the parts":

> Mrs. Gurley-Kane is something entirely different from the "reader" or "elocutionist." Her entertainment includes so much of acting and her representation of so many characters reveals much more than the gift of reading.[216]

Her programs continue this illusion, some devoting an entire page to the "Cast of Characters," consisting of the Shepherds of Judea, Tirzah, Ben Hur, Messala, Captain of Soldiers, Rabbi Joseph, Decurion, Quintus Arrius, Hortator, Simonides, Esther, Malluch, Drusus, Flavius, Iras, a Tribune, Gesius, and the Widow of the Prince of Hur. The entire performance was accompanied by music. Indeed, the Washington performances were accompanied by the U. S. Marine Band.

The performance began with the Annunciation, or "The Prayer in the Desert," which the current chaplain of the Senate delivered in at least one Washington performance. There followed four acts, including Tirzah singing on the Roof Garden of the House of Hur (I), two scenes involving the galley and the rescue of Arrius (II), the initial meeting with Simonides, Messala's revelry, and the Chariot Race (III), and the Release of Prisoners, Healing of Mother and Sister, and Reuniting of the Family, concluding with "Holy. Holy. Holy." (IV). The Washington performances began with introductions by distinguished members of Congress and a tribute to the late General Wallace, whereupon Gurley-Kane entertained the distinguished audience with the assistance of not just the Marine Band but also a chorus of nine women.[217]

Two years later, Jane Taylor Miller published *The Christmas Story: A Group of Tableaux* with the National Board of the Y.W.C.A.[218] She explains in the preface that "The Christmas Story" was adapted from Book First of *Ben-Hur: A Tale of the Christ* and presented "in one of the large southern colleges for women." She was encouraged to publish the libretto because some of the audience thought it could be adapted for the regular Sunday school observance of Christmas and, through repetition, make the familiar story of the advent of the Christ child "more real and potent." The tableaux are structured in six scenes, each following a substantial but edited excerpt from the novel, with no copyright license mentioned in the prefatory material, nor even Lew Wallace's name. Each tableau is accompanied by a two-stanza rhyming chorus and very detailed stage instructions of the sort we wish we had for the Clark & Cox representations:

> STAGE DIRECTIONS FOR SCENE III
> Half way down the stage a screen, five or six feet high, runs straight across. In front of it, to the left, is the shepherds' fire.
> The six shepherds are seated or lying about the fire. Three on the left might be reclining. All faces are turned toward Gabriel and their hands are held up in fear. Let the three on the right hold their crooks aloft.
> The watchman, in costume like his fellows, stands just in front of the shepherds at the right. In place of a crook he has a heavy staff, which he holds up.
> Gabriel stands in center waist high above the screen. In his right hand is a silver wand, surmounted by a star.
> Six other angels are grouped back of Gabriel, making a double line to the right, the second two a little higher than the first, the last two still higher. They stand with arms outstretched toward the men.
> Six other angels stand at right on the floor before the screen.[219]

Her guidelines seem similar to Bradford's directions in several details. For instance, she recommends in the Appendix that the reader, who is "the voice of the whole," should sit at a desk placed to the side of the stage.[220] Further on she recommends that the time for holding each tableau should be from one and one-half to two minutes, so long as the chorus lasts: "This will not be difficult since the poses are all natural and easy." She even specifies why just two rehearsals are sufficient. The first is to learn the poses and stage positions, the second, a dress rehearsal, so that the posers can hear the readings and "catch the spirit of the characters." Lastly, she offers some advice about casting:

For the choice of characters careful selection should be made. Not one girl in fifty will be able to portray Mary. Herod should be chosen with the idea that anyone who sees him will recognize him as a Herod.[221]

Indeed, for the 1925 MGM film hundreds of women were interviewed or tested for the role of Mary.

There was limited carry-over in the next few years, whether in the United States or abroad. The subsequent record includes "'The Christmas Story,' taken from Ben Hur" performed in Salisbury, North Carolina, in 1923,[222] and the National Library of the Netherlands website (Delpher) lists a Ben-Hur pageant for Christmas, 1914.[223] And, although it was not for general public consumption, the approximately hundred thousand men and women who joined the Tribe of Ben-Hur over the next few decades performed an initiation ritual that was very much like a reading with pantomime, as we will see in the chapter on commerce. Nonetheless, the heyday of the *Ben-Hur* stage tableaux had passed and would soon give way to genuine drama and then moving pictures.

NOTES

1. Letter from Lawrence Barrett to Wallace (August 31, 1882), IHS.
2. McKee 130 and 175.
3. *An Autobiography* 1001.
4. Letter from Alexander Salvini to Wallace (May 31, 1895); Letter from W. M. Wilkinson to Wallace (August 30, 1895), LL.
5. M&M 453–6; Morsberger and Morsberger, "'Christ and a Horse-Race'," 489–92; Lighty, *The Fall and Rise of Lew Wallace*, 79–81; Preston and Mayer, *Playing Out the Empire*, 191; and McKee 175–6.
6. Russo & Sullivan 327.
7. Letter from Josef J. Reinisch to Wallace (January 21, 1895), LL.
8. Letter from W. W. Allen to Wallace (October 26, 1898), LL.
9. Letter from Harper & Brothers to Mrs. Albert W. Berg (February 13, 1889), LL; Morsberger and Morsberger, "'Christ and a Horse-Race,'" 490.
10. *The Churchman* 88 (July 4, 1903) 17; *Woman's Who's Who of America, 1914–1915*, 96.
11. Henderson, *The City and the Theatre*, 134–5. This theater at Broadway and 30th Street was otherwise known as [Lester] Wallacks' Theatre but currently was leased to Albert M. Palmer.
12. Letter from Wallace to Ruford Brauer (April 11, 1896), LL; M&M 454–5.
13. *NYT* (March 12, 1889) 1.
14. Letter from Wallace to W. W. Allen (November 15, 1898), LL.
15. *WP* (December 7, 1890) 13.
16. *WP* (August 8, 1899) 10.
17. E.g. *The Century Magazine* 48 (June, 1894) 217; "I Come, O Blessed Lord, to Thee," in Sankey, et al., *Christian Endeavor Edition of Sacred Songs*, 92 [#83].
18. *WP* (December 7, 1890) 13.

19 *DFP* (May 16, 1891) 5.
20 Ibid., 5; cf. *Boston Daily Advertiser* (February 28, 1889) 8; *Boston Daily Advertiser* (May 3, 1890) 4
21 E.g. *The Vermont Watchman* (October 24, 1888) #43; cf. *The Atchison Daily Globe* (April 24, 1889) 4.
22 *The Vermont Watchman* (October 24, 1888) #43; *Atchison Daily Champion* (April 21, 1889) 4; *The [Raleigh] News and Observer* (February 24, 1892) 1.
23 *PI* (April 23, 1890) 4; (January 24, 1891) 3.
24 *BG* (February 28, 1889) 2: the business was managed by Boston's Merton [E.] Shedd and A. K. Young.
25 *BE* (May 1, 1890) 1; *Boston Daily Advertiser* (May 3, 1890) 4.
26 *TBS* (March 9, 1889) 4.
27 *StLPD* (April 5, 1889) 4.
28 *DFP* (May 19, 1891) 7.
29 *WP* (April 18, 1890) 4; (April 14, 1890) 4; cf. *AC* (June 8, 1890) 15.
30 *The Original Evening With Ben-Hur*, program for April 17 and 18 [1890]. Performing Arts Library, New York Public Library.
31 *TBS* (March 9, 1889) 4.
32 Ellen Knight Bradford, *Selections from 'Ben-Hur' – Adapted for Readings with Tableaux* (Washington, DC: n.p., 1887). The name "Susan Wallace" is written on it but not in her own hand.
33 *The Hartford Courant* (April 28, 1888) 8; *The Congregationalist* (May 3, 1888) 4.
34 *WP* (April 18, 1890) 4; *Iowa State Reporter* (April 4, 1889) 1, reports that this was read before "a scenic picture by [George] Clausen, the British artist."
35 *BE* (May 1, 1890) 1.
36 Bradford's libretto adds (32) "Orchestra" after Judah's mother and daughter are released from prison and then "Stop Orchestra" when Judah recognizes Amrah (34). There may have been more information in Bradford's *Directions for Preparatory Work and Materials Needed for Producing the "Ben-Hur" Tableaux* (Washington, DC: R. H. Darby, 1888), and *Directions for Producing "Ben-Hur" Tableaux* (Washington, DC: R. H. Darby, 1889), but the only catalogued copies are reported as "lost" by the Library of Congress.
37 *WP* (December 12, 1890) 8.
38 *BE* (May 1, 1890) 1.
39 *TBS* (March 6, 1889) 6; *The North American* (April 17, 1890) 4.
40 *BG* (February 28, 1889) 2.
41 *The Hartford Courant* (April 28, 1888) 8.
42 *DFP* (May 19, 1891) 7, reports that some of the noise backstage between acts interrupted her several times.
43 *PI* (January 24, 1891) 3; *AC* (June 6, 1890) 5. McKee 175, seems to conflated her work with Louisville's 1890 "Satellites" celebration (below).
44 *The [Raleigh] News and Observer* (February 27, 1892) 1.
45 *StLPD* (March 24, 1889) 21; *The [Raleigh] News and Observer* (March 1, 1892) 1.
46 *BE* (March 27, 1890) 1.

47 *BG* (February 28, 1889) 2. Cf. "the most beautiful society girls" in *BE* (March 27, 1890) 1.
48 *WP* (April 18, 1890) 4.
49 E.g. *BE* (April 27, 1890) 3; *The Vermont Watchman* (October 17, 1888) [#42]; *The [Raleigh] News and Observer* (February 25, 1892) 1.
50 *AC* (June 6, 1890) 5.
51 *WP* (December 12, 1890) 8.
52 *BE* (April 27, 1890) 2.
53 *CT* (December 17, 1887) 6. The church was the Trinity Methodist Church.
54 *The Milwaukee Sentinel* (April 7, 1889) 11.
55 *The Richmond Dispatch* (April 12, 1888) 1.
56 *The Vermont Watchman* (October 3, 1888) #40.
57 *Indianapolis Press* (May 13, 1888) 3; Letter from Wallace to Harper & Brothers (June 27, 1888), UVA.
58 *Indianapolis Sun* (May 28, 1888) 4.
59 Letter from Harper & Brothers to Wallace (January 29, 1889), LL.
60 *TBS* (March 6, 1889) 6.
61 *The News and Observer* (February 17, 1892) 1. Because of the more relaxed schedule in 1892, Bradford consented to an encore Raleigh performance at reduced rates.
62 Letter from Harper & Brothers to Wallace (August 7, 1889), LL.
63 *The Daily Inter Ocean* (January 1, 1888) 14.
64 *Logansport Journal* (November 21, 1888) 8.
65 *Logansport Journal* (November 21, 1888) 8.
66 *The Galveston Daily News* (April 24, 1892) 2.
67 *The St. Paul Globe* (July 26, 1896) 9.
68 The program, in the possession of the author, is unprovenienced. Cf. an amateur production by The King's Daughters in Pottsville, Pennsylvania listed in *PI* (January 29, 1899) 12.
69 *Oakland Daily Evening Tribune* (October 9, 1894) 5.
70 *Oakland Daily Evening Tribune* (October 12, 1894) 6.
71 *Oakland Tribune* (November 10, 1894) 8.
72 *Oakland Daily Evening Tribune* (October 12, 1894) 6.
73 *The Fort Wayne Sentinel* (May 13, 1889) 3; *Bangor Daily Whig and Courier* (May 14, 1889) 2.
74 *PI* (November 17, 1888) 3.
75 *HW* (October 11, 1890) 794.
76 *Frank Leslie's Illustrated Newspaper* (October 11, 1890) 172–5, with illustrations.
77 *HW* (October 11, 1890) cover and 794.
78 *StLPD* (October 4, 1891) 25, which includes two illustrations of the Wallace floats. The text is confused in labeling Messala a Christian.
79 Reply from Harper & Brothers, April 11, 1899, BL.
80 Gen. Lew Wallace, *Life of Gen. Ben Harrison* (New York: W. A. Houghton, 1888) 6.
81 M&M 372.
82 *CJ* (November 8, 1888) 4.

83 *Winchester [IN] Journal* (July 4, 1888) 5.
84 *Logansport [IN] Journal* (November 14, 1888) 3; *CJ* (November 17, 1888) 4; Caldwell, *The Golden Age of Indianapolis Theaters*, 67.
85 *Logansport [IN] Journal* (November 21, 1888) 8.
86 *NYT* (September 30, 1942) 23. There is scant evidence about Clark's background, but the 1880 United States Census online includes a Walter C. Clark from Pewaukee, born in c. 1854, who listed his occupation as "singer."
87 *The [Benton Harbor] News-Palladium* (September 29, 1942) 1 and 3.
88 Dunn, *Indiana and Indianans*, 5:2206–8.
89 *The Rocky Mountain News* (May 6, 1894) 12.
90 Ibid., 2206.
91 *The [Benton Harbor] News-Palladium* (September 29, 1942) 3; *The Ottawa Journal* (November 12, 1896) 7.
92 *CJ* (November 9, 1888) 4; (November 10, 1888) 4; (November 17, 1888) 4.
93 *CJ* (December 5, 1888) 4. For Watson, see *The Crawfordsville Star* (August 14, 1884) 1.
94 Reprinted in *Morning Oregonian* (January 11, 1889) 7.
95 E.g. *CJ* (December 5, 1888) 4.
96 *CJ* (December 15, 1888) 4; (December 19, 1888) 4.
97 Ibid., 4.
98 *CJ* (December 18, 1888) 4.
99 *The Morning Oregonian* (January 11, 1889) 7.
100 According to Bartlett, *An Evening of Statuary and Tableaux*, 11–12, those representing statuary should be dressed mostly in white cotton, their eyes should remain closed, the background should be draped in white, and "a good effect is produced by showing them first on a dark stage, and turning on the gas very slowly until it is quite light. They come out very strongly under this treatment."
101 For a preannouncement of the live horses, see *CJ* (December 15, 1888) 4.
102 *CJ* (December 18, 1888) 4.
103 E.g. *CJ* (December 24, 1888) 4.
104 *CJ* (November 8, 1888) 4.
105 *CJ* (November 15, 1888) 4; November 20, 1888) 4.
106 E.g. *NYT* (December 24, 1888) 3.
107 *Elkhart Daily Review* (May 13, 1889) 2.
108 *CJ* (December 8, 1888) 4.
109 *CJ* (December 19, 1888) 4.
110 Russo and Sullivan 327.
111 *Logansport Pharos Tribune* (January 30, 1889) 3.
112 *CJ* (November 4, 1890) 4.
113 <http://www.loc.gov/resource/rbc.2012gen23734/?sp=7>
114 In the Consent to Transfer, April 1, 1889, LL, Wallace gives written consent to have Harry Pontious, also of Crawfordsville, replace Albert Miller.
115 Contract (January 15, 1889), LL.
116 Reply by Harper & Brothers (April 11, 1899); Contract for Theatrical Version of his *Ben Hur* (February 14, 1889), BL; Letter from Harper to Wallace (February 14, 1889), IL. Glued onto the back of a handwritten version of

this February 14 document was a copy of the *New York Times* review of the Palmer's Theatre presentation.
117 Patent Number 349526, issued September 21, 1886; *AC* (July 21, 1891) 6; and *Oshkosh Daily Northwestern* (November 4, 1893) 1.
118 *Oshkosh Daily Northwestern* (November 4, 1893) 1.
119 *Cleveland Leader* (April 27, 1896) 12.
120 *The World* (March 15, 1889) 10; cf. Iliff, *The Lost Tribe of Ben-Hur*, 16, reports that fifty members of the (as yet unformed) Tribe of Ben-Hur were in attendance.
121 *New York Daily Mirror* (March 23, 1889) 1.
122 *The Evening World* (May 9, 1889) 2.
123 *The Evening World* (May 18, 1889) 3; *StLPD* (May 17, 1889) 9.
124 Letter from Wallace to Zara McCosh (January 31, 1889), LL.
125 Letter from Wallace to Major Pond (July 8, 1895), IHS.
126 *NYT* (March 15, 1889) 4.
127 *Hamilton [OH] Daily Democrat* (March 21, 1889) 3.
128 *Cedar Rapids Evening Gazette* (April 20, 1889) 4.
129 *Cincinnati Enquirer* (April 9, 1889) 5; *Miami Helmet* (May 9, 1889) 5; *Piqua Daily Call* (May 4, 1889) 1; *Lima Daily Times* (May 8, 1889) 4; Program for May 2, 1889, in the possession of the author.
130 *The Daily Inter Ocean* (July 21, 1889) 12.
131 Stanton, et al., *History of Woman Suffrage*, 6:541. The co-authored novel is *Koradine: A Prophetic Story* (Chicago: Alice B. Stockham, 1893).
132 *The Daily Inter Ocean* (July 21, 1889) 12.
133 *Hamilton Daily Democrat* (March 20, 1889) 3.
134 *Cincinnati Enquirer* (April 11, 1889) 8. Cf. *Miami Helmet* (May 9, 1889) 5.
135 *The Daily Inter Ocean* (July 21, 1889) 12.
136 *Hamilton Daily Democrat* (March 20, 1889) 3.
137 *Miami Helmet* (May 9, 1889) 5.
138 *Hamilton [OH] Daily Democrat* (March 21, 1889) 3.
139 *Cincinnati Enquirer* (April 11, 1889) 8.
140 *Piqua Miami Herald* (May 2, 1889) 5.
141 *Piqua Miami Herald* (May 2, 1889) 5.
142 *Hamilton Daily Democrat* (March 21, 1889) 3.
143 Ibid., 3; *Lima Daily Times* (May 9, 1889) 4.
144 *The Writer* 17 (May, 1905) 107–8.
145 *The Daily Inter Ocean* (July 21, 1889) 12; cf. *Middletown [NY] Daily Argus* (December 19, 1895) 8.
146 *Miami Helmet* (May 9, 1889) 5.
147 *The Chautauquan* 10 (March, 1890) 768.
148 <http://laserweb.redondo.org/WebLink/0/doc/21698/Page74.aspx>
149 *The Los Angeles Herald* (August 3, 1890) 5.
150 *LAT* (August 3, 1890) 6; (November 4, 1891) 8.
151 *LAT* (August 2, 1890) 4.
152 *The [Ann Arbor] Chronicle-Argonaut* (January 17, 1891) 153; *Indiana Evening Gazette* (March 21, 1933) 6.
153 *Pittsburgh Dispatch* (August 8, 1890) 4.

154 *Pittsburg Dispatch* (August 9, 1890) 5.
155 *AC* (July 19, 1891) 2.
156 *AC* (July 12, 1891) 18.
157 *AC* (July 19, 1891) 2; (July 22, 1891) 2.
158 Letter from Mary Bonsall to Wallace, September 13, 1890, LL.
159 *The Public School Journal* 9 (May, 1890) 448; *Cincinnati Enquirer* (November 9, 1890) 18.
160 <http://sdrcdata.lib.uiowa.edu/libsdrc/details.jsp?id=/benhur/1&page=1>
161 Agreement between Harper & Brothers and Wallace for *Ben-Hur in Tableaux and Pantomime* (September 25, 1890); Copyright Deposit (September 27, 1890), LL.
162 There is a copy in the Special Collections at the Regenstein Library, University of Chicago.
163 Agreement (March 19, 1891); and Letter from W. C. Clark to Wallace (October 2, 1894), LL; Contract (April 16, 1891), BL.
164 Program for *Ben-Hur* at Bleecker Hall, Albany, January 19–23, 1892, in the possession of the author.
165 Letter from Walter C. Clark to Wallace (October 2, 1894), LL;
166 The program for the Corry, Pennsylvania, performances of November 13–15, 1895, does not include the usual copyright statement but reverts instead to a simple printing of the copyrights of the novel and libretto, as stipulated in the April 16, 1891, agreement.
167 Contracts for Buffalo Star Theatre (December 16, 1897), LL.
168 Program (March 16–17, 1899) at Pottstown, Pennsylvania.
169 *Amsterdam Daily Democrat* (May 9, 1894) n.p. Cast lists include also pairs or trios of chaperones for all the groups of young women.
170 *The Wichita Daily Eagle* (January 12, 1893) 5.
171 *The Wichita Daily Eagle* (January 12, 1893) 5.
172 *The Milwaukee Journal* (November 19, 1893) 1.
173 *MS* (November 24, 18 93) 3.
174 The January 19–23, 1892 Albany program inserts the lyrics to Tirzah's song "Wake not, but hear me, love!" within the synopsis for Iras's song; cf. *Mitchell [North Dakota] Daily Republican* (October 6, 1886) 4.
175 *The Milwaukee Journal* (November 19, 1893) 1.
176 The January 19–23, 1892, Albany program, in the possession of the author; C. Lance Brockman, "Creating Scenic Illusions for the Theatre and the Fraternity," in Brockman, ed., *Theatre of the Fraternity*, 93–109.
177 The December 26–30, 1894 Grand Rapids program, in the possession of the author.
178 *Oshkosh Daily Northwestern* (November 7, 1893) 8.
179 *Oshkosh Daily Northwestern* (November 7, 1893) 8.
180 *Decatur Daily Review* (April 21, 1893) 3.
181 *Amsterdam Daily Democrat* (Maya 8, 1894) n.p.
182 The May 2, 1889, program was sponsored by the Manhattan One Price Clothing Company of St. Paul; *St. Paul Daily Globe* (April 18, 1888) 8.
183 Cf. *Goshen [IN] Democrat* (June 23, 1880) 2.
184 *Warren [Ohio] Ledger* (December 4, 1891) 12.

185 *AC* (April 22, 1898) 10.
186 *The Milwaukee Journal* (November 17, 1893) 2.
187 *Oshkosh Daily Northwestern* (November 4, 1893) 1.
188 *The Milwaukee Journal* (October 10, 1893) 1; Letter from Walter C. Clark to Wallace (February 22, 1897), and Receipts (February 18–20, 1897), LL. These performances drew audiences of 494, 636, 530, and 721 patrons, most of them paying fifty cents to one dollar, some paying two dollars for a box seat.
189 Letter from Wallace to Harper & Brothers (April 7, 1899), LL.
190 Contract between Wallace, Harper, and Klaw & Erlanger (April 11, 1899), BL.
191 *New York Herald* (April 17 1899) 5.
192 E.g. *WP* (April 17, 1899) 1; *CT* (April 17, 1899) 1; *[San Jose CA] Evening News* (April 17, 1899) 1.
193 *LAT* (April 17, 1899) 1 and 2.
194 *Wilkes-Barre Weekly Times* (April 7, 1899) 6.
195 Letter from W. C. Clark to Wallace (April 19, 1899), BL. Cf. *New York World* (April 18, 1899) 9; *Middletown [NY] Daily Argus* (April 11, 1899) 1.
196 Letter from Wallace to Walter C. Clark (April 20, 1899), BL. The previous autumn Clark had pleaded with Wallace, who was threatening to abrogate the contract, to grant him a personal interview to explain several "unfortunate circumstances." Cf. Letter from Walter C. Clark to Wallace (September 26, 1898); Letter from Wallace to Clark (October 1, 1898), LL.
197 Letter from W. C. Clark to Wallace (April 23, 1899), BL.
198 *Harrisburg [PA] Telegraph* (February 1, 1899) 2.
199 Letter from Wallace to Harper (April 20, 1899), BL.
200 *Bangor Daily Whig & Courier* (May 1, 1899) 6.
201 Letter from Harper to Walter C. Clark (April 24, 1899); *Middletown [NY] Daily Argus* (April 11, 1899) 1; *The Hartford Courant* (May 12, 1899) 10.
202 *Des Moines Daily News* (January 20, 1899) 4.
203 Letter from Saidee Vere Milne to Alfred Smiley (May 25, 1901), personal collection of the author, found by Diane DeBlois.
204 *Columbus Daily Enquirer* (January 6, 1901) 10.
205 *Trenton Evening Times* (March 27, 1911) 10.
206 *Dallas Morning News* (November 13, 1904) 7.
207 *WP* (May 10, 1912) 5; (February 18, 1914) 2.
208 *WP* (January 30, 1914) 4; Barbee, "President Lincoln and Doctor Gurley," 3–5.
209 *WP* (February 7, 1914) 7.
210 Program for *Ben Hur: The Noted Gurley-Kane Arrangement* (February 11, 1919), LoC.
211 *Cedar Rapids Evening Gazette* (April 1, 1902) 4.
212 Program for "Evelyn Gurley-Kane in General Lew Wallace's Play *Ben Hur*," August 20, 1909, University of Iowa, Special Collections; *Cedar Rapids Evening Gazette* (August 27, 1909) 7; cf. *Monroe [Missouri] City Democrat* (July 15, 1909) 1.
213 *WP* (September 24, 1913) 7.
214 *Adams County News* (July 12, 1913) 1; *The Gettysburg News* (July 23, 1913) 2.

215 *SFC* (March 28, 1915) A3; (April 8, 1915) 5. Cf. *The Washington Times* (February 17, 1914) 5.
216 *Cedar Rapids Evening Gazette* (August 27, 1909) 7.
217 *WP* (February 18, 1914) 2.
218 Miller, *The Christmas Story*.
219 Miller, *The Christmas Story*, 30.
220 Miller, *The Christmas Story*, 31.
221 Ibid., 31.
222 *Luther League Review* 35 (March, 1923) 33.
223 *Nieuwe Tilburgsche Courant* (January 9, 1914) 3.

8 Ben-Hur *in Song and Instrumental Music*

The concentrated burst of enthusiasm for *Ben-Hur: A Tale of the Christ* in the mid-1880s inspired a number of songs and musical compositions that belonged to a spectrum of musical genres and were played or performed in a wide range of venues.[1] The reader may be surprised to learn that the initial musical forays were almost all in the field of the classical art-song. Some of America's most respected late nineteenth-century composers set lyrics that Wallace had included within his novel. John Philip Sousa, who was equally respected but composed popular music, was inspired by Wallace's chariot race to compose a descriptive piece for his band. Then, less surprisingly, a lowbrow but particularly energetic and cleverly marketed creation caught a wave of popularity and cashed in on perfect timing. E. T. Paull's "The Chariot Race or Ben Hur March" not only sold well as sheet music but proliferated in all the newly invented means of automatic mechanical and recorded music. Like Wallace's novel, the piece became an early icon of popularity and played a lasting role in the development of commercially popular music at the turn of the century. This chapter will examine most of the published pieces of music that were inspired by Wallace's novel from the late 1880s into the third decade of the twentieth century. It will not include the music written for dramatic renderings of the novel in public recitations or for the Clark & Cox *Ben-Hur, in Tableaux and Pantomime*, none of which seems to have been published separately or survives in manuscript format. Nor will it include the music for the Klaw & Erlanger production or the two MGM films, which were published separately and will be treated in subsequent chapters.

CLASSICAL ART-SONGS AND PARLOR SONGS

The earliest published work inspired by *Ben-Hur: A Tale of the Christ* was George L. Osgood's 1886 setting of "Wake not, but hear me, Love," not performed publicly until 1895.[2] The words for his text are the first of three lyric passages in the novel. It occurs near the beginning of the central story

(2.6), where Wallace introduces Judah's sister Tirzah. It brings to conclusion a peaceful moment – the last one before catastrophe strikes. Judah has had his quarrel with Messala and then asked his mother's permission to become a soldier in the service of the Lord against Rome. The direction of the teenager's life now determined in one emotional afternoon, Judah falls asleep after all the turmoil, and as we wakes he sees the sun in the sky, the gleaming wings of birds, and the golden temple in the distance. In this somewhat dreamy state he hears his younger sister, "scarcely fifteen," playing a *nebel* resting on her knee and singing, as Wallace designates it, "THE SONG":

> "Wake not, but hear me, love!
>   Adrift, adrift on slumber's sea,
>   Thy spirit call to list to me.
> Wake not, but hear me, love!
>   A gift from Sleep, the restful king,
>   All happy, happy dreams I bring.
>
> "Wake not, but hear me, love!
>   Of all the world of dreams 'tis thine
>   This once to choose the most divine.
> So choose, and sleep, my love!
>   But ne'er again in choice be free,
>   Unless, unless – thou dream'st of me."

Wallace wrote much more poetry than he ever published, particularly in his youth, but some of it was to be used for song lyrics. The reader may recall, for instance, that while encamped in Cincinnati in 1863, Wallace was challenged by some of the city's artistic elite to compose a ballad "suited for the camp." The result was "The Stolen Stars; an Hysterical Ballad," in fifteen eight-line stanzas. This ballad was soon published on the cover of *Harper's Weekly*, issued as a broadside "dedicated to the soldiers of the union," and then rendered as the lyrics of the song "The Stolen Stars; or, Good old Father Washington," with music adapted and arranged by R. Hastings and published by A. C. Peters & Brothers in Cincinnati.[3] In his novels, other than the three lyrical segments inserted into *Ben-Hur: A Tale of the Christ*, he inserted only one poem in *The Fair God*, a single stanza of a Spanish ballad.[4]

Charles Laurie Osgood represents the quintessential American art-song composer of the 1880s in that he was American born, European trained, and then found teaching positions in the United States while adapting contemporary classical style to American taste. He was born in Chelsea, Massachusetts, into a colonial-era Puritan family, graduated from Harvard in 1866, and then traveled to Germany. There, in Berlin and Halle, he studied for over two years under some of the most prominent teachers of the period, particularly composition with Karl August Haupt and art-song [lieder] with Robert Franz, and then studied voice for two additional years in Milan with Francesco Lamperti. Performing as a tenor, he toured central Europe in 1871 before returning to the United States where he toured with the highly respected Theodore Thomas, later the founder of the Chicago Symphony Orchestra. He then became established in Boston as a teacher and director/conductor of the acclaimed vocal choir known as the Boylston Club, and in 1874 he published his *Guide in the Art of Singing, Based on the Reliable Tradition of the Italian School of Vocalization and Practical Developments of Modern Science*. He composed over fifty songs, church anthems, and choruses.

With a copyright entry date of June 28, 1886, "Wake not, but hear me, Love" was published by Oliver Ditson Company of Boston in the key of A♭, "for Soprano and Tenor," F "for Alto and Baritone."[5] The cover of the six-page publication specifies, "Words from 'Ben Hur' by Lew Wallace," as does the attribution below the title on the sheet music itself, but there is no evidence of any license, or even any attempt to ask for permission, from Wallace or Harper. The copyright concerns of Wallace and Harper focused almost entirely on the sale of illegal copies of the entire novel, not musical adaptations of mere excerpts. The lyrics of the song comprise only seventy-seven words, plus repetitions, but the guideline of "Fair Use" would not yet be incorporated into United States copyright law for many decades. Osgood's copyright was renewed in 1913.[6]

The song itself is brief and simple, consisting of twenty-three measures for each of the two stanzas. Written in an elegant 9/8 and marked adagio with the vocalist encouraged to sing "tenderly," the piece begins with a melodic motif accompanied by a major arpeggio, builds in intensity to a musical climax on the last three lines of each stanza, culminating with a crescendo, rallentando, and fermata before resolving to the original motif for the last three words. The work received some high praise from Louis Elson in his comprehensive 1904 *The History of American Music*:

> Osgood is one of the finest melodists that America has ever possessed. . . . His part-song, "In Picardie," his "Wake not, but here me, Love," may be cited as examples of the sweetness which does not cloy, and which is not akin to musical vulgarity. Few composers have so tastefully united the popular and classical as this excellent musician.[7]

Of equal interest to us is that when it was published in Louis Dressler's 1897 anthology of *Favorite Masterpieces*, much more space was devoted to a biography of Lew Wallace than to Osgood.[8] It even includes a large photograph of Wallace.

The publication of a different setting of the same lyrics by E[rnest] R[ichard] Kroeger in the same year, 1886, provides further demonstration of how pivotal that year was. Contemporary with the skyrocketing sales of the novel, the licensing of *Seekers After the Light*, and Wallace's breakthrough visit to Chautauqua, now the burgeoning *Ben-Hur* phenomenon was proliferating in the musical world and inspiring different composers from different backgrounds. Kroeger's musical training and career was quite different from Osgood's. Thoroughly American, Kroeger was born, trained, and worked in St. Louis, where he served as church organist, teacher, and co-founder of the American Guild of Organists. Three of his six dozen songs were settings of lyrics written by Lew Wallace. Collected as a suite named "From the Orient," he published them with the Kunkel Bros, Charles and Jacob, who like Kroeger belonged to a German-American family. As established music publishers, they published not only new American music in sheet-music formats but also in their monthly magazine, *Kunkel's Musical Review*.[9]

The trio of works are dedicated, unofficially, "To Gen. Lew Wallace," which is printed at the top of the cover page. Below "From the Orient" are listed the three songs, "Kapila," "Wake Not," and "The Lament," "Words From Lew Wallace's 'Ben Hur.'" Again, this is probably not an attempt at claiming they had acquired a copyright license but an example of the prestige Wallace's name suggested in 1886. Also, in the publication of these art-songs it is not so much a matter of the familiarity with Wallace's name and novel, let alone the marketability they might provide, but the assumption at least by prominent members of the musical community that he had provided them with bona fide, literate American poetry. This is not so surprising for musicians from the Midwest but it is for those in New England, where Wallace was being snubbed by the Boston literati in December, 1886.

Kroeger's "Wake not," subtitled "Poem by Lew Wallace," unfolds as a lullaby in E♭ major in 6/8. Either his or Osgood's setting may have been the piece sung at a "Ben Hur" stereopticon performance in Montreal. A tantalizing piece of ephemera preserved at the University of Virginia Library is the program for the Thursday, December 5, 1889, premier at Windsor Hall, the grand venue used for some of Montreal's most illustrious events.[10] The program is marked "Opening Week," presumably of the Winter Carnival that attracted many celebrities, so this seems to have been an important booking. The last page of the bi-fold informs the audience that "Miss Tessier will sing 'Wake not, but hear me, love,' Tirzah's song in 'Ben-Hur' and other songs." As we will see repeatedly, this was not at all the only cross-referencing of Ben-Hur products in the late 1880s. Of course, because the reading was to take place in Canada, no copyright clearance or permission from Wallace or Harper was required.

The first piece in Kroeger's collection is "Kapila." Not including representations in the *Ben-Hur* tableaux of the next few years, settings of "Kapila" as an independent song seem to be a rarity. Wallace would have known of the Vedic sage Kapila from his readings about Hindu philosophy and theology, which may have included the *Bhagavata Purana*. He mentions him first in the initial speech by Melchior (1.4), and then has Iras sing a song entitled "Kapila" to Judah (5.3). She does this the day after she sang "The Lament" by the lake, which brought Book Fourth to a close (4.17), and it precedes the lengthy, six-part Egyptian story of Ne-Ne-Hofra, which is the symbolic, non-lyrical, narrative that brings the chapter in which "Kapila" is sung to a close. These elements will help redeem Iras in future representations of *Ben-Hur* in that they emphasize her characterization as an enchanting Egyptian songstress much more so that as a dangerous femme fatale and Messala's spy and agent.

Iras says she learned this song from "the daughter of the Ganga" on a street corner in Alexandria:

I.
Kapila, Kapila, so young and true,
   I yearn for a glory like thine,
And hail thee from battle to ask anew,
   Can ever thy Valor be mine?

Kapila sat on his charger dun,
   A hero never so grave:
"Who loveth all things hath fear of none,
   'Tis love that maketh me brave.
A woman gave me her soul one day,
The soul of my soul to be alway;
   Thence came my Valor to me,
   Go try it – try it – and see."
II.
Kapila, Kapila, so old and gray,
   The queen is calling for me;
But ere I go hence, I wish thou wouldst say,
   How Wisdom first came to thee.

Kapila stood in his temple door,
   A priest in eremite guise:
"It did not come as men get their lore,
   'Tis faith that maketh me wise.
A woman gave me her heart one day,
The heart of my heart to be alway;
   Thence came my Wisdom to me,
   Go try it – try it – and see."

Kroeger sets this in E minor. Without adding an introduction, he uses syncopation in the base, the overlying melody unfolding in syllabic style. Here the ascending/descending stepwise melody makes a syncopated leap from G to C to emphasize the words "young and true" and then does the same with "ask anew" in the repetition of the melody for the third and fourth lines. The effect would have seemed characteristically Eastern and mysterious in the 1880s.

Kroeger's setting of Iras's "The Lament" brings out some of the same dreamy quality infused into the lyrics of "Wake not, but hear me, Love!" but with a clear Egyptian emphasis enhanced by geographical references to Memphis, the Nile, and Simbel. The poem is found almost exactly halfway through the novel, at the end of the fourth of eight books, where Judah finds himself in a state of confusion. He has spent an entire evening listening to Balthasar's lengthy discourse on the coming of a new King of the Jews, a spiritual king of an eternal kingdom. As Judah steps out into the night and ponders the advent of a new religion, he hears the angelic singing of Iras from her small boat on a lake. Now he finds himself doubly confused, torn spiritually between his traditional Judaism and the advent of the Messiah, and romantically between the Egyptian temptress Iras and the faithful Jewess Esther.

THE LAMENT.
(Egyptian.)
I sigh as I sing for the story land
   Across the Syrian sea.
The odorous winds from the musky sand
   Were breaths of life to me.
They play with the plumes of the whispering palm
   For me, alas! no more;
Nor more does the Nile in the moonlit calm
   Moan past the Memphian shore.

O Nilus! thou god of my fainting soul!
   In dreams thou comest to me;
And, dreaming, I play with the lotus bowl,
   And sing old songs to thee;
And hear from afar the Memnonian strain,
   And calls from dear Simbel;
And wake to a passion of grief and pain
   That e'er I said – Farewell!

To convey the mood Kroeger uses the key of $F\sharp$ minor, the piano accompaniment accentuating the melody's mostly descending scalar chromatic movement. The broken chord pattern in the left hand beats out the piece's incessant 4/4 rhythm while the right glides downward with symmetric triadic structures. He prefaces the song with an eight-measure introduction broken into two parts, each of those also broken into two repeating or echoing parts. He repeats the melody of the first two lines of text for the next two, and at "They play" and the beginning of the fifth line, he uses A major to brighten the song for a few measures and then returns to the minor chromatic movement. He does not reuse the same music for the second stanza as he had for "Wake not, but hear me, love." Instead, he repeats the eight-measure introduction to separate the two and then after restating the primary melody brings the piece to its musical climax on the word "wake" in a brief excursion into D major, ultimately modulating back into $F\sharp$ minor for "I said farewell," repeating the final word two more times in another descending but diatonic pattern.

Another prominent classical composer was G. W. Chadwick, whose art-song version of "The Lament" was published in 1887.[11] His life and training parallel Osgood's in that he was born in Lowell, Massachusetts, studied in Leipzig and Dresden, and then returned to the United States to take up a position at the New England Conservatory in 1880, the year *Ben-Hur: A Tale of the Christ* was published. The careers of Chadwick and Lew Wallace were chronologically analogous also in that in 1887 both were rapidly becoming well-established artists. As one of America's foremost and versatile composers, he set lyrics on exotic Eastern subjects written by three contemporary American authors: Henry Wadsworth Longfellow's "Allah," Thomas Bailey Aldrich's "Song From the Persian," and "The Lament" from Wallace's *Ben-Hur*. In contrast to Aldrich's failure to meet Wallace in Boston in December, 1886, in Chadwick's estimation during approximately the same period, Wallace was a distinguished contemporary American author.

The full title of Chadwick's song is "The Lament: Egyptian Song From Ben Hur – Poem by Lew Wallace." There is no equivalent mention of Harper & Brothers. The song was published three times, first as an independent art-song, published by A. P. Schmidt in Boston in 1887, second, as one of "Fifteen Songs for Soprano or Tenor," a collection which included pieces set to works by Aldrich, Longfellow, Heine, Arlo Bates, and others, also apparently published in 1887, and much later as one of "Seventeen Songs for Alto or Baritone" published in 1918.[12]

The piece itself has a 9/8 time signature and begins with a three-measure introduction descending to the key of the piece, C minor. Two ninth chords give this introduction color and foreshadow some of the harmonic depth that will develop further on. The chordal accompaniment is more independent than in the previously described pieces. The range is much larger, too, stretching more than an octave from middle C to g. The melodic phrases are considerably longer as well, always beginning with a descending direction but developing into waves that echo the geographical beckoning of the text. Appropriately, the words "[no] more" and "[Memphian] shore" are held for a dotted half note, adding to the emotional desire inherent in the lyrics. After the latter, the accompaniment descends in a triple figure for two measures into a time signature of 12/8 which will last the duration of the song. This establishes a more majestic setting for the second stanza filled with twelve chords per measure, each beat with an ostinato pattern. To give the nostalgic quality of the final four lines particular poignancy, Chadwick modulates into C major and changes the rhythmic ostinato into arpeggiations, culminating in dotted half notes for the final phrase, "I said – Farewell!"

"The Lament" was performed publically several times, including an April 4, 1888, benefit concert in Los Angeles, sung by Charles M. Byram, and a May 9, 1888, recital at the Boston Orchestral Club in Music Hall.[13] Garner S. Lamson, a baritone, who often chose songs from Chadwick's repertoire, was the vocalist. There was also a performance on July 30,

1890, at the Freyeburg (Maine) Chautauqua, sung by the local contralto Jennie King [Morrison], soloist for the Cecelia Quartet.[14] In the February, 1896, issue of the popular *Godey's Magazine*, Rupert Hughes, a versatile author, composer, and Hollywood writer and film director, as well as one of Chadwick's rivals at the New England Conservatory, attacked Chadwick's work in general, finding him an inferior composer when compared to the likes of Edward MacDowell.[15] Hughes praises some of Chadwick's works, but when he gets to the "Lament" he calls it "trash of the purest ray serene," using with irony the expression from Thomas Gray's "Elegy Written in a Country Churchyard."

Like Kroeger, the Baltimorean Harry G. Martin was American born and trained, and, working as a church organist and piano soloist and accompanist, he was well integrated into the Baltimore music establishment.[16] He represents a different type of composer in that his compositions belong almost entirely to the popular sphere. One of his earliest compositions was "Wake Not, But Hear Me, Love!" which he published with another Baltimorean musician, Otto Sutro, in 1888, and he dedicated the work to "Miss Grace Cassard," a local debutante.[17] The ascription to Wallace is of particular interest in that the cover of the sheet music displays as a subtitle, "Serenade – Words from 'Ben Hur' by Gen. Lew Wallace." Three other composers will apply the term "serenade" to a setting of Tirzah's lyrics even though Wallace does not describe or term it as such in the novel. A local reviewer for *The Sun* described his music as "full of rich harmony and modulation, yet catchy and full of sprightly rhythm."[18] His "Serenade" is written in E major with a 6/8 time signature but modulates to B major at the words "A gift." His uses thirds and sixths to create a brighter tone than in other versions, and to provide additional interest he shifts between major and minor ("A gift from sleep"), inserts several fermatas ("hear ... happy ... dreams"), and employs chromaticisms ("dreams I bring").

Another version of "Tirzah's Serenade From 'Ben Hur'; words by Gen. Lew Wallace," was by Annie M. Lyon, presumably the same who finished her formal musical training at the University of Wisconsin School of Music more than a decade after its publication in 1888.[19] Published by George E. Marshall of Chicago, this setting is in E♭ major, as was Kroeger's, in 6/8 time. After a simplistic five-measure introduction, the beginning of the text is marked *"con tranqillaza"* and does not stray from the tonic and dominant as it wends its way to a fermata, a series of rests, and a ritard at "Adrift, adrift on slumber's sea." Then at "Thy spirit call," the dynamic marking changes to *"animato"* and alternates between E♭ and F major as the accompaniment is reduced to the "om-pah-pah" triple rhythm so common for popular music at the time. Along with Annie Lyon, Lillian Bissell was one of the few other women to attempt a *Ben-Hur* composition. She also trained in Germany, and then as a teacher at the Hartford

Ben-Hur *in Song and Instrumental Music*

Figure 8.1 Four of the many songs inspired by *Ben-Hur*, the top two setting lyric passages in the novel, the bottom two inspired by its story and imagery.

School of Music she would become a leading advocate for the value of a music in primary levels of education.[20] Her lone published composition was her 1895 setting of "Wake not but hear me Love." According to the cover, the song was printed "by permission of Harper Bros." and attributed to Lew Wallace. As for the third *Ben-Hur* serenade, the lyric poet and composer Frank E. Sawyer wrote it as the second part of his "Three Songs with Pianoforte Accompaniment," published with Edward Schuberth & Company of New York.[21] Harry Pepper, a balladeer as well as a tenor, performed the cycle for the Manuscript Society of New York, January 4 and May 5, 1893.[22] The fourth was an undated, unpublished version in A minor sent to Wallace and surviving in the Lilly Library's "Collection of Musical Compositions Based on Works by Gen. Lew Wallace: 1886–1900."[23]

On July 31, 1889, Henry Pettit of 118 South 19th Street in Philadelphia sent Wallace a four-page letter describing his three settings of poems from "Ben-Hur."[24] Pettit humbly describes himself as being "but an amateur," but a historical search clued by his Philadelphia address reveals him to be the distinguished architect and civil engineer who designed the Main building and Machinery Hall for Philadelphia's Centennial Exposition in 1876 and supervised the buildings constructed by the United States for the Paris Exposition Universelle in 1879.[25] His prominence as an architect gives some credence to the statements he makes in his letter about his role as a composer setting Wallace's lyrics, a rare exposition of an artist's intentions and goals for minor works of art like these. He begins with a compliment, praising "the suggestiveness and adaptability of the words, to say nothing of their rhythmic and melodic impulse." Pettit explains that he has traveled in Egypt and India, and that "although the melodies are purely Anglo-Saxon in their motives, if the songs are intelligently sung, by one who grasps the musical conception, an Eastern impression may be produced upon the hearers." He offers a much more detailed analysis of his setting of "Song of the Nile":

> The singer is first musing, and after formulating her wishes in a simple strain breaks out in her prayer to Nilus, and just as her outburst is developed she hears the god's answer by the same strain in the dominant key, with which she is carried on by the words until she awakens to find it but a dream – and closes with her original longing, ending in a loftier aspiration.

As a composer Pettit explains here that his initial "simple strain" is intentional, as is the repetition in the dominant key at the end of the piece, as we have seen in several of the pieces already described. When describing his setting of the "Song of Tirzah," he makes clear that his simplicity was intended to preserve the historical authenticity so many readers associated with Wallace's novel:

> As to the "Song of Tirzah," the strikings of the strings of the nebel have suggested the treatment and controlled the movement. There are many piano movements,

embracing arpeggios, for instance, which might be exquisitely rendered to your words, but I have kept strictly to the chords, thinking that such treatment was suggested by the context. Tirzah no doubt had much sentiment and feeling for expression, but I have doubts about her appreciating the style of the modern virtuoso.

Another composer, Herbert Sparling, sent Wallace a copy of his pre-published manuscript setting of "The Lament," which is now found in the Lilly Library at Indiana University. It is a relatively sweet composition in F major beginning in 4/4 and finishing in 6/8 with a bright emphasis from a D♭ major chord near the conclusion. M. Witmark & Sons of New York and Chicago published the piece in 1900. Two of his ten song settings written around the turn of the century were published in London, so it is quite likely that he was the same Herbert Sparling who as a singing actor created the role of Marcus Pomponius in *A Greek Slave* at its London premiere and then reprised the role at New York's Herald Square Theatre on November 28, 1899 – just one night before the premiere of the Klaw & Erlanger *Ben Hur*.

In 1893 a different version of "The Lament" was set by Leandro Campanari, the Italian-born violinist, conductor, and composer who had come to Boston in 1881 to head the Violin School of the New England Conservatory for five years. After his stint in Boston, Campanari returned to Europe but then came back to America, this time to serve as professor of violin at the Cincinnati College of Music from 1890–6. It was during this second American sojourn that he composed his "Egyptian Song." Actually, the sheet music published by The John Church Company of Cincinnati, New York, and Chicago has a longer title on the cover page: "Egyptian Song: From 'Ben-Hur' by permission of Gen'l Lew Wallace," and on the inside cover the entire text of "Egyptian Song (The Lament)" is printed, again with a citation that it is from "'Ben Hur' by Lew. Wallace." Without any mention of Harper & Brothers, this did not constitute a full copyright clearance. At best Wallace gave Campanari permission in a letter, as he would Victor Kemp [Harry Girard] and E. T. Paull, but no such letter has been discovered.

The cover is illustrated with a watercolor depicting a Nilotic scene, with a woman, i.e. Iras, in a small skiff and with an island like Philae in the background. The title of the piece atop the music itself is "I Sigh As I Sing." The piano accompaniment imitates the strumming of a harp. The reviewer in the February, 1894, edition of *Music*, presumably the editor W[illiam] S [Smyth] B [Babcock] Matthews, describes this and several other Campanari songs as "above average."[26] He explains, "The Egyptian song runs to queer melodic skips and rhythms, suggestive of something foreign, which may as likely be Egyptian as anything else."

One of the more elegant settings of "The Lament" was set by Victor Kemp, the name Harry Girard used for his publications, in 1896, published with Schuberth in 1900. Written in C major, the melody undulates as the triplet accompaniment proceeds through some relatively sophisticated broken chord progressions, culminating in a G seventh chord and fermata on "Memphian." The "O Nilus" passage then shifts into an ostinato accompaniment, returning to the prior motifs into the conclusion and its penultimate augmented A♭ seventh chord. The copy preserved in the Lilly Library is quite important for our understanding of the relationship between Wallace and these musical settings of his poetry. It is the copy Girard sent to Wallace, and on the cover page he "respectfully" thanks Wallace for granting him "permission to use the words herein set to music." This, confirmed by the 1895 letter written by Wallace to E. T. Paull, demonstrates that Wallace did not object to the use of his poetry by classical, parlor-song, and popular composers. This was still the same decade in which he denied permission to a number of potential impresarios, producers, and artists, but he seems to have been quite pleased to provide professional and amateur composers with poetic inspiration without demanding any remuneration.

The reader may want to take notice of one additional setting, that by C. E. Merrifield, an Indiana businessman who self-published his own setting of "The Song of Tirzah" in 1897, arranged by the German-born musician Henry D. Beissenherz. While neither the melody or accompaniment of the two-page, F major setting warrants careful scrutiny, the cover illustration is the same bicycle-wheel framed medallion image of a chariot race used by the Central Manufacturing Company of Indianapolis to advertise their Ben-Hur Bicycle after 1895. This provides another early example of a commercial by-product enjoying the use of the *Ben-Hur* name that did have to seek permission or a license from Wallace or Harper because they could not trademark their intellectual property in the 1880s or 1890s.

The many non-copyrighted editions of *Ben-Hur: A Tale of the Christ* sold in England during the 1880s and 1890s planted the seed for a lesser *Ben-Hur* phenomenon to develop there during the first years of the twentieth century. The arrival of the Klaw & Erlanger production in 1902 provided a secondary impetus. In 1909, Pierre Mellarde (a pseudonym for R. Price of Halesworth, Suffolk), who had published several works for violin and piano with French titles, published another setting of "Wake Not, But Hear Me, Love," with Weekes & Company in London and distributed through Chicago's Clayton F. Summy in two editions (C and E♭).[27] The cover carries the subtitle "Slumber Song" along with an ascription to Lew Wallace, and the next page of the folio includes the lyrics of the two stanzas of the "Slumber Song" attributed to Lew Wallace, specifically citing "Ben Hur, Bk. 2, Chap. 6."

By far the most ambitious musical *Ben-Hur* composition on either side of the Atlantic was *Ben-Hur, a Dramatic Cantata* (1903).[28] This comprehensive adaptation published in London by J. Curwen & Son contains ten pages of dialogue and 145 pages of score as well as a full-page summary of the story preceded by a page (iii) that lists the dramatis personae (including Judah's mother "Jerusha") and scene locations and describes costumes in very specific detail, even differentiating changes of costume between acts. The lyrics were written by M. C. Gillington [Byron]. Publishing elsewhere under her nom de plume Maurice Clare and her married name May Byron, May Clarissa Gillington Byron wrote a number of poems and books. She became popular by writing about and imitating famous composers, authors, and poets, many in the "Days With the Great . . ." series. Of particular interest here is that in the 1920s, near the end of her career, she published several adaptations of J. M. Barrie's Peter Pan publications, e.g. *J. M. Barrie's Peter Pan in Kensington Gardens,* as "retold for little people with the permission of the author." Peter Pan, introduced in 1902, was one of the turn-of-the-century characters in popular art that engendered great commercial success to rival that of *Ben-Hur* during the twentieth century, but Gillington wrote her *Ben-Hur* libretto more than twenty years earlier than her Peter Pan books, and *Ben-Hur, A Dramatic Cantata* is a much more serious work. Her subtitle includes the attribution, "Founded On Lew Wallace's Novel."

A note on the title page suggests that the work may be performed without costumes and scenery and that the accompanying dialogue can be read aloud, but the advertisement in London's *The Musical Herald* suggests rather that it can be "staged with costume and action." That the cantata, staged or not, was created seventeen months after the Klaw & Erlanger production premiered in London makes it a *Ben-Hur* by-product of a *Ben-Hur* by-product. The ad therefore notes that "great popularity is predicted for this work, owing to the story being so well known." In an additional suggestion for staging, the libretto (ii) recommends using "a boy" for Act I, which begins with Judah's quarrel with Messala and ends with his arrest; "an older youth" for Acts II and III, which take place along the wharf in Antioch, outside the Ilderim's tent in the Orchard of Palms, and inside the Palace of Idernee; and "a man, tall and bearded" in Act IV, which takes place outside the Palace of the Hurs. The chariot race is omitted from the action except for threatening words before the race and Judah's being crowned with flowers afterwards. However, the fight with Thord's companion is supposed to take place on stage. The figure of Christ is not staged, of course, but his healing of Tirzah and Jerusha as well as his crucifixion are included within the dialogue towards the end of Act IV. The dialogue itself paraphrases Wallace's prose, borrowing some imagery, e.g. Messala's circle in the sand, and conflates several scenes. Iras's final threats to Judah, for instance, are interrupted by news that the Nazarene has been arrested. As in many dramatic adaptations of *Ben-Hur: A Tale of the Christ*, the dialogue fails to stay within its proper parameters, at times sounding too archaic and biblical, at times sounding too crass:

> Ben-H [sic]: Mother, have I no secret ambitions. Think you, no bitter thoughts smouldering like a hidden fire? Has not the Roman iron entered into the soul even of us, the wealthiest and lordliest in Jerusalem?
> Jerusha: Alas, my son!
> Ben-H: How can I enjoy lands, riches, splendour; of what avail are they to me, while my country lies under the heel of a conqueror? Never will I desist from my one sole aim – never will I rest till we can drive Rome out!

Gillington's libretto was set by Thomas Facer, a British organist and teacher who since the early 1890s had been composing a number of songs, anthems, cantatas, and operettas of both a serious and comic nature. There are ten principals, five males (Judah Ben-Hur, Messala, Balthasar, Ilderim, Thord) and five females (Jerusha, Tirzah, Amrah, Esther, Iras), and the score consists of twenty-seven numbers. There are some discrepancies between the list of Gillington's text and Facer's score. In the former the name "Ben-Hur" is always hyphenated and his mother is named Jerusha, but not in the score. Similarly, in the former the role of Judah is listed as a baritone and Messala a tenor, but No. 2 in the score is a baritone solo for Messala, and No. 3, a duet between "Ben Hur and Mother," calls for a tenor and a contralto. These assignments do not change when Judah matures. The penultimate song, No. 26, is a tenor solo for Ben Hur: "I have seen the King of kings."

The music is quite unadventurous in its simple melodies, mostly major harmonies punctuated by traditional and predictable sequences and cadences, with uneventful rhythms. Nonetheless, Facer demonstrates no lack of ability in creating songs that are appropriate for such varied soloists as Messala, Iras, Thord, and Balthasar and choruses as the Slaves of Lebanon, Roman Soldiers, Seamen, Pilgrims of Daphne, and Little Children. And the lyrics, while bombastic, create sharply differentiated characters. Messala's solo (No.2), for instance, emphasizes his desire for conquest and power while employing Wallace's much quoted demarcation between Eros and Mars:

> The world has climes unconquered;
> The sea has isles unknown:
> No mountain range but may be
> The pathway to a throne,
> The pathway to a throne.
> ...
> The Fates that rule our follies
> Shall urge my car along:
> Farewell to puling Eros,
> And hail to Mars the strong!
> And hail to Mars the strong!

The performance by the teachers and pupils of St. Joseph's Convent Bandra, near Mombai – the first of two performances of *Ben-Hur* music in India to be mentioned in this chapter – required a cast of from "fifty to sixty."[29] The summation in *The Times of India* said that "the cantata provides excellent scope of histrionic and musical expression."

JOHN PHILIP SOUSA'S "THE CHARIOT RACE"

The most widely recognized celebrity composer who found inspiration in *Ben-Hur* was John Philip Sousa. Unlike Chadwick, Kroeger, and Campanari, who as classical art-song composers were inspired by Wallace's poetry, Sousa, a popularizing but serious-minded composer, was inspired by Wallace's vivid prose description of the chariot race. Sousa's output was prodigious. He composed not only nearly twelve dozen marches, several of which would become iconic in American popular culture, but also orchestral and band fantasies, operettas, humoresques, waltzes, and songs, as well as dozens of popular band arrangements of nineteenth-century European classical music favorites. The fact that he also wrote several novels demonstrates his appreciation for literature as well. He composed three "descriptive pieces," as his biographer Paul Bierley catalogs them, one derived from Bulwer-Lytton's *The Last Days of Pompeii* (1893), another derived from Thomas B. Read's *Sheridan's Ride* (1891), and his first, "The Chariot Race" (1890).[30] At a later date Sousa would say that he was particularly interested in American subjects, as his marches would demonstrate clearly, so the choice of two novels set in the ancient Roman Empire says much about the power of its allure to this high-profile American artist.[31]

Sousa's immediate inspiration was Hannah Harris, a Philadelphia educator, who organized a successful campaign in 1890 to bring Sousa's band to Philadelphia, where he would eventually give many concerts at nearby Willow Grove Park, and suggested the *Ben-Hur* chariot race as a subject for a new composition, "speculating that it would be a success because of the current popularity of *Ben Hur*."[32] Sousa's handwritten orchestral score proves that he originally designated this work as a "symphonic poem," and he originally gave it the title "The Chariot Race."[33] But the name would appear in programs variously as "The Chariot Race," "The Ben Hur Chariot Race," "Ben Hur's Chariot Race," and "The Chariot Race, from Ben Hur" (with or without the comma).[34]

The orchestral score (in B♭ major) includes parts for all the customary symphonic band instruments as well as one originally marked "Tympani in B♭ and F" written on the top stave and "The Chariot Race" on the second stave. But the words for the first stave have been crossed out and in the top margin is written instead: "Horses behind the Stage," suggesting that employing the sound of horses hooves was not part of his original orchestration. At measure #13, where the piece becomes "più vivo," the "Horses" have a solo, consisting of an ostinato pattern of an eighth-note followed by two sixteenth notes. Nine measures later the word "Drum" is written to differentiate it from the horse sound. Where the piece is marked "furioso," "Horses" have another solo, and under the stave written in pencil are the numbers "1 – 32," the larger number no doubt designating the number of hooves participating in a race with the two *quadrigae* of Messala and Judah Ben-Hur. Nine measures further there is a designation for "Whips."

To help clarify the sections and effects of his symphonic poem for audiences, a detailed synopsis was often included on a printed program.[35] Every word of it comes directly from the novel (5.13–14). There are six passages. The first is described as when "The trumpeters blew a call at which the absentees rushed back to their places." Sousa scored this as a four-measure trumpet solo "off stage," culminating in a B♭ major chord. Second is Wallace's description of "the trampling of the eager horses and the voices of the drivers ... heard behind the stalls," followed by the trumpets sounding again. Sousa realized this passage with tuba playing close intervals very softly, with a "short and sharp" call from a B♭ cornet. Third, beginning with "Again the trumpets blew," continues with Wallace's description of the charge towards the starting rope, followed by "the trumpeter by the editor's side blew a signal vigorously." It is at this point that the listener understands that Sousa's "The Chariot Race" is indeed a "descriptive piece" or "symphonic poem" and not at all a verbatim musical rendition of Wallace's text. The text calls for a trumpet/cornet passage, a "horse" passage, and another trumpet/cornet passage, but Sousa's music follows the opposite pattern once the più vivo passage has begun. More specifically, Sousa scores solo cornet where Wallace says "the trumpets blew." After eleven measures there is another cornet blast, and two measures later the dynamic marking changes to maestoso, with the "horses" still running accompanied by a descending melodic line led by the cornet in a dotted rhythm. After ten more measures there is an allegro furioso passage: "There was a crash, a scream of rage, and fear, and the unfortunate Cleanthes fell under the hoofs of his own steeds." The fifth quotation begins with "Above the noises of the race there was but one voice, and that was Ben-Hur's." This passage is not marked separately in the score, but twenty-nine measures later there is a pronounced B♭ major theme announced with a half-note chord and then resolving in the next measure in a dominant seventh. This alternates with a more subdued passage before building through a passage rising stepwise in a series of measure-long descending chromatic scales to a sudden jolt, created by an accented diminished chord on the back beats, repeated over three measures. This is a musical interpretation of Wallace's description of how Messala's chariot "went to pieces." Perhaps the musical repetition even designates "a rebound as of the axle hitting the hard earth; another and another." Sousa moves out of this by returning to the stepwise rising movement, now diatonic and modulating between major and diminished, building and repeating, culminating a sixth higher. This in turn begins a furioso passage in which the entire band plays triplets, descending a full three octaves to the rousing five final notes played in unison, representing Wallace's "AND THE RACE WAS WON."

Unlike some of the previous examples, this program does not claim that permission was granted by Wallace, and there is no record of Sousa ever contacting Wallace or Harper to obtain permission even though almost two dozen sentences of the prose text were printed in the program, and from the most popular part of the novel. And Sousa's concerts were only occasionally designed as charity benefits. Two piano reductions of the score were published. The first was arranged by Henry Xander and published with Oliver Ditson Company in 1892, and the second further transcribed by Launce Knight and published by Ditson in 1896.[36] Neither publication makes any mention of Harper or Wallace, but they do not include any text either. Interestingly, Sousa never allowed a full band score to be published because he did not want to reveal his "instrumental tricks."[37] Nor did he allow the piece to be recorded.

It is important to realize that Sousa did not have full legal custody of his own work, for it helps to demonstrate by comparison how diligent Wallace was with his. Both men created extremely popular works which had an enduring effect. For Sousa, suffice it to be said that Congress made his "Stars and Stripes Forever" the official march of the United States of America.[38] In 1892, Sousa resigned as director of the U. S. Marine Band, a post he had taken up in 1880 (when he composed "President Garfield's Inauguration March"). He then entered into an agreement with David Blakely as his newly formed popular band's manager. By contract he was to be paid $6000 per year. In 1895 the band played 644 concerts. In contrast, that was just two years before Major Pond offered Wallace $4000 to give twenty lectures, and Wallace turned him down. Blakely voluntarily gave Sousa thousands more than that from royalties, but when Blakeley died unexpectedly in 1896, his widow, who claimed that she inherited her husband's position as manager, refused to continue that practice. She and Sousa battled in court for four years with the result that Sousa had to pay her $30,000 and lost the right to any royalties from the works he composed while under contract. Article 12 of that contract specifies:

> and in case of any musical compositions by said Sousa during or prior to said period, the profits of the sale or negotiations of any such musical compositions, and all other music now controlled by the said Sousa, or composed by him during or prior to this engagement, including his "Sheridan's Ride," "Ben Hur," etc. (already composed), shall be divided equally between the parties of this agreement.[39]

The next article stipulates that Sousa was to transfer and deliver his original scores and music to Blakely, and the next that he could not engage in any other musical work not connected with Blakely. Again for comparison's sake, during those same years Wallace was not only receiving his book royalties – as much as 30 percent for the *Prince of India* – but had also negotiated and was receiving additional royalties from both the *Ben-Hur, in Tableaux and Pantomime* and the Klaw & Erlanger production, over which he maintained much artistic control as well as the right to abrogate the agreement.

Also unlike Wallace, Sousa discussed his legal and financial turmoil in the press. Wallace always safeguarded his reputation and authority. In contrast, Sousa consumed one and one-half columns on the second page of the April 12, 1897, *Washington Post* explaining and lamenting his current difficulties.[40] In the article, aptly named "Harmony Took Flight – Upon the Death of Sousa's Business Manager," Sousa even admits he lacked foresight and business acumen:

> After some correspondence a contract was drawn up and signed by both. I considered it at the time a one-sided affair, but neither of us had any idea of the success to be achieved by the band.

Of course there was and still is a significant difference between the professions of musician and author, but the reader can only imagine the demands Lew Wallace might have made had he written "Stars and Stripes Forever" and "The Washington Post March," or given over six hundred performances per year.

Sousa's "The Chariot Race" was very popular from the outset. The audience response in Philadelphia on March 14, 1891, was exceptionally positive:

> Sousa's symphonic poem, "The Chariot Race," in Ben Hur, was received with unstinted applause, and the band was obliged to repeat some sections of the piece before the audience would be contented. The instruments produced a wonderful effect in representing incidents in "The Chariot Race," the clatter of the horses feet being remarkably realistic.[41]

A month later after a concert at Music Hall in Boston, the *Globe*'s incredulous reviewer had to admit to the popular appeal of recreating Ben-Hur's chariot race with musical effects:

> There is something unique, even inspiring in such a descriptive piece as that in which Mr. Sousa tells, in resonant and varied tones, the story of the chariot race from "Ben Hur." A man brought up on Bach fugues might find some objection to the simulated shouts of the multitude and the cleverly managed effect of the clattering horse hoofs. But the great public emphatically likes "that sort of thing," as the enthusiastic redemand by M. Sousa's audience, yesterday evening, made evident enough.[42]

A year later, in Salt Lake City on April 2, 1892, "The Chariot Race from Ben Hur" was:

> ... the advertised feature of the programme. To every one who is familiar with that thrilling chapter of "Ben Hur" the idea of the chariot race set to music was quite enough to arouse keen anticipation, which was, I think, fully realized. From the

time the trumpeters called the steeds to the race until Messala, crushed and bleeding, saw Ben Hur win the race, the audience was lost in the music.[43]

Even eight years later, a writer for the *San Francisco Chronicle* reporting on Sousa's visit to Paris described the effect of Sousa's "Chariot Race" with such vividness – "past pillar and post the music takes them, and then the chariots whirl by in great but terrible splendor; faster and faster they fly and louder and louder become the cheers" – that by the end of his paragraph there is nothing left but to paraphrase Wallace's "The race is won!"[44] Sousa performed the piece as late as 1908 – for a benefit held at the Metropolitan Opera House in New York.[45]

A reviewer in the *Washington Post* said the piece was "so realistic that the running is certainly heard and almost seen."[46] The *St. Paul Globe* said the work "is descriptive, in the highest sense of that much-abused word, and its effect on the hearer is dazzling."[47] Similarly, the *Washington Herald* wrote that "the sounds from the track and the enthusiasm of the onlookers are plainly depicted."[48] Another reviewer summarized, "What Lew Wallace has done in word-painting for the Roman pastime, Sousa has done in music and with greater effect."[49] Clearly audiences not only enjoyed the experience immensely but found the symphonic poem to provide a powerful and stimulating inspiration to abandon their historical present. As we have seen, unaccompanied recitations and declamations of the *Ben-Hur* chariot race had a somewhat similar effect on contemporary audiences, and the various *Ben-Hur* tableaux of the same period would do the same. In fact, chariot racing itself would become all the rage in the next decade, particularly on stage in the Klaw & Erlanger spectacular but also in real, live chariot racing outdoors. This compelling effect on the imagination served the *Ben-Hur* phenomenon in two ways, that is, in helping to make *Ben-Hur: A Tale of the Christ* much more than just a novel that would continue to sell tens of thousands of copies each year but also in establishing it as a symbol of thrilling action, daring, and triumph that fed into the burgeoning American juggernaut of industrialization, invention, and consumerism. We have seen a few examples of American patriotism inspired by *Ben-Hur* before. Another case in point would be the performance at Ford's Grand Opera House in Baltimore on May 10, 1898, just nine days after Dewey's victory at Manila Bay, the first triumph of the Spanish-American War. Sousa's concert, "The Trooping of the Colors," inspired "a riotous exhibition of patriotic fervor" that included uniformed military on stage, flag waving, and exuberant renditions of "The Stars and Stripes Forever" and "The Star-Spangled Banner."[50] The piece played just before the jingoistic part of the program commenced: "The Chariot Race."

Sousa played hundreds of concerts per year all over the country, at venues ranging from huge metropolitan opera houses to county fairs. It should be remembered that in addition to the thousands who heard his band play at traditional indoor venues, there were perhaps hundreds of thousands who may have heard him at outdoor venues. More than one million people attended the California Midwinter International Exposition in San Francisco's Golden Gate Park in the spring of 1894, and the *Chronicle* devoted almost a half column to printing the entire "The Chariot Race" synopsis described above.[51] The first page of the 1895 Thanksgiving Day issue of *The Atlanta Constitution* printed the entire synopsis as well, for Sousa's concert was a featured part of that day's events of the Cotton States and International Exposition.[52] What this meant for the developing *Ben-Hur* phenomenon was exposure, whether from the newspaper, from the daily programs, from the performance itself, or from excitement shared after the performance. Moreover, after Sousa sold Xander's arrangement of the score to Ditson in 1892 "at a handsome figure," the piece was available in that format not only to individuals as a retail item but also to other band leaders.[53] Patrick Gilmore's band, for instance, performed the piece in May, 1891, as a tribute to Sousa and to the delight of the Washington, DC audience.[54] In addition, as the phenomenon proliferated, different aspects could occasionally reinforce each other. In the visual arts, a *Los Angeles Herald* ad for the Sousa concert to be held on Wednesday, April 13, 1892, at Hazard's Pavilion incorporated into its large, 10in.×4in. format an etched rendition of Alexander von Wagner's painting of *The Chariot Race*. Sousa's band would also employ the newly invented means of recording music with their 1902 and 1912 recordings of "The Ben Hur Chariot Race." However, their recording was not of Sousa's own composition. It was a recording of the equally or perhaps even more popular march by E. T. Paull.

E. T. PAULL'S "THE CHARIOT RACE OR BEN HUR MARCH"

The Original Sheet Music
Edward Taylor Paull was born and raised in Virginia and began his composing and publishing career in Richmond. Compensating for what he lacked in classical training and professional experience was his mastery of marketing. He issued more than two hundred popular piano pieces with such descriptive titles as "The Midnight Fire Alarm March and Two Step" and "Napoleon's Last Charge."[55] To excite potential buyers he sold his piano pieces in brilliant multi-color covers, most by them printed by the A. Hoen Lithograph Company of Baltimore, one of the leading chromolithography companies in the United States at that time.

Appropriately, his first marketed composition was "The Chariot Race or Ben Hur March," published in 1894. Trade-mark laws of the late nineteenth century could not prevent him from using the name Ben-Hur or any chariot race imagery from the novel. For the cover Paull chose to use a dazzling, five-color chromolithographed composite of elements from both Checa and Wagner. Because they were both European, they did not have any copyright protection in the United States. Similarly, because Paull was not using any of the text from the novel, he was not required to get copyright permission from Wallace. Nonetheless, in another smart marketing ploy, at the top of the cover Paull boldly displayed "RESPECTFULLY INSCRIBED TO GEN. LEW WALLACE, AUTHOR OF 'BEN HUR,'" giving the vague impression that this was part of an apparent *Ben-Hur* franchise. Wallace himself had as yet had no imput into Paull's publication, but, uncharacteristically, even though Paull had not written him first, Wallace wrote Paull a letter on March 8, 1895:

> I have just heard the March called *Chariot Race or Ben Hur*, and make haste to congratulate you upon the composition. I think it most admirable. You are at liberty to say so in any form.
> Very Truly,
> Your Friend
> Lew Wallace

Paull printed a facsimile of this letter on the inside of a new version of the sheet music issued through the Richmond Music Company until 1897, to demonstrate that Wallace had essentially given his endorsement.

Like so many commercialized popular art productions that bore the name of *Ben-Hur* in the 1890s, Paull's "The Chariot Race or Ben Hur March" was a smashing success. This was particularly true for performances that highlighted the thrilling chariot race, whether in public readings and recitations, the Bradford tableaux and the *Ben-Hur, in Tableaux and Pantomime*, or the Klaw & Erlanger dramatic adaptation. We just saw that the newspaper advertisement for Sousa's April 13, 1892, performance at Hazard's Pavilion in Los Angeles included a small black-and-white etching of Wagner's painting next to an image of Sousa and large font performance particulars. Going further, Paull displayed the Checa-Wagner composite image in brilliant color, in a larger format, and on a cover page that included eye-catching large font names like "Ben-Hur" and "Gen. Lew Wallace." And now the consumer could purchase it and take it home.

The music itself is a formulaic but energetic ragtime piece. The beginning of the piece is marked *con spirito*, and the time signature is 2/4. An eight-measure introduction features a two-octave descending figure resolving into the E♭ major theme that is repeated multiple times, followed by a Trio where the melody is in the base, a paraphrase of the introduction, more repetitions of the first two themes, and then a fortissimo, fifteen-measure, extended cadence culminating in three E♭ major chords separated by rests, as if the player had just finished a piano concerto. As with many products of popular art, the attraction of Paull's march is not so much in its accuracy in musically recreating a chariot race – as was Sousa's – or even its impressionistic quality but in its rousing start,

Figure 8.2 In 1894 E.T. Paull created his first commercial success with this vivid chromolithographed cover adapting elements from both the Wagner and Checa compositions and "respectfully inscribed to Gen. Lew Wallace, Author of 'Ben Hur.'"

simple and memorable melodic themes, incessant repetitions of rhythmic motifs, and an equally rousing conclusion.

With Wallace's blanket statement of permission, Paull proceeded to relate his composition even more closely with the novel. In the Richmond printing that included the facsimile of Wallace's letter, he placed lines from the text (5.14) below the title but above the top stave on the page:

> On Atair! On Rigel! What, Antares! Dost thou
> Linger now? Good horse – Oho, Aldebaran!***
> **
> 'Tis done! 'Tis done! Ha, Ha! We have overthrown
> the proud. **** ours the glory! Ha, Ha!
> The work is done. Soho! Rest!
> [sic]

Some later printings fill the entire inside cover by summarizing the novel's account of the chariot race, quoting Messala's "Down, Eros, up, Mars" and Judah's exhortation quoted above, part of which Sousa also used in his synopsis.

In 1899 Paull collaborated with H. A. Freeman, a minor lyricist, in publishing the march with a "descriptive song," a term that echoes Sousa's generic term of a "descriptive piece." These sophomoric lyrics are constructed in rhyming couplets in a loose iambic trimeter. At the end the content becomes crudely descriptive.

> 'Mid dust and din and rattle
> Six gallant teams give battle;
> As round the circus dashing
> Six chariots go crashing.
> The frenzied crowds rejoicing;
> Their exultation voicing,
> Greet with cheers the charioteers
> As each in turn appears.
> . . .
> [TRIO]
> Brave Ben Hur,
> Prince of his race!
> Godlike in form,
> Godlike in face.
> Skilled and strong,
> He'll stand the pace
> Till the race is done.
> . . .
> And the crowds go wild and shout their fierce applause
> And greet with mad huzzas, the champion of their cause.
> For Ben Hur has brought the proud patrician low,
> Messala lies a crushed and bleeding heap of pain and woe.
> For the Prince of Judah, idol of the town,
> Has cut the Roman down, and gained the victor's crown;
> And the race is run and victory is won!
> The grandest race the sun e'er shone up-on.

Paull, self-described as "The New March King," issued many other editions of the march, including some with blue and white or monochrome covers and also full color covers not printed by Hoen and lacking significant detail. By 1896 he had prepared versions in two different printing formats, larger and smaller, and a variety of arrangements for two hands, four hands, and "simplified," and for different instrumental ensembles, including orchestra (ten parts and full), military band (thirty-one parts), fife and drum band,[56] mandolin solo, mandolin and guitar, two mandolins and guitar, mandolin and piano, guitar solo, banjo solo, banjo and guitar, violin and piano, and cornet and piano. At some point, apparently after 1902, he began printing "Played by Sousa's Band" on the cover. And Paull's march remained in print for decades. In 1922, when he was serving as Secretary of the Music Publishers' Association of the United States, Paull himself recopyrighted and reprinted the work both as a single composition and in a collection of works. Paull died in 1924, and in 1932 the copyright was officially assigned to Paull-Pioneer Music Corporation of New York.

By this time Paull was remembered as the founder of the descriptive march. The dust cover provided with the Edison 1913 recording offers the following printed text:

> E. T. Paull is recognized throughout the entire country as being one of the greatest descriptive march writers of the present time. He practically originated this style of composition. . . . All his writings are wonderfully stirring, catchy, and inspiring.

The term "descriptive," recalling Bierley's designation for Sousa's symphonic poem, will appear two decades later in a new edition issued by the Paull-Pioneer Music Corporation. Inside the monochrome color is a full page of prose with the subtitle: "Descriptive March-Galop Explanatory." The new editor now relates Paull's piece even more closely to Wallace's book, perhaps inspired by the success of the 1925 MGM film adaptation and particularly its rerelease with sound in 1931. The rest of the text paraphrases "the great race . . . fully described by General Lew Wallace in his world renowned book, 'Ben Hur.'" It offers a description of Antioch, the circus, the procession, and then the race itself, concluding that this "short description of the race" inspired "Mr. Paull" to compose the "'Ben Hur Chariot Race,' March-Galop, which has become one of the most popular selling numbers ever published."

This paraphrase then yields to a prose account of the seventeen "descriptive headings" that will appear throughout the score. The introduction was labeled with "The Trumpets Call" and "Dash For Position." The main theme was labeled "The Race" and "Round the Arena Six Chariots Go Crashing." The *brillante* passage was labeled "Like Whirlwinds Madly Rushing" and "Like Mountain Torrents Gushing." The introduction to the trio then brings "The Swish of the Lash," followed by "Racing Side by

Side" and "Flying Like the Wind," and the same motif at a higher tessitura is said to represent "Loud Huzzas of the Crowd" and "With Every Muscle Straining." The paraphrase of the introduction is labeled "Their Lightning Pace Maintaining." For the final repetitions of the two main themes the editor assigns "Like Eagles Swiftly Flying," "Fast They Come and Faster," and "One More Round To Go." The first part of the extended cadence proclaims "Ben Hur Wins the Race," and the final few measures read: "The Crowds Go Wild With Applause." The expansive text on the inside cover then concludes with these instructions for enhancing the player's interest and enjoyment:

> If the performer will keep these descriptive headings in mind while playing the piece and try to reproduce the ideas the headings are supposed to represent musically, it will make the playing of this composition specially interesting.

Paull's "Chariot Race and Ben Hur March" was also incorporated into a number of collections. In 1925 it was included in Carl Fischer's "E. T. Paull – Loose Leaf March Folio," which included the piece arranged for a concert orchestral ensemble.[57] In 1928 Paull-Pioneer Music Company issued a collection of nine marches with two variant titles, *Paull's Famous Marches* and *E. T. Paull's March Folio*.[58] The "Chariot Race of Ben Hur March" appears first, of course. Actually, on the cover is a reduced image of the original chromolithographed covers of all the marches, including "Chariot Race of Ben Hur March," but in the table of contents the march is listed as "Ben Hur Chariot Race March," recalling the inconsistent titles assigned to Sousa's symphonic poem. Another printing of this collection was issued in 1938, and still another in 1960.[59] In 1956 alone, by which point the original copyright had expired, both the Chart Music Publishing House in Chicago and Belwin of Rockville Centre, Long Island published modern editions. The latter was a new arrangement of the piece by Wesley Schaum, a simplified piano reduction in F major with no repeats or secondary motifs. In the renascence that followed the release of MGM's 1959 film adaptation of the novel, Paull's four-hand arrangement was the basis for the "piano duet" issued by Century Music of New York in 1961, and additional reprints were issued by Larrabee Publications and Shawnee Press of Delaware Water Gap, Pennsylvania. In 1963 the piece was included in Albert Gamse's collection of *World's Favorite Marches*, in 1964 in Century Music Publishing's *Most Popular Piano Pieces*, which was also copyrighted in Britain, and in 1973 in Sandy King's *A Selective Musical Collection of the World's Greatest Hits of the March Kings*.[60] Columbia Pictures Publications issued still another reprint in 1977. As we will see, these were recommended by piano teachers all along the way.

All these editions were for sale, of course, and the number of copies that survive in libraries and throughout the ephemera networks demonstrate how widely they were distributed and sold. And they were used, as Elizabeth Axford eloquently surmises in her *Song Sheets to Software: A Guide to Print Music, Software, and Web Sites*: "Though his covers are more prevalent than Norman Rockwell's, they are considered in the scarce category, often found dirty and torn due to their popularity."[61]

As Paull published and advertised more compositions, he inevitably identified himself as the composer of the "Chariot Race or Ben Hur March," and advertisements of his works for sale almost always listed the "Chariot Race or Ben Hur March" first. Even the announcement of the aforementioned "America Forever March" reminds the reader that the composer "is also the author of the 'Ben Hur Chariot Race March.'"[62] In 1907 he published Harry J. Lincoln's "The Midnight Fire Alarm – March and Two Step," and on the top of the chromolithographed cover is printed "Companion Piece To The Celebrated Ben Hur Chariot Race March." Almost the entire left half of a company envelope postmarked 1897 contains a large engraving of his signature cover version of the Checa and Wagner compositions, beneath which is printed "Publishers of the Great Ben Hur Chariot Race March – Price, 50 cts. by mail post paid." And as as late as 1911 a bordered list on the E. T. Paull & Company letterhead has the "Ben Hur Chariot Race March" on top.

Paull used it to propel his business forward. In announcing his expansion into the phonograph manufacturing business in the trade journal *Electrical Age*, he made clear both the source of his success and his impressive sales figures:

> The E. T. Paull Music Company are [sic] one of the largest and most successful music publishing firms in New York City, and as such are known all over the United States by the music dealers. Mr. E. T. Paull, the head of the concern, has the reputation of writing the most popular marches of the present day. He has won pronounced fame on his "Ben Hur Chariot Race March," "Charge of the Light Brigade March," "America Forever March," and other marches, the sales of which run largely in the hundreds of thousands.[63]

Just before the turn of the century Paull began to focus on the expanding market provided by music teachers. The copy in the series of ads used for a campaign in *The Etude*, a magazine for the "teacher, student, and lover of music," begins with a "Special Offer for Music Teachers Only."[64] The E. T. Paull Music Company then states that they want every music teacher in the country "who uses a good grade of popular music teaching pieces" to employ copies of their marches, two-steps, and waltzes. The first one listed is the "Ben Hur Chariot Race March" by E. T. Paull; (the company published works by other authors as well). The copy continues:

> This is without exception one of the best and most popular marches of the present day. A splendid teaching piece, now being used by thousands of teachers. A universal favorite. Fine base solo. Try it.

One year later a briefer ad in *The Etude* lists the "Ben Hur Chariot Race March" first (of fifteen) and briefly summarizes: "The great seller.

Universal favorite. Best march published."[65] The aforementioned 1911 letterhead claims, "The World's Greatest Edition of Teaching Pieces."

By targeting this increasingly popular demographic, Paull built up a clientele who in turn would recommend or even require their students to purchase the piece. The campaign worked. Even ten years later, *The Etude* in 1909 reports that the piano recital programs of Mrs. G. Bellm and Miss Edith W. Page included the "Ben Hur Chariot Race," as did the "musicale" by the pupils of Nellie Treuholtz two years later in Oakland, California.[66] Decades later the members of the Happy Hour Piano Club of the International Institute in Lowell, Massachusetts, began their June, 1945, recital with Paull's march.[67] And still two decades after that, in addition to the 1963 recital by the students of Mrs. Avis M. Jensen in Albert Lea, Minnesota, *The Wellington (Texas) Leader* reports recitals by the students of Mrs. J. L. Harper in 1966 and then again in 1973.[68]

Paull's early advertising campaigns had their effect on musical directors as well, so concert performances of the march were presented by soloists, bands, orchestras, and a variety of ensembles played by amateur, professional, and military instrumentalists from coast to coast. Newspaper accounts describe concerts by an 1897 "Sunday-school orchestra of twenty-two pieces," a 1899 Guitar and Mandolin orchestra, a 1910 concert by a college ensemble in Holt County, Oregon, and another by the Fort Bliss military band in El Paso.[69] The flexibility of the piece allowed for ever more rearrangements. Online catalogues include an arrangement for salon orchestra by Voelker in 1895, and another with xylophone obligato performed as part of the musical program for E. H. Sothern's *Captain Lettarblair* in the same year.[70] Ephemera include a copy signed by the vaudevillean accordionist, Carlo Restivo.

Band concerts remained quite popular during the first few decades of the twentieth century, and in many instances the piece was used to open or close the program. It was the "Ben Hur Chariot Race March" that opened the twenty-first season of Selbert orchestral concerts at Conover Hall in St. Paul in 1895 and the third annual Concert and Ball under the auspices of Company G, 2nd Regiment, of the National Guard, State of Maine [N.G.S.M.] in Bangor in 1896.[71] It was used in 1896 as well to celebrate a grand opening of the Buffalo Woolen Company of Los Angeles, and for the inaugural appearance of the De La Salle Literary Society in Washington, DC.[72] It was also the "Ben Hur Chariot Race March" that closed a Westlake Park concert in Los Angeles in 1896.[73] Such popularity continued well into the following decades. The piece opened the Long Beach Marine Band's Pavilion Sunday afternoon concert and the Third Infantry's band concert in Cincinnati in 1903, closed the concert by the Seventy-First Regiment Band in New York's Central Park in 1904, was featured for the formal opening of Edison's Little Thimble Theatre on Fifth Avenue in 1915, and opened the final orchestral concert of the season for the First Methodist Episcopal Church in Los Angeles in 1924.[74]

A copy of Paull's "Ben Hur Chariot Race March" purchased directly from Paull cost 50¢. But Paull apparently understood – as did Henry Wallace – that after initial sales had reached their peak, volume sales at a fraction of the original retail price could attract an even wider audience. By 1898 advertising in the ephemera record begins to show secondary outlets offering Paull's marches for 10¢ for the "regular" version, 15¢ for the "special."[75] Ten years later, Paull's ad in *The Etude* still has the list price of 50¢ but offers readers any single march for 25¢, three for 60¢, and six for $1.00, while an ad for The Fair Store in the *Chicago Tribune* offers this and other popular sheet music for 10¢ each.[76]

Nor was the popularity of Paull's march confined to the United States. In 1894 he published a version in England through C. Sheard & Company. Over the years Paull collaborated with a number of other publishers in not only New York, Chicago, Boston, and San Francisco but also Toronto, Ceylon, and Australia, that is, across the British Empire. There were at least two early Australian editions by Nicholson's (1894) and J. Albert & Son (1896), both in Sydney. *The Times of India* reports a performance by the Victoria String Band at Pyrke's Apollo restaurant along with other descriptive pieces on October 17, 1906.[77] (Europeans only were admitted.) Between 1929 and 1936 an edition was published in Spain by La Garriga (Barcelona) Rollos Victoria. Shortly before this, Julius S. Seredy, the Hungarian-born composer, director, arranger, and pianist, issued it as part of his collection of silent film scores through the State Theatre in Sydney. Paull's "Ben Hur Chariot March" was used for silent films in the United States as well. In fact, the piece was played during a 1988 silent film retrospective at Lincoln Center.[78]

Neither the huge initial sales nor the continuing volume sales of Paull's "Ben Hur Chariot Race March" provided any royalties for Lew or Henry Wallace. Nonetheless, this was an authorized expansion of the phenomenon personally approved and encouraged by the original author. As a secondary vector separate from the contemporary *Ben-Hur, in Tableaux and Pantomime* and the Klaw & Erlanger dramatic production, it became a discrete but significant part of the *Ben-Hur* phenomenon. It could attract those more interested in popular music than literature or drama, and it helped establish the popularity of *Ben Hur* for the younger demographics of the next several generations. When MGM produced its new film version in 1959, despite the acclaim for and availability of Miklós Rózsa's soundtrack, Paull's more pianistic march experienced a modest revival, as evidenced by the aforementioned publications and recitals in 1963, 1966, and 1973.

Recorded Music

As a result of Paull's marketing skill, the "Ben Hur Chariot Race March" achieved robust and continuing sales. As it turned out, the timing of its success could not have been better. Its popularity was surging just as recording technologies were being patented and made available for the home and commercial markets, and this created additional consumers and auditors who could thereby enjoy Paull's music whether they played piano or not. This differentiates Paull's piece from all the other *Ben-Hur* adaptations of the period. None of the authorized or unauthorized *Ben-Hur* tableaux, pantomimes, readings, recitals, or pageants of the period were recorded. Images from the Klaw & Erlanger dramatic production were photographed, but only static stage tableaux and individual or groupings of actors in costume. This was by design. Klaw & Erlanger, like most dramatic producers, used these photographs as a means to advertise their product or give departing customers a memoir of their experience. Sound recordings were – and are – different. Just because the sheet music or orchestral parts have been made available does not mean the consumer can recreate the sound of the product played by professional musicians. This was especially true around the turn of the century when hearing recorded music was still a novelty and purchasing the equipment to play a recording was a household status symbol.

Paull's piece was ideal for the burgeoning recording industry. It had a vivid, impressive, and memorable title. It offered a popular, rhythmically catchy, and harmonically simple composition. It was consistently loud and therefore relatively easy for primitive recording devices to pick up. And it was flexible in length, depending upon whether any or all of the many repeats were taken or omitted, so it could fit onto a variety of recording media. As a result, it would become one of the signature works in the proliferation of the *Ben-Hur* phenomenon. Decades before the advent of radio or television, and also a few years before the development of moving pictures as a bona fide attraction for the popular consumer, the late 1890s offered consumers this other, albeit drastically transformed and severely limited in size, version of *Ben-Hur*. And this craze would last for decades.

Music Boxes and Band Organs

Even before the introduction of the Aeolian Company's pianola in 1897, a number of mechanical recording methods and devices played on hand-cranked equipment were and would continue to be developed and then mass-produced for the next three decades until the disk format emerged triumphant in 1929, when Edison halted production of its amberol cylinders. In this sense and indirectly, Gustave Brachhausen, the president of the Regina Music Box Company, Edwin Votey, the developer of the mass-marketed pianola, and Thomas Edison, along with their many competitors, played an essential role in the mechanical dissemination of the music of the *Ben-Hur* phenomenon.

The music box and band organ created the first commercially successful response to the public's fascination with automatic musical instruments. The former, a cabinet-device that played recordings stamped out on large zinc or steel disks ("tune sheets"), created via small metal tubes an ethereal sound reminiscent of a metallic harp. Although relatively expensive, American consumers bought tens of thousands of music boxes, and a variety of recordings of Paull's "Ben Hur Chariot Race" appeared in the years just before and after the turn of the century. These included a Regina 15½ inch tune sheet of Paull's march [#1409] and a Stella 17-inch version [#768]. Companies released their products on more than one label, and copyright laws did not prescribe exclusivity at the time, and so the Swiss Mermod Frères company that produced the Stella also sold a 12-inch Mira version which was produced differently and played on different equipment, and additional versions could be played on The Olympia Self-Playing Music Box or a German Symphonion.[79] Because the disk could be played for only one revolution, the duration of the piece was limited to approximately one minute. The Stella version, for instance, omits the introduction, plays the main and second theme only once, and then the trio, also without repeats, and omits the final returns and the coda entirely. The Mira does include the introduction but only at the expense of the much shortened second theme and second half of the trio.

The insistent rhythm, featured base solo, wide tessitura, and simple but memorable melodic lines, not to mention Paull's own arrangements for band, orchestra, and various ensembles, made for an easy transition to band organ. Band organ rolls brought this secondary segment of the *Ben-Hur* phenomenon beyond the home market to ever more casual listeners, establishing an ambient connection between Paull's march and thousands of people enjoying their leisure time at fairgrounds and other outdoor venues. Because the player machines were designed to play loud and raucous music, horn, drum, and xylophone parts were added to the original composition, and rolls were made that played in a variety of Wurlitzer organs from the relatively small Tonawanda Military Band size to the huge Wurlitzer 164 with its twenty-eight wood and brass trumpets.

Player Pianos

The piano roll market was quite competitive, as thousands of titles were issued among a plethora of start-up companies. None were able to acquire copyright protection, especially in that the United States Supreme Court in 1908 unanimously confirmed the status quo.[80] Like so many products associated with the veritable *Ben-Hur* brand name, *Ben-Hur* proliferated in this newly invented medium for the home market. With the shortened title "Ben Hur Chariot Race," Paull's march was issued on piano rolls sold under such labels as Aeolian 88 Note, Arto, Gulbransen Music, Harmony, Ideal, Imperial, MelOdee, Melographic Roll Company, P. A. Starck Piano Company, Perfection, Pianostyle, Playrite, QRS, Supertone, United States Music Company, Universal (owned by The Aeolian Company), Vocalstyle, and Connorized Music Company's "88 Note."[81] All these rolls are marked as marches, except for the QRS #30886, which is labeled as a "Two Step." Only the Playrite and Vocalstyle rolls list the performers, Albert Delhi and William Hartman, respectively, although the QRS #1606 box is marked "played by E. T. Paull." The rolls issued by Pianostyle, P. A. Starck, and United States Music Company, and perhaps several others recorded four-hand arrangements, and one of the QRS versions printed Freeman's lyrics along the right side of the roll to enable a sing-along. Paull's "Ben Hur Chariot Race" is one of several dozen rolls used as an enticement to purchase a player piano in a 1913 ad in *The Oakland Tribune*.[82]

From the early 1900s to the late 1920s, nearly two million player pianos were sold in the United States,[83] and to meet the demand piano roll manufacturers and distributors created and packaged and bought and sold under different names. Supertone, for instance, was sold exclusively through Sears, and Harmony was sold through Montgomery Wards, while QRS and Aeolian in particular distributed several different labels. But most of the important national concerns offered a version of Paull's "Ben-Hur March," and they did so over a number of years. Most of these releases are difficult to date, but the 1915 Connorized catalog lists both "Ben Hur Chariot Race – March" [#213] and "Two Step Special, No. 3," which included both the "Ben Hur Chariot Race" and Paull's "Burning of Rome" [#457]; the QRS "Blue Bird Ballads" box is printed "Words Copyrighted 1921 by Q R S Music Co.," and the Gulbransen roll is advertised in a 1929 periodical.[84] The latter demonstrates the longevity of Paull's composition in the era of automatic musical media.[85]

Early Recordings
Both of the contemporary systems for recording and reproducing a musical performance, Edison's phonograph cylinder and the disk-shape gramophone, offered versions of Paull's "Ben Hur Chariot Race March" for the home market. Band music and solo performances were ideal for both systems because, lacking microphones and amplification, acoustical recordings had difficulty in picking up the dynamic range of a stringed orchestra. A case in point is one of the earliest recordings of Paull's march, which was by Joe Belmont, a popular whistler known for both his solo whistling accompaniments and bird-call imitations.[86] After recording the "Whip-poor-will Song," Robert Browne Hall's "Independentia March," and Septimus Winner's "The Mocking Bird" the previous December, Belmont made his first master recording of an arrangement of Paull's "Ben Hur Chariot Race" on May 19, 1902, in Philadelphia.[87] This was released as

a 7-inch disk [Victor #1396]. A day short of one year later he seems to have made another master [Matrix #B-23] which was then released on a different 7-inch disk [Victor #3237]. The latter runs a little over two and one-half minutes after Belmont, as usual, introduces himself and the title of the piece in his speaking voice. As the piano accompaniment plays the piece quite rapidly, taking three of the repeats, Belmont whistles the first melodic motif, the repeat much embellished by warbling; the secondary motif he tweets and warbles, usually warbling through the endings. In the trio he ad-libs a piccolo part, as it were, and he warbles through most of the prestissimo finale. Belmont seems to have made another recording on May 11, 1905 [Matrix B-2546], and this was released on Victor's 10-inch Monarch label [#2327].

Sousa's Band and Victor Recordings

As the reader already knows, the band of the genuine "March King," John Philip Sousa, recorded Paull's march in 1902 and again in 1912. The Victor Talking Machine Company held its first session devoted to recording Paull's march in Philadelphia on January 7, 1902 [Pre-matrix A-1196]. The result was released in the United States in both 7-inch [Victor #1196] and 10-inch [Monarch #1196] formats and in Canada as well [Berliner #704].[88] It is very doubtful that Sousa himself conducted the band at this session.[89] In 1906 he would publish his article, "The Menace of Mechanical Music," in which he maintained that recordings were no substitute for live performances. He published this shortly after testifying at the June 6 hearings on revising the Copyright Act held by the Joint Congressional Committee on Patents.[90] There he spoke against the recording of music but also complained that the Copyright Act did not provide any remuneration for the composer of a recorded composition. Interestingly, it may well have been at this point that another form of synergistic advertising was applied to the *Ben-Hur* phenomenon when Paull issued new printings of his sheet music with "PLAYED BY SOUSA'S BAND" printed in red ink.

Arthur Pryor had for many years served as Sousa's featured trombonist and assistant director. But in 1903 he left Sousa to form his own band, and he wholeheartedly embraced the recording of musical performances. He recorded Paull's "Ben Hur Chariot Race March" for Victor on April 25, 1904 [Matrix B-1260] in Philadelphia. This was then issued as a single-faced black label disk [Victor #4085]. Around 1910 Pryor became a staff conductor for the Victor Talking Machine Company in Camden, New Jersey, and there in 1912 Pryor again conducted Sousa's Band again in a recording of Paull's piece in a May 16 session [Matrix B-12025].[91] Taking the first four repeats but then omitting the secondary introduction and the final two repeats, this recording lasts for 2'53". The recording was issued in August on two different double-faced, 10-inch disks. Victor #17110 contained Paull's march and Alvin Willis's Irish novelty called the "March Shannon," played by Arthur Pryor's Band, recorded on April 9, 1912 [Matrix #B-11836].[92] Victor #63866 contained Paull's march and Perucho Figueredo's "Himno Bayamés," aka "La Bayames," the national anthem of Cuba, played by the in-house Victor Band, which had been recorded on August 6. This disk was marketed in Latin America with the Spanish title of Paull's march, "Carrera de carrozas 'Ben Hur': Marcha." Victor #17110 was included in a 1918 Victor collection of 10-inch disks.

Edison and Columbia Recordings
In addition to the recordings on the Victor label, the consumer had a choice of purchasing disks and cylinders from Edison and Columbia. As early as April, 1901, Edison issued a Brown Wax Cylinder recording with Joe Belmont [#7772]. In 1905 Edison put onto the market a Gold Moulded Record cylinder with a version played by the Seventy-First Regiment Band of New York [#7282]. In 1913 Edison offered a version recorded by the New York Military Band on May 16, 1913 [#2291]. They released this on one of the two faces of Edison Diamond label #50085 [L], and then in 1916 as an Edison Blue Amberol [#2810].[93] This recording is distinguished by the percussion recreating the sound of hoof beats – à la Sousa's piece – during the trio.

In 1902 Columbia also issued a brown wax cylinder version played by their in-house Columbia Band, with Joe Belmont whistling as a solo performer [#1015]. Columbia then discontinued brown wax cylinders in 1903 or 1904, selling the remainder of their stock through Sears, Roebuck. In 1908 Prince's Military Band, a group frequently recording on the Columbia label formed by Charles A. Prince in 1905, made a recording of Paull's "Ben Hur Chariot Race March." This was released on a two-faced 10-inch disk with the recording by Belmont on the other face [#3549], and then sold, minus the initial spoken announcement, on their single-sided Lakeside label [#70057] through the Montgomery Ward mail-order catalogue.[94] In September, 1913, Prince's Military Band made another recording [Matrix 77337-1]. This was released on the Columbia Graphophone Company label [A-2848], and rereleased in September, 1919.[95]

Pirated Recordings
The New York firm of Leeds & Catlin launched several new labels in 1905 in spite of impending legal redress by Victor for patent infringement.[96] Leeds & Catlin did not print their own name on the labels but issued Paull's "Ben Hur Chariot Race March" on their Imperial [#44604] and The Silver Star [#B4604] labels. So as not to reveal the source of the recording, in both instances the performer is listed as simply "Orchestra Selection." In the same period the American Record Company (ARC) issued copies of Columbia's Belmont recording under their own label [#030497].[97] But then the legal dispute, Leeds & Catlin Company v. Victor

Figure 8.3 Paull's brief piano piece was recorded on different sizes and labels of vinyl and metal disks, Edison amberol cylinders, and a variety of player-piano rolls.

Talking Machine Company and United States Gramophone Company, reached the United States Supreme Court in January, 1909, just a little more than two years before the Kalem Company v. Harper Brothers case determining the legality of making the first film adaptation of Wallace's novel without obtaining prior permission.[98] Just as in the Kalem case, the court ruled in favor of the respondent and enjoined the petitioner, so Leeds & Catlin terminated their Imperial and The Silver Star labels, and the American Record Company went out of business.

The releases of Paull's march by Leeds & Catlin were not the central focus of this legal dispute over recorded sound. They were just a few of hundreds of pirated releases. But much like the Kalem v. Harper case, this roughly contemporary case helps to illustrate the business climate in which the various *Ben-Hur* by-products were being created and released. New inventions were pushing many legal barriers regarding both patents and intellectual property not yet modernized with updated legal precedents, so many of the decisions rose to the Supreme Court level where very basic, technical definitions had to be determined, e.g. what constitutes a recording, and what constitutes a moving picture, and what is the relationship between the original music and the secondary recording, and what is the relationship between the original novel and a moving picture that tells the same story.

Paull's "Chariot Race or Ben Hur March" was extremely popular at its release in 1894 and maintained a presence through the 1910s to be recorded in a variety of media and by a number of different artists. As the recording industry itself and its retail models evolved, Paull's march was marketed continually. In the decade after this particular legal dispute, the virtual monopoly by the larger, more established companies was giving way to competition from retailers who could sell in greater volume at cheaper prices. From a September, 1917, recording, Victor Hugo Emerson, Edison's former co-worker who had been a manager at Columbia for two decades, issued a licensed recording of Paull's march on his own Emerson Records [#2713].[99] Little Wonder Records sold its copy of the "Ben Hur Chariot Race March" played by Prince's Band [#329] for just 10¢, often through the Sears and Wards catalogs.[100] This was not a pirated recording: it was recorded separately, with fewer repeats and at a quicker tempo so as to last only 1'33". Recordings of Paull's march were also distributed overseas. The German website musiktiteldb.de lists both an Odeon recording of January 15, 1909, and an Edison Bell 78 that was recorded by the London Regimental Band in 1902.

ADDITIONAL POPULAR MUSIC

Paull was not alone in writing *Ben-Hur* instrumental compositions for the popular market, although he was one of the first and certainly the most commercially successful by far. The *Catalogue of Title-Entries of Books and Other Articles Entered in the Office of the Librarian of Congress at Washington Under The Copyright Law* lists John C. Querrie's "Ben Hur Quickstep" for band (1891), W. I. Peters' "The Chariot Race" (1892) for orchestra, and F. A. Hall's "Ben Hur March" (1892).[101] That Hall's march was published by Thomas Goggan and Brothers in Galveston, Texas, suggests that he composed it for the newly founded Ben Hur Shrine Temple in Austin.[102] In 1895 Richard J. Carpenter, known for his expertise in playing and teaching mandolin, composed "The Chariot Race" (Opus 19) for a series of mandolin and guitar arrangements published by the Denver Music Company. He divides the piece into three parts: "Entrance March of the Charioteers," "The Race," and "Finale." Like Paull, the publishers sent a copy to Wallace (which is the copy held by the Lilly Library at Indiana University) inscribed "With Compliments," and atop each of the parts is printed in italics, "Dedicated with gratitude to General Lew Wallace." Below the title appear the final lines of Book Fifth, Chapter 13 of Wallace's novel: "The race was on; the souls of the racers were in it; over them bent the myriads – Ben-Hur."

It was in 1895 that the Ben-Hur Bicycle Company of Indianapolis began using the medallion featuring the chariot from Wagner's painting for their advertisements. The next year they offered for free (plus postage) "A copy of the Popular Ben-Hur March." The potential customer might assume this was a copy of Paull's "popular" march, but after the word "March" in small font and in parentheses is printed "Key of F." This was not Paull's popular march (in E♭) but a modest composition written by the obscure John H. Cody, arranged by the more published Chas. W. A. Ball, printed by William B. Burford, Indianapolis's most prominent printer, and distributed "Compliments of" Central Cycle Manufacturing Company.[103] Not surprisingly, the white cover of the sheet music bears a large gray-scale version of the Ben-Hur Bicycle medallion. The composition itself, like most ragtime pieces of the day, is formulaic. But when considered in connection with the Merrifield setting of "The Song of Tirzah," it shines some light on the kinds of commercial synergies that were being developed in the mid-1890s, in this instance fusing the new-found popularity of the safety bicycle with the ongoing popularity of *Ben-Hur*, chariot racing, and ragtime music. In fact, in 1896 Paull himself published his timely "New York and Coney Island Cycle March Two-Step."[104]

Such ongoing popularity produced additional chariot-related compositions even more than a decade later. Fredrick [aka Frederick] Messick, who published several works in the early 1890s, attempted a return to the public eye in 1909 with his "Ben Hur's Ride," a ragtime *marceau characteristique* for solo piano, published in Chicago by Windsor Music Company.[105] Two years later, Glenn W. Ashley published his four-page, large-format march and two-step, "The Charioteer" with Frank K. Root & Company of Chicago and New York.

In 1900 Chas Hoffman created a different kind of imagery in his "Ben Hur Waltzes" published by Shapiro, Bernstein & Von Tilzer of New York and Chicago. His formulaic music, arranged for piano by Frank David, is divided by four numbers in bold print and runs for a full eight pages. Much more distinctive than the composition, the artwork by the prolific Edgar Keller, is striking. Thirty bronze-tinted, halftone etchings are scattered throughout the large-format (13½in. × 10¼in.) pages. They depict Greco-Roman coins, costumed women, vases, and chariots and stretch into the margins and overlap the musical staves as well, not unlike the arrangement of Johnson's images in the Garfield edition of *Ben-Hur: A Tale of the Christ*. Emerging from the green-bordered cover is a gold circle filled with a large image of a dynamic four-horse chariot taken directly from Wagner's painting. There is no mention of an arrangement with Harper or Wallace.

Aubrey Stauffer's "Ben-Hur Overture" for mandolin solo (1906) provides still another perspective from which to understand the popularity of the alluring name *Ben-Hur*.[106] The influx of Italian immigrants in the late nineteenth century provided the climate for the popularity of the mandolin, and just as *Ben-Hur* items were included in various genres of popular music and most of the new recording technologies, they were added into mandolin literature as well. This chapter has already touched upon six compositions or arrangements of *Ben-Hur* songs and music designed for the instrument, four by Paull alone and another by Carpenter, who later as a Professor at the University of California at Berkeley directed its Mandolin and Guitar Club. Stauffer's composition was originally for mandolin solo, but subsequently it, too, would be played by mandolin ensembles and issued for banjo as well.

Meanwhile the *Ben-Hur* phenomenon had spread to Australia, in part from the impact of the novel itself (which was advertised in the *Sydney Morning Herald* already by April, 1881, and then inspired recitations and declamation contests as well), in part from the sale of Seredy's edition of Paull's march in 1900, and in part from the performances of the Australian Klaw & Erlanger production in 1902 and 1912.[107] Dudley T. Satchwill published his three-page "Ben Hur March," a ragtime in 6/8, with Allan & Company around the turn of the century. This also featured a chariot race on the cover, this one more reminiscent, but not a direct copy, of Checa's painting. W. H. Paling, the leading musical publishing house in Sydney, issued three additional Australian *Ben-Hur* publications: the "Ben Hur March – Two Step – Piano Solo" by Edward H. Saull, the "Ben Hur March" by Edward H. Morse, and "Three Dances From Ben Hur."[108] It is not clear how or why Paling published the first two as discrete pieces, for the music itself is exactly the same four-page rag-style march in F major. Although apparently issued in the same year, their appearance and packaging is different in that the cover of the Morse march is plain with blue borders and the inside covers include excerpts from other Paling piano pieces, while the Saull cover illustration displays a chariot race again reminiscent of but not a direct copy of Checa's painting. The Morse also bears its copyright date of 1916 printed at the bottom of the first page. The titles at the top of the first page of both pieces read "Ben-Hur: March – Intermezzo – Two Step; Op. 25," and both claim that the composer is also the composer of "Charge March." The Library of Congress *Catalogue of Copyright Entries* of 1916 lists both the "Charge March" and "Ben-Hur: March-Two Step" under the name of Edward H. Saull.[109]

The "Three Dances from Ben Hur" has a small chariot silhouette on the cover. Paling issued it as part of its "Charming" series. Just as Paull targeted the music teacher and student demographics, Paling sold six different books of "dainty piano solos suitable for all tastes, invaluable to teachers, students, and lovers of music" from "Robin Hood," "The Arabian Nights," and other popular subjects, including "Ben Hur," the fifth in the series. The nine folio pages are divided into the "Roman Dance," "Egyptian Dance," and "Dance of the Slaves," each beginning with a sketch of an ancient scene at the top and along the sides of every page border decorations representing ancient fluted candelabra.

Still another impetus for producing *Ben-Hur* music was the Tribe of Ben-Hur. In 1909 Bernard C. Owen of Crawfordsville, the home office of the Tribe, copyrighted his "Tribe of Ben-Hur March." Arranged for piano, this is a rag-style march in B♭ major. He dedicated the piece to David Gerard, the co-founder of the company. In addition, the Tribe of Ben-Hur issued a book of "Odes," a collection of songs to be song during Ben-Hur meetings. This was an eighteen-page booklet with a deep-red cover. The first piece consists of a simplified version of "America the Beautiful," but the following pages contain three different "Opening" odes, three "Closing" odes, one "Initiatory" ode each for men and women, two "Funeral" odes, an "Anthem," and the hymn "Holy! Holy! Holy!"

This chapter comes to a close as the era of the popular march was coming to an end. Nonetheless, still two additional *Ben-Hur* marches were composed in 1923 and 1925. The first was H. E. Baxter's "Ben Hur Patrol."[110] Despite the fact that this was published by Orville C. Walden in New York, it was written for the Ben Hur Patrol, a nearly one hundred man drill team, with drum and bugle corps, of the Ben Hur Shrine in Austin.[111] Baxter played the cornet and was the director of the forty-seven piece Ben Hur Band. The second, José Armándola's German *Ben-Hur Marsch*, was composed in conjunction with the 1925 MGM *Ben-Hur* film.

While new editions, printings, and recordings of Paull's march would continue to be issued and reissued over the next half century, the thirty-five years that had produced all the *Ben-Hur* music catalogued and described in this chapter also saw popular music in America develop into a major consumer industry that would continue to expand with the advent of radio. Of course the *Ben-Hur* phenomenon would reach into this new medium as well, but the near half-century that had to this point produced so many individual *Ben-Hur* songs would now give way to more complete film and dramatic scores of the later twentieth and twenty-first centuries.

NOTES

1. Cf. Solomon, "The Music of *Ben-Hur*," 153–78.
2. *Werner's Magazine* 17 (April, 1895) 322.
3. *HW* (August 22, 1863) 529–30; Moore, *The Rebellion Record*, 8:32–3.
4. After Wallace had become a successful novelist, he returned to poetry and composed *The Wooing of Malkatoon*, a 78-page epic poem which appeared in *Harper's Magazine* in December, 1897.
5. *Catalog of Copyright Entries: Musical Compositions, Part 3*, #14838; *Mitchell [SD] Daily Republican* (October 6, 1886) 4.
6. *Catalog of Copyright Entries: Musical Compositions, Part 3*, renewal #4879, December 13, 1913.
7. Elson, *The History of American Music*, 251.
8. Dressler, *Favorite Masterpieces*, 230–1.
9. *Kunkel's Musical Review* 9 (October, 1886) 387–9.
10. Broadside 1889.B45, UVA.
11. *BG* (December 11, 1887) 10.
12. Faucett, *George Whitefield Chadwick*, 193–4. The original publication is dedicated "To James Means, Boston," presumably the successful shoe manufacturer.
13. *Los Angeles Daily Herald* (April 4, 1888) 4; Faucett, *George Whitefield Chadwick*, 188–9; *The Musical Year-Book of the United States* 7 (1889–90) 82.
14. *Bangor Daily Whig & Courier* (August 1, 1890) 1; cf. *Lewiston Evening Journal* (February 12, 1972) 4A.
15. *Godey's Magazine* 132 (February, 1896) 199.
16. *TBS* (March 24, 1893) 8.
17. *TBS* (January 19, 1889) 4.
18. *TBS* (March 30, 1895) 10.
19. *The Mount Vernon Signal* (September 30, 1904) 3; *[Madison] Capital Times* (November 24, 1923) 9.
20. Bissell, *Music in Cultural Education*.
21. *Catalogue of Title-Entries of Books and Other Articles* 15.1 (Washington, DC: Government Printing Office, 1898) 45 [#301]. The songs were: No. 1: To Sigfride, Swedish Love Song, Words by F. Peterson. No. 2: Serenade. From Ben Hur. No. 3: Sylvia. Many online references omit "From Ben Hur."
22. Wilson and Cady, *The Musical Yearbook of the United States* 10, 103.
23. OCLC #122404122.
24. Letter from Henry Pettit to Wallace (July 31, 1889), LL.
25. E.g. *The Catalogue of the Members of the Fraternity of Delta Psi* (June, 1889) 46.

26 *Music* 5 (February, 1894) 494.
27 Russo & Sullivan 334.
28 OCLC #498692253; this printing includes Tonic Sol-fa notation, as does the 1930 reprint. OCLC #42223145, also published by Curwen Inc., in Germantown, Pennsylvania, cites Florence Hoare as author of the libretto, but her name does not appear in the advertisement in *The Musical Herald* (September 1, 1903) 272.
29 *ToI* (February 18, 1933) 16.
30 Warfield, "The March as Musical Drama and the Spectacle of John Philip Sousa," 289–318, esp. 302.
31 *WP* (November 26, 1893) 14.
32 Bierley, *John Philip Sousa*, 87.
33 Sousa Archive, University of Illinois Library.
34 *Pittsburg Dispatch* (April 19, 1891) 5; *The Sunday [Washington] Herald* (May 10, 1891) 3.
35 *StLPD* (October 22, 1893) 11; *AC* (November 18, 1895) 5; cf. Newsom, *Perspectives on John Philip Sousa*, 73.
36 <http://www.loc.gov/search/?q=sousa%20chariot%20piano&fa=digitized:true>
37 Cf. Newsom, *Perspectives on John Philip Sousa*, 73.
38 Bierley, *The Incredible Band of John Philip Sousa*, 20.
39 Bierley, *The Incredible Band of John Philip Sousa*, 22.
40 *WP* (April 12, 1897) 2; *TBS* (April 13, 1897) 6.
41 *The [Philadelphia] North American* (March 16, 1891) 5.
42 *BG* (April 4, 1891) 8.
43 *Salt Lake City Daily Tribune* (April 2, 1892) 3.
44 *SFC* (June 10, 1900) 31.
45 *NYTr* (November 1, 1908) 8.
46 *WP* (May 5, 1891) 1.
47 *St. Paul Globe* (March 12, 1897) 4.
48 *The Sunday [Washington] Herald* (May 10, 1891) 3.
49 Press Clipping from New Britain, University of Illinois, Sousa Archive.
50 *TBS* (May 10, 1898) 7.
51 *SFC* (April 15, 1894) 12.
52 *AC* (November 28, 1895) 1.
53 Bierley, *John Philip Sousa*, 87; *Salt Lake Herald* (July 24, 1892) 12.
54 *WP* (May 25, 1891) 6.
55 *Omaha Daily Bee* (February 19, 1899) 13.
56 OCLC #498235766.
57 In the possession of the author.
58 OCLC #6492189 and #79208756.
59 OCLC #30617378; and #14635210.
60 Gamse, *World's Favorite Marches*; OCLC #39396425.
61 Axford, *Song Sheets to Software*, 21.
62 *Book Notes* 2 (January, 1899) 63.
63 *Electrical Age* 24 (August 12, 1899) 7.
64 *The Etude* 16 (March 1, 1898) 3.

65 *The Etude* 17 (March 1, 1899) 96.
66 *The Etude* 27 (September 1, 1909) 209 and 643; *Oakland Tribune* (June 4, 1911) 11.
67 *The Lowell Sun* (June 27, 1945) 9.
68 *Albert Lea Tribune* (May 5, 1963) 8; *The Wellington (Texas) Leader* (May 19, 1966) 5; (May 17, 1973) 5.
69 *LAT* (March 8, 1897) 10; *The St. Paul Globe* (February 17, 1899) 8; *Holt County Sentinel* (September 9, 1910) 3; *El Paso Herald* (May 30, 1910) 5.
70 OCLC #429672180; OCLC #755005573.
71 *St. Paul Daily Globe* (November 17, 1895) 16; *Bangor Daily Whig & Courier* (May 2, 1896) 1.
72 *Los Angeles Herald* (September 13, 1896) 12; *WP* (March 23, 1896) 4.
73 *LAT* (August 23, 1896) 11.
74 *LAT* (June 7, 1903) C3; *CE* (August 28, 1903) 9; *NYT* (June 18, 1904) 9; *NYT* (August 3, 1915) 9; *LAT* (July 5, 1924) 11.
75 *StLPD* (April 24, 1898) 3.
76 *The Etude* 26 (November 1, 1908) 11; *CT* (May 24, 1908) E6; *TBS* (February 6, 1909) 5.
77 *ToI* (October 17, 1906) 4.
78 *NYT* (March 1, 1988) C17.
79 *The Black Cat* (December, 1898) ii.
80 *White-Smith Music v. Apollo* [209 U.S. 1 (1908)].
81 Arto #86424; Harmony #10048 and #15440; Ideal #S1088 and 1253; Imperial #512480-70; Melodee #300297; P. A. Starck Piano Company [of Chicago] #X5065; Perfection #86424; Pianostyle [of Brooklyn] #45767; Playright #486A; QRS #30886 and #1606: "words copyrighted 1921 by Q. R. S. Music Co."; Supertone #10079 and #40049; United States Music Company #6139 and #[6]6139D; Universal #300297; Connorized Music Company's "88 Note" #213. Some recordings were duplicated and released under different names while maintaining similar catalog numbers, e.g. Melodee and Universal #300297. Not all roll numbers are available or legible. Cf. <http://launch.groups.yahoo.com/group/EliteSyncopations/message/9975>
82 *The Oakland Tribune* (August 29, 1913) 8.
83 Bowers, *Encyclopedia of Automatic Musical Instruments*, 255.
84 *Presto-Times* (January 19, 1929) 15.
85 *Connorized Guaranteed Music Rolls for 88 Note Player Pianos, August 1915* (New York: Connorized Music Company, 1915) 25 and 133.
86 Cf. *Bangor Daily Whig & Courier* (December 14, 1889) 1.
87 The Encyclopedia of Victor Recordings, maintained on the University of California, Santa Barbara website [victor.library.ucsb.edu] reports that the Philadelphia location is unconfirmed.
88 Bierley, *The Incredible Band of John Philip Sousa*, 440. Bierley's catalogue lists this as Sousa's composition.
89 <http://www.newworldrecords.org/liner_notes/80282.pdf>
90 Sousa, "The Menace of Mechanical Music," 278–84.
91 Bierley, *The Incredible Band of John Philip Sousa*, 454.
92 *Honolulu Star-Bulletin* (August 12, 1912) 11.

93 The other face [50085-R] has Clark's "Belle of New York," recorded by the New York Military Band on August 11, 1913.
94 OCLC #432665568; Sutton, *American Record Labels and Companies*, 113; <http://launch.groups.yahoo.com/group/EliteSyncopations/message/9944>
95 Brooks and Rust, *The Columbia Master Book Discography*, 2:228; cf. Barr, *The Almost Complete 78 rpm Record Dating Guide II*, 25.
96 Allan Sutton, *Directory of American Disc Record Brands and Manufacturers, 1891–1942* (Westport, CT: Greenwood Press, 1994) 79 and 139.
97 <http://www.angelfire.com/or/settlet/AmericanMatrix.htm>
98 Leeds & Catlin Company v. Victor Talking Machine Company and United States Gramophone Company [213 U.S. 301]; cf. Sutton, *Directory of American Disc Record Brands and Manufacturers, 1891–1942*, xv.
99 OCLC #82712502; cf. <http://www.ehow.com/info_11402100_emerson-records-phonographs-history.html>
100 Sears Catalog #135 (1917) 840; cf. <http://www.littlewonderrecords.com/little-wonder-history.html>
101 *Catalogue of Title-Entries of Books and Other Articles Entered in the Office of the Librarian of Congress at Washington Under The Copyright Law From August 31 to September 5, 1891* (Washington, DC: Government Printing Office, 1891) 17 [176]; *Catalogue . . . December 12 to December 17, 1892*, 20 [585]; and *Catalogue . . . October 10 to October 15, 1892*, 15 [348]. Cf. William H. Rehrig (Paul E. Bierley, ed.), *The Heritage Encyclopedia of Band Music* (Westerville, OH: Integrity Press, 1991–6) 2:611 and 2:311. Cf. *SFC* (December 16, 1895) 10.
102 *Denver Post* (July 16, 1899) 18.
103 OCLC #247503690; cf. McKee 186; M&M 496.
104 <http://www.thewheelmen.org/sections/memorabilia/covers/music_index.pdf>
105 OCLC #244286854.
106 *Catalogue of Title-Entries of Books and Other Articles Entered in the Office of the Librarian of Congress at Washington, First Quarter, 1906*, 981.
107 *The [Adelaide] Advertiser* (March 14, 1901) 6, (August 19, 1901) 7; *The [Adelaide] Register* (September 11, 1901) 8.
108 OCLC #219869462, #222701061, and #221543477. Morse's piece was #31 of Paling's March Series.
109 *Catalogue of Copyright Entries, Part 3: Musical Compositions* (1916) 1095 and 1100.
110 *Catalogue of Title-Entries of Books and Other Articles Entered in the Office of the Librarian of Congress at Washington, Part 3: Musical Compositions, Last Half of 1923* (1924) 1314; cf. OCLC #449242254; and Rehrig, *The Heritage Encyclopedia of Band Music*, 52.
111 Baxley, et al., *Shrine Patrol*.

9 "My God! Did I Set All This Into Motion?": The Klaw & Erlanger Ben-Hur

The Klaw & Erlanger *Ben-Hur* was by contemporary and historical accounts one of the most spectacular and spectacularly successful Broadway productions ever mounted. The *New York Times* labeled the stage production "the grandfather of all spectacles,"[1] and Ray and Pat Browne in their *Guide to United States Popular Culture* described it as "one of the most spectacular theatrical productions ever."[2] Within the context of the *Ben-Hur* phenomenon it was surpassed by only the novel in terms of the number of years it retained a dynamic presence in its genre, and by only the 1959 MGM film in terms of its sustained profitability as popular entertainment. The numbers are not precise but overwhelming: approximately 6000 performances witnessed by well over ten million people who paid over $10 million as the production traveled coast to coast. It was a notable presence on the American theatrical landscape from 1899 to 1920. After its initial record-breaking runs in the East Coast cities and Chicago, it took to the road. The dozen or so freight cars that carried the massive amounts of patented electrical and mechanical equipment and miles of rigging as well as racing horses, a camel, and a cast and crew of several hundred people represented one of the largest traveling productions ever put on the road. And when *Ben-Hur* arrived in new venues, city after city like St. Louis, Cincinnati, and San Francisco proudly boasted that more people had purchased tickets to see *Ben-Hur* in their city than anywhere else, and that full-house runs of two or more weeks meant that they, too, like New York, Boston, and Chicago, had now finally become major theatrical centers. Record-breaking productions were also mounted in London and Sydney, so that at one point in 1902, three separate *Ben-Hur* companies were employing about 1200 people around the world. When King Edward VII of England sat in a specially constructed box to watch the live, onstage chariot race, it was global news, and even after Her Majesty's Theatre in Sydney was closed because of an outbreak of bubonic plague, just one week later patrons clamored to get into the building to watch *Ben-Hur*. And when the show went dark in 1920, its producer, Abraham

Erlanger would be the person who sold the film rights to Hollywood for more than $1 million, thereby providing the means to carry the torch further for decades.

Despite its tremendous success, the Klaw & Erlanger *Ben-Hur* has long needed a lengthy scholarly study.[3] There is much more to be done than this chapter, lengthy as it is, can accomplish. But here at least is a chronological survey of the inception, production, and touring of the Klaw & Erlanger production derived primarily from hundreds of contemporary newspaper reviews, press releases, articles, and features, and a reconstruction of the play itself derived from William Young's published dramatization of the novel, Edgar Stillman Kelley's published musical score, and Joseph Byron's black-and-white stage-production photographs.

THE CLASH OF THE TITANS: ERLANGER AND WALLACE

In the early 1880s, Abraham Lincoln Erlanger was in his early twenties and working as a road manager for Joseph Jefferson, the actor celebrated for his popular portrayal of Rip Van Winkle.[4] Erlanger later recalled that he picked up a copy of *Ben-Hur: A Tale of the Christ* at a bookstand, read most of it during a twelve-hour train ride, and remarked to Jefferson: "You may smile, Mr. Jefferson, but some day I am going to own that book and produce it."[5]

His travel circuit interconnected with that of Marc Klaw, a contemporary who had abandoned both his native Kentucky and the legal profession to become a theatrical advance man for Effie Ellsler, the locally beloved Cleveland actress.[6] By 1886 the two men had formed a partnership to be known for decades as "Klaw & Erlanger." Revising the chaotic, ad hoc method of theatrical booking, they established a centralized system that enabled them to develop into two of the wealthiest and most powerful men in American theater.[7] When Klaw died in 1936, his obituary in the *New York Times* says of the partnership: "They reached a peak with 'Ben Hur,' probably the greatest road show of them all."[8] At the time of Erlanger's death in 1930, his worth was estimated to be as much as $75 million. Far from being remembered as a kindly or beloved impresario or patron of the arts, even his first-page obituary in the *New York Times* stated:

> Mr. Erlanger was called "the little Napoleon of the theatre" and the title fitted. He was a fighter and made many enemies, but even his enemies respected his ability, his tactics and his driving, positive personality. In the days when he was the undisputed czar of the stage, it was his boast that his word was as good as his bond.[9]

By the mid-1890s Klaw & Erlanger were producing very popular plays and had formed, with Charles Frohman and several other theatrical managers, the Theatrical Syndicate, which for many years monopolized bookings across the United States, particularly in the metropolitan centers. Understanding that Erlanger was the American theatrical world's equivalent of a late nineteenth-century industrial mogul, the reader, already knowing how resistant Lew Wallace was to the dramatization of his novel, will now find of particular interest how relatively ineffective Erlanger's Napoleonic, Czar-like manner was when confronted with General Wallace's demands for artistic control and financial remuneration, how Wallace ultimately found the dramatic adaptation of his novel so sufficiently appropriate, not to mention lucrative, that he gave it his heartiest public endorsement, and, in a later chapter, how Erlanger would ultimately shepherd Wallace's valuable literary property into the hands of MGM.

The thread resumes in 1895, when Jefferson Patten, a Brooklyn inventor who had developed a theatrical horse-racing mechanism for Neil Burgess's 1889 version of Charles Barnard's play, *The County Fair*, attempted to bring an injunction against Burgess for insufficient payment and breaking their verbal contract. He secured the services of an attorney and prepared to sell his device to another production company to "incorporate in a play his great Roman chariot scene."[10] The attorney was Mitchell L. Erlanger, the elder brother of Abe, and the production company was Klaw & Erlanger. Although Klaw & Erlanger seem to have had *Ben-Hur* in mind around 1890, this particular play was *The Year One*, another Barnard play reflecting contemporary interest in ancient Roman culture and particularly chariot racing.[11] With a reliable chariot-racing mechanism in hand and Klaw & Erlanger still eager to expand their domain, the prospect of staging Wallace's novel became even more desirable.

To put the chronology into perspective, it was in 1895 that Alexander Salvini and Josef J. Reinisch made their unsuccessful proposals to Wallace. That same year Major Pond, according to his autobiography, brought the initial proposal from Klaw & Erlanger.[12] A few more years passed, and it was in 1898 that Wallace wrote to W. W. Allen, "In my view, the subject ought not to be put on the stage; that would be profanation, not of the book, but the most sacred of characters to which it must be considered dedicated; especially would that be the case if given in ordinary dramatic or spectacular form." A letter dated January 4, 1899, preserves the earliest evidence of a second proposal from Klaw & Erlanger arranged through Harper & Brothers, although at that point Harper had notified Wallace only that some "responsible theatrical managers" had contacted them.[13] Even in the spring of 1899, while he was negotiating with Klaw & Erlanger, Wallace received a proposal from William Gillette, the actor who created the modern iconography for the dramatized Sherlock Holmes, another from Jeannette L. Gilder, editor of *The Critic*, another from Esther Lyons, "The Klondike Girl," and still another from Elisabeth

Marbury, who was well connected with the Theatrical Syndicate and its European network.[14]

Erlanger trumped them all by sending his trusted associate, director Joseph Brooks, to Crawfordsville.[15] Brooks must have addressed Wallace's long-held objection to having the Christ portrayed on stage or represented in any inappropriate manner.[16] His solution was to simulate the presence of Christ with a very intense shaft of light, an idea reportedly inspired by sunlight striking down on him while lying down on his couch one afternoon at his home in Somerville, New Jersey.[17] With assurances from his head mechanic that such a light could be reproduced onstage, Brooks presented the concept to Wallace. When the producers later issued a statement to the public, they affirmed that "the religious features of the famous book will be carefully safeguarded when rendered on the stage.... General Wallace ... is now satisfied this can and will be done."[18] This became the stuff of legend. Sixty years later, Groucho Marx in his autobiography credited Erlanger with "one of the greatest comebacks of all time" when asked in a face-to-face interview if he believed in Jesus Christ: "Well, frankly I don't. My partner, Klaw, does – but he's up in Boston!"[19]

Wallace's other general concern was that the action of the novel could not be translated to the stage. To address this, Brooks accompanied Wallace, now nearly seventy-two years of age, back to New York so he could examine in person a number of scale models of the proposed stage sets and the treadmill mechanism. *Harper's Weekly* later published a drawing of Wallace examining the model of the chariot race set.[20] Meanwhile, Klaw & Erlanger awaited Wallace's final approval. The reader already knows that Wallace innately had the eye of an artist. In the early 1890s he had also demonstrated his mechanical know-how by developing a few patented inventions, including a fishing reel and then a combined joint-bar and railway tie.[21] The Klaw & Erlanger presentation satisfied him on both accounts, and he gave his consent. Wallace's comment at the time, "You now have a subject, which, properly outfitted, will last your lives, longer in fact than Uncle Tom," makes clear the level of expectations he had for the production and its success.[22] He would not be disappointed with either.

This is an important turning point in the development of the *Ben-Hur* phenomenon and for that matter a notable episode in the marketing of popular culture. Already at the cutting edge of establishing high-water marks for successful synergies in the budding consumer culture, the *Ben-Hur* phenomenon thus far had produced a number of by-products ranging in genre and type from classical art-songs to safety bicycles and an interstate insurance network, and while the Bradford tableaux, authorized *Ben-Hur, in Tableaux and Pantomime*, Sousa symphonic poem, Paull march, and Tribe of Ben-Hur were each played to or were enjoyed or joined by thousands and even hundreds of thousands of people, the Klaw &

Erlanger *Ben-Hur* would be the first *Ben-Hur* by-product to reach millions of viewers and earn millions of dollars.

No contract had been signed yet. Klaw & Erlanger misjudged Wallace's business acumen and, more importantly for him and also for the argument of this book, sorely underestimated the worth of his artistic property. Already in the January 10 letter, just after he asks Harper who these "responsible theatrical managers" are, he asks in quick succession who will own the manuscript copyright, can it be incorporated into their original publishing agreement, will the royalties be calculated by net instead of gross receipts, will Harper be "at charges" and what would those charges be, will he have approval of the manuscript, and what percent of the gross receipts will Harper charge the managers. The answer to the last question proved to be the sticking point. Klaw & Erlanger made Wallace and Harper their standard offer of a little over a 3 percent royalty.

Even though Klaw was originally from Kentucky and Erlanger had spent years in Cleveland, they seem to have treated Wallace as a greenhorn Midwestern artist grateful for the opportunity to see his work mounted upon a New York stage. But Wallace was already sensitized to East Coast snobbery, he was not at all desperate to have his novel dramatized and staged, he was receptive to entertaining competitive offers from Gillette and Marbury, and financially he was already quite well off from book sales. In this new venture, however, it was not Wallace who was being compensated so much as his novel, and if his novel was not properly valued, he would not come to terms. Insulted by the offer Klaw & Erlanger extended at first, he wrote to Harper on February 11, "the savages who sell things of civilized value for glass beads live further west than Indiana."[23] Already receiving 5–6 percent from *Ben-Hur, in Tableaux and Pantomime*, accustomed to the standard literary royalty of 10 percent, and having demanded and received an extraordinary 30 percent for *The Prince of India*, Wallace countered with a demand of 10 percent. On March 1 Klaw & Erlanger upped their offer to 4 percent of the first $10,000 per week and then 6 2/3 percent on any amount above $10,000. They insisted that this amount was "a hundred percent in excess of price ever paid to dramatize [a] book and that is all we are paying, for there will be additional author's fee for the dramatist."[24]

By March 6 Harper had advised Wallace to accept this new offer, causing the author to accuse his publisher of collusion with the producers.[25] Harper resented such "unjust inferences," but Wallace made his final offer, 7 percent of the first $10,000 and 10 percent thereafter, one third of this sum going to Harper, two thirds to Wallace.[26] When negotiations stalled in mid-March, Brooks wrote to Henry Wallace, now and for many years thereafter a participant in the legal arrangements, to move the process along.[27] The producers finally succumbed, and on April 11, 1899, Wallace returned from a hunting trip along the Kankakee River to sign two contracts, the first with Harper & Brothers as well as Klaw & Erlanger, the second with Harper alone.[28]

The agreement between all three parties restates the agreement between Wallace and Harper stipulating that the latter held the copyright of the novel while the former as author reserved "certain rights in respect to dramatization." It extends Klaw & Erlanger exclusivity in producing the dramatized version of the novel internationally and in any language, but in exchange the first article stipulates that Klaw & Erlanger must pay for the dramatization, submit it to Wallace and Harper for approval, in writing, and then forbids them from changing the text without approval. This demonstrates once again that Wallace's primary concern was in maintaining artistic control over the use of his property. The third requires "the proper . . . atmosphere and the scenic character of the story" to be exhibited only in first-class theatres in cities of no less than 10,000 inhabitants. Although Klaw & Erlanger certainly had no intention of taking their *Ben-Hur* to villages and hamlets, Wallace wanted to make sure that his property not only enjoyed a very high level of production but also played in large and important venues. There were a few additional points. Klaw & Erlanger had to pay Harper the cost of publishing the manuscript, of which they permitted no more than 250 copies to be printed, and a small purchase fee. And, of course, Wallace insisted that the agreement stipulate that "the character of Christ shall not be personated, nor shall the crucifixion scene be represented." Wallace also demanded that royalty payments be made every week no later than Wednesday, that he and Harper maintain the right to revoke the agreement, as in the contract for the *Ben-Hur, in Tableaux and Pantomime*, if Klaw & Erlanger failed to produce exhibitions over the course of one year, and that Clark's permission to exhibit the *Ben-Hur, in Tableaux and Pantomime* would be revoked. The second, much briefer contract established a schedule for Harper to divide the weekly payments and forward Wallace his portion.

The contract that awarded a number of guarantees to Wallace and Harper while saddling Klaw & Erlanger with cost outlays, potential liabilities, and the risk of having their agreement unilaterally terminated, was hammered out at the expense of two of the most successful and powerful men in the theater industry. It therefore provides an updated witness that in the year 1899 Lew Wallace reaffirmed legal corroboration of his position as the author of one of the most valuable properties ever created. As it would turn out, this agreement would be operative for the ensuing two decades, long after Lew's death, under the watchful eye of his son Henry, who signed the second contract as a witness.

A brief mention in the "Plays and Players" section of the *Los Angeles Times* puts this into perspective. Just a few months after the Klaw & Erlanger *Ben-Hur* premiered, Broadway also witnessed the premiere of a dramatized version of *Quo Vadis?*, the other very popular paleo-Christian novel circulating at the turn of the century. As a novel, Sienkiewicz's property was an international success, and as a play it ran for several years, attracting many of the same demographic elements as *Ben-Hur* both in the United States and Italy. But in London in 1900 a dramatic adaptation failed miserably,[29] and the brief note in the *Times* points out the important difference in copyright protection between the *Quo Vadis?* and *Ben-Hur* properties:

> "Quo Vadis" has made a triumphal march through the Italian cities. It was performed fifty times in Naples and 100 in Rome. The author has had little or nothing from the play, as the novel was not protected by copyright.[30]

The official announcement about the agreement between Wallace and Klaw & Erlanger was carefully crafted and came from New York and Crawfordsville direct to the *New York Herald*, where Walter C. Clark read the headline, "'Ben Hur' at Last Is To Be Staged," much to his dismay.[31] The news soon spread nationwide. The *Los Angeles Times* and *San Francisco Chronicle* ran "Direct Wire" and "Special Dispatch" reports on their second page. In addition to reassuring the industry and the public that the religious features of the book would be "protected" and were non-denominational, this initial press release makes it clear that Klaw & Erlanger wanted to publicize Lew Wallace's wholehearted endorsement for the scenic aspects of the project:

> "Yes, I have acceded to the request of Klaw & Erlanger," said Gen. Wallace tonight. "Their design of production was altogether new and attracted me at once. The dignity of the story, as I conceive it, was carefully preserved and due regard shown to religious opinion of all who might attend the performance.
> . . .
> The play will deal with the love story of Ben Hur, the galley fight, the chariot race and the spectacular scenes in the Grove of Daphne, all this without detracting from the religious atmosphere which pervades every chapter of the book.

PREPRODUCTION

By May 1 Klaw & Erlanger had already hired William Young to dramatize the work.[32] Like Klaw, the Chicago-born Young had studied law but by his mid-twenties began establishing himself as a theatrical writer. Edwin Booth produced Young's first play, *Jonquil*, and Lawrence Barrett, who did not produce Wallace's play *Commodus*, did produce Young's blank-verse historical tragedy *Ganelon* in 1889.[33] In a subsequent interview with the *Boston Globe*, under the apt headline "How He Wrote Ben Hur," echoing Wallace's "How I Came to Write *Ben-Hur*," Young offered some details about his process of adapting the novel.[34] He explains:

> I took the book home and read it most carefully. Play writing and novel writing are two distinct arts. My first endeavor was to find my play in the book. I saw it there.

Every character, every scene, what is called the "gist of the play" appeared to me. There I had my dramatic machinery.

He recounts that it took him one week to develop his scenario, "incessant and exhausting" work because Klaw & Erlanger gave him a looming deadline. But by the end of that week he had mapped out every scene and character, every entrance and exit, and the substance of every speech. His next step was "to take it to General Wallace." Presumably this was now mid-May. This is of particular interest because there is an otherwise undated photograph of Lew Wallace sitting in his Crawfordsville study, flanked by Young, Brooks, and his son Henry. Young also tells us that he spent ten weeks writing the dialogue and delivered his manuscript to Klaw & Erlanger on September 1. That would suggest that the photograph was taken between the second week of May and the third week of June, 1899. However, on July 4, 1899, Wallace wrote a note to Thomas B. Nicholson of Crawfordsville granting him permission "to make a book of photographs of my Study." One of the last photos printed in that book, *The Home of Ben Hur* (1900), is similar in that it pictures Young, Wallace, and Brooks without the presence of Henry. This could mean that the photograph was taken after the July 4 permission note and that Young might have been wrong in his recollection as to how long it took him to prepare the manuscript or when he delivered it. If so, this would agree with the recollection of Walker Whiteside (discussed below) that he received the script in October.

After receiving Wallace's approval, Young continues:

> I began putting the flesh on this skeleton in the form of dialogue. Before writing the dialogue I completely saturated myself with Gen. Wallace's literary style, endeavoring to follow as closely as I might all of the peculiarities and excellences of his form of composition, so that those who had read the book should not be disturbed by the introduction of anything that would tend to modify or amend this impression of the original novel. As there are not more than 50 lines in the entire play taken directly from the book, you can easily see that this part of the work took more time and care than appears on the surface.

He goes on to explain that he considers the writing of dialogue to have been the most difficult aspect of the task because "it has to have the pulse-beat, in a rhythmic sequence." Making it very clear that he was writing this as a popular work designed to please a broad spectrum of audience types, he adds, "A violation of this grates upon the ears of the uneducated as quickly and as surely as upon the learned." Young finishes the interview by revealing that he wrote the first two acts last.

Meanwhile Klaw & Erlanger were casting the play and keeping the newspaper theater columns buzzing before, during, and after the off-season with periodic updates. On May 5 Grace George was announced as their selection to play the role of Esther.[35] As part of a May 14 *New York Times* piece on the 1898 theater season, the most lucrative on record, and the general optimism for the 1899 season, Klaw & Erlanger announced that William Young would write the dramatization, E. Hamilton Bell would oversee the "designs, costumes, archaeological researches, etc.," and Edgar Stillman Kelley would compose the incidental music.[36] Originally they had asked Edward MacDowell, but he in turn recommended Kelley.[37] On May 23 they announced that they had engaged Henry Lee for the role of Simonides.[38] William S. Hart was then engaged to play Messala.[39] On May 28 they announced that Walker Whiteside would play the title role, and on July 1 they specified that the young Whiteside had been signed for three years.[40] On September 7 Mary Shaw was announced as their selection to play Amrah.[41]

Whiteside was from Logansport, and McKee reports that not only did Wallace prefer this fellow Hoosier after seeing him perform the role of Hamlet (in New York) but that Whiteside may have been influential in convincing Wallace to accept Klaw & Erlanger's proposal to dramatize his novel.[42] Now Whiteside anchored his 25-foot naphtha launch at the Tower Ridge Yacht Club at Hastings-on-Hudson and awaited the arrival of Young's script.[43] He claimed he did not receive it until October, but even so he found it quite "strong" and looked forward to playing the role. When he arrived in New York for a reading rehearsal one week later, he "found that prime and principal consideration was to be given to the scenic part and the acting was minor, subsidiary":

> For instance, public interest, of course, centers around the chariot race for which the book is famous. During that scene not a word is spoken . . . Then, take the other scenes – the visit of the wise men to the manger in Bethlehem, Ben Hur hurling tiles from the house top to the street below, the arrest of Ben Hur, the galley fight at sea, the sinking of the galley, the grove of Daphne with countless numbers in the ballet, the scene with Iras where Ben Hur follows her as she rides away on a camel, the catching by Ben Hur of the two running horses driven by Messala, the healing of the lepers where 250 people assemble, singing, and numberless changes of scene. It is a gorgeous pageant, superb, magnificent, but it is no place for acting to be foremost, the actor must submerge himself in the scenic effects.[44]

Whiteside quit the cast in late October, but already by November 1, the premiere twenty-eight days away, Klaw & Erlanger had worked out a deal with Daniel Frohman for the loan of the English actor, Edward Morgan.[45] Morgan was very much in demand. The previous season Frohman had loaned him to create the starring role for the premiere of *The Christian*, and Frohman then had him playing the role of Lefarge in *The Only Way*, and now he was to create the role of Ben-Hur.

Klaw & Erlanger took measures to make sure this sudden late change of a major cast member did not become fodder for gossip columnists and interfere with the public's anticipation of this extraordinary theatrical production. They issued a formal press release:

> Mr. Whiteside reported for rehearsals, but after two rehearsals came to the conclusion that he was temperamentally unsuited for the role, and so notified his

managers. This statement is made so that there may be no misapprehension as to the causes which brought about the change.[46]

Similarly, Grace George bowed out and Gretchen Lyons was cast as Esther during the final week of rehearsals.

What the pre-publicity lacked in innovation it made up for in high-profile concepts and placement in the major urban newspapers. Yet, the hyperbole was almost restrained. At least, in predicting great success for a spectacular production, they did not make claims that turned out to be inaccurate. *The Washington Post* began their two-column preview and full synopsis by describing the production as a "massively ornate spectacular" that "will completely eclipse anything ever seen in a theater, either in this country or abroad."[47] The article emphasizes that "real camels" will be used in the production and then invokes not just the name but the endorsement of General Wallace by detailing his enthusiasm about the prospects for extraordinary success. Indeed, Wallace's fame, earlier reluctance to permit a dramatization, and subsequent endorsement of the Klaw & Erlanger production became an important component of the pre-publicity. On November 5, after previewing the chariot race, Wallace issued a full statement in the *New York Herald*, under the headline, "How General Lew Wallace's Famous Novel Was Turned Into a Religio-Historic Spectacle":

> For years I had my misgivings about the practicability of placing the chariot race described in "Ben-Hur" on the stage. In spite of the marvelous progress in stage mechanical effects I could not conceive how two chariots, each driven by four horses, could bring about anything like a realization of the described race. This was one, among other reasons, why I could not consent to have the novel dramatized. When Messers. Klaw & Erlanger, through Mr. Joseph Brooks, submitted to me their ideas for staging "Ben-Hur" I was at once interested in their plan for the general treatment of the play, and saw the possibilities of the chariot race as it was then outlined to me. Since I have been in New York and have seen the action of the horses, I myself, for the first time, began to realize that the chariot race could and would be given to the satisfaction and surprise of the readers of the novel. The work of the horses, as I saw them this morning, impressed me with the hope that this scene will be presented in a most stirring and [dramatic] manner.[48]

McKee reports that it may have been at this time that Wallace made his much-quoted remark to Kelley, "My God! Did I set all this into motion?"[49] The *New York Times* announced Wallace's return to New York on November 23 and the November 29 arrival of his retinue of distinguished guests from Crawfordsville, including John Wingate, the Indiana State Tax Commissioner, in addition to "fifty members of the fraternal order of 'Ben-Hur,'" that is, from the Supreme Tribe of Ben-Hur.[50]

Publicity involving the chariot race was designed to impress the public with its many mechanical and electrical marvels and behind-the-scenes technical achievements. In addition to Wallace's endorsement, Klaw & Erlanger advertised that they had completely reconstructed the stage of

Jacob Litt's Broadway Theatre and had spent some $15,000 on this part of the production alone, and that the horses had been training for two months on the stage of the Broadway Theatre in a daily run the equivalent of one mile.[51] They also let the public know how prepared they were by training three extra horses in case one or more of the eight became ill or incapacitated. And Klaw & Erlanger took an important step toward fulfilling their prediction that this would "completely eclipse anything ever seen in a theater, either in this country or abroad" by anticipating any challenge to their English rights for the play by putting on a copyright performance at the Duke of York Theatre in London the previous Saturday afternoon, where *The Christian* was being performed.[52]

THE PLAY

Because *Ben-Hur* was such an exclusive production, and because recording Broadway shows was a rarity at the time, there are no audio or filmed recordings of a performance, although there was at least a contract drawn up in 1915 granting Selig Polyscope Company, for a fee of $75,000, a license to make and distribute a filmed version of the production.[53] Klaw & Erlanger did shoot publicity photos of staged tableaux, and these were included in the *Souvenir Album*, the December, 1900, issue of *Werner's Magazine*, and Harper's "The Player's Edition" of the novel.[54] Numerous newspaper accounts briefly describe favored scenes, a cover article in *Scientific American* details the mechanical effects of the chariot race, as did the *New York Times*,[55] and Commissioner Wingate wrote an eyewitness account of the premiere in the December, 1899, issue of *The Chariot*, the newsletter of the Supreme Tribe of Ben-Hur.[56] The printed program for the Drury Lane production in London lists the timings of the intermissions. All these sources, along with the published versions of Young's script and Kelley's score, preserve the original dialogue, verbal descriptions, musical cues, and staged tableaux well enough to inform the following summary of a performance, at least in the early years.[57] Unfortunately the visual and aural spectacle itself, which by almost all accounts was the most impressive aspect of the production, remains in the past and cannot be recovered.

Young assigns twenty speaking parts, from the mandatory "Ben Hur, Judah, Son of Ithamar" and "Mother of Hur," Tirzah, Amrah, Messala, Drusus, "Arrius the Tribune," Simonides, Esther, Malluch, Sanballat, Balthasar, Iras, and Ilderim, to such lesser figures as Hortator, Metellus, Cecilius, Khaled, Centurion, and Officer of the Galley. Young's published text of the play runs 114 pages and was designed to be read in about two hours. With the dance and action scenes punctuated by intermissions, performances usually lasted just under three hours.[58] The premiere performance, interrupted by many curtain calls, especially after the Act V chariot race, lasted three hours and twenty-nine minutes.[59]

(The reader may have noticed already that the name "Ben Hur" lacks the hyphen in the "List of Characters in the Drama," as it did, curiously, in the contracts signed by Lew Wallace. Although Young employs the hyphen on the title page of his published text, within the publication thereafter the hyphen never appears in his scene descriptions or in the dialogue. Press releases, reviews, and programs often omit the hyphen as well, but there is no consistency. In this chapter the hyphen will be used in the title of the play and the name of the character. As in the rest of the book, the hyphen will be omitted in direct quotations that originally omitted it.)

Prelude
The front curtain is lifted after the orchestra begins to play the *lento maestoso* Prelude in which trumpets and trombones announce the "The Prophecy" theme. The audience looks first upon a painted house-drop "symbolic of Rome and Jerusalem."[60] The off-stage chorus of as many as 180 joins in singing the prophecy itself, the lyrics derived from Isaiah 1: 2 ("Hear O Heavens and give ear, O Earth; for the Lord hath spoken") and Isaiah 60: 1 ("Arise, Shine, for thy light is come and the glory of the Lord is risen upon thee"). The melodic theme Kelley establishes here he will employ again in Act I and near the end of the play.[61]

The drop rises to reveal a pantomime of the three Wise Men played out in front of a desert scene. The audience sees the three Magi, Balthasar's camel, and the luminous star in the heavens, its bright light muted and colored by layers of gauze, increasing in size and shooting forth rays of light. Young (5) describes all three Wise Men already in place, although at least one newspaper preview describes Gaspar as "riding" on his camel to join the other two [property] camels.[62] Kelley's second number, "The Approach of the Magi," imitates the gait of a camel and perhaps Gaspar's approach by using a rhythmic imitation while the melody ascends via a sequence of bassoon, base clarinet, clarinet, and violin solos.[63]

Kelley's published score gives some other details of the pantomime not found elsewhere. The third number, "The Star in the East," begins with Balthasar, Gaspar, and Melchior "in eager conversation. Balthasar motions towards the south as he indicates the direction from whence he came." In the ensuing *lento maestoso* section ("They speak about the Messionic [sic] Prophecy"), Kelley repeats the melody of "The Prophecy." Then a *poco agitato* section colors "shimmerings of light" that "indicate the presence of the star in the East." A slow but continually rising motif corresponds to the moderato maestoso passage: "The star begins to rise and grows in intensity until the end of the scene. Filled with religious fervor the three Wise Men exchange salutations and reverently kneel in prayer." The Klaw & Erlanger tableau photographed for the *Souvenir Album* depicts this final kneeling posture.

Act I

Act I is set on the roof-terrace of the Palace of Hur, furnished with a divan, decorated with a wood trellis, and open to an expansive view of the Jerusalem rooftops and distant hills beyond the balustrade under the open sky. Young immediately establishes anti-Roman sentiment in a conversation between Simonides and Mother. The merchant then offers her the vast fortune he has amassed over the past twenty years, but she urges him to keep it safe in Antioch. Ben-Hur and Messala enter, and Mother quickly whisks Tirzah away to escape Messala's insulting comments. Then the quarrel between Ben-Hur and Messala, which was of course the first episode in the novel, grows in intensity very quickly, depending on such paraphrases of Wallace's novel as "Mars reigns – Eros hath found his eyes" and "I will succeed Cyrenius – and thou shalt share my fortune." Wallace did not use the archaisms nearly so often as Young. Young also creates the phrase "Forget thou art a Jew," which will reappear in the intertitles of the 1925 MGM silent film version. (Wallace (2.2) says only: "By the drunken son of Semele, what it is to be a Jew! All men and things, even heaven and earth, change; but a Jew never.") There are additional differences between the script and the text of the novel. Young characterizes a darker Messala who accuses Ben-Hur of treason and of rejecting his friendship, while in the novel it is Judah who is the first to anger and refuses to shake Messala's hand. By shifting characterizations and rearranging sequences and text in this way, Young continues to build his dramatic arc by having Mother fill her son's ears with anti-Roman curses ("Ruthless robbers!") and encourage him to become an anti-Roman soldier in preparation for "When the King cometh."

Unlike the novel and some of the musical compositions derived from it, Tirzah does not play the nebel and sing her song. Instead, just as Mother is counseling her son to rely on Simonides for advice, trumpets blare, Ben-Hur runs upstage to look over the parapet at the Roman procession below and then accidentally knocks a tile that falls towards the street, hitting the procurator Gratus. Ben-Hur immediately realizes the catastrophe this will cause for his family. Kelley provides some ominous background music as Messala and Centurion rush into the house.

In adapting Wallace's novel for dramatic presentation, Young here expands the action while quoting and adapting the original prose, adding detailed stage directions:

> *Messala (speaking as he enters, and pointing to* Ben Hur*).* That is he.
> *Centurion.* What? That the assassin? He is but a boy.
> *Messala.* His was the hand that did it. I saw him throw the tile.
> *Ben Hur (stepping towards* Messala*).* Oh! Thou – (*Turning suddenly, he appeals to the* Centurion). But hear me –
> *Centurion (interrupting).* Seize – bind him!
> [*Soldiers spring forward to seize* Ben Hur.]

> *Mother (frantically interposing).* No! No! Ye shall not. He is guiltless. It was an accident – accident, I say! Will ye not hear his defence?
> *Centurion.* The women, too! Bind them all!
> [*Soldiers lay hands on the* MOTHER *and* TIRZAH.]
> SERVANTS *shriek in terror. At the same instant* BEN HUR *is seized.*
> *Ben Hur (shaking off the grasp of the soldiers).* God! Hast thou forsaken us? Messala, by the memory of our childhood! If, indeed, thou wast witness, thou knowest how guiltless I am. Speak the word of truth. (MESSALA *averts his face.*) Thou wilt not? Then acquit these (*pointing to his* MOTHER *and* TIRZAH) and save them! For thou canst. They, at least, have never offended thee! Oh, in the name of thine own mother –
> *Messala (to Centurion).* I can be of no more service to thee. There is better entertainment in the street.
> [*He turns and exit. With cry of rage* BEN HUR *springs towards the retreating* MESSALA.
> *Centurion.* Secure him! To the Tower with the women!
> [*Soldiers throw themselves upon* BEN HUR. *Others drag the* MOTHER *and* TIRZAH *towards the entrance.*

By writing that the "soldiers throw themselves upon Ben Hur," Young introduces action into the arrest scene that Wallace had used to explain the instant Judah "had put off childhood and become a man" while surrendering without a struggle. Cinematic adaptations of the arrest scene will introduce even more physicality.

Young then incorporates Amrah into the scene, with the Centurion calling her a "hag," throwing her to the floor, and ushering the others out. The last line of dialogue in Act I is from the novel, where Ben-Hur says from a kneeling posture, "O Lord, in the hour of thy vengeance, *mine* be the hand to put it upon him!" Here Kelley introduces another musical theme, an ostinato musical passage (*allegro con fuoco*) to convey the message and bring the act to a close.

7 minute Intermission

At the beginning of Act II, Kelley recreates musically the strokes of the Roman galley oars by repeating a pattern of descending couplets of half-note chords in a long prelude. After sixty-one measures, the curtain rises and reveals an impressive set in the interior of the Roman galley. Lanterns are lit. Nearly fifty slaves man multi-tiered oar banks on both sides of the stage and rise above the height of a number of helmeted Roman guards. From ceiling to floor in the center of the stage sits the massive 3-foot diameter base of the mast. At its base sits the hortator. Seated on a dais above him, Arrius barks out an order and the hortator slackens the pace of the rowing. Young continues the military regimen by having Arrius question the officer Metellus about the young rower, number sixty. Arrius then interviews the rower, establishing that he knew his father Ithamar, and suggesting that his claim of innocence may be of merit. To reinforce Ben-Hur's steadfast commitment to familial piety, Young has Ben-Hur offer this passionate plea from his knees:

My mother! Tirzah! Oh, noble Tribune! Think of me what thou wilt; but if thou knowest aught of my mother or sister, tell me – I beseech thee, tell me! The horrible day is three years gone – three years, O Tribune! – and every hour a lifetime, in a bottomless pit, with never a word, a whisper to tell me of their fate. Oh, if I could but shut it from mine eyes! That sight – my sister torn from me – my mother's last look. I have heard the tempest lashing the seas; I have felt the plague's breath, and the shock of ships in battle; but that horror hath quelled all others – their shrieks have rung the loudest. Oh, if thou canst give me no better comfort, tell me they are dead, and I will bless thee – dead, and at peace from the woes I brought upon them.

This speech is crafted from Judah's address(es) to Arrius in the novel (3.3), but the critical insertion point where Judah and Jesus meet at the well could not be staged according to not only Wallace's insistence but the producers' sense of public propriety. Instead, during this interview the music, which has been absent since the act's prelude, returns as Ben-Hur remembers that "a boy, by a well, blessed me, and gave me a draught of water. How beautiful his face! With what light of heaven his eyes shone." The musical theme Kelley introduces here is the leitmotif labeled "This is Jesus of Nazareth." It will be reprised and featured in Act VI just after the dazzling shaft of light representing the power of Christ heals Ben-Hur's mother and sister.[64]

Moments later the enemy is sighted. Arrius immediately orders Metellus to leave Ben-Hur unshackled during the impending battle. The battle itself is highlighted by syncopated orchestral music, individual trumpet blasts, onstage and offstage shouting ("Now pull! Full speed! Faster!"), and two distinct collisions enhanced by the sound "of rending timbers," perhaps produced by a hand-cranked "crash machine" that turned a cogged cylinder against slats of resonant wood. Arrius fights desperately while encouraging his men, and when he is struck on the helmet and reels backwards, Ben-Hur breaks off a piece of his oar and uses its jagged edge as a weapon against the pirates while catching Arrius in his arms. After a third collision, the stage lights go out.

Unseen by the audience, the side scenes are quickly folded in and collapsed onto the floor as the trireme benches and mast base are pushed to the sides and the galley backdrop is lifted to reveal the seascape backdrop already in place. Just as quickly, the men portraying the galley slaves lay their backs on the floor while stagehands from the rear pull a cloth painted to look like the sea's surface and fasten it to a batten near the footlights. The flotsam to which Arrius and Ben-Hur will cling has been concealed under the dais and pinned to the stage floor. It is now uncovered and unpinned as the two actors take their places.[65] As the lights come up for the second scene of Act II, the men under the cloth push it up and down in movements coordinated with the stagehands in the wings to give the appearance of wave action. As they speak and act, Arrius and Ben-Hur make the flotsam move up and down on its flexible hinges. Kelley scored the entire scene with a melody that echoes the initial galley theme above an undulating base.

Feeling hopeless and defeated, Arrius has given Ben-Hur his ring so he can obtain his freedom. But Ben-Hur has sworn an oath to save Arrius, so he tosses the ring into the water. Just then they sight a Roman ship, and Kelley's score begins a crescendo of ascending brass, again echoing the Roman galley theme. The photograph of this scene shows a series of choppy, white-capped waves populated with the flotsam of warships. Half in the water, Arrius with his left hand clutches a beam of wood while grasping with his right onto Ben-Hur who kneels above him and extends his arm to signal an approaching Roman ship. Young's script (31) continues:

> *Arrius* (*excitedly*). Lift me up! (*All his spirit returning.*) Jove with us! A Roman! We are saved. Thank thy God! – and call to them!
> *Ben Hur* (*hailing*). Help! Help!
> *Arrius.* Wave thy hand! Fortune hath not deserted me. The victory shall yet be mine. And thou – I knew thy father – thou shalt be my son. Call to them! Shout!
> *Ben Hur* (*hailing and waving his hand*). Help! Help! Ho!
> [*An answering hail is heard at a distance. On from R., in middle distance, sweeps a Roman galley.*]

5 minute Intermission

The first scene of Act III in the House of Simonides in Antioch features the disabled Simonides, who scoffs at his Roman tormentors and brags that his wealth has enabled him to purchase the confiscated Palace of Hur in Jerusalem from "the master-robber, Caesar." He has installed Amrah as its caretaker. His extensive search for the family of Hur has been to no avail, but his agents Malluch and Sanballat have traced Messala to Antioch. Enter Ilderim, eager to find a charioteer for the upcoming race. He informs Simonides that Balthasar, one of the three Wise Men who had come to him for protection years ago, has returned to his Orchard of Palms and proclaimed that the King of the Jews will establish his kingdom within the year. As Simonides and Ilderim reconfirm their anti-Roman sentiment, "a Roman" enters, unbeknownst to all until he reveals himself as Judah, son of Ithamar. Ben-Hur recounts his experiences of the past few years, then the conversation focuses on Messala and the impending chariot race. After he leaves, Simonides reveals to Esther that Ben-Hur's family owns them as slaves. Esther assures her father that Ben-Hur will free them both. The curtain drops.

Kelley (17–19) covers the extensive scene change with three pages of transition music leading into the much more expansive and celebratory scene in the Grove of Daphne. Young (45) then describes processions of boys and girls along with Priests of Daphne, worshippers bearing offerings, singing girls, and Devadasi (Priestesses of Daphne) beneath layers of leafy green bowers and downstage from a garlanded Greek façade featuring four caryatids. They sing choral arrangements of Young's pagan hymnal lyrics. However, here the texts and sequence of songs and dances in Young's published text and stage directions differ from those in Kelley's published score. That the printer inserts the beginning of Scene 2 before the last page of Scene 1 is just one of the discrepancies. Here follows Young's arrangement and text.

Young begins with a hymn to Apollo of the grove of Daphne:

> Daphne! Daphne! Whilst above,
>   Beams the Sun-God in his power,
> Still the earth his warmth shall prove,
>   Still the bee shall seek the flower,
> And the bird his mate; and love
>   Still shall be the maiden's dower.
>   Follow we
>   Bird and bee,
> Whilst the earth is still in flower!
>   Heigho! Heigho!
>   Ho, for the bridals of Daphne!

A young man and maiden then perform a pantomime of Apollo chasing Daphne. A second singing chorus enters from the right followed by Eros:

> Prithee, maiden, why so coy?
>   What is here to hurt or harm thee?
> What to vex thee, or annoy?
>   What to flutter, or alarm thee?
> Eros – rosy little boy!
>   Let his smiling looks disarm thee!

In the pantomime the maiden yields to Eros.

> Cometh here
> One as fair
> As Apollo's self to charm thee!

After youths carrying hoops of flowers erect a moving bridal bower, the chorus sings a final "Heigho! Heigho! On to the Temple of Daphne!" A trumpet passage precedes an *aulos* player leading a group of shepherds and shepherdesses. All enter the Temple of Daphne.[66]

Ben-Hur and Malluch enter. The despair felt by Judah at this point in the novel is nowhere to be found, nor is he tempted in the slightest by Daphne's pagan Greek delights the audience has been enjoying. He wants to find the chariot course to espy Messala. Some transitional dialogue, accompanied by unadorned incidental music, leads him and Malluch into Scene 3, where the reveling chorus accompanying the young couple sings another ode. The maiden now "joins with the youth at last in the wild abandon of the dance." They finish with:

> For a day,
> While we may,

Quaff the cup and tread the measure!
Heigho! Heigho!
Ho, for the revels of Daphne!

Kelley (40–2) scores this passage first for basses and tenors, then for sopranos and altos. The Devadasi lead a wild dance, and pressing through the throng Ben-Hur and Malluch now find the stadium they had been seeking.

At this point Ben-Hur sees Ilderim's magnificent horses and is tempted when Khaled, Ilderim's agent, proclaims aloud his need for a charioteer. Enter a large, white camel, and from its howdah emerges first Balthasar and then his daughter Iras. Ben-Hur is immediately struck by her beauty and fetches her a cup of water. Revelers return and sing another chorus of "For a day, While ye may." All of a sudden, with rhythmic musical accompaniment, Messala's chariot charges in, disperses the revelers, and rushes directly towards Balthasar and Iras. Ben-Hur brings the chariot to a halt and glares at Messala. In the novel (4.8), Ben-Hur does glare at Messala as the Roman utterly ignores him and flirts with Iras. Young condenses and transforms the passage by having Messala very briefly question Ben-Hur and then just as briefly attempt to charm Iras:

> *Messala.* What is thy quarrel with me? Have I seen thee before? Or wouldst thou shine as a protector of beauty?
> *Iras* (*low, to* BEN HUR). For my father's sake! For mine!
> *Messala* (*again laughing lightly*). None the less, fair mistress, thou wilt smile upon me yet . . . Till another day!

Messala drives off stage. Extremely agitated, Ben-Hur agrees to drive Ilderim's horses against the Roman.

The revelers return with a substantial choral song, "The Spinning of Arachne," representing "the spinning of the web to entangle men's souls." It is composed in modal form (Kelley 43–56), and a "wild dance" brings the act to a close as Iras remounts the camel and from her howdah exchanges smiles with Ben-Hur.

5 minute Intermission

Act IV takes place within Ilderim's tent. Kelley (57–60) imbues his prelude to the "Forest of Palms" with an oriental flavor. Ben-Hur enters, having just finished training his horses. Iras playfully teases him, and then another Roman stranger is brought in. It is Drusus, whom Messala has sent to find out the identity of Ilderim's driver and ask Iras to wear his emblem – a knot of scarlet and gold ribbon. Iras places it "against her breast coquettishly and defiantly." Balthasar enters, speaks about his lengthy pilgrimage, and says, "The hour is at hand." Simonides and Esther enter with papers to prove that Ben-Hur is worth 673 talents and that he owns them in perpetuity as slaves. Simonides credits Esther with convincing him to make these revelations as Iras looks her over and, in an aside, engages the audience in their rivalry. ("So! There is a daughter. Thou art in high favor, it seems.") In contrast Esther affirms her loyalty and embraces her father. After all the other principals exit, Ben-Hur delivers a soliloquy, representing the passage in the novel (4.17), that conflates Judah's attempt to comprehend Balthasar's extended prophecies and his attraction to Iras's allurements. Young uses this moment to bring together diverse thoughts as well about Ben-Hur's family, Esther, and his newfound wealth.

> Wealth, boundless wealth, and "wealth is a means to every end." Spake he the truth? Means, then, to compass justice and vengeance not only for myself, but – dare I think of it? – mayhap for my mother, my sister – my whole race. Oh, vision too dazzling! And Esther – that to her I should owe it all! How sweet her face, how pure, how fair! Like a lily against the other's gorgeous beauty. And yet, were that other at the feast, would I linger? (IRAS *is suddenly heard singing* "The Lament." BEN HUR *pauses, arrested by the sound*.) The nightingale! (*The song of* IRAS *swells and sinks*.) Of what – for whom – doth she sing? (IRAS *executes a brilliant passage*.) Splendor – and power – and passion!

An Ethiopian messenger enters and hands Ben-Hur Messala's emblem. Understanding Iras's signal, Judah goes out to her as the stage becomes dark and Iras continues singing. Kelley's "Song of Iras" resembles the many art-songs that were composed in the previous decade only in using the same lyrics from Wallace's novel ("I sigh as I sing"). The song itself, which Kelley published separately, is a rhythmically and melodically uncomplicated 6/8 *andantino* with rising melodic line, accompanied by open chords, arpeggios, and a scalar passage. As expected, at the foot of Kelley's score (61) appears "Words by Lew Wallace; Copyright 1881–1899 [*sic*] by Harper Bros."

Scene 2 takes place under the moonlight by the edge of the lake. Iras lounges in an elegant loveseat as Ben-Hur leans towards her. Behind them the lake seems to extend back to the horizon. Mesmerized, Ben-Hur kisses Iras and declares his love, but she demands complete devotion and steps into her curved Egyptian shallop. Casting aside devotion to duty, he follows her. As the boat recedes and Iras reprises her song, Simonides and Esther see them from across the stage. Young says that Esther "utters a moan and covers her eyes with her hands."

8 minute Intermission

The first scene of Act V is set before Doric columns and a large arch leading into the Antioch Circus. Facing the audience, the interior wall of the arch displays a banner. Here Young writes unusually detailed stage directions that even cite the correlating passage from the novel: "A BANNER, DISPLAYING THE PROGRAMME OF THE RACE – SEE NOVEL, BOOK 5, CHAPTER 10." Consequently, on the banner below Messala's name the audience could read, as it says in the novel, "BEN HUR – A JEW, DRIVER." The orchestra plays Kelley's prelude, a ¾-time processional designed to represent the power of Rome, as a grand cavalcade crosses the stage. Young explains that the crowd of spectators should enter the Circus, cross the back of the stage, and then return as "newcomers," some wearing the scarlet and gold colors of Messala and others the white emblem of Ben-Hur, and many shouting the name of their favorite, all the while creating the illusion that there are thousands of eager, boisterous spectators.

Cecilius, a half-drunken Roman, is wagering with local citizens. When all have entered the circus and exited the stage, Messala says (to Drusus) of Ben-Hur that he "will humble him in the dust; in the game of love, too, will I break and beggar him." The two Romans hide behind a column as a litter brings in both Iras and Esther. Iras is "gorgeously attired" and Esther "modestly garbed and veiled," but when Messala sees Iras wearing Ben-Hur's white emblem, he curses her: "Pluto take her!" Citizens stare at the unveiled Iras, and Ben-Hur chastises her as well. She instinctively turns this against him: "Did I promise to guard what thou callest my beauty, solely for the delight of *thine* eyes?" She rips off his emblem, and he exits. Messala makes advances upon her. Sanballat conducts his aggressive wagering campaign, stunning Messala by proving that he represents fifty talents. Messala responds, as in the novel, by offering odds of six to one, "the difference between a Roman and a Jew!" A trumpet sounds, the stage goes dark:

> Through the period of darkness the tumult of the crowd heard – shouts of "The Roman!" "The Roman!" "Jove with us!" and "Ben Hur!" "Ben Hur!" Then the thunder of hoof and wheels.

These pre-race encounters involving Messala, Drusus, Ben-Hur, Iras, and Esther have taken place downstage. Meanwhile stagehands have been preparing for Scene 2, the chariot race. Behind the Antioch Circus exterior drops, hostlers were putting into place the racing horses they had retrieved from the stables a few blocks away ten minutes earlier, and the equipment has all been readied. The drops are lifted from the dark stage.

In the darkness the audience hears the thundering hooves and shouts. As the lights come up Messala and Ben-Hur are already driving their *quadrigae* at full gallop. Ben-Hur shouts out "On, Atair! On, Rigel! Antares! Oho, Aldebaran!" The lead changes hands several times until, after a little over one minute, "*the wheel rolls from* MESSALA'S *chariot, and* MESSALA *falls, as* BEN HUR *draws past him. Stage dark. Change.*"

As the lights come back up, Ben-Hur is standing in his chariot before the consul's seat in the interior of the Circus. He receives the victor's crown to the sound of "shouting, cheering, and trumpet calls" and Kelley's triumphal victory march.[67]

10 minute Intermission

Act VI opens in a Palace of Hur interior room. The dome-shaped roofs of Jerusalem are visible through a large window in the back. Simonides, with Esther ever at his side, is instructing a servant to bribe off-duty Roman guards for more information about the two women rumored to have been found in a secret cell in the Tower of Antonia now that Pontius Pilate has taken command. Ben-Hur enters. He has been with the Nazarene at Bethpage and has mustered his three legions of Galileans. Now he recalls encountering the Nazarene as a boy: "That face I have seen again. It is the face of the man – if He be a mere man – who resteth to-night at Bethpage." Young describes that face, as he suggested in the *Boston Globe* interview, in Wallace's style but not his words:

> The same eyes, so full of pity, so mystic, so far-seeing! The same brow, about which a halo seemed to shine! But the face of a king? No! Meek, with the meekness of a woman! Sorrowful, with the fore-knowledge of a martyr! The face of one born, not to rule, but to suffer and, I fear, to die!

As Ben-Hur then describes the miracles he has seen him perform, Amrah, who alone knows the whereabouts of Ben-Hur's mother and sister, rushes out to inform them. In a surprising turn, Ben-Hur also announces that Balthasar's daughter has abandoned him and gone to Messala. Simonides is wheeled off-stage, leaving Ben-Hur and Esther alone. Ben-Hur confesses his love for her:

> I admit the Egyptian wove a spell about me. She had a serpentine power of fascination that took away my reason ... (*taking her hand*) I have to tell thee now, Esther, that the glamour is gone, and I see with my natural eyes. Her beauty had in it a taint of poison; thine is the beauty of the rose just breaking into bloom, pure of itself, and doubly pure of the morning dew upon it. Oh, sweet Esther, I love thee!

A veiled woman enters, and Esther immediately leaves. It is Iras, sent by Messala, who now attempts to blackmail Ben-Hur by threatening to inform Sejanus, as she does in the novel (8.6), except that in the novel it is to inform him that "Arrius" is an escaped Jewish galley slave and here it is that Ben-Hur has trained three legions "to seize the Roman governor and enthrone the son of the Carpenter of Nazareth." Ben-Hur steadfastly refuses to submit and, paraphrasing the novel, offers Messala only Iras: "I send him thee, whom he shall find the sum of all curses."

Here Young notes that *"the whole scene from this forth should be played with the utmost rapidity."* In short order Amrah reports that Ben-Hur's mother and sister are alive in the Vale of Hinnom, so Ben-Hur rushes out to find them, with Esther close behind, but not before addressing Iras as "thou vile woman!" Simonides orders Iras to leave. As the latter acts out Young's instructions ("Iras with face bowed in abject defeat, moves towards the door"), the orchestra plays Kelley's "The Fall of Iras," an *allegro con fuoco* segment that elaborates on the musical theme introduced at the end of Act I when Ben-Hur swears, "Oh, Lord, in the hour of thy vengeance, mine be the hand to put it upon him!"

Kelley begins Scene 2 with "The Vale of Hinnom" prelude "suggestive of the misery of the lepers."[68] Amrah tells Tirzah and Mother about Ben-Hur and the Nazarene, and in a much beloved sentimental tableau, the two women come upon Ben-Hur, who, fatigued and in despair, has fallen asleep, dreaming of them.

As the three women make their way to the Mount of Olives, the instrumental and choral music, like "the choiring of angels," begins to play and continues until the end of the act. Kelley here composed a series of eight-part choral settings of the appropriate passages in Matthew 11: 10 and 21: 9 ("Hosanna in the highest") and Luke 19: 38 ("Blessed be the King that cometh"), where Christ and his disciples have made their way to the Mount of Olives.

Into this final setting a chorus enters, singing repeatedly in a fugal arrangement, "Who is this? Why this tumult?" (Revelation of Stephen or Psalm 2). From the other side of the stage a chorus of children enters holding palms and singing as a response, "This is Jesus of Nazareth of Galilee!" in 9/8 time featuring triplet patterns. They are joined by a chorus of the "multitude" and then a soprano chorus repeats "Blessed be the King that cometh." As the base movement quickens and trumpets and trombones introduce and then repeat a triplet pattern:

> Suddenly, from above, a dazzling radiance pours upon the kneeling women; the palms wave, the anthem swells, and touches its culmination. The drop becomes opaque, but the chanting continues, again distant, and low.

The strings play a tremolo pattern of swelling chords combined with the brass triplet pattern and the chorus singing "Hosanna in the highest." Ben-Hur awakes and soon encounters Esther, Malluch, and Amrah, who lead him to the Mount of Olives where he finds his mother and sister now cured of their leprosy by the Nazarene. The leitmotif "This is Jesus of Nazareth" representing Christ and Redemption is heard again. As the Hur family embrace one another and then fall upon their knees, the chorus sings the *Nunc dimittis* from Luke 2: 29–32: ("Lord, now lettest thou thy servant depart in peace ... A light to the revelation of the Gentiles, and the glory of Thy people Israel"). Young concludes: "*the music swells into a joyous and triumphant strain.*"

BEHIND, BENEATH, AND IN FRONT OF THE STAGE

Audiences in 1899 expected this high-profile dramatization of *Ben-Hur: A Tale of the Christ* to be faithful to the novel. Young accordingly gave all the major characters in the novel speaking parts, fleshing out a few minor characters like Cecilius and the hortator to connect and render into dialogue format some of the disparate events described in prose in the novel. The drunken, wagering Cecilius serves also to characterize Roman decadence. Young invented Khaled to consolidate Ilderim's search for a charioteer and his negotiations with Judah by having him read aloud (for the audience's benefit) a public proclamation. Young also changed some details of the novel to shape the story as a drama. To create more tension on the stage, he fully develops the rivalry between Esther and Iras. They repeatedly eye each other, and Iras mutters a number of sarcastic asides. The Circus prelude brings the two of them as well as Ben-Hur and Messala together in the same time and place. Wallace's Esther never speaks harshly to Iras and in fact invites her to stay at their house at the end of the novel, but in the play the tension between her and Iras builds throughout, leading to Iras's demise. Also, Young complicates the relationship between Arrius and his adopted son by having Ben-Hur claim that he feels like a prisoner in Rome. This symbolic parallel is not found in the novel.

> Nothing did he deny me, save the one thing my heart most hungered for – leave to search for my people. That, with more than a father's jealousy, and with all his Roman pride, he forbade. And so close were the bonds in which he held me that while he lived, Rome was my prison. He is dead – and my search is begun.

Nor is the novel's description of Judah's unfamiliarity with the power of wealth. Here Judah immediately decides to use his 673 talents as a means "to compass justice and vengeance." Similarly, in observance of the original agreement between Wallace and Klaw & Erlanger, Young brought the play to its conclusion before the Crucifixion. This required making a significant change to Wallace's sequence of events. In the novel Balthasar died on the day of the Crucifixion, and that is when his daughter Iras left to join Messala. In the play Young has Iras abandon her father and flee to Messala earlier and for purely romantic reasons.

In rendering novel to stage, Young necessarily had to reduce or eliminate most of Wallace's lengthy and detailed explications. Where Wallace gave Balthasar several chapters to expound his prophetic theology (4.15–17), Young writes a compact speech of a single paragraph in the first scene of Act IV:

> One more stage hath my pilgrimage. Long hath been my time of waiting and wandering since I fared with Gaspar and Melchior, and, led by the Star, we three, from the three ends of the earth, found in the manger of Bethlehem, the Holy Child, before whose throne all kings shall bow. Thirty and more years ago! But never hath my faith wavered. And now the Child is a man. Soon. If ever, He must declare himself, and stand forth and reign. And He will. A voice telleth me the hour is at hand.

To concentrate the visual and action elements of the story, Young condensed the novel's eighty-one chapters and many excursions back and forth from city to desert and Rome to Judea into a prelude and six acts consisting of thirteen scenes.[69] Bethlehem and Misenum had to be omitted, as did the Palace at Idernee and the entire scene with Thord as well as the Palace of Hur in its desolate state. The requirements of dramaturgy allotted Young much less time to develop Judah's suffering. Nor could he fully develop Simonides' back-story. On the other hand, by eliminating

Judah's participation in the advent of Christ and the Crucifixion, Young could move the chariot race closer to the end of the story and make it more climactic, thereafter literally urging the director to hurry along the ensuing scenes. To reincarnate Wallace's preference for intrigue and mystery, characters sometimes appear on stage before the other characters or even the audience learn their identity. This helps integrate the argument Ben-Hur and Iras have about her not wearing a veil, and it integrates as well the mystery of the Nazarene, who of course is never seen.

The play incorporates most of the major elements of Wallace's narrative. The Wise Men gather, and Ben-Hur develops into an anti-Roman crusader, is assisted by the young Jesus, rescues Arrius and obtains his freedom, seeks revenge against Messala, reacquires his wealth from Simonides, finds his mother and sister, and embraces Christ. This is accomplished in a visually and aurally spectacular production that features the Star of Bethlehem, the Roman naval battle and sea rescue, the choral singing and "wild dances" at Daphne, the moonlit lake with Iras's song, the chariot race, and the Revelation that cures Ben-Hur's mother and sister. Such a visually complicated production required ninety-five drops, and many reviewers commented very positively on the scenery, particularly the perspective scenes of Jerusalem rooftops stretching out into the distance, the atmospheric and moody moonlit scene by the lake of the Orchard of Palms, and the gloomy Vale of Hinnom, visually splendid scenes not diminished by the spectacular action events. The artists who originally created these highly praised visions were Ernest Albert and Ernest Gros. Both were already established by 1897, and they often worked together for Klaw & Erlanger until separating in the late 1910s. Their designs for *Ben-Hur* were used for many years, but in 1909 Oliver P. Bernard was also credited in programs.[70] For the London production in 1902 the designs were painted by T. R. Ryan, Bruce Smith, and McCleery of London, and after that engagement this same scenery would be shipped to the United States and used for the New York Theatre engagement in the fall of 1903.[71] From the final year of performances, a program from the Baltimore Academy of Music printed for the March, 1920, engagement, attributes the scenery entirely to Frank Platzer.[72]

The spectacular elements were thoroughly planned in advance, demanded huge cost outlays, and were executed night after night without major mishap. The use of Burgess's horse-racing system remained at the core of the production. Even the 1920 Baltimore program cites:

> Messrs. Klaw & Erlanger acknowledge their indebtedness to Mr. Neil Burgess for some of the patented appliances used in the Chariot Race.

For *The County Fair* and *The Year One*, Burgess had placed his horses facing the drop-off at the edge of the stage and the dark vacuum behind it, which tended to frighten the horses.[73] For the Klaw & Erlanger production the horses were turned towards the wings of the stage, and Claude L. Hagen developed many additional innovations and enhancements. Our best source here is the August 25, 1900, *Scientific American* that featured Hagan's electro-mechanical designs and illustrated them in three engravings, and this article was redacted three years later in several newspaper publicity features.[74] While the wagering and romantic flirtations were taking part in the front of the Circus exterior set, stagehands behind the false façades were removing a number of large panels from the stage flooring and placing them in the wings. Soon the eight horses were secured by chains and cables on the treadmills, which remained locked until the scene began. The treadmills themselves were 12-feet long, 2 ½-feet wide, and made of 2-inch hickory slats covered with rubber.[75] The chariots did not sit on the stage floor or a treadmill but on a cradle and short poles that kept the wheels above the floor level. Electric motors, plugged into floor sockets, made the wheels turn. Once the race began, stagehands below poured dried vegetable-matter into fourteen conduits that blew clouds of "dust" behind the chariot wheels. The chariots were attached to sliding platforms so Messala could alternately race in the lead or behind Ben-Hur.[76] At a given signal, a spring mechanism forced Messala's wheels to pop off and tilted the chariot over, and the whole cradle assemblage supporting the chariot structure, the four treadmills, and all four horses, slid back 15ft on the platform to give the illusion that Ben-Hur had toppled his rival's chariot, pulled into the lead, and won the race.

The 1920 Baltimore program still cites Hagen's "moving floor effects panoramas." This patented system showed the audience three large aprons, canvases measuring 96ft × 25ft and painted to represent the tiers of seats at the Antioch Circus from the track-level view. (The *Souvenir Album* did not show this but substituted a perspective painting from the race-level point of view between the *spina*, decorated with obelisks, and the seats, topped by a massive Corinthian porch.) One canvas stretched along the back of the stage behind the chariots, the other two along the wings. They were coordinated by a series of below-stage electric motors and belts and above-stage hangers, gears, and pulleys to roll along in unison at the speed of 2000ft per minute, creating the illusion of the chariots whizzing passed the stands filled with spectators. George W. Enright was later credited with this design.[77] Before the scene began, the side panoramas that had been folded in against the central one, were now unfolded and locked into place. When Ben Teal, the stage manager, signaled a stagehand operator with an electric lamp, the latter manually started the motor.[78] Another feature was attached along the flooring of the stage, where the arena sands were simulated by a number of like-painted canvas strips that were also moved on a series of belts to create the illusion of forward motion. This effect was so sophisticated that differently sized belts allowed the "sand" to move increasingly more slowly towards the rear of the stage. All these

Figure 9.1 The secrets of the Klaw & Erlanger chariot race treadmill and cyclorama were revealed in 1900 issues of *Scientific American* and *St. Nicolas*.

strips were installed so they could be removed immediately after the completion of the scene and leave a level stage floor.[79]

The *Scientific American* article states that it took eight minutes to set up the scene:

> In that time the side panoramas are folded out into position, the sections of floors are removed, and the chariots are rolled into position and adjusted. The horses are hitched to the chariots, connections are made with the belts for giving the effect of moving ground, and the dust arrangements are put in place.

The $15,000 cost of this elaborate machinery was only a fraction of Klaw & Erlanger's initial outlay of approximately $70,000 that included completely remodeling the stage of the theater.[80] Eager to promote their hit play by impressing audience members with the sheer size of their "stupendous production," for the next season's Boston premiere Klaw & Erlanger made sure to list prominently in the program some impressive numbers, e.g. the 900 amperes of incandescent lamps and 400 of electric calciums, the 102,740 square feet of canvas drops, the 2½ tons of scenery ("exclusive of the chariot apparatus"), and the 10¼ miles of rope along with the forty men required to set and clear the stage during just thirty-four minutes of intermissions.[81] They also boast that the chariot race covers 1,320ft.

From the thousands of performances at approximately 200 venues over two decades, there were relatively few reports of stage mishaps, especially considering that the production required the synchronized movements of many machine parts, more than eight horses, a camel, and over 100 onstage extras. Oddly, only the reviewer for Milwaukee's *Sentinel* reported that for the premiere performance at the Broadway Theatre in 1899, Messala's chariot did not collapse, and that this necessitated an early curtain drop.[82] Even Clement Scott, who wrote a six-paragraph critique of this method of recreating the chariot race, preferring Barnum's circus variety, did not mention this, nor did the eyewitness reviewer for the *New York Times*.[83] Apparently there were glitches when the play opened at the newly remodeled Academy of Music in Baltimore in 1902, though the hint in *The Sun* is counterbalanced in the same issue by a printed statement from Claude Hagen, affirming that "everything was absolutely perfect."[84] When problems appeared before the premiere at London's Drury Lane in late March, 1902, the opening was delayed until April 3 rather than risk a problem during the performance. The *New York Times* reported that one night in 1903 the stagehands mistakenly lowered a drop in front of Ben-Hur's chariot leaving Messala appearing as the only contestant.[85]

There were a few incidents involving the animals. Two days after the show moved from the East Coast to Chicago's Illinois Theatre on September 3, 1901, two of the horses, already dressed in race regalia, shied when faced with the relatively unfamiliar theater entrance and ran from Michigan Avenue to Lake and Dearborn before several neo-Ben-Hurs grabbed their bridles and brought them to a halt.[86] Reportedly "nearly every chorus girl" fed the beloved camel Bluch so many sweets in Baltimore in 1902, that he died suddenly.[87] William Farnum reportedly had himself "vaccinated" because eight times per week he handled horses on stage and fought a dozen pirates in hand-to-hand combat.[88] In his 1929 autobiography, William S. Hart recalls that on opening night, towards the end of the scene in which he rode his chariot into the crowd at Daphne, he had to jump back on his chariot prematurely because the costumed horse handler developed stage fright and lost control.[89] Hart also famously claims that one night at Boston's Colonial Theatre his horses defeated those of Ben-Hur, then played by William Farnum, much to the latter's embarrassment with many of Farnum's friends and relatives from Bucksport, Maine, in attendance. His anecdote has no contemporary or independent corroboration, and given that the winner of the race at each performance was determined by not the relative speed of the horses but the sliding rail mechanism below stage, this is difficult to believe. Accounts of the incident written decades later (in association with the release of the 1959 film) specified that Ben-Hur's treadmill broke, ignoring the fact that each of his four horses had its own treadmill.[90] This is not the only spurious story associated with *Ben-Hur*. A verifiably false legend persisted for years that the old Fort Worth Opera House had to close because the weight of the horses, treadmills, and chariot race mechanisms had caused the stage to collapse during a performance.[91]

For some, the real onstage heroes were the horses themselves. Even Farnum said in an interview, "When I get through I feel that I am the victor, but when the audience applauds I do not like to bow, for I feel that the applause is for the horses."[92] In 1929 Hart recollected the name of one of Ben-Hur's horses, Monk, and the names of his quartet – Tom, Jerry, Rosie, and Topsy, the former pair being white, the latter two black, conforming to Wallace's description of their colors.[93] But more contemporary was the 1902 article in *The Minneapolis Journal* that reported the names of Ben-Hur's quartet as Monk, Jacko, Nellie, and Emma, and Messala's as Tom and Whitie (white), and Phil and Dollie (black).[94] Tom must have been the original "Old Tom" described in a newspaper feature in 1903.[95] This was the thoroughbred Hagan used to demonstrate his original treadmill mockup for Wallace. The feature does not specify whether Wallace witnessed the treadmill trial before or after he signed the April 11, 1899, contract with Klaw & Erlanger, but if it had been before and if Tom had failed, there may never have been a Klaw & Erlanger *Ben-Hur*. The original treadmill was only 27 inches wide, but Tom was said to be a "very close" runner. The article also reports that Tom helped train other thoroughbreds and that he would make his own way from Hagen's shop to the stables. Of the four horses used for Messala's chariot on stage, Tom was always closest to the audience, and by at least as late as 1903 Tom had not missed a single performance.[96] Several different eyewitness accounts tell us that Tom and the other horses were capable of waiting calmly behind stage when stagehands were scurrying about preparing for the race scene in the darkness before the race began, and even after the canvas behind them started whirring, it was not until they "heard their cue" that they became excited and ready to leap into action.[97] They also knew when the race had been won and it was time to stop.[98] Their trainers for many years were Frank Engels and Dr. William H. Potter, a veterinarian who worked in Boston.[99] The former insisted on taking the original horses to England for the 1902 Drury Lane production because he believed that American horses, unlike their "slow-witted" English cousins, could "learn tricks faster than any other equine nationality."[100] By 1902 there were reported to be over fifty horses in use, with full complements for the American circuit, the London production, the Sydney production, and even more in training for the proposed engagements in Paris and St. Petersburg.[101] The single original camel was purchased from Ben Wallace's Circus in Peru, Indiana.[102] It was injured in a sleet storm in New York, so a replacement was purchased from Sells Brothers Circus in Columbus, Ohio, and later a second camel was purchased from the Hagenbeck circus in Hamburg. An earlier report claims that Klaw purchased two camels in Hamburg, but a later feature article on the *Ben-Hur* animals specifies just one Hagenbeck camel, "Ben," a Siberian white.[103]

The incidental music composed by Edgar Stillman Kelley helped establish the emotional content for the intimate scenes, provided historical authenticity, and brought the performance to a powerful and inspirational conclusion. Like several of the most distinguished composers discussed in Chapter 8, Kelley spent several years in England, France, and Germany studying harmony, composition, piano, and organ, returning to the United States, like Chadwick, in 1880. After establishing his theatrical reputation with the music he composed for McKee Rankin's 1885 production of *Macbeth* in San Francisco, he took up professorial positions on the faculty of the New York College of Music and New York University.[104] By the time his music for *Ben-Hur* was published, he had been named Acting Professor of Musical Theory at Yale, replacing Horatio Parker. Musicologists have recognized Wagnerian influence in his music in that he takes "the most pertinent phrases in the text for illustration" and establishes leitmotifs that echo pertinent themes in various parts of his scores.[105] In *Macbeth*, for instance, he had a theme for Ambition, while at the end of Act I in *Ben-Hur* he introduced a theme for Vengeance where Ben-Hur says "O Lord, in the hour of thy vengeance, *mine* be the hand to put it upon him!" He reprises this leitmotif in "The Fall of Iras" at the end of Act VI, Scene 1. He establishes another leitmotif for Christ's

Redemption (Act II), which is recalled throughout the inspirational final minutes of the drama in Act VI.

Kelley infused historical authenticity into his score. In constructing the "The Approach of the Magi" in the Prelude, he employed "the ancient musical scale peculiar to the Semitic peoples – Arabs and Hebrews," that is, pentachords featuring the augmented 2nd.[106] As a professor of music theory and ethnomusicology, Kelley was familiar with a number of elements of ancient Greek music theory, the most important and distinct feature of which was their harmonic system. Ancient Greek music theory had become an area of concentrated study in the 1890s. In 1894 D. B. Munro published the first important work on the subject in English, *The Modes of Ancient Greek Music*, and during the 1890s a number of fragments of Greek music written on papyrus and inscribed in stone had been discovered, analyzed, and published as academic studies circulated in professional journals.[107] In 1902 Kelley was invited to lecture on Chinese and Greek music at Yale, Columbia, and elsewhere, demonstrating that American institutions of higher learning were now generally interested in ancient and ethnic musical studies, and that Kelley was considered an authority.[108] For the Chorus of Girls passages near the beginning of the Daphne section, Kelley incorporated his studies by employing the Greek Dorian scale.[109] To represent the ancient Dionysian *aulos* preceding "The Spinning of Arachne," Kelley composed a lively passage of eighth and sixteenth notes and limited each musical phrase to the range of a Greek tetrachord. To imitate "some of the meters peculiar to the Greeks," he inserts triplet clusters in otherwise duple constructions. "The Spinning of Arachne," particularly the penultimate section (*allegro con moto*), lacks a key signature and builds on brief Greek modal segments of limited range, usually a pentachord, even if to the untrained ear it just sounds like an elegant choral hymn.[110] Technical and arcane as all this may seem, the result was effective. *Werner's Magazine*, the monthly publication of the Music Teachers' National Association, describes the music in the Daphne Grove scenes as "unusual" but only because Kelley draped these historical authenticities "with modern clothing."

REACTIONS AND REVIEWS

Wingate reports that the theater was packed from boxes to balcony to standing room. Erlanger later reflected that this was the first "national opening," with many national and international critics in attendance, as were a host of influential theater managers and impresarios, including Florenz Ziegfeld, who many years hence would be involved with licensing the 1925 MGM *Ben-Hur*.[111] Wingate describes an air of "expectancy" when the curtain rose promptly at 8:00 p.m., and writes that the "spectacular genius" of the "beautiful and expressive" desert scene with the pulsating star created an initial positive impression among the audience members, who whispered their approval to each other. He very much appreciates Young's "actual and honest portrayal of character; Jew is to be Jew, and Roman to be Roman." Similarly, in the relationship between Arrius and Ben-Hur he sees "the certainty of the appreciation of real worth, somewhere along the pathway of life, whether it lie in laborer or Ruler." He finds the scenic effect after the naval battle to be particularly impressive, pointing out that the Roman ship that comes to rescue Arrius and Ben-Hur bears a beautiful star, "bright as polished gold," on its topmost sail. Of the third act in the Garden of Daphne Wingate makes clear that Kelley's "Chorus of Girls" passages overwhelmed him with their authentic ancient conception and that Young's use of the continuously circling crowd had its desired effect even though the viewer understood the stagecraft that produced it:

> Two hundred and sixty chorus girls of almost all ages, in modest dress, nothing nude, just beautiful, that's all. . . . The chorus girls marched in and about the garden which was thickly set with trees covered with exquisite foliage and blooming vines, together with the undulation of the ground enabling them to appear and reappear until you were ready to believe there were a thousand of them.[112]

He also praises the scenic effect of the moonlit lake, the parallax effect of watching the chariot horses gallop in one direction while the arena [circus] scenes move in the opposite direction, and the multitude of people assembled on the Mount of Olivet. At the conclusion of the performance, he adds, the audience cheered for twenty minutes.

Wingate was from Crawfordsville. His positive reaction was expected. But even the critic for the *New York Times*, after identifying the play as "ordinary melodrama," lambasting Hart for being "as crudely violent and incoherent as ever," and criticizing the religious scenes that he thought would "undoubtedly shock many persons," he praises the spectacle of the presentation ("beautiful beyond expectation"), the visual splendor of the Daphne revelry and the moonlit lake ("all superb"), and even the scenes with Simonides, which "have a poetical quality."[113] He also praised the production itself, pointing out that even for an opening night of such a complicated presentation there seemed to be no mistakes during the scene changes or in managing the various lighting effects.

The veteran Willie Winter, drama critic for the *New York Tribune* since 1865, wrote the harshest review. He unloaded a general attack against all attempts at rendering popular novels into stage plays. Rightly, he argued that the printed page and the live stage have very different requirements. But beyond the generic objections, he also disapproved of the *Ben-Hur* adaptation specifically:

> There is not a single essentially dramatic situation in the piece . . . It is a languid story and it has been languidly told. No attempt is made to develop character.[114]

He cared not a whit for *Ben-Hur*'s modernized spectacular effects, and he, like the *Times* reviewer, objected to the religious component, arguing that even modern dramatic effect cannot recreate biblical reality:

> Men may come and men may go, as the poet Tennyson has comprehensively remarked, but the atmosphere of that weird, mysterious, and sublime night, when the shepherds were watching their flocks and the awful portent of revealed Divinity flamed in the wintry sky, can never be expressed by canvas and calciums.

Nevertheless, most national and international reviews were effusively positive. Papers like the *St. Louis Post-Dispatch* and *Chicago Daily Tribune*, quoting Sidney Sharp's syndicated review in *World*, declared that the New York performance was "a memorable event in stage history."[115] And in describing the audience's reaction to the chariot race, they said: "Wilder enthusiasm than that which followed the scene has seldom manifested itself in a theater." Leander Richardson, another well-established drama critic, wrote in London's *Daily Telegraph*:

> I have been going to theaters for a good many years now, but I never saw a success upon the stage in this or any other country that compared in even a remote degree with the one which went on record last evening.[116]

Certainly the most accurately prophetic review was syndicated from the *New York Dramatic News*:

> "Ben Hur" has come. It's going will be a matter of years, for it is a play that will outlive the oldest play now on the stage of modern times and its stay at the Broadway theater is sure until the hot weather drives it out.[117]

None of these reviewers advanced the argument that *Ben-Hur* was a great drama, but that was never the strength of *Ben-Hur*. As a theatrical spectacle, it was indisputably stupendous. Despite their thoughtful criticisms, both *The Times* and *World* reviews predicted great popular success for the play. And as it turned out, their objections to the religious component of the drama would rapidly become obsolete. Within months *Werner's Magazine* would publish still photographs of Anton Lang portraying Jesus, Anna Flunger as Mary, and three additional photographs of actors portraying biblical characters in the Oberammergau Passion Play of 1900. Klaw & Erlanger themselves were pioneers in producing film versions of the Oberammergau Passion Play as well as original productions of the Passion of Christ.[118] These would be widely distributed in the United States in just a few years and by comparison make the religious imagery in the Klaw & Erlanger *Ben-Hur* seem modest and reserved, even quaint and tasteful. Seven years after the Klaw & Erlanger production went dark in 1920, Cecil B. DeMille would make one of the most widely distributed and watched films ever made – *The King of Kings* – in which H. B. Warner vividly portrayed Christ on the screen for most of the film's two and one-half hours. Whatever quibbles or fundamental quarrels some critics may have had with the dramaturgy or religious propriety of the

Klaw & Erlanger *Ben-Hur*, the public and most critics agreed that they had witnessed an innovative theatrical experience that would prove to be an unparalleled success.

The production played at the Broadway Theatre every night at 8:00 p.m. with 2:00 p.m. matinees on Wednesday and Saturday, and a special matinee on New Year's Day. As they did during pre-production, Klaw & Erlanger frequently updated the theater world about their progress, but now they were usually trumpeting the length of the run to entice additional patrons. The ad on the theater pages of the January 21 *New York Tribune* was standard size and unadorned. Thick block letters stated simply "9th WEEK – BEN-HUR."[119] This same week they announced that Daniel Frohman was taking back Edward Morgan to open a new comedy, so they had engaged Emmett Corrigan, who had been playing Ilderim, to play the role of Ben-Hur.[120] The ad in February featured the words, "ALL ROADS LEAD TO THE BROADWAY – 4th MONTH – 114 TIMES – BEN-HUR."[121] They ran these kinds of ads repeatedly until the end of the season.[122]

In March Klaw & Erlanger announced in the *New York Times* that they had made an "important and effective improvement" in the chariot race, the mechanisms described above which moved along the stage floor to resemble the moving ground, as well as "a low, front wall of stonework."[123] Constantly developing means of urging the public to purchase tickets, the same week they announced that theatergoers in many cities were forming "Ben-Hur Clubs." Members of these clubs would contribute a set fee each week so they could accumulate enough to pay for the trip to New York to see *Ben-Hur*.[124] This was not mere hype: for two decades *Ben-Hur* would consistently generate extra-urban excursions, although they were usually arranged and encouraged by local theater managers, with the assistance of the Klaw & Erlanger advance agents.

When the season finally closed on May 12, a performance graced with a congratulatory telegram from Lew Wallace, the *New York Times* reported in a comprehensive, season-end summary that several New York productions ran longer and netted more money than in any recent years and that "the most important among them" was *Ben-Hur*.[125] It reports the astounding figures: 194 performances played to over 400,000 people, with regular receipts of over $18,000 per week. Shortly after, Klaw & Erlanger circulated a report about Wallace's $30,000 royalty.

The close of the first season did not at all put a halt to the publicity or marketing of *Ben-Hur*. June reports followed Klaw's European travels as he was now reported to be in Hamburg purchasing two trained camels for the play.[126] Just one week later the "Theatrical Notes" section of *The Washington Post* had three separate items to report: Ben Teal would begin rehearsals August 6 for the September 3 reopening, "the well-known character actor" George Osborne would play the role of Simonides, and

William Farnum had been engaged to play the title role for the next three years.[127] The last note details that Farnum was young (twenty-six) and tall (5'11") and had a build to be compared favorably with that of Samson and Sandow: "An actor who can look Ben-Hur as well as act the part is a valuable acquisition to this play." A July column in the *Los Angeles Times* announced that Klaw had engaged the young English actress Nellie Thorne to play Esther, and that additional improvements have been made to the chariot race "which will greatly add to its remarkable realism."[128]

THE METAMORPHOSIS OF LEW WALLACE

The audience at the premiere Broadway Theatre performance in November, 1899, burst into spontaneous applause after the Act V chariot race. During the one dozen or so curtain calls, they called for Wallace to speak. Reluctant at first, Wallace acquiesced and was guided by Erlanger from his lower box to the stage, where the aging author apologized and said he did not "have the voice to make a speech."[129] According to *The Sun*, at some point that evening he was quoted as saying:

> I take this lesson from the performance of this evening – that we are no longer dependent upon London or Paris, but that here in America there is at command the genius to undertake every theatrical necessity.[130]

William S. Hart recounts that after the performance Wallace told him, "Young man, I want to thank you for giving me the Messala that I drew in my book."[131] Still another source reported that Wallace remarked, "Without the religious music of Mr. Stillman Kelley, the stage production of *Ben-Hur* would have been an impossibility."[132] Delivering a prepared statement the next day, he expressed his own sense of wonderment at cutting-edge stagecraft and its ability to enhance the simulation of antiquity:

> It far surpasses my expectations. The staging is something wonderful, and I am free to say that every idea has been more than carried out. The meeting of the wise men in the desert is a beautiful piece of stagecraft, and shows how modern electricity can successfully be utilized to illustrate an ancient happening.[133]

By all accounts Wallace was quite satisfied with both the adaptation and the performance. His comments were reported nationwide, the press now providing Klaw & Erlanger with the ultimate endorsement for their production:

> After nearly 20 years of reluctance to have the scenes and incidents described in my book of "Ben Hur" translated to the stage, it is with a spirit of considerable relief that I am able to make acknowledgement now that final acquiescence was not an error. Yet I do not regret the hesitation, because I doubt if 10 years ago theatrical invention and ingenuity had reached a point where adequate production of "Ben Hur" could have been made within the limitation of a stage covering an area of 40×70 feet.[134]

Even ten weeks later the *New York Times* thought it worthy to report that when Wallace arrived in town with almost the entire Indiana Congressional delegation and their wives to see a February performance, Klaw & Erlanger sent each of the wives a large corsage bouquet of white roses with a card attached, saying, "Wear Ben-Hur's colors."[135] Inspired as a poet and author, Wallace wrote to Kelley on April 15, 1900, about setting the music to a libretto for an opera based on *Ben-Hur: A Tale of the Christ*.[136] Wallace wrote that he was "ready to begin" writing the libretto as soon as he heard back, but there is no mention of the project thereafter.[137]

Wallace's celebrity and his full endorsement of the play as well as his appreciation for the "tact and sensitiveness displayed in the treatment of the religious episodes" meant as much for the Klaw & Erlanger production as it did for the *Ben-Hur* phenomenon for the next two decades. It would be two years later that Wallace would endorse John Holland Fountain Pens. He had by now been gradually but thoroughly transformed into a commercial author and celebrity. His age was too advanced for him to produce any more writing for the general public. It would be Susan and then Henry along with Harper and Erlanger who would carry on his professional and commercial legacy to the next stages. Instead the reader should regard this as the final stage in the growth of a frontier child and an adult public servant with a passion for writing, a talent for evoking a distinguished popular image, a penchant for business, and a strong sense of self worth and the value of his literary gold mine.

During the twenty years from the publication of *Ben-Hur: A Tale of the Christ* to the Klaw & Erlanger premiere on November 29, 1899, the climate of American commerce, industry, and consumerism had changed, and concepts of religious propriety were evolving. As the new century emerged, the dramatic adaptation of *Ben-Hur*, dependent upon mechanical and electrical devices, ready to tour the country, was a modern adaptation in harmony with this new world.[138] Just as the original novel was released into the lengthy boom of the American economy after the 1873 crash and delighted the developing consumer culture with its action sequences, religious positivism, and eloquent but accessible literary style, the Klaw & Erlanger production flourished during the golden age of American invention, industrialization, and consumer expansion with its state-of-the-art stagecraft, religious nostalgia, and powerful dramaturgical spectacle. The "stupendous" production of the Klaw & Erlanger adaptation of *Ben-Hur* would from this point become a regular part of the American theatrical landscape.

Lew Wallace would receive hundreds of thousands of dollars in royalties. As already mentioned, at the conclusion of the first season Klaw & Erlanger circulated a report that the royalty paid out to Wallace for the season was $30,000.[139] Klaw & Erlanger promoted this as positive publicity, but a comment in the *Cincinnati Enquirer* version, under the headline, "Wallace's 'Ben Hur' Royalties," reveals the naivety, and perhaps envy, of a segment of the contemporary public that had not yet come to understand the implications of a burgeoning shift in the economics of artistry, copyright, and popular culture.

> General Lew Wallace made an independent fortune out of the novel of "Ben Hur," and it appears likely that he will acquire another by the stage version of his book. Klaw & Erlanger have just paid him $30,000 in royalties for the six months the play has been running at the Broadway Theater, the gross receipts for that period being $450,000. General Wallace was not required to write anything for this money. All that he did for it was to sign a contract giving William Young permission to dramatize it for the use of Klaw & Erlanger. It looks as if the play would last for several seasons, and it is possible that General Wallace will receive at least 10 times $30,000.

This telling statement observes incredulously that Wallace did not have to "write anything" to earn this enviable sum of money. All he had to do "was to sign a contract," as if that was a simple route to fabulous riches. Despite his Civil War patina, Midwestern background, religious aura, and elderly stature, Lew Wallace as a popular commercial author was a pioneer in safeguarding, guiding, promoting, licensing, and profiting handsomely from a literary creation.[140]

SECONDARY SALES

Joseph Byron's Stage-Production Photographs

Klaw & Erlanger issued photographs of the production in several different types of publications. This was not common practice at the time, when it was only studio portrait photographs of actors that circulated either separately or assembled in albums depicting a group of cast members or selected celebrity thespians, and when photographs were only occasionally reproduced or rendered as engravings or photogravures in newspapers. But Klaw & Erlanger had a special property on their hands, and as the reader knows, the early *Ben-Hur* successes tended to proliferate and create by-products in other media or genres. Klaw & Erlanger were pushing the envelope of normal procedure and investing substantial sums into first producing and now promoting *Ben-Hur*. The photographs themselves were flash-light photographs taken by Joseph Byron. Associated with Daniel Frohman since 1889, Byron had developed a reputation for being Broadway's leading stage-production photographer.[141] He usually shot his stage-production photographs during dress rehearsals, but to light a big stage covered by a large cast, Byron had to employ a synchronized array of seven different lamps containing magnesium powder ignited with a blow torch, and for the camera to gather enough light for the image, the actors had to hold their poses for as long as forty-five seconds. Consequently, the poses have a staged look, and in *Werner's Magazine* they were actually labeled and critiqued not as dramatic stills but static tableaux.

The published photographs encompass tableaux from all six acts and thirteen scenes, beginning with an image of the Wise Men Prelude, the Act I roof-terrace of the Palace of Hur, the Act II galley interior and sea rescue, the Act III room in the House of Simonides, Temple of Apollo at Daphne, and Fountain of Castalia, the Act IV dower of Ilderim in the Orchard of Palms as well as the moonlit lake, the Act V Circus exterior and interior, and the Act VI room in the Palace of Hur, Vale of Hinnom, and Mount Olivet. There are two different tableaux each on the roof-terrace of the Palace of Hur and the dower of Ilderim, three at the Fountain of Castalia. The photograph of the Circus interior in Act V depicts Ben-Hur receiving the victor's crown, not the chariot race itself.

Seventeen of these photographs appeared from mid-July to mid-August, 1900, in the *Concord Enterprise* as halftone illustrations.[142] In this way, "through the courtesy of Messrs Klaw & Erlanger" the Massachusetts newspaper heralded the opening of *Ben-Hur* at Boston's Colonial Theatre, which, as we shall see, was considerably delayed. The captions are quite fulsome, describing the setting, scene, story, and musical accompaniment.

The illustrations in the December, 1900, issue of *Werner's Magazine* served a different purpose. They had prepared their readership for the play in the October issue, which included the *Scientific American* cut-away illustrations of the chariot race and sea rescue scenes. Now they offered their readers seventeen of the Byron photographs as well as a summary of the plot, photographs of Wallace, Young, and Kelley, and a brief discussion of the latter's music along with three printed (not manuscript) excerpts of his score – brief selections from the Wise Men Prelude, the Christ theme from Act II (although described only as "Dialogue between Ben Hur and Arrius"), and "The Spinning of Ariadne." The captions for the photographs do not focus on the drama. The editors of a magazine that frequently featured articles related to declamation and elocution instead offer their critique of the individual posing and group arrangements. A review in the *St. Paul Globe* explained that one reason the tableaux are particularly valuable is that they indicate "how to reproduce them on the amateur stage or parlor":

> Much of stage-technique and of what to look for in the dramatic value of stage-scenes, also of artistic draping and posing, may be learned from these tableaux.[143]

There is some historical irony in the magazine's approach. The staged poses of the Klaw & Erlanger drama were demanded by the requirements of Byron's camera and not fully developed (other than the crowd scenes at Daphne) as tableaux. In contrast, the fully developed and road-tested poses of the authorized *Ben-Hur, in Tableaux and Pantomime* were never photographed, even though the company had been disbanded only a few months earlier.

In May, 1901, Meyer Bros. & Co. in New York began publishing *The Theatre*, the first illustrated magazine in the United States devoted to theater and music. Meyer Bros. also published the related supplemental series, *Our Players' Gallery*. The first number of this "Edition de Luxe" quarterly included dozens of studio portraits of dramatic artists, but the second also included a small selection of stage-production photographs of scenes from four contemporary plays, all of them photographed by Byron. One of these was *Ben-Hur*, of course, and included the Byron photograph of the Antioch Circus exterior centering upon the veiled Esther and unveiled Iras.[144] The photograph was not touched up, still displaying the Byron inventory number [8196]. *The Players' Gallery* offered these photographs for sale, one of the first of many separate commercial synergies derived from the Klaw & Erlanger *Ben-Hur*. In a separate bit of commercial synergy, a dozen of the photographs were assembled as the "Ben-Hur Calendar," advertised in October, 1900, as one of "the best calendars published."[145] The same month Dodge Publishing Company advertised a boxed version of the calendar "with scenes from the play – mounted on dark gray board."[146] The price was $1.00, and it was advertised again the following year in *The Dial* along in the "Holiday Gift-Books, Calendars" section.[147]

Souvenir Album
On a much larger scale, Klaw & Erlanger published twenty sepia prints of the Byron photographs in their *Souvenir Album: Scenes of the Play*, published in 1900. These were sold at the theatrical performances – by the tens of thousands. The photographs are credited to both Byron and Hall's Studio in New York, the latter specializing in celebrity photographs and their mass production and distribution. The *Souvenir Album* was a large format booklet (12in. × 10in.) held together with red ribbon tied through three punched holes on the left side less than half an inch from the edge. The cardstock cover had "Ben-Hur" printed in a heavily ornamented, green serif font reaching almost from margin to margin. Above in smaller fonts were printed "Souvenir Album – Scenes of the Play." Beneath the lettering was an interesting watercolor illustration in that it depicted two charioteers, the one on the left much like Checa's left charioteer, the one on the right much like Wagner's right charioteer, with a small number of people on a segment of a circus *spina*. The inside cover, and the reverse of every page were left blank. The rear cover displays a symbolic engraving of a Roman shield and short sword, shackles, and a palm frond.

The title page includes a George Rockwood photograph of Lew Wallace, a facsimile of Wallace's signature, and the names and offices of all the major figures in charge of the production and the booklet – Klaw, Erlanger, Young, Teal, Kelley, Brooks ("Business Direction") and Byron. Not counting the title page, there are twenty pages with plates, unnumbered, each of them noting: "COPYRIGHTED, 1900, BY KLAW & ERLANGER." Two plates contain two photographs – the Roof-Terrace of the House of Hur contains a large plate of the Hur family and Messala and a small, turban-shaped cropped insert including photos of Ben-Hur, his Mother, and Tirzah; and The House of Simonides appears in a large plate with Simonides, Esther and Ben-Hur, and a smaller one with Simonides, Esther, and Ilderim. However, later variants by the Courier Company and J. W. Clement inserted below the Roman galley plate a second, smaller photograph of Arrius interrogating Ben-Hur from the dais. The scene depicted in front of the Antioch Circus is different from the two published in *Werner's*. One of these features Simonides and Balthasar facing each other in a double litter resting between two black slaves, Ilderim standing to the rear between them, the veiled Esther and Iras to their right, Messala and Drusus standing besides the columns to the left. The other depicts Messala on his knees before Iras as Drusus looks on. The *Souvenir Album* photograph of the Circus exterior features Esther and Iras in the center, Messala and Drusus by the columns on the left. The plate pages are each preceded by a verbal quotation from the play, novel, or New Testament printed on tissue pages. The margins of the sepia photos are decorated with simple but apt sketches, e.g. waves and gulls for the raft photo, and racing chariots for the circus exterior. Three pages contain brief passages from a manuscript (not printed) version of Kelley's score, twenty measures from "Star of Bethlehem" before the first photo, fourteen measures from "The Spinning of Arachne," and seven measures from the "Musical Theme – Jesus of Nazareth," that is, the three-note Christ motif arranged to the syllables of "Hosanna," sung at the outset of Act VI.

The design of the *Souvenir Album* changed little over its twenty years of use. The copyright date of 1900 is never updated, but a few copies in library archives and in the ephemera network were dated by their original owners, either by writing the precise date they saw the play or inserting the free daily program they received upon entering the theater. According to this meager evidence, American Colotype Company of New York and Chicago seem to have been the original printers of the album, followed by The Courier Company of Buffalo no later than 1910/11, and then J. W. Clement, Co., Buffalo possibly as late as 1920. The Clement printing eliminated the tissue pages and placed the quotations on the plate pages instead, sometimes requiring shrinking the size of the font and replacing parts of the sketched illustrations. The Courier printings changed the photograph used to illustrate the galley scene, demonstrating that the galley set was considerably redesigned after the first season(s). Most notable is the expansion of the oar banks protruding from the hull on both

Figure 9.2 Hundreds of thousands of copies of the *Souvenir Album* containing Joseph Byron's photographs set amidst engravings like those in the Garfield edition were sold at performances of the Klaw & Erlanger *Ben-Hur*.

sides of the stage, not to mention an unidentified blond actor playing the role of Ben-Hur. This photograph was reused in the Clement printing. The latter two also changed the photograph of the Temple of Apollo and the Fountain of Castalia tableaux, the scene in the Dowar of Ilderim, and the quotations used to precede the Daphne and Mt. Olivet photographs. The Fountain of Castalia scene looks much the same and continues to use the caryatid façade, but the original photograph depicts Balthasar, Iras, and Ben-Hur from a different angle, the camel is kneeling, and the costumes are considerably different as well. In the Courier and Clement printings the dark-haired actor who plays Ben-Hur is different from the blond depicted in the galley scene, neither of them being Edward Morgan who is depicted in all the original photographs. (Once *Ben-Hur* became a roadshow, a number of different actors played the part.) Nonetheless, the copyright date on all photographs was still 1900.

The *Souvenir Album* did not include any advertising print, and no ephemera evidence has been found to suggest that it was marketed outside the theater. Nor do any of the extant examples bear a price tag, although newspapers report the retail cost of 25¢. Compared to many of the *Ben-Hur* generated dollar amounts scattered throughout this book, 25¢ might seem insignificant. But the *Souvenir Album* was extremely popular among audience members, and the few newspaper articles that happen to mention the sales figures as an aside report astounding sums. For instance, the *St. Louis Post-Dispatch* reported in late 1901 that on the East Coast an average of 3000 "librettos" per week were sold in New York, and that in St. Louis in the third season about 4000 per week were sold.[148] The even more successful four-week engagement in San Francisco in the fall of 1903 generated still greater sales amounting to $5000, that is, 20,000 copies.[149] Needless to say, photographs of the stage production were only rarely printed in the free programs available to the millions of audience members who attended over the years, the most notable exception being the celebratory program for the inaugural of Cincinnati's New Grand Opera House in 1902. It included five of Byron's stage-production photographs.

The Player's Edition
By far the greatest number of Byron's stage-production photographs, along with a number of studio portraits in costume, appeared in "The Player's Edition" of *Ben-Hur: A Tale of the Christ*, distinguished by its dark-green cloth cover decorated with a light-green and orange art-deco design incorporating two tragic masks and a cropped sepia photograph of William Farnum posing as Ben-Hur in a short tunic, arms crossed, and holding a whip. The retail cost of this upgraded edition of the original novel was $2.50, and it came in a decorative box. Other printing features have been described in Chapter 5.

Below the colored title and author line of the title page is printed "illustrated with scenes and characters from the play." This is an apt description of the thirty-one scenes from the play and another seventeen character portraits scattered throughout the book. In addition, there is a frontispiece displaying the whole photograph of Farnum, followed by tissue paper. As in the Garfield edition, there is a Table of Contents that includes all the chapter headings, but following this now is also a list of illustrations, divided by book number and cited by the number of the page it faces. There are many more illustrations in Book Fourth (17), including several tableaux that do not appear in the other publications cited above. The placement of the illustrations is not consistent. Some are placed exactly where they belong in the text of the novel. When the Wise Men declare "The Star! The Star!" at the end of 1.5, that is precisely where Byron's photograph of the Star of Bethlehem appears. Similarly, where Judah and Messala begin their discussion that will turn into a quarrel (2.2), that is where a studio photo of William S. Hart and William Farnum shaking hands is positioned. However, a photo of Ben-Hur and Iris – as her name is spelled in every caption – appears right in the middle of Messala's letter to Gratus (5.1).

The name of the play [hyphenated] and the names of Wallace, Klaw, Erlanger, Young, Kelley, Teal, and Brooks are listed on the last page of the book, as is the date of the original Broadway Theatre performance. However, Harper & Brothers had no legal obligation to cite either the photographer or the actors, so their names are not mentioned. All the captions name only the characters portrayed, not who portrays them. Part of the reason for this is that the studio photographs depict cast members hired after those who performed at the Broadway Theatre. William Farnum, of course, was one of these, and he appears on the cover, in the frontispiece, and in a few of the character portraits, but the stage-production photographs inside the book depict Edward Morgan as Ben-Hur. More than half of the stage-production photographs duplicate those published elsewhere. Some of those not published elsewhere include the following, which helped us flesh out our skeletal image of the play. They are listed in order, with the "Facing Page" and original captions (again with the name of Iras misspelled throughout), and a brief description.

> Facing page 92 – MOTHER, SIMONIDES, TIRZAH, AND AMRAH: In the opening scene of the play, the (ambulatory) Simonides kneels before the Mother of Ben-Hur and kisses her robe. This episode is invented by Young, though it will be loosely adapted for several film versions. In the novel Simonides does not appear until Book Fourth.
>
> Facing page 120 – BEN-HUR'S PROTEST: A second image of the arrest scene. Here instead of Messala pointing accusingly at Ben-Hur or gesturing to have him taken away, Ben-Hur is making a gesture of appeal towards Messala, who has his back turned to him and faces the audience.
>
> Facing page 136; IN THE GALLEY, ARRIUS NOTICES BEN-HUR: A unique shot of the galley scene. The hortator wears a Roman cuirass, and the face of Ben-Hur is cropped off at the far right, his position at the front of the oar banks.
>
> Facing page 214 – BEN-HUR STOPS MESSALA'S CHARIOT: A quintessential scene in which Ben-Hur and Messala encounter each other for the first time since the former's imprisonment, and both meet Balthasar and Iras for the first time, creating a romantic triangle between Ben-Hur, Iras, and Esther, and establishing Iras as a wicked agent for Messala.

Facing page 236 – SIMONIDES AND ESTHER IN DOUBT: Esther rests on Simonides' knee. Reviews make clear that Henry Lee portrayed the role of Simonides very effectively, as did several of his successors.

Facing page 292 – BEN-HUR AND IRIS ON THE LAKE: This tableaux comes later than the one more frequently published. Iras is now reclining in the boat, with Ben-Hur kneeling before her. At the same time on the shore Simonides and Esther see them and shield their eyes. The illusionistic palm orchard scene-painting is more visible here.

Facing page 346 – WAGERING ON THE RACE: Sanballat and Drusus are featured in this tableau.

Facing page 476: – IRIS APPEALS TO BEN-HUR TO SAVE MESSALA: Another pivotal scene that in the novel leads to a display of Esther's clemency but in the play demonstrates her hatred for Iras.

Facing page 490 – AMRAH TELLING OF THE HEALING OF BEN-HUR'S MOTHER AND TIRZAH; and Facing page 522 – AMRAH TELLING BEN HUR'S [sic] MOTHER AND SISTER OF THE NAZARENE'S POWER: These two captions tell the story in reverse order.

Throughout the decade, as *Ben-Hur* continued to play before capacity houses, all three versions continued to appear. Werner's released a separate album of the December, 1900, feature in their "Special 1907 Catalog of Plays and Entertainments," which included an offer of "Ben-Hur Tableaux." Maintaining their approach to the dramatic arts, Werner's advertised this "profusely illustrated" collection of stage-production photographs, that is, a reprint of their December, 1900, illustrated feature, as "entertainment" in which the consumer could read the lines and display the images, or read the text while recreating the tableaux with a group of participants. New printings of Harper's "The Player's Edition" were issued no earlier than 1908, when Henry Wallace's copyright renewal begins to appear on the copyright page. And ten years after it was first issued, the *Souvenir Album* was recommended in *The Story of Paul of Tarsus: A Manual for Teachers* for studying the Roman pastimes of St. Paul, where it is assumed the student can obtain a copy fairly easily.[150] Indeed, there are hundreds of original copies still in circulation even today, demonstrating not only how many were originally sold but the care their owners took to preserve them.

Kelley's Music
Werner's Magazine sold selections from Kelley's "Song of Iras" (75¢), "The Prophecy," chorus for men's voices (12¢), and "The Fulfillment" – "Hossana to the Highest" chorus (40¢).[151] Such supplemental sales helped to extend the commercial applications of *Ben-Hur*, even if they were beyond the control of Wallace and Harper, not subject to their copyright, and miniscule by their profit standards. Kelley's music was also released selectively for sale in several different formats. In 1900 Kelley's "Song of Iras (From 'Ben Hur')," Opus 17, was published by the John Church Company of Cincinnati, a prominent music publisher that had

agreements with distributors in New York, Chicago, London, and Leipzig. Following the same courtesy procedure of many of the art-song composers discussed previously, Kelley immediately sent a copy to Wallace with a warm and respectful handwritten note on the cover:

> For Gen. Lew Wallace,
> In remembrance of the many pleasant hours spent in reading his inspiring book, and also as a relic of the months of labor in setting portions of the same to music.[152]

The following year, a New York firm, Towers and Curran, published a twelve-page edition of selections reduced to a piano score, and then in 1902 they published a more complete score edited by Charles Feleky, who had been the conductor for the original New York performances. Many years later, in 1930, Miessner Music Company of Chicago reprinted the "Sacred Choruses," consisting of the music for the prelude ("The Prophecy") and the last scene of the last act ("On the Mount of Olives.")

THE SECOND SEASON, 1900–1

For the next season, Klaw & Erlanger had scheduled *Ben-Hur* as the inaugural production of Boston's Colonial Theatre in an arrangement with its lessees Charles Frohman, another original member of the Syndicate, and Rich & Harris. However, construction delays forced them to take the play elsewhere.[153] This did not present a problem to New York's most powerful booking agency that had the city's most popular play to book. So they opened the second season with a limited five-week engagement at the Broadway Theatre, again averaging some $19,000 per week.[154] Then they moved the play to Nixon & Zimmerman's Chestnut Street Opera House in Philadelphia, which had to be refurbished with a new electrical plant and extensive alterations to the stage.[155] The *Philadelphia Inquirer* reported that the work under the stage took fifteen men over four weeks to complete.[156] In addition to several pre-publicity articles about the size of the production, newspaper advertisements were of normal size but added this intriguing notice, variants of which would be used for many years to make sure that every performance ran like clockwork and the audience entered the theater with a reverent attitude:

> Messrs. Zimmerman & Nixon respectfully request patrons of Klaw & Erlanger's "Ben-Hur" to be seated BEFORE 8 O'CLOCK P.M., as the play begins sharply at that hour with the beautiful opening scene of the "Wise Men of the East" and "Star of Bethlehem." During the progress of this scene the auditorium is in entire darkness.[157]

The *Inquirer* criticized the play itself, the acting of Farnum and Hart, and the dancing and singing at Daphne, but the chariot race and "the stagewright's art achieved a notable triumph."[158] Klaw & Erlanger responded by placing their own review, although not announced as such, highlighting the "sumptuous presentation" and the "beautiful picture of light and effect" on the Mount of Olives.[159] Fully realizing the allure of the hitherto unlikely pairing of Christ and a chariot race, they added that the "shaft of light symbolical of the Messiah is a tasteful expedient which removes all possibility of offense to the church goer," and that the chariot race is "nightly greeted with vociferous applause."[160] Weekly reminders of this sort, with statements that "the demand for seats represents almost every town within a radius of one hundred miles" helped to expand their audience geographically and encourage the various suburban and rural populations to attend.[161] To accommodate them, special train excursions were arranged for specific dates, for instance, from Millville and Salem, New Jersey, on November 14.[162] Over the course of the play's two-decade run, in addition to the aforementioned "Ben-Hur Clubs," small groups who participated in such excursions were sometimes noted in local newspapers as "'Ben Hur' theatre parties."[163]

The engagement in Philadelphia was held over for two additional weeks because the Colonial Theatre was still not readied.[164] Reconfiguring this into a public offering and continued profits, Klaw & Erlanger claimed to bestow upon the Quaker City an extra matinee on Thanksgiving, although extra holiday matinees, particularly towards the end of an engagement, would become standard practice throughout the two-decade run of *Ben-Hur*.[165] More important for the reader is that in making the announcement Klaw & Erlanger expressed two important factors in the popularity of *Ben-Hur*. One was that in addition to the "marvelous" scenic and mechanical effects and the "sumptuous" scenes,

> the impression that lasts and lives is the beautiful fervent and highly dramatic story so forcibly enacted and so realistically told with all its endowment of grand music and other impressive accessories.

Allowing for standard promotional speak, Klaw & Erlanger were trying to impress upon Philadelphians that, more than just "Christ and a chariot race," this was a multifaceted production that could create pleasurable memories for a variety of people for a variety of reasons. In confirming this approach they added the second factor, that members of the clergy and church circles, some of whom had never before paid for a theater ticket, were making the trip to the city to see *Ben-Hur*. As the Philadelphia engagement was approaching its extended final date of December 15, 1900, receipts for the previous week were $20,400, reported to be the largest amount ever netted in any theater in the United States.[166]

Meanwhile, finishing touches had been put on the Boston venue, so now the December 19 inaugural was firm, and tickets went on sale December 12.[167] Probably because building the Colonial had run into so many delays, and perhaps because they had already focused on the refurbishing of the Chestnut Street Opera House, Klaw & Erlanger now listed in the press the sheer mass transported during the three-day move to Boston to impress potential ticket buyers. Even by today's standards, the numbers they quote are indeed impressive, saying that three chartered trains would include ten 60ft freight cars for the scenery, nine for the camels, horses, chariots, and the mechanical equipment, and an unspecified number to carry the 425 people employed in the production, including a reported 200 chorus members and 75 stage machinists, carpenters, scene shifters, property men, and electricians.[168] Wary of ticket speculators, they refused to fill pre-opening mail orders and limited at ten the number of tickets they would sell to any single purchaser.[169] Much more so than for the New York and Philadelphia openings, the pre-publicity seems to have been designed to ward off religious resistance. One of their initial forays in the *Boston Globe* assured the public:

> Those who expect to have their sensibilities shocked are most pleasantly surprised. From the opening to the close, in every act, scene and tableau, the highest Christian sentiment is most carefully guarded and preserved. The climax of the play comes with the great chariot race ... But the deeper and more profound impression is made in the final scene of the great play. No word is spoken, but the beautiful significance of the scene is conveyed in the most lucid and reverent manner.[170]

In February, during the tenth week of the engagement, ads in the *Boston Globe* contained an endorsement from Rabbi Samuel Hirshberg, who found the play particularly helpful in "combating the prejudices of which his people are but too frequently the objects at the hands of the non-Jewish world."[171]

Press releases also addressed the literary culture of New England that Wallace's novel had originally failed to impress. It was therefore at this point that Young gave the *Boston Globe* the aforementioned detailed interview with the appropriate Wallace-like headline, "How He Wrote 'Ben Hur.'"[172] At least one of Boston's musical writers was very impressed with Kelley's music. This was William P. Apthorp, who regularly annotated the programs for the Boston Symphony. He expressed the modern quality of the harmony, melody, and coloring, comparing Kelley to such contemporary European luminaries as Chabrier and Richard Strauss. He was also the first to recognize the Wagnerian quality of the entire presentation, and in saying so he expressed in a single complex sentence one of the most important elements that made sitting in the dark theater and watching *Ben-Hur* with its pagan, Christian, and action elements such an engrossing experience for the members of the audience:

> They did not listen to the music at all, but to the play; they heard the music, though subconsciously, and could not but feel how it intensified and illustrated the dramatic action on the stage.[173]

The run in Boston lasted until April 20, 144 performances, as Klaw & Erlanger proudly calculated.[174] Meanwhile they had negotiated important future engagements. Already by mid-March they announced that Arthur Collins, the director of the Drury Lane Theatre in London, had secured the British rights from them and that they would have a company ready by late the following season.[175] On March 24 they announced that the domestic season would finish at the Columbia Theatre in Brooklyn and that the 1901–2 season would be played entirely at Chicago's Illinois Theatre. (As it turned out, the latter would be changed into a limited engagement.)[176] On April 22, the day before the Brooklyn opening, they announced an agreement with J. C. Williamson, who secured the Antipodean rights and planned for an Australian production the following March/April simultaneous with the London production.[177]

It was no accident that *Ben-Hur* was booked at some of the largest venues in the country – the Broadway in New York, the Chestnut Street Opera House in Philadelphia, the Colonial in Boston, the Columbia in Brooklyn, and the Illinois Theatre in Chicago. Besides the fact that their size could handle the enormous stage, backstage, and audience seating requirements, bookings for these important venues, and a few dozen others, were all channeled through the Syndicate, which was at the height of its power, crowding out independent works and essentially blackballing feisty actors like Minnie Maddern Fiske who defied them.[178] Theater managers like Nixon & Zimmerman and Charles Frohman's partners, who owned or leased the large metropolitan venues, preferred to fill their stages, and therefore their seats, with hugely popular productions that would have lengthy runs. This desire to build large-concept stage productions, create innovative visual and aural effects, and reap record profits was the goal of many involved with the Syndicate at the turn of the century, and none of their popular productions was bigger, more spectacular, longer lasting, or more profitable than *Ben-Hur*. Despite the long run of George Lederer's musical *The Casino Girl* in New York and London, for instance, management did not extend the engagement through the summer because they wanted to ready their theater for *Ben-Hur*.[179]

Despite some rain, long lines formed as soon as the box office opened for the Brooklyn engagement. The *Brooklyn Eagle* reviewer who attended the April 24, 1901, premiere expected therefore to see a packed house but recorded seeing "significant rows of empty seats downstairs," attributing that to the high ticket prices.[180] Nonetheless, what had originally been scheduled as a two-week engagement ultimately had to be held for an additional two weeks.[181] Unknown to the *Eagle* reviewer, *Ben-Hur* engagements often did not hit their peak attendance until after the first few days.

The review itself was one of the most insightful of the contemporary newspaper analyses. Moved by the impact of Kelley's music, much more so than by the dialogue, the reviewer understood the success of the production as part melodrama, i.e. drama with music, and part Wagnerian *Gesamtkuntswerk*:

> The production is an effort to realize Wagner's idea of a union upon the stage of the arts of drama, music and painting with incidental aid from sculpture. But in this case painting comes first. The scene painter is a more important person than the dramatist and the characters, the text and the music are merely contributory figures to a great historic spectacle of Judea at the time of the coming of Christ. . . . The talk, too, is in the pseudo-classic style, which was once considered the only appropriate vehicle for tragedy, and it drags rather more heavily upon a sensitive ear for that reason. . . . Mr. Young's play has one great merit for which critical observers will excuse the talk and pompousness of its earlier scenes. In the last act, when it deals with the healing of the lepers and approaches the presence of the Saviour, its stilted tone is dropped, its melodrama falls away, its feeling becomes genuine and its effect profoundly moving.

Klaw & Erlanger released the final figures at the end of this second season – $915,000 in aggregate receipts.[182] They used this as the initial part of their pre-1901–2 season publicity, along with a reasonably detailed description of the treadmill system as well as what they now call the "cyclorama" representing the interior of the Antioch Circus. This seems to have been by design, for the more technical *Scientific American* article had been issued the previous August, just before the 1900–1 season and reprinted in *Werner's Magazine* the following October.[183] The 1901 pre-publicity concluded with high praise for the last act:

> In a larger and better sense the sixth act is the chief excellence of this memorable production. Here is represented the healing of the lepers on the Mount of Olives. Hundreds are assembled to worship Him. His bodily presence is not attempted, but His immediate nearness is suggested impressively by a peculiar white light. As treated it is an incident of extraordinary dignity and reverence.

In making such statements in print, Klaw & Erlanger have in a dramatic sense become an extension of Lew Wallace by emphasizing his original demands, namely, that they make the chariot race realistic and maintain the religious miracle of the Revelation amidst the atmosphere of first-century Judea without representing the figure of Christ himself.

BEN-HUR TOURS THE MIDWEST, 1901–2

An important component of Klaw & Erlanger's pre-season publicity for 1901 was keeping the American newspaper theater columns filled with reports of their international networking. Their longer-term intention was to expand American offerings abroad and bring English productions to the United States. In doing so, *Ben-Hur* was their pilot project. A case in point is the July 7 theater page of the *Cincinnati Enquirer Sunday Olio*.[184] Klaw & Erlanger figure in six different items, three of those involving *Ben-Hur*. One was the announcement that Joseph Brooks was returning from London with the manuscript, costume sketches, and music for *The Sleeping Beauty and the Beast*, the "musical extravaganza" that was part of the reciprocal agreement with Arthur Collins to acquire *Ben-Hur*. The second was the announcement that still another improvement had been made to the chariot race for the Chicago season by adding a concealed fan to create a wind for the garments of the charioteers and the manes of the horses.[185] And third was a lengthy paragraph announcing that *Ben-Hur* would be offered in three countries during the upcoming season – in Melbourne's Princess Theater from Christmas week and then Sydney and elsewhere in Australia, at London's Drury Lane commencing March 31, and at the Illinois Theater in Chicago from September 2 – and that negotiations were ongoing to bring the production to Paris and elsewhere:

> The negotiations mentioned concern Paris, so the French people will also have an opportunity of enjoying a play which will soon have an international fame. Unlike other plays which have been offered in all the countries on the map, Klaw & Erlanger retain an interest in the productions wherever made, and it will not take long before Germany and Italy will have this drama in its theaters.[186]

On August 4 they printed a follow-up announcement that Brooks had also been working on the upcoming *Ben-Hur* production in London, and now that Brooks had returned, Marc Klaw was sailing to Europe and would spend most of his two months there further arranging matters in London.[187] In September the Russian city of St. Petersburg was added to the list, along with the clarification: "All foreign presentations of this drama will be made under the direction and control of Klaw & Erlanger."[188]

When *The Sleeping Beauty and the Beast* was ready to open at the Broadway Theatre on November 4, Klaw & Erlanger released a straightforward public statement about their reciprocity agreement with Collins. Marketing *Ben-Hur* as "the best American example of romantic drama and advanced stagecraft," they declared that this would mark "the first direct exchange of attractions ever made between American and English managements."[189] Once again a *Ben-Hur* product was at the forefront of expanding the parameters and practices of popular art and commerce. In its wake, *The Sleeping Beauty and the Beast* would earn more money at the Broadway Theatre than *Ben-Hur*, at least $1000 more per week, and it had a longer run at the Broadway, thirty weeks instead of twenty four.[190] But, after requiring the excavation and blasting of a 40ft×20ft pit, 24ft deep, to accommodate the "Chrystal Palace" scene, the British import would not return to the New York stage repeatedly, nor the other major cities in the East Coast, nor would it tour the Midwest, South, and West for the next two decades as did *Ben-Hur*.[191] To the contrary, at the close of its 1904 tour, its magnificent glass palace set, consisting of seven tons of molded Venetian blue, red, and amber glass, was broken up into small fragments, crated, and shipped back to England for junk.[192] For *Ben-Hur*, thousands of performances still lay ahead. For that matter, by frequently reporting these kinds of developments in such papers as the *Cincinnati Enquirer*, Klaw & Erlanger were demonstrating that their geographical targets had shifted not only east to Europe but west across the United States. During these early years of the new century, Midwestern theater critics, columnists, and aficionados were doing their best not just to develop and appreciate their local talent but elevate themselves by demonstrating their capacity for appreciating imported East Coast and European talent. And now the American production of *Ben-Hur* was to be performed in Chicago, and then St. Louis and Pittsburgh.

After three weeks of rehearsals in Chicago, the Midwestern tour opened on September 3 at the Illinois Theatre. The *Tribune* reviewer had high praise for the dramatic adaptation itself, and that may have been in part, as he explains, because the cast was almost entirely new, except for Mary Shaw (Amrah) and Mabel Bert (Mother of Hur), both of whom had already received the approval of the East Coast critics. Demonstrating further the international flavor of American Midwestern theater in the early years of the century, Messala was now the English-born George Alison, and Simonides the Australian Henry Jewett, in that sense reciprocating the London and Melbourne productions of *Ben-Hur* that would begin in the spring. Ads began to appear in the *Tribune* less than one week in advance, as was the norm.[193] All seats for the "Stupendous Production – Gen. Lew Wallace's BEN-HUR" were reserved, and prices were 50¢, 75¢, $1.00, $1.50, and $2.00, with boxes costing $7.50, $10.00, and $15.00.

Meanwhile the Olympic Theatre in St. Louis had been completely remodeled with a larger stage, set upon newly poured concrete foundations, and equipped for electrical machinery.[194] The public was being primed with exuberant testimonials from Chicago audiences.[195] The day after the November 18 Olympic premiere, the reviewer for the *St. Louis Post-Dispatch* was so impressed by the music that it was likened to an oratorio.[196] Then there was "the immensity of the whole":

> What "Ben Hur" the book is to literature, that "Ben Hur" the play is to the stage. It stands alone. It is unique in its conception and massive in its construction. In fact the massiveness is the particular feature of the production that makes it remarkable. It's the biggest thing ever put on the stage. Even if one were disposed to criticize some of the dramatic details, such criticism would fall flat because these details are of so little importance. They are lost sight of in the immensity of the whole.

Ben-Hur played in St. Louis until the first week of December. It followed the usual weekly schedule, with performances every day but Sunday, matinees Wednesday and Saturday. The second week it collected $22,658.[197] The third, aided by an extra Friday matinee, is reported to have collected $27,000.[198] The Olympic, with a seating capacity of 2400, was slightly larger than the previously played venues, and the capacity seating did not include the standing-room patrons who numbered in the hundreds. The *Post-Dispatch* reported that eight performances the second week averaged an attendance of 3000 each, and that although house seats were $2.00, the average price for admission was approximately 90¢.[199] In addition, about 4000 "librettos" sold each week.

The *Post-Dispatch* boasted that "St. Louis broke a national theatrical record," and it identified the city's capacity to fill the Olympic from floor to galleries for *Ben-Hur* as a turning point. On page 1 it ran the headline, "St. Louis as a Theatrical City, As Shown by 'Ben Hur' Engagement, Is Out of One Week Stand Class," and beneath it was a large photograph of a long line of ticket buyers standing outside the theater.[200] This represents a significant change in American theatrical attendance that accompanied and was attributed to the tour of the Klaw & Erlanger *Ben-Hur*. The article in the *Post-Dispatch* continues:

> It was not so long ago that St. Louis was a two-shows-a-week city. When the theaters changed to one show for a whole week, it was considered a good deal of an undertaking. The transition to the several weeks for one attraction promises to be easy. The engagement of "Ben Hur" in St. Louis will be the biggest three weeks the attraction has ever played to.

The Klaw & Erlanger *Ben-Hur* had the same effect on other cities far from the East Coast. Local managers and newspaper editors embraced this unparalleled urgency to purchase tickets and throng their showcase urban theaters to see *Ben-Hur* as justification for civic pride. Two years later as part of its first swing to the far West, for instance, *Ben-Hur* played in San Francisco. The huge receipts from thirty-three performances in four weeks amounted to $128,000, including a record-breaking $38,453 the final week. Haughtily dismissing the previous record-breaking but smaller receipts from St. Louis, Chicago, New York, and Boston, the *San Francisco Chronicle* declared their civic pride by stating:

> The financial success of the run in this city has broken all records for dramatic productions in the history of theatricals in this or any other country.... These figures are with doubt the largest ever secured in four weeks by any dramatic attraction, and will place San Francisco at the head of the theatrical cities of the world.... San Francisco's reputation for being a great show town will now rest upon the phenomenal showing made during the just closed run of "Ben Hur."[201]

Charles F. Towle, Klaw & Erlanger's road manager, suggested that the record numbers of people coming to see the play were doing so because so many of them had read the book. A subsequent article in the *Post-Dispatch* seems to attribute the huge attendance to interest in outlying small towns, detailing the route and passengers of the special train bringing 375 patrons to St. Louis from as far as Vincennes, Indiana, approximately 150 miles away. As we have been seeing, this extra-urban demographic purchased thousands of tickets for each engagement. The *San Francisco Chronicle* reported over $25,000 in mail orders, with hundreds of orders left unfilled.

Of course these are not the sole reasons for the record attendance, nor can *Ben-Hur* alone be said to have transformed American theater. On this grand stage of mass American enculturation in which *Ben-Hur* played a significant and multifaceted supporting role, operatic performances were earning huge receipts, as were the 1902 musical adaptation of *The Wizard of Oz* and such contemporary plays as *Peggy From Paris* and *Mr. Blue Beard*, one of the Klaw & Erlanger British imports. On the other side of the ledger, some theaters and productions suffered if they were not offering the new style of productions. The last day of the *Ben-Hur* engagement in St. Louis, for instance, the *Post-Dispatch* reported that all the other theaters in St. Louis suffered poor attendance.[202] But in setting American records for attendance and profits and in the sheer immensity of a spectacular production that toured for years in succession, *Ben-Hur* was indeed "the grandest, most impressive, instructive and stupendous indoor entertainment ever offered the public."[203] That was the perception at the time among the Eastern, Midwestern, and far Western crowds who flocked to buy tickets when the show came to town.

Ben-Hur was credited also with helping to increase the size of American stages from the traditional smaller European and colonial American type, thereby increasing the availability and popularity of large-scale melodrama and, indirectly, the size of American theaters. A three-column article in the *New York Times* in 1909 on "Three Cycles of Scenic Melodrama" pinpointed *Ben-Hur* as "a unique American production ... which was so decided a departure":

> To take this play on tour Klaw & Erlanger were forced to make places for it. After "Ben-Hur" had toured the country there were stages in all the principal cities to accommodate so large a production, and it served a purpose in this respect alone. In the principal cities the modern theatres are all fitted out with stages that now make room for the biggest kind of productions.[204]

After the record-breaking engagement in St. Louis, *Ben-Hur* then moved to Nixon & Zimmerman's Alvin Theatre in Pittsburgh.[205] Receipts there amounted to more than $90,000.[206] Then it returned to Philadelphia's Chestnut Street Opera House, opening on January 13, 1902.[207] The *Philadelphia Inquirer* reviewer found the chariot race "vastly improved by the complete turning around of the horses after the victory, so hotly contested, is won by Ben Hur."[208] Then came its first appearance at Washington's National Theatre, with its reconstructed stage.[209] Advertisements in *The Washington Post* emphasized the size of the cast and chorus "350 – PEOPLE – 350."[210] Expecting a broader demographic in the capitol city, Klaw & Erlanger gave *The Washington Post* a brief account of the 1876 encounter between Lew Wallace and Robert Ingersoll,[211] balanced on a different page with an assurance that Christ was not portrayed on the stage.[212] During the February 10–22 engagement *The Washington Post* ran a personal interview with Lew Wallace, paragraphs of praise for both Kelley's score and William Farnum's suitability for the role, and notes in the theatrical pages about the intimate friendship between

Farnum and Alison in addition to Alison's account of how well the horses knew their cues and enjoyed running on the treadmills as much as the audience enjoyed watching them.[213] Opening night was a sell-out and a critical success. Fittingly, the review in *The Washington Post* concludes with the distant but relevant news that the same day *Ben-Hur* premiered so successfully in Washington, DC, Klaw & Erlanger received a cablegram from Sydney: "'Ben-Hur' a complete success. Grand production; hitchless performance; splendid notices."[214]

On to Baltimore, where the pre-publicity for the Academy of Music premiere on February 24 now stated that the cyclorama had 3,600 feet of canvas and that an additional chariot had been added.[215] Klaw & Erlanger put out a call for twenty additional men to apply for short-term employment in the crowd scenes.[216] Again, because of the uniqueness and enormity of the production, simply its relocation was regarded as a news event and a spectacle. *The Sun* reports that a crowd of people watched as the horses and camels were led from the train yard to the stable near the theater, and that it took almost ten hours to unload the ten cars of equipment and transport it to the theater, drawing another crowd, and then for some sixty men to install the miles of ropes, over 100,000 square feet of canvas, and the chariot race mechanisms.[217] Klaw & Erlanger offered two additional matinees during the final week to accommodate the demand, which came not only from the urban population but also the 200–300 daily mail orders sent from Maryland, Pennsylvania, North Carolina and the Virginia coast, and a number of pre-planned train excursions from various towns in Maryland and Pennsylvania.[218] *The Sun* reported that they were setting attendance records despite turning away "fully 1,000 people."[219] And *The Sun*, like the *St. Louis Post-Dispatch*, took pride in the fact that for the first time ever their city was able to draw crowded houses for a three-week engagement.[220] Advertised ticket prices, were $2 and $1.50 for Lower Reserved, $1.50 for Balcony, and 75¢ and 50¢ for Gallery.

Ben-Hur returned to Boston's Colonial Theatre March 17 to finish the 1901–2 season with a six-week engagement.[221] The pre-publicity again noted the addition of a third chariot.[222] The *Boston Herald* reported that clergymen seemed to prefer Monday nights for seeing the play.[223] The same day the *Boston Daily Globe* surmised that the large audiences consisted of patrons who missed the play the previous year, giving no indication that some audience members might have been seeing the performance for the second time.[224] Yet even for the original Broadway Theatre production in New York two years earlier, *The Cast*, a weekly theatrical publication listing the casts of all current plays and adding a few introductory tidbits, comments:

> A great many theatre-goers like all of "Ben Hur," a great many more like a lot of it, while everybody likes it well enough to go to see it at least twice, hence it is that

over 300,000 people have already paid to see the hair-raising chariot race, etcetera, etcetera.[225]

Subsequently an unabashedly pro-American report assumed that many of the Americans who had witnessed *Ben-Hur* in New York also attended the premier in London.[226]

BEN-HUR IN AUSTRALIA

From the outset Klaw & Erlanger had promised that *Ben-Hur* would "completely eclipse anything ever seen in a theater, either in this country or abroad" and developed plans to establish their beachhead in Europe with *Ben-Hur*. As we have seen, when *Ben-Hur* was playing at the Colonial, the *Boston Globe* was frequently alerting their readers as to the forthcoming production in London.[227] Klaw & Erlanger issued updates repeatedly to American newspapers as their newly made celebrities Brooks and Klaw crossed the Atlantic to make preparations with Arthur Collins, one of Britain's leading producers. Meanwhile, J[ames] C[assius] Williamson, American-born but now Australia's equivalent to Erlanger and Collins, had spent six months traveling in England and the United States to secure agreements with Klaw & Erlanger as well as Charles Frohman and others "representing immensely powerful theatrical syndicates in the United States," as he boasted to the Australian press covering his trans-oceanic return in August, 1901.[228] Williamson added that he would produce *Ben-Hur* before it appeared on the stage at London's Drury Lane Theatre. This he did. Oh, but read on!

He spent £6000 to prepare Her Majesty's Theatre in Sydney, £1500 to rebuild the stage to accommodate the chariot race.[229] He imported a mostly British cast, and their arrival from England on the *Oruba* two weeks before the premiere was reported in the papers.[230] The mayor of Melbourne initially feted Williamson's "Ben Hur Company" at Town Hall before they sailed on to Sydney, where they were similarly honored.[231] Williamson appointed his associate H. H. Vincent, who had observed the production of *Ben-Hur* for one week in Chicago, as manager.[232] Some of his first tasks were to purchase an appropriate white camel from a herd in New South Wales and find suitable horses.[233] Six of the horses were seriously injured during training and had to be destroyed, which created an undercurrent of discontent among those promoting animal welfare.[234] Meanwhile, Williamson custom-ordered 50,000 paper-bound copies of Wallace's novel from Ward, Lock & Company.[235] On the cover was an illustration of the chariot race, and the frontispiece contained an illustration of Ben-Hur's gladiatorial combat with Thord, even though it is not enacted or referred to in the play. More pertinent were advertisements for the production, includ-

The Klaw & Erlanger Ben-Hur

Figure 9.3 Harper's "Player's Edition," Williamson's Australian edition, Kelley's piano/choral reduction, and a 1901 program for the Illinois Theatre in Chicago.

ing a portrait of Williamson and, on the end papers, illustrations of a theater in Sydney and Her Majesty's Theatre in Melbourne, to which the production would be traveling next.[236] The book was to be sold at the theater and elsewhere.

"The American Invasion," as the Australians termed it, had been launched.[237] When the London production opened in seven weeks, that meant that the American dramatic adaptation of *Ben-Hur* would be simultaneously employing 1200 people in three continents.[238] Already in the summer *The Brisbane Courier* remarked that *Ben-Hur* "was the greatest theatrical presentation ever given to the American public, which is saying a great deal."[239] When Vincent ran his first ad in *The Sydney Morning Herald*, his description of how the American production of *Ben-Hur* overwhelmed Williamson is filled with many superlatives in all caps:

> The extraordinary magnitude and immensity of the production, the originality and completeness of the entire conception, and the tremendous scope for marvelous spectacle, coupled with the high literary qualities of the work, attracted and impressed Mr. Williamson, and he was determined that he should be the means of introducing so remarkable a play to Australian patrons.[240]

Although the actors were predominantly British and the chorus held over from Williamson's productions of Italian opera, Vincent employed an Anglo-American actor, Conway Tearle, to play the role of Ben-Hur, as well as an American horse trainer and machinist.[241]

The premiere on February 7, 1901, was a great success, and the first item addressed in the first paragraph of the review in *The Sydney Morning Herald* was its American origins:

> No higher praise can be given the drama ... than to say that in its religious aspect – upon which many playgoers who remembered the American source were uneasy – the wisest reticence, the greatest possible tact, has been observed.... For whatever conclusion we may come to upon "Ben Hur" as a drama, it is unquestionably the most superb and artistic spectacle ever presented in Australia.[242]

As always with *Ben-Hur* products, it is the popular response that is the most important barometer of success. And here the reviewer informs us that the response to the chariot race in particular "caused a fresh sensation, and the cheering can only be described as frantic." As at the New York premiere, the audience did not cease their outburst until Williamson and Vincent responded to several curtain calls by introducing the American trainer and machinist ("Mr. Watson").[243] Perth's *Daily News* concurred: "After the first act the audience began to cheer and applaud until it culminated in a terrific uproar at the conclusion of the great chariot race."[244]

Australia was inflamed with *Ben-Hur* fire. The *Daily News* in Perth commented that "wherever you go the novel and the play are topics of conversation, and in ordinary society you are pretty sure to hear as much about 'Ben Hur' as about cricket."[245] The *Clarence and Richmond Examiner* concurred:

> The book is read, reviewed, criticized, and even preached about.... You hear at almost every street corner hoarse cries of "Ben Hur-r-r, nine pence." You see your fellow travellers in tram, boat and bus, poring [sic] over the books – and if a man

says he read it eleven years ago, he is looked at as though he has committed a sort of sacrilege.[246]

Within just a few days Williamson sold every copy of the novel he had ordered, and there were reportedly no copies left in the country.[247] As in the United States, "theatre parties" were being formed to bring in patrons from beyond Sydney.[248] The Australian clergy embraced the movement. On March 2 the Rev. George Walters' sermon at Sydney's Australian Church was "Ben Hur: the Book and Play."[249] Williamson and Vincent inserted into their newspaper ads extracts from several laudatory sermons. One ad quotes the prominent Rev. E. Tremayne Dunstan, who at the time resided in Australia but later would lecture on the Chautauqua circuit and then remain in the United States until his death: "The story of 'Ben Hur' is one which helps us to a stronger faith. Those who are responsible for the production are to be congratulated."[250]

Soon Williamson went to Perth with plans to build a theater large enough to stage *Ben-Hur*, continued on to Adelaide with the same purpose, and publicly announced his plan to import more American productions like it.[251] But Williamson was not alone in trying to exploit his success. C. H. Walther and Co., the harness maker who provided the trappings for the play, began to advertise this in *The Sydney Morning Herald*.[252] As the reader knows, this was normal *Ben-Hur* business practice, but a few individuals quickly began to arrange their own performances and presentations of *Ben-Hur*.[253] Alfred Dampier "possessed a version of 'Ben Hur'" and offered to produce it on a Sunday night in Kalgoorlie.[254] *The Cumberland Argus and Fruitgrowers Advocate* advertised Albert Lucas's suburban tour of "The History of Ben Hur."[255] And in Granville the Rev. A. E. J. Ross used lantern slides to lecture on "The Wonderful Story of 'Ben Hur'" and inspire his audience to purchase the "cheap editions of the work" he offered for sale.[256] Alarmed at such independent entrepreneurs taking advantage of his production, Williamson issued a warning in several newspapers to those who violated his rights:

> The sole right of producing a play founded upon General Wallace's famous book entitled "Ben Hur" was purchased from the author by Messrs. Klaw and Erlanger, New York, from whom Mr. Williamson has acquired the sole liberty of representing or causing the play to be represented throughout the Australian Commonwealth and New Zealand. Notice is hereby given that any person infringing upon these rights will be prosecuted to the utmost vigour of the law.[257]

Due to three catastrophes almost biblical in nature, the success of the 1902 Australian production was short-lived. On Sunday, February 16, a boy who had been selling fruit at Her Majesty's Theatre developed "a suspicious case of sickness" that health authorities discovered to be bubonic plague.[258] Williamson immediately closed the theater. After a week of disinfecting and fumigating it and reassuring the public that none of the cast or crew had been taken ill and that performances would resume soon, Williamson reopened the following Saturday.[259] *The Brisbane Courier* observed that the public's attraction to *Ben-Hur* was little diminished by even an outbreak of plague, and indeed "a vast throng of people . . . quickly filled every part of the great playhouse." Despite having to absorb that week's losses, Williamson then voluntarily cancelled the regular Wednesday matinee on February 26 in observance of the national Day of Humiliation and Prayer for the perennial drought.[260] Less than one month later, on March 22–3, late Saturday night and early Palm Sunday morning, a fire destroyed Her Majesty's Theatre and with it the *Ben-Hur* scenery, costumes, and equipment.[261] Insured for only £2000, having lost the signature scenery and mechanisms of *Ben-Hur*, and thousands of miles away from Klaw & Erlanger, Williamson had no choice but to cancel all remaining *Ben-Hur* performances in both Sydney and Melbourne, and many other productions besides.[262] He dismissed the company, putting about 400 people out of work, although he helped some of them find employment by placing them in his other productions elsewhere, or at least by giving them one week's severance pay.[263]

Unlike all but one major production in the entire duration of the *Ben-Hur* phenomenon, the 1902 Australian venture lost a considerable portion of its initial investment. This evoked at least one belated prophecy. The *Clarence and Richmond Examiner* stated:

> All the curious superstitions to which theatrical folks and sailors are alike so addicted have been revived with medieval gusto, the most curious coincidence being that "Ben Hur" dramatized concludes on Palm Sunday, and so evidently did the Sydney life of the play.[264]

The same writer suggested that the horses were "whinnying for joy" in recompense for the cruelty they had suffered during training. Nonetheless, the *Ben-Hur* phenomenon in Australia marched on. The Rev. Walters revived his sermon on "Ben Hur: the Book and the Play."[265] Pastor Warboys in Parramatta, just a few kilometers west of Sydney, advertised that he was "resuscitating" *Ben Hur* by delivering a lecture with lantern slides: "Those who put off seeing the play will now have the opportunity of getting an idea of what it was like."[266] And less than ten weeks after the catastrophe, the theater column in *The Brisbane Courier* assured its readers that Arthur Collins would shortly be producing *Ben-Hur* in both Paris and Berlin.[267] There is no evidence that those plays were produced, but ten years later Williamson would have much better fortune producing *Ben-Hur* again in Sydney as well as Melbourne, Perth, and Adelaide, not to mention several cities in New Zealand.

BEN-HUR IN LONDON

American theater columnists had been following the development of the *Ben-Hur* production in London since at least April, 1900, when near the close of the first season the *Boston Globe* reported that Klaw would sail to England on May 30 to arrange "some of the details" in connection the English production of *Ben-Hur*, and that the lead role would be played by "one of the best known stars in Great Britain."[268] Eleven months later these plans were reconfirmed when in March, 1901, Arthur Collins sailed back to London having finalized his agreement with Klaw & Erlanger.[269] Collins was a crucial element in the arrangement because he was the manager of the relatively cavernous Drury Lane Theatre, with its seating capacity of over 3000. Benjamin Wyatt, the architect of Drury Lane, must have had a production like *Ben-Hur* in mind a century earlier when he said:

> I was aware of the very popular notion that our theatres ought to be very small; but it appeared to me that if that very popular notion should be suffered to proceed too far it would in every way deteriorate our dramatic performances depriving the proprietors of that revenue which is indispensable to defray the heavy expenses of such a concern.[270]

The New York Times reported again that Collins was seeking to secure "a prominent British actor" to play Ben-Hur. But four months later Collins signed Robert Taber, an American, the *Boston Herald* highlighting the irony that Morgan was English and Taber American.[271] J. E. Dodson, who would play Simonides, was the only other American actor.[272] But most of the technical directors and artists, including Claude Hagen and Theodore Bendix, who would serve as the Musical Director, were Americans as well, as were the horses and their trainer, Frank Engel.[273] The most notable of the English directors was the ballet master John d'Auban, best known for his Gilbert and Sullivan choreography. But even he had spent a week in Chicago observing the production.[274] Indeed, the *Boston Herald* termed it the "Big American Invasion."[275] Brooks and Klaw had sailed to England to arrange the production in previous years and months, Ben Teal sailed in mid-February to direct rehearsals, and now Erlanger sailed to England on March 8 for the premiere scheduled for March 31, Easter Monday.[276] Reports circulated that even Lew Wallace was to be in attendance.[277] Denying that rumor, Erlanger nonetheless commented at the time that the most attractive thing he saw in London was the American flag flying on the Drury Lane Theatre. By March 23 the advance sales had already topped $20,000.[278] Two of the Byron photographs filled an entire page in *Black & White*, Britain's popular weekly illustrated periodical.[279] *Ben-Hur* was set to open, but mechanical problems forced a postponement until Thursday, April 3.[280] The only remaining obstacle was the bastion of London theater critics.

In that Collins was introducing this new, major *Ben-Hur* by-product into the most experienced and demanding theatrical center in the English-speaking world, the response of the British critics was instructive, as was the audience response.[281] Many of the critics expected very little from an overwrought Drury Lane melodrama, but even then they found *Ben-Hur* deficient. *The Times* reviewer reduced the melodrama to trite foundations – a wrongfully accused hero, two women competing for his affections, one fair, one dark-spirited, a villain who loves the latter and is ultimately defeated by the hero, and "the usual complement of aged fathers, faithful nurses, and so on."[282] He found the last act tedious and remarked that it caused a disturbance among the audience. After suggesting that the play would have been better if it had ended after the chariot race, the reviewer suggested dispensing with the dialogue altogether and – the reader will see the irony here – presenting the story as a series of *tableaux vivants*. The reviewer for *The Manchester Guardian* compared *Ben-Hur* unfavorably to other Drury Lane melodramas: "We have seen better sea-pictures before now on the Drury Lane stage."[283] And the reviewer for *The Observer* not only lambasted in general and specifically this attempt at transferring a novel to the stage but also thought the religious element of the play was irrelevant:

> The tale of the young Jewish prince Ben Hur . . . would have been quite complete without any reference either to the Star of Bethlehem or to the miracle of Mount Olivet. Even the fact that Ben Hur becomes a convert to Christianity has no effect upon his career as it is set out before us; and the only purpose served by what may be described as the religious prologue and epilogue, is that of incidental impressiveness and solemnity.[284]

Despite the disdain for Collins, his Drury Lane melodramas, and adapting plays for the stage and the American *Ben-Hur* in particular, these and many other criticisms might have been more influential or relevant if the subject had not been the Klaw & Erlanger *Ben-Hur*. *The Observer* even went so far as to say that "critical disapproval extended in many quarters to the methods of [Drury Lane's] art will be no new experience to the management of this theatre, where the penalty of popularity has necessarily to be paid upon a large scale." If *Ben-Hur* would prove anything performance after performance in scores of cities in a number of countries, it was that critical rejection would rarely inflict a penalty. To the contrary, the next week Drury Lane shares advanced on the London Stock Exchange, which the *Daily Telegraph* attributed to the success of *Ben-Hur*.[285] Even many of the British critics observed that the audience reacted with "wild enthusiasm" and "loud and hearty" cheering, and that, after the chariot race, the applause did not cease until Collins brought Hagen out for a curtain call, perhaps a first in the history of London theater.[286] The reporter from the *New York Herald* timed the final applause at ten minutes, invoking six curtain calls, and added that "the handclapping continued after the lights of the theatre were turned out."[287]

We might note that in the United States a syndicated report circulated that there was booing and hissing during the religious finale.[288] But in quoting *The Times* review, suggesting that the play should end with the chariot race, the review offers no evidence of an eyewitness report but seems to have sensationalized the original *Times* remark that "the applause was no longer unanimous, and at the close the verdict was not entirely favourable." Apparently trying to interpret the mixed signals, a different syndicated report from The New York Herald Company surmised that the intense discussion about the final act stimulated additional ticket sales.[289] One month later, another report circulated that Americans who witnessed the premiere denied hearing any "hisses and boos."[290]

Counterbalancing the critical consensus and the alleged religious shock was the favoritism shown by the royal family. Less than two weeks after the premiere, King Edward VII announced he would be attending the play.[291] Rather than seating him in his traditional royal box, Collins had a custom box hastily constructed in the middle of the front row so the king could have "the best view" of the chariot race.[292] Edward reportedly rose from his golden armchair and loudly applauded the scene.[293] He personally congratulated Collins and Brooks. Edward soon developed a particular liking for American plays, and at least one influential contemporary reviewer cited Edward's presence as a major factor in the play's continuing popularity.[294] Queen Alexandra attended on May 5 and invited a royal party that included Prince and Princess Charles of Denmark.[295] They, too, sat in the specially constructed box, but Charles was escorted to the wings where he could watch the race head on.[296] Described as "an extremely pious woman," Alexandra congratulated Collins and added, "I think General Wallace deserves great praise for the great reverence with which he has treated a religious theme."[297] She even said that although she rarely visited the theater, she would see *Ben-Hur* again if possible. On May 13, barely one week later, she returned, again with the Danish guests as well as the Prince and Princess of Wales, the future King George V, who shushed the audience for cheering too loudly.[298] These well-publicized, positive appearances by English royalty further inspired foreign royalty to attend subsequent performances.[299]

Meanwhile the first twenty performances drew in nearly $50,000.[300] Nancy Sykes was reporting that the play was drawing $3000 per night, and advance sales for the next two months approximated $100,000.[301] On behalf of Klaw & Erlanger, she sarcastically thanked the British journalists "who are so generously rendering to them their kind sympathies. It's so American, you know." The two Saturday performances took in over $6000, and weekly receipts were uniformly over $25,000.[302] This was the greatest financial success London theater had ever experienced.[303] On July 2 there was a celebration for the 100th performance, the longest run in the ninety-two year history of the theater.[304] Finally, at the traditional midsummer end of the season, the run came to an end in its sixteenth week, adding even more to its record receipts with four extra performances. The simple recognition in the American press read, "These facts quite strikingly indicate the great success 'Ben-Hur' has made on the other side."[305] At least one final summation in the British press suggested that *Ben-Hur* was a huge English production tailor-made for Americans.[306]

Particularly after Edward's widely reported visit to *Ben-Hur* in April, reports again began to circulate about negotiations for Continental productions of *Ben-Hur* in Paris, Berlin, and Vienna.[307] Reports focused on Brooks, who "visited the principle theatres of Paris and Berlin with a view to studying their stability for the French and German productions of 'Ben Hur' which are in contemplation."[308] In late May, just before his departure, reports became a little more specific, for instance, examining Continental venues like the Hofburg Theatre in Vienna which had a large capacity and up-to-date mechanical equipment.[309] The bibliographical record does preserve a mostly favorable review of the Drury Lane production in the French journal *L'Art Dramatique et Musical au XXe Siècle*.[310] The reviewer, Osman Edwards, observed that instead of the ancient Roman "bread and circuses," the English public enthusiastically calls for "Christ and circuses." It is hard to tell if Edwards was just playing with words and Juvenal's famous phrase or if he was demeaning the British for embracing *Ben-Hur* and its action melodrama in the same way the ancient Romans were so easily pacified by the public grain dole and idling their time with public games. In either case, there does not seem to be any record of performances in Paris, Berlin, Vienna, or St. Petersburg. And despite its tremendous success at Drury Lane, *Ben-Hur* would not return to London, or to Australia, for ten years. *Ben-Hur* was predominantly an American phenomenon with a persistent influence abroad that periodically blossomed into enormous successes, as it did in 1902 and 1912–13, and then again in 1926, 1931, and 1959 with the MGM films, and yet again with the popular French and English dramatic productions of 2006 and 2009.

BEN-HUR ON THE ROAD

In the United States, after its initial twenty-four weeks at the Broadway Theatre, over the next two seasons *Ben-Hur* had been engaged at the largest East Coast and Midwest venues for a number of weeks – New York (5), Philadelphia (10), Boston (18), and Brooklyn (4) in 1900–1, and Chicago (11), St. Louis (3), Pittsburgh (5), Philadelphia (4), Washington (2), Baltimore (3), and Boston (6) in 1901–2. The third season had taken the play to the largest Midwest metropolitan centers, and now for the 1902–3 season Klaw & Erlanger arranged an ambitious itinerary that continued the expansion of their *Ben-Hur* property by reaching into the three other relatively large cities in the Midwest (Cincinnati, Cleveland, Indianapolis) and additional cities in the upper Midwest (St. Paul, Minneapolis), upstate New York and New England (Rochester, Buffalo, Albany, Springfield [MA], Providence, Hartford), and the Deep South (Birmingham, New Orleans, Atlanta, Louisville).

Although there were many variables involved in scheduling, the touring production first and foremost required a large venue in terms of stage size and seating capacity, as well as a reliable and extensive rail network. At the time many American cities already had the physical theater requirements, whether originally built as a theater, opera house, or meeting hall. At the turn of the century these cities now found themselves in competition with one another for visitor dollars, and therefore local leaders urged on the process of urban expansion and modernization, particularly when it involved the installation of electricity. But no matter the status of the theater venue, a team of Klaw & Erlanger carpenters, mechanics, and electricians had to arrive in advance of a *Ben-Hur* engagement to prepare the stage and ensure the proper electrical voltages were accessible.[311] In many instances, as we have seen but as would continue to be necessary, the stage had to be substantially rebuilt. Some of the mechanisms employed were so complicated, particularly the Antioch Circus panorama, that Klaw & Erlanger ordered a second one that could be installed ahead of time in the next city before the previous engagement had come to an end.

Klaw & Erlanger sent ahead to each city an advance agent, usually Edward G. Cooke, their general manager of sixteen years, to make arrangements several weeks before the performance.[312] Hotels were booked in advance not only for the players and crew, of course, but for out-of-town patrons as well. The agent oversaw the hiring of local "supes" to fill the crowd scenes, including as many as twenty children.[313] Along with the theater manager and ticket agents, he also arranged for the train excursions from the outlying towns up to a radius of approximately 150 miles, whether for every night of the engagement, or specifying a particular route for a particular night.[314] A few newspaper announcements preserve details. During the second week of the Cleveland engagement, for instance, the newly built and consolidated Baltimore & Ohio offered a train nightly from October 13–18 departing from Akron's Union Depot at 4:53 p.m. and leaving Cleveland twenty minutes after the curtain went down.[315] The $1 fare was an integral part of how the arrival of the Klaw & Erlanger *Ben-Hur* in the vicinity indirectly increased the coffers of many related businesses and helped spread still another layer of the *Ben-Hur* phenomenon across much of the United States. The arrival of the Klaw & Erlanger play in town meant increased profits and visibility and more business synergies. Shops, hotels, and trains all benefitted from the arrival of *Ben-Hur*.

The publicity campaign was never exactly the same in any two cities. By 1902–3 the company had built up an array of publicity pieces they could release locally to weekly theatrical columns and features, such as paragraphs describing the beauty of the performance or the religious propriety of the play. The features included brief or detailed synopses of the drama itself, short pieces on Wallace, the meeting between Wallace and Ingersoll, explanations of the chariot race mechanisms, and occasionally biographies of players, particularly if they were local, as Farnum was in New England. Occasionally a photograph depicting a player was included in feature-type pieces.

Generally after an announcement was made months in advance that *Ben-Hur* was coming, the newspapers were quiet until a week or so ahead of the initial performance. The public's enthusiasm repeatedly demonstrated that there was no need to hype *Ben-Hur*. As soon as Klaw & Erlanger announced that ticket sales were about to begin, long lines formed at the box office and mail orders from the 150-mile radius began to pour in. Other than calling the production "stupendous," which by all contemporary standards it was, the newspaper ads were neither large nor complex. Most often they were simple boxed ads on the theater page placed alongside all the other local theater offerings. The *Ben-Hur* ads were distinguished mostly by the block lettering of the symmetrically divided six-letter name – always an important element in advertising any *Ben-Hur* product. If the ad had an extra line, it would include the name "Gen. Lew Wallace." If additional lines, then the names of Young, Teal, and Kelley were listed. As the multi-week engagements progressed, the ad often notified the public as to whether it was the second or third week, or the "final" week. Unlike the first two seasons, however, these engagements did not run weeks and months on end, nor did the carefully pre-arranged travel schedule allow them to extend the engagement. The only possibility was to add an extra matinee, which warranted an additional announcement or ad in the local newspaper.[316]

Part of the reason for informing the public about the length and weekly status of the engagement was that early on Klaw & Erlanger, like the *Brooklyn Eagle* reviewer who recorded seeing on opening night "significant rows of empty seats downstairs," observed that the first week often drew the poorest attendance because potential patrons assumed it would be the heaviest.[317] Patrons tended to wait for the final week, hence the extra matinee, and usually receipts were highest then. Consequently, Klaw & Erlanger placed notices in newspapers. Many were simply informational, saying that advance ticket sales had been very large but that there were still many good seats left, or citing specific excursion trains from distant towns. Some were aimed at procrastinators and therefore designed to establish a sense of urgency, warning that this would be the last time *Ben-Hur* would be seen in the area for a long time.[318] The October 22, 1903, notice in *The Newtown Register*, for instance, suggested to residents of suburban New York that "[these] will undoubtedly be the last times this remarkable production will be seen in New York for many years, if ever again."

Of course this did not apply to the smaller venues where the company performed for one week or less. Klaw & Erlanger's commitment to expanding their market into new territories necessitated many of these shorter engagements, as befitted the smaller population centers. Cities like St. Paul, Minneapolis, Omaha, Birmingham, Atlanta, Louisville, Toledo, Syracuse, Albany, Springfield, and Hartford were scheduled for one week only, with performances from Monday evening to Saturday evening, matinees Wednesday and Saturday, and the option of an additional matinee on Friday.[319] This meant they had to break down, load, travel, unload, and install in about twenty-four hours from Saturday night into Sunday. Klaw & Erlanger boasted that its dozen or more specially arranged and equipped trains cars carrying the equipment, animals, and personnel amounted to the largest organization ever sent on tour.[320] Monday was reserved for a full dress rehearsal to ensure that all the timings and equipment were running correctly and give the chorus and orchestra an opportunity to fine tune.[321] Sometimes there were two dress rehearsals, one Sunday night and another Monday afternoon.[322] The *Ben-Hur* company would follow this rigorous schedule for most of the next two decades.

A CASE STUDY:
BEN-HUR IN CINCINNATI, SEPTEMBER, 1902

The Cincinnati engagement in the fall of 1902 was atypical in that it was one of only two engagements that lasted three weeks that year, but the longer engagement followed the same progression and produced some of the same types of incidents and problems that occurred elsewhere, *mutatis mutandis*. In June the *Cincinnati Enquirer* announced that *Ben-Hur* was coming to their newly rebuilt Grand Opera House in September.[323] The original Grand had been destroyed by fire the previous year, and on August 17 the *Enquirer* announced *Ben-Hur* would inaugurate the New Grand during the city's annual two-week Fall Festival and continue for an additional week. The announcement added that the "'Ben Hur' people" would arrive one week early to prepare the stage, and that the new stage would surely be put to the test with production involving over 360 people.[324] To accommodate the expected extraordinarily high demand for seats for the inaugural evening, John Havlin, who co-managed the Grand, announced on August 19 that he would distribute those tickets in an auction.[325] On August 24 came another announcement that in eight days the "advance guard" would arrive to prepare the stage. Along with this came Klaw & Erlanger's promise that Cincinnati, as the ninth city to host *Ben-Hur*, would witness a production "on a scale similar to that which marked its long run in New York City."[326] The first newspaper ad appeared on

August 31.³²⁷ The top of the ad lists the Grand, its managers (Bainforth & Havlin), the opening date (September 15), and the names of Klaw & Erlanger, Gen. Lew Wallace, *Ben Hur*, Young, Kelley, and Teal, along with the phrase "Stupendous Production." Below those are the starting times, 8:00 p.m. "precisely" and 2:00 p.m. matinees on Wednesday and Saturday, and the advisory: "No Sunday Performances." The bottom lists the ticket prices, which range from the usual gallery for 50¢, balcony for $1 and $1.50, and lower floor for $1.50 and $2 to boxes for $15 and $20. In between, considerable space is given to explaining the rules of the ticket auction, although not very many cities followed this particular procedure. Usual practice was to include simply a few lines about mail-order procedures.

Once the performances began on September 15, no review was necessary in the local papers. The production was indeed the same that had already been reviewed in New York, Chicago, and elsewhere and distributed to papers in smaller cities over the course of several years. Newspapers continued to run simple classified ads. When luminaries attended performances, local papers took note. In this instance, on September 18 Albert White, the Governor of West Virginia, along with his wife, made an excursion to see a performance even though the purpose of his trip was ostensibly to inspect the troops he had deployed to monitor a local miners' strike.³²⁸ On September 21 the *Enquirer* ran the results of the first week's attendance. Here Klaw & Erlanger made clear that the Fall Festival may have interfered with attendance the first few days, but by Thursday, September 18 "the spacious new Grand was packed to the doors."³²⁹ They assured the public that attendance during the first week is always the poorest, adding brief descriptions of some of the beautiful aspects of the play, and thanking the public for heeding their request to be seated promptly by 8:00 p.m. and 2:00 p.m.

Thus far press reports would make the casual reader assume that *Ben-Hur* was not a tremendous success in Cincinnati, suggesting perhaps that Klaw & Erlanger's claim that ticket sales would improve in the second and third weeks was little more than box-office hype. But the former assumption would have been incorrect, and when it came to Klaw & Erlanger *Ben-Hur* "hype," they were merely advising the public as to what they had already experienced in city after city. Now the box-office crush was happening in Cincinnati, and we learn this not from Klaw & Erlanger but from accounts of a natural disaster and an emergency meeting of the Cincinnati Board of Legislation. On September 24 there was a power outage in the theater district.³³⁰ Most of the theaters had to turn away their patrons and promise to refund their money. The newly constructed Grand included its own electrical plant for the front part of the building, but the stage area still depended on city power. Bainforth & Havlin were assuring the eager crowd that they would find a solution, when a local shop owner offered them his supply of electrical cable. While J. C. Griffith, the Ben-Hur Company electrician, and the Grand crew then worked to establish power, the audience waited for two hours in the rain. The *Enquirer* commented, "It was a noticeable fact that the audience waited patiently for the delay to be remedied, and the house filled rapidly when the doors were finally opened." As the third and final week approached, Klaw & Erlanger as often announced that ticket sales had broken records and that an extra Friday matinee for October 3 would be the last chance for most to see *Ben-Hur*.[331] Tickets went on sale on Monday, September 29. They sold out in thirty-five minutes. But soon after, ticket speculators across the street were re-selling the $2 seats for $5.[332] That night Police Judge William Lueders made a "scathing denunciation" of speculators before Cincinnati's Board of Legislation. The reader will take special notice of the portion of Lueders' speech where he talks of "a show of great attraction at one of our theaters":

> A number of our best citizens, aided by the Mayor, through the means of the Fall Festival, brought thousands of visitors to Cincinnati. During the Festival, and continuing still, is a show of great attraction at one of our theaters, and a number of persons have conspired together to victimize and pilfer from the pockets of the public money to which they have no right.... I am informed that during the three weeks' engagement the receipts of the house from tickets will be $60,000, or $20,000 a week. In addition to this an extra sum of $10,000 has gone into the pockets of the speculators. I say that this is nothing less than robbing the public.

Feeling compelled to take concrete action before the Friday matinee, Board member Michael Mullen proposed a license fee of $1000 for ticket speculators, and another member proposed to amend that to $3000.[333]

The urgency to solve the scandalous *Ben-Hur* tickets problem spilled over to a meeting of businessmen on Wednesday, October 1. It was the focus at the monthly meeting of the Cincinnati Hotel Men's Association.[334] They considered this scalping to cause serious injury to their out-of-town patrons. They had already planned on obtaining tickets for their patrons who had booked rooms in advance and were willing to pay them an extra fee. They added that it would take a long time for the city to recover from "the rapacity worked by the speculators upon the people [who do not live] here." Meanwhile, to accommodate this crush for tickets, Towle and Bainforth & Havlin announced another extra matinee to be given on Thursday, October 2, stipulating that the number of tickets sold to any individual would be limited to two.[335] An eyewitness reported that after purchasing their two tickets, some patrons would immediately rejoin the line at the back and repeat until they had acquired ten tickets.[336] Despite the limitations on the number of tickets sold to each patron at the ticket window, the extra matinee was sold out before noon.

Most often the *Ben-Hur* production left town without fanfare. The 1902 Cincinnati engagement was no different except that the furor over the ticket scalpers and the decision to schedule still another matinee on Thursday elicited another press release. As usual, Klaw & Erlanger press releases promoted *Ben-Hur* by releasing information designed to impress the public with the size and complexity of the production and its operation, providing us as well with a deeper layer of information about the inner workings of the *Ben-Hur* tour. In this instance, they announced that all tickets had been sold for another "packed house," but then assured the public that they were one of the few companies that gave extra compensation to its members and recognized the "rather arduous" work and technical ability expected of them.[337] They finished with a paragraph outlining their Sunday morning departure for Cleveland on two special trains, the first departing at 5:00 a.m. with eleven baggage cars, one stock car, and a sleeper for the crew, and the second at 8:00 a.m. with the cast, chorus, and orchestra, arriving in time for a Sunday evening dress rehearsal, followed by a second dress rehearsal Monday morning. The last sentence reads, "Manager Towle received word from there yesterday saying the first day's sale had been the largest ever known in that city."

The *Cincinnati Enquirer* on its own printed a human interest story about Ben Mears, who at this time was playing the role of Sanballat and would a decade hence play Simonides.[338] He was a native of Cleveland, and his mother, Sadie Mears, had stayed the week at Cincinnati's Sterling Hotel to watch her son perform. Her son left with the company on the 8:00 a.m. train, and as she was preparing to follow, she suddenly took ill, was taken to a nearby hospital, and died during surgery. Cleveland's *Plain Dealer* ran an additional story during the subsequent engagement in that city, highlighting in the headline that a quartet of actors in the *Ben-Hur* company sang at her funeral and admiring her son's ability to perform his role despite his loss.[339]

BEN-HUR HEADS SOUTH, 1902–3

The rest of the fall and winter consisted of an unbroken string of engagements in the Midwest, including three weeks surrounding Thanksgiving in Indianapolis,[340] Milwaukee,[341] and the Christmas and New Years weeks in the Twin Cities at the Metropolitan in St. Paul and the Lyceum in Minneapolis.[342] These engagements each brought in over $17,000 per week. The beginning of 1903 found the company making a swing further West to Omaha, where the advertising included a halftone illustration of a chariot race, assisting in establishing box-office records at Boyd's the second week of January,[343] followed by another record-breaking engagement at the Willis-Wood in Kansas City and a repeat engagement of two weeks at the Olympic in St. Louis.[344]

The company then headed south in early February. Four cities were originally scheduled – Memphis, New Orleans, Atlanta, and Louisville, but during the season Birmingham was substituted for Memphis.[345] H. L. DiCive, manager of Atlanta's Grand Opera House, saw such an overwhelming number of out-of-town ticket inquiries before the engagement began that he used the *Atlanta Constitution* to urge regular patrons to secure seats early.[346] Elsewhere in a feature titled "Ben-Hur Comes Like a Circus," the *Constitution* details the rapid trains which transported the equipment the 175 miles from Montgomery to Atlanta in four and one-half hours, more than an hour faster than the fastest regularly scheduled train.[347] The paper also mentions that this engagement will include the 1000th consecutive performance by Monk but adds that unfortunately William Farnum would not be appearing because of his mother's fatal illness. As often, the paper made the initial figures available – $6330 the first day, which is compared to Kansas City's $9100, Birmingham's $4572, and New Orleans' $6289.[348] And it reports a story about a speculator to whom two police detectives replied to his offer of two tickets for sale, "We won't take the tickets but we will take you."

THE *BEN-HUR* AUDIENCE: TURNING CHURCHGOERS INTO THEATERGOERS

When Lew Wallace first submitted the manuscript of *Ben-Hur: A Tale of the Christ* to Harper & Brothers in the spring of 1880, the publisher considered the novel's religious subject matter to be a potential liability. Many of the initial book reviewers concurred with Harper's assessment, as did the world press nineteen years later when reviewing its most important scion, Klaw & Erlanger's *Ben-Hur*. The London critics expressed this same concern. But the most significant portion of the public not only did not consider the religious element a liability but fully embraced it and particularly its dramatic and spectacular rendering in the final act of the drama. A feature article in 1907 *Macon Telegraph* recognized the impact the play was having around the country.[349] Introduced by the telling headline, "Gen. Lew Wallace's Mighty Play Has Changed the Attitude of the Church Against the Playhouse," the article details how the play will encourage audiences to attend additional religious plays. It explains that it is "only a step from the present mixed dramas of religious and secular to the works of religious import purely, and it is certain that such works, if written in exalted spirit, would continue to attract a large portion of the regular theatergoing public."[350]

After the one-week 1903 Atlanta engagement was finished, the immediate estimate was that over 25,000 people had seen the production.[351] The article in the *Constitution*, "'Ben-Hur' Seen By Thousands," concludes with an interesting paragraph exposing one of the apparent paradoxes within the *Ben-Hur* phenomenon – the apparent lack of enthusiastic responses from an audience.

While it is true that no great amount of enthusiasm was shown by those who had the opportunity of seeing "Ben-Hur," it is equally true that no expressions of disappointment were heard. As the result of extensive advertising on the part of the company coupled with a widespread knowledge of General Lew Wallace's novel, the public expectation was high, and it was greatly to the credit of the production that the public expectation was in no way disappointed. The only note or regret heard during the week was that William Farnum, the leading man, failed to appear with the company.

More than a decade after the Atlanta engagement, the *Seattle Daily Times* would offer an explanation for of this kind of audience reaction:

> "Ben-Hur's" strength is not after all in its heavy production and its chariot races and the masses of its participants, but in the direct appeal it makes to the religious beliefs of all Christian nations. . . . "Ben-Hur" is not only enjoyed, but it is reverenced.[352]

This would apply particularly to the people who were attending such a spectacle for the first time and in all likelihood seeing a religious drama for the first time out of a church context, where of course fulsome applause was not encouraged. The Seattle paper continues:

> Because of "Ben-Hur's" religious quality, its audiences have always been of unusual makeup. It draws its tens of thousands of nontheatregoers. There are each night in the audience scores of people who were never in a theatre before, who go to nothing but "Ben-Hur." There wasn't the amount of demonstrative applause last night that there is at an ordinary success. Doubtless more than one timid stranger there last evening figured that he would be put out if he made too much noise with his hands.

In 1922 The *Indianapolis Star* recalled the cultural achievements of the play:

> Season after season for more than twenty years it has played all over America to enormous audiences, made up in large measure of persons who had never been inside a theater before and who regarded their visit to "Ben Hur" very much in the light of a religious ceremony, and as one of the most interesting events of their lives.[353]

The next year in "'Ben-Hur' Passes Over to the Movies," a lengthy, illustrated article promoting Erlanger's film production of Wallace's novel, the *New York Times* similarly reviewed the impact of *Ben-Hur* on rural audiences:

> Edward Cooke, advance agent for sixteen years, called it "the awakening of America to the possibilities of super stage spectacle," and I guess that statement goes. It was a snowball of advertising that grew and grew. Seeing "Ben-Hur" became a deed of merit. The "Ben-Hur" audience was unlike any other audience in the country. Deacons and deaconesses from backwoods hamlets; professors and parsons, their families and disciples from mid-continent seats of culture; the educated, the self-educated, the thrill-hungry, music lovers, dance devotees, "Rubes" and small-town sports, those who had learned from the Bible in youth, and those who sought escape from Puritanism in the theatre, all this motley throng were there, all of them united by the flavor of culture and romance and pietistic tradition.[354]

The *Times* also makes clear that "the show broke down the imaginary barrier between Church and drama," and that it was the Tribe of Ben-Hur that paved the way. Throughout the 1890s, tens of thousands of people gathered in small, self-supervised groups, participated in public *Ben-Hur* readings that were sacred to their society, dressed in costumes, and acted out parts for their initiations and other rituals. Community theatrical and church dramatizations of the New Testament narrative were the natural outgrowth, and the next step was attending the wholesome big-city spectacle that required only a discounted ride on a train excursion.

The modern reader eager to dismiss the importance of this contribution to American culture as a pointless expansion of crude popular culture will benefit from hearing the brief recollection of just such a rural person, who in this instance happened to be none other than William Faulkner. As a young boy he traveled with his father to Memphis from Oxford, Mississippi, a trip of about eighty miles, and there he saw a performance of the Klaw & Erlanger *Ben-Hur*. Many years later, when students at the University of Virginia asked the acclaimed author about the influence of drama on his writings, Faulkner replied that he had only seen a handful of plays in his entire life, and that one of them, *Ben-Hur*, he particularly remembered because "it had live horses in it and a camel and I'd never seen a camel before."[355]

In the wake of the 1874 Swing heresy trial, the *Chicago Tribune* had long ago identified the potential relationship between religion and commerce with this witty comment: "The theological market may be quoted as fairly active, with brisk inquiries as to futures."[356] With *Ben-Hur* it had become a blue-chip equity.

TRAVERSING THE COUNTRY WITH TWO *BEN-HUR* COMPANIES

If the reader will consider the expenses involved in traveling from city to city with several hundred actors and extras, a dozen or more thoroughbred horses and a camel, and an additional crew charged with rebuilding stages and preparing equipment, and the need for not just the citizens of each new city but also those of the surrounding towns and smaller cities to fill the largest theater in the city, and then consider as well that *Ben-Hur* came to many cities two, three, four, or more times over two decades, it is quite remarkable that at no point along the way did a few municipalities fail to fill the venue adequately and thereby cause a series of losses that amounted to a sum sufficient for Klaw & Erlanger to shut down the production. But as we have just seen, the momentum behind this dramatic spectacle continued to thrive and draw excellent attendance and even capacity crowds almost every day and everywhere. There did not seem to be any geographical pockets of disinterest, new areas of the country meant new markets, and a return engagement attracted those who wanted to relive the experience as well as those who regretted missing it previously.

The Klaw & Erlanger management calculated the tour so as not to overstay their welcome, despite the expense of moving. Problems arose frequently, as the 1902 Cincinnati account suggested. But they were always relatively minor in the realm of an international dramatic juggernaut, and often the result of its own success. In Memphis in February, 1904, for instance, the *Ben-Hur* company was sued for violation of contract and the court went so far as to attach the scenery until payment was made.[357] The dual complaint was that (1) the company did not give the Arkansas newspaper editors the complimentary tickets they were promised, to which the company replied that the crush for ticket purchases had been even greater than anticipated, and (2) eight local children were paid only 40¢ instead of 50¢, for which, as compensation, the court demanded payment of $100.

In the 1903–4 season, in fact, the momentum was strong enough to support two separate production companies. The original company which had been on tour for the past three seasons continued to explore new territory. This included cities in the mountain states (Denver, Salt Lake City, Butte)[358] and the West Coast (Seattle, San Francisco, Portland),[359] as well as southern, Midwestern, east coast cities not yet visited (e.g. Memphis, Lexington, Detroit, South Bend, Grand Rapids, Duluth),[360] as well as Worcester, Portland, Bangor, and Lewiston.[361] This company carried 226 people, including 180 singers and dancers, plus the working staff of 73.[362] William Farnum sometimes played the lead role, as did Alphonz Ethier, who had played the role of Messala for two years, and Wilfred Payne.[363] In the heartland the publicity sometimes re-emphasized the reverent and inspiring religious nature of the drama along with its wholesomeness. Before the September 14–19, 1903, Grand Rapids engagement, which also coincided with a local fair that brought in additional rural patrons, the *Muskegon Chronicle* ran this paragraph:

> "If the American drama had done absolutely nothing worthy in its long career but this; had its fame to rest solely upon this one noble product of Messrs. Klaw & Erlanger," says an advance notice, "it has justified its existence; for in this at least, it has shown that the stage may be given over to uses wholly worthy, highly commendable, and which cannot fail to exert the greatest possible blessing on mankind – that of bringing home with immense force and dignity the eternal truth and verity of the birth into the world of the Savior of mankind.
>
> To every man, no matter what his conditions, 'Ben Hur' has its appeal. It appeals to the deep-grained, firm-rooted religious feeling in the human heart and brings back with great directness, the simple lessons and divine truths that every man born in a Christian land learned at his mother's knees."[364]

Such a press notice, whether read by true believer or skeptic, reflects the unique status of this well-publicized *Ben-Hur* by-product.

This West Coast tour, as we have seen in the results from the San

Francisco engagement, faced a clean slate of patrons not unfamiliar with the *Ben-Hur* product.[365] Portland was just as excited and proud. The *Oregonian* describes lines of people sitting on wooden cracker boxes and camp stools while waiting in line for tickets. The paper listed its single week results – eight performances, $23,000 in receipts, 18,000 patrons, and 125 local "supes" hired for the engagement.[366] Putting this into perspective, the report added that it cost $1000 per day to produce the play, suggesting to the public the size of their undertaking rather than the enormous profit margins they were reaping. The tour was scheduled for four cities – two weeks in Denver, five nights in Salt Lake City, four weeks in San Francisco, and one week in Portland, and then a direct return to St. Paul. But Cooke filled still unscheduled time with a one-week engagement at the Grand in Seattle (December 7–12), and instead of heading directly back to the Midwest he scheduled a stop in Butte for an engagement November 18–19.[367] This would turn out to be an innovative type of engagement in that it proved that the touring Ben-Hur company could profitably offer engagements of reduced length in smaller towns so long as $10,000 could be netted.[368] The company would do this between major venues. Two months after Butte, for instance, the company offered a compact four-day, six-performance Christmas engagement at the Lyceum in Duluth, December 23–6, with matinees on both December 25 and 26.[369] For the duration of the existence of the Klaw & Erlanger *Ben-Hur*, this option for a shorter engagement allowed the production to reach smaller localities with greater frequency. In 1907 the company played two smaller Pennsylvania venues in Allentown and Scranton, the first October 7–9, the second October 10–12.[370] In the 1913–14 season the tour reached over sixty venues. It may be coincidence, but perhaps the short engagements put some additional pressure on the company to add another wrinkle to their advertising. For the brief Saginaw engagement in the late fall of 1906, advertising boasted that not just Edward VII but President Theodore Roosevelt and Pope Leo XIII had seen the drama.[371] The tour returned from the West and then in the 1904–5 season swung into Texas and introduced *Ben-Hur* to audiences in Dallas, Austin, San Antonio, Galveston, and Houston in the late fall, followed by a return in December, 1904, through the same southern cities visited in the early spring of 1903 with such actors as Alphonz Ethier, Lionel Adams [Moise Hirsch], and Orrin Johnson playing the lead role.

Klaw & Erlanger had announced already the previous May that they planned to reuse the Drury Lane equipment and scenery to form a second company to play the East Coast metropolitan centers, beginning with New York City.[372] The role of Simonides was reprised by J. E. Dodson, who had played the role in London, but he and the scenic equipment were the few London holdovers.[373] When this company inaugurated the newly rebuilt New York Theatre on September 21, 1903, Ben-Hur was played by

Henry Woodruff, a company newcomer and a Harvard graduate.[374] Mabel Bert, who had created the role of Mother in 1899, had played in 1071 performances.[375] By far the most spectacular new feature was the addition of two more chariots.[376] The New York Theatre offered the usual eight performances per week, plus a Sunday evening performance, since no traveling or concern for religious observances was involved, from September 21 until December 12.[377]

This doubling of the company confused the public. Rumors circulated that the two companies were "No. 1 and No. 2," suggesting that one company was preferable to the other. Klaw & Erlanger took measures to counter this misperception, printing in local papers statements of this sort:

> Klaw & Erlanger's special company to present the London Drury Lane production of "Ben Hur" at the New York Theatre in September will begin rehearsals next Monday. The original "Ben Hur" organization has been in rehearsal two weeks and will open at South Bend, Ind., September 7. Several dramatic writers have referred to these two companies as "No. 1" and "No. 2" Ben Hur companies. The management says no such distinction should be made, as each is the equal of the other in both cast and equipment. The company that opens its season in South Bend, Sept. 7, and which will tour the west and the Pacific coast is the original organization which first presented "Ben Hur" at the Broadway Theatre in November, 1899.[378]

After New York, the Drury Lane company moved to Philadelphia in late December. William Farnum was once again scheduled to play the role of Ben-Hur when the production was preparing to move to Chicago's Iroquois Theater. But on December 30, 1903, the Iroquois was destroyed by fire, with hundreds of lives lost. Performances by the second company seem to have come to an end in Philadelphia on December 28, 1903, but the Drury Lane scenery would be used for several more years, e.g. for the "Special Production" that ran for the entire two-month duration of the St. Louis World's Fair in the fall of 1904.[379] And in 1912 there would again be multiple companies playing on three continents.[380]

BUSINESS AND ADVERTISING SYNERGIES

Never before had such a popular contemporary novel been so successfully adapted for the stage on such a huge scale in terms of the size and scope of the production, the breadth of its distribution, and the durability of its popularity. Unaware of the word "synergy," Thorold's 1901 *Our Players' Gallery* nonetheless recognized the process in this way: "The greatest novel of the greatest century resulted in the greatest drama of the new era ... an achievement unprecedented in the united dominion of the theatre and literature."[381] And while this metamorphosis of a bestselling novel into an equally lucrative drama should be recognized as a landmark example of cross-pollination between popular literature and popular theater, the Klaw & Erlanger *Ben-Hur*, like the novel and some of its previously discussed by-products, encouraged a number of businesses to participate in or benefit from its fame and visibility.

The novel itself was both a benefit to ticket sales and a prime beneficiary for book sales. Despite their long-standing attempts at confining the *Ben-Hur* name to traditionally reputable applications within the publishing world, Wallace and Harper had gradually become leading innovators in rejecting a narrow business perspective and exploiting commercial popularity. The creation and repeated printings of "The Player's Edition" testifies to this, as does J. C. Williamson's order for tens of thousands of copies of the novel specially designed for his Sydney and Melbourne productions.[382] A few years later, on March 13, 1907, Harper contacted Susan Wallace to relay Klaw & Erlanger's desire to give away copies of the novel during that year's Holy Week and to ask her willingness to waive her royalty on a few hundred copies.[383] Wallace replied by telegram, authorizing them to give Klaw & Erlanger no more than one thousand copies.[384] Either circumstances changed or Klaw & Erlanger had reason to suspect that Susan would not cooperate in their promotional scheme, which was to distribute copies of "The Player's Edition" to every woman in attendance at New York's Academy of Music to mark the 2500th performance of the production.[385] Press releases at the time made no mention of Holy Week. Instead, in a bold synergy with the publisher, the release stated, "It is not recalled that a copyrighted book of a representative American author has ever before been made a souvenir of a theatrical performance." For some of the roadshow stops in 1906–7, Harper arranged special local promotions and offered the novel for sale in conjunction with the play.[386] It was in the following year that Harper published *The Chariot Race*, another edition excerpted from the original.[387]

As they did when Lew Wallace was alive, Harper frequently coordinated its serial publications with the Klaw & Erlanger production as well. In addition to the *Harper's Weekly* article on Hagen's specially designed treadmill that preceded the New York premiere in mid-November, 1899, they advertised the new "Player's Edition" of the novel in both their weekly and monthly magazines in the spring of 1901.[388] In 1902 they published an announcement of the first London production and then the inaugural of the new Grand Opera House in Cincinnati.[389] In 1907 they published a unique stage-production photo of Arrius fighting the pirates aboard his galley along with a photograph of the scene before the Temple of Apollo at Daphne. And in January, 1912, they announced the opening of the New Amsterdam Theatre on Broadway, illustrated with three principals in costume, including Richard Buhler as Ben-Hur.[390]

Relevant ads appeared in both local newspapers and the gratis programs handed out to audience members. Harper placed an ad for a boxed edition of the novel in the *New York Tribune* on the day of the Broadway Theatre premiere, November 29, 1899.[391] In the initial programs for that historic New York engagement, E. T. Paull placed a prominent half-page ad for "THE GREATEST SONG EVER WRITTEN – THE BEN HUR CHARIOT RACE SONG."[392] To fill the space, Paull printed the thirty-four lines of H. A. Freeman's lyrics in two columns, followed by a description of the "handsomely lithographed" title page and information on how and where to purchase the piece and other selections in Paull's catalogue. A few pages later, Harper & Brothers displayed a half-page ad for a "special two-volume holiday edition" of the Garfield edition. Taking advantage of the premiere of the play during the Christmas season, they offer this version of *Ben Hur* [sic] as "An Ideal Book for a Holiday Gift," two volumes in a box for $4.00. In the new year, Harper placed a different half-page ad in the January 15, 1900, program.[393] Omitting any reference to the holiday season, they offer the same two-volume set at the same price by specifying the connection to the play: "General Lew Wallace's BEN HUR, from which the play is adapted, is now in its 679th Thousand. In order to meet the still pressing demand a new 2 volume edition has just been published."

Of course, when the touring *Ben-Hur* was scheduled to arrive in a city, local merchants sometimes ran ads targeting the thousand of patrons who would be attending the play. The same day the *Cincinnati Enquirer* announced that the "'Ben Hur' people" would be arriving one week early to prepare the stage, The Fair, the city's largest department store at the time, ran a typical, large, illustrated display ad listing many items, but they placed the "special sale" of two discounted editions, *Ben Hur* (95¢) and *Ben Hur Player's Edition* ($1.75), in the prime, top-left location.[394] When the play opened on September 15 to inaugurate the city's New Grand Opera House, the celebratory program handed out to members of the audience included a large but simple ad, "ASK YOUR GROCER FOR BEN HUR FLOUR," placed directly next to the aforementioned Byron stage-production photographs. In preparation for the December 16–17, 1912, Ogden engagement, Wright's Big Store placed a large ad in *The Evening Standard* beginning with a prominently placed "Notice To Out-of-Town Patrons." They informed them of the dates and venue of the engagement as well as the size of the production, and then announced their "Mammoth 'Ben Hur' Feature Sale."[395] The ad encouraged their patrons to take advantage of the railroad excursion rates, shop, save money, and enjoy Christmas, all as the prelude to seeing *Ben-Hur*:

> During the dates mentioned the Ogden Rapid Transit and the Salt Lake & Ogden Railroad, beginning at noon, will make the above round trip rates over their respective lines. In connection with the above WRIGHT'S BIG STORE will hold a Mammoth "Ben Hur" Feature Sale and by taking advantage of the Excursion Rates, given by the railroads and of the unheard-of-reduction in prices made for this special sale, you will be enabled to save a large amount of money on your Christmas purchases as well as witnessing one of the World's most famous plays.

Above this notice to the Out-of-Town Patrons, the ad on the far left includes photographs of Simonides, Balthasar, and Tirzah, and to the far right are individual special sales for candies, watches, gloves, and garments, all marked "Ben-Hur Sale."

Just as local shops and companies employed advertising copy that used the name Ben-Hur in connection with their ads placed in programs for the *Ben-Hur, in Tableaux and Pantomime*, the top of the first page of the program for the Hinton Theatre in Muskogee, Oklahoma, dated February 9, 1911, begins with this tie-in advertisement from The G. M. Burcham Furniture Store: "The 'Ben Hur' Production Makes a Hit with the Theatre Goers – The Low Prices on Furniture and Rugs makes a Hit with the Muskogee Buyers."[396] A few pages later there is a full-page ad for The Tribe of Ben-Hur: "19,805 new members added to the Tribe of Ben Hur during 1910." Comprising an even larger scope was the 4½-inch ad placed in the program for St. Louis' Olympic Theater engagement commencing on Monday, October 17, 1904.[397] The ad was not for a retail item or company but an announcement from the Olympic for the "Tribe of Ben Hur Day" at the World's Fair the following Thursday (October 20) and an extra matinee to be offered that afternoon. The same ad appears again in the final pages of the program. The cover for one of the appearances at Syracuse's Wieting Opera House featured a reproduction of Wagner's painting on the cover. This was relatively rare for the Klaw & Erlanger production, but the same image was quite familiar in commercial advertising at the time, as we will see in the next chapter. Charles A. Marshall, the manager of Duluth's Lyceum Theatre, made an arrangement with *The Duluth Evening Herald*, and for two weeks in advance of the March 22–4, 1909, performances the paper ran a contest that awarded 150 tickets to the school pupils who wrote the 150 finest essays about *Ben-Hur*.[398] In conjunction with this the paper epitomized the story of the play in five installments.[399]

Separate from the program advertisements was the ad in the *New York Times* less than one year after the Broadway Theatre premiere.[400] Along with a sale of Renaissance doylies, centerpieces and scarfs came an offer for pillow tops to be embroidered in various designs. Among the "latest designs" was the Ben Hur.

PARODIES, BURLESQUES, VAUDEVILLE, AND SPIN-OFFS

Although the religious aspects of Wallace's story for the most part provided it with an air of sacrosanctity that insulated it from burlesque and parody, the popularity of the Klaw & Erlanger production and the fame of the chariot race made it an obvious target. An interesting indicator of the impact the *Ben-Hur* production made on Philadelphia theater was that the listing for a farcical "Ben Her," performed by Frank Dumont's Minstrels, appeared one page before the Klaw & Erlanger announcement. It jokingly promised that the "wild horses attached to the chariots for the great sensational race are in daily training and fed on scrapple and horse shoes for strength and endurance."[401] In early October, 1901, W. S. Cleveland, the proprietor of Cleveland's Minstrel Theater in Chicago, developed a racy parody called "Her Bun."[402] Of course he feared an injunction from Klaw & Erlanger, but an initial press release stated positively that the latter would not hinder Cleveland's project, "despite the dislike with which it was viewed."[403] And even though several weeks later Judge Kohlsaat of Chicago had issued a restraining order, he ultimately refused to enjoin the enterprise.[404] In 1903 the Bohemian Club of San Francisco announced that former California Governor Pardee and other distinguished speakers would be present and then entertained the group with "a genial burlesque of 'Ben Hur,' one of the most captivating sketches ever placed on the stage of Bohemia."[405] On a more grandiose scale, at least in terms of advertising imagery, the High Rollers Extravaganza Company's poster for its burlesque "Bend Her" displayed two large and statuesque women charioteers, one of them equipped with a whip.[406] Robert C. Allen in his book, *Horrible Prettiness: Burlesque and American Culture*, appropriately articulated the social politics of the poster when he wrote:

> What is most striking about these posters is their celebration of charismatic female sexual power. Several posters represent this power through inversion, by placing burlesque-costumed women in traditionally masculine roles.

Ben-Hur ran for so many years that it extended well into the Vaudeville period of American popular theater. At that point Charles Robinson, with "His Big Parisian Flirts," billed himself as "The Ben Hur of Burlesque."[407] In a slightly different vein, this aspect of the *Ben-Hur* phenomenon seems also to have inspired the creation of at least one performance troupe in the 1910s, the Ben Hur Company of Albuquerque.[408] A Vaudeville program listed in *The San Bernadino County Sun* in 1914 included a skit, "A Slave of the Galleys," that promised:

> It takes one back to the old Roman days, the barbarous times when slaves were chained to the Roman triremes and forced to work at oars to propel the war craft of those days.
> "The Slave of the Galleys" is a distinct novelty, unusual in every way. It is an act that stand in a class by itself, unlike anything else offered as a vaudeville attraction.[409]

And lastly, in 1915 the *Oregonian* and *Boston Herald* make mention of the Frey Twins, an athletic and handsome duo known as the "Ben Hur and Messala of Vaudeville."[410]

Though the Klaw & Erlanger *Ben-Hur* paved the way for such a Christian oriented and spectacularly staged production as *Quo Vadis?*, its most elaborate and costly spin-off was the Klaw & Erlanger production of Wallace's *Prince of India*. Wallace wrote Joseph Brooks on April 10, 1903, from his location "On the Kankakee River, Indiana" to grant the permission Klaw & Erlanger requested, agree to 7 percent of the gross receipts as a royalty, and make it clear that he would not pay the dramatist.[411] Because it was designed to surpass even *Ben-Hur* in preparations, it took two years for the production to be mounted, costing over $100,000.[412] Much of the expense was lavished on over 100 historically accurate painted backdrops and over 800 costumes modeled after authentic artifacts from the British Museum. Horatio Parker himself was comissioned to compose the entr'acte and incidental music, and, leaving little to chance judging by past performance, William Farnum was secured to create the protagonist role.[413] After a half-year in New York through the fall of 1906, *The Prince of India* then toured the country in 1907.[414] But unlike its cousin and like *Quo Vadis?* and most other lavish productions of the era, it did not thrive beyond these initial successes.

THOUSANDS OF PERFORMANCES

Newspaper entries in the second decade of production do not read very much differently than those from 1900, with the exception that along with emphasizing the size of the production they highlighted how many times the production had visited their city. Portland's *Oregonian* in 1913 boasted:

> Last night this spectacular religious drama came on its fourth visit to Portland and played to a capacity audience. ...Thirteen years of constant repetition have not dimmed any of the glories of this dramatization of General Lew Wallace's immortal story. Its appeal was as powerful last night and as undoubted in its sway over the entranced spectators as on its first visit at the old Marquam nine years ago.[415]

Clearly part of the allure was that the production had not at all grown tired, nor audiences tired of it. The announcement in the *St. Louis Post-Dispatch* for the 1908 production stated:

> During the nine years that have passed since its first production at the Broadway Theater in New York, its owners have not only kept it up to the high standard originally set, but have elaborated it until it stands unrivalled in beauty and impressiveness.[416]

In praising the 1911 version of the production, Henry Wallace commented:

> The play "Ben-Hur" ... is improving each year, and only the finest actors and best scenery are allowed in its production. This year the sinking of the galley during the sea fight has been so improved that the ship actually goes down before the eyes of the audience.[417]

Still six years later, the pre-publicity announcement in *The Atlanta Constitution* boasted:

> "Ben Hur," now in its eighteenth year, is beyond question the most successful and popular play ever produced in this country. One reason for its continued

remarkable favor is that Klaw & Erlanger have never allowed the play to run down, and in fact, this year, with its powerful company of 250 people and twenty horses, the production is practically a new one.[418]

The production's reputation and its original "high standard" remained an integral part of its continued attraction. The public all knew this was a spectacular, or inspiring, or exciting yet reverent show, and as time and the production marched on, nearly one out of every ten people in the United States had seen a performance.[419]

We have already read in the *Seattle Times* that audiences in 1913 were quite fond of the religious component of the performance. And as we are seeing, for the action-loving segment of the audience Klaw & Erlanger had increased the number of horses and chariots. The announcement for the opening at New York's New Amsterdam Theatre on December 23, 1911, stated that in their "new" production Ben-Hur (Richard Buhler) would race against four other chariots.[420] Smaller venues would see three chariots, or the original two.[421] Addressing a different segment of their audience, and probably a large one, they focused on their longest continuing star and sentimental favorite, Monk. By the end of the 1916 season the brown gelding, now twenty-two years of age and still winning the race for Ben-Hur on a daily basis, had developed such a close relationship with Richard Buhler that at the end of the season Buhler purchased him so that he could someday retire to Buhler's farm near Paw Paw Lake in Michigan.[422] Far from ready for retirement, however, the next fall Monk was winning races for the next Ben-Hur, A. H. Van Buren.[423]

By the mid-1910s, Klaw & Erlanger's production was competing against moving pictures. In their ad for performances at New York's Manhattan Opera House in early November, 1916, they emphasize "350 REAL PEOPLE – 20 REAL HORSES."[424] Elsewhere they used the wording, "Not a Moving Picture – The Century's Greatest Play."[425] That same month Klaw & Erlanger took out a copyright on "Ben Hur, the World's Greatest Play."[426] These ads, and those for the engagement at the Boston Theatre in January, 1915, all advertise "popular prices," again in competition with the cost of new forms of dramatic entertainment. The most expensive floor seat was $1.[427] Reduced prices were not the norm, however, nor ideal for their bottom line. For the final Indianapolis engagement in the spring of 1920, ticket prices ranged again from 50¢ to $2.50, and the ad can now be read almost like a movie poster: "KLAW & ERLANGER COLOSSAL NEW – BEN-HUR; 300 PEOPLE IN THE MIGHTY SPECTACLE – 300."[428] For religious approbation, they added a quote from Billy Sunday: "I wish 100 million people could see it, and I should like nothing better than to talk to 50,000 men and women just after they had seen 'Ben Hur.'"[429]

The Klaw & Erlanger production of *Ben-Hur* performed at least once and often repeatedly in over 175 cities in almost every one of the United States. Philadelphia and Columbus hosted the *Ben-Hur* production nine times, Pittsburgh, Baltimore, and Washington eight times. Using weeks of engagement as a measure, *Ben-Hur* played in Philadelphia for fifty-six weeks, more than an entire year. Similar numbers can be calculated for New York and Boston, and the combined engagements in Chicago and St. Louis also add up to more than one year. *Ben-Hur* was featured at the St. Louis World's Fair in 1904, at the Lewis and Clark World's Fair Exposition in Portland, Oregon, in 1906, the Jamestown Exposition in Norfolk in 1907, and a decade later at the West Coast Panama-Pacific Exposition.[430] (To put this in chronological perspective, Mckee reports that the record-breaking production at the San Francisco Panama-Pacific Exposition in 1915 coincided with an independent performance by Evelyn Gurley-Kane.)[431] *Ben-Hur* also appeared in Canada, England, Australia, and New Zealand.[432] There were later reports of appearances in Holland.[433] And with the return to England in 1912, there were performances "in the provinces" in Manchester, Ireland, and Scotland as well as another attempt at arranging a production of *Ben-Hur* in Germany and Austria.[434] There is at least one report of a "Ben-Hur" performance at Juneau's Orpheum Theater in 1915, although it is attributed to the Belasco & Robson Ben Hur Company.[435] The only interruption in their record string of engagements was the hiatus of 1918–19, during which *Ben-Hur* played for only two weeks. Because the United States had entered World War I and nationalized the railroads, transporting the company from one venue to another became impractical.[436]

The number of performances kept mounting, and as had been Klaw & Erlanger's preference all along, many milestones were shared with the public. We have already marked Mabel Bert's 1071st performance as Ben-Hur's Mother as well as the distribution of a copy of "The Player's Edition" to every woman in attendance at New York's Academy of Music to mark the 2500th performance.[437] Harper marked the occasion with a paragraph in *Harper's Weekly* by estimating that one million people had seen the play in New York City, where the play had been performed some 450 times, and six million nationwide.[438] For scale, in 1908 the entire population of the Pacific Coast had not yet reached six million.[439] When the production returned to Boston for the sixth time in 1915, it marked the 4500th performance. Klaw & Erlanger's press release calculated that "more than 12,000,000 people have watched with breathless interest the unfolding of the play's story."[440] They do not report on their total receipts or profits, but they do estimate that they had spent more than $1 million in preparing stages and electrical systems for the production. Nor did the public's appetite seem to diminish. There was such a demand for tickets at a New York performance at the Manhattan Opera House in November, 1916, that at 8:30 the management had to call for the police because the crowd clamoring for seats was so unruly.

At the beginning of the final season, *The New York Clipper* labeled the Klaw & Erlanger *Ben-Hur* a "dramatic institution."[441] A feature in Cleveland's *Plain Dealer* looked back at its origins. In addition to reviewing Wallace's reluctance and the first few seasons on the East Coast, the piece offered a retrospective:

> It must be remembered that the mechanics of the stage had not reached anything like present high developments, any more than steamships, automobiles, and wireless telegraphy had. ... The public outside of the national metropolis was quite unfamiliar with the colossal theatrical companies which would soon make annual tours from coast to coast – grand opera organizations, "Garden of Allah" companies, even bands of vaudeville performers moving on special trains and requiring the largest theaters and convention halls to accommodate their machinery and their audiences. So "Ben Hur" was a sensation even before the curtain went up for the first time on the opening night. It was heralded as the biggest play ever attempted and that it justified expectations is proved by its longevity and present ratings.[442]

As artistic, commercial, and popular attention began to focus on shifting the play to cinema, the *New York Times* described the many contributions it made to American theater, commerce, and culture:

> The possibilities of a play (American style) were first illustrated by "Ben-Hur," for it perfected dramatic and fathered "movie" spectacle, formed the theatre's right wing in echelon with the Church, got the parson to acting, put its signs in the sky and its name on every lip, linked business and the theatre, developed "circusing" and national propaganda, and finally became an institution that fully 12,000,000 Americans attended as a solemn duty.[443]

The paper reports that there had been 42,200 performances, a preposterous number. McKee estimated that by the time of the last performance in the spring of 1920, the Klaw & Erlanger *Ben-Hur* had been performed 6000 times before twenty million people who paid some $10 million for tickets. He may have found this number in the widely circulated Erlanger publicity connected with the purchase of the film rights for *Ben-Hur*.[444] The total number may be a little less.[445] According to Klaw & Erlanger's press releases, the 1071st performance came at the completion of 1903, the 2500th performance in March, 1907, and the 4500th performance in January, 1915. That means it took eight years to produce 2000 performances between early 1907 and the end of 1914. *Ben-Hur* ran until the end of the 1920 season, minus the 1919 season, so if it continued to play some 250 performances per year for the final five years, that additional 1250 performances would make the total approximately 5750. Klaw & Erlanger do not report if these numbers include the performances under the management of Collins and Williamson in England and Australia/New Zealand. If they do not, the total would be over 6000. Similarly, if 4500 performances produced $12 million, then the additional 1250 performances would produce over $3 million more for a total of over $15 million. It is not known if these amounts include the sales of the *Souvenir*

Album. And although the profit margins are unknown, the *New York Times* did report that the 1919 production cost $207,000.[446]

Ben-Hur outlasted many of its creators. Lew Wallace died in 1905. Edward Morgan became a morphine addict and caused his own asphyxiation in 1906.[447] Charles Towle resigned in 1913 and died in 1914.[448] In September, 1914, Joseph Brooks quit Klaw & Erlanger over differences with the latter, although he did comment to the *New York Times* that he was "still interested in several ventures with Klaw & Erlanger, notably 'Ben Hur,' which has been running for many years."[449] He committed suicide in 1916.[450] Ben Teal died in 1917.[451] And Klaw & Erlanger dissolved their partnership in the summer of 1919.[452] This was another reason the production did not go on tour the following season. And yet, several rehearsals had been held, the initial engagement for the Manhattan Opera House had already been booked, and there were several different announcements about plans for future tours, "since it is recognized that it has far from exhausted its popularity."[453]

The dramatic version of *Ben-Hur* they created was a spectacular, groundbreaking achievement. It attracted millions of people from a wide range of demographics to see pagan and Christian splendor performed by hundreds of singers, dancers, and an orchestra, and a thrilling chariot race. They ingeniously transferred Lew Wallace's conception to the theater, and the same degree of popularity that the general public willingly granted to the original novel they just as willingly and perhaps even more eagerly heaped upon the Klaw & Erlanger *Ben-Hur*. Central to Wallace's story was the chariot race of revenge, and Claude Hagen, just like Yakima Canutt after him, rendered a literary description of an action scene into a fully realized artistic version that fooled the eye and stirred unbounded excitement among common Americans and European royalty alike. To make this happen, the construction units built large, electrically updated, and physically durable stages all over the United States and, like Johnny Appleseeds, helped to spread the Wallace seeds of energetic, tense action sequences throughout the American theatrical psyche. *Ben-Hur* was the longest-running, most widely viewed, most spectacular, and most commercially lucrative theatrical property America had ever seen. And even as the show was finally going dark in 1920, Erlanger and his associates were already taking steps to make an even more expensive and more spectacular *Ben-Hur* on film.[454]

The Klaw & Erlanger *Ben-Hur* left quite a legacy. The first chapter of this book cited the story of how the founder of Ben Hur Construction Company saw a performance at the 1908 St. Louis engagement and, according to the company's online centennial video, was "very impressed with the character of this guy Ben-Hur," so much so that he named the company after him.[455] The classical composer G. W. Chadwick, who had composed his setting of Iras's song as "The Lament" in 1887, was eager to compose the music for the Broadway show *Everywoman* because the producer assured him it would be "another *Ben-Hur*."[456] And at the beginning of this chapter, Marc Klaw was said in his 1936 *New York Times* obituary to have reached a peak with *Ben-Hur*. In addition, the careers of Teal, Brooks, Towle, and other behind-the-scenes managers reached their zenith during the many years spent working behind the scenes of *Ben-Hur*.[457] Many of the actors who portrayed Ben-Hur – Morgan, Corrigan, Farnum, Ethier, Tearle, Tabor, Buhler, Van Buren, and Woodruff as well as Robert Frazier, William J. Kelly, Orrin Johnson, Henry Basil Gill, and Thurston Hall – helped cement their acting careers and were recognized for their service. Emmet Corrigan, for instance, was headlined in 1909 for his role in Paul Wilstach's *Keegan's Pal* as "Emmet Corrigan of Ben Hur Fame," and even in 1915 William Farnum was advertised for his performance in William Fox's film, *A Wonderful Adventure*, as "Creator of the title roles in the stupendous Klaw & Erlanger Productions 'Ben Hur' and 'Prince of India.'"[458] Several went on to play leading roles in silent films, particularly Farnum and Tearle as well as William S. Hart, who became one of the first movie cowboys. Thurston Hall, who played the lead role of *Ben-Hur* as early as 1907, had a long career in film, first as Mark Antony in Theda Bara's *Cleopatra*, and much later as a blustery businessman in films of the 1940s and 1950s.[459]

The Klaw & Erlanger *Ben-Hur* left different kinds of traces in the cinema of the 1920s and 1930s. Erlanger's name appears prominently on one of the initial title screens of the MGM film adaptation released in 1925. As we will see in greater detail in the chapter on the 1925 film, Erlanger played an important role in shepherding the novel, and to a certain extent, his play, into another spectacular dramatic presentation. And the film played through the second half of the 1920s and was released again in 1931 with a soundtrack. Just three years later in the Ray Enright/Busby Berkeley film *Dames* (1934), when Joan Blondell's character (Mabel Anderson) figures out a scheme to make money, she exclaims with great excitement: "I'll walk out of there with enough money to finance *Ben-Hur* with gold horses!" The same year in *Search for Health* we hear the line, "You've got to have that stadium. . . . You might as well stage *Ben-Hur* without the chariots." Five years later, in 1939, in *It's a Wonderful World*, a stagehand describes the sound effects created by beating drums, a siren, and a shooting pistol as the "noisiest backstage since *Ben-Hur*." From our perspective a century later, we lament that the Klaw & Erlanger *Ben-Hur* production was so carefully managed that it was never captured on film, and so expensive that it could not be revived, but the 1925 MGM film would replace it soon enough.

NOTES

1. *NYT* (January 7, 1923) SM4.
2. Browne and Browne, *The Guide to United States Popular Culture*, 79.
3. Earlier, briefer studies include Morsberger and Morberger, "'Christ and a Horse-Race, 489–502; Preston and Mayer, *Playing Out the Empire*, 1–29.
4. Hirsch, *The Boys from Syracuse*, 22–6; Avery, *A History of Cleveland and Its Environs*, 544–6.
5. *NYT* (January 31, 1926) X5; McArthur, *The Man Who Was Rip Van Winkle*, 340.
6. *NYT* (March 8, 1930) 1.
7. *The Billboard* 33 (December 17, 1921) 43.
8. *NYT* (June 15, 1936) 21.
9. *The Billboard* 33 (December 17, 1921) 43.
10. *BE* (November 21, 1895) 16; cf. *CPD* (May 30, 1920) 77.
11. *NYT* (October 10, 1895) 10. Letter from Klaw & Erlanger to Wallace (April 1, 1899), LL, mentions that they "had the idea in mind eight or nine years."
12. Pond, *Eccentricities of Genius*, 466.
13. Letter from Harper to Wallace, January 4, 1899; Wallace to Harper (January 10, 1899), LL; Lillian Gary Taylor Letters, UVA.
14. M&M 457; Letter from Maurice Thompson to Wallace (March 20, 1899); Letter from Esther Lyons to Harper (March 18, 1899); Letter from Wallace to Harper (February 14, 1899), IHS.
15. *NYT* (January 31, 1926) X5; Letters from Brooks to Wallace (February 17 and 21, 1899), LL.
16. *NYT* (January 31, 1926) X5.
17. *NYT* (January 7, 1923) SM4.
18. Cf. *NYT* (January 31, 1926) X5.
19. Marx, *Groucho and Me*, 178–80.
20. *HW* (November 18, 1899) 1167–8. The portraits are inaccurate, and the course of the chariot race is depicted as moving from right to left.
21. Cf. Letter from Lew Wallace, Jr. to Aunt Sue (March 6, 1904), IHS.
22. Letter from Wallace to Klaw & Erlanger (March 25, 1899), LL; cf. McKee 176.
23. Letter from Wallace to Harper (February 11, 1899), LL. Wallace edited his original text, "The Indians who give jewels for glass beads..."
24. Letter from Klaw & Erlanger to Wallace (March 1, 1899), LL.
25. Letter from Wallace to Harper (March 6, 1899), LL.
26. Letter from Klaw & Erlanger to Wallace (March 16, 1899); Letter from Harper to Wallace (March 21, 1899), LL.
27. Letters from Joseph Brooks to Henry Wallace (March 22, 1899; March 30, 1899), LL.
28. Letter from Wallace to Harper (April 7, 1899); Agreements (April 11, 1899), LL.
29. *PI* (June 24, 1900) 6.
30. *LAT* (July 15, 1900) III:2. *PI* (November 4, 1900) 16.
31. *New York Herald* (April 17 1899) 5; cf. Letters from Klaw & Erlanger to Wallace (April 3; April 11, 1899), LL.

32 *Bangor Daily Whig & Courier* (May 1, 1899) 6.
33 Cf. *DFP* (October 22, 1899) D7.
34 *BG* (December 31, 1900) 9.
35 *NYT* (May 5, 1899) 7.
36 *NYT* (May 14, 1899) 25; *The Ohio State Archaeological and Historical Quarterly* 49 (1940) 68–77; Rivenberg, "Edgar Stillman Kelley," 118; "Great Yesterdays in Music," *The Etude*, 152.
37 *Etude Magazine* (March, 1944) 152; cf. Schleifer, *American Opera and Music for the Stage*, 8–9.
38 *NYT* (May 23, 1899) 7.
39 Hart, *My Life East and West*, 147.
40 *BG* (May 28, 1899) 18; *Waterloo Daily Courier* (December 23, 1899) 1 and 4.
41 *DFP* (September 7, 1899) 4.
42 *Logansport Pharos Tribune* (December 1, 1898) 8.
43 *The Hastings [on-Hudson] Echo* (July 1, 1899) 1.
44 *Waterloo Daily Courier* (December 23, 1899) 1.
45 *NYT* (November 1, 1899) 7.
46 *WP* (November 13, 1899) 7.
47 Ibid., 7.
48 *New York Herald* (November 5, 1899) 4:7.
49 McKee 188.
50 *NYT* (November 24, 1899) 5; (November 29, 1899) 4.
51 *TBS* (November 8, 1899) 9; *WP* (November 13, 1899) 7.
52 *The [London] Times* (November 16, 1899) 8.
53 Unsigned contract, William Selig Folder, HL.
54 E.g. *Werner's Magazine* 26 (December, 1900) 313–31; *Overland Monthly* 36 (July, 1900) 38–46.
55 *NYT* (November 5, 1899) 18.
56 Cf. M&M 460–4.
57 Young, *Lew Wallace's Ben-Hur*; Kelley, *Words and Music*; cf. Preston and Mayer, *Playing Out the Empire*, 189–290; Schleifer, *American Opera and Music for the Stage*, 6–99.
58 *PI* (November 11, 1900) 15.
59 M&M 464.
60 *The [San Diego] Evening Tribune* (November 11, 1905) 3.
61 *Concord Enterprise* (October 19, 1900) 6; *The [Perth] Daily News* (February 21, 1913) 7. The program printed for the November, 1912, performances at Chicago's Colonial Theatre lists the size of the orchestra as twenty-four out of 300 total in the production.
62 *DFP* (December 2, 1899) 4.
63 *TBS* (November 8, 1899) 9.
64 *Concord Enterprise* (October 19, 1900) 6; cf. *The [Perth] Daily News* (February 21, 1913) 7.
65 *MS* (December 1, 1899) 3; *NYT* (September 5, 1909) X4.
66 Kelley's published score (20) begins with the Chorus of Girls singing in unison: "For today we take or give; For today we drink and live; For today we beg or borrow; Who knoweth of the silent morrow." Then (21–6) a four-part

chorus sings a different hymn about Apollo and Daphne: "Daphne! Daphne! Daphne through this haunted grove, Where thou fledst the fair Apollo, Where the song and sigh of love, Breathe from ev'ry leafy hollow, Wander we, and fain would prove, Whether still the god will follow. Heigho." After the incidental music for the dialogue between Ben-Hur and Malluch (26–7), he offers additional transition music (27–8) and then Chorus III (28–32), which uses Young's initial lyrics ("Daphne! Daphne! Whilst above . . .") and a Chorus of Revelers ("Prithee, maiden . . .") (33–4), followed by the Pantomime "Eros and the Maiden" (35–8) designed "for a few voices only." Once the revelers enter the Temple of Daphne, a trumpet solo and then an aulos solo (38–40) lead a group of shepherds and shepherdesses into the temple.

67 *Concord Enterprise* (October 19, 1900) 6; cf. *The [Perth] Daily News* (February 21, 1913) 7.
68 *Concord Enterprise* (October 19, 1900) 6; cf. *The [Perth] Daily News* (February 21, 1913) 7.
69 Cf. *TBS* (February 9, 1902) 8; (February 18, 1902) 7; *The West Australian* (February 15, 1913) 2.
70 Program for *Ben-Hur*, The Auditorium, Chicago, November 1, 1909; Hinton Theatre, Muskogee, Oklahoma, 1910/11.
71 Program for *Ben-Hur*, New York Theatre, New York, October 19, 1902.
72 Program for *Ben-Hur*, Academy of Music, Baltimore, March 8, 1920.
73 *WP* (December 10, 1899) 26, reports that Burgess declared bankruptcy as a result.
74 *Scientific American* (August 25, 1900) cover and 119; *Riverside Independent Enterprise* (October 31, 1903) 3; *AC* (February 22, 1903) C5. Cf. *New York Herald* (November 5, 1899) 4:7, *NYT* (November 5, 1899) 18; Vardac, "Filmed Scenery on the Live Stage," 556–8; Huhtamo, *Illusions in Motion*, 123 and 126.
75 *Riverside Independent Enterprise* (October, 31, 1903) 3.
76 *NYT* (October 11, 1903) 21.
77 *NYT* (August 1, 1929) 27.
78 Henderson, *Theater in America*, 101.
79 Cf. Kimberly Poppiti, "Galloping Horses: Treadmills and Other 'Theatre Appliances' in Hippodramas," 50
80 Nancy Sykes [*DFP* (December 2, 1899) 4] reported the amount as $70,000. Wingate and "*Overland Monthly* 36 (July, 1900) 38–46, $71,000. Erlanger [*NYT* (January 31, 1926) X5] later claimed $100,000.
81 Program from the December 17, 1900, *Ben-Hur* at the Colonial Theatre, Boston, 13; cf. *TBS* (February 24, 1902) 7.
82 *MS* (December 1, 1899) 3.
83 *Boston Daily Advertiser* (December 1, 1899) 4.
84 *TBS* (March 4, 1902) 7.
85 *NYT* (October 11, 1903) 21.
86 *CT* (September 5, 1901) 3.
87 *TBS* (March 22, 1902) 7.
88 *WP* (February 16, 1902) 30.
89 Hart, *My Life East and West*, 152-3.

90 E.g. *BH* (November 5, 1959) 54; *[New Orleans] Times-Picayune* (March 12, 1960) 38.
91 Jones, *Renegades, Showmen, & Angels*, 112–13.
92 *[New Orleans] Times-Picayune* (April 13, 1902) 21.
93 Hart, *My Life East and West*, 151.
94 *The Minneapolis Journal* (December 30, 1902) 6.
95 *Salt Lake Telegram* (October 28, 1903) 6.
96 Ibid., 6.
97 *St. Nicholas* 28 (November, 1900) 45–9; *WP* (February 23, 1902) 30.
98 *The Minneapolis Journal* (December 30, 1902) 6.
99 *Pearson's Magazine* 24 (July, 1910) 73.
100 *The Minneapolis Journal* (December 30, 1902) 6.
101 *BG* (March 10, 1902) 11.
102 *PI* (October 28, 1900) 14.
103 *WP* (June 10, 1900) 24; *The Minneapolis Journal* (December 30, 1902) 6.
104 Beasley, *McKee Rankin*, 211–12; <http://staff.lib.muohio.edu/westernarchives/kelley/bio2.php>
105 Beasley, *McKee Rankin*, 211–14.
106 *Concord Enterprise* (October 19, 1900) 6; cf. *The [Perth] Daily News* (February 21, 1913) 7.
107 Solomon, "The Reception of Ancient Greek Music in the Late Nineteenth Century," 497–525; cf. *NYT* (October 27, 1895) 8.
108 *Worcester [MA] Daily Spy* (February 19, 1902) 7.
109 Cf. *WP* (February 16, 1902) 30.
110 *Werner's Magazine* 26 (December, 1900) 331.
111 *NYT* (January 31, 1926) X5. *WP* (April 17, 1927) F4, says that Frank Currier, who would play Arrius in the 1925 film, was in attendance.
112 M&M 461.
113 *NYT* (November 30, 1899) 7.
114 *NYTr* (November 30, 1899) 7.
115 *World* (November 30, 1899) 12; *StLPD* (November 30, 1899) 5; *CT* (November 30, 1899) 8.
116 *CE* (December 1, 1899) 3.
117 *The Salt Lake Tribune* (December 10, 1899) 22.
118 Niver, *Klaw & Erlanger*, 1–27.
119 *NYTr* (January 21, 1900) 12.
120 *NYT* (January 30, 1900) 2; *WP* (January 28, 1900) 24. Emmett Corrigan was the stage name for Antoine Zittes; *PI* (November 18, 1900) 16.
121 *NYTr* (February 25, 1900) 12.
122 *NYTr* (March 18, 1900) 12: "17th Week, 138 times."
123 *NYT* (March 9, 1900) 7. According to Poppiti, "Pure Air and Fire," 172, Hagen's patent [#653,997] for this new mechanism was granted on July 17, 1900, one month before his patent [#656,969] for the moving panorama was granted on August 28.
124 *WP* (March 11, 1900) 24.
125 *NYT* (May 13, 1900) 8.
126 *WP* (June 10, 1900) 24.

127　*WP* (June 17, 1900) 24.
128　*LAT* (July 15, 1900) III2.
129　*World* (November 30, 1899) 12.
130　*TBS* (November 30, 1899) 1. Wallace thanked also Young, who "adhered so scrupulously to the text and incidents of the book," and the scenic artists, Ernest Albert and Ernest Gros.
131　Ibid., 148.
132　Rivenberg, "Edgar Stillman Kelley," 118. Mckee 177, reports that Wallace "successfully defended the music against abridgment by Klaw and Erlanger."
133　*CE* (December 1, 1899) 3; *CT* (November 30, 1899) 8.
134　*StLPD* (November 30, 1899) 5.
135　*NYT* (February 11, 1900) 4.
136　Letter from Wallace to Edgar Stillman Kelley (April 15, 1900). Miami University, Kelley Collection.
137　King, *Edgar Stillman Kelley*, 69–70.
138　*TBS* (February 24, 1902) 7.
139　*CE* (May 20, 1900) 26; *SFC* (May 18, 1900) 1; *LAT* (June 3, 1900) III1; *CE* (May 20, 1900) 32.
140　*BG* (March 17, 1902) 9.
141　*American Annual of Photography* 37 (1923) 178–83.
142　*Concord Enterprise* (July 19, 1900) 4 and 6; (July 26, 1900) 6; August 2, 1900) 6; et alibi; cf. *Overland Monthly* 36 (July, 1900) 38–46.
143　*The St. Paul Globe* (November 30, 1900) 4.
144　*Our Players' Gallery* 2 (1901) n.p.
145　*The Book Buyer* 21 (October, 1900) back ads.
146　*PW* 58 (October 13, 1900) 931; cf. *A Cumulated Index to the Books of 1900* (Minneapolis: H. W. Wilson, Publisher, 1901) 36, 59, and 352.
147　*The Dial* 31 (September 16, 1901) 203.
148　*StLPD* (December 27, 1901) A6.
149　*SFC* (November 29, 1903) 34.
150　Atkinson, *The Story of Paul of Tarsus*, 23–4; cf. *Religious Education Through Graded Instruction* (Chicago: University of Chicago Press, 1911) 23 and 92.
151　*Werner's Magazine* 26 (December, 1900) 331.
152　Manuscript with Inscription (April, 1900), LL.
153　*StLPD* (October 27, 1901) A6.
154　*BG* (December 2, 1900) 18; *NYT* (September 27, 1900) 7.
155　*PI* (September 2, 1900) 6.
156　*PI* (September 21, 1900) 16.
157　*PI* (October 6, 1900) 9.
158　*PI* (October 9, 1900) 2. The cast lists Corrigan in the role of Simonides.
159　*PI* (October 14, 1900) 12.
160　Cf. *PI* (October 30, 1900) 14.
161　*PI* (November 4, 1900) 16.
162　*PI* (November 11, 1900) 15.
163　E.g. *The [Chicago] Inter Ocean* (October 13, 1906) 6; *Harrisburg Telegraph* (October 25, 1913) 2.
164　*StLPD* (October 27, 1901) A6.

165 Cf. *PI* (November 25, 1900) 16.
166 *StLPD* (December 9, 1900) 22.
167 *BG* (December 2, 1900) 18.
168 Ibid., 18; cf. *AC* (March 2, 1903) 6.
169 Cf. *BG* (December 16, 1900) 18.
170 *BG* (December 9, 1900) 18.
171 *BG* (February 17, 1901) 19.
172 *BG* (December 31, 1900) 9; *NYT* (May 18, 1900) 7.
173 Program of the Boston Symphony Orchestra (December 28–9, 1900), 340, Miami University, Kelley Collection; King, *Edgar Stillman Kelley*, 69.
174 *BG* (March 24, 1901) 18.
175 *NYT* (March 9, 1901) 7; *CE* (March 11, 1901) 6.
176 *BG* (March 24, 1901) 18; *Chicago Tribune* (June 1, 1901) 16; <http://www.loc.gov/pictures/collection/var/item/var1993000020/PP>
177 *CE* (April 22, 1901) 6; Columbia Theatre Program, April 23, 1901, Brooklyn Public Library [#PP-0215].
178 *CT* (January 11, 1901) 1; cf. *LAT* (September 8, 1901) C2.
179 *CT* (June 23, 1901) 50.
180 *BE* (April 23, 1901) 6.
181 *BE* (May 19, 1901) 4, reports that Emmett Corrigan [Simonides] was arrested after the two performances on May 18.
182 *DFP* (August 22, 1901) 4.
183 *Werner's Magazine* 26 (October, 1900) 161–6.
184 *CE* (July 7, 1901) B3.
185 *TBS* (February 23, 1902) 6.
186 The Australian schedule was later changed, opening first (and only) in Sydney.
187 *BG* (August 4, 1901) 18
188 *DFP* (September 16, 1901) 4; *WP* (September 15, 1901) 26.
189 *WP* (October 27, 1901) 30.
190 *[New Orleans] Times-Picayune* (June 1, 1902) 21.
191 *CE* (July 14, 1901) B3; *New Orleans Item* (July 28, 1902) 3.
192 *The Washington Times* (December 18, 1904) 8.
193 *CT* (August 27, 1901) 5.
194 *StLPD* (November 8, 1901) 3.
195 *StLPD* (September 4, 1901) 3.
196 *StLPD* (November 19, 1901) 4.
197 *DFP* (December 1, 1901) 3.
198 *StLPD* (December 1, 1901) A11; (December 9, 1901) 3.
199 *StLPD* (December 27, 1901) A6.
200 *StLPD* (November 27, 1901) 1.
201 *SFC* (November 29, 1903) 34.
202 *StLPD* (December 8, 1901) B1.
203 *Riverside Independent Enterprise* (October 19, 1903) 2.
204 *NYT* (September 5, 1909) X4.
205 *Indiana [PA] Democrat* (January 8, 1902) 1.
206 *TBS* (January 19, 1902) 6.

207 *Lebanon Daily News* (January 6, 1902) 2.
208 *PI* (January 15, 1902) 4.
209 *WP* (February 6, 19021) 8.
210 *WP* (February 2, 1902) 31.
211 Cf. *WP* (February 9, 1902) 14, for the report that Wallace and Ingersoll were on a train to Chicago; cf. *WP* (February 23, 1902) 20.
212 *WP* (February 11, 1902) 3.
213 *WP* (February 23, 1902) 20; (February 16, 1902) 30; (February 23, 1902) 30.
214 *WP* (February 2, 1902) 31.
215 *TBS* (February 9, 1902) 8. Cf. *The San Francisco Call* (January 3, 1909) 25: "a little over one minute"; *St. Nicholas* 28 (November, 1900) 45–9: "not very much more than two minutes"; *The Minneapolis Journal* (December 30, 1902) 6: "They run about a minute and a half."
216 *TBS* (February 21, 1902) 10.
217 *TBS* (February 24, 1902) 7; *AC* (March 2, 1903) 6.
218 *TBS* (March 9, 1902) 6; (March 2, 1902) 6; (March 3, 192) 10; (March 7, 1902) 7.
219 *TBS* (March 12, 1902) 12.
220 *TBS* (March 8, 1902) 1.
221 *BG* (March 15, 1902) 12. Ticket prices cost $1.50, $1.00, and 50¢.
222 *BG* (March 23, 1902) 33.
223 *BH* (March 30, 1902) 35.
224 *BG* (March 30, 1902) 33.
225 *The Cast* (April 9, 1900) 4.
226 *BH* (April 6, 1902) 7; *Dallas Morning News* (April 6, 1902) 3.
227 *BG* (March 9, 1902) 29; cf. *TBS* (January 19, 1902) 10.
228 *The Sydney Morning Herald* (August 2, 1901) 8. Cf. *The [Adelaide] Register* (June 22, 1901) 6.
229 *The [Adelaide] Register* (August 21, 1901) 7; *The [Adelaide] Advertiser* (January 25, 1902) 5.
230 *The [Adelaide] Advertiser* (January 15, 1902) 5.
231 *The [Adelaide] Advertiser* (January 15, 1902) 5; *The Sydney Morning Herald* (January 18, 1902) 10.
232 *DFP* (December 2, 1901) 4.
233 *The Sydney Morning Herald* (January 25, 1902) 4; *The [Perth] Daily News* (February 1, 1902) 3.
234 *Queensland Figaro* (February 27, 1902) 7.
235 *The Sydney Morning Herald* (January 18, 1902) 7.
236 *Australian Town and Country* (February 1, 1902) 57.
237 *The [Adelaide] Advertiser* (January 25, 1902) 5.
238 *The [Launceston] Examiner* (June 29, 1901) 3.
239 *The Brisbane Courier* (August 10, 1901) 9.
240 *The Sydney Morning Herald* (January 27, 1902) 2.
241 *The Sydney Morning Herald* (February 10, 1902) 3.
242 Ibid., 3.
243 Ibid., 3.
244 *The [Perth] Daily News* (February 22, 1902) 3.

245 *The [Perth] Daily News* (March 8, 1902) 3.
246 *Clarence and Richmond Examiner* (February 25, 1902) 4.
247 *The West Australian* (February 12, 1902) 9.
248 *Australian Town and Country* (January 25, 1902) 41.
249 *The Sydney Morning Herald* (March 1, 1902) 7.
250 *The Sydney Morning Herald* (March 4, 1902) 2.
251 *The West Australian* (February 12, 1902) 9.
252 *The Sydney Morning Herald* (February 11, 1902) 6.
253 *The Cumberland Argus and Fruitgrowers Advocate* (February 1, 1902) 9.
254 *The [Perth] Daily News* (October 26, 1901) 3.
255 *The Cumberland Argus and Fruitgrowers Advocate* (February 1, 1902) 9.
256 *The Cumberland Argus and Fruitgrowers Advocate* (February 8, 1902) 2; (February 1, 1902) 9.
257 E.g. *The West Australian* (February 11, 1902) 1.
258 *Launceston Examiner* (February 17, 1902) 6.
259 *The Sydney Morning Herald* (March 1, 1902) 7; *The Brisbane Courier* (March 1, 1902) 9.
260 *The Brisbane Courier* (March 8, 1902) 9; *The Sydney Morning Herald* (February 25, 1902) 9.
261 *The Sydney Morning Herald* (March 24, 1902) 7; *Australian Town and Country* (March 29, 1902) 45.
262 *The [Adelaide] Advertiser* (March 25, 1902) 4.
263 *The Sydney Morning Herald* (March 26, 1902) 7; and (April 5, 1902) 7.
264 *Clarence and Richmond Examiner* (March 29, 1902) 4.
265 *The Sydney Morning Herald* (April 5, 1902) 12.
266 *The Cumberland Argus and Fruitgrowers Advocate* (March 29, 1902) 4.
267 *The Brisbane Courier* (May 31, 1902) 9.
268 *BG* (April 22, 1900) 18.
269 *NYT* (March 9, 1901) 7; *CE* (March 11, 1901) 6.
270 Mackintosh, *Architecture, Actor and Audience*, 331.
271 *CT* (July 28, 1901) 36; *BH* (March 23, 1902) 35.
272 *NYT* (January 14, 1902) 6.
273 *The Minneapolis Journal* (December 30, 1902) 6; *BH* (March 9, 1902) 17. Cf. *[San Diego] Evening Tribune* (September 1, 1902) 3.
274 *DFP* (December 2, 1901) 4.
275 *BH* (March 24, 1902) 8.
276 *BG* (August 4, 1901) 1; *Jackson [MI] Citizen Patriot* (February 15, 1902) 9; *NYT* (April 11, 1902) 8.
277 *NYT* (April 11, 1902) 6.
278 *Boston Journal* (March 23, 1902) 4.
279 *Black & White* (March 29, 1902) 445. A full-page Langfier photograph of Esther [Nore Kerin] and Simonides [J. E. Dodson] appeared in the May 3, 1902 issue.
280 *BH* (March 30, 1902) 10. *Boston Journal* (March 23, 1902) 4.
281 *BH* (April 13, 1902) 42.
282 *The [London] Times* (April 4, 1902) 4.
283 *The Manchester Guardian* (April 6, 1902) 6.

284 *The Observer* (April 6, 1902) 6.
285 *TBS* (April 13, 1902) 5.
286 Ibid., 5; *NYTr* (November 14, 1920) E12; Grau, *The Business Man in the Amusement World*, 169.
287 *TBS* (April 4, 1902) 9.
288 *Omaha World Herald* (April 6, 1902) 7; *CPD* (April 6, 1902) 4; *Duluth News-Tribune* (April 6, 1902) 6.
289 *TBS* (April 13, 1902) 5; *BH* (April 13, 1902) 8.
290 *Sagninaw [MI] News* (May 17, 1902) 4.
291 Subsequently circulated reports [e.g. *The [Ogden] Evening Standard* (December 12, 1912) 5] that the 1902 London production closed because of the death of Queen Victoria on January 21, 1901, are inaccurate, as is the report [*NYT* (September 1, 1911) 7], that claimed that the "illness of King Edward interfered with the business of the theatres ... at Drury Lane in 1901"; cf. *The Times* (June 25, 1902) 9.
292 *TBS* (April 15, 1902) 1; *Cleveland Leader* (April 15, 1902) 5. *[San Diego] Evening Tribune* (July 17, 1902) 5, reported that the box was Brook's idea.
293 *BH* (April 27, 1902) 42.
294 *Munsey's Magazine* 29 (April, 1903) 364–8, esp. 367; *The Saturday Review* 93 (April 19, 1902) 490.
295 *TBS* (May 6, 1902) 8.
296 *NYTr* (May 6, 1902) 5.
297 *BG* (May 11, 1902) 5.
298 *TBS* (May 14, 1902) 9; *CPD* (April 11, 1920) 85.
299 *The [London] Times* (May 22, 1902) 4; (June 3, 1902) 9; (June 9, 1902) 11.
300 *Sagninaw [MI] News* (May 17, 1902) 4; *Salt Lake Herald* (October 23, 1903) 8.
301 *[New Orleans] Time-Picayune* (April 27, 1902) 22.
302 *Sagninaw [MI] News* (May 17, 1902) 4.
303 *TBS* (May 18, 1902) 8.
304 *New Orleans Item* (July 13, 1902) 22.
305 *Riverside Independent Enterprise* (August 10, 1902) 7.
306 *PI* (September 3, 1902) 8.
307 *Fort Wayne Journal Gazette* (April 20, 1902) 2.
308 *Salt Lake Herald* (June 29, 1902) 10.
309 *TBS* (May 26, 1902) 2.
310 *L'Art Dramatique et Musical au XXe Siècle* 2 (1903) 240.
311 *[Lexington] Morning Herald* (February 17, 1904) 4.
312 *Grand Rapids Press* (August 26, 1903) 2; *Omaha World Herald* (September 10, 1903) 3.
313 *AC* (March 4, 1903) 12; *AC* (March 2, 1903) 6.
314 *The Lehi [Utah] Banner* (October 15, 1903) 2.
315 *Akron Daily Democrat* (October 14, 1902) 6.
316 *CE* (October 3, 1902) 7, points out that the players and crew were paid for these extra performances.
317 *CE* (September 21, 1902) A1.
318 *The Newtown Register* (October 22, 1903) 8.

319 *AC* (February 21, 1903) 9.
320 *[Harrisburg] Patriot* (July 12, 1902) 8.
321 Cf. *AC* (March 2, 1903) 6; *StLPD* (November 17, 1901) A2.
322 *CE* (October 3, 1902) 7.
323 *CE* (June 8, 1902) B6.
324 *CE* (August 17, 1902) B6.
325 *CE* (August 19, 1902) 3.
326 *CE* (August 24, 1902) A1.
327 *CE* (August 31, 1902) 3.
328 *CE* (September 18, 1902) 7.
329 *CE* (September 21, 1902) A1.
330 *CE* (September 24, 1902) 3.
331 *CE* (September 28, 1902) A1.
332 *CE* (September 30, 1902) 12.
333 *Cincinnati Post* (September 30, 1902) 6.
334 *CE* (October 1, 1902) 5.
335 *CE* (September 30, 1902) 3 and 7.
336 *Cincinnati Post* (September 30, 1902) 6.
337 *CE* (October 3, 1902) 7.
338 *CE* (October 6, 1902) 5.
339 *CPD* (October 13, 1902) 5.
340 *Logansport Reporter* (November 13, 1902) 3; *Connersville Evening News* (November 17, 1902) 1; *AC* (January 25, 1903) 5.
341 *AC* (January 25, 1903) 5.
342 *St. Paul Globe* (November 30, 1902) 13; *The Minneapolis Journal* (January 5, 1903) 11.
343 *Malvern [IA] Leader* (January 1, 1903) 1; *Omaha World Herald* (January 1, 1903) 5.
344 *AC* (January 25, 1903) 5; *StLPD* (January 22, 1903) 6; (February 1, 1903) A19B.
345 *[Harrisburg] Patriot* (July 12, 1902) 9.
346 *AC* (February 22, 1903) B4.
347 *AC* (March 2, 1903) 6.
348 *AC* (February 27, 1903) 9.
349 *Macon Telegraph* (December 29, 1907) 5.
350 *CE* (November 21, 1909) B7.
351 *AC* (March 8, 1903) B9.
352 *Seattle Daily Times* (February 4, 1913) 9.
353 *Indianapolis Star* (June 17, 1922) 10.
354 *NYT* (January 7, 1923) SM4.
355 Blotner and Gwynn, *Faulkner in the University*, 285; Humphreys, *Faulkner on Stage*, 2–12.
356 Hutchison, *The Modernist Impulse*, 60.
357 *Salt Lake Telegram* (February 26, 1904) 2.
358 *Denver Post* (September 27, 1903) 19; *Salt Lake Telegram* (October 3, 1903) 5; *Anaconda [MT] Standard* (November 27, 1903) 7.
359 *Seattle Daily Times* (November 19, 1903) 33; *SFC* (November 29, 1903) 34; *[Portland] Oregonian* (December 1, 1903) 9; (December 6 1903) 12.

360 [Lexington] Morning Herald (February 25, 1904) 8; [Lexington] Morning Herald (February 17, 1904) 4; Detroit Free Press (March 4, 1904) 4; Decatur Daily Review (August 16, 1903) 2; PI (July 12, 1903) 11; Grand Rapids Press (August 26, 1903) 2; [Sault Ste. Marie, MI] Evening News (December 3, 1903) 2.
361 Riverside Independent Enterprise (April 15, 1904) 4.
362 Elkhart [IN] Daily Review (August 22, 1903) 2.
363 StLPD (October 30, 1904) 5; PI (July 12, 1903) 11.
364 Muskegon Chronicle (September 9, 1903) 8.
365 [Portland] Oregonian (December 6, 1903) 12; cf. CPD (May 3, 1903) 35; BH (May 3, 1903) 3; The San Francisco Call (May 10, 1903) 48.
366 [Portland] Oregonian (December 6, 1903) 12.
367 Anaconda [MT] Standard (November 27, 1903) 7.
368 NYT (January 7, 1923) SM4.
369 [Sault Ste. Marie, MI] Evening News (December 3, 1903) 2; Duluth News-Tribune (December 15, 1903) 4.
370 The Billboard 19 (October 12, 1907) 45.
371 Saginaw News (November 26, 1906) 8.
372 The San Francisco Call (May 10, 1903) 48; PI (May 31, 1903) 16.
373 BH (June 7, 1903) 38; PI (July 12, 1903) 11.
374 NYT (September 22, 1903) 6.
375 Jackson [MI] Citizen Patriot (December 30, 1903) 3.
376 New Orleans Item (September 27, 1903) 12.
377 NYT (September 14, 1903) 12; NYTr (December 12, 1903) 16.
378 Omaha World Herald (August 23, 1903) 14. Cf. Decatur Daily Review (August 16, 1903) 2; Daily Illinois State Register (August 15, 1903) 7.
379 StLPD (October 2, 1904) 7B; (November 20, 1904) 3B.
380 E.g. [Perth] Sunday Times (February 23, 1913) 16; cf. NYT (January 4, 1912) 14; TBS (February 18, 1912) 8.
381 Thorold, Our Players' Gallery, n.p.
382 The West Australian (February 12, 1902) 9.
383 Letter from Harper to Susan Wallace (March 13, 1907), BL.
384 Response from Susan Wallace to Harper (March 20, 1907), BL.
385 Trenton Evening Times (March 24, 1907) 15.
386 Cf. Loney, "The Heyday of the Dramatized Novel," 198.
387 The Manuscripts Department of at Lilly Library at Indiana University preserves a copy of Nat Ward Fitz-Gerald's "Ben-Hur: A Poem Written on the Play by Hon. Nat Ward Fitz-Gerald, Charlestown, West Virginia." The poem consists of eight stanzas of an exclusively Christian nature.
388 HW 43 (November 18, 1899) 1167–8; 45 (April 6, 1901) 352; Harper's Monthly Magazine 102 (May, 1901) 18.
389 HW 46 (May 24, 1902) 673; HW 46 (August 30, 1902) 1211.
390 HW 56 (January 13, 1912) 20.
391 The NYTr (November 29, 1899) 8.
392 Program from December 18, 1899, NYPL.
393 Program from January 15, 1900, NYPL.
394 CE (August 17, 1902) 5.

395 *The [Ogden] Evening Standard* (December 12, 1912) 5.
396 Program from the Hinton Theatre, Muskogee, Oklahoma, February 9, [1911], in the possession of the author.
397 Program from the Olympic Theatre, St. Louis, Missouri, October 17, 1904, in the possession of the author.
398 *The Duluth Evening Herald* (March 8, 1909) 3.
399 Ibid., 8.
400 *NYT* (October 28, 1900) 5.
401 *PI* (November 25, 1900) 15.
402 *NYT* (October 22, 1901) 1.
403 *Chicago Daily Tribune* (October 4, 1901) 2.
404 *NYT* (October 23, 1901) 9.
405 *San Francisco Call* (December 20, 1903) 44.
406 Allen, *Horrible Prettiness*, 205–14.
407 *Springfield Daily News* (January 26, 1918) 7.
408 *Albuquerque Journal* (February 7, 1917) 4.
409 *The San Bernadino County Sun* (May 5, 1914) 5.
410 *[Portland] Oregonian* (April 13, 1915) 16; *BH* (June 13, 1915) 32.
411 Letters from Wallace to Joseph Brooks (April 10, 1903; February 26, 1904; March 5, 1904), IHS.
412 *Springfield [MA] Republican* (February 4, 1906) 19.
413 *El Paso Herald* (November 24, 1915) 2 and 4.
414 *The Fort Wayne News* (January 31, 1907) 6.
415 *[Portland] Oregonian* (January 28, 1913) 10.
416 *StLPD* (October 4, 1908) 9.
417 *Indianapolis Star* (December 3, 1911) A3.
418 *AC* (November 3, 1917) 7. An eyewitness [*New Mexico Historical Review* 36 (January 1, 1961) 66] saw only a pair of two horse-chariots without the Hagan backdrop in 1908/9 performance at Milwaukee's Davidson Theatre.
419 *BG* (January 4, 1915) 12.
420 *NYT* (December 17, 1911) X1.
421 *Seattle Daily Times* (February 4, 1913) 9.
422 *TBS* (April 9, 1916) SO10.
423 *NYT* (November 7, 1916) 7.
424 *TBS* (November 7, 1916) 5.
425 *BH* (January 10, 1915) 33; cf. *NYT* (January 7, 1923) SM4.
426 *Catalogue of Copyright Entries, Part 1, Group 2* (Washington: Government Printing Office, 1916) #26481. Cf. *The Billboard* (October 29, 1921) 9.
427 *BG* (January 5, 1915) 3.
428 *Indianapolis Star* (March 7, 1920) A2.
429 *Trenton Evening Times* (January 15, 1917) 7; (January 22, 1917) 7. Cf. *[Canton OH] Repository* (September 19, 1933) 5; Lindvall, *Sanctuary Cinema*, 107.
430 *BG* (January 4, 1915) 12; Harlowe R. Hoyt, *CPD* (April 11, 1920) 85.
431 Mckee 185; *SFC* (March 28, 1915) A3; (April 8, 1915) 5.
432 *[Perth] Sunday Times* (February 23, 193) 16.
433 Davis, "The Most Successful Play Ever Produced," 45; *CPD* (April 11, 1920) 85; *WP* (October 3, 1926) SM5; Slater, "The Vision and the Struggle," 64. An

extensive search in Delpher, the online newspaper database of the National Library of the Netherlands failed to confirm these reports.

434 *TBS* (February 18, 1912) 8; *NYT* (September 1, 1911) 7; *The Manchester Guardian* (February 4, 1913) 6; *NYT* (January 4, 1912) 14.
435 *Daily Alaska Dispatch* (December 12, 1915) 8.
436 *The New York Clipper* (January 9, 1918) 5; *CPD* (April 8, 1920) 16.
437 *Trenton Evening Times* (March 24, 1907) 15.
438 *HW* 51 (April 6, 1907) 490; cf. (February 23, 1907) 277.
439 *Montgomery [AL] Advertiser* (August 30, 1908) 20.
440 *BG* (January 4, 1915) 12. *The New York Clipper* (January 28, 1920) 4, reports the number as "more than 10,000,000 people."
441 *The New York Clipper* (February 4, 1918) 1; (December 17, 1919) 8.
442 *CPD* (April 11, 1920) 85.
443 *NYT* (January 7, 1923) SM4.
444 *NYT* (April 8, 1921) 23; *NYTr* (April 8, 1921) 10; *LAT* (October 4, 1924) C19.
445 Cf. King, *Edgar Stillman Kelley*, 68, n. 4.
446 *NYT* (January 7, 1923) SM4.
447 *NYT* (March 11, 1906) 9.
448 *BG* (May 11, 1915) 62; *New York Times* (December 3, 1914) 13.
449 *NYT* (September 27, 1914) 15.
450 *NYTr* (November 28, 1916) 3.
451 *The Washington Times* (April 21, 1917) 8.
452 *The New York Clipper* (August 6, 1919) 1.
453 *NYT* (October 17, 1920) X1; (April 8, 1921) 23; *Indianapolis Star* (November 2, 1921) 10.
454 *SFC* (July 16, 1922) D4; *NYT* (January 7, 1923) SM4.
455 <http://www.benhurconstruction.com/AboutUs/BenHurConstruction CentennialVideo/ATimetoRemember/tabid/205/Default.aspx>. The present owner recalls that the performance was at the Old American Theater, but it was not built until 1917.
456 Faucett, *George Whitefield Chadwick*, 256.
457 *The Washington Herald* (August 24, 1913) 8.
458 *Boston Journal* (September 2, 1909) 10; *El Paso Herald* (November 24, 1915) 2.
459 *[Harrisburg PA] Patriot* (September 17, 1907) 2.

10 *"Ben-Hur Flour Has The Go To Make The Dough": Early Ben-Hur Commerce*

INTRODUCTION

This chapter documents for the first time and demonstrates thoroughly and conclusively the unprecedented and unparalleled impact *Ben-Hur: A Tale of the Christ* and its major artistic by-products made on the world of commerce beginning from the mid-1880s. With multiple and often significant entries in such a wide range of categories as manufacturing, construction, mining, petroleum products, shipping, railroads, automobiles, bicycles, hardware, insurance and fraternal organizations, tobacco, groceries, personal care products, shoes and clothing, as well as toys, games, and leisure and amusement activities, the *Ben-Hur* phenomenon was embraced by an extraordinarily broad spectrum of industrial, corporate, and individual businesses from multi-million dollar regional and national operations to local establishments, and it did so for many decades and continues today, albeit much reduced in scope. Its huge compass of commercial activity makes the *Ben-Hur* phenomenon unique. The name of a book or a fictional character has never been used by so many companies, entrepreneurs, businessmen, or retailers.

In 1888, when Coca-Cola was in its infancy, still lacking its famous trademark and limited to Atlanta, Ben-Hur had already provided its exotic but memorable hyphenated bisyllabic name to a variety of successful business applications, including a large freighter working along the Ohio River Valley, Ben-Hur Flour in Colorado, fraternal organization chapters in Kansas and Illinois, and Detroit's Ben-Hur Cigars. Some of these ran considerably large operations: by 1892, for instance, Moebs in Detroit had already manufactured and sold well over thirty-five million Ben-Hur Cigars. Three years later The Tribe of Ben-Hur had already subscribed 8801 members in fifteen states. And these include only business concerns that had developed within just the first few years after the novel became popular. The next four decades would continue and expand manifold upon this energetic beginning. (Subsequent chapters will continue the study from the mid-1920s to the present.)

This aspect of the *Ben-Hur* tradition, as much as any discussed in this book, distinguishes it from its popular contemporaries. Far exceeding companies or products associated with such popular properties as Alice in Wonderland, Peter Pan, the Wizard of Oz, and Tarzan, Ben-Hur represented a much wider range of commercial offerings and a more sophisticated imagery. It did not represent juvenile fantasy, wicked demons, imaginary lands or primitive jungles. Thematically speaking the language of contemporary advertising, Ben-Hur represented images of success, victory, and quality embodied in its much admired youthful male champion and, at least for the first three decades of Ben-Hur business, the much admired General Wallace. That Judah Ben-Hur was a Jew made no difference at all. In the public image he was not a Jew but a Christian or even a Roman who won a chariot race. Of equal importance is that the name Ben-Hur came ready-made with visual images of a chariot race, whether they were renditions and variations of Wagner's painting or Checa's print.[1] For advertising purposes they both provided a dynamic image that was easily available and free of copyright. Chariot races were not only a thrilling vestige of yesteryear, popular and positive remembrances of the mighty Roman Empire, they also struck an immediate response among a public that was still using horses for local transport. And then as horse travel was rapidly abandoned during the first two decades of the twentieth century, chariot racing enjoyed a renascence both in imagery and in reality, whether realized on a huge, crowd-thrilling electrical sign in New York, imitated in roller-coaster rides in Coney Island, Baltimore, Kansas City, and Ocean Park, or actually recreated in the New Year's Day races in Pasadena before tens of thousands of cheering spectators.

Lew Wallace did not create in *Ben-Hur: A Tale of the Christ* a modern popular property that lorded legally over a vast empire of commercial tie-ins. As we have seen, that concept was not yet established, nor practicable, nor legally protected. But Wallace, along with Harper, did control the literary and dramatic rights to his novel and negotiated licenses. It was his literary and then dramatic juggernauts that spread across the country, inspiring entrepreneurs and managers to create or brand a slew of Ben-Hur companies and products, many of which made large fortunes and in turn helped to spread and reiterate the name Ben-Hur across the country for many decades. As it entered the world of commerce in so many ways and at so many different times, whether advertised in print copy or images or on radio or television, the name Ben-Hur would become a powerful icon that reached tens of millions of customers from a wide variety of demographic groups and generated hundreds of millions of dollars. In the opening paragraphs of this book we saw this process develop in the founding of the Ben Hur Construction Company, and in this chapter we will see it repeated time and time again.

The late nineteenth century produced a historic expansion in most branches of American commerce.[2] Leaving behind the eras of the Civil War and Reconstruction and transforming itself with newly patented inventions, the nation coalesced through rapid forms of communication and transportation and the creation of incorporated business structures. In the epicenter of this period that transformed the United States into an industrial giant and a mecca of consumerism, Ben-Hur became a veritable brand name that would represent numerous enterprises. In terms of sales and distribution, Lew Wallace's novel and its artistic progeny benefitted directly from the expansion of the entrepreneurial-minded segment of the population, with its freshly stimulated desire to start up new business enterprises, and the consumer class, with its access to greater amounts of disposable income and the consequential desire to purchase new inventions and quality products and indulge in new forms of leisure activities.[3]

This new economic environment contributed to not only the nationwide success of such diverse popular artistic products as Wallace's novel, Paull's "Chariot Race or Ben-Hur March," and the Klaw & Erlanger *Ben-Hur* but also a variety of consumer products not designed for the world of popular art. Technical innovation would become one of the signatures of the years bracketing the turn of the century, and from phonographs and player pianos to bicycles and automobiles, consumer-oriented inventions were embraced by the American public in rapid succession, and millions of people throughout this period would be introduced to the spectrum of Ben-Hur brands and products.[4] Similarly, this was the period in which advertising fully matured. Companies now regularly hired or contracted with professional designers to develop effective programs, and while the companies and their agents implemented aggressive newspaper and magazine campaigns, employing elaborate and colorful graphics and offering enticing sales ploys, Ben-Hur brands and products could promise a high degree of quality and superiority supported by colorful images of a racing chariot or a victorious charioteer, thereby attracting and reassuring potential consumers with positive messages. Millions of consumers could instantly recognize and associate with the positive energy, moral strength, and triumphant superiority of the Ben-Hur concept as well as two additional concepts that distinguished Ben-Hur – speed and durability, which were employed in the various modes of transportation associated with the Ben-Hur name.

FRATERNAL SOCIETIES

Shrines

On September 2, 1888, thirteen Freemasons residing in the Argentine area southwest of Kansas City, Kansas, held an organizational meeting that focused on the allure of Ben-Hur's heroism and philanthropy. On March 2, 1889, they received a letter of dispensation from the Grand

Lodge of Kansas, which issued the charter for Ben Hur Lodge No. 322 A.F. & A.M. in mid-February, 1890, identifying Wallace's hero as "a soul who exemplified all that is true of brotherly love, relief and truth."[5] In the following year they officially changed the name of their associated women's Chapter of the Order of the Eastern Star from the more generic Old Testament name Leah to Tirzah, the name of Judah's sister. As more than a century has passed, Ben Hur Lodge No. 322 built its Temple at the corner of 30th Street and Connor in 1923, organized fundraisers nicknamed "the Chariots" to raise the money to install air conditioning in the Lodge Hall in 1984 and for the Down Syndrome Guild of Great Kansas City in 2011, and recently held its 125th celebration.[6] Today they operate an active Facebook page.

The year after the Argentine charter, the Ben Hur Temple of the Nobles of the Mystic Shrine in Austin, Texas, was issued a dispensation to organize on June 2 and then instituted on October 8, 1891.[7] To celebrate its 100th anniversary, the Ben Hur Shrine Temple issued a commemorative booklet in which Robert Emrie, Potentate, gave a current status report of 2173 members participating in twenty or more parades annually, sponsoring the annual circus, and funding the Houston Orthopaedic Unit and the Galveston Burn Institute.[8] Still very active, on January, 2015, the Ben Hur Shrine of Austin hosted its sixty-seventh annual Shrine Circus, and their monthly newsletter, *The Chariot*, is available online.[9] The initial membership of the Austin Shrine, consisting of fifty Knights Templars and Masons of the thirty-second degree, celebrated their inaugural by dressing in costume and parading through the Austin streets. They initiated thirty more members in March, 1892, and another fifty the following October.[10] The *Dallas Morning News* made clear that these were the "leading men of the state in all the business avocations."[11] As Freemasons, part of their initiation celebration included a visit to admire the masonry of the dam on Lake McDonald, the magnitude of the project, and its "prospective benefits to the city." Just a few years later the lake and dam would be the regular home of a Ben-Hur paddle-wheeler and its beloved musical excursions. The Austin Ben-Hur Temple, Mystic Shrine, expanded aggressively for a number of years. In late August, 1906, they even sent a degree team to Mexico City to initiate Mexican President Porfirio Diaz into their order.[12]

At least seven other chapters or lodges having associations with the Ben-Hur name have been organized under the umbrella of fraternal organizations. The Ben Hur Lodge No. 818 of Arlington Heights in the Chicago area, was chartered on October 5, 1892.[13] This Masonic lodge is still active as well, meeting the first and third Thursday evening every month.[14] June 28, 1888, was a "great day in Pythian circles" in Evansville, Indiana, being the institution of the new Knights of Pythias Lodge "Ben Hur," No. 197.[15] The same year, or perhaps the following year, the Ben Hur Lodge 870 of the Independent Order of Odd Fellows was already operating in Vandalia, Illinois.[16] As recently as 2005 Ben Hur Lodge #870 purchased new property and runs a pancake breakfast the first Sunday of each month.[17] In 1901 The Foresters of America initiated a Ben Hur Circle in Boston that was still active through World War II.[18] In 1894 the Dramatic Order Knights of Khorassan, a branch of the Knights of Pythias, was established in Tulsa, Oklahoma. The Knights of Pythias base their ideals of friendship and loyalty on a different ancient story, but on Facebook they continue raising money through Ben Hur Temple No. 131.[19] J. F. Diffenbacher's 1895 Pittsburgh *Directory* includes the Ben Hur Commandery within the Ancient and Illustrious Order of Knights of Malta, reporting that the Commandery met at Malta Hall on South Sheridan the second and fourth Friday of every month.[20] Similarly, a list of York Rite Bodies of Oklahoma lists the Ben Hur Commandery No. 14 in Ponca, Oklahoma.[21]

The oriental mystique that helped make *Ben-Hur: A Tale of the Christ* such a success in the mid-1880s was integral to the rapid growth of the Shrine movement during the same period. Following the custom established in the 1870s by Walter Fleming and William [Billy] Johnson, the founders of what was more formally labeled the Ancient Arabic Order of the Nobles of the Mystic Shrine,[22] their costumes would continue to feature Arabic and ancient Egyptian themes, including the red fez decorated with the traditional scimitar, crescent, and star.[23] But in the next decade some of the annual awards given by the Austin Shrine also included a racing *quadriga*. These were brass medals, consisting of two parts attached by a metal link. The upper piece features one or two scimitars with the location and date of the meeting (e.g. Atlantic City, 1904; St. Paul, 1908). The lower portion contains a 1 1/2 in. disk depicting in relief a racing chariot underneath the words "Ben Hur Temple."[24]

Obituaries and biographies from the period illustrate how a single prominent person often belonged to more than one such organization. Just to cite one example, Dr. Andrew Jackson Colburn of Pennsylvania ran several businesses and served as a postmaster before becoming a physician and establishing membership in the Independent Order of Odd Fellows, Knights of Malta, Fraternal Order of Eagles, Fraternal Order of Owls, the Royal Arcanum, Knights of the Maccabees, Knights of the Mystic Senate, and Children of Ben Hur.[25] Such a proliferation of fraternal orders created a concordant proliferation of names. In addition to "Children of Ben Hur," collected biographies and extant pieces of ephemera make reference to the "Society of Ben Hur" as well as the "Ben-Hur Union."[26]

The Tribe of Ben-Hur
The economic expansion and infusion of immigrants during the latter third of the nineteenth century helped to instigate the "coming of age" of the American insurance industry.[27] Following the model of John

Upchurch's Ancient Order of United Workmen founded in 1868, many fraternal societies organized to spread risk and accumulate life insurance protection for their members. Of the approximately 600 fraternal beneficiary societies active in the United States around the turn of the century, contemporary sources distinguish between those that provided remedial relief and those that were fundamentally different in that they bound themselves with their members by contract, the latter to pay a set fee, the former to pay the beneficiary a predetermined sum in the event of such contingencies as sickness, disability, or death.[28] One of the leading entrepreneurs in the fledgling insurance industry in the Midwest was David W. Gerard.[29] Seventeen years younger than Lew Wallace, Gerard grew up just after the last days of the frontier in Miami County, Ohio, where his grandfather had been killed by Indians. Gerard married into the Krug family of Montgomery County, and shortly after relocating to Crawfordsville, he and his partner Frank L. Snyder formed the successful and long-lasting Indiana [and Ohio] Live Stock Insurance Company. Eventually he would become the director of the Elston family bank. Then in 1893 he turned his attention to establishing a national fraternal insurance society based in Crawfordsville. Collaborating primarily with Snyder and Crawfordsville's former mayor, Samuel Voris, Gerard led an embassy to his friend, neighbor, and occasional business associate Lew Wallace, whose novel had inspired him with its vivid descriptions of "the uplift of the Lowly Nazarene."[30] The meeting is said to have taken place underneath the famous beech tree where Wallace penned much of the novel before departing for Santa Fe.[31] The timing was propitious. This was the year Harper published *The Prince of India*, for which Wallace received a huge royalty, and he was turning his mind towards traditional business investments. Most evident from this period, remaining to this day, is the Blacherne in Indianapolis, the seven-story apartment building Wallace began constructing in 1893.[32]

Wallace supported the fraternal movement. Just three weeks after the incorporation of the Supreme Tribe of Ben-Hur in Crawfordsville, he participated in an "Authors' Reading" Benefit for the Booksellers' and Stationers' Provident Association of the United States in New York.[33] In fact, he was the first author to read that evening, raising nearly $1000 for a contingency fund to help take care of members during illness.[34] Later the New York Life Insurance Company boasted that Wallace was one of their first celebrity agents.[35] More directly, he approved the idea of establishing a fraternal insurance society named after the protagonist of his novel, which would provide a fundamental distinction between the society and its many competitors. When Gerard first proposed the name "Knights of Ben-Hur" to Wallace, the author reportedly placed his hand on Gerard's shoulder and said:

> Well, my dear boy, there were no knights in those days. Tribes there were, however, so why wouldn't it be well to call it the "Tribe of Ben-Hur"?[36]

Wallace was presumably referring not to the equestrian order of ancient Roman society, an entire class of "knights" that produced Cicero and the emperor Augustus, but the "lost tribes of Israel," a concept that appealed to cultural and even national political interests at the time.[37] The unique term "tribe" would also help distinguish the new order from the names of such other contemporary fraternal organizations as the Knights of Pythias, the Knights of Honor, the Knights of the Maccabees, the Knights of Malta, and the Catholic Knights of America.

The new Ben-Hur organization benefitted from instant name recognition, for which Harper also granted permission, and its association with Lew Wallace, although the author never engaged in the operations of the business itself or received a royalty or fee. A widely syndicated announcement highlighted these advantages for potential recruits:

> The society was christened by Gen. Lew Wallace, the author of the famous book, "Ben Hur," and was organized with the full consent and permission of Harper Brothers, the publishers of Gen. Wallace's works, who have the copyright on the book and its title. The ritualistic features are founded upon the principles laid down in the beautiful story of the "Tale of the Christ."[38]

In addition, by evoking the name "Ben-Hur," the new society was able to evoke a thoroughly embedded theme of Christian reverence and morality.[39] Gerard expressed this later in a historical context, asserting that Ben-Hur was a witness to the earthly existence of Jesus:

> You should study the Holy Bible and the book "Ben-Hur" that you may catch the spirit and emulate the example of the grand men and women who, from the manger to the cross, knew the World's Redeemer.[40]

A lead article in *The Chariot*, the newsletter of the organization managed for years by Gerard himself, described the Tribe of Ben-Hur in a religious context, as if the novel were "a book of sermons":

> At Covington, Kentucky, recently where 250 members of the Tribe of Ben-Hur sat down together at a banquet, the honored Chief of one of the Courts said, "About all the religion I have is Ben-Hur. . . . It has helped me to understand that General Wallace was a preacher, that Ben-Hur is a book of sermons, and that the Leadership of the Divine Spirit, the Influence and Blessedness of Prayer, the Immortality of the Soul, the benignant graces of Sympathy and Charity, all of which the book teaches, and more, is the creed of the Tribe of Ben-Hur.

The same blend of religious spirit pervades the lyrics of the first stanza of the "Opening Ode" printed in their *Odes* pamphlet (6), and therefore sung by tens of thousands of members on countless occasions:

> In the "Tribe of Hur" we glory,
> With its principles divine,
> All the light of sacred story
> Sheds upon our work sublime

The articles of incorporation for The Supreme Tribe of Ben-Hur (the order's governing body) were finalized on January 9, 1894. The initial press release specified the fraternal themes inspired by the novel, albeit here tempered with contemporary Midwestern prejudice:

> The objects as set forth in the articles are to unite in bonds of fraternity and benevolence all acceptable white persons of good character and sound bodily health who believe in the Supreme Being, to educate and improve its members morally, socially, and intellectually.[41]

Women were welcome to the organization from the outset. This was one of the organization's most progressive features and frequently advertised for the next few decades. In contrast, the limitation to whites only would not be lifted until 1970.[42]

In reporting the formation of The Tribe of Ben-Hur, a number of contemporary newspaper accounts state that Wallace had taken on the task of developing the new ritual adapted from his novel.[43] In an era in which approximately one in four adult male Americans belonged to a fraternal organization, this ritual would have the unique advantage of being written by the local celebrity author of *Ben-Hur: A Tale of the Christ*.[44] In his book on Victorian secret rituals, Mark C. Carnes specifically cites the Supreme Tribe of Ben-Hur for its colorful ritual derived from the novel. In 1897 Gerard, who was elected Supreme Chief in 1896 and repeatedly thereafter, copyrighted an 87-page *Court Degree Ritual* bound in cloth containing full texts of the opening and closing ceremonies as well as initiation ceremonies for the "sons and daughters of Hur."[45] These texts, officially revised in 1914, incorporate lengthy dialogues with roles for Ben-Hur, his mother, Arrius, and Balthasar. The relationship between the New Testament and the novel is carefully nuanced. The former is quoted, the latter re-enacted.

During the "Obligation" (14–15), the Teacher addresses to the newly sworn inductees:

> Let me impress you with the language of Ben-Hur when pleading for the life of his mother and sister: "God is just, he will give you mercy for mercy."
>
> [All are seated.]
>
> ... Our order is founded upon a "Tale of the Christ," and the teachings of the Nazarene are its chief corner stone. As His ministry of three years on earth was expressed by the words, "He went about doing good," so we, as "Sons and Daughters of Hur," purpose by thus binding ourselves together, to aid each other in the great work of Fraternity and Benevolence.
>
> To this end you should study well the Holy Bible, and the book "Ben-Hur," that you may catch the spirit and emulate the example of the grand men and women who, from the manger to the cross, knew the World's Redeemer.
>
> We are informed by the eminent author of the book "Ben-Hur" that he was first induced to write this wonderful book by reading the first two verses of the second chapter of Matthew ...

("He went about doing good" is a quotation from Acts 10: 38.)

The "Ceremony for Ladies" (18) begins with a procession to "where the Mother of Hur and Tirzah stand behind the wall of the cell." (A diagram in the book [62] shows the arrangement of chairs.) The Mother of Ben-Hur reviews her family history:

> Tirzah and myself were imprisoned for eight years in cell number six in the Tower of Antonia; our son, and brother, Ben-Hur condemned to the galley, and our property confiscated by order of our enemy, Messala.

The male candidates interview with Arrius, reviewing the attack on Gratus and the former's familiarity with Judah's father. One by one they are seated on a makeshift galley, given a cape with the number 60, and handed Ben-Hur's oar. The judge pounds out a hortatory beat with his gavel, and at a given signal the Master of Ceremonies pulls a chord that causes the "galley" to collapse. After the candidate is helped to his feet, he pays homage to the Bible and the American Flag before the final steps of induction. As we have seen, some years later the *New York Times* would credit these Tribe of Ben-Hur rituals for playing an initial role in breaking down the barrier between church and drama.[46]

In addition, it was Wallace who selected the Tribe's first medical examiner, his former legal and political associate Jesse Franklin Davidson.[47] That seems to have been the extent to which Wallace involved himself in the operations of the Tribe of Ben-Hur, although in 1904 Wallace wrote a personal appeal urging delegates to the national meeting to vote against the proposal that would move the company headquarters to Ohio.[48] More in accordance with his innate talents, Wallace made a lasting artistic contribution to the Tribe by sketching a Roman galley that would serve, along with a seven-pointed star, as the society's insignia on letterhead, publications, pins, and medals for many decades to come.

The Supreme Tribe of Ben-Hur held its first official session on January 16, 1894, and then Simonides Court No. 1, was formed on March 1 with 422 participants, amidst a grand gala in Crawfordsville.[49] Ira Chase, the outspoken former governor of Indiana known for making a campaign speech in the morning and preaching a sermon later the same day, was elected Supreme Chief, Frank Snyder Supreme Scribe. Gerard, as a member of the Executive Committee, devoted his time and energy to growing the society. He appointed local agents, targeted local markets with newspaper ads, and judiciously employed the name of General Lew Wallace. In May, for instance, he spread five different ads or notices on the back page of the *Sandusky Register*.[50] At the top of the page "BEN HUR!" appears in 32-point bold type and again a few inches below, only slightly smaller. When Simonides Court No. 2 was initiated in Sandusky, Ohio, in early June, the report he placed in the local paper made clear the association with Wallace's novel:

This is a social and beneficial order and is founded on the novel of Gen. Lew Wallace, of Crawfordsville, Ind. It has already several thousand members since its organization January last.[51]

Even when the organization had grown considerably, newspaper announcements could still make this association, whether in Sacramento:

The Tribe of Ben-Hur, a society which has taken for its foundation that wonderful story of "Ben-Hur," written by General Lew Wallace, met Friday night...[52]

or Los Angeles:

The ritualistic work could not be more interesting, as it clearly acts forth the characters in the wonderful book, "Ben Hur."[53]

Growing the business beyond the traditional Midwest region, Gerard concentrated his efforts in Nebraska during the spring of 1895. He spent over six weeks in Omaha, collecting a list of the leading businessmen of the city, especially those already active in secret societies. In print announcements, even before praising the economic benefits of the order over competing fraternal insurance orders and the social benefits of an order which women were eligible to join, he invoked the name of Wallace twice, first as author of the book that inspired the fundamentals of the order, and then as a citizen of Crawfordsville, the home of the order.[54] Within two years the membership had swollen to 8801 members in 306 subordinate lodges and chapters in fifteen states.[55] After it had spread to California, *The San Francisco Call* of April 11, 1897, reported that in its thirty-third month the order had issued 13,600 certificates covering $16 million in insurance, having paid out $49,250.[56] A decade later there were 92,500 members, and in 1910, the year David Gerard died, there were 104,250 members with some 1400 courts in twenty-nine states.[57] The following year a group of dignitaries led by Governor Thomas R. Marshall of Indiana laid the cornerstone for the Tribe's new five-story, air-conditioned, fireproof headquarters, with its distinctive white and emerald terracotta façade, at the corner of Main and Water Streets in Crawfordsville, where it still stands.[58] After the ceremony the dignitaries visited the nearby home of Lew Wallace with its "historic relics."

The more the society membership increased, the more the society could advertise itself. In 1915 the company ran a large ad in the *Indianapolis Star* celebrating twenty-one successful years and boasting of more than 100,000 members in thirty-eight states with over $14 million paid in benefits.[59] In 1917 alone the society added 32,827 members in nearly 100 courts.[60] They had grown large enough to develop a political voice, providing a sufficient number of responses to a 1907 Indiana newspaper poll to convince the legislature to vote for a statue of Wallace to be the state's second representative in Statuary Hall in Washington, DC.[61] Needless to

Figure 10.1 Over 100,000 people joined The Tribe of Ben-Hur, which reproduced Wallace's depiction of a Roman galley for their logo and adapted his novel for their initiation rituals.

say, this is the only statue of a popular author in the nation's Capitol. In 1917 Roy Gerard, David Gerard's son, served as president of the National Fraternal Congress of America and met with President Woodrow Wilson to discuss what assistance fraternal societies could provide to the war effort.[62] In 1921 the order established a college scholarship fund providing $500 for its younger members, a new venture for fraternal societies in the field of philanthropy.[63] The booklet published to celebrate the first year of Ben-Hur Scholarships in 1922 still describes the importance of Wallace and his novel as central to the original conception and continuing themes of the society, labeling his novel a "masterpiece" and his house a "shrine sacred to American literature."[64] At this time the Tribe of Ben-Hur also purchased the home of Lew Wallace, the booklet makes clear, to preserve it and open it to the public. To members of the Tribe of Ben-Hur, the Wallace Home was "a Mecca to be seen at least once during a lifetime."

As Lew Wallace himself had learned, with fame come accusations and legal entanglements. In 1908 the Tribe, facing solvency issues because of their fixed-fee policy, created a second class of membership (Class B) with different rate structures, and then in 1912, under the leadership of Roy Gerard, began converting original members (Class A) to the new structures. This created enough dissatisfaction among the membership to warrant a class-action suit in 1913, led by George Balme of Kentucky. Balme was joined by 523 other members representing fifteen different states and Canada, but none of them lived in Indiana, so the suit was dismissed in 1915. But when Indianans, led by Aurelia J. Cauble, filed an ancillary suit in 1919, this created a jurisdictional problem for the Montgomery County Circuit Court in applying a ruling about exclusively non-Indiana residents bringing suit against a fraternal society organized under Indiana law to exclusively Indiana residents who belonged to the same society. Like the suit that embroiled Kalem's 1907 film adaptation of Wallace's novel, this commercial application of a Ben-Hur product was brought before the United States Supreme Court [Supreme Tribe of Ben-Hur v. Cauble, 255 U.S. 356 (1921)]. The decision established a precedent for jurisdiction in class-action cases, has been cited numerous times, and was as recently as 2006 described as a decision that remains "vital to this day."[65]

The legal dispute interfered little with the growth of the society. In 1931, the company, as of 1930 officially renamed Ben Hur Life Association, issued a card listing the Total Admitted Assets beginning in 1894 with $2,660 and ending with $10,113,255 in 1931. The continued success and growth of the Tribe of Ben-Hur meant that more than 100,000 people across the United States not only belonged to a Ben-Hur organization and had commerce with and dependence on a Ben-Hur business, but that they had even portrayed Judah Ben-Hur himself or a member of the Hur family in a solemn ritual attended by dozens, if not hundreds of fellow Ben-Hur members. The society offered much more. Many of the activities that took place during less formal gatherings and picnics of Ben-Hur chapters were designed to provide community and social engagement through sporting contests, dances, musical performances, and other kinds of recreational activities. Within a ten-day period in August, 1899, for instance, the Astrea Court No. 64 of Cleveland hosted both a formal meeting and a "social meeting" offering a choice of musical selections, recitations, card games, and dancing as well as a picnic offering boat rides, bathing, football, baseball, tennis, croquet, and dancing.[66] Highland Court, No. 3, offered motion pictures and illustrated songs to the citizens of Baltimore on November 9 and 10, 1903.[67] Usually these meetings and activities were advertised in local newspapers, perpetuating the seeming ubiquitousness of the name Ben-Hur ever further in thousands of instances over the years, as did *The Chariot*, which was recognized as one of the leading papers of the fraternal press.[68]

The Tribe membership was growing throughout the period in which millions of people were also paying money to see the various *Ben-Hur* tableaux, stereopticon lectures, and the Klaw & Erlanger production as well as purchasing copies of Paull's piano piece, not to mention the million people who would purchase the Sears edition of the original novel. The concurrence of these various *Ben-Hur* products, by-products, and experiences cross-bred the various Ben-Hur businesses. The reader already know of the fifty members of the Ben-Hur Tribe accompanying Wallace to the 1899 New York premiere of the Klaw & Erlanger production, and then there was "Tribe of Ben Hur Day" at the 1904 St. Louis World's Fair. The former was worthy of several notices in the *New York Times* and inspired *The Chariot*'s lengthy account of the premier of the Klaw & Erlanger *Ben-Hur*.[69] The latter was advertised in *The St. Louis Post-Dispatch* and memorialized on a souvenir pin with a tricolored ribbon attached to a stamped button depicting a color version of Wallace's Roman ship with "T B H" printed on its sail.[70] Such synergies had the potential to impact ever-increasing numbers of society and audience members. It was not coincidence that the February 9, 1911, program for the performance at Muskogee's Hinton Theatre ties in the visiting Klaw & Erlanger production with a local furniture Store ("The 'Ben Hur' Production Makes a Hit with the Theatre Goers / The Low Prices on Furniture and Rugs makes a Hit with the Muskogee Buyers") as well as the subsequent full-page Tribe of Ben-Hur ad boasting of 19,805 new members added during 1910. Surely some audience members noticed this triple infusion of *Ben-Hur*-related by-products and ads.

In California a postcard was used to publicize the 1909 Tribe of Ben-Hur entry in the Pasadena Tournament of Roses. The reverse of the card printed by Benham Indian Trading Company of Los Angeles describes the scene:

> A chariot bedecked in red and white roses against a background of green, drawn by four horses abreast. The idea founded on the ancient Roman fashion was especially appropriate.

Of course most of the floats in the parade were drawn by horses, but none of the others had a male and female charioteer dressed in Roman costume and riding on a chariot, from the rear of which emerged a banner with the company name and seven-pointed star emblem.[71] And as we will see below, this same day in Pasadena would see living "Ben Hurs" perform in actual chariot races.

In an unprecedented concentration of commercial synergies, during its first two years of publication *The Chariot*, circulated to ever-increasing thousands of members and filled with encomia of Lew Wallace, included advertisements for *Ben Hur* stereopticon lectures in individual courts, Ben-Hur Bicycles, and even such souvenirs as leaves from the "Old Beech tree under which the book, 'Ben-Hur,' was mostly written."[72] Single leaves were mounted beneath a photogravure made from a sketch of the tree, and this was "approved by the author and whose certificate and signature accompany the leaf." There were also strong suggestions to read "the matchless book, *Ben-Hur* ... the most popular book in the world – save the Bible ... and the printing presses of Harper Bros. are constantly turning out edition after edition to supply the ever-increasing demand."[73] In the same issue, the official ad of the organization states in very large font, "THE TRIBE OF BEN-HUR – Founded on the Book Ben-Hur, A Tale of the Christ."[74] The third issue includes an endorsement for the readings by Professor Charles Montaville Flowers in that they will benefit the court and membership:

> The book, "Ben-Hur," affords the best possible field for delinators of character, and among them there stands none higher than Prof. Charles Montaville Flowers, teacher of elocution in the Cincinnati College of Music. He will give a reading at the Y.M.C.A. Hall, Crawfordsville, on the evening of November 18. Simonides Court, No. 1, T.B.H., of this city, will attend in a body as well as the Supreme Officers of the Order. The entertainment is highly commended by the press generally, and THE CHARIOT suggests that our various Courts arrange to secure Professor Flowers during the coming winter to give public readings. It will not only delight all who attend, but add to the treasury of any court that may be fortunate enough to secure a reading. For terms and date address Inter-State Lecture Bureau Station H., Cincinnati, O.[75]

Professor Flowers' monologue presentation of *Ben-Hur* will be discussed in the next chapter, as will the other types of stereopticon lectures. The latter were designed both for the membership and to help in recruitment. Created by George W. Bond & Company in Chicago, the set consisted of thirty-five slides, thirty of them portraying scenes from the novel, and five of them advertising the Tribe itself, including text slides as well as images of Wallace and the seven-pointed star emblem.

Also in Crawfordsville there was an issue of photographs and postcards depicting the inner offices of the Tribe of Ben-Hur and the exterior of their headquarters building. These provided some of the few opportunities for other businesses to cash in on the Tribe's name. The headquarters building was used in 1929 for a full-page ad in *The American Architect* advertising steel heating boilers manufactured by Heggie-Simplex of Joliet, Illinois.[76] A large photograph of the building, identified clearly as the "Supreme Tribe of Ben-Hur, Crawfordsville, Ind. Building," dominates the page. A panel of text contains a statement of endorsement from J. C. Snyder, Supreme Chief of the Supreme Tribe of Ben-Hur, averring that by installing two steel Heggie-Simplex oil boilers he has saved over $2000 per year in heating costs. This sort of secondary synergy produced at least one additional outlet. In a 1917 ad in the *Indianapolis Star*, the Dictating Machine Company of Columbus, Ohio, cited the Supreme Tribe of Ben-Hur as one of its major clients.[77]

For decades the Tribe of Ben-Hur issued thousands of certificates, pamphlets, and promotions that included graphics depicting either Wallace's Roman galley or the image of a charioteer and his *quadriga* adapted from Wagner's painting, with the color of the horses changed to brown. Its core business was insurance, but the Tribe of Ben-Hur issued as well a variety of publications in addition to *The Chariot*. Some of these were limited to officers, e.g. the 1906 pamphlet outlining "Drill Tactics" for the use of the Ben-Hur Marine Guards and Ladies' Drill Platoons, which in turn often appeared in public. More widely available were the musical publications, particularly the piano sheet music for Bernard Owen's "Tribe of Ben-Hur March," copyrighted in 1909, and the book of "Odes." They sold a small number of Tribe souvenirs like gold or black decks of playing cards with a drawing of the headquarters building on the back. *The Chariot* itself continued to serve as a vehicle for this kind of synergy, advertising for sale in 1902, for instance, copies of Edgar Cameron's painting, *The Ben Hur Chariot Race*, for $2.[78] In 1928 they sold *The Boys' Ben Hur*, Harper's newly published abridged version of Wallace's novel.[79] The Tribe of Ben-Hur also commissioned leather billfolds and stationery wallets as well as mantel clocks with a galloping *quadriga*. These were distributed as gifts for members and retiring chiefs. They sent silver spoons – decorated with a racing chariot – to newborns in Ben-Hur families.[80] Hundreds of Tribe items like these and gift paraphernalia, particularly award medals, buttons, and pins, now appear regularly in the online ephemera networks. A patent was issued in 1902 for Julius A. Oswald, who designed and patented a souvenir spoon with representations of a chariot race and General Wallace as well as the beech tree.[81]

The increase in membership in the Tribe of Ben-Hur also paralleled the release of the MGM film. The Tribe sponsored the use of one of the chariots used in the film for the parade of the Pacific Southwest Exhibition at Long Beach in 1928.[82] During the 1930s depression, the Ben-Hur Life Association continued to thrive by absorbing or merging with other companies. Over the next few decades, however, membership declined as the fraternal movement had lost its turn-of-the-century energy and modern insurance products became more competitive. Finally, in 1988 the venerable fraternal society was transformed officially into a mutual insurance company known as USA Life Insurance Company.[83] Two years later the name was modified to USA Life One Insurance. Although the latter's website says they have been providing life insurance and annuity products since 1894, the name Ben-Hur is not included.

THE EARLIEST BEN-HUR BRANDS AND PRODUCTS

The reader might recall that in his autobiography Wallace said, "The name Ben-Hur was chosen because it is Biblical, and easily spelled, printed, and pronounced." Almost immediately as *Ben-Hur: A Tale of the Christ* was becoming an astounding success in 1885 and 1886, several businesses unrelated to the world of popular arts began to employ the name Ben-Hur to increase the visibility of their product and give potential customers that much extra promise of quality. Particularly because it was not a genuine, proprietary trademark or brand name and therefore lacked any legal restrictions other than representing the novel and its dramatic scions, the name Ben-Hur was available for adoption as a company or brand name or as the name of a product or product line. The reader has already read about the license Harper granted to George R. Lockwood & Son in the fall of 1886 for the publication of *Seekers After "The Light" From "Ben-Hur."* This gave Lockwood the opportunity to create a Ben-Hur gift for the next two Christmas seasons in a quasi-literary venture never straying far from the watchful eyes of Wallace and Harper & Brothers. Similarly, the "Ben-Hur Calendar" was composed of scenes from the fully authorized Klaw & Erlanger production of *Ben-Hur*, much like the souvenir booklet sold to tens of thousands attending the play. Although he did not issue a license, Wallace granted permission to several composers to set his poetry to music or compose a piece inspired by and named after the chariot race. And as just described, Wallace played an advisory role in the formation of the main Ben-Hur fraternal organization. But the rest of this chapter will now focus on the non-literary, non-dramatic, unlicensed, and unauthorized commercial employment of the name Ben-Hur in the first few decades following the publication of the novel.

A Note on Methodology
Many of the materials assembled and researched for the rest of this chapter differ from those employed up to this point in the book. Such ephemera as programs and piano rolls, copyrighted texts and musical compositions, and newspaper and magazine accounts, and, of course, archive library materials, have provided ample information for describing the various Ben-Hur artistic products and their historical and cultural contexts. The desire to increase membership as well as pride and tradition inspired the

officers of most of the chapters of the various Ben-Hur fraternal societies to record the story of their foundation, growth, and planned events in booklets, pamphlets, and newspaper and online announcements. In contrast, a century ago industrial and commercial companies often came into business, bought or merged with other companies, and went out of business without necessarily leaving behind a full accounting of their presence and activities. Unless there was an extraordinary advertising campaign, legal dispute, or bankruptcy, their activities only rarely warranted newspaper coverage. Commerce at the time warranted for the most part only a few pages of statistics in the major urban newspapers. A dedicated paper like *The Wall Street Journal* had a relatively small circulation. In 1902, for instance, it had a mere 7000 subscribers.[84] That number of people attended performances of the Klaw & Erlanger *Ben-Hur* every week. In most industries, particularly at the retail end, there was as yet no regularized process or tax code that necessarily required recording or auditing by local, state, or federal offices. Many were at most entered into handwritten logs. Of those that were put into print, many have not been properly indexed, let alone digitized. Such disconnected threads of information allow for a number of permutations. Such gaps in source materials require caveats. What appear in our sporadic and incomplete sources to be two products or brands may actually be found to be one. Products and brands may have changed hands without leaving obvious traces of the transactions. Lack of ephemeral evidence and advertising does not necessarily mean a product did not yet exist. And if products surfaced briefly and then seem to have disappeared, it does not necessarily mean that they had already ceased to be manufactured, distributed, or sold.

Despite our incomplete information, it is indisputable that out of the thousands of brands and products being manufactured and sold during the period, dozens upon dozens of Ben-Hur products and brands emerged from the masses and almost by nature lent themselves to high-profile advertising and commercial success in one or more regions of the country. The spillover was considerable, and some of the companies, brands, and products to be discussed here, particularly in the rapid growth and ultimate longevity of Ben-Hur Cigars, Ben-Hur Flour, Ben-Hur Coffee & Spices, Ben Hur Construction, and the Tribe of Ben-Hur, not only resemble the original novel, the *Ben-Hur in Tableaux and Pantomime*, the Klaw & Erlanger *Ben-Hur*, Sousa's "The Chariot Race," and Paull's "The Chariot Race or Ben Hur March" in terms of success but were surely in several ways the result of it or at least part of the same extraordinary phenomenon.

Cigars
The cigar business flourished in the 1880s. Nearly every state had hundreds of factories, the more populated states several thousand.[85] The German-born George Moebs had begun his career importing and man-

ufacturing cigars in the early 1870s.[86] Moebs began producing Ben-Hur Cigars in 1886. Predictably for us, despite widespread competition, the Ben-Hur brand of cigar immediately caught the attention of consumers, and sales flourished over three decades. Moebs reported that in 1886 they sold 3,487,275 Ben-Hur cigars, in 1888 over five million, and in 1891 6,983,207.[87] Meanwhile Moebs himself, recognized as one of the leading cigar manufacturers in the West, rose to prominence as chairman of the conference committee of both manufacturers and journeymen formed to represent the industry before the United States government.[88] His factories on Woodward Avenue were recognized as the heart of economic activity in the "Havana of the North."[89] The original Ben-Hur cigar retailed at 10¢ each, or three for 25¢, and they were sold throughout the Midwest and upper Atlantic states through sales agents and licensed distributors and retailers.[90] In fact, even in Denver an extant piece of letterhead for Harvey & Parker Wholesale Cigars and Teas lists as a specialty Ben Hur Cigars.[91]

Moebs supplemented the visual familiarity of the name Ben-Hur with the image of the chariot. Chromolithograph cardboard advertising printed by the Calvert Litho Company of Detroit and marked with a copyright date of 1886 displays a cropped version of Wagner's painting that isolates the left, foremost charioteer, renders all four of his horses in white, and changes the stadium background.[92] Above the scene it says, "SMOKE BEN-HUR CIGARS." Then for the Detroit International Exposition and Fair of 1889, Moebs hired a circus driver, dressed him in a tin Roman helmet, and instructed him to advertise his product by driving around in a white chariot drawn by four black horses.[93] The next year he did the same at a fair in Saginaw.[94]

A print ad, a newspaper halftone version of the Wagner adaptation in the *Omaha Daily Bee* of Sunday, June 4, 1900, is noteworthy for two reasons. The image eliminates the entire background, replacing it with the words "Mild" and "Aromatic" on either side. The copy both advertises the same Ben-Hur cigar for 10¢ and now also introduces the Little Ben-Hur ("same quality, smaller size") for 5¢. Ads were frequently accompanied by the slogan – "Made on Honor – Sold on Merit," capitalizing on the good reputation of both Moebs and Ben-Hur. By 1904, the retail price for the original Ben-Hur cigar was now listed as 5¢.[95] This is the price that appears in a print ad with German copy targeting the growing German immigrant population in the Midwest.[96] The ad is unprovenienced and undated, but the reader may recall that the Chicago Public Library purchased the Hammer German edition of Wallace's novel in 1891, and the America German edition of *Ben-Hur: A Tale of the Christ* was published in 1895.

This change took place around the time the company was inherited by the next generation of Moebs. George Moeb had died in 1893, leaving the enterprise to his sons William D. C., George, and Gustave. By July, 1903, Gustave had taken the reins and changed the name of the company

Figure 10.2 Moebs of Detroit manufactured and sold Ben-Hur Cigars from 1886 until 1913.

to Gustave A. Moebs & Company.[97] He had already begun to take legal and fiscal steps necessary to meet the many challenges beginning to overwhelm the competitive cigar industry and small businesses in general during the early years of the new century. He first trademarked the name Ben-Hur in 1903.[98] Then he responded to the 1905 revised trademark law requiring a distinct form of lettering. The June 18, 1907, publication by the U.S. Patent Office contains approved serial numbers (27469, 27470) for both the BEN-HUR logo (all caps, bold) and the chariot logo, now entirely without Wagner's original background. By at least 1901, Moebs was offering both full-size and "Little Ben Hur Cigars" otherwise packaged as "Perfectos."[99] In 1907 an announcement in *Trade* stated that the cigar was now sold in one shape only, the "New Ben Hur."[100] In print the name now frequently appeared without the original hyphen.

Reinvigorated, the company displayed its image on a huge sign atop its five-story factory on Woodward Avenue, which was depicted on contemporary postcards.[101] It also advertised on small enamel signs. Boasting about their longevity, a print ad placed in the *Detroit Medical Journal* in 1907 proclaimed, beneath the chariot logo:

> The Ben Hur Cigar has met the requirements of critical professional men for a score of years. Today its reputation is unshaken and men who are posted on cigar goodness have no hesitancy in giving them first preference and handing them to their particular friends. All dealers sell them.[102]

Nonetheless, most of their later advertising programs seem to have abandoned the ancient emblems. A four-panel brochure printed a lighthearted modern story, and their giveaway 3-inch glass paperweight and iron ashtrays bear such slogans as "Wise Men Smoke Ben Hur Cigars" and "Get the Habit," all unrelated to the original conception of the product. Meanwhile the company was having labor disputes, and in 1909 they claimed that their competition was exploiting this to put them out of business.[103] That same year Moebs was issued a patent for a shaping machine, but in November, 1913, in concert with the surging popularity of cigarettes, the *Detroit Free Press* advertised a receiver's sale for Moebs' entire plant and equipment.[104]

The online ephemera sites carry a number of lithographed images of a cigar box inner label with Moebs' cropped adaptation of the Wagner painting emerging from a blue background. Along the top it says "Ben-Hur," and along the bottom in fine print it reads that "Wm. Tegge & Company of Detroit has registered this with the U. S. Patent Office." This was in 1929, when in the midst of a general decline in the cigar industry Thomas P. Jackson, formerly of Detroit's Webster Cigar Company, reorganized Tegge into the Tegge-Jackman Cigar Company and continued the Ben-Hur Cigar legacy.[105]

There was also a brand of Ben Hur chewing tobacco, although less well documented. The online John B. Capewell Glass Negative Collection of Westville, New Jersey, contains an image of several unidentified men lying prostrate on the ground. One of them, with his bowler hat beside him, is taking a chew from a bag of Ben-Hur Scrap.[106] The date of the negative is reportedly 1908, but the Moebs name, a likely candidate, is not visible on the print.[107] A separate piece of ephemera is an undated "Ben-Hur Scrap Coupon," the text of which says that it was issued by Vincent Brothers of 42 State Street, Rochester, New York, and printed by Scotten, Dillon Company of Detroit. It lists sixteen items available for redemption, ranging from twelve Ben-Hur Cigars for fifty coupons to a "Ben-Hur, Weathered Oak Wall Clock" for two hundred.[108] Scotten-Dillon was indeed a Detroit chewing tobacco manufacturer. In addition, there are extant examples of Ben-Hur tobacco pins that may have belonged to chewing-tobacco bags.[109] Both pin types are round. One is painted yellow with a red circumference and red stripe across the middle. In large black, block letters is painted "BEN-HUR" in two registers. There are numerous extant examples of these. Less commonly found today are examples of the embossed, unpainted type, which have small arcs above and below each register of "BEN-HUR."

There is another interesting connection between the novel *Ben-Hur: A Tale of the Christ* and cigar manufacturing. Forgotten for the most part until recently were the cigar-factory lectors who read out loud to the workers in the factories. Often they read newspapers and lighter fair, but they also read excerpts from novels.[110] Quite popular were the works of Victor Hugo, Alexandre Dumas, and Leo Tolstoy, but according to a 1929 *New York Times* article, the most popular book among lectors around the turn of the century was *Ben-Hur*:

> General Lew Wallace had an enthusiastic following, and his "Ben-Hur" is still described as having the greatest vogue of any book read in the cigar-making factories.[111]

Flour
Several different flour companies targeted housewives and their families as well as farmers and breeders, quite different demographics from the consumers who purchased Ben-Hur brand cigars.[112] The water-powered Lindell Mills of Fort Collins, Colorado, which dated back to 1868, were destroyed by fire in July, 1886, just one year after being acquired by the Colorado Milling and Elevator Company.[113] The mills were rebuilt and reopened in July, 1887, as The New Lindell Mills. Some of this information is printed on an extant example of their letterhead, dated November 19, 1888, describing the company as wholesalers of flour and grain as well as "Manufacturers of Defiance, Ben-Hur & Other Brands." Later the company was renamed the Fort Collins Flour Mills and manufactured such additional brands of flour as Jack Frost, Snow Trader, Snowflake, and

Pride of Colorado.[114] According to the list of "Trade Marks Filed" in the 1898 *Biennial Report of the Secretary of State of Colorado*, the Colorado Milling and Elevator Company filed trademarks for Ben Hur, Defiance, and Jack Frost on June 7, 1897.[115]

Several Ben-Hur Flour products were sold out of the Minnesota twin cities of Minneapolis and St. Paul just after the beginning of the century. In December, 1902, the Loftus-Hubbard Elevator Company, with elevators and mills located in St. Paul, Duluth, and Stillwater, received a laudatory write-up in *The St. Paul Globe* describing the company as a "young giant" and crediting them with such innovations as sending out agents to build market relationships and establishing feed mills in St. Paul.[116] The third and final paragraph of the article reads:

> The company manufactures ground feed, cornmeal and other products of course [*sic*] grain, and have recently become the exclusive distributors of the famous Ben Hur flour. This flour really needs no introduction to St. Paul householders, and it will require only the pushing qualities of the Loftus-Hubbard company to make a place for it in the provision room of every home in St. Paul.

An aggressive advertising campaign aimed at the retail market followed this standard type of product launch. On January 18, 1903, the entire upper third of a page in *The St. Paul Globe* was covered by a halftone adaptation of Checa's version of the chariot race, surrounded by copy on all four sides and a border.[117] The largest type is beneath the graphic, reading "'BEN-HUR' FLOUR – THE WINNER," capitalizing on the racing motif. Next largest, the upper headline boasts that "'two sacks' Ben-Hur Flour," reduced to smaller type, "will give more satisfaction than three sacks of ordinary flour." The left panel re-emphasizes the economy of buying Ben-Hur Flour, its extraction from "the choicest grain grown in the great Northwest," and the care with which it is inspected "by intelligent men of life-long experience," while the right panel suggests superior taste, versatility, and fair price. These target the frugal and concerned housewife, but an additional note placed between "'BEN-HUR' FLOUR – THE WINNER" and the large "LOFTUS-HUBBARD ELEVATOR CO." targets parents, particularly mothers:

> A BEAUTIFUL PICTURE BOOK, in full bright colors, with story and illustrations so arranged as to entertain and delight the children, will be sent to any woman who will send us before March 1st, 1903, two two-cent stamps and the card or bill-head of one retail grocer in her town who does not sell BEN-HUR FLOUR.

The ad does not elaborate, but we will do so further on.

Surrounding the entire complex of chariot race illustration and print columns are images of twenty-seven S & H Green Stamps. The Sperry & Hutchinson Company Green Stamps, which would thrive for many more decades, were relatively new at the time and represented an innovative method of attracting loyal customers.[118] Their newness is evidenced by the fact that in 1904 their total capitalization was only $1 million.[119] Loftus-Hubbard's participation in the S & H Green Stamp program demonstrates their aggressiveness, although this developed into a controversy within the local Retail Grocers' Association. This warranted newspaper coverage, which makes clear that Ben-Hur Flour was at the center of the controversy, since one firm in the city was selling it at a lower price than all the others.[120]

This ad appeared in the Sunday edition of the paper. Loftus-Hubbard placed a different ad the next Sunday. This January 25 ad was two columns wide, featuring a large, lidless flour barrel on its side, spilling out both flour and a *quadriga* – a freely adapted version of the Wagner painting, although the charioteer wears a white tunic and all four horses are black.[121] On the side of the barrel it says, appropriately, "HIGH QUALITY WINS." Probably contemporary were their Ben-Hur Flour larger-format (5½ in. × 3½ in.) trade cards, with a chromolithographed chariot race à la Wagner and "HIGH QUALITY WINS" on the front, and basic bread and pastry recipes on the back. On February 8 another ad portrayed Ben-Hur, again in white, his arms outstretched and holding the reins of his four horses.[122] They all face the reader, and no chariot is visible. The slogan below reads, "Ben-Hur Flour – It has won the race on quality and economy." At the bottom of the ad it promises, "You get the original S. & H. Green Trading Stamps with every sack of Ben Hur Flour."

A few weeks later Loftus-Hubbard sponsored a fundraiser that created another double Ben-Hur synergy. The winter of 1902/3 brought famine to Scandinavia, and the Norwegian and Swedish populations of Minnesota helped raise millions of dollars in relief. On February 27 the First Swedish Methodist Church of St. Paul hosted a lecture on *Ben-Hur* attended by more than 500 people. Savannah-born actor, Brock Beckwith, supplemented the lecture with stereopticon slides "illustrating Ben Hur's famous chariot race and other incidents from the famous work of Lew Wallace."[123] Loftus-Hubbard paid all of Beckwith's expenses, enabling the entire proceeds to be contributed to the famine fund.

Even more aggressive in their advertising was The Royal Milling Company of Minneapolis.[124] An extant piece of Royal Milling Company's letterhead, dated December 4, 1903, displays an etching of the Minneapolis mill itself, and to the left is a circular emblem depicting in color two *quadrigae* in an ancient circus setting. In late 1902 Royal Milling began an intensive advertising campaign for Ben-Hur Flour which would provide business cards, trade cards, letterhead, envelopes, advertising displays, posters, and even printed store awnings for individual retailers throughout the Midwest and in the Mid- and North Atlantic states. Each business card contained the image of a three-dimensional ceramic image of a *quadriga*, the same used for the aforementioned spilled-barrel image in the Loftus-Hubbard newspaper graphic, again identifying with the iconic scene in the novel. All had in red the slogan "BUY IT – TRY IT," and many had a simulated handwritten note from a local grocer, whose name and address were printed on the right, often beneath a photograph of the purveyor.[125]

Royal Milling also distributed their trademark on such everyday items as bill holders, matchsafes, and blotters. The blotters were particularly colorful, with a reproduction of Wagner's featured *quadriga* set before an ancient circus background, albeit with the horse image reversed and rendered in brown, the charioteer remaining right handed, and the *spina* architecture rearranged as well. In three different locations the copy includes the name "BEN HUR" in large print. They also issued postcard-size advertisements. One displayed their brand name and the aforementioned slogan "High Quality Wins" placed above a colorful illustration of a chariot race freely adapted from Wagner.[126] On the reverse side were two recipes, one for bread, the other for pastry. Another type of postcard advertisement takes advantage of contemporary interest in the Holy Land and seems to target in particular consumers of German heritage. Printed on the front of an extant example postmarked December 11, 1902, was the Germanic phrase "Private Post-Karte" written in Gothic script, as if to resemble a postcard sent from abroad, albeit with American postage affixed. The back of the card has a photo of "An Ancient Church in Jerusalem" on the left, and the following paragraph printed in cursive:

> This traveling is certainly grand. The scenes around here make me think of Ben Hur and that reminds me of the appetizing bread and pastry mother baked from Ben Hur Flour. I hope you are carrying this flour in stock because we want to trade with you and must have it. If your jobber does not handle it write to the Royal Milling Co., Minneapolis, Minn., the makers. They will tell you where you can get it. Ben Hur Flour is –
>
>   Simply,
>   L E Gant[127]

Royal Milling initiated their most visible program, a series of distinctive print advertisements, during the fall of 1902. Achieving greater levels of penetration than advertisements for any other commercial Ben-Hur products, the company placed vivid ads in such widely circulated magazines as *Ladies' Home Journal* (where William Martin Johnson had just recently served as Art Editor), *The Saturday Evening Post*, *Munsey's*, *Colliers*, *Century*, *Leslie's*, *McClure's*, *Youth's Companion*, and, appropriately, *Harper's*. They launched their campaign near the end of the first decade of the "Magazine Revolution" that featured low-price, high-volume magazines subsidized by advertising revenues, many of them targeting a variety of consumer demographics.[128] This was precisely the year in which most of these magazines began featuring muckraking articles, and Cyrus Hermann Curtis, the publisher of *Ladies' Home Journal*, stated that his readership consisted largely of urban, suburban, and small-town professionals.[129] His editor, Edward Bok, aimed at reaching a "broad middle-class" audience. Circulation numbers were rapidly increasing at the time. In 1895 *Ladies' Home Journal* had a circulation of 715,000. In 1903 it became the first magazine to reach one million readers.[130] Ben-Hur Flour ads began to appear in the October, 1902, issue of the *Ladies' Home Journal* with a quarter-page ad featuring two racing chariots à la Wagner, and then in the November issue with a handsome, robed male standing in front of an Ionic column beneath the statement that "bread is the pillar of strength."[131] In January, 1903, the issues of McClure's that contained the third installment of Ida Tarbell's articles on Standard Oil also contained a version of the two-sack/emerging chariot ad.[132] A few months later Ben-Hur Flour placed an ad on the rear cover of *Harper's Weekly* (June 13) and *The Saturday Evening Post* (July 18), adding nearly another million to the number of people exposed to this Ben-Hur commercial product.[133] Dominating this graphic is a bright red banner displaying the brand name above and behind a racing chariot viewed from the side, a cloud of dust rising from beneath it. Two sacks of Ben-Hur framing the upper part of the banner are themselves illustrated with medallions depicting an adaptation of the Wagner painting wide enough in scope to encompass two racing *quadrigae*. The copy specifically reflects the racing motifs: "BEN-HUR FLOUR is in the race to win your favor."

The advertising industry took particular interest in these Ben-Hur Flour ads. Harold Dwight's essay in the trade journal *American Printer and Lithographer* noted that these ads were "conspicuous" and "striking":

> Among the various magazine work, the designs placed by the Royal Milling Company are conspicuous. The great flour interests have awakened to the fact that they must resume advertising or permit the numerous new food preparations being given wide publicity to run away with the market. The Royal Milling Company seems to have come to a realization of this fact, and its magazine campaign exploiting the merits of Ben Hur flour is the result. The designs being used are striking, the chariot and horses having been adopted as the principal feature. The treatment is excellent.[134]

Earlier in the article Dwight stressed the relatively new concept of making an advertising campaign "unique and distinctive in itself" and that new ideas were at a premium in the expectation of avoiding monotony, so Royal Milling paid for more than a dozen different advertisements, each of them employing chariot imagery in a relatively astounding series of evocative images, especially when one considers that the purpose was to sell bread and biscuit flour. The entire back cover of the December 27, 1902, *The Saturday Evening Post* fills the rectangular frame with a newly conceived *quadriga* charging out at the reader from between two large sacks of flour, both of them with depictions of racing chariots adapted from the Wagner painting. The graphic is particularly large, measuring 12¼ inches wide by 9¼ inches tall. The ad in the February 28, 1903,

Figure 10.3 Colorful Ben-Hur Flour ads in national magazines, reaching several million subscribers monthly throughout 1903, always featured the concept of the victorious charioteer.

issue of *Harper's Weekly* depicted a ceramic chariot carved in relief onto a medallion, much like the business-card graphic.[135] The entire width of the rear cover of the March 14, 1903, issue of *Collier's* is filled with a four-horse chariot charging out at the viewer. At the top of the ad, shaded in blue, is the slogan, "A penny saved is a penny made," followed by: "Your savings will be counted by dollars if you use BEN-HUR FLOUR," implying that the victory the consumer would achieve would be economic. At the bottom is the offer for "Ben-Hur Dough Boys." The same ad was placed on the April 4, 1903, issue of *The Saturday Evening Post*. An ad that ran in the November, 1902, issue of *Munsey's Magazine*, which in 1903 had a circulation of 634,000,[136] has racing chariot horses and a profile of a charioteer, presumably Judah Ben-Hur, crowned with a laurel wreath aside a collection of slogans: "A portion of your income must go into flour. That portion will be small if you use Ben-Hur Flour. Every batch of Bread good. No waste. We're in the race to win your favor. Try Ben-Hur; Don't allow a substitute. All grocers sell it."[137] The quarter-page ad just inside the cover of the August 1, 1903, *Saturday Evening Post* presented a newly conceived image of a victorious charioteer, his horses facing away as he turns towards us, casually grasping the reins with his extended arm. The *Saturday Evening Post* had a circulation of 512,000 in 1903.[138]

As we are seeing, many of their ads made a verbal reference to racing or victory. 425,000 weekly subscribers saw the slogan "THE WINNER-ON QUALITY" atop a 6-inch ad prominently displayed just inside the cover of the January 3, 1903, *Saturday Evening Post*.[139] Below there was an illustration of a large sack of flour containing a circular view of two racing *quadrigae*, above which Ben-Hur stands triumphantly in front of his own team of black horses, behind all of which is still another sack of flour with its own illustration of a chariot race. A similar ad had appeared in the November 27, 1902, issue of *Youth's Companion*, just nine weeks before the heavily promoted issue that published Wallace's "How I Came to Write *Ben-Hur*."[140] An ad Royal Milling Company placed in both *McClure's* and *Munsey's* as early as November, 1902, showed two Wagner-like chariots at the top and an oval-shaped cameo of a togaed Roman wearing a victory wreath, along with the text, "We are in the race to win your favor." Another ad in the same magazines in the same month depicted Mowbray's victorious charioteer from the Garfield edition, holding one of his spirited horses by the reins. Here the copy says, "BEN-HUR FLOUR 'Has The Go To Make The Dough.'" Nearly one year later, the rear cover of *Harper's Weekly* of September 5, 1903, depicted a *quadriga* atop a globe of the earth, the copy here reading "BEN-HUR FLOUR – THE BEST ON EARTH."[141] Another *Harper's* advertisement with a single chariot and two bags with two chariots each reads, "BEN-HUR FLOUR – WINS THE RACE." Still another *Harper's Weekly* rear-cover ad depicts the youthful charioteer holding back his team of horses while standing atop a bag of Ben-Hur Flour.[142]

At the bottom of many of the Royal Milling Company ads the reader saw an offer similar to the one in the Loftus-Hubbard ads, promising a "beautiful picture book . . . to entertain and delight the children." This picture book featured the Ben-Hur Dough Boys, playful cartoon creatures made of flexible dough, their arms circling around, intertwining, and stretching in various elastic configurations. This belonged to a particularly innovative type of campaign strategy for home products that would become ever more important in the ad campaigner's portfolio throughout the following decade, preceding both Grace Weidersein's well-known "Campbell's Kids" of 1904 and Jell-O's famed "Kewpies" of the following decade.[143] The back covers of the May 16, 1903, issue of *The Saturday Evening Post* and the April 25, 1903, issue of *Harper's Weekly*, picture "The Dough Boys' Chariot Race" alongside the following poem. The illustration features a race between two chariots, each pulled by three wooden horses on wheels and driven by a whip-cracking, doughy charioteer, and a new-fangled automobile-like vehicle rolling on thread spools and manned by goggled and gloved driving enthusiasts. At the finish line one of the charioteers stretches his doughy neck forward thirty times its normal length to win the race "by a neck."

> The sportive Dough Boys planned a race
>   Their nimble steeds to try:
> For they enjoyed a track event
>   As well as you or I.
> The day had come, the track was fine,
>   No clouds hung o'er the sky.
>
> Their horses were but wooden toys;
>   You might have thought them slow,
> For you have really, truly nags
>   Which can like lightning go.
> But wooden horses are the things
>   For little boys of dough.
>
> Each charioteer made up his mind
>   That he would not be last.
> Clang! Clang! Rang out the starter's bell,
>   Off sped the racers fast;
> When, like a streak, a spool-mobile
>   With Dough Boys two whizzed past.
>
> The hindmost racer saw a chance
>   To have a bit of fun.
> Beneath the "chuffer's" arm he tucked
>   His head, as by they spun.
> Out stretched his neck across the line –
>   Thus, "by a neck" he won.

Seven different short-poem stories appeared in a blotter series.[144] These begin with the creation of the Dough Boys when "careless Bob" spilled

Figure 10.4 The innovative Ben-Hur Flour Dough Boys targeted young families and preceded Grace Weidersein's "Campbell's Kids" and Jell-O's famed "Kewpies."

water into a sack of Ben-Hur Flour. Others illustrate two dough boys joining and stretching their arms to make a jump rope for a Ben-Hur Dough Girl, the Dough Boy who slept on a hammock on a summer's day, another who fell from a tower but did not hurt his doughy body, and so on. The "beautiful picture book" itself was a 6¾in. × 9¼in. booklet that contained illustrations of the same stories in a larger, two-page format, although substituting for the first story about careless Bob is another about Dough Boy Joe who ate too much yeast. The final two pages contain a message from The Royal Milling Company, affirming the quality of Ben-Hur Flour and the process by which it is milled, and a polychrome version of the red-banner ad described above, so while the booklet is designed to delight children, it is still designed to sell Ben-Hur Flour to their parents.

The copy on many of these same ads made direct appeals to efficient and frugal housewives. The back cover of the April 4, 1903, *Saturday Evening Post* contains the slogan, "'A penny saved is a penny made': Your savings will be counted by dollars if you use BEN-HUR FLOUR." An important part of this aspect of the campaign was to expand the Ben-Hur retail network by encouraging women to notify the company of retailers who did not carry their product. To accomplish this, a paragraph at the bottom of these magazine ads promised housewives that they would be sent a free kitchen utensil, like a branded mixing spoon, matchsafe, or flat-iron holder, or a coupon for a free bag of flour "to any woman who will send us the card or bill-head of one retail grocer in her town who does not sell BEN-HUR Flour."[145] Making a more personal appeal to the homemaker, Royal Milling placed an ad that contained the endorsement of Susan Wallace. Appropriately, they placed this ad in the April, 1903, issue of *Harper's*. The upper copy reads, "BEN HUR FLOUR – Proves Itself – 'Worthy the Fame of a Famous Name,'" and in place of chariot imagery is a facsimile of a handwritten letter addressed to Royal Milling Company and sent from Crawfordsville, dated November, 1902, quite early on in the Ben-Hur Flour ad campaign of 1902–3:

> I have pleasure in commending your Ben-Hur Flour. It is white, sweet, wholesome in whatever shape it may be used.
> Susan E. Wallace
> (Mrs. Lew Wallace)[146]

Including the endorsement ad by "Mrs. Lew Wallace," this means that within the space of approximately one year, the Royal Milling Company launched at least five different Ben-Hur Flour advertisement concepts, one attempting to make the consumer associate the product with the Holy Land and *Ben-Hur: A Tale of the Christ*, a second celebrating the victorious Judah Ben-Hur and thereby connecting culinary triumphs with the thrill and victory of the novel's protagonist in the iconic chariot race, a third aimed at thoughtful housewives who ran their food budgets efficiently and frugally, a fourth targeting young families who would delight in the charming Dough Boys chariot racing, and a fifth connecting the fame of Lew and Susan Wallace with the Ben-Hur brand name.[147]

These five marketing strategies reflect the epitome of advertising in 1903, which turned out to be a pivotal year. In his study of the development and importance of *The Saturday Evening Post*, Jan Cohn points out some of the major changes taking place in that year.[148] Like Dwight, although decades later, Cohn takes particular interest in the Ben-Hur Flour ads, observing that the January 3, 1903, issue of *The Saturday Evening Post* was the first to demonstrate fully the shift in emphasis from the household demographic to the magazine's newly targeted audience, the young male interested in business. Ben-Hur Flour was the only household product advertised in that issue, and this trend would continue. But our more comprehensive examination of the Ben-Hur Flour ad campaign in 1902–3 has shown that it was targeting not only the traditional housewife demographic interested in good value and a quality food product but also (predominantly) men interested in competition and success in business, a demographic more apt to be lured by its chariot imagery and slogans emphasizing racing and triumph. In addition, it targeted parents who wanted to delight their children, as well as those who might be persuaded by a celebrity endorsement. The advertising campaign for Ben-Hur Flour, like its popular artistic predecessors, operated along the cutting edge of the rapidly developing consumer market and addressed a variety of demographic targets.

We should not underestimate how extraordinary this advertising campaign was. It was only in 1905 that Earnest Calkins, who would pioneer psychological targeting, consumer engineering, and the sophisticated use of artistic images, published *Modern Advertising*, his first treatise on scientific management.[149] And it was not until 1910 that *Printers' Ink* admitted that psychological targeting was anything other than "horse sense."[150] Royal Milling with its Ben-Hur Flour brand was well ahead of the curve. They marketed their product as aggressively, attractively, and intelligently as any regional or national competitor in the first few years of the new century. Before the era of radio and television, the weekly and monthly periodicals were the most colorful and impressive means of reaching the masses. During its year-long period of national magazine exposure, Ben-Hur Flour stood out as one of the most effectively advertised household products in the country, its famous name and recognizable imagery reaching several million readers each month, helping to ingrain its fame, commercial viability, and claims to excellence among men, women, and children.

Ads for Ben-Hur Flour appeared in newspapers as well, whether placed by Royal Milling Company or co-sponsored by wholesalers or even individual distributors and grocers. The halftone ads that ran in local papers were contemporary with the national magazine programs and employed similar imagery and theme. In the January 13, 1903, *Oshkosh Daily Northwestern*, a victorious charioteer holds his horses by the reins, and the surrounding copy reads, "ASK YOUR GROCER FOR – BEN-HUR FLOUR – It has won the race on quality and economy."[151] More than a year later the *Monticello Express* and *The Sumner Gazette* of Iowa ran large ads depicting a chariot, a sack of flour with the company chariot logo, and a lengthy text, including the offer for the "Ben-Hur Dough Boys."[152] Even so, the graphics were quite different from one another in design and composition, the former co-sponsored by the distributor George Stuhler & Sons, the latter by J. H. Noon. In 1903 advertisements for both the Klaw & Erlanger *Ben-Hur* and Ben-Hur Flour so frequently filled advertising sections of local newspapers that they inevitably sometimes appeared on the same page.[153]

Although this Ben-Hur Flour advertising blitz came to an end at the beginning of 1904, extant ephemera like bills of sale, letterhead, envelopes, and trade postcards displaying a barrel of Ben-Hur Flour as well as photos of store fronts displaying "We Sell Ben-Hur Flour" signs demonstrate that the product was still sold well into the next decade.[154] The 1907 Food Show at Mechanics Hall in Worcester, Massachusetts, included a huge display composed of several dozen of these distinctive Ben-Hur Flour barrel-top chariot logos arranged in an elaborate design.[155] In 1909 Ben Hur Flour won a prize at the Seattle Fair.[156] An envelope bearing the postmark of March 5, 1915, states that Gross Bros. of Toledo, Ohio, are "Distributors of BEN HUR FLOUR."[157] Newspaper ads, appearing sporadically when the product was put on sale, continue to offer the product as a fine grain bread flour for nearly three decades.[158] An ad in the *Miami Daily News Record* from 1946 specifies that the Ben Hur Flour they sold was "Made by Makers of Red Star," based in Wichita, Kansas.[159]

A number of official reports by state and university agriculture offices confirm that the name and brand carried on for decades milled as several types of feed. Royal had been producing Ben Hur feed since at least 1903.[160] In 1908 the Van Eyck-Weurding Milling Company was advertising its own Ben-Hur brand flour in the local, Holland, Michigan, Dutch-language newspaper, *De Grondwet*.[161] The Department of Agriculture of New York included in its 1917 report of feeding stuffs a Ben-Hur Horse & Mule Feed manufactured by Golden Grain Milling Company of East St. Louis, Illinois, and Ben Hur Horse Feed manufactured by Metropolitan Mills of New York City.[162] Many mills of this sort were united under one umbrella when General Mills, Inc. consolidated them in 1928, and then in 1931 General Mills was granted trademark registration for "Ben Hur," which did not expire until 1992, as well as a patent.[163] Similarly, on May 6, 1948, federal trademark registration [#71556319] was filed for "Ben-Hur" by The Colorado Milling & Elevator Company.[164] The trademark, which includes a *quadriga* racing from right to left in front of an ancient circus wall, expired also in 1992. But the legacy continues: at PizzaMaking.com, General Mill's Ben Hur unbleached flour is still recommended for use in making commercial pizza dough.[165]

Coffee, Teas, Spices, and Baking Powder
The Emporium, a popular department store in St. Paul, promoted a free weekly cooking school in their basement kitchen, and on Monday, June 8, 1903, the featured demonstration on Breakfast Dainties used exclusively "Ben Hur Flour and Ben Hur Baking Powder."[166] All attendees were to receive a free loaf of bread, and "every lady" was urged to "be sure and secure a Ben Hur Dough Book illustrated for children." From this isolated source of information alone it seems that this promotion was sponsored by Royal Milling Company and that the company also produced a baking powder under the same label as its high-profile flour product. Similarly, throughout 1904 Schoch's, another local Twin Cities retail store, ran ads including listings and prices for Ben Hur Baking Powder sold in one-pound cans.[167] A decade or so later, there was a second Ben Hur Baking Powder manufactured in the Midwest prepared, as the label on an extant jar specifies, "expressly for Albert Hildreth, Dealer in General Merchandise" in Mahomet, Illinois, and marketed by Geiger-Tinney Wholesale Coffee & Spices Company of Indianapolis.[168] It was sold in a #5 Ball aqua mason jar, identified by the embossed, cursive "Ball" name [Type 2-L], and these were not manufactured until 1910.

The baking powder industry was a very competitive market, and these were just two of the many manufacturers at the time.[169] In the same year another Ben-Hur Baking Powder was advertised in the Los Angeles area. The Thomas J. Barkley Company, incorporated in April, 1903, placed a series of extraordinary ads in the *Los Angeles Herald* in the fall of 1904.[170] The Sunday, September 18 ad covered an entire page with a large black-and-white reproduction of the Wagner painting beneath the headline, "BEN-HUR Baking Powder WINS."[171] Below and on the left is a text of "The Chariot Race," or more precisely, a condensed version of the already condensed version of Wallace's description printed by Sousa in some of his programs and newspaper announcements.[172] As with the Sousa selections, there is no evidence of a license granted for printing excerpts from the novel. Nonetheless, it provides another example of a second layer of borrowing, a process more frequently and easily enabled when a property has already been widely disseminated and adapted. Below some additional copy claiming the health benefits of cream-of-tartar-style baking powder is this additional allusion to a chariot race:

> In the Race for Popular Favor
>   Ben-Hur Baking Powder Has a Long Lead!
>   It is Unquestionably the Best

Figure 10.5 Beginning with Thomas J. Barkley in 1903, Ben-Hur Coffee, Teas, Spices, & Extracts products were advertised in the *Los Angeles Times* regularly for fifty years, as was the unrelated product sold as Ben-Hur Soap.

The Sunday, September 25 ad also consumes an entire page, but here the main chariot in Wagner's painting has been extracted in a halftone rendering that looks very much like the logo of Ben-Hur Cigars.[173] The copy follows the same tact as one of the programs of Ben-Hur Flour in directly targeting the smart consumer. Here the promise is that the chef will save money by using a smaller amount of Ben-Hur Baking Powder, much preferred to the "so-called 'Absolutely Pure' Baking Powders":

> If every woman in Los Angeles knew just how good Ben-Hur Baking Powder really is, there would be more Ben-Hur sold than of all the other brands put together.

At the bottom left, the company reintroduces the racing motif by matching Ben-Hur Spices with its own Ben-Hur Baking Powder:

> Ben-Hur Spices couldn't be any better than the Ben-Hur Baking Powder, but it's a pretty close race for supremacy.

At the bottom right Ben-Hur Extracts are then said to "rival" Ben-Hur Baking Powder. The name Ben-Hur occurs with great frequency, appearing twelve times in twelve headlines and sentences.

The October 2 full-page ad returns to the whole Wagner depiction of a chariot race, this time under the appropriate headline "Ben-Hur Leads."[174] Again touting the quality of Ben-Hur Baking Powder, a boxed insert quotes an endorsement by J. A. Fazenda, President of the Los Angeles Retail Grocers' Association. In this ad the name Ben-Hur appears fifteen times, including Ben-Hur Coffee and Ben-Hur Tea as well as Ben-Hur Extracts and Ben-Hur Spices. Before incorporating his own company, Barkley had previously co-managed the Barkley-Stetson-Preston Company, a wholesaler of coffee, tea, and spices, products that were typically packaged, distributed, sold, and advertised together in the late nineteenth century.[175]

Thereafter their concentration of newspaper advertisements devolved to occasional ads featuring the extracted Wagner chariot and, of course, the name Ben Hur, often without the hyphen.[176] By the time the company was reincorporated in 1910 as the Joannes-Splane Company, ads included halftone illustrations of their cans, the labels of which depicted the extracted chariot and company name, now more regularly with the hyphen restored.[177] Readers of *Home Helps*, the 1910 cookbook compiled by the First Baptist Church Ladies' Aid Society of Whitier, California, were reminded on every page of Ben-Hur products, although without the logo. At the top of each open pair of pages were slogans like:

> – NEVER TOO OLD TO BEGIN . . . TO DRINK BEN-HUR COFFEE
> – GOOD SEASONING IS MOST ECONOMICAL . . . USE BEN-HUR HIGH GRADE SPICES
> – IF INVITED TO TAKE TEA . . . SAY, BEN-HUR SUITS ME
> – YOU MAY THINK OTHERS NICE . . . BUT THERE'S NOTHING LIKE BEN-HUR SPICE[178]

The entire back cover of the 1911 *Los Angeles Times Cook Book – Number Four* displayed an advertisement for Ben-Hur products, with images of five packages and tins displaying chariot logos as well as the verbal headline with another chariot racing motif, "Always Leads."[179]

Two years later, when Vice-President John R. Splane died, the company was renamed the Joannes Brothers Company. Following the precedent set by Barkley, Joannes Brothers would continue to maintain their high visibility in the Los Angeles area for decades.[180] One of their most successful products was Steel-Cut Coffee sold in blue tins. "BEN-HUR" was printed in large white letters across the top, and in a circle was a colorized image of the isolated Wagner chariot. Although the chariot logo endured and was eventually trademarked, it was not as important in their advertising as the omnipresence of the Ben-Hur name. Illustrating an endorsement of Ben-Hur Steel Cut Coffee by hundreds of attendees at Parmelee-Dohrmann's Fourth Annual Household Show, for instance, was simply a halftone depiction of a woman holding a cookbook in her hands.[181] Engaging in a popular type of advertising scheme to sell their Steel-Cut Coffee, the company created a graphic mascot, Coff E. Bean, not at all a Roman charioteer but a coffee bean with anthropomorphic legs and arms. Nonetheless, the messages he conveyed always carried the name Ben-Hur. In a number of ads in the *Los Angeles Herald* he spouted rhyming jingles like "Of course, BEN-HUR's a welcome guest in homes that always want the BEST," and "Bring in the coffee pot so bright, BEN-HUR, of course, we'll serve tonight."[182] In 1914 the company even invested in a 12-foot electric sign at 4th and Broadway displaying Coff. E. Bean holding a cup over his head, the steam rising from the cup forming the words "Coff. E. Bean says – Ben Hur Steel Cut Coffee – Satisfies," written out in script and finishing with a big flourish and a coffee pot underneath.[183] Creating effects like those of the heralded chariot displays in New York, Detroit, and Ocean Park (described below), the sequencers made Coff E. Bean appear to have six different facial expressions, and eight movements of the eyes.

For decades the company and their number one product were generally called and advertised as Ben-Hur Coffee. As such, Ben-Hur Coffee played an integral role in a number of bread and baking contests for such local stores as Hamburger's and Brent's by outright sponsorship or providing branded supplies.[184] They also sponsored or participated in cooking schools,[185] demonstrations,[186] and local household shows,[187] and through the *Los Angeles Times* they recommended banquet menus that of course included Ben-Hur products,[188] and they ran sales contests.[189] Their almost daily presence in the *Times*, whether through these independent features or ads for grocery stores, helped make them a fixture in Southern California. In 1915, for instance, the *Times* ran a Prosperity and Trade Contest in which consumers were asked to bring receipts and empty product containers to The Times Building. On the Fourth of July the paper ran a photo of Harry L. Joannes, one of the three brothers and secretary of the company, standing in front of a massive, "veritable mountain" of Ben-Hur Coffee cans.[190] The page-long article begins:

> The Prosperity and Trade Contest is finished. The contest office is closed. The contestants come no more to the second floor of The Times Building and only one thing remains, on this same floor, to indicate that a Trade Contest has ever been – the huge pile of Ben Hur coffee, tea and spice cans.

With considerable fanfare in the local business community, the company in 1917 opened a new five-story headquarters and factory at 800 Traction Street, which is still extant.[191] The write-up in the *American Globe* details their line of spices and extracts, all of them packaged in small canisters, tins, jars, bottles, and boxes marked with the chariot logo and distributed in California, Arizona, Nevada, New Mexico, and Texas. To the south, their logo was painted and is still visible on an exterior brick wall at the corner of Ivy and India Streets in San Diego.[192]

Additional Food, Beverage, and Liquid Medicinal Products
Although they were not nearly so widely advertised and distributed as Ben-Hur Flour or Ben-Hur Coffee, Tea, and Spice products, the record shows still more food products for sale during the first decades of the twentieth century. Ben-Hur Oranges were shipped in crates identified by a brilliant label depicting Wagner's main charioteer racing out of a yellow background alongside a Sunkist orange wrapped in thin paper.[193] These oranges were grown and packed by the Redlands Co-Operative Fruit Association in California.[194] A Ben Hur brand of Sunkist Washington Navels, omitting the hyphen in "Ben Hur" and depicting Checa's main charioteer instead of Wagner's, was shipped in a bluish label.[195] A contemporary history of Southern California reports that 1350 acres of orchard acreage were purchased by Charles Joannes in 1904, still several years before he became president of the forerunner of Ben-Hur Coffee.[196] Fruits produced in the orchard were shipped to the East. Already by December an ad for "the celebrated Ben Hur brand seedless oranges" appeared in Michigan,[197] and in 1907 the Papworth stores in Syracuse were running this ad in local newspapers:

> We have some of those famous oranges for all of you. Rich, juicy, finely-flavored highland fruit. Call for Ben Hur.[198]

In 1908 and 1909 the *Los Angeles Herald* was meticulously reporting the number of shipments and relative prices in New York, St. Louis, and Cleveland, along with the weather conditions, especially during the winter months.[199]

Three-pound cans of Ben Hur Tomatoes were advertised in the Midwest between 1895 and 1902.[200] A much wider range of Ben Hur canned vegetables, seafood, and meats were sold in Manitoba from the 1910s to the 1930s, most notably catsup and several varieties of salmon.[201] Also, in the 1910s Washington's J. L. Smiley & Company produced Alaskan coho salmon under the Ben Hur brand.[202]

There are several known examples of beverage and liquid medicinal products. Rhomberg Distilling Company of East Dubuque, Iowa, produced both "the celebrated" Ben-Hur Whiskey and Ben-Hur Rye from around 1899 to 1909.[203] Croll & Huber of Tchoupitoulas Street in New Orleans, distributors for Ben Hur Bitters, ran a series of local newspaper ads in June, 1908.[204] The ads urge:

For Your Stomach's Sake
A Drink of BEN HUR BITTERS Take

Collectors also make reference to a Ben Hur Kidney & Liver Bitters.[205] The Fort Pitt Brewing Company, flourishing from 1908 to 1956, produced a brand of Ben Hur Beer during an as yet unspecified period.[206] During some of that period there was also a European brand of Ben-Hur food products, headquartered in Antwerp and selling margarine, pudding, biscuits, and the like.[207]

PERSONAL CARE PRODUCTS

Soap
Newspaper ads for a Ben-Hur Soap began appearing along the West Coast from San Diego to Seattle in 1905.[208] By 1907 grocery stores in Duluth carried the product, and by 1909 Washington, DC.[209] Made from vegetable oils, this was a cold-water, white bleaching bar-soap to be used for bath, laundry, and dish washing. It was sold in convenient bars sized to fit in the hand and capable of floating. Ad copy emphasized that it was pure and sanitary as well as economical, but as a grocery store non-food item, there was little opportunity for graphic images in cramped newspaper ads, especially in the early 1900s. In May, 1914, the Peet Bros. of Kansas City, soap manufacturers since 1872, trademarked the name Ben-Hur with a prominent curl attached to the initial 'B.'[210] That fall ads began to display the trademark above a line-rendering of the Wagner chariot race, although Wagner's rightmost charioteer is now on the left, and the prominent charioteer used by so many other companies is reversed in a mirror image and completely white.[211] They would print this on the bar wrappers as well. When Peet Bros. merged with Palmolive in 1926, the new Palmolive-Peet Company of Chicago issued tokens to attract consumers for their collective products, including a hexagonal Ben Hur token.[212] Ben-Hur Soap was advertised regularly through 1944, although at that time, even after the 1928 Palmolive-Peet merger with Colgate, it was often advertised as a Palmolive product.[213] Even later than that, in 1950 Colgate-Peet-Palmolive Company introduced a "'Ben Hur' all-purpose synthetic detergent cleaning compound."[214]

Perfume

In 1872 Andrew Jergens formed a soap company in Cincinnati.[215] Three decades later, The Andrew Jergens Company filed the name "Ben-Hur" with the Manufacturing Perfumers' Association,[216] and by 1901 retail stores began to advertise Ben-Hur Perfume.[217] Distribution seems to have been wide in that Ben Hur Sachets were sold in Hawaii in 1906.[218] However, there is a long gap in advertising between 1907 and 1919.[219] Thereafter the product was marketed with reinvigorated energy. A 1921 ad for Gold's Rexall stores in Newark describes it as "a new creation which jumped into fame over night."[220] It was usually listed as a sale-counter item among an abundance of inexpensive "toilet goods," as they were often categorized during that period, and it was sold in a variety of sizes, including perfume nips and 2-dram bottles.[221] But according to a 1922 distributor's catalog, Ben Hur (now without the hyphen) was categorized

Figure 10.6 Jergens sold Ben-Hur [Ben Hur] Perfume in attractive packaging throughout the 1920s.

as a "fancy package perfume." Many were elegantly presented in frosted French bottles, often with a gilt label and an embossed, frosted stopper attached by silk floss. These were packaged in a variety of arrangements and presentations in a spectrum of silk-lined, jewel case boxed sets sold as Christmas and novelty gifts.[222] The sets were advertised with such names as the "Elfin Package," "Jewel Case," and, most appropriately for a Ben-Hur product, "Victory Box."[223]

Razors
The Shumate Razor Company formed around 1900 in Austin and sold the Shumate Dollar Razor.[224] It then moved to St. Louis around 1904, the year of the World's Fair and a visiting engagement by the Klaw & Erlanger production, at which point the company began to produce a Ben-Hur straight razor.[225] They marketed it nationwide though traveling salesmen until 1920.[226] In 1920 the company changed its name to Shumate Cutlery

Figure 10.7 American and German as well as British companies manufactured Ben-Hur straight and safety razors from the turn of the century until the 1930s.

and went out of business in 1932 during the Depression. Americans also had the opportunity to purchase imported Ben-Hur razors from overseas.[227] From 1909 M. L. Brandt Cutlery, with production in New York and Germany, produced several Ben-Hur brand straight razors, including #107 of magnetic steel,[228] and a handle featuring a molded Roman motif of vines and scrolls.[229]

SHOES AND CLOTHING

Ancient Roman dress is a facet of Ben-Hur imagery that in the modern world generally signals costume togas and sandals or, appropriately modified, high fashion. Therefore Ben-Hur clothing was rare. In this era there was almost none, although that did not prevent a few clothiers, like Eph Joel in Crawfordsville in 1888 or the Gibson Bros. in Schenectady in 1894, from capitalizing on local tableaux performances, as we have seen. This was also true of accessories, but New York's J. Lynn & Company extensive 1914 catalog prominently displayed The Ben Hur Purse.[230] Just above it on the same page is the more expensive White Star Purse "called after the White Star Line of steamers" without mention of the *Titanic* disaster two years earlier. The purse is described as 3½ inches wide and made with black kid. Much more appropriate was the "Ben Hur" horsehair lap robe.[231] The date is not specifiable, but "buggy blankets" made to warm passengers in horse-drawn carriages (and early automobiles) were generally manufactured between 1890 and 1920.

There seems to have been more leeway in the shoe market. In the fall of 1896 the Boston Store of Kansas City advertised a men's Ben Hur Shoe for $1.29.[232] Not at all an ancient Roman *caliga*, the ad simply describes this as a "good quality" satin calf shoe. M. C. Frohman & Son of English, Indiana, advertised a Ben Hur men's shoe for $2.75 in 1903.[233] Though not identified as such, this seems to be the earliest example of the Ben-Hur Shoes sold and distributed by John J. Schulten & Company, an established Louisville business since 1867.[234] The earliest piece of extant Schulten ephemera listing Ben-Hur Shoes dates from the following year in the form of a text-only advertisement, but because it was mailed from Louisville to Kossuth, Indiana, we might assume that their Ben-Hur Shoes were already for sale in 1903.[235] The center of the reverse side of an extant Schulten envelope postmarked September 30, 1913, contains an ovoid engraving of the Wagner painting.[236] The following year the shoes were being sold at a substantial price ($4.50) and used to entice customers to the opening of The Louisville Clothing Store in Ewing, Indiana.[237] As if filling in a vacuum, a Ben Hur Manufacturing Company located at 493 Washington Street in Portland, Oregon, advertised an "absolutely waterproof" Ben Hur Shoe Polish in 1909.[238]

Figure 10.8 John J. Schulten of Louisville sold Ben-Hur Shoes for over a decade from approximately 1903 to 1914, freely using the Wagner painting, as on the reverse of this advertising envelope.

MODES OF TRANSPORTATION AND RECREATIONAL VEHICLES

Boats

In 1894 a writer for the *New York Tribune* dubbed one of the Harvard crew "a regular Ben Hur." Because the most memorable action sequence in the story other than the chariot race involves Quintus Arrius' Roman galley and its protagonist galley slave, the name Ben-Hur had well-established maritime claims. Not a large amount of information is available for all the boats christened *Ben-Hur*, but there were dozens of them and of many different types. They can be identified now a century or so later more or less in proportion to their size. The registration and movements of such larger vessels as paddle-wheel steamers and schooners were recorded more frequently than those of small yachts and sloops, with rowboats barely making a mark on the commercial and ephemera records. But, whereas regular sailings and disembarkations were not always noteworthy, unfortunately for their owners accidents, groundings, founderings, and wrecks were officially reported or made local headlines.

Earliest and most prominent was a stern-wheel river packet *Ben Hur*. Famed for its "sweet and pleasing" whistle, the packet's 29-year career is reasonably well attested.[239] It was built in 1887 at the Knox Boat Yard in the Harmar area of Marietta, Ohio.[240] With a wooden hull of 165-feet long,

30.5-feet wide, 4.8-feet deep, and a gross tonnage of 284, it was relatively large for river traffic.[241] Captain Sanford Cramer placed the vessel in service along the upper and lower Ohio in the Portsmouth and Cincinnati trade, the Huntington, Pomeroy, and Cincinnati trade, the Wheeling, Marietta, and Parkersburg trade, and also as an independent.[242] It carried such varied freight as coal, lumber, water pipes, and barrels of fruit.[243] "Loaded to the guards," the *Ben-Hur* was the first packet to deliver coal from Pittsburg to Cincinnati in the late fall, 1895.[244] The *Ben Hur* frequently carried passengers as well.[245] Ironically, it had a documented but tangential connection with show business, for in March, 1888, John Robinson chartered the packet for the summer to carry his menagerie and circus along the Ohio River and play a number of riverside towns.[246]

Variations in water levels along the Ohio River system created problems for a vessel the size of the *Ben Hur*. It was taken out of commission during the low-water summer season of 1890.[247] During the droughts of 1899 and 1900, it had to lay up at Parkersburg and ran aground in the Ohio River,[248] and then in 1904 it was again taken out of commission.[249] Winters presented different difficulties, as gorges suspended the packet in Pennsylvania and Ohio during January, 1903, and put it on dry ground in December, 1903.[250] In addition, the narrow straits of the river system caused several collisions, one in 1892 with the Volunteer, and another in 1898 with the Raymond Horder.[251] In 1906 it hit the tugboat *Tom Rees* No. 2, sinking one of its barges, smashing the guardrail, and "otherwise injuring the packet."[252]

The Brown Collection at the Ohio County Public Library possesses a vintage photo [#77] of the packet tied up on Water Street in Wheeling, Ohio, during the flood of 1891.[253] In June, 1909, *The Paducah Evening Sun* reported that the "*Ben-Hur*, a fine appearing packet boat" had left the upper Ohio and was bound for the upper Mississippi, and the Minnesota Historical Society preserves a photograph dated July 16, 1911, picturing the *Ben Hur* at Stillwater.[254] That summer for the Mississippi River Amusement Company of St. Paul it made excursions from Red Wing to Stillwater along the St. Croix River between Minnesota and Wisconsin.[255] At the end of the 1911 season it took a load of 2500 barrels of apples down the Mississippi, pausing at St. Louis in November and arriving at Natchez on November 26.[256] It had a new Calliope installed and served in the excursion trade first in New Orleans harbor and then along Bayou Teche. In 1912 it was sold again and spent the year in Vicksburg for the Vicksburg-Greenville trade.[257] Finally it foundered at Duckport, Mississippi, on March 20, 1916.[258]

The reader can now appreciate the following humorous story repeated in a 1906 newspaper entry:

> As they were walking along the river front approaching the [Wheeling] depot Bill saw a stern-wheel steamer plowing its way up the muddy stream. On its sides,

painted in letters large enough to be read half a mile away, appeared the boat's name, "Ben-Hur."

"Funny name for a river craft," said Bill, "Ben-Hur."

"Yep," he replied. "It does beat the very devil himself how Klaw and Erlanger advertise."[259]

From 1893 the triple-decked, side-wheel steamer *Ben Hur* traversed the dammed Colorado River's Lake McDonald in Austin, Texas.[260] The $20,000 vessel was built by the Lake Navigation Company,[261] and it was captained by Elisha P. Bartlett.[262] As many as 1500 people at a time, at a cost of 50¢ each, could cruise for three and one-half hours while enjoying dinner service, dancing, and vaudeville presentations composed and arranged by the German-born Carl William Besserer. Otherwise the *Ben Hur* shuttled over to Camp Chautauqua.[263] Several photographs and postcards of the *Ben Hur* are extant.[264] At least one of the postcards is at present viewable online.[265] One photo commemorates an 1895 excursion on the riverboat by the Stuart Female Seminary group, consisting of two dozen women, several teachers, and the Rev. John M. Purcell, the seminary president.[266] The *Austin Weekly Statesman* of May 28, 1896, waxed poetic in its description of the previous evening's excursion:

> The excursion on the steamer Ben-Hur last night was attended by about 400. It was one of the most delightful excursions of the season. The full moon shining from an unclouded sky shed its silvery rays over hill top and dale and made the winding river a glittering sheet of silver. The view from the hurricane deck of the steamer was entrancing and many spent the entire evening up there. Dancing was, as usual, the order of the evening, and many enjoyed the excursion to the limit. In addition to the large number of regular patrons in attendance, the young ladies of Stuart seminary, some thirty strong, were also on board and enjoyed the run immensely.[267]

On April 7, 1900, after five inches of rain and resultant inundation throughout the area, flood waters crested eleven feet above the dam, and the dam burst, destroying the *Ben Hur*, along with the Ben Hur wharf.[268]

A schooner named *Ben-Hur*, 130 feet in length, had a newsworthy collision with the steamer *Passaic* and a string of barges in 1890.[269] Henry McMorran of Port Huron had purchased the schooner for the recently formed [Thomas] Murphy Salvage Company. On the dark, squally night of November 8, 1890, the *Ben-Hur* had anchored in the St. Clair River, near Lake Huron, to remove the wreck of the *Tremble*, which had sunk two months earlier. The *Passaic* had already headed upstream to the lake but unfavorable weather conditions forced it to turn around and return downstream. Along the way the fourth of its barges collided with the *Ben-Hur* on the port bow and sank it. Murphy sought damages, but the case was ultimately adjudicated only partially in their favor by the New York District Court the following October.[270] Shortly after the incident the upper works were dynamited to clear the navigation channel, but the hull of the *Ben-Hur* remains on the river bottom as an attraction for local divers.[271]

Twenty-five additional vessels named *Ben-Hur* are less well attested.

The 1910 *Blue Book of American Shipping* lists a different schooner built in 1888, with a length of 81 feet and a tonnage of 84, based in Castine, Maine.[272]

The Library of Congress possesses the January 1, 1899 to June 8, 1901 account book of a tugboat named *Ben Hur*.[273]

The 1900 *Annual Report of The Operations of the United States Life-Saving Service* reported the raising of a sloop *Ben-Hur* that had capsized and sunk in Muscle Ridge Channel in Maine in April, 1900.

Other volumes report rescues of a catboat named *Ben-Hur* off Point of Woods, New York, in August, 1901, and a sloop named *Ben-Hur* that had been dragged while anchored near City Point, Massachusetts, in June, 1903, and then capsized with two boys on board (subsequently rescued) in May, 1906.[274]

Still another disaster occurred to a launch named *Ben Hur* at the St. Clair Flats near Detroit.[275] On the evening of September 5, 1905, about thirty passengers returning from a dance had to leap overboard when a drunken passenger kicked open a cock on the engine and carelessly lit a cigar and tossed a match onto the spilled gasoline. Four of the passengers drowned.

The Congressional list of *Foreign Vessels Admitted to American Registry* lists a *Ben-Hur* with a gross tonnage of 314 authorized on September 12, 1888.[276]

An 89-ton, 82-foot schooner named *Ben-Hur* was built in Phippsburg, Maine, in 1888, and a 12-ton, 40-foot steam-screw towing vessel was built in Portland, Maine, in 1889.[277]

The annual *Merchant Vessels of the United States* and Lloyd's *Register of British and Foreign Shipping* list a single-deck, 105-ton, 84-foot wooden sailing schooner named *Ben Hur*.[278] Built in 1889 in Essex, Massachusetts, and registered at Gloucester, this is the fishing vessel that wrecked off Barrington in Nova Scotia on January 1, 1890.[279] It had picked up about 45,000 pounds of halibut but ran aground, some of the crew remaining in the rigging until their rescue at daylight.

Later annuals listed a 10-ton, 49-foot sloop built in Champ, Maryland, in 1896, and a 46-ton, 76-foot, steam-powered stern-wheeler passenger ship built in Nome, Alaska, in 1906.[280]

When new kinds of engines were being developed during the first two decades of the new century, the Ben-Hur group added at least seven new vessels to the list. There were:

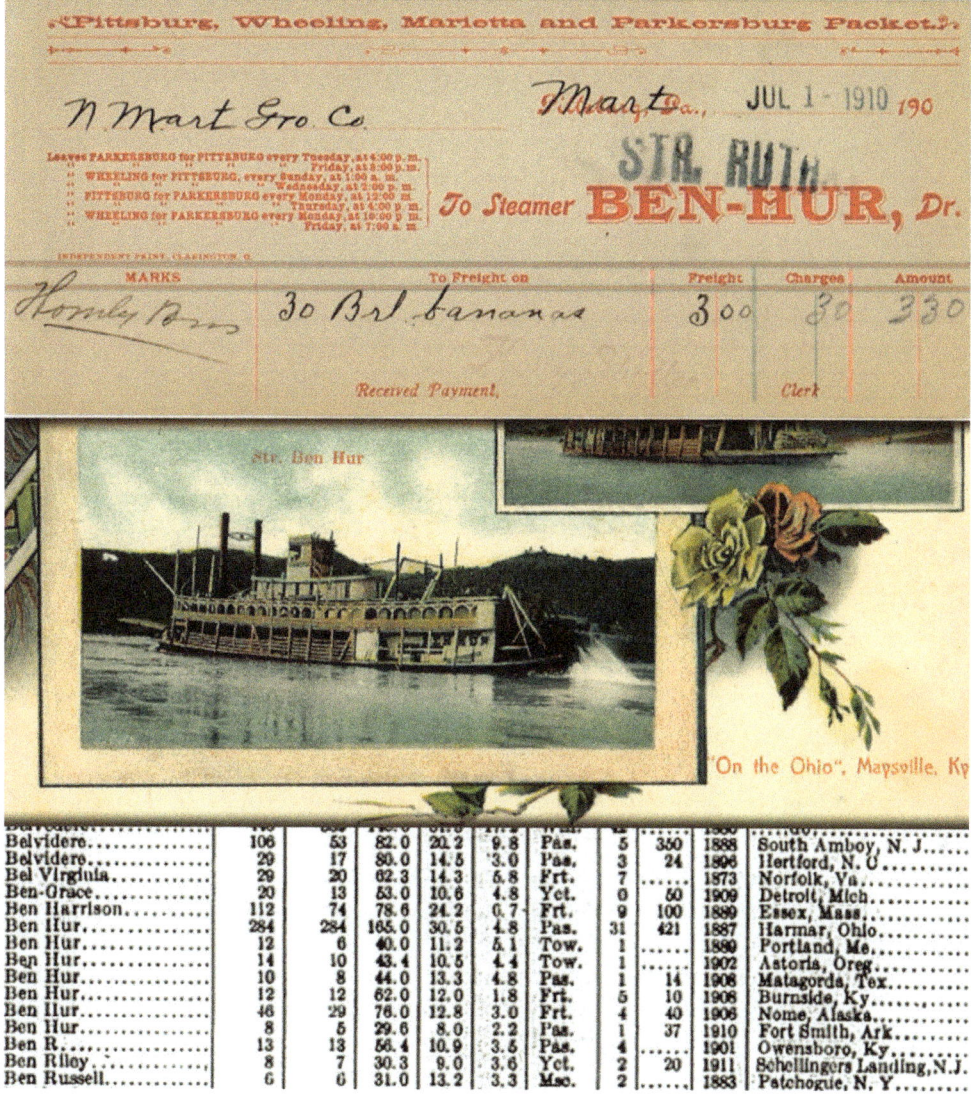

Figure 10.9 More than two dozen large boats named *Ben-Hur* carried freight and passengers or sported along America's rivers and shores for many decades.

- a 14-ton, 43-foot, gas-screw towing vessel built in 1902 in Astoria, Oregon;
- a 10-ton, 44-foot, gas-screw passenger vessel built in 1908 in Matagorda, Texas;
- a 12-ton, 62-foot, gas-powered stern-wheeler freighter built in 1908 in Burnside, Kentucky;
- an 8-ton, 30-foot, gas-powered, side-wheeler passenger ship built in 1910 in Fort Smith, Arkansas;[281]

- a 12-ton, 52-foot, gas-powered stern-wheeler passenger ship built in 1912 in Clarington, Ohio;[282]
- an 8-ton, 45-foot, gas-powered stern-wheeler towing vessel built in 1915 in Knoxville, Tennessee;
- and a 13-ton, 61-foot, gas-powered stern-wheeler passenger ship built in 1917 in Burnside, Kentucky.[283]

Just as the *Ben-Hur* phenomenon established a notable presence in new technologies developed in the musical recording industry and the production of packaged grocery-store products, so did it infiltrate early on the newly developed technology of gas-powered engines designed for the individual consumer. The Ben Hur Motor Company was incorporated in 1906 with $50,000.[284] Founded by J. Herbert Hopp, Albert A. Barrett, and C. Glenn Moats, and with its headquarters on Randolph Street in Chicago, the company designed, manufactured, and sold gasoline engines made of highly polished, close-grained iron.[285] These ranged from one to eight cylinders and from 3 to 75 horsepower and were designed for both motorboats and cars. Joining the new craze for gas-engine boats, they began advertising in just the third volume of the twice-monthly trade journal, *The Motor Boat*. The company placed an ad in anticipation of the second annual Boat Show in Chicago.[286] The ad displays a cutaway illustration of an engine cylinder, not a chariot and charioteer, but they do promote their "SPEED." The company apparently made considerable impact at the Chicago show, where they displayed models that offered "accessibility without sacrifice of strength."[287]

While the historical record by necessity catalogs usually only the hard facts about these boats named *Ben-Hur* and makes no room for connecting the name with its literary or dramatic origins, the public, as we see in Clara R. Lain's letter on behalf of Ben-Hur Coffee, probably made these associations on a regular basis. In addition to the 1894 Harvard allusion mentioned at the beginning of this section, an 1893 article in a Sunday edition of the *Boston Globe* provides some additional anecdotal testimony.[288] "Jolly Girls A-Yachting" is an unsigned piece describing the overnight voyage of three friends on an unnamed 70-footer along the Atlantic Coast. On the first morning they are resupplied with water:

> Then the "Ben Hur" comes steaming and puffing alongside and supplies us with water in answer to a bucket hung in our crosstrees as a signal. "Ben Hur!" Shades of Gen. Lew Wallace!

Appropriately, a number of smaller boats named *Ben-Hur* were used for racing.

The February, 1898, issue of *Outing* lists a *Ben-Hur* as part of the fleet of fliers sponsored by the Excelsior Ice Yacht Club of Minneapolis.[289]

One of the yachts entered in the Citizens' Yachting Regatta of Detroit in 1893 was named *Ben-Hur*.[290]

At least three of the many well-heeled individual consumers who joined the craze for gas-powered boats named theirs *Ben Hur*. One was merely listed as a sale item in *Forest and Stream*.[291]

Another is evidenced only by an unpostmarked photo postcard picturing the *Ben Hur* amidst a half-dozen small craft at the boat landing on James Lake, Indiana.[292]

The third was well publicized. Walter B. Wilde of the Illinois Valley Yacht Club entered his motorized *Ben Hur*, a 28-foot cruising launch with a 4-cycle automobile motor, in a local competition along the Illinois River near Peoria.[293] True to its namesake, this *Ben Hur* won the three-mile Senachwine Trophy Cup in June, 1907. Although the *Ben Hur* did not fare as well in the first annual 33.7-mile Webb Endurance Race, it should be noted that none of the other thirty-nine entrees listed were named after a fictional character of popular literature. The monthly periodical, *Fore 'N' Aft*, also covered this race and printed six photographs of individual boats, including the *Ben Hur*.[294]

Two years later, motorboat races were held on July 4 at Palacios, Texas.[295] Although none of the entrants piloted a racer named *Ben Hur*, forty spectators were carried to Palacios from the town of Matagorda on the aforementioned gas-screw passenger *Ben Hur* built in Matagorda in 1908. In fact, by 1909 businesses along the Matagorda Peninsula were promoting barbecues, ball games, swimming, and fishing along Ben Hur Beach, and sailboats would regularly transport tourists to the beach from across the bay.[296] By 1912 *The Texas Magazine* was promoting the nearby Ben Hur Inn,[297] and the 1924 *Yachtsman's Annual Guide and Nautical Calendar* lists as one of the country's yacht clubs the Ben Hur Beach and Boat Club of Matagorda.[298]

Lastly, it will come as no surprise to read that Henry Wallace, the general's son and heir, owned a boat named *Ben-Hur*, but even this might have passed unnoticed except that in 1920 a gale forced the motor launch onto the rocks on Burt Lake, Michigan.[299] Aboard were Wallace, the wife of Judge Kenesaw Mountain Landis, and fifteen other guests, all of whom were forced to wade ashore and telephone for dry clothing and transportation.

Trains

Trains, the most prevalent form of intercity transportation from before the time Lew Wallace wrote his novel until the predominance of the automobile a decade or two after his death, were an important component of the *Ben-Hur* phenomenon. According to the tradition discussed earlier, *Ben-Hur: A Tale of the Christ* was born on a train. Wallace, and many after him, frequently related the story that it was his encounter with Robert Ingersoll in 1876 on a train from Crawfordsville to Indianapolis that inspired him to write the novel itself. Three to four decades later, many newspapers regularly reported on the movement of the many train cars that carried the machinery, props, costumes, animals, cast, and crew of the Klaw & Erlanger *Ben-Hur* from venue to venue. A report like "Ben Hur Passes South" in the *Los Angeles Herald* helped sell tickets by calling the assemblage of thirteen cars "the largest theatrical train that has ever passed through Los Angeles."[300] The arrival of the train was reported in local papers,[301] some of which referred to a Ben Hur "special" train,"[302] a designation sometimes used also for the hundreds of excursion trains scheduled specifically to bring audience members from smaller cities and towns to the urban venues of the Klaw & Erlanger production, or a train that was carrying notable individuals from smaller localities to a nearby city to see a performance, not to mention the trains scheduled specifically to bring Ben Hur Shriners to meetings, conventions, and other excursions.[303] As with some of the Ben-Hur boats that collided, ran aground, or sank, the "Ben Hur Special Train" carrying the Klaw & Erlanger company from Portland to Seattle made local front page news on January 24, 1909, when it crashed into a freight train at Castle Rock, Washington, turning one of the freight cars "into kindlingwood" and tossing its cargo of flour and feed, household furniture, and livestock down an embankment.[304] *The Seattle Star* reported that the "monster Ben Hur special train" pulled into the Union depot eight hours late "a little worse for a collision at Castle Rock."[305] Subsequently several photocards of the incident were circulated.[306]

Fittingly in two respects, there was also a Ben-Hur train line that represented a new technology, and it ran to and from Crawfordsville. The invention of the electric traction motor in 1895 allowed for a network of interurban lines connecting rural and smaller towns in Ohio and Indiana.[307] In 1907 the Indianapolis, Crawfordsville & Western Traction Company opened up a direct line from Indianapolis through Crawfordsville all the way to the Illinois state line. The section between Indianapolis and Crawfordsville was known as the "Ben-Hur Route." The line was heavily used, especially to carry passengers to the most famous race in America at the time, the Indianapolis 500. For the 1914 race, forty-eight cars were readied to carry fans to the venue in Indianapolis.[308] In 1919 they used fifty cars.[309] And even more so than with the Ben-Hur Coffee and the "Jolly Girls A-Yachting" essay, the Indiana customers of the Ben-Hur line were adamant about making the association between the interurban and their local literary hero. Shortly after the line was sold in 1912 to the Terre Haute, Indianapolis & Eastern Traction Company, T. H. I. & E. officials decided to remove the name Ben-Hur from the cars.[310] It was not just passengers who objected. The Commercial Club of Crawfordsville also investigated the feasibility of boycotting the company's freight service. According to the reporter in the *Indianapolis Star*, part of the anger directed at the company derived from the fact that the tracks passed directly in front of the recently deceased Wallace's house:

The tracks pass the home of Gen. Lew Wallace on Wabash Avenue who was the author of "Ben-Hur." The book title has also been used by several manufacturing concerns here and the citizens have made an effort to maintain the connection between the well-known novel and the name of the city.

The decision was reversed, and the line did not close until 1930. Not only do extant photos of abandoned cars display the label BEN-HUR, but the car pictured in William Helling's book on Crawfordsville was a special chair car that bore the name "Esther."[311]

Two years after the Crawfordsville line came into being, a gasoline-powered trolley named Ben-Hur was added to the Lakewood Park and Scenic Railway in Mineral Wells, Texas. 1909 was the only year it was in operation. A photograph of the trolley is available online from websites specializing in Texas history.[312]

Bicycles

The development in the mid-1880s of the modern safety bicycle with two equal-sized wheels and secure sprocket action initiated the boom in manufacturing and sales during the next decade. As traction trains provided a new means of transportation in the decades before the automobile became dominant, bicycles provided both transportation and recreation and soon became one of the most desirable consumer items in the United States. The Monarch Bicycle Company of Chicago, for instance, incorporated in 1892, sold 1200 bicycles in 1893, and 50,000 in 1896.[313] The popularity of the bicycle as a recreational means of transportation challenged the equestrian culture in particular, and here the image of Ben-Hur riding in a chariot surfaced in a newspaper comparison between the two, placing Ben-Hur as a historical figure in the realm of Napoleon and George Washington. We will see such analogies again.

> Bicycles may be very nice to ride, and they have the advantage of not needing anything to eat but a little machine oil occasionally, yet a man can never make the same impression riding on a bicycle as when mounted on a prancing steed. Then is when you think of heroes . . . imagine Napoleon on a bicycle riding to Waterloo; think of a statue of Washington mounted on a bicycle, or Ben Hur.[314]

Even Lew Wallace, now at the height of his celebrity, issued a public comment about the popularity of bicycles among women, and the *Chicago Daily Tribune* filled in the de rigeur reference to chariot racing:

> Gen. Lew Wallace says the future of the bicycle depends on the woman riders. "If the use of wheels were confined to the men," he says, "the fad might spend itself in a season. But when the women take hold of the bicycle its future is secure." Gen. Wallace believes bicycle racing will eventually supersede horse racing, but never of course chariot racing of the Ben Hur kind.[315]

By the mid-1890s there were ten million bicycles in America, and 10 percent of all newspaper and magazine advertising was being paid for by manufacturers and retailers of bicycles, parts, and accessories. From the 300 bicycle manufacturers, two Ben-Hur brands appeared on the market in 1891 and 1892. The first was manufactured by the Central Cycle Manufacturing Company of Indianapolis, the second by Luburg Manufacturing of Philadelphia. Luburg manufactured various kinds of rolling chairs and lounge chairs in the 1880s and then expanded to include folding beds, library desks, and even refrigerators and ice chests as well as baby buggies, tricycles, and bicycles.[316] They sold their manufactured goods directly to the public, thus undercutting other manufacturers. Their cross-frame Ben Hur model bicycle cost only $65, but it seems to have been retailed only in 1892 and was not widely distributed.[317] Their advertising notified the public of such safety improvements as a puncture-proof tire,[318] and, interestingly, to do this effectively they placed a magazine ad headline specifically contrary to the Ben-Hur mystique: "NEVER WON A RACE."[319]

Central Cycle's Ben-Hur had a much longer run and a wider distribution. Under the stewardship of Lucius M. Wainwright, the company began advertising the Ben-Hur Sulky Wheels in *Printers' Ink* in 1892, and by 1893 they were already recruiting agencies across the country.[320] In Utah's *The Lehi Banner*, an advertisement for The Ben-Hur Safety Bicycle with either cushion tires or pneumatic included the notice, "Agents Wanted."[321] In 1892 they sold through The A. O. Very Cycle Company in Boston and Thorsen & Cassaday in Chicago,[322] and the following year they received an order for 100 "safeties" from the Charles H. Sieg Manufacturing Company in Illinois.[323] In 1895 Davis Brothers of San Francisco boasted in large type that "We have also secured the Agency of the BEN=HUR [sic],"[324] and in 1897 H. A. Straight secured the agency for Ben-Hur bicycles in Minneapolis and St. Paul, where the year before a different Ben-Hur agency had sponsored a baseball club in the Twin City Junior Base Ball League.[325]

Here, too, the copy of most of Central Cycle's ads for their Ben-Hur did not capitalize on the racing and victory motifs, emphasizing quality instead. Assuming that the speed of Ben-Hur's chariot and his racing triumph were implicit in the brand name, the company offered its consumers the feeling that they were buying a quality safety bicycle enhanced by modern improvements.[326] A statement printed in 1895 in the *New York Times*, for instance, assured readers that their agents, the Park Row Bicycle Company, had "not heard a complaint" despite selling the Ben-Hur to customers who weighed as much as 220 pounds.[327] Nonetheless, the image attached to most of their ads was their trademarked "nameplate" reproducing a section of the Wagner painting – a halftone rendition of the featured charioteer and circus venue background.[328] Central Cycle's letterhead used a broader section of the painting depicting the two main charioteers with the name "BEN-HUR" printed at the bottom.[329] The cover

Figure 10.10 The Central Cycle Manufacturing Company of Indianapolis trademarked this circular adaptation of Wagner's painting for its Ben-Hur Bicycle logo in the mid-1890s.

of their 1897 catalog features a large watercolor enlargement of Wagner's main charioteer and three of his horses, now completely white. Most interesting was their 1896 catalogue. In an attempt to evoke the allure of the exotic and historical, the catalogue resembles the 1991 Garfield edition of Wallace's novel by having line drawings of ancient Rome and Egypt on every page snaking around illustrations of their new model bicycles. In addition to their large logo on the inside cover and a mythological Roman relief on the opposite page, the back inside cover contains a black-and-white rendition of the Checa painting.

There were suggestions of Ben-Hur racing and even wagering motifs in an ad placed in Seattle's *Trade Register* in 1896.[330] The copy in large font reads on the bottom, "Use the same judgment as if buying a horse," and on the right side, "You are safe to bet your bottom dollar on the Ben-Hur." As we have seen, Central Cycle also employed a different kind of Ben-Hur synergy in 1896, one that bypassed the novel itself and advertised both the Ben-Hur Bicycle and another Ben-Hur by-product. They did this by offering readers of such national magazines as *McClure's Magazine* and *The Review of Reviews* a free copy of John H. Cody's "Ben-Hur March" mailed in exchange for two 2¢ stamps.[331] Printed at the top of the cover page of the sheet music is a dedication to Wainwright. The center features a large, tinted version of the Ben-Hur Bicycle trademark, juxtaposing the words "Ben-Hur March" with the large image of a racing *quadriga* in an ancient circus.

This is an important point of convergence within the Ben-Hur ephemera. The lynchpin connecting Cody's Ben-Hur March, Paull's "Chariot Race or Ben Hur March," and Ben-Hur Bicycle was primarily but simply the name "Ben-Hur." The name of the novel's protagonist inspired both popular artists and commercial entrepreneurs. All of their products featured the name, while many of their advertisements bore proudly the name of the eponymous victor of one of the most famous action passages in popular American literature and the dynamic images created by European artists that were available without restriction in the United States. As we have seen with the commercial products already discussed in this chapter, one can probably presume that the potential customer regularly made these associations. Cody's "Ben-Hur March" was no exception. The cover page contains the name Ben-Hur twice, once pertaining to the musical composition, once pertaining to the bicycle company. The inside of the cover contains a full-page ad for quality Ben-Hur Bicycles, "BETTER THAN EVER." Featured is the Ben-Hur Tandem and "four elegant models" that "represent the highest stage of the art and are beyond compare." The back cover again displays in large type the name Ben-Hur and "BETTER THAN EVER." Although it was quite the fashion at the time to associate bicycles with songs – the most famous of those songs was, of course, "Daisy Bell" ["Bicycle Built For Two"] – the special commercial synergy here is relatively ambitious.[332]

In the January 28, 1896, *Intersocialities*, the newsletter of the local Y.M.C.A., Central Cycle announced the opening of a new store in downtown Indianapolis,[333] and in 1897 the company made sure to include in every ad their trademarked nameplate and the statement, "This name plate is on every genuine Ben-Hur."[334] But at the height of its expansion the company began to experience some imbalances. Problems with East Coast suppliers and its recently failed manufacturing associate in Chicago took their toll. The company even tried a different kind of advertising campaign that eliminated the chariot nameplate and instead featured the face of a mime.[335] But the fiscal problems proved insurmountable, and on July 3, 1897, the Ben Hur Bicycle Company found itself in court and placed in the hands of a receiver.[336] The receivership was discharged six months later when the entire plant, including the building, machinery, models, stock on hand, and Ben-Hur trademark, were sold to the Van Camp Hardware Company of Indianapolis, which vowed to maintain production and put a new model on the market the following year.[337] To be sure, the June 8, 1898, *Scranton Tribune* advertises a "Ben-Hur Bicycle Contest" in a local hardware store.[338] Thereafter the brand is rarely mentioned.[339] *The Seattle Star* offers a used Ben-Hur Bicycle for sale in 1909,[340] but otherwise the trail goes cold for two decades.

Roller Coasters
The novel's renowned chariot race gave the name Ben-Hur the implication of speed and the spirit of competition. For gentler folk, Ben-Hur chariots were installed as carousel rides, particularly in England in the 1890s.[341] And for the more daring, in 1908 the Ben Hur Race, a roller coaster ride, was installed along Surf Avenue in Luna Park, "the heart of Coney Island."[342] William Johnson owned the building,[343] and the reputable W. F. Mangels Company built the ride using the third-rail electric system and Westinghouse motors.[344] That it was their only construction billed as a "Double Road," suggests that it was a particularly ambitious project. A lithographed 3-inch disk, thought to be an entrance ticket, depicts two competing charioteers. The leader in the foreground drives three horses (white, black, and brown). Block lettering says: "THE MODERN BEN HUR RACERS."[345] The back gives the location on Surf Avenue near Culver Depot and depicts a large crowd of people, a huge entrance arch, and a massive roller coaster behind it. Sometimes called "The Ben Hur," the installation was demolished in 1923 when Coney's streets were widened.[346] Vintage postcards depicting the Ben Hur Race are widely available.

Ben-Hur's presence was felt nearby as well. Claude Hagen, highly regarded for his stage effects in the Klaw & Erlanger production, designed "Fighting the Flames." In describing this entertainment the June 23, 1907, *New York Tribune* inserted the name "Ben Hur" three times and made reference to the chariot race, always of interest to the public:

> In the spectacle "Fighting the Flames," at Coney Island, Mr. Hagen, the manager, has introduced one of the horses which was in "Ben Hur." Mr. Hagen constructed the mechanical effects for "Ben Hur" when it was produced at the Broadway Theatre several years ago. In "Fighting the Flames" the same effect is obtained when the engines are dashing to the burning building where the hero fireman's family is in danger as in the "Ben Hur" chariot race.[347]

Two pages later in the same issue, a pictorial article on the "Attractions at Brighton Beach" highlights a different kind of Ben-Hur-related feature.[348] There "an attraction which the management believes will please is the pictorial views showing Biblical scenes from 'Ben Hur,' the Passion Play, etc." These were stereopticon slide lectures. The reader may recall that eleven weeks earlier, on April 2, 1907, the New York Academy of Music marked the occasion of the 2500th performance of the Klaw & Erlanger *Ben-Hur* by giving patrons a copy of Wallace's novel.[349] And nearly two months after that, on May 30, 1907, 25,000 New Yorkers entered William J. Warner's Golden Gate amusement park in Canarsie by passing beneath the 100-foot entrance arch above which was a sculpture of the Ben-Hur chariot race.[350] Clearly during the spring and summer of 1907 New Yorkers could experience the *Ben-Hur* phenomenon in a number of different genres and venues. Also, this was the year in which Kalem shot their film version of *Ben-Hur* near Coney Island. A few years later, chapters of the Tribe of Ben-Hur had gatherings at Coney Island worthy of announcing or reporting in newspapers.[351]

In 1913 Kansas City installed a "'Ben Hur' Racing Coaster" at its Electric Park, "Kansas City's Coney Island."[352] This was one of the main features of the newly refurbished park. The *Kansas City Star* described the new ride as "unusually spectacular."[353] By 1915 Baltimore's River View Park also has amusements that "smack of Coney island," including the "Ben Hur Races" ride.[354] But the most famous of the Ben Hur roller coasters would turn out to be Alexander Fraser's "Ben Hur Racer" at Ocean Park near the Venice Beach area of Santa Monica, California, "the Coney Island of the Pacific."[355] In September, 1912, a restaurant fire fanned by the Pacific breezes had severely damaged Fraser's Million-Dollar Pier, an integral part of the popular amusement complexes along the Ocean Park, Venice, and Santa Monica beaches. Two years of court battles over ownership of the ocean front forced Fraser to build pilings well out into the water, but this was turned into a promotional bonanza in that patrons of the Ben Hur Racer found themselves riding as much as 100 feet above the ocean waters for well over 600 feet.[356] Designed and constructed by the William H. Labb Company in 1914, the dual-track racer ran for 4200 feet along the north side of Fraser's refurbished Ocean Park pier. A contemporary postcard printed in Los Angeles depicts the entrance of the Ben Hur Racer lit against the night-time sky.[357] Yellow and red "Ben Hur" pennants, as well as two American flags, unfurl in the wind atop the wooden

Figure 10.11 A postcard of the Ben Hur Racer at Ocean Park, California, c. 1914, preserves a night-time photograph of the entrance, electric-light chariot display, and two Ben Hur pennants.

construction as crowds mill about. Above the bandstand on the right shines a large electric sign depicting Ben-Hur and his chariot wheels illuminated by red bulbs, the horses by white bulbs. The back of the postcard identifies this as:

> Ben Hur Races (Over the Sea on Santa Monica Bay)
> The safest, fastest and most exhilarating ride ever constructed.

Unfortunately, another fire broke out on Fraser's pier in late December, 1915, and at least one third of the Ben Hur Racer was immediately destroyed.[358] Fire Chief Hubbard of Venice told the *Los Angeles Times* that a secondary fire fueled by an oil tank further destroyed the wooden structure.[359] J. W. Hughes, receiver of the Ben Hur Racer, which was owned by the Ben Hur Racing Coaster Company, soon called a meeting of his creditors and hoped to begin rebuilding immediately. No further developments were reported.

Automobiles
We noted already that the Ben Hur Motor Company of Chicago manufactured gasoline motors for both marine and automobile use. In 1916 stock was issued in Delaware for a different Ben Hur Motor Company formed in Willoughby, an eastern suburb of Cleveland at that time the second most productive car manufacturing city after Detroit. The incorporation announcement in *Motor Age* lists only the names Ferris Giles, K. M. Dougherty, and L. S. Dorsey, but the *Standard Catalog of American Cars, 1805–1942* says that L. L. Allen of Allen Motors, another Ohio manufacturer, desired to have a brand with "a more dramatic name" than his own.[360] Although the incorporation announcement specified that the company would "manufacture, sell, and deal in and with bicycles, motor cars, etc.," it immediately set about assembling medium high-end automobiles designed by B. P. Babgy and featuring a Buda motor, Bosch magnets, and a Westinghouse electrical system. Ben-Hur sold four models – a 4-passenger Cloverleaf roadster, a 5-passenger touring car, a 7-passenger touring car, and a 7-passenger sedan – ranging in price from $1875 to $2750.[361]

They introduced their cars to the industry and public at the annual National Automobile Show in New York's Grand Palace the second week of January, 1917,[362] and they also exhibited a few weeks later at the Chicago National Show.[363] As in the early years of bicycle manufacturing, there were many competitors. Nearly 100 American automobile manufacturers exhibited that year in Chicago. Attempting a different kind of enticement at the subsequent Cleveland show, the company staged a special exhibit by converting their own showrooms at 1900 E. 13th Street into a "virtual garden" decorated with trellised vines, arbors, and flowers.[364] But the original Ben-Hur theme was never lost, as evidenced by the company's emblem. This was a circle with the motto "Form – Endurance

– Speed" printed along the curve of the circumference. An image of an automobile sits atop the circle just above the name "BEN-HUR." And the rest of the interior of the circle contains a chariot racing from right to left, with horses rearing and the charioteer's cape blowing behind him. Another emblem that appears in advertisements was the name BEN-HUR resting atop four charging horses and a charioteer.[365] The Ben-Hur concept remained essential in advertising the product. At the top of an ad in the December, 1916, issue of *Motor* appears their racing chariot logo (in profile), with the motto "FORM – ENDURANCE – SPEED" surrounded by two bundles of Roman *fasces*.[366] The chariot, racing right to left in profile, is painted to look like a relief sculpture on a marble slab with two victory wreaths on the sides. At the bottom is the slogan, as if carved onto a stone scroll:

THE SPIRIT OF THE GREAT CHARIOTEER IS BACK OF THIS CAR.

As suggested by several other examples in this chapter, the public certainly inferred an association between the racing Ben-Hur and an automobile. At least the *Automobile Trade Journal* included the word "racy" in its review of the 4-passenger Cloverleaf Ben-Hur roadster.[367]

Their ad campaign, designed to attract dealers, emphasized the superiority and the high degree of quality often associated with Ben-Hur brands, and each of the four pages inserted into the January 25, 1917, issue of *The Motor Age* displayed the "Ben-Hur" graphic with four white steeds and a white-robed charioteer charging directly at the reader.[368] The graphic on the first page consumes the entire top half of the page, addressing "BEN-HUR and The Automobile Merchant."

In March, 1917, with an additional office already opened in St. Louis for the Ben Hur St. Louis Motor Company, they planned a further expansion, proposing to stockholders a capital stock increase of $5 million and the erection of two more buildings that could produce 100 cars per day as well as engine and body plants.[369] However, by May the company was in receivership, so this was the only model year for the Ben-Hur, although gear parts were still being sold more than a decade later.[370] The 1929 catalog of *Republic Quality Gears* still lists prices for seventeen gear-related parts. Even though barely 100 cars had been sold, the name lived on indirectly through their factory located along Willoughby's adjacent, eponymous Ben Hur Avenue. Immediately after the company ceased operations, the factory was used to manufacture the poisonous gas Lewisite during World War I.[371] Thereafter the site along Ben Hur Avenue was used to manufacture tires for Ford, eventually to become the Ohio Rubber Company, and finally be declared a superfund site.[372]

Even before the Willoughby version of the Ben-Hur Company was incorporated in the fall of 1916, David F. Reid, President of Chicago's recently organized Speedway Park Association, announced in April of that year that he was building several "Ben Hur" cars in preparation for the upcoming Indianapolis and Chicago endurance races.[373] The announcement in *Motor Age* made immediate use of the familiar chariot imagery:

> It is announced that the purple, white and gold banners of the Chicago Speedway Association will be carried by a racing team to be known as the Ben Hur Special, whose chariots will be three of the classiest ever put on tires in America.

Reid was secretive about the name of his engineer, but he claimed he had already designed an oscillating-valve motor capable of maintaining a speed of 125 mph. He also claimed that he would produce street versions employing the same chassis and engine.[374] *Motor Age* reported that the first Ben Hur was scheduled to race at the Chicago Speedway's 250-mile Grand American on October 14 with Louis Chevrolet at the helm, but Chevrolet was also obligated to Frontenac.[375] No matter, on race day "the Ben Hur ... was not in shape to start."[376]

In addition to mentioning frequently both of these Ben-Hur automobile concerns, the trade journal *Motor Age* also made reference to the novel itself. "Our Orient – New Mexico," an article aimed at enticing the reader to drive for pleasure in the recently ratified state, focuses on the historical atmosphere:

> There is a section with the coloring of the Orient, with a setting older than that of Babylon or Damascus, and having something of that intangible air of mystery that the Moors brought from the Far East.[377]

After two paragraphs of such enticements, the article makes reference to part of the mythology surrounding the writing of *Ben-Hur: A Tale of the Christ*:

> Those of you who have read "Ben Hur" should remember that Lew Wallace had not seen Palestine when he wrote his famous book, but drew his pictures of the Orient from the familiar surroundings of Santa Fe.

The Ben-Hur automotive spirit seems also to have affected subsidiary industries. *Motor Age* reported that even when the Ben Hur Rubber & Tire Company was acquired by a consortium in 1916, the plan was to maintain the brand name.[378] A Ben-Hur Metal Polish Company even popped up in Crawfordsville, evidenced in catalogs from 1918 to 1922.[379]

Other Ben Hur Vehicles

The Henry Ford Museum preserves a bandwagon named "Ben Hur."[380] Preceding Ford's industrial innovation and built during the horse-drawn age, this 17-foot long, 8-foot high bandwagon contains four benches with backs to hold as many as a dozen musicians with a driver. The colorfully painted sides display the name "BEN HUR," and the rear panel depicts a chariot race. According to the museum notes, this bandwagon was used originally at the 1901 Pan-American Exposition in Buffalo, then as a sightseeing bus at Niagara Falls, and then as a bandwagon in Ypsilanti. It is unknown if the Buffalo venue concurred specifically with "Ben Hur Day," August 27, 1901, in connection with the local chapter of The Tribe of Ben-Hur. An extant program from that day includes a multitude of activities ranging from traditional musical performances at the Temple of Music to "The Golden Chariots – Music by the famous $10,000 Orchestrion" to "Jerusalem and the Crucifixion, a marvelous scenic and electrical exhibition; a vial of water from the river Jordan given with every ticket."[381] Another of the many highlights of the 1901 Buffalo Exposition was Frederick Roth's sculpture, "The Chariot Race," which was depicted in the current *Harper's Weekly*.[382] Here again we see that the public perceived this as a Ben-Hur product. The print on an extant Exposition postcard says the sculpture was located in the Horticultural Exhibit area, and on the back of the postcard written in pen is "Ben Hur's Horses, Pan Am Expo."[383] Typically for the period, a Ben Hur Match Company is listed as well as an exhibitor on page 145 of the Official Catalogue and Guide.[384] Adding to this impressive convergence of Ben-Hur activities, Lew Wallace himself had been booked to speak at this same Expo. But President William McKinley was assassinated there at the Temple of Music on September 6, causing Wallace, this being the third presidential assassination in his adulthood, instead to publish an essay, "Prevention of Presidential Assassinations," in the *North American Review*.[385]

The racing component of the *Ben-Hur* phenomenon spread into different parts of the American landscape, including the home market. The 1913 Sears sale, following close upon the inception of the Parcel Post system, also coincided with a new infusion of Ben-Hur scions and mail-order campaigns. Boston's Perry Mason company was the publisher of *The Youth's Companion*, the same publication that had printed Wallace's "How I Came to Write Ben-Hur" in 1893. Now in 1912–13 they were promoting The "Ben Hur" Steel Racing Car. Advertising copy specifically targeted speed, asserting that the design of the all-steel racer was like that of "racing motorcars":

It is long, low, racy, easy to run, and very fast, being geared for speed.

Perry Mason used the allure of speed to attract members of their target demographic – boys aged eight to fourteen. Ads for the Ben Hur Racer targeted them either to purchase The "Ben Hur" Steel Racing Car, or to obtain one for free by signing up five more subscribers to *The Youth's Companion*. The headline of catchy ads placed in the magazine from 1912 into 1913 asked, "Are You the Boy?" or asserted, "We Want One Boy Owner for This Car in Every Community."[386] Collecting the largest amount of Ward-Owsley Bread labels could win a racer in Aberdeen, South Dakota.[387]

The Ben Hur Racer was sold in several parts of the country. In the Midwest Hugh Hill of Anderson, Indiana, sold the vehicle as part of his

Irish Mail line, and Perry Mason offered to pay the freight charges to any shipping office east of Colorado.[388] In their large-format, bi-fold mailer offering dealers their Hoosier velocipedes and tricycles as well as various sorts of wagons, sidewalk sulkies, and wheelbarrows, by far the largest featured item, centered on the double-wide obverse side, is the Ben Hur Racer.

Chariots

In his biography of Lew Wallace, Irving McKee remarked, "Chariot races became a part of American life – not plain chariot races, but 'Ben-Hur chariot races.'"[389] In fact, chariot races, not so much a novelty as a test of training, skill, and speed in the days of horse-drawn transportation, had taken place in American venues decades before Wallace wrote his novel. In 1853, for instance, Franconi's Hippodrome, a "restoration of the festivals, games and amusements of the ancient Greeks and Romans" included "Daring Chariot Races" for the matinee, and the "Grand Chariot Race" for the evening performance.[390] More novel were the women charioteers who in Philadelphia drew "an immense crowd" in the summer of 1866.[391] Similarly in 1874, when Lew Wallace was writing his novel, P. T. Barnum opened his Great Roman Hippodrome in New York with a number of entertainments, including a Roman chariot race "between three ladies driving two horses each, and one between two driving four horses each."[392]

In the Ben-Hur era, the Ringling Brothers show for the 1892/3 season featured a "Real Roman Hippodrome" with both two- and four-horse chariots.[393] In the same season Sells Brothers Circus introduced "The Terrific Roman 4-Horse Chariot Race" with acrobats serving as charioteers.[394] As usual there is anecdotal evidence that the public perceived these prominent chariot races as Ben-Hur races. A visitor to Sydney Australia in 1892, for instance, looked at posters advertising that evening's performance of Sells Brothers Circus and remarked:

A prominent feature of the bills was the chariot race scene in Ben Hur.[395]

"The granddaddy of them all" was the annual New Year's Day chariot race in Pasadena, California.[396] In 1902 Pasadena had hosted the first post-season college football game, but the lopsided 49-0 victory over Stanford by Michigan's undefeated, unscored-upon, "point-a-minute" squad left the 8000 spectators dissatisfied.[397] In the fall of 1903, Charles D. Daggett, that year's president of the Tournament of Roses, suggested "a Roman chariot race," arguing that the expense of hosting another Eastern football team, especially if the game was so lopsided, would be much greater than a chariot race with cash prizes of $500 or $600.[398] Daggett made it clear to the reporter for the *Los Angeles Times* that Ben-Hur was the model:

The requirements of the race will be of the strictest, relative to the war cars themselves, the costumes of the drivers and the method of racing. From start to finish the race will be run in strict conformity to the famous chariot race in Ben Hur, even to the dropping of balls as the circuit of the course is made. Such an event, if successful once, would undoubtedly become an annual event, and would prove far more popular than any bull fight or football game.

Daggett promised a regional contest that would be won by the local "champion who will stand forth for Pasadena against all comers in the four-horse chariot race, and see to it that he wins the victor's crown and the plaudits of our people."[399] It took longer than expected, but enough contestants paid the $100 deposit, and Superintendent of Streets C. C. Brown oversaw the construction of the 50-foot wide, nearly half-mile long course and a grandstand with a seating capacity of 4500.[400] As the day neared, the *Los Angeles Times* even saw fit to report the arrival of the costumes appropriate to Ben-Hur:

> Among the events of the afternoon the chariot race easily holds first place in interest. The contestants will race in the costume which has been made famous to all who have read "Ben Hur." The costumes have arrived from New York, and the drivers of the two chariots that will be in the parade will wear them.[401]

And indeed the *Los Angeles Times* not only compared the local victor, "Mac" Wiggins, to Ben-Hur and declared Pasadena superior to ancient Rome but actually lamented the fact that Wiggins was unable to race against Ben-Hur, as if the latter had been a real person who lived and raced in ancient Rome:

> Yet, glorious as it all was – the blue skies, the ravishingly beautiful girls, there is still the shadow of one great regret hovering above it, and that is that Ben Hur himself could not have been there – there in the flesh and his abbreviated toga to try it out against Wiggins. Oh, but wouldn't that have been a show for your life; to settle once and for all that old claim that the men of former days were superior in prowess to our men of today? Ben Hur and Wiggins on the same track . . .
> Alas, however the question must forever remain unsettled. Ben Hur is long since commingled with the dust of his ancestors and Rome is nothing now but a place of ancient art galleries and faded memories. On the other hand, Pasadena is flourishing like a green bay tree, and it stands to back Wiggins against the world.[402]

The following year the prize money was raised to $1000, and the Tournament of Roses Association adopted as their letterhead a locally designed image of a Roman charioteer and his chariot amidst roses, palms, and mountains.[403] They also sponsored a parade of the chariot contestants to Los Angeles.[404] Ticket prices for the races, now held in three heats, ranged from 50¢ to $2.00, costing as much as tickets for the Klaw & Erlanger *Ben-Hur*.[405] On race day in 1905, one of the chariot teams ran out of control, and when a local cowboy came to the rescue, the *Times* not only called him a hero but declared in the secondary headline "Cowboy Plays Finer Part Than Ben Hur's in the Wild Chariot Race."[406] Especially with this added excitement, the event was so successful that a local businessman hoped "to enlist the enthusiasm of several of the Ben Hurs" to race on Washington's birthday.[407] Instead, in mid-March Wiggins challenged P. B. Michel, 1905's victor, to a grudge match on a longer course.[408] For 1906 the PTRA adapted the Checa painting – surrounded by roses – for their advertising poster, expanded the number of entries, the grandstands, and the size of the track, and they negotiated special travel arrangements with Santa Fe and other railroads, advertising in national magazines.[409] An ad placed in *Harper's Weekly* in December enticed visitors to take the Santa Fe's California Limited across the continent "to see many unique floral features and chariot racing."[410] The copy is set against a watercolor of lofty mountains issuing forth the racetrack, the filled grandstands, and two *quadrigae* racing directly towards the reader. In reviewing the spectacle here, too, Santa Fe employees were told:

> For a few hours the excited multitude apparently lived again the time of Caesar and Ben Hur.[411]

Even an ad for *The Pacific Garden* journal, "devoted to the art of gardening," featured a disk depicting "ROMAN CHARIOT RACES" at the "Grand Floral Pageant" of the Tournament of Roses, 1911.[412]

The 1908 races had "a thrilling accident, very like the one in Ben Hur."[413] The *Times* used the Ben-Hur imagery several times in their coverage this year because Michel was disqualified for steering his chariot into his opponent's "using the tactics made famous by Ben Hur." Similarly, when there was a mishap during one of the 1912 heats before a crowd of some 30,000, the *Times* vividly described the scene in the first paragraph of a two-page description accompanied by three photographs:

> When Ben-Hur, tearing at the bits of his Roman steeds to avert a collision with the racing chariot of his proudly-sneering rival while straining, white-faced Roman patricians looked anxiously down at the tragic scene before their eyes, the thrills that stirred them were no more keen than those which shook the 30,000 people gathered at the Pasadena Tournament Park, when C. E. Post, young son of a Chicago millionaire, striving his every nerve to carry his colors to victory, ran his chestnut four full tilt into the chariot of Albert Persons.[414]

In 1914 the *Times* writer mused over two anachronisms that contrasted with "the traditions of Ben Hur":

> The chariot races always are the chief feature of the afternoon events at Tournament Park. The costumes of the charioteers – with the exception of the goggles – and the chariots and the management of the race are true to the traditions of Ben Hur. When an airship appeared on the scene during the Roman chariot races there was a pleasing blending of the classic and the cosmopolitan.[415]

The 1915 chariot races also drew an audience of over 20,000.[416] In 1916, a few years after the formation of the NCAA, Pasadena opted to return to college football, even though rainy weather kept the crowd down to 7000

Figure 10.12 Between 1904 and 1915, the Pasadena New Year's Day "Roman Chariot Races" attracted crowds of 20,000 or more, consistently evoking the name Ben-Hur and its familiar imagery.

that year. The year after the chariot races were terminated, a 1917 issue of *Popular Mechanics* included a California photograph of "an impersonator of Ben Hur" clad in a Roman toga standing on a chariot pulled by four motorcycles elaborately decorated with flowers and greenery.[417]

The historical record would continue to show that chariot racing in Pasadena from 1904 to 1915 was associated with Ben-Hur. The same year John W. Wood's history of Pasadena commented, "It was a 'Ben Hur' episode brought down to date."[418] As the decades passed, retrospectives on the heralded annual Rose Bowl football game would frequently include recollections of the "Ben Hur" chariot races in Pasadena.[419] In fact, the spectators were standing on them: the bleacher floor of the original Rose Bowl stadium, opened in 1922, was made of the wood from the chariot race grandstands.[420] And one source adds that revenue from the chariot races helped fund the building of the stadium.[421]

Quite frequently the simple mention of horses and racing in a newspaper inspired the writer to make reference to *Ben-Hur*. A lawsuit involving an altercation at a horse race led the editors of the *National Corporation Reporter* to summarize the pertinent actions of the case by identifying them with those in the novel.

> **Intimations of Ben Hur** – Ben Hur – the famous chariot race – the breaking of the wheel – the winning of the race – are all brought back to mind in the case of Carleton v. Fletcher, 85 Atlantic reporter, 395, a horse race case. In the 2:20 race three horses were entered, Kohl, Sidnut and Roanbird. ... As they went down the turn a modern Ben Hur, Roanbird's driver, touched her with the whip and swung up against Sidnut's wheel and on to his legs, causing him to break and run. Thereupon Roanbird's driver pulled away. ... Upon this occurring, Sidnut's driver appeared before the judges and attempted to explain the incident according to the facts as claimed by him. As a reward for his explanation he was knocked down by "Ben Hur" in the presence of the judges and beaten and bruised until he was unconscious.[422]

The story was syndicated in newspapers as well as volumes of court reporters.[423]

Electric and Print Chariots

It was not only the speed of a chariot but also the size and spectacle that connected the public with *Ben-Hur*. A 1944 Ford Motor Company ad placed prominently in *Life*, *Popular Mechanics*, and a number of other national magazines illustrated a street crowd looking up at a large billboard with a roadster zooming along an open road. Below, the Ford motto, "WATCH THE FORDS GO BY," is spelled out by light bulbs.[424] The headline above the ad says:

> AS EXCITING AS THE RACE IN "BEN HUR"!

The rest of the copy vividly describes the June night in 1908 when Ford, as part of its preparations to introduce the Model "T" to the public, erected a "spectacular sign with 2000 twinkling light bulbs" atop the Wonderland [Temple Theatre] in Detroit:

> "It's exciting as the race in 'Ben Hur'," said an onlooker. The newspapers thought so, too.[425]

Four years before the installation of the large electric sign sitting atop the bandstand next to Ocean Park's Ben Hur Racer, there were crowd-dazzling electric signs of racing chariots in New York and Detroit. The earliest and largest was supported by a structure 90-foot wide, 72-foot high on the roof of New York's Hotel Normandie in Herald Square.[426] Elwood E. Rice and his Rice Electric Display Company sequenced 20,000 incandescent lamps, ranging in size from 2 to 32 candle power, and connected by a reported ninety-five miles of wire to create a 20-foot tall charioteer holding the reins as his horses appear to be galloping around the *spina*, and behind him to the left and further up the track his competitors approach in pursuit. This electrical *trompe l'œil* even seemed to create spirals of dust swirling up from the track, and the horses' manes and tails as well as the Roman's robes seem to blow in the wind.[427]

When the display was lit for the first time on June 18, 1910, the *New York Times* called it "A Roman chariot race,"[428] as did a feature piece in *Scientific American* and a 1911 *National Magazine* article singing the praises of the proliferation of electric signs in America's largest cities:

> Perhaps the most interesting electrical display advertising is that of the animated sign, and the perfection which has already been attained is astonishing. Chicago has a number of very attractive animated signs, but the Chariot Race display on the Hotel Normandie, New York, is perhaps the most elaborate and most interesting conception which has so far been the product of the electrical sign designer's brain.[429]

Perhaps Rice and the print reporters and publicists were too well aware that the previous year the local Circuit Court of Appeals had upheld the legal finding that Kalem had violated Wallace's copyright by creating a version of *Ben-Hur* in "moving pictures," so they carefully avoided the use of the name. But the July 14, 1910, *Printers' Ink* saw the sign for what it was, describing the "Ben Hur sign" as being without rival.[430] Two months later the *Cincinnati Enquirer* made a more specific identification with the Klaw & Erlanger chariot race just below a printed photograph of the sign:

> The picture is that of a chariot race, very similar to the one enacted in the stage version of "Ben Hur," and it is made to move in much the same manner.[431]

In 1914 the *Electrical Review and Western Electrician* also described the sign as "the chariot race scene from Ben Hur, which was the distinguishing feature and the principal attraction of a very large electric advertising display in New York City."[432] And certainly much of the public perceived it this way. A Yonkers resident sending a postcard postmarked on August 22, 1913, and depicting a daytime view of the sign on the front of the card and labeled on the back simply as "THE GREAT WHITE WAY, BROADWAY, NEW YORK CITY," wrote:

> This is Ben Hur's chariot race on an electric sign. It looks like the real thing when lighted up.[433]

Like so many Ben-Hur inspired products and by-products, the sign was spectacular and wildly popular. The *Times* reported that the police had difficulty keeping order among the thousands who had gathered to see the display. *Printers' Ink* said, "This 'flaming chariot' sign is the most unique and intrinsically interesting illuminated sign yet devised."[434] And, like so many Ben-Hur inspired products and by-products, the sign also served a commercial purpose and earned steady revenue. The large panel between

Figure 10.13 Contemporary with Pasadena's live chariot races, spectators recognized Elwood Rice's "A Roman Chariot Race" atop the Hotel Normandie in Herald Square, one of the first icons of "The Great White Way," as "Ben Hur's chariot race on an electric sign," as described on one of these postally used cards from 1913.

the header and the chariot displayed illuminated advertising messages in 4- to 5-inch letters, changing every fifteen seconds and cycling over a period of three quarters of an hour.[435]

By 1911, a few years after the Ford Model T display had been erected on the Temple Theatre, Detroit enjoyed another large electric sign.[436] This one was located opposite the Pontchartrain Hotel in the business district nearby the Campus Martius – an appropriate Roman place name for a chariot installation. Again attuned to commerce, Rice announced his plan in early 1912 to turn the light panel above "the famous Chariot Race" into a Convention & Auto Bulletin, that is, a message board that would update convention information for visitors.[437]

Of course local lore recognized the sign as representing the Ben-Hur race. A night-time postcard postmarked August 25, 1914, captures the image of the sign that reaches some four stories above the fifth floor of the building on which it rests.[438] Above the charioteer, racing from left to right, additional lights spell out: "IN DETROIT LIFE IS WORTH LIVING." The printed identification on the back of the card reads:

> The second largest electric sign in the world showing the Chariot Race in a scene from Ben Hur, where thousands gaze on it day and night.

The printed identification on the back of a postcard depicting a daytime scene and postmarked 1920 describes it this way:

> The electric sign on top of building [sic] is one of the finest in the west and when in action gives a description of the Chariot Race of Ben Hur.[439]

The Detroit sign also represented a *Ben-Hur* triple synergy. A newspaper anecdote about the manager of the Detroit Opera House said that he jokingly claimed to have arranged the sign to advertise the visit of the Klaw & Erlanger production during the 1911–12 season but then explained that it was actually an advertisement for Ben-Hur Cigars![440]

Chariots appeared also on a variety of printed and painted surfaces during this period. When the city of Wichita built its enormous 5000-seat Forum, the $1200 fire-curtain was painted with an image of a chariot race adapted from Wagner.[441] Checa was the model for the curtain of the Metropolitan Theatre in St. Paul.[442]

CONSTRUCTION AND INDUSTRIAL COMPANIES

Several dozen additional Ben-Hur companies, brands, and products developed in the late nineteenth century or the first few decades of the twentieth. These need not be described in great detail, and some of them are too obscure for even modern research techniques to identify securely. On the other hand, a major company like Ben Hur Construction is reasonably well documented because of its long-lasting success, and they have a company history tab on their website. Yet what is really relevant here about such a large and successful company is both simple and quintessential: (1) at his wife's instigation W. N. Brown attended a performance of the Klaw & Erlanger production in St. Louis in 1908 and admired the protagonist so much he named the company after him, (2) Ben Hur Construction has become a multi-million dollar company with offices in four states, (3) it still thrives more than a century later, and (4) the logo on their website is a stylized chariot, horse, and helmeted charioteer.[443]

Mining
The most populated single category of Ben-Hur business concerns was mining, and these mining companies, mines, and claims were located in many different states. Ben Hur Leasing Company of Spokane, Washington, began mining gold at the Republic Mine in 1897 or 1898.[444] Stock certificates still exist from the Ben Hur Mining Company in the Ojo Caliente area of what was then still the Territory of New Mexico, still in the shadow of Lew Wallace, which filed for incorporation with $1.5 million in capital stock on April 14, 1898.[445] Colorado had at least two, the Ben Hur Mining and Milling Company, which issued stock as early as 1901,[446] and the Ben Hur Gold Mining Company in Teller County, in operation by at least 1905.[447] Perhaps related or perhaps a third Colorado concern, the Grass Roots Gold Developing & Mining Company of Denver claimed in April, 1906:

> We Are Sacking Ore on the Ben Hur Claim[448]

South Dakota had a Ben Hur gold and silver mine in the Bald Mountain area by 1904.[449] Utah's Boston Consolidated opened two Ben Hur tunnels in 1905.[450] Frank Bell incorporated the Ben Hur Mining Company of Saltese, Montana, in April, 1907, and the company operated until 1925 and was not finally dissolved until 1940.[451] The Ben Hur section of the Fife Mines in British Columbia were in operation in 1910.[452] Volume 14 of *The Mines Handbook* lists both the Ben Hur Divide Mining Company and the Ben Hur Extension Mining Company in Tonopah, Nevada, founded in 1918 and 1919, and the North Ben Hur Divide Mining Company in Goldfield, Nevada.[453] Frank C. Schrader's 1923 U.S. Geological Survey of the Jarbridge mining district of Nevada also described the earlier Ben Hur Prospect gold and silver mine in Eklo, Nevada.[454] Oklahoma had at least two mines, the Ben Hur Fairview Mining Company near Guthrie in operation by 1911,[455] and the Taylor Ben Hur Coal Company near Henryetta founded in 1927.[456] The latter was involved in a legal dispute as late as 1957.[457]

Because of the nature of the mining industry, these companies had little reason to launch an advertising program, let alone sport a chariot logo. However, the Ben Hur Mining Company of New Mexico certificates contain an illustration of the three Wise Men in the desert,[458] and the upper portion of extant Ben Hur Mining and Milling Company stock certificates from Colorado, dating from March 6, 1901, features a copy of the main Wagner *quadriga*.[459] In 1915 the Meister Coal Mining Company of Bridgeport, Ohio, advertised "Ben-Hur Genuine Black Band Splint – The Big Blocky Coal," taken from their mine in Kanawha County, West Virginia.[460] The upper half of the poster illustrates a straining team of horses – Checa's version but with two white and two black horses – pulling its charioteer over and above the large, red, block-lettered "BEN-HUR" name.

Petroleum Exploration
There have been at least six Ben Hur companies drilling, refining, or selling oil and gasoline. Newspaper searches alone have identified the first Ben Hur Oil & Gas Company. The earliest notice records that Emil W. Luffer filed for incorporation in Clarington, Ohio, in 1911.[461] Several 1913 want ads clarify that the company had located its headquarters in Chickasha, Oklahoma.[462] These want ads, placed as far afield as in the *Atlanta Constitution*, were for live agents to sell stock in the company, claiming nearly 1000 acres in the Comanche oil field and promising $50 to $100 per week. As we will see, additional Ben Hur oil companies would emerge decades later.

ADDITIONAL PRODUCTS, BRANDS, AND COMPANIES

Hardware
Hardware stores at the turn of the century were expanding their inventories with stocks of sporting goods equipment that had become increasingly popular. According to a contemporary article in *The Atlanta Constitution*, this included "fine fishing tackle, baseball goods and athletic supplies."[463] The reader will find a number of sports teams bearing the Ben-Hur name, and at least one baseball glove, made in Indianapolis, has surfaced with the name BEN HUR at the base of the pocket.[464]

Fly reel collectors have safeguarded more information about William H. Talbot's Ben Hur fly reels. Talbot worked out of Nevada, Missouri, from 1895 to 1913, and his reels, made of aluminum and German silver and strengthened by Talbot's patented design and "shouldered" pillars, and accordingly priced at $10, remain much prized for their durability and workmanship even today. [465] At a 2007 auction one reel sold for $8900.[466] The ad for the Ben Hur fly reels in the 1907 Abercrombie & Fitch catalogue solidified two different connections to *Ben-Hur* and Lew Wallace.[467] The ad includes an apparently unsolicited testimonial from a customer, Ben P. Mayer:

Your reel is well named, carrying out strength and durability, as the strength and endurance is portrayed in men of the era General Lew Wallace so illustriously pen-pictures in "Ben Hur." Besides, I understand General Wallace is a great lover of fly fishing.

In fact, in 1891 Lew Wallace had patented a fishing rod, and the *Indianapolis Star* later reported on a Ben-Hur Fishing Club, but Wallace's invention was never named "the Ben Hur."[468]

In more traditional retail interests, shortly after Van Camp purchased Central Cycle's brand of Ben-Hur Bicycle in the late 1890s, they issued a line of Ben-Hur sewing machines. An undated catalog of Ben-Hur Sewing Machines issued by Van Camp Hardware & Iron Co. is listed in WorldCat, but an extant advertising card bears a postmark of July 6, 1901.[469]

The George Worthington Company, Cleveland's pioneer retailing firm established in 1829, also sold products with a Ben-Hur brand until it became exclusively a wholesaler and discontinued its retail business in 1920.[470] Worthington made effective use of Ben-Hur imagery. Their letterhead in 1912 featured a 2-inch, oval emblem filled with the main charioteer of the Wagner painting.[471] At the four cardinal points are "The – G – W – Co," and printed at the bottom along the curve of the oval is "BEN HUR." This emblem is labeled as a registered trade mark, and beneath the emblem are listed:

BEN-HUR LINES
BLANKETS-ROBES
HARNESS-WHIPS

Appropriately, the company issued a 55-page catalogue of "BEN HUR – HARNESS AND WHIPS for 1908/9.[472] An enlarged version of the trademarked emblem sits prominently in the center of the cover. The 1941 Geo. Worthington Company Distributors Catalog still offers a Ben Hur Team Harness, marked by the familiar Ben-Hur chariot logo.[473]

Fencing

To corral Ben-Hur's horses one would need a wire fence, or at least it was so advertised in an oversized advertising card issued by the Page Woven Wire-Fence Company of Adrian, Michigan, in the 1890s. The front of the card has two chromolithographed images. On the top is an innovative image labeled "Ben-Hur Chariot Race." A charioteer is driving four white horses towards a wire fence. The bottom image depicts the horses crashing against the fence, their forward progress immediately halted, and the charioteer being flung over their heads. The caption here says, "Up against it." The back of the card contains extraordinary copy that both highly praises and yet utterly rewrites the story of the chariot race. It begins with a large headline, "Down Eros, Up Mars!"

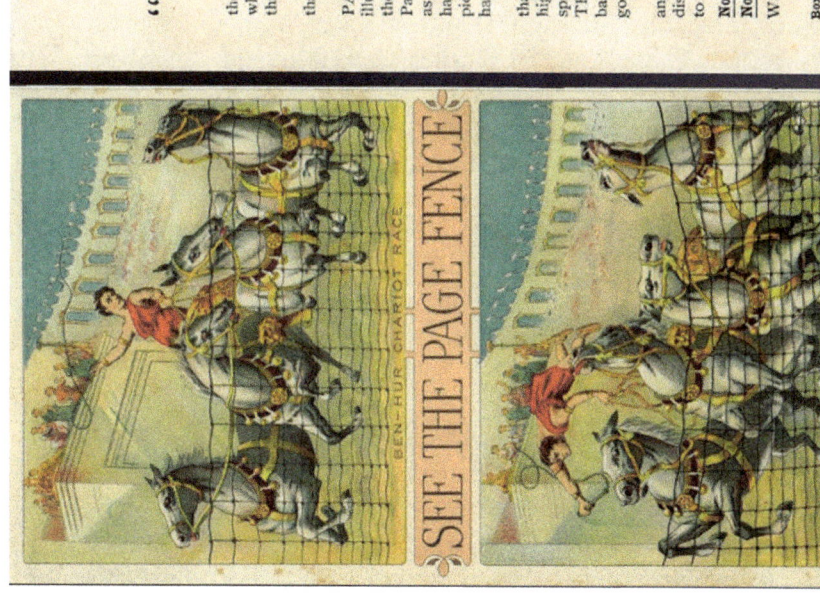

Figure 10.14 This 1890s advertising card for the Page Fence depicts a surprising variant to the Ben-Hur chariot imagery on the front. On the reverse is printed: "Down Eros, Up Mars!" from *Ben-Hur*, "the most fascinating book ever written."

It has been said that the book "Ben-Hur" is the most fascinating book ever written, and its whole teaching has caused the civilized world to think profoundly.

The Chariot Race has been more talked of than any other horse race in the world.

We have taken the liberty of incorporating a PAGE 13-Bar, 58-inch STOCK FENCE into the illustration of the Ben-Hur Race, to show what the result would have been, provided that such a Page Fence had been stretched across the course, as shown in the upper picture, and how it would have appeared a moment later, in the lower picture. Neither the team nor the fence would have been hurt.

If Ben-Hur's Arabs and Chariot had struck that PAGE STOCK FENCE at the moment of highest speed, the elasticity in those long coil spring horizontal wires would have let out, and then THEIR RECOIL would have thrown the horses back on their haunches, and the driver would have gone into the air, as shown in the picture.

The story of Ben-Hur is wonderfully fascinating and interesting to its readers. The original and distinct features of Page Fence should be interesting to any man who thinks, and has use for fencing.

Clocks and Watches

In the late 1910s the Western Clock Company of LaSalle, Illinois, manufacturer of Westclox clocks, had introduced their Big Ben and Baby Ben models of wind-up alarm clocks named after London's famous Big Ben.[474] In mid-February, 1927, they complemented these earlier Ben products with a Ben Hur model, their first clock with a metal base.[475] That year both newspaper retail ads as well as the wholesale catalogs of the W. Bingham Company of Cleveland (715) and The Smith Bros. Hardware Company of Columbus offered a choice of a white plain or a black luminous dial with a nickel case.[476] By the fall of 1928, the newspaper and magazine ads as well as the Belknap Hardware & Manufacturing Company catalog were also offering the Ben Hur in cases painted in Nile green, old rose red, and blue.[477] The 1930 catalog (1276) of the Blish, Mize & Stillman Hardware Company of Atchison, Kansas, pictured a full-page color ad. The 1931 Frankfurth Hardware Company catalog offered an orchid color as well, as did the Shapleigh Hardware Company of St. Louis,[478] but Westclox ceased selling the Ben Hur the next year.[479]

In August, 1926, during the release of the MGM *Ben-Hur*, the Gruen Watch Company of Cincinnati, one of the largest in the country, sold a wrist attachment for their watches known as the Ben Hur bracelet.[480] Manufactured by Wadsworth, this was "a perfectly smooth, gold-filled, single-piece flexible metal strip with a concealed clasp." A local Pennsylvania newspaper ad depicts a crudely drawn charioteer raising his whip over two galloping horses' heads.[481] The copy makes the connection clear:

> The Ben Hur Band once drew the eyes of thousands to a winning arm. Nowadays the *new* Ben Hur Band on a Gruen strap is also widely admired – for both style and beauty.

Figure 10.15 Westclox produced the Ben Hur model wind-up alarm clock as a companion to their Big Ben and Baby Ben in 1927, contemporary with the New Haven Clock Company's Ben Hur Dollar Pocket Watch. Bulova advertised their Ben Hur wristwatch in the late 1930s, as did Elgin.

Zell Bros. Jewelers & Platinumsmiths placed a much more elaborate ad in the *Oregonian*.[482] Four columns wide, the upper third of the nearly full-page length, delicately bordered presentation depicts in bold halftone Wagner's main charioteer on the right. To the left are tall ancient candelabras on either side of an entrance tunnel, emerging from which is a huge rendition of a state-of-the-art Gruen Quadron Watch with its Ben Hur Band. On the opposite side of the tunnel arch lies a chariot wheel drawn much in the manner of the Garfield edition etchings.

The New Haven Clock Company, which had been in existence even before the Civil War, manufactured a non-jeweled Ben Hur Dollar Pocket Watch in the 1920s.[483] Ben Hur was clearly written in cursive on the dial, but neither it nor the case bore any logo.

Arcade and Board Games
Four different manufacturers have produced Ben-Hur models in the mechanical games category. The Caille Brothers Company of Detroit belongs to the era under discussion. They introduced their Ben Hur slot machine in 1908, advertised as one of "the smallest slot machines with automatic payout."[484] This wheel-type machine was designed as a tabletop model standing only 21 inches high. The International Arcade Museum reports that a Caille Brothers catalog suggested to potential buyers living in towns where taller machines were prohibited that this smaller type machine could be easily whisked away and hidden under the counter if necessary.[485] Nothing on the machine seemed to convey the imagery appropriate to the Ben Hur name.

There have also been a number of board games and puzzles, manufactured and sold mostly in connection with the two MGM films. But long before those *Ben-Hur* tie-ins, McLoughlin Brothers, Inc., America's leading children's book and game publisher since 1828, sold a Ben Hur game in 1890.[486] It was designed for two to four players and came with a large board, four wooden pawns, and two spinners. The New York Historical Society preserves an example of Chaffee & Selchow's "Ben Hur, or The Chariot Race," issued in 1899.[487] This one consisted of a board chromolithographed with a four-lane track "that represents the interior of a Roman arena with chariot drivers around the track and spectators in the stands." The box cover depicted a chromolithographed charioteer with a winged helmet, a second driver, and four black horses set amidst a circus filled with spectators. Emil Voellmy's "The Ben Bur Chariot Race – A New And Absorbing Game" appeared among magazine advertisements in 1911.[488] It consisted of simply a full-page oval filled with forty-eight orange and white, numbered rectangles arranged around four tracks.

Also in this category belongs a set of Movie Souvenir Playing Cards displaying the "53 most prominent Stars in Filmdom," made by the M. J. Moriarty Card Company of Cincinnati, Ohio.[489] Individual black-and-white photos of the faces of early film stars like Blanche Sweet and Ruth Roland replace the usual geometrical arrangements of suits on the front of the fifty-two cards, with Charlie Chaplin as "The Tramp" on the joker card. The back of each card contains a color reproduction of the Checa chariot race, almost an exact duplicate of the Sears advertising postcard that had been widely distributed three years earlier. Two of the actors used within have *Ben-Hur* connections: William Farnum, who played Judah in the Klaw & Erlanger production, and George Walsh, who would be initially cast for the Judah role in the 1925 MGM film.

Lesser Manufacturers and Products
Other commercial enterprises left a lesser imprint. These are businesses or products that emerge only for a moment, or leave behind nondescript ephemera, and they do not generally belong to the same categories as other items. They include the following:

– There have been at least three different Ben-Hur composition books. The first contains "Useful Information" on the back cover that lists as the superior example of velocity the speed of a steamboat, making the date no later than approximately 1905.[490] The cover depicts two filleted Ben-Hur profile medallions facing each other. The second is datable by its contents to 1916, the cover featuring a racing *quadriga* in a circus setting, albeit running counterclockwise.[491] We also hear that the Tayloe Paper Company, established in 1923, issued a Ben Hur Composition Book of "extra quality," distributed in at least Indiana.

– The Ben-Hur Manufacturing Company, Limited, of Toronto, was incorporated with $25,000 in 1903.[492]

– The Ben Hur Mfg. Co. of Crawfordsville advertised Clark's Hog House and a cafeteria feeder for hogs in a Midwestern agricultural trade magazine in the 1910s. These advertisements span from 1914 to 1919.[493]

– A pattern of Ben-Hur sterling, a Whiting Division Louis XV spoon with a gold-washed bowl, can be dated to 1891.[494] If the date is correct, it predates the formation of The Tribe of Ben-Hur.

THE NAME BEN-HUR

People
The most prominent Ben-Hur was the eminent Ben Hur Lampman, Poet Laureate of Oregon, who won the O. Henry Award in 1943.[495] He was born in Wisconsin in 1886, the year that *Ben-Hur: A Tale of the Christ* emerged as a super-bestseller. Another artist was *Esquire*'s illustrator Ben-Hur Baz, known for his pin-up creations in the 1940s and 1950s. He was born in Mexico in 1906. Lesser known was Ben-Hur Chastain, born in Tennessee in 1889, a military officer who led American guerilla forces in the Philippines, served time as a prisoner of war in Japan, and then

became a professor of military science and tactics at Penn State.[496] All three of these men were given the name Ben-Hur by their parents, who apparently admired the name and presumably the character.

Two others adopted the Ben-Hur as stage names. They both seemed to have chosen the name consciously as symbols of strength and victory. Little is known about the bodybuilder Ben Hur. A photograph of him carrying a sack of sand weighing 330 pounds is included in an article on rationale dietetics in 1904 issue of *Health and Strength*.[497] Of particular interest was the Australian 20-year-old, 5ft 5in. athletic showman who promoted himself as "Ben Hur, the Pocket Hercules."[498] His real name was reported to be "N. Evelyn."[499] He was said to "rival Sandow in muscular development" and known for "His Graceful Poses and Marvelous Dance of the Muscles."[500] To prove his strength and make his mark, on August 7, 1907, he challenged to throw anyone in a catch-as-catch-can wrestling match within twenty minutes, or he would pay him £5. That night he defeated two men in consecutive bouts without resting between matches.[501] The next night he defeated Ned Pickup, who outweighed him by about 30 pounds.[502] The Australian papers followed his progress with interest for more than a year, after which this Ben Hur began a lucrative tour of Singapore, Sumatra, China, and India.[503]

Animals

A number of breeder and show animals were named Ben-Hur, including bulls,[504] pigs,[505] sheep,[506] goats,[507] dogs,[508] a 30-foot python,[509] and, of course, horses.[510] A few were even related to the book. Sells-Floto, for instance, advertised as part of their 1907 Managerie-Museum and Circus the "Ben Hur Herd of Arabian Stallions."[511] The earliest of the horses seems to have been a trotter in the Watertown, New York, County Fair in 1885.[512] Another competed at the first annual meeting of the Independence Driving Park and Fair Association in 1888.[513] Perhaps this was the same horse that was scheduled to compete in the Stallion Stakes in Lexington, Kentucky, on October 8, 1888.[514] Even if it were, the Pedigree Online All Breed Database lists twenty-five horses named Ben Hur, ranging chronologically from 1888 to 2001 and including five thoroughbreds, three Arabians, two Swedish Warmbloods, a prominent quarter horse,[515] an appaloosa, and a dozen other breeds.[516] Interestingly, the earliest in this list was sired by Bend Or. The name sounds similar, but he was sired already in 1877, three years before the initial publication of *Ben-Hur: A Tale of the Christ*, and documented back to a generation foaled before Lew Wallace was born.[517] Curiously, in July, 2006, Vimeo listed a postcard depicting a white stallion with the following caption: "Ben Hur: The great reading, writing, spelling and mathematical horse, 16 years a diving horse; foaled June 12, 1880." The steed's unparalleled intellectual gifts aside, the novel was not published until November, 1880, but the name could certainly have been applied after its gifts were identified. The most famous of the horses named Ben-Hur was Zack Miller's show stallion, an integral part of his famous 101 Ranch.[518] A 1903 Ringling Brothers program lists Ben Hur as a horse in the Ladies' Jockey Race.[519] The practice of naming animals Ben-Hur continued for decades. An 1898 issue of *Field and Stream* offered a two-column eulogy of a hunting dog named Ben Hur,[520] and the cover of a 1917 issue of *The Breeder's Gazette* depicted the Aberdeen-Angus bull, Ben Hur of Lone Bell, the winner of nineteen champion ribbons.[521] Another was listed in *The Ayrshire Record* of 1922.[522] In the plant world there was also a hybrid of gladiola named Ben Hur.[523]

Businesses
The name "Ben-Hur," as always with or without the hyphen, was so well known and so positively identified that still other businesses and business-minded communities embraced it as their own, even if the connection was simply that the name was illustrious and represented an admirable concept, or was the result of nominal coincidence. In 1913, for instance, Dave and Bessie Kaplan opened "Kaplan's" department store to serve the rural farming communities surrounding Houston. They later started an adjacent five-and-dime store for their two sons, Bennett and Herman, and the entire operation was later named after their consolidated names – Kaplan's Ben Hur.[524] That Houston landmark at 2125 Yale remained in operation until January 7, 2006, when Martin, grandson of Dave and Bessie, succumbing to competition from big box stores, closed it.[525]

Three different grocery stores chose the name. Denver had a Ben Hur grocery at 1901 Champa Street in 1907; Huntington, Indiana, had one in the 1910s; and the Ben Hur Grocery in Emporia, Kansas, began placing ads in 1921 and was still operative in 1940.[526] St. Louis had a Ben Hur Bazaar at 604–606 South 4th Street. Extant artifacts include two advertising calendars. The earliest is a 1911 McNicol plate, with each month printed around the rim alternating with floral bouquets.[527] The second is a die-cut plaque featuring an embossed lithograph with gold glitter.[528] It depicts a saloon girl wearing a showy red dress and a red-plumed hat, sitting on a small hallway table, and answering the telephone, saying, "Hello. Give Me Olive 3770." Beneath her is a paper calendar pad for 1914. In addition to the phone number on the plaque, both advertise Ben Hur Bazaar by printing the name of the establishment, the address, and the names of the proprietors, Adamie & Shelbey.

The reader will not be surprised to learn that there was a Ben-Hur Hotel in Indianapolis, or that Lafayette, Indiana, still has a Ben Hur Tavern, and that elementary school #107 in Indianapolis was named after Lew Wallace.[529] Local Hoosier homages to Wallace and his famous creation were to be expected, and there would be others. But the name Ben-Hur was also applied to four additional hotels, two metropolitan apartments on each coast, and more than a dozen municipal meeting halls.

Roughly contemporary with the Ben Hur Inn in Matagorda was Goshen's Ben Hur Hotel in northern Indiana, which was operating at least as early as 1896.[530] The Ben Hur Hotel in City Island in the Bronx remained a local landmark for several decades, and 1922 witnessed the deadly destruction by fire of the Ben Hur Hotel in Portland, Oregon.[531]

As for the apartments and meeting halls, at the turn of the century the *New York Times* ran sporadic advertisements for vacancies in the Ben Hur Apartment building at 2643 Broadway, and even now one can still live in the Ben Hur Apartment building at 400 Hyde Street in the Tenderloin district of San Francisco.[532] This structure, built in 1926, features festooned blue chariots on the spandrel panels.[533] Incidentally, Wallace himself built the first major apartment building in Indianapolis, but he named it "Blacherne" after the Byzantine palace in Constantinople.[534] The many Ben Hur Halls were built by, associated with, or rented by fraternal organizations in Logansport and Indianapolis as well as Chicago, Atlanta, Oakland, Seattle, Omaha, Tulsa, Waterloo, St. Louis, Louisville, and Nashville.[535] Chicago also had a Ben Hur Theatre on South Cicero Avenue, and so did Fort Wayne.[536] Bob Pastor, a heavyweight boxer in preparation for a title bout against Joe Louis at Briggs Stadium in Detroit, trained at the Ben Hur Farm in Brighton, Michigan.[537] The Ben Hur Farm and Forest is still being used for research by Louisiana State University in Baton Rouge.

In the category of business establishments in the hospitality industry, there was a restaurant, a club, and a café in Tijuana. In the 1920s Walter "Smoke" Schulz and Jessie H. Scott of Sycamore, Illinois, married and then ran Smoke's Ben Hur Soda Grill for twenty-two years.[538] On an extant shot glass, below the name printed in red, a *quadriga* also printed in red races from left to right, and below that is printed Smoke's feisty motto: "The Customer is Never Right."[539] Also in the 1920s, Gus Schulte ran a club named Ben Hur at the Hotel Ben Hur In City Island.[540] A great distance away in Tijuana, Mexico, during the economic boom initiated by the racetrack and casinos that lured southern Californians to cross the border in the late 1920s and early 1930s, Wulfano and Umberto Ruiz opened up their Ben Hur Café on the main street.[541] The name was no doubt inspired by the 1925 MGM film starring Ramon Novarro, a Mexican by birth. Several postcards preserve images of the storefronts on Calle Principal from different angles and several years apart, judging by the automobile models and the design of the storefronts. One in particular, looking south, shows a large sign with "RUIZ BROS" and "BEN HUR CAFE" in large letters at the top, Mexicali Beer advertised below, and "OPEN ALL NIGHT" at the bottom.[542] As with the Ben-Hur ships, newspapers paid attention only for paid ads or newsworthy catastrophes. In an instance of the latter, Salvator Carioti, an Ensenada businessman came to the Ben Hur Café one

Figure 10.16 The name Ben-Hur was given to animals (Zack Miller's show stallion), restaurants (Tijuana's Ben Hur Café), sports teams, roadways, and even municipalities, as well as businesses and people, from the 1890s and continuing for more than a century.

Saturday in mid-December, 1927, to dissolve his partnership but ended up shooting and killing his former business associate with a revolver later in the evening.[543] There were additional incidents in subsequent years.[544] Hollywood engineer Herman J. Schultheis, known later for his work on *Fantasia*, photographed a crowd in front of the café in 1937.[545]

Sports Teams
A number of sports teams and clubs named themselves after the hero of the novel. These ranged from amateur baseball teams like the aforementioned belonging to the Twin City Junior Base Ball League to the Brooklyn's Ben-Hur Athletic Association, founded in 1895, which also fielded a baseball team that played at least until 1905.[546] In 1903 Detroit produced an amateur Ben-Hur baseball club "ready to book games with strong local teams."[547] The following year Watertown, New York, formed a Ben Hur team.[548] The indoor baseball leagues of the Kalamazoo Y.M.C.A. included a Ben Hur team in 1914.[549] A junior team of Ben Hurs was playing in Portland, Oregon, in 1916.[550] And these were in addition to the baseball games sponsored by various local chapters of the Tribe of Ben-Hur,[551] or played by the stagehands of the Klaw & Erlanger production.[552]

In addition, Omaha's Ben Hur Pleasure Club Juniors played football in 1901,[553] as did the Hartford Ben Hurs in 1913.[554] The 1905 Ben Hurs of Reading, Pennsylvania, competed in a basketball league.[555] The Ben Hur A. C. Soccer Football Club of Kearney claimed the juvenile championship of New Jersey in 1907.[556] At the time of the release of the 1925 MGM *Ben-Hur*, a Ben Hur bowling team was active in Baltimore.[557]

Places
Not unexpectedly, into the 1920s one of the major roads leading northeast into Crawfordsville, the Rockville-Rosedale Road, was aptly named the Ben Hur Highway,[558] and the *Rand McNally Official 1923 Auto Trails Map of District Number 1* included the Ben Hur Trail, predating the system of numbered highways.[559] But in addition at least a dozen municipalities named roadways after Wallace's celebrated creation. A Google Maps search will show that many of these names are still being used: Ben Hur Road (Baton Rouge; Mariposa, California), Ben Hur Street (Pittsburgh), Ben Hur Drive (Brighton, Michigan; Spring Valley Village, Texas; San Antonio; Santa Fe, New Mexico), Ben Hur Avenue (Whittier, California; Willoughby, Ohio; Indianapolis; Knoxville, Tennessee), and Ben Hur Lane (Rose Bud, Arkansas), not to mention several in Crawfordsville. A postcard from Chillicothe, Missouri, postmarked in 1926, depicts the Old Graham Bridge and Mill on Ben Hur Highway.[560] And in Pennsylvania both a Ben Hur Bridge was located on the campus of the School for the Deaf in Mt. Airy, near Philadelphia, and there is still the Ben Hur Camp in Elk County.[561]

On a larger scale, municipalities have been named Ben-Hur in several states. The *Pittsburgh Dispatch* from Friday, August 18, 1899, captured at least one of these in development. A large halftone reproduction of the Checa painting is surrounded by copy offering "FREE EXCURSION, DANCE AND BARBECUE" on Saturday to entice buyers to take the boat up the Monongahela River to Ben Hur, Blair, and purchase one of the several hundred lots laid out in a plan reproduced at the bottom of the page. The other Ben Hurs are in Newton County, Arkansas, in the Ozark Highlands,[562] and Mariposa County, California.[563] The latter is better remembered.[564] At least we know that when the Quick Ranch grew large enough to warrant a post office in 1890, the name "Ben Hur" was chosen simply because of the popularity of the novel. The post office, located along Route 5 between Mariposa and Raymond, was closed in 1951. This short list does not include the mining areas in the Western states that have already been mentioned. The two best known today are the Ben Hur in Lee County, Virginia, and Ben Hur in Limestone County, Texas. A. T. Derden was the person responsible for naming the latter town, formerly known as "Cottonwood," after Wallace's hero in 1895.[565] As for the former, *Life* included it in a list of "wonderful" names in the state of Virginia, including Ambrosia, Bias, Coffee, Joker, Skinquarter, Scruggs, and Waggy. Needless to say, this was the one named derived from popular literature.[566] On one side of a Civil War Centennial matchbook issued by the Americana Best Accommodations Series [#193] in 1962 reads:

Greetings from the town of
BENHUR
Virginia
Reminiscent of the fabulous Chariot Races.[567]

SUMMATION

For more than a century the popular arts have been producing concepts, vocabulary, and images that have entered the mainstream of American life, whether for months or years. No one wants to do business with a "Mickey Mouse" operation, and everyone has heard of but never been to Wonderland, Neverland, or Oz. The town of Tarzana is almost a century old. But no other blockbuster of contemporary popular culture so permeated the American psyche in the late nineteenth and early twentieth century as did *Ben-Hur: A Tale of the Christ*. In this chapter alone – there is more to come – the reader can find varying amounts of information on ten fraternal organizations, two tobacco companies, three flour companies, three baking powder labels, a coffee, tea, and spice company, independent brands of oranges, tomatoes, salmon, bitters, whiskey and rye, beer, and margarine, pudding, and biscuits, soap, perfume, two brands of razors, clothing, shoes, and shoe polish, over two dozen boats named *Ben-Hur*, two different motor companies, three different kinds of cars, trains, bicycles, carousel and four different roller coaster rides, two bandwagons, circus and festival chariot races, four images of chariot races in electric lights, a steel construction company, well over a dozen mining and petroleum operations, such hardware as tools, wire fencing, and gear for horse riding, fishing, and baseball, a clock, a watch and a watch band, arcade and board games, composition books, and a few more, not to mention a few prominent people, dozens of farm and competition animals, five private businesses, five hotels, two apartment buildings, a dozen meeting halls, eating establishments, sports teams, and more than a dozen roadways and places named Ben-Hur. This amounts to over 100 real world applications of the name, most of them chosen consciously and many of them repeatedly employing Ben-Hur imagery in advertising. While the process of selecting the name has been lost to us in almost every instance, the few anecdotes that have survived fail to reveal any profound psychological keys to the reasons individuals embraced and adopted the Ben-Hur name. What we take from this entire process instead is that the sheer numbers of propagations of the Ben-Hur name in dozens of different applications, remembering the tens of millions of people exposed or impacted and the millions of dollars that changed hands along with the wealth that was created, represents a societal process of familiarity, acceptance, and tacit approval as both the name and the chariot imagery became a permanent strand in the fiber of contemporary popular culture.

NOTES

1 There were also images by E. Cameron and Carlo Ademollo. The Library of Congress [Control No. 95521691] estimates that Cameron's chromolithograph *The Ben Hur Chariot Race* was executed by 1890. It uses the same perspective as Wagner's painting and follows the outline of its composition but changes almost all of the details. Ademollo's follows Checa in showing a crash, although here the overall composition and details are unique.
2 Gordon, *Empire of Wealth*, 205–39; Bensel, *The Political Economy*, 19–100; Brands, *American Colossus*, 43–103.
3 E.g. Hoganson, *Consumer's Imperium*, 1–12.
4 Cf. Grossman, *Labeling America*.
5 Lietzen, *Ben Hur Lodge*, ix and 5; <http://www.mypresentpast.com/home/towns/kansas/argentine-kansas-masons.html>
6 <https://www.facebook.com/BenHur322?rf=289815137769009>
7 Root, *The Ancient Arabic Order*, 79; *The [Fort Worth] Gazette* (October 9, 1891) 6.
8 *Ben Hur Shrine Temple, A.A.O.N.M.S.* (Marceline, MO: Campus Photo, 1992) 5.
9 <http://www.benhurshrine.org/chariot>
10 *Forth Worth Gazette* (March 5, 1892) 2.

11 *Dallas Morning News* (October 8, 1892) 2.
12 *The Guthrie Daily Leader* (August 20, 1906) 2.
13 <http://benhur818.org>
14 <http://www.benhur818.org>
15 *Evansville Courier and Press* (June 29, 1888) 4.
16 Palmer, *The Bench and Bar of Illinois*, 2:870; cf. *Official Record of the Proceedings of the Grand Lodge of Illinois Knights of Pythias* (Chicago: Geo. Gregory, Printer, 1896) 249.
17 <http://www.richmondil.com/oddfellows.html>
18 *BG* (September 30, 1945) D10.
19 <http://www.facebook.com/pages/Dramatic-Order-of-the-Knights-of-Khorassan/192589354128138>
20 J. F. Diffenbacher, *Diffenbacher's Directory of Pittsburgh and Allegheny Cities, 1895/1896* (Pittsburgh: Diffenbacher & Thurston, 1895) 65. The commandery was installed in March, 1892; cf. *The [Chicago] Inter Ocean* (February 28, 1892) 28.
21 <http://www.okcyorkrite.org/home/packet/page4>
22 For the history, see Root, *The Ancient Arabic Order*, 9–29.
23 E.g. Edwards, *Noble Dreams, Wicked Pleasures*, 216–23.
24 The 1908 medal was manufactured by the Charles M. Robbins Company of Attleboro, Massachusetts. The 1904 example contains the Shrine signature "A.A.O.N.M.S. Austin, Texas."
25 John W. Jordan and James Hadden, eds, *Genealogical and Personal History of Fayette County, Pennsylvania* (New York: Lewis Historical Publishing Company, 1912) 2:520.
26 White, *Our County and Its People*, 2:479; Nancy Bateman and Paul Selby, eds, *Illinois Historical: Crawford County Biographical* (Chicago: Munsell Publishing Company, 1909) 788; a 1 1/4 in. red/cream/black pin advertising the Ben-Hur Union Picnic at Island Cottage on August 4, 1904, is in the possession of the author.
27 Jonathan Levy, "The Mortgage Worked the Hardest," in Zakim and Kornblith, *Capitalism Takes Command*, 52–61; Miller, *Men in Business*, 238.
28 E.g. Meyer, "Fraternal Insurance in the United States," 232–51.
29 Dunn, *Memorial and Genealogical Record of Representative Citizens of Indiana*, 295–309; Zach, *Crawfordsville*, 58–9.
30 Dunn, *Memorial and Genealogical Record of Representative Citizens of Indiana*, 297–8.
31 Iliff, *The Lost Tribe of Ben-Hur*, 2. Iliff is the great grandson of Tribe co-founder David Gerard.
32 Ray Boomhower, "Wallace, Lewis (Lew)," in David J. Bodenhamer and Robert Graham Barrows, eds, *Encyclopedia of Indianapolis* (Bloomington: Indiana University Press, 1994) 1408.
33 *The Critic* 21 (February 3, 1894) 72.
34 *The Critic* 21 (February 10, 1894) 102.
35 *BG* (April 13, 1944) 12. <http://www.newyorklife.com/nyl/v/index.jsp?vgnextoid=2e272f5a919d2210a2b3019d221024301cacRCRD>

36 Dunn, *Memorial and Genealogical Record of Representative Citizens of Indiana*, 298; *Crawfordsville Daily Journal* (December 29, 1905) 1.
37 E.g. Poole, *Anglo-Israel*.
38 *The Evening World* (January 10, 1894) 1; *St. Paul Daily Globe* (January 10, 1894) 4.
39 *The Chariot* 11 (February, 1906) 1.
40 Iliff, *The Lost Tribe of Ben-Hur*, iii.
41 *CT* (January 17, 1894) 3.
42 Iliff, *The Lost Tribe of Ben-Hur*, 16.
43 *Louisville Courier-Journal* (January 10, 1894) 2; *SFC* (January 17, 1894) 2; *CT* (January 17, 1894) 3.
44 Carnes, *Secret Ritual and Manhood*, 1–6.
45 *Court Degree Ritual of the Tribe of Ben-Hur, Containing the Opening and Closing Ceremonies* (n.p.: The Ben-Hur Press, 1897).
46 *NYT* (January 7, 1923) SM4.
47 Iliff, *The Lost Tribe of Ben-Hur*, 2.
48 Iliff, *The Lost Tribe of Ben-Hur*, 5.
49 Cf. <http://wallacestudy.blogspot.com/2011/09/look-back-tribe-of-ben-hur.html>
50 *Sandusky Register* (May 2, 1894) 6.
51 *Sandusky Register* (June 6, 1894) 5.
52 *The [Sacramento] Record-Union* (December 4, 1898) 4.
53 *LAT* (July 27, 1897) 7.
54 *Omaha Daily Bee* (April 23, 1895) 8.
55 W. A. Northcott, ed., *Statistics of Fraternal Beneficiary Societies*[3] (Davenport: Egbert, Fidlar, & Chambers, 1897) 52–3.
56 *The San Francisco Call* (April 11, 1897) 30.
57 Meyer, "Fraternal Insurance in the United States," 250; Dunn, *Memorial and Genealogical Record of Representative Citizens of Indiana*, 299; cf. *Indianapolis Star* (January 1, 1913) A9.
58 *Indianapolis Star* (April 7, 1911) 5.
59 *Indianapolis Star* (December 31, 1915) B8.
60 *Indianapolis Star* (February 19, 1917) 4.
61 *Indianapolis Star* (March 11, 1918) 3.
62 Iliff, *The Lost Tribe of Ben-Hur*, 22; cf. *Indianapolis Star* (January 14, 1918) 3.
63 *The Fraternal Monitor* 31 (November, 1920) 9–10.
64 *The Ben-Hur Scholarships: A Memorial in Honor of David W. Gerard* (Crawfordsville: n.p., 1922) 22–32.
65 Freer, *Introduction to Civil Procedure*, 741.
66 *CPD* (August 13, 1899) 7.
67 *TBS* (November 9, 1903) 1.
68 *The Fraternal Monitor* 32 (September, 1921) 39.
69 *NYT* (November 24, 1899) 5; (November 29, 1899) 4.
70 *StLPD* (October 17, 1904) 3.
71 *SFC* (April 23, 1915) 5: Six years later the Tribe represented itself at the meeting of the Fraternal Orders of the World in San Francisco with a float representing a Roman galley on the open sea.

72 *The Chariot* 1 (November, 1896) 3.
73 *The Chariot* 1 (August, 1896) 2.
74 Ibid., 7.
75 *The Chariot* 1 (November, 1896) 8.
76 *The American Architect* 135 (April 20, 1929) 10.
77 *Indianapolis Star* (March 28, 1917) 16.
78 Iliff, *The Lost Tribe of Ben-Hur*, 17; <http://hdl.loc.gov/loc.pnp/pga.00454>
79 Iliff, *The Lost Tribe of Ben-Hur*, 27.
80 Iliff, *The Lost Tribe of Ben-Hur*, 28.
81 #35,573, issued January 14, 1902.
82 Iliff, *The Lost Tribe of Ben-Hur*, 27.
83 <http://nationalheritagemuseum.typepad.com/library_and_archives/supreme-tribe-of-ben-hur/>
84 *WSJ* (August 1, 2007) B1.
85 Cooper, *Once a Cigar Maker*, 12.
86 *DFP* (April 18, 1873) 1.
87 *Bay City [MI] Times* (March 16, 1892) 4.
88 *DFP* (October 18, 1887) 5.
89 Rice, *Digital Detroit*, 57.
90 Leonard, *The Industries of Detroit*, 131.
91 Letterhead, January 31, 1889, in the possession of the author.
92 Two examples are in the author's personal collection.
93 Bak, *Detroit Land*, 10–11.
94 *Saginaw News* (September 23, 1890) 7.
95 *Brownsville [TX] Daily Herald* (June 6, 1904) 1.
96 <http://atdetroit.net/forum/messages/6790/156450.html>
97 Clarence Monroe Burton, ed., *The City of Detroit, Michigan, 1701–1922* (Detroit: The S. J. Clarke Publishing Company, 1922) 5.240–1.
98 *Annual Report of the Secretary of the Commonwealth to the Governor and General Assembly for the Year Ending September 30, 1903* (Richmond: n.p., 1903) 42.
99 A Little Ben Hur box in the possession of the author preserves its tax stamp from the state of Michigan dated March 2, 1901. The label in the inside of an undated box of "Ben-Hur Juniors," i.e. cigarillos (two for five cents), identifies "Wm. C. Mithoefer, Cincinnati 13, Ohio," presumably the retailer. However, the bottom of the box displays the seal of the city of Tampa, and there are no chariots or any other tell-tale Moebs signatures.
100 *Trade* 14 (September 25, 1907) 43.
101 Detroit Historical Society Historical Digital Collection (#2011.036.072).
102 *Detroit Medical Journal* 7 (1907) vii.
103 *Cigar Makers' Official Journal* 28 (December 15, 1903) 13; *DFP* (October 9, 1909) 3.
104 *DFP* (March 18, 1909) 8; (November 9, 1913) B6.
105 *Printers' Ink* 148 (July 18, 1929) 155; Grossman, *Labeling America*, 136. Cf. *Vendre* 10 (March, 1929) 209.
106 <http://pinterest.com/willceau/the-capewell-glass-negative-collection>
107 <http://willceau.com/news/2012/04/05/bowler-hats-ben-hur-scrap>

108 In the possession of the author.
109 Storino, *Chewing Tobacco Tin Tags*, 32 [B-293, B-294].
110 Tinajero, *El Lector*, xiii.
111 *NYT* (February 3, 1929) 130.
112 Sivulka, *Stronger Than Dirt*, 61–2.
113 *Galveston Daily News* (July 12, 1886) 2.
114 <http://www.ranch-way.com/company>
115 <http://eadsrv.denverlibrary.org/sdx/pl/doc-tdm.xsp?id=WH259_doe33&fmt=text&base=fa>
116 *The St. Paul Globe* (December 21, 1902) 4.
117 *The St. Paul Globe* (January 25, 1903) 14.
118 *The Philistine* 18 (February, 1904) 64; (April, 1904) 160.
119 *Printers' Ink* 46 (January 13, 1904) 9.
120 *The St. Paul Globe* (January 22, 1903) 5.
121 *The St. Paul Globe* (January 25, 1903) 14.
122 *The St. Paul Globe* (February 8, 1903) 14.
123 *The St. Paul Globe* (February 28, 1903) 2.
124 <http://www.generalmills.com/~/media/Files/history/history_book.ashx>; cf. Groner, *The History of American Business and Industry*, 170.
125 Cf. Bertholf and Dorflinger, *Blairstown and Its Neighbors*, 46.
126 eBay #130154261445, ended September 23, 2007.
127 Cf. Hassan, *Immigrant Narratives*, 24.
128 Waller-Zuckerman, "'Old Homes, in a City of Perpetual Change,'" 715–56.
129 Schneirov, *The Dream of a New Social Order*, 97 and 202–6.
130 Damon-Moore, *Magazines for the Millions*, 1; cf. Wood, *Magazines in the United States*[3], 94–6.
131 *Ladies Home Journal* 19 (October, 1902) 33; (November, 1902) 36.
132 *McClure's* 20 (January, 1903) n.p.
133 *HW* 47 (June 13, 1903) 1004; *The Saturday Evening Post* (July 18, 1903) n.p.
134 *American Printer and Lithographer* 35 (January 3, 1903) 446.
135 *HW* 47 (February 28, 1903) 368; (August 15, 1903) 1352.
136 Schneirov, *The Dream of a New Social Order*, 265.
137 Presbrey, *The History and Development of Advertising*, 374–87.
138 Schneirov, *The Dream of a New Social Order*, 265.
139 *The Saturday Evening Post* 175 (January 3, 1903) inside cover.
140 *Pittsburgh Dispatch* (December 22, 1892) 12.
141 *HW* 47 (September 5, 1903) 1460.
142 *HW* 47 (January 31, 1903) 208.
143 Cf. *The American Magazine* 62 (October, 1906) 570; Cleary, *Great American Brands*, 55; Pavlik and McIntosh, *Converging Media*, 390; O'Neill, *The Story of Rose O'Neill*, 94–5; Strasser, *Satisfaction Guaranteed*, 131 and 166–70.
144 <http://greatriversnetwork.org/index.php?q=ben-hur%20dough%20boys&websites=no&historicgroup=all>
145 *HW* 47 (September 5, 1903) rear cover.
146 *New Outlook* 73 (April 25, 1903) n.p.
147 Strasser, *Satisfaction Guaranteed*, 118–21, 145, and 182–3.
148 Cohn, *Creating America*, 69.

149 Calkins, *Modern Advertising*. Cf. Boradkar, *Designing Things*, 182; Cross, *An All-consuming Century*, 34, 82, and 272.
150 *Printers' Ink* 71 (May 4, 1910) 22.
151 *Oshkosh Daily Northwestern* (January 13, 1903) 2.
152 *Monticello [IA] Express* (January 28, 1904) 8.
153 E.g. *The St. Paul Globe* (December 29, 1903) 10; *Malvern [IA] Leader* (January 15, 1903) 4; cf. *CE* (January 13, 1903) 5; (January 15, 1903) 5.
154 Wolf, *West Warwick*, 51.
155 Kemp, *Worcester II*, 109.
156 *Benton Harbor [MI] News Palladium* (October 20, 1959) 2.
157 In the possession of the author.
158 *The Mahoning [OH] Dispatch* (December 9, 1910) 3; *Daily Leader Grand Rapids Wisconsin* (March 14, 1919) 2; *Titusville [PA] Herald* (January 19, 1929) 4.
159 *Miami Daily News Record* (September 5, 1946) 8; cf. *Report of the Kansas Board of Agriculture* 47 (Topeka: Kansas State Board of Agriculture, 1928) 213.
160 *Hatch Experiment Station of the Massachusetts Agricultural College – Bulletin No. 93* (Amherst, MA: Press of Carpenter & Morehouse, 1903) 18 and 21.
161 *De Grondwet* (September 15, 1908) 7.
162 *Twenty-Fourth Annual Report of the Department of Agriculture* (Albany: J. B. Lyon Company, 1917) 77 and 82.
163 Gray, *Business Without Boundary*, 52–3; <http://www.trademarkia.com/benhur-71312181.html; http://img02.mar.cx/us/285170.png>
164 <http://www.legalforce.com/benhur-71556319.html>. In 1942, *A List of Flour Mills in the United States and Canada* (Minneapolis: The Northwestern Miller, 1942) 45, lists the trade name "Royal Milling Company" of Kalispell, Montana, under the "Central Division of General Mills, Inc."
165 <http://www.pizzamaking.com/forum/index.php?topic=18407.200>
166 *The St. Paul Globe* (June 7, 1903) 22.
167 E.g. *The St. Paul Globe* (February 11, 1904) 10; (December 4, 1904) 27.
168 In the possession of the author.
169 Morrison, *The Baking Powder Controversy* (Volume 2), *passim*.
170 Edrick J. Miller, *The Ben Hur Memorabilia Check List* (Santa Ana, CA: n.p., 1994) 7–8.
171 *Los Angeles Herald* (September 18, 1904) 10.
172 E.g. *AC* (November 18, 1895) 5.
173 *Los Angeles Herald* (September 25, 1904) 9.
174 *Los Angeles Herald* (October 2, 1904) 12.
175 *Simmons' Spice Mill; Dedicated to the Interests of the Coffee, Tea and Spice Trades*; *LAT* (March 30, 1902) 8; (March 6, 1902) A5.
176 *Club Women of California Official Directory and Register* (1906–7) 132.
177 *Out West* 1 (December, 1910) 80; (January, 1911) 5; (February, 1911) 5.
178 *Home Helps* (Bedford, MA: Applewood Books [reprint]) 1–8.
179 *LAT Cook Book – Number Four* (Los Angeles: The Times-Mirror Company, 1911).

180 *LAT* (August 7, 1904) A12.
181 *LAT* (April 14, 1915) II10.
182 *Los Angeles Herald* (February 17, 1913); (February 19, 1913) [clippings].
183 *Journal of Electricity, Power and Gas* 32 (May 30, 1914) 482.
184 *LAT* (May 13, 1914) II12; (November 22, 1914) IIA5; (April 19, 1915) III16.
185 *LAT* (November 23, 1915) II2.
186 *LAT* (April 19, 1914) III16.
187 *LAT* (April 14, 1915) II10.
188 *LAT* (July 8, 1911) I14;
189 *LAT* (May 28, 1915) II10.
190 *LAT* (July 4, 1915) I9.
191 *American Globe* 15 (October, 1918) 3–4.
192 <http://visualingual.wordpress.com/2012/06/18/ben-hur-coffee-ghost-sign-in-san-diego>
193 eBay #150073982623, ended February 21, 2007; McClelland and Last, *California Orange Box Labels*, 128; cf. 42–51 and 71.
194 Cf. *Catalog of Copyright Entries: Musical Compositions* (Washington, DC: U.S. Government Printing Office, 1953) 317.
195 eBay #7209031919, ended April 2, 2006.
196 Eugene L. Menefee and Fred A. Dodge, *History of Tulare and Kings Counties, California* (Los Angeles: Historic Record Company, 1913) 63.
197 *Ironwood [MI] News Record* (December 24, 1904) 11.
198 *Syracuse Journal* (March 21, 1907) 5; *Syracuse Herald* (March 21, 1907) 8.
199 *Los Angeles Herald* (February 25, 1908) 7; (May 25, 1909) 6.
200 *StLPD* (March 10, 1895) 6; *CT* (November 17, 1895) 16; *Elkhart [IN] Daily Review* (April 19, 1899) 3; and *StLPD* (November 16, 1902) A7.
201 *The Shoal Lake [Manitoba] Star* (February 1, 1912) 1; *[Winnipeg] Manitoba Free Press* (December 5, 1918) 18; (March 18, 1933) 6.
202 Hunt and Kaylor, *Washington*, 2:457.
203 *Dubuque Sunday Herald* (November 26, 1899) 10; *Columbus Evening Dispatch* (July 8, 1909) 9.
204 *New Orleans Item* (June 3, 1908) 11.Cf. Richard E. Fike, *The Bottle Book: A Comprehensive Guide to Historic, Embossed, Medicine Bottles* (Salt Lake City: Peregrine Smith Books, 1987) 154; Richard Watson, *Bitters Bottles* (New York: Thomas Nelson & Sons, 1965) 63.
205 R. Barlett Saalfrank and Carlyn Ring, *For Bitters Only* (Wellesley Hills, MA: The Pi Press, 1980) 78.
206 *National Labor Tribune* (April 30, 1908) 1; *Boston Traveler* (October 18, 1956) 50.
207 <http://www.zazzle.com/vintage_ben_hur_1920s_advertising_poster-228561708503112214>
208 *[San Diego] Evening Tribune* (January 31, 1905) 5; *Seattle Daily Times* (March 15, 1906) 7.
209 *Duluth News-Tribune* (March 16, 1907) 4; *[Washington, DC] Evening Star* (October 22, 1909) 4.
210 #71078505, issued May 23, 1914.
211 *Seattle Daily Times* (August 9, 1914) 8.

212 *CT* (December 22, 1926) 29; cf. <http://www.ebay.com/itm/CIRCA-1927-PALMOLIVE-PEET-COIN-MEDAL-TOKEN-LOT-5-NEW-OLD-STOCK-/261022110074>
213 *Emporia [KS] Gazette* (August 17, 1944) 7; cf. *NYT* (July 23, 1928) 29; *[San Diego] Evening Tribune* (March 18, 1932) 34.
214 *Soap, Cosmetics, Chemical Specialties [Soap & Sanitary Chemicals]* 27 (May, 1951) 145; (December, 1951) 57.
215 Cox, *Sold on Radio*, 88–9.
216 James E. Davis, ed., *Proceedings at the Ninth Annual Meeting of the Manufacturing Perfumers' Association* 3 (1903) 165.
217 *CT* (November 3, 1901) 15.
218 *The Hawaiian Gazette* (August 28, 1906) 4.
219 *Washington Times* (March 4, 1919) 11.
220 *Jersey [City] Journal* (December 19, 1921) 2.
221 *Jersey [City] Journal* (December 14. 1921) 4; *[Canton OH] Repository* (December 7, 1923) 32.
222 *[Canton OH] Repository* (December 19, 1924) 34; (December 4, 1925) 25.
223 *Photoplay* 29 (January, 1926) 91.
224 *Palestine [TX] Daily Herald* (September 5, 1903) 3.
225 *The Houston Daily Post* (August 14, 1902) 12.
226 *The Salt Lake Herald-Republican* (October 8, 1909) 11; *Flint [MI] Journal* (August 10, 1917) 4.
227 *The Circle* 5 (May, 1909) 257.
228 *El Paso Herald* (July 19, 1910) 3.
229 eBay #180313138905, ended December 17, 2008.
230 In the possession of the author.
231 In the possession of the author.
232 *Kansas City Daily Journal* (November 29, 1896) 2.
233 *English Crawford County [IN] Democrat* (March 5, 1903) 2.
234 <eris.uky.edu/catalog/xt7xok26bf4b_92/text>
235 eBay #160043683338, ended October 29, 2006.
236 In the possession of the author.
237 *Brownstown [IN] Banner* (September 9, 1914) 8.
238 Advertised in *The Oaks* playbill (1909) 3; eBay #190107409626, ended May 6, 2007.
239 *The Waterways Journal* 71 (April 20, 1957) 10; *The Waterways Journal* 89 (January 3, 1976) 8.
240 *The Waterways Journal* 71 (April 6, 1957) 10; *S & D Reflector* 13 (June, 1976) 8.
241 *Report of the Commissioner of Corporations on Transportation by Water in the United States – Part I* (Washington, DC: Government Printing Office, 1909) 231.
242 *[Maysville, KY] Evening Bulletin* (April 18, 1904) 2; *[Maysville, KY] Daily Public Ledger* (March 7, 1904) 3; (August 10, 1904) 2; (August 15, 1904) 3; (April 17, 1905) 3; cf. *[Maysville, KY] Daily Public Ledger* (September 13, 1906) 3; *Blue Book of American Shipping* 15 (Cleveland: The Penton Publishing Co., 1910) 498; *The Waterways Journal* 71 (April 6, 1957) 10.

243 *DFP* (November 11, 1889) 2; *The [Maysville, KY] Evening Bulletin* (May 13, 1904) 3; invoices from J. B. Sheppard of Wheeling, WV, March 4, 1892, and from the Pittsburgh, Wheeling, Marietta, and Parkersburg Packet, July 1, 1910, both in the possession of the author.
244 *[Maysville, KY] Daily Public Ledger* (November 29, 1895) 3.
245 *The [Maysville, KY] Evening Bulletin* (May 13, 1904) 3.
246 *The [Maysville, KY] Evening Bulletin* (March 29, 1888) 3; *New Albany [IN] Daily Tribune* (June 1, 1888) 4; cf. *Annual Reports of the War Department* (1901) 4:2621; (1904) 7:2415; (1905) 6:1814.
247 *Steubenville [OH] Herald* (July 18 1890) 5.
248 *Marietta [OH] Daily Leader* (June 29, 1899) 3; *[Maysville, KY] Daily Public Ledger* (July 21, 1900) 1.
249 *Brooksburg [IN] Sun* (August 11, 1904) 1.
250 *[Maysville, KY] Daily Public Ledger* (January 14, 1903) 3; (December 23, 1903) 2.
251 *The Waterways Journal* 71 (April 6, 1957) 10.
252 *[Maysville, KY] Daily Public Ledger* (December 7, 1906) 3; *The Waterways Journal* 120 (December 4, 2006) 14.
253 <http://wheeling.weirton.lib.wv.us/history/photos/brown/BROWN77.HTM>
254 *The Paducah Evening Sun* (June 18, 1909) 8; MNHS #3162-A; Runk Collection #1989, #1990, and #1992.
255 *Blue Book of American Shipping*, 12. See also, Shawn Perich and Gary Alan Nelson, *Backroads of Minnesota: Your Guide to Minnesota's Most Scenic Backroad* (Stillwater, MN: Voyageur Press, 2002) 141; and Kathryn Strand Koutsky and Linda Koutsky, *Minnesota Vacation Days: An Illustrated History* (St. Paul: Minnesota Historical Society, 2006) 145; postcard [eBay #270034019294, ending October 4, 1906].
256 *The Waterways Journal* 71 (April 13, 1957) 15.
257 *CE* (March 16, 1913) 25.
258 *The Waterways Journal* 71 (April 13, 1957) 15.
259 *CE* (January 14, 1906) B2.
260 <http://www.austinpostcard.com/gdam.html>; and <http://www.i35austin.com/newsletters/vol7/vol7.pdf>. The Austin Ben Hur Shrine claims no connection with the "pleasure boat."
261 Cf. *The Southwestern Reporter* 30 (1895) 832.
262 <http://genealogytrails.com/tex/hillcountry/travis/1897city_directory.html>; <http://richardzelade.com/daysof.htm>; David Dettmer, *The Texas Book Two: More Profiles, History, and Reminiscences of the University* (Austin: University of Texas Press, 2012) 24; Karen R. Thompson and Kathy R Howell, *Austin, Texas* (Charleston, SC: Arcadia Publishing, 2000) 38. Cf. Don Martin, *Austin* (Charleston, SC: Arcadia Publishing, 2009) 105.
263 Chandra Moira Beal, *Splash Across Texas: The Definitive Guide to Swimming in Central Texas* (Austin, TX: La Luna Pub., 1999) 142 <http://www.texasescapes.com/AustinTexas/LakeAustin/LakeAustin.htm>
264 <http://www.austinlibrary.com/ahc/photo.htm>

265 <http://www.chase-1.com/historic%20photos%20austin.htm>
266 Thompson and Howell, *Austin, Texas*, 24–5.
267 *Austin Weekly Statesman* (May 28, 1896) 3.
268 William Keith Guthrie, *An Environmental History of Flooding in Texas* (PhD diss., University of Kansas, 2006) 255–62.
269 James L. Donahue, *Schooners in Peril* (Holt, MI: Thunder Bay Press, 1995) 72–3; Cris Kohl *Shipwreck Tales: The St. Clair River (to 1900)* (Chatham, ONT: Cris Kohl, 1987) 131–6.
270 *The Federal Reporter* 76 (St. Paul: West Publishing Co., 1897) 460–4.
271 Donahue, *Schooners in Peril*, 73.
272 *Blue Book of American Shipping* 15 (Cleveland: The Penton Publishing Co., 1910) 12.
273 OCLC: 190787370.
274 *The Annual Report of the Operations of the United States Life-Saving Service* (1901) 64; (1903) 166; (1906) 152.
275 *WP* (September 5, 1905) 8; *CE* (September 5, 1905) 1; *BG* (September 5, 1905) 9.
276 E. T. Chamberlain, ed., *Foreign Vessels Admitted to American Registry* (Washington, DC: Government Printing Office, 1915) 11.
277 *Merchant Vessels of the United States* (Washington, DC: Government Printing Office, 1894) 74 and 276; (1911) 138.
278 *Merchant Vessels of the United States* (Washington, DC: Government Printing Office, 1889) 45; *Lloyd's Register of British and Foreign Shipping* (London: Lloyd's Register of Shipping, 1893) 73.
279 <http://www.wrecksite.eu/wreck.aspx?32843>
280 *Merchant Vessels of the United States* (1907) 17.
281 *Merchant Vessels of the United States* (1911) 138.
282 *S & D Reflector* 3 (June, 1966) 26.
283 *Merchant Vessels of the United States* (1919) 202.
284 *The Motor Boat* 3 (October 10, 1906) 38.
285 *Automotive Trade Journal* 11 (April 1, 1906) 296.
286 *The Motor Boat* 4 (February 10, 1907) 59.
287 *The Motor Boat* (March 10, 1907) 21.
288 *BG* (April 13, 1893) 27.
289 *Outing* 31 (February, 1898) 523.
290 *Detroit Free Press* (June 10, 1893) 8.
291 *Forest and Stream* 62 (May 21, 1904) 425.
292 eBay #250176606922, ended October 22, 2007.
293 *The Motor Boat* 4 (June 25, 1907) 29–30.
294 *Fore 'N' Aft* 3 (July, 1907) 28032.
295 *The Motor Boat* 6 (July 25, 1909) 41.
296 Matagorda County Museum Association, *Matagorda County* (Charleston, SC: Arcadia Publishing, 2008) 125.
297 *The Texas Magazine* 6 (September, 1912) 436–7.
298 *Yachtsman's Annual Guide and Nautical Calendar* (1924) 257.
299 *[Rockford IL] Register Gazette* (September 1, 1920) 7.
300 *Los Angeles Herald* (November 16, 1905) 8.

301 *Omaha Daily Bee* (December 6, 1912) 7.
302 *The Green Book* 11 (1913) 43, 45; cf. *Medford [OR] Mail Tribune* (January 28, 1914) 4.
303 *Monroe City Democrat* (December 5, 1901) 4; *The San Francisco Call* (May 10, 1912) 12.
304 *Centralia [WA] Daily Chronicle* (January 25, 1909) 1.
305 *The Seattle Star* (January 25, 1909) 6.
306 In the possession of the author.
307 *Indiana Magazine of History* 20 (September, 1924) 221–79; Nye, *Electrifying America*, 117–20; *Brill Magazine* 5 (September, 1911) [*Electric Railway Historical Society Bulletin* 34 (n.d.)] 18–19.
308 *Indianapolis Star* (May 29, 1914) 1.
309 *Indianapolis Star* (May 30, 1919) 20.
310 *Indianapolis Star* (February 7, 1913) 11.
311 William P. Helling, *Crawfordsville* (Charleston, SC: Arcadia Publishing, 2011) 44. Cf. Robert Reed, *Central Indiana Interurban, Indiana* (Charleston, SC: Arcadia Publishing, 2004) 108.
312 <http://texashistory.unt.edu/explore/partners/BDPL/oai/?verb=ListRecords&metadataPrefix=oai_dc>
313 *McClure's Magazine* 8 (December, 1896) 100; Crown, *No Hands*, 18–19; Epperson, *Peddling Bicycles to America*, 242.
314 *St. Paul Daily Globe* (August 13, 1893) 4.
315 *CT* (July 27, 1895) 16.
316 *The Churchman* 55 (March 19, 1887) 337; *The Ladies Home Journal* 8 (May, 1891) ii.
317 *The Wheel and Cycle Trade Review* 8 (February 12, 1892) 859.
318 David Beecroft, *The History of the American Automobile Industry* (n.p.: lulu.com, 2008) 86; <http://books.google.com/books?id=3A4CTZbOemcC&pg=PP2&lpg=PP2&dq=beecroft+automobile&source=bl&ots=NKtdxH5mJp&sig=xZ-pHghCPZI5qRx6ZPQlnb_a2W8&hl=en&sa=X&ei=AjE2Ue6ANcHL2QX_hoDwBQ&sqi=2&ved=0CEQQ6AEwBA#v=onepage&q=luburg&f=false>
319 *The Wheel and Cycling Trade Review* 10 (October 21, 1892) 25.
320 *Printers' Ink* 7 (October 5, 1892) 420. An advertising envelope postmarked September 2, 1892 is labeled "'BEN-HUR' SULKY WHEELS, Central Cycle Mfg. Co., Indianapolis."
321 *The Lehi [UT] Banner* (October 19, 1893) 1.
322 *The Wheel and Cycle Trade Review* 8 (January 8, 1892) 636; *The Wheel and Cycle Trade Review* 8 (February 12, 1892) 871.
323 *The Wheel and Cycling Trade Review* 10 (February 10, 1893) 30.
324 *The San Francisco Call* (May 5, 1895) 16.
325 *St. Paul Daily Globe* (February 26, 1896) 5; and *St. Paul Daily Globe* (April 4, 1897) 8.
326 *Outing* 29 (March, 1897) 606; cf. Epperson, *Peddling Bicycles to America*, 238–41.
327 *NYT* (April 19, 1895) 6.
328 *Youth's Companion* (May 13, 1897) 230; *The San Francisco Call* (May 5, 1895) 16.

329 Invoice, dated July 6, 1895, and envelope, postmarked May 28, 1894, are in the possession of the author.
330 *Trade Register* 4 (April 25, 1896) 11.
331 *McClure's Magazine* 7 (June, 1896) 79; *The Review of Reviews* 13 (June, 1896) 54.
332 <http://www.thewheelmen.org/sections/memorabilia/covers/music_index.pdf>
333 *Intersocialities* (January 28, 1896) 4.
334 *McClure's Magazine* 8 (March, 1897) 32; (April, 1897) 30.
335 *McClure's Magazine* 8 (May, 1897) 36.
336 *CT* (July 16, 1896); (July 4, 1897) 14; *Louisville Courier Journal* (July 4, 1897) A3.
337 *Hardware Dealer's Magazine* 9 (January 1, 1898) 89.
338 *The Scranton Tribune* (June 8, 1898) 6.
339 *Bridgeton [NJ] Evening News* (April 15, 1899) 2.
340 *The Seattle Star* (July 19, 1909) 2.
341 <http://www.carouselworld.com/carousel_world_014.htm> – no longer accessible. Photos in the possession of the author.
342 <http://www.westland.net/coneyisland/articles/independentrides.htm>; Register, *The Kid of Coney Island*, 161.
343 *Annual Report of the Board of Health of the Department of Health of the City of New York* (New York: Martin B. Brown Company, 1909) 461–2.
344 Jim Futrell, *Amusement Parks of New York* (Mechanicsburg, PA: Stackpole Books, 2006) 51; W. F. Mangels Co., Carousell Works: *Catalogue #4* (n.d.) 15; <http://www.coneyislandhistory.org/voices/index.php/ObjectDetail/Show/object_id/70/search_mode/search>; *The Billboard* 20 (December 5, 1908) 102.
345 eBay #160151117383, ended September 1, 2007.
346 *The New York Clipper* (July 16, 1919) 17; (June 27, 1923) 28.
347 *NYTr* (June 23, 1907) B6.
348 Ibid., B8.
349 *Trenton Evening Times* (March 24, 1907) 15.
350 <http://lostamusementparks.napha.org/Articles/NewYork/GoldenCity-NY.html>; cf. *NYT* (July 1, 2007) O4.
351 *Cincinnati Post* (July 15, 1911) 3.
352 *Kansas City Star* (May 25, 1913) 7.
353 *Kansas City Star* (May 11, 1913) 4.
354 *TBS* (August 21, 1915 1; *Baltimore American* (July 1, 1917) 9; (August 17, 1919) 8.
355 Jeffrey Stanton, *Venice of America: 'Coney Island of the Pacific'* (Los Angeles: Donahue Publishing, 1987) 55; <http://madeinvenice.net/history-of-venice>; <http://www.westland.net/venicehistory/articles/cc.htm>
356 *Los Angeles and Vicinity, California*, (San Francisco: Cardinell-Vincentt Company, n.d.) 45.
357 In the possession of the author.
358 *LAT* (December 27, 1915) I1.
359 *LAT* (December 28, 1915) II3.

360 *Motor Age* 30 (October 12, 1916) 54; Beverly Rae Kimes and Henry Austin Clark, Jr., *Standard Catalog of American Cars, 1805–1942* (Iola, WI: Krause Publications, 1885) 111.
361 *Motor Age* 31 (January 11, 1917) 21.
362 *The Horseless Age* 39 (January 1, 1917) 17–20; *Motor Age* 31 (January 4, 1917) 25.
363 *The Horseless Age* 39 (January 15, 1917) 18.
364 *The Horseless Age* 39 (January 15, 1917) 52; *Motor Age* 31 (January 25, 1917) 8.
365 <http://earlyamericanautomobiles.com/americanautomobiles20.htm>
366 *Motor* 25 (December, 1916) 124. *The Fourth Estate* #1192 (December 30, 1916) 25, reports that the director of advertising was Franklin C. King.
367 *Automobile Trade Journal* 21 (February 1, 1917) 255.
368 <http://www.hcfi.org/read.php?doc=../Library/The_Motor_Age/1917/01/25/page_0243.pdf&fromSE=GoogleREFERRED>
369 *Motor Age* 30 (October 26, 1916) 54; *Motor Age* 31 (March 1, 1917) 16.
370 *Motor Age* 31 (May 17, 1917) 10. The single model year was not a stock scam, e.g. in *Wall Street Journal* (August 23, 1957) 1.
371 *Richmond Times Dispatch* (July 27, 1919) 39; Hershberg, *James B. Conant*, 47.
372 Richard Wager, *Golden Wheels: The Story of the Automobiles Made in Cleveland and Northeastern Ohio, 1892–1932* (Cleveland: The Western Reserve Historical Society and The Cleveland Automobile Club, 1975) 283–4.
373 *Motor Age* 29 (April 6, 1916) 24.
374 *Motor Age* 29 (April 13, 1916) 17.
375 *Motor Age* 30 (October 12, 1916) 10.
376 *Motor Age* 30 (October 19, 1916) 20.
377 *Motor Age* 31 (March 15, 1917) 17.
378 *Motor Age* 30 (December 7, 1916) 39.
379 *The Automobile Trade Directory* 16 (October, 1918) 486; *Chilton Hotel Supply Index* 1 (May, 1922) 270.
380 Ford R. Bryan, *Henry's Attic: Some Fascinating Gifts to Henry Ford and His Museum* (Detroit: Wayne State University Press, 2006) 83.
381 In the possession of the author, with gratitude to Rob Harris and Diana DeBlois for the program.
382 *HW* 45 (April 20, 1901) 405.
383 In the possession of the author.
384 <http://books.google.com/books?id=Sg0aAAAAYAAJ&pg=PA145&lpg=PA145&dq=1901+Pan+American+Exposition+Buffalo+ben-hur&source=bl&ots=9cc-cK-iGP&sig=8F-hAp9iHtYCEnUPBSXdopQe68U&hl=en&sa=X&ei=oPZDUc3xOqOEygHnz4H4BA&ved=0CCoQ6AEwAA#v=onepage&q=1901%20Pan%20American%20Exposition%20Buffalo%20ben-hur&f=false>
385 Lew Wallace, "Prevention of Presidential Assassination," *The North American Review* 541 (December, 1901) 721–6.
386 *The Youth's Companion* (October 24, 1912) 592; (October 31, 1912) 599.

387 *Aberdeen [SD] Daily News* (June 29, 1912) 3.
388 In the possession of the author.
389 McKee 186.
390 *NYTr* (May 9, 1853) 1.
391 *NYT* (June 20, 1866) 5.
392 *NYT* (April 28, 1874) 5.
393 Kotar and Gessler, *The Rise of the American Circus*, 319.
394 Doss, *Memorial Mania*, 271.
395 *[Chicago] Daily Inter Ocean* (January 4, 1892) 4.
396 Michelle L. Turner and Pasadena Museum of History, *The Rose Bowl* (Charleston, SC: Arcadia Publishing, 2010) 25.
397 *LAT* (January 2, 1902) A4.
398 *LAT* (November 4, 1903) A7; James Miller Guinn, *Historical and Biographical Record of Southern California* (Chicago: Chapman Publishing Company, 1902) 1072; John Windell Wood, *Pasadena, California: Historical and Personal* (Pasadena: J. W. Wood, 1917) 440–1.
399 *LAT* (November 11, 1903) A7.
400 *LAT* (December 21, 1903) 15.
401 *LAT* (December 31, 1903) A7.
402 *LAT* (January 3, 1904) A4; cf. (January 2, 1904) A1.
403 *LAT* (October 22, 1904) A9.
404 *LAT* (December 24, 1904) A1.
405 *LAT* (December 23, 1904) A11.
406 *LAT* (January 3, 1905) II1.
407 *LAT* (January 31, 1905) III11.
408 *LAT* (March 18, 1905) II5.
409 *LAT* (November 24, 1905) I6; cf. Fried, *Appetite for America*, 165.
410 *HW* 51 (December 14, 1907) 1854.
411 *Santa Fe Employes' [sic] Magazine* 4 (January, 1910) 110, 112.
412 Unprovenienced, in the possession of the author.
413 *LAT* (January 2, 1908) II1, 3.
414 *LAT* (January 2, 1912) II2.
415 *LAT* (January 2, 1914) II5.
416 *International Railway Journal* 21 (November, 1913) 20.
417 *Popular Mechanics* 27 (April, 1917) 524.
418 Wood, *Pasadena, California*, 441.
419 *BG* (December 15, 1963) A9; *LAT* (December 30, 1971) A1.
420 Myron Hunt, *Myron Hunt, 1868–1952* (Santa Monica: Hennesey & Ingalls, 1984) 65.
421 Turner and Pasadena Museum of History, *The Rose Bowl*, 2.
422 *The Virginia Law Register, 1913–1914* 19 (March, 1914) 877–88.
423 *Lexington [KY] Herald* (October 19, 1913) II4.
424 *Life* 17 (November 13, 1944) 3; *Popular Mechanics* 82 (December, 1944) 163.
425 David L. Lewis, *Ford Country* (Sidney, OH: Amos Press, 1999) 136; cf. *Cycle and Automobile Trade Journal* 13 (August 1, 1908) 116.
426 *Scientific American* 103 (July 9, 1910) 28–9; *National Magazine* 34 (May, 1911) 153–60.

427 Nye, *Electrifying America*, 52–3.
428 *NYT* (June 19, 1910) 8.
429 *Scientific American* 103 (July 9, 1910) 28; *National Magazine* 34 (May, 1911) 157.
430 *Printers' Ink* 72 (July 14, 1910) 193–4.
431 *CE* (September 25, 1910) 20.
432 *Electrical Review and Western Electrician* 64 (April 25, 1914) 819.
433 In the possession of the author.
434 Cf. F. Scott Fitzgerald, *This Side of Paradise* (New York: C. Scribner's Sons, 1920) 20.
435 Presbrey, *The History and Development of Advertising*, 618; *Scientific American* 103 (July 9, 1910) 28.
436 *Automobile Topics* 24 (December 23, 1911) 306.
437 *Automobile Topics* 24 (December 23, 1911) 306.
438 In the possession of the author. Cf. Jenkins, "The 'Signs' of the Times," 157.
439 In the possession of the author.
440 *NYT* (January 7, 1923) SM4.
441 Jane G. Rhoads, *Kansas Opera Houses: Actors and Community Events, 1855–1925* (Wichita, KS: Mennonite Press, 2008) 144.
442 *St. Paul Dispatch* (March 28 1902) n.p. [eBay #160149938576, ended August 28, 2007].
443 <http://www.benhurconstruction.com>
444 Edward M. Walter and Susan A. Fleury, *Eureka Gulch; the Rush for Gold* (Colville, WA: Don's Printery, 1985) 68–71; Waldemar Lindgren and Howland Bancroft, "The Republic Mining District," in Howland Bancroft, *The Ore Deposits of Northeastern Washington* (Washington, DC: Government Printing Office, 1914) 163.
445 *Report of the Secretary of the Territory, 1903–1904, and Legislative Manual, 1905* 3 (Santa Fe, The New Mexican Printing Company, 1905) 187.
446 *WSJ* (January 8, 1902) 6; *Denver Post* (April 3, 1899) 2.
447 *The Pacific Reporter* 85 (June 18–August 13, 1906) 1006.
448 Paper ephemera [eBay #260045746682, ended November 5, 1906].
449 J. D. Irving, S. F. Emmons, and T. A. Jaggar, Jr., *Economic Resources of the Northern Black Hills* (Washington, DC: Goverrnment Printing Office, 1904) 150; Francis Church Lincoln, Walter G. Miser, and Joseph B. Cummings, *The Mining Industry of South Dakota* [South Dakota School of Mines, *Bulletin No. 17*] (1937) 94.
450 *WSJ* (August 11, 1906) 7.
451 <http://www.lib.uidaho.edu/special-collections/Manuscripts/dmginv/mg284.htm>
452 *The Mining World* 32 (January 22, 1910) 240.
453 Walter Harvey Weed, *The Mines Handbook* 14 (New York City: W. H. Weed, 1920) 1128 and 1152. Cf. *NYT* (February 11, 1926) 31.
454 <http://pubs.usgs.gov/bul/0741/report.pdf; cf.. http://mineral-resources.findthedata.org/l/44529/Ben-Hur-Prospect>
455 *Fourth Annual Report of the Corporation Commission of the State of Oklahoma* 4 (1911) 539.

456 Utility Coal Co. v. Rogez [1934 OK 754].
457 242 F.2d 481 (1957).
458 In the possession of the author.
459 In the possession of the author.
460 In the possession of the author. For Meister's Ben Hur mine, see *West Virginia Annual Report of the Department of Mines* (1930) 28–9.
461 *Mansfield [OH] News* (December 19, 1911) 1.
462 *Ada [OK] Evening News* (July 7, 1913) 4; *AC* (November 18, 1913) 17.
463 *AC* (November 22, 1896) 5.
464 In the possession of the author.
465 Patent #666,398, issued January 22, 1901; A. J. Campbell, *Classic and Antique Fly-Fishing Tackle: A Guide for Collectors and Anglers* (New York: Lyons & Burford, 1997) 186–7; <http://luresnreels.com/talbot.html>
466 eBay #290083673020, ended February 21, 2007.
467 *1907 Catalogue and Price List* (New York: Abercrombie & Fitch, 1907) 231.
468 #460,272, issued September 29, 1891; *Indianapolis Star* (January 9, 1913) 10.
469 OCLC #62502374; the card is in the possession of the author.
470 <http://ech.case.edu/ech-cgi/article.pl?id=GWC>
471 In the possession of the author.
472 In the possession of the author.
473 eBay #280000535592, ended June 28, 2006.
474 *The Farm Journal* 43 (July, 1919) 38; *Cosmopolitan* 70 (February, 1921) 3.
475 *Printers' Ink* 138 (January 27, 1927) 138.
476 *CT* (April 2, 1927) 9.
477 *CT* (September 24, 1928) 18; cf. *Collier's* 81 (January 7, 1928) 3.
478 Catalog pages, dated July 30, 1931, in the possession of the author.
479 <http://clockhistory.com/o/westclox/series/series-31-1/style-68-1.html>
480 <http://www.pixelp.com/gruen/1922.html>; cf. *[New Orleans] Times-Picayune* (August 3, 1926) 4.
481 *New Castle [PA] News* (September 21, 1926) 3; cf. *Seattle Daily Times* (April 14, 1927) 22.
482 *[Portland] Oregonian* (September 5, 1926) 12.
483 eBay # 281596408922, ended February 16, 2015.
484 Dieter Ladwig, *Slot Machines* (Secaucus, NJ: Chartwell Books, 1994) 73.
485 <http://www.arcade-museum.com/game_detail.php?game_id=947>
486 Bill Alexander, Anne D. Williams, and Richard W. Tucker, *The Game Catalog: U.S. Games Through 1950*[8] (AGCA, 1998), 74; <http://boardgamegeek.com/boardgame/21515/ben-hur>
487 #2000.361; see also, Alexander, Williams, and Tucker, *The Game Catalog*, 35.
488 eBay #7759368195, ended April 21, 2006.
489 <http://www.wopc.co.uk/usa/movie-souvenir.html>
490 In the possession of the author.
491 In the possession of the author.
492 *Sessional Papers [Volume c45 XVI—Part IX] Second Session of Tenth Legislature of the Province of Ontario* (Toronto: L. K. Cameron, 1904) 116.

493 *Berkshire World and Corn Belt Stockman* 6 (January 1, 1914) 31; 11 (January 1, 1919) 24.
494 In the possession of the author.
495 <http://en.wikipedia.org/wiki/Ben_Hur_Lampman>
496 *The Pittsburgh Courier* (November 10, 1945) 2; *NYT* (February 10, 1945) 5; *WP* (June 20, 1948) M18.
497 *Health and Strength* 9 (1904) 223.
498 *Kalgoorlie Miner* (August 7, 1907) 7.
499 *Bunbury Herald* (November 9, 1909) 3.
500 *Kalgoorlie Miner* (August 8, 1907) 6.
501 *The [Perth] Daily News* (August 9, 1907) 7.
502 *The [Perth] Daily News* (August 8, 1907) 6.
503 *The Singapore Free Press and Mercantile Advertiser* (July 15, 1908) 1; *De Sumatra* (September 2, 1909) 6; and *Port Pirie Reporter and North Western Mail* (December 15, 1909) 6.
504 *The American Galloway Herd Book* 4 (1889) 322; *The American Aberdeen-Angus Herd Book* 28 (1918) 636; *American Short-Horn, Herd Book* 103 (December 11, 1919) 774.
505 *The Standard Polad-China Record* 12 (Maryville, MO: The Press of James Todd, 1898) 46–7 [#18321]; *The Dominion Swine Breeders' Record* 18 (1907) 1:10; *National Duroc-Jersey Record* 61 (1919) 405.
506 *The American Sheep-Breeder and Wool-Grower* 29 (1909) 546.
507 *The American Milch Goat Record* 40 (1921) 73.
508 *Forest and Stream* 26 (May 20, 1886) 334; *The Field Dog Stud Book* 6 (1906) 440; *The Dog Fancier* 21 (July, 1912) 38.
509 *Boston Daily Globe* (August 14, 1904) 22.
510 *Wallace's American Trotting Register* 13 (1895) 381; *The Register of the American Saddle-Horse Breeders' Association* 2 (1909) 396; *The Morgan Horse and Register* 2 (1905) 442; cf. *Denver Rocky Mountain News* (August 23, 1914) 15.
511 *Idaho Statesman* (May 26, 1907) 8.
512 *Watertown [NY] Daily Times* (September 17, 1885) 4.
513 *Kansas City Times* (October 5, 1888) 3.
514 *CPD* (October 7, 1888) 3.
515 <http://www.cnrquarterhorses.com/quarter-horse-legends.htm; *LAT* (December 22, 1929) E8>
516 <http://www.allbreedpedigree.com/index.php?query_type=check&search_bar=horse&h=ben+hur&g=5&inbred=Standard>
517 Cf. G. H. Dawkins, *Present Day Sires and the Figure System* (London: Horace Cox, 1897) 15–16.
518 *American Cowboy* 10 (January/February, 2004) 52; Wallis, *The Real Wild West*, 356.
519 <http://www.circushistory.org/History/Ringling1903.htm#PROGRAM>
520 *Field and Stream* 50 (March 12, 1898) 213; cf. *CPD* (January 21, 1890) 5.
521 *The Breeder's Gazette* 73 (August 30, 1917) cover; cf. *Berkshire World and Corn Belt Stockman* 11 (February 1, 1919) 42.

522 *The Ayrshire Record* 37 (Bellows Falls, VT: P. H. Gobie Press, Inc., 1922) 28, 84, and 107.
523 *National Stockman and Farmer* 21 (May 6, 1897) 102.
524 Anne Sloan, *Houston Heights* (Charleston, SC: Arcadia Publishing, 2009) 86.
525 <http://www.chron.com/neighborhood/heights-news/article/Kaplan-s-Ben-Hur-bids-farewell-1932394.php>
526 *Denver Post* (December 8, 1907) 39; The Huntington [IN] Press (March 29, 1913) 4; *Emporia [KS] Gazette* (September 15, 1921) 5; (April 4, 1940) 10.
527 eBay #250253155555, ended June 4, 2008.
528 <http://www.liveauctioneers.com/item/3341797>; eBay #180098812021, ended April 28, 2007.
529 <http://www.collegebarscene.com/bar/Ben-Hur-Tavern/867>; eBay #320318 221344, ended November 24, 2008.
530 *Goshen [IN] Daily News* (July 17, 1896) 1; *The Indianapolis Morning Star* (April 11, 1905) 10.
531 *Jersey Journal* (November 9, 1911) 1; *[Portland] Oregonian* (November 22, 1921) 19; *CPD* (December 2, 1922) 15.
532 E.g. *NYT* (May 8, 1909) 15; *New York Blue Book* (New York: Dau's Blue Books, 1911) 17 and 749; <http://www.apartments.com/ben-hur-apts-san-francisco-ca/jteo5j5/>
533 <http://www.flickr.com/photos/anomalous_a/4236511826>
534 David J. Bodenhamer and Robert Graham Barrows, eds, *Encyclopedia of Indianapolis* (Bloomington: Indiana University Press, 1994) 1408; Letter from Henry Wallace to Frederick A. Duneka (May 19, 1908), Morgan Library, New York; *The Bookman* 28 (1909) 339; <http://www.vanrooy.com/blacherne/history-2>
535 *Longansport Reporter* (November 24, 1899) 11; *Indianapolis Star* (September 6, 1908) 5; *Chicago Star Publications* (October 10, 1907) 4; *AC* (June 7, 1921) 10; *Oakland Tribune* (May 28, 1903) 4; *The Seattle Daily Times* (November 29, 1903) 21; *Omaha World Herald* (September 17, 1918) 4; *Tulsa World* (August 2, 1911) 2; *Waterloo [IA] Evening Courier* (April 1, 1925) 7; *StLPD* (September 22, 1905) 2; *[Louisville] Courier-Journal* (October 15, 1922) B7; *Nashville Tennessean* (December 6, 1921) 3.
536 *TFD* 26 (November 2, 1923) 6; *Albion [IN] New Era* (March 7, 1906) 4.
537 *NYT* (July 29, 1939) 15.
538 <http://www.findagrave.com/cgi-bin/fg.cgi?page=gr&GRid=21933172>
539 eBay #110091663415, ended February 19, 2007.
540 *The New York Clipper* (June 28, 1922) 28; (May 9, 1923) 28; (June 27, 1923) 28. The hotel was sold in the 1930s; cf. Catherine A. Scott, *City Island and Orchard Beach* (Charleston, SC: Arcadia Publishing, 2004) 37; <http://www.ouroldneighborhood.com/bxpc/bxpc10/benhur.jpeg>; *NYHT* (March 10, 1936) 16; *The New York Sun* (March 10, 1930) 39.
541 Vanderwood, *Juan Soldado*, 104.
542 Cf. <http://www.etsy.com/listing/102019318/mexicali-mexico-1930s-alcohol>
543 *Oakland Tribune* (December 15, 1927) 5; *LAT* (January 25, 1928) A10.
544 *LAT* (September 19, 1931) 4.

545 OCLC: #827801061.
546 *The Brooklyn Daily Eagle Almanac* (1899) 105; *Omaha World Herald* (May 8, 1905) 5; cf. *The [New York] Sun* (June 26, 1897) 8.
547 *DFP* (March 22, 1903) 8.
548 *Watertown [NY] Daily Times* (February 16, 1904) 4.
549 *Kalamazoo Gazette* (April 25, 1914) 7.
550 *Oregonian* (August 16, 1916) 14.
551 *Baltimore American* (August 19, 1907) 10.
552 *Trenton Evening Times* (April 15, 1904) 1.
553 *Omaha World Herald* (October 14, 1901) 2.
554 *Springfield [MA] Union* (January 18, 1913) 17.
555 *[Harrisburg] Patriot* (February 23, 1905) 6.
556 *Jersey [City] Journal* (February 12, 1907) 7.
557 *TBS* (December 13, 1925) 55; (January 1, 1926) 12.
558 <http://www.coveredbridges.com/index.php/covered_bridges>
559 eBay #270105133422, ended April 8, 2007; cf. *Official Automobile Blue Book, 1922* (New York & Chicago: Automobile Blue Book, 1922) 576.
560 In the possession of the author. Cf. *Highways Green Book*[3] (Washington, DC: American Automobile Association, 1922) 419.
561 <http://digitalcollections.philau.edu/cdm/compoundobject/collection/postcards/id/1285/rec/7>; eBay #180111697896, ended May 4, 2007; <http://www.eachtown.com/places/Ben-Hur-Camp;1209414.html>
562 *Scouting Magazine* (March–April, 2002) <http://www.scoutingmagazine.org/issues/0203/a-five.html>; <http://www.fs.fed.us/outernet/oonf/ozark/recreation/ohteast.html>
563 Mildred Brooke Hoover and Douglas E. Kyle, *Historic Spots in California* (Palo Alto: Standford University Press, 1990) 201.
564 Shirley Sargent, *Mariposa County Guidebook* (Yosemite, CA: Flying Spur Press, 1984) 37–9.
565 <http://www.tshaonline.org/handbook/online/articles/hlb25>
566 *Life* 4 (June 27, 1938) 32.
567 In the possession of the author.

11 Ben-Hur *in Moving Pictures: Stereopticon Lectures and the 1907 Kalem* Ben-Hur

The unique popularity and adaptability of *Ben-Hur: A Tale of the Christ* would eventually lead to the first cinematic rendering of Wallace's story by the fledgling Kalem company in 1907. But during the transitional period from verbal presentations and staged dramatic performances to moving picture representations, optical manufacturers were employing new combinations of oxygen, hydrogen, and calcium to create a more powerful lamp and turn the centuries-old magic lantern concept into the stereopticon technology that projected crisp, detailed images over large distances. Comfortable with the technology and eager to employ the new formats for educational entertainment, churches, schools, and other institutions and societies as well as individual entrepreneurs purchased the relatively inexpensive apparatus and filled darkened halls and auditoriums with audiences eager to gaze at beautiful and spectacular "views" while listening to a descriptive lecture. *Ben-Hur: A Tale of the Christ* was the best-known and most profitable literary property during this period and provided both secular and religious subject matter as well as beautifully portrayed exotic settings and locations.

This same popularity and adaptability that made *Ben-Hur* such a desirable property for both the stereopticon and film formats put it on an inevitable collision course with the legal agreements uniquely and carefully monitored by Lew Wallace and Harper & Brothers and produced two important copyright challenges that ultimately affected the development and future of the entertainment industry. Indeed, the companies that were profiting from the new technologies specifically targeted *Ben-Hur* for test cases and even paid for most of the legal expenses. The copyright battles consumed nearly two decades, at the end of which the judicial process finally established the legal distinctions between literature, drama, photographic representations, and moving pictures. As the predominant property during the first great age of American consumer commercial expansion, *Ben-Hur*, perennially popular and profitable and with a copyright so carefully guarded in both literary and dramatic applications, had an enormous impact on the business of artistic entertainment. This is one of *Ben-Hur's* most important legacies.

STEREOPTICON PRESENTATIONS
The Reading Tradition Continues
During this important and transformative period from the 1890s into the first two decades of the twentieth century, when developing technologies were integrated into methods for exhibiting and marketing popular culture, Ben-Hur commerce kept expanding into many sectors of the public economy, and various tableaux presentations and then the Klaw & Erlanger production continued to entertain audiences across the country, as did Sousa's and Paull's chariot race music. Meanwhile the novel *Ben-Hur: A Tale of the Christ* had by no means fallen from public consciousness. It continued to permeate the public through continued book sales plus countless readings and declamations of sections of the novel and lectures and sermons that analyzed its story and focused on its morality. These kinds of representations, many of them raising money for charitable causes or individual profit, continued for decades, be it the Rev. Johnston's sermon on Lew Wallace and *Ben-Hur* at the First Congregational Church in Springfield, Illinois, in 1905,[1] the "Detroit Sorosis" fundraiser in 1909,[2] the graduation sermon for the Mansfield [Ohio] High School in 1911,[3] the 1901, 1907, and 1929 Christmas programs at the Grand View Presbyterian Church in Los Angeles, the Methodist church in Nashua, Iowa, and the Lutheran Church in Reno, Nevada,[4] or the series of "Ben Hur" lectures delivered in Appleton, Wisconsin in 1938 and an evening church lecture in Harrisburg, Pennsylvania in 1939, just to cite a representative and chronologically wide-ranging series of examples.[5] Some of the presentations were enhanced. In 1897 a "recital" given by Mrs. Henry A. Powell and witnessed by "many prominent eastern district women" in the music room of Brooklyn's Knapp mansion consisted of six scenes "selected for interpretation," including "Messala and the Roman youth at a midnight revel, when it is revealed to Messala that Ben Hur is alive," each of the scenes interspersed with piano solos.[6] One year earlier Anna Lee Darnbrough began "The Angel and the Shepherd" with a backstage chant that "produces a strong effect on the audience."[7] Her brief write-up in *Werner's Magazine* adds:

> The arrangement is original with her and cannot be published, owing to the owners of the copyright refusing to have such extracts made from the book.

As we will see shortly, this announcement comes within one month of the lawsuit Wallace and Harper brought against Riley Brothers for distributing a printed lecture on *Ben-Hur*.

The novel was now sometimes recognized as a classic, and the public was expected to be familiar with its details. Tom Fitch's 1910 op-ed in the *Los Angeles Times*, for instance, assumed his readers knew – thirty years after publication – that Judah alternated rowing on the left and right sides of the galley:

> Education helps the laborer. . . . The ignorant galley slave, who always labored at an oar on the same side of the vessel went back into the world deformed when his term of service expired; but educated Ben Hur preserved his manly proportions by being granted the privilege of daily changing sides. The college graduate who knows how to handle his flexors and extensors will drill more cubic feet of rock in a day than will the cockney miner.[8]

The novel even made the news in 1922, when Edward Meagher, "the world's fastest reader," was reported to have read it in just five hours (although usually reported as ten).[9]

Charles Montaville Flowers was so successful at giving readings of *Ben-Hur* that he, much like E. T. Paull and Klaw & Erlanger, created a *Ben-Hur* product and remained associated with it for several decades. He claimed to have given as many as 300 presentations in a single tour,[10] and like many other Ben-Hur speakers, he lectured in the Y.M.C.A., Lyceum, and Chautauqua circuits.[11] Even as late as 1919, after he had become a political essayist and campaigned (unsuccessfully) for California's 9th Congressional seat in 1918, his publicity brochure not only listed his earlier literary lectures but advertised that "he is willing, under special arrangement," to give his Ben-Hur lecture.[12] In 1930 he is listing his Ben-Hur presentation as a "milestone."[13] In organizing his presentation, Flowers divided the novel into four "acts," the first on the parapet of the House of Hur, the second depicting the conversation between Judah and Arrius, the third the chariot race, and the fourth the final visit of Iris after the death of Messala.[14] Much like Gurley-Kane, he impersonated fifteen different characters from the novel, changing his voice and making a variety of facial expressions and body movements:

> Now he was the young Ben-Hur, now the haughty Roman conqueror, now the shrinking, fearful, pleading Tirzah, fearing in sisterly fashion for Ben-Hur's life. Later he became the abrupt but honest Roman sea fighter, the Quintus whose adopted son Ben-Hur became, then each of the characters came on in turn and each was real – Iris, Simonides, Sheik, Ildrahim [sic], Esther, the timidly loving Jewish girl; the still haughtier Messala of the days before the chariot race, then the old servant, Amrah; the leprosy stricken mother and sister and lastly the Christ.
> The chariot race at Antioch, in his interpretation as well as in the theatrical productions, was the most powerful part. With fierce intensity and passion, his monologue brought the whole action to the highest point of realism, following out Gen. Wallace's description to the fullest. There were other scenes full of the same fire and intensity, and through it all the spirit of the story and of the times was preserved in extraordinary fashion. The entertainment was a most unusual one and most excellent.[15]

Born in Ohio and a graduate of the College of Music of Cincinnati, the early part of his career he spent in educational administration and developing his technique. Already he had lectured on "Ben-Hur – a Study in Plot-Construction."[16] Just a few months after he published a didactic article for *Werner's Magazine,* he began presenting *Ben-Hur* late in 1896.[17] Already by January, 1897, he featured the following claim in his ad for an appearance at the Sixth Street Methodist Church in Portsmouth, Ohio:

> At Crawfordsville, Ind. a few months ago Gen. Lew Wallace, the author of "Ben Hur," was the first person to congratulate Mr. Flowers when he had finished rendering this great monologue.[18]

He continued making this claim for years. The pre-publicity for a number of his appearances offered this expanded version:

> Gen. Lew Wallace said of Montaville Flowers' work: "It was a most excellent arrangement of Ben Hur and Mr. Flowers displayed splendid judgment in his adaptation. His elocutionary power is admirably suited to the work. He presents the scenes and incidents of the plot in a charming manner, and his work in the adaptation was by far the best I ever heard. Mr. Flowers' work has my most hearty approval. It is the revival of the ancient eastern custom of story telling. It is a re-creation of the lost art. It is in safe hands with this young man and will prove an attractive form of high-class platform work. I wish him success."[19]

Corroborating evidence for Flowers' claims is non-existent, and some of his other pre-publicity citing the *Cincinnati Enquirer* and *Nashville Sun* are difficult to verify.[20] Moreover, considering Wallace's copyright concerns at the time – he had recently rejected Salvini's requests in the summer of 1895, it would seem highly unlikely that Lew Wallace would have given his "most hearty approval" to anyone, even to a talented young Ohioan attempting to earn a living by rendering the plot and characters of his novel in a public performance, especially in the fall of 1896, when Judge Lacombe imposed an injunction upon Riley Brothers for adapting Wallace's text for lecture purposes, as we will see presently.

Stereopticon Slide Sets
Stereopticon lectures illustrating the story of *Ben-Hur: A Tale of the Christ* began to appear in 1889. This was relatively late in the popularization of stereopticon presentations, but Wallace's property was nonetheless one of the first novels to be adapted. The narration for the notable, December 5, 1889, performance in Montreal that included Miss Tessier's melodic rendition of "Wake Not, But Hear Me, Love" was given by L[ouis] O[livier] Armstrong. An extant broadside tells us that "he tells the story and illustrates it in such a manner that it rivets and retains the interest of every one present."[21] His slides were a hodgepodge of photographic copies of "masterpieces" by Rubens, Raphael, Doré, Wagner, Scheffer, Delaroche, and others, landscape and travel photos "from nature," and others "transformed into copies of the originals by an eminent artist." Unlike most subsequent *Ben-Hur* stereopticon lectures, Armstrong's went well beyond the chronological period covered by the novel, for it included the life of St.

Paul and even the opening of the Colosseum. Like Flowers, the program claims that Armstrong had Wallace's permission:

> All the most striking portions of Gen. Lew Wallace's book – "Ben-Hur" – are illustrated (by his kind permission).

This cannot be corroborated either, but neither Wallace nor Harper could have had much recourse in Canada anyway.

Genuine sets dedicated to *Ben-Hur* appeared even later. T. H. McAllister's *Catalogue and Price List of Stereopticons, Dissolving-View Apparatus, Magic Lanterns, and Artistically-Colored Photographic Views on Glass*, dated February, 1887, lists a few thousand views of historical sites, geological wonders, and famous sculptures.[22] Because churches represented their broadest customer base, the first and largest groups of slides consist of some 200 Old Testament, New Testament, and specialized biblical scenes as well as moralizing "Tales of Temperance" and selections from Bunyan's *Pilgrim's Progress*. A few pages further along are the brief lists of limited numbers of slides representing more contemporary literary works, twelve for *Uncle Tom's Cabin*, six for *Rip Van Winkle*, and twelve for two poems by Robert Burns. The only large set associated with a literary work contains the fifty views of Milton's *Paradise Lost*, but these were less for the poem and more for the fifty illustrations Gustav Doré executed for the 1866 edition of the poem. For comparison, the 1895 *Illustrated Catalogue of Stereopticons* issued by the McIntosh Battery and Optical Company of Chicago lists several thousand more slides, mostly travel slides, which include eighty-seven views of the 1890 Passion Play at Oberammergau, more Doré illustrations, series on Napoleon and the Crusades, children's stories like *Cinderella* and *The Three Bears*, and more. But other than a few new Dickens' entries with six, twelve, and twenty-five slides each, the only large literary set is the "New Ben-hur Set" [sic] with sixty slides. Eventually *In His Steps* warranted an even larger set of 150 slides listed in the 1902 Kleine catalog, but Sheldon's bestseller was not published until 1897, a year or so after *Ben-Hur* stereopticon lectures had already taken a solid foothold. In February, 1897, for instance, two different churches in neighboring Michigan cities were simultaneously offering *Ben-Hur* lectures.[23] Being first in a new category is often vital to becoming a permanent fixture in the popular culture.

This set of sixty slides was painted by the Philadelphian Joseph Boggs Beale, a pioneer magic lantern artist with over 600 religious images to his credit, and originally executed for C[aspar] W[arren] Briggs Company, also of Philadelphia.[24] Beale did not work in a painterly style. His lines are precise with a minimum of shading, and his images tend to fill the slide, often cropped into a circle. His painting of the galley, for instance, depicts three rows of oarsmen in loincloths, viewed from a frontal perspective reaching back from the right side of the slide to the center, where there is a Roman standing before a door at the back of the galley. The left is filled with a series of mast bases, again in vanishing perspective, in front of which sits the beating hortator and red-cloaked Arrius. His cloak trails to the floor, pointing towards the distinctively dark-haired slave at the head of the second row, presumably Judah Ben-Hur. The effect such images beaming in the dark had on audiences was considerably more powerful than modern audiences can appreciate. One account tells us:

> Images of a chariot race elicited cheers, and images of Jesus giving Ben-Hur water to drink awed and electrified congregations in to a palpable hush.[25]

The McAllister Company of New York introduced its set of sixty *Ben-Hur* slides in their October, 1894, catalog.[26] The same set was also sold by Williams, Brown, and Earle of Philadelphia.[27] They also sold a nearly identical "Economic Series" in 1895.[28] The McAllister catalogs offered both uncolored ($30) and "finely colored" versions ($90).

McIntosh/McAllister:
1. The Meeting of the Three Wise Men
2. The Joppa Gate
3. Mary, the Mother of Christ
4. The Way to Bethlehem
5. Cave of the Kahn at Bethlehem
6. The Field of the Shepherds
7. "While Shepherds Watched their Flocks"
8. Angel Appearing to the Shepherds
9. In the Cave
10. Wise Men Arriving at Jerusalem
11. Herod
12. Adoration of Wise Men
13. Ben Hur before Arrius
14. A Judean Home, exterior
15. A Judean Home, court
16. Mother of Ben Hur
17. Tirzah
18. The Tile Falling From the Roof
19. Son of Mary
20. Arrius Going to Sea
21. Ben Hur before Arrius
22. Sea Fight
23. Celebrating Victory of Arrius
24. Warehouse of Simonides
25. Ben Hur's First Interview with Simonides
26. Grove of Daphne
27. Procession in the Grove
28. The Stadium
29. Orchard of Palms
30. Sheik Ilderim
31. The Arabs
32. Iris [sic]
33. Morning of the Games

34. Circus at Antioch
35. Chariot Race
36. Chariot Race, Messala down
37. Chariot Race, Ben Hur wins
38. Messala Carried from the Circus
39. The Combat in the Palace of Idernee
40. Tower of Antonia, Exterior
41. Tower of Antonia, Dungeon
42. Tower of Antonia, Tirzah and Mother
43. Jerusalem
44. Leper's Dwelling Places
45. Amrah Taking Food to her Mistress
46. Group of Lepers
47. At Bethabara
48. "Behold the Lamb of God"
49. The Coming of the King
50. Ben Hur and his Mother
51. Gethsemane, Betrayal
52. Gethsemane, Christ Taken Prisoner
53. The Going to Calvary
54. Nailing Christ to the Cross
55. Christ on the Cross
56. "It is Finished"
57. Ben Hur's Home
58. Ben Hur and Esther
59. The Catacombs
60. Ecce Homo

In addition, a *Ben-Hur* set of twenty-four slides was sold by the [George] Kleine Optical Company of Chicago.[29] According to the George Eastman House, this set was also originally published by C. W. Briggs and painted by Beale, again in a precise style.[30]

Kleine:
1. Balthazar in the Desert awaiting the arrival of the Wise Men
2. The Wise Men Relating their Histories
3. Joppa Gate
4. Wise Men conferring with Herod
5. Adoration of the Wise Men
6. Ben Hur and Messala
7. Ben Hur and his Mother
8. The Tile Falling from the Roof
9. Jesus gives Ben Hur to drink
10. Ben Hur before Arrius on the Galley
11. Ben Hur Saves Arrius in the Sea Fight
12. Ben Hur's First Visit to Simonides
13. Ben Hur checks Messala's Steeds
14. The Gambling Party. A Roman Orgie
15. Ben Hur and Iris on the Lake
16. Ben Hur training the Arabs
17. Chariot Race – the Overthrow
18. The Wrestling Scene in the Palace of Idernee

19. Tirzah and her Mother in the Dungeon
20. Ben Hur views Jerusalem
21. Ben Hur Discovered by his Mother and Tirzah
22. Amrah giving Food to her Mistress
23. Ben Hur Finds his Mother
24. Ben Hur and Esther

The October, 1899, McAllister catalog offers five of the Kleine slides (#1, 11, 13, 14, 21) in addition to the complete set of sixty.[31]

In January, 1896, the English Riley Brothers began selling their set of seventy-two slides in the United States, and they immediately took out a copyright on "The Stereopticon Illustrator of 'Ben Hur' A Tale of the Christ By General Lew Wallace – 72 Lantern Slides Pictures by Eminent Artists."[32] Costing some $5000, ambitious in scope, execution, and distribution, and aggressively advertised, Riley issued a flyer that explains the division of labor between two artists, Frank F. Weeks [Francis Frederick Theophilus Weeks] and Nannie Preston.

> This important and realistic set of pictures have been prepared with considerable labor, and at an enormous cost. The commission being first entrusted to the Patent Novelty Lantern Slide Co., under the management of Mr. F. F. Weeks, but the slow progress made with the work, and the enormous cost of the process led us to transfer the commission when the first 25 pictures had been *completed*, and the whole of the slides, from the picture numbered 22, have been drawn by the celebrated Artist who designed the set which has elicited so much praise from all who have seen it on the "Pilgrim's Progress" and the six Sermons on the same subject. It will be seen that these pictures fully uphold this artist's already high reputation.[33]

Weeks' heavily etched, atmospheric style does seem to yield to the less populated vistas of Preston at the twenty-fifth slide, #22: Arrius on the Mole.[34] Riley sold through other companies as well. Williams, Brown, and Earle sold slides depicting Riley images and maintaining the Riley sequence numbers but labeled as their own.[35] In addition, the George Eastman House in Rochester contains an uncolored set of Riley slides that they attribute to P.N.L.S. Company.

Riley:
1. Introductory
2. Balthasar in the Desert
3. Balthasar and Melchior Embracing
4. The Conference in the Tent
5. Melchior kneeling before the Star
6. Following the Star
7. Joseph and Mary leaving Jerusalem
8. Joseph pleading with the Gatekeeper
9. An Asylum in the Cave
10. The Sheep-fold near Bethlehem
    10A Effect – The Affrighted Shepherds
    10B Effect – The Angelic Visitant
    10C Effect – The Host of Angels

11. Adoration of the Shepherds
12. The Magi approaching Jerusalem
13. Herod before the Sanhedrim
14. The Magi before Herod
15. The Watchman observes the Star
    15A Effect – The Adoration of the Magi
16. Messala and Ben Hur
17. Ben Hur and his Mother
18. Tirzah [Amrah] and Ben Hur
19. The Accident to Valerius
20. Ben Hur made Prisoner
21. The youth Christ gives Ben Hur to drink
22. Arrius on the Mole
23. Arrius watching Ben Hur at the oar
24. Ben Hur before Arrius
25. Ben Hur holds Arrius to the plank
26. Ben Hur before Simonides
27. Simonides tells his Story to his Daughter
28. Ben Hur gives the Cup to Balthasar
29. Ben Hur and Sheik Ilderim
30. Malluch before Simonides
31. Simonides and Esther
32. Messala and the Romans
33. Ilderim and his Guests
34. Ira[s] and Ben Hur on the Lake
35. The Rage of Ilderim
36. Simonides gives Document to Ben Hur
37. Ben Hur and Esther on the Terrace
38. Sanballat receives the Wagers
39. The Chariot Race
40. Messala Overthrown
41. Attempted Assassination of Ben Hur
42. Tirzah and her Mother in the Dungeon
43. Gessius discovers the Captives
44. Freedom!
45. Ben Hur Gazing on Jerusalem
46. Tirzah and her Mother bending over Ben Hur
47. Amrah brings provisions to the lepers
48. Ben Hur fights with the Centurion
49. The Party at the Fountain
50. Ben Hur and Iras in the Desert
51. John the Baptist and Jesus
52. Ben Hur tells of the Miracles of Christ
    52A Effect – Touching the Garment's Hem
    52B Effect – Giving Sight to the Blind
    52C Effect – Raising the Widow's Son
53. Amrah and the Lepers
54. The Lepers wait for Christ
55. Christ heals the Lepers
56. Ben Hur embraces his Mother
57. Ben Hur and the perfidious Egyptian

58. Christ Betrayed
59. Jesus and Ben Hur
60. Ben Hur fleeing – naked
61. The Raising of the Cross
62. The Death of Balthasar
63. Iras kissing Ben Hur's Children
64. On the Housetop
65. The Catacombs of San Calixto

Additional sets were specially ordered and manufactured. The Tribe of Ben-Hur employed a set of thirty-five slides created specifically for the organization by the George W. Bond & Company of Chicago.[36] The Bond set is eclectic. After the initial colored portrait photograph of Lew Wallace and another of him sitting under the beech tree, the next image, the three Wise Men under the tent, is a Briggs slide painted by Beale, as is the slide of Ben-Hur training the Arabs.[37] The two slides of the chariot race are derived from the Checa and Wagner paintings. The rest derived from still other photographic and painted sources. This may have been the set used by the Rev. W. H. Kerr of Crawfordsville. In the second issue of *The Chariot*, to which he was a contributor, a paragraph served as an advertisement for his stereopticon lecture, describing him as "a close student of the book Ben-Hur" and his target audience as "Courts of our Order desiring to give an entertainment that will delight and entertain all classes."[38]

The largest known *Ben-Hur* set was created for John P[hilip] Clum. An announcement published in *The Washington Post* explains:

> The lovers of English literature and art should surely not miss the opportunity that is afforded them at Carroll Institute Hall this evening when Mr. John P. Clum, of California, will deliver that ever interesting story of "Ben Hur." Much time and money have been expended to make the lecture complete in every respect. It is illustrated with over 150 highly-colored views. They are the work of a Washington artist, and are conceded to be the most complete set obtainable.[39]

Elsewhere in the same issue it says that the lecture would be "profusely illustrated with 200 colored views." Another announcement specifies that the views were created "under Mr. Clum's personal supervision."[40] In an otherwise undocumented but extraordinary instance, Klaw & Erlanger created a version for a one-night performance in Crawfordsville in 1901:

> The stereopticon views to be shown have never been seen on canvas before. Klaw & Erlanger, who own the dramatic rights of Ben-Hur have granted permission for their use for this occasion only and the plates are to be destroyed after this lecture.[41]

Many years later, around 1920, Willis F. Hume, a pastor in Tonawanda, New York, retired in Oberlin, Ohio, and spent the remaining fifteen years of his life giving religion-oriented stereopticon lectures.[42] His lectures do not surface in the newspaper archives, but an eBay auction in 2006 offered a vintage carrying case of stereopticon slides from various sources. Tellingly, the heavy case, with the label "Penetrating Africa," contained

Figure 11.1 Stereopticon views illustrated popular, commercial, and spiritual *Ben-Hur* readings and lectures for three decades. The two large slides demonstrate the different styles employed by the artists for Riley (L: Ben Hur tells of the Miracles of Christ) and Briggs (R: Ben Hur Discovered by his Mother and Sister).

slides of Africa, Japan, India, European sites, Chicago, Wisconsin, a number of religious slides depicting the Ten Commandments, an old blind leper, and other slides typical for the period. As often, the only non-religious, non-travel slides were five representing *Ben-Hur*.[43] Hume's slides are identified with "REV. WILLIS F. HUME-COLORED SLIDES-OBERLIN, O" printed in small font. Above are the titles:

#8: Summit of Mt. St. Elias
#20: Ben Hur at Bethlehem
#62: Grove of Date Palms
#85: [Amrah] Fell at Feet of Her Old Mistress"
#95: [Jesus] Sank Under His Burden

The first three of these are simply contemporary photographs of the Holy Land.

Lastly, a 1919 issue of *The Expositor* included a personal ad selling a set of *Ben-Hur* Viopticon slides.[44] The Viopticon was a portable unit developed by the Victor Animatograph Company in the 1910s.

The Kleine set of twenty-four necessarily omits much that the larger sets contain, devoting five slides to the Nativity, McAllister twelve, and Riley fifteen plus the three images that dissolved onto #10: The Sheepfold near Bethlehem (#10A Effect – The Affrighted Shepherds, #10B Effect – The Angelic Visitant, #10C Effect – The Host of Angels) and another onto #15: The Watchman observes the Star (15A Effect – The Adoration of the Magi). The next three Kleine slides illustrating Ben-Hur's family and arrest lack several of McAllister's and Riley's intimate domestic scenes. All three sets, of course, have a slide of Jesus giving the drink to Ben-Hur by the well and also the scene of Ben-Hur being discovered by his mother and sister, both of which were popular also in public readings and in the contemporary *Ben-Hur, in Tableaux and Pantomime*, as well as the chariot race.[45] While the Riley set greatly expands its number of illustrations of the Nativity scenes, the McIntosh/McAllister set establishes a different sense of religious tone by incorporating several slides quoting scripture (#7: "While shepherds Watched their Flocks"; #48: "Behold the Lamb of God; #56: "It is Finished") as well as a final slide (#60: Ecce Homo) that does not illustrate a scene from the novel. Featuring the two most popular subjects in the stereopticon slide catalogs, in addition to the biblical slides, the McIntosh/McAllister also inserts exotic scenic views of the Holy Land (#2: The Joppa Gate, #4: The Way to Bethlehem, #14: A Judean Home, exterior, #15: A Judean Home, court, #40: Tower of Antonia, Exterior, #43: Jerusalem, and #47: At Bethabara). This reduces the number of slides directly related to the novel.

Although the McIntosh/McAllister set inserts two slides illustrating the novel's Daphne episode that are not included in the other two sets, in general the Riley set pays the most attention to the details of the story.

Kleine, for instance, allots just five slides to the pre-chariot race encounters with Simonides and Esther, Balthasar and Iras, and Messala, while Riley allots thirteen, adding Malluch, Sanballat, and several events from the novel not normally represented visually, e.g. #36: Simonides gives Document to Ben Hur. Most important, in illustrating the post-chariot race events of the novel with just seven slides, the Kleine finishes without showing an image of Jesus or the Crucifixion. In contrast, Riley offers twenty-five and here inserts three dissolving slides for religious allure (#52A Effect – Touching the Garment's Hem, #52B Effect – Giving Sight to the Blind, #52C Effect – Raising the Widow's Son).

The Suit Against Riley Brothers
The most critical difference between the sets was not the images but the accompanying text. So far as the extant evidence suggests, most of the *Ben-Hur* sets did not include a text to be read while the images were projected. The 1895 McIntosh catalog (126) offered to provide some information, though apparently more for biblical and travel slides:

> Descriptive Readings or "Lectures" of any series of slides not accompanied with a printed lecture, will be furnished by us in manuscript at 40 cents per slide, or in typewriting at 50 cents per slide. The large public library of this city enables us to obtain any information of "data" published upon almost any subject.

Of course, no *Ben-Hur* stereopticon lecture was too far removed from the book. None are known to have modified the story drastically or supplemented it with new characters or events. Some mentioned or even focused initially on Lew Wallace, but the only substantial narrative modifications were in the treatment of the Christ. Moreover, the novel was an integral part of both the advertising and the public's relationship to the presentation. An announcement in the *San Francisco Chronicle* from June, 1895, concludes with:

> It is a rare opportunity to become thoroughly familiar with a book that has attracted unusual attention in these days of prolific bookmaking.[46]

Another newspaper ad for a presentation included a notice that "a great many people are now reading Ben Hur preparing for Rev. McButt's illustrated lecture."[47] The Rev. E. Homer Wellman, a pastor in Brooklyn who boasted about his Ph.D., gave a *Ben-Hur* lecture illustrated with slides depicting "eighty of the most beautiful pictures by celebrated foreign artists shown on the canvas as huge oil paintings."[48] His lecture lasted nearly two hours, and recounted the story of the novel in great detail. The last line of Wellman's notice reads:

> The dramatic form of the story cannot be realized from a resume like this, but to those who know the work, it will be quite explanatory; and to those who do not, the above sketch cannot but be interesting.

The Riley lecture soon came to Wallace's attention. The text may have begun with "I can give but a brief outline of the story, but the book may be read by all," but Riley was unique in offering a free, printed text with the purchase of a *Ben-Hur* slide set. The cover of the British version contains the title:

A TALE OF THE CHRIST
Abridged from the well-known book by Lew Wallace
ADAPTED AS
A LECTURE
TO ACCOMPANY A SERIES OF
Magnificent Transparencies
FOR THE LANTERN.

The text is long, spreading over twenty printed pages, devoting a distinct, well-marked paragraph to each slide. It is a conscious paraphrase, that is, often using the same words and even whole phrases, albeit much condensed, or substituting a simple synonym for one of Wallace's original words. Wallace's description of the scene at the well in Nazareth (2.7), for instance includes: [my italics]

A *prisoner* whom the horsemen were guarding was the object of curiosity. He was afoot, *bareheaded*, half naked, *his hands bound behind him. A thong fixed to his wrists* was *looped over the neck of a horse*. The dust went with the party when in movement, wrapping him in yellow fog, sometimes in a dense cloud. He drooped forward, footsore and faint. The villagers could see *he was young*.

The equivalent Riley "Reading":

Their pitying eyes fell upon a *prisoner* who walked *bareheaded, his hands bounds behind him, a thong fixed to his wrists* and *looped over the neck of a horse*. He *was* very *young*.

Wallace: he was *stooping over the prisoner*, and offering him *drink*.
Riley: *Stooping* down *over the prisoner* he gave *him* a *drink*.

Wallace: And *so, for the first time,* Judah and the son of Mary *met and parted*.
Riley: *So for the first time* Ben Hur and the Christ *met and parted*.

In contrast, the Riley lecture modifies the end of the chariot race, removing any possible blame from Judah and thus palliating the revenge motif:

And now they are about to make the turn, and Messala draws in his left-hand steeds. His spirits are high, 200 yards away are fame and fortune. But at that moment those in the gallery saw Ben Hur lean forward – out flew his lash, and, and in the language of the Arabs he urged on his willing steeds. There was a loud crash as the noble animals bounded forward, and a thrill ran through the circus as the Roman's chariot went to pieces, and Messala, entangled in the reins, pitched headlong forward.

The flyer says that this "Reading" was available from Riley's offices in New York and Bradford, England, as well as "any optician or lantern slide" dealer or agency in the United States, including Kansas City, Minneapolis, Chattanooga, San Francisco, Portland, Chicago, and Boston, or Great Britain, Canada, Australia, New Zealand, South Africa or India. Despite the international coverage, it was simply in Pewaukee, Wisconsin, where Walter Clark and David Cox of the *Ben-Hur, in Tableaux and Pantomime* took objection.[49] February 8, 1896, four weeks after Riley Bros. filed for their copyright, Wallace sent a letter to Harper along with a copy of the flyer ("a prospectus of pictures"), concluding that, "For my part, I cannot avoid a feeling that, while they advertise, they cheapen the work."[50] Harper did not respond to Wallace but sent the flyer to Clark. Clark went to Augustus T. Gurlitz, his attorney in New York, who wrote a letter on his behalf to Wallace on March 21, which happened to be the same day that Wallace posted his follow-up letter to Harper.[51] Comparing it unfavorably to the Wellman Readings, Gurlitz described the Riley slide set and lecture as "an enterprise which will probably destroy the pantomime and tableaux exhibitions of 'Ben-Hur' unless steps are taken promptly to suppress it." Indeed, when Clark purchased a set, he learned that the company could not keep up with the demand. Gurlitz warned further that "the country will be overrun with these performances." Clark even offered to pay half the legal expenses. Wallace's letter to Harper included the "reading" Gurlitz had sent him and made a formal request that they begin action against Riley, reminding them that they were contractually obligated to do so.[52] Wallace and Harper filed suit on April 26, claiming damages of $10,000.[53]

Legal challenges on behalf of his own interests were not new to Wallace. He had sued the United States in the 1880s in a salary dispute arising from his service as minister plenipotentiary to Turkey [133 U.S. 180: Wallace v. United States], and he appealed the decision in 1890. And he along with Harper had acted in 1890 to protect his *Ben-Hur* copyright when a Minneapolis newspaper attempted to serialize the novel in Norwegian.[54] But this was his first legal challenge to protect a derivative *Ben-Hur* product. On April 26, sixteen days after Riley was issued a copyright by the Library of Congress, Wallace and Harper brought suit against the firm of Herbert J. Riley Bros.[55] Because it involved such a popular property, a "Special Dispatch" to the *Cincinnati Enquirer* informed readers that upon publication Wallace and Harper had reserved all rights to the publication and dramatization of the novel, that they had sold the dramatization rights to Clark and Cox, and that Wallace and Harper now "claimed to have been damaged to the extent of $10,000." The case was adjourned until May 1, and at that point the story was syndicated nationwide.[56] The report reached England as well, adding that Herbert Riley had already sailed for the United States to defend his firm in the American court system.[57] *The Optical Magic Lantern Journal and Photographic Enlarger* inserted into the syndicated announcement that this suit "certainly puts the American copyright law in a very unfavourable light" and appended an editorial comment:

> In this country it might seem absurd to claim that a lantern entertainment is in effect a dramatic representation. The action is a novel one, and is regarded as a test.

The complainants argued that live models had been used for the production of some of the slides, and therefore when the slides were projected they seemed to reproduce the same effect as their *Ben-Hur, in Tableaux and Pantomime,* and this they claimed was a "dramatic representation" and infringement of the dramatic rights that had been sold to Clark.[58] As a point of fact, in 1894 Weeks and Joseph Riley had taken out a patent [#8615] on their lantern slide process that began by photographing "living figures or models against a plain background."[59] The Riley Brothers' attorney, M. D. Wilber, argued that a drama, according to "any author of any dictionary in the English language," required "representation by living actors" with "living voices and movements."[60]

After several more months of "prolonged legal warfare" and "skirmishing," the case was further postponed until October, but during the interim, on September 2, Judge Emile Lacombe of the U.S. Second Circuit Court in New York, issued a preliminary injunction restraining Riley from selling, advertising, or distributing "copies of any compilation or epitome of the dramatic scenes and incidents of 'Ben Hur'" as well as copies of "any summarized reading of 'Ben Hur.'"[61] This gave Wallace and Harper cause for optimism, for they had successfully found legal redress to the copyright infringement insofar as their novel was concerned. New York's *Evening Telegram* and *Tribune* both ended their reports by writing, perhaps paraphrasing the plaintiffs' attorney:

> This, it would seem, will put an end to "Ben Hur" stereopticon lectures, excepting those authorized by General Wallace, until the lawsuit is decided.

This was wishful thinking. Writing his decision in late September, Judge Lacombe left the injunction but ruled in favor of Riley insofar as granting permission for them to sell their *Ben-Hur* slide sets, and he awarded no damages to the plaintiffs.[62] Ruling in favor of the defendants, Lacombe stated that he could not be certain that the life models or drawings were originally prepared specifically for the purpose of illustrating the novel, and, even if they had been, "it would hardly be contended that no one, except with permission of complainants, might produce and sell copies of drawings, the *motif* of which was suggested in the novel." *The Optical Magic Lantern Journal and Photographic Enlarger* commented that the decision was in harmony with the dictates of common sense, but it also reiterated that "this case has excited the utmost interest in the United States, where it was regarded as a test case."[63] In November the *Journal* published a study of Weeks' methodology and made it very clear that he did indeed use live models in his studio where he maintained a supply of costumes, backdrops, and other related paraphernalia.[64] And in their statement published by the *Journal*, Riley Brothers admitted the judge's point in saying "that if we have been setting it forth in the 'Vitascope,' where there is such a real representation of life," he could have understood the argument by the plaintiffs. This will soon take us to the next *Ben-Hur* test case, the Kalem case more than a decade hence, which, unlike this one, did involve living actors and movements but did not involve a printed "compilation or epitome." In between came a less problematic encounter between Klaw & Erlanger and a Ben-Hur lodge in Indiana.[65] Their Tribe of Ben-Hur initiation rituals had become so "spectacular" that Klaw & Erlanger regarded them as an infringement on their theatrical rights. The lodge complied without objection.

Meanwhile the Riley *Ben-Hur* stereopticon presentations continued apace. The next year Lebanon, Pennsylvania, heard a *Ben-Hur* stereopticon lecture using seventy-two slides,[66] and even in 1901 there is a record of Riley's 72-slide set being used in a Christmas celebration at the Boston Baptist Bethel on behalf of navy seamen.[67] And whether consisting of Riley slides or not, as we shall see, *Ben-Hur* stereopticon lectures continued well into the twentieth century. Wallace himself received two requests for stereopticon slides of himself just weeks after the Riley decision was handed down, one from G. N. Buzby of Merchantville, New Jersey,[68] the other from a Bostonian, A. Dobbins, requesting a stereopticon slide for his own presentation, "'The Two Princes,' partly taken from the story of Ben-Hur."[69] Meanwhile in England, *The Optical Magic Lantern Journal and Photographic Enlarger* had already reported that the pending decision in the U.S. "[does] not in any way affect sales in this country."[70] In fact, *The Journal* suggests, the publicity may have helped sales.[71]

Notable Stereopticon Lecturers
Because announcements for stereopticon presentations were usually local affairs written on a chalk board, printed on a paper circular, or spread by word of mouth, modern electronic archives preserve only a proportionally small number of stereopticon announcements and advertisements printed in newspapers of the period.[72] One of the earliest notices for a *Ben-Hur* presentation surfaces in Watertown, New York, in December, 1890, where a "goodly-sized audience took in some measure of the interest and spirit of Gen. Wallace's great book."[73] One half year later another turns up on the West Coast. On June 6, 1891, the Rev. George L[orin] McNutt of the Sacramento Congregational Church advertised in the local newspaper that he would "tell the wonderful story of Ben Hur, using over fifty views of great paintings with the stereopticon."[74] Three days later the paper included a simple announcement that proceeds were for the benefit of the Sunday school. That this was followed by an independent

review one night later reflects the novelty of the presentation, the paper's reviewer being quite aware that this was a coordinated visual and verbal adaptation.[75] The review informs us at the outset that this was "one of the largest audiences ever gathered in the very large auditorium," in fact the largest in the city,[76] and that the "very beautiful stereoptican [sic] views [were] shown in an admirable manner – indeed we do not remember ever having seen finer views thrown up by the magic lantern process." But McNutt was roundly criticized for speaking too rapidly, and the reviewer makes a specific comparison to another rendition of Wallace's material:

> He attempted to read the celebrated "Chariot Race" extract from General Wallace's book. But it was a total failure. The audience before him heard it read not long ago by an artist who, without stereopticon aid, made the recital so vivid, and so graphically depicted the dramatic scene that the auditors fairly held their breath as the recital proceeded. . . . "Ben Hur" is a story that must be told with deliberation and emphasis, and with the dramatic spirit predominant. Mr. McNuttt has voice enough, sufficient literary finish and enthusiasm, but he cannot carry an audience through such a recital as "Ben Hur" necessitates, at lightning speed.

Indeed, the previous December the *Sacramento Record-Union* reported a fine rendition of the "Chariot Race" by the recitationist Lura Barden, in a performance for the Sacramento Lecture Association.[77] It says much to the argument of this book that the city of Sacramento had the luxury of comparing oral *Ben-Hur* renditions.

Apparently not deterred, McNutt gave at least one additional presentation in San Bernadino the next year,[78] and at least two more in Indiana in 1893, but these hardly elicited high praise either.[79] McNutt was a native of Indiana and a much-traveled crusader for temperance and social causes, widely known as the "Dinner Pail Man."[80] These incidences of a renowned minister and social reformer disappointing local audiences and reviewers who attended specifically to witness a novel method of delivering *Ben-Hur*, again helps us appreciate the relatively high level of execution and expectations that had come to be associated with the contemporary pre-stereopticon recitations of *Ben-Hur*, including not just the public readings and declamations but the *Ben-Hur, in Tableaux and Pantomime* as well.[81] It was a local Huntington, Indiana, newspaper ad for McNutt's presentation that claimed "a great many people are now reading Ben Hur preparing for rev. McButt's illustrated lecture."[82] Whether or not this was fact or suggestion, it still reveals the high level of expectation. McNutt also gave the presentation in Davenport, Iowa, in May, 1893, and the Davenport newspapers also record *Ben-Hur* performances in June, 1892 (graduation recitation),[83] and a visit by the *Ben-Hur, in Tableaux and Pantomime* in April, 1893,[84] not to mention the announcement that the eleventh grade literature class "has now dropped Bryant's poems and have taken up *Ben-Hur*," familiarizing the next generation with the novel.[85] Clearly, by the early 1890s *Ben-Hur* had become an extraordinarily popular and adaptable text.

McNutt seems to have been the exception, perhaps in part because he was one of the first to present a *Ben-Hur* stereopticon lecture. Much more successful were A. G. Rogers, Captain J. A. Rider, and John Wilder Fairbank. These three men represent the diversity of appeal and complexity of the *Ben-Hur* property in that Rogers was a clergyman, Rider an actor and retired adventurer, and Fairbank a published historian and naturalist.[86]

The Rev. Dr. A. G. Rogers, previously of Salem, Massachusetts, was at the time pastor at the Universalist Church of Our Father in Washington, DC and a strong advocate for Universalism, the tenets of which were well served by Wallace's Christology.[87] In January, 1896, he began giving his lecture, "Ben Hur," with eighty slides and musical effects, as part of "The People's Course."[88] The start date and number of slides suggest that he used a Riley set. Announcements in *The Washington Post* described the event as a "stereopticon spectacle," "a stereopticon novelty," and a lecture featuring "one of the finest collections of stereopticon slides in existence."[89] This was a huge success, warranting numerous repetitions throughout the spring, establishing his reputation as a clergyman willing to enter the public arena.[90] The advertisement for his seventeenth and eighteenth presentation in April boasted of having already attracted over 10,000 spectators.[91] By April the lecture included "musical effects."[92] These refer to not just some [unnamed] vocal songs but to Constance Hurworth's whistling rendition of "the celebrated 'Ben Hur March,'" most likely the Paull march. This was six years before Joe Belmont recorded his whistling rendition of Paull's march for Victor, and another fine example of Ben-Hur synergy. In this instance a minister narrates Wallace's tale of the Christ while displaying a set of *Ben-Hur* stereopticon slides accompanied by a whistled rendition of E. T. Paull's "The Chariot Race or Ben Hur March." Rogers continued to give the lecture through the season, repeating it several dozen times, raising as much as $100 for a single charity in one evening.[93] He earned enough to fund a trip to Europe during the summer, his purpose being to procure more images. As it turned out, his lectures were so successful that he inspired notable competitors, for instance, Charles P. Lincoln, the former U.S. Consul to China, who gave multiple performances.[94]

Rogers introduced the 1896/7 season with an expanded version that employed 120 views.[95] He celebrated his fiftieth presentation in January, 1897, by engaging the services of a full orchestra.[96] The following season he moved on to other literary subjects like Edward Eggleston's *The Hoosier Schoolmaster* and Hawthorne's *The Scarlet Letter*, but even then his reputation as a lecturer rested upon his "Ben Hur."[97] The Rev. Rogers was removed from his Washington appointment in 1897,[98] but in March, 1901, he returned to Washington's Columbia Theater with another presentation.[99] The reviewer in *The Washington Post* for that presentation particularly enjoyed Rogers' depiction of Judah's search for his mother and sister, his meetings with Iras, and the healing of the lepers.

Captain Rider changed careers several times, preserving the title from the years he transported British troops to the Crimean War, and then gaining theatrical experience with Lester Wallack's company in New York.[100] Despite being just a few years younger than Lew Wallace and hampered by health issues possibly associated with alcoholism, he and his *Ben-Hur* stereopticon lecture begin to appear in newspaper announcements in 1896, in this instance appropriately under the auspices of the Grand Senate of the Knights of the Ancient Essenic Order in New Orleans.[101] The announcement for a 1898 presentation in Charleston, South Carolina, specifies that the slides were "100 hand painted pictures made in Europe for this subject," so it would seem that the Riley set was used and then supplemented to make a custom arrangement.[102] The review of his New Orleans presentation mentions that he included a slide "representing the head of Jesus crowned with thorns." The newspaper trail also shows that he gave the lecture in different venues in Lexington, Kentucky, the first week of December, 1898, at State College on Friday, at Hamilton College on Saturday, and at the Y.M.C.A. the following Monday.[103] An appearance in Atlanta on December 2, 1897, warranted this positive review, which was circulated in several other papers:

> The lecturer made a pleasing impression from the start and for two hours the audience listened with rapt attention to the unfolding of one of the most interesting stories ever written. The stereopticon views were grand, the chariot race being wonderfully realistic. Captain Rider certainly did full justice to his subject. He is fluent, perfectly at ease and handles his subject most pleasingly.[104]

Fairbank was a noted historian and lecturer long associated with the Y.M.C.A.[105] Based in Boston, his lecture to the local Y.M.C.U. in December, 1898, had the unique printed title, "The Son of Hur of the Tribe of Judah; a Tale of the Christ."[106] He maintained a busy travel schedule and often lectured on consecutive nights, sometimes in a series of lectures. His 1902 lecture on Ben-Hur to the Reading, Pennsylvania, Y.M.C.A., for instance, was the fourth of five, the first being derived from *In His Steps*, the last from Wilson Barrett's *The Sign of the Cross*.[107] The report on the latter says he used slides "chiefly taken from life models with others from the masters added," which may explain why the Boston report says he used 110 slides for the *Ben-Hur* lecture. The announcement preceding his 1899 Boston lecture for The People's Star Course included him among luminaries, including Major J. B. Pond.[108] Fairbank kept the *Ben-Hur* lecture in his portfolio for many years, traveling coast to coast. In 1894 a local newspaper announced that Fairbank's lecture that evening at the Unity Auditorium in Olympia, Washington, had been preceded by successful shows in Seattle and Tacoma.[109] In 1905, while serving as superintendent of the Puget Sound Chautauqua Assembly, he offered the *Ben-Hur* lecture for the Star Course at the San Francisco branch of the Y.M.C.A.[110] That same year he lectured to the Odd Fellows at the Grand Opera House in Atlanta.[111] The announcement in *The Atlanta Constitution* reports that Fairbank[s] had given the lecture more than 400 times. Even six years later, in 1911, he gave an impressively advertised presentation to the "Men of Trenton" at the Y.M.C.A.:

> Mr. Fairbank is one of New England's most talented lecturers and his "Ben Hur" has drawn immense audiences wherever it has been given. The pictures he brings are said to be remarkable for their beauty. Mr. Fairbank is always in great demand all over the country for this lecture on Easter Sunday and it was only by securing the date months ago that the Trenton Association was able to have him.[112]

There were still others who gave *Ben-Hur* stereopticon lectures on multiple occasions in addition to Charles P. Lincoln and Wellman, the latter giving his lecture numerous times over the course of seven years.[113] As early as January, 1895, the Rev. Dr. N. W. Tracy of Philadelphia gave his already "celebrated" lecture, illustrated with 126 stereopticon views, on "Ben Hur, or the Tale of the Christ" at Simpson's Tabernacle in Los Angeles in 1895,[114] and eight years later Tracy's *Ben-Hur* surfaces again during a series of tent lectures in Harrisburg, Pennsylvania.[115] Interestingly, an 1897 announcement in *The Washington Post* for a lecture by Dr. Thomas J. Jones includes the title "Ben Hur – a Tale of the Christ," quite similar to Tracy's 1895 lecture on the West Coast, as was the number of stereopticon views (125).[116] Some were less well traveled. Kerr seems to have remained near the Crawfordsville area, giving his presentation again in Logansport as the evening culmination of "'Ben Hur' Day" during the Baptist Young People of Ohio Festival in the summer of 1896.[117] Prof. Kanoga gave his lectures to "overflowing audiences in the largest churches in Chicago,"[118] Dr. J. M. Cromer gave his in Kansas City,[119] Thomas J. Jones in Washington, DC,[120] and the Rev. C. H. McIntosh as well as Lucy A. Andrews, an elocutionist and one of the few women to give *Ben-Hur* stereopticon lectures, in the Milwaukee area.[121] Another, Eliza Warren, offered her stereopticon illustrated "Evening with 'Ben-Hur'" in Cleveland.[122] And across the Pacific, Albert Lucas gave multiple presentations in the Sydney area.[123]

Much more worldly, Clum was founder and editor of the *Tombstone Epitaph* in the Arizona Territory during Lew Wallace's tenure as governor of the New Mexico Territory, where he himself served as a representative of Wallace's predecessor, Marsh Giddings, in the early 1870s, and even in the same room in which Wallace finished his famous novel.[124] Returning to the East in the 1890s, Clum was invited by Rogers to give two presentations during The People's Course in Washington, one of them titled "Santa Fe Trail," in January, 1896.[125] That was when Rogers introduced his *Ben-Hur* lecture, and it was just two months later that Clum ordered his own set of 130 slides and gave lectures announced in *The Washington Post* and *Alexandria Gazette* in March 1896 and 1897.[126] Even after Clum was appointed postal inspector of Alaska during the gold rush in 1898, he returned to the East Coast in 1899 to give his own course of four lectures "America Picturesque," in which the first three were on the West, the Northwest, and Alaska and the fourth on *Ben-Hur*.[127]

The Rev. Earl Wilfrey, who spent part of his life in Crawfordsville, gave a *Ben-Hur* lecture to all the courts of the Tribe of Ben-Hur located in the Cincinnati and northern Kentucky area,[128] and five years later at Washington's Vermont Avenue Christian Church he gave a similar lecture to the Indiana Society of the Knights of Pythias.[129]

The *Boston Herald* informed its readers that W. H. Josselyn gave "his celebrated colored glass slide-presentation of *Ben-Hur*" many nights consecutively at Boston's Theatre Premier in January, 1908, and assured them that though the moving pictures shown as part of the program changed weekly, Josselyn's *Ben-Hur* was "still remaining as the feature."[130] The reason for this assurance may have been related to his encounter with Klaw & Erlanger and Harper & Brothers. in July, 1907.[131] The latter parties advised him to abandon using the name *Ben Hur*, threatening legal action if he did not. The notice in the *Boston Herald* makes it clear that he did not, and there is no record of legal action. Tellingly, the July, 1907, legal notice in *Moving Picture World* is followed by a defiant statement confirming the persistence, pervasiveness, and success of *Ben-Hur* stereopticon presentations:

> William H. Josselyn, who for seven years has been presenting as a vaudeville feature a pictorial panorama of "Ben Hur" all over the country and is now exhibiting the same at Brighton Beach, Brooklyn, N.Y., is in trouble. Klaw & Erlanger and Harper & Bros. . . . have notified Mr. Josselyn to abandon the name "Ben Hur" in connection with his enterprise, threatening legal steps if he does not. The notification comes rather late, the Brighton Beach manager thinks, as he has given his show in every State in the Union repeatedly, without legal interference, although such steps have been threatened several times.

Ben-Hur Stereopticon Programs

Programs varied greatly. As we have already seen, a setting of "Wake not, but hear me, Love" may have been the piece sung at the Montreal *Ben-Hur* stereopticon performance in 1889. Rogers added music, and preceding Fairbank's presentation in Trenton a forty-piece orchestra played "special music" for one half-hour. Jones' lectures in June and December, 1897, included two songs with organ music, albeit with different musicians,[132] while for his April lecture he gave the role of reading the chariot race to Miss Emily Sauter.[133] Still another Washingtonian, the Rev. Mr. Skellinger, gave a 1902 *Ben-Hur* stereopticon lecture and incorporated vocal renditions of "Redemption" and "Calvary" as well as a piano rendition of Paull's "Chariot Race or Ben Hur March."[134] A 1900 Boston presentation of *Ben-Hur* was illustrated by 90 stereopticon views, some of them "throwing upon the screen" the music and words of hymns that were sung along with the lecture.[135]

In addition to musical numbers, other presentations were sometimes supplemented with an additional feature, like a one-act play.[136] The Central Picture Play Company offered "illustrated recitals" of both *Ben-Hur* and *In His Steps* when invited to perform in churches,[137] and a July, 1909, presentation in Tyrone, Pennsylvania, was part of a triple bill that included *The Prodigal Son* and other illustrated songs, stories, and anecdotes.[138] Two of the most synergistic of these complex programs were offered in St. Paul in 1903 and at Cincinnati's Music Hall in 1905.[139] The former was the fundraiser on behalf of the Famine Fund for Sweden held at the First Swedish Methodist Church and sponsored by the early distributors of Ben-Hur Flour, Loftus-Hubbard.[140] The program included two vocal solos and drew over 500 people. Cincinnati's "literary and musical entertainment" was also well attended, providing a *Ben-Hur* combination of the Rev. Earl Wilfrey's *Ben-Hur* lecture illustrated by stereopticon views and an address by D. W. Gerard, Supreme Chief of the Tribe of Ben-Hur, as well as music by the Orpheus Quartet, an organ recital, and recitations. The 1908 Woonsocket & Pascoag, Rhode Island, broadside lists the title as "Ben Hur: In Picture, Song and Story." The program began with "Eighty Beautiful Dissolving Colored Views" accompanied by songs like "Bethlehem" and "The Palms," "Moving Pictures from 'The Passion Play'" accompanied by "appropriate music," followed by the McAllister *Ben-Hur* set for the finale. As mentioned in a previous chapter, the 1904 Fourth of July gala held in Eau Claire, Wisconsin, sponsored by Congregational, Presbyterian, and Baptist churches featured a *Ben-Hur* stereopticon presentation projected upon a 15-foot square screen, preceding patriotic songs accompanied by additional stereopticon views and sung by the combined church choirs.[141]

Clum's lectures always used his proprietary 130 slides, but the number of views used in the independent presentations otherwise varied greatly.[142] In 1904 a presentation in Bemidji, Minnesota, used seventy-six stereopticon views,[143] a 1906 presentation in San Francisco used 100,[144] a 1907 a presentation in Riverside, California, used 114,[145] and the next year San Francisco witnessed a presentation expanded to 150 views.[146] The Tyrone triple bill of lectures used 200, as did a similar complex program offered in Princeton, Minnesota.[147] Lecturers commonly intermixed sets, adding or subtracting as befit their purpose, time constraints, or budget. Many extant slides have a printed number from a set overwritten or supplemented by a different handwritten number. Riley, in fact, produced a twenty-slide set called "The Story of the First Christmas." Fourteen of the twenty slides were from the *Ben-Hur* set, so their ad advises customers that the additional six slides "can be had at the same time so as to complete both sets." Even the number of slides used by the Tribe of Ben-Hur varied. In

1916 Harry Michaels, "Supreme Lecturer" and a native of Crawfordsville, gave a presentation consisting of 150 slides to three local courts, far more than the original thirty-five the Tribe had ordered from the George Bond Company.[148]

Characteristically for the *Ben-Hur* phenomenon, measurements of popularity include a frequent presence in both small towns and large cities, crowded halls, sizable receipts, repeated performances, and many years or even decades of success. There was a small, rural tent-Chautauqua in Elyria, Ohio, in 1904,[149] and, in contrast, at a Cincinnati Chautauqua in 1906 a "Ben-Hur" stereopticon lecture reportedly drew 6000 patrons.[150] A Plattsmouth, Nebraska, presentation in 1903 "filled the church to overflowing,"[151] and "The house was crowded" was the final comment in a report from Anaconda, Montana,[152] while in New Orleans a presentation "was one of the best attended for some time,"[153] *The Minneapolis Journal* reported in 1904 that "a course of six lectures on 'Ben Hur' using stereopticon views ... is drawing large crowds,"[154] and a presentation in Washington, DC gathered "a large audience."[155] And a "Special Notice" ad in *The Sun* claimed that "25,000 people in Baltimore enjoyed 'Ben Hur' last year," recalling Rogers' numerous full houses.[156]

Rogers, Fairbank, Captain Rider, and Josselyn made their reputations through multiple presentations and generated money, whether for charity or personal profit. When admission was charged, the usual price was 25¢, 15¢ for children.[157] Clum charged 35¢ for his lecture at Lannon's Opera House in Alexandria, Virginia.[158] A notice in the Lincoln (Nebraska) *Courier* adds to their report on a *Ben-Hur* presentation at the opera house in Denver that it "cleared a neat little sum" for the Woman's Club.[159] Similarly, the "large audience" that attended a presentation in Kansas City earned $34.50 to be "applied to liquidation of the long-standing church debt."[160]

This is not to suggest that the *Ben-Hur* stereopticon slide sets generated numbers like the Klaw & Erlanger production. There was no single manufacturer or sponsor, but they served countless churches, schools, and societies for many decades, even the generation that was growing up with silent films. Just as in the 1890s and early 1900s, *Ben-Hur* continued to provide inspiration for student presentations in the following decades. In 1913, for example, *The New York Times* reports two illustrated lectures by Henry R. Rose.[161] In 1917 students gave "a most thorough and artistic presentation of *Ben-Hur* with the aid of stereopticon views of the play" in Ogden, Utah.[162] In 1921 a religious school in Oregon sponsored the presentation of a 25-slide version at a local Y.M.C.A.[163]

The phenomenon continued even beyond the Klaw & Erlanger era. In 1924 Dr. Ira W. Barnett had to place chairs in the aisles and accommodate a standing-room crowd at his Calvary Presbyterian church in Riverside, California.[164] He supplemented the *Ben-Hur* stereopticon lecture by outlining as well the life of Lew Wallace and "how the writing of the book made him a Christian." He added the singing of several hymns and an "organ recital by Marguerite Hyde, in which she rendered numbers adapted to the dramatization of 'Ben Hur,'" suggesting another example of inter-*Ben-Hur* synergy four years after the Klaw & Erlanger production had closed. Hardly newsworthy in this late stage, the Rockford, Illinois, *Republic* nonetheless gives notice of a *Ben-Hur* stereopticon presentation along with readings and musical numbers in 1929,[165] and Athol, Massachusetts, was entertained with another in 1935.[166]

The transitional period that led to cinema produced a number of entertainment variations and experimental terms to describe them. The terms "moving pictures" and "motion pictures" had several different meanings, one of which was the effect of "dissolving" stereopticon views. The second page of a Montgomery Ward *Catalogue of Magic Lanterns, Stereopticons, and Moving Picture Machines* from the late 1890s defines a "Moving Picture Machine" as a combination of a single magic lantern and a mechanical attachment that can show both lantern views and "flexible films by means of which are produced the celebrated moving pictures."[167] The same catalog (10) advertised an Optiscope to employ both technologies. Indeed, Kleine's June, 1902, catalog advertises a top-of-the-line exhibition outfit that contained or could accommodate everything from tickets to a large Edison cylinder record player, a dissolving view magic lantern/motion picture projector, and a large variety of slides and films. This new flexibility enabled further variations in *Ben-Hur* presentations. The management of Burton Holmes, the inventor of the "travelogue," explained the transformation to readers of the *Cincinnati Enquirer* who would otherwise expect to see only stereopticon still views:

> The management announces that during the coming season they will make a distinct innovation in the illustration of Mr. Holmes's lectures by inserting the motion pictures into the very body of the lecture, just as has always been done with the stereopticon views heretofore. Of course, they will continue to use the latter views also, beautifully colored and from original negatives.[168]

As early as 1903, the same year as Edwin S. Porter's *The Great Train Robbery*, *The Minneapolis Journal* reported that Josephine Bonaparte Rice would "read" *Ben-Hur* and that "175 stereopticon views illustrating the story will be shown together with motion pictures."[169] Perhaps the motion pictures in question included segments from Lumière's 1898, short film, *La vie et la passion de Jésus-Christ*. Also at Tracy's series of tent lectures in Harrisburg:

> A large audience [was] present to hear and see the life of Christ as illustrated in "Ben-Hur." The stereopticon and moving pictures were among the best ever shown in the city.[170]

Around the same time W. S. Kelly, a Methodist clergyman who was one of the first to include cinematic presentations in his church in Petaluma, purchased a set of *Ben-Hur* stereopticon slides along with a copy of Pathé's *Life of Christ*, a 1903 film that was released in the United States in 1904.[171] A flyer announcing the Saturday night entertainment for the first annual assembly of the Tuscarawas County Chautauqua held at Reeves' Grove, New Philadelphia, Ohio, from August 4–13, 1906, climaxed with "Ben Hur (Moving Pictures)."[172] An undated flyer advertised Theodore Holman, "Dramatic Reader, Press Correspondent, and Condenser of Popular Works of Fiction," who included *Ben-Hur* as one of the ten novels he had condensed and committed to memory.[173] However, the flyer continues:

> Introducing Ben Hur in the Great Chariot Race, in addition to three thousand feet of selected Motion Pictures.

This was in addition to Charles Gelton Pidgen's *Quincy Adams Sawyer*, which was published in 1904, and later he would offer four reels of *Quincy Adams Sawyer* "presented and talked by Theodore Holman."[174] The December 28, 1907, issue of *The Moving Picture World* contains a small ad for "Pictures adapted from Gen. Lew Wallace's famous book – for rent or on a percentage" by E. Eichenlaub of Chillicothe, Ohio.[175] This ad appeared just three weeks after Kalem first advertised their version of *Ben-Hur*, and it was placed on a page advertising kinetoscopes, films, lanterns, vaudeville songs, and more. It would seem to refer to the Kalem film, but a list of dozens of "Film Renters" on the previous page does not include Eichenlaub.[176] In January, 1908, four weeks after the release of the Kalem film, the *Boston Daily Globe* announced a "moving picture production of 'Ben Hur' at the Theatre Premier every day from 9 a.m. to 2 p.m."[177] But what sounds like a continuous theatrical showing of the Kalem black-and-white film turns out to be a "magnificent colored scenic novelty ... 108 separate scenes from the play." Also in 1908, Edward G. Cooke, the general manager of Klaw & Erlanger, even used the term to describe their staged version of chariot race as "this hitherto unequaled stage moving picture."[178] This was the same year that Kalem's moving picture of *Ben-Hur* was being exhibited, and making headlines.

THE KALEM *BEN-HUR* (1907)

Just as the offerings in the stereopticon catalogues in the first years of the twentieth century included relatively few substantial literary works except for *Ben-Hur* and other biblical novels like *In His Steps* and *Quo Vadis?*, so too the number of films based on classic or bestselling literary works was very limited. The film technology and distribution systems available at the time, not to mention the concept of cinematic dramaturgy, did not yet accommodate well the length and intricacies of a novel. A short-story adaptation like Vitagraph's *Adventures of Sherlock Holmes; or, Held for Ransom* (1905) was better suited for the limited capabilities of the early days of cinema, but even the handful of American films that did represent well-known novels, like Edison's *Uncle Tom's Cabin* (1903), directed by Edwin S. Porter, and Biograph's *20,000 Leagues Under the Sea* (1905), were quite short and heavily abridged. And again the copyright holders of these properties either did not have an American copyright or were allowing theirs to lapse. *The Moving Picture World* of December 7, 1907, the same day Kalem's *Ben-Hur* was released for distribution, lists more than 300 films from Actograph, Biograph, Essanay, Gaumont, Goodfellow, Kalem, Lubin, Méliès, Miles Bros., Pathé, Selig, Cines, Urban-Eclipse, Vitagraph, and Williams, Brown and Earle, and very few of them were based on an American copyrighted book or play.[179] Once again *Ben-Hur* would provide the ideal test case, for Harper and now Henry Wallace would not abide what they considered an egregious infringement of their literary and dramatic copyright which, following current law, would be coming up for renewal the very next year. Now twenty-seven years past the initial publication date, *Ben-Hur* was not only continuing to make its mark among booksellers and on stage and in the lecture hall, it was also appearing in Coney Island, Ocean Park, and elsewhere across the country in various guises and reinterpretations. This would be the year in which *Ben-Hur: A Tale of the Christ* would also become the first bestselling novel to be adapted for film and require suitable compensation.

Kalem's Production of *Ben-Hur*[180]

When the Brooklyn-based Kalem produced *Ben-Hur* in the late fall of 1907, it was still a young company, incorporated six months earlier by two Biograph managers, Samuel Long and Frank J. Marion, along with George Kleine, the Chicago optical camera equipment manufacturer who had already issued a *Ben-Hur* stereopticon set.[181] They soon hired actor Sidney Olcott as a director,[182] and then Marion turned the job of scenario writing over to actress Gene Gauntier (*née* Genevieve Liggett).[183] Gauntier is particularly important in the history of the *Ben-Hur* phenomenon not only as an important contributor to the early days of American cinema who wrote and acted in the first cinematic *Ben-Hur* but also in that she included her recollections of the *Ben-Hur* production in an autobiographical essay published in *Woman's Home Companion*, although this was not published until 1928, a few years after the release of the first MGM film adaptation.[184] Some of Olcott's recollections were also published, where he recalled that the task of writing the "scene and story sequences" was usually assigned to Gauntier. Kalem had been one of the first studios to shoot their films with a pre-approved script, and this provided in advance the logical continuity found in many of their films, including *Ben-Hur*.[185]

The Supreme Court will find this aspect of their production process to be of prime importance, too.

Too often brief descriptions of the *Ben-Hur* production are derived not from these eyewitness accounts but the court materials related to the subsequent trial. Unfortunately, the Supreme Court cited promotional material from Kalem that was filled with false claims and exaggerations inserted for effect. There is no corroborating evidence for Kalem's claims, for instance, that the Third Battery of Brooklyn was involved, or that the costumes came from the Metropolitan Opera Company,[186] or that the supers belonged to Pain's Fireworks Company,[187] or, for that matter, that the film was shot at Coney Island.[188] Similarly, the written decision of the Supreme Court depended on the erroneous assumption that it was "a man" who wrote the *Ben-Hur* scenario. And even the International Movie Database is certainly incorrect in saying that the part of Messala was played by William S. Hart.[189] Hart, the future screen cowboy star, opened the part of Messala for Klaw & Erlanger in 1899 but did not begin working in the film industry until 1914.[190] Neither his biography nor autobiography says anything about a role in Kalem's film.

Gauntier's recollection was that in October, when Pain's Fireworks Company was shutting down its summer pyrotechnical spectacle installation at the Sheepshead Park racetrack, Marion thought that this was "a great opportunity to produce Ben Hur using the Pain Company's props, supers and standing scenery."[191] She specifically recalled that this was in October because "the fall rains might begin at any time," and so Marion wanted the scenario in just two days. She continues:

> Mr. Olcott and I went to the racetrack, found the props impossible and the supers inadequate, hurried back to Swain's Agency and interviewed people for the cast and for extras, and late in the evening rushed down to [Gus] Elliott's and remained until after midnight selecting props and hundreds of costumes.

Olcott and Gauntier may well have replaced Pain's scenery and supers, but they did in all probability use Pain's chariots. This was the original incentive for shooting the film at their Sheepshead Park racetrack, and Frank Oakes Rose's credited participation as co-director makes it almost a certainty, for Rose was the stage manager for Pain's spectacular dramaturgy.[192] Similarly, Harry Temple was credited in the Kalem ads as a director, and he was on the Board of Directors of Pain's Fireworks. Kalem advertising makes two different claims, that the chariot race was re-enacted by the "3d Battery, Brooklyn" and "the trained four horse teams of the 13th Heavy Artillery of Brooklyn," which makes both claims suspect.[193] Complicating matters is that Henry Pain's 1935 *Time* obituary mentions that he had produced "The Chariot Race of Ben Hur."[194] Although the Lilly Library does preserve a copy of the scenario, the reader knows that Harper and Henry Wallace would never have licensed such a chariot race or ignored such a high-profile copyright infringement, especially in the New York area.[195]

Gauntier also explains that Rose did not realize the significant differences between directing a crowd before a huge, live audience and doing so in front of a stationary moving picture camera:

> The weather turned cold with a biting wind coming in from the sea, and the people had been called for eight o'clock in the morning. When I arrived a little before noon they were shivering in their thin Roman costumes and nothing had been accomplished. Not a scene had been taken. Chaos reigned and Mr. Rose was like a madman. He had never even seen a motion picture taken, knew nothing of technique or camera limitations, and had reduced Max Schneider, our cameraman, to despair with his impossible suggestions. Olcott sat on the fence of the racetrack kicking his heels . . .
> At last Marion came to him, almost with tears in his eyes. "For the love of Mike, Sid, get into this and get something done. That man doesn't know the first principles of pictures."
> Sid twitched his eyebrows and laughed but he jumped down from his perch, which was promptly taken by Mr. Rose who was wiping nervous perspiration from his brow.
> "Gad, that's the hardest thing I was ever up against," said the man who had produced a dozen spectacles. And there he sat for the rest of the day, learning how moving pictures were made.
> Fast and furiously Olcott drove his crowds and they, sensing an intelligent guiding hand, ceased milling and stampeding and settled down to constructive action. Three days it kept up and at the end of that time, exhausted but happy, we had the picture "in the box." And the next day it rained.

Confirming Gauntier's account, the data recorded by the New York Central Park Tower station for October, 1907, show that temperatures began to dip into the 30s after October 18, creating the chilly mornings she describes. There was only a trace of precipitation leading up to October 26. On the twenty-seventh and twenty-eighth over two inches of rain fell. Therefore, the shoot must have been on Thursday, Friday, Saturday, October 24–6, with the chariot race sequence probably occurring on the last day.[196]

For backdrops, Olcott used the same wall that provided the background to the chariot race to shoot the initial crowd sequence of a Jerusalem angry mob engaging in an anti-Roman demonstration. He shot two scenes in front of a two-story "House of Hur" that included a parapet and a broad, open entry way. For the house of Arrius, he used a set equipped with a broad stairway and a colonnaded porch. And for the challenge between Judah and Messala, he used a backdrop of a multi-tiered fountain complex intended to evoke architecturally the atmosphere of Daphne.

Post-Production, Release, and Advertising

During the early period of narrative film in 1907, Kalem was still a fledgling company in the process of establishing itself by turning out a new

Figure 11.2 Kalem advertised their unauthorized *Ben-Hur* in 1907 as "Positively the Most Superb Moving Picture Spectacle Ever Produced in America." This ad contains much of the information used by the U.S. Supreme Court. The three screen grabs show Judah pushing the tile from his parapet, confronting Messala at Daphne, and being declared victor after the chariot race.

release every week, as was the industry expectation at the time. In 1910 Kalem would be the first American company to release a film shot overseas, and Olcott's subsequent five-reel *From the Manger to the Cross* would be a veritable epic. But in 1907 Olcott was still limited by a small budget, a single reel of film, and a short production schedule. To compensate, Kalem was innovative in its use of intertitles.[197] They inserted eight into the *Ben-Hur* footage, and each included one of Kalem's signature "cartoons." To give the short film the appearance of including more events from the novel, they inserted an intertitle in silhouette labeled simply, "BEN HUR TO THE GALLEYS." It included an image of a Roman galley at sea with a Roman fleet in the distance. The footage this intertitle preceded was not shot on a galley or by the sea but simply continued the tile incident scene shot at the House of Hur set, with Messala periodically pointing into the distance to illustrate that the Hur family was being led away. Kalem further expanded this misrepresentation in their advertising, claiming in *The Billboard*, for instance, that one of the scenes was "Ben Hur in Chains to the Galleys."[198]

Similarly, the ads that appeared first in such trade publications as *The Moving Picture World* and *The Billboard* and later in local newspapers claim that there are "Sixteen Magnificent Scenes with Illustrated Titles." This may have been another intentional exaggeration, or it may have been the inevitable result of a harried forty-day period between shooting and exhibition, but only fifteen scenes are listed in the ads. The name of Arrius is misspelled, the intertitles "AN UNFORTUNATE ACCIDENT" AND "WOUNDING OF THE PROCURATOR" describe the same incident, and in the film "The Dash for the Finish" is difficult to differentiate from "The Finish." Also, in that the final "lap" is a repeat of the footage of the first, perhaps Olcott did not shoot enough footage of the racing chariots.

JERUSALEM REBELS AT ROMAN MIS-RULE
THE FAMILY OF HUR
AN UNFORTUNATE ACCIDENT
WOUNDING OF THE PROCURATOR
BEN HUR IN CHAINS TO THE GALLEYS
BEN HUR ADOPTED BY ARRIAS AND PROCLAIMED A ROMAN CITIZEN
BEN HUR AND MESSALA – THE CHALLENGE
THE CHARIOT RACE:
   1. GRAND TRIUMPHAL ENTRY OF CHARIOTS AND ATHLETES
   2. THE START
   3. FIRST TIME BY
   4. SECOND TIME BY
   5. THE RACE FOR THE FINISH
   6. THE FINISH
BEN HUR VICTOR

The film itself, which was being released in early December along with these advertisements, contains only eight intertitles, eliminating entirely the subdivisions of the chariot race. Some of the other titles differ from the ad versions, too. For instance, the ad's BEN HUR ADOPTED BY ARRIAS AND PROCLAIMED A ROMAN CITIZEN appears in the film as BEN HUR – RESCUER OF ARRIUS – ADOPTED AND FREED FROM SLAVERY.

Although crude by modern standards, the strength of the film, given the challenge of designing a mute drama played out upon just a few sets and limited to 1000 feet, derives from Gauntier's scenario. She reduced the enormous plot of Wallace's novel by eliminating entirely the religious element, Sheik Ilderim and the Orchard of Palms, and the Galilean sojourn and concentrated on highlights, attractions and "textual fragmentation."[199]

The opening scene establishes the anti-Roman sentiment expressed by the crowd on the street in Jerusalem. It also introduces Ben Hur as the protagonist who seems to be inciting the populace to express their disdain for the Roman military procession that passes by. The second intertitle establishes the tranquility of the family as it introduces a scene in which Ben Hur is caressed by his mother on the upper level of their house. He washes his hands and converses with her. The third intertitle introduces the tile incident, which begins with Ben Hur addressing the crowd in the street below. This, and the action in the film, which depicts Ben Hur crouching behind the loose tile, suggests that Gauntier wanted her Ben Hur to push the tile onto the procurator's head intentionally. There follow no gestures of denial, and the act incites a street riot well before the next intertitle, "BEN HUR TO THE GALLEYS." At first the camera focuses the action on only the upper patio, showing the Romans arriving, Messala pointing at Judah, and a subsequent struggle. Then a second shot, focusing on only the entry doorway, depicts Ben Hur's mother and sister (played by Gauntier) as well as Amrah and finally Ben Hur himself being dragged away to prison by Roman soldiers, with Messala gesturing them away on the right side of the shot.

Ben Hur's imprisonment and escape at sea is then encapsulated in the fifth intertitle, BEN HUR – RESCUER OF ARRIUS – ADOPTED AND FREED FROM SLAVERY. The scene looks very different. No longer showing a street in Jerusalem filled with an angry mob, the camera now transports the viewer to the exterior porch of Arrius' elegant house in Rome. A four-horse chariot rides past, a beggar sits in front of the steps to the portico and is given some alms, two couriers appear and run up the steps, and a crowd gathers as Ben Hur and Arrius appear on foot and mount the steps. Arrius addresses the saluting crowd and then places a medallion around Ben Hur's neck. He bows and the crowd hails him repeatedly.

The grandeur of Rome then shifts to the scene at the Fountain of Castalia outside Antioch. The intertitle "BEN HUR AND MESSALA – THE CHALLENGE" does not suggest the presence of Balthasar and Iras, but the crowd bows before the former when he raises his arms. Iras merely stands to the side. But then, much abbreviating the events in the book, Messala's chariot races towards the crowd, Ben Hur grabs hold of the reins, and stands defiantly as Messala dismounts and points into the distance, presumably to the circus. In the penultimate scene an official box sits even with the finish line. The crowd salutes a procession carrying crudely painted Roman standards and soldiers, followed by four four-horse chariots. They complete a full circle, and the standard-bearers and soldiers then line the track. The race begins with two chariots abreast in two rows. The sole stationary camera locks onto the cheering crowd as the chariots pass by six times at irregular intervals of approximately 10–20 seconds, the last pass being a repeat of the starting footage. There is no crash. Instead, in the final vignette [BEN HUR VICTOR] Messala is carried in on a stretcher and gestures, perhaps salutes, as Ben Hur kneels and is crowned in front of the viewing stand, his triumph over the mean-spirited Roman complete.

Just as the film offered a number of discrete events to potential exhibitors and patrons, Kalem crammed many details and superlatives into the advertisement they placed in fledgling trade papers like *The Moving Picture World* and *The Billboard*. In addition to listing the sixteen "Magnificent Scenes with Illustrated Titles," the phrases "A Roman Spectacle" and "Positively the Most Superb Moving Picture Spectacle Ever Produced in America" appear in large fonts. Another selling point, one the reader has seen already in reference to other items associated with *Ben-Hur*, was the name of Lew Wallace, again in large font. And, as usual, there are images of chariot racing individually designed for each publication. A few pages afterwards Kalem placed the name *Ben Hur* at the top of the list of its current twenty-five films. It was the only one listed as long as 1000 feet, and one of only eleven films of such length out of the approximately 300 films in release during early December, 1907. Another nearby page contains Kalem's two-paragraph summary of the film, again suggesting that the film includes a galley scene and again misspelling the name of Arrius:

> Ben Hur is consigned to the galleys, where he is loaded with chains. Here he signalizes himself by saving the life of Arrias [sic], who publicly adopts him.[200]

Because films were just beginning to be recognized as an accepted form of dramatic entertainment, newspaper advertising of new releases, especially because they were being produced and introduced on a weekly basis, was not common. But this was a film version of *Ben-Hur*. Over the next nine weeks ads popped up in newspapers in many localities in the U.S. and Canada.[201] Some ads, like those for the Bijou in Watertown, New York, the Star Theatre in Ann Arbor, and the Empire Theatre in San Diego used some or all of Kalem's wording: "A Roman Spectacle ... Pictures Adapted From Gen. Lew Wallace's Famous Book, Ben Hur."[202] An ad in Aberdeen, South Dakota, did not even use the name "Ben Hur," stopping after "Wallace's Famous Book."[203] Not surprisingly, others highlighted the chariot race. The Paris Moving Picture Theatre in Springfield, Illinois, for example, did so and also associated the film with both the original novel and the Klaw & Erlanger production, while also claiming the length of the film to be extraordinary:[204]

> Paris Moving Picture Theatre
> Will Exhibit a Special Added
> Attraction
> Gen. Lew Wallace's Famous
> **BEN HUR**
> And His Great Chariot Race.
> This picture is the original production, taken from the Famous Play, which was produced throughout the United States and Europe. It lasts One Hour, and is worth $1.00, but our price remains the same – 5c to all.

The New Star Theatre ad in the *Pawtucket Times* used the Kalem phrasing and also included the full list of scenes, even the misspelled Arrias.[205] The Theatorium in Macon, Georgia, did all of the above while promising a "superb film, unquestionably the greatest ever brought South."[206] Of special interest is the unique claim that "the pictures are highly finished and colored." In contrast, the *Daily Herald* of Biloxi advertised the film as "thrilling."[207]

Many of these advertisements are for three-day engagements, including a New Year's matinee in San Diego. A January 15 ad for The Marvel in Winston-Salem announced that this would be the last day of the engagement, succinctly boasting of "Introducing the Famous Chariot Race" of "Gen. Lew Wallace's Powerful Drama."[208] An interesting variation and an expected synergy with the Tribe of Ben-Hur appeared in the *Saginaw News*, urging that "every Ben Hur in the city should attend Thursday."[209] At the time film exchanges handled the distribution, and within three weeks the O. T. Crawford Film Exchange Company of St. Louis listed "Pathé's Life of Christ, Ben Hur, and Parsifal" as their most attractive products in their trade ads.[210] These kinds of ads appeared well into February.[211] The list of the latest releases from all the film companies in *The Moving Picture World* of February 15 still contains *Ben Hur* among twelve Kalem releases.[212]

Movie reviews were rare in early 1908. But a few newsworthy accounts are preserved from late February. This is from the "Trade Notes" column of *The Moving Picture World*:

> Have one on us, Kalem! A Western newspaper in commenting on a local show refers to "Ben Hur" as "a wonderfully realistic and pleasing presentation of Lew Wallace's famous story and a triumph of the kinetoscopic art.[213]

A report on the Augusta, Georgia, premiere says that the movie evoked spontaneous applause at the end of the chariot race:

> The most striking feature of the program was a reproduction of the dramatization of the famous Ben Hur by General Lew Wallace. The leading events of this great masterpiece were faithfully depicted, and the grand climax when Ben Hur wins the

chariot race was applauded as heartily as if the stage had been a real one instead of a canvas sheet.[214]

The Ben Hur Case
The importance of the suit filed on March 14, 1908, by Harper & Brothers, Klaw & Erlanger, and Henry Wallace (representing the estate of Susan Wallace, who had died in October, 1907) against Kalem was the direct result of the unparalleled success of the *Ben-Hur* property. There was not another work of contemporary popular art that had made and was continuing to make such a large impact on both the literary and dramatic worlds while still being controlled by the original literary contract's representatives (the Harper management and the Wallace estate) and the signatories (Klaw & Erlanger) for the subsequent contract assigning dramatic rights, and now it had been translated into a high-profile 1000-foot film without seeking copyright clearance or a license from either. The *New York Times* reported that Kleine Optical Company, responsible for the machines that exhibited "the play in cheap theatres in this city," was also named in the suit.[215] The plaintiffs were seeking damages and an injunction as well as a temporary restraining order against selling or exhibiting this "Roman Spectacle" while the litigation was pending.[216] According to the *New York Tribune*, Klaw & Erlanger claimed that staging *Ben-Hur* cost $300,000 and that Wallace had been paid $200,000 in royalties,[217] but the amounts claimed by the plaintiffs were actually $100,000 and $300,000.[218]

The industry-friendly *Variety*, which only recently had begun to include expanded film coverage, downplayed the impact of the legal action.[219] Reducing the contest to "an interesting point," the article begins by dismissing the film as an ephemeral event that "has long since outlived its usefulness." This would apply to most films of the era, but not a *Ben-Hur* product. Characteristically, the film would still be exhibited for several more years, despite the legal encumbrances. A Kalem spokesperson quoted in the article addressed Harper's insistence on declaring the film a drama and therefore subject to their copyright:

> It must be clear to anyone who is familiar with past litigation that a moving picture film is neither a book nor a drama, but is a photograph, coming clearly under the provisions of the copyright law, which provides protection for photographs. When I was with the Biograph Company we made a determined effort to have the Librarian of Congress recognize a moving picture as drama in order that we might have protection of dramatic copyright ... but the Librarian after careful investigation decided moving pictures were plainly photographs.[220]

Although assuring readers that Kalem has "nothing to lose in the present case," the article warns:

> Should such a point be decided against the moving picture manufacturers it would be impossible to reproduce scenes from any copyrighted book or dramatic performance without consent.

The United States Circuit Court heard the arguments on April 10.[221] David Gerber of Dittenhoefer, Gerber, & James represented the complainants. The *New York Times* reported his argument:

> Mr. Gerber argued that the representation of moving pictures of scenes from "Ben Hur" violates the clause of the copyright law which interdicts "printing, reprinting, copying, publicly performing, or representing" the copyrighted book or play.[222]

On behalf of Kalem and Kleine, Drury W. Cooper of Kerr, Page, & Cooper, a firm that still specializes in intellectual property cases, argued that a moving picture did not constitute a dramatic performance, for no words were spoken.[223] (The *Times* reports his name as Henry L. Cooper, contradicted by all the legal documents.) In turn, Gerber emphasized the phrase "or representing," inserted into the Act of 1856 copyright revision (169), as inclusionary of the new technology.

The decision was issued May 6.[224] Judge Lacombe once again presided over a case involving copyright, as he had done not only in the Riley case but also in the Daly v. Webster case, ultimately upheld by the U.S. Supreme Court in 1896, in which the court found that imitating a scene from a copyrighted play was an infringement.[225] Using the analogy of pantomime, which does not require the use of the spoken word, Lacombe focused on the capability of the moving picture medium to represent a story, in this instance one which had been copyrighted as a book and then authorized by the author and publisher as a play:

> The result obtained when the moving pictures are thrown upon the screen is, within Daily vs. Webster, an infringement of various dramatic passages in complainants' copyrighted book and play. To this result, defendant, the Kalem Company, undoubtedly contributes. Indeed, it would seem that it is the most important contribution.

A letter written on May 19, 1908, by Henry Wallace to Frederick Duneka of Harper & Brothers comments, "We must all congratulate ourselves on these conclusions which might have opened up new fields full of trouble."[226] Because it involved not only a federal court decision but also a bestselling book and highly successful dramatic production, the *Times* concluded that this decision would have "a most important effect on the moving picture business" not just in the New York area where many of the early films were being made but all over the country where films of popular plays like *The Merry Widow*, *Dr. Jekyll and Mr. Hyde*, *William Tell*, and *Parsifal* were already in circulation or in preparation. By October, the size of the impact of this decision had become apparent. A report circulated that at least 1000 venues had to pull their exhibitions of films portraying previously written material, and that "the entire map of the moving picture business is altered."[227] The report, with the headline "No More Moving Pictures of 'Ben Hur,'" then clarifies that the decision primarily affected *Ben-Hur* and estimates that "about 800" prints had to be withdrawn. The appellate brief would say that "at least 500 exhibitions" had been given, and both of these numbers suggest that this first cinematic *Ben-Hur* might have achieved greater sales and penetration than almost any of its competitors in 1907–8. Further evidence comes from the autobiography of King Vidor, who recollected that as a young projectionist in Galveston, he played the film twenty-one times a day over the course of its seven-day run – 147 times.[228] And that was just one of the 500 exhibitions.

After the decision, Cooper told the press he would confer with his clients, who opted to appeal. It was at this point that Edison and the newly formed Motion Picture Patents Company, of which Kalem was a member, collaborated by helping to underwrite the remaining legal expenses.[229] As for legal representation, Cooper teamed with Frank L. Dyer in representing the appellants, and Gerber, originally Klaw & Erlanger's attorney, worked with John Larkin for the other appellees, Harper & Brothers and Wallace, although the official court report lists Larkin as attorney for Lew Wallace, not Henry. This decision [Harper v. Kalem Co., 169 Fed. 61] was written by Judge Henry G. Ward and dated March 16, 1909.[230] He begins with "The late Gen. Lew Wallace wrote a story called 'Ben Hur,'" and proceeds to account for the Harper & Brothers copyright and Klaw & Erlanger's sole right of producing the story upon the stage, and adds:

> The defendant the Kalem Company also employed a writer to read the story, without having any knowledge of the copyrighted drama, and to write a description of certain portions of it.

It was important to the court that Kalem was accused of dramatizing Wallace's novel, not the Klaw & Erlanger drama, and Gautier's account of writing the scenario in two days, without recourse to Young's dramatic adaptation, accords with the judge's text. Interestingly, when qualifying the extent to which Kalem infringed, the court did not differentiate between the film itself and Kalem's publicity, most notably by including the galleys:

> The defendant did not reproduce the whole story, but only certain of the more prominent scenes, such as the wounding of the Roman procurator, Ben Hur in the galleys, the chariot race, and others.

While mentioning several more times that the *Ben-Hur* property was protected as both novel and drama, Ward makes reference to Kalem's extensive distribution, expanding his legal argument by suggesting that the scope of Kalem's moving picture was large enough to warrant such consideration by the court. In doing so he discounted Kalem's argument that they could not be held accountable because the film was "capable of innocent use, e.g. exhibitions for private amusement":

> Inasmuch as it advertises the films as capable of producing a moving picture spectacle of Ben Hur, and sends its advertisements to proprietors of theatoriums with

the expectation and hope that they will use them for public exhibitions, charging an entrance fee, and inasmuch as many of these proprietors have so used them, the defendant is clearly guilty of contributory infringement.

The last paragraph addresses the constitutional issue advanced by the appellants. They had argued that the assignment of congressional powers in Section 8, Article 1, was limited to "authors ... and their respective writings" and therefore that copyright protection could not apply to a filmed performance of *Ben Hur*. He cited the copyright laws of 1856 and 1870, which extended coverage to dramas and photographs and many other artistic products:

> The construction of the word "writings" to cover these various forms of expression, and also to cover the right of giving public performances, has been acquiesced in for over 50 years. In view of this fact, we have no difficulty in concluding that moving pictures would be a form of expression infringing not the copyrighted book or drama, but infringing the author's exclusive right to dramatize his writing and publicly to perform such dramatization.[231]

In the spring and summer, the trade papers summarized some of the arguments and several aspects of the decision.[232] *The Virginia Law Register*, for instance, duly reported the setback for the industry as an infringement of the right to dramatize a book, failing to see merit in Ward's observation that "when the film was thrown upon a sheet reproducing the action of the actors and animals, it became a dramatization and infringed." The following September, *The Nickelodeon*, still in its first year of publication, was calling it "The Ben Hur Case" and published not only a summary but also a feature article by K. S. Hover, "The 'Ben Hur' Copyright Case," that included a complete version of Ward's decision preceded by a brief and non-committal introduction.[233] Even as late as 1924, *The Film Daily* was still calling it "The Ben Hur Case."[234]

Of course viewings overseas were not affected, and by no means did the appellate court's decision put an end to exhibitions of the Kalem *Ben Hur*.[235] Within weeks of the original court injunctions, Elmer Blue, manager of the Williamsport [Indiana] Theatorium (formerly the Nickelodeon), that is, in Henry Wallace's backyard, so to speak, boasted in the local paper that he would be exhibiting the Lyceum Bio-Scenograph Company's "realistic productions of moving pictures ... 'Ben Hur,' the most superb moving picture spectacle ever produced in America."[236] Typically for Chicago's Lyceum Bio-Scenograph presentations, lectures and "explanations" accompanied the showing of their religious films. Similarly in 1910 Dwight, Illinois, enjoyed a Lyceum Bio-Scenograph program that featured *Ben Hur* and the Ambrosio/Maggi Italian import, *The Last Days of Pompeii*.[237] The next year Klaw & Erlanger took matters into their own hands. Not satisfied to have "'Ben-Hur' Pirates" pay the $100 fine mandated by the copyright law for the first offense and $50 for each subsequent offense, they made sure that in May, 1911, Charles E. White, manager of the Lyceum Bio-Scenograph Company, was imprisoned for sixty days.[238] Their syndicated press release gave this dire and lengthy warning:

> This is the opening gun in a campaign instituted by Klaw & Erlanger against the motion picture pirates. As fast as violations of this most sweeping injunction are reported instant arrest and prosecution will follow. Judge Killett's action clearly indicates that it is the intention of the court to deal out terms of imprisonment to all found guilty of violating the injunction. The case of Klaw & Erlanger against the Kalem company was bitterly fought and the injunction was issued only after a series of exhaustive hearings and arguments. It resulted in a complete victory for Klaw & Erlanger, and most of the "Ben-Hur" films were withdrawn from the motion picture houses. There were, however, several fugitive films and these have been exhibited from time to time. ... There will be no let-up in this campaign. Klaw & Erlanger have determined to stop this form of fraudulent amusement and it is quite evident the United States courts have placed an ugly weapon in their hands. Their agents everywhere have been ordered to institute criminal proceedings instantly upon the discovery of any violation of the injunction and to urge upon the United States courts to inflict prison sentences in all convictions.[239]

In *The Moving Picture World* of October 21, they announced that they had brought suit against the Aladdin Amusement Company of Springfield, Missouri.[240] The company admitted to only two exhibitions and therefore a penalty of $150, but the warning continued in the national trade journal:

> No doubt every exhibitor throughout the United States is aware of the prohibition of the use of this film, but it seems that some promoter sooner or later gets foolish and is caught in the bargain. This is not the only suit brought about by K. & E., as other like cases are pending in courts of various states.[241]

Klaw & Erlanger also began taking action against John Noonan, proprietor of the Virginia Theatre.[242] When he then claimed that he did not know about the copyright, Klaw & Erlanger also went after his distributor, Harry K. Lucas of Charlotte, North Carolina.

The newspaper record shows that some of the exhibitors chose *Ben-Hur* specifically for its associated high moral standing and Christian values. Already in May, 1908, the Ladies Guild of the Church of the Good Shepherd in Columbia, South Carolina, arranged a program that featured *Ben Hur*, and this program was to run continuously from five o'clock in the afternoon until 10:30 at night.[243] In October, 1909, one of the largest churches in Jonesboro, Arkansas, posted a notice for *Ben Hur*, causing the local paper to criticize the pastor for his earlier sermon denouncing the moving picture shows in the city.[244] Presumably the pastor thought *Ben Hur* was morally acceptable. The manager of the theater decided to run *Ben Hur* for another whole week, "it having proved very popular last week and creating much comment." The first church in Los Angeles to claim that it was employing "the motion picture as a means of arousing interest in religious work" was the Salem Congregational Church. The story was syndicated nationwide.[245] In 1911 the church exhibited such films as *Ben Hur* and *Uncle Tom's Cabin* to "aid in the elimination of indecent pictures from theaters and to give the people a place where they may find good, clean amusements." Similarly, the Majestic Theatre in Ada, Oklahoma, advertised "High-Class Pictures – Nothing But The Best" and praised *Fires of Fate*, a 1911 Vitagraph film about the early days of Christianity, as being "in a class with Ben Hur."[246] A few months later, in mid-November, the *Tampa Tribune* ran an ad for the local Kinodrome: "Motion Pictures taken from Gen. Lew Wallace's Famous Book – BEN HUR."[247] This was the week after the U.S. Supreme Court upheld Kalem's final appeal.

Kalem Co. v. Harper Brothers [222 U.S. 55 (1911)] was argued before the Supreme Court on October 31 and November 1. A Canadian report later described the case as "the first theatrical litigation which has been passed upon by the United States Supreme Court."[248] No doubt the phrase "theatrical litigation" was intended to establish a historical perspective, but a reporter in the courtroom on October 31 described the scene as "a miniature production of 'Ben-Hur'" and then elaborated:

> In the course of the argument counsel displayed a book of films, showing the chariot race and other spectacular scenes, the exhibition attracted considerable interest, not only among the members of the Supreme Court bar and the few visitors in the courtroom, but interested the justices of the court.[249]

Of the thousands of churches, lecture halls, auditoriums, theaters, opera houses, boardrooms, schoolrooms, factories, racetracks, stadiums, and many other types of venues that witnessed *Ben-Hur* readings, performances and adaptations, certainly this was the most prestigious, and unique. And the fact that everyone in the courtroom was interested is a testament to the novelty of the film and the effectiveness of Olcott's adaption, not to mention the lure of a visual adaptation of *Ben-Hur*.

Joining Kalem's legal representation now was John W. Griggs, former United States Attorney General, but the result, encapsulated in the decision written by Oliver Wendell Holmes, Jr. on November 13, was the same.[250] In summarizing the pleadings and facts used in the previous appeal, Holmes also begins by referring to "the late General Lew Wallace's book 'Ben Hur'" and then differentiates "moving-picture films," as a widely applicable means of reproduction, from this particular Kalem film, apparently not having been informed that Gene Gauntier was a woman:

> The defendant employed a man to read Ben Hur and to write out such a description or scenario of certain portions that it could be followed in action; these portions giving enough of the story to be identified with ease.

Confirming Ward's analogy to pantomime, Holmes succinctly tied up the greatest issue by citing the relevant passage from the 1891 Revised Statutes and thereby declaring the film a drama:

> Authors have the exclusive right to dramatize any of their works. So, if the exhibition was or was founded on a dramatizing of Ben Hur, this copyright was infringed. We are of the opinion that Ben Hur was dramatized by what was done.

The court upheld Ward's decision and awarded $25,000 in damages, based on the assumption that the film had been exhibited some 500 times. This made the Kalem *Ben Hur* the costliest film of its era, just as the two subsequent MGM films would be the most expensive films to produce in their respective eras.[251]

The decision was publicized widely and had a much greater impact than the decisions of the lower courts. As legal analysts explored the ramifications, a widely syndicated newspaper report assumed that this victory in "a contest over the copyright of Gen. Lew Wallace's 'Ben Hur'" was "a blow to moving picture show promoters."[252] Interestingly, the *Los Angeles Times*, just a few years before Los Angeles would become the home of the motion picture industry, independently left out the initial sentence about this being "a blow" to the industry.[253] However, the trade newsletter *Motography* recognized the importance of this "test case,"[254] and *The Moving Picture World*, representing a much more positive industry perspective, immediately broadcast the decision's broader applications:

> By thus defining the status of the motion picture, the Supreme Court has performed a distinct service for the picture manufacturers of the country since it places their productions in the same class with other dramatic productions and entitles them to the same protection under the copyright laws.[255]

They also featured a forum on "The Scenario Writer" to give advice regarding copyright to professionals.[256] Nonetheless, in 1914 they placed an advertisement in their own publication offering to purchase second-hand moving picture films, and first on the list was *Ben Hur*.[257]

Within weeks the House Committee on Patents was holding hearings that included Edward W. Townsend, a New Jersey congressman and an author himself, the president of Edison Electric, a representative of the M.P.P.C., a representative of the Society of American Dramatists and Composers, the Librarian of Congress, and the Register of Copyrights. By the end of the winter, Townsend submitted legislation that ultimately went into effect on August 24, 1912, providing for the separate copyrighting of motion pictures, previously registered as photographs.[258] As a result of "The Ben Hur Case" and now the Townsend Bill, *The Moving Picture World* considered this essential issue resolved:

> The Edison Company has arranged with the publishers for the use of some O. Henry stories, but we have seen some other photoplays that came dangerously close to thefts from that versatile writer and others. But with the settlement of the Ben Hur case and the passage of the Townsend Bill we think publishers will find that it pays to watch production and this, in its turn, will make some editors more careful in their selection. In any event it will not pay a photoplaywright to become identified with thefts.[259]

The status of scenario writers like Gautier and many others would be changed forever, as would the relationship between film producers and the authors of magazine stories and novels.[260] Here the reader can appreciate in particular the transformation in American popular culture that had taken place over the course of the first three decades of the *Ben-Hur* phenomenon and especially the irony in that the novel Lew Wallace for so long protected from any attempt at dramatization had now become the subject of the test case that would help establish the relationship between literature, drama, and film for the next century, at least.[261]

The Kalem *Ben Hur* eventually disappeared from exhibition. Understandably, even the Library of Congress did not retain a copy. Kemp R. Niver, who catalogued the Paper Print Collection in the Library of Congress in the 1980s, labeled its lone, 93-foot film segment as *The Chariot Race* and suggested that the rest of the original Kalem film was lost.[262] There is a single newspaper entry that states clearly that the Film Society of London screened a copy of the film in 1928.[263] We know that this was the Kalem film and not the 1925 MGM film from the description:

> This "Ben Hur" lives by its brevity, which telescopes "the Hur family – an unfortunate accident" into one unintended sub-title and skirts the famous chariot race with two shots."

This description suggests that their copy of the film was severely edited, as is the otherwise superior copy presently housed at the Cineteca di Bologna.[264] There are less than a half-dozen prints in existence today, although a digitized version is now available online.

The precedent-setting decision accordingly figured into numerous subsequent disputes and legal cases. The 1924 dispute over the Newton Bill, which would have exempted movie theaters and radio stations from paying license fees to composers whose works they used, invoked this response from Nathan Burkan, the attorney for the American Society of Composers, Authors, and Publishers:

> The pending bill is promoted by purely selfish interests who are seeking to secure, for the purpose of profit, the works of American composers without any return. The moving picture owners have amassed tremendous fortunes. The principal part of their programs consist of musical features. This industry began as a parasitic industry taking novels, stories and plays for reproduction in pictures without leave or license until it was stopped by the Supreme Court in the "Ben Hur" case.[265]

The New York Clipper quoted Burkan in saying:

> Piracy is what they want. The motion picture producers stole every story in sight until the Supreme Court stopped them with their decision in the "Ben Hur" case.[266]

The high-profile cases include those litigating Mutual Film Corporation censorship,[267] The Lone Ranger scripts,[268] and, most notably, the 1984 Sony Corp. of America v. Universal City Studios, Inc. battle over home-video tape recorders.[269] This case will be discussed in the final chapter of the book, but it is worth pointing out here that as history would prove, by fighting against the new technology, Universal paralleled Lew Wallace in his initial refusals to dramatize his novel: both Wallace and the moving picture industry would reap great profits from what they had vigorously opposed.

These cases involve film, television, radio, music, computer software, video games,[270] and news distribution[271] – wherever the precedents of derivative copyright apply. They continue a century later, e.g. 2005's Metro-Goldwyn-Mayer Studios Inc. v. Grokster, Ltd.[272] The Kalem Co. v. Harper Brothers decision has also been cited in federal cases involving the sale of petroleum fuel, the sale of real estate, and a fatal railroad accident for which the court said that "a distinction has been taken between sales made with a view to a certain result and those made simply with indifferent knowledge that the buyer contemplates that result."[273] Modern legal and academic scholarship has produced a modicum of scholarship.[274]

In addition, apart from its legal significance, the film left a legacy that occasionally surfaces in our extant sources. *The Moving Picture World* published an editorial cartoon in 1916 to accompany their five-year campaign to support the legal right of exhibitors to show motion pictures on Sunday in New York.[275] The cartoon features a man wearing an ancient Roman military costume, and above and behind him is a poster for *Ben-Hur* displayed on the wall leading into the "Moving Picture Theater." *The Life of Moses* (1909) is listed as well as *Quo Vadis?* (1913). Interestingly, the *Ben-Hur* poster says the film is in four reels (nearly the size of *The Life of Moses*). Another editorial cartoon appeared in the *Los Angeles Times* in 1930.[276] This one accompanies the article, "Litigation Swells Cost of Early Epic," that remembers the Kalem *Ben Hur* for its unprecedented expense. The cartoon depicts a Roman, his cape labeled "KALEM," driving a chariot as an Uncle Sam figure yelling, "In the name of the law!" The article is subtitled "Expensive 'Ben Hur' of Twenty Years Ago Ran Into Big Money Largely Through Litigation." Two years later, Lee Shippey in his column offered a survey of Christian films, and he devotes a paragraph to the Kalem *Ben Hur* between Gaumont's *Life of Christ* and *The Life of Moses*.[277] He mentions Harper, the Wallace estate, the litigation, and the $25,000 fine. And even as late as 1958, in pre-publicity for the 1959 MGM film, paragraphs here and there were devoted to remembrances of the Kalem film and the copyright challenge.[278]

In general the film today is remembered for the controversy it engendered and the important judicial precedent that it set. But in light of the present examination, we can identify the film in another way, as a daring – albeit to the point of futility – attempt at a synergy between one of the bestselling novels of the late nineteenth century and the visual narrative medium of commercially profitable popular film. Supported by the masters of the fledgling motion picture industry, in Kalem's willingness to press the legal proceedings through appellate courts all the way to the Supreme Court – arguing that the film was "merely a series of photographs" – we may see an insistence not on breaking the law but fighting for the right of film-makers to adapt and recreate a work of literature in a different medium with very different demands, techniques, and results. The step that Kalem did not take was to secure permission to recreate the *Ben-Hur* story in a motion picture play. Not fully realizing that they were at the dawn of a new age, Marion and Olcott believed their project was beyond the reach of copyright law, and they paid the price. So did the public in that they did not have the opportunity to make the Kalem *Ben Hur* into a success like its *Ben-Hur* cousins. Reading between the lines, the reader may assume that much of the reason for the major role that the Kalem *Ben Hur* played in the development of commercial cinema was that the courts and the industry knew well that this was not just a film, it was a film featuring the *Ben-Hur* property still well within its prime and enjoying one of its many peaks of popularity. It was just a little over one year after the Supreme Court battle that Sears, Roebuck and Company would purchase their one million volumes, and Klaw & Erlanger would continue their production for another nine years and even add to its spectacle.

Two weeks after the Supreme Court decision, Henry Wallace, in an interview with the *Indianapolis Star*, proclaimed, "no motion picture company will be allowed to produce in films the story of 'Ben-Hur.'"[279] Much like his father, Henry would eventually change his mind. This did not happen until after years of legal battles and contract negotiations, but ultimately he, too, would succumb to the advances of Abraham Erlanger.

NOTES

1 *The [Decatur IL] Daily Review* (February 20, 1905) 4.
2 *DFP* (December 19, 1909) C2.
3 *Mansfield [OH] News* (June 5, 1911) 2.
4 *LAT* (December 23, 1901) 10; *The Nashua [IA] Reporter* (December 19, 1907) 6; *Reno Evening Gazette* (December 21, 1929) 3.
5 *The [Appleton WI] Post-Crescent* (February 1, 1938) 4; *Harrisburg [PA] Telegraph* (March 4, 1939) 2.
6 *BE* (January 20, 1897) 2.
7 *Werner's Magazine* 18 (February, 1896) 180.
8 *LAT* (July 3, 1910) V16.
9 International Newsreel Photo # 184834; cf. *Newark Advocate* (December 15, 1922) 1.
10 *[Boise] Idaho Statesman* (April 14, 1908) 3.
11 *[Boise] Idaho Statesman* (April 11, 1908) 5; *[Cumberland MD] Evening Times* (October 25, 1911) 8; *Muskegon [MI] Chronicle* (July 31, 1913) 4.
12 <http://apps.its.uiowa.edu/libsdrc/details.jsp?id=/flowers/5&page=4>
13 <http://apps.its.uiowa.edu/libsdrc/details.jsp?id=/flowers/8>

14 *Riverside Daily Press* (March 14, 1903) 10.
15 *Dallas Morning News* (December 10, 1913) 13; cf. *[Louisville] Courier Journal* (January 5, 1897) 2.
16 *Werner's Magazine* 18 (June, 1896) 616.
17 *Werner's Magazine* 18 (August 1, 1896) 603 and 709–13; *Evansville [IN] Courier and Press* (November 2, 1896) 1.
18 *Portsmouth [OH] Daily Times* (September 30, 1897) 10.
19 E.g. *Riverside Daily Press* (February 16, 1906) 6; *[Boise] Idaho Statesman* (April 12, 1908) 3.
20 *Riverside Daily Press* (March 14, 1903) 10; cf. *[Cumberland MD] Evening Times* (October 25, 1911) 8.
21 Broadside for Miss Tessier, December 5, 1889, UVA.
22 <http://archive.org/stream/cataloguepricei100thmc#page/no/mode/2up>
23 *The Advance* 33 (February 4, 1897) 162.
24 <http://magiclantern.chcs.biz/about-magic-lanterns/lantern-slides/j-b-beal>; <http://www2.hsp.org/collections/manuscripts/b/Beale2007.html>; cf. Lindvall, *Sanctuary Cinema*, 48.
25 Lindvall, *Sanctuary Cinema*, 48.
26 *Catalogue of Stereopticons and Magic Lanterns* (October, 1894) 1 and 17; cf. <http://www.geh.org/ar/strip66/htmlsrc/m198903750005_ful.html#topofimage>
27 <http://www.artfact.com/auction-lot/81-ben-hur-magic-lantern-glass-slides-45-c-58ce84d951>; eBay #6265514890, ended April 1, 2006.
28 eBay #181336627614, ended March 5, 2014.
29 *Complete Illustrated Catalogue of Moving Picture Machines: Stereopticons, Magic Lanterns, Accessories, and Stereopticon Views* (June, 1902) (Chicago: Kleine Optical Co., 1902) n.p.
30 <http://www.geh.org/ar/strip56/htmlsrc/briggs_sum00018.html#86:0808:0027>. The Eastman House online catalog does not recognize these as belonging to the Kleine set, nor do the sequence numbers match up, but the depictions match the Kleine titles and not the McAllister or Riley titles.
31 McAllister *Catalogue of Stereopticons and Magic Lanterns* (October, 1899) 237.
32 A copy is in the Lilly Library, Indiana University.
33 *CE* (April 27, 1896) 9.
34 Henry, "Ben-Hur, 3–4; David Robinson, Stephen Herbert, and Richard Crangle, *Encyclopedia of the Magic Lantern* (London: Magic Lantern Society, 2001) 240 and 320.
35 The eBay sale number cannot be retrieved.
36 Malamud, *Ancient Rome and Modern America*, 133.
37 George Eastman House #86:0808:0001 and 86:0808:0031.
38 *The Chariot* 2 (February, 1896) 7.
39 *WP* (March 15, 1897) 2, 7.
40 *[Washington, DC] Evening Star* (March 16, 1896) 10.
41 *The [Crawfordsville] Daily News-Review* (November 19, 1901) 1.
42 <http://images.library.yale.edu/divinitycontent/beard/Beard1901.pdf>
43 eBay #230050213537, ended November 17, 2006.

44 *The Expositor* 20 (May, 1919) 696.
45 *The St. Paul Globe* (February 28, 1903) 2.
46 *SFC* (June 25, 1895) 7.
47 *The [Huntington IN] Daily Democrat* (January 16, 1893) 3
48 Flyer, Wallace Collection, IHS; cf. *BE* (December 31, 1895) 5.
49 *PW* 49 (May 2, 1896) 768.
50 Letter from Wallace to Harper (February 8, 1896), IHS.
51 Letter from A. Gurlitz to Wallace (March 21, 1896), LL.
52 Letter from Wallace to Harper (March 21, 1896), LL.
53 *CE* (April 27, 1896) 9.
54 Letter from Harper to Wallace (October 30, 1890), LL.
55 *CE* (April 27, 1896) 9.
56 *[St Joseph LA] Tensas Gazette* (May 1, 1896) 94; *The Publishers' Weekly* 49 (May 2, 1896) 768.
57 *The Optical Magic Lantern Journal and Photographic Enlarger* 7.85 (June, 1896) 92–3.
58 *The Optical Magic Lantern Journal and Photographic Enlarger* 7 (October, 1896) 166–7.
59 Henry, "Ben-Hur", 4–5. Cf. *Optical Magic Lantern Journal and Photographic Enlarger* 6 (July, 1895) 119.
60 Ibid., 2–3.
61 *The [New York] Evening Telegram* (September 2, 1896) 3; *NYT* (September 3, 1896) 9; *NYTr* (September 3, 1896) 12.
62 *The Photographic News* 40 (September 25, 1896) 618.
63 Cf. Robinson, *From Peepshow to Palace*, 171.
64 Henry, *The New Magic Lantern Journal*, 2–3.
65 *Logansport Journal* (February 4, 1908) 4.
66 *Lebanon [PA] Daily News* (March 1, 1897) 1; (March 3, 1897) 1.
67 *BG* (December 23, 1901) 5.
68 Letter from G. N. Buzby to Wallace (November 13, 1896), LL.
69 Letter from A. Dobbins to Wallace (December 14, 1896), LL.
70 *The Optical Magic Lantern Journal and Photographic Enlarger* 7.88 (September, 1896) 138.
71 Cf. *The Sydney Morning Herald* (December 25, 1901) 6.
72 Cf. *[Washington, DC] Evening Star* (January 16, 1896) 12.
73 *Watertown [NY] Daily Times* (December 4, 1890) 5.
74 *The Sacramento Record-Union* (June 6, 1891) 2; (June 9, 1891) 6.
75 *The Sacramento Record-Union* (June 10, 1891) 6.
76 <http://freepages.genealogy.rootsweb.ancestry.com/~npmelton/sacpi049.htm>
77 *The Sacramento Record-Union* (December 3, 1890) 3.
78 *The [San Bernadino] Daily Courier* (April 28, 1892) 3.
79 E.g. *The [Huntington IN] Daily Democrat* (January 24, 1893) 3; *Logansport Pharos-Tribune* (May 3, 1893) 16.
80 *The [Springfield] Illinois State Journal* (January 8, 1911) 13.
81 Cf. *The Davenport [IA] Daily Republican* (April 11, 1893) 4.
82 *The [Huntington IN] Daily Democrat* (January 16, 1893) 3.

83 *The Davenport [IA] Daily Leader* (June 30, 1892) 4.
84 *The Davenport [IA] Daily Leader* (April 13, 1893) 4.
85 *The Humboldt [IA] Republican* (January 19, 1893) 5.
86 Cf. John Wilder Fairbank, *Various Papers from the Fairbanks Family in America, Inc.*, (Boston: Fairbanks Family in America, 1904–5); and Fairbank, *Coaching and Camping in the Yellowstone* (St. Paul: Chas. S. Fee, 1898).
87 E.g. *WP* (January 3, 1897) 19.
88 *[Washington, DC] Evening Star* (January 25, 1896) 12.
89 *WP* (January 16, 1896) 10.
90 *WP* (January 11, 1897) 4.
91 *WP* (April 20, 1896) 9.
92 *WP* (February 4, 1896) 8; (April 19, 1896) 20.
93 *WP* (May 28, 1896) 7; (June 22, 1896) 10; (July 5, 1896) 14.
94 *WP* (April 11, 1896) 2; (April 12, 1896) 10. Cf. *WP* (May 9, 1896) 10.
95 *WP* (October 17, 1896) 10. Cf. Pentz-Harris, et al, "Screening Male Sentimental Power in *Ben-Hur*," 119.
96 *WP* (January 17, 1897) 22.
97 *WP* (April 19, 1896) 20.
98 *WP* (April 4, 1897) 22.
99 *WP* (March 20, 1901) 8.
100 *The Scranton Republican* (April 17, 1905) 1.
101 *The [New Orleans] Times-Picayune* (September 11, 1896) 3.
102 *[Charleston, SC] Evening Post* (April 5, 1898) 10.
103 *[Lexington KY] Morning Herald* (December 5, 1898) 4.
104 *AC* (December 3, 1897) 7.
105 Lorenzo Sayles Fairbanks, *Genealogy of the Fairbanks Family in America, 1633–1897* (Boston: printed for the author by the American Printing and Engraving Company, 1897) 446. <http://www.archive.org/stream/genealogyfairbaoofairgoog/genealogyfairbaoofairgoog_djvu.txt>; cf. <http://www.findagrave.com/cgi-bin/fg.cgi?page=gr&GRid=98110280>.
106 *Report of the Young Men's Christian Union for the Year Ending March 31, 1899* (1899) 107.
107 *Reading [PA] Times* (October 21, 1902) 5; (October 30, 1902) 1.
108 *Cambridge Chronicle* (October 21, 1899) 11.
109 *Morning [Olympia WA] Olympian* (January 24, 1894) 12.
110 *The San Francisco Call* (March 30, 1905) 11; *The San Francisco Call* (August 4, 1895) 6.
111 *AC* (March 9, 1905) 2.
112 *Trenton Evening Times* (March 24, 1910) 115.
113 *BE* (December 28, 1895) 9; (December 19, 1896) 10; (December 16, 1897) 6; (March 29, 1900) 9; (December 28, 1901) 13; (March 1, 1902) 8.
114 *LAT* (January 3, 1895) 10.
115 *Harrisburg [PA] Telegraph* (June 16, 1903) 1.
116 *WP* (June 6, 1897) 2.
117 *Logansport [IN] Journal* (July 10, 1896) 8.

118 *Oak Park [IL] Vindicator* (January 20, 1899) 5.
119 *The Kansas City Star* (March 1, 1896) 12.
120 *WP* (April 9, 1897) 7.
121 *Milwaukee Sentinel* (May 27, 1894) 19; *The Advance* (July 1, 1897) 26; *Yenowime's Illustrated News* (December 20, 1896) 6.
122 *Werner's Magazine* 18 (January, 1896) 84 and 1198.
123 E.g. *The Sydney Morning Herald* (December 25, 1901) 6; (February 3, 1902) 3; cf. *The Cumberland Argus and Fruitgrowers Advocate* (February 1, 1902) 9.
124 Clum, *Apache Agent*, 118–19; Ledoux, *Nantan*, 32.
125 *[Washington, DC] Evening Star* (January 16, 1896) 12.
126 *[Washington, DC] Evening Star* (March 16, 1896) 10; *Alexandria Gazette* (February 11, 1897) 3; *WP* (March 15, 1897) 2.
127 *Trenton Evening Times* (March 24, 1899) 8.
128 *CE* (November 26, 1905) A8.
129 *WP* (November 22, 1910) 9.
130 *BH* (January 7, 1908) 8.
131 *Moving Picture World* 1 (July 7, 1907) 311.
132 *WP* (June 6, 1897) 2; (December 18, 1897) 2.
133 *WP* (April 9, 1897) 7.
134 *Alexandria [VA] Gazette* (April 11, 1902) 3.
135 *BG* (April 2, 1900) 5.
136 *Athol [MA] Daily News* (January 28, 1935) n.p.
137 <http://apps.its.uiowa.edu/libsdrc/details.jsp?id=/centralp/1&ui=1>
138 *Tyrone [PA] Daily Herald* (July 8, 1909) 8.
139 *CE* (November 26, 1905) A8.
140 *The St. Paul Globe* (February 28, 1903) 2.
141 *The [Eau Claire WI] Daily Telegram* (July 1, 1904) 7.
142 E.g. *Trenton Evening Times* (March 24, 1899) 8.
143 *The Bemidji Daily Pioneer* (December 5, 1904) 4.
144 *The San Francisco Call* (March 20, 1906) 7.
145 *Los Angeles Herald* (August 4, 1907) 5.
146 *The San Francisco Call* (June 15, 1908) 9.
147 *The Princeton [MN] Union* (July 15, 1909) 4.
148 *Rockford [IL] Republic* (October 20, 1916) 4.
149 *The [Elyria OH] Chronicle-Telegram* (July 6, 1906) 1.
150 *The Elyria [OH] Republican* (June 21, 1906) 1; cf. *Chicago Tribune* (August 8, 1897) 14.
151 *The Omaha Daily Bee* (November 8, 1903) 3.
152 *The Anaconda [MT] Standard* (January 30, 1898) 12.
153 *[New Orleans] Times-Picayune* (April 1, 1899) 10.
154 *The Minneapolis Journal* (February 10, 1904) 17.
155 *[Washington, DC] Evening Star* (April 8, 1897) 12.
156 *The [Baltimore] Sun* (November 21, 1896) 4.
157 *The [Louisville KY] Courier-Journal* (April 7, 1899) 3; *The Ligonier [IN] Leader* (May 6, 1909) 5; and *Logansport Pharos-Tribune* (February 7, 1893) 11.
158 *Alexandria Gazette* (February 11, 1897) 3.

159 *The [Lincoln NE] Courier* (February 12, 1898) 12.
160 *[Dodge City KA] The Globe Republican* (April 2, 1896) 3. "The stereopticon plates, the only set in the West, were loaned by a Kansas City gentleman."
161 *NYT* (March 1, 1913) 21.
162 *The Ogden [UT] Standard* (November 10, 1917) 12.
163 *St. Johns [OR] Review* (May 20, 1921) 3.
164 *Riverside [CA] Daily Press* (December 29, 1924) 12.
165 *[Rockford IL] Republic* (May 23, 1929) 4.
166 *Athol [MA] Daily News* (January 28, 1935) n.p.
167 <http://archive.org/stream/catalogueofmagic00mont#page/no/mode/2up>
168 *CE* (November 19, 1899) 33.
169 *The Minneapolis Journal* (March 14, 1903) 7.
170 *Harrisburg [PA] Telegraph* (June 16, 1903) 1.
171 *The Expositor* 20 (May, 1919) 650–1.
172 In the possession of the author.
173 In the possession of the author.
174 *Middlebury [VT] Register* (June 6, 1913) 8.
175 *The Moving Picture World* 1 (December 28, 1907) 709.
176 *The Moving Picture World* 2 (January 18, 1908) 49.
177 *BG* (January 5, 1908) 24.
178 *Colorado Springs Gazette* (November 22, 1908) 23.
179 *The Moving Picture World* 1 (December 7, 1907) 654.
180 Solomon, "The Kalem *Ben-Hur* (1907), 189–204.
181 Rita Horwitz and Harriet Harrison, eds, *The George Kleine Collection of Early Motion Pictures in the Library of Congress: A Catalog* (Washington, DC: Library of Congress, 1980) xiii–xiv; Harner, "The Kalem Company," 188–90; Slide, *Early American Cinema*, 47–64. Cf. *NYT* (April 30, 1907) 12.
182 Jacobs, *The Rise of the American Film*, 122–5.
183 Menefee, *The First Female Stars*, 71–82; Azlant, "Screenwriting for the Early Silent Film," 237–9.
184 Gene Gauntier, "Blazing the Trail," *Woman's Home Companion* 55 (October, 1928) 7; cf. <http://www.cinemaweb.com/silentfilm/bookshelf/4_blaze2.htm>
185 Foster, *Stardust and Shadows*, 226.
186 *New York Magazine* (December 29, 1975) 47.
187 Cf. *BE* (June 20, 1902) 10.
188 *The Billboard* (December 7, 1907) 74.
189 <http://www.imdb.com/title/tt0000582/fullcredits?ref_=tt_ov_st_sm>
190 Davis, *William S. Hart*, 58–67.
191 Gauntier, "Blazing the Trail," 7; *NYT* (March 14, 1908) 7.
192 *BE* (August 2, 1898) 5.
193 *The Moving Picture World* (December 7, 1907) 651; *The Billboard* (December 7, 1907) 74.
194 *Time* (February 25, 1935) = <http://www.time.com/time/magazine/article/0,9171,754576,00.html>
195 <http://www.indiana.edu/~liblilly/lilly/mss/index.php?p=wallace2>
196 *BE* (October 26, 1907) 7.

197 "Production as the Nickelodeon Era Begins: 1905–1907 – New Production Companies," *The Encyclopedia Britannica*, 1911 ed., = <http://encyclopedia.jrank.org/articles/pages/1923/Production-as-the-Nickelodeon-Era-Begins-1905-1907.html>
198 *The Billboard* (December 7, 1907) 100.
199 Hovet, "The Case of Kalem's Ben-Hur," 284–7; Fell, "Motive, Mischief, and Melodrama," 272–83.
200 *The Moving Picture World* 1 (December 7, 1907) 651.
201 *The Moving Picture World* 2 (February 1, 1908) 80.
202 *Watertown [NY] Daily Times* (December 18, 1907) 10; *Ann Arbor News-Argus* (December 20, 1907) 8; *San Diego Union* (December 29, 1907) 5. Cf. *Evansville [IN] Courier and Press* (December 12, 1907) 9.
203 *Aberdeen American* (January 9, 1908) 5.
204 *Daily [Springfield] Illinois State Register* (December 21, 1907) 8.
205 *Pawtucket [RI] Times* (December 19, 1907) 3.
206 *Macon [GA] Telegraph* (December 20, 1907) 1.
207 *[Biloxi MS] Daily Herald* (February 3, 1908) 1.
208 *Winston-Salem Journal* (January 15, 1908) 6.
209 *Saginaw [MI] News* (January 1, 1908) 2.
210 *The Moving Picture World* 1 (December 28, 1907) 651.
211 E.g. *The Scranton [PA] Republican* (February 18, 1908) 5 and 8.
212 *The Moving Picture World* 2 (February 15, 1908) 126.
213 *The Moving Picture World* 2 (February 25, 1908) 159.
214 *Augusta [GA] Chronicle* (February 8, 1908) 6.
215 *NYT* (March 14, 1908) 7. "Cheap" encompasses non-legitimate theaters.
216 *Moving Picture World* 2 (March 21, 1908) 233.
217 *NYTr* (March 14, 1908) 6.
218 *Kansas City [MO] Star* (October 22, 1908) 71.
219 *Variety* 10 (March 21, 1908) 14.
220 Segrave, *Piracy in the Motion Picture Industry*, 47–8.
221 *NYT* (April 10, 1908) 13.
222 *NYT* (May 6, 1908) 5.
223 <http://www.ilntoday.com/files/2012/03/Cooper-and-Dunham-125-Years-of-Intellectual-Property-Law.pdf>
224 *Variety* 10 (May 9, 1908) 11.
225 163 U.S. 156.
226 Letter from Henry Wallace to Frederick A. Duneka (May 19, 1908), Pierpont Morgan Library.
227 *Kansas City [MO] Star* (October 22, 1908) 4.
228 Vidor, *A Tree Is a Tree*, 18–21; cf. M&M, 468–9.
229 Bordwell, et al., *The Classical Hollywood Cinema*, 131.
230 *United States Circuit Courts of Appeals Reports* (Rochester: Lawyers' Co-operative Publishing Co., 1910) 94:429–33.
231 Cf. *The Virginia Law Register* 15 (September, 1909) 405.
232 E.g. *The Nickelodeon* 1 (May, 1909) 124; *Variety* (August 21, 1909) 17.
233 *The Nickelodeon* 2 (September, 1909) 72 and 81–2.
234 *The Film Daily* 28 (May 9, 1924) 1.

235 E.g. *Soerabaijasch Handelsblad* (May 13, 1908) 7; (May 14, 1908) 7; (May 23, 1908) 8.
236 *Williamsport [IN] Warren Review* (May 21, 1908) 1.
237 <http://dwight-historical-society.org/Star_and_Herald_Images/1910_Star_and_Herald_images/029_0001.pdf>
238 *Springfield [MA] Daily News* (May 11, 1911) 10.
239 Cf. *Richmond [IN] Morning News* (May 13, 1911) 4.
240 Also in *The Winnipeg Tribune* (May 20, 1911) 25.
241 *Moving Picture World* 10 (October 21, 1911) 198.
242 *The Billboard* (September 30, 1911) 14.
243 *[Columbia SC] State* (May 25, 1908) 8.
244 *Jonesboro [AR] Weekly* (October 20, 1909) 2.
245 E.g. *Macon [GA] Telegraph* (July 2, 1911) 12.
246 *The [Ada OK] Evening News* (August 14, 1911) 3.
247 *Tampa Tribune* (November 18, 1911) 4.
248 *The Winnipeg Tribune* (November 23, 1911) 2.
249 *WP* (November 1, 1911) 2.
250 Ibid., 2.
251 Cf. *LAT* (June 1, 1930) B9.
252 *University of Pennsylvania Law Review and American Law Register* 60 (February, 1912) 347–8; *SFC* (November 15, 1911) 5; *DFP* (November 14, 1911) 8; *Grand Forks [ND] Herald* (November 16, 1911) 3.
253 *LAT* (November 14, 1911) 3.
254 *Motography* 6 (November 11, 1911) 207.
255 *The Moving Picture World* (November 25, 1911) 644.
256 *The Moving Picture World* 11 (January 13, 1912) 118; cf. 13 (August 31, 1912) 875.
257 *The Moving Picture World* 19 (March 14, 1914) 1424.
258 *Report of the Librarian of Congress and Report of the Superintendent of the Library Building and Grounds* (Washington, DC: Government Printing Office, 1912) 137–41; cf. Frohlich and Schwartz, *The Law of Motion Pictures*, 510–12; Maras, "In Search of 'Screenplay'," 347.
259 *Moving Picture World* 13 (August 31, 1912) 875.
260 *Moving Picture World* 10 (November 25, 1911) 644; Loughney, "From 'Rip Van Winkle' to 'Jesus of Nazareth'," 285–6; Van Nostrand, "Making and Marketing Fiction," 152.
261 Bordwell, et al., *The Classical Hollywood Cinema*, 129–32; Azlant, "Screenwriting for the Early Silent Film," 238–42; Caidhyanathan, *Copyrights and Copywrongs*, 93–6; Allen, "Copyright and Early Theater, Vaudeville and Film Competition," 10–11.
262 Kemp R. Niver (Bebe Bergsten, ed.), *Early Motion Pictures: The Paper Print Collection in the Library of Congress* (Washington, DC: Library of Congress, 1985) 52.
263 *The Manchester Guardian* (April 2, 1928) 11.
264 My special thanks to Andrea Meneghelli.
265 *TFD* 28 (May 9, 1924) 1.
266 *The New York Clipper* (May 15, 1924) 39.

267 236 U.S. 230 (1915); cf. *The Motion Picture News* 9 (April 18, 1914) 19–20; *The Moving Picture World* 19 (February 28, 1914) 1075.
268 740 F.2d 718 (1984).
269 464 U.S. 417 (1984).
270 964 F.2d 965 (1992).
271 E.g. 248 U.S. 215 (1918).
272 545 U.S. 913 (2005).
273 280 U.S. 390 (1930); 235 U.S. 99 (1914); and 242 U.S. 13 (1916).
274 E.g. Ginsburg, "Creation and Commercial Value," 1887–8; Wu, "Copyright's Communications Policy," 302, n. 80; Fearing, "Research, Journals, Etc.," 318–24.
275 *The Moving Picture World* 27 (February 5, 1916) 825.
276 *LAT* (June 1, 1930) B9; cf. *The Film Daily* 29 (December 14, 1924) 1 and 10.
277 *LAT* (November 4, 1932) A4.
278 E.g. *NYT* (August 10, 1958) X5.
279 *Indianapolis Star* (December 3, 1911) A3.

12 "The Greatest Motion Picture Property in the History of the Screen": The 1925 MGM Ben-Hur

THE DISPUTE OVER THE MOTION PICTURE RIGHTS

Although the 1911 Supreme Court decision in Kalem Co. v. Harper Brothers proved in many ways to be a milestone for the cinema industry, it did not quell the desire to represent the story of *Ben-Hur* on film.[1] Less than two years later rumors began to surface that Klaw & Erlanger were producing their own film version of *Ben-Hur*.[2] As the first theatrical entrepreneurs to involve themselves in film production and distribution, Klaw & Erlanger had already in 1897, even before producing the staged version of *Ben-Hur*, established their claim by financing Walter W. Freeman's production of the Horitz Passion Play, the first shown in the United States.[3] Now in the early 1910s many theatrical moguls sought some degree of vertical integration by producing their own films. After months of denial Klaw & Erlanger announced in June, 1913, that they had come to an agreement with the Biograph Company.[4] Together they would form the Protective Amusement Company as "an exclusive service of copyrighted plays" that would "produce the more prominent of the latter's theatrical successes in motion picture form." One of their partners, Albert H. Woods, another New York theatrical manager, had reportedly paid $32,000 "for the American rights to the 'Ben-Hur' motion pictures,"[5] and this was reinforced by a subsequent July, 1913, syndicated report that they had already completed *The Road to Yesterday* and *Ben-Hur*.[6] *The Road to Yesterday* they did make, along with twenty-five other films, before ceasing production in 1914.[7] *Ben-Hur* they did not make. In 1915 *Variety* reported that "Klaw & Erlanger may have a picture production of 'Ben Hur' made this summer,"[8] but despite Klaw & Erlanger's exclusive contractual control over the play, they did not have the legal rights to produce a film adaptation.

Henry Wallace had written to Harper in 1912:

> I will oppose in every way possible all attempts to produce any of General Wallace's works in moving pictures. The reason is because moving picture shows are wretched exhibitions utterly unworthy of dignified consideration.[9]

The capabilities of film at the time did not meet the standard he envisioned for a new conception of *Ben-Hur*. He despaired also of incompetent projectionists, films in a state of disrepair, and the lack of synchronized music and color. During the summer of 1913, Klaw & Erlanger were telling him that Italian, English, and German companies were mounting film versions of *Ben-Hur*, George Kleine was reportedly interested, and two years later Harper and Wallace received requests from Rex Beach and even William Farnum.[10] Wallace steadfastly refused. His attitude did not apply to *Ben-Hur* alone but to requests for filming *The Fair God* and *The Prince of India* as well. Correspondence with Houghton Mifflin records that in 1915, D. W. Griffith desired to produce *The Fair God* as a comprehensive historical epic set in Mexico. But when he had to abandon this project he instead turned to *Intolerance*, which, although not a financial success, did set high-water marks for a film set in the ancient world.

Finally, impressed by the technical achievements of Griffith's *The Birth of a Nation* in 1916, Wallace became willing to negotiate the motion picture rights to *Ben-Hur*.[11] He and Harper had already been challenging Klaw & Erlanger's attempt at producing a film adaptation of *Ben-Hur*, again in the United States District Court for the Southern District of New York [232 F. 609 (1916)].[12] On January 6, 1916, they were granted an injunction against Klaw & Erlanger. In his decision, Judge Charles M. Hough re-examined the Kalem case and inserted a note questioning Klaw & Erlanger's participation: in his opinion they had no moving picture rights to be infringed upon. That right belonged to Wallace and Harper, but this forced the judge to issue a double injunction, explaining that if Harper produced or distributed a film version of *Ben-Hur*, "the market for the spoken play would be greatly impaired, if not destroyed."[13] A follow-up report in *The Moving Picture World* added that Klaw & Erlanger would not be permitted to produce a motion picture version of *Ben-Hur* until the resolution of "the question as to whether the dramatic rights purchased by them some years ago covers the rights to produce a picture."[14] This question would not be resolved until well after the war years.

In 1919 Klaw & Erlanger began the lengthy and complicated process of dissolving their partnership.[15] Erlanger immediately formed a new partnership with two other theatrical titans, Florenz Ziegfeld, Jr. and Charles B. Dillingham.[16] *The Atlanta Constitution* pointed out that "in the matter of finances and prestige this triumvirate is likely to prove the biggest firm ever organized in the theatrical world."[17] They immediately set about building a dozen modern theaters in large cities like New York, Philadelphia, Boston, Chicago, and Detroit, where they would "embark upon the production of plays on a stupendous scale" that would run year round.[18]

Early in 1919 Selig offered $200,000 for the rights to *Ben-Hur*.[19] Klaw & Erlanger's response was that "the picture rights could not be purchased for anything like that sum." As negotiations continued into 1920, Judge Hough suggested that the litigants reach an agreement regarding the value of the picture rights, but the film rights could not be sold until Klaw's holdings were legally disentangled from Erlanger's.[20] Erlanger was under additional time constraints. According to the original contract with Wallace and Harper, if he and Klaw did not produce the play for an entire season, the agreement would be abrogated, leaving him with no dramatic rights to sell.[21] And then in the spring of 1921, *The Film Daily* reported that Italy's Ultra Company had already acquired the funding for their own extravagant version of *Ben Hur*, with the chariot race to be shot in the Colosseum.[22]

In February, 1920, Wallace and Harper tried unsuccessfully to dissolve the cross injunction and strip [Klaw &] Erlanger from the bidding by making a formal charge that they had not produced a sufficient number of performances the preceding year.[23] It was apparently at this point that competing offers came in from powerful forces. Klaw advised First National Pictures to offer a guaranteed purchase price of $250,000 for the screen rights and a fifty–fifty split on profits, but the offer was rejected by not only Erlanger but also Wallace, who was demanding at least $400,000 for his one-third share.[24] United Artists submitted a package that would cast Douglas Fairbanks as Judah Ben-Hur and Mary Pickford as Esther, with Griffith directing, but they, too, balked at paying $1.2 million to Wallace, Erlanger, and Harper.[25] Months later, Erlanger reportedly agreed with Adolph Zukor to have Max Reinhardt, the highly regarded German theatrical producer, direct a film costing some $3 million – $1 million for the rights, $1.5 million for the production, and another $.5 million for advertising and exhibition – referred to commonly in the 1920s as "exploitation."[26] Some of this information did not become public until months after the completion of the litigations, but meanwhile rumors abounded in the press, erroneously claiming that a group of Indianans had paid $1 million;[27] or that the court decided upon $500,000, a sum Griffith refused to pay;[28] or that Griffith had already paid $1.5 million.[29] The names of Marcus Loew,[30] Rex Ingram, and Marshall Neilan were bandied about.[31] Even silence from John Larkin, Wallace's attorney, when asked for any details, was worthy of a press report.[32] "Ben Hur" was current currency. J. Gordon Edwards inserted a chariot race into his newest big-budget film, *The Queen of Sheba*, and *King Queen Joker*, a Sidney Chaplin Paramount comedy, was advertised as "the 'Ben Hur' of screen comedy."[33]

On June 24, 1921, Justice Edward G. Whitaker of the New York Supreme Court signed off on a stipulation that legally separated Klaw's interests in a *Ben-Hur* film from Erlanger's,[34] so finally, on July 22, Wallace and Thomas B. Wells, the Harper representative, signed an agreement with Erlanger.[35] Lew Wallace was well represented in spirit, for Erlanger agreed to pay his son (and grandson, Lewis, Jr., who was a signatory) the unprecedented sum of $600,000 for the film rights.[36] Like Lew Wallace's royalty percentages for *The Prince of India* and the Klaw & Erlanger *Ben-Hur*, this was an extraordinary amount, more than three times the $175,000 Griffith paid for Lottie Blair Parker's play, *Way Down East*. According to the second stipulation in the agreement, neither Christ nor the Crucifixion scene could be portrayed. The agreement also assured that Wallace, or one of the other parties, would extend the novel's copyright for another fourteen years.

The reader can appreciate here a quantitative leap in the perceived and real value of Lew Wallace's unique property. Now forty-one years past its original publication, the novel, along with the Klaw & Erlanger play, had earned millions of dollars for Lew, Susan, and Henry Wallace, Harper, Klaw, and Erlanger. And even after thriving throughout those four decades, its capacity for popular and commercial success was surely far from spent. In fact, already having proved itself to be the most lucrative work of popular literary art in theatrical history, the film industry, baited throughout its formative years with the prospect of filming *Ben-Hur*, demonstrated the property's massive appeal to entrepreneurs not just in the endless rumors of heretofore unimaginable amounts of money but in the legally binding agreement that in actuality established a high-water mark for the industry. More than a decade later David O. Selznick would reportedly pay only $50,000 for the rights to *Gone With the Wind*.[37] And in agreeing to maintain the deceased author's insistence on representing Christ "by symbolic representation, but not in action," this generation of *Ben-Hur* guardians demonstrated their reverence not only for the subject matter but for Lew Wallace as well, adding an additional layer of respect and prestige atop the fantastic profitability.

Two newspaper entries make it clear that contemporaries were well aware of the significance of these two aspects of the *Ben-Hur* phenomenon. As for the financial aspect, an editorial comment in *The Film Daily* sees *Ben-Hur* as the harbinger of a welcome relationship between literary artists and the film industry:

> Two recent news articles give a hint as to the trend of the screen. One is the reported sale of the motion picture rights to "Ben Hur" for a million dollars. That proves that no material will be overlooked because of expense. . . . In every issue of the trade papers one finds an announcement of a new literary light who is turning toward the screen as his medium.[38]

The respect and prestige aspect was embraced by Erlanger. Consenting to a lengthy interview with the *New York Times* in connection with the New York premiere of the film, he reflected upon his long-standing relationship with both Lew Wallace and *Ben-Hur* after saying that the stage royalties paid to Wallace and his estate "have been in the neighborhood of $1,000,000."

After the death of General Lew Wallace I felt strongly and continue to feel that the financial side is entirely secondary to the sacred trust he laid on me to preserve the nobility and reverence and essential greatness of his work.... "I want you to handle the picture," said Mr. [Henry] Wallace, "because of your intimate knowledge of the subject and your respect for the ideals of my father. One of the last acts of Henry L. Wallace before his death was to give his approval of the picture as now shown.... After seeing the film production running in one of my theatres, my only regret is that my old friend Lew Wallace has been dead these many years; that his son, Henry L. Wallace, outlived the opening of the picture but a few days, and they cannot personally share in the joy of this wondrous development.[39]

In fact, Henry Wallace had traveled to New York to attend the premiere of the film and died a few days later in the home of his son, Lewis, Jr., in Rye.[40]

This sense of respect and prestige extended to the next producer as well, for Marcus Loew, Erlanger's successor, reportedly told Erlanger:

> I do not care how much the picture costs. I am going to produce it the way you want it.

Of course anything Abraham Erlanger and Marcus Loew said to the press must be scrutinized carefully. But even the most cynical reading that discounts these statements as mere theatrical hype and perfunctory public sentiment still leaves respect for the late general, dedication to his popularly beloved novel, and reverence for its theological tone as some of the primary themes they used to sell their valuable property.

Before Judge Whitaker could sign off on the stipulation that legally separated Klaw's interests from Erlanger's, both had to submit an affidavit affirming that they had come to an agreement with Wallace and Harper concerning the picture rights for *Ben-Hur*.[41] This agreement seems to have been reached by April 8, when variations of the following press release began to appear nationwide in newspapers and trade journals.

> A. L. Erlanger, Charles B. Dillingham, and F. Ziegfeld, Jr., yesterday acquired the production rights of every kind to "Ben Hur," the famous play by William Young, founded on the novel of Gen. Lew Wallace. Included in the transaction are the motion-picture rights for which the price alone is to be $1,000,000.
> This deal, one of the biggest and most important ever made in the theatrical world, is the culmination of eight years of negotiations and conflict in the courts, and by its consummation the three associated managers come into undisputed possession of all the stage and screen rights to the story that have heretofore been vested in Henry Wallace, the son of the author and the representative of the estate; in Harper Brothers, the publishers of the novel, and in various other persons.[42]

The *New York Times* and *New York Tribune* added:

> It is the intention of the present owners to make an annual production of the play and also to present a screen version, ... since it is recognized that it has far from exhausted its popularity.[43]

The reader will note here that the original conception of the film was that it would be a filmization of the play, not the novel.

The July 22, 1921, signed agreement stipulates that the motion picture rights were to be sold for $600,000, not $1,000,000; the rights were granted in the agreement to Erlanger, not his consortium; it granted rights only insofar as a motion picture was concerned, not necessarily "production rights of every kind"; and the play never toured again. Clearly the pre-publicity for a stupendous cinematic adaptation of *Ben-Hur* film was already being carefully crafted by an experienced theatrical master, but as with Klaw & Erlanger's boastful press releases and advertising for their Broadway production, most of the claims would prove to be accurate. Erlanger would eventually reap much more than $1,000,000 from the transfer of the movie rights. He and the exclusive Classical Cinematograph Corporation, incorporated that same day by such wealthy financiers as Vincent Astor and Robert W. Goelet, would over the next few years reap more than $2,750,000 from the cinematic *Ben-Hur*.[44] When the certificate of copyright extension was issued to Henry Wallace the following October, he immediate transferred the copyright to Erlanger, Dillingham, and Ziegfeld.[45] And even Henry Wallace used the ploy of promising another season of the stage play in order to increase interest in the film rights.[46]

These were the preliminary salvos for what was soon to become a most ambitious, complicated, and nearly catastrophic but hugely successful film production. *The Billboard* articulated the prospects and put it into historical perspective:

> This valuable piece of property – it has grossed close to ten million during its stage career – has at last been secured for motion pictures. ... This is perhaps the biggest transaction in film circles ever recorded. It is the culmination of years of litigation and at last all the interests vested in the heirs of the author, in Harper Bros., publishers of the book, have been bought outright by the new owners. The moving picture rights to the story have been sought after for years – even while the author himself was alive, but he regarded his work as too sacred, too reverential, too potential for the then limited scope of the screen. But today all things are possible in the cinema.[47]

Although eight years had passed, it would still take another four years before this already expensive but eagerly awaited project would consummate in a film release. And the path from Lew Wallace and Harper and then Henry Wallace to Erlanger and his two consortia would still experience more twists and turns before ending up in the hands of one of the most capable film producers of the 1920s, MGM's Irving Thalberg.

MAKING THE FILM

Sources
Problematic, expensive, and time-consuming, the production itself is a monument of the *Ben-Hur* phenomenon separate from the actual release print of the film. The press and the public expected this cinematic adapta-

tion of *Ben-Hur* to be both spectacular and inspirational, and, as we have seen, many Hollywood businessmen and many of its greatest talents had wanted to take on the challenge, and responsibility, of making that a reality. Later labeled "the heroic fiasco" by Academy Award-winning silent-film preservationist and film historian Kevin Brownlow,[48] this $4 million project intersected with the formation of Metro-Goldwyn-Mayer and the careers of such titans and luminaries of the cinema in the 1920s as Samuel Goldwyn, June Mathis, Marcus Loew, Louis B. Mayer, Irving Thalberg, Rudolph Valentino, Ramon Novarro and several others.

Fortunately for our understanding of this material, some of the scholars who have written biographies of these film industry giants accessed face-to-face interviews, personal letters, and oral histories that enabled them to build more detailed narratives than the sources for the earlier dramatic representations in the *Ben-Hur* tradition were able to provide.[49] However, the interviews and anecdotes are often unverifiable, incomplete, and subject to the imperfections of human memory and bias. Some are utterly contradictory. Samuel Marx, who worked for Louis B. Mayer and Irving Thalberg for a number of years and wrote a book about them, expressed it well in his Foreword:

> I dipped only sparingly into books by previous biographers. Their inaccuracies leap off almost every page. I prefer to make my own mistakes rather than propagate theirs.[50]

If one were to construct a narrative from the comments of George Walsh and Francis X. Bushman, the result would be an indictment of MGM for breach of contract, fraud, animal cruelty, and perhaps even negligent homicide. In stark contrast, a narrative constructed from the pronouncements of Marcus Loew, Louis B. Mayer, and Irving Thalberg would follow them as they rescued this project misconceived by Erlanger and the Goldwyn company and mishandled by the Italians but ultimately created a unique, authentic, and thrilling adaptation of Wallace's beloved novel without serious harm to any animal or human. Taking a different approach, Italian scholarship has focused on the political struggle between Fascists and anti-Fascists in a period of extraordinary turmoil in their history that had direct consequences for the American company producing a "grand reconstruction of the film *Ben-Hur*."[51] In addition, Hollywood biographies rarely cite their sources sufficiently and, typically, are too often ill-informed about the novel. To pick the most egregious examples, Mark Vieira in his book on Irving Thalberg wrote that Lew Wallace was a confederate general, and André Soares in his book on Ramon Novarro said that after the Ingersoll encounter "the embarrassed dilettante devoted the next three years to studying the Bible."[52] Almost everyone refers to the Antioch racing venue as the Circus Maximus, except for Louis B. Mayer, who in a telegram called it the "Circus Maximum."[53]

Two types of sources for the 1925 *Ben-Hur* are more reliable, the transatlantic cables and the frequent press releases. As for the first, the attempt at shooting the film in Italy, which seemed for months to be a strategic catastrophe, generated dozens of printed cables and telegrams sent back and forth from California and Italy. These enabled later film historians like Brownlow, Rudy Behlmer, and Charles Higham to follow the frequent mishaps and personnel problems from crisis to crisis. If the film had been shot entirely in Culver City, most of those "conversations" would never have been committed to print, and if the film were not *Ben-Hur*, no one would have preserved them. But this was the most prestigious and expensive literary property to acquire and the costliest film to produce, all contributing to the significance of the film in the eyes of MGM's most powerful forces at the time. Consequently, the cables – whether referring to Mussolini's politics or Francis X. Bushman's divorce – besides giving us inside information have also helped to increase the production's legendary status. From a source perspective, the cables are not unlike the reports about some of the boats named *Ben-Hur*: they entered the historical record most frequently when they were in distress, ran aground, or sank. Metaphorically speaking, the production in Italy did all three. As for the press releases, the nearly two decades of film production after the 1907 Kalem film generated several different trade and fan periodicals as well as regular newspaper coverage that gave film companies ample opportunity to inform the industry and publicize their productions. Reports on the *Ben-Hur* production appeared regularly, particularly in *The Film Daily* and the *Los Angeles Times*, and some of their reporters sailed along with MGM brass to Italy. Of course the studio dictated much of what the press reported, but that gives us reliable coverage of their promotional campaigns. Again, if this were any other film, it would be just disposable noise, but *Ben-Hur* in its day was from the outset intended and designed to be, promoted as, and in actuality became the biggest, most expensive, most aggressively promoted film ever made.

The purpose of this chapter is to refocus this fascinating material on the *Ben-Hur* phenomenon, which has never been done sufficiently.[54] This will provide a comprehensive narrative of the *Ben-Hur* production as it follows the lineage of production companies and executive decisions that controlled the fortunes of the *Ben-Hur* property once it was sold by the Wallace estate, highlights descriptions of the size and cost of the production and the persistent desire to make a unique film, canvasses the publicity that built upon the *Ben-Hur* tradition and attracted the interest of additional millions of potential spectators, examines the transfer of Wallace's story to the silent-screen format, demonstrates how the exhibition of this film differed from most of its contemporary releases, reviews statements about the impact the MGM film had on Hollywood and the film industry, and collects references to and puts into perspective various commercial tie-ins and business synergies. By the end of this chapter, the reader will understand just how difficult this film was to make, how successful it became worldwide, and how integral it is within the *Ben-Hur* phenomenon.

Goldwyn Publicity
Along with Erlanger's rumored million-dollar-plus asking price, the nationwide economic recession of 1920–1 and coincidental slowdown in the burgeoning film industry may have slowed negotiations but did not by any means scuttle the project.[55] In January, 1922, Marcus Loew, the theater-chain magnate who had recently purchased Metro Pictures, had apparently entered into an agreement with Erlanger's Classical Cinematograph Corporation and held an option on the screen rights to *Ben-Hur*.[56] He had reportedly promised Rex Ingram, who had just directed Valentino in *The Four Horsemen of the Apocalypse* (1921), that he would direct the film, and he also announced that some of the film would be shot overseas.[57] Meanwhile, one of the film production companies most affected by the current economic climate was Goldwyn Pictures. In 1920, Samuel Goldwyn's East Coast investors forced him to bring in as the new studio chief Frank Joseph Godsol, an American-born French citizen whose superior business acumen was matched by his checkered reputation.[58] Successfully selling everything from cheap diamonds and fake pearls to French military vehicles, *The Washington Post* featured an article about "his remarkable money-making exploits."[59] Godsol's interest in film production began in Italy, where he had a hand in the successful international distribution of the 1913 *Quo Vadis?* By March, 1922, he was in charge of Goldwyn Pictures and wanted to produce an even bigger film.[60]

On June 15, 1922, the major daily newspapers announced an agreement:

> Goldwyn Pictures Corporation has acquired picture rights and one half dramatic rights for story of "Ben Hur" from A. L. Erlanger for a sum stated to be in excess of $1,000,000. Production will be filmed partly in Italy and Palestine and at Goldwyn studios in California.[61]

Godsol and Goldwyn celebrated their acquisition in a full-page ad in *The Film Daily*, labeling their prize "The Greatest Motion Picture Property in the History of the Screen," again boasting about the million-dollar price tag, and putting it into context by describing the long run of the Klaw & Erlanger play, the novel as "the world's best seller," and then promising:

> We will make "Ben Hur" the greatest, the most colossal motion picture of all time.[62]

The announcement in the *Los Angeles Times* evaluated the novel:

> No novel ever written has, it is believed, achieved a greater popularity than "Ben Hur." It has been translated into many languages, and it has been read by millions

of persons in all parts of the globe. . . . It is impossible to give any definitive idea of the large amount of money derived from the sale of the novel published by Harper and Brothers. The story, one of the most romantic ever told, lends itself particularly to presentation on the screen.[63]

The New York Tribune, rather shocked at the "magnitude" of the project and the amount of money changing hands, stretched further back to bring Lew Wallace into the financial equation:

When a stack of gold like that is pushed across the table before a scenario even is begun, let alone a camera crank twisted, it is only natural for a number of questions to pop into the mind. Who will be the director? Who will be in the cast? And, for the love of Pete, how much more will be spent on the actual production? That's not mentioning the most interesting query either. That is, what would General Lew Wallace think now? . . . It is fair to assume he didn't know he was doing [this] much with his pen.[64]

Goldwyn's announcement ginned up the rumor mill. *The Film Daily* said that Edgar Stillman Kelley would provide a musical score.[65] In a Special Dispatch to the *Los Angeles Times*, Frederick James Smith guaranteed that D. W. Griffith, for a long time eager "to do the Wallace story in celluloid," would be Erlanger's choice to direct.[66] Just days later *The Film Daily* reported that Marshall Neilan would direct.[67] But Erlanger, who had approval over the choice of scenario, cast, and other production details, made it clear that no director or cast member would be selected until the scenario was completed.

A mid-July report in the *San Francisco Chronicle* began with, "Active preparations have already been begun by Goldwyn for filming the world's most widely read novel."[68] It continues:

There is no doubt that the screen version of "Ben Hur" will be the biggest motion picture ever produced. It is to be done on a scale as magnificent as the broad sweep of the novel itself, and in keeping with the world-wide appeal of General Wallace's famous story. . . . The entire resources of the Goldwyn organization will be bent for the coming year on a production that will far exceed the expectations that the public will naturally have formed of a film version of "Ben Hur." Steps are already under way for an expedition to Palestine, where most of the action takes place, to film the exteriors. Entire temporary cities will be built there in order to reproduce the ancient and civic architectural features of Palestine in the time of Christ. General Wallace wrote his novel only after long and patient study of manners and conditions of that age, and Goldwyn will endeavor to make the details of its screen version of the story as true to historical fact as is the novel itself. An army of experts will be employed for the purpose.

Once again these kinds of statements were as much show-business hype as they were bona fide claims reflecting genuine ambition and actual success. Much of Goldwyn's resources would indeed be spent on the film, they did film abroad in Italy and Tunisia, and Sophie Wachner's costume designs were based on her research.[69] Perhaps most important here is the statement that the "production that will far exceed the expectations that the public will naturally have formed of a film version of 'Ben Hur.'" This sentence alone demonstrates that the forthcoming film adaptation of Wallace's novel had to be "big" because that is what the producers assumed the public expected of them, and they were willing to spend the money to deliver it.

The June Mathis Scenario
As soon as he signed the agreement in mid-June, Erlanger ordered his staff to compile a synopsis of the novel.[70] In mid-September it was announced that the writing assignment was given to June Mathis, one of Hollywood's most successful scenario writers.[71] She had demonstrated an innate movie-making instinct by targeting Rudolph Valentino for stardom in her adaptation of *The Four Horsemen of the Apocalypse*, earning some $4.5 million for Metro Pictures. She was soon being paid $75,000 in annual salary to work as head of Goldwyn's story department, editorial director, and production supervisor, in what the *Los Angeles Times* identified in a headline as the "Most Responsible Job Ever Held By a Woman."[72] Mathis may have actually played a larger role than was reported in the press. She may have been one of the voices urging Godsol to acquire the rights to *Ben-Hur* in the first place, and she along with Erlanger seem to have been the forces insisting on shooting the film in Rome.[73] Now assigned the daunting task of adapting Wallace's novel, and to some extent Young's play, into a silent film scenario for the "world's biggest picture," Goldwyn reportedly had her insured for $1 million.[74] Mathis' appointment gave rise to still another name as a possible director, Fred Niblo, who had worked together with her and Valentino on *Blood and Sand*.[75]

Given considerably more time to prepare the scenario than Gene Gautier had been given for the Kalem scenario, and much more publicity, Mathis completed the task on December 1. She then attended a Culver City meeting with Godsol, Erlanger, and Goldwyn vice-presidents Major Edward Bowes and Abraham Lehr.[76] This initiated a new round of national press releases, a feature on Mathis as a "Woman Pioneer,"[77] the aforementioned feature "'Ben-Hur' Passes Over to the Movies,"[78] and two large Goldwyn ads in *The Film Daily* for "the Great and Only BEN HUR."[79] New rumors began to surface for what the *Los Angeles Times* labeled "the monster production of 'Ben-Hur.'"[80] Now Frederick James Smith was suggesting that Mathis was pushing to have Erich von Stroheim direct. Von Stroheim, recently under a Goldwyn contract, was already preparing his own epic production set in the American desert.[81] Smith also said that Mathis wanted Valentino to play the starring role, but Valentino was under legal obligation to Famous Players-Lasky.[82] (Later Valentino was said to have rejected the role because of *Ben-Hur*'s prestige: "Where can I go after Ben-Hur? I have no place to go but down."[83]) Erlanger left Los Angeles without making any announcement.[84]

With the approval of Erlanger, Mathis created a scenario quite faithful to Wallace's novel and Young's play, so it was comprehensive, if not indulgent.[85] It consisted of 190 pages and 1722 scenes [shots]. Pages 1–12 treated Book First of the novel, i.e. the story of the Wise Men, but through the vision of Young and Erlanger:

> We open the picture with the curtain going up on a dark stage and very soft music begins to sound, of the "Prophecy of Isaiah" from the play. Gradually the stage lights go up and we Fade In on the screen a mountain height with a valley beyond. In the vast loneliness upon a rock, stands Isaiah, with his arms upraised to heaven, – then slowly a light appears and the Angel Michael, in armour, in his hands the symbols of the sword and scales, appears. Isaiah falls upon the rock before the Angel who speaks; slowly we Fade Out.

These opening pages include scenes of Balthasar in Alexandria, Melchior in India, and Gaspar at a temple at the base of Mt. Olympus. The influence of Young continues in the very next scene with Simonides and Judah's mother (Act I, Scene 1) and in Judah's reply to Messala, "Forget thou art a Roman!" In addition, at the end of the film Mathis uses stage lighting effects and choral music:

> [The procession continues] as though following the Light, which comes directly into the camera and the entire scene is illumined – very similar to the effect of the Star of Bethlehem in the first sequence. FADE. The music ends with the words: "Hosanna! Hosanna!"

In between, some fifty pages are spent on the desert scenes developing the relationships between Judah and Iras, Esther, and Ilderim. For the chariot race she maintains Wallace's vengeance motif by having Judah crash Messala's chariot. The copies preserved in the Cinema Arts Library of the University of Southern California and the Herrick Library, dated December 1, 1922, bear Erlanger's signature. The theater mogul recommended several edits that demonstrate his cinematic limitations. On page 120, for instance, he writes, "Cut out wreck of Greek chariot." However, he soon relinquished his initial demand to have approval of the final release print, and from this point he will retreat to the background as Mathis and her successors take control of making the film.[86] Erlanger, along with J. J. and Lee Shubert, would lend his expertise to exhibiting the film, initially by modifying a number of their first class theaters to accommodate a *Ben-Hur* roadshow with ticket prices at a premium.[87]

Production in Italy

A number of months passed as the Goldwyn top brass, led by Major Bowes, scouted Italian locations, where Goldwyn hoped to lower its projected production costs of $1–1.5 million by negotiating a five-million-lire working agreement with the Unione Cinematografica Italiana.[88] Finally in late September, 1923, came the announcement that the entire production would be filmed abroad and directed by a former colleague of Mathis, Charles Brabin, the British-born director who had begun directing for Edison already in 1908, later moved from Fox to Goldwyn, but was more usually identified as the husband of Theda Bara.[89] Although later Hollywood gossip would characterized Brabin as an alcoholic and mediocre director,[90] he had recently directed and independently produced *Driven* (released by Universal in 1923), which drew high praise from many quarters.[91] Mathis said she liked him for this project because he was knowledgeable about the Bible and familiar with Europe.[92] More importantly, he shared Mathis' vision for *Ben-Hur*. Bosley Crowther, while serving as the film critic for the *New York Times* in the mid-1960s, wrote:

> Nothing would do, she insisted but that [*Ben-Hur*] be produced in Italy, the only place where the spirit and atmosphere of the Roman Empire could be obtained.[93]

Her concept of recreating an authentic Roman imperial backdrop for the film began to come to fruition in the ambitious set-building program Brabin initiated at the start of production. On the ship crossing the Atlantic in early October, 1923, he told Bowes that he planned to build the Joppa Gate three times higher than the original.[94] The purpose was to create a symbol of Rome that would dwarf the crowd of people filling the Jerusalem streets during the march to Calvary.

At the end of September, the first rumors began to appear that George Walsh, 6-feet tall with an athletic build and reportedly Mathis' romantic partner, would play the role of Judah, and indeed, out of ten actors tested, he was the one selected.[95] By the beginning of 1924 several other actors had been announced, most notably Carmel Myers, who had a reputation for playing vampish women, to play Iras, and Francis X. Bushman, a screen idol of the early 1910s, to play Messala.[96] Bushman provides another example of continuity between the stage and film productions, for Brownlow records part of a conversation he had with Bushman about the role of Messala with William S. Hart, the first Klaw & Erlanger Messala:

> They didn't ask any questions, they just offered me the part. But I'd always played a hero, and I was afraid of it. I went to Bill Hart, who'd played Messala on the stage for years, and I said, "Bill, do you think I ought to do this filthy Roman?"
> "Frank," he said, "that's the best goddamned part in the picture." He told me how they once got him to play Ben-Hur, and he got sick, longing to be back playing Messala. So he sold me on it, and I accepted.[97]

While the Goldwyn production was unfolding slowly, DeMille released *The Ten Commandments* in 1923. Goldwyn denied that this was a competitive concern for their own ancient film property.[98] On the contrary, they reasserted their commitment in *The Film Daily*:

> There is an axiom in the picture business that no company is really a great company until it produces an unusually great picture. "The Four Horsemen" and what

it did for Metro is cited as an example. And those who carry the Goldwyn production banner say "Ben Hur" will prove the axiom for Goldwyn.[99]

MGM Assumes Control

From this point weekly press releases announced every time Mathis, Bowes, Goldwyn staff, production crew, or cast members sailed to or from Rome or traveled elsewhere in the United States or Europe. Filming had begun in March,[100] but despite denials along the way,[101] Goldwyn was foundering, and by late December, 1923, Godsol had already entered into merger negotiations with Marcus Loew and William Randolph Hearst.[102] On April 15, 1924, almost two years after negotiating for the film rights to *Ben-Hur*, Goldwyn was merged with Marcus Loew's Metro Pictures Corporation and Louis B. Mayer Productions, forming Metro-Goldwyn.[103] The merger incorporated hundreds of theaters in the major cities across the United States and in Canada, the capacious 40-acre Goldwyn Studios in Culver City, and several ongoing productions, the two most important of which were von Stroheim's *Greed* and *Ben-Hur*, not to mention the fifty–fifty agreement with Erlanger.[104] Loew appointed Mayer as first vice president and general manager, and his 24-year-old assistant, Irving Thalberg, as second vice president and supervisor of production, and a few months later, at Loew's suggestion, the company was renamed Metro-Goldwyn-Mayer.[105] At first Loew did not put *Ben-Hur* under the control of "the Mayer group" but kept it separate under the umbrella of the Classical Cinematograph Corporation.[106] It remained Mathis' project, and the merger now gave *Ben-Hur* the backing of a $65 million corporation capable of absorbing the huge production costs and eager to expand its reputation by doing so. According to Crowther:

> Marcus Loew seemed to feel the foreign venture was a challenge to his new company's prestige. There was also the little matter of the agreement with Abe Erlanger.[107]

Production continued slowly as the merits of shooting in Rome were debated.[108] Bowes claimed that the film could be produced in Italy for $600,000, but when questioned how that could be possible he responded, "That's the director's worry."[109] Thalberg asserted that he could make the film in Culver City for $800,000 and that there was no need to shoot in Italy.[110] In May J. Gordon Edwards and D. W. Griffith toured the available facilities in Rome and visited Brabin's production. When Griffith returned to New York, he stated that he found the studios to be languishing in pre-war condition with inadequate electricity and barely cost effective.[111] Just days after Griffith's return, Bowes had to deny rumors that adverse weather conditions in Italy had slowed the set construction so severely that he was about to bring the production home to the United States even as he affirmed that the Wise Men scenes had been shot in Tunis.[112] Others reported factional struggles between Fascist workers and Socialists.[113]

Edwards' return generated a headline that read "Praise for Brabin" in *The Film Daily*.[114] In the article Edwards praised the atmospheric conditions in Italy, the beautiful natural scenery, the low cost of production, and the charm of the Italian people who very much appreciated the benefits American film productions brought to their country.[115] However, the interview reads like a sympathetic apology, he contradicts his own statement about cost savings, and he concludes by addressing currently circulating rumors that Brabin will be removed from the project:

> The construction work on the big sets, the Circus Maximus, the ships, and other sets is taking time and costing a lot. The lighting plant put in must have been very costly. They had to erect a studio; because the studios obtainable were too small. They were held up on the costumes which were made in Germany. It has been a trying job for the director. But I am convinced that Brabin is doing very good work; he is whole souled about the task, and is living with it day and night. I doubt if anyone could do better. Certainly it seems inadvisable to make a change in the direction of this production unless it cannot be avoided.

In fact, Fred Niblo and Marshall Neilan were already on route to Rome.[116]

Firing Mathis

Mathis had now had the project in her hands for eighteen months, spent a reported $3 million with very little result, and even lost control over Brabin.[117] He had been in Italy since October, 1923,[118] and when she arrived the following February, he immediately made it very clear that he would not allow her to interfere.[119] The production had split into Mathis and Brabin factions.[120] When the first rushes arrived from Italy in the spring of 1924, the home office was horrified.[121] In a 1964 letter to Brownlow, Mayer's daughter described her recollection of the initial screening with adjectives like "terrible," "awful," and "cheesy."[122] Loew demonstrated his unswerving belief in the property by immediately reassigning *Ben-Hur* to the Mayer group despite their warning that it could cost another $1.5 million to complete the film.[123] Mayer and Thalberg had Niblo examine all the relevant written materials, and on May 20 he handed in a critical analysis.[124]

Niblo first addressed Mathis' fidelity to Wallace's novel from a film director's perspective, describing her work as "a beautiful continuity of the terribly long story of Ben Hur as Lou Wallace wrote it" and "impossibly long." This recalls Joseph Young's comment that a novel cannot be translated one for one into a drama. Mathis had had success with her adaptation of Blasco Ibañez's *The Four Horsemen of the Apocalypse*, which was almost equal to *Ben-Hur* in length. But now she had millions of dollars to lavish on potentially the greatest film ever made, and her vision was accordingly huge but without proportional cinematic results.

Niblo then focuses on "Research":

> This is very important. Don't forget Miss Mathis and her assistants have spent months and months on research and correct data covering every angle of this period. . . . Who has it and where is it? This is something to be thought of. It will take time to get hold of this or start new research.

Here he replicates Wallace himself in "How I Came To Write *Ben-Hur*" by anticipating criticism for producing any historical or visual inauthenticities. To make such a historically accurate work, Niblo recommended securing the research material, putting a halt to the production, preparing a new script, and making necessary cast and staff changes, adding that taking the extra time now would save as much as $2 million in the end. Then he finishes with a statement worthy of a commercial artist who would be chosen to carry on the *Ben-Hur* torch into the mid-1920s:

> Ben Hur can be the biggest thing that has ever been done. It can also be the biggest flop.

Far removed from the Wallace estate and from Erlanger, the future of the *Ben-Hur* cinematic property was now in the hands of a committee of picture studio executives – MGM's Loew, Mayer, Thalberg, Nicholas Schenck, and Harry Rapf.[125] Mayer and Thalberg also consulted with Schenck's brother Joseph, the head of United Artists and one of Loew's former partners. He concurred that Mathis and Brabin would create "either absolute failure or at best a tremendous waste of money." In his telegram of May 2 to Loew, who had adamantly opposed the transfer, Schenck explained why the company should be brought home and why Erlanger should be left out of the deliberations:

> REMEMBER ALL THIS EXPENSE YOU CAN ONLY GET BACK FROM FIFTY PERCENT OF GROSS AND THAT ERLANGER DOES NOT OBJECT TO YOU SPENDING HUGE SUMS WHETHER NECESSARY OR UNNECESSARY AS HE IS NOT INTERESTED THAT PHASE AND HE WILL NATURALLY THINK HE WILL GET MORE BECAUSE INEXPERIENCED PICTURE PRODUCER FIGURES THE MORE YOU SPEND THE BIGGER AND BETTER THE PICTURE IS stop
> . . .
> YOU WILL NO DOUBT ENCOUNTER DIFFICULTIES WITH ERLANGER WHO IS SOLD ON JUNE MATHIS BUT YOU MUST BE FIRM NOW BEFORE ITS TOO LATE stop THE WORST ERLANGER COULD DO WOULD BE TO CANCEL CONTRACT FOR PRODUCTION BEN HUR WHICH PROBABLY WOULD BE VERY BEST THING FOR YOU NOTWITHSTANDING THE LOSS YOU WILL INCUR IN PRODUCTION COSTS ALREADY INVESTED[126]

The rule of thumb is not to throw good money after bad money. In following that rule, MGM concurrently had another runaway production in von Stroheim's *Greed*, which at over nine hours of running length the director insisted should be exhibited over two consecutive nights of four-plus hour shows. Under Thalberg's insistence *Greed* was cut to less than two hours; the rest of the footage was intentionally destroyed. In sharp contrast, at a May 1 meeting in Culver City, it was agreed to destroy most of the Italian *Ben-Hur* footage but completely reshoot the film, a daring decision and testimony to the prestige of *Ben-Hur* in that they could already calculate that after splitting the receipts with Erlanger's Classical Cinematograph Corporation they would have to bring in at least $7 million just to break even.[127]

In an attempt to conceal from the industry and the public what they hoped to be a temporary failure and maintain the prestigious status of the *Ben-Hur* production, the MGM executives held private meetings, issued misleading press releases, and gave staff secret assignments.[128] They claimed that Brabin was ill, and Niblo was said to be scouting exteriors for a different film. They hired Novarro but ordered him to tell no one.[129] But the trades knew something was happening, even if it was erroneous. They rumored that Brabin had resigned, that the project had cost "$200,000 or more," and that Mathis was about to marry Walsh.[130] What matters to us in all this is that the project was still generating so much interest. Amidst columns of gossip, *Photoplay* editorialized:

> The excitement surrounding the making of "Ben Hur" in Italy goes on and is about as interesting to the film colony in Hollywood as the picture itself is likely to be. If they wanted to make the title of "Ben Hur" better known to the public by this mystery and manipulation, that object has certainly been accomplished.[131]

Taking it upon himself to fire Mathis and Brabin in person, Marcus Loew embarked from New York on June 15 and "confirmed" to the press that Brabin was ill and might be replaced by Niblo.[132] Thalberg had long ago secretly assigned veterans Carey Wilson, a Goldwyn holdover, and Bess Meredyth, former actress and freelance writer, the task of preparing a new scenario and continuity,[133] so the *Leviathan* passengers included Loew, his attorney J. Robert Rubin, Niblo, Wilson, and Meredyth as well as Denny from *The Film Daily* and Herbert Howe from *Photoplay*.[134] It had been Howe just a few months earlier who had quipped that *Ben-Hur* might be finished in 1940 with an elderly Jackie Coogan playing the lead.[135] By mid-July not only had Brabin been replaced, assigning the blame for "a general condition of the chaos and futility" on the Italian syndicate, but he immediately filed suit for breach of contract and sought $500,000 in damages, which the court ultimately rejected.[136] As for Mathis, by the end of August she had signed with First National.[137] To the press asking about her departure she ironically commented, "Naturally, I didn't expect a new director coming in to take entirely my point of view."

Fred Niblo as Director

The burden of making *Ben-Hur* a success now fell on the shoulders of primarily Fred Niblo, who along with such capable assistant directors as Al Raboch and Christy Cabanne, had the full support of MGM and a proven ability to marshal its enormous corps of artists, technicians, and staff.[138]

This was in Rome. Back in Hollywood Thalberg would delineate clearly his understanding of the importance of *Ben-Hur* and his confidence in Niblo in his September 23 letter to the latter:

> Naturally, "BEN HUR" is the big ace in the hole. It, and you, and all of us, are probably the subject of more conversation in Hollywood and New York than anything else. Certainly we have got to come through with the picture – and certainly, I am sure that you will.[139]

This is the letter containing Thalberg's much quoted reaction to watching the original rushes from Rome:

> I inwardly breathe a prayer of relief that we have taken the hysterical action that was necessary to make a change, when I saw the stuff that had been made. It is almost beyond my conception that such stuff could have been passed by people of even moderate intelligence – that June Mathis, in fact any one over there, could have allowed [it] to pass, for one single day.

Meanwhile Mayer had also assigned General Manager Harry Edington to supervise the production in Rome, instructing him on July 5 in the grammar of a cablegram, "Niblo likes battle he knows value of argument; my directors have respect for management you are my business representative."[140]

After Niblo arrived in Rome, he reported that there was still much preliminary work to be finished, including leasing 400 acres of land for the construction site and building dressing rooms, restaurants, and an infirmary capable of accommodating thousands of extras.[141] Despite all the problems, delays, unexpected costs, and personnel issues, Lou Marangella, recently put in charge of press releases for "the 'Ben Hur' company" and shipped off to Rome in July, emphasized the visible, physical achievements in *The Film Daily*:

> Outside of Rome. On a splendid plateau. Within sight of the aqueduct and city walls. There arises probably the largest set ever built for a picture: the "Joppa Gate" through which streamed the populace; the goats, the cows, the camels, a living pulsating throng. In which Lew Wallace graced his hero with every trick of imaginable melodrama.
>
> And it's more than that. Remember the big sets of "Intolerance"? remember the huge walls of "Robin Hood" – did you see the big set in "The Queen of Sin" which was made in Austria under the name of "Sodom and Gomorrah"? Well, they were big sets. All of them. Each of them. But this "Joppa Gate" is something to remember alongside of these. It rises to over 150 feet. Imagine how it appears, or rather, how it will, when it is "dressed."[142]

A series of releases to *The Film Daily* maintained continuity. One addressed Niblo's concerns over building the "Circus Maximus ... ten stories in height" and the number of low-cost extras required to fill it.[143] Another announced that important passages in the film would be in [two-strip] Technicolor, at that time still a rarity.[144] Later *Photoplay* ran a two-page spread with the title, "The Fiasco of 'Ben Hur,'" although clearly the source of the critical report was Walsh, who complained of having had nothing to do for four months.[145] Despite the title of the article, even the author, A. Chester Keel, quipped: "If a bad beginning makes a good ending, 'Ben Hur' will be the greatest picture of all time." Upon his return from Europe in mid-August, Loew assured everyone that Niblo was "working at top speed" and expecting completion around the end of the year.[146] Competitors in the film industry exploited the summer delay by creating their own chariot motifs. Paramount-Famous Players advertised *The Ten Commandments* by filling the marquee above New York's Criterion Theatre with depictions of thirty chariots, and Enrico Guazzoni inserted into *Messalina* a four-minute, seven-lap chariot race, filmed with several shots taken from the perspective of a ground-level camera.[147]

The casting of the lead role used up additional ink. Thalberg had been looking for an actor who either looked Jewish or could handle horses.[148] Fan letters made it clear that audiences expected the lead to have a body type similar to that of many of the Klaw & Erlanger leads, hence Mathis' decision to use the athletic Walsh.[149] But Wallace's protagonist was not designed with the cinema in mind. The novel begins with Judah at age seventeen, and he is slightly shorter than Messala, age nineteen. Judah is "slighter in form," but three years at the oar bulked him up considerably. Wallace writes that the young Judah had a face that was "rich and voluptuous," and, less concerned with the body, Thalberg recognized in the Mexican Novarro a dark complexion and a face that MGM wanted the public to adore. Novarro was considerably shorter than Walsh, whom Mathis had preferred in part because he matched Bushman's height.[150] Lifts were added to his sandals, and he had to complete a rigorous exercise regime to build up his physique.[151] Confident in his ability and adaptability, Novarro later claimed that he knew years in advance that this role would someday be his.[152]

In December, 1924, Louis B. Mayer returned from his visit to Italy promising that the "mammoth picture" would be finished in March or April and boasting about the twenty-five galleys built for the naval sequences shot off Livorno and the circus extending over 1000 feet in length:

> I don't like to use superlatives in describing any picture, but really, it is impossible to do justice to "Ben Hur" without talking press agents' language. It is a picture that will outlive this generation and future generations.[153]

The film itself confirms that the construction of seven life-size ships was only part of what was required to shoot the demanding sea battle sequences. Our world now accustomed to the frequent use of CGI and miniatures cannot begin to comprehend the physical and organizational effort Niblo had to oversee. He said in an interview printed just a few days after the New York premiere of the film:

In the sea fight episode there were fourteen vessels, seven of which were good-sized ships. There were others, about a dozen, which were camouflaged for distant effects. We had about 2800 men in the sea scrap, and as many as 300 galley slaves on one of the vessels. Perhaps this was the most difficult stretch to picture.... This fight was filmed in the Mediterranean, virtually on the original location of the conflict. We had to get out to sea, and it was necessary to be sure of the weather, as we had a number of cameras – there were twenty-eight cameras employed there – some on the vessels, others on the decks of boats, and still others on floats. The apparatus on floats, in several cases, were mounted on towers more than sixty feet high. It was another example in which we had to grind out a lot of negative and take our chances of catching something that happened which was not mapped out in the scenario but which contributed in a spontaneous way to the effect of the whole.[154]

Of course neither Mayer nor Niblo said anything about the alleged, near, or real, disasters that occurred during the filming of the action scenes. Not reported in the industry controlled press, several horrifying stories circulated later about the first batch of newly constructed galleys being unseaworthy and sinking almost immediately,[155] and a fire blazing out of control on the principal 250-foot galley manned by hundreds of Italian extras, many of them unable to swim, who had to jump ship.[156] Recollections by Bushman, Samuel Marx, and Enid Bennett (Niblo's wife), varied as to whether three, two, or one of them drowned or was at least reported missing, while according to Novarro and MGM, not one Italian was killed on that day.[157] The very fact that such horror stories continued to fester provided fodder for the growing legendary status of this production. That these alleged mishaps took place in Italy, and especially out on the Adriatic Sea, increased the mystery all the more. There were also later reports of an accident during an attempt at filming the chariot race. Bushman's chariot crashed into Novarro's, and for a moment everyone there thought Novarro must have been killed.[158] The letters Crowther solicited from members of the cast and crew decades later contradicted one another as to the veracity of the story.[159] Ironically, the actor who played the evil Messala insisted that many horses were destroyed during the filming of the chariot race, while the actor who played Judah Ben-Hur, along with MGM, denied any serious injuries during the production.[160] A. Arnold Gillespie, long-time special effects master of MGM who was in charge of and actually aboard the burning ship at the time of the accident, explained that the three missing extras were picked up by fisherman, feted and feasted in a nearby village while still wearing their ancient costumes, and then returned to claim their street clothes a few days later only to find that Adolph Sidel, MGM's wardrobe assistant, had burned the clothes to destroy any evidence of their demise.[161]

Six months after the overhaul, the film looked as if it would be completed by April, 1925, although Loew and Mayer decided that a fall premiere would better serve their conception of a New York theatrical opening.[162] This was not going to happen.

Moving to Hollywood

At the time the galley sequence was being filmed off Livorno in early October, 1924, Marangella sent a number of photographs to Thalberg "to use judiciously in the Coast newspapers."[163] These were probably the images released to the *Los Angeles Times* for its full-page feature of January 7, 1925, "Ben Hur is Sailing Along Now," an ebullient text laid out amidst five production stills of the naval scenes. This was just part of the cover for Mayer and Thalberg to bring the production home. The extant cablegrams from MGM's Parisian office manager, Alexander Aronson, to Thalberg, Mayer, and Rubin contain numerous paragraphs of complaints about the lack of progress, problems with the lighting facilities and equipment, the malaise of the cast, and the inefficiency of Niblo's direction.[164] Meyer seized an opportune moment in history to make yet another "hysterical action." Rome had been experiencing political turmoil for many months, exacerbated by the assassination of socialist leader Giacomo Matteotti in late May and perpetuated by fist fights in parliament in the summer. By December 24, when Mussolini seized power, factional militias were filling the streets of Rome.[165] Mayer let the press know that he had ordered the "Ben Hur company" to return to the United States immediately.[166] The MGM transatlantic communications say nothing about Mussolini or the political situation in Rome, but that was the story fed to the press. Niblo stayed in Rome until mid-February, and when he returned home he had only positive comments about the quality of the Italian facilities, the work of the Italian extras, and the Italian government insofar as extending them "every courtesy and cooperation."[167] He would later nuance his description of the situation:

> It is all very well in picture making to have an occasional disagreement, but when you have 1000 men of one political adherence and 1000 of another, you may be apt to dread any hostilities between the rival factions. We had no trouble with the Italians, but we could not afford the trouble they had among themselves.[168]

At the same time in Italy, MGM cordially invited both the King of Italy and Mussolini to visit the production site, but the latter declined the invitation.[169]

Once it was removed to California, the production would finally be under the close supervision of the 25-year-old Irving Thalberg, who would finally bring the multi-million dollar production to completion, albeit not before causing him to suffer a heart attack. Interior scenes were shot in Culver City throughout the spring of 1925. This relatively standard mode of filming did not warrant much publicity. Even so, every issue of *Photoplay* and *The Film Daily* managed to mention *Ben-Hur* several times. (By comparison, MGM's other very successful 1925 release, *The Big Parade*, warranted mentions only about half as often.) Most revealing was Niblo's feature essay in *The Film Daily*, "Difficulties Encountered in

Making Ben Hur."[170] Among other matters, he discussed the wide-ranging search for an actress to play the role of the Madonna. Casting this role was of course essential for establishing the spiritual reverence associated with *Ben-Hur* and the authenticity of the Nativity sequence, and in the silent era, when "faces" were such an essential element of screen presence, the casting choice was all the more vital.

The reader will see here that Niblo was confronted with a decision similar to those confronting Wallace when he was researching historical sources in the 1870s and trying to reproduce biblical scenes accurately. The kinds of sources Wallace (1.8) used, like the New Testament and Josephus, do not contain a description of Mary:

> She was not more than fifteen. Her form, voice, and manner belonged to the period of transition from girlhood. Her face was perfectly oval, her complexion more pale than fair. The nose was faultless; the lips, slightly parted, were full and ripe, giving to the lines of the mouth warmth, tenderness, and trust; the eyes were blue and large, and shaded by drooping lids and long lashes; and, in harmony with all, a flood of golden hair, in the style permitted to Jewish brides, fell unconfined down her back to the pillion on which she sat. The throat and neck had the downy softness sometimes seen which leaves the artist in doubt whether it is an effect of contour or color. To these charms of feature and person were added others more indefinable – an air of purity which only the soul can impart, and of abstraction natural to such as think much of things impalpable. Often, with trembling lips, she raised her eyes to heaven, itself not more deeply blue.

Niblo does not mention this. Reflecting current practice for biblical productions in the 1920s, he makes reference to iconic scenes painted by European masters. First he had to establish the correct prototype, ultimately rejecting the common conception of the brunette "Sistine Madonna," that is, Raphael's *La Madonna di San Sisto*. After months of research "it was decided" that they were looking for an actress that instead resembled "Tissot's prototype," that is, James Tissot's *Holy Virgin As a Girl*: "a slight and very young girl with blue eyes, a blonde." This, of course, much more closely resembles Wallace's description, but here the process diverges entirely from Wallace's single-authored decision. Film-making required matching the prototype with an actual person, an actress, perhaps even a "movie star," and amidst an ironically cantankerous struggle between several men, each forwarding their own Madonna types, hundreds of women were interviewed and screen tested.[171] The names of Lillian Gish, Greta Garbo, and Myrna Loy all appear in our sources.[172] Ultimately Betty Bronson, who had the preceding year played the lead in the Famous Players-Lasky *Peter Pan*, was chosen as the best match.

Reflecting upon the many months he had spent in Italy, and certainly encouraged by the home office, Niblo emphasized both the international appeal of the *Ben-Hur* story and the importance of portraying the novel accurately. Millions of members of the audience would expect the latter:

Probably no other story now in print demands as much attention to detail as does "Ben Hur."

    For this there are two reasons. One – it is a story of antiquity. The other – it is a tale with which at least twenty million people of our nation, alone, are familiar.

. . .

    "Ben Hur" is a story dear to the hearts of the peoples of many nationalities. To film it incorrectly would be a keen disappointment to them and would call for much adverse criticism. For that reason we have endeavored to faithfully portray it on the screen.[173]

Niblo adds that the film would be educational:

The public will learn more about the world in the first century in the short time necessary for the picture to be unreeled than one could possibly learn by studying for months. Facts and fiction have been so carefully separated – and so thorough has been the process of weeding out all that smacks of unauthenticity – that the action that will take place on the screen will virtually be the visualization of life in the first century as it actually existed.

Part of a media blitz, Niblo's essay was published on June 7, the same day as Whitney Williams lengthy feature in the *Los Angeles Times*, "Filmdom's 'Big Ben,' After Much Winding, Is About to Strike."[174] After announcing that the film will be ready by the first of the year, Williams sarcastically describes the film as "somewhat of an achievement in the art of wasting time and money." But thereafter he follows the press release script and describes the value of the film's authenticity, which is attributed to several esteemed Italian archaeologists, "Professor Angeli, the celebrated archaeologist of Rome and Prof. Della Horti of the Pompeian museum," who were said to have spent months performing research before the production began and to have remained thereafter to critique and correct any deviations or anachronisms.[175] Of these the latter is undoubtedly Matteo Della Corte, author of *Pompeii, The New Excavations*.[176]

Filming the Chariot Race

This brought the public up to date and bought MGM the three months required for the crew to edit the enormous amount of captured footage, for Mayer to arrange the premiere around Christmas Day, and for Cedric Gibbons, Horace Jackson, and their technical team to rebuild entirely the "Circus Maximus," one of the largest sets ever built, this time not a few miles southeast from the Circus Maximus in Rome along the Appian Way but at the intersection of Venice and La Cienega Boulevards.[177] Rather than return to Italy to use the enormous set built by the Italians at such great cost and effort, Thalberg authorized yet another $300,000 to build the set. For a contemporary comparison, the original Yankee Stadium was built in 1922–3 at a cost of $2.5 million,[178] but that construction remained in service for eighty-five years: this one would be used for a few weeks. When Thalberg looked at the preliminary sketches, he thought the visual concept translated onto film would look "fake," so he ordered in addition "some statues, huge statues we can place the extras beside so the audience will get a sense of scale."[179] He had German-born sculptor Eugene Maier-Krieg build the two colossi to be situated at the ends of the *spina*, beyond where Wallace (5.12) and our ancient sources place the three signature sculpted columns:

> ... three low conical pillars of gray stone, much carven. Many an eye will hunt for those pillars before the day is done, for they are the first goal, and mark the beginning and end of the race-course.[180]

Upon completion MGM publicity distributed a photo of Carmel Myers (not in costume) standing at the base of one of the 20-foot statues. *The Seattle Times*, for instance, ran the caption, "'Ben Hur' Has Massive Sets."[181] Such colossi would appear again in the 1959 version.

The chariot race was scheduled for shooting on Saturday, October 3.[182] This was a legendary day for Hollywood, and it should warrant another entry in the ongoing list of *Ben-Hur* milestones. Across the continent even the *New York Times* began its description with two different superlatives:

> Most of the Hollywood picture folk recently took a day off to witness the filming of the most expansive motion picture scene on the largest set ever constructed.[183]

Thalberg had a viewing platform constructed where a number of contemporary stars watched the race, including Douglas Fairbanks, Mary Pickford, Lillian Gish, Harold Lloyd, John Gilbert, Marion Davies, and John and Lionel Barrymore, not to mention Sid Grauman and Sam Goldwyn.[184] Lloyd later said, "It was the most exciting event he had ever witnessed or was ever likely to witness."[185] Although not even of interest at the time, costumed and photographed were such future MGM stars as Myrna Loy and Clark Gable.[186]

The actual seating capacity of the constructed site allowed for about 10,000 "costumed, bearded, and bewigged" extras, and Hollywood legend has it that Thalberg ordered his assistant to go out into the streets of Culver City to fetch more bodies to fill out the crowd.[187] Frank William's hanging miniature effects added the upper seating areas to create a circus that appeared to seat some 60,000 spectators.[188] Niblo directed from a 100-foot tower, using a semaphore system as well as thousands of feet of telephone wiring to send instructions to several dozen togaed assistant directors, some of them borrowed from other companies, including Universal's William Wyler, the future director of the 1959 version of the film.[189] In the crowds and on the sands there were police and military units, the latter being Troop B, Eleventh Cavalry, from the Presidio in Monterey.[190] The four dozen soldiers, all of similar height and weight, were loaned by the commander of the Presidio and brought with them their bays and equipment by special train to play the Roman horse guards and buglers.[191] To create an authentic-looking race, a $150 bonus was offered to the winner, and the several thousand spectators wagered amongst themselves.

Capturing the race were forty-two, state-of-the-art Bell & Howell and Akeley cameras hidden behind shields, within the colossal statues, under the track, on top of a soaring tower built behind the stands, and even higher in a biplane, although there is no evidence of the latter in the film.[192] It is doubtful that any shoot in film history has used more cameras.[193] Ten of the twelve chariots were driven by stunt men, and even if Novarro (Ben-Hur) and Bushman (Messala) were not involved in the "real" race, no stunt doubles were used.[194] Although MGM denied it, Bushman later said that at least five horses were killed in a single crash, and that as many as one hundred were destroyed.[195] The presence of the S.P.C.A. without complaint adds some weight to MGM's denial,[196] as does a later eyewitness account from Rosamunde Rae Wright, President of the American Animal Defensive League, President of the California Anti-Vivisection Society, and then a deputy sheriff of Los Angeles County.[197] However, she does thoroughly condemn the production for inflicting multiple lacerations, torn mouths, and skinned legs upon the horses, and she reports that at least one horse had been killed during rehearsal, even if no animals were killed in the great crash during shooting.

Four more weeks were needed in the empty circus, where second-unit director B. Reaves Eason filmed additional shots from a high tower placed in the *spina* and action close-ups using an innovative, skid-proof Packard Eight, specially configured with cameras on its three different platforms to capture the horses at leg level, the drivers at face level, and whole *quadrigae* from above.[198] And then the tens of thousands of feet of film shot by the forty-two cameras had to be edited down to 750 feet. Brownlow praises the final result:

> But those seven hundred and fifty feet are among the most valuable in motion-picture history. For this was the first time that an action director, realizing the potential of the cinema, had possessed courage and skill enough to fulfill it.[199]

The day after the race was shot, the Sunday *Los Angeles Times* ran a sizable headline superimposed over a large photo of two chariots racing in the circus, "History of Stupendous 'Ben Hur' Screen Production Brings New Triumph to Hollywood as Film Capital."[200] In his accompanying feature Bill Henry concludes by stating that the entire experience proved once and for all that the only place to make a film was Southern California. As if to prove the point, on December 8 MGM announced that they had included 500 local school children as part of the legions that gathered after the Crucifixion.[201] The company reported to the *Times* that they had hired dozens of teachers to give the children their academic lessons throughout the day, and assigned Boy Scouts to marshal the youngest forces.[202] Henry also announces plans for the roadshow presentations, which will include a traveling corps of musicians and technicians as well as stage effects, screens, and projectors.

The last few weeks before release were pressure-filled. Lloyd Nosler was the chief editor, but Thalberg supervised very closely.[203] His biographers follow him as he sends specific instructions about special effects for the Nativity scene, fights with the New York office about the representation of Christ's hand and arm, and even takes time to remind his staff to pay the organist at the December 20 preview in Pasadena.[204] The relentless schedule and mental stress was so great that the young Thalberg, already of delicate constitution and working day and night against a deadline, suffered a heart attack. Thalberg recovered gradually, but even before he was allowed to get out of bed, he was reportedly critiquing the rushes of *Ben-Hur* projected onto the ceiling of his room.[205]

THE FILM AS A VERSION OF *BEN-HUR*

From Novel to Film

Finally completed, the film presented a narrative designed to remain as faithful to Wallace's venerated novel as the medium would allow while generating as much cinematic romance, spectacular action, and spiritual reverence as the medium could provide. Wallace tended to unfold parts of his narrative through mysteries like the status of Simonides within the House of Hur, the identity of Judah in Antioch, the purpose of Judah's wanting to know the height of Messala's axle, and, more importantly, the fate of Judah's mother and Tirzah and the identity of the new king of the Jews. Elsewhere he painted some events with relatively few strokes, for instance, the adoption of the young Arrius and the murder of Messala by Iras. In picturizing a historical epic, the film medium does not easily lend itself to portraying either vagueness, since it by nature depicts established events, or to inexplicable actions that might distance an audience from the story. This is by no means a hard and fast rule, but it does apply in particular to a multi-million dollar Hollywood production targeting a huge, general audience and even more so for a picturization of a story known to so many millions of prospective moviegoers.

Thalberg along with Nosler and the team of Katherine Hilliker and H. H. Caldwell, who crafted the intertitles, kept those mysteries and imprecisions to a minimum. They managed to unfold the complicated epic at an efficient and insistent pace, conflating or omitting a number of scenes from the novel and pausing only for the romantic scenes between Judah and Esther and, especially, the traditionally beloved scene outside the palace of Hur where Judah's mother watches over her sleeping son. The latter lasts over five minutes and is interrupted by only two intertitles, one in which Judah in a dreamlike state utters the word "Mother" and the other in which his mother tells Tirzah, "Not a sound! He belongs to the living – we to the dead!" Of course the chariot race and the sea battle warrant extensive coverage, and they last approximately fourteen minutes each, one fifth of the entire length of the film. In consequence, Balthasar has only a few minutes on screen, but they make the most of it. He appears first as one of three Wise Men in the desert and at the Nativity in the cave, and then, nearly two hours later, in Ilderim's tent. The silent film medium cannot preserve the long theological disputations he delivers in the novel's Orchard of Palms interlude, so instead here he concisely announces the impending downfall of Rome in one intertitle, the realization that the child of Bethlehem is indeed the Messiah and the new king in another, and then that "He alone can save the world from the bondage of Rome!" The latter he says directly to Judah in their only face-to-face exchange in the entire film. But this provides strong motivation for Judah who becomes passionately re-energized, decides to leave Antioch so he can raise legions for the new king, and commits his entire fortune to the anti-Roman cause. There follow less than half a minute of brief exits from and entrances into the frame by Balthasar, Ilderim, Simonides, Sanballat, and Esther, but then the latter remains with Judah for almost two minutes as they make somber vows to each other and depart after a warm, long embrace. Far from dying on the day of the Crucifixion, as he does in the novel, Balthasar substitutes for Ben-Hur when he appears before the two advancing legions in the penultimate scene of the film, delivering the message that their dead king "bade us hold our peace – forgive our enemies – love one another – and pray."

The novel does not require its audience to have a lengthy explanation of how Judah spent his time in Rome or why he wanted to return to his homeland to find his mother and sister. Wallace allotted only four paragraphs to narrating the rescue of Arrius, his unexpected victory, his Triumph in Rome one month later, and his subsequent adoption of Judah as son and heir. Previous to that, however, he spends several pages describing the scene on the flotsam in which Arrius offers Judah his ring that Judah then tosses into the sea. The film is apportioned with reverse emphasis, for two men floating upon the sea does not carry the same visual impact as a screen filled with a few hundred armed men bustling about a fully manned Roman galley, lowering a net ladder over the side, and hailing their victorious commander in unison motion, then focusing on the half-naked hero climbing up the ladder while facing his past in the countenance of a pitiable galley slave staring at him through the porthole, and then less than a minute later entering his future in a magnificent, Technicolor Roman Triumph – the only non-biblical Technicolor sequence that remained in the release version of the film – featuring shimmering rose petals, long festoons, topless flower girls, prancing horses, uniformed soldiers marching with banners, and the handsome hero bedecked in the finest Roman dress, a dynamic *tableau vivant* of Lawrence Alma-Tadema's *Spring*.[206]

Jerusalem, the Nativity, and the House of Hur

The intertitles often drive the story with concise but powerful statements. At the beginning of the film they establish the turbulent political setting so essential to Wallace's conception of a land abandoned by its old god and in much need of a new one.

> Pagan Rome was at the zenith of her power. The tread of her iron legion shook the world; and from every land rose the cries of captive peoples – praying for a deliverer.

Without interruption a second intertitle asserts that Judea's glory was "scattered in the dust" and Jerusalem conquered. These few words encapsulate in a few seconds Wallace's first chapter (2.1). As in the novel (2.2), this leads directly to the population of Jerusalem and a survey of its many ethnicities, but the filmmakers, as we have seen, much preferred to emphasize the height of the walls and the size of the crowd as well as the calendar date – December 24. Even more, as was the cinematic style at the time, the Jerusalem street scene then continues with some light fare as a young family with a tall father, a shorter mother, and then three decreasingly smaller children in stair-step order pause for the fourth, a little toddler with a bright smile, a funny waddle, and an even smaller dog on a leash. Onlookers smile, and then two older men shake their heads as make-up is applied to a woman's face. A Roman soldier mischievously steals an apple by stabbing it with his sword behind the vendor's back. The apple vendor accuses an innocent passerby, and the Roman and his comrades laugh as the vendor submissively forces a smile at them. This returns the audience to the political reality of the day, and it becomes more seriously engaged as a Roman savagely tugs at a young woman's hair and brutally tosses her to the ground.

This brief series of vignettes, shot by assistant directors Cabanne and Raboch in Rome during August, 1925, prepares the audience for the entrance of Joseph and Mary on a donkey. Again, there is no reference to Wallace's detailed history of the Jewish traditions but an invented sequence in which Mary lovingly strokes a nearby baby's head: the infant's mother immediately angers at the intrusion but almost as immediately relents and smiles as she gazes upon the angelic face of the Madonna. Thus far the film has used the first few minutes to set its own tone, much simplifying the novel, redirecting the larger clashes of culture and religion, taking them down to the street level of observable human interactions, and counterbalancing Roman oppression with the power of Mary's gentle countenance. Mary has a similar effect on the innkeeper who would turn Joseph and Mary away until he and the camera gaze upon her, and this graceful portrait culminates in the subsequent Technicolor shot showing a halo shimmering behind her head, recalling and animating the aforementioned paintings. Meanwhile, using the medium to full advantage, the interwoven Star of Bethlehem sequence employs over the course of four minutes several different matte paintings, processed shots, tinting, unique lighting and film effects (by MGM art director Ferdinand Earle), and crowd scenes to coordinate the heavenly phenomenon and its effect on the people and the surrounding desert.

Wallace begins the primary narrative of his novel with a progression from the quarrel between Judah and Messala (2.2), to the consolation the servant Amrah and the historical lecture his mother give Judah (2.3–5), to Tirzah's song and the tile incident (2.6). Joseph Young's dramatic adaptation began by immediately introducing Simonides about to depart for Antioch to protect the Hur fortune from the hated Romans. The film narrative, as Mathis had originally outlined, follows Young's innovation but without the dramatic dialogue and is instead designed to initiate the romance that will blossom as the film proceeds. The anti-Roman exchange between the "Princess of Hur" (as Judah's mother is called in the initial title card and the first few intertitles) and Simonides, citing Gratus' arrival as the cause for Simonides' immanent departure, leads neatly to the introductions of their teenage children, Judah and Esther. With even greater expediency the intertitles make it clear that Simonides has not seen Judah since he was a little boy and remains a slave of the House of Hur only because the law does not allow otherwise. This helps to simplify the complicated conditions of servitude Wallace applied to Simonides' backstory, makes him much more approachable to the audience than was the secretive miser of the novel, and prepares the audience also for how Judah will deal with Simonides and Esther's status later on.

This elegant but compact exposition also enables a series of scenes that are not in the novel and would have been nearly impossible to create in the stage play. Simonides' departure moves the action through the gate and outside the palace of Hur, puts Esther on a donkey (an echo of Mary), and elicits a wave from the upper balcony, whence soon the tile will be dropped on Gratus' head. Now out to the main street of Jerusalem amidst hundreds of people going about their various businesses and heading in both directions, we are introduced to young Judah, who after watching Romans march in formation espies Esther purchasing a white dove (another echo of Mary). She does not hold onto this delicate creature for long, though, and after Judah spryly chases and recaptures the bird, he presents it to Esther, their eyes and gestures already supplying the audience with a budding romance. Like Judah's heart, the camera tracks Esther as her mount slowly leads her away from him. Wasting no time, the story moves on as the preoccupied Judah backs into a Roman soldier, who calls his race "backward." Judah glares briefly but asks for Messala, who does not acknowledge Judah until they go around a corner. Messala's welcoming smile is long in coming, but after just one dialogue intertitle, Judah invites him to see his mother and sister. From the fateful balcony the camera observes them approaching the palace of Hur.

As in the Kalem film, we already see the loose tile foreshadowing their impending fate.

The Quarrel, Tile Incident, and Arrest
Most of this is new and gives a logical coherence and emotional key to the narrative, and it injects human sweetness into a story that is otherwise consistently somber. And yet, the sweetness will begin to dissipate along with the friendship in literally one minute, deteriorate further in two and three minutes, and end forever in four. First Messala rejects the sweets offered him by Amrah, who has a much reduced role. Then he insists that the Jews are conquered and therefore need to understand their Roman masters. Judah stands back and explains that Messala seems a stranger, in fact, as Messala boldly asserts, "A Roman! ... And why not? To be a Roman is to rule the world! To be a Jew is to crawl in the dirt. Forget you are a Jew!" The reader may recall that this very powerful phrase comes from Young, not Wallace, who gave a much more nuanced and geo-political argument in his early chapter. Reducing into just a few lines of dialogue Wallace's carefully drawn out argument in Book Second demonstrates how thoroughly Carey Wilson and Bess Meredyth rewrote not only Wallace's initial chapters and the first act of Young's play but also important sections of Mathis' faithful but lengthy scenario.

As in the novel, Judah backtracks and reminds Messala of their friendship, but just then trumpeters are edited in, so Messala turns away, warns Judah about speaking treason "even to a friend," and storms out, the camera not tracking along with his departure but following it for a long time from behind, both as he exits the door to the house and then the main gate. As in the novel, Judah's mother succeeds in comforting him, but rather than filming the novel's long discourse on Romano-Jewish relations, Judah here gives a predominantly Christian message:

> The Holy Child of Bethlehem you told me of – prophesied to be the Messiah! If it were true, He could save us from Rome!

A semi-circle of trumpeters begins the procession of Gratus. This segment was shot in Rome, and it clearly retains Mathis' conception of an impressive Roman component as well as her efforts to replicate the book on film. Gratus wears the laurel wreath that Wallace describes. Amidst the pomp and multiple camera angles Judah points out Messala: "Caesar himself is not more kingly!" The reader will recall that in the novel Messala had no official military position, nor was he in the procession, let alone visible to Judah. Inadvertently Judah leans on the tile and reaches after it much as Wallace describes in the novel, although the cinematic Judah's movement had not "served to push the descending fragment farther out over the wall." When Gratus is struck on the head, it is Messala who is seen next to him to determine his condition, and then Messala rides his horse into the house to make his accusation against Judah. As in the Kalem film, Judah pleads to free his mother and sister and struggles to get free, but ultimately he follows Wallace in proclaiming, although now lacking the leitmotif Kelley had provided for the stage play, "Oh, Lord, in the hour of thy vengeance – mine be the hand to put it on him!"

The Well in Nazareth

Just as abruptly as in the novel, but absent from the stage play, Judah suddenly finds himself crossing the desert on his way to the galley. For the encounter with Jesus at the well in Nazareth, respecting Wallace's and Erlanger's prohibitions, but because Thalberg insisted on showing at least part of his body, the camera shows us the arm of the carpenter's son sawing wood, and this arm and hand give Judah water from a gourd and stroke his hair. More than mere refreshment, the encounter gives Judah renewed commitment "to fight for the King when he comes!" and thereby helps to drive the plot in the second half of the film. The scene ends with another glimpse of the arm and hand sawing. Creating a sharp contrast, the intertitle immediately following reads: "The vengeful arm of Rome had reached forth to Simonides – " and we see a few seconds of Simonides being tortured on the rack. And again just as abruptly, the film moves to the galley sequences.

The Galley Scenes

These sequences shot by Niblo off the coast of Tuscany render some spectacular action and in that sense realize Wallace's words not literally but in cinematic spirit. The novel describes only what Judah can see and ascertain from below the deck:

> Smoke lay upon the sea like a semitransparent fog, through which here and there shone cores of intense brilliance. A quick intelligence told him that they were ships on fire. The battle was yet on; nor could he say who was victor. Within the radius of his vision now and then ships passed, shooting shadows athwart lights. Out of the dun clouds farther on he caught the crash of other ships colliding.

Amidst pervasive smoke, Niblo picturized Wallace's ramming ships – both the Italian life-size ships and model galleys photographed later in a Culver City tank – manned by asymmetrical masses of soldiers. He inserted a number of gruesome close-ups – the pirate leader Golthar holding a speared Roman head, a Roman carrying a dead pirate on his spear, and men using fire to drop soldiers held in a suspended basket down to the deck – that recall motifs used by Griffith in the siege of Babylon in *Intolerance*, and the bodies and limbs of struggling galley slaves below fill the screen like a DeMille composition. Niblo also added into the ubiquitous swordplay a glass jar filled with snakes catapulted onto a Roman deck, fiery ballistas, three banks of galley slaves pushed to breakneck speed in battle, a slave hanged by his own chains, a huge burning timber seemingly crashing down onto Novarro's head, and the scores of men in the sea swimming away from the (actually) burning galley. Although it would later be overshadowed by the chariot race, this is some impressive footage and, along with the Jerusalem scenes, demonstrates that some of Niblo's Italian footage assisted immeasurably in making *Ben-Hur* come alive on screen in spectacular fashion.

Return to the East
Revealing in an intertitle that the "mysterious miser at Antioch" is Simonides and showing Judah's mother and sister alive but in prison, the film in a few seconds further frees the audience from Wallace's ongoing mysteries and drives a clearer narrative that portrays Simonides as Esther's devoted father and Judah's trusted ally and allows the audience to pity Judah's loss and celebrate the anticipated anagnorisis of the Hur family at the end of the film. Now based in Antioch, this condensed portion of the film integrates the stories of Judah, Simonides, Esther, Sheik Ilderim, Iras, and Messala without forcing them to travel back and forth across the desert as they do in the novel.

Ilderim and Iras
Ilderim was tailor-made for the screen, an exotic ethnic with many visually fascinating trappings, a large number of attendants, and a huge tent in the desert amidst an orchard of palms. As in the novel, it is he who charges Sanballat with luring the Romans into huge wagers, and the cinematic Ilderim equally worships his horses as demigods. Freed from the limits of the stage, Niblo, as Wallace described (4.13), brings the four white horses into Ilderim's tent for Judah to admire, making a memorable screen event, as it would be in the 1959 version.

Omitting Wallace's poetry, song, and even the moonlit boat ride used so effectively in the Klaw & Erlanger production, the film introduces Iras as a screen vamp with a blond wig, feather and bejeweled headdresses, and pearls adorning her scanty but lovely outfits. She charms Judah with her looks, incense, perfume, and flattery, using a comparison ("Almost I am convinced you are Apollo himself.") that in the novel she applies to Messala (5.13). When Ilderim brings the horses into the tent, she whispers to Judah: "Flashing eyes and milk-white bodies! Beauty to be tamed! Does it not thrill you?" She is well integrated into the plot. Wilson and Meredyth have her embraced and almost kissed by Messala before he sends her to find out the name of Ilderim's driver, embraced and almost kissed by Judah before he stops himself (Iras: "If you are as slow in the race tomorrow as you are in love today, Messala may drive snails and win!"), embraced again and kissed by Messala after Simonides unknowingly reveals Judah's identity, and then present a striking figure in her box at the chariot race, costumed by Erté.

The Wagering Scene
Messala dismisses the possibility that Judah is still alive, making all the more powerful the wagering scene, which had already been a highlight of the Klaw & Erlanger production, with Judah, Esther, Iras, and Messala on stage at the same time. At the climax of the scene, when Messala is shaking and strangling Sanballat after he offered 6–1 odds, angrily asking who has the 10,000 pieces of gold to bet at those odds, Judah appears out of nowhere, grabs Messala's arm, and answers: "The Unknown Jew, Messala! I have that amount and more! And I want no odds!" They glare at each other for two and a half minutes. Messala threatens to kill Judah during the race and taunts him for being a Jew, but he hesitates to sign for an amount greater than his entire fortune. Now Hilliker and Caldwell echo the intertitles they composed for the initial quarrel between Judah and Messala, for Judah says, "Do you forget that you are a Roman – and that I am only a Jew?" This forces Messala finally to sign the wager, which he does without ever taking his piercing eyes off Judah. Again Messala threatens Judah's life, so Judah responds: "So be it! To the death! But one of us shall leave the course alive!" This utterly recasts Wallace's concept of premeditated murder and palliates his Old Testament revenge motif. It has now become a duel to the death, a Hollywood staple that has not lost its effectiveness in nearly a century of exploitation and variation.

The Chariot Race
Trumpets put an end to this intense scene, leading to the chariot race. After some exterior shots of the masses filing in between several towering columns and litter-borne aristocrats settling into their boxes, a memorable tracking shot takes the viewer out into the circus and pans up to its huge victory columns and along to its thousands of spectators. The reader may recall Wallace's considerable efforts, relying upon Smith's dictionaries, at describing the ancient venue accurately, while the emphasis here is on size and pomp. Two rows of two dozen plumed horses comprise the military guard that performs its orchestrated drills and again signals with its several dozen trumpets. Locating their presence in the seats, the camera shows Esther and the Erté-bedecked Iras eyeing each other. By necessity Eason eliminated Wallace's chalk-line starting system and replaces it with cinematically effective shots of nervous, rearing horses from below and the side. One chariot's wheel is pulled onto the axle of the next chariot, foreshadowing Messala's demise, although not as Wallace described it. The race itself follows Wallace's outline insofar as the Greek's crash, despite Erlanger's criticism, and Eason uses this to great effect. He places the crash directly in front of Judah's chariot. Judah tries to pull his team to the right but runs right over [a ramp placed behind] the wreck. Then a rescue crew runs out onto the track to clean up the wreckage, and Eason creates further excitement by having them clear out of the way just in the

nick of time as the other chariots are charging upon them. In addition, Hilliker and Caldwell insert the only intertitles in the race here to further prepare for Messala's demise. The first has the Greek shouting to Messala, "You're fouling me, Roman dog!" to which Messala responds, "Yes, and I'll wreck you, Greek, to smash the cursed Jew behind you!" Messala here is a study of anger and intolerance.

Eason designed Messala's crash to be obvious and deserved. Wallace wrote that the spectators could not see the "the cunning touch of the reins" that "caught Messala's wheel with the iron-shod point of his axle, and crushed it," and he does not explain this until after the fact. Moreover, Wallace thought it horrible enough that earlier in the race Messala had lashed Judah's Arabs, for they had never been whipped before. The cinematic Judah whips his own horses throughout the race – it creates exciting motion – but Eason further indicts Messala in the eyes of the audience by having him turn his whip on Judah as he pulls up next to Messala nearing the last turn of the race. Judah determinedly grabs Messala's whip and tosses it aside. As if this were the last straw, Judah maneuvers his left wheel inside Messala's right wheel, here perhaps illustrating in motion Wallace's phrase, "Ben-Hur's inner wheel behind the other's car." Judah stretches both axle lengths to capacity and then cracks his whip twice. His horses leap forward and pull Messala's wheel off. In a quick blur we see the following team [the Sidonian team in the novel] run Messala over, and this is the point at which Eason had as many as six teams pile onto Messala's wreckage. Judah continues down the course one last time to victory, his cape blowing behind him as he is photographed from a camera positioned high above the circus spectators. Perhaps taking a cue from the Kalem film, Eason has Judah ride up to the tribunal to declare victory and includes in the same shot the bloodied Messala being carried on a stretcher.

The Narrative Arc and the Final Thirty Minutes

The narrative arc of *Ben-Hur* is unlike that of many modern novels. It establishes its characters and their career paths early on, but then the critical chariot race takes place not even two-thirds of the way through, putting aside the personal revenge motif and leaving a large portion of the narrative subject to a different motivation. Of course this was by design since Wallace's initial concept of a book about "a Jewish boy whom I have got into terrible trouble, and must get out of it as best I can" was supplanted by his tale of the Christ. The narrative arc now ranged chronologically from the Nativity to the Crucifixion. Having diminished the menace of Messala, Judah takes on two missions, one to discover and reunite with his mother and sister, the other to find and fight for the new king of the Jews. As it happens, he will reunite with his family on the very day that the new king will be led to his Crucifixion. In the meanwhile Judah becomes an eyewitness to the Passion of the Christ and then a soldier who will ultimately lay down his arms in his name.

To render all this cinematically in a silent presentation that would last a little over two hours challenged Wilson and Meredyth, for again they had to balance what the audience expected with what the audience would appreciate. The most prominent incidents of *Ben-Hur* had proven themselves over four decades to be the gathering of the Wise Men, the Star of Bethlehem, the quarrel, the tile incident, the encounter at the well, the galley sequences, Daphne, the chariot race, the lepers gazing upon Judah sleeping, Christ's curing them, the family's reunification, and the Crucifixion. Of the dozen, all are included in the film except the Daphne episode, which is listed on MGM's Shot List but did not make it into the release version. The first eight in the 1925 film adaptation consume almost one hour and fifty minutes. The final thirty minutes move rapidly, pausing to dwell on only one scene – the lepers watching over Judah sleeping.

Some of the novel's other events, the encounter with Thord, the political confrontation instigated by Pontius Pilate's ensigns, and the struggle against Pilate's hidden thugs, are jettisoned. Immediately after the conclusion of the chariot race scene, we see a brief snippet of Judah's mother and sister in their dungeon, and because the audience can now be sure that they are alive, more energy and time can be spent on different matters – Christ protecting Mary Magdalene, the Palm Sunday advent, and the trial before Pilate. All those scenes are in Technicolor, but much of what follows – the scenes in the dungeon, outside the palace of Hur, and in the Valley of the Lepers – take place at night or in dark interiors thereby contrasting the lighting and tone of the scenes. After Judah awakens, Balthasar's aforementioned re-emergence quickly stirs Judah to action and the gentle farewell with Esther. Judah rides off on horseback to form two legions. Meanwhile the advent of Palm Sunday is conflated with Pontius Pilate's decree of amnesty, so Judah's mother and sister are freed at the time of the Last Supper (depicted in a Technicolor tableau recreating Da Vinci's painting) and Judah returns to Jerusalem on horseback to enable the sleep scene and once again profess his love for Esther. Another abrupt announcement, that the king has been seized, incites Judah to ride off, causing his mother to swoon, which in turn convinces Esther to guide them to Jesus. While he is carrying the cross through the streets of Jerusalem, as in the novel, across the street stands Judah ready to fight on behalf of the new king. When Christ passes by Judah's mother and sister, the audience watches their leprous skin miraculously heal, an effect cinematographer Karl Struss accomplished by sliding a red filter across the lens to cancel out their red make-up.[207] Judah now sees them, and the family is reunited. This means that it is left up to Balthasar to climb upon a rock plateau to dismiss Ben-Hur's legions but only after Roman soldiers draw lots for Jesus's robe and the Jerusalem "Senate Building," symbol of Roman dominance, crumbles into a heap. The final tableau finds Judah in civilian clothes embracing his mother and Esther.

While it contains night photography, horse mounts, dismounts, and galloping, Technicolor for the Palm Sunday, robe, and final sequences, and some convincing matte work for the collapse of the Roman praetorium as well as the large crowd scenes along the Via Dolorosa and meeting of the legions, this concluding half hour is a dizzying whirlwind devoted to fitting in as much of the novel as practicable, and one that may reflect the rushed and extremely stressful conditions under which Thalberg and Nosler found themselves during the last weeks of December, 1925. Nonetheless, contemporary critics and audiences did not seem to object, balancing the thrills of the previous sections of the film with the Technicolor beauty and spiritual satisfaction experienced near the end of the film.

EXPLOITATION

New York Premiere
Even as late as December 13, 1925, MGM was still expecting to open the film on Christmas Eve in New York and was already running a still photo of Betty Bronson as the Madonna in the *New York Times*.[208] A December 21 announcement postponed the opening until "next week,"[209] and then on December 26 Marcus Loew himself, crediting the talents of Erlanger, Mayer, Thalberg, and Niblo, announced that the film had been completed and that a print was being shipped to New York for a December 30 roadshow premiere.[210] The very next day newspaper publicity employed some proven selling points in highlighting the *Ben-Hur* tradition of successes. A headline in *The New York Herald* and *New York Tribune* cited the popularity of the book that had been "Blessed by Pope, Translated Into Arabic."[211] The copy surveyed the history of the book through the million-dollar agreement with "a mail order house in Chicago" and the twenty-one years of the Klaw & Erlanger production, while the papers also featured new photos of the sea battle, chariot race, and Romans entering the "Gate of Jerusalem."[212] Nonetheless, the reception in the papers was relatively subdued because the New York papers at the time were chafing at the number of Hollywood blockbusters usurping their legitimate theater houses to put on elaborate roadshow productions.[213] Concurrently *The Merry Widow* was at the Embassy, *The Big Parade* at the Astor, and *His Secretary* at the Capitol, and *The Birth of a Nation* was being revived at the Cameo. Now *Ben-Hur* was coming to the Cohan. Singling out the Cohan were 5-foot high, neon-lit letters spelling out B-E-N-H-U-R, the first large neon sign installation in Times Square.[214] Although the premiere on December 30 was not as gala as one might expect, Marcus Loew,

Niblo, Bushman, May McAvoy [Esther], and Henry Wallace were all in attendance.[215] Novarro was not because he had reportedly taken ill on the train, but many years later he would attend the 1959 premiere.

The film itself was very well received. Mordaunt Hall's review in the *New York Times* begins:

> As a film spectacle it is a masterpiece of study and patience, a photodrama which is filled with so much artistry that one would like to ponder over some of the scenes to glean all that is in them, instead of seeing just that passing flash. Ordinary conventional methods have for the most part been discarded by Fred Niblo, the director, who, while he has availed himself of every iota of photographic worth in the thrilling episodes, nevertheless finds it pleasant to get in trenchant streaks and positively sublime poetic touches. And when the march to Calvary is depicted it is done with such solemnity and quiet respect that one feels impelled to bow one's head.[216]

Without saying it, he praises the two scenes that Niblo filmed with multiple cameras explicitly to capture unscripted actions, describing the sea battle as "a stupendous photographic feat [with] scores of men's heads dotting the sea as they swim for the grinding cameras" and highlighting the great crash and pile up in the chariot race. He was awed by the grand scope of the setting:

> The arena in which the race takes place is enormous, and from some of the camera shots the horses look like mere mice pulling on nutshells with a fly for a driver. About thirty horsemen could ride abreast in the narrowest section of this amphitheatre, and when the signal is waved for the race to start one can't help but be impressed by the space.

Hall also noted that the race "evoked no little applause" from the New York audience, and Ralph Flint in *The Christian Science Monitor* described the "cheers and plaudits" of the audience as Ben-Hur crossed the finish line.[217] Several times the latter felt compelled to compare the film, "a thing of authentic beauty and power," to the Klaw & Erlanger stage production, using it as proof of the superior advancement of the cinematic arts and particularly this film, not to mention the bold innovation characteristically required by the *Ben-Hur* property for advancement from one genre to the next:

> It is a triumph of the new art of the twentieth century, and in the light of the original stage version, stands out an artistic achievement of a new order. Where the "Ben Hur" of the stage dwelt in picturesque confinement amid its canvas waves and revolving platforms, the "Ben Hur" of the screen takes to itself the wings of the morning and moves where it will over land and sea. . . . In "Ben Hur" the screen takes on new justification. When the play was first put on at the Broadway Theater in New York, nearly two score years ago, who then ever imagined such a spectacle as is now being unfolded at the Cohan Theater, with its vast pageantry, its stirring sequences of battling ships of war and of racing chariots? And who would willingly return to the cumbersome treadmills and painted trappings of the vintage of 1899 after the winged steeds and far-flung settings of today? "Ben Hur" fully justifies the

prodigious labors and expenditures of its makers. It stands high among the finest pictures as yet brought to the screen.

Danny of *The Film Review*, who knew first hand how difficult it had been to produce this film, went a step further by calling the stage play a "pigmy" when compared to this new version, concluding that *Ben-Hur* was a "monument" to the film industry.[218] Assuming that it, like the stage play, would attract audiences on the basis of its religious message and thrilling action, and echoing the sentiments of those who have cited Wallace's novel and Klaw & Erlanger's production as lures to rural residents unfamiliar with or even antagonistic to plays and drama, he described *Ben-Hur* as superb entertainment with an evangelical message:

> Millions . . . who have never seen a motion picture will forever preach the gospel of the motion picture.

The film had a long and successful exclusive engagement at the Cohan for the twenty-week duration of its contract.[219] Elaborate advertising was unnecessary in New York. Even during the first week the *New York Times* ran only Niblo's interview and this large print ad:

> The Magnificent Chariot
> Race and Galley Scenes
> (The greatest thrills of all time)
> with the immortal love story of
> BEN-HUR *and* ESTHER
> Make
> BEN-HUR
> the Outstanding Attraction now
> being presented in New York[220]

On May 23, at the end of the season, it moved to the Embassy theater, where it would play for another thirty-one weeks.[221] On July 17 the theater celebrated its 400th showing.[222] The Embassy manager joked to the press, "Ben-Hur is going to run at the Embassy until the horses get tired." That did not happen until December 22, when MGM replaced it with *Tell It To the Marines*.

J. J. McCarthy's Roadshows

In the mid-1920s, the most exceptional cinematic properties were exhibited in roadshows. From the industry's perspective, the practice was designed to generate high profits by introducing the product as a legitimate theatrical entertainment shown in a first-rate venue on an exclusive and limited basis, with top-of-the-line ticket prices of $2.00 paid in advance. To maintain an aura of exclusivity, these agreements also prohibited exhibitors from negotiating advertising tie-ins, which at the time did not generate any significant income for the film industry. In 1926 *The Film Daily* ran a series on "Know Your Own Industry: How Super-

Pictures Are Nationally Presented," where the practice was lauded for providing uniform entertainment, especially the synchronized orchestral accompaniment.[223]

MGM signed a $3 million agreement with Joseph Jefferson McCarthy to arrange the roadshows for their two biggest hits of the year, King Vidor's *The Big Parade* and Niblo's *Ben-Hur*.[224] J. J. McCarthy had invented the concept, cutting his teeth on local exhibitions of the ground-breaking Italian blockbusters *Quo Vadis?* and *Cabiria*, and then exhibiting *The Birth of a Nation*, bringing in $4 million, followed by such successes as Griffith's *Way Down East* and DeMille's *The Ten Commandments*.[225] Independent from Erlanger and the Shuberts, he managed only films that promised spectacular results, taking 5 percent of the gross for making arrangements. He also produced the orchestral accompaniments, most often composed by William Axt and David Mendoza of the Capitol Theater, whose scores were reportedly rehearsed by each traveling company for two weeks before being sent out to perform.[226] He was also entirely in charge of publicity. It was his idea not to advertise heavily in New York but simply print the name of the film and the pertinent practical information.[227] In doing so he claimed that Lew Wallace had left instructions in his will that "methods of advertising used should always be entirely reverent and free from sensationalism," although in other cities McCarthy could not resist offering a display of the twelve chariots used in the film.[228]

Early in 1926 the *Ben-Hur* roadshow opened at only three additional locations – at the Woods in Chicago (February 8), at the Colonial in Boston (February 22), and then the Forrest in Philadelphia (April 19).[229] Pre-publicity was again minimal. The review of the Chicago premiere in Evanston's *Daily Northwestern* captured the atmosphere by putting the film into cinematic historical perspective:

> "Ben-Hur" suggests hurtling chariots as inevitably as "Uncle Tom's Cabin" suggests blood hounds, so it is fitting that the greatest scene in this great picture should be the chariot race. If anything as rousing and exciting and breathtaking has been filmed before it has not been my good fortune to see it. Only one other time – and that was at "The Birth of a Nation" – have I seen a motion-picture audience turn into a crowd of screaming, cheering maniacs like the one at the Woods when the madly streaking chariots, more terrible than so many cars of Juggernaut, swerved around bends and thundered down the stretch.[230]

The reader may recall that Klaw & Erlanger disseminated an extra degree of information before premiering in Boston. McCarthy did the same for the film's premiere at the Colonial, the same theater where the Klaw & Erlanger play had opened in 1900. The day before the premiere, the *Boston Globe* carried four different pieces (as well as an everyday ad for Jergen's Ben-Hur brand Talcum Powder on page A10).[231] On page A48 appeared an interview with the Broadway producer, George W. Lederer, who recounts in some detail how when Abraham Erlanger convinced Lew Wallace to produce *Ben-Hur* as a play, American theater and the business of American theater were in their infancy, and that Erlanger had also spearheaded the movement to render *Ben-Hur* as a moving picture.[232] On page B12 Francis X. Bushman regaled the *Globe* reporter with stories of working on a 6000-acre set with reconstructions of Jerusalem, Antioch, the Circus Maximus, and the Joppa Gate populated by some 2000 extras who took their work so seriously that as many as 190 of them would visit the infirmary in a single day for kicks, camel bites, and even broken bones from the chariot race, finishing with, "But we loved the risks because we were confident the result would be worth everything."[233] The regular MUSIC – DRAMA – PICTURES column on B13 includes three separate items about *Ben-Hur*.[234] The first tells of Wallace's encounter with Ingersoll, the second points out that Claire McDowell plays the protagonist's mother in both *The Big Parade* at the Majestic and *Ben-Hur* at the Colonial, and the third states:

> "The Antioch arena is the largest ever built for a picture scene. . . . As this, like most of the great Roman arenas, was free to the populace, the presence of a massive audience was necessary to preserve historical accuracy. In this scene there were estimated to have been at least 100,000 in the seats surrounding the arena.

And then page B14 offers a somewhat more responsible review of the history of Wallace's novel, the Klaw & Erlanger play, and the cost and effort that went into the production of the film, although it still reports that 100,000 extras filled the Antioch circus and nearly two million feet of negative were exposed, as the MGM pressbook reiterated. Erlanger himself attended the premiere on February 22, and that occasioned his reminiscing about opening the Colonial with his *Ben-Hur* twenty-five years earlier and explaining how he cherished his collection of *Ben-Hur* memorabilia, especially the letter from Garfield and a dozen giant volumes of scrapbook materials.[235]

The day after the premiere came an anonymous review that praised Novarro's ability to portray Judah's development from an innocent teenager to a determined and mature soldier, as well as the excitement of the audience at seeing the book come to life on the screen:

> The chariot scene, in which the hero, Ben-Hur, wins from his great enemy, Messala, was accompanied by hand-clapping, excited squeals from the women of the audience and a triumphant burst of applause at the conclusion. So excited did the audience become that one might have believed that the actual race was being run off on the stage of the Colonial Theatre, instead of just a pictorial representation of it.[236]

Bostonians were given repeated doses of interesting publicity thereafter, including an article detailing Niblo's sojourns to tribal Africa, his father's being wounded at Gettysburg, and his mother's French ancestry,[237] a MUSIC – DRAMA – PICTURES paragraph about Roman triremes,[238] an article on Ferdinand Earle and his "miracle effect" of the Star of Bethlehem,[239] an interview with Niblo about his Italian experiences,[240] an article on Iras and ancient Egyptian cosmetics,[241] and an interview with Carey Wilson about the sleepless weeks of work he had to put in while finishing the scenario on a European typewriter.[242] And early on in its run, there was one notable movie-page ad, filled with not photos and brief blurbs but fairly lengthy quotations from local reviews and one large bold statement:

> **FOUR MILLION DOLLAR CHEER**
> *Thundered from Two Thousand Throats at the*
> *Colonial Theater Last Night!*
> **'BEN-HUR' IS THE BIGGEST THING TO DATE IN THE FILM WORLD. AUDIENCE ACTUALLY ROSE TO CHEER ITS CHARIOT RACE SCENES.**
> **GORDON HILLMAN in the ADVERTISER**[243]

Home to Los Angeles

McCarthy's plan for the 1926–7 season was to send out twelve companies for *Ben-Hur*, eight for *The Big Parade*.[244] Selected cities included Los Angeles, Ottawa, Detroit, Newark, Columbus, Pittsburgh, Norfolk, Washington, San Francisco, Toronto, Cleveland, and New Orleans, all of them to open in August and September, and each assigned thirty-five people, including a twenty (or twenty-six) piece orchestra and a corps of projection experts as well as all the stage and electrical effects required to make the presentation – as it was advertised – "in exact replica of those at the Embassy Theater, New York."[245] The first of these, at Erlanger's Biltmore in Los Angeles, warranted special attention amidst a constant barrage of publicity, for only Los Angeles could claim that *Ben-Hur* was coming home, and, as with the Klaw & Erlanger roadshows decades before, the city took additional pride in its ability to compete in its appreciation for a major motion picture event. The caption for an August 26 publicity still of Novarro and May McAvoy specifies "its splendor in completed form has delighted those residents of Los Angeles who witnessed the making of some of its scenes."[246] Under the headline, "'Ben Hur' Places Los Angeles in Long-Run Ranks," the *Los Angeles Times* pointed out that the thirteenth week of the engagement surpassed the runs in Chicago, Philadelphia, and Boston and "puts Los Angeles forward as the second city of the land in theatrical importance."[247] The article points out that the engagement was also superior in box-office receipts because of the large capacity of the Biltmore.

The review of the premiere by Edwin Schallert of the *Los Angeles Times*, who would remain a constant champion of the film for years, described the film as the ultimate achievement in filmmaking:

> It typifies, in a way, the vast resources of the pictures thrown into a single accomplishment. Veritably, in this respect, it is a sort of huge melting pot for all that

pictures have won and conquered, brought together for a dazzling culmination. It is the victory of technique and of physical daring, of prodigal beauty in photography and of settings and investiture unrivaled in imposingness and grandeur; of mobs and supermobs, and of perfection remarkable in many ways in individual characterization.[248]

Schallert also observed that the thrilling chariot and galley scenes as well as the tasteful spiritual scenes were "following the best 'Ben-Hur' traditions." He writes that both major aspects of the story moved even veteran Los Angeles movie connoisseurs:

> Even the hardy first-nighter, and the individual doubter, was changed into a new being – momentarily becoming a fan breathless with excitement at the chariot race and the galley, and deeply moved by rare spiritualized influences of the story laid in the days of the Christ, as it has been brought to the screen from the pages of Lew Wallace's celebrated novel.

As the film continued with twice daily shows at 2:20 and 8:20, the *Times* produced new pieces marking each week of exhibition.[249] The fifth week, for instance, produced a brief statement on the superiority of the cinema over the printed page or spoken drama.[250] The sixth week occasioned an accounting that the film was now in its ninth month in New York.[251] The tenth week was headlined, "Bible Pictured in 'Ben Hur.'"[252] It described the biblical Technicolor scenes, the "terrific cataclysm of nature" that occurred at the end, and especially the final scene of the women kneeling at the foot of the cross as "one of the most reverent and beautiful ever staged." The article also pointed out that among the patrons were many who rarely went to the theater but were familiar with General Wallace's book and may have been patrons of the play some years earlier. Another contained an anecdotal account of shooting the raft sequence off the coast of Livorno, concluding that because of the cold water Frank Currier said to Novarro, "Hereafter, my boy, I play only bankers."[253] Other articles featured Francis X. Bushman discussing the "scanty costumes" worn by the ancient Romans,[254] various methods of representing Christ in the visual arts and Lew Wallace's "explicit instruction" to Erlanger not to do so in the dramatization of his book,[255] reminiscences of the actors who starred in the Klaw & Erlanger production,[256] and production stills[257] or photos of the actors out of costume (most were already appearing in films produced after *Ben-Hur*), one caption lamenting that Carmel Myers did not have the opportunity to employ "all her seductiveness" in her role as Iras.[258] One repeated theme was that *Ben-Hur* was attracting patrons "of widely divergent tastes" and nationalities, with local Mexican residents of Los Angeles enamored of Novarro, Italians pining over scenes of their homeland, and Jews interested in seeing "the glories of ancient Jerusalem depicted with historical accuracy."[259]

By now the *Los Angeles Times* was boasting that in a few short years Los Angeles had become the home to 85 percent of the $100 million American film industry, and, as we have seen, it was the overseas production costs and difficulties of *Ben-Hur* that convinced MGM to film all of their productions in Los Angeles.[260] As a result of the immediate success of *Ben-Hur* along with *The Big Parade*, MGM very rapidly became the largest film company, more than doubling its production program for 1926–7 to the sum of $25 million. Films like these were causing a paradigm shift in the industry (keeping in mind that in the 1920s the word "pretentious" was not a pejorative term):

> The current trend is toward few and better pictures. The notable success of some of the larger and more pretentious films during the past six or eight months has led several producers to devote more attention to this type of production, ... The rise of Metro-Goldwyn-Mayer to first place this year is one of the most spectacular advances ever made by any of the major organizations. Due to the success of such films as "Ben Hur," "The Big Parade" and other specials, this firm plans to devote much of its effort to the making of large road-show productions.

Citing the unparalleled track record of the novel and play and glorying in the advantages of the roadshow, the *Times* added the prediction that the film version of *Ben-Hur* would be the most successful ever:

> It is the opinion of substantial authorities that "Ben Hur" as a picture will out-live any other cinema effort ever made. These experts contend that it will duplicate the wide vogue of the book and the great popular appeal of the play even to a more far-reaching degree as a picture. Evidence of this thought is to be found in the fact that the Metro-Goldwyn-Mayer Corporation has turned this great work over to the exclusive direction of Messrs. A. L. Erlanger, C. B. Dillingham, and F. Ziegfeld, Jr., to tour as a special road-show attraction in leading legitimate theaters for three years.[261]

Some of this was certainly generated by Erlanger himself. A few weeks after the August 2 premiere, he publically affirmed the superiority of the cinematic medium and the newest Ben-Hur, Ramon Novarro.

> The picture is mightier than the play, even as the new medium is so much more world-wide than the other. I have employed a dozen or more Ben Hurs, including some very distinguished names in theater history; but to my mind Ramon Novarro is the greatest of them all.[262]

Two days later he was joined in this estimation by Marcus Loew and veteran actor David Warfield, who wired Novarro his personal congratulations.[263] In late October, Erlanger announced that he would rearrange his bookings so that *Ben-Hur* could be held beyond its original twelve-week engagement, and added that because the West Coast had its own *Ben-Hur* roadshow company, the film might return to Los Angeles the following year.[264]

Ultimately the Biltmore engagement ran sixteen weeks and played to well over 300,000 ticket buyers, reportedly setting a record for playing to "the greatest box-office receipt figures ever known for a picture offered purely as a legitimate theater attraction and with no attendant stage production."[265] These qualifiers distinguish *Ben-Hur* from *The Big Parade*, which by February had already attracted nearly one half-million people to Grauman's Egyptian and would continue its run there into May,[266] but these qualifiers were an integral part of Erlanger's calculation. The stage presentations or "prologues" that preceded each performance at Grauman's were often innovative, star-studded, and lengthy.[267] They offered an additional attraction to those who thought that the entertainment value of a film alone was not proportionate to the high prices normally charged for legitimate theater tickets. Grauman was not alone. Many theaters at the time used prologues. Erlanger rejected the practice, so a controversy over prologues flared up at the time of the Los Angeles premiere of *Ben-Hur* as the two MGM blockbusters played simultaneously in two of Los Angeles' most prominent theaters, one with a prologue, and one without.

In his glowing review of the August 2 Los Angeles premiere of *Ben-Hur*, Schallert had pointed out the potential detriment of opening the film in a traditional theater rather than a movie palace, especially being devoid of a prologue, and observed a remarkable success:

> The whole undertaking was viewed somewhat in the light of a very questionable experiment, and incidentally some doubt was also felt over the absence of embellishments, like the stage prologue which here apparently, no matter what the film, is outstandingly popular. It was amazing with what speed all this diminished and ultimately vanished with the starting of the showing.

Less than one week later in a piece on "The Prologue Controversy," he was singing the praises of Grauman and assuring his readers that in the face of change Grauman would be innovative.[268] Indeed, having maintained the practice throughout the transitional period, Grauman then introduced the Vitaphone system into his theater the following October.[269]

Three weeks later, Katherine Lipke of the *Times* supported the local Grauman against the New Yorker Erlanger with the headline, "Prologue Is Here To Stay?" She specifically cited *Ben-Hur* as a film with unique reasons for popularity, not the least of which was Erlanger's "propaganda":

> There seems to be little probability that the "Ben-Hur" experiment of giving a picture without a prologue will cause a reversion to the old days when people went to the theater to see the picture and nothing else. "Ben-Hur" is able to draw the crowds sans prologue because there are thousands who wish to see the picture, either because of the expensive propaganda circulated about it, or because of Lew Wallace's original story – or yet again because of Ramon Novarro. However, there are not many pictures which can draw people as can "Ben-Hur."[270]

Taking the opposing view was acclaimed comedy producer Hal Roach. He likened "atmospheric prologues" to a "hodge-podge" of bicyclists, jugglers, "child wonders," and other amateurish distractions that do not give the audience what they came for, which is generally a love of motion pictures or an actor or actress, or "some certain story interpreted."[271]

Making the latter allusion specific, he concludes his entire statement with this:

> The truth of this statement is effectively illustrated by the fact that during the past year some of the most sensationally successful motion pictures have been enthusiastically received by the public, with no pretense at presentation, atmospheric or otherwise. One current notable example is "Ben Hur."

At the tail end of the exchanges in the press, an anonymous paragraph in *Photoplay* corroborated Schallert's observations:

> "Ben Hur" took us to the downtown section of Los Angeles where a legitimate theater was converted into a motion picture house and somebody forgot all about arc lights. No matter arc lights and lack of prologue, no matter beautiful dresses, unsullied by spotlights, everyone forgot the pomp of a premiere as they sat, rapt and tense, watching the gradual unfolding of the great picture. Gasps of admiration, breathless silences broken by sporadic applause that grew suddenly deafening, murmurs of appreciation. It was more emotional than fashionably dazzling, that premiere. It was splendid.[272]

Once again a *Ben-Hur* production had become, albeit unofficially, a test case. In the summer of 1925, Grauman had already signed a contract with MGM to have the world premiere of *Ben-Hur* at his Hollywood theater for "the greatest sum of money ever paid by a single exhibitor for a single production," and it was to continue playing there for an entire year.[273] Witnessing the signing was none other than the "Czar of Filmdom," Will Hays, and as late as March, 1926, the *Times* and *The Film Daily* were still reporting that *Ben-Hur* would replace *The Big Parade* at the end of its historic run at the Egyptian.[274] But, in actuality, *The Big Parade* was replaced by a Douglas Fairbanks/Mary Pickford double feature of *The Black Pirate* and *Sparrows*, both fitted with prologues, and *Ben-Hur* went to the Biltmore without one.[275]

Roadshows Elsewhere
Los Angeles was a unique venue. For other cities, the arrival of *Ben-Hur* inspired different associations. The first bit of local pre-publicity to appear in *The Washington Post*, for instance, compared it to the "old-time stage show":

> Instead of eight horses and the old-time mechanical illusion of the stage show the new and greater "Ben Hur" shows twelve teams of four horses each racing the seven laps of a great arena with all the hairbreath escapes and spills incident to the struggle.[276]

Similarly, John J. Daly, the local "Stage and Screen" columnist for the *Post*, compared the limitations of the stage with the expansiveness of cinema:

> In the film version of the play and novel, the chariot race is put on in just such a stupendous and startling scenic study as might be expected, where there are no

four dimensions, no narrow confines of stage and theater, and where the great open spaces were at the command of men and machinery – and money, too – to make a Roman holiday.[277]

Harold Phillips of the *Evening Times* focused on the young generation:

> Not to see this picture of Ben-Hur is a misfortune. Not to have your children see it is an injustice.[278]

The film's arrival in Cleveland on Labor Day might have been marred somewhat by Karl K. Kitchen's review in the *Plain Dealer*. He complained about the scope:

> The dramatic story of Lew Wallace has been so swamped with huge mobs of extras and overbuilt settings that the result is a super film spectacle with the characters of the story mere puppets in the background.[279]

But he admits that the film will "add enormously to the prestige of the Metro-Goldwyn-Mayer company" and that it will be showing "in Yazoo, Mississippi and Medicine Hat long after most of its artistic rivals have been forgotten." In his own city the engagement ran eight weeks and sold an estimated 160,000 tickets.[280]

For the San Diego premiere at Spreckels Theater in November, McCarthy expanded the pre-publicity again for Southern Californians more keenly interested in film production. An article in the *Evening Tribune* somewhat overstates the case in declaring that "the camera is an instrument demanding absolute truth," explaining that where Wallace could get away with giving "a vague description," Niblo was "obliged to reproduce the actual circus," but the basic premise is an important one for understanding the growth of the *Ben-Hur* phenomenon from book to stage to screen.[281] The piece lists ten cinematic innovations, thereby effecting McCarthy's desire to promulgate the prestige of *Ben-Hur* not only in size, cost, length, and spectacle but in the "new modes of technique that 'Ben Hur' has evolved." The ten include directing "immense crowds" of 20,000 extras "by the modulated thunders of a myriad-horned magnavox," full-coverage photography, automobile photography, photography through gauze and glass, sea photography from above a floating platform, importing thousands of costumes from Germany, and "the ceaseless experimentation whereby 1,900,000 feet of film were cut and recut into an evening's entertainment." Elsewhere, in claiming that the $4 million film employed nearly 150,000 extras and 100 ships, we encounter some exaggerated numbers that would continue to be quoted in the publicity for many years.[282]

The premiere at Ford's Theater in Baltimore in mid-December, 1926, brought out a lengthy article on the production of the film, recounting the history from Brabin's arrival in February, 1924, and introducing the detail that the fighting in the galley sequence was so furious because the Florentine, Pisan, and Livornian extras were Fascists, the Romans anti-Fascists.[283]

As McCarthy scheduled repeat engagements in thirteen cities,[284] the April return engagement at Washington's National Theater evoked new newspaper articles that focused on *Ben-Hur*'s presence in the nation's capital, saying that "like the sublime theatrical contribution of Mrs. Stowe, the Wallace opus presently assumes the proportions of a national institution," and that the stage play "raised more dust and noise in the opera houses of the republic than was consistent with dignified drama."[285] Putting that aside as history and claiming that the film achieves what would be impossible on any stage, the article points out is appropriateness for Easter week:

> It is happily fitting that the National Theater should choose Gen. Wallace's epic tale for an Easter season presentation. Holy week observance had an appreciable effect on last night's audience – and if any offering is destined to weather this period of penitence it is such an offering as "Ben Hur."

To this day Turner Classic Movies usually broadcasts a version of *Ben-Hur* during Easter season.

Because the huge moneymakers *Ben-Hur* and *The Big Parade* were being booked exclusively in legitimate theaters, it raised an outcry from general film exhibitors just before their annual April, 1927, convention in Columbus.[286] They claimed they owned dedicated movie theaters better equipped for film showings but were presently excluded from the sizeable revenues. McCarthy justified the practice in *The Film Daily*, pointing out that if movie-theater owners charged roadshow ticket prices they would lose their regular patrons to the competition across the street, and that his roadshows attracted new movie patronage, "building a prestige for the motion picture in general that helps every exhibitor box-office." Echoing his logic was Griffith Grey, the roadshow manager at Famous Players-Lasky.[287] He told *The New York Times* that the roadshow programs stimulate business for the entire industry. They allow producers to film ambitious projects with the knowledge that roadshow exhibition can return their investment within a year, and "then afterward the subject goes to the picture houses with the enhanced value of this special exploitation." Nonetheless, in May Louis B. Mayer used the annual Metro-Goldwyn-Mayer sales convention to announce that *The Big Parade* and *Ben-Hur* would soon be offered at regular cinema theaters.[288] He used the same forum to announce that foreign receipts for their films had increased from 15 percent of their total income to 45 percent.[289] In doing so, he specified that *Ben-Hur* was doing particularly well abroad. This was because *The Big Parade* was set during the great European war, so its American perspective did not play as well there as it did in the United States.[290]

International Distribution

When Marcus Loew traveled to Europe in the summer of 1924 to fire the principals of the first Ben-Hur company, his itinerary included London, where he had recently purchased the Tivoli Theater to increase the international distribution of his films.[291] Unreported at the time was his agreement with Paramount and the powerful German production company Ufa to form Parufamet, a mutual distribution agency that encouraged Loew to make Berlin the site of *Ben-Hur*'s first international exhibition.[292] In attendance at the September, 1926, premiere at Ufa's Theater am Nollendorfplatz were Chancellor Wilhelm Marx, United States Ambassador Jacob Gould Schurman, one half-dozen cabinet ministers, and other local celebrities.[293] Unlike the U.S. premieres, this one was a cause for a major gala that included a battery of powerful searchlights outside the theater and a full press corps. The thousands of people in the crowd necessitated calling in the police reserves to keep the proceedings orderly. According to the *New York Times*, this was "absolutely new to Berlin," but the reader knows that *Ben-Hur: A Tale of the Christ* had sold very well in Germany and was not at all unknown to the German public.

From the outset *Ben-Hur* did very well. The German receipts were cause for recalculating the ultimate financial success of the film. When Loew's Incorporated reported in November that it expected to net $1 million from the German exhibition of *Ben-Hur* alone, stock in the company instantly became a buy.[294] By January, 1927, the theater was awarding a prize to its 100,000th customer,[295] and Loew himself gave a lengthy interview to Schallert of the *Times*.[296] Quite optimistic, he upped the estimate to $1.25 million for German receipts, musing over a report that in one smaller German city the demand to see the film was so great that the engagement had to be extended to a second theater.[297] Schallert exuberantly prophesized:

> That in itself is a forceful argument to prove the enormous fortune that "Ben Hur" will roll up, and beside that the length of time that it may be shown is absolutely indefinite.

Ben-Hur opened at Loew's Tivoli Theatre in London on November 9, 1926, replacing *The Big Parade* after its twenty-fifth week. As with the Klaw & Erlanger premiere at the Drury Lane Theatre twenty-four years earlier, the British reviews were not at all effusive. *The Observer* concluded that while it is "not a masterpiece of art, we still feel that it is anybody's money's worth."[298] The review makes clear a dislike for the Old Testament turned Christian morality of Wallace's story as "being founded on humbug":

> The novel's moral is that vengeance, wreaked spectacularly upon evil-doers, is splendid. To offer us a vision of Calvary when we finish glorying in blood-lust, is to

Figure 12.1 MGM promoted their 1925 *Ben-Hur* along with Parufamet in Germany and via this educational leaflet in the U.S. The leaflet was "to be used only for recitations," not "amateur entertainments or performances."

reduce the world's greatest doctrine to the sentimentality of the satiated. Like the novel, the film is only healthy when feverish.

But, as with the Klaw & Erlanger premiere, the lack of critical support did not affect the opinions of the royalty, high-profile government officials, or the public. As the *London Evening Standard* reported on November 18:

> Within five days, two queens, three princesses and the Duke and Duchess of York have seen "Ben Hur" at the Tivoli. The Princess Royal was there the night before last. The previous evening the Duke and Duchess of York sat in the circle, while Princess Marie Louise and Princess Victoria were in the stalls. On Sunday night the Queen of Spain was present and a day or two earlier the Queen of Norway was among the spectators.[299]

The following April, nineteen members of the Tivoli Theatre orchestra accompanied a performance at Windsor Castle for King George, Queen Mary, and their guests.[300] *Ben-Hur* was the first film wartime Prime Minister Lloyd George ever saw in a theater.[301] Former and future Prime Minister Ramsay MacDonald, when visiting Boston a few months later, was asked about American movies. His response was that he did not see many, did not care for the ones he had seen, but he did like *Ben-Hur*.[302] Back in England a political joke was that the voters of one town "prefer 'Ben Hur' to Mr. Ramsay MacDonald."[303]

Meanwhile the public kept pouring into the Tivoli. *The Observer* had to admit in February, 1927, that the chariot race was "still the most talked about sight [in pictures]," and by March there were already predictions that the engagement would break the long-standing record of *The Four Horsemen of the Apocalypse*.[304] That actually happened in July during its thirty-fifth week, when after 500 performances *Ben-Hur* also surpassed the number of performances given by any play in the legitimate theater.[305] In mid-September the one millionth ticket was sold, and at the end of the month, now in its forty-eighth week, the run was nearing its New York mark but was released "to the provinces."[306] The next month, the London correspondent for the *New York Times* pointed out in retrospect that American films generally did not find great favor in England:

> Exception must of course be made of some of the better class of American films. The phenomenal run of "Ben-Hur," for instance, is proof sufficient that a good film will draw, whatever be its country of origin.[307]

This was the same month in which *Ben-Hur* opened in Dublin, where the Capitol Theatre boasted of an expanded orchestra of twenty-five playing for three performances daily.[308] Two weeks later the film had already been seen by 70,000 people and was being held over for an additional week with expectations of reaching another 30,000 at least.[309]

Paris gave the film its own record-breaking reception. Premiering at the Cinéma Madeleine in early April, 1927, with English and French intertitles, the film garnered positive reviews and did not finish its engagement until sixteen months later.[310] Not only had no film ever run for more than one year in Paris, according to *The Billboard*, but this was the longest engagement in Continental motion picture history.[311] Along with the film, Ramon Novarro became very popular in Paris.[312] This exacerbated a pre-existing anti-American sentiment and a chauvinistic movement towards French films. In July there was a movement to establish a National Film Week in which only French films could be exhibited, but the argument was advanced that no country in Europe could produce films of similar quality.[313] France had the artistic talent, of course, but it lacked the industrial organization, especially on such a prodigious scale.[314] As with the London engagement, after the run at the Madeleine finished, the film was exhibited elsewhere in Paris and in the outlying areas.[315]

In addition to the lobby cards and programs that were printed for most of these transatlantic presentations, card sets containing dozens of publicity stills from *Ben-Hur* proliferated in Europe and elsewhere. Sets were issued by Ross Verlag in Berlin (in conjunction with Parufamet), Iris Verlag in Vienna, and Cinémagazine in Paris in different sizes and in black and white, color, and tinted. J.R.P.R. in Paris issued cards with Novarro and Bronson in character. At the Tivoli Theatre on The Strand in London, one could purchase a packet of twelve green-tinted postcards. The Madeleine commissioned postcards with the phrase, "Le Triomphe du Cinéma Madeleine" printed on the back.[316] The back of the Madeleine card also contains a price schedule for a Lethielleux edition of the novel (translated in 1913 by Phillippe Mazoyer, a specialist in early Christianity), a full 692-page edition illustrated by P. Rousseau, a deluxe edition in half-marbled sheepskin, and an abridged edition, ranging from three to twenty-eight francs. In reverse synergy, on the back cover of the latter, published in 1928, were advertisements for the MGM film at the Cinéma Madeleine in Paris and for the complete 692-page edition.[317] Another new French publication was a photoplay edition by Jules Tallandier of Paris, which included sixty-four pages of still images from the MGM film, some full page. In Spain cards were issued advertising E. Juncosa Chocolate. The 1925 *Ben-Hur* was also represented in color on the Cinema Cavalcade series issued in English and Afrikaans by Max ciarettes in Johannesburg.

The other major markets open to American films in the 1920s were China, Australia, and India.[318] *Ben-Hur* opened for extended runs in Melbourne and Sydney in July, 1927, and nine months later at the Carlton Theatre in Shanghai, followed by the Isis, and then the Peking at the end of the year.[319] The Australian market was particularly receptive. Part of the reason for this was its fondness for Niblo, who had worked as a live stage performer in Australia for several years before the war and then married the Australia actress Enid Bennett. One newspaper write-up even claimed that he was an Australian native.[320] The feeling was mutual. Niblo sent a cablegram to the theater manager to be read at the opening gala:

Figure 12.2 At least a half dozen different sets of trading cars extended the reach of MGM's 1925 *Ben-Hur* overseas. Pictured here are three cards from Ross Verlag in Berlin (in conjunction with MGM/Parufamet), both sides of a tinted card from the Tivoli in London, a J.R.P.R. card from Paris, and a colored Afrikaans MAX Cinema Cavalcade cigarette card. In its initial release the film earned $4 million domestically, $5 million overseas, far exceeding any other film of its era.

To the enjoyment of my friends in Australia, I humbly dedicate my picture, "Ben Hur." Hope they will like it."[321]

The premiere at Sydney's Prince Edward Theatre was a festive gala complete with a prologue consisting of orchestral selections from Tannhäuser, a rendition of the show tune "Melody of Love" on the organ, and the operatic tenor John Priors singing "Star of Bethlehem in an effective stage tableau."[322] Similar to the accounts of premieres elsewhere, the crowd at the Prince Edward was "so carried away by the realism of the chariot race that they cheered as enthusiastically as if they were watching a real race being run."[323] The engagements in the two largest Australian cities lasted for several months, and then the film enjoyed an equally popular "country release" commencing in October. The limited number of prints limited the engagements to at most several nights each, but *Ben-Hur* was shown frequently from Lismore, Newcastle, and Camden in the east, to Canberra in the south and Perth in the west into January, 1928.[324]

In India *Ben-Hur* was an instant success, playing twice a day in J. F. Madan's signature theater in Bombay [Mumbai] in September, 1927.[325] In a brief essay lambasting American film exports, the correspondent for *The Times of India* singles out *Ben-Hur* as an exception:

> There has been a good deal of perfectly legitimate criticism of some of the trashy stuff forced on exhibitors by the great monopolistic concerns in the United States. But let us be fair even to the Americans! The productions of Hollywood are intended primarily for American audiences and therefore are not always suitable to countries of differing traditions and outlook. Agreed! But I wonder if a finer film will ever come to this country than 'Ben-Hur' (an American masterpiece) now drawing two packed houses daily to the Madan Cinema here?

The film was so popular that Madan felt compelled to take out an ad in *The Times* claiming exclusive rights for India, Burma, and Ceylon and warning – as Wallace, Harper, and Erlanger had all done – about infringement of copyright.[326] In mid-November the film began a four-week, thrice daily, record-breaking run at Madan's Empire Theatre, and thereafter the "twelve thundering reels" of "this mastodonic screen epic" were moved to the Empress.[327] Such phrases are typical of the newspaper advertising for these engagements. The most elaborately illustrated pressbook ads were quite popular overseas.[328] Unique in this advertising is the note that says the festal virgins parading topless in the Technicolor Triumph scene were hired from the Folies-Bergère in Paris,[329] but this assertion is corroborated in a cablegram from Niblo to MGM, and Ertè, it should be pointed out, used to design costumes for the Folies-Bergère.[330]

Ben-Hur "at Popular Prices"

After Mayer announced that he was releasing *Ben-Hur* and *The Big Parade* for regular distribution for the 1927–8 season, Alexander Pantages soon put in a $26,000 guaranteed bid to exhibit both films at popular prices.[331]

He was in the process of changing the content of his West Coast theater empire from vaudeville to film, and these two films would provide an auspicious beginning. But MGM was temporarily keeping the films in-house. In the Midwest, Loew's Stillman Theater in Cleveland began advertising *Ben-Hur* "at popular prices for the first time anywhere" in mid-August.[332] The cost was now 75¢ for adults, 40¢ for children, and 40¢ and 25¢ for matinees. But this did not mean that the film was not distinguished from the dozens of relatively ephemeral products coming off the movie assembly line. The original roadshow effects and the musical score remained part of the exploitation, and the Stillman offered a "sensational extra!" This was the exclusive opportunity to view the actual chariot and white horses used for filming the chariot race sequence. They were presented "on stage and in action." The theater offered six showings per day, although the 9:30 a.m. morning show was omitted on Sundays. To maintain the image of *Ben-Hur* as an inspiring and educational film, Loew's arranged for an exhibition in the main Cleveland Public Library, and many of its branches displayed books on the Holy Land and the life of Jesus as well as still photos from the production.[333]

Back in Los Angeles, Grauman's Million Dollar Theater displayed Novarro's leather racing costumes, his whip, Arrius' Roman staff, weapons, and trumpets, and two model galleys.[334] This was just part of his campaign. Because exhibitors were not required to employ the Axt-Mendoza score, he hired Leo Forbstein, at the time the leader of a local theatrical orchestra, to prepare a musical pastiche.[335] Grauman also submitted new newspaper entries on Niblo's love for old musty books,[336] Frank Currier's desire to film Shakespeare,[337] and the location for the Triumph sequence.[338] The latter was the garden in Frascati on the property that used to be owned by Kaiser Wilhelm but was then bestowed upon the poet-soldier Gabrielle d'Annunzio. In contrast, the return engagement at New York City's Capitol Theater exhibited only the film and published only a few plain ads as well as very specific start times.[339] The latter specified five showings from 1:00 p.m. to 11:50 p.m., allotting only two hours and five minutes for an abridged cut of the film plus a four-minute orchestral prelude.[340]

The advertising now advances the *Ben-Hur* tradition another step. It no longer recalls the nostalgia and spectacle of the Klaw & Erlanger stage play but instead highlights the romance and spectacle of the film that had premiered more than one year earlier.[341] Also, because the story was so well known from the book and play as well as the film, some of the advertising copy does not hesitate to review the plot. One example for Loew's in Canton, Ohio, derived from the pressbook, describes in detail the end of the film:

> Mother and Tirzah find the youthful Ben-Hur asleep on a bench outside the disused Palace of Hur. The sister kisses his shoe but the mother does not dare to touch him. Silently they go away to save him from the ruin which is theirs.

There are few dry eyes during the enactment of this scene. But the sorrow is turned to joy after Esther discovers the outcasts in the Vale of Hinnom, takes them to the Divine Healer, whose benediction cures them, and the happy four are reunited.[342]

In October MGM took out a two-page color advertisement in *The Film Daily* to announce to theater owners the nationwide release of *Ben-Hur* on October 10.[343] Again, despite specifying the "release at popular prices," the concept of prestige was not to be forgotten:

You will show it in October and your audiences will remember it forever. By playing "Ben-Hur" in your theatre, you are proving the greatness of your theatre. The final flower of motion picture creation has been achieved – on your screen – when you play BEN-HUR. Be first in the hearts of your public with Metro-Goldwyn-Mayer.

In late September, a front-page, boxed note in *The Film Daily* had announced that Loew's was considering eliminating vaudeville acts during all the runs of *Ben-Hur* and *The Big Parade*.[344] But once the film was released to the smaller theaters not directly answerable to the company, the methods of presentations depended more on the individual theater owners. Even a week before the film was moved from New York's Capitol to Loew's State and Metropolitan theaters, the "Gossip of Vaudeville" column in the *New York Times* reported that an "a la Carte" act, Powers and Wallace, would be at Loew's State.[345] The write-up in the *Richmond Times Dispatch* concludes that the length of the film made it an excellent idea to eliminate the usual comic prologue, adding, "even the news reel makes the show long for one sitting."[346] But the Valencia in Baltimore advertised in addition to a guest conductor and an organist "other screen specialties," suggesting perhaps comic shorts.[347] Despite this initial independence, the local theaters inevitably include a write-up with the phrase, "a Metro-Goldwyn-Mayer production made by special arrangement with A. L. Erlanger, Charles B. Dillingham and F. Ziegfeld, Jr.," the same that appears on the title card that introduces the film itself.[348]

Keeping abreast of current trends typified by local exhibitions of *Ben-Hur*, *The Film Daily* began running an "Exploit-O-Grams" column where owners could read and exchange homegrown ideas. An entry from Marion, Illinois, said that the Lyric Theater ran a "Do You Know Contest" for a week in advance of the initial *Ben-Hur* play date, using the local paper to ask twenty-four questions relevant to *Ben-Hur*, the winners getting free tickets.[349] The theater manager also illuminated a 24-sheet poster of the chariot race on his marquee. The manager of the Rialto in Butte, Montana, ran a contest through the local newspaper, in which the readers fill in the missing words from a summary of the plot of *Ben-Hur*.[350] A similar contest was held in Rockford, Illinois,[351] and another in Springfield, Illinois.[352] Even MGM got into the spirit, sponsoring a contest in *The Film Daily* for which first prize was a check for $50 and Ramon Novarro's whip.[353] The manager of the Pantages Theater in Salt Lake City, gave a KSL radio announcer a microphone and a box seat from which he narrated the entire film as if a live event.[354] Thousands of letters came to the theater and the radio station as a result. In Columbus, Georgia, the owner of the Grand hitched two ponies bearing banners that said "Grand – Ben Hur – Now Playing" to a chariot and drove it through the streets.[355] A similar gimmick was enacted in nearby Macon, where the wintering Spark's Circus had a chariot to lend the manager for free.[356] The Forest Templin Theater owner in Alliance, Ohio, reprinted an image from the MGM pressbook and distributed thousands of copies on a number of rural free delivery routes.[357] Having a more urban constituency to attract and targeting those who had not attended the roadshow, Loew's Grand in Atlanta offered a midnight premiere, albeit without the usual vaudeville prologue on account of the late hour.[358] This was in addition to a string of superlatives that attempted to summarize the success of the *Ben-Hur* property:

> Massive as a story, massive as a stage play, the screen version of General Lew Wallace's masterpiece is even greater than massive, it is stupendously massive and is by far the greatest picture, in many respects, ever conceived in the mind of man.[359]

Because Wallace's novel was now generally considered a classic work of modern American literature, several theater managers appealed to schools. The manager of the Colorado Theater in Pueblo encouraged high-school officials to preview the film and then talk to their students in school assemblies.[360] In Alliance, Ohio, the superintendent of schools announced in every class from seventh to twelfth grades that there would be a special student matinee for a mere 25¢.[361] In Greeley, Colorado, grade schools were even dismissed early one day so that the children could attend a matinee.[362]

Even more significant was the relationship between some theater managers and local clergymen. The owner of the Capitol Theater in Aberdeen, South Dakota, much as did the owner of the Garrick in Duluth and the Hippodrome in Waco, wrote letters to clergymen of every denomination describing the film and inclosing two free tickets, and he sent them on a Thursday so there would be ample time for them to speak about the film to their congregations on Sunday.[363] A minister in Greeley encouraged his congregation to see the film and then wrote a letter of endorsement to the Sterling Theater manager who in turn used it for a newspaper ad.[364]

The film industry and the Religious Motion Picture Foundation along with Will Hays had begun making religious films in 1926,[365] and just as we saw with the *Ben-Hur* stereopticon lectures, some churches were willing to introduce the new technologies into their buildings. There was an early experiment in 1927, when the Wesley Methodist Church of Worcester, Massachusetts, the largest Methodist church in New England at the time, inaugurated a Sunday night picture club that would conduct services "entirely from the screen," along with a brief prayer.[366] The two films mentioned are *The Ten Commandments* and *Ben Hur*. The Greater Pittsburgh Inter-Club Council held an April, 1928, Monday evening showing of *Ben-Hur* to raise money for their scholarship fund.[367] One of the ads in *The Pittsburgh Courier* focuses on the "magnificent plot, fine characterization and beautiful love story" rather than the sea battle or chariot race, and it also uses the copy from the pressbook describing the pitiable night-time scene outside the Palace of Hur.[368] The same month the Congregational Church of the Pilgrims in Brooklyn ran an advertisement for a showing,[369] as did Washington's Unitarian All Souls' Church.[370] Two years later a showing at a Manassas, Virginia, church was advertised in the *Afro-American*,[371] while the *New York Times* advertised another at the Broadway Temple at 174th Street, this one accompanied by a sermon, "Does Right Win?"[372] A few months later, the first page of the November 3, 1930, *The Film Daily* ran the following in a box:

> Two years ago the Sunday evening services of St. Peter's Episcopal Church were attended by an average of a dozen persons. Now that the church conducts its services almost entirely on the screen, attendance invariably exceeds 400. Among films shown already are "Ben Hur," "Sorrel and Son," "Rich People," and "Tale of Two Cities."[373]

Synchronized Sound Added

In December, 1926, Schallert predicted that "the final reel of 'Ben Hur's' history will not be unspun until five years from now or longer."[374] By mid-1928, *Ben-Hur* had been playing in multiple theaters simultaneously in multiple cities for over six months.[375] In Chicago alone eight different theaters were playing *Ben-Hur* in February.[376] New bookings probed neighborhoods and communities that had not yet seen the film, and then the popularity of the film inspired repeat bookings. In Minneapolis the manager of the Logan Theater filed this report:

> Despite the fact that it was a fourth run in the zone and that others had played it at 10 and 20 cents, W. A. Steffes booked "Ben Hur" at the Logan for five days, changed to a reserved seat policy at 20 cents straight, and set a new all-time record for the theater. The run could have been extended.[377]

But by mid-1929, three and one-half years after release, even neighborhood showings had been reduced to a trickle as sound and "talkies" were beginning to consume the film industry. A single page of *The Atlanta Constitution* from October 28, 1928, advertises the opening of *Ben-Hur* at the Cameo directly between the opening of *The Melody of Love*, Universal's first "100 per cent talking picture," at Loew's Capitol and Loew's Grand presentation of Al Jolson in *The Jazz Singer*, which co-starred May McAvoy.[378] (Jolson's next sound hit, *The Singing Fool*, co-starred Betty Bronson.) The new technology had penetrated into the old-fashioned neighborhood theaters as well, the showing of *Ben-Hur* at the National Theatre in Boston's South End being sandwiched between *Fancy Baggage,* a film with Vitaphone sound, and four vaudeville acts.[379] Before converting the Capitol Theatre in Cornwall, Ontario, exclusively to "talkers," the manager presented *Ben-Hur* as the first of his "farewell to silent pictures" program.[380] The showings at churches and schools continued, as evidenced further by the showing at Howard University in January, 1930, under the auspices of the school's Committee on Religious Life.[381] Meanwhile the film was also still being shown overseas, where a reprise at Paris's Maillot-Palace warranted a billing in *Le Temps* as "le plus beau film du monde."[382]

Already there was a movement to create a sound version of *Ben-Hur*. In March, 1929, MGM reported that its fan mail preferred two films in particular for "talkifying and sounding," and they were of course *The Big Parade* and *Ben-Hur*.[383] One year later the Associated Press disclosed that "plans were being made" to refilm *Ben-Hur* as a talkie. Despite its original cost and profit-sharing obligation, the film was now reaching the $10 million mark in gross receipts, with foreign sales ongoing.[384] Nonetheless, with the Depression setting in, MGM decided simply to rerelease *Ben-Hur* with "a synchronized score and excursions in sound," much as had been done with *The Birth of a Nation*, by most accounts the most successful film of the silent era, in 1930.[385] No doubt this is what Fred Niblo had recommended, for he, too, had contributed a column in *The Film Daily* to the debate over silent films versus talkies:

> I would suggest that we go in for sound pictures before embarking upon talking pictures. Reproduction of sounds may be very effective. I would have liked sound effects for such scenes in "Ben-Hur" as the galley-fight and the chariot race.[386]

MGM assigned Howard Dietz of its New York office to manage the publicity.[387] He distributed a seven-page pressbook that contained promotional write-ups, reviews, ideas for local publicity, illustrated ads, photographs, and a number of items for sale, including lobby cards, posters, large marquee banners, block letters to line curb, and, significantly, an ad for the Grosset & Dunlap edition of the novel. Typical for the *Ben-Hur* tradition, he specifically targeted churches, schools, and libraries. The copy cemented the claims that 1.9 million feet of film were exposed and 850,000 printed, "more than double the entire footage of *The Big Parade*," that the production employed 150,000 extras, 100,000 in the Antioch Circus alone, and that the sea battle employed 100 ships. Of course there were numerous variations on the fact that this was "the most spectacular and most expensive picture ever made," but new was the validation from the National Board of Review:

> In the opinion of our review group, the revival of this film, which belongs as rightfully among the classics of the screen as General Wallace's novel does among the

classics of literature, has been successfully elaborated with music and sound. As a spectacle it is still one of the most thrilling of its kind, and it is a kind improved rather than hurt by the lack of dialogue. The historical elements which make the bulk of the film are solid and imposing, the fight between the Roman galleys and the pirates, and the chariot race at Antioch, retaining unimpaired their perennial vigor and thrill. The most up-to-date processes have made no improvement on the New Testament sections done in color. The film, which was exceptional when new, is well worth reviving not only for new audiences but for those who, having seen it before, will be surprised how much they like seeing it again.

The synchronized sound version of *Ben-Hur* was released first in London in mid-June, 1931.[388] Mark Forrest in *The Saturday Review* complained that the synchronized score was no improvement over the live orchestral music played during the original roadshow presentations, and that the synchronization, for instance, to the beating of the hortator, was off.[389] He also found the acting style to be a bit artificial and the Technicolor scenes harsh and disruptive to the narrative. However, he has considerable praise for the film when comparing it to current talking films:

> Apart from these criticisms, however, the picture stands out as a great contribution to the cinema; it has action, that essential ingredient of which the talking films have largely deprived the public. "Ben Hur" was seen by over a million people when it was first shown, but if there should be some who have not witnessed the battle of the triremes and the fate of Messala they should rush to have a change from racketeers, American newspaper reporters, gold-diggers and vulgarities.

The reviewer in the *Wall Street Journal* had a similar reaction, describing the film as a study in the transformation of acting styles caused by the use of dialogue, making *Ben-Hur*'s pantomimes of emotion obsolete.[390] A similar analysis by Robert E. Sherwood declared that the five years had brought such "amazing differences in technique that tempo and silence – and subtitles – seem ancient" by comparison.[391] Nonetheless, they all agreed with the reviewer for *The Manchester Guardian*, who named the rerelease of *Ben-Hur* "one of the most interesting cinema events that have happened for some time."[392]

When the sound version of *Ben-Hur* was released in the United States the following December, it evoked a similar kind of curiosity. The reviewer in the *Dallas Morning News* much preferred the sound version of *Ben-Hur* to the sound version of *The Birth of a Nation*, "merely a museum piece."[393] He also compares it favorably to Chaplin's *City Lights*, a silent film produced and released in the sound era, and the sound version of *The Big Parade*, which he describes as more drama and less action and therefore a better test case for the new trend.

As we have seen in this chapter already and elsewhere in the book, the evaluations of critics and public perception were rarely in agreement. But a May, 1932, report from Baton Rouge suggests that audiences felt the same way.[394] The local audience "laughed" at the romantic scenes when

Novarro and McAvoy "made eyes" at each other and expressed their emotions through subtitles, although they found the action scenes as impressive as ever. One of the patrons at the Rialto in New York was Ramon Novarro, who in the meanwhile had established his credentials in sound films by singing "Pagan Love Song," and he said he felt embarrassed and wondered "why the audience wasn't laughing at him strutting and puffing across the screen."[395]

The action scenes evoked an entirely different reaction. Like Forrest, a local writer in Ohio welcomed the opportunity to see thrilling action of the sort that no longer appeared in films:

> At the time of its original release "Ben Hur" came when spectacle was at its highest favor on the screen. It was bigger and better than the others but audiences had been accustomed to things of the same general type. Then the coming of the talkies did away with all this. For years the screen has been concerned with its drama and dialog and it is a thrilling thing to see gigantic spectacle again. ... At times the drama is not as subtle as the work of today, ... but the tremendous spectacle and sweeping action has not been excelled and "Ben Hur" still holds its place as the biggest thing ever brought to the screen.[396]

The published criticisms were not universally disapproving of the refurbishing. *The Billboard* commented that the film "still stands as one of the finest silent pictures ever made" and that the new version improved the viewing:

> The sound actually aided the production vastly, particularly in the choral ensembles, in the grunting and groaning of the galley slaves and the crashing and crunching of the chariot wheels in the big race.[397]

When the film came to the Columbia Theater in Washington, DC, the anonymous account in *The Washington Post* dismissed the Klaw & Erlanger version as ridiculous. He, too, vilified the pantomimic style of the 1925 film but found the old-style action not only refreshing compared to current fare but uniquely exciting, concluding with his identification of the film as a milestone in the history of cinema:

> The rest of the cast has suffered by the half decade or so that has spun away since Lew Wallace's tried and trusted tome was amplified through the lens, and taken once and for all from the ridiculousness of the stage's meager treadmills. The remaining characters are outdated: puppets of the era when each character was armed with a bucket of subtitles and the elocutionary motions of an unsymmetrical windmill.
>
> But what was it that made your hair stand on end when first you saw "Ben Hur"? It was the immemorial size of everything; the seeming millions of people; the greatest race of all time, with the same old-nerve-jangling doubt that Ben-Hur would win, and still-frightening galley slave scenes and eerie Valley of the Lepers shots. They are all here, improved for the greater part by the addition of sound.
>
> If you are among the few who have not seen "Ben Hur," be quick about it. It's more than an outstanding picture. It's a hall-mark, a monumental milestone in the history of moving pictures. It is a revelation, at this late date, not only by dint of its

own greatness, but because it is about the only picture you have seen in three years or so, wherein your eye has been free to roam farther stretches than the corners of a drawing room.[398]

MGM had announced high hopes for the rerelease, but the disappointing reaction to the sound version of *The Big Parade* caused them to hesitate and convinced them to exhibit the new version of *Ben-Hur* in mostly secondary houses.[399] It was still playing at Seattle's Rex Theatre early in 1933, while several churches in Portland held evening showings.[400] It lasted even longer abroad, where the ephemeral record shows that the film was playing in Bombay in 1932,[401] Kingston, Paris and Shanghai in 1933,[402] and Kalgoorlie in southwest Australia in 1934,[403] with periodic revivals in Paris, Bombay, Manchester, and the Hague as late as 1942.[404] As Schallert had pointed out already in 1930, "'Ben Hur' has gone farther in round-the-world distribution probably than any other [film]."[405]

THE IMPACT ON THE FILM INDUSTRY

Ben-Hur remained a high-profile film for many years. As we have just seen, the films produced over the next few years were smaller in terms of scope, budget, length, and, in many instances, familiarity. The technical achievements of the film and the extraordinary ways in which it was exhibited made it exemplary, and the reverent spirit underlying the subject of the film gave it a place in other rare categories. These and other aspects of the 1925 *Ben-Hur* would make the film a standard for reference and comparison as well as a lightning rod for controversy, especially in Italy and China where it could be viewed as both anti-Fascist and anti-revolutionary Christian propaganda.

Of course contemporaries often placed *Ben-Hur* high on their annual lists of best films.[406] Reflecting the film's staggered release schedule, *The Film Daily* poll of 280 screen critics placed it high on their lists for both 1926 and 1927.[407] Over the next few years, the name *Ben-Hur* continued to identify the film's producers, director, players, and crew in their various endeavors. Whether Ramon Novarro was featured as one of the first film vocalists or as an ambitious 33-year-old interested in directing, he was inevitably identified as the star of *Ben-Hur*.[408] Whether Reeves Eason signed on to a Western like *Cimarron* (1931) or a horse racing film like *Racetrack* (1933), he was remembered as the director of the *Ben-Hur* chariot race, and the spectacular land rush opening of the former certainly bears its signature.[409] Even relative trivialities like Niblo's collection of "'Ben Hur' period" furniture that he accumulated while shooting in Italy, or his wife Enid Bennett's European matches tipped in custom colors to match her gowns, kept the name *Ben-Hur* in the newspapers.[410] Three decades after the release of the film, the 1957 *Boston Globe* obituary of Louis B. Mayer lists *Ben-Hur* before any other film, even *The Big Parade*,

Grand Hotel, and *The Wizard of Oz*.[411] The names of the Wallace scions also appeared frequently. After the untimely death of Henry Wallace, his son Lew Wallace, Jr., makes the news when he retires from one Wall Street firm,[412] announces that he will head a new one,[413] and when he buys an exchange seat and receives a round of applause from the floor of the exchange.[414] In these business news articles he is described as "the son [*sic*] of the late General Wallace, author of 'Ben Hur,'" or "grandson of the late General Lew Wallace, author of 'Ben Hur' and famous Indian fighter," or, more accurately as "grandson of Gen. Lew Wallace, author of 'Ben Hur.'" Lew's centenary in 1927 was a serendipitous cause for celebration,[415] and periodically there were brief histories of the *Ben-Hur* property and accounts of "How 'Ben-Hur' was Written,"[416] or accounts of people who came into Wallace's orbit, like the German-born Willi Spiegelberg to whom Wallace showed his original *Ben-Hur* manuscript when they were both working in New Mexico early in 1880.[417] Erlanger's name also resurfaced when he bought film options on both *The Fair God* and *The Prince of India* in 1927, although nothing came of this before he fell ill and passed away in March, 1930.[418]

A few lesser players used the name to advertise themselves. The choreographer Josephine McLean, for instance, included in her press résumé that she staged all the dance numbers for the *Ben-Hur* production in Italy.[419] Eva Farren, one third of The Three Farrons Vaudeville group, traveled to Java, Sumatra, and Singapore before arriving in Shanghai, where, exploiting the popularity of the film there, placed ads in *The China Press* for their "Nights of Gladness." Readers were reminded that she "did her Danse Orientale in 'Ben Hur.'"[420] One write-up claimed:

> Miss Eva Farren is the dancer who, when performing her "Danse Orientale" in Rome was seen by the famous producer, Fred Niblo, and he was so struck by her fine work that he promptly engaged her to go to New York so that this dance could be incorporated in the film of "Ben Hur" which was being made.[421]

As subsequent high-profile films were released in the late 1920s well into the 1930s, they were frequently compared, favorably or unfavorably, to *Ben-Hur*. This was of course true for other Ancients. *The Evening World* published a verbal endorsement for the recent Italian adaptation of *The Last Days of Pompeii* that mentioned *Ben-Hur* five times,[422] and *Ben-Hur* was said to have blazed a trail that led to DeMille's *King of Kings*.[423] As a drama *Ben-Hur* was also compared to DeMille's adaptation of *The Squaw Man*.[424] In adapting John Erskine's novel, First National intended *The Private Life of Helen of Troy* to be "a second 'Ben Hur.'"[425] To make this a reality they hired both Carey Wilson and Horace Jackson for the project. When General Sir Ian Hamilton, Commander of the British expeditionary force at Gallipoli, urged the British film industry to outdo the American by making a film version of Homer's *Iliad*, he specified that the sacrifice of Iphigenia "could easily eclipse the finest scene in 'Ben

Hur.'"[426] And the major press release for the independent Mormon film, *Carianton*, described the religious project "as the successor to 'Ben Hur,'" and Edgar Stillman Kelley was hired to compose the music.[427]

In terms of cost, length of production, and potential profitability, *Ben-Hur* was compared to Howard Hughes' multi-million *Hell's Angels*.[428] The Biltmore in Los Angeles compared the remarkable initial success of *Wings* to that of *Ben-Hur*,[429] and *The Big House* was advertised as "the biggest production since 'Ben Hur' or 'Big Parade.'"[430] Schallert likened the big scenes in Universal's *Uncle Tom's Cabin* (1927) to those in *Ben-Hur*.[431] *Michael Strogroff* was expected to be "bigger than 'Ben Hur.'"[432] MGM claimed that *The Trail of '98* was as "mammoth as 'Ben Hur,'"[433] and the studio also called *The Trail of '98* "as romantic as 'Ben Hur.'"[434] When inventor and theater magnate Ludwig Blattner announced his plans to build a British Hollywood, the future Elstree Studios, he boasted that it would produce any size of production "from a British 'Ben Hur' to a one-act farce."[435] Even when MGM was planning its adaptation of *Quo Vadis?* in 1950, *Ben-Hur* was recalled as the last film to be of such scope, cost, and grandeur.[436]

Because of its origins, size, and success, *Ben-Hur* figured into the most spirited cinematic debates of the day. Even before the Depression set in, the industry debated the merits of small productions versus big, where *Ben-Hur* had established the high-water mark. Both DeMille and Schallert included the film in observing that it was only the epoch-making features that were leaving deep impressions on the industry.[437] Kenneth MacGowan in the *New York Times* emphasized the financial returns in saying that despite their huge costs, films like *Ben-Hur* and *Grand Hotel* "did very nicely in spite of the many scenes and costumes that their producers had to pay for."[438] In fact, this aspect of Loew's investment in a film as costly as *Ben-Hur* even reached the financial pages of *Barron's*.[439] To make the point, after a year without a "big" release, Schallert wrote:

> The screen has the gift of motion; it can portray with magical sweep nature's cataclysms, the hughest tides in human events and affairs, the imaginary and fantastical. Yet only too seldom is this power used to its full advantage.
> The reason is that it costs. The picture that involves the imaginary of the unusual runs to hundreds of thousands of dollars. From "Cabiria" to "Intolerance;" from "Intolerance" to "Robin Hood;" from "Robin Hood" to "The Ten Commandments" and from "The Ten Commandments" to "Ben Hur;" and from "Ben Hur" to "Wings" is a pathway strewn prodigally with gold.
> The lean years of the movies may be identified by their lack of great photographic glamour. . . . yet the golden pathway of the "big show" is by far the screen's most enticing, whether in the now [or] in retrospect. The eye must be satisfied; and it is seemingly only fully satisfied with the production that literally jangles with coin of the realm.[440]

A *Variety* article in 1932 printed the box-office figures.[441] The top three domestic grossing silent films were *The Birth of a Nation* ($10,000,000),

The Big Parade ($6,400,000), and *Ben Hur* ($5,500,000). Later, including overseas sales, reports were that *Ben-Hur* generated over $11 million.[442] Publicity for the 1959 *Ben-Hur* usually reported the figure as $9.3 million.[443] Decades later, the Eddie Mannix ledgers were made available through the Herrick Library, and they contained more precise figures.[444] The production cost $3,967,000, had a domestic gross of $4,359,000, and an international gross of $5,027,000, for a total of $9,386,000. The synchronized sound rerelease cost $36,000 and earned only $199,000 domestically but another $1,153,000 abroad, for a total of $10,738,000, the largest worldwide gross until *Gone With the Wind* replaced it at the end of the 1930s. Because of the original contract with Erlanger, the initial release lost $698,000. With the sound rerelease the film earned a profit of $81,000. Undoubtedly MGM accountants calculated slightly different numbers, but the bottom line certainly seems to be that *Ben-Hur* cost more to produce and generated a larger gross than any film of the silent era.

Other debates that featured *Ben-Hur* were those over the merits and finances of the roadshow for "superproductions,"[445] prologues,[446] literary adaptations,[447] synchronized sound and talkies,[448] Technicolor,[449] historical films,[450] and religious films.[451] Ed Sullivan's 1938 feature article on screen rights said that Lew Wallace "tops all authors in a single picture revenue," estimating that the Wallace estate garnered close to $2 million.[452] The article includes pictures of both Ramon Novarro as charioteer and Lew Wallace, with the caption: "Gen. Lew Wallace's book holds the record for movie earnings."

The prominence of the film also made it a magnet for controversy. The Westerner's Protective Association, an organization of cowboy motion picture actors and extras, lodged a formal protest against the United States government for allowing the film industry to employ active troops.[453] Their complaint charged that the troops from the Presidio in Monterey were illegally dressed in Roman costumes instead of their regulation uniforms, and that they were riding trained government horses and using government equipment, exposing federal property to risks in private enterprise, and keeping their members out of work. They also claimed that the members of their organization were responsible for the success of such films as *Ben-Hur* and *Beau Geste*. As a result, Brigadier General Lutz Wahl, the Adjutant General of the U.S. Army, issued an order forbidding his post commanders from lending troops to moving picture companies.[454]

In England the "Quota Bill," as the 1927 Film Bill in the House of Commons was known colloquially, addressed the common practice of "blockbooking" that allowed American films "of the vulgar and knockabout sort" to dominate the local market, but *Ben-Hur*, *Beau Geste*, and *What Price Glory?* were exempted from the restrictions.[455] A controversy erupted in July, 1931, over showing "sex-appeal" films on Sunday.[456] The consensus in the House of Commons gravitated towards "films of religious or instructive character," and *Ben-Hur* was cited as a commercial film that might be allowed. Lord Eustace Percy evoked laughter from the members when he mused that "the result would be to invite kinema magnates to produce semi-Biblical films like 'Ben Hur,' and I suppose there would be a film of David and Bathsheba." Similarly, in 1931 Thomas Ince's 1916 film *Civilization* was banned by the Entertainments Committee of the London Council Committee for its representation of Christ.[457] *Ben-Hur* was not banned, of course, because of its tactful representation, although DeMille's *King of Kings*, inexplicably, according to *The Manchester Guardian* report, was not banned either.

There were more profound controversies on the Continent. In France there was a movement to exclude foreign pictures altogether.[458] In Poland, when the film was playing at the Cinema Apollo in Bialystok in January, 1927, it was denounced in one of the city's many synagogues as "an insult to the Jewish race," inciting a riotous crowd of several thousand Orthodox Jews to storm the theater, beat the Jewish manager, and burn the film in a bonfire in the street.[459] Reportedly the theater itself was burned to the ground.[460] In Italy the government had made a show of their appreciation for the production by presenting Harry Edington with the official decoration of Cavaliere of the Order of the Crown of Italy in 1926. Receiving the honor at his office in Hollywood, Edington described Mussolini as "the greatest man Europe has seen in many ages."[461] Later the Italian release of the film was delayed by several pending lawsuits against Metro-Goldwyn-Mayer, and then two weeks after the Christmas Eve premiere at twenty-four theaters, the police suspended further performances and confiscated the prints, excepting only the houses that were showing the film for charitable purposes.[462] No official explanation was issued, but foreign correspondents surmised that Fascist officials in the Ministry of the Interior were offended by the unfavorable light in which Messala and the ancient Romans were portrayed.[463] Shortly thereafter Mussolini revoked the ban and ordered the prints to be returned to the theaters, albeit disallowing any additional engagements.[464] In China, where *Ben-Hur* had been playing so successfully in Shanghai, the film was reportedly banned in Canton, the center of Kuomintang control during a period of considerable political, religious, and ethnic turmoil.[465] A more reliable report specifies that the Bureau of Education ordered only "objectionable and superstitious" parts of the film to be removed, namely, all the miraculous Christian scenes, including the Star of Bethlehem at the beginning of the film and the resurrection of the child, the curing of the lepers, and the earthquake near the end of the film.[466] Addressing both the objectionable theology and the cinematic power of *Ben-Hur*, the official statement from the Bureau was as follows:

These things are not only absurd and fictitious but also tend to beguile people to believe in superstition. Moving pictures such as "Ben Hur" have a powerful effect on social education. They tend to undermine social progress and promote superstition. The whole picture is nothing but Christian propaganda, absurd in the extreme.

ARTISTIC AND CULTURAL IMPACTS

The Novel

The MGM film adaptation of *Ben-Hur* re-energized the *Ben-Hur* phenomenon, beginning with the novel itself. Harper included photos of the MGM 1925 "photoplay" in its reissue of the 1922 edition of the novel, wrapped in the illustrated dust jacket from the Sears release. Sears put Wallace's novel back in its catalogue. Both Harper & Brothers and Grosset & Dunlap authorized an educational pamphlet that included the text of Wallace's chariot race from the latter's edition along with a black-and-white version of the Checa painting, and two photographs from the film. This was distributed at theaters and "specially designed for the use of pupils who are chosen each week for individual recitations before the assembled classes." However, the front cover makes it clear that this could be used "only for recitations. Amateur entertainments or performances in which this material is used must not be presented." Libraries monitored the increase in popularity of *Ben-Hur*. Eleanor Ledbetter, an official representing the American Library Association said specifically that "The 'Ben-Hur' film has greatly increased the demand for that work in all languages in American libraries."[467] Three years later the A.L.A. endorsed the novel's inclusion in the Friendship Book Lists published in *The Christian Science Monitor*.[468] Across the Atlantic, Herbert Alden, Chairman of Simpkin, Marshall and Company, described the "tremendous demand" for the novel in England after a recent lull.[469]

The popularity of the novel was being continued in the younger generation as well. A 1927 poll of high-school students taken by *Current Literature* and reported in the *New York Times* found *Ben-Hur* to be one of the books they considered to be the most influential, behind *Little Women*, the Bible, *Pilgrim's Progress*, Helen Keller's *Story of My Life*, Eleanor Porter's *Pollyanna*, and two others less remembered today, and the next year *The Atlanta Constitution* reported that the principal of a private school in Atlanta listed *Ben-Hur* as one of the most desirable novels for her school library.[470] A survey taken among Pittsburgh school teenagers from 1928–31 confirmed the continuing popularity of Wallace's novel, albeit behind *Treasure Island* and *Ivanhoe*.[471] In 1929 an English professor writing in a professional teaching journal prescribed *Ben-Hur* for students at technical high schools, calling it a fine example of "thrilling adventure."[472] Reading these tea leaves, in 1928 Harper & Brothers released its new edition of the novel, *The Boys' Ben-Hur: A Tale of the Christ*.[473] Targeting juvenile readers, this edition was illustrated and abridged by Virginia Kirkus, who at the time was the children's books editor at Harper. This was the edition of the novel that was also sold directly by the Tribe of Ben-Hur. Coincidentally, The Tribe of Ben-Hur was itself making headlines at the time because John C. Snyder was currently serving as president of the National Fraternal Congress of America.[474]

Writing an essay for the *Los Angeles Times* in February, 1929, J. A. Graves offered his view of the roaring twenties by reflecting upon a quote from Wallace's novel (4.11), where Simonides says to Malluch:

> The curse of the time is prodigality. The poor make themselves poorer as apes of the rich, and the merely rich carry themselves like princes.[475]

Even Walt Mason's 1929 essay assailing popular novels and describing *Ben-Hur* as a "waste of precious time," admitted:

> Year after year this "Ben Hur" sells to children, matrons, graybeards, belles, to folks in robes and rags; best sellers have their little day, from time to time, and fade away, but "Ben Hur" never sags.[476]

Henry James Forman's 1934 book, *Our Movie Made Children*, examining the influence filmed novels had on young people declared that a film like *Ben-Hur* had a "powerful effect ... and a proportional influence upon their conduct."[477] He quoted one young man who said that seeing the film three times inspired him to live "an unselfish, self-sacrificing life," albeit only for two or three weeks afterwards.

The renewed popularity of Wallace's novel continued the processes of transforming the author from a living artist to a legend of the past, his famous protagonist from a literary character into a historical figure, and his novel from a very popular book to a classic. The *New York Times* preserves examples of all three. A travel piece on Constantinople corroborates the misconception that Wallace's inspiration for the chariot race came from his on-site examination of the ruins of the Hippodrome, and another on Antioch states:

> The outstanding feature of the new city was the four-mile main street that connected the east and west gates. On each side rose double rows of lofty marble columns between which Ben Hur drove his chariot and Caesar paraded in triumph.[478]

And a previously cited Bertram Reinitz piece on cigar-factory readers singled out *Ben-Hur* as "having the greatest vogue of any book" that was read out loud to factory workers.[479] Similarly, the *Boston Globe* contained a travel piece on Santa Fe in which the author suggests that Wallace was appointed to the governorship in Santa Fe specifically to finish his novel and that "the Mexican *carretas* thundering around the plaza" were the inspiration for the chariot race.[480]

Just as the initial success of *Ben-Hur: A Tale of the Christ* inspired other authors to write similar paleo-Christian novels, the production of the film seems to have inspired Edmund H. Sears' *Zatthu: A Tale of Ancient Galilee*, published in 1925. The *New York Times* advertised the story about "the unrest of the Jewish people under Roman rule and vividly narrates the exciting experiences of a would-be deliverer . . . who becomes a follower of Jesus of Nazareth."[481] The review in the *Brooklyn Daily Eagle* made the obvious comparison to *Ben-Hur*. Sears had listed a similar novel, *The Son of the Prefect: A Story of the Reign of Tiberius*, in 1914, the year after the million volumes of *Ben-Hur: A Tale of the Christ* were sold to Sears, Roebuck and Company. The introduction of another new novel, Louis Tucker's *When He Came to Himself*, published in 1928, specifically cited *Ben-Hur* and informs his readers that his book is "a tribute to the genius of General Lew Wallace" and that his plot was deliberately parallel to that of Wallace's novel.[482] Both protagonists go to Rome and then the Syrian province and come upon the Messiah. Quoting the author and then adding their own observation, the *New York Times* explains one obvious difference:

> "The divergence is due to the difference in character of the two men." Also there is no chariot race![483]

In 1930 William L. Beaumont published *Ben Ezra; Or, The Midnight Cry*.[484] This was "intended to be a sequel to *Ben-Hur*."[485]

Drama, Film and Music
The film also inspired a number of artistic creations and performances, the grandest of which was the Hollywood Art Theater's production of Shakespeare's *Julius Caesar* at the Hollywood Bowl in September, 1926. The stage setting was reportedly a city block in width, and when Julius Caesar triumphantly entered at the Feast of the Lupercal (1.2), he rode the chariot and drove the white horses Novarro had used for the race one year earlier.[486] This performance took place at the same time as the very successful Biltmore engagement, and some of that same vociferous enthusiasm was heard at the Hollywood Bowl:

> Most of the costumes, the paraphernalia and other impediments of the production came from the same source, wherefore they were authentic and impressive. Because of the bigness of the scheme it easily aroused enthusiasm among the audience with frequent bursts of applause and even some cheering.

The review published in the *New York Times* described the triumphal entry of Caesar as "one of the features of the evening."[487] It was not coincidental that the role of Marcus Antonius was played by William Farnum. He was a charter member of the Hollywood Theater Arts Alliance.[488] It may have been coincidence, however, that the ad for the production in the *Los Angeles Times* sat right above the ad for the Biltmore *Ben-Hur*.[489]

Just over one month later, on November 1, 1926, Bud Fisher, the cartoonist who created Mutt and Jeff and, in his private life, was a successful racehorse owner, released *A Roman Scandal*, a seven-minute cartoon version of an imperial Roman chariot race. It has a number of allusions to the race in *Ben-Hur* including a wager, which in this instance is for the entire empire. During the race the "Ben-Hur" figure, Jeff, driving white horses, has to use a variety of innovative strategies to compete, like pulling his own chariot and dividing it in half to go around the impeding champion. Then the Messala figure, who drives black horses, begins whipping Jeff, much as in the MGM film. Here, though, Jeff ultimately wraps and ties Messala up in the whip and tosses him out of the chariot. Emperor Mutt takes the reigns, and to defeat him Jeff puts up a sail and floats to victory, but not before there is the obligatory *Ben-Hur* crash at the penultimate turn.

In live-action film, Zion Myers, Carmel's brother, and Jules White, later of The Three Stooges fame, were developing a series of comedy shortfilm "barkies" for Metro-Goldwyn-Mayer designed to parody high-profile Hollywood films. They listed as one of their projects a parody of *Ben-Hur*, but it does not seem to have been made.[490] The live stage offered the Ben Hur Ponies in 1929. This was part of George Washington Dewey's Vaudeville act, "They're Off."[491] Details are sparse, but the advance ads stated that "a real race will be run on a revolving stage."[492]

The film also inspired a new entry into the list of many musical works resulting from the *Ben-Hur* phenomenon. José Armándola's "Ben-Hur Marsche" in E♭, is a German march published in 1926, not surprising considering the gala opening and grand reception given to the film in Berlin in September of that year. Indeed, the wording under the title on the colorful cover of the sheet music, featuring a charging chariot pulled by white horses, states specifically (in German) that the work "was inspired by the presentation of Metro-Goldwyn-Mayer's film 'Ben-Hur.'"[493] On the left side of the chariot is the logo of Metro-Goldwyn-Mayer, on the right the logo of Parufamet. Of course, the Axt-Mendoza score was published at the time, too.[494] Axt also adapted his score in the "Capitol Photoplay Series" published by Robbins Music Corporation of New York, including "The Toilers. ... Originally introduced in the N. Y. presentation 'Ben-Hur.'"[495]

Radio
Radio as a regular form of popular entertainment flourished in the mid-1920s just as *Ben-Hur* was playing its first roadshows. This new medium naturally accommodated local and network *Ben-Hur* programming, whether the impetus came from MGM personnel as a means of advertising their film or their players, or from unassociated artists newly inspired by the story and imagery of *Ben-Hur*. Because the scope of the *Ben-Hur* phenomenon was so broad, there was room for a variety of programming in different formats.

Original local programming designed to advertise the popular film adaptation of *Ben-Hur* found a perfect outlet in the aforementioned radio program in which an announcer for KSL in Salt Lake broadcast his description of the film live over the radio.[496] MGM's Major Bowes, acting as the manager of New York's Capitol Theatre, exploited radio's capacity as an aural medium by creating a Sunday evening broadcast concert of the Axt-Mendoza incidental music scored for the film, played by 193 musicians in his theater.[497] Meanwhile MGM's youngest representative, their "Million Dollar Baby" 6-year-old Joyce Coad, read juvenile versions of *Peter Pan* and *Little Red Riding Hood* over the radio in 1925 and 1926, and she was reportedly preparing a version of *Ben-Hur* in 1926 for KHJ in Los Angeles.[498] Whether that materialized or not, MGM publicity spread around the story that she was the guest of Francis X. Bushman at the filming of the chariot race "and was so thrilled with the picture that she decided to tell the whole world about it."[499] Bushman himself reprised the various characters he had portrayed in his nearly 400 films, beginning with Messala, in a series of ten programs for WBZ of Boston.[500] This turned out to be the inaugural of a radio career for Bushman that would serve him well into the next decade.[501] Similarly, Ben Mears, who had played Simonides in the Klaw & Erlanger production, performed on WOR in New York. For both actors newspaper descriptions usually recalled their roles in *Ben-Hur*.[502]

On several occasions this new delivery system supplemented the hundreds of live *Ben-Hur* readings that had been offered in schools, churches, and auditoriums for the past four decades. WPCH in Boston offered "a treat for listeners" when actor A. Winfield Hoeny offered a "vivid verbal description" of the chariot race from *Ben-Hur* "taken from the play by Lew Wallace."[503] A harpist accompanied his presentation. A few years later Charles Frederick Lindsley, a professor of public speaking at Occidental College and part-time actor, gave a similar reading, now with an organ accompaniment, on KHJ in Los Angeles.[504] Christmas was represented on WEAF in New York which had a Broadway performer, Lucille Husting, read "The Birth of Christ" from *Ben-Hur* on Christmas Eve at 4:45 p.m.[505] *The Manchester Guardian* reports a similar type of reading in London, where fifteen minutes of programming in June, 1927, was allotted to actress and radio narrator Dorothy Freshwater's reading of "The Chariot Race from 'Ben Hur.'"[506] More ambitious was WEAF in Baltimore. After a radio performance of Shakespeare's *Julius Caesar* in October, 1926, *The Sun* announced that "Ben Hur" was one of the productions they were planning for the near future, although there is no subsequent notice in the paper archives.[507]

Representing the educational aspect of the *Ben-Hur* tradition was a 1931 KHJ broadcast of Columbia's "American School of the Air."[508] This was in the second year of the series that had commenced in February, 1930, with fifteen half-hour radio broadcasts about literature and culture financed by the Columbia Broadcasting System and the Grigsby-Grunow radio manufacturing company, and approved by the Secretary of the Department of the Interior and the Federal Commissioner of Education.[509] The broadcasts were supplemented with a printed *Teacher's Guide and Manual* that was sent upon request, and an integral part of this interactive program was to have students and faculty write letters back to Columbia for evaluation.

Radio musical programming periodically revived some of the old music that the novel had inspired. A rendition of Paull's "Ben Hur Chariot Race March" was played on the Acousticon Hour by WEEI in Boston.[510] The theme of the show was the horse, recalling "the good old days when hitching racks were as common as traffic lights are today – a musical memorial to a good and faithful servant of 25 years ago." Paull's march was featured on WEEI for the Jenney Concert the following year by Walter Smith and his band.[511] A "Chariot Race" from *Ben-Hur* was also played for a radio recital in Adelaide, but the newspaper announcement does not specify which one.[512]

Radio also inspired some novelty *Ben-Hur* programming. At the local level there are printed schedules that include a program that ran for at least four weeks during the winter of 1928/9 on WCLB of Long Beach, Long Island. They list the otherwise unknown "Prince Ben Hur, Mental Genius," who came on the air at 7:00 p.m. on a Saturday or Sunday night for one hour.[513] A little more information survives about the *Ben-Hur* "spectacle" played during the Halsey Street Playhouse on WOR in New York in December, 1928.[514] This was a parody of the chariot race with "several novelties arranged" by station manager Leonard E. L. Cox, whose other productions included "Custer's Last Stand" and "Napoleon's Retreat From Moscow."[515] At the network level, two years after he had broadcast the 1928 World Series for NBC, sports announcer (and future executive) Phillips Carlin provided the lead voice for "Ben Hur Drives a Mean Chariot," another humorous rendition of the chariot race.[516] This was the premiere of "Hysterical Sportcasts," a series of broadcasts burlesquing sporting events in history, sponsored by the Hickok Manufacturing Company.[517] This sketch was broadcast Friday evening, May 16, 1930, at 8:30 p.m. from WJZ in New York and carried to numerous affiliates on the NBC network. The ad in the *Chicago Daily Tribune* said simply, "It's a scream." In Baltimore *The Sun* had a lengthier write up that included a number of sports metaphors and chronological anachronisms:

> The program will feature Phillips Carlin in detailed descriptions of ancient sports in modern fashion.
> "Ben Hur Drives a Mean Chariot" has been chosen as the subject of the premiere broadcast. It will be nothing less than wheel-by-wheel description of the famous race between Ben Hur and Messala, which took place at Antioch, Ben's home grounds, on June 14, 305 A.D.

Radio audiences will hear the heroes cheered, the pounding of horses' hoofs, and when the race is over the victor will say a few words to listeners.

The premiere broadcast will be introduced by Raymond Knight, while incidental music is to be furnished by an orchestra directed by Joe Rines.[518]

Another radio parody of chariot racing appeared in San Francisco, where the "Cecil and Sally" radio show, produced from 1928 to 1933, starred Johnny Patrick [aka John Patrick Goggan], as Cecil. Cecil's car was named, aptly, Ben-Hur.

Chariot Racing

As we are seeing, the 1925 film bolstered especially the continuing renown of the *Ben-Hur* chariot race. Now a generation past the regular use of horses for transportation, the general populace found use for chariot race imagery as a popular metaphor, and it inspired a number of people in several different countries to involve themselves in actual chariot races of various sorts. In the theatrical world, references to the Klaw & Erlanger treadmill still arose whenever a production included horses. "The World's Greatest Entertainer" in 1926 was Al Jolson, and the publicity for his new musical show *Big Boy*, where in black face he plays the role of a stable boy who rides the winner in the Kentucky Derby, serves as an excellent example. A December, 1926, pre-publicity write-up in *The Washington Post* concludes with a brief description of the "most outstanding feature" of the production, "the track scene in which four thoroughbreds compete in the most thrilling stage race since "Ben Hur."[519] When the production moved to the West Coast more than five months later, these same words were echoed by the *Los Angeles Times*.[520] And with good reason: one of the horses they used was from the Ben Hur Stables in New York and a stage veteran of twenty-four years, no doubt having done service for the Klaw & Erlanger *Ben-Hur*.[521] For comparison, in January, 1927, before the Jolson show moved to Los Angeles, Fox Pictures released a new Tom Mix Western, *The Last Trail*, based on the 1909 novel by Zane Gray. The film reviewer in *The Christian Science Monitor* clearly references the MGM *Ben-Hur* chariot race in his description, as does the film itself with its exciting stagecoach race:

> "The Last Trail" is distinguished by a regular Ben-Hur finale, with the open desert serving as Circus Maximus, Mr. Mix as Hur, and a typical Deadwood stagecoach as chariot. A race has been arranged to prove the relative merits of the local stage drivers, and a half dozen four horse outfits take part.[522]

Actual chariot races and imitations popped up seemingly everywhere, beginning in Los Angeles on February 4, 1926. That year the "WAMPAS Frolic," the annual celebration hosted by the Western Association of Motion Picture Advertisers, was held at the Shrine, which featured what was claimed to be the largest stage in the world.[523] That made it possible to bring in the horses and chariots from *Ben-Hur*, and there, under the direction of Sid Grauman, as the publicity in the *Los Angeles Times* promised, "one of the big moments in the chariot race between Ben Hur and Messala will be reproduced with the addition of numerous thrills."

In 1927 chariot races were held at more unusual venues. In June, Griffith Stadium, home of the Washington Senators as well as the annual Masonic and Eastern Star field day, featured a chariot race with Nick Altrock, the long-term coach of the Senators, dressed in charioteer attire along with his usual baseball socks and cleats.[524] There were 24,000 people in attendance. In Paris, not only did the Madeleine management send a chariot out into busy traffic every day to advertise the film,[525] but in August ten young girls rigged up teams of "fuzzy poodle dogs to tiny wicker chariots" and held a chariot race driven by Ramon Novarro dolls.[526] Metaphors also appeared in various contexts. In September, Frank Getty described the last days of the 1927 National League pennant race as "nearly neck and neck as the four horses of Ben Hur's chariot,"[527] and when newsreel cameras came to the Georgia Tech football practice two weeks later, the team "reproduced the scene of the chariot race from Ben Hur – but Bill [Fincher] used seven linemen as horses and a bucking dummy for a chariot."[528] One month later a pageant of students in the streets of Dublin, Ireland, recreated chariots with "cabs and jaunting cars" to head the procession to the Parnell Monument.[529] While some of these instances are local and relatively trivial, they still require someone to think up a *Ben-Hur* chariot allusion, others to join in, and then make enough splash for the press to cover it, fully appreciating on their own the *Ben-Hur* imagery. And, as often, there are not just one or two examples but many over a course of several years.

In 1928 the fever seemed to strike Great Britain, where the queen purchased a model of the *Ben-Hur* chariot as a gift for the royal children.[530] Anne St. John, a 15-year-old contestant in the 1928 Royal Drawing Society competition for children, won a prize for her studies of horses. When asked about her inspiration, she replied that it was images from the circus and the "Ben Hur" chariot race.[531] In May "the smallest ponies in the world," Lizzie and Bronte, were cheered by 10,000 people attending the opening of the 45th Royal Tournament as they were hitched to the 17/21st Lancers' chariot covered on both sides with large letters spelling the name "Ben Hur."[532] A political issue arose in County Clare, Ireland, where the Board of Health brought public attention "to the 'chariot races' now being held along most of their public roads,"[533] referring to rival bus companies racing against one another. At the end of the year a report was circulating in England that chariot racing might become an official sport.[534] When asked about the rumors, an unnamed official of the British Dirt Track Racing Association said that the present tracks were too narrow to accommodate such "wild horse shows" with four chariots and eight horses trying to round a bend at the same time. No doubt referring to the

1925 MGM *Ben-Hur*, the report concludes: "And, after all, the 'pictures' do these things infinitely better."

Back in the United States, at the end of August the annual Asbury Park baby parade, admired by a reported 150,000 spectators, saw the Princess Cinderella Prize awarded to Robert Bates, the 4-year-old son of a Jersey City family, dressed as the charioteer Ben-Hur.[535] The following month paired Governor Fred B. Balzar of Nevada against Lieutenant Governor Morley Griswold in a chariot race at a rodeo.[536] Harry Crocker spent some of his family fortune collecting film memorabilia for a private museum in Hollywood, and in the front window he placed one of the model galleys from *Ben-Hur*, and in the center of the floor was Ben-Hur's chariot.[537] No wonder the book editor of *The Youth's Companion* in the same period praised *The Boys' Ben-Hur* for offering "the most famous race in the history of the world."[538] It was coincidence – but rather fitting – that the Ben Hur mine near Tonopah, Nevada, was concurrently producing increasing amounts of gold and silver.[539]

The same years produced print and conceptual allusions to chariot racing, most notably in a lengthy feature piece in the *New York Times*, signed by author and critic R[obert] L[uther] Duffus.[540] There he writes that the competition between General Motors and Ford has been "as spectacular as the chariot race in 'Ben-Hur'" and continues the allusion for several paragraphs as he describes the companies vying for the lead in automotive output. In April, 1927, the Rogers Peet Company placed a cartoon ad in the *Boston Globe* depicting a chariot driving into a columned building with the inscription "R-P" above, the purpose, as the copy explains, to pick up his new spring clothing.[541] The text begins:

> If Ben Hur were driving today, we'd suggest he change his last name to Hurry and quickly drive his chariot in here for his chauffeurs' Spring livery.

Still another example was the focus of an advertisement for Oboy Bread, sold by the Stone Baking Company.[542] Their large ad begins with the caption, "The Oboy Gang – THEY DRAMATIZE THE CHARIOT RACE FROM "BEN HUR." The cartoon below has two children's wagons, both ridden by girls who hold poles from which dangle loaves of Oboy Bread in front of the two boys eagerly pulling the wagons to catch up to the loaves.

A chariot race parody committed to print in 1927 resembled some of the radio parodies discussed above. H. I. Phillips devoted his entire column in the *Boston Globe* to reporting on the "Big Chariot Race Scandal."[543] He joked throughout by claiming that Ben Hur and Messala had been barred from circuses everywhere because the Corinthian Commissioner of Public Games had discovered in a "sweeping probe" that their race was fixed, that the two competitors were actually good friends and spent much time together, and that Messala's chariot had been fitted in advance with a defective axle. Coincidentally, a future issue of *Photoplay* included a photograph of Messala's wrecked chariot in the film along with a caption explaining that the axle "was sawed with careful calculation to break at the turn."[544]

Allusions to physical chariot racing continued into 1929 and 1930 when the film was only rarely being exhibited. The National Motor Board Show in New York in January, 1929, included a ski-board propelled by an outboard motor. *The Atlanta Constitution* depicted two of them with riders and printed the caption, "Ben Hur's Race Modernized."[545] One month later *The Manchester Guardian* likened motorcycle racers to Ben-Hurs.[546] Baltimore's newly appointed coroner assigned specifically to automobile accidents wrote a lengthy essay in *The Sun* urging his fellow citizens to halt the "Daily Race of Death" and, especially when making turns, "slow down considerably, and if need be stop, rather than wheel around the corner like Ben Hur's chariot."[547] A photo of mule chariot races with the caption, "BEN HUR A LA MISSOURI" appeared in the *Chicago Daily Tribune* in January, 1930.[548] When Dartmouth College celebrated its Winter Carnival in February, 1930, the winners of the team races were said to have skied "skillfully in Ben Hur fashion."[549] In covering the opening day of the Bay State horse racing circuit the following June, Frank G. Trott in the *Boston Globe* began, "Horse racing has come down through the centuries from Ben Hur's time with its major appeal unchanged."[550] In the late summer the mayor of Boston organized a fair to educate the city's youth on the danger of automobile traffic.[551] The first and largest photo in the *Boston Globe*'s coverage was of a chariot race in which boys pulled the chariots driven by charioteers named Nero, Caesar, and Ben Hur. Even in 1932 we find the *Globe* adding a caption to a photo of a young man driving a sled pulled by two dogs that says: "Roxbury 'Ben Hur' and His Dog Chariot."[552] Also making international headlines that year was a British sculpture made entirely of colored sugar reconstructing the *Ben-Hur* chariot race.[553] It was displayed at the Confectioners and Bakers Exhibition held at the Agricultural Hall in London.[554] And a 1932 Mack Sennett short, *Speed in the Gay Nineties*, which featured a primitive automobile race, includes a verbal allusion to Ben-Hur.

After the first few months of 1932, the decreased visibility of the sound version diminished its impact on contemporary popular culture. But as late as March, 1932, the *Los Angeles Times* ran a large action photo of the chariot race with the caption:

> Will you ever forget the chariot race in "Ben Hur," with Ramon Novarro enacting the title role? It provided one of the most exciting scenes in screen history.[555]

Ben-Hur was represented in racing without a chariot, too, as one new horse named Ben Hur was entered into thoroughbred races on each coast over several years.[556] One show horse at least was an Arabian,[557] and the lineage of a prize-winning show horse and a dog as well is traced to a Ben

Hur.⁵⁵⁸ This was true also overseas, where an Irish "jumping horse,"⁵⁵⁹ an Irish blue terrier,⁵⁶⁰ and a Tasmanian thoroughbred – all named Ben Hur – appeared during this period.⁵⁶¹ The association between horse racing without chariots and Ben-Hur was easily made and, as we have seen, already part of the cultural tradition. In an article describing the new three-decked clubhouse at Saratoga Springs, New York, W. J. Macbeth described the local press agent as being "familiar with every course and every horse since Ben Hur got away with his foul against the patrician Messila [sic]."⁵⁶² Along the same lines, when greyhound races were introduced in Tijuana in 1927, an advertisement in the *Los Angeles Times* called upon that city's frequently demonstrated interest in all things Ben-Hur:

> When Ben-Hur made chariot-race history, dog racing was already a famous pastime. Starting July 2nd at Tijuana this royal and ancient sport will be staged in renewed glory for 64 days by the nation's largest and fastest field of racing greyhounds.⁵⁶³

Nostalgia

Although the film is set in the ancient world, the modernity of the production sometimes evoked a nostalgia for the Klaw & Erlanger production and the earlier days of the *Ben-Hur* phenomenon. This was in addition to the dozens of comparisons between the new film and the old stage play written up in pre-publicity and reviews of the film. A 1930 article in the *New York Herald Tribune* recalled the old Ben Hur Stables on Seventh Avenue,⁵⁶⁴ and another in 1932 sang the praises of the horse Althea, a thespian of twenty-three years that "made her stage debut as one of the three white steeds harnessed to the chariot of Ben Hur in the play of that name."⁵⁶⁵ The article says that at the time her name was changed to Katie, but neither name is recalled in other lists of the names of the horses used in the Klaw & Erlanger production. This nostalgia was heightened with the sale and demolition of two monuments of the bygone era, the Ben Hur Hotel on City Island and the Broadway Theatre.⁵⁶⁶ On January 2, 1929, the Broadway Theatre, where *Ben-Hur* premiered in November, 1899, went dark.⁵⁶⁷ It was scheduled for demolition and to be replaced by a 33-story skyscraper. The *New York Times* began reporting on this in May, 1927, when the theater was purchased for a reported $1 million.⁵⁶⁸ Each report recalled the production of *Ben-Hur* as a monument of its history, for example:

> The theatre opened in 1888 with the first American production of "La Tosca." On its stage Edwin Booth and Sir Henry Irving made their farewell Broadway appearances. One of the biggest attractions to be staged there was "Ben Hur."⁵⁶⁹

> "Ben Hur" was quite an undertaking – forty stage carpenters, ten property men and ten clearers were required to handle the production, and there were eighty singers and 180 extra people on the stage at every performance.⁵⁷⁰

The nostalgia incorporated other elements of the *Ben-Hur* phenomenon, beginning with the success of the original novel. An essay by novelist and literary critic Malcolm Cowley in 1930 lamented the state of the current book market.[571] After a one paragraph introduction, he delves immediately into the success of *Ben-Hur*, citing the statistics that by the 1890s it had already sold one million copies and that it was purchased by one family out of every thirteen in the nation. He adds that contemporary publishers would consider such numbers "almost fabulous" and that the most successful book of the past decade, Sinclair Lewis's *Main Street*, had sold fewer than 600,000 copies. The following year the *Los Angeles Times* thought it newsworthy to report that a first edition of Wallace's novel was now worth as much as $400–$500.[572] Examples of thoughts of yesteryear for other Ben-Hur items include a syndicated 1929 retrospective of old automobile manufacturers that recalled the "fanciful" name of the 1916/17 Ben Hur,[573] and a detailed description of New York's "Great White Way" and the electric "Ben Hur Chariot Race" above the Hotel Normandie.[574] The latter was published in Ireland, and at approximately the same time the British Beltona Records released a recording of the Paull march.[575]

COMMERCIAL SYNERGIES

By the mid-1920s, some of the kinds of business synergies that the *Ben-Hur* phenomenon had been commercially pioneering and legally challenging for decades had become common practice. It was now the norm for the dramatic rights of a novel to be sold for theatrical and cinematic adaptation, although rarely both, and rarely with as much faithfulness to the original as to *Ben-Hur: A Tale of the Christ*. In one of the early issues of H. L. Mencken's *American Mercury*, he observed the effects of this transformation, naming *Ben-Hur* as one of the paragons of the commercially successful novel.[576] And it had become common for literary, theatrical, and cinematic properties to advertise aggressively, and companies eagerly looked for luminaries and stars to endorse their products. *Ben-Hur* was not unique in having printed programs or tobacco and trading cards associated with the release of the film. Similarly, the Ben Hur Movie-Land Puzzle issued by Milton Bradley in 1926 and the Ben Hur Pastimes Puzzle issued by Parker Bros. in 1934 do not make *Ben-Hur* a unique film, although the former was a very early entry into the movie-picture image puzzle craze of the Depression era.[577]

Ben-Hur was, however, a uniquely proud name that represented a tradition of success and righteousness, ripe for the taking by new business concerns, and maintained by some of the thriving Ben-Hur companies, brands, and products that had formed in the previous decades. No other cinematic property had that kind of applicability, certainly not its comparably profitable cinematic competitors like *The Birth of a Nation*, *The Big Parade*, *Way Down East*, *The Ten Commandments*, *The King of Kings*, and *Wings*, which were limited in this by the nature of their plots and were either new fiction, war stories, or biblical tales that did not lend themselves so easily to commercial applications. In addition, none of these properties were created by a nearly contemporary author so admired as Lew Wallace. For instance, Wanamaker's placed a column-one ad in the *New York Times* during the 1928 Christmas season.[578] It consisted entirely of quotations about motherhood "From the Founder's Writings," that is, from John Wanamaker, and the third of three paragraphs includes a quotation from *Ben-Hur: A Tale of the Christ* (4.9):

> President Harrison's old Indiana friend, Lew Wallace, who wrote "Ben Hur," once said: "God may have thought He could not be everywhere, there He made mothers."

Jergens created the most explicit advertising synergies with the 1925 film. In Boston, the initial appearance of publicity for the film's engagement at the Colonial Theater coincided with an ad for Jergen's Ben-Hur Talcum Powder in the *Boston Daily Globe*.[579] That was nearly inevitable because of the frequency of the Jergens ads. But almost as soon as the film began its first exclusive roadshows in January, 1926, Jergens placed a full-page ad featuring Carmel Myers in that month's *Photoplay*.[580] There are large photos of three different boxed arrangements of Ben-Hur Perfume and another of Myers leaning against an enormous, ornate Roman column and dressed in the blond wig and pearl-adorned outfit she wears to seduce Ben-Hur in Ilderim's tent. The caption here reads:

> CARMEL MYERS – as the beautiful Egyptian princess, Iras, in the Metro-Goldwyn-Mayer spectacle, "Ben Hur," by her interpretation of the role, more than justifies the prediction of success voiced by her thousands of admirers.

The copy begins with a quoted endorsement signed with Myers' signature in black pen. The alluring photo of Myers and the frequent suggestion that these Ben-Hur packages make charming gifts demonstrates that the ad was targeting both female and male demographics. To drive the association home, the rest of the ad uses the name "Ben Hur" eight times (without the hyphen), all in connection with the perfume or other beauty products.

In addition, the company distributed in theaters thousands of blotter samples in 2in. × 3in. glassine packets. They had the following printed on the back:

> This Blotter is scented with Ben Hur – the Perfume preferred by CARMEL MYERS – featured in the Photoplay Ben-Hur.[581]

The name of the theater was often printed on the reverse side of the blotter.

At the same time Jergens advertised the perfume nationwide in newspaper ads that sometimes mentioned the Metro-Goldwyn-Mayer film by name but always contained the endorsement, "Preferred by Carmel

Myers."[582] As it turned out, Myers later became the sole American importer of Zizanie perfume, and reportedly it was only because the chauvinistic French owner remembered her performance as Iras in *Ben-Hur* that he signed the deal with an American.[583]

It is not clear why this particular tie-in was allowed as early as 1926. But Jergens signed similar endorsements with McAvoy and Novarro, although these did not appear until the fall. Comparable ads with McAvoy and Novarro pictured in costume appeared in the October and November issues of *Photoplay*.[584] McAvoy's includes the name of the film but fails to mention Metro-Goldwyn-Mayer. Novarro's does, where the copy emphasizes Novarro's image as the romantic lead in the film:

> Ramon Novarro as the adventurous young hero Ben Hur, in the Metro-Goldwyn-Mayer spectacle of that name.
> Writing of Ben Hur Perfume, this great romantic actor says, "Perfume is not for men, but we must admit its seductive sway when combined with the beauty of women. Women have praise for Ben Hur Perfume, as it seems to distill the romance which its name has typified."

In December Jergens placed the fourth and final ad in the series, a two-page ad including all three *Ben-Hur* principals.[585] At the top of the first page appear three photographs, Novarro's being an action photo from the chariot race. The film benefits from such caption phrases as "great picture spectacle" and "breath-taking scene of the chariot race." The headline is the epitome of *Ben-Hur* synergy in not only including the name "Ben Hur" in both its cinematic and brand-name contexts but matching them up to sit one atop the other:

> THREE GREAT STARS
> appearing in Ben Hur tell why
> they admire BEN HUR PERFUME

The second page of the ad juxtaposes large images of Ben Hur combination boxes ("Carre," "Le Coucher du Soleil," and "Le Cadeau") as well as an action photo of the chariot race with the caption, "the great dramatic climax of Ben Hur, and one of the most thrilling scenes ever staged for the silver screen."

In December, 1926, one year after the premiere of the film, Jergens introduced Ben-Hur Face Powder and sold it individually as well as combined and neatly arranged with a bottle of Ben-Hur Perfume in a decorative pink, silk-lined, gift box.[586] The Clark W. Thompson Company in Galveston offered a discount on both Ben-Hur Perfume and Ben-Hur Face Powder:

> Special Introductory Offer On the Perfume Preferred by Carmel Myers

> Carmel Myers, featured as Iras in the Metro-Goldwyn-Mayer Spectacle, "Ben-Hur," admires this exotic perfume of the same name.

So that the Thompson store patrons, too, may enjoy the mysterious charm, we are making the following, attractive offer, for this week only . . .[587]

In 1927 *The Baltimore Sun* ran a display ad for a bottle of Ben Hur Perfume with the added line: "Preferred by Carmel Myers."[588] The same year Jergens began to offer both toilet water and perfume strengths.[589] With the film still in high-profile release, souvenir bottles of Ben Hur perfume were reserved for women attending the Monday and Tuesday showings in Omaha during the second week of its "record-breaking run."[590]

Bell & Howell also exploited the use of their new model cameras in the production of the film and especially the shooting of the chariot race. In 1927 they ran an ad containing a touched-up image of the production showing the Packard truck specially configured with platforms holding two cameramen filming Bushman's racing chariot.[591] Arrows point to the Bell & Howell cameras, and the caption reads:

FILMING of the chariot-race in *Ben Hur*. Here you see BELL & HOWELL professional movie cameras in use. Nearly all great productions are made with them.

The purpose of the ad is to demonstrate the twenty years of professional experience Bell & Howell has brought to the production of their Automatic Filmo 16mm camera designed for the amateur market. The same photograph (untouched) of the filming of the chariot race from the truck was used by Quaker Oats to advertise an entirely different product, breakfast cereal. In an ad placed in the April, 1928, issue of *Ladies' Home Journal*, for instance, the caption below the photo reads:

Francis X. Bushman, star of Metro-Goldwyn-Mayer's super-film "Ben-Hur," says "Hot oats for physical fitness and clear brain."[592]

Throughout the period of its theatrical release, the *Los Angeles Times* contained not just publicity pieces, pictorial ads, and theater listings for the MGM *Ben-Hur* but also daily ads for products produced by Ben-Hur Coffee, Tea, and Extracts, Ben-Hur Soap, and Ben-Hur Perfume and Powder. While this was certainly due to coincidence, its effect was not lost on a contemporary writer for *Photoplay*, who observed the two-way process already in August, 1925:

The only persons who have profited thus far by the production of "Ben Hur" are the manufacturers of Ben Hur coffee and Ben Hur soap. This reverses the normal course of publicity. The soap and coffee being good, may sell the picture.[593]

Ben-Hur Coffee in particular maintained a frequent and conspicuous local profile by sponsoring contests, generating weekly cooking hints and menu plans by Noni, then Sallie, and in 1932, Marian Manners, the head of their Home Service Bureau, and placing elaborate ads with letters, testimonials, and endorsements, mostly for their Drip Coffee.[594] Often these ads were in the same issue as an ad or listing for the MGM *Ben-Hur*,

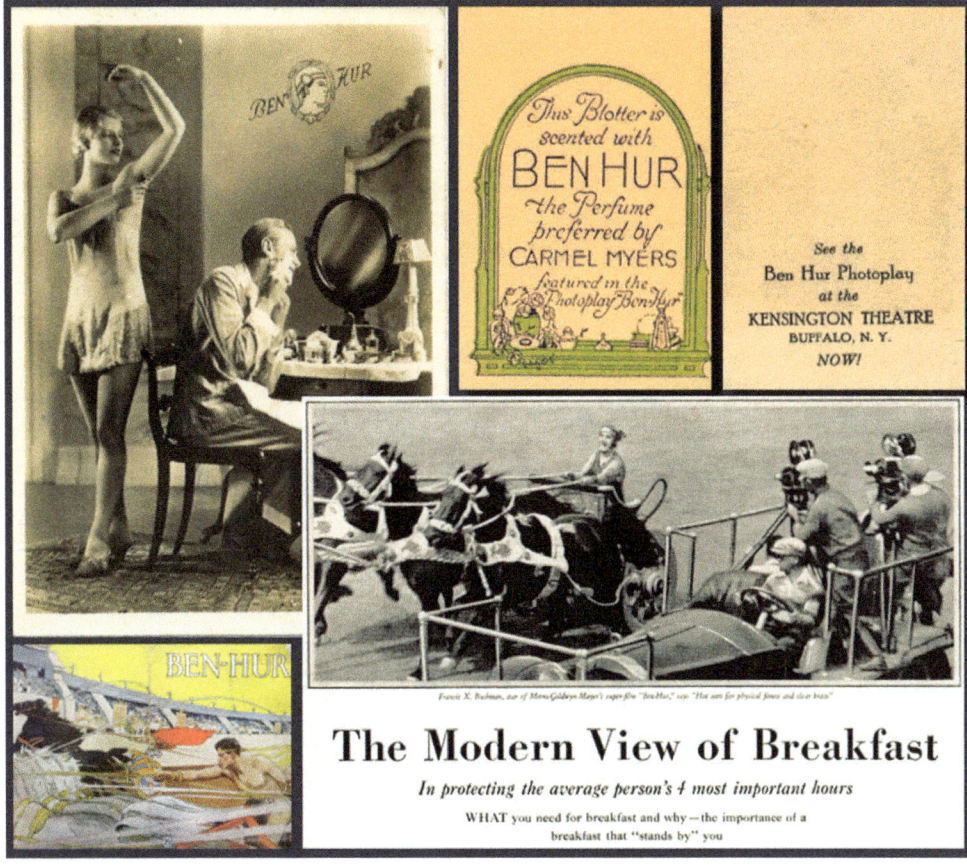

Figure 12.3 Commercial applications of the 1925 MGM *Ben-Hur* included a Portuguese postcard containing an ad for Solingen Ben Hur razors, Carmel Myers-endorsed samples of Jergens' Ben Hur Perfume distributed at local theaters, and a production shot used in a Quaker Oats ad for a national magazine.

and sometimes they appeared on the same page as, and a few times even juxtaposed with, ads for other Ben-Hur products.[595] Indeed, the regularity with which they appeared made it likely that there would be multiple appearances within single issues, and, to be sure, an ad for Ben-Hur Pure Flavoring Extracts appeared while the film was being advertised at the Million Dollar Theater.[596] Probably not so coincidental was that shortly after the release of the film early in 1926, Ben-Hur Coffee employed the chariot imagery more than usual in a few of their newspaper ads.[597]

Because McCarthy's exclusive roadshow agreements prohibited exhibitors from negotiating advertising tie-ins, it was impossible for the company to pair with MGM at the outset. As a result, in 1930 they signed an agreement with United Artists to serve their coffee at the local United Artists Theatre. In one of their most elaborate newspaper ads they depicted Fannie Brice and Harry Green, stars of United Artists' *Be Yourself*, both with cans of Ben-Hur Drip Coffee, and even included one staff of a musical jingle from the film, "Cooking Breakfast for the One I Love."[598] In the same year Ben-Hur Coffee placed an ad connected with the film *Hit the Deck*, much of which takes place in Looloo's Coffee Shop.[599] It depicts Polly Walker [Looloo] and Jack Oakie holding a Ben-Hur Drip Coffee maker and can, respectively, and explains in the extensive copy that Ben-Hur Drip Coffee is served at the Orpheum Theatre where the film is playing.

The most thoroughly integrated synergy Ben-Hur Coffee developed with MGM is evidenced in a full-page ad with an action photo of the chariot race covering the upper third of the page, above which is written "BEN-HUR *Wins!*" and credit to MGM Studios prominently placed. The copy below contains the endorsement of Percy Hilburn, one of the four credited cinematographers for *Ben-Hur*. There he writes:

> During "time off" and in the intermissions between the shooting of pictures, many of the cameramen and technicians, as well as the actors, have found Ben-Hur Drip Coffee a truly refreshing drink . . . void of unpleasant after-effects, and at the same time easily prepared and an excellent "conclusion" to any meal . . . be it sandwich or the most sumptuous repast. I most heartily endorse Ben-Hur Drip Coffee.

Unfortunately the ad, found online, is unprovenienced, but because the copy cites two other credits for Hilburn, *The Rogue Song* and *The Unholy Three*, the ad can with some certainty be dated to 1930, the same year as the previous two synergistic film ads. This was the same year that Ben-Hur Coffee merged with Puritas Coffee and Tea Company and was renamed Coffee Products of America.[600] That merger was finalized in June, and there is no evidence of the name change in the ad. In November of that year, the company placed an ad for Ben-Hur Tea that depicted Lupe Valez, star of *East to West*, which was currently playing at the R-K-O Theatre.[601] There the company was offering Ben-Hur Tea to patrons "in keeping with the oriental atmosphere."

Start-Up Companies
The release of the film inspired the creation of a number of new companies, brands, and products, slowly at first but then gaining momentum by 1929, particularly in the New York area. A mechanic in Reading, Pennsylvania, began advertising a local Ben Hur auto repair company already in the spring of 1926.[602] A few months later Chas. A. Steven & Bros in Chicago advertised a Ben Hur Bracelet for sale,[603] and then the "Ruth Goes Shopping" column in *The Atlanta Constitution* included a fashion-drawing silhouette of the "Ben Hur helmet" . . . a popular chapeau – tailored and plain."[604] Gruen introduced into its Guild Watches line the Ben Hur Band in the fall of 1927.[605] Gruen appropriately advertised the Ben Hur Band in a film-fan magazine, *Photoplay*, although the text does not make any mention of the film. Just the same, it speaks to the increasing resurgence of the *Ben-Hur* phenomenon during this period that

the Gruen ad appeared just a few pages after the Jergens Ben Hur Perfume ad featuring May McAvoy. It was in February, 1927, that Westclox introduced the "Ben Hur" alarm clock as the companion model to their "Big Ben" and "Little Ben."[606] In the summer the Ben Hur Realty Corporation of Bronx County as well as a local Ben Hur Construction Company surfaced in the New York papers, albeit because of legal judgments.[607] The latter company was not the same as the extant, St. Louis-based Ben Hur Erection Company, as it was known then, which was being awarded major new contracts.[608] Meanwhile in France someone was producing those Ramon Novarro dolls that served as "drivers" of the chariot race staged in Paris's Bois de Boulogne in the summer of 1927. According to the author of the syndicated article, Glenn Pullen:

> Ramon Novarro dolls are making their appearance in the shop windows, as the Josephine Baker "golliwog" dolls did last year when [that] American entertainer was the idol of Parisian theatergoers.

Now begins a dizzying pace of Ben-Hur start-ups, especially in the clothing industry, prefaced by the incorporation of the Ben Hur Clothing Company located at 1440 Broadway in New York.[609] With few exceptions these companies appear once or twice on the business pages of the *New York Times* or *New York Herald Tribune* but leave no other record behind. Within the final six months of 1929 and in New York alone the Ben Hur Blouse Company, Inc., leased a floor at 33 West 26th Street,[610] the Ben-Hur Clothing Company, Inc., leased a floor at 826 Broadway,[611] the Ben Hur Sportswear Corporation leased part of the 16th floor at 240 [or 248] West 35th Street,[612] and a new Ben-Hur insurance company, Ben Hur Recreation, was incorporated in Brooklyn with offices at 1560 Broadway in Manhattan.

The following January, 1930, the nylon industry adopted a color named Ben Hur.[613] Some of these small new companies lasted for at least a few years in the depths of the depression. Ben Hur Blouse Company increased its capitalization from $10,000 to $50,000 at the end of 1930,[614] and it kept advertising in the *Daily Boston Globe* in 1931 and 1932,[615] as did Ben Hur Sportswear in the *New York Times*.[616] The year 1931 almost kept pace, with Ben Hur Drinks, in the refreshment stand category,[617] and the Ben Hur Hat Corporation of 205 West 34th Street.[618] The *Times* also lists a new, $50,000 incorporation of a Ben-Hur Products company in 1931.[619] Located at 521 Fifth Avenue and founded by S. H. Birnbaum, this does not seem to be the same as the New York Ben-Hur Products Company at 11 West 42nd Street, also known as Ben-Hur Industries, Inc. and manufacturer of the Quadro-Gammon game, also in 1931. That company was founded in 1923 by Behr and Hirtenstein and will be surveyed further in the next chapter. One more product was manufactured in 1932, a 16-inch long, 8¾-inch high Ben Hur Chariot Clock, notable for its bright gold finish and team of only three horses.[620]

FINAL ASSESSMENT

The 1925 cinematic adaptation of *Ben-Hur: A Tale of the Christ*, was a fitting heir to the record-breaking Klaw & Erlanger spectacle and the greatly revered novel from which it was derived. The number of human talents involved in creating it were legion, from the Wallaces and Erlanger to Godsol, Mathis, Loew, Mayer, Niblo, and Thalberg, to the two companies and enormous crews in Italy and California and the thousands of extras in both locations. The locations were filled with gargantuan city walls, life-sized Roman galleys, and two full-sized Roman circuses and were filmed through dozens of state-of-the-art cameras that exposed from one to two million feet of film, all costing unprecedented sums of money. The distribution of the film was equally "mammoth," beginning with exclusive roadshows at legitimate theaters and filtering down months later to local neighborhood movie theaters and churches while filling movie palaces abroad from Berlin to Shanghai for many years, ultimately recouping much more than the initial cost of production. Usually accompanied by a symphonic score and "a car load of scenery and special stage effects,"[621] audiences rose to their feet and cheered at the chariot race. In that the film industry and the public taste were rapidly turning towards sound just as the film was hitting its stride, *Ben-Hur* still had time to establish itself as one of the great films of the silent era and one of its last hurrahs.

Metro-Goldwyn-Mayer made sure that the many serious problems encountered during its extraordinarily lengthy production were regarded as a positive. Newspaper ads for the next seven years claimed with pride that the film had cost $4 million. Even the MGM souvenir booklet for the 1959 production restated that the 1925 production had cost $4 million. The film's restorer, Kevin Brownlow, regarded the entire process as one of the film's greatest successes:

> Courage displayed under controlled conditions is impressive enough. Under conditions of chaos it becomes heroic. The technicians and players who worked on *Ben-Hur* – enduring seemingly endless hazards, and supporting men who were bewildered and confused – displayed courage on a level almost unparalleled in film history. They established the production as a sort of Dunkirk of the cinema: a humiliating defeat transformed, after heavy losses, into a brilliant victory."[622]

During its release, the film, like the novel and stage play, appealed to different demographics in various ways. Advertisements highlighted the spectacle of the chariot race and sea battle, the size and cost of the production, the star power of Ramon Novarro, the romance between Novarro and May McAvoy, the novelty of the Technicolor scenes, the respectful presentation of Christ, or the film's educational appeal or historical authenticity. A major factor, of course, was the name Ben-Hur and the story so familiar to millions of people. But just as the success of *Ben-Hur* cannot be attributed to any single attraction or audience demographic, it cannot be attributed to any single artist or manager. It was the quintessential studio production. Edwin Schallert first called it an "organizational picture," and the cooperation within the organization as well as its profound internal disagreements testify to the accuracy of his evaluation.[623] This applies from the pre-production decisions made by Erlanger and the Goldwyn Company in 1922 and 1923 through its roadshow and local theater releases in 1927 and 1928 and the sound releases of 1931 and 1932. As we have just seen, the multi-year success of *Ben-Hur* unleashed a new impetus for Ben-Hur commerce and helped re-establish the broad cultural linkage between *Ben-Hur* and chariots, racing, and spectacle as well as reverence and prestige.

In 1933 Irving Thalberg co-authored an article in *The Saturday Evening Post* with the title, "Why Motion Pictures Cost So Much."[624] In addressing the multi-million dollar price tag of *Ben-Hur*, which he says along with *The Big Parade* had solidified the superior status of Metro-Goldwyn-Mayer, he concluded by making clear the unique significance of the *Ben-Hur* property:

> A poor picturization of Ben Hur would have cost us in prestige far more than the half million dollars' worth of junked film. The good picturization, which we did finally make, not only earned back the huge sum of money it cost but it built up a goodwill the value of which is almost impossible to estimate.

NOTES

1. *Positif* 468 (February, 2000) 91–6.
2. *Kansas City [MO] Star* (August 7, 1913) 14.
3. *NYT* (November 23, 1897) 7; Grace, *The Religious Film*, 17–19; Musser, "Passions and the Passion Play," 435–9.
4. *The Billboard* 25 (June 28, 1913) 17.
5. *Seattle Daily Times* (March 26, 1913) 8.
6. *[New Orleans] Times-Picayune* (July 25, 1913) 5.
7. Niver, *Klaw & Erlanger*, 121–4; Tibbetts, *The American Theatrical Film*, 71–7.
8. *Variety* 38 (March 5, 1915) 20.
9. Letter from Henry Wallace to Harper (May 6, 1912), LL.
10. Slater, "The Vision and the Struggle," 76–7; M&M 469–70.
11. Boomhower, *The Sword and the Pen*, 141–2.
12. <http://www.indiana.edu/~liblilly/shorttitle/wallace.html>
13. 232 F. 609 (1916).
14. *The Moving Picture World* 27 (February 5, 1916) 752.
15. *The New York Clipper* (June 9 20) 6.
16. *NYT* (August 7, 1919) 8; *The New York Clipper* (August 6, 1919) 1.
17. *AC* (August 17 19) D8.
18. *NYTr* (August 7, 1919) 11; *NYT* (August 10, 1919) XX2; *CE* (August 17, 1919) B2. This was not the Classical Cinematograph Corporation; cf. *NYT* (August 7, 1919) 8.

19 *TFD* 7 (January 9, 1919) 1.
20 *TFD* 16 (June 24, 1920) 2.
21 *TFD* 14 (November 19, 1920) 1 and 4.
22 *TFD* 16 (May 24, 1921) 1 and 4; (June 4, 1921) 1.
23 *The New York Clipper* (February 25, 1920) 30.
24 *TFD* 11 (February 19, 1920) 4; cf. Slide, *American Racist*, 74, and Wade, *The Fiery Cross*, 123–4, for Thomas Dixon, who sold the screen rights to *The Clansmen* for only $2500 and one fourth of the profits of *The Birth of a Nation*, which earned some $4 million.
25 *TFD* 20 (June 15, 1922) 1–2.
26 *Duluth News-Tribune* (July 3, 1921) 2.
27 *TFD* 11 (February 6, 1920) 1.
28 *TFD* 14 (November 19, 1920) 4.
29 *TFD* 11 (October 25, 1920) 1.
30 *[Portland] Oregonian* (January 29, 1922) 3.
31 *The Kansas City Star* (July 20, 1919) 12.
32 *TFD* 14 (November 19, 1920) 4.
33 *TFD* 15 (January 26, 1921) 4; *TFD* 16 (April 18, 1921) 2.
34 *TFD* 16 (June 24, 1921) 2.
35 Agreement (July 22, 1921), LL. Cf. 272 F. 894 (1921).
36 *Trenton Evening Times* (November 26, 1939) 15, and *Variety* 215 (August 12, 1959) 76.
37 *NYT* (July 11, 1936) 11.
38 *TFD* 16 (April 24, 1921) 79.
39 *NYT* (January 31, 1926) X5.
40 *NYT* (January 10, 1926) 29.
41 *TFD* 16 (June 24, 1921) 2.
42 *LAT* (April 9, 1921) II7.
43 *NYTr* (April 8, 1921) 10.
44 *NYT* (July 22, 1921) 22; *New York Supreme Court: Appellate Division – First Department: In the Matter of Proving the Last Will and Testament of Abraham L. Erlanger, Deceased* (1930) 67–8; cf. Crowther, *The Lion's Share*, 92–3; *NYT* (July 22, 1950) 13.
45 *The Billboard* 33 (October 29, 1921) 9.
46 Letter from Henry L. Wallace to Thomas B. Wells, Harper & Bros. (October 11, 1919), LL.
47 *The Billboard* 33 (April 16, 1921) 99.
48 Brownlow, *The Parade's Gone By . . .*, 385.
49 E.g. Eyman, *Lion of Hollywood*; Vieira, *Irving Thalberg*; Soares, *Beyond Paradise*.
50 Marx, *Mayer and Thalberg*, viii.
51 E.g. Quargnolo, et al., "The Heroic Fiasko," 1–7.
52 Vieira, *Irving Thalberg*, 48; Soares, *Beyond Paradise*, 69. Vieira says the novel was published in 1867, Altman [*Hollywood East*, 129] in 1890.
53 Brownlow, *The Parade's Gone By . . .*, 393; Flamini, *Thalberg*, 5; Eyman, *Lion of Hollywood*, 107; Altman, *Hollywood East*, 129; Telegram from Louis B. Mayer to Alexander Aronson (January 5, 1925), HL.

54 M&M 471–9, citing almost exclusively Crowther and Brownlow.
55 Eyman, *Lion of Hollywood*, 71.
56 Crowther, *The Lion's Share*, 92–3; *[Portland] Oregonian* (January 29, 1922) 3.
57 Soares, *Beyond Paradise*, 72; Brownlow, *The Parade's Gone By . . .*, 391.
58 *NYT* (October 31, 1920) X2.
59 *WP* (May 12, 1918) 5.
60 Birmingham, "The Rest of Us," 197–200.
61 *NYT* (June 15, 1922) 26; *WSJ* (June 16, 1922) 3; *TCSM* (June 16, 1922) 8; cf. Eyman, *Lion of Hollywood*, 71.
62 *TFD* 20 (June 20, 1922) 4.
63 *LAT* (June 16, 1922) II 11; *Indianapolis Star* (June 17, 1922) 10.
64 *NYTr* (June 18 22) D2.
65 *TFD* 20 (June 15, 1922) 1–2.
66 *LAT* (June 25, 1922) III 27.
67 *TFD* 20 (June 30, 1922) 1.
68 *SFC* (July 16, 1922) D4.
69 *Nashville Tennessean* (November 19, 1922) A5.
70 The Synopsis, dated June 17, 1922, and preserved in the USC Cinema Arts Library, misspells the names "Simondes," "Iris," and "Mallush" throughout.
71 *TFD* (September 8, 1922) 1; *LAT* (September 15, 1922) II 11. Cf. Slater, "June Mathis's *Classified*," 3–14.
72 *LAT* (June 3, 1923) III 13.
73 Eyman, *Lion of Hollywood*, 71; Crowther, *The Lion's Share*, 93–6; Soares, *Beyond Paradise*, 71.
74 *Arizona Republican* (December 10, 1922) A6; *Photoplay* 24 (October, 1923) 63.
75 *LAT* (September 15, 1922) II 11; cf. *TBS* (October 1, 1922) MS7.
76 *NYT* (December 10, 1922) 100; *SFC* (December 17, 1922) D1; *TBS* (December 24, 1922) P2S11.
77 *DFP* (December 31, 1922) C14.
78 *NYT* (January 7, 1923) SM4.
79 *TFD* 23 (February 1, 1923) 10; (February 21, 1923) 2.
80 *LAT* (December 30, 1922) 87.
81 *LAT* (December 10, 1922) III 33.
82 Leider, *Dark Lover*, 237–8.
83 Brownlow, *The Parade's Gone By . . .*, 390.
84 *LAT* (December 13, 1922) II 11.
85 Slater, "The Vision and the Struggle," 63–78.
86 Soares, *Beyond Paradise*, 71.
87 *The New York Clipper* (June 13, 1923) 7.
88 *NYT* (May 19, 1923) 16; *TFD* 25 (July 29, 1923) 1; cf. *NYT* (April 26, 1923) 40; *TFD* 24 (April 27, 1923) 1; 26 (November 14, 1923) 1; Brownlow, *The Parade's Gone By . . .*, 389.
89 *TFD* 25 (June 22, 1924) 55 and 57; (September 30, 1923) 1 and 11; *Pictures and Picturegoer* 5 (December, 1923) 80; cf. Higham, *Merchant of Dreams*, 76.

90 Higham, *Merchant of Dreams*, 76; Flamini, *Thalberg*, 62.
91 Brownlow, *The Parade's Gone By . . .*, 391.
92 Ellenberger, *Ramon Novarro*, 28.
93 Crowther, *The Lion's Share*, 93.
94 Crowther, *The Lion's Share*, 94; TFD 25 (September 30, 1923) 1.
95 TFD 25 (September 30, 1923) 11; 26 (October 18, 1923) 4; Higham, *Merchant of Dreams*, 76.
96 TFD 26 (December 28, 1923) 7; (January 2, 1924) 6.
97 Brownlow, *The Parade's Gone By . . .*, 390.
98 TFD 26 (November 2, 1923) 1.
99 TFD 26 (November 2, 1923) 1.
100 TFD 27 (March 25, 1924) 1.
101 TBS (November 18, 1923) MS6.
102 Higham, *Merchant of Dreams*, 66–8; and Pizzitola, *Hearst Over Hollywood*, 216–17.
103 NYT (April 18, 1924) 21; TFD 28 (April 16, 1924) 1 and 6–7.
104 Eyman, *Lion of Hollywood*, 72.
105 Marx, *Mayer and Thalber*, 56.
106 Ibid., 47–8; Flamini, *Thalberg*, 61; Crowther, *The Lion's Share*, 95.
107 Crowther, *The Lion's Share*, 95.
108 Brownlow, *The Parade's Gone By . . .*, 109.
109 Crowther, *The Lion's Share*, 94.
110 Vieira, *Irving Thalberg*, 48.
111 TFD 28 (May 9, 1924) 1–2.
112 TFD 28 (May 12, 1924) 1–2.
113 Higham, *Merchant of Dreams*, 80; Brownlow, *The Parade's Gone By . . .*, 393 and 397.
114 TFD 28 (June 10, 1924) 1–2.
115 TFD 28 (June 22, 1924) 98.
116 TFD 28 (June 8, 1924) 1 and 3.
117 Eyman, *Lion of Hollywood*, 99, reports that by April, 1924, the production had consumed $167,307 of its allotted $750,000; Vieira, *Irving Thalberg*, 48, reports that she had spent the original budget of $1.25 million in two months.
118 TFD 25 (September 30, 1923) 1; TFD 26 (October 28, 1923) 10.
119 TFD 27 (February 6, 1924) 6.
120 Letter from Fred Niblo to Louis B. Mayer (July 21, 1924), HL.
121 Cf. Higham, *Merchant of Dreams*, 68; Brownlow, *The Parade's Gone By . . .*, 394
122 Brownlow, *The Parade's Gone By . . .*, 395.
123 Marx, *Mayer and Thalberg*, 56.
124 Letter from Fred Niblo to Louis B. Mayer (May 20, 1924), HL.
125 Higham, *Merchant of Dreams*, 76.
126 Telegram from Joseph Schenck to Marcus Loew (May 2, 1924), HL.
127 LAT (October 4, 1925) C19.
128 Crowther, *Hollywood Rajah*, 107; Brownlow, *The Parade's Gone By . . .*, 394–6.

129 *Photoplay* 26 (August, 1924) 95; Ellenberger, *Ramon Novarro*, 3–4.
130 *Photoplay* 26 (August, 1924) 98; (September, 1924) 133.
131 *Photoplay* 26 (September, 1924) 90.
132 *TFD* 28 (June 15, 1924) 1 and 4; *LAT* (June 15, 1924) B13; Marx, *Mayer and Thalberg*, 57–8.
133 *TFD* 29 (August 15, 1924) 1; Crowther, *The Lion's Share*, 95–6.
134 *Photoplay* 26 (October, 1924) 37. Soares, *Beyond Paradise*, 79; Flamini, *Thalberg*, 64–5.
135 *Photoplay* 26 (May, 1924) 57.
136 *TFD* 29 (July 10, 1924) 1–2; 30 (November 24, 1924) 2.
137 *LAT* (August 28, 1924) A9.
138 Brownlow, *The Parade's Gone By . . .*, 413.
139 Letter from Irving Thalberg to Fred Niblo (September 23, 1924), HL.
140 Cable from Louis. B. Mayer to Harry Edington (July 5, 1924), HL.
141 *LAT* (February 15, 1925) 34.
142 *TFD* 29 (July 11, 1924) 3; *TFD* 28 (July 13, 1924) 1 and 4.
143 *TFD* 29 (July 30, 1924) 5.
144 *TFD* 29 (August 12, 1924) 1; cf. Bohn and Stromgren, *Light and Shadows*, 81, 194, and 200.
145 *Photoplay* 26 (November, 1924) 32–3 and 101.
146 *TFD* 29 (August 14, 1924) 1.
147 Ibid., 1; (August 27, 1924) 5.
148 Marx, *Mayer and Thalberg*, 57; cf. Scodel, "The 1925 *Ben-Hur* and the 'Hollywood Question,'" 313–29.
149 Soares, *Beyond Paradise*, 82.
150 *Photoplay* 26 (November, 1924) 101; Soares, *Beyond Paradise*, 75.
151 Soares, *Beyond Paradise*, 72–3, describes the process of selection.
152 Soares, *Beyond Paradise*, 72 and 80.
153 *TFD* 30 (December 11, 1924) 1 and 5. Cf. *LAT* (March 1, 1925) 17.
154 *NYT* (January 3, 1926) X5.
155 Marx, *Mayer and Thalberg*, 63.
156 Crowther, *Hollywood Rajah*, 109 and *The Lion's Share* 97; repeated by Brownlow, *The Parade's Gone By . . .*, 397 and 401.
157 Kevin Brownlow, "Ben-Hur: The Heroic Fiasco," 31; Marx, *Mayer and Thalberg*, 63.
158 Flamini, *Thalberg*, 63.
159 Brownlow, *The Parade's Gone By . . .*, 396–401.
160 Cf. *NYT* (January 3, 1926) X5.
161 Gillespie, "Remembrances of Ben Hur," 38–40; Riley and Welch, *The Wizard of MGM*, 37.
162 *LAT* (January 7, 1925) C4.
163 Letter from Lou Marangella to Irving Thalberg (October 2, 1924), HL.
164 Higham, *Merchant of Dreams*, 77 and 101.
165 *NYTr* (January 9, 1925) 3.
166 *LAT* (January 10, 1925) A1 and A6; *TFD* 31 (January 19, 1925) 1; Telegram from Louis B. Mayer to Alexander Aronson (January 5, 1925), HL.
167 *LAT* (February 15, 1925) 34.

168 *NYT* (January 3, 1926) X5.
169 Quargnolo et al., "The Heroic Fiasko," 1–2.
170 *TFD* 32 (June 7, 1925) 23.
171 Higham, *Merchant of Dreams*, 92.
172 *TFD* 31 (March 27, 1925) 1; *TBS* (May 3 25) R5; Eyman, *Lion of Hollywood*, 107; Higham, *Merchant of Dreams*, 84; *LAT* (July 15, 1934) A5; Leider, *Myrna Loy*, 49–50.
173 *TFD* 32 (June 7, 1925) 139.
174 *LAT* (June 7, 1925) 17–18.
175 *AC* (February 9, 1927) 16.
176 Matteo Della Corte, *Pompeii, The New Excavations* (Valle di Pompei: F. Sicignano, 1925).
177 *TFD* 33 (September 18, 1925) 9; (September 20, 1925) 3; (September 21, 1925) 1; Brownlow, *The Parade's Gone By . . .*, 35–6.
178 *NYT* (April 19, 1923) 1.
179 Thomas, *Thalberg*, 72–3.
180 *LAT* (July 12, 1931) B12. [Canton OH] *Repository* (September 4, 1927) 21, attributes some of this artwork to Carmelo Barbara and "Carlo[s] Romonelli."
181 *Seattle Daily Times* (November 8, 1925) 68.
182 *TFD* 34 (October 2, 1925) 1.
183 *NYT* (November 1, 1925) X5.
184 Brownlow, *The Parade's Gone By . . .*, 408; Thomas, *Thalberg*, 73; Eyman, *Lion of Hollywood*, 108; Higham, *Merchant of Dreams*, 97.
185 *Photoplay* 29 (March, 1926) 100.
186 Quirk, *The Films of Myrna Loy*, 38–9. Cf. *CT* (November 4, 1934) G8.
187 Thomas, *Thalberg*, 73; Higham, *Merchant of Dreams*, 97.
188 *Photoplay* 29 (April, 1926) 28–31 and 114–15; cf. *Science and Invention* 13 (March, 1926) 986–8; Eyman, *Lion of Hollywood*, 108.
189 Brownlow, *The Parade's Gone By . . .*, 36.
190 *NYT* (November 1, 1925) X5.
191 Crowther, *The Lion's Share*, 98; *Philadelphia Tribune* (September 4, 1926) 3; Herman, *A Talent for Trouble*, 71–2.
192 Higham, *Merchant of Dreams*, 98; *American Cinematographer* 6 (January, 1926) 5–6; Raimondo-Souto, *Motion Picture Photography*, 135–6; *TFD* 34 (October 6, 1925) 1, reports thirty-five cameras and 7500 people.
193 <http://dfphotography.wordpress.com/2010/02/13/53>
194 Higham, *Merchant of Dreams*, 98.
195 Brownlow, *The Parade's Gone By . . .*, 403.
196 Crowther, *The Lion's Share*, 100.
197 *Vegetarian and Fruitarian* 28 (February 1, 1929) 19.
198 *TFD* 34 (November 1, 1925) 1; *LAT* (November 15, 1925) G6 (with photo).
199 Brownlow, *The Parade's Gone By . . .*, 36.
200 *LAT* (October 4, 1925) C19.
201 *LAT* (December 9, 1925) A11.
202 *LAT* (December 13, 1925) C27.
203 *American Cinematographer* 6 (January, 1926) 12 and 16.
204 Flamini, *Thalberg*, 67–8; Higham, *Merchant of Dreams*, 101.

205 Thomas, *Thalberg*, 75–6; Higham, *Merchant of Dreams*, 101.
206 Raimondo-Souto, *Motion Picture Photography*, 135; Blom, "Quo Vadis?," 281–96.
207 *American Cinematographer* 80 (March, 1999) 193.
208 *NYT* (December 13, 1925) X7 and RPB3.
209 *TFD* 34 (December 21, 1925) 5.
210 *LAT* (December 27, 1925) C27.
211 *The New York Herald* (December 27, 1925) D3.
212 *NYT* (December 27, 1925) X5.
213 *NYT* (January 1, 1926) 18.
214 *NYT* (November 13, 1938) 152.
215 *Photoplay* 29 (March, 1926) 49.
216 *NYT* (December 31, 1925) 10.
217 *TCSM* (December 31, 1925) 7.
218 *TFD* 34 (December 31, 1925) 1 and 5.
219 *NYT* (February 14, 1926) D4; *The New York Herald* (February 21, 1926) D5.
220 *NYT* (January 3, 1926) X4.
221 *TFD* 34 (May 13, 1926) 2.
222 *NYT* (July 18, 1926) X2.
223 *TFD* 37 (August 1, 1926) 4.
224 Eyman, *Lion of Hollywood*, 111; cf. Holston, *Movie Roadshows*, 45–6.
225 *TFD* 37 (August 1, 1926) 4.
226 *NYT* (December 27, 1925) X5.
227 *TBS* (July 11, 1926) MP6.
228 *LAT* (August 29, 1926) C16; *TFD* 34 (December 2, 1925) 1 and 3.
229 *TFD* 35 (January 27, 1926) 1; *BG* (February 22, 1926) 18; *Brooklyn Daily Star* (April 24, 1926) 18; *PI* (April 19, 1926) 16. Cf. *TFD* 35 (February 25, 1926) 4.
230 *Daily [Evanston IL] Northwestern* (February 23, 1926) 2.
231 *BG* (February 21, 1926) A10.
232 *BG* (February 21, 1926) A48.
233 *BG* (February 21, 1926) B12.
234 *BG* (February 21, 1926) B13.
235 *BG* (February 22, 1926) 18.
236 *BG* (February 23, 1926) 18.
237 *BG* (February 28, 1926) B14.
238 *BG* (February 28, 1926) B15.
239 *BG* (March 14, 1926) B1.
240 *BG* (April 4, 1926) B11.
241 *BG* (April 11, 1926) B10.
242 *BG* (April 18, 1926) B18.
243 *BG* (February 24, 1926) B14.
244 *TFD* 37 (August 1, 1926) 4.
245 *TFD* 37 (August 3, 1926) 1 and 5; *WP* (September 26, 1926) F1; and *LAT* (September 23, 1926) A9.
246 *LAT* (August 26, 1926) A9.
247 *LAT* (October 27, 1926) A11.
248 *LAT* (August 3, 1926) A11.

249 According to *LAT* (July 14, 1926) A9, the orchestra was under the direction of Clarence West.
250 *LAT* (September 2, 1926) A11.
251 *LAT* (September 5, 1926) C15.
252 *LAT* (October 6, 1926) A9.
253 *LAT* (September 8, 1926) A10.
254 *LAT* (August 22, 1926) C19.
255 *LAT* (September 5, 1926) C15.
256 *LAT* (September 26, 1926) C26.
257 *LAT* (August 26, 1926) A9; (October 18, 1926) A9.
258 *LAT* (August 22, 1926) I2; (September 15, 1926) A11; (October 11, 1926) 11.
259 *LAT* (September 12, 1926) C21.
260 *LAT* (May 2, 1926) C27.
261 *LAT* (October 17, 1926) C21; cf. (October 13, 1926) A9.
262 *LAT* (August 20, 1926) A11.
263 *LAT* (August 22, 1926) C19.
264 *LAT* (October 24, 1926) C21.
265 *LAT* (November 4, 1926) A8; (October 31, 1926) C25.
266 *LAT* (February 21, 1926) 24.
267 *LAT* (August 8, 1926) C23.
268 *LAT* (August 8, 1926) C23.
269 *LAT* (October 21, 1926) 11.
270 *LAT* (August 29, 1926) C19.
271 *LAT* (October 3, 1926) C29.
272 *Photoplay* 29 (November, 1926) 124.
273 *LAT* (August 1, 1925) A1; Brownlow, *The Parade's Gone By . . .*, 405.
274 *LAT* (March 18, 1926) A9; *TFD* 35 (March 24, 1926) 2.
275 *LAT* (May 2, 1926) C24.
276 *WP* (September 23, 1926) 14.
277 *WP* (September 27, 1926) 5.
278 *WP* (October 7, 1926) 12; cf. (April 17, 1927) F2.
279 *CPD* (January 10, 1926) 66.
280 *TFD* 38 (October 21, 1926) 11.
281 *[San Diego] Evening Tribune* (November 25, 1926) 3 and (November 20, 1926) 7.
282 *[San Diego] Evening Tribune* (November 14, 1926) 23.
283 *TBS* (December 19, 1926) MF5.
284 *TFD* 40 (April 12, 1927) 7.
285 *WP* (April 10, 1927) F1.
286 *TFD* 39 (March 30, 1927) 1.
287 *NYT* (March 13, 1927) X3.
288 *LAT* (May 25, 1927) A13.
289 *TFD* 36 (May 4, 1926) 1–2.
290 *CPD* (August 17, 1927) 19; *LAT* (May 6, 1928) C11.
291 *TFD* 28 (June 18, 1924) 1; cf. (August 14, 1924) 1.
292 *NYT* (September 7, 1926) 44.
293 *TFD* 38 (October 12, 1926) 1; *TBS* (January 9, 1927) RM5.

294 *WSJ* (November 24, 1926) 20.
295 *TFD* 39 (January 3, 1927) 7.
296 *LAT* (January 16, 1927) C25.
297 *TBS* (January 9, 1927) RM5, reported that "in towns throughout Germany ... it is being exploited in the same manner as a circus."
298 *The Observer* (November 14, 1926) 15; cf. *The Manchester Guardian* (November 9, 1926) 5.
299 *NYT* (January 16, 1927) X5.
300 *NYT* (April 8, 1927) 2.
301 *LAT* (December 13, 1926) 1.
302 *BG* (April 18, 1927) 2.
303 *The Manchester Guardian* (January 20, 1928) 10.
304 *The Observer* (February 6, 1927) 20; *TFD* 39 (March 27, 1927) 30.
305 *TFD* 41 (July 24, 1927) 5.
306 *TFD* 41 (September 16, 1927) 2; (September 25, 1927) 12.
307 *NYT* (October 23, 1927) X7.
308 *The Irish Times* (October 3, 1927) 5.
309 *The Irish Times* (October 18, 1927) 3.
310 *Le Petit Parisien* (April 8, 1927) 4; cf. *Le Temps* (April 21, 1928) 4.
311 *NYHT* (May 12, 1928) 7; *The Billboard* 40 (December 1, 1928) 25.
312 *LAT* (January 22, 1928) B4.
313 *TFD* 41 (July 17, 1927) 10; *LAT* (January 22, 1928) B4.
314 *NYT* (June 23, 1929) X4.
315 *TFD* 46 (October 17, 1928) 11.
316 Postcard in the possession of the author.
317 P. Lethielleux Libraire-Edition. The translator is credited as Philippe Mazoyer.
318 Cf. *LAT* (May 6, 1928) C11.
319 *TFD* 41 (July 31, 1927) 8; *The China Press* (March 10, 1928) 3; (June 10, 1928) 4; (December 30, 1928) A7.
320 *The [Perth] Daily News* (December 2, 1927) 10.
321 *The [Victoria] Horsham Times* (July 16, 1927) 4.
322 *[Sydney] Evening News* (July 7, 1927) 6.
323 *Sydney Sunday Times* (July 3, 1927) 2.
324 *Lismore [NSW] Northern Star* (October 15, 1927) 4; *Newcastle Morning Herald & Miners' Advocate* (January 6, 1928) 6; *Camden News* (December 29, 1927) 10; *The Canberra Times* (October 7, 1927) 9; *The [Perth] Daily News* (December 2, 1927) 10.
325 *ToI* (September 22, 1927) 5.
326 *ToI* (November 9, 1927) 6.
327 *ToI* (November 19, 1927) 3; (November 23, 1927) 5; (December 30, 1927) 4.
328 E.g. *ToI* (November 19, 1927) 3; (November 23, 1927) 7; *The China Press* (March 18, 1928) C8; (June 10, 1928) A4.
329 *ToI* (November 25, 1927) 8; cf. *Playboy* 12 (June, 1965) 158; "Ben Hur (1970) Scrapbook" 3, New York Public Library.
330 Blom, "*Quo Vadis?*," 285.
331 *TFD* 41 (August 2, 1927) 6.

332 *CPD* (August 7, 1927) 72; (August 14, 1927) 64.
333 *CPD* (August 21, 1927) 68.
334 *LAT* (August 30, 1927) A11.
335 *LAT* (September 8, 1927) A9. Cf. (May 4, 1935) 5; Behlmer, "'Tumult, Battle and Blaze,'" 25–7.
336 *LAT* (September 11, 1927) C13.
337 *LAT* (September 18, 1927) 15.
338 *LAT* (September 11, 1927) C15.
339 *TFD* 41 (September 20, 1927) 3–4.
340 *WSJ* (September 12, 1927) 3.
341 *[Canton, OH] Repository* (September 5, 1927) 3.
342 *[Canton, OH] Repository* (September 11, 1927) 11; cf. *Rockford [IL] Register Gazette* (December 19, 1927) 9.
343 *TFD* 41 (September 20, 1927) 3–4.
344 *TFD* 41 (September 28, 1927) 1.
345 *NYT* (October 2, 1927) X2.
346 *Richmond [VA] Times Dispatch* (October 11, 1927) 12.
347 *TBS* (November 8, 1927) 6.
348 *WP* (October 9, 1927) F4.
349 *TFD* 42 (October 2, 1927) 10.
350 *TFD* 42 (December 27, 1927) 7.
351 *Rockford [IL] Register Gazette* (January 5, 1928) 28.
352 *TFD* 43 (February 6, 1928) 8.
353 *Photoplay* 32 (November, 1927) 120.
354 *TFD* 42 (October 5, 1927) 4.
355 *TFD* 42 (October 13, 1927) 6.
356 *TFD* 43 (January 16, 1928) 2.
357 *TFD* 42 (October 28, 1927) 7.
358 *AC* (October 29, 1927) 10; (October 30, 1927) F5.
359 *AC* (October 30, 1927) F4.
360 *TFD* 43 (January 11, 1928) 7.
361 *TFD* 42 (October 28, 1927) 7; (November 15, 1927) 6.
362 *TFD* 43 (January 6, 1928) 2.
363 *TFD* 42 (October 10, 1927) 8; (October 23, 1927) 2; (December 1, 1927) 10.
364 *TFD* 43 (January 6, 1928) 2.
365 *LAT* (August 1, 1926) X2.
366 *TFD* 42 (October 26, 1927) 4.
367 *The Pittsburgh Courier* (April 14, 1928) 6; (April 28, 1928) 7.
368 *The Pittsburgh Courier* (April 21, 1928) 12.
369 *NYHT* (April 14, 1928) 9.
370 *WP* (December 2, 1928) 10.
371 *Afro-American* (June 7, 1930) 12.
372 *NYT* (June 15, 1930) N20.
373 *TFD* 54 (November 3, 1930) 1.
374 *LAT* (December 26, 1926) C25.
375 *NYT* (October 8, 1927) 15; *CPD* (October 29, 1927) 17.

376 *CT* (February 16, 1928) 12. Cf. *CPD* (October 23, 1927) 61; *LAT* (January 28, 1928) A6; (February 3, 1928) A6; (April 28, 1928) 6.
377 *TFD* 44 (April 6, 1928) 2.
378 *AC* (October 28, 1928) 4G.
379 *BG* (June 1, 1929) 4.
380 *TFD* 49 (July 1, 1929) 7.
381 *WP* (January 19, 1930) 41.
382 *Le Temps* (March 29, 1930) 6. Cf. *ToI* (August 2, 1930) 5; (September 21, 1929) 19.
383 *The Billboard* 41 (March 16, 1929) 21.
384 *WP* (March 30, 1930) A4; *TBS* (April 20, 1930) M1; cf. *WSJ* (May 14, 1930) 2: $8 million.
385 *LAT* (September 30, 1930) 13; cf. *The Saturday Review* 151 (June 6, 1931) 829.
386 TFD 45 (September 16, 1928) 9.
387 MGM *Ben-Hur* Pressbook, undated, 4–5, British Film Institute Library.
388 *TFD* 55 (June 18, 1931) 1.
389 *The Saturday Review* 151 (June 6, 1931) 829.
390 *WSJ* (December 7, 1931) 4.
391 *TBS* (December 13, 1931) MR1.
392 *The Manchester Guardian* (December 29, 1931) 11.
393 *Dallas Morning News* (January 18, 1932) 4.
394 *[Baton Rouge] State Times Advocate* (May 12, 1932) 4.
395 *NYT* (January 3, 1932) X7.
396 *[Canton, OH] Repository* (December 21, 1931) 18.
397 *The Billboard* 43 (December 12, 1931) 18.
398 *WP* (December 19, 1931) 14.
399 *TFD* 57 (December 16, 1931) 1.
400 *Seattle Daily Times* (February 16, 1933) 14; *[Portland] Oregonian* (February 5, 1933) 41; (May 6, 1933) 7.
401 *ToI* (September 17, 1932) 5.
402 *Kingston Gleaner* (January 12, 1933) 4; *Le Figaro* (July 17, 1933) 4; *Le Temps* (September 22, 1933) 4; [cf. *NYT* (December 6, 1931) X6]; *The China Press* (December 7, 1933) 5.
403 *Kalgoorlie Miner* (April 12, 1934) 1.
404 *The Manchester Guardian* (March 25, 1937) 12; (May 15, 1937) 13; *Het Vaderland* (June 12, 1937) 1; *ToI* (July 20, 1937) 3; (December 23, 1937) 4; *L'Humanité* (July 29, 1938) 7; *ToI* (August 24, 1942) 3.
405 *LAT* (April 6, 1930) B11.
406 *LAT* (February 6, 1927) C19; *TBS* (January 9, 1927) RM5.
407 *TBS* (October 3, 1926) SM5; *NYT* (February 5, 1928) 112; *LAT* (February 26, 1928) C13.
408 *LAT* (January 24, 1930) A11; *The China Press* (February 8, 1930) 10; *AC* (February 16, 1930) 4G; (December 7, 1931) 4; *NYT* (June 19, 1932) X2.
409 *NYHT* (June 25, 1932) 10; (September 19, 1931) 8.
410 *LAT* (March 30, 1927) A9; (March 27, 1927) C16.
411 *BG* (October 30, 1957) 27.

412 *NYHT* (January 8, 1930) 37.
413 *NYHT* (January 19, 1930) D5.
414 *CT* (January 28, 1927) 5.
415 *NYT* (April 10, 1927) XX13; *LAT* (June 25, 1927) A4.
416 *WP* (November 6, 1927) F3.
417 *NYT* (February 1, 1929) 18.
418 *The Billboard* 40 (November 10, 1928) 6 and 22; *NYT* (November 4, 1928) 123; (March 8, 1930) 1.
419 *LAT* (October 25, 1927) A11; (October 27, 1927) A9.
420 *The China Press* (July 28, 1927) 4.
421 *The China Press* (July 26, 1927) 3.
422 *TFD* 36 (April 23, 1926) 3.
423 *TBS* (July 11, 1926) MP7.
424 *Afro-American* (November 14, 1931) 2.
425 *BG* (February 25, 1928) 4.
426 *NYT* (January 4, 1928) 4.
427 *TFD* 54 (November 9, 1930) 4.
428 *BG* (April 11, 1929) 14; (October 19, 1930) 50; *CT* (June 28, 1931) C10. Cf. *Variety* 107 (June 21, 1932) 1.
429 *LAT* (April 15, 1928) C20.
430 *CT* (August 15, 1930) 15.
431 *LAT* (December 25, 1927) J3.
432 *Afro-American* (July 30, 1927) 6.
433 *LAT* (June 19, 1927) 33; *CT* (March 8, 1929) 34.
434 *LAT* (June 19, 1927) 33; *CT* (March 8, 1929) 34.
435 *The Irish Times* (December 31, 1927) 7.
436 *San Diego Union* (February 27, 1943) 9; *Omaha World Herald* (March 1, 1943) 11.
437 *LAT* (November 6, 1927) C13; cf. *TFD* 60 (November 23, 1932) 5.
438 *NYT* (January 3, 1932) X2.
439 *Barron's* (May 17, 1926) 15.
440 *LAT* (October 28, 1928) C11.
441 *Variety* (June 21, 1932) 1.
442 *AC* (March 3, 1940) 10.
443 *Dallas Morning News* (December 13, 1959) 5.1.
444 Glancy, "MGM Grosses, 1924–1948," 127–31.
445 *LAT* (Dc 13 25) C29; *TFD* 37 (August 1, 1926) 4; *WSJ* (June 23, 1927) 1; *The Billboard* 40 (February 11, 1928) 7; cf. Gomery, *The Coming of Sound*, 69.
446 *LAT* (Ot 3 26) C29.
447 *TBS* (October 17, 1926) MO3.
448 *TFD* 45 (September 16, 1928) 9; *NYHT* (March 16, 1930) G3; *ToI* (January 24, 1931) 14.
449 *NYHT* (April 3, 1927) E3; (March 16, 1930) G3.
450 *WP* (August 2, 1926) 7; *NYHT* (February 5, 1928) F3.
451 *The Independent* (May 28, 1927) 565.
452 *CT* (January 23, 1938) F2.
453 *Philadelphia Tribune* (September 4, 1926) 3.

454 *Afro-American* (August 28, 1926) 4.
455 *WSJ* (April 25, 1927) 17; cf. *ToI* (April 2, 1927) 14.
456 *The Manchester Guardian* (July 10, 1931) 8 and 13.
457 *The Manchester Guardian* (May 7, 1931) 8.
458 *Forum* 80 (September, 1928) 364.
459 *Jewish Advocate* (January 27, 1927) 2.
460 *TBS* (February 3, 1927) 10.
461 *LAT* (September 21, 1926) A22.
462 *The Irish Times* (January 9, 1932) 6.
463 *TBS* (January 7, 1932) 12.
464 Cf. *LAT* (January 7, 1932) 1.
465 *Philadelphia Tribune* (January 19, 1929) 5.
466 *The China Weekly Review* (January 19, 1929) 347.
467 *TCSM* (December 22, 1926) 4A.
468 *TCSM* (January 31, 1929) 7.
469 *The Observer* (December 18, 1927) 12.
470 *NYT* (March 22, 1927) 7; *AC* (October 14, 1928) 9M.
471 *TCSM* (May 22, 1931) 16.
472 Rose M. Cox, "The Individual and the Reading Course in a two-Year Technical High School," *Teachers College Journal* 1 (November, 1929) 46.
473 *NYHT* (September 2, 1928) J12; *WP* (September 30, 1928) S9; *The North American Review* 226 (December, 1928) 15.
474 *TBS* (August 22, 1926) 4.
475 *LAT* (February 1, 1929) A4.
476 *LAT* (July 6, 1929) A4.
477 Forman, *Our Movie Made Children*, 170.
478 *NYT* (June 17, 1928) 45; (July 31, 1932) RE11.
479 *NYT* (February 3, 1929) 130.
480 *BG* (February 12, 1928) C8.
481 *NYT* (December 20, 1925) BR25.
482 *NYHT* (June 3, 1928) K15.
483 *NYT* (May 6, 1928) 61.
484 William L. Beaumont, *Ben Ezra; Or, The Midnight Cry* (Boston: The Stratford Company, 1930).
485 *NYT* (December 28, 1930) BR11.
486 *TCSM* (September 28, 1926) 10.
487 *NYT* (September 19, 1926) 28.
488 *LAT* (August 1, 1926) B8.
489 *LAT* (September 9, 1926) A9.
490 *LAT* (May 25, 1930) 89.
491 *BG* (October 13, 1929) A52.
492 *TBS* (November 24, 1929) AT4.
493 "Herausgegeben anlässlich der Aufführung des Filmes 'Ben-Hur' der Metro-Goldwyn-Mayer."
494 Mendoza and Axt, *Music Score*.
495 Axt, *The Toilers*.
496 *TFD* 42 (October 5, 1927) 4.

497 *NYT* (September 3, 1927) 18; the announcement says that the music was arranged also by Major Bowes, soon to be a radio star on his own.
498 *ToI* (December 9, 1925) 10; cf. *The San Bernadino County Sun* (March 4, 1926) 8.
499 *El Paso Herald* (August 11, 1928) 9.
500 *BG* (July 10, 1931) 23.
501 *NYT* (September 7, 1947) X7.
502 *The Billboard* 41 (June 1, 1929) 35.
503 *BG* (May 8, 1927) 54.
504 *LAT* (July 9, 1930) A7.
505 *NYHT* (December 23, 1928) G2.
506 *The Manchester Guardian* (June 18, 1927) 14.
507 *TBS* (October 17, 1926) RA7.
508 *LAT* (March 4, 1931) 22.
509 William C. Bagley, "Radio in the Schools," *The Elementary School Journal* 31 (December, 1930) 256–8.
510 *BG* (January 6, 1929) B11.
511 *BG* (September 14, 1930) 62 and 63.
512 *The [Adelaide] Register* (January 16, 1926) 12.
513 E.g. *NYHT* (December 29, 1928) 17; (January 20, 1929) G8.
514 *NYHT* (December 9, 1928) G2.
515 *NYT* (October 28, 1928) 154.
516 *CT* (May 16, 1930) 28.
517 *NYT* (May 11, 1930) 150; (May 16, 1930) 28.
518 *TBS* (May 11, 1930) MR10.
519 *WP* (December 12, 1926) F1.
520 *LAT* (May 22, 1927) 17; (May 29, 1927) C11; cf. LAT (January 30, 1927) C19.
521 *LAT* (June 5, 1927) C14.
522 *TCSM* (January 27, 1927) 10.
523 *LAT* (January 21, 1926) A10; (February 3, 1926) A9.
524 *WP* (June 25, 1927) 13; (June 26, 1927) 1.
525 *NYHT* (June 19, 1927) E3.
526 *CPD* (August 17, 1927) 19.
527 *AC* (September 4, 1927) B3.
528 *AC* (September 17, 1927) 8.
529 *The Irish Times* (October 31, 1927) 11.
530 *The Manchester Guardian* (February 22, 1928) 6.
531 *The Manchester Guardian* (April 14, 1928) 10.
532 *The Manchester Guardian* (May 25, 1928) 10; *BG* (July 1, 1928) 11.
533 *The Irish Times* (September 8, 1928).
534 *The Manchester Guardian* (December 12, 1928) 13.
535 *NYT* (August 30, 1928) 10.
536 *AC* (August 23, 1928) 24.
537 *Photoplay* 35 (December, 1928) 64–5; *BG* (September 16, 1928) B3; cf. *LAT* (May 18, 1930) J10; *CT* (April 28, 1929) Picture Section, Part 2.
538 *The Youth's Companion* 102 (November, 1928) 604.
539 *LAT* (e.g. September 26, 1927) 16; (October 29, 1927) 16.

540 *NYT* (November 18, 1928) XX4.
541 *BG* (April 8, 1927) 29.
542 *AC* (February 9, 1929) 4.
543 *BG* (January 22, 1927) 14.
544 *Photoplay* 32 (November, 1927) 33.
545 *AC* (January 20, 1929) E15.
546 *The Manchester Guardian* (February 25, 1929) 11.
547 *TBS* (January 19, 1930) 89.
548 *CT* (January 26, 1930) C4.
549 *BG* (February 8, 1930) 8; *NYT* (February 8, 1930) 16.
550 *BG* (June 11, 1930) 30.
551 *BG* (August 29, 1930) 15.
552 *BG* (March 27, 1932) A40.
553 E.g. *[San Diego] Evening Tribune* (October 20, 1932) 12; *Sheboygan Press* (December 29, 1932) 3.
554 *Look and Learn Magazine* (September 24, 1932) 3.
555 *LAT* (March 13, 1932) 14.
556 *NYHT* (June 9, 1928) 17; (September 27, 1930) 26; *NYT* (May 20, 1930) 39; (June 4, 1932) 12; *LAT* (December 22, 1929) E8.
557 *LAT* (July 20, 1930) A1.
558 *NYHT* (September 13, 1931) 89; *NYT* (April 16, 1929) 38.
559 *The Irish Times* (August 7, 1930) 5; (May 26, 1927) 11.
560 *The Irish Times* (June 30, 1932) 5; (May 26, 1927) 11.
561 *The [Hobart] Mercury* (February 8, 1926) 4.
562 E.g. *NYHT* (January 11, 1928) 20.
563 *LAT* (June 21, 1927) B2.
564 *NYHT* ((March 26, 1930) 16.
565 *NYHT* (February 14, 1932) F5.
566 *NYT* (March 9, 1930) 170.
567 *NYT* (January 3, 1929) 33.
568 *NYT* (May 19, 1927) 3; cf. *CT* (December 30, 1928) F1.
569 *NYT* (January 3, 1929) 33.
570 *NYT* (January 6, 1929) 118.
571 *Forum and Century* 84 (September, 1930) 167.
572 *LAT* (May 11, 1931) 6.
573 E.g. *TBS* (March 24, 1929) S10.
574 *The Irish Times* (May 25, 1929) 4.
575 *The Nation & Athenaeum* 43 (September 1, 1928) 712.
576 Cf. *The Manchester Guardian* (September 6, 1927) 8.
577 Anne D. Williams, *Jigsaw Puzzles: An Illustrated History and Price Guide* (Radnor, PA: Wallace-Homestead Book Company, 1990) 214–15.
578 *NYT* (December 18, 1928) 32.
579 *BG* (February 21, 1926) A10.
580 *Photoplay* 29 (January, 1926) 91.
581 eBay #320013757953, ended September 2, 2006.
582 *TBS* (November 27, 1927) SF13.
583 *NYT* (April 23, 1959) 24.

584 *Photoplay* 30 (October, 1926) 89–90; (November, 1926) 109–10.
585 *Photoplay* 30 (December, 1926) 97–8.
586 *[New Orleans] Times-Picayune* (December 18, 1926) 18.
587 *Galveston Daily News* (December 5, 1926) 10.
588 *TBS* (November 27, 1927) SF13.
589 *Omaha World Herald* (March 12, 1926) 6.
590 *Omaha World Herald* (October 10, 1927) 13.
591 *National Geographic* 51 (May, 1927) 17.
592 *Ladies' Home Journal* 45 (April, 1928) 80.
593 *Photoplay* 28 (August, 1925) 110.
594 E.g. *LAT* (April 27, 1929) 3; (December 6, 1929) 7; (December 30, 1929) A6; (June 7, 1932) Part 2, page 7.
595 E.g. *LAT* (November 19, 1928) A3.
596 *LAT* (September 13, 1926) A15.
597 E.g. *LAT* (January 19, 1926) A8.
598 *LAT* (April 14, 1930) A9.
599 *LAT* (January 18, 1930) 3
600 *LAT* (June 24, 1930) 12.
601 *LAT* (November 15, 1930) 2.
602 *Reading Times* (April 9, 1926) 22.
603 *CT* (July 21, 1926) 13.
604 *AC* (February 27, 1927) C2.
605 *Photoplay* 30 (October, 1926) 99.
606 E.g. *CT* (February 28, 1927) 11; and *WP* (March 5, 1927) 3.
607 *NYHT* (July 10, 1927) B20; *NYT* (July 11, 1927) 35; (June 13, 1927) 36; (July 20, 1927) 39; (September 3, 1927) 50; *NYHT* (July 30, 1930) 28.
608 *Railway Age* 88 (June 21, 1930) 1492; 91 (September 5, 1931) 382.
609 *NYT* (January 8, 1928) 48.
610 *NYHT* (June 4, 1929) 45.
611 *NYHT* (October 19, 1929) 29.
612 *NYHT* (July 4, 1929) 26; *NYT* (February 5, 1932).
613 *CT* (January 19, 1930) F3; *NYHT* (January 19, 1930) 7.
614 *NYT* (December 31, 1930) 36.
615 *BG* (September 25, 1931) 14; (March 4, 1932) 7.
616 *NYT* (March 2, 1931) 42; (February 5, 1932) 38.
617 *NYT* (January 22, 1931) 44.
618 *NYT* (July 7, 1931) 43.
619 *NYT* (March 26, 1931) 50.
620 *The Billboard* 44 (September 24, 1932) 75.
621 E.g. *Milwaukee Journal* (November 28, 1926) 9.
622 Brownlow, *The Parade's Gone By . . .*, 386.
623 *LAT* (December 19, 1926) C21; cf. Brownlow, *The Parade's Gone By . . .*, 411.
624 *The Saturday Evening Post* 206 (November 4, 1933) 10 and 83–5.

13 Between the MGM Films

THE TRADITION CONTINUES

Throughout its history, *Ben-Hur* had introduced, solidified, or extended a variety of popular trends. Wallace's novel, for instance, introduced popular fiction to new demographics, was a model for copyright protection, and re-energized the trend in historical novels set in biblical antiquity. *Ben-Hur, in Tableaux and Pantomime* inspired new kinds of synergistic advertising. The Klaw & Erlanger production, in establishing a high-water mark for box-office receipts and touring longevity, expanded the audience for live popular drama as well as the size of stages and theaters across the country. In music, purveyors of new technological advancements eagerly and repeatedly recorded Paull's "The Chariot Race or Ben Hur March," and comprehensive *Ben-Hur* literary sets were the first to appear in stereopticon catalogs. In the film world, the Kalem *Ben-Hur* venture brought about new and enduring definitions of cinematic copyright guidelines, and MGM's 1925 film thoroughly expanded the international market for *Ben-Hur*. As new popular trends emerged in the commercial world, here, too, there were Ben-Hur products, as in the insurance industry and electrical outdoor display lighting, while Ben-Hur Flour furthered several advertising trends with its campaigns targeting housewives and children in prominent national weekly and monthly magazines.

The *Ben-Hur* property would continue to find a variety of outlets in the popular arts and commerce during the 1930s, 1940s, and early 1950s as new trends would dictate. Radio listeners heard a half-dozen different dramatized versions on national networks, a serialized syndicated graphic depiction of the story was published in newspaper comic pages coast to coast, and several types of comic-book adaptations were published as well. Pageants and parades exploited *Ben-Hur* themes, and frequent retrospectives featuring Wallace, his novel, the Klaw & Erlanger adaptation, and the 1925 MGM film appeared in newspapers. Some of the latter's stars, like Novarro, Bushman, and Myers, found second careers in radio and television, and publicity usually cited their role in the well-remembered *Ben-Hur* film. In the business world many Ben-Hur companies and products continued through the worst depression years of the early 1930s or emerged shortly after. One supplied an award-winning Ben Hur Trailer to the U.S. Army during World War II and then helped to pioneer the home freezer market. Ben-Hur Hair products and nylons tinted with Ben-Hur color appeared in newspaper advertisements in all three decades almost as frequently as did ads for Ben-Hur Soap and Ben-Hur Coffee products. All these and much more were produced before MGM announced their plans to remake *Ben-Hur* late in 1952.

Radio
After MGM pulled the domestic release of its film in 1933, Francis X. Bushman carried the torch as he developed a second career in radio, first hosting a daily morning program on WGN in Chicago. He "reenacted his ride in the chariot race in *Ben-Hur*" late in 1933 and repeated it "by popular demand" in January, 1934.[1] That same month the American School of the Air performed a dramatized version of the novel over the Columbia network.[2] Three months later Bushman staged a theatrical sketch at the Oriental Theater preceded by a retrospective that included a trailer from the MGM *Ben-Hur*.[3] His role in the film was invoked repeatedly in publicity releases. When the Mutual Broadcasting system advertised a new radio play, *Make Believe*, in 1940, it carried a contemporary photograph of the actor and boasted, "Among Francis X. Bushman's great triumphs was 'Ben Hur.' This epic took years to make and is still being shown in some parts of the world."[4] Besides Chicago, Baltimore was another city that embraced the early silent-film star once it was revealed that he had been born there. He was the subject of several newspaper features in 1947,[5] and in August, 1951, when he received a key to the city, there were several extensive pieces in *The Sun*.[6] One of them highlighted his visit as part of a promotional tour for his role as King Saul in Daryl F. Zanuck's *David and Bathsheba*, one of his first movie roles in more than a decade. The feature finished with the line, "Baltimoreans past the age of thirty will doubtlessly remember Mr. Bushman for his memorable performance as Messala in 'Ben Hur.'"[7] In the same year, Bushman appeared in *Hollywood Story* along with other silent-film stars, including William Farnum, the original Klaw & Erlanger Ben-Hur.[8] In each of these instances and still others, *Ben-Hur* is almost always a primary identifier. As we will see, Bushman's name would return to the limelight several more times later in the decade as the release of the 1959 film approached.

The 1933 adaptation was relatively early in radio broadcasting. It was not until 1936 that radio programming began to include substantial numbers of newly written dramatic works. Again at the forefront of technological and popular cultural advancement, *Ben-Hur* was adapted already in 1937 as the eleventh script of the *Treasures Next Door* series produced by the Office of Education of the U.S. Department of the Interior.[9] Because the scripts were designed to dramatize the works of "great American novelists" and "bring you fifteen minutes with an important writer,"[10] it was probably intentional that the government script was anonymous. Unlike some of the subsequent adaptations of Wallace's novel in the 1930s and 1940s, this one neither emphasizes nor avoids the religious aspects of the story. Fulfilling its designed purpose, it encourages the radio listener to read the end of the story in the original novel.

The script begins with an announcer detailing some of Lew Wallace's accomplishments, concluding with, "though he wrote one of the greatest religious stories of all time, he was never a church member!" There follows an imaginary scene in the Wallace home where Susan ["Mrs."] Wallace has just finished reading her husband's manuscript, a labor of seven years finally dedicated "To the wife of my youth who still abides with me." As the reader may be observing, the script seems to reflect accurately what is known about the writing of *Ben-Hur: A Tale of the Christ*, but Wallace then tells his wife that the Madonna was modeled after her. The music swells and brings us to the tile incident in ancient Jerusalem and Judah and Tirzah discussing his quarrel with Messala: "I found a haughty Roman stranger wearing Messala's face. . . . He told me to forget Moses and turn to Mars!" Quoting from the novel, he concludes, "What has been will be again."

Crowd interaction enlivens the experience for the listener. Two women in the crowd at Nazareth observe Jesus giving Judah a drink:

> 1st Woman: "You're taller. Can you see what's happening, Rachel?"
> 2nd Woman: "That young carpenter in Joseph's shop laid down his saw and is filling a pitcher at the well . . . Now he's holding it to the prisoner's lips for him to drink."
> 1st Woman: "Oh yes – I know whom you mean. A young man with such kind eyes. What is his name?"
> 2nd Woman: "Jesus, Jesus of Nazareth . . ."

The narrator describes the transitions to the galley and then back to Judea, but despite the time limit, the listener still gets to hear an informative interview between Arrius and Number Sixty, the galley engaging in battle and sinking, and Ben-Hur rescuing Arrius at sea. Unique in the penultimate Judean scene is that Iras completely replaces Esther, who does not appear at all, and expedites Ben Hur's participation in the chariot race against Messala. The chariot race is then almost entirely allotted to crowd reactions, and near the climax the announcer intervenes:

> What happened? Who won the race? Did Ben Hur humble his enemy in this public place? Did Ben Hur ever find his mother and Tirzah? Did his path ever again cross that of the carpenter's boy who held a pitcher to the lips of a galley slave? Those of you who have read Ben Hur once will want to re-read it and refresh your memory

of its wonders. If you have never read it, ask you own public library for this book, and others by the same author.

The four final pages of the script are devoted to descriptions of the characters' voices (e.g. Iras: "A woman's voice, sweet as a caress") and to the production of background noises and sound effects.

Elphie A. Ellington's more widely publicized "radioization" followed in 1940.[11] This installment of *Command Performance* starred the youthful Frankie Thomas, Henry Hull, and Del Casino, and was broadcast over the Mutual Broadcasting System.[12] This was a thirty-minute broadcast scheduled to coincide with the Easter season, as was the *Star-Spangled Theater* presentation, starring Bert Lytell, Jean Muir, and Judith Allen, broadcast the following year on Easter Sunday, 1941.[13] These half-hour formats challenged the writer to produce incisive characterizations and swift action. Flashbacks, summary narrations, and very brief expository scenes often assisted in condensing much longer originals.[14] Norman Weiser, dramatic editor of *Radio Daily*, specifically chose Ellington's "Ben-Hur" as one of only ten, out of some 9000 hours of dramas broadcast in 1940–1, to be included in his anthology of "outstanding plays," *The Writer's Radio Theater, 1940–41*.[15] He wrote at the time:

> "Ben Hur" illustrates one of the newer techniques in radio writing, the tying in of the narrator's role with the starring character to enhance the word pictures painted by the actors. This technique, although tried in earlier years, was one of the outstanding developments of 1940, when it really came into its own.

He also praised Ellington's script for successfully transplanting the written narrative into dialogue form.

Like the federal government's anonymous author, Ellington also begins with a prologue, this one in an imaginary bookshop, where the owner, Mr. Meggs, holds up a copy of *Ben Hur* and asserts its relevance to the rise of the Nazi empire, the first of many associations between *Ben-Hur*, the Nazis, and World War II:

> Ben Hur, a young man who lived in an age when the world was in just about the state it is today. There were wars, heavy taxes, religious persecution. A single empire had risen in strength until it was practically dictator of the world. This empire had a fierce and bigoted hatred of all nations and peoples but its own. Particularly did they have contempt for the children of Israel who dared believe in the existence of only one god. These people had heard that a child had been born, and they waited patiently for the day when he would show himself and lead them into Freedom.

Music then leads us into the quarrel with Messala, conversation with his mother, and tile incident. The dialogue includes several lines from Wallace's text ("There is richer entertainment ..."; "Down Eros, up Mars!"), although Ben Hur's signature oath of vengeance is omitted. As in the previous example, the scene at the well is described by unnamed onlookers, and the galley sequence consists of discussions between the hortator and Arrius, and Ben Hur and Arrius. Then we return to the bookshop characters for a description of the naval battle, enhanced by sound effects. Extended scenes with Simonides, Esther, and Malluch recreate the mystery and intrigue of the original novel, and it is left mostly to Simonides and an adoring Esther to describe the chariot race, backed up by crowd voices and specific studio instructions:

> ESTHER: Father, the chariot of the Greek driver is overtaking the Roman!
> SIMONIDES: Quickly, daughter, cover thine eyes; Messala is driving the Greek to the wall!
> **SOUND OF CRASH ... VOICES UP ... SCREAMS**
> SIMONIDES: The dog has killed the Greek!
> ESTHER: He will do the same to Hur. Watch, Father, now he is forcing him to the wall!
> SIMONIDES: Prayers for him, my daughter, prayers!
> **MUSIC: INCREASE IN TEMPO**
> VOICE: (*Over crowd*) Speed, Messala – give them the rein!
> 2ND VOICE: (*Over crowd*) Look – Ben Hur has made the turn.
> ...
> SIMONIDES: Our master's Arabs run side to side with Messala!
> ESTHER: He's trying to pass!
> SIMONIDES: Messala refuses to give way!
> ESTHER: His wheel, his wheel! It is locked in that of Ben Hur's!
> **SOUND OF CRASH – SHOUTING**
> SIMONIDES: The Roman lies in the dust!
> ESTHER: Our master tries to free himself!
> SIMONIDES: He is free! Here he comes! He wins! He wins!
> **BIZ: SHOUTS OF "BEN HUR! BEN HUR!"**
> **MUSIC: UP TO CLIMAX. CROSS-FADE TO MR. MEGGS' THEME.**

Mr. Meggs narrates briefly the transition to the leprosy of Ben Hur's mother and sister and Ben Hur's and Simonides' search for "the king." From a distance the latter two witness the lepers being miraculously cured and then the Crucifixion scene punctuated by sounds of human gasps and sobbing. Celestial thunder then returns the listener to the modern bookshop. Mr. Meggs concludes, again emphasizing the modern relevancy of the story:

> The world has never needed crusaders as it does right now. There are plenty of heroic deeds to be done, but we need men with faith to do them. ... [Faith] was the cure in the age of Ben Hur, and it can be again. You see it's when we lose faith that things happen. ... They'll have to fight with a different artillery, use truth instead of bullets. ... They must be soldiers of the spirit!
> **MUSIC: UP BIG AND OUT**

The producer of this "Ben-Hur," Ted Lloyd, told Weiser that this radio adaptation was so popular that he was "besieged" by requests from schools and colleges nationwide to utilize the script in radio and dramatic workshops.[16]

Four more radio plays would be produced. In 1948 alone two different dramatizations were broadcast, a *Tell It Again* presentation in May, and a *My Favorite Story* version in August, starring John Beal as Judah Ben-Hur and Marvin Miller as Messala, and narrated by Ronald Colman.[17] The *My Favorite Story* series that ran from 1946 to 1949 dramatized literary works selected by celebrities and luminaries and then adapted by Jerome Lawrence and Robert E. Lee. "Ben-Hur" was selected by Clyde Beatty, the lion tamer and circus impresario. The next year the British United Press announced that Vatican radio would broadcast a serialized version of *Ben-Hur*.[18] On April 10, 1952, the CBS network reused the Lawrence and Lee adaptation for its *Hallmark Playhouse* series (#162), featuring Jeff Chandler as Judah and Bill Conrad as Messala.[19]

Lawrence and Lee framed their script, which is preserved in the Special Collections Library at The Ohio State University, with dialogue between Judah, his mother, and Judah's newly invented son David. This enabled much of the story to be narrated in flashbacks interspersed with brief dialogue exchanges, some of it taken from the novel itself, colored by background sound effects and David Rose's musical flourishes. Their version of the story necessarily narrows the number of characters, so Balthasar replaces Amrah and Esther in locating Judah's leprous mother and sister, and Judah's narration to David says only that he escaped from a Roman galley and had a long journey back home. As in the novel, Judah is slow to embrace the message of the child Balthasar describes in some detail, focusing the drama on the spiritual themes of the novel, even if Christ's name is not mentioned. The story concludes with the message, "Where there is love, there is god."

While such companies as Ben Hur Products [Coffee, Tea, and Spices] and Ben Hur Manufacturing [Freezers] continued to sponsor a number of shows and radio advertisements,[20] Wallace's fame as the author of *Ben-Hur* inspired several additional broadcasts. While touring New Mexico in 1940, Bob Ripley narrated several stories featuring the former governor "who wrote *Ben-Hur*."[21] The next year, Ted Malone's visit to Wallace's home in Crawfordsville was broadcast on the NBC-Blue network.[22]

Comics

The story of *Ben-Hur: A Tale of the Christ* was also redacted in graphic form. *Popular Comics*, published monthly by Dell, ran a seven-part series from May through November, 1939.[23] It was one of the first comics drawn and inked by Erwin L. Hess, known later for his own cartoon series, *The Good Old Days*, that was syndicated from 1947 to 1981.[24] Compared to the painterly style of many of the *Ben-Hur* stereopticon slides, most of Hess's cartoon panels offer challenging perspectives penciled with detailed linear textures. As we see Judah and Tirzah watching from their "window," more than a dozen Roman soldiers march below, each of them discretely drawn. Similarly, each wooden plank is visible in the drawings of the Roman galleys. Some of the imagery derives from the 1925 film, for instance, Judah's conical helmet (in the first panel of the first issue) and the pirate chief who holds a Roman head pierced by his sword. The story, which unfolded on twenty-eight pages of six panels each, four pages per issue, is entirely devoid of the Christian element. Judah does not encounter the Christ on his trek across the desert to the galleys, there is no Crucifixion, and Judah's mother and sister do not even contract leprosy. After Pontius Pilate releases them from prison, they choose not to allow Judah to see them only because of their "weakened" condition and then in the final three panels ultimately reunite with him through Amrah's intercession.

Beginning in April, 1940, during the first year of publication, *Flash Comics* included short book reviews and synopses. The first was of *Robinson Crusoe*, followed by various works of Jules Verne, Mark Twain, Charles Dickens, and others. *Ben-Hur* was reviewed in the February, 1941, issue by Mollie Zisser, whom U.S. Census records identify as a septuagenarian.[25] She introduces a few minor inaccuracies, e.g. placing Ben-Hur's initial re-encounter with Messala in the great circus at Antioch, and simplifies Wallace's theological excursions while at least preserving the Christian events of the novel. In the penultimate paragraph she writes:

> By now, Jesus Christ was going throughout Judea, teaching gentleness and mercy. When Ben-Hur saw Jesus, he recognized Him as the boy who had given him a drink of water when he was a galley-slave! Ben-Hur became a follower of Jesus Christ.

From August 29 to November 14, 1943, the Bell Syndicate serialized *Ben-Hur: A Story of the Christ* in twelve installments for Sunday newspaper comic pages, e.g. the *Dallas Morning News*. This series belonged to Bell's *Famous Fiction* series and was illustrated by "Chad" Grothkopf, an animation artist also known for his *Sandman* work.[26] Some of the installments included an added bonus of paper doll cut-outs along with appropriate clothing, e.g. a tunic and sandals for Ben-Hur and a robe and headdress for Amrah.[27]

Each page was divided into six half panels, some of them further divided, providing eight, nine, or ten scenes per page. The first page, for instance, dedicates two full and two half panels to the Nativity, one full and two half panels to the quarrel between Judah and Messala, and two half panels to the conversation between Judah and his mother, concluding with her permitting Judah to become a soldier to "serve the Lord instead of Caesar." Each subsequent installment begins with a full panel summarizing the events of the previous installment. Grothkopf created several panels illustrating an angel announcing the birth of a savior and Jesus is embellished with a halo, but the rest of the scenes illustrate Wallace's narrative quite faithfully. The galley sequence, the fourth installment, for instance, consists of a full panel showing Ben-Hur at the oar, four half panels illustrating the conversation between Ben-Hur and Arrius, a full panel showing the ship being rammed, three half panels showing Ben-Hur and Arrius in the water, and a final half panel showing Arrius saying, "You saved my life! You shall no longer be a slave, but my adopted son."

Because of the limited space allotted to telling such a complex story, the sequence of events moves rapidly and the dialogue is abbreviated, much as in the Lawrence and Lee radio script. But rather than relying on flashbacks and narration, the visual component allows Grothkopf to present more of the story in vivid detail. The chariot race, for instance, contains a half panel showing a close up of Messala in the lead ("Ha, Ben-Hur, so we meet again, and you shall see that a Jew is no match for a Roman!"), a full panel with a broader view showing Messala and his *quadriga* in the foreground, a more distant team, and part of a *spina* with columns and spectators behind. Another full panel shows a close up of chariot wheels spinning in the dust, with Ben-Hur's feet on the chariot platform between them. The caption reads, "Then on the final turn, Ben-Hur executes a lightning maneuver." One half panel shows an axle hub crashing into a spinning wheel, and another shows a close-up of horses galloping above the fallen Messala's head. Ben-Hur's *quadriga* extends across the length of the final panel. He raises his right arm in triumph, and word bubbles among the crowd in the background read, "Ben-Hur wins!" and "Hurrah! Ben-Hur!" The eleventh installment has several depictions of the Crucifixion, and the twelfth concludes when Simonides (in a wheelchair) suggests that Ben-Hur donate his wealth for the burial of the Christians persecuted by Nero, with a penultimate half panel of Esther and Ben-Hur standing in front of a huge sunrise across a broad horizon. The final half panel has text only, reading:

> THUS THE FORTUNES OF BEN-HUR WERE PUT TO THE SERVICE OF A NEW, ALL-INSPIRING FAITH. WITH THEM BEN-HUR BUILT THE CATACOMBS OF ROME, AND OUT OF THOSE VAST TOMBS A NEW RELIGION AROSE TO LIGHT THE WORLD, AND THAT RELIGION WAS ... CHRISTIANITY!

In one of several interesting departures for the *Ben-Hur* tradition to be described here, "Ben Hur Wins a Race" presented a comic version of a chariot race starring the comedy duo Doc and Fatty.[28] It was penciled and inked by Howard Sherman and published in the May–June, 1949, issue of DC's *World's Finest Comics*. Doc, who is tall and wears a suit, top hat, and spats, and Fatty, who is rotund and wears a vested suit several sizes too small, have a "Time Typer" that sends them back to an ancient Roman stable. There they are accused of stealing horseshoes, so Nero sentences them to the dungeons, where they meet Ben Hur, a square-jawed athlete in a short white tunic. They say to him, "You're a famous chariot racer – or maybe you don't know it yet." Ben Hur explains that he has never won a chariot race and needs to do so to earn his freedom. After digging themselves out of the dungeon, Doc and Fatty earn enough money to buy him a chariot and horses by inventing and selling "Red Hot Roman Dogs." To help Ben Hur win the race, the time travelers give cheap cigars to the other drivers. Incensed, they chase Doc and Fatty, but Ben Hur hands them their Time Typer and they escape in the nick of time. The final panel shows Doc and Fatty reading a "History of Rome" on a modern park bench. Doc reads, "and then Ben Hur won his freedom and all was well!" Fatty comments, "Now take the average man: he'd never believe **we** won that race would he?"

Famous Authors Illustrated offered a graphic version of the novel in 1951. Modeled after Gilberton's *Classics Illustrated* [aka *Classics Comics*] series and similarly designed to bring literature to young people, this monthly series began with adaptations of such popular adventure tales as *The Scarlet Pimpernel*, *Captain Blood*, and *She* in the *Fast Fiction* series.[29] *Ben-Hur* was the eleventh release, issued in January, 1951. Adapted by Dana E. Dutch and illustrated by Gustav Schrotter, this 44-page "comic-book" version was just the first of a number of juvenile adaptations to appear later in the decade in concert with the release of the MGM film.

The first page announces the theme of the story, Ben-Hur's metamorphosis from a youthful and rebellious "prince of Jerusalem" to a man of peace blessed with "fame and fortune." Dutch then divides the story into four parts, although Part I does not have a subtitle. Part III ("The Long Road to Vengeance") includes a five-page flashback illustrating "Balthasar's Story." The page after the conclusion of Part IV adds a large drawing of a piece of parchment on which is printed a lengthy prose explanation of "What Became of Ben-Hur's Great Wealth," without illustration, concluding with several quotations from the last pages of Wallace's novel. The bottom of the page contains a footnote describing the Roman catacombs. Not nearly so constrained as the thirty-minute radio scripts or serialized comics, Dutch had the luxury of spreading his adaptation over 250 panels. The initial quarrel between Judah and Messala fills two entire pages and contains more dialogue than in Act I of Young's script for the Klaw & Erlanger play and, of course, the intertitles for the 1925 film. The second page includes most of Wallace's arguments, Messala's desire to have Judah join him, and Ben-Hur's insistence that his people will withstand the Roman occupation. A few of the phrases derive directly from the novel.

> Ben-Hur: "I've taken enough of your insults, Messala! There was no such poison in our nature before you left for school in Rome five years ago."
> Messala: "Of course I'm different! All men change, but a Jew never! ... Wait a minute! I haven't finished with you!"
> Ben-Hur: "No, we had better part. Your Roman boasting drives me to hate you!"
> Messala: "Don't be a fool, Ben-Hur! Cast aside these Jewish traditions and be like me – a Roman! You don't have to be an underdog!"
> Ben-Hur: "You are the bigger fool, Messala! There were masters of Judea before the Heathen Romans came, but Judea has outlived them all! What has been will be again!"

> Messala: "Impossible! Rome is now the world. Join with me and become a soldier of the empire. We'll rise to power and mastery over millions of your people!"
> Ben-Hur: "Never! As a Roman you may fight for Rome. I am a Jew and all Romans are my enemies. I fight against Rome – for freedom!"
> Messala: "Stubborn fool! I offer you friendship and you leave me a bitter foe. Soon you will be down on your knees, begging for mercy! Watch out, Ben-Hur! I'll put you in your place!"
> Ben-Hur: "You too, Messala! Let Rome beware the vengeance of a persecuted people. The day will come when Rome will be no more, and the chosen race of God shall rule once more as is our right!"

Similarly, the story spends fifteen panels for the tile incident and arrest, and fourteen for the naval battle, raft, and rescue scenes. Schrotter varied the layouts from page to page, employing a number of differently shaped panels. He carefully conceals the face of the Christ from view by placing him in the distance or, where he cures Ben-Hur's mother and sister, covering his face with the narration box.

One battle page consists of two half-page panels filled with blue sky and sea, the red Roman galley, two yellow pirate ships, grey smoke, and white plumes of sea water. The sails, ropes, oars, and wood planks contain much linear detail. The upper hull of the Roman galley, for instance, shows a lantern, a bust of the emperor, an iron ring, and embossed shields. "Balthasar's Story" contains several notable panels that illustrate the shepherds tending their sheep during the night, a choir of singing angels, and the three shepherds running from the glimmering, radiant light. The chariot race panels employ full *quadrigae* differentiated by the colors of the horses. The climax, where Ben-Hur splinters Messala's spokes and Messala is pinned beneath the wreckage, are laid out on a double-wide page, the former wide enough to show their *quadrigae* side by side, the latter to show the fallen Messala, his fallen team of black horses on the left and Ben-Hur driving his white horses to victory on the right. In the final part Ben-Hur dismisses the ambitious Iras as a "vain and selfish creature," and the penultimate two pages consist of single panels illustrating Ben-Hur, Esther, and Balthasar lamenting the impending Crucifixion and Ben-Hur, amidst his friends and with Golgotha in the background, admitting:

> At last, Oh Christ, I understand how I can serve thee – forever banish thought of hate and vengeance from my heart and help me build thy kingdom through mercy and forgiveness.

The last page celebrates the Resurrection of the Christ three days later.

"The Hot-Rod Chariot Race!" employed Ben-Hur as a featured character in a time-traveling Superboy story published in Dell's *Adventure Comics* in June, 1952.[30] The cover, designed by DC artist Win Mortimer, depicts Superboy pulling a modern teenager on a chariot ahead of two other two-horse chariots, crammed Roman circus section on the right and the *spina* platform holding a few more Romans on the left. The tease reads, "It's Superboy against Ben Hur in 'The Hot-Rod Chariot Race!'" The twelve-page story begins in Smallville, where Superboy tasks himself to teach Victor Varley, a red-head teenager, not to drive his hot rod so recklessly, and to save Professor Whitley's reputation. Whitley claims that he has excavated the helmet of "the greatest chariot racer of them all – Ben Hur," but a "group of experts" has declared the helmet to be a fake and Ben Hur a fictional character. Whitley insists, "Ben Hur *must* have been a real person! His feats may have caused exaggerated stories to be written about him, but he was real!" The bad publicity could cause Whitley to be fired, so Superboy takes Varley back in time to ancient Rome in the year 50. There he searches for Ben Hur in vain while Varley enters into a chariot race, which turns out to be fixed by a shady Roman named Festus. The race is preceded by a gladiatorial contest between a young Quintus Arrius and a lion, which Festus again tries to fix by filing Arrius' sword. Superboy saves him, but the latter now needs money for the entry fee for the chariot race. Superboy invents and then sells popcorn and ice cream to raise the cash. Meanwhile Superboy is still searching in vain for Ben Hur. Festus and his fellow gamblers have tampered with the chariots, so both Arrius and Varley have to stop, but Superboy fashions a jet engine for Arrius because "the rules say that chariots may be driven by *any* means!" Arrius wins, the judges send the gamblers to prison, and Arrius' name is about to be inscribed on the victory monument when he reveals that his real name is Ben Hur. He changed his name "to trap these gamblers whose tricks killed my father in a race years ago." Having found the "real" Ben Hur, Superboy returns Varley, who vows never to drive recklessly again, to Smallville and informs Whitley precisely where to excavate the inscribed victory monument to prove Ben Hur's existence.

In 1953 a French adaptation was serialized in the Canadian magazine, *Le Samedi*. Published in Montreal and copyrighted by Opera Mundi, the black and white adaptation was drawn by Carlo Raffaele Marcello, aka Ralph Marc, the Parisian artist who specialized in adaptations of popular novels.[31] Each episode consisted of a single page divided into three registers of four panels each. Between the panels are extensive prose descriptions of the narrative, which the panels then illustrate.

The series ran for more than five dozen episodes from late 1952 to early 1954.[32] This extensive coverage of the story allowed for extraordinary narrative detail. Episode #51, for instance, covers only the period after the chariot race from the announcement that Messala was injured so severely during the chariot race that the doctors have determined that he will not walk again, to Judah's lonely arrival at the Palace at Idernee.[33] We read in some detail that the debts that Messala and Drusus are refusing to pay Sanballat will be adjudicated by an imperial representative. In Episode #57 there is a panel devoted to Ilderim presenting Aldebaran to Judah.[34] There are even a few details that Wallace did not clarify, e.g. that Cleanthes was killed in the chariot race.

The Novel
While the plot and episodes were being adapted and recreated in the rapidly developing fields of radio and popular comics, the original novel remained in public consciousness in a variety of ways. New editions of the novel continued to be issued by some publishers under different imprints and in collections of famous books. In 1934 The Modern Library included *Ben-Hur* in its full-page, *New York Times* advertisement for its "Distinguished List" of the World's Great Books.[35] *Ben-Hur* belonged to such other series as The Spencer Press's World's Greatest Literature (1936), Grosset & Dunlap's Novel's of Inspiration (1946/7), Literary Classics (1947), and the Fountain Press's World's Greatest Literature edition illustrated by Louis Dechmann (1949). New editions included Webster Publishing Company's edition adapted by William Kottmeyer and illustrated by James Cummins (1949), and Dodd, Mead & Company's edition (1953), which added an introduction by Basil Davenport and sixteen illustrations, among them several photos of Wallace and one of F. M.'s sketches from *Seekers After "The Light" From "Ben-Hur."*

Books listing American bestsellers often placed *Ben-Hur* near the top of their lists, including Edward Weeks' "Sixty-five American Best Sellers" in 1934,[36] Alice Hackett's *Fifty Years of Best Sellers: 1895–1945*,[37] Luther Mott's *Golden Multitudes: The Story of Best-Sellers in the United States* in 1947,[38] and the American Bookseller's Association report of 1949.[39] It was Mott's publication that "explodes the myth" that *In His Steps* had sold eight million copies,[40] which puts the *Wall Street Journal*'s ranking of America's bestsellers since 1875, published in April, 1934, into the proper perspective.[41] There *Ben-Hur* (1.95 million copies sold) follows only *In His Steps* and Gene Stratton Porter's *Freckles* (two million). The novel ranked high even when contemporary books were compared. George Gallup conducted a survey in 1938 and listed *Ben-Hur* seventh, remarkable considering that the top six included the Bible and otherwise only 1930s bestsellers (*Gone With the Wind* [1936], *How To Win Friends and Influence People* [1936], *Anthony Adverse* [1933], *The Citadel* [1937], and *The Good Earth* [1931]).[42]

The reader should keep in mind here that during the 1930s the MGM *Ben-Hur* would remain near the top of *Variety*'s list of top-grossing films, and the Klaw & Erlanger production would be remembered as the greatest roadshow of all time. Even if no one seems to have commented at the time, when a July issue of *Motion Picture Herald* published a list of all-time bestselling books, films, and plays, *Ben-Hur* was third in each category.[43] No other literary property had that kind of multi-generic success.

The novel continued to be praised by individuals of considerable public influence. New York Governor Herbert Lehman listed *Ben-Hur* as one of his ten favorites to initiate a humanitarian book drive.[44] A biographical work on Franklin Roosevelt reminded *New York Times* book reviewer John Chamberlain of Garfield's admiration for *Ben-Hur*.[45] In 1933 Winston Churchill (with Eddie Marsh) published an abridged version of the novel as one of "The World's Great Stories."[46] The abridgement, which included references to Gibbon and the historical Messala, was syndicated through *News of the World* and premiered in American papers early in 1933.[47] Not surprisingly, in 1949 Frank N. McGill included a three-page abridgement of *Ben-Hur* as one of his popular "Masterplots."[48] For young readers, Whitcombe's Story Books issued a 168-page abridged version of *Ben-Hur* in 1946 [#622] in New Zealand. Self-described as being designed for 10- to 12-year-olds, it included a map, two illustrations of the chariot race, and a glossary explaining ancient and technical terms.

Positive reminiscences of the novel and its author appeared in more than a dozen newspaper features,[49] while a milestone like the 125th anniversary of Harper & Brothers occasioned more coverage,[50] as did the obituaries of Garfield edition illustrator William Johnson and Harper editor Lewis Rosenquist.[51] When novelist Lloyd C. Douglas, author of *The Robe*, died in 1951, the *New York Times* obituary remarked that his audience was "the same audience, or the grandchildren of the same audience, which delighted in the religion and the melodrama of Gen. Lew Wallace's 'Ben Hur.'"[52] Douglas's own memoires were published a few months later, instigating another round of reports that his father had read *Ben-Hur* to him in 1887 when he was nine years old.[53] Douglas added, in his contemporary voice, "I am sure I have General Lew Wallace's *Ben Hur* to thank for much of [my] early preoccupation with the Roman Empire."[54]

Because it had set precedents in book promotion and resale marketing, *Ben-Hur: A Tale of the Christ* also was featured as well in newspaper articles about the publishing business.[55] One of these included a lengthy review of the industry by Henry Steele Commager.[56] And because Wallace originally inscribed the novel "To the Wife of my Youth" and thereby confused the public, necessitating the additional phrase "Who Still Abides With Me," his novel also figured in at least one article about book inscriptions.[57] Another feature pointed out that this made the authentic first edition of *Ben-Hur* even more highly valued by collectors.[58]

The diversity of topics written about in Wallace's novel and the variety of demographic groups it reached perpetuated its memory throughout these decades, particularly in churches and schools. Whenever a new religious, adventure, or historical novel was published, *Ben-Hur* was identified either in advertisements or reviews as one of its comparanda, be it Douglas's *The Robe* (1943) and *The Big Fisherman* (1948),[59] or bestsellers like *Anthony Adverse* (1936) and *Gone With the Wind* (1936),[60] or such lesser-known novels as *Tros of Samothrace* (1934),[61] *Goodbye To the Past*

(1934),[62] *Festival at Meron* (1935),[63] *In the Years of Our Lord* (1942),[64] *Charioteer* (1946),[65] *The Herdsman* (1946),[66] *Gentleman's Agreement* (1947),[67] *The Robber: A Tale of the Time of the Herods* (1949),[68] *The Chain* (1949),[69] *The Unknown Disciple* (1950),[70] and *The High Calling* (1951).[71] In the 1950s the book editors of the *Chicago Daily Tribune* and *Boston Globe* each recommended, albeit eight years apart from one another, reading a chapter or two of *Ben-Hur* to children at bedtime.[72]

Sunday School features in newspapers featured either the novel's story or its description of Antioch and Daphne ("famed seat of licentiousness"), and from the 1930s into the 1940s the *Los Angeles Times* ran a series of Sunday School Lessons by William T. Ellis that reflected upon such diverse items as Daphne and Judah's Galilean legions.[73] Church readings were often promoted through newspaper announcements,[74] while the obituary of Trenton's the Rev. James L. Gardiner cites his widespread popularity as a public lecturer who "gave 'Ben Hur' many times."[75]

Ben-Hur had long since become a Christmas staple, and this continued into the 1950s. On December 24, 1935, for instance, *The Christian Science Monitor* printed Wallace's lengthy description (1.9) of the Cave of David.[76] At a 1937 woman's club annual musicale in New York, the "Christmas Story" from *Ben-Hur* was read aloud along with instrumental recitals and sung carols.[77] The "Nativity Story" was read for the Wadsworth Baptist Church in New York in 1939, and then almost a decade later a similar reading took place at the Central Eleanor Club in Chicago in 1948.[78] On December 24, 1950, another commentator recommended reading chapter 1.11 of *Ben-Hur* instead of Luke if the latter seemed "too much like church."[79]

During the war, the entertainment at a December, 1943, meeting of the Atlanta chapter of the D.A.R. featured "a reading, 'The Angels and the Shepherds,' from Ben Hur."[80] Similarly, in Baltimore's *Afro-American* in 1944, Dwight Holmes recommended *Ben-Hur* in a Christmas message:

> I would advise everybody to read "Ben Hur," not merely as an interesting story, but of an interpretation of the meaning of Christ's earthly ministry. Personally, I think that General Lew Wallace, the author, did an excellent job. Although a soldier himself, he realized fully that Jesus was the Prince of Peace and that His kingdom was the Kingdom of Love.[81]

The presence of *Ben-Hur* during the war will be discussed more fully below.

Notably lacking during these years were public readings of the chariot race. No doubt the vivid realization of the race in the 1925 film replaced the thrill listeners used to find in that activity.[82] But schools and institutions of higher learning still regarded *Ben-Hur: A Tale of the Christ* as a popular and therefore valuable resource. An experimental study in 1934 by the National Council of Teachers of English reported that two-thirds of the six million high-school students in America preferred books like

Cimarron, Tom Sawyer, and *Ben-Hur* because of their popular film adaptations.[83] School libraries continued to track the popularity of the novel as a "classic,"[84] and they also purchased popular anthologies that targeted the younger audience, like *The Story Behind Great Books* (1946), many of which included sections on *Ben-Hur* and Lew Wallace.[85] Essays on religious novels inevitably invoked *Ben-Hur: A Tale of the Christ*,[86] too, as did a baccalaureate sermon for the 1936 commencement of the Catholic Georgetown Preparatory School.[87] The reader will remember the *Ben-Hur* recitals that were being given already in the late 1880s, and at least twice newspapers offered features on reminiscences of such *Ben-Hur* recitals.[88] Although less frequent than in previous decades, school presentations of *Ben-Hur* continued to appear, mostly at the college level.[89] In 1943 Jeannette Temple included "The Crucifixion" as part of her "Masterpieces Made to Live" presentation at the theater at Bennett College.[90] For her "speech recital relating the story, 'Ben Hur,'" performed at the Wheaton College chapel in 1945, Ellen Ruth Wagner enacted several of the principal characters and was accompanied by an organist and vocal quartet.[91]

Lew Wallace
Lew Wallace's versatility as an author, soldier, administrator, businessman, and diplomat made a rather extraordinary imprint on history. His activities and accomplishments in each of these professions provided material for newspaper entries decades after his death, and every one of the following instances – and many others not included here – was accompanied by a phrase like, "author of *Ben-Hur*" or "best-known for writing *Ben-Hur*," [almost always without the hyphen]. This included short pieces and features about his education,[92] the Mexican War,[93] Monocacy,[94] Lincoln assassination,[95] Billy the Kid,[96] Benjamin Harrison,[97] and late nineteenth-century Republican presidential politics.[98] Most of these subjects were revisited in each of the three decades, and a number of the newspaper features included a photograph of Wallace.[99] When William Gilbert, the last surviving Union soldier to guard Lincoln's coffin, visited the Roosevelt White house, the entire final third of the feature article focused on Lew Wallace's role at Monocacy, finishing with the sentence, "Gen. U. S. Grant later asserted that [Wallace's] stand was one of the main factors in saving Washington."[100] When *The Sun* ran a feature on Annapolis graduations, the 1894 commencement address by Lew Wallace ("noted Civil War general and author of 'Ben Hur'") was said to be "an inspirational talk that is still remembered by those that heard it."[101] In 1940 the *Chicago Tribune* printed as an example of "Gems of American Eloquence" a lengthy excerpt of Wallace's July 4, 1866, post-Civil War address to his fellow Indianans.[102] Indeed, when Indiana University began to show its dominance in basketball in the early 1950s, Wallace was invoked as a prime example of Hoosier genius.[103] He was portrayed on radio, impersonated on

parade floats, and was one of the twenty-eight great Americans profiled in the book *There Were Giants in the Land*.[104] MGM even rumored it was contemplating a film on the life of Lew Wallace, focusing on his experiences as the Territorial Governor of New Mexico, where "he brought law and order to the old West."[105] When MGM's *The Wizard of Oz* went into production, Wallace, like L. Frank Baum, was cited as an author who had another profession while writing his bestseller.[106] Wallace did appear as a historical character in the 1955 Greer Garson film *Strange Lady in Town*. Garson plays an independent and modernized physician who has moved to Santa Fe in the 1870s when Wallace was governor. At a reception she attends to Wallace who is seems to be suffering from a heart problem, but she traces the cause of his discomfort to a stiff collar.[107] Wallace is said to be working on *Ben-Hur*, and Susan appears in the scene as well.

Special attention in advertisements, announcements, and reviews focused on Wallace when Irving McKee published his biography in 1947.[108] Headlines like "Lew Wallace: A Showman of Literature" and "Indiana's Perennial Best Seller" demonstrated that Wallace's *Ben-Hur* creation was now being recognized for the unique phenomenon that it had become.[109] More unique was McKee's public invitation to those who could provide him with information about performances of the Klaw & Erlanger production of *Ben-Hur*. This appeared in the *New York Herald Tribune* five years before the biography was published:

> To the Editor of BOOKS:
>   Any one who recalls the date, place and other important details of a stage performance of "Ben-Hur" is invited to send the information to Irving McKee, Culver, Ind. Dr. McKee is completing a biography of Lew Wallace, author of "Ben-Hur," the novel.
>
>   IRVING McKEE[110]

McKee seems to have received ample responses, for his book lists scores of cities that hosted the Klaw & Erlanger *Ben-Hur*.

Travel pieces on Santa Fe, New Mexico,[111] and on Civil War battle sites,[112] as well as reports about Flora Spiegelberg, who claimed as the first Jewish woman in the New Mexico Territory to have been closely connected with Wallace,[113] inevitably brought up Wallace's name and therefore his novel.[114] That was in 1950. In 1951 the Santa Fe Fiesta featured a float pairing Wallace, "frowning over his palace desk," with Billy the Kid.[115]

In 1941 the Lew Wallace Study in Crawfordsville opened, producing even more national publicity.[116] There were pieces on his 1868 house,[117] and even his birthday.[118] There were also occasional pieces on his extended family, including Zerelda Wallace,[119] his grandson Lew Wallace, Jr.,[120] his granddaughter Margaret,[121] and his great-granddaughter Susan Wallace. When the latter became engaged, got married, and had a child, each announcement warranted a separate celebrity announcement.[122]

The wedding announcement, just to cite one example, listed the people involved in the wedding and then concluded with:

> The bride is a great-granddaughter of the late General Lew Wallace, lawyer, soldier, diplomat and author of "Ben-Hur" and other books.

His name and the name of his novel appeared also in announcements involving author Meredith Nicholson,[123] and when his violin maker, John Joseph Hornsteiner, turned eighty, the feature in the *Chicago Daily Tribune* noted that he had made a copy of the King Joseph Guarnerius for Wallace.[124]

There were a two notable erroneous claims.[125] Arch Crawford of the *Chicago Tribune* asserted that Wallace wrote most of the novel while acting as commanding officer of the Union's Paducah supply base following the Battle of Shiloh,[126] and radio commentator Lowell Thomas claimed that Wallace wrote the book while staying at the Mizzentop Inn in Pawling, New York.[127]

Lastly, there is an interesting use of the novel in Raymond Chandler's mystery novel, *The Big Sleep* (1939). His protagonist detective Philip Marlowe suspects that Geiger's bookstore is a front for an illegal operation. He tests the woman at the desk:

> "Would you happen to have a Ben Hur 1860?"
> She didn't say: "Huh?" but she wanted to. She smiled bleakly. "A first edition?"
> "Third," I said. "The one with the erratum on page 116."
> "I'm afraid not – at the moment."
> Across the street he does this again at a genuine bookstore.
> I said: "Know anything about rare books?"
> "You could try me."
> "Would you have a Ben Hur, 1860, Third Edition, the one with the duplicated line on page 116?"
> She pushed her yellow law book to one side and reached a fat volume up on the desk, leafed it through, found her page, and studied it. "Nobody would," she said without looking up. "There isn't one."
> "Right."
> "What in the world are you driving at?"
> "The girl in Geiger's store didn't know that."

These same scenes are included almost verbatim in the 1946 film of *The Big Sleep*, and slightly modified in the 1978 version.

TURN OF THE CENTURY *BEN-HUR* BY-PRODUCTS

Older by-products of the *Ben-Hur* legacy evoked their own varieties of nostalgia. In the *New York Herald Tribune* in 1939 Walter Cameron claimed to have been one of the charioteers in the 1907 Kalem film,[128] and elsewhere DeMille was said to have been part of the production. However, both accounts placed the production in Los Angeles.[129] In music, E. T. Paull's "The Chariot Race or Ben Hur March" was reprinted several times, played in recitals, and revived periodically as a nostalgic novelty even after the popularity of ragtime and march music had waned in the 1920s.[130] Decca, for instance, in its second year of operation in the United States, held a recording session for the Perry Brothers Trio on April 14, 1935, and released the Paull recording on a disk paired with Juventino Rosas' well-known 1888 "trapeze" waltz, "Over the Waves" [#39479].[131] Twenty years later the *Los Angeles Times* featured Robert Huish, a mechanical music aficionado who knocked out a ceiling in his house to install one of the few existing German orchestrion machines.[132] After thirty years of collecting mechanical musical machines and rolls, and after an eighteen-month building renovation and installation process, he christened the huge orchestrion with champagne and played "The Chariot Race or Ben Hur March," his favorite piece. The piece was cited by even the most sophisticated listeners. *New York Times* dance critic John Martin cited it as an example of a descriptive and popular work of art,[133] and Paul Bowles, music critic of the *New York Herald Tribune*, when pressed to criticize Alexander Borovsky's Town Hall recital of Bach piano pieces, said that "its frantic tempo belonged to the 'Ben-Hur Chariot Race' as much as anything."[134] Meanwhile the electrical installation atop the Normandie Hotel in New York was the subject of two different syndicated newspaper pieces in the 1930s.[135] And, separately, in October, 1935, *The Washington Post* ran a full-page retrospective on stereopticon slide painter Joseph Beale that included a large reproduction of his much-admired Roman galley scene.[136] The same year but on the West Coast, a Seattle reverend gave a *Ben-Hur* stereopticon presentation at his church.[137]

The Klaw & Erlanger Production
The Klaw & Erlanger play evoked various types of recollections as well. As with the novel, the obituaries of Kelley, Marc Klaw, William Farnum, William S. Hart, Thurston Hall, Orrin Johnson, Dodson Mitchell [Simonides], Adeline Adler [Tirzah], and the horse named Anna fondly recalled their roles in the Klaw & Erlanger production.[138] The same was true when vintage theaters like New York's New Amsterdam, Boston's Colonial, and Chicago's Illinois, celebrated anniversaries or were sold or demolished.[139] A feature article celebrating the Colonial pointed out that the blueprints for the chariot race machinery were still on the wall of the property room.[140] Indeed, any mention of onstage treadmills or animals evoked anecdotes, mostly of questionable historicity, from "the good old days" of live theater.[141] One of the many Klaw & Erlanger Ben-Hurs, A. H. Van Buren, for instance, told the *New York Herald Tribune* that he used to travel overnight in the train with two of his horses, George M. Cohan and Washington.[142] He said that Washington once tried to reciprocate by visiting his dressing room but got stuck in the door, requiring the local fire department to extract him. He also reported that one night, when as many

as five chariots were competing onstage, one charioteer's whip flicked off another charioteer's toupee.

Brownie, at age thirty-nine in 1934, was the last survivor of the Ben-Hur horses.[143] He still resided at the Ben Hur Stables, managed by Edward Fills and located for many years at 156 East 30th Street and 322 West 48th Street.[144] Fills provided various types of animals for plays and operas. Beginning in 1942, Ben Hur Stables began raising race horses as well, including a steed appropriately named Thespian.[145] Similarly out in Hollywood, the aforementioned Walter Cameron, who had played the sheriff in *The Great Train Robbery*, owned and operated the Ben Hur Stables in Culver City from the early 1920s until 1942.[146] He provided horses for the 1925 MGM film as well as the white jumping horse for *Gone With the Wind*.[147] Other cities had Ben Hur Stables, too, including Baltimore and San Francisco.[148]

Although legal restrictions and outmoded technology prevented the play itself from revival, Kelley's music appeared in several concerts in 1939.[149] The most significant of these were given for the National Association for American Composers and Conductors in April, 1940,[150] and at the convention of the National Federation of Music Clubs in Baltimore with delegates representing 4800 affiliated clubs.[151] The agenda of the organization was to promote American classical music, and the climax of the concert program was a performance of the "Sacred Choruses" from *Ben-Hur*, for which Kelley, "dean of American composers," composed a "special festival ending." Anticipating the multitude of musical performances at the New York World's Fair of 1939, *New York Times* music critic Olin Downes devoted most of his feature on Kelley, now eighty-two years old.[152] Regarding the score for *Ben-Hur*, Downes notes that while Kelley was paid a minimal amount of money, "the score has gone on to enduring success and enduring replenishment of others' coffers." A highlight of this resurgence in 1939 was a performance at the World's Fair as the finale of a program sung by mixed choruses from across the country.[153] An enthusiastic review of the opening of the Fair helps to demonstrate how pervasive was the association between a huge production and *Ben-Hur*, especially when it was not exactly clear whether the reference was to the Klaw & Erlanger play or the MGM film. Printing Inez Robb's report from the International News Service, *The Washington Post* first-page report begins:

> Bigger than Ben Hur, better than Barnum, a brave new World of Tomorrow marched across time to Flushing Meadows today, where President Roosevelt officially opened New York's $156,000,000 World's Fair of 1939, and 1940, too.[154]

The 1925 *Ben-Hur*

As MGM continued to screen *Ben-Hur* in India and rereleased the synchronized sound version in England,[155] and while Mussolini was building Cinecittà on the site of the Italian production of *Ben-Hur*,[156] American reports on movie rights often included lists and reminded readers that *Ben-Hur* was the most expensive literary property ever purchased,[157] or one of the longest film productions ever,[158] or one of the longest film releases ever,[159] and many others included it in reports that discussed huge domestic box-office grosses, usually rounding off *Ben-Hur* at $4 million,[160] although *The Atlanta Constitution* correctly reported that the sum was $11 million, $6 million of it from overseas.[161] Early reports were that the filmization of *The Robe* would be on a bigger scale than *Ben-Hur*,[162] and when J. Arthur Rank's *Caesar and Cleopatra* premiered in London in December, 1945, the lead paragraph of the Tribune Company's coverage began by declaring that *Ben-Hur* was no longer the costliest production ever:

> Bernard Shaw's "Caesar and Cleopatra," which has been made into a film by Gabriel Pascal – with more of J. Arthur Rank's money than was ever spent on a film before, including "Ben Hur" [and] "Gone With the Wind". . . – opens here tomorrow night.[163]

Industry debates about roadshows in legitimate theaters and double features continued to cite *Ben-Hur* as a monument of the past,[164] as did nostalgic retrospectives of silent cinema,[165] the development of Technicolor,[166] and the first neon signs displayed in New York.[167] Because the 1925 production had so many important facets, it was associated with many other types of films for a variety of reasons. In every instance, *Ben-Hur* was the identifier. *National Velvet* (1945), for instance, promised "one of the most thrilling races since 'Ben-Hur,'" as did *Broadway Bill* (1934).[168] Large crowd sequences requiring more than a thousand extras, as in MGM's *Tale of Two Cities* (1935) and RKO's *The Hunchback of Notre Dame* (1939), claimed to break the record set by *Ben-Hur*.[169] Descriptions of such action films as Warner Brothers' *The Charge of the Light Brigade* (1936) and *Air Force* (1943) and David O. Selznick's *Duel in the Sun* (1947) all referenced *Ben-Hur* because Reeves Eason directed the second unit.[170] An overseas production like *The Search* (1948) or a spectacular like the 1951 Italian production of *Fabiola* recalled *Ben-Hur*,[171] as did the gala New York premiere of Warner's *A Midsummer Night's Dream* (1935).[172] MGM advertising proudly placed some of their high-profile new films, like *Mutiny on the Bounty* (1935), *Romeo and Juliet* (1936), *Captains Courageous* (1937), and *Northwest Passage* (1940), within the studio tradition, highlighting *Ben-Hur* and now regularly listing it before *The Big Parade*.[173] Of course, the release and record-breaking ticket receipts of *Gone With the Wind* in 1939, decidedly surpassing *Ben-Hur*, resulted in numerous box-office comparisons.[174]

Religious films from DeMille's *Sign of the Cross* (1934) to MGM's *Quo Vadis* (1950) inevitably evoked comparisons to *Ben-Hur*, often with the expressed approval of religious leaders.[175] Indeed, the *Quo Vadis* project was compared to *Ben-Hur* already in 1939, a decade before it went into production,[176] in 1949 when it was determined to film in Rome,[177] and again later when it became clear that the budget and scope of its production would surpass those of *Ben-Hur*.[178] MGM publicity made sure to point out that some of the chariots used in *Quo Vadis* were those tailor-made for the 1925 *Ben-Hur*.[179] And MGM's twentieth anniversary in 1944, twenty-fifth in 1949, and thirtieth in 1954 warranted special recollections as well, whether for the general public or business sales meetings.[180] For the silver anniversary the studio prepared *Some of the Best*, a cinematic retrospective that began with *Ben-Hur* and *The Big Parade*.[181] Ed Sullivan showed an excerpt on CBS-TV in 1954.[182] In addition, Cecil B. DeMille praised the film in 1934,[183] and Hedda Hopper's syndicated column gave us a good indication of the status of the film in 1949 at the time of the release of DeMille's *Samson and Delilah*:

> Into "Samson and Delilah" Cecil B. DeMille has put all the knowledge, showmanship, and ability he's acquired in 38 years of picture making. It's a knockout. The Bible story you know. The sex impact of Hedy Lamarr, Victor Mature, and George Sanders you can imagine. Technicolor is glorious; and the background shots of Egypt are Egypt. DeMille's made many fine pictures, but this is his best. Hollywood's always said, "Let's make one bigger than 'Ben-Hur.'"[184] DeMille made it.[185]

Sullivan and Hopper, along with Edwin Schallert of the *Los Angeles Times*, were three of the most powerful voices in the national entertainment media, and they were all influential champions of *Ben-Hur*, inserting references to the film and expressing awe at its size and praise for its qualities whenever practicable.[186]

In 1938 Francis X. Bushman, between show-business jobs, owned and operated a roadside lunch stand in Los Angeles. A *Los Angeles Times* photo superimposed the familiar still of him as Messala embracing Carmel Myers as Iras in the 1925 film.[187] The photo was superimposed on top of a photo of the restaurant. In addition to the frequent publicity Bushman elicited, the press followed Ramon Novarro from exhibitions of his *Ben-Hur* chain mail and other props at the L.A. Museum of History, Science, and Art in 1936 and 1939 to his 1940 auto accident and subsequent professional comeback in 1948.[188] He took on additional film roles in the early 1950s,[189] culminating in television appearances,[190] early rumors of a role in the 1959 remake,[191] and a Golden Globe Special Achievement Award, along with Bushman, for their roles in the 1925 film.[192] Of course all these reports included the *Ben-Hur* name, which also followed Fred Niblo through the years and editor Lloyd Nosler as well.[193] Carey Wilson perpetuated the name in the publicity that accompanied his association with the Andy Hardy films and *The Postman Always Rings Twice* (1945).[194] This was also true when those associated with the well-publicized production got married (Myers),[195] or arrested (Key),[196] or passed away (Thalberg, J. J.

McCarthy, Edington, Cabanne, Eason, Mayer).[197] When television enticed Carmel Myers out of retirement in 1950, Walter Ames' announcement in the *Los Angeles Times* provided the usual type of reminder:

> One of the real old timers of the movie industry is coming out of retirement tomorrow to start her career anew in the blooming infant television industry. She's Carmel Myers.
> It has been a long time since she made such triumphs as "Ben Hur" and other great silent pictures. In fact, it has been almost two decades ago but she's still a stunning woman who draws second glances in the swankiest of restaurants.[198]

The *London Sentinel* list of "milestone films" placed *Ben-Hur* among its top five.[199] But because MGM was no longer exhibiting its prints, The Roosevelt University Film Society of Chicago chartered a bus to Rochester, New York, where the Eastman House screened eighteen hours of silent films, beginning with *Ben-Hur*.[200] The successful transfer from stage to screen was featured in a widely distributed academic study by Nicholas Vardac, who praised the 1925 rendition of the chariot race as an example of "convincing realism and magnitude of the spectacle."[201] And the sea battle was featured in the film, *Unreeling History*, which received syndicated newspaper publicity.[202] Churches continued to offer limited showings of the film for a few years,[203] although, as in every era, newspaper reports sometimes leave us unclear as to the medium used to present *Ben-Hur*. A 1934 ad in the *Boston Globe* invited readers to a church to "see Ben Hur Illustrated with a trio by Mrs. George Jeter on the piano, Adabeth Sizoo with the violin and Rev. Bascom with the saw."[204] At least one of these rental prints was alleged to have been exhibited illegally and was the first of the "hot" films the *Herald Tribune* listed as part of a federal investigation in New York.[205]

A few humorous recollections depended upon or exploited the monumental status of the film. As air-conditioned neighborhood movie theaters beckoned patrons during the summer of 1940, one Chicago resident reportedly said, "I'm going to the Esquire tonight even if they're showing *Ben Hur*."[206] Bob Hope joked that his ambitious benefit for the Cerebral Palsy Fund at the Hollywood Bowl in August, 1950, would be "bigger than 'Ben Hur.'"[207] Ironically, *The Billboard* review of Hope's *Star-Spangled Revue* broadcast on NBC television the previous June said that it began with "the longest credit list since Ben Hur."[208] Lastly, the MGM *Ben-Hur* was alluded to in one of the most popular television shows of the era, *I Love Lucy*. In "The Handcuffs," originally broadcast on October 6, 1952, Lucy [Lucille Ball] responds to a question about when she last saw a movie, "You know how long it's been since I've seen a movie? . . . Well, I can't remember the title, but there was a guy named Ben that won a chariot race."

WORLD WAR II AND ITS AFTERMATH

When the United States entered World War II, this put *Ben-Hur* into different perspectives. Although war-related issues and icons diminished its prevalence, it demonstrates how deeply and thoroughly *Ben-Hur* had penetrated into the American psyche as a moral touchstone. The president of Morgan State College recommended that young recruits should put a copy of the novel in their knapsack.[209] In addition, the book's desert descriptions were applied to the North African theater. Ernie Pyle reported from Algeria that Oran looked "like Ben Hur but a disappointment to Yankee soldiers."[210] A syndicated report said that "British forces have taken Bengasi, with the Axis troops taking a Ben Hur across the desert."[211] *Ben-Hur* provided not only geographical and historical reference points but various forms of horse and chariot imagery, particularly in connection with the Axis powers in Rome. A report from Rome referring to "a searchlight high up above the Circus Maximus, where, it is said, Ben Hur won his chariot race," suggests that there was still a segment of the population that thought of Ben-Hur as an historical personage.[212] An impending assault on Mussolini's Rome in 1943 reminded the reader of the ancient catacombs that he is said to have funded:

> Mussy had kind of counted on being able to scream about the statues and the things in the Eternal City and escape a bombing, but now he knows the Allies meant it when they told him to quit the war activity there or be blown into Trajan's Tomb. As one ruin among a lot of others, Mussy doesn't know where to go to escape retribution. . . . In the days of Ben Hur, the catacombs of Rome were a good place in which to hide, in these days even the other rats wouldn't welcome Mussolini down there, it would pollute the social atmosphere.[213]

Months later a report of "an epidemic of horse-stealing" in the vicinity of Rome caused the *Boston Globe* to quip, "If you hear of a chariot heading north, the driver won't be Ben Hur."[214]

Even the struggle against the Nazis evoked Ben-Hur lore and imagery. When eight Nazi saboteurs were to be put on trial in the summer of 1942, a half-page feature in the *Boston Globe* discussed Wallace's roles on the military commissions appointed to adjudicate the Lincoln assassination conspirators and Andersonville commandant.[215] Of course the feature introduced him as "Gen. Lew Wallace, known to most Americans as the author of 'Ben Hur.'" That same summer one of the ten soldiers who crash-landed in an undisclosed Latin-American jungle published his diary in *Yank*, the official U.S. Army newspaper, before it was syndicated nationally.[216] Their ten-day ordeal included days of rowing a native boat:

> July 21 – Paddling from dawn to dusk. Empty river except for a boat manned by three boys. We hire it, tying our rafts on behind. We paddle, which Lieutenant Grenfell says he feels like Ben Hur on a Roman slave ship.

In 1944 the United Press circulated a report that American bombers and a ground assault by the U.S. First Army on an undisclosed German town forced German draft horses to "charge like the steeds in a Ben-Hur race, galloping crazily to escape from their own mental torment."[217] That same year the American Bar Association put a Civil War photographic portrait of Wallace on the cover of its journal and ran a feature article inside as part of its series on soldier-lawyers.[218] When the allies were heading towards Berlin in April, 1945, the drive across the northern German plain by the "hell on wheels" division of the U.S. Ninth Army was described as a race under the headline, "'Ben Hur' Shadowed."[219] Meanwhile, when Paris was liberated in 1944, GIs, WACs, and French citizens alike stood in line to see old prints of films like Chaplin's *Gold Rush* and the Marx Brothers' *Monkey Business*, and *Ben-Hur* was soon to follow.[220] Two years later, British patrons were weary of old American imports and complained about the age of their film libraries and how currency fluctuations were preventing them from importing new films.[221] Harold Wilson, then president of the Board of Trade, remarked sarcastically, "We are paying for the privilege of seeing ... 'Ben Hur' for the twenty-third time."[222] In France, the expression *"arrête ton char Ben-Hur,"* i.e. "hold on," began to appear in print, for instance as the title of a mystery novel by Ange Bastiani [Victor Marie LePage].[223]

Stateside, at Ft. Benning, Georgia, a training exercise was said to consist of "the chariot race from 'Ben Hur' without the whips."[224] The story of *Ben-Hur* was also occasionally used to raise money for the war effort. Proceeds from the aforementioned reading at the 1943 Atlanta D.A.R. meeting went to a local mobile blood-plasma unit. For the 4th of July during the first summer of the war, St. John's A.M.E. Church in Norfolk advertised a "Dramatic and Musical Recital" that included a rendition of the Crucifixion from *Ben-Hur*.[225] All proceeds from Aileen Mize's "dramatic interpretation" of *Ben-Hur* for the Maryland chapter of the International Federation of Catholic Alumnae were to be used for the USO and the nearby Officer's Candidate School.[226] Mize, director of speech and drama at the College of Notre Dame of Maryland, offered a monologue in three acts, and she represented twenty different characters, much as Gurley-Kane and Flowers had done in the distant past.[227] She had already given the presentation at Catholic University and at the dedication of the college library.[228] Elsewhere, *Ben-Hur* was on the minds of government officials and served on at least one occasion as a jovial palliative that was syndicated nationwide. Elmer Davis, Director of Office of War Information and a native Indianan, quipped at a high-level Washington, DC banquet that Wendell Willkie, another Indianan and author of the currently bestselling *One World*, "threatens to outsell Ben Hur, even without a chariot race."[229]

An interesting phenomenon took hold near the outbreak of the war. In the wake of the creation and proliferation of such radio quiz programs as "Dr. I.Q." and "Information Please" during the late 1930s, newspapers began to run periodic literary quizzes.[230] Not surprisingly, Lew Wallace and his novel often provided questions, answers, and distractors for these popular educational exercises.[231] The name Ben-Hur was used also in newspaper Bible quizzes and anecdotes like the "Bible Briefs" that ran in *The Atlanta Constitution* during the war.[232] Occasionally *Ben-Hur* was the subject of prize-winning literary essays submitted by newspaper readers.[233] And because each of the names Ben, Hur, and Lew has only three letters, they were also frequently linked in crossword puzzles as clues and answers.[234] Sometimes the clues demanded more information and thought, e.g. "Ben Hur's brother?" and "What Ben Hur wore."[235]

Ben-Hur was not forgotten in the political upheavals that followed the war years. A Cold War report from England on the drabness of Leipzig behind the Iron Curtain described the shortage of farm machinery, precision instruments, and vehicles:

> Bicycles on view were ten years out of date, the only motor-cars came from other zones, and some farm-carts were built on the same all-wooden basis as Ben Hur's chariot.[236]

The creation of Israel elicited a *Jewish Advocate* historical review of American relations with Jews and the Palestine region, including Wallace's "vigorous actions against the threatened expulsion from Jerusalem of sundry naturalized American Jews" during his tenure in Constantinople.[237] A Dan Dowling political cartoon in the *New York Herald Tribune*, with the caption "Ben Hur Took That Corner on One Wheel," depicted a togaed Harry Truman driving a chariot labeled "State of the Union Message" and crushing "VOTES" under his spinning chariot wheel.[238] Another with the caption "There Won't Be Much Time for That Ben Hur" depicted an empty *quadriga* with "Legislative Program" written on the platform and a togaed elephant ("Second Session") and two other characters ("Extraneous Issues," "Investigations") plotting in the foreground.[239] In these two instances, Dowling assumed that his readers would understand the allusions to the Ben-Hur chariot. The same could be said for comedian Bob Hope who called the 1952 presidential race "a sort of 'Ben Hur' with dark horses."[240]

We need to pause here in mid-chapter to emphasize the historical context of these hundreds of new references and allusions to *Ben-Hur*. The continuing presence of the name Ben-Hur and allusions to Wallace or the chariot race demonstrate not the current popularity of the novel, Klaw & Erlanger drama, or MGM film. Of course they had been extremely popular in their day, but this chapter is covering a period that postdates the publication of the novel by more than a half century, the premiere of the play by more than thirty years, and the release of the MGM film by ten to thirty years. What this chapter is demonstrating is how *Ben-Hur* had by now thoroughly entered the vocabulary, mindset, and imagery of American popular culture. The early emergence of *Ben-Hur: A Tale of the Christ* as a bestseller and its proliferation into so many other aspects of the arts and commerce gave it a permanence afforded to few other properties. And making it all the more pervasive and seemingly ubiquitous were the many facets included within the *Ben-Hur* tradition, like the Civil War, Lew Wallace, Christ, chariot racing, galley slaves, and stage treadmills, just to name a few. More so than any of its competitors, *Ben-Hur* had age, depth, and breadth.

COMMERCE – CONTINUITIES

The name Ben-Hur became well established in the business world already in the 1880s and 1890s and thrived, as the reader already knows, into the 1930s. By then, especially after the MGM film began to disappear from the horizon, the impetus to create a Ben-Hur business or product had diminished, and now the economy was suffering through a decade of depression. Even so, such established icons as Ben-Hur Coffee would continue to advertise regularly in the newspapers, and we have already seen that the Tribe of Ben-Hur would continue to flourish. The commerce of Ben-Hur found new champions, too. Few would rival the early successes, but Milwaukee's Ben Hur Manufacturing and Ben Hur Hair Products would develop into industry standouts, and from the beginning of the 1930s depression into the mid-1950s, long before the 1959 film was put into production, an amazing array of other companies, products, and special applications would perpetuate this widely recognized name and exploit its familiar imagery in the banking, real estate, mining, fossil fuels, clothing, advertising, transportation, and leisure industries, especially, of course, horse racing.

Ben-Hur Coffee

The Joannes Brothers Company changed its name to Coffee Products of America in 1930 after the merger with Puritas, and then finally to Ben-Hur Products, Inc. in 1940.[241] In all its formulations the company found a number of ways to display the name and logo of Ben-Hur in a proliferation of products. It continued to be one of the most frequent and consistent advertisers in the *Los Angeles Times*, warranting a feature about the company in the early 1940s and a notice in 1948 that the company's association with Ralph's was approaching fifty years.[242] It still sponsored or participated in local shows,[243] demonstrations,[244] and sales contests run through the *Times*.[245] By advertising their name in this way, their distinctive chariot logo returned even more eye-catching dividends. *My Best Recipes*, Kate Brew Vaughn's 1929 cookbook, contained only one

Figure 13.1 The exploitation of the Ben-Hur name in commerce continued from the 1920s into the early 1950s with elaborate print ads and New Year's Day Parade floats sponsored by Ben-Hur Coffee, with additional appropriations by Green Giant peas and Ben Hur Salmon.

fold-out ad.[246] On it the reader saw a tempting graphic of a decorated layer cake sitting on a doily. Racing around the cake plate as if on a circus track is the familiar Wagner image of the racing chariot. "BEN-HUR Wins Again" declares the headline. The company continued to sponsor Marian Manner's *Times* columns and culinary classes through the 1940s into the 1950s as well as contests and charm lessons.[247] The *Times* even reported when the company began supplying an airplane for its salesmen, the first food-services company to do so.[248]

The familiar chariot logo was always illustrated on product containers. Sometimes the chariot became part of the message. A 1934 ad placed the logo at the top with the headline, "Ahead of the Procession!"[249] One of the most impressive ads of 1941 featured the chariot riding across a radiant sky above suburban-style homes, accompanied by the motto: "IT'S SWEEPING ACROSS THE WEST!"[250] During the war they ran a print ad that greatly enlarged the size of the chariot.[251] Accompanying the expanded Wagner *quadriga* was the large slogan, "Win with America!" The ad also urged, "Save metal for Defense!" Like many manufacturers during the war years, Ben-Hur Coffee switched from its red coffee tins to glass jars – with the chariot logo now displayed on the paper label.

The name Ben-Hur and the chariot logo were printed on other types of containers and materials as well. In 1930, Coffee Products of America struck an agreement with the prominent Ohio Fraunfelter China Company of Zanesville to manufacture a brand of Ben-Hur china and a Ben-Hur Coffee pot specifically designed for the new Ben Hur family-size drippers.[252] The company also issued advertisements on porcelain signs, and locally famous in Los Angeles was the huge rooftop Ben-Hur Coffee pot atop the Wilshire Coffee Pot restaurant, several photographs of which are viewable online, although not the chariot logo.[253] In 1935 the company built a pavilion at the San Diego Exposition. Extant postcards of the "Globe – Ben Hur Spanish Patio" depict the adobe-style Food Building identified by conspicuous Ben-Hur Coffee and Globe A1 Flour signs, and many of the variously colored ceramic ashtrays given away as free gifts are still extant as well. Perhaps as part of the educational interests piqued by the San Diego Exposition, in April, 1937, the company co-sponsored the traveling "Gas Cookery School" and advertised that they were using "twelve *recognized* and *named* Ben-Hur garden-grown varieties to meet every taste for finer teas."[254] In the 1940s Ben-Hur Products sought out a celebrity endorsement for product placement, signing an exclusivity agreement with the Del Mar Turf Club when Bing Crosby was president and advertising on the back of their paper programs.[255]

Ben-Hur Coffee also advertised on radio. Already in 1924 Joannes Brothers sponsored an evening program of popular classical music, including Spanish guitar music designed to "stir the pulses of the adventurous" in reminiscences of coffee plantations, followed by a segment in which Eugene C. Joannes, company vice-president, spoke about "the romance of coffee."[256] The program warranted a very positive review in the *Los Angeles Times*, particularly Joannes' lecture that "served to illustrate the truth that the great men of commerce are those who carry in their hearts the flame of romantic beauty in which to envelop the prosaic affairs of the day."[257] Joannes went a step further than Lew Wallace in relying upon not translations of ancient texts but original manuscripts from the Bibliothèque Nationale in Paris. Here, too, was further evidence for the company's penchant for educational and developmental programming. Nightly programming for the 1935 *Food and Household Show* featured film star Dick Powell on Campbell Soup Night and Jack Benny sponsored by General Foods, but Ben-Hur Coffee Night featured Harry H. Balkin, a "vocational guidance and character analysis expert."[258]

In continuing radio sponsorships, in 1940 the company appropriately co-sponsored "Insomnia Club of the Universe" on KFAC, an all-night talk and music show that ran from midnight to 6:00 a.m. seven days a week.[259] In 1941 and 1942 they were still purchasing forty-two spots per week on KFI in Los Angeles, and another 101 announcements on KPRO, Riverside.[260] They would later advertise on KQW in San Francisco as well.[261] In 1943 Ben-Hur Coffee bought sponsorship of the talent competition show, "Hollywood Showcase: Stars Over Hollywood," starring Mary Astor and broadcast on KNX.[262] At the end of the year Janet Gaynor took over as emcee of the popular program, followed by none other than Hedda Hopper, who would then emerge as a champion of the *Ben-Hur* films.[263] In 1944 Ben-Hur Coffee sponsored a new show, "Aunt Mary," broadcast on NBC in California and Arizona.[264] Although these audio presentations could not convey the image of the chariot race as specifically as the Wagner extract logo, anecdotal ephemera suggests that consumers did not forget the association between the name Ben-Hur and Wallace's story. In a 1941 ad-writing contest run through the newspaper, the *Times* chose to print the following:

Dear Editor:
I'm just a simple housewife, and can't write that many ads. So please believe me when I say that BEN-HUR ALWAYS WINS. A long time ago, he won a chariot race – and today, at our house, BEN-HUR beats all the other coffees.
Yours very truly: Clara R. Lain 2317 Juliet[265]

In the post-war period, Ben-Hur Coffee joined in the celebration at Pasadena's New Year's Tournament of Roses parade in 1946, the first held since 1943. In anticipation the *Los Angeles Times* ran a photo of the "Ben Hur chariot horses, which have appeared in almost every Rose Parade."[266] Reflecting that year's post-war parade theme of "Victory, Unity, Peace," the company entered a float, "STILL FIRST," which featured a yellow floral *quadriga* riding in front of three Roman columns.[267] At the front is the word "VICTOR" and on the sides are large signs for "Ben-Hur Products." The float won a prize for outstanding merit.[268] One of fourteen postcard photographs assembled as a souvenir packet of the Tournament of Roses pictures the Ben-Hur Coffee float.[269] Along the same lines, their 1949 float was labeled "A Roman Holiday."

The financial health of Ben-Hur Products, Inc. flourished immediately after the war. Sales in 1946 showed a 25 percent increase over 1945, and its stock, listed in the over-the-counter market, paid regular dividends.[270] In addition to its typical print ads and radio sponsorships, the company advertised on outdoor billboards, and from December, 1946 through 1947, they ran a newspaper ad campaign in California, Arizona, Idaho,

Washington, and Oregon featuring George Lichty cartoons.[271] These cartoons employed modern themes and images, yet as always the name Ben-Hur was used repeatedly in the accompanying copy – except in the latter two states where the brand name was Golden West. One example from 1947 depicts a housewife reclining on a comfy chair as her husband runs towards her with her slippers and the newspaper in his hands, as if he were the stereotypical pet dog.[272] The caption has the wife saying:

> Nothing's too good for me since I started serving him Ben-Hur Coffee. Not just any coffee, dearie, but Ben-Hur, richer in those rare, fine-flavored coffees from Central America.

After a few years of inconsistent growth,[273] Ben-Hur Products under the leadership of Walter Emmerling (Eugene Joannes had died in 1943) reported that sales and profits in 1950 were the highest in the company's forty-seven years of existence.[274] Gross sales reached $9.4 million.[275] That same year they bought the General Foods Building in Los Angeles, availing the company of some 150,000 square feet of office and factory space.[276] In 1951 they expanded their radio advertising to the ABC Pacific network news broadcast, "Bob Garred and the News," and they renewed this sponsorship into 1953.[277] That same year Ben-Hur Coffee sponsored its first television program, Betty White's "Hollywood on Television" on KLAC-TV.[278]

A very successful company that dominated its Western territories, Ben-Hur Products, Inc. averaged more than $8 million annually for the last five years of its existence.[279] As we will continue to observe, the mid-1950s were a relative low point in the visibility of the *Ben-Hur* tradition, the 1959 version still being in the process of development but not yet fully in the public consciousness. Consequently, when the outstanding shares of Ben-Hur Products, Inc. stock were acquired by McCormick & Company, Inc. of Baltimore in the fall of 1953, on the West Coast the name Ben-Hur had to be shared with "Schilling," the company McCormick had acquired in 1947. A November, 1954, ad in the *Los Angeles Times* urges readers to "Look for Schilling or Ben-Hur Pure Vanilla."[280] The brand name Ben-Hur would soon disappear altogether from shelves, advertisements, and sponsorships.[281] In 1957 Wellman's Coffee bought the Los Angeles plant, and Emmerling retired as vice-president of the new company a few months later.[282] One of its only product legacies seems to have been a 1957 patent on a method of preparing colored potato chips that refers to the coloring or dyeing operation as "Ben Hur liquid food color."[283] However, also in 1957, as the MGM film was gearing up for production, Ralph's regular list of products on sale included: "COFFEE – BEN HUR – It's Back!"[284]

Fraternal Organizations
The fraternal organizations associated with the Ben-Hur name continued to hold regular meetings and events, most of them announced and reported

in local newspapers. By this point in the twentieth century, the Ben-Hur name had long been associated with halls, lodges, courts, clubs, circles, groves, groups, and associations.[285] The *Boston Globe*, for instance, routinely circulated announcements about the local Ben Hur Circle of the Companions of the Forest of America from the early 1930s until the end of the war.[286] Usually meeting in Roxbury, the Ben Hur Circle held whist parties, pie socials, and dances, and public condolences were expressed on behalf of lost members.[287]

The Tribe of Ben-Hur was by now a hoary institution. In January, 1941, the Congressional Court No. 809 maintained its local tradition by electing Eugene B. Bell financial scribe for the forty-second consecutive year. During the war the most active chapters were those located in Washington, DC. By 1942 the Washington members had already formed Victory, State, War, and Navy courts to consolidate with the original United court,[288] and that same year the United Court voted to invest all their surplus money in defense bonds. Nonetheless, they had not forgotten their roots and as a matter of course sent representatives to the biennial convention in Crawfordsville.[289]

As for Shriners, their international convention in Washington, DC, in the spring of 1935, featured a Lew Wallace float that led the entire procession up Pennsylvania Avenue.[290] The page-one story in the *Washington Post* made clear the continuing impact of *Ben-Hur*:

> Henry M. Folmer, teacher at Elliott Junior High School will have the difficult task of portraying Lew Wallace, the author of Ben Hur, who also wrote the shrine ritual. The float in which the character of Wallace appear will lead the pageant Thursday night as it rolls down Pennsylvania avenue and will include the delivery of the prologue by Folmer and the much-anticipated chariot race. Chariots used in the motion picture production of "Ben Hur" have been secured for the race.

Ben-Hur Perfume

1929 saw the introduction of Jergens' Ben Hur Talcum.[291] An ad in New Orleans' *Times-Picayune* offering "Colgate's Ben Hur Perfume Set" with talcum powder, perfume, and face powder, suggests that Ben Hur Perfume products and Ben-Hur Soap were produced by the same company.[292] They were not. In 1929 only Ben-Hur Soap was made by Colgate. This is a rarity, but at least one person seems to have been under the impression that there was a single Ben-Hur company issuing several different products. Prices of these products soon dropped significantly with the onset of the economic depression. A boxed Christmas set was sold as a two-for-one or for as little as a fourth or fifth of its mid-1920s prices.[293] Nonetheless, in December 1930 and 1931 newspapers were filled with listings for Ben Hur gift boxes, albeit without any reference to the propriety of the novel as a Christmas gift. Then again, the 1931 rerelease of the 1925 film with a soundtrack might have led some retailers or consumers towards this association. A new gift set, a set with perfume, toilet water, and face powder, was packaged for the 1932 Christmas season.[294] By 1935 the product seems to have been discontinued and remaindered.[295]

The next turn of events is a rarity in the world of Ben-Hur products. Ben-Hur Perfume resurfaced in discount stores in the 1950s.[296] As an enticement, Shop-N-Save Markets in Cleveland offered free bottles of "the famous perfume" to the first 300 women who asked.[297] However, at that time the scent of the old-fashioned fragrance made it subject to popular ridicule as a cheap perfume. In a chit-chat column, one Iowa paper referred to "Freshmen girls wearing carnations reeking with Ben Hur perfume,"[298] and another paper listed as fourth of the ten most unpleasant sensations:[299]

1. The suspicion that you have just swallowed a fly.
2. Finding a mouse's calling card in the silver-ware drawer.
3. A cold sore.
4. The smell of Ben Hur perfume generously doused on a little girl's hair.

Despite the negative journalistic topos, the 1959 MGM film revived sales into the 1960s,[300] and at that point the product was sometimes associated with a strong sense of nostalgia. A Montana paper noted that "We can guess how old you are if ... the first girl you ever dated wore 'Ben Hur' perfume."[301] Even today, the website of The Vermont Country Store advertises a 1.7 oz. bottle of Ben Hur Eau de Cologne, "Back at Your Request," by appealing to nostalgia:

If beauty had a scent of its own, it would be that of Ben Hur, the 1904 fragrance that brings to mind the unforgettable allure of a rose garden. With subtle top notes of ylang-ylang and base notes of tonka, this sweet musky scent is always captivating and never overpowering ... Surprise her with Ben Hur Eau de Cologne and watch the memories come flooding back.[302]

MANUFACTURING

The Ben Hur Manufacturing Company

The Ben Hur Manufacturing Company of Milwaukee was originally a division of the Lavine Gear Company established in 1911.[303] Under the direction of Herman Ühlein, who served also on the board of his father's Schlitz Brewing Company, the company changed its name to Ben Hur and manufactured "scientifically engineered" all-steel trailer frames and sold them through Montgomery Ward retail outlets and mail-order catalogs.[304] They supplied the one-ton G518 Ben Hur trailers to the United States military during World War II,[305] and the company won an Army-Navy production award for outstanding performance in 1943, the year after Ühlein died.[306] The G518 became such a standard that similar models manufactured by more than two dozen other companies were commonly referred to as "Ben Hur trailers."[307] They served a variety of purposes, including the hauling of fire pumps, generators, and mobile kitchens. After the war the company reconfigured the trailer as a pop-up "Jiffy Camper,"[308] and this model, too, became so familiar that Sears sold a version manufactured by David Bradley but still labeled as a "Ben Hur."[309] The Ben Hur trailer has not been forgotten even several generations later. Model enthusiasts can purchase replicas of this very popular unit. A 1/72 resin miniature of the Ben Hur 1-ton trailer from Al.By [#911] is sold in the United States.[310] The 1/72 Kit Planet model [MV087] is manufactured in the Czech Republic,[311] and the 1/48 full resin kit is sold by Czech Master's Kits [8041].[312] U-Models sells a 1/35 reproduction [UM221] in the United Kingdom.[313] And SHQ also sells a 1/72 die-cast miniature.[314]

After the war Ben Hur's engineers helped to pioneer the manufacture of home freezers.[315] In 1953 they issued a consumer-friendly publication, *The ABCs of Food Freezing*, to encourage the growth of the home market. Again, they manufactured private labeled residential freezers for Sears (Cold Spot), Admiral, and Gibson.[316] It was around this time that the advertisements they placed in newspapers and national magazines employed the hyphen in their name and introduced an innovative five-sided logo with a *quadriga* galloping left to right.[317] They molded relatively large, three-dimensional versions of this and placed one on every model. A particularly interesting example appeared at the bottom of an ad placed in *McCall's* in 1954.[318] Against an aqua watercolor wash, a woman in an elegant gown and full-length evening gloves stands next to a Ben-Hur Freezer. The copy begins with "America's Finest" written in elegant script.[319] Promoting the quality built into their product, they offered a ten-year warranty. Interestingly, ads placed after the release of the 1959 MGM film seem to lack the chariot logo.[320] However, even though the son of Herman Ühlein, now regularly spelled "Uihlein," left the company in 1962 to start up his equally successful U-Line business, the company website includes as the first of its key milestones, "1962: Henry Uihlein, Sr. founds U-Line Corporation as an outgrowth of Ben-Hur."[321]

Ben Hur Products, Inc.
Having incorporated in 1923, between the end of the Klaw & Erlanger production and the MGM film, Siegfried Behr and Max Hirtenstein introduced their "Quadro-Gammon," a four-player version of backgammon, eight years later.[322] "A 'Ben-Hur' product" is printed on the board, along with the copyright date of 1931. The following year they introduced boxed versions of bagatelle, chess, and "Polly Woggle."[323] Beginning in the mid-1930s, Ben-Hur Products, Inc. took out a number of patents on such hair ornament products as a winged clamping comb,[324] comb and casing,[325] barrettes,[326] and various clutches, claws, hairpins, and tiaras

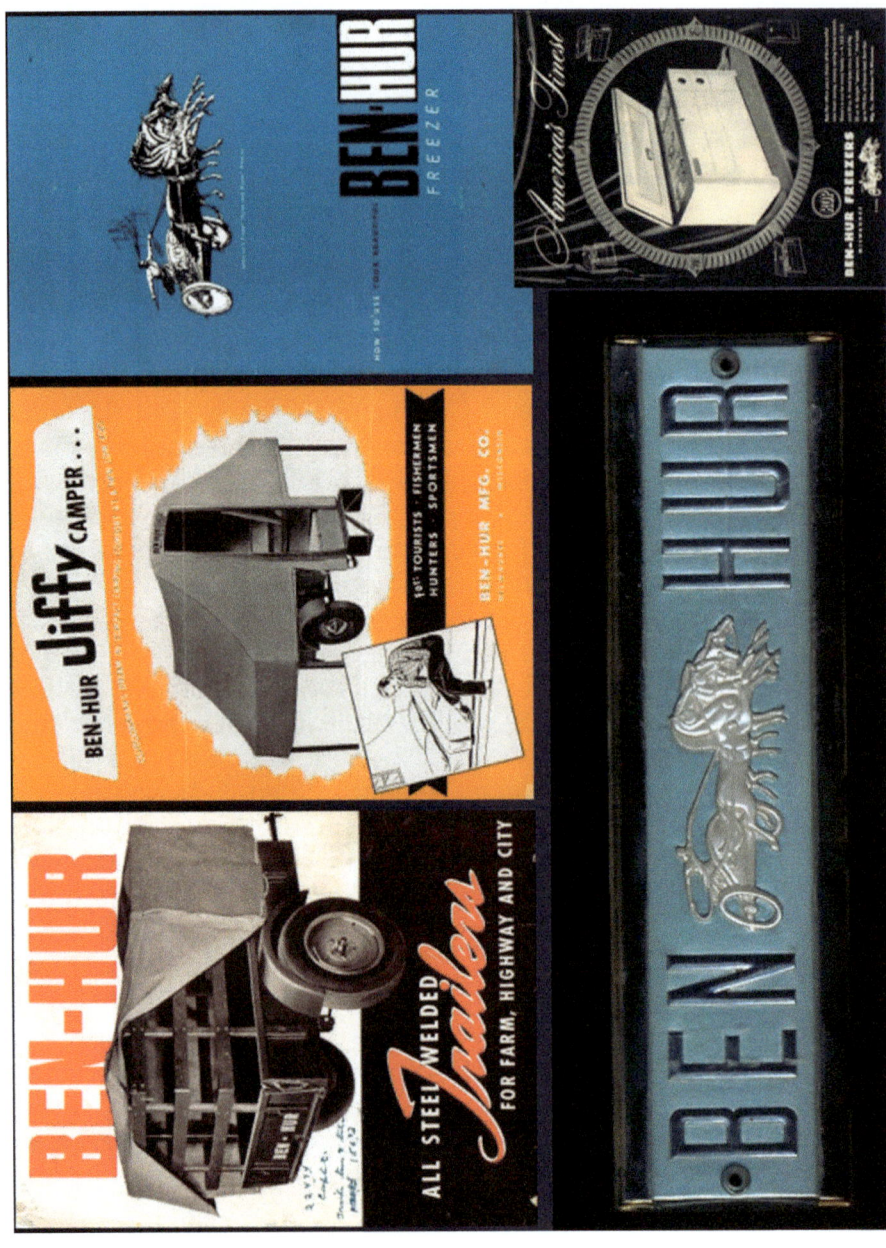

Figure 13.2 Ben-Hur Manufacturing Company of Milwaukee produced the "Ben-Hur" supply trailer during World War II, refitted it as the Ben-Hur Jiffy Camper in the late 1940s, and in the 1950s sold the Ben-Hur Freezer, complete with chariot logo.

as well as a Streamline Hair Curler and sunglasses,[327] using such plastics as celluloid and Ivorene decorated with rhinestones, which were much in fashion in the 1940s and 1950s.[328] Newspaper ads begin to appear in 1934, when a full-page ad for Marshall Field in Chicago listed and illustrated black foundations by Bien Joie on the right, hand-tailored initial handkerchiefs on the left, and three different Ben Hur hair ornaments in the center.[329] The catch-line read, "New Ornaments Give a Brilliant Turn to Your Head," and below the copy next to three silhouettes continued, "This exciting collection, styled by Ben Hur, assures a smart gaiety in Chicago's formal season." The three illustrations depict the "Juliet Cap," "Widow's Peak," and "Beatrice," the latter with four adjustable, rhinestone bands.

By 1937 they had appointed Gussow, Kahn & Company to handle their advertising account.[330] During the war they placed one ad with six photographs of different hairstyles held in place by barrettes sold at Saks Fifth Avenue and B. Altman.[331] A *New York Times* ad featured the Ben Hur bandeau, "crusted with silvery beads and finished at either end with beaded tassels that act as earrings."[332] Expanding after the war by adding a number of staff, including a store demonstrator,[333] the company achieved sufficient visibility for Behr's son Fred, now president of Ben Hur Products, to be elected to the board of the National Notion Association in 1947 and then president in 1948.[334] Over the next decade and beyond, fashion shows and advertisements often included Ben Hur hair accessories, whether a $40 "After Dark" dress with a $15 Ben Hur rhinestone tiara for Saks in a two-page layout in *Vogue*,[335] or a *New York Times* fashion feature on summer costume jewelry,[336] or a nationwide campaign to be a "Queen for the Night" a few months after the televised coronation of Queen Elizabeth II.[337] The queenly tiara was modeled (and credited) in ads for other products as well, e.g. Ronson lighters ("How to Give Like a Queen"),[338] and Maidenform bras ("I Dreamed I Lived Like a Queen in my Maidenform Bra").[339] Annual six-figure net losses in 1951 and 1952 led the company to reconfigure its products,[340] despite a small ad placed in *Life*.[341] By 1955 they were emphasizing scaled-down pieces for one or two dollars at urban department stores like the May Store in Los Angeles and Lord & Taylor in New York.[342] It was just a few months before the release of the 1959 film that the company began selling a new model of sunglasses – with a hairband attached.[343]

Their last patent for a Ben Hur barrette was issued in 1961,[344] but they issued an elaborate catalogue of Ben Hur Hair Accessories in 1964, describing their offices at 302 Fifth Avenue as "The Hair Accessories and Sunglasses Headquarters."[345] They often advertised in the trade journal *Chain Store Age*,[346] and although their advertising seldom makes any reference to the character Ben-Hur or chariot racing, a rare but unprovenienced box of ten hairpins from Ben Hur is distinguished with a maroon, wrap-around label and gold printing that depicts a two-horse chariot riding from right to left.

Hardware
After Van Camp's purchased Central Cycle's brand of Ben-Hur Bicycle, they also issued a line of Ben-Hur tools and hardware products. Ben-Hur brand tools included chisels, drills, screwdrivers, draw knives, hatchets, hammers, planes, wrenches, and tin snips. Made of metals and woods, many examples still survive among collectors and are exchanged via the internet. The hardware products also include volatile compounds and pressure sprayers, which are less likely to survive for so many decades. Despite their being simple hand tools, they represent the *Ben-Hur* tradition in that a full-page ad placed in the December, 1935, issue of *Hardware Retailer* features their quality and is presented with elegant imagery.[347] A fine border surrounds the text block placed in the center of the page, its gently spaced copy decorated with cursive script and surrounded by wide margins. Four Ben Hur emblems with a single racing *quadriga* each mark the corners, and the top line reads, "QUALITY WITHOUT EXTRAVAGANCE." Van Camp Hardware & Iron Company assures the reader that their tools are made of high quality materials, cost effective, and much in demand by repeat customers.

Like many major hardware retailers, Van Camp did not manufacture all their own products. Various pages in their wholesale catalogs list different varieties for sale. For instance, a page in an unprovenienced catalogue – but no doubt from the 1930s – pictures and describes 1 Vanco, 1 Plumb, 2 Van Camp, and 2 Ben Hur half hatchet models sold a half dozen in a box. The more expensive, drop-forged Ben Hur model displays the familiar charioteer both on the haft and the blade. The same and other catalogs contain Ben Hur models of iron-block planes (page 41), chromium-plated electric irons (854), cotton clothes lines (1357), washboards (1358), and several models of bicycles (2053).[348] Van Camp was probably the distributor of the Ben-Hur roller skates that display the patent date of September 12, 1922.

In 1928, as well as in 1934 and 1935, Van Camp Hardware and Iron Company issued several different advertisements for their new manifestation of the Ben-Hur Bicycle.[349] Appealing specifically to nostalgia for the "Gay Nineties," Van Camp took out a full-page ad in the 1935 *Hardware Retailer* with the grab-line:

> WAY BACK IN THE "GAY NINETIES"
> DAD RODE A BEN HUR BICYCLE

The ad is aimed at retailers interested in establishing an exclusive agency in their locality. And emphasizing the image of "BEN HUR – The Best for Forty Years" are four repetitions of the chariot logo from the original company of the 1890s. Van Camp continued to sell the Ben-Hur through the 1930s. Their 1939 catalogue includes several models of Ben-Hur sleds and a Ben-Hur ice-cream maker.[350]

Clothing
The clothing industry applied the name Ben-Hur to a variety of products. "'Ben Hur' shirts" were advertised in New England from 1933 to 1937.[351] Their logo was an octagon divided into two halves.[352] The upper half contained a two-horse racing chariot driven by a charioteer brandishing a whip lashed into a decorative curl. The text of the bottom half began, "Mightier Than Ever! A Genuine Ben-Hur Boy's Shirt." In 1947 Gude's in Los Angeles advertised a pebble crepe woman's sleeved shirt with French cuffs, pearl studs, an adjustable collar, and a Ben-Hur print design featuring a racing chariot, classical column, and stylized whip.[353] The Ben-Hur print was etched on a choice of white, pink, or aqua. The choice of colors might otherwise be immaterial, but it was in 1930 that the nylon industry adopted the color named Ben Hur.[354] These light taupe nylons were available through such high-end department stores as Saks, which seems to have introduced it, Macy's, Marshall Field, and Henri Bendel.[355] They advertised in the major urban newspapers throughout the 1930s and 1940s until at least 1959.[356]

There are additional but relatively isolated bits of evidence that together help to demonstrate the broad application of the Ben-Hur name in the clothing industry. Ben Hur Blouse Company, that had leased space at 33 West 26th Street in Manhattan in 1929,[357] announced a move in January, 1937 to 44 West 25th Street,[358] but no other information has turned up. In 1941 the *Chicago Daily Tribune* advertised Ben Hur muslin.[359] In 1946 John Wanamaker advertised Ben Hur indoor clothes dryers.[360]

There were also additional Ben-Hur accessories. In the spring of 1937 Bonwit Teller sold a style of Ben Hur shoe. Made by Palter DeLiso, the open-toed Ben Hur Oxford was made from Mexican leather and offered in a variety of colors.[361] The year before, a report on Paris fashions said a "Ben Hur" model hat with a high crest had the look of a Roman helmet.[362] Another accessory was a Ben-Hur model watch. As wristwatches became popular in the 1930s, Bulova produced a Ben Hur wristwatch made with twenty-one jewels.[363] The focus of one newspaper ad was appropriate in that it was "a real gift watch for his Christmas gift."[364] The Bulova model was manufactured from 1936–9.[365] There was also a 17-jewel, Swiss-movement Lady Elgin model of Ben Hur wristwatch.[366] And at the end of the shopping trip, so to speak, consumers could transport their purchases home in a Ben Hur shopping bag made of vinyl and rolled along on four ball-bearing wheels, a mail-order item advertised in the *New York Herald Tribune* during the 1957 Christmas shopping season.[367]

Food Products

From the late 1930s until at least 1949 the Oceanic Sales Company of Seattle sold Ben Hur Salmon from Alaska.[368] The can labels feature the words "BEN HUR SALMON" printed in a circle. On one side there is a leaping salmon in the center of the circle, on the other a modified version of the Wagner charioteer. A more accurate rendition of the same Wagner charioteer filled the label of the Ben Hur Tomato Catsup canned by the Winona Preserving Company of Ontario, which was in business by 1926.[369] An extant isolated product is a soda bottle labeled "Ben Hur Beverages" and produced by Ben-Hur Bottling Company of Wallingford, Connecticut. The name Ben Hur (without the hyphen) is printed in red across the label of an extant a 26-ounce bottle, while the bottle has the name Ben-Hur (with the hyphen) raised in the molded glass above the label.[370] Likewise, the name Ben Hur is molded at the bottom of the bottle. Above the name Ben Hur on the label is an emblem of a spread eagle with a circled BH in the center. The font and style of labeling and molded glass suggest the 1930s or 1940s.

Miscellaneous Manufacturers

Chicago's Pace Manufacturing Company introduced their mechanical Ben Hur pinball machine in 1933.[371] Unfortunately, although listed on all the comprehensive pinball and arcade-game website catalogs, there are no descriptions of the game or the cabinet relevant to the Ben-Hur motif. Another elusive company was the manufacturer of Ben-Hur Bakelite. The surviving examples are mostly holders for miniature cocktail recipe booklets, suggesting that they postdate the end of Prohibition era in December, 1933.[372] The Bakelite holders were molded in a variety of animal and human shapes ranging from roosters to giraffes and a donkey kicking a human in the rear.

In 1940 the Ben Hur Wire Fence was revived, now manufactured by the Mid-States Steel & Wire Company of Crawfordsville. In 1955 they registered the name as a trademark.[373]

In the late 1940s, another Ben-Hur Products, Inc., also self-identified as Ben-Hur Industries, Inc., with an office at 11 West 42nd Street in New York, manufactured such decorative and juvenile wares as a 17-inch electric clock decorated with a dark-brown molded plastic depiction of a modern sailboat on a mountain lake;[374] bendable and washable latex foam-rubber clown toys, and a blue "kiddie juke box" that included an electronic phonograph, an illuminating light, a 5-inch speaker, and a red top that rendered it useful as a stool.[375] This company placed short, catch-all classified ads in the *New York Times* and *Los Angeles Times* to purchase electrical appliances and housewares at close-out prices.[376]

European Products

The unparalleled and continuing success of the 1925 MGM film overseas inspired a few manufacturers and retailers outside of the United States. In 1929 the May Company sold a sculpture titled, "Broken Chariot Wheel or Ben Hur," imported from Dux, Czechoslovakia.[377] Costing $29.95, it was the most expensive of the nine items listed in its category.

Friedrich Herkenrath of Solingen-Merscheid, a German company, produced a Ben-Hur straight razor in 1932.[378] Herkenrath and apparently others also sold a safety razor in a travel case. In Sheffield, England, Kayser Ellison & Company, Ltd., manufactured a silver steel brand of Ben Hur safety razor blades in the 1930s.[379] Twelve packages of their Ben-Hur blades were attached to a large display featuring their "silver steel" logo – the profile of a Roman with a shiny silver helmet – and placed on store counters. Beneath the blades, "known the world over" was printed, and indeed they were sold as far away as Portugal, as evidenced by a Gabriel de Carvalho postcard recently offered on eBay,[380] and in several Shanghai newspapers well into the 1930s.[381]

In 1936, Ben Hur Sigarenfabrieken of Zeist in the Netherlands produced a Ben Hur brand of cigars.[382] The product was manufactured for only one year, but the company produced a handsome lithographed label featuring a Roman wearing a plumed helmet.[383]

PETROLEUM EXPLORATION, FOSSIL FUELS, AND MINING

Major newspapers reported that oil drilling began in Ben-Hur, Louisiana, in 1933 and in Ben Hur, Virginia, in 1947.[384] Also in 1947, a legal claim for a Ben Hur Oil Company was filed in Indiana,[385] and two years later the company was co-sponsoring a local golf tournament.[386] A neighborly newspaper announcement saying that a cloth money bag with $73.04 had been lost near the company location near North 3rd Street in Logansport, Indiana,[387] makes clear that this is not the same contemporary Ben Hur Oil Company advertised on an extant book of matches listing an address at Route 45 and Piatt Ave in Matoon, Illinois.[388] This establishment carried White Rose Gasoline and Enarco Motor Oil,[389] but no doubt it was the Logansport owner who dubbed it a "Ben Hur" business: his name happened to be Lew Wallace. In 1949 the *Los Angeles Times* began reporting on drilling operations by the Ben Hur Refining Company, Ben-Hur-von Glahn Sydicate, and Ben Hur-Imperial Development Company in the Signal Hill, Sand Canyon, and Lopez Canyon areas of Los Angeles.[390]

At the user end, from 1948 into the 1950s the Ben Hur Oil Company of Los Angeles and New Orleans sold Ben Hur Premium Motor Oil as well as a Unity Oil brand.[391] The Ben Hur Premium Motor Oil cans included a depiction of a charioteer with raised whip, printed in white against a

Figure 13.3 George Urich, who pioneered discount, self-service gas stations throughout Southern California, produced the most colorful logo among many Ben-Hur products, companies, and claims in the petroleum and mining industries.

red background. Unlike most Ben-Hur logos and the Wagner and Checa models, this one keeps three contiguous horses' heads at the same height. George Urich, the independent Los Angeles gasoline station owner who opened the first discount, self-service station in 1947 and soon expanded the concept,[392] owned over twenty locations in Southern California where he sold a 101-Octane Ben Hur Aviation Ethyl – Superior Gasoline in 1959, probably in conjunction with the new MGM film.[393] His chariot logo employed a reverse image of the Wagner model. The horses are all brown, however, with white and red harnesses, and lines suggesting their exhalation emerge from their noses. The charioteer is white. Behind the entire chariot assemblage is a blue, cloud-like background.[394]

As for mining concerns, in the 1930s the *Los Angeles Times* reported that the California Ben Hur gold mine was sold to a South African company, and that the Ben Hur Divide Company was working a group of silver and gold claims in Tonopah, Nevada.[395] Following union struggles in 1948, the *New York Times* and *Wall Street Journal* as well as papers in Ada, Miami, and Ardmore, Oklahoma, reported on the local dispute between the family-owned Ben Hur Coal Company and Starr Coal Company.[396] In 1954 Ellis, Gene, and Amy Taylor launched a $769,000 lawsuit against Starr's Earl Wells for underpricing their Henryetta domestic stoker coal and forcing closure of their Atlas Mine.[397] Ben Hur lost the case, and an appeal to the 10th Circuit of the federal courts in February, 1957, was unsuccessful, as was their final appeal to the U.S. Supreme Court, as reported in the *New York Times* later that year.[398] Nonetheless, the *Wall Street Journal* reported that Ben Hur resumed operations at its Blackstone coal mine in 1959.[399]

BANKING AND REALTY

Although the Ben Hur Savings & Loan at 1650 South Pulaski Avenue was only one of seventy-nine S&Ls in the Chicago area in the early 1950s, the uniqueness of its name is instructive.[400] As so often, none of the other names derive from a novel, play, movie, or any other kind of artistic product, and none are named after a famous person. Two have Greek mythological names (Apollo, Triton) and a few are named after their chief executive officer, but otherwise their names reflect their street address or neighborhood, or they use such generic names as American, Capitol, Colonial, and Equitable. Six years later, after the association had expanded considerably, the only "historical" names added are Lincoln and Ben Franklin.[401] As the reader knows well, the name Ben-Hur claimed a unique position in popular culture in the late nineteenth century, and now more than seven decades later it still maintained that special evocative power.[402]

The real estate business also exploited the popular allure of the Ben-Hur name. In the 1930s and 1940s, Ben Hur Homes operated in the Jamaica Estates area of Queens in New York (just a few miles from Little Neck, where Bushman used to live),[403] and Manhattan still had the Ben Hur Apartments on Broadway.[404] Representing the post-war suburban expansion in California, and reflecting the trend towards contemporary domestic ranch architecture, Earl P. Snyder and Kenneth P. Schmidt of the Kenbo Corporation announced in May, 1951, their planned $1.5 million Ben Hur Estates development in East Whittier.[405] The eighty-one three-bedroom and two-bedroom-and-den houses sat on terraced view lots, were offered for just under $20,000, and were financed by the FHA. Ben Hur Estates appeared frequently in the *Los Angeles Times* in advertisements, photographs, and progress announcements until May, 1952, when the last few lots were prepared for building.[406] Halfway through the project the National Association of Home Builders selected Ben Hur Estates as one of five winners in the NAHB Neighborhood Development contest.[407] On a much smaller scale, Ben Herz and others incorporated their Ben Hur, Inc. in Seattle in 1934,[408] and the Ben Hur Garage, Inc. maintained property on 47th and 48th streets in Manhattan from at least 1936 until 1940.[409]

Crawfordsville sprouted the Ben Hur Drive-in, operating from 1949 to 1956,[410] and the General Lew Wallace Motor Inn at 309 West Pike Street, serving primarily Wabash College, and in operation until just recently.[411] There is also an extant matchbook cover from Spence Steinmetz's Ben Hur Sports Shop at 109 North Green Street in Crawfordsville.[412] No later than 1953, the locally prominent Republican Clyde R. Black was operating the Ben Hur Motel and Dining Room on Hi-Way 24 in Logansport.[413] A number of postcards survive depicting both the dining room and motel.[414]

ADVERTISING

Advertisers used some of the images and imagery associated with Ben-Hur to promote products that were not named Ben-Hur. At least one local newspaper ad preceded the national proliferation of the comic book characterizations of Ben-Hur. In 1933 Schwegmann's Grocery and Delicatessen in New Orleans placed an ad depicting a race between a chariot and contemporary racing car.[415] The charioteer, his cape flowing behind him, his hands holding his head in disbelief, says:

> "So This is Technocracy," says Ben Hur. "Guess I'll have to junk my chariot. What chance have I up against machinery of such speed and power and precision?"

In 1934 Minneapolis-Honeywell placed a large ad with a chariot motif in *Fortune Magazine*.[416] It featured a powerful charioteer reining in his four horses, as the headline reads: "CONTROLLED in one harness – the six climatic factors of true air conditioning."

During and after the war a number of Ben-Hur-themed ads were aimed at national readership. It was during the war in 1944 that the Ford Motor Company placed their "Watch the Fords Go By" ad in a number of popular national magazines and newspapers, featuring the headline, "It's exciting as the race in 'Ben Hur.'"[417] Two years later the Minnesota Valley Canning Company ran a series of ads featuring the Green Giant as famous figures in history, and one of these presented "The Green Giant as Ben Hur," depicting the Green Giant as the charioteer in the Wagner painting.[418] In 1947 Standard Oil Company ran a large newspaper display ad featuring the publicity-still depicting Novarro grabbing onto Bushman's whip. This chariot race photo from the 1925 *Ben-Hur* was used to demonstrate how comparatively low gasoline prices had become.[419] The caption below says, "How Old Are You? – Old enough to remember Francis X. Bushman and Ramon Novarro in 'Ben Hur'?"

The chariot race imagery continued in the early 1950s but without photos from the MGM film. Instead, cartoons were used. In 1951 a nearly full-page ad for Ballantine Beer began with the headline:

> Ben Hur's the boy the Roman horde
> Would always bet across the board.[420]

This is illustrated with four chariot race cartoon panels and finishes with the rhyme:

> This beer is always first, you know,
> It never takes a place or show.

A 1952 magazine advertisement for Reo Motors, Inc., of Lansing, Michigan, featured a cartoon mascot named Benny.[421] After the name Benny the copy adds, "(Ben Hur, that is)." This ad, which belonged to a campaign that used the Sphinx and other cartoon images, was for their Gold Comet truck engines.[422] Benny is pictured twice. He wears a green victory wreath on his head and a red cloak fastened at the front of his neck. The entire upper half of the ad depicts him standing on the rear axle of a truck drive-train, greaves on his legs, reins in his right hand, whip in his left. The speed of the drive-train is noted by the use of motion lines, and behind him are three trailing contemporary racing cars. In an insert at the lower right, there is the second depiction of the smiling Benny and a quotation: "This Reo Gold Comet puts other truck engines in the same class with my old hayburners that I discarded centuries ago." A full-page, 1949 ad in *Life* for the Sanforized, anti-shrinking process depicts a young man, "Ben Hur(ts)," standing on a wheelbarrow, no doubt an ersatz chariot.[423] Holding an ax, he cannot get any work done because he is busily tugging at his shrunken collar. In 1953 Pacific Telephone placed a three-panel cartoon, "Ben Hur Gets Straight Steer" to advertise the Yellow Pages. The panels progress from depicting Ben Hur fretting because he is anxious to get to Rome but his chariot has a broken wheel, to Ben Hur looking through the handy Yellow Pages, to Ben Hur happily driving into Rome in a new automobile.[424]

TRANSPORTATION

Just as in the earlier era, there was a Ben Hur train in the 1930s, although in this instance it was a freight train.[425] At the end of a lengthy decade of depression, the *New York Herald Tribune* finished a feature on the economy and the nation's rail system by listing "fanciful titles" for trains and concluding:

> The traditional hobo who, at least in fiction, always "grabs a rattler," may now perhaps be more selective and, spurning the Vegetable Special, prefer to come into town on Ben Hur.

Twenty years later the *New York Times* confirmed that there was at least one other Ben Hur freight train in service:

> If he is a serious student of freight trains he may know also that "Abe Martin" is a nickname for a Chicago, Indianapolis and Louisville freight between Chicago and Indianapolis, or that "Bean Train" is the official name of a freight on the Southern from Jacksonville to Potomac Yard, Va., or that there are listed two freight trains named "Ben Hur," neither serving the same cities. But this is highly specialized knowledge [for] the average commuter.[426]

A 1949 article, "A Nod to Ben Hur," reprinted in *The Train Dispatcher*, even traced the gauge of modern railroad tracks back to ancient Roman chariots and therefore, of course, Ben Hur:

> Strange as it may seem, historians claim that the clearance between the wheels of Ben Hur's chariot was the same as that which now exists between the wheels of a modern Canadian National Railways locomotive, passenger or freight car ... and the distance between the wheels of a Roman chariot was established by Julius Caesar.[427]

On the road, Hartley's Ben-Hur Transfer, which was a local and long distance moving company in Oklahoma City, was ambitious enough to advertise in *The Christian Science Monitor* in 1942.[428] In addition, a few newspaper articles recalled the 1916/17 Ben Hur automobile for the novelty of the name, one in response to the production of Ford's Edsel,[429] and long after Van Camp revived the Ben-Hur Bicycle in the 1930s, the Columbia brand advertised bikes for young children "with 'Ben Hur' side wheel stabilizers," i.e. training wheels.[430] It is important to note that this particular allusion predates the iconic blades adorning Messala's chariot in the 1959 MGM film.

On the water, from 1940 to 1946 a yacht named *Ben Hur* competed in more than a dozen summer races in the Boston area, all duly reported in the *Boston Globe*. Registering his racer in the Hustler Class,[431] Dr. Al Stanley from Savin Hill occasionally sailed to victory, although there are no recorded remarks relevant to the yacht's namesake.[432] Among non-racing boats, a *Ben Hur* tugboat operated in Portland Harbor on the West Coast until 1937,[433] and the 1941 *Pacific Motor Boat* lists a tugboat *Ben Hur* belonging to C. Lloyd Munson with the call-name WNZW.[434] A French fishing barque was newly christened *Ben Hur* in or shortly before 1936.[435] In that year, the three-masted vessel was rescued in the Atlantic by the ocean liner *City of Baltimore*. In gratitude, the crew gave a gift of salt cod to the Americans, whose menu the next day, according to the *New York*

Herald Tribune, featured "Salt Cod à la Ben Hur." (Other examples of *Ben-Hur* menu items: the October 26, 1957, menu for the Cunard Line's Queen Mary features a "Ben Hur Entrecote Steak";[436] and the May 7, 1957, lunch menu includes a "Kebab Ben Hur."[437]) In 1939 the *Ben Hur* caught fire, and the entire crew had to be rescued by the liner *Duchess of Bedford*.[438] Just three weeks later, the U.S. Coast Guard cutter *Champlain* sighted "two dories marked Ben Hur" and reported their precise locations.[439]

LEISURE ACTIVITIES

The reader has observed repeatedly the popular association between *Ben-Hur* and chariot racing. As we have reached well into the period when horses were no longer used for regular transportation or transport, the concept of chariot racing, its periodic recreation, and its metaphorical application, as well as its visual imagery represented not just a nostalgic recreation of an exciting institution of yesteryear but a universally recognized *Ben-Hur* reference point that could be applied to almost any kind of vehicle or animal racing, competition, or driving, whether in the real world, live entertainment, or movies.

Ben-Hur in Sports

Sportswriters frequently made reference to Ben-Hur whether as a historical ancient Roman champion, a movie racer, or the protagonist of Lew Wallace's novel. United Press distributed a syndicated piece on Cavalcade, the winner of 1934's Kentucky Derby, that began:

> Webster's big dictionary says Cavalcade is derived from the Latin word, Caballus, meaning an inferior horse. Back when Ben Hur was a hero at the Roman race tracks, the Latin Cavalcade might have been a selling plater, but since then there's been a lot of improvement in his breed.[440]

Here he is represented as a historical hero, but a United Press prelude to the next year's Kentucky Derby promised "something on the order of Ben Hur, only quite a bit more Cecil de Millish."[441] The 1939 Derby even inspired the *Kansas City Star* to run an excerpt from Wallace's novel. The introduction preceding the excerpt articulates the assumption that the famous predecessor to the most prominent American races of any type was the chariot race in *Ben-Hur*:

> Another great race was run at Churchill Downs Saturday in the Kentucky Derby. Still another great race will be run at Indianapolis at the end of this month when the motor cars dash over the speedway in the annual Memorial Day classic. Since history began, men have thrilled to the contest of speed, and the vast crowds at the competitions of 1939 share an ecstasy that was experienced by multitudes in the ancient world. As spectacular in their time as the turf, speedway and aerial races of today were the chariot races of the Romans. Among the great pieces of descriptive literature is that of the chariot race in "Ben Hur," by Gen. Lew Wallace.[442]

The third "jewel" in the Triple Crown inspired yet another comparison,[443] and a similar allusion was applied to the 1951 Hambletonian.[444] An earlier steeplechase event inspired this introductory paragraph in the *Boston Globe*:

> "The glorious uncertainties of horse racing is what makes it the king of sports." This is as true now as some 1900 years ago when Ben Hur was, as fiction records, the top race driver.[445]

In 1946 the *New York Times* was nostalgic for turn-of-the-century buggy races "as exciting as Ben-Hur's chariot race" in Madison Square Garden,[446] and even a hurdle race at Belmont Park evoked a photo headline in the *New York Herald Tribune*, "Jumpers Aligned in a Ben Hur Chariot Race Setting at Belmont."[447] When *Chicago Tribune* sports columnist Edward Burns responded to a reader's question about which sporting event in all of history he would like to have seen, he wrote:

> That chariot race between Ben Hur and the haughty Messala almost 1900 years ago! . . . Incidentally, Ben Hur drove without a whip and never doped a horse.[448]

The *Times* horse-racing editor, Joe H. Palmer, wrote that he remembered receiving Wallace's novel as a Christmas gift when he was a boy, although he admits to receiving only "low pleasure from the chariot race."[449] Nonetheless, two years later he cited *Ben-Hur* as an authoritative text on Arabians.[450] Red Smith wrote a syndicated piece in 1956 describing the throng at Hialeah as "the scene of the wildest charge since Ben Hur was known as the Eddie Arcaro of the chariot races."[451] It was a matter of course, then, when Santa Anita Race Track ran an illustrated ad in the *Los Angeles Times* that included a sketched portrait of a Roman horse named Ben Him wearing a laurel wreath and toga.[452]

Ben-Hur was also applied to non-equestrian sports. Henry McLemore, sports columnist for the United Press, humorously undercut his prediction on an upcoming 1935 Joe Louis heavyweight boxing match by commenting:

> Gents in all parts of the country will start writing me letters discrediting all the McLemores clean back to the original one, H. Peabody McLemore, who was fed to the lions for picking Ben Hur to finish no better than third.[453]

The imagery of the Ben-Hur chariot race and the motifs of speed and victory filtered even into baseball. In the lead-up to the 1932 World Series, the *Cleveland Plain Dealer* ran a five-column-wide editorial cartoon featuring Babe Ruth wearing a leather vest while driving a chariot.[454] His three horses kick up dust as they knock baseball opponents off the track and into the air, and on the rim of his chariot are printed the dates of the ten World Series Ruth's teams have won. Above the illustration, spanning the entire length of the cartoon, runs the headline: "Ben Hur of World Series Classics Is Mighty Bambino."

Team sports seemed to be particularly appropriate. A syndicated short story in 1936 compared Ben Hur and his galley slaves to a football team, and later that year Ben Hur was in fact the name of an amateur football team in Cleveland.[455] In 1946, five years before he wrote that he would rather see the Ben-Hur chariot race than any other sporting event in history, Edward Burns compared Chicago Cubs manager Charley Grimm to Ben Hur "and other famed bullwhip practitioners."[456] Either Burns or one of his staff writers wrote that polo incorporated "the racier aspects of Ben-Hur."[457] The *New York Herald Tribune* found a New York Giants baseball player getting a clutch hit worthy of the Ben-Hur sobriquet,[458] as did the *Boston Globe* in describing hockey players chasing after a puck.[459]

In a serious and quasi-historical evocation of the whole Ben-Hur chariot racing complex, the *New York Herald Tribune* and *New York Times* printed a major news story about the 1947 Queens County Grand Jury's recommendation that Governor Thomas Dewey make off-track bookmaking legal in the state of New York.[460] The second paragraph of the Grand Jury's statement to the governor said, "The urge to bet is as old as the human race itself, and its existence is even more widespread today than it was in the days of Ben Hur."[461] Ironically, in the late 1950s MGM, searching for people named Ben-Hur as part of a publicity campaign for the film, would locate a pari-mutuel ticket seller named Ben Hur living in Jamaica, New York.[462]

Of course there were racing horses named Ben-Hur in this era. In addition to Ben Hur Stables' Thespian, a trotter named Ben Hur raced in the summer of 1937,[463] and another was active between 1940 and 1945.[464] This one, owned and driven by Albert A. Pratt of Massachusetts, won the Coldstream Cup and the Adirondack feature race for 4-year-olds at Empire City in 1943.[465] Another thoroughbred named Ben Hur entered and won several races at Belmont, Aqueduct, and Jamaica in the New York area as a 2-year-old in 1945.[466]

In other equestrian events, in 1934 and 1935 Pauline Scovern entered her Arabian Ben Hur in the Salinas rodeo,[467] Pauline Yetten her Ben Hur in a gymkhana in Dover, Delaware,[468] Reginald Auchincloss, Jr., his chestnut gelding Ben Hur in the Tuxedo Horse Show in New York,[469] and a bay colt Ben Hur was consigned in Kentucky.[470] At the Pasadena New Year's parade in 1934, Ben Wilson rode his thoroughbred Arabian Ben Hur, "one of the most handsome steeds in the pageant."[471] In 1939 Marcia Daughtrey was in the mainstream when McClure syndicated her short story about a chestnut gelding racer named Ben Hur,[472] and still another steed named Ben Hur took third at the Royal Winter Fair Horse Show in Toronto in 1954, where two other horses had names derived from popular culture, Peter Pan and Flash Gordon.[473]

In other uses of the name, in 1946 the *New York Herald Tribune* called the Madison Square Garden Rodeo a "western Ben Hur show."[474] And

Ben Hur Farms in Portland, Indiana, produced a prize-winning Arabian, Aarafla, that took the special Arabian Stake Challenge Trophy, awarded by King Farouk of Egypt, at an international horse show in 1950.[475] Aarafla won several more competitions until at least 1957,[476] by which time MGM was already searching for "Arabians" for the remake.[477]

Chariot Racing
In 1950 actual chariot races with toga-draped drivers were held every night for one week in Brighton, England, to celebrate their ancient Roman heritage,[478] and, on a grander scale, in 1954 nightly "'Ben Hur' spectacles" were scheduled at the 5000-seat arena in Fort Lauderdale, Florida.[479] Other Ben-Hur-related chariot races included those at the Maine State Fair in 1934,[480] the 1935 Southern California Shriners pageant in the L.A. Coliseum,[481] the annual round-up of the Y.M.C.A. Pioneer Clubs in Southern California in 1936,[482] not to mention a local elementary-school carnival.[483] To promote the release of its 1940 film, *The Boys of Syracuse*, Universal contemplated running a chariot race from San Francisco to Syracuse, New York. Hedda Hopper commented with a Ben-Hur neologism:

> I suggest they have special truck built with a treadmill and let the horses gallop on the treadmill through the towns, but rest on the truck through the wide-open spaces in between. Horses, like people nowadays, have grown soft. Can you see the populace in the various towns, with horses "Ben-Hur-ing" their way from coast to coast?[484]

One of the papers carrying her syndication was the *Washington Post*. Two pages after the one carrying her column, resident columnist Nelson B. Bell began his version of the same press release this way:

> Those oldsters of the theater who remember the treadmill chariot race in "Ben Hur" as the ultimate spasm in thundering excitement "ain't seen nuthin' yet," as Al Jolson would say, until they have viewed the closing sequences in Universal's picturization of George Abbott's successful stage musical, "The Boys From Syracuse."

As we have seen, not all chariot races or allusions involved Roman-style chariots, or horses. In 1935 the Lake Forest, Illinois, Winter Club featured a chariot race on the snow, promising that "the 'Ben Hur' sleds have been improved over those used in seasons past."[485] A harsh criticism of the ice revue "Alaskan Stampede" lamented that "the dog team race was no hullabaloo of an Alaskan Ben Hur and his rival in furs."[486] North of the United States, "Ben Hur and his chariots had nothing on" the nightly Chuck Wagon races at the Calgary Stampede in 1939, and at the Military Tatoo in Dublin two motorcycles were hitched side by side and controlled from behind, as headlined in *The Irish Times*, "In the Wake of Ben Hur!"[487] Mimi Garneau advertised the smallest chariot race in history as she toured the country in the 1940s with her trained flea circus and "Ben Hur, Champion Roman Chariot Racer."

Entertainments and Pageants

The following passages will demonstrate as thoroughly as any in the book just how variegated Ben-Hur associations had become. As at Coney Island, Ocean Park, and elsewhere just after the turn of the century, public entertainments simulated chariot racing activity on a large scale, but now in England, R. J. Lakin & Company of Besley Street in south London (Streatham) introduced the Ben Hur Ark, an undulating merry-go-round, in 1935.[488] This was in response to the success of their rival, Orton & Spooner, who had been building German-style "Arks," merry-go-rounds with animal themes. Lakin was enamored of the Wagner painting in the Manchester Art Gallery, and so he affixed horses and chariots on his ark, reproduced the dramatic scene – four panels high – on the marquee of the ride, and had some of the chariots carved as dragons or sea horses.[489] Britain's National Fairground Archive website describes many such machines, including a 3-hill built in 1937 and photographed in 1949, and the Coronation Ben Hur Ark built in 1937 and photographed in 1947. A machine with twenty-one platforms, built in 1935, was in use into the 1980s. In all, the website includes photographs of nearly a dozen Ben Hur Arks.

Circuses frequently invoked images of Ben Hur horses or chariots, often associated with the initial parade.[490] Describing the opening performance by Ringling Brothers and Barnum & Bailey Circus at Madison Square Garden in 1935, the *New York Herald Tribune* said that "'Aida' never had more elephants ... nor did 'Ben Hur' have as many horses."[491] In 1935 the sweepstakes-winning float at Seattle's August Potlatch celebration featured Queen Juno, Cupid, and Ben Hur, who "step out of the pages of history into real life."[492] In 1940 New Orleans hosted a pageant featuring a Ben-Hur theme. The annual Virgilians' Ball included staged tableaux of the Wise Men, the Palace of Hur, the tile incident, and the chariot race.[493] All the members of the court were clothed in Roman costumes. As a celebrity King of the Ball, New York Giants first baseman Zeke Bonura represented Ben-Hur and rode the four white horses in the race.[494]

In the arts, when in 1936 the *Chicago Daily Tribune* published a copy of Jan Styka's monumental painting *The Crucifixion* [*Golgotha*], the key to the characters in the painting included Ben-Hur, Esther, and Simonides.[495] Another columnist described a painting of an American Indian standing "à la Ben Hur" on a cow.[496] In the movies, a review of the 1935 Warner Brothers' *Red Hot Tires*, a film about a car racer, says that in the lead role Lyle Talbot plays "a modern Ben Hur, gets his Messala, and gets him so good that he's given a 10-year manslaughter stretch."[497] The *Los Angeles Times*' Philip K. Scheuer, Schallert's replacement, wrote that at the raucous chuck-wagon chase climax of Red Skelton's *Texas Carnival* (1951), the winner "comes in riding the buckboard's shafts as proudly as, and even more surprised than, Ben Hur."[498] In 1941 long-time New York drama critic Charles Darnton interviewed Lionel Barrymore about his technique of acting in a wheelchair.[499] Darton comments at the end of the second paragraph, "As a scene-stealing device, it is the biggest thing since the winning chariot in 'Ben Hur.'"

For children, a 1934 Seattle exhibition of gadgets included a toy chariot designed so that "every young fellow of three summers can be his own Ben-Hur."[500] The rivalry at the annual Soap Box Derby in 1937 was said to be "as keen as witnessed in any race since Ben Hur drove the Arab steeds around the ancient hippodrome."[501] A 1952 juvenile circus in Oak Park was headlined as "Shades of Ben Hur."[502] Just two days later, veteran *Chicago Tribune* columnist Will Leonard, pondering why children were so fascinated by old-fashioned cowboy heroes, wondered what passed for nostalgia back in the 1890s: "Then we remembered – they went for the chariot race in 'Ben Hur.'"[503] That same year, which was two years after the release of MGM's *Quo Vadis*, a mail-order house in Chicago sold English sculpted, hand-painted, miniature "Racing Roman Chariots . . . From the Times of Quo Vadis and Ben Hur."[504]

Chariot racing also provided an apt metaphor for driving in modern automobile traffic. In 1942 *The Christian Science Monitor* gave praise for a friendly bus driver because "his skill in directing his chariot surpasses that of any Ben Hur."[505] When traveling in Ireland in 1943, the aforementioned Henry McLemore began his syndicated essay with this extended allusion to Ben-Hur:

> I never met Ben-Hur, he being slightly before my time, but I hope to run across him some day and swap experiences. He will undoubtedly have some thrilling stories to tell of his chariot-driving days. But even Ben and any of his contemporaries who happen to be about will stop and listen when I tell them of riding jaunting cars in Ireland.[506]

In a 1955 syndicated essay on "Civilization Sickness," Pulitzer Prize-winning journalist Hal Boyle said driving through Sunday traffic to the beach makes one "feel like a charioteer in 'Ben Hur,'"[507] much as did Timothy G. Turner in the *Los Angeles Times* when describing the perils of being a pedestrian in that city.[508]

The metaphor applied not only to the building of the Rome subway below the original Circus Maximus and a speeding taxi ride in Baltimore,[509] but also a runaway junk wagon in the same city,[510] a Boston police circus,[511] a debate on the trustworthiness of women drivers,[512] a farmer with a new tractor who was as proud "as if it were Ben Hur's chariot,"[513] a quartet of tugboats "working abreast something like the chariot horses in 'Ben Hur,'"[514] and even to an incident in which the *Tribune*'s Lucy Key Miller observed a mother pushing two baby strollers "with the agility of Ben Hur driving in the chariot race."[515] A summer fashion feature in the *New York Times* described the contemporary resort beach scene, where:

> Strolling on the sands any morning one is liable to run into young Ben Hur, set for a chariot-race with Neptune's steeds, draped in a toga and headband of flame-rose fine wool with fringed edges, created by Dilkusha.[516]

And the reporter who covered the June 3, 1937, wedding of Wallis Simpson to the Duke of Windsor, former King Edward VIII of the United Kingdom, described the event as "the biggest event up to that time since the chariot race in 'Ben Hur.'"[517]

In his extensive eastern Mediterranean wanderings in the late 1940s, travelogue author Robert Wilkin Blake walked into Antioch, describing it as:

> The city where Anthony [sic] and Cleopatra kept their second rendezvous, the city of St. Paul's first ministry, the city where the term "Christianity" was first used, the city where Ben-Hur was supposed to have run his famous chariot race.[518]

He spent the rest of his column describing his individual quest to find the stadium and his satisfaction in doing so.

THE NAME BEN-HUR

There was a new generation of Ben Hurs. In addition to the pari-mutuel ticket seller in Jamaica, New York,[519] there were also the fashion model Jorge Ben-Hur,[520] another Ben Hur in Bethesda, Maryland,[521] a Denver cult limousine driver,[522] a Virgin Islander Ben Hur Brad,[523] and a Ben Hur Lawson in Los Angeles.[524] A nationally syndicated piece told of the Fort Worth, Texas, municipal "toyrarian" – a librarian that distributed toys – known as Mrs. Ben Hur.[525]

The name Ben-Hur also attracted canine lovers. Besides a best of breed Collie and a puppy-class winner in the New York area,[526] *The Manchester Guardian* listed pedigree Kerry Blue terrier puppies by Ben Hur for sale.[527] Usually only show, breed, and competitive animals appeared in newspaper accounts, but a tour of a sprawling estate in the Seattle area listed a round stone house for a Sealyham named Banker's Ben Hur.[528]

And for garden enthusiasts there was the Narcissus Ben Hur, commonly called the Ben Hur Daffodil, a large-flowered cultivar.[529]

BEN-HUR IN HUMOR

Because Ben-Hur remained active within the vocabulary of contemporary popular culture, it remained a target for humor of various sorts. In addition to the Bob Hope and Henry McLemore quips already cited, newspapers periodically thought additional off-the-cuff remarks involving Ben-Hur would be of some interest and amusement to their readership. We read in the *San Diego Union* that when a defendant in California in 1942 told a federal judge that he had been in jail more than ten months awaiting trial, the judge remarked, "Some one should read *Ben-Hur*."[530] When Mrs. Dorothy Mary Stokes of London was granted a divorce in 1948 on grounds that her husband made her drive him about like a horse hitched to a chariot and beat him, *The Washington Post* added the headline, "Wife Was Forced To Play 'Ben Hur.'"[531] A widely syndicated Nina Wilcox Putnam short story in 1942, "Undercover Man," punned on the name and that of French painter, Rosa Bonheur.[532] Cleaning an overpainting and discovering a Bonheur original, one character says to the other, "Under this modern atrocity is a famous Rosa Bonheur." Her companion replies, "Rosa Ben Hur? I thought that was a book." And a pre-war syndicated cartoon depicted an American husband and wife riding in a Japanese rickshaw.[533] The husband stands up, and the wife hollers, "Sit down, Ben Hur, before you fall out!"

There were two printed anecdotal stories, both during the war. One involved an insurance salesman who said that when he seemed to be losing a prospect, he would intentionally leave behind items like a cheap umbrella or a used book. The next day or a few days later he would return ostensibly to retrieve the item but actually to resume the sales pitch. He said he did this for over twenty years:

> An old copy of "Ben Hur," for which I had paid thirty-seven cents, helped revive a deal which I was sure, at the time, was as hopelessly dead as Cock Robin. I brought it back to life and earned a commission of $23,000, thanks to "Ben Hur." I've always credited that commission to "Ben Hur."[534]

The other recorded the account of a traveling salesman from Athens, Georgia. While traveling he used to hide his cash each night, and usually he had no trouble the next morning remembering where he had hidden it. However, on one occasion he hid two $100 bills and could not remember where he put them. He says he had to leave the money behind and that he never hid his money again. However, *The Atlanta Constitution* continues:

> A few nights ago as he was sitting in the library of his home here, his mind fell to pondering again about those two $100 bills. His eyes vacantly ran along a bookshelf and then he jumped about four feet out of his chair, into the middle of the room.
> Rushing to the telephone he put in a long distance call to a boarding house in Charleston, S.C., got the landlady on the wire and identified himself. Yes, she remembered him and his loss.
> He asked if the bookcase still was in his old room. It was. Was the copy of "Ben Hur" still in it? It was. Would she look in the book at page 99 and tell him if she found anything? She would. In a few minutes the landlady was back on the phone. She had found the two $100 bills. Two days later he received the postal money order.[535]

Throughout all three decades newspapers and radio broadcasts periodically circulated variations of a joke about the proverbial cat or dog or goldfish called Ben Hur but originally named Ben, until she was discovered to be a female.[536] A 1939 example in the *Wall Street Journal* uses the punchline, "I wanted to name [the dog] after our hired man, Ben; and when I found it was a her, I just called it Ben Hur."[537] Six years later the *Jewish Advocate* offered this version:

> "What's the cat's name?"
> "Ben Hur."
> "How'd you happen to choose that?"
> "Well, we called him Ben till he had kittens."[538]

Ten years afterwards, the *Chicago Tribune* offered the punchline, "Originally we named the cat Ben, but after she had kittens we added the Hur."[539]

A new round of Ben-Hur jokes began to appear in the late 1950s as the production of the 1959 film approached. In one of them Charlton Heston, accounting for his roles in both *The Ten Commandments* and *Ben-Hur* remarked, "It's getting so that I feel uncomfortable wearing pants."[540] In another he explained why he was chosen for the lead role: "I happen to be one of the only two men in Hollywood who can drive a chariot. Francis X. Bushman is the other, but he's over seventy!"[541]

That is as good an exit line that the ephemeral record can provide. Francis X. Bushman has taken us from start to finish and sufficiently paved the way to the next chapter and "the world's most honored motion picture."

NOTES

1. *CT* (January 21, 1934) NW4.
2. *[Canton OH] Repository* (January 16, 1934) 8; *TCSM* (January 16, 1934) 4.
3. *CT* (April 22, 1934) S6.
4. *CT* (March 10, 1940) N6.
5. *TBS* (December 7, 1947) MS13; cf. *NYT* (September 7, 1947) X7.
6. *TBS* (August 20, 1951) 9 and 30.
7. *TBS* (August 20, 1951) 9.
8. Cf. *NYHT* (June 3, 1951) D3; *TBS* (January 28, 1951) FT8.
9. <http://babel.hathitrust.org/cgi/pt?id=wu.89097385371;view=1up;seq=366>
10. *WP* (January 18, 1937) 20.
11. E.g. *TBS* (April 21, 1940) M12; *BG* (April 26, 1940) 29; *WP* (April 26, 1940) 32; *NYT* (April 21, 1940) 129, (April 26, 1940) 44.
12. *[Baton Rouge] Advocate* (August 31, 1941) 30.
13. *NYHT* (April 13, 1941) E9; *NYT* (April 13, 1941) X11.
14. Cf. *NYT* (November 2, 1941) X12.
15. *WP* (October 19, 1941) L7; Weiser, *The Writer's Radio Theater*, 1–6 and 47–68.
16. Weiser, *The Writer's Radio Theater*, 47.
17. *WP* (May 9, 1948) L4; *NYHT* (May 9, 1948) C6; *NYHT* (August 15, 1948) C6; OCLC #40695407.

18 *The Manchester Guardian* (November 3, 1949) 2.
19 *NYT* (April 10, 1952) 43; OCLC #53277993; cf. <http://www.digitaldeliftp.com/DigitalDeliToo/dd2jb-Hallmark-Playhouse.html>
20 *NYHT* (September 24, 1946) 41; *Broadcasting* 50 (March 5, 1956) 24.
21 *WP* (May 24, 1940) 34.
22 *TCSM* (April 4, 1941) 8.
23 E.g. <http://comicbookplus.com/?dlid=36594>; <http://comicbookplus.com/?dlid=31399>
24 http://thelivingshadow.wikia.com/wiki/Erwin_Hess>
25 *Flash Comics* 14 (February, 1941) 46; cf. Tilley, "Superman Says," 251–63.
26 Mike Conroy, *500 Comic Book Action Heroes* (Hauppage, NY: Barron's, 2003) 160; Ron Goulart, *The Great Comic Book Artists* (New York, St. Martin's Press, 1989) 2.54–5.
27 <http://mostlypaperdolls.blogspot.com/2012/06/ben-hur-and-amrah-cut-outs.html>
28 *World's Finest Comics* 40 (May–June, 1949).
29 Cf. William B. Jones, Jr., *Classics Illustrated: A Cultural History*[2] (Jefferson, NC: McFarland & Company, 2011) 335.
30 *Adventure Comics* #177 (June, 1952).
31 <http://www.lambiek.net/artists/m/marcello_rc.htm>
32 *Le Samedi* (January 31, 1953) 32.
33 *Le Samedi* (October 17, 1953) 31.
34 *Le Samedi* (November 28, 1953) 32.
35 *NYT* (January 21, 1934) BR24.
36 *[New Orleans] Times-Picayune* (May 20, 1934) 26.
37 *NYT* (June 24, 1945) 75.
38 *NYT* (October 29, 1947) 25.
39 *CT* (June 5, 1949) H4.
40 *NYHT* (July 13, 1947) E10.
41 *WSJ* (April 18, 1934) 6.
42 *NYT* (January 15, 1939) BR2.
43 *TBS* (July 10, 1934) 8.
44 *NYT* (April 14, 1936) 19.
45 *NYT* (October 29, 1934) 15.
46 *Finest Hour* 152 (2011) 58. Text: Wolff, *The Collected Essays of Sir Winston Churchill*, 4.157–66.
47 *[Portland] Oregonian* (January 5, 1933) 3.
48 McGill, *Masterpieces of World Literature*, 66–8.
49 *BG* (February 25 39) 10; *NYT* (August 6, 1944) BR7.
50 *NYHT* (October 6, 1941) 11; *BG* (Dc 17 50) A41.
51 *NYT* (October 2, 1942) 25; (February 9, 1945) 13.
52 *NYT* (February 14, 1951) 29.
53 *NYHT* (October 12, 1951) 17; *Los Angeles Time* (October 7, 1951) D6.
54 Douglas, *Time to Remember*, 167–8.
55 *TBS* (February 14, 1937) SC7.
56 *NYHT* (September 17, 1950) E1.
57 *Trenton Evening Times* (February 5, 1937) 14.

58 *LAT* (May 11, 1931) 6; cf. <http://www-personal.ksu.edu/~rcadams/first.html>
59 *NYHT* (June 6, 1943) F24; *NYT* (November 16, 1948) 27.
60 *NYT* (September 20, 1936) BR19; *AC* (December 13, 1936) 8A.
61 *NYHT* (December 30, 1934) F6.
62 *NYT* (September 9, 1934) BR7.
63 *NYT* (September 25, 1935) 21.
64 *NYHT* (April 5, 1942) H6.
65 *NYT* (September 29, 1946) 162.
66 *NYT* (November 10, 1946) G9.
67 *NYT* (May 27, 1947) 52.
68 *NYHT* (July 10, 1949) D8.
69 *WP* (April 10, 1949) B7.
70 *NYT* (July 9, 1950) BR11.
71 *WP* (June 17, 1951) B6.
72 *CT* (December 3, 1950) F32; *BG* (August 11, 1958) 16.
73 *[New Orleans] Times-Picayune* (August 13, 1933) 65; *[Boise] Idaho Statesman* (October 14, 1933) 4; *LAT* (June 17, 1934) A5; (August 19, 1939) A2; (November 29, 1941) A3.
74 *Trenton Evening Times* (November 2, 1933) 10.
75 *Trenton Evening Times* (September 15, 1944) 21.
76 *TCSM* (December 24, 1935) 9.
77 *NYHT* (December 12, 1937) D2; cf. *NYT* (December 23, 1939) 10.
78 *NYT* (December 23, 1939) 10; *CT* (December 5, 1948) K5.
79 *LAT* (December 24, 1950) C10.
80 *AC* (December 8, 1943) 12.
81 *Afro-American* (December 30, 1944) 4.
82 *WP* (March 14, 1937) S6.
83 *NYHT* (September 19, 1934) 15.
84 *CT* (March 2, 1947) SW5.
85 Montgomery, *The Story Behind Great Books*, 193–7.
86 *NYHT* (March 22, 1934) 19; (July 30, 1944) E14; *NYT* (February 9, 1945) 13; *WSJ* (March 14, 1945) 6; *WP* (December 1, 1948) C1.
87 *WP* (June 1, 1936) X11.
88 *The Chicago Defender* (February 10, 1940) 12; *TCSM* (January 29, 1949) 8.
89 *CT* (April 6, 1949) A6.
90 *Greensboro [NC] Daily News* (March 27, 1943) 3.
91 *CT* (May 6, 1945) NW3.
92 *TCSM* (April 11, 1939) 21.
93 *NYT* (August 27, 1944) 5.
94 *WP* (February 13, 1935) 18; (August 5, 1959) B2; *NYT* (November 28, 1952) 27.
95 *LAT* (May 5, 1935) H3; *BG* (April 19, 1949) 21; *Newsday* (December 29, 1950) 32.
96 E.g. *BG* (April 19, 1949) 21; *LAT* (August 19, 1953) A5.
97 *NYT* (June 5, 1959) 26.
98 *CT* (June 18, 1944) F6.

99 E.g. *CT* (June 18, 1944) F6.
100 *CT* (February 13, 1935) 3.
101 *TBS* (August 11, 1940) MA8.
102 *CT* (September 1, 1940) G2.
103 *CT* (December 31, 1950) C5.
104 *NYHT* (September 13, 1942) F5.
105 *LAT* (February 28, 1940) 12.
106 *LAT* (August 19, 1934) 3.
107 *NYT* (May 21, 1955) 11.
108 *LAT* (December 14, 1947) H6.
109 *CT* (December 28, 1947) G3; *NYHT* (December 28, 1947) E2.
110 *NYHT* (May 3, 1942) H22.
111 *TCSM* (November 21, 1934) WM8; *BG* (March 8, 1939) 14; *CT* (April 5, 1941) 15; *NYT* (October 18, 1953) BR44.
112 *LAT* (July 29, 1935) 4; *BG* (March 8, 1939) 14; *CT* (April 5, 1941) 15; (May 29, 1949) F13; *NYT* (June 2, 1957) 145.
113 *Jewish Advocate* (March 24, 1936) 4; *NYT* (September 6, 1936) N2; *NYHT* (December 9, 1943) 26A.
114 *CT* (July 30, 1950) S C9.
115 *CT* (August 26, 1951) E10.
116 *NYT* (November 16, 1941) XX3; cf. *CT* (September 20, 1953) 28.
117 *CT* (July 16, 1937) 22.
118 *CT* (April 10, 1946) 10.
119 *CT* (December 10, 1939) G4; *Trenton Evening Times* (September 21, 1941) 34.
120 *NYT* (April 28, 1949) 31.
121 *NYHT* (September 20, 1942) E1; cf. *NYT* (March 7, 1953) 18.
122 *NYHT* (October 29, 1948) 23; (February 1, 1949) 19; *NYT* (June 25, 1957) 33.
123 *NYHT* (December 3, 1948) 26; (December 22, 1947) 18.
124 *CT* (December 13, 1942) NW1.
125 *BG* (April 11, 1934) 14.
126 *CT* (February 19, 1950) E9.
127 *WP* (June 28, 1948) 1.
128 *NYHT* (May 14, 1939) E3.
129 *CT* (December 30, 1950) A3; *NYHT* (March 21, 1943) E3.
130 *Atlanta Daily World* (August 26, 1953) 5.
131 <http://settlet.fateback.com/Dec5000.htm>
132 *LAT* (March 27, 1955) H1.
133 *NYT* (December 11, 1938) 196.
134 *NYHT* (April 22, 1943) 19.
135 *Morning Olympian [WA]* (December 20, 1934) 4; *NYT* (November 19 1937) 22.
136 *WP* (July 2, 1939) A4.
137 *Seattle Daily Times* (March 30, 1935) 7.
138 *NYHT* (November 13, 1944) 14A; *NYT* (June 15, 1936) 21; (June 6, 1953) 17; *LAT* (June 24, 1946) 1; (February 21, 1958) B1; *NYT* (November 25, 1943) 25; *NYT* (June 3, 1939) 20; (June 5, 1958) 31; *NYHT* (March 23, 1940) 1.

139 *NYT* (July 4, 1937) H1; *NYHT* (November 4, 1957) 16; *CT* (December 15, 1950) A41.
140 *BG* (November 18, 1951) A12.
141 *TBS* (March 19, 1945) 12; *CT* (May 27, 1946) 27; (February 26, 1951) 16; *BG* (September 26, 1943) B18; *LAT* (October 6, 1957) E1.
142 *NYHT* (January 26, 1941) E5.
143 *[Baton Rouge] State Times Advocate* (January 15, 1934) 6.
144 *NYHT* (May 3, 1940) 23.
145 *NYT* (December 9, 1942) 41; (December 13, 1942) S1; cf. (April 2, 1941) 42.
146 *Culver Historical Highlights* 20 (1999) 3.
147 *AC* (December 14, 1929) 5K.
148 *TBS* (March 19, 1945) 12; *San Francisco-Oakland Directory, 1907* (Oakland, CA: Walter S. Fry Co., 1907) 802.
149 *NYT* (May 22, 1938) 156.
150 *NYHT* (March 31, 1940) E6.
151 *TBS* (February 26, 1939) MM5; (May 15, 1939) 18.
152 *NYT* (April 23, 1939) 129.
153 *NYHT* (February 5, 1939) E6.
154 *WP* (May 1, 1939) 1.
155 *ToI* (July 20, 1937) 3; (December 12, 1941) 2; (September 2, 1944) 3; *The Manchester Guardian* (March 25, 1937) 12; (May 15, 1937) 13.
156 *TCSM* (November 2, 1938) 10.
157 *BG* (October 25, 1937) 15; *WP* (January 28, 1940) A1; *LAT* (March 23, 1941) C3; (March 29, 1942) C3.
158 *LAT* (January 26, 1943) 20.
159 *NYT* (February 18, 1945) SM10.
160 *NYHT* (August 5, 1934) D3; *CT* (December 7, 1938) 21; *BG* (March 20, 1944) 4; *LAT* (August 14, 1935) 7.
161 *AC* (March 3, 1940) 10.
162 *AC* (February 2, 1944) 14.
163 *NYHT* (December 13, 1945) 23A; cf. *NYT* (February 16, 1941) X4.
164 E.g. *LAT* (April 28, 1935) A1.
165 *LAT* (January 3, 1950) D129; (July 22, 1951) B5.
166 *LAT* (January 5, 1936) H16.
167 *NYT* (March 29, 1954) 19.
168 *WP* (April 17, 1945) 7; *Life* 18 (February 12, 1945) 47; *NYHT* (December 9, 1934) E1.
169 *LAT* (August 2, 1935) A11; *NYHT* (September 30, 1939) 8.
170 *CT* (December 5, 1936) 24; *LAT* (January 24, 1943) H7; *NYHT* (April 20, 1947) C3.
171 *LAT* (June 22, 1948) 22; (June 11, 1951) B9.
172 *LAT* (October 13, 1935) A3.
173 *WP* (September 8, 1935) SM1; *CT* (March 22, 1936) E10; *BG* (June 2, 1937) 29; *LAT* (May 29, 1937) 19; (January 28, 1940) C1.
174 *CT* (January 6, 1940) 13; *TBS* (April 19, 1942) SM7.
175 *BG* (April 29, 1951) AA19; *LAT* (March 28, 1949) A7; *NYHT* (July 11, 1934) 14; (July 24, 1934) 10.

176 *Box Office* 35 (August 26, 1939) 25.
177 *LAT* (February 25, 1949) 18.
178 *NYHT* (May 7, 1950) C5.
179 *BG* (December 9, 1951) B6.
180 *Box Office* 55 (March 14, 1949) 19; *CT* (July 9, 1944) C4; (February 15, 1954) C4.
181 *CT* (January 4, 1949) 14; cf. *BG* (March 8, 1936) 34.
182 *NYHT* (February 17, 1954) 25.
183 *LAT* (August 4, 1934) 5.
184 Cf. Hopper, *Under My Hat*, 137; *LAT* (July 5, 1949) 26, quoting Frances Marion.
185 *CT* (October 15, 1949) 15.
186 *LAT* (August 20, 1939) C2; (October 6, 1941) 22; (July 5, 1949) A6; cf. (January 18, 1938) 13, and *BG* (February 17, 1954) 14.
187 *LAT* (January 10, 1938) 20.
188 *TBS* (March 15, 1936) M7; *LAT* (March 5, 1939) C4; *NYHT* (December 14, 1940) 30; (September 23, 1948) 23; *ToI* (May 9, 1948) 5.
189 *LAT* (April 4, 1955) 13.
190 *BG* (February 15, 1959) A20.
191 *Variety* 192 (November 4, 1953) 5.
192 Ellenberger, *Ramon Novarro*, 165.
193 *LAT* (September 13, 1935) 15; (May 28, 1940) 12; *NYHT* (October 4, 1942) E3; (October 24, 1937) F3.
194 *NYHT* (June 8, 1941) E5; *LAT* (July 15, 1945) C1.
195 *Box Office* 60 (November 3, 1951) 13.
196 *LAT* (June 6, 1941) 3.
197 *NYHT* (September 15, 1936) 22A; (February 26, 1937) 16; *Box Office* 54 (March 19, 1949) 45; *LAT* (October 17, 1950) A2; (June 12, 1956) A7; *NYT* (October 30, 1957) 29.
198 *LAT* (October 23, 1950) 22; cf. *NYHT* (June 3, 1951) D5.
199 *CT* (July 15, 1934) D1.
200 *CT* (May 14, 1959) C12.
201 Cf. Charles McGaw, *Educational Theatre Journal* 2 (1950) 88–9.
202 *The Kansas City Star* (March 24, 1935) 56; *BG* (March 8, 1936) 34.
203 *LAT* (August 11, 1934) A2; *WP* (October 8, 1938) X10.
204 *BG* (May 2, 1934) 18.
205 *NYHT* (February 2, 1941) 34.
206 *CT* (July 27, 1940) 9.
207 *LAT* (July 27, 1950) B10.
208 *The Billboard* 62 (June 10, 1950) 8.
209 *Afro-American* (August 14 1943) 6.
210 *BG* (December 24, 1942) 16.
211 *BG* (December 27, 1941) 10.
212 *NYHT* (June 16, 1940) 1A.
213 *LAT* (July 20, 1943) A4.
214 *BG* (January 25, 1944) 12. *NYT* (November 11, 1946) 25.
215 *BG* (July 12, 1942) D2.

216 *WP* (August 14, 1942) 12.
217 *NYT* (November 17, 1944) 1.
218 *American Bar Association Journal* 30 (December, 1944) 681–2 and 721.
219 *AC* (April 3, 1945) 13.
220 *CT* (November 27, 1944) 17.
221 *BG* (August 11, 1946) A25.
222 *NYHT* (April 12, 1948) 13.
223 Bastiani, *Arrête ton char Ben-Hur!*, 158; cf. <http://www.expressions-fran caises.fr/expressions-a/425-arrete-ton-char.html>
224 *CT* (April 4, 1943) D2.
225 *[Norfolk] New Journal and Guide* (July 4, 1942) B9.
226 *TBS* (April 11, 1943) CS16; (April 13, 1943) 6.
227 *TBS* (April 8, 1943) 24.
228 *TBS* (March 28, 1943) CM6.
229 E.g. *NYT* (May 19, 1943) 22; *WP* (June 1, 1943) B7.
230 E.g. *CT* (May 16 43) D15.
231 E.g. *AC* (April 4, 1941) 30; *TBS* (May 24, 1942) MA9; *CT* (May 16, 1943) D15; (September 26, 1943) E16; (November 13, 1944) 14.
232 *AC* (June 21, 1942) 2D.
233 *[New Orleans] Times-Picayune* (September 15, 1935) 44.
234 E.g. *TBS* (May 24, 1942) MA9; (May 31, 1942) MA9; *NYT* (December 20, 1942) SM22; *AC* (December 8, 1942) 19.
235 *NYT* (July 2, 1944) SM44; (November 10, 1946) SM62.
236 *The Manchester Guardian* (March 25, 1947) 8.
237 *Jewish Advocate* (January 1, 1953) 1A.
238 *NYHT* (January 10, 1948) 10.
239 *NYHT* (January 19, 1954) 20.
240 *Variety* 187 (July 23, 1952) 2.
241 Edrick J. Miller, *The Ben Hur Memorabilia Check List*, 8; *Tea and Coffee Trade Journal* 101 (November, 1951) 76.
242 *LAT* (February 2, 1941) D8; (June 3, 1948) B6.
243 *LAT* (May 12, 1930) 8.
244 *Covina [CA] Argus Citizen* (April 9, 1937) 2; *LAT* (November 30, 1941) D8.
245 *LAT* (July 23, 1940) 18; (August 4, 1940) C6.
246 Kate Brew Vaughn, *My Best Recipes* (Los Angeles: K. B. Vaughn, 1929) 18–19.
247 E.g. *LAT* (June 8, 1941) 14; (April 9, 1950) B10; (March 28, 1939) A8; (November 3, 1940) A13.
248 *LAT* (April 17, 1934) A18.
249 *LAT* (October 12, 1934) B2.
250 *LAT* (November 23, 1941) D11.
251 *LAT* (April 19, 1942) C8.
252 *San Diego Union* (May 18, 1930) 54.
253 <http://pinterest.com/pin/53128470574617400>; <http://lahistory.tumblr.com/image/10806702133>
254 *Riverside Daily Press* (April 14, 1937) 1 and 7; *[San Diego] Evening Tribune* (October 1, 1931) 7.
255 *LAT* (April 19. 1941) 11.

256 *LAT* (July 9, 1924) A5.
257 *LAT* (July 10, 1924) A3; (November 4, 1935) A1.
258 *LAT* (November 3, 1935) 30; (November 4, 1935) 13.
259 *Broadcasting* (June 15, 1940) 45.
260 *Broadcasting* (November 24, 1941) 40; *Broadcasting* (April 6, 1942) 36.
261 *Broadcasting* (August 7, 1944) 54.
262 *The Billboard* (January 30, 1943) 6.
263 *The Billboard* (December 4, 1943) 5. Jane Powell won the competition when Gaynor was serving as host. The show was broadcast in CBS Studio A at the Columbia Square Playhouse, 6121 Sunset Boulevard – the old CBS studio.
264 *Broadcasting* (February 7, 1944) 60; *The Billboard* (July 1, 1944) 7.
265 *LAT* (January 23, 1941) A3.
266 *LAT* (December 8, 1946) 7.
267 Cf. *LAT* (January 2, 1946) 2.
268 *LAT* (January 3, 1946) A1.
269 In the possession of the author.
270 *Tea & Coffee Trade Journal* 92 (March, 1947) 60; *LAT* (August 9, 1947) A7; (June 29, 1949) 22.
271 *Tea and Coffee Trade Journal* 92 (April, 1947) 14; cf. *LAT* (February 7, 1947) 7.
272 *LAT* (February 7, 1947) 7.
273 *LAT* (August 8, 1948) 27.
274 *Tea and Coffee Trade Journal* 92 (March, 1947) 60; *LAT* (April 24, 1949) A9; *Tea and Coffee Trade Journal* 100 (May, 1951) 78.
275 *LAT* (March 6, 1951) A8.
276 *Tea and Coffee Trade Journal* 100 (January, 1951) 50.
277 *Tea and Coffee Trade Journal* 100 (March, 1951) 55; *Broadcasting-Telecasting* 21 (January 21, 1952) 14.
278 *Tea and Coffee Trade Journal* 105 (July, 1953) 50.
279 *WSJ* (March 11, 1954) 21.
280 *LAT* (November 22, 1954) B9.
281 *Tea and Coffee Trade Journal* 105 (October, 1953) 101; *Tea and Coffee Trade Journal* 105 (November, 1953) 144.
282 *Coffee & Tea Industries and The Flavor Field* 80 (May, 1957) 115; *Coffee & Tea Industries and The Flavor Field* 80 (September, 1957) 93.
283 #2,789,056, submitted August 19, 1955; patented April 16, 1957.
284 *Los Angeles Sentinel* (July 18, 1957) B5.
285 Cf. *[New Orleans] Times-Picayune* (February 16, 1934) 2.
286 *BG* (January 24, 1932) A46; (September 30, 1945) D10.
287 *BG* (September 13, 1940) 30.
288 *WP* (December 27, 1942) R8.
289 *WP* (March 8, 1942) L8; (October 18, 1942) L6.
290 *WP* (June 9, 1935) 1 and 3.
291 *Oregonian* (June 2, 1929) 3.
292 *[New Orleans] Times-Picayune* (November 29, 1929) 7.
293 *[NO] Times-Picayune* (December 11, 1930) 19; *Omaha World Herald* (December 6, 1930) 16.

294 *[NO] Times-Picayune* (December 9, 1932) 19.
295 *[Canton OH] Repository* (July 7, 1935) 22.
296 E.g. *Kerrville [TX] Mountain Sun* (October 26, 1950) 3; *The Brownsville Herald* (October 26, 1950) 22.
297 *Cleveland Call and Post* (February 3, 1951) 5B.
298 *Albert City [IA] Appeal* (May 14, 1953) 4.
299 *Algona [IA] Upper Des Moines* (November 2, 1961) 17.
300 *Farmington [NM] Daily Times* (May 21, 1959) 4; cf. *Financial World* 117 (February 28, 1962) 13.
301 *Billings [MT] Gazette* (September 21, 1962) 2.
302 <http://www.vermontcountrystore.com/store/jump/productDetail/Health_&_Beauty/Health_&_Beauty/Ben_Hur_Eau_de_Cologne/53406>
303 *Automotive and Aviation Industries* 88 (May 1, 1943) 54.
304 *Carroll [IA] Times Herald* (August 24, 1942) 6; *Gettysburg Times* (June 9, 1938) 6.
305 <http://www.cckw.org/Ben_Hur_Story.htm>
306 *Manitowoc [WI] Herald Times* (April 5, 1943) 1; <http://www.slahs.org/uihlein/family_history1.htm>
307 <http://www.coachbuilt.com/bui/i/ionia/ionia.htm>; <http://www.cckw.org/Ben_Hur_Story.htm>
308 *Connellsville [PA] Daily Courier* (April 22, 1947) 10.
309 *The Milwaukee Journal* (April 29, 1948) 24.
310 <http://www.onthewaymodels.com/kitlists/albykits.htm>
311 eBay #310629049, ended April 13, 2013.
312 eBay #111216798934, ended February 13, 2014.
313 <https://www.whiteensignmodels.com/p/UModels+135+Ben+Hur+Trailer+UM221/16818/#.UV78Vr992ao>
314 Cf. <http://aeif.scalemodel.net/fsid.aspx?id=140933666817&sid=0>
315 Strasser, *Never Done*, 272-7.
316 <http://www.legacy.com/obituaries/jsonline/obituary.aspx?pid=153421274#fbLoggedOut>
317 *The Milwaukee Journal* (September 5, 1954) 19; cf. *Good Housekeeping* 96 (March, 1953) 118; 97 (September, 1953) 177.
318 *McCall's* 81 (March, 1954) 77.
319 *Life* 33 (September 29, 1952) 116.
320 *Life* 50 (May 19, 1961) 146.
321 <http://www.u-line.com/about-us/anniversary>
322 *Chain Store* 23 (June, 1947) 13; cf. *Chain Store* 25 (January, 1949) 7; *BG* (December 10, 1925) 30.
323 Bill Alexander, Anne D. Williams, and Richard W. Tucker, *The Game Catalog: U.S. Games Through 1950*[8] (AGCA, 1998) 16.
324 #1,998,699, patent issued April 23, 1935.
325 #2103930, patent issued December 28, 1937.
326 #D129739, patent issued September 30, 1941.
327 #2,172,959, patent issued September 12, 1939.
328 *NYT* (November 3, 1950) 23.
329 *CT* (October 15, 1934) 13.

330 *NYT* (January 9, 1937) 22.
331 *NYT* (July 30, 1944) SM25.
332 *NYT* (March 11, 1944) 16.
333 *NYT* (April 10, 1945) 27; (July 19, 1945) 37; (September 19, 1945) 39; (April 9, 1946) 29.
334 *NYHT* (February 1, 1947) 19; *NYT* (February 1, 1948) F7.
335 *Vogue* 114 (October 15, 1949) 106–7.
336 *NYT* (May 9, 1951) 38.
337 *LAT* (November 23, 1952) J22; *TBS* (November 23, 1952) WM16.
338 *Life* 36 (March 22, 1954) 11.
339 *Ladies' Home Journal* 70 (June, 1953) 20.
340 *NYT* (May 21, 1953) 47.
341 *Life* 37 (December 6, 1954) 180.
342 *LAT* (November 4, 1956) H2; *NYHT* (June 19, 1957) 4.
343 *LAT* (May 22, 1959) I32.
344 #D190, 216, patent issued April 25, 1961.
345 eBay #280131089983, ended July 10, 2007. [In the possession of the author.]
346 E.g. *Chain Store Age* 25 (January, 1949) 16.
347 *Hardware Retailer* 49 (December, 1935) 72.
348 In the possession of the author.
349 *Van Camp Catalogue* (1928) 1955; *Hardware Retailer* 48 (August, 1934) 55; (May, 1935) 8; (December, 1935) 72.
350 Van Camp Hardware & Iron Co., Catalog (1939) 1662 and 1793.
351 *Lowell [MA] Sun* (January 24, 1933) 37.
352 *BG* (April 23, 1936) 45.
353 *LAT* (June 15, 1947) B3.
354 *CT* (January 19, 1930) F3.
355 *NYT* (May 5, 1935) 25; (January 16, 1955) 2; *CT* (May 20, 1935) 11.
356 *NYT* (September 13, 1959) 20.
357 *NYHT* (September 11, 1937) 28.
358 *NYHT* (January 11, 1937) 28.
359 *CT* (June 5, 1941) 16.
360 *NYHT* (July 31, 1946) 20.
361 *NYT* (March 18, 1937) 5; (June 15, 1937) 4; *NYHT* (January 5, 1937) 5.
362 *ToI* (September 29, 1936) 12.
363 E.g. *The Saturday Evening Post* (October 23, 1937) 72; *Richmond Times Dispatch* (December 12, 1937) 19.
364 *[Canton OH] Repository* (December 14, 1937) 3.
365 <http://www.mybulova.com/bulova-models>
366 eBay #8934447265, ended May 14, 2006.
367 *NYHT* (December 8, 1957) F22.
368 *Report of the North Dakota State Laboratories Department* 53–58 (c. 1939) 10.
369 *The Canadian Patent Office Record* 54, Part 2 (1926) iii; <http://trade.mar.cx/CA275470>
370 eBay #231468157235, ended February 7, 2015.

371 <http://www.arcade-museum.com/game_detail.php?game_id=11154>; <http://www.ipdb.org/machine.cgi?id=2854>
372 Cf. Matthew L. Burkholz, *The Bakelite Collection* (Atglen, PA: Schiffer Publishing Co., 1997) 74–9.
373 *Hardware Age* 146 (1940) 663; Patent #0618082, registered December 27, 1955.
374 eBay # 370110677640, ended November 12, 2008.
375 *The Billboard* (April 19, 1947) 112.
376 *LAT* (November 14, 1948) B5; *NYT* (June 5, 1949) F9.
377 *LAT* (May 26, 1929) 29.
378 John Walter, *GermanBladesmiths* (Hove, UK: Nevill Publishing, 2012) 18.
379 eBay #130037135082, ended October 21, 2006. The Wellington Cutlery [eBay #170075415175, ended February 3, 2007] with a chariot race molded onto the handle, and another engraved onto the blade between "BEN" and "HUR," remains undated.
380 eBay #380628502154, ended October 29, 2013.
381 *The China Press* (July 27, 1931) 2; (September 14, 1931) 3; *The North China Herald and Supreme Court & Consular Gazette* (April 18, 1934) 86.
382 <http://www.delpher.nl/nl/boeken/view?identifier=MMMVC01%3A00000029%3A01281&query=ben-hur+sigarenfabrieken&page=1&coll=boeken>
383 <http://cigarboxlabels.com/gallery2/main.php?g2_itemId=14644&g2_page=8>
384 *[Baton Rouge] State Times Advocate* (August 24, 1933) 1; *WP* (May 4, 1947) M1.
385 *Logansport [IN] Press* (February 27, 1947) 11.
386 *Logansport [IN] Press* (September 18, 1949) 6.
387 *Logansport Pharos Tribune* (September 22, 1949) 6.
388 eBay # 1096004996, ended April 28, 2002.
389 Cf. *The Corunna [MI] News* (August 26, 1948) 3.
390 E.g. *LAT* (May 30, 1949) 11; (October 15, 1949) 12; (January 6, 1950) 18; (May 19, 1950) A11. Cf. *Life* 23 (March 10, 1947) 15.
391 The printing on an extant can of the latter, in the possession of the author, gives the 1948 date.
392 William Kaszynski, *The American Highway: The History and Culture of Roads in the United States* (Jefferson, NC: McFarland & Co., 2000) 176.
393 *LAT* (February 6, 1959) C7. Cf. eBay #7230055093, ended April 2, 2006.
394 eBay #270005321274, ended July 13, 2006. [In the possession of the author.]
395 *LAT* (January 19, 1935) 11; (January 23, 1935) 12; (February 5, 1934) 13.
396 *Ardmore [OK] Daily Admoreite* (March 16, 1948) 1; (September 29, 1954) 11; *Ada [OK] Evening News* (September 29, 1954) 1; *Miami [OK] Daily News Record* (September 29, 1954) 4.
397 242 F.2d 481 (10th Cir. 1957).
398 *NYT* (June 11, 1957) 71.
399 *WSJ* (August 6, 1959) 3.
400 *CT* (May 4, 1953) A6.
401 *CT* (January 4, 1959) G8.

402 *CT* (November 2, 1949) 20, and *WSJ* (February 18, 1954) 1, nostalgically recall an automobile named after Peter Pan.
403 *NYT* (August 2, 1938) 33.
404 *NYT* (April 2, 1940) 47; (February 18, 1942) 34.
405 *LAT* (May 27, 1951) E1–2.
406 *LAT* (May 4, 1952) E9.
407 *NYT* (December 23, 1952) R1; *LAT* (January 13, 1952) E8.
408 *Bellingham [WA] Herald* (April 9, 1934) 13.
409 *NYHT* (August 14, 1936) 35; (August 6, 1940) 27.
410 *Box Office* 54 (May 21, 1949) 34; *Variety* 205 (December 5, 1956) 30.
411 <https://www.facebook.com/pages/General-Lew-Wallace-Inn/115840651770287>
412 In the possession of the author; cf. *LAT* (July 3, 1959) 16.
413 *[Logansport] Pharos Tribune* (March 3, 1953) 1.
414 eBay #6278345635, ended May 14, 2006; eBay #290104027313, ended April 17, 2007.
415 *[New Orleans] Times-Picayune* (August 5, 1933) 16.
416 *Fortune Magazine* 10 (September, 1934) 145.
417 E.g. *CT* (November 19, 1944) G6; *Jewish Advocate* (December 14, 1944) 3.
418 E.g. <http://www.ebay.com/itm/1946-Green-Giant-Ben-Hur-Niblets-Food-Retro-40s-Kitchen-Art-Le-Sueur-MN-Print-Ad-/150998451642?pt=LH_DefaultDomain_0&hash=item23283585ba>
419 *CT* (October 26, 1947) 32.
420 *Newsday* (April 21, 1952) 51.
421 *Life* 32 (June 30, 1952) 5.
422 E.g. *Life* 32 (April 21, 1952) 21.
423 *Life* 26 (March 21, 1949) 5.
424 *LAT* (January 28, 1953) 18.
425 *NYHT* (May 28, 1939) A15.
426 *NYT* (February 12, 1959) 26.
427 *The Train Dispatcher* 31 (April, 1949) 167.
428 *TCSM* (June 24, 1942) 17.
429 *WSJ* (August 23, 1957) 1.
430 *Newsday* (May 4, 1951) 41.
431 *BG* (November 10, 1946) D26.
432 *BG* (August 16, 1943) 6; (September 3, 1944) D6.
433 *Trenton Evening Times* (December 28, 1937) 1.
434 *Pacific Motor Boat* 33 (May 31, 1941) 189.
435 *NYHT* (September 18, 1936) 32.
436 In the possession of the author.
437 <http://menus.nypl.org/menu_pages/61052/explore>
438 *Trenton Evening Times* (June 12, 1939) 12.
439 *NYHT* (July 1, 1939) 26.
440 *[Baton Rouge] State Times Advocate* (June 4, 1934) 12.
441 *Bellingham [WA] Herald* (May 2, 1935) 9.
442 *Kansas City Star* (May 8, 1939) 16.
443 *LAT* (March 31, 1935) 16.

444 *Newsday* (August 9, 1951) 75.
445 *BG* (June 19, 1935) 20.
446 *NYT* (November 11, 1946) 25.
447 *NYHT* (October 6, 1944) 22.
448 *CT* (November 29, 1951) D7.
449 *NYHT* (December 11, 1950) 30.
450 *NYHT* (August 4, 1952) 17.
451 *TBS* (February 19, 1956) 6D.
452 *LAT* (April 19, 1952) A6.
453 *Trenton Evening Times* (November 15, 1935) 29.
454 *Cleveland Plain Dealer* (September 4, 1932) 3B.
455 *WP* (September 20, 1936) PY7; *Cleveland Call and Post* (October 14, 1937) 10.
456 *CT* (March 8, 1949) B4.
457 *CT* (December 3, 1949) 15.
458 *NYHT* (August 12, 1934) B1,
459 *BG* (November 25, 1942) 8.
460 *NYHT* (August 14, 1947) 1; *NYT* (August 14, 1947) 2.
461 Cf. *NYT* (July 1, 1958) 40.
462 *CT* (April 27, 1959) D6.
463 *NYT* (July 29, 1937) 26.
464 *BG* (October 17, 1940) 16.
465 *BG* (October 9, 1942) 32; *NYT* (September 7, 1943) 27; (November 28, 1945) 24.
466 *NYT* (July 6, 1945) 16; (August 8, 1945) 26; *NYHT* (July 27, 1945) 18; (August 8, 1945) 25.
467 *LAT* (July 26, 1934) 7.
468 *BG* (September 30, 1934) A28.
469 *NYHT* (June 2, 1934) 19; (June 9, 1935) B9; (June 6, 1936) 21.
470 *NYHT* (November 28, 1935) 31.
471 *LAT* (January 2, 1934) A1.
472 *BG* (February 25, 1939) 13.
473 *NYT* (November 19, 1954) 31.
474 *NYHT* (October 27, 1946) SM8.
475 *NYT* (October 29, 1950) 149.
476 *NYT* (November 13, 1957) 44.
477 *Variety* 195 (August 4, 1954) 4. *The Arabian Horse* 7 (June/July, 1955) 11.
478 *BG* (December 5, 1950) 17.
479 *NYHT* (December 12, 1954) G3.
480 *BG* (September 6, 1934) 19.
481 *LAT* (October 17, 1935) A8.
482 *LAT* (April 26, 1936) A6.
483 *LAT* (March 31, 1935) 16.
484 *WP* (July 31, 1940) 14 and 16.
485 *CT* (February 2, 1935) 17.
486 *CT* (June 17, 1944) 11.
487 *The Irish Times* (February 6, 1939) 4; (September 8, 1945) 6–7.

488 <http://fairground-heritage.org.uk/learning/fairground-people/robert-lakin-company>
489 <http://cdm15847.contentdm.oclc.org/cdm/search/collection/p15847coll3/searchterm/chariots>
490 E.g. *WP* (April 4, 1940) 9.
491 *NYHT* (April 12, 1935) 3.
492 *Morning [WA] Olympian* (August 9, 1935) 1.
493 *[New Orleans] Times-Picayune* (January 9, 1940) 7.
494 *CT* (January 10, 1940) 24; *WP* (January 19, 1940) 21.
495 *CT* (March 1, 1936) F4.
496 *CT* (December 6, 1949) A1.
497 *[New Orleans] Times-Picayune* (June 23, 1935) 41.
498 *LAT* (September 27, 1951) A6.
499 *NYHT* (January 26, 1941) E3.
500 *Bellingham [WA] Herald* (April 2, 1934) 5.
501 *AC* (July 19, 1937) 4.
502 *CT* (August 3, 1952) W8.
503 *CT* (August 5, 1952) A7.
504 *CT* (November 23, 1952) 22.
505 *TCSM* (April 13, 1942) 12.
506 *LAT* (July 6, 1943) 6; *BG* (July 6, 1943) 13.
507 *Trenton Evening Times* (September 26, 1955) 13.
508 *LAT* (June 15, 1950) A5.
509 *TCSM* (April 22, 1947) 11; *TBS* (October 20, 1936) 12.
510 *TBS* (January 6, 1957) 15.
511 *TCSM* (September 23, 1940) 12.
512 *NYT* (March 27, 1955) SM26.
513 *BG* (February 17, 1943) 15.
514 *BG* (February 17, 1946) C3.
515 *CT* (September 27, 1950) A8.
516 *NYT* (June 23, 1935) X8.
517 *Trenton Evening Times* (December 12, 1950) 27.
518 *CPD* (May 26, 1947) 5.
519 *CT* (April 27, 1959) D6.
520 *Afro-American* (October 17, 1959) 16; *Bay State Banner* (October 2, 1965) 7.
521 *WP and Times Herald* (February 15, 1956) 19.
522 *[Baton Rouge] Advocate* (April 4, 1937) 24.
523 *Afro-American* (June 27, 1959) 6.
524 *LAT* (May 22, 1954) 12.
525 *WP* (May 26, 1941) 6.
526 *NYT* (September 10, 1939) 58; *NYHT* (August 10, 1944) 14; *NYT* (September 12, 1950) 38.
527 *The Manchester Guardian* (September 10, 1934) 2.
528 *Seattle Daily Times* (July 29, 1934) 13.
529 *NYT* (April 25, 1954) X37.
530 *San Diego Union* (November 10, 1942) 12.
531 *WP* (December 9, 1948) 18.

532 *LAT* (November 1, 1942) H4; *NYHT* (November 1, 1942) H4.
533 *Trenton Evening Times* (August 23, 1938) 4.
534 *NYHT* (June 6, 1943) C4.
535 *AC* (May 17, 1943) 12.
536 *WSJ* (January 17, 1939) 4; *BG* (June 3, 1947) 1; (November 11, 1951) A38; *TCSM* (June 9, 1956) 19.
537 *WSJ* (January 17, 1939) 4.
538 *Jewish Advocate* (November 1, 1945) 6.
539 *CT* (February 26, 1955) 5.
540 *TBS* (July 27, 1958) F9.
541 *NYHT* (July 18, 1958) 10; *TBS* (May 25, 1958) FA9.

14 "The World's Most Honored Motion Picture": The 1959 MGM Ben-Hur

Now that we have made a beachhead on the decade of the 1950s, we will focus on what many people often assume is the only *Ben-Hur*, the 1959 MGM epic. Even this common misperception provides testimony to the tremendous success of this genuine Hollywood icon. Similar to and in some respects even more so than its dramatic and cinematic predecessors, this version of *Ben-Hur* was an enormous enterprise that entailed a record-sized budget, a very lengthy pre-production process, eager public anticipation, gala premieres, enormous profits, critical acclaim and controversy, worldwide visibility, and exceptional longevity. By marketing everything from paperback editions and stereo LPs to *Ben-Hur* helmets, swords, clothing, board games, puzzles, and coloring books to chariot race decorated cookie tins, participating manufacturers and MGM profited considerably from officially licensed tie-ins, and unlike the early ventures into *Ben-Hur* synergies pioneered by Wallace and independent entrepreneurs, this new version of *Ben-Hur* mania was engineered by experienced, professional exploiteers hired by MGM to take this uniquely successful popular literary, dramatic, and silent-film property into areas of transmedia merchandising never before so saturated by a major Hollywood release.

PRE-PRODUCTION

The process had begun almost immediately after MGM took out its two-page color advertisement in *The Film Daily* announcing the film's nationwide general release of *Ben-Hur* on October 10, 1927. This occurred just four days after the New York premiere of *The Jazz Singer*.[1] The resulting synchronized sound version of *Ben-Hur* released in 1931 had a modicum of success despite its inherent technological limitations, but soon after it was withdrawn from American distribution in 1933, the call by newspaper columnists and industry insiders for a genuine sound remake would then resurface several times over the next two decades.

Early in 1934, Universal's Carl Laemmle, Jr. announced plans to remake *The Hunchback of Notre Dame*. In breaking this news, *Los Angeles Times* columnist Edwin Schallert began with this sentence:

> It is natural that in the due course of events some of the great silent pictures should be made as talkies. One can imagine "Ben Hur" being done again and plenty of royalties will doubtless be paid for that. Perhaps the "Big Parade" could be reproduced.[2]

The Big Parade was never remade, but just six months later Schallert sounded the drums again, this time under the headline, "All Signs Point to Remake of 'Ben Hur.'"[3] Confident that a contemporary religious film like DeMille's *Sign of the Cross* provided the answer to the movement spearheaded by the Catholic Legion of Decency and culminating that year in the stricter enforcement of the Hays [Motion Picture Production] Code, Schallert offered "a prophecy" that *Ben-Hur* would be remade. After explaining that despite the great costs the film had not only turned profitable but was in fact continuing to provide a profit overseas, he hoped that the "Wallace-Erlanger group" might be willing to change their 50 percent arrangement, and added that studio efficiency might make the film less expensive to produce. In 1936, at least according to those responsible for the preliminary plans to build Cinecittà on the site where "you Americans" had chosen to film the 1925 *Ben-Hur*, Thalberg was contemplating a remake of *Ben-Hur* there, as would happen, albeit more than two decades later.[4] Schallert revisited the idea in 1940 when he suggested that Errol Flynn reprise the role played by Ramon Novarro.[5] During the war, in 1943, Hedda Hopper was more accurately prophetic by reporting that Lloyd C. Douglas's recently published *The Robe* and a remake of *Quo Vadis* would be produced as films before a remake of *Ben-Hur*.[6]

It took almost another decade, but by the early 1950s the film studios were responding to the encroachment of television and the loss of their theater circuits by issuing a new crop of lavish, color, historical epics like MGM's $6.5 million production of *Quo Vadis* and *Ivanhoe* and employing widescreen presentations like Fox's CinemaScope adaptation of *The Robe*.[7] As *Quo Vadis* was about to be released in 1951, MGM president Dore Schary said he was also contemplating a remake of *Ben-Hur*.[8] Underestimating the viewing capacity of American audiences, *Chicago Tribune* television critic Larry Walton warned:

> A supercolossal spectacle about once in 5 years is enough for many people. "Quo Vadis" will lure lots of viewers away from TV for one night, but the next evening they'll be ready for Red Skelton.

It was finally in early December, 1952, that MGM issued a brief press release – special to the *New York Times* – that it would indeed be making a new, Technicolor version of *Ben-Hur*, and that it would be filmed in Italy "to take advantage of the old Roman atmosphere required by the story," and, added the *Times*, to give Metro an opportunity to draw on some of its earnings frozen in Italy after the *Quo Vadis* production.[9] In the fall of 1953, MGM agreed to assign Sam Zimbalist, who had satisfactorily seen the *Quo Vadis* production through to its completion, to produce this new big-budget project,[10] and Karl Tunberg to write the screenplay.[11] They were to confer in London and then scout locations in and near Rome.[12] Schary announced that the remake of *Ben-Hur* would be MGM's "biggest production" of 1954,[13] and *Variety*, reporting on the current industry trend of producing remakes to fill out the studios' relatively thin production schedules, said that in 1954 alone Hollywood had committed to spending $35 million on remakes, the most expensive being Paramount's *The Ten Commandments* and MGM's *Ben-Hur*.[14] Hedda Hopper put the project in perspective:

> See where Metro will remake "Ben Hur." That picture set the studio back many years because every story on the sound stage had to be better than "Ben Hur." They even tried with "Quo Vadis." It not only wasn't better; it wasn't as good.[15]

1954 was MGM's thirtieth anniversary year. That fledgling company that inherited Goldwyn's problematic *Ben-Hur* production in the early 1920s and turned it into its first "colossal" achievement had continued on its stellar trajectory, grown Loew's into a $100 million corporation, and produced some 1600 films in the interim.[16] Now it had come nearly full circle, and although producing the remake of *Ben-Hur* would not be without its own problems, delays, and record-setting costs, the studio would by no means have to relive the catastrophic Italian production of 1923–4. The most serious problems it faced were corporate and financial. A bitter struggle between Joseph R. Vogel and Louis B. Mayer for control of the divested MGM put the project on hold for several years. But soon after Vogel successfully re-established his position as president, he green lighted the production of *Ben-Hur* in August, 1956, with a projected start date of March, 1957.[17] Then MGM suffered a loss of nearly $16 million in 1957, causing another delay. But Vogel announced in January, 1958, that MGM had lost only $1 million for the previous quarter,[18] and he was optimistic about a new crop of scripts, prime among them being *Ben-Hur*.[19] Once again, MGM was embarking upon a production of *Ben-Hur*, budgeted at a larger amount than any film in history, when it was least able to afford it.

Emerging from periods of turmoil and financial distress, and eager, if not nearly desperate, for a huge success, MGM's confidence was high in the property, and that confidence was generated originally from Schary and then continued by Vogel, Sol Siegel, and Zimbalist, who paid the ultimate price before filming was completed. From its inception, the film was conceived as a project of enormous proportions that would be continuously managed by veterans of a mature studio. Focusing its decades of collective production experience on *Ben-Hur* for two full years, MGM would support the production with its vast artistic and technical resources. In 1963, when *Ben-Hur* had become one of the top three money-earners in film history, the *New York Times* analyzed infamously problematic projects that amassed huge cost overruns, like Fox's *Cleopatra* and Universal's *Spartacus* along with MGM's notorious *Mutiny on the Bounty*, and concluded that inadequate pre-production planning and confusion during production laid the foundations for later difficulties.[20] In comparison, *Ben-Hur* was a model project in many ways, and unlike its contemporary problematic epics, its $15 million budget generated many times that amount in revenue, earned the final product an unprecedented eleven Academy Awards, and produced one of American cinema's most heralded action sequences. As a mid-century paradigm of a successful popular culture product, *Ben-Hur* accomplished exactly what MGM intended. As ever, *Ben-Hur* was treated as a very special, if gigantic, project.

After lengthy negotiations, in October, 1957, the same month Mayer passed away, Metro signed an agreement to employ, indeed consume, the underused Cinecittà facilities in Rome, where the company would spend much of its *Ben-Hur* budget over the course of the two years.[21] This time the Italian production would not have to be scrapped, nor would the director or star, who were both carefully chosen. Zimbalist had earlier offered the directing job to Metro veteran Sidney Franklin, who was reluctant to go abroad, so he instead courted William Wyler, one of Hollywood's most respected directors. Wyler objected that he had never directed an epic and proposed to direct only the chariot race, but Zimbalist and Vogel wanted him to focus on the drama and give it depth and intimacy. The rest was "second-unit stuff." Wyler was signed in June, 1957.[22] Like Wallace and Erlanger, he negotiated an extraordinary deal that included 8 percent of the gross revenues or 3 percent of the net profits, whichever was greater, in addition to his salary of $350,000.[23]

Charlton Heston, despite his success in playing Moses in DeMille's remake of *The Ten Commandments* and his work with Wyler on *The Big Country*, was not at all the first choice any more than Novarro had been. In the initial press release to the *New York Times*, the names immediately suggested were Robert Taylor and Stewart Granger.[24] Then Marlon Brando and Paul Newman were considered.[25] During the summer of 1957, MGM was negotiating a four-picture deal with Burt Lancaster's independent production company, Hecht-Hill-Lancaster, with the expectation that Burt Lancaster would star in *Ben-Hur*. Rock Hudson seemed to be Hedda Hopper's favorite. She reported that MGM was willing to pay as much as $750,000 as a buyout from Universal.[26] And in the months before the signing, Wyler had encouraged Heston to play the role of Messala.[27] But in January, 1958, MGM made several announcements, one of them that Heston had been selected for the lead role.[28] Others included the readiness of stunt coordinator Yakima Canutt and second-unit director

Andrew Marton, already in Rome and soon to be joined by cinematographer Robert Surtees, for the targeted March start date,[29] the preparation of the Roman galley models to be shot in tanks in both the MGM back lot in Culver City and at Cinecittà,[30] and, demonstrating the degree of detail that was already decided upon, that the official spelling of the name of the film would always include the hyphen.[31]

Other principle actors were signed over the next few months, Jack Hawkins [Arrius] in March, Steven Boyd [Messala], Sam Jaffe [Simonides], Finley Currie [Balthasar], and Cathy O'Donnell [Tirzah] in April, and Haya Harareet [Esther] and Hugh Griffith [Ilderim] in May.[32] Demonstrating how important he thought the musical score would be, Zimbalist had already assigned Miklós Rózsa to compose the music in July of 1957.[33] Rózsa, too, would spend time in Rome. He later told the anecdote that one Sunday morning he was walking along the Palatine, lost in musical thought, subconsciously striding in cadence with the march he was composing in his mind.[34] Two young Italians saw him and thought he was crazy, "but with my insanity was born the 'Parade of the Charioteers.'"

THE SCRIPT

None of the aspects of the production generated as much controversy as the script. More than five years in development, Tunberg's script was subsequently edited by four highly respected playwrights as well as Zimbalist, Wyler, and other MGM staff. So heavily layered, the final screenplay became the subject of a lengthy, public quarrel involving the Screen Writers Guild, making it the only major aspect of production that did not win an Academy Award. While all the major participants in that controversy have passed on, the task remains here to identify as best as possible each of the many hands that crafted the version of the *Ben-Hur* story that the next two generations would recognize as the standard by which to compare all other versions of *Ben-Hur*, including Wallace's novel. Fortunately, many dated and attributed extant versions of the script have been preserved, and they provide a documented history of the script development up to the version of January, 1958, that was distributed to the cast and crew for use in Italy. Once the production commenced overseas, however, the arrival of Gore Vidal and Christopher Fry, under constant supervision by Wyler and Zimbalist, greatly complicated the historical record. The inaccessibility of typed and dated records from this crucial period, along with the conflicting accounts given later by the participants in the controversy, have made it much more challenging to determine who was responsible for the many rewritten lines and scenes that made it into the final release version of the film that despite or because of the many hands turned out to be such a great success.

Tunberg, a studio and independent screen writer since the 1930s, had conferred with Sidney Franklin early on, and he was scheduled to take a section of his initial version of the script to New York in early March, 1954.[35] After several additional installments, he submitted his first composite script on June 17 and a complete script the following February 18, 1955. MGM submitted this information to the Writers Guild of America in 1959 when the organization was in the process of assigning authorship.[36] Listed in their submission were the 1957 and 1958 scripts co-edited by Maxwell Anderson and S. N. Behrman as well as early contributions by Franklin and later additions by Leroy Linick, Jan Lustig, and Robert Wyler, the director's brother. Of note also were such early versions of the chariot race as Canutt's action breakdowns of September 1, 1955, and April 18, 1957, along with Marton's version dated March 25, 1958. Archival searches have identified additional script variants, but we will concentrate our survey on five stages of script development: Tunberg's original script that he wrote in 1954 and revised in 1955; the November, 1957, version revised by Tunberg and Anderson; the January, 1958, version by Tunberg and S. N. Behrman that was taken to Rome by the cast and crew;[37] Vidal's contributions of the spring of 1958 recorded in his script now housed at the Harvard Library; and Fry's contributions from the spring of 1958 to the summer of 1959 that were clumsily collected by MGM for submission to the Writers Guild of America.

Tunberg's 1954 and 1955 Scripts
Although today we inevitably compare Tunberg's original drafts to the release version of the film, here we should focus first on how he adapted Wallace's novel. De rigueur were Wallace's scenes featuring the Wise Men and Nativity, the quarrel between Judah and Messala, the tile incident and arrest of the Hur family, the encounter at the well in Nazareth, the galley, naval battle, and raft sequences with Arrius, Judah's return to the East and the subsequent introduction of Simonides, Esther, Balthasar, and the Sheik and his reacquaintance with Messala, the chariot race, Judah's search for his mother and sister, their plight in the Valley of the Lepers and subsequent healing by Christ, the Crucifixion, and the reunification of the Hur family. Essential to Wallace's narrative was also his method of temporarily making mysterious characters out of the young Arrius, Simonides, and the Messiah as well as creating a mystery out of the condition of Judah's mother and sister. The technical requirements, audience expectations, and style of a 1950s Technicolor and sound film in the biblical epic genre were necessarily quite different from those facing William Young, June Mathis, Beth Meredyth, Carey Wilson, and other earlier adaptors, but they had already moved the introduction of Simonides' anti-Roman advocacy and the romance between Esther and Judah into the early parts of the story, reduced Amrah's role in rescuing Judah's mother and sister and Judah's role in raising three anti-Roman legions in Galilee,

and eliminated the Thord assassination episode. And dramaturgical limitations had generally raised the ages of Judah and Messala from teenagers to more mature adults (except in the *Ben-Hur Cantata*).

While preserving many of these plot points and signature events of the novel, Tunberg broadened its characterizations. The 1954–1955 script fleshes out the Hur family by creating light dialogue between Judah and Tirzah about marriage:

> BEN HUR
> I don't intend to get married. A married man is like a camel – always a burden on his back.
> TIRZAH
> [And] the man I marry will be ten times as rich as you, and –
> BEN HUR
> Old and fat.

Tunberg chose not to revive Tirzah's "Wake not, but hear me love," Wallace's lyrics that had been set to music by a number of late-nineteenth century composers. Perhaps he did not want to duplicate the Christian song voiced by Carol Richards for Betta St. John [Miriam] in *The Robe*, released the year before Tunberg began writing his first draft. One of his most important contributions here was focusing the tile incident on Tirzah, making her the person who last touches the loose tile. In the novel this is Judah, and because he reaches after it, he looks as if he threw it. In Tunberg's script, and in the film, she sees where the loose tile goes, is horrified, screams, cries, and pleads her innocence. This enables the viewer to feel confident that Judah and the Hur women are innocent of any conspiracy charge, adds an additional layer of pity for an innocent who inadvertently causes her family's demise, and ennobles Judah by taking the blame onto himself as a prelude to Christ taking on the sins of humankind.

Like Mathis many decades earlier, Tunberg saw the need to establish firmly the renewed friendship between Judah and Messala. Now assigned the rank of tribune, Messala has more scenes in Tunberg's original script, including a gambling scene in which Drusus calls Messala a "Jew-lover" for being fond of Judah, "an old friend, and a rich one." Tunberg elaborated upon the initial quarrel between Messala and Judah, here called a prince, a title Wallace assigned only to Judah's father, Ithamar:

> BEN HUR (*quietly*)
> I should have known that it couldn't be the same after such a long time, Messala. We've traveled different roads.
> MESSALA
> If you'd ever looked beyond the shadow of your Temple, you would have discovered that all roads lead to Rome.

> BEN HUR (*smiling*)
> The time may come again when they will lead elsewhere.
> MESSALA (*ominously*)
> Dangerous talk, my Prince of Jerusalem.
> BEN HUR (*coldly*)
> Make of it what you will, Tribune.
> *He turns and starts to leave.*
> MESSALA
> Judah!
> *Ben Hur turns back. Messala goes up to him.*
> MESSALA
> If I've ~~hurt~~ wounded you, it was only because I want to help you. There's a new world, Judah, a Roman world. If you want to <u>survive</u> live in it, you must become a part of it.
> (*significantly*)
> Be wise, Judah.
> *Ben Hur steps over to the oak beam and pulls out the javelin from it. He turns back to Messala.*
> BEN HUR
> Do you remember, Messala, when we used to hunt lions with these in the hills of Galilee? I had hoped we would do it again. Now I see I shall have to hunt alone.
> *He hurls the spear at the opposite wall. It sticks into an oak beam and quivers there. Then he walks out. Messala stands looking after him.*

The reader can already see the foundations of the initial scene between Judah and Messala as it would appear in the film.

In another scene Messala disputes Judah's innocence with Esther.

> MESSALA
> No woman thinks ill of the man she loves.
> ESTHER
> I first met Judah only a few days ago. We did speak of love – his love for you. Surely you still bear some affection for him. He said you had been like brothers.

Further on, Messala takes on the characterization of Wallace's haughty Messala:

> MESSALA
> Is one man's life to be so prized? You'll find another to bed with and to sire your children. But take care to bring them up to serve the emperor.
> ESTHER
> They will serve God – the God you will face one day.
> MESSALA
> We Romans have already faced the Druid gods of

> Britain, the shady deities of the Northmen, the crocodile divinities of Egypt.
> (*sarcastically*)
> Your one, meager God will not prevail against the Gods of Rome.

At the end of the scene Esther runs to Judah as he is being led away in manacles, but a centurion forces her out of the courtyard. Messala responds to Judah's threat, which is simply, "If I live, I will kill you," with "If you live." This would be paralleled in the release version of the film, where Judah threatens, "My God grant me vengeance, I pray that you live till I return," and Messala responds, simply, "Return?"

Like the novel, this version also introduces Messala to Iras after he almost runs over Balthasar with his chariot. Drusus wants to blame the "desert goat," but Messala eyes Iras and says, "This desert goat has done us a service!"

Tunberg's most important plot modifications involving Messala occur during the chariot race. Wallace had made Judah the vengeful aggressor and had him defeat but only disable Messala in the race, using him subsequently to hire the assassins, steal Iras away from Judah and Balthasar, and even attempt blackmail by an appeal to Sejanus. Tunberg decided to eliminate all of these plot points by making Messala the aggressor in the race, killing him off, and focusing the latter parts of the film on Judah and his family. He creatively enables this by beginning Judah's search for his mother and sister in Messala's villa, where he makes a surprise, pre-race visit as "Young Arrius" and gives Messala the gift of an exquisite dagger. Now threatened by the son of a Roman consul, Messala commences the search that leads to the shocking prison discovery of the lepers, and it allows Messala to reach a climactic peak of villainy when in the Circus infirmary he tauntingly informs Judah to look for his family in the Valley of the Lepers:

> You may not recognize them immediately, but you will find them!

In the first versions of the script, Messala then picks up the bejeweled dagger Judah had given him and plunges it into his own chest.

In contrast, Judah in Tunberg's early versions of the script speaks of tolerance and leniency towards Messala and even Gratus, who confiscated much of his wealth and property, and he has a much closer relationship and greater admiration for Arrius than in the novel, and this remains in the final release version of the film. As in the film, Judah tells Messala he can keep the exquisite dagger as a gift if he restores his mother and sister to him. But at this stage of the writing Simonides chastises him for this:

> SIMONIDES
> It was not the hand of a Roman which saved you
> – it was the hand of our Lord.

> BEN HUR
> Should we not honor the hand chosen by our lord?
> SIMONIDES
> Your love for Arrius does you credit, and yet it disturbs me. You must never allow your loyalty to one Roman to make you loyal to Rome.
> BEN HUR
> My loyalties are the same as yours, Simonides. Arrius would be the first to understand that.

Tunberg's Judah is also more dynamic. In Rome he is somewhat of a womanizer. To a friend named Fabricius he describes an admiring woman as "a simple, innocent child of nature – passionately fond of laurel." When Esther asks him what kept him alive, he says "hate," foreshadowing Arrius' "Hate keeps a man alive." Yet this hate is misdirected, for Judah again insists that "there are good and bad Romans, as there are good and bad Jews." This will remain a constant in Tunberg's scripts. As suggested in the novel, Simonides encourages Judah to use his Roman military training to lead a rebellion against the Romans, but Judah's goal in the early script, after using Messala to find his mother and sister, is to return to Rome where he had pledged his faith "to the man I now call father." Not fully accepting Balthasar's preaching, he muses, "If his God intends to deal with Messala on the Judgment Day, surely He can't blame me for dealing with him now." Accordingly, Judah premeditates killing Messala during the race with the deadly hub of his Greek chariot. After winning the race, he receives official word from Rome that Quintus Arrius has died and that the emperor has declared young Arrius a freeman. This enables Judah to focus on the political issues of his homeland. He accompanies Jesus to Cana, offering him military protection and money, and then he unsuccessfully pleads with Pilate to save Jesus.

Around this point Tunberg inserted a note:

> I have taken it for granted, in planning the following outline, that certain changes will be made in the first 145 pages. Without going into detail, I suggest that the character of Ben Hur can be sharpened in the opening scenes to provide a better motive for Esther's falling in love with him, but when he returns from Rome, she finds him a changed man, a violent man with murder in his heart. Her attitude is that the man she loved died in the galleys and has been replaced by a man she could never love. Thus they break.

Although modified, this is how his relationship with Esther develops in the filmed version as well.

The minor characters are more lively as well. Simonides becomes so frustrated at Judah's tolerance for the Romans that he rises from his chair and then collapses onto the floor! Gratus, not Pilate, presides over the chariot race. Even the Roman decurion at the well in Nazareth taunts Judah, saying, "I forgot. You're an assassin. You don't drink anything but blood." Iras plays a full role, including the boat scene, delivers her Egyptian parable, and claims to have had the emperor as a lover. Like the novel's Iras, she says that striving for love is ecstasy, achieving it is disaster, and much like the Klaw & Erlanger Iras, she taunts Esther. To Judah she complains, "I wish you had told me you were going to free [her]. She would make an excellent hand-maid." Tunberg also creates a much needed father-daughter exchange between Iras and Balthasar.

> BALTHASAR
> His heart is full of bitterness, revenge, and violence. There may be no room for love.
> IRAS
> There is always room for love in a man's heart.
> BALTHASAR
> Perhaps I have instructed you better than I know.
> IRAS
> No, father. Don't give me credit for virtues I don't have. I think there is love in his heart – but for someone else.
> BALTHASAR
> He has never mentioned anyone but a mother and a sister.
> IRAS
> I've looked into his eyes.
> BALTHASAR
> If you are sure of this, you should not covet what isn't yours.
> IRAS
> I've always wanted most the things that weren't mine.

As in the novel, Balthasar dies during the Crucifixion, so it is Judah who delivers a strong Christian message at the end of the script:

> He died for this. To prove that truth will never die. It will live in us, in our children and our children's children, and it will grow and multiply as the grain in the fields grows and multiplies, until all men believe – and then there will be no evil in the world, and no death.

This version was completed in June, 1954. By September Tunberg had already made a number of revisions.[38] Simonides complains that Judah "is more Roman than a Roman," walks out on him, taking Esther with him. They are reconciled, however, and appear together in the new ending:

> BEN-HUR
> But why Esther? Why? Why must there be evil and death
> ESTHER
> I don't know but all things are possible to Him. He will return and help us. I know that – as a

> child afraid in the dark knows its cries will bring the father.

Tunberg made additional changes the following year, more of the scenes now appearing as they would in the film, except for dialogue changes.[39] This version of the script opens with the hand of Augustus Caesar signing an "impressive document" as a narrator says, "At the beginning of the first century a decree of Tiberius Caesar changed the lives of an entire nation." The census registration scene is already fully formed, but it is followed by dialogue among the Wise Men, particularly Gaspar's account of his conversion as in the novel, and Joseph's bargaining with the innkeeper at Bethlehem. The description of the Star of Bethlehem and the sound of the shofar dissolving to the next scene are similar to their final form, but the shofar sound, along with "ominous thunder," dissolves not to the title of the film but a Roman legion marching through Nazareth many years later. The Nazareth scenes are fully formed. The reader would recognize lines like "My table is not finished" and "He said to me, 'I must be about my father's business.'"

The scenes in the Tower of Antonia are quite developed, too. After marching through the Joppa Gate, Messala ("When I was a boy, I used to pretend I was commander of this garrison.") argues with Sextus about how to "arrest an idea." Messala advises Sextus ("Go to Capri ... and forget that 'God is in every man.' There is divinity in only one man.") just before the centurion announces a visitor who "says he's a prince." Messala's ensuing dialogue ("Then treat him like one!" "Don't forget this was his country before it was ours." ". . . with another idea.") remains in the film, although this extended speech does not:

> We were like brothers. No. There's usually a natural rivalry between brothers. There was none between us. We were closer than brothers.

As in the film, Messala and Judah stand at opposite ends of the armaments corridor, and they are "delighted" to see each other, "holding each other at arm's length, smiling with the unspoken affection of old friends reunited." There is still no cross beam for the javelins, but they do proclaim "Down Eros! Up Mars!" Messala adding, "I'm afraid I can't 'Down Eros' with much conviction anymore. I've met too many charming ladies to go about insulting the god of Love." [The reader can access a screen test of this scene played by Cesare Danova and Leslie Nielsen.[40]]

Tunberg's most important contributions in these early scenes of this version of the script is to develop further the quarrel between Judah and Messala. Whereas Wallace's Judah developed his anger quite abruptly, and the quarrel in the 1925 film develops within two minutes, Tunberg inserted leisurely moments of humor, genial political banter, and a genuine warmth shared between Judah and Messala. When Messala asks if Tirzah is married, Judah replies, "The suitors march in with gifts. Her nose stays in the air. They march out again – leaving the gifts behind, of course." Messala earnestly seeks to use Judah's influence to save his people. After cornering Judah to provide the names of the "rabble-rousers" ("Yes, Judah, who are they?"), Messala makes a full speech:

> The informer is the patriot when he saves his people. These few violent men will destroy your people, Judah. They will bring down Roman swords on all of you. Isn't it better that the few be removed so the many can live in peace?
> *(intensely)*
> You can save your people. You can weed out these maniacs who defy the Emperor. You better than anyone.
> *(getting closer to Ben Hur)*
> You inherited more than a seat on the Sanhedrin from your father – you inherited an empire of commerce. You have warehouses and banks and caravans all over the eastern world; your ships sail from Alexandria to Antioch. Let your empire of commerce serve Caesar's empire.
> *(excitedly)*
> You can be my eyes and ears, Judah. We can go forward hand in hand. There's no limit to where we can go!
> *(triumphantly)*
> One day we'll sit next to Caesar and help him rule his troubled world. The future belongs to those who are strong enough to take it. We must be strong, Judah!

Film scholars no doubt assume correctly that the specific reference to "the informer" would have struck a nerve in the mid-1950s political climate shaped by Senator McCarthy and HUAC.[41]

Tunberg also fleshes out Judah's mother, given the name Miriam, by writing her a precis of the chauvinistic speeches she makes in the novel (2.5):

> MIRIAM
> Let us give the Romans their due. They are superior to us – but only in making war. In no other way do we suffer by comparison with them. History proves otherwise. We were a great nation, blessed by God, when Rome was still a village in the swamps of the Tiber, debasing itself before pagan idols!
> ...
> Our prophets have promised we will be free. They spoke the word of God.

> BEN HUR
> Did they, mother? Then perhaps God has forgotten us.
> MIRIAM
> No. It is not true. Sometimes we have forgotten God, but Rome has never known Him.

In the exchange with Messala during the arrest, Judah finishes with what Wyler will display visually:

> It was an accident! I was watching the governor. I rested my hands on the ledge. A stone was loose – it gave way under my hand – you can see for yourself – the mortar is loose –

Similarly, there is extended dialogue in the climactic Tower of Antonia scene that will be edited down later. Holding a spear, Judah both threatens and pleads with Messala:

> BEN HUR
> Is it possible for you to do this – to a family you've known and loved? Are you a monster? Are you debased beyond all feeling?
> *(brokenly)*
> Messala – have pity on them!
> MESSALA *(evenly)*
> A door must be open or shut. You shut it yourself, Judah. I offered to share my future with you if only you would serve Rome. You refused.
> *(cynically)*
> Now you will serve Rome in another way. You will be an example to those who would defy the Emperor.
> BEN HUR
> I am innocent.
> MESSALA *(harshly)*
> It does not matter. Innocent or not, you are responsible. Innocent or not, you must be an example.
> BEN HUR
> Surely one example is enough! I no longer care about myself. But my mother and sister – surely you can show them leniency –
> MESSALA *(levelly)*
> To show leniency is to encourage rebellion. The Jews must be taught a lesson. You and your family are that lesson.
> ...
> Drop the weapon, Judah. I am going to call the guard. Drop the weapon, and you will be allowed to live.
> BEN HUR *(wildly)*
> I will live! Do you think a few crumbs of life matter now? A great boon, Tribune! You will let

> me live, so I can die in the galleys. I would rather die now and take you with me!
>   MESSALA (*hard*)
> And your mother and sister? Throw it, Judah! Drive the spear through me, and your mother and sister will not die one day in prison. They will die today – nailed on a cross – in front of your eyes. Throw it, Judah!
> *He throws it into the wood beside Messala. The Roman sits without moving.*
>   BEN HUR (*in a choked voice*)
> Messala, the God of my fathers permits vengeance! I will pray with every breath I draw this vengeance will not be delayed too long!

Tunberg's early versions of the script contain more dialogue than the release form of the film, but most of these passages contained nuggets that would be mined and modified by Vidal and Fry during production in Rome. Vidal's retrospective claims in the media that Tunberg's script was "awful" or that the first third had to be completely rewritten ignore the degree to which the finished product reflected Tunberg's earliest screen adaptations of the novel and speak more to the polished quality of the release version of the film and Vidal's own self-promotion. Wyler's later statement that Tunberg had written only the three words "The Chariot Race" without any further details were also utterly inaccurate.[42] In addition to the 1955 and 1957 Canutt "action breakdowns," Tunberg's 218-page script contains more than twenty-five pages describing the race: the Sheik warning Judah that Messala is driving a Greek chariot (but not the serrated blades), the pre-race festivities, each of the laps marked by a dolphin, three crashes, Messala's attempt at crashing Judah, his wheel coming off, and Judah's glancing back at "the Roman's scarlet and gold figure" being dragged by his reins and then trampled by the next team of horses.

Many segments of Tunberg's earliest adaptations of Wallace's novel survived the entire editing process. He invented Sextus to put Messala's understanding of Judea and Judeans into a more favorable perspective, and he made Drusus into an obedient and loyal companion to Messala, just as he rendered the Sheik as a much more genial and less militaristic companion to Judah. In addition to the lines already quoted, more of the poignant lines from the film are already written in final or semi-final form, including:

> Messala to Gratus: "Jerusalem's welcome will not be a warm one – But I pledge my lord it will be a quiet one."
> Sextus to Messala: "How do you arrest an idea?"
> Judah to Simonides: "Once a year you bring your accounting, and once a year I find myself wealthier."
> Arrius to Judah: "Nothing could make stronger the bond between us. . . . The formalities of adoption have been completed."

Judah to Arrius: "It is a strange destiny . . . a new home, a new father. . . . I shall always try to wear this ring as the son of Arrius should wear it – with honour."
Simonides to Judah: "We were released on the same day – Malluch without a tongue and I without legs. But I have been his tongue , and he has been my legs. Together we make a whole man. . . . Judah – Judah Ben Hur . . . I would like to laugh, Judah, Let us laugh again."

The galley scenes are also fully formed in the script. The well scene in Nazareth immediately dissolves to ships on the sea, the pounding of the hortator initially establishes the tone of the galley interior, the imperial barge brings Arrius, no longer duumvir but consul, aboard. He immediately reviews the galley slaves, asking "how many rowers? And reliefs?" He hears the response, "of forty, every hour," and he continues to examine the slaves: "This man is ill. Replace him."; "That will stop"; "What service have you seen?"; "In this ship – one month lacking a day."; "You keep an exact account." "You have the spirit to fight back, but the intelligence not to. Your eyes are full of hate, Number Forty One. That's good. . . . Hate keeps a man alive. It gives him strength." Arrius announces that the emperor "has honoured us with the task of seeking out and and destroying" the enemy, and he tests the rowers through increasing speeds (battle – attack – ramming) while carefully eyeing Ben-Hur. Also, Tunberg has already changed Wallace's Number Sixty into the more sonically explosive Forty-One.

As in the novel, Arrius invites Judah to a private meeting that cements the special bond between the two, and Tunberg condenses Judah's explanation of his extrajudicial imprisonment into a single exchange. Much of this dialogue is also in its semi-final form:

>ARRIUS
>Your Jehovah has forsaken you. He has no more power than the images I pray to. . . . Your Jehovah will not help you. I might. Does that interest you, Number Forty One? I see that it does. I am a fighting man by profession
>. . .
>You do not say you were innocent.
>BEN HUR
>Would it do any good to say it again?
>ARRIUS
>No.
>(significantly)
>Think carefully of what I have offered. You'll never escape while we're victorious. If we're not, you'll sink with this ship, chained to your oar.
>(he pauses)
>You'd find it easier to breathe in the arena.
>BEN HUR
>For awhile, perhaps, I'd sink just as surely in the end.

And so on through unchaining Judah ("Once before a man helped me"), viewing the attacking ship through the oar hole ("We're going to be rammed!"), Judah throwing the spear to save Arrius on deck, and sighting the square sail ("It's a Roman sail."). As we will see, some of the dialogue will be modified or deleted. Some details of the battle will have to conform to accommodate the actualization of the action scenes, and Arrius' on-deck augury and prayer to Neptune will be deleted, and, of course, Rózsa's memorable music sets the tone for much of the galley sequence.

Arrius' original speech to the galley slaves was designed to help characterize him as the thoughtful, cultured Roman:

> ... Hate keeps a man alive. It gives him strength.
> (*ironically*)
> I would rather see them full of love. The poets tell us that is the strongest of all emotions. How wonderfully a ship would sail – propelled by love!

The same is true for this version of his conversation with Judah in his private quarters:

> I pray only because it is expected of me. It comforts the men. Religion is necessary as long as men fear.
> (*bitterly*)
> But there is no need for intelligent men to delude themselves. My Gods will not help me. Your God will not help you. I might.

On the raft, Tunberg prepares for Judah's adoption by creating another glimpse of Arrius' human side:

> Once I had a son. He didn't grow to be as high as my sword.
> (*harshly*)
> Were he here in your place, I would ask him to let me die.

Like most of the galley scenes, Judah's visit to Messala upon his return to Judea remains intact. Judah gives Messala the dagger and the conversation continues as in the film ("and from a man I've never met."; "You're wrong, Messala."; "By what magic do you bear the name of a consul of Rome?"; "You were the magician, Messala.. . . . You know the mark of Arrius?"; "Your gift is exquisitely appropriate, Young Arrius. Is it your intention to use this on me, or are you suggesting I use it on myself?"; "Find them, Messala. Restore them to me, and I will forget the pledge I made with every stroke of my oar."; "I'm not the Governor of Judea. I can't give you what you want without Gratus' approval."; "Get it. I will come back tomorrow. Don't disappoint me, Messala."). Omitted later is the line Tunberg uses to close the scene, when Messala confesses to Drusus: "The

Jew who survives in a Roman world might be better than a Roman." Both these scenes were shot in the fall of 1958, three years later.[43]

On the other hand, some of the 1955 script had to be extensively edited later. Today's reader would surely not find those sections unrecognizable, but they tend to be verbose and political. After Tirzah's hand sets loose the tile that wounds Gratus, for instance, she repeatedly says she was innocent, Judah repeatedly claims it was his hand and insists, "You can't think me mad enough to commit such a stupid, criminal act," to which Messala responds, "I know you hate Rome!" The scene closes with the pathos of Judah's dog Shep whimpering alone in the deserted House of Hur – very different from Messala's inspection of the parapet in the release version of the film. As in the novel, it is Sanballat, not the Sheik, who visits the Romans to wager for the race. In the aftermath of the race, Messala commits suicide with the dagger Judah had gifted him upon his return to Judea, and Pilate, who plays a greater role, informs him that the emperor has bestowed citizenship upon him and urges him to return to Rome:

> At this moment a rabble-rouser called the Messiah goes about Galilee stirring up rebellion. Many already hail Him as the King of the Jews. You are a Jew and a prince. If you stay here, you must become part of this tragedy. Go back to Rome, Young Arrius, while you can go with honor. You have had your revenge. The man who destroyed those you love is dead.

Judah responds angrily and blames Rome and the Roman occupation:

> Rome made Messala evil and cruel! Rome destroyed him and my family – as it destroys everything! ... Messala was not my enemy – Rome was my enemy – and always will be!

In obeisance to the novel, Tunberg turns Judah into a military captain, but Esther tries to convince him to submit to the Romans. She even talks back to her father:

> You were tortured in the dungeons, but this time you will die in them. [to Judah] You were tortured in the galleys, and this time you will die. Are you so in love with death? ... Can you defeat Rome – the whole world? Your desert tribes, your angry Galileans, your Zealots plotting in Jerusalem alleys – can they really sweep the Roman legions into the sea? ... A woman does not fear submission. It is her whole life.

Tunberg uses Esther's sober assessment of Judea's realpolitik as the opportune moment for Judah to profess his love for her to Simonides:

> The stone that fell from this roof so long ago is still falling – still smashing lives. It must stop. ... She is my slave as my heart is my slave. She is my property, and no man ever was as rich. She has served me, and those I love, with her love. And if I have the good fortune to live, Simonides, I will spend my days serving her.

Still not pacified, however, Judah and the Sheik lead the troops to a camp, much as in the 1925 film, amidst desert rocks. Here Ben-Hur greets Ilderim and prepares to ride into Jerusalem to take Simonides and Esther to safety. Meanwhile Esther, not Amrah, fearlessly and faithfully leads Miriam and Tirzah from the Valley of the Lepers to the Bethany Road to be healed by Christ. Finding Balthasar in the city, Judah witnesses the silent procession along the Via Dolorosa and swears a new target for vengeance:

> I did not come to mourn a king. But I will mourn a Man and a Jew. And I will pledge myself to avenge Him and all others the Romans have murdered.

Here Balthasar surprises Judah by informing him that the Christ healed Miriam and Tirzah, so Judah hastens to the citadel to plead for Jesus's life, and, failing there, reunites with his family. He delivers a message of love and forgiveness, and the camera tilts towards the sky as the Voice of the Christ concludes the script: "Lo, I am with you always, even unto the end of the world."

As we have seen, Tunberg's original adaptation of Wallace's plot would in many scenes remain essentially intact throughout the process. But the difference between a competent screenplay and a great one can rest on a few memorable phrases or moments, and *Ben-Hur* would have many more of them in its 212 minutes.

The Tunberg/Anderson 1957 Script

In a summary dated June 21, 1957, Jan Lustig, who had specialized in writing screenplays for historical romances, suggested that Judah be portrayed even more as a political radical who has shaken off his apathy to challenge Roman domination.[44] Later in the year MGM narrowly circulated a "Complete" script by Tunberg and Maxwell Anderson, although subsequent reports claimed that Anderson had been too ill to participate.[45] This script promotes more concise or more poetic dialogue, eliminating lines that repeat ideas already expressed and reversing word order. It omits, for instance, the second sentence of Messala's, "Either you are for me or against me. Nothing else is possible." Instead of "My gift to Esther will be her freedom," Judah now says, "Her freedom will be my gift to Esther." Judah's final line in Messala's office has been changed from "I will pray with every breath I draw this vengeance will not be delayed too long!" to, "I will pray that you live till I return." The decurion at the Nazareth well now says "No water for him!" instead of "No water for that one!" And when Messala receives the dagger from young Arrius, he asks simply, "Is it your suggestion that I use it on myself?"

As for the narrative, the initial night-time roof scene between Judah and Esther is completely rewritten so that now Esther gives Judah her slave ring and he promises to wear it "until there is someone else." This revised script inserts an additional romantic scene to complement this one. When Judah returns to Judea and the House of Hur to reunite with Simonides and Esther, he and Esther again meet on the parapet in a night scene. She asks about the slave ring, and he shows her that he still wears it, although the polish is now "dull from sea-water and verdigris." Because this is one of the few new scenes in the script and its language, style, and fresh approach seem to bear witness to a different hand, perhaps both scenes with Esther and Judah can tentatively be ascribed to Anderson.

The final third of the script has been substantially revised to have Judah's anti-Roman politics stand in starker contrast to the effect Jesus will have on the Hur family. During the night scene Esther still lies to Judah about the deaths of his mother and sister, but she warns him that if he kills Messala, it will also bring death upon Simonides. Later, returning from the Valley of the Lepers, Judah, Esther, and Malluch meet up with Balthasar and a blind man cured by Jesus. Still not believing in the power of Jesus, Judah is abruptly summoned before Pilate, who informs him that the emperor has granted him citizenship. Judah, like the Judah Wallace modeled after Judas of Galilee, threatens Pilate:

> BEN HUR
> A great many will die, Lord Pilate, and they will not all be Arabs and Jews! I take pleasure in that thought! If we die we shall make sure of some Romans to share our graves!
> PILATE
> You do choose death then. I'm sorry. I'd rather you were my friend.

These scenes replace the argument between Esther and Simonides and Judah's confession of love for her with a different encounter between Judah and Esther. She meets him after the interview with Pilate and they kiss for the first time. But because Judah has threatened Pilate, he considers himself "an outlaw" and will join the rebel forces organized by her father and the Sheik. Esther protests, pointing out that rebellion will be hopeless ("bloodshed will not end bloodshed") and fearing that she will never see Judah again. The scene dissolves directly to the Valley of the Lepers, where, despite Miriam's protests, Esther leads her and

Tirzah to Jesus, streamlining the convergence between her and Judah in Jerusalem.

Silent no longer, the crowd witnessing the judgment and procession of Jesus now contains groups shouting in anger and others singing hymns. Judah no longer disputes with Balthasar, but a careful look at Jesus creates "an amazing change" on the face of Judah. This brings him back to a hardened Pilate who argues that "a new faith can be a very dangerous thing" and that "an occasional crucifixion helps keep order." Meanwhile Jesus passes by Esther and the Hur women on the street, and as soon as Tirzah says, "When I saw his face I believed," she discovers that she and her mother have both been instantly healed. At the end of the script, Judah finally reveals the effect Jesus has had on him when he confesses that he feels pity for Pilate. The camera tilts upwards, and now Esther brings the story to a close:

> There is one thing Jesus said – and I get comfort out of remembering it: He said: "Lo, I am with you always, even unto the end of the world..."

In January, 1958, production manager Henry Henigson circulated this same script with a four-page list of changes, mostly minor dialogue edits and modified descriptions of the naval miniatures (which were already being built) and interiors, except for an expanded role for Iras. The latter appears in the Tunberg/Behrman script.

The Tunberg/Behrman 1958 Script

The early scenes still include the autobiographical speeches by Balthasar and Gaspar, and most of the script remains unchanged until the dialogue exchanged by Messala and Judah in the Antonia fortress. The 1957 script had added some years to Wallace's teenage and twenty-something protagonists, changing Messala's absence of eight years to fifteen. Building on this, when Judah points out, "You have changed, Messala," Messala says, "I have grown up," emphasizing their mature adult status. Consequently, the current political situation is made to seem more dire. The following speech, for example, has been made more intense:

> Persuade them their resistance to Rome is stupid and futile. It can end only in suffering and bloodshed – for your people.

> Persuade them their resistance to Rome is stupid. It is worse than stupid – it is futile. It can end in only one way – extinction for your people.

The following passage is equally fortified and helps to demonstrate how Tunberg's 1954 and 1955 drafts were crafted into their more powerful final form in 1958:

1955:	1957:	1958:
Messala Don't be a fool! Are the lives of a few Jews so dear to you? Ben Hur What they believe in is dear to me. I'm against violence, Messala, but I believe in the past of my people – and in their future. Messala What future? You're a conquered people. You have no future. Ben Hur You've conquered the land and the bodies of a nation, but you haven't conquered our minds or our spirits. Messala A speech worthy of the High Priest himself! You cling to a tree that's dead. You walk in a circle around the memory of your past – like a blindfolded donkey plodding around a waterwheel. Wake up, Judah! The glory of Solomon is gone. Do you think it will come again – that a warrior king will spring up out of fire and lead you? No Judah. The mighty have fallen! Moses is dead! Joshua will not rise again to save you – nor David.	Messala Don't be a fool! Are the lives of a few Jews so dear to you? Ben Hur I'm against violence, Messala, but I believe in the past of my people – and in their future. Messala What future? You're a conquered people. Ben Hur You've conquered the land and the bodies of a nation, but it will rise again. Messala You cling to a tree that's dead. Wake up, Judah! The glory of Solomon is gone. Do you think it will come again? No Judah. Moses is dead! Joshua will not rise again to save you – nor David.	Messala Don't be a fool! Are the lives of a few Jews so dear to you? Ben Hur If I cannot persuade them that does not mean that I will consent to murder them. Besides – you must know this, Messala – I believe in the past of my people and in their future. Messala That is not a belief. That is a dream. You are a conquered people. Ben Hur You may conquer the land. You may slaughter the people. But that will not be the end. We will rise again. Messala You live on dead dreams. You live on the myths of the past. The glory of Solomon is gone. Do you think it return? No Judah. Moses is dead! Joshua will not rise again to save you – nor David.

Accordingly, when their quarrel turns their friendship into an open declaration of enmity, the termination of their personal relationship is attributed to political factors. From Tunberg's original:

> I thought – my friend has been to Rome, but he has returned. I was wrong. We'll never be friends again.

the Tunberg-Behrman script develops:

> I thought it was my friend who returned – and I came here with my heart full of joy. But I was wrong. It is not my friend who has returned. It is a tribune of Rome – it is a conqueror who has returned. It is an enemy who has returned.

In contrast, Messala makes psychoanalytical remarks during the arrest. The exchange:

> BEN HUR
> You can't think me mad enough to commit such a stupid, criminal act.
> MESSALA
> I know you hate Rome!

now develops into:

> BEN HUR
> You can't think me so insane that I would do a thing like this openly.
> MESSALA
> Hatred often leads to insanity. But this act was inspired not by your hatred of Rome, but by your hatred of me to destroy my authority here.

Tirzah now talks about Messala as her childhood hero, so she suffers even greater disappointment when Judah tells her Messala has become his enemy. In exchange, the pro-Judean politics espoused by Judah's mother in Wallace's novel and greatly reduced in previous versions of the script are now eliminated entirely. The initial romantic encounter between Judah and Esther is again completely rewritten, adding to the slave ring motif that Esther does not "feel free" and introducing the exchange:

> BEN HUR
> If you were not a bride I would ask to kiss you goodbye.
> ESTHER
> If I were not a bride I would not deny you.

This scene also introduces Esther's early memory of the hunting incident involving "that Roman – your friend" and praying for the injured Judah not to die, her clear confession that she has been attracted to her master ever since childhood.

The official Triumph in Rome was an innovation of the 1925 film that Tunberg incorporated for its visual splendor, if only thus far in a one-paragraph description, followed by an interview in the Palantine [sic] Palace. An additional scene in the 1958 script attempts to develop the relationship between Judah and Arrius. Inserted between the nautical rescue and Roman party scenes, the new dialogue remarks upon Judah's good fortune in rescuing Arrius and offers Judah an update on the emperor's decision. The scene addresses Judah's uncertain status after saving Arrius. In the novel Arrius adopts Judah immediately after their return to port at Misenum in the final paragraphs of Book Third, thereby enabling Wallace to commence Book Fourth with Judah already sailing towards Antioch. Wallace wrote no intervening scenes set in Rome. In the 1925 film Arrius claims Judah as his son almost as soon as they board the rescue ship. Following this are two Technicolor scenes in Rome (not found in Mathis' treatment) – the Triumph and, after an intertitle explaining that Judah is distraught about his mother and sister, a scene in an exterior colonnade where Judah informs Arrius that he must leave Rome to find Simonides. There are narrative problems here. Not only are Judah's emancipation and adoption abrupt and unrealistic, but his long sojourn in Rome living the life of an aristocrat seems unconscionable for a man whose mother and sister are presumed to be suffering.

Tunberg accounts for the time delay by having Arrius petition the emperor for Judah's personal and political freedom. Tiberius gives Judah to Arrius as his personal slave but refuses to allow Judah to return to Judea because "to reopen the case is to undermine my personal authority in Jerusalem." Tunberg also interweaves the character of Pontius Pilate into this. He was presumed to be made governor of Judea, which his good friend Arrius took to be a positive sign and reason for Judah to be patient. This new scene leads the way to the final solution that accounts for Judah's delayed return to the East. In the final release Tiberius would comment on the case at both the triumph and the subsequent audience with Arrius, where he would insist on being "generous." This is not yet developed. In the imperial audience scene in this semi-final script Tiberius says only, "He tries to kill one Roman, save another. Very inconsistent."

At the party in "the classically beautiful atrium of Arrius' home in Rome," Ben-Hur is accompanied no longer by Fabricius, as in the earlier scripts, but by a young woman named Flavia:

> FLAVIA
> I will have that girl whipped.
> BEN HUR
> Why?
> FLAVIA
> She looked at you. I hate every woman who looks at you. Yesterday I could have killed all those women who cheered you at the Colosseum [sic].

Still searching for romance, when Arrius announces his adoption of Judah, Flavia says she hopes that will be reason for him to remain in Rome.

There is considerable light conversation, as when Arrius and Pilate discuss the Carthaginian dancers, introducing the type of witty repartee Pilate will offer in the film.

> ARRIUS
> This is a fertility rite.
> PILATE
> No wonder Carthage is over-populated.
> ARRIUS
> That is General Vitruvius' daughter, with Ben Hur.
> PILATE
> I see a decided impulse toward fertility there, too.

Three other characters play expanded roles, Iras, The Sheik, and Ben-Hur's dog, now named Siva. When Ben-Hur returns to his house in the evening, he is first recognized not by Esther but Siva, and Siva will pose a threat when Miriam and Tirzah are released from prison and come by stealth of night to the House of Hur. They have to warn Esther not to let Siva touch or reveal them.

Iras plays a more integral role at the Orchard of Palms. In this version of the script it is she, for instance, to whom Ben-Hur says that the Sheik's horses will not hold the turn during a practice run, and it is she, not Balthasar, who reports this to the Sheik. This portion of the script introduces her this way:

> Iras is a ravishingly striking brunette, with magnetic eyes that see all and an expression of inscrutability. Her voice is low and uninflected. There is about her an air of deep reserve, as if she has learned that it is dangerous to say too much.

Later Iras reveals that she has been Messala's lover for three years and now hates him, encouraging Judah to enter the race to defeat him. This scene includes a characteristic moment for Iras when she tells Judah:

> To be the daughter of a saint puts a burden on me – that I have always found difficult to bear....
> My father dreams of happiness in the next world.
> I dream of happiness in this.

She then kisses Judah "full on the mouth." She kisses him again in an extended night scene. At this point in the script development, Judah has romantic associations with three women, again, without knowing the whereabouts or condition of his mother or sister.

This version of the script adds several scenes that further bathe Tunberg's anti-Roman political Sheik in the kind of genial humor that would help Hugh Griffith win his Academy Award. One in particular plays off Tunberg's original lines in which Messala taunts Judah for believing in only one god. This occurs when Judah tells the Sheik he is going to kill Messala and asks him to protect Simonides and Esther:

> THE SHEIK
> Because it is a Roman you will kill, you are twice welcome. And your wives? I should like to offer them my hospitality also.
> BEN HUR
> I have no wives.
> THE SHEIK
> Sure you have <u>some</u> wives!
> BEN HUR
> Not one.
> THE SHEIK
> I have six wives, no, seven. That is because I am traveling. At home I have more. It is a great advantage, believe me my friend, to have many wives.
> BEN HUR
> Some day I hope to have one.
> THE SHEIK
> One wife! One God – that I can understand. But one wife – that is uncivilized!

Many accounts state that Tunberg did not work on the script after the company departed for Rome in the late winter of 1958, but a letter from Wyler to Fry dated June 19, 1959, refers to his limited participation during post-production, when Wyler was attempting to make adjustments to the Crucifixion scene:

> I asked Tunberg to write something, but I am not satisfied with the words, although I think the thought is quite good. Meanwhile, Joe Cohn brought me some of your penciled notes from the Cavalry scene, and we found references to the pain of childbirth which disappears and all that remains is the joy that man is born into the world. I am enclosing these notes of yours to refresh your mind.[46]

Vidal's Contributions

Gore Vidal had signed a four-year contract with MGM in 1956, and, wanting to terminate the agreement prematurely, agreed to serve as a script doctor for *Ben-Hur* in the spring of 1958 in exchange for abandoning the remaining two years of the contract. He arrived in Rome on April 23, a week before Fry, and departed either in late May, according to his memoirs, or on June 24, according to MGM records.[47] Like Fry, Vidal would not receive a writing credit for his numerous changes to the script, but Wyler, Heston, and MGM would promote Fry's contributions as worthy of official recognition while Vidal's were discounted and even rejected, according to Heston during their public quarrel in the 1990s. After his death in 2012, Vidal left his papers to Harvard Library, among which was his personal copy of the January 28, 1958, script that included his numerous edits and annotations in pencil. The (incomplete) script is accompanied by a two-page, undated cover letter written on the stationery of New York's Hotel New Weston.[48] The letter, similar in content to that sent to William Morris in 1959, states that he rewrote the script from the beginning through the chariot race, made an important structural change to the original script, and rewrote "nearly all of the dialogue."[49] He concludes, "I should say a third of the picture shot is my dialogue."

The accompanying screenplay cannot verify these claims. His revisions for the initial census scene in Jerusalem were rejected, he made no changes at all to the subsequent speeches by Gaspar and Balthasar, nor did he make any for the introductory Bethlehem scenes. The chariot race scenes have relatively little dialogue anyway, and his edits do not extend that far. They conclude with the desert scenes between Judah and Iras, which were never filmed. Also, if Vidal's recollection that he departed from Rome in late May is correct, it contradicts his claim that he was writing pages for each day's filming, for principle photography began on May 20.

On the other hand, Vidal did make an important structural change to the initial scenes involving Ben-Hur, Messala, and Esther. Tunberg had moved Wallace's initial quarrel in a palace garden on Mt. Zion to the interior of the Castle of Antonia, where he placed the conversations between Messala and the invented Tribune Sextus, and Messala and Judah. Vidal divided the latter into two discrete segments, adding the segment in the garden of the House of Hur and the horse Judah gives to Messala. (Vidal also claims that the gift of the brooch Messala brings for Tirzah was his, but Tunberg's script already mentions a gift.) Vidal's ear for dialogue evidences itself in several passages. Where Tunberg had Judah say to Simonides "Your presence is the best gift of all, Simonides," Vidal rewrites as "And the best gift of all, your presence, Simonides." Where Tunberg had Simonides say, "Esther has a question to ask," Vidal writes, "Esther wishes to speak to her master." And where Tunberg had Ben-Hur say, "You wish to marry, Esther?" and Esther respond with "My father wishes it," Vidal writes, "You are eager to marry, Esther?" and "It is my father's wish." Similarly, in the galley scenes Vidal rhythmically alters Tunberg's "In this ship – one month less a day" and "Other ships – for three years" by reversing the phrase order. He strengthens the following exchange and increases its efficiency.

ARRIUS I own some of the best athletes in Rome – gladiators, wrestlers, charioteers. Would you like to become one of them? BEN HUR As your slave? ARRIUS Better my slave than chained below these decks the rest of your life. BEN HUR I hope not to be here the rest of my life.	ARRIUS I own some of the best athletes in Rome – gladiators. Would you like to become one of them? BEN HUR To die as your slave? ARRIUS Better than live chained below these decks. BEN HUR I will not be here forever.

Vidal also made a clever and lasting suggestion that brings the galley sequences to an end. When Arrius, after being rescued from the flotsam, learns that he has won a victory, Tunberg had Arrius turn to Judah and say, "Some debts are impossible to repay. But I would like to try. Come with me to Rome. You will have a friend there." Vidal leaves that speech in but precedes it with an ironic admission that decidedly demonstrates Arrius' increasing fondness for Judah and amused tolerance for his Jewish faith: "Apparently, in saving you, your God has saved the Roman fleet, Judah!" Like many of Vidal's edits, this last one was not used verbatim but did lay the foundations for one of the film's most irony-filled lines.

Fry's Contributions
The highly respected English playwright Christopher Fry arrived in Rome on April 29, 1958, to begin work on the script. He worked throughout the filming process from May 20, 1958, when principle photography commenced, until its completion on January 19, 1959, remained in Rome through June,[50] and then worked with Wyler again during post-production from June to October. In addition, Fry and Heston developed a strong friendship during their time together in Rome. The differences between the January 8, 1958, script and the release version of the film make it clear that the final form of the dialogue owes much to Fry's efforts, as does the quality of the film. Countless anecdotes about William Wyler make it clear that he often did not know exactly how he wanted a scene shot ahead of time, so he rethought and adjusted them as the day proceeded. When he did, it was usually Fry who made the necessary dialogue adjustments to nuance the scene. On the other hand, Heston's diary recorded on September 30: "Willie fixes script."

At the time, no script was printed that bore Fry's name, making it difficult for us to attribute his contributions with confidence. However, the controversy over assigning screen credit generated several additional documents that distinguished Fry's (and Vidal's) work from Tunberg's and are preserved in the Herrick Library. On June 1, 1959, for instance, Rudi Monta, representing MGM's legal arm, sent to the WGA several typed pages listing Fry's contributions, adding that inasmuch as Tunberg went off this assignment on May 5, some of the lines in the June, 1958, script were Fry's as well even if they were not clearly identified as such. These include:

SEXTUS It's something you can't put your finger on. There are strange spirits at work. There's a man who goes about the country – a carpenter's apprentice, they say. He preaches and teaches some new idea – MESSALA There's always some sort of rabble-rouser going about stirring up trouble. SEXTUS This man is different. He teaches that God is not a long way off, but near – in every man. MESSALA Go to Capri, Sextus. Bathe and rest – and forget that God is in every man.	SEXTUS O, you don't know. There's nothing you can put your finger on. I tell you, there are strange forces at work here. For instance, there's this Messiah business – MESSALA Oh, I know. I know! There was one predicted when I was a boy. SEXTUS Yes. A king of the Jews! Who will lead them all into some sort of anti-Roman paradise. Huh! Makes your head spin. And there's a wild man in the desert named John, who drowns people in water. There's a carpenter's son who goes around doing magic tricks. Miracles they call them! MESSALA There's always some sort of rabble-rouser going about stirring up trouble. SEXTUS Um no, no, no. This man is different. He teaches that God is near, in every man. MESSALA Hah! SEXTUS It's actually quite profound, some of it. MESSALA You've been too long away from Rome. Go back, Sextus. Go to Capri! Bathe! Rest! Lie by the sea and forget that "God is in every man."

In December, 1959, after the Screen Writers Guild had already determined to award Tunberg sole credit, MGM veteran J. J. Cohn wrote a six-page letter to Wyler specifying the numerous script innovations that had been developed in Rome without Tunberg's input.[51] He lists nine "New Scenes," including the exchange between Tiberius and Arrius during the triumph and Messala's examination of the loose tiles, as well as such substantial revisions as Ben-Hur's giving a stallion to Messala and the substitution of the Sheik for Sanballat in the wagering scene, although some of these cannot be attributed directly or solely to Fry. The entire second half of the letter focuses on Fry's extensive rewriting of the post-chariot race portion of the film. When Fry and Vidal were both doctoring the script in late April, 1958, this was Fry's assignment, and this is where the most extensive changes were made.[52] As we have seen, Tunberg, in part following Wallace but also trying to portray the protagonist as a diplomatic hero, places Judah with Balthasar at the Crucifixion and then has him summoned to a final audience with Pilate while on a "cobbled street" Jesus passes by

CENTURION A Jew to see you, Tribune. MESSALA Who is he? CENTURION He says he's a prince – the Prince of Hur. MESSALA Then treat him like one. Tell him I'll join him. CENTURION Yes, Tribune. MESSALA One moment, Centurion . . . Don't forget this was his country before it was ours. CENTURION Yes, Tribune. MESSALA The Prince of Hur is the head of one of the greatest families in Judea. He is – SEXTUS I've met the Prince. He is a reasonable man. MESSALA We were friends as boys. SEXTUS How strange. MESSALA The distinctions which separate men make little difference to boys. We were like brothers. (*He moves towards the door.*) Sextus, you asked how you arrest an idea – with another idea.	CENTURION There's a Jew outside. He wants to see the Tribune Messala. MESSALA I assume he has a name? CENTURION He says he's a prince – Prince Judah Ben Hur. MESSALA Then treat him like one. Tell him I'll join him. CENTURION Yes, Tribune. MESSALA Centurion . . . This was his country before it was ours. Don't forget that. CENTURION Yes, Tribune. SEXTUS Very wise! This Ben Hur is the richest man in Jerusalem. MESSALA And the head of one of the greatest families in Judea. We were friends as boys. We were like brothers. Sextus, you asked how to fight an idea. Well, I'll tell you how. With another idea.

Miriam and Tirzah and miraculously heals them. Fry changed the late audience with Pilate, places Miriam and Tirzah in a cave where they find themselves healed at the moment of Christ's death on the cross, utterly rewrote the dialogue for the Golgotha scene, and added the earth-cleansing rain near the end of the film. During post-production Wyler and Fry developed these final scenes further, making Miriam and Tirzah suffer sudden physical pain as part of the healing process.[53]

THE PRODUCTION

For two years MGM had been preparing the Cinecittà sets, signed labor agreements, and scouted other locations outside Rome, most of it effectively managed by Henry Henigson.[54] By the time filming began in May, 1958, half a square mile of the Roman studio had been populated with Jerusalem building fronts, rooftops, the Via Dolorosa, the Fortress of

MESSALA Your gift is exquisitely appropriate, young Arrius. Is it your suggestion I use it on myself? BEN HUR You enjoy expensive things, Messala. That's worth more than you realize. Keep it with the rest of your treasures. MESSALA I'm sure you'll allow me to give you something in return. BEN HUR Yes, give me back my mother and my sister. MESSALA I fear it is not in my power. BEN HUR Find them, Messala. Restore them to me, and I will forget the pledge I made with every stroke of my oar. Restore them to me and keep that as a token of my forgiveness and good will. MESSALA I'm not the Governor of Judea. I can do nothing without Gratus' approval. BEN HUR I will come back tomorrow. Don't disappoint me, Messala.	MESSALA Your gift is exquisitely appropriate, young Arrius. Do you suggest I use it on myself? BEN HUR What has become of my mother and my sister? MESSALA It is not my duty to keep track of prisoners. BEN HUR Find them, Messala. Restore them to me, and I will forget what I vowed with every stroke of that oar you chained me to. MESSALA I am not the Governor of Judea. I can do nothing without Gratus' approval. BEN HUR Then get it! I will come back tomorrow. Don't disappoint me, Messala.

SHEIK You've a keen eye. Where did you acquire it? BEN HUR In the Circus Maximus in Rome. SHEIK You have driven in the Circus Maximus? BEN HUR Yes. SHEIK Tell me, my young friend, could you make my four run as one? BEN HUR You have a driver. SHEIK I will cut his throat this minute if you will take his place.... Stay, my friend. Stay here as my honoured guest.	SHEIK You've a keen eye. Where did you acquire it? BEN HUR In the circus in Rome. SHEIK You have driven in the great circus? Tell me, my friend, could you make my four run as one? BEN HUR No, I'm on my way to Jerusalem. SHEIK But, your caravan rests until daylight tomorrow! We have time to eat, drink, and talk! Come into my tent and refresh yourself, and let me hear how you raced in Rome.

Antonia, and the House of Hur. Behind was the eighteen-acre circus with 1500-foot straightaways and a proportionally huge *spina* (more than twice the size of Wallace's *spina*) decorated with crouching figures, one of which stands guard outside the Cinecittà to this day. Next to the circus was a huge practice track. As for the Klaw & Erlanger and 1925 MGM productions, the company circulated the mega-numbers to the press – 1,000,000 pounds of plaster, 40,000 cubic feet of lumber, 250 miles of metal tubing for the circus stands, and 40,000 tons of sand.[55] Later press releases claimed that 10,000 costumes and over one million props had been made, and that 4000 pounds of hair had been woven into wigs and beards.[56]

Much of this was studio business that need not be described here, but, fortunately, we do have descriptive accounts of some of the filming from three of the most important contributors to the drama and the action – the man who designed the chariot race, the actor who portrayed Judah Ben-Hur, and the film's principle director.

Canutt

In his autobiography, Yakima Canutt describes participating in a 1958 screening of the 1925 *Ben-Hur* along with "most of the M.G.M. studio brass."[57] These included Henigson and "The Fixer," the infamous Eddie Mannix. The latter asked him, "Can you beat that?" Impressed by "Breezy" Eason's work but much more safety conscious, Canutt responded, "Give me cooperation and the tools I need." These included not just the seventy-eight Lipizzaners and Arabians [Andalusians] from Yugoslavia and Spain and several Italian drivers, but Hollywood drivers familiar with horses and film-making, a special horse trainer, Glenn Randall, to "high school" the four white horses assigned to Ben-Hur, and gooseneck tongue fittings and swivel connectors for the chariots "so they could hug the end of the *spina* in fast, skidding turns" and flip over and over after a crash. Mannix asked, "Just what the hell is a *spina*?"

Standing his ground against the MGM reps, Canutt negotiated hard for sufficient funds and equipment, battled with Henigson about how to prepare the track surface, and he chafed at having to work under second-unit director Andrew Marton. But by late May, 1958, the circus surface, equipment, and all the horses and drivers were ready for filming, and the three crashes and various special effects had all been mapped out in a 61-page script.[58] $1 million was allotted to the chariot race alone, and Marton and Canutt were supplied with three of the six 65mm cameras in existence.[59] Unlike the 1925 production, the entire race would be filmed in Rome.

Heston's Diary

We learn from Charlton Heston's diary that he arrived in Rome by train on April 13, 1958, and that the next day Canutt was introducing him to driving a *quadriga*. Not a novice, Heston had driven a two-horse chariot in *The*

Ten Commandments, but he still had trepidations. Canutt assured him, "You just learn to drive the team. I guarantee you'll win the damn race."[60] Commenting on the physical aspects of the role, much like Walker Whiteside when he read through the Klaw & Erlanger script, Heston remarked on May 22, "Rather tricky driving, but not much acting." When we read of a costume problem like Messala's painful contact lenses [June 17] or technical mishaps like the failed javelin rigging for Judah and Messala [May 30], we might compare the approximately 6000 performances of the Klaw & Erlanger *Ben-Hur* that rarely suffered a glitch. These kinds of anecdotes make for interesting reading, but as Heston's diary follows his progress up the professional ladder of film acting success from 1956 to 1976, it also bares an actor's intentions, anxieties, and challenges when playing Wallace's protagonist as well as the tensions involved in an ensemble production trying to reconstitute the story of *Ben-Hur: A Tale of the Christ* as an epic motion picture:

> May 15: Today we rehearsed Vidal's rewrite of the crucial scene with Messala. Indeed, the crucial scene of the whole first half of the story, since it contains the seed of so much that follows. This version is much better than the script scene, and Willy brought its virtues out in his usual manner as we worked: picking, carping, cutting, finding a reading here and a gesture there till you're smothered by his concept, which then proves to be excellent.
>
> June 2: The final quarrel with Messala in the garden, which is the first time Judah really admits they're at odds, shaped up. I sense Willy ... thinks I'm too flat through the opening scenes.
>
> June 6: Sixteen takes for me to say "I'm a Jew!" Maybe because I'm not, I damn near decided I never would say it right.

Heston, Wyler, and the others were clearly wrestling with character relationships that Wallace sketched out and were then revised and shaded by several highly respected playwrights. It was enough for the novel that Judah and Messala had been friends and, after one political and cultural argument and a physical accident, became enemies. Much of this was due to Judah's youth and Sadducee upbringing, but neither of these translated onto the script or film set. Heston records elsewhere:[61]

> Willy was ready to shoot the scene Vidal had tried to fix: Judah and Messala meeting for the first time since boyhood. Fry had reworked it by then, and we'd read it through in the office. ... We dug away at it for two long days, but when we wrapped late Saturday night, Wyler was clearly not satisfied.
>
> "I've got to see how strong this friendship is. The audience has to believe you as friends. In the next scene you quarrel, and for the rest of the movie you're trying to kill each other. The audience has to remember this scene. They have to know it's real.

Heston then spent his free Sunday writing several hundred words of backstory, attempting on his own to fill in what Wallace, Tunberg, and the others had omitted. This actually angered Wyler, who wanted Heston to act, not write, but Wyler also admitted that he had no ready solution to offer. Ultimately it was Wallace's story and the tile incident which made their enmity so convincing.

Heston also discusses the difficulties the production had with the love scenes that are much less pronounced in the novel.

> June 23: We continued to circle around that damn love scene like wolves closing in on a fallen elk, but we never actually got to it. We did everything you can possibly do with the entrances and exits, and we did the little bit with Simonides afterward, but Willy is apparently not sure what he really wants to do with the scene itself.

This was largely because Fry preferred to diminish its importance in the story:[62]

> If I were writing an original screenplay instead of adapting a semiclassic novel, I wouldn't have the girl's role in the story at all. The significant emotional relationship is the love/hate between Messala and Ben-Hur. The audience knows this, and they're not interested in the Ben-Hur/Esther story.

Heston coincidentally provides us with a sketch of the shooting schedule, thereby helping us attribute the script changes. He records that filming during the last week of May concentrated on the pre-race assemblage, including the new (but anachronistic) Star of David scene that introduces the race with themes of ethnic pride and anti-Roman bravado. This is the week that Vidal later remembered marked his departure from the production, but that seems highly unlikely. In early June the first unit worked on the recognition and quarrel scenes between Ben-Hur and Messala in the Tower of Antonia. This was followed by the scenes with Esther and Simonides in the House of Hur. In mid-June they were shooting the quarrel scene in the garden, followed by the introductory scenes with Esther and Simonides. No doubt, by the time filming moved on to Judah's imprisonment, escape, and confrontation with Messala in the Tower of Antonia, that is, from June 26 to July 4, Vidal had departed.

Although all of these scenes come early in the script and the Crucifixion scenes were shot last, the shooting schedule did not follow in sequence. July 5–6 they shot the award ceremony after the chariot race, and July 22–3 they were shooting the earlier Nazareth sequence in Fiuggi [Arcinazzo]. August 9 marked the conclusion of filming the chariot race, August 25 the triumph in Rome, and August 30 the adoption scene at Arrius' party. The galley sequences, directed in part by Richard Thorpe, began filming on September 8. On September 21 the production moved to Nettuno for the desert oasis scenes, although Heston returned to the second unit on the last day of September to film the ramming speed test and naval battle. The first week of October, Heston recorded that Glenn Randall had done a remarkable job training the four white horses, no doubt for their charming performance in the tent interior. The leper scenes were shot later in October outside Rome. After Zimbalist suffered his fatal heart attack in early November, production concentrated on finishing up the galley and desert sequences. The final scenes shot in Rome in early January were of the Crucifixion. Additional filming resumed in Los Angeles the following July with extra coverage of the Sheik's feast and the Golgotha scene. These studio shots give those portions of the film a very different look.

In the shooting script of 1958 there are many inserted pages marked with separate dates between May and December. Many of the lines are now edited to what we see in the release version, some of them on the typescript. When the rower next to Judah whispers, "Why – did they unchain you?" a notation in pen changes it to "Why did he do that?" After being rescued from the raft, on a page dated September 15, Arrius now quips, "It would seem that in his eagerness to save you, your God has also saved the Roman fleet." Tiberius now says to his aide that to kill a Roman governor but save a Roman consul is "somewhat unpredictable and inconsistent," and then says to Arrius, "Allow us to be generous," as in the film, adding the stipulation that he is never to return to Judea. The banter at Arrius' party now concerns a Numidian, not Carthaginian, fertility rite, and Pilate, observing Ben-Hur and Flavia, says that "the dance has apparently made its meaning clear." Concerning his appointment to the governorship of Judea, Pilate had remarked that it was "hopelessly provincial." Here he refers to "scorpions and prophets." In this version Iras's name is crossed out in the chariot practice sequence, Balthasar's used instead. Interestingly, Judah recommends that Antares, the slow horse, should run on the outside, but this has been crossed out and changed to the inside.

Wyler

Wyler's initial reluctance to take on the directorial assignment and the amount of remuneration he was offered demonstrate how anxious MGM's top officers were to produce a commercially successful film that also perpetuated the company's reputation for Hollywood artistry. As we saw in the reconstruction of the 1923–5 production, those that were disaffected or detached from the production have negatively colored the retrospective accounts more than seems warranted. Vidal's and Wyler's biographers seem to sensationalize, for instance, Wyler's dissatisfaction with the script. In *A Talent for Trouble*, Jan Herman wrote:[63]

> Wyler finally agreed to look over the script and concluded that the story wasn't bad but its quality was still out of the question for him. The screenplay, written by Hollywood veteran Karl Tunberg, was "very primitive, elementary" – no better than good hack work. It lacked feeling for character, as well as dramatic nuance. ... Apart from the spectacle, all *Ben-Hur* had were cardboard figures, "villains and heroes," he said. ... One of the best things about the screenplay, he joked, was its brevity on the subject. Tunberg had written just three words – "The Chariot Race" – leaving the rest to the director's imagination.

Many of these problems derive from Wallace's novel, and the reader has already seen that Tunberg took great pains to flesh out many of its sharp characterizations, smooth its abrupt transitions, and resolve its minor mysteries. Contrary to this statement, the release version of the film that Wyler directed, even after the subsequent script edits by skilled hands, still preserves much of Tunberg's dialogue and characterizations. Elsewhere Wyler claimed as his own the idea of having the charioteers parade around the stadium before the race, but the reader knows he would have seen this in the 1925 film.[64] Indeed, having served as one of the dozens of assistant directors for the 1925 near-legendary Hollywood shoot of October 3, 1925, Wyler certainly had a special place in his heart for the chariot race, but his statement about the three-word chariot race sequence, as we have seen, is wholly inaccurate.

As it turned out, the production was so massive that Wyler had very little to do with the chariot race, assigning almost all responsibility to Marton and Canutt, both of whom received screen credit as second-unit directors. Wyler did not even look at the dailies until they had been assembled into a rough cut. He had much to do elsewhere, reportedly working twelve to fourteen hours a day six days a week.[65] And when Zimbalist died on November 4, he had to take on many of the additional duties of producer.[66] With costs mounting to some $15 million, the MGM home office applied additional pressure. It was at this point that the infirmary doctor began to give Wyler injections of "Vitamin B."[67] Typically, he postponed any decisions on how to handle the Crucifixion sequence:[68]

> I spent sleepless nights trying to find a way to deal with the figure of Christ, ... the best-known man who ever lived. Everyone already has his own concept of him. I wanted to be reverent, and yet realistic. Crucifixion is a bloody, awful, horrible thing, and a man does not go through it with a benign expression on his face. . . . It is a very challenging thing to do that and get no complaints from anybody.

As we have seen, he was still reformulating the final scenes of the film as late as the summer of 1959.

Wyler did much more than hold the production together, however. His repeated insistence on perfecting individual scenes elevated a number of vital passages, most notably the encounter with Jesus at the Nazareth well. This was a pivotal point for Wallace's narrative structure, where it not only bridges the gap between the nativity scenes in the beginning of the film and the crucifixion scenes at the end but also begins to establish the savior parallel between Jesus and Arrius. Where Wallace (2.7) had focused on the face of Jesus "shaded by locks of yellowish bright chestnut hair, a face lighted by dark-blue eyes, at the time so soft, so appealing, so full of love and holy purpose, that they had all the power of command and will," Tunberg's script, following Wallace's strictures, focused not on Jesus's face but on the reaction of the Roman decurion in charge of the desert march:

> As he comes closer, the figure of Ben Hur's benefactor rises in the foreground, holding the gourd. The young man has glowing, chestnut-coloured hair, and wears

a simple peasant's woolen tunic, but his face cannot be seen. He stands there, back to CAMERA, watching the approaching Roman. Suddenly the Roman stops.
CLOSE SHOT – THE DECURIAN [sic]
He seems spellbound, perplexed, confused. Slowly he lowers the whip. For a moment he stands irresolutely, his glance riveted on the unseen figure. He moves backward a step or two, awkwardly, still staring. Then he moves backward another step or two. . . . The decurian continues to stare at the son of Joseph. Finally, with an effort, he frees his glance.

The scene was shot in Fiuggi, approximately fifty-five miles east of Cinecittà. When it came time for the close-up, Wyler noticed that they were not using the actor he cast, the expatriate American Remington Olmsted.[69] While the entire cast and crew were waiting, Wyler insisted on locating Olmsted in Rome and had him driven to the site. It was estimated this cost MGM $15,000, but the reaction shot speaks volumes about the power of Jesus's visage and Wyler's determination to capture on film a scene that met his standards.

Wyler's directorial signature is clearly present where Judah and Messala throw javelins into the symbolic cross beam, in Messala's hesitation in handing Judah the wine cup when he says, "You're very cruel to your conquerors," in Messala's silent examination of the roof tiles followed by an echo and horse whinny as the tile he loosens spills onto the back end of the Roman parade below,[70] in the Sheik's deep probing of the chest of gold coins, and in Tiberius looking darkly at the slave who fails to place Arrius' victory baton directly in his hand and then silencing a crowd of thousands with a simple gesture of his hand. Wyler gave some of the credit for these ideas to Fry,[71] but the aerial shots framing the tile incident certainly match those used for the fatal rooftop plunge of Humphrey Bogart (Baby Face Martin) in Wyler's *Dead End*.

Wyler and Fry collaborated on some of the verbal and visual threads and echoes that have the effect of tying disparate sections of the story together and thereby help the viewer negotiate the lengthy, complicated film. Wallace made limited use of the technique in the novel. He introduces the phrase "Down Eros, up Mars!" early in the initial quarrel between Judah and Messala, has Messala repeat the phrase as the last line of that chapter, and then has him say it again, twice, in the chariot race. He provides non-verbal parallels when Jesus gives Judah water in Nazareth and then Judah reciprocates on the Via Dolorosa, and when Arrius saves Judah by unshackling him on the galley a few minutes before Judah reciprocates in the sea. In the film, Fry and Wyler gave Arrius the line, "We keep you alive to serve this ship," and Judah repeats it to Arrius on the raft. Judah begs Messala to free his mother and sister, to which Messala replies, "Didn't I beg you?" Pilate repeats the phrase "one true god" to Judah, and the camera focuses on the Antonia Fortress cross beams in two different scenes. The beams foreshadow the Crucifixion, of course, as does Messala's threat of crucifying Judah's mother and sister. Judah wears Esther's slave ring as a sign of love and foreshadowing his imprisonment, and he accepts Arrius' ring as a symbol of adoption, and this is what he shows Messala to demonstrate his status as the son of a Roman consul. The quadruple echoes of the Arabian steed Judah gives to Messala early in the film will ultimately defeat him in the chariot race.

Other, more minor variants were changed during the filming process. At the chariot assembling, for instance, Messala is number six in the script, not five as in the film. "Five" sounds better when shouted in an English accent, just as "forty-one" sounds better than "sixty." Similarly, in the release version Judah is horrified to learn that he is being sent to Tyrus, not the Caesaria [sic] of Tunberg's script.

Extras

On July 2 Heston wrote, "I won the race today. Thundering past those screaming extras over the finish line was as thrilling as anything I've done in pictures." As many as 6000 extras were used for the circus crowd alone, yet another *Ben-Hur* record, not including Roman soldiers, Jerusalemites, Nazarenes, and Romans attending the Triumph.[72] Familiar with a practicable mass employment system from *Quo Vadis*, MGM built a labyrinth of fences to channel the lines of day laborers passed the processing gate into the costuming area and then the circus stands, and then back out again to exchange the costumes for their street clothes and ultimately their wages of 1500 lire ($2.50).[73] For lunch MGM provided a cafeteria with coke, coffee, fries, and macaroni. The day laborers were organized into groups of thirty, each with a leader, and men were divided from women. The system kept fraud to a minimum, making it difficult to obtain more than one pass or obtain a pass and then disappear until it was time to get paid. Assistant directors helped control potential anachronisms by inspecting the costumed workers for sunglasses, watches, and drink containers, and monitoring cigarette breaks. An independent account from Patricia Hall reported that the chariot race segment she observed in person had to be completely reshot because one of the extras was seen wearing a handkerchief on his head for relief from the oppressive summer heat.[74]

While the MGM production was ongoing, NBC sent a television crew to Rome to film an episode of Chet Huntley's Sunday news magazine, *Outlook*, aired in July, 1958. The episode fictionalized a story about three young Italian extras who during the lunch break hop the fence, don Roman costumes, see sculptures under construction, and visit Glen Randall while instructing the white horses and Yakima Canutt "who is said to be able to back a four-horse chariot into a tight parking spot and then have the lead horse put a nickel in the meter." They wander into various sets in Jerusalem, including the House of Hur. At this point Huntley reviews the story by "General Wallace" and reads a few brief passages from the novel. The three youths continue on to see a galley under construction and the hydraulics that provide a rocking motion and sit on the rowing benches. Inside a sound stage they catch a glimpse of Wyler, Heston, Cathy O'Donnell, and Martha Scott. Finally they climb onto a chariot as Huntley reads again from the novel, and a mounted camera tracks them from above. Huntley remarks that Wallace had exclaimed, "My God, did I set all this in motion?" to which he adds, "He could say that again in 1958!" The listing in the *Chicago Tribune* read, "Three Italian youths, hired as extras for 'Ben Hur,' romp thru the largest movie set ever built."[75]

The MGM production poured much of its $15 million budget into the Italian economy and added as many as 10,000 people to the Italian labor force in 1957 and 1958.[76] The construction of the eighteen-acre circus alone took 750 men almost a year and the sculpture department at Cinecittà employed another 200.[77] In the midst of a local economic depression even a call for bearded extras one day brought some 2000 to the gates. But the daily call varied, and in early June, 1958, on a day when the call was limited to 1500, several thousand Romans denied a day's work swarmed around the employee entrance, shouted insults, and threw stones.[78] When the riot police arrived, it took an hour to restore order. The syndicated UPI report stated that "some 3000 Romans threw stones and staged a brawl that was not in the script."

PUBLICITY

On his way to Rome in the late winter of 1958, Charlton Heston visited several European cities for interviews, marveling that MGM had arranged a full schedule of pre-publicity more than eighteen months before the film was to be released and before principle photography had commenced.[79] In fact, by February, 1958, MGM had officially announced its ambitious plan to make the press and public highly aware of *Ben-Hur* long before photography had been completed or the film released. At the same time *The Billboard* reported that to promote the film MGM would sell the soundtrack separately through MGM Records as a corporate tie-in.[80] MGM also wanted to make it clear to the industry that they intended to exploit this film thoroughly.

Once photography had commenced, an endless stream of VIPs, including the American Ambassador to Italy James Dunn and much of Rome's diplomatic corps, movie industry magnates and stars,[81] and over 1000 members of the American and European press, visited the Cinecittà complex.[82] Hedda Hopper was among them, and she wrote of the "thrill" she had riding beside "Ben Hur" as Heston drove her around the track in his *quadriga*.[83] When Vogel arrived the next day, Hopper asked him if he would take a ride, to which the manager of the entire project joked, "I couldn't afford it." Hopper, whose 1959 greetings card depicted her and

Heston standing on the *quadriga*, syndicated several items, including her meeting with Harareet, who had spent two years in the Israeli army but chose to hide her eyes (like Esther in the novel) when the two of them watched the filming of chariot mishaps.[84] She also reported that Wyler received letters from cast members of the 1925 production – Novarro, Bushman, Myers, Bronson – offering their services to advertise the film.[85] The *Los Angeles Times* ran a feature with photographs of the chariot race and impressive statistics, including the estimated $15 million budget.[86] Towards the end of June, TWA was advertising their Showplane to Europe, a 17-day tour that included the opportunity to visit the set and wear a costume.[87] Around the same time, Beth Hollinger, associate producer of NBC's *The Price is Right*, announced unique prizes for one lucky contestant – a horse and chariot plus a role in the *Ben-Hur* production.[88]

Throughout the summer, Hopper and other movie columnists, e.g. Hy Gardner of the *New York Herald Tribune*, circulated Heston's joke about his getting the role because Bushman was over seventy."[89] It did not hurt matters in July when Wyler asked Martha Scott to play the role of Miriam. The newspapers reveled in the idea that Scott had already played Heston's mother in *The Ten Commandments*.[90] This is also when Heston connected the two epic Ancients by saying that "It's getting so that I feel uncomfortable wearing pants."[91] Hiring Les Ballets Africans for the Arrius party sequence provided more fodder for the columnists,[92] as did hiring the tall operatic heldentenor Claude Heater to portray Jesus,[93] and the Italian starlet Marina Berti to take the role of Flavia.[94] Even Glenn Randall made the newspapers in August when asked if it had been difficult training the chariot horses:[95]

> Naw. Don't forget that I'm the guy who trained Trigger for Roy Rogers. I had to teach Trigger to count, dance the polka, and take bows. All these horses have to do is pull chariots that are equipped with ball bearings and hydraulic brakes.

Morgan Hudgins, MGM's public-relations rep stationed in Rome for the duration, forwarded to the *New York Times* that not only was this "the costliest movie ever made" but also "the most ambitious project ever undertaken by any film company anywhere."[96] Hudgins also reminded the public of the history of the property on the stage and screen, citing at his conclusion the long-term influence of the Kalem lawsuit.[97]

Through the AP MGM was already circulating pressbook features about the $1 million chariot race, Heston, and Harareet.[98] The *Chicago Tribune* advertised one of these features the day before its publication with alluring copy:

> Israel Beauty to Play Esther in "Ben Hur"
> One of the top movie roles of the year has gone to a rifle-carrying marine. Haya Harareet, a slow-eyed temptress type, has been cast to play Esther in a $14,000,000 new production of "Ben Hur." She served for two years in the Israeli marines and can handle a machine gun like a pro.[99]

Separately MGM sent special color postcards depicting Heston aboard his chariot to more than 20,000 exhibitors and press,[100] and an AP wire photo pictured a "modern chariot," Heston and Boyd riding on a Vespa. The good publicity created a new optimism. Loew's stock rose on the New York exchange, particularly when "annuity values," i.e. future rereleases, were factored in,[101] and in the next quarter Loew's would run a $2.6 million profit. In October MGM brought out newspaper features on Fry, explaining that he was on the set to doctor the script every day and arguing that he should therefore receive screen credit along with Tunberg.[102] Following the death of Zimbalist in November, MGM kept the show going by promoting Yakima Canutt's chariot race as "Rome's Big Wild-West Show,"[103] and over the next two months they produced features on the young Italian actress playing the Madonna (José Greci) and even on the dismantling of the set.[104]

At their annual meeting in February, 1959, Loew's officially announced that the film cost approximately $15 million.[105] This was more than $1 million over the previously announced budget, but Wyler explained that producing the film in California would have cost an additional $7 million.[106] But now that the money had been spent, the goal was to get it back, and more. At first, and in general, MGM publicity focused primarily on the artistic prestige of the film. They commissioned six paintings from the popular illustrator, Ben Stahl, and exhibited them at museums around the country, and distributed small replicas in a folder decorated with a panorama of the Antioch Circus and chariot race.[107] They laid plans to have a special ceremony at Wallace's statue in the Capitol's Statuary Hall on the general's 122nd birthday.[108] They announced through the movie columnists that they were looking to purchase copies of the first edition of the novel to use in theater displays.[109] Predictably, because of the confusion surrounding the first state binding of the first edition and the omnipresence of subsequent copies, they immediately received some 3000 responses – more than the number printed in 1880 – compelling them to issue an explanation of how to correctly identify the rare first edition of *Ben-Hur* with its floral cover, and listing at the end all the printed editions of the novel planned for 1959.[110] In another appeal to the novel's highly respected source, the company let it be known through Hopper that Crawfordsville was to be renamed Lew Wallace during the two weeks of the New York and Los Angeles premieres.[111] In early July, production chief Sol Siegel announced that as part of MGM's "tremendous exploitation program" the company planned a documentary short subject titled *Two Magic Words* to be filmed in Crawfordsville.[112] Cities like Oklahoma City and Minneapolis were offered an art exhibit of pre-production pencil sketches.[113]

Over the summer, as the 1.25 million feet of film were being cut to a little over four hours, the company itself took on a more commercial guise. Phone calls were being answered, "MGM, good afternoon, *Ben-Hur* is coming."[114] William Robinson, Chairman of Coca-Cola, agreed to let MGM use its 110-foot sign along the New Jersey Turnpike for the message, "Ben-Hur is coming!"[115] And on July 26, Ed Sullivan showed a film clip of his chariot ride with Heston on his highly rated television variety show on CBS.[116] Sullivan would reuse the footage to introduce his Christmas show on December 27, 1959. The latter, following the release of the film, featured Heston reading passages from "The Five Books of Moses."[117] Addressing the press, Vogel described the progress of Loew's overseas arrangements:

> Plans now being worked out between our London organization and the home office for the launching of "Ben-Hur" abroad are of a stature commensurate with the size of the attractions, and when they are ready for announcement they will fit into the category of "They said it couldn't be done."[118]

By the end of August, MGM moved "into high gear."[119] They underwrote a Sindlinger & Company survey to confirm that 534 of every 1000 people "knew about" *Ben-Hur*, the highest percentage ever recorded for an upcoming film. The same survey found that 42.2 percent of respondents preferred a religious theme over either romance or action/vengeance, and that over 50 percent preferred the use of the subtitle "A Tale of the Christ."[120] Addressing the educational and religious attraction to *Ben-Hur*, MGM inserted the subtitle in their advertising, targeted public and parochial schools by commissioning a secular study guide, written and co-edited by Joseph Mersand, then president of the National Council of Teachers of English, and the *Catholic School Supplement "Ben-Hur" Study Guide* by the Rev. Dr. Leo J. McCormick.[121] The former included a list of questions for discussion, while the latter was a fold-out format that displayed eight stills of religious scenes in the film, plus five of Stahl's paintings on the other side. A boxed announcement on the rear labeled "School Theatre Parties" encourages arranging extra morning showings at a reduced rate for students. It also suggests celebrating the eightieth anniversary of the novel in their schools and libraries, and writing the Educational Division, BEN-HUR, in New York. They also planned to provide adult groups with lecturers. As in 1925, when Loew's helped local librarians to display copies of *Ben-Hur: A Tale of the Christ*, the Boston Public Library arranged an exhibit of translations of the novel.[122]

Once theater managers booked roadshow engagements, they were assisted by an MGM Field Press Representative in planning their promotional campaign through the National Screen Service, MGM, and the pressbook. Thick, detailed, and comprehensive, printed in an exceptionally large format and updated as the film gained in prominence, the 37-page pressbook ("Exhibitor's Promotion Portfolio") contained much more than the usual announcement and feature stories, captioned photographs, and newspaper layouts. There were nearly fifty layouts and mats ranging from one to six columns, Julius Kroll caricatures, and a 1300-word "Facts and Figures" column. Exhibitors were offered lobby and window cards, flags, valance

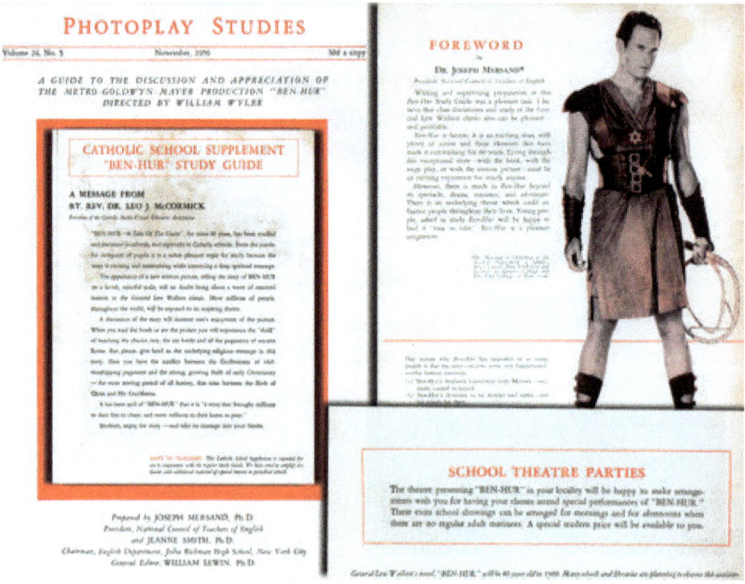

Figure 14.1 MGM marketed *Ben-Hur* as an educational product to public and private schools and churches by printing study and teaching guides.

and streamer displays, copies of the Ben Stahl paintings, and brown prints reproducing many of the original production sketches. One of the featured items was the giant standee that won first prize in the National Off-set Lithographic Awards Competition.[123] It stood 10-feet high and 8-feet wide at its base, with a blend of Stahl paintings surrounding the unique, colossal *Ben-Hur* stone typography and lit by lights from below. Throughout the pressbook are numerous versions of the iconic stone typography Joseph J. Smith developed for the film.[124] The more elaborate version piled the syllable BEN- upon HUR in a monumental, three-dimensional structure appearing to be chiseled from stone of such colossal size that it incorporated a massive colonnade and supported throngs of spectators looking down upon the chariot race and one of the equally iconic *spina* sculptures. Many printings of this logo include Smith's signature along the lower left part of the ground line. Another, more commonly printed version arranged the syllables horizontally following a stereoscopic convex curve, precluding the spectators above. These stone logos appeared in newspapers throughout the country for many years.

The pressbook gave detailed suggestions on how to ensure a successful presentation by checking the projection equipment, curvature of the screen, house and stage lights, and the sound system, especially the balance of the rear speakers enabling the "surround speaker effects" from the fourth sound track on even 35mm prints, beginning the 3-hour, 50-minute presentation (with the 6-minute overture and 15-minute intermission) on

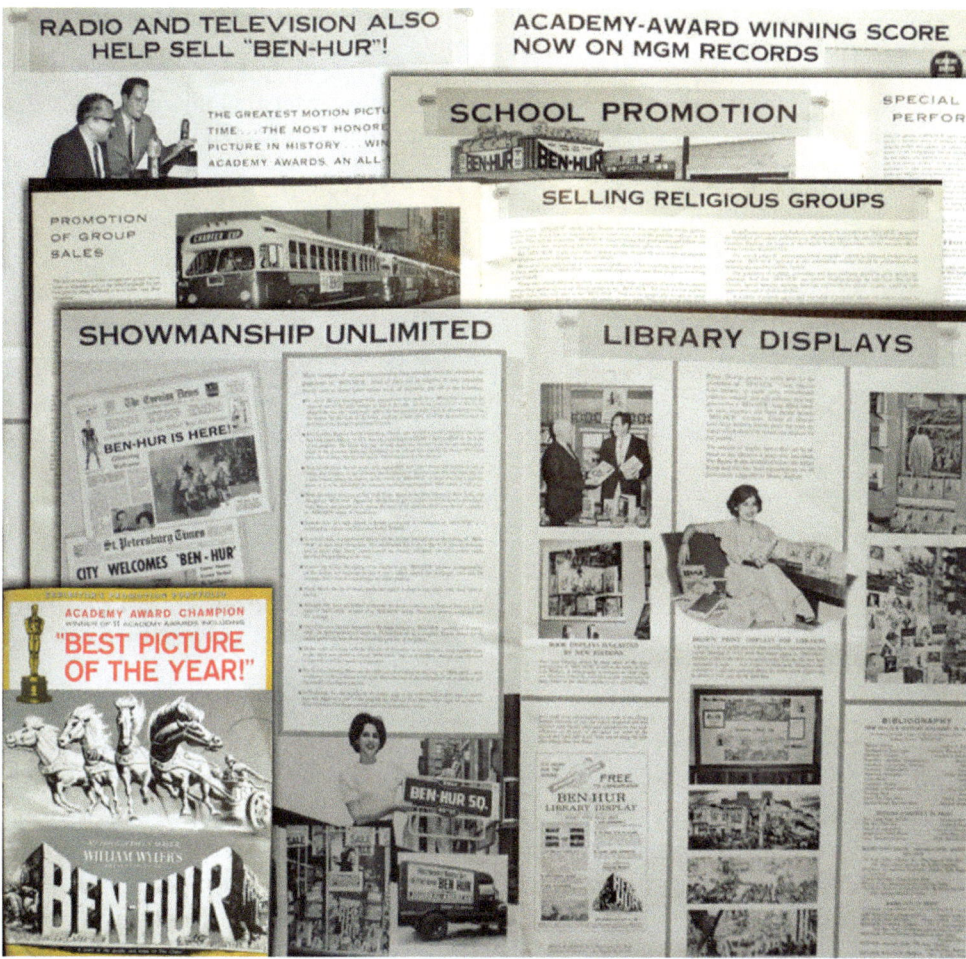

Figure 14.2 The large-format MGM Pressbook assisted exhibitors in promoting the film in contemporary media with innovative schemes while also marketing to institutions and groups.

time, and being "certain to use a hyphen between Ben and Hur" on the marquee. As in the Klaw & Erlanger performances, theater managers were instructed not to allow any seating during the 7-minute Nativity scene. And they insisted that no other music be played at any time during the engagement other than what was on the sound track: "To do so would completely destroy the mood established by the Academy-Award winning composer, Miklós Rózsa."

MGM made it very clear that this was not standard procedure. The first page of the pressbook says:

> Generally speaking, BEN-HUR will attract not only your regular patrons, but those who attend only the very best of any form of entertainment. Your entire staff

should be briefed on handling the huge attendance that will suddenly fill your house within a twenty-minute period prior to advertised performance times....

The magnitude, the dignity, the importance of "BEN-HUR" must all be expressed in your front. And the display matter prepared by Metro-Goldwyn-Mayer will enable you to create a front of unusual magnificence at nominal cost to you.

The pressbook also sought to inspire creative managers to arrange a special edition of a local newspaper covering the entire front page with *Ben-Hur* headlines, photos, and features (London; St. Petersburg), stage chariot races for youths (Pittsburgh), set up lobby displays in resort hotels (Miami), and coordinate with the local Chamber of Commerce to place the *Ben-Hur* logo in members' shop windows (San Francisco). The pressbook offered additional full-page instructions and suggestions for advertising beyond the usual newspaper outlets and to various groups of potential patrons. Radio and television spots were still a relatively untapped media for film promotions, so MGM offered four transcribed interview records with Heston, Hawkins, and Harareet as well as 20-, 30-, and 60-second spots. They suggested television round-table discussions with a clergyman, school principle, civic personality, and a movie critic, and providing *Ben-Hur* licensed toys as prizes for kiddie shows. An entire page was devoted to books and library displays, another to recordings and sheet music of Miklós Rósza's score along with the names, addresses, and phone numbers of three dozen distributors of MGM Records, and still another to "off-theatre" pages emphasizing Jewish and Christian history for church listing pages, the size of the 70mm image for television pages, chariot race imagery for sports pages, and the love story for women's pages. Whole pages were also devoted to group sales, particularly schools and religious groups. MGM recommended contacting superintendents, principles, and mothers superior, and distributing as promotional material the specially prepared educational pamphlets by McCormick and Mersand. They also prepared an educational 35mm film strip for use at schools, churches, and civic club luncheons.[125] After the film won so many Oscars, a new edition was issued, perpetuating MGM's direct intervention for another half year. A separate British pressbook recommended offering group sales to factories and Boy Scout and Girl Scout groups. It also contained a "painting block" outline of a chariot race still for distribution in schools, libraries, bookshops, and recreation areas, recommending advertising a painting contest in local newspapers.

MGM appointed Howard Strickland to oversee their $1,750,000 newspaper ad budget, $200,000 of that targeted for the November 18 New York premiere alone. The general public was soon bombarded with newspaper features, press interviews, and radio and television appearances by Heston, Boyd, and Harareet, "a heavenly body going into orbit."[126] The latter appeared on NBC's *Today* the week before the premiere.[127] Jack Hawkins was given a newspaper feature asserting the authenticity of the film's naval battle.[128] Martha Scott discussed her hairdo.[129] Other features focused on the chariot race, whether in the form of a personal account by Heston,[130] or a narrative disclaimer that none of the drivers, spectators, or horses had been injured during filming.[131] (Joe Canutt's accident was not acknowledged until later.)[132] Boston in particular received a blitz. Prior to its November 24 premiere at the Saxon, there were articles in the *Boston Globe* on November 1, 4, 5, and 15. The last of these was a large pictorial with six photos related to the chariot race.[133] On November 2 Heston came to the city for press interviews and to address Boston University and Harvard students on "Motion Pictures as an Art and Career."[134] The day after the Saxon premiere, MGM scheduled him to appear as Santa Claus for Hollywood's Thanksgiving parade.[135] None of this was standard procedure for a movie release in 1959.

Wyler, dispatched to Boston, Philadelphia, New York, and London, presented the larger perspective, assuring readers that he would not have made the film if it were only a spectacle that could not engage an audience:

> The spectacular sequences ... take up only about 45 minutes of the film. They are great because by the time they come the audience cares terribly about what happens to Ben-Hur because of the story with which they've become emotionally involved. It's basic that spectacle for the sake of spectacle means absolutely nothing. When "Ben-Hur" has spectacle, it means much – to the story, the characters, and, most important, to the audience.[136]

In contrast, across the Atlantic, *The Guardian* featured Christopher Fry and simply his happy return to traditional theater as soon as he finished his work on *Ben-Hur*.[137] *The Irish Times* published a still photo from the Via Dolorosa sequence, making sure to say in the caption, "Throughout the film the face of Christ is never seen nor His voice heard."[138]

Other features reviewed the history of the Ben-Hur tradition from the novel to the Kalem film to the 1925 film.[139] In three separate articles *American Cinematographer* examined the skill applied by Robert Surtees, Piero Portalupi, and Harold E. Wellman in adapting the Panavision cameras, their lenses and filters, and the Eastman Color film to the variable light quality of the Roman sun, the shifting color temperatures, and challenging action sequences.[140] The week before the premiere, Earl Wilson in his nationally syndicated column, "It Happened Last Night," suggested as a publicity slogan: "'Ben-Hur' will be the greatest thing since 'Ben-Hur.'"[141] Wallace's participation was frequently invoked. The pictorial in the November 8 *New York Times* was introduced by the quote, "My God! Did I set all this in motion."[142] With intended irony under the headline "Clouded Crystal Ball," *Variety* reminded readers that Lew Wallace had said that he wished it understood that *Ben-Hur* would not be dramatized and that "it is not likely that I will ever sell such a privilege."[143] The reader may find additional irony in a *New York Herald Tribune* note reporting that MGM used three indicators to track the success of their publicity campaign: (1) ticket sales at Loew's State and elsewhere, (2) the number of phone calls to ticket offices, and (3) the regularity with which newspapers correctly included the hyphen in the name Ben-Hur.[144]

EXHIBITION PREPARATIONS

As in the early 1920s, Goldwyn and then MGM assumed *Ben-Hur* to be worthy of epic treatment, and now in the 1950s MGM was again handling it as an extraordinary property. Normal industry or company business models would not provide a satisfactory exhibition scheme suitable for such a unique blockbuster. In the 1950s this meant employing a technical system that would make *Ben-Hur* appear larger than life, indeed, of epic proportions. Before shooting began, Zimbalist tempted future audiences by suggesting that the chariot race might be shot in Cinerama: the film would be shown in the widescreen format until the chariot race scene, when two extended screens would be opened up.[145] Eventually he decided upon the 65mm Panavision system that had been used to film MGM's *Raintree County*, although that film had been exhibited in the usual 35mm. The Camera 65 system could produce sharp close-ups and stunning widescreen effects in the theater, although, as we will see, it would take a major investment on the part of theater managers to accommodate it.[146]

The huge scope of a *Ben-Hur* filmed and projected in a newly developed widescreen format was designed in part to lure homebound television audiences to the theater. When asked about the difference between television and widescreen films, Zimbalist commented in April, 1958, "'Ben-Hur' on a small screen would seem ridiculous."[147] Similarly, when asked if *Ben-Hur* might be presented on television some day, Wyler commented, "I hope I never live to see the day."[148] Rod Serling elsewhere added that television could not provide the physical scope for such an epic.[149] It would seem that the two types of media could not be further apart when it came to exhibiting *Ben-Hur*, but in the summer of 1958 David Suskind, the leading television producer in New York, announced that his production company, Talent Associates, was preparing a two-hour, live television performance of *Ben-Hur* at a cost of some $450,000 and that it would be broadcast before the MGM film was released.[150] This turned out to be a negotiating ploy, but MGM succumbed to the threat and gave Suskind what he wanted – the rights to a dozen or so MGM properties, like *Ninotchka* and *Mrs. Miniver*.[151] Almost as immediately as it was reported in the press, came an announcement that Suskind's project had been canceled,[152] but in the years in which Hollywood films only occasionally appeared on television, this new arrangement enabled him to expand his empire considerably. Although not initiated by MGM, this unexpected synergy demonstrates both the anticipation and the special circumstances that this MGM *Ben-Hur* would inspire and occasion for an entire decade.

Exhibitor interest was already so strong that theater owners willingly paid for extensive and costly renovations so they could show the film with state-of-the-art 70mm equipment that projected the 65mm film and played the additional 5mm magnetic soundtrack in six-channel stereophonic sound.[153] Loew's State Theatre on Broadway was renovated at a cost of $800,000 specifically to accommodate *Ben-Hur*, and the manager of the United Artists Theatres Circuit signed a contract with Siegel to guarantee that the film would play at the Hollywood Egyptian Theater for two years,[154] as did Boston's Saxon Theatre,[155] reported as the longest guaranteed first run in movie history.[156] Benjamin Sack, owner and operator of the Boston venue, boasted, "You will see a new look very soon. . . . The Saxon Theater sign will be replaced by one heralding the coming of 'Ben-Hur.' It will be a flashing sign and it will be there months before the film is shown."[157] As part of its remodeling plans, the Egyptian Theater forecourt would now include a museum to display weapons, set decorations, costumes, and jewelry from the *Ben-Hur* production. Helping to generate additional audience enthusiasm, MGM was shipping eight of its chariots back from Rome to display in such promotional venues.[158]

Other major metropolitan theater managers emulated these flagship theaters. The Columbia Theater in Washington, DC underwent $900,000 worth of rebuilding. As with local bookings of the Klaw & Erlanger *Ben-Hur* at the turn of the century, signing long-term exhibitor contracts with MGM became a matter of local pride. When a two-year deal was signed with Philadelphia's Boyd Theatre, the *Philadelphia Tribune* pointed out that Philadelphia had been a leader in the sales of the original novel, made history with its bookings of the Klaw & Erlanger production, and proclaimed that the deal to play the highly anticipated MGM *Ben-Hur* involved "more money, longer playing time, and greater long-range preparation than any similar deal in local amusement history."[159]

Much more so than in 1925, MGM's initial planning included an ambitious international program. Already during the preparation for post-production, Vogel flew to the West Coast in early February not only to view four hours of footage and consult with Siegel about editing and scoring, but also to lay the groundwork for international distribution to be discussed at meetings that would be held in Madrid, Tokyo, and Mexico City in April.[160] By July the Famous Players chain in Canada announced that they had booked *Ben-Hur* for exclusive one-year engagements in Toronto, Montreal, and Vancouver,[161] and that Vancouver's Capital Theater had to be closed for extensive renovations.[162] The same was true for Tokyo's Urakuza.[163] MGM paid for similar kinds of alterations to its Empire Theatre in London.[164] To accommodate the widescreen there, seating capacity had to be drastically reduced by 72 percent, but the company was confident that the long run of *Ben-Hur* – ultimately seventy-six weeks – would more than compensate. More so than for any prior film, theater bookings were long term, international, and worthy of general press releases in addition to numerous trade announcements.

Some smaller exhibitors were so eager to sign a deal that they were ready to print up reserved-seat tickets and sell them months in advance,[165] this despite a preliminary warning to its members by the Theatre Owners of America that relatively few 65mm and 70mm features were in the pipeline.[166] MGM countered confidently. They announced in late June that they would set up ticket offices at New York's Times Square and Los Angeles' famed intersection at Hollywood & Vine to accommodate the thousands of summer travelers visiting those two tourist-filled cities.[167] Visitors interested in seeing *Ben-Hur* in their local theaters could give their names and addresses to the MGM ticket reps, and then MGM would turn these lists over to local theater managers back home. This petition system was designed to supply managers with signatures from thousands of committed ticket buyers, who in turn would receive preferential seating treatment. By August, theaters in thirteen cities had committed to long-term exclusive contracts, and many of them aggressively sought group sales.[168] Boston, where the John Hancock insurance company pre-purchased 5000 tickets as subsidized entertainment for its employees, had a group-bookings phone number,[169] and MGM would soon establish a special nationwide sales promotion unit targeting "fraternal, social, industrial, educational, and business organizations."[170]

As another indicator of the heightened anticipation on the part of theater managers, in June Chicago's *Daily Defender* proudly announced that Chicago would be one of the first cities to see the five-year, $15 million production.[171] At the time, pickups were still being shot,[172] and although booking arrangements were not at all settled, the paper boasted that the film would arrive "some time between Thanksgiving and New Year's ... on a road-show, reserved-seat basis ten times per week with matinees Wednesdays, Saturdays, and Sundays and additional morning shows for theater parties booked in advance." Three months later several Chicago theater managers were still bidding against one another, including the Balaban & Katz Theater that had previously maintained a standing aversion to roadshow arrangements.[173] The Todd Theater won the bidding, and then, like the venues in other cities, immediately had to go dark for several months while being renovated for 70mm.[174] Meanwhile, the release of *Spartacus*, also in 70mm, had to be delayed because of all the prior, exclusive *Ben-Hur* engagements.[175]

MGM had let it be known during the summer of 1959 that there would be no sneak preview until Rózsa's score was recorded. Often sneak previews were accompanied by canned music, but MGM was insisting on treating the score as both integral to the film and a separately marketable product.[176] Rózsa recorded the score in eleven sessions of three days separated by two weeks during the months of June, July, and August, 1959.[177]

In September, when the film had been edited and Rózsa's score laid on the 5mm tracks, the company announced it would offer only the "sneakiest sneak" to be disclosed only a few hours before showing.[178] In mid-September they offered sneaks in Denver and Dallas (Palace), and then a third at the Capri Theater in San Diego – to a standing-room-only audience.[179] Dozens of local theaters in Texas agreed to run *Ben-Hur* trailers even though the film would be exhibited as a roadshow in only a single urban venue.[180] There was an additional recording session on October 9 to adjust the score to Wyler's late changes,[181] including the aforementioned pickups shot in the Arizona desert and at the Metro studios,[182] and then MGM turned over the approximately 19,000 feet of *Ben-Hur* to the Technicolor laboratories to prepare the release prints, which had been edited to a reported three hours, thirty-seven minutes, three minutes less than *Gone With the Wind*, two less than *The Ten Commandments*.[183] (Subsequently the running length would be reported as 213 and ultimately 212 minutes.)[184]

At this point ads for tickets began to appear in the New York papers,[185] although more than 20,000 tickets had already been sold for Loew's State in New York.[186] The Variety Club of New York alone had bought out the entire house for November 20,[187] and MGM agreed to show the film on November 24 at the Egyptian Theater as a black-tie benefit for the Medical School Scholarship Fund of the University of Southern California.[188] Without a dress code, a special New York showing on November 19 was for the benefit of the Police Athletic League.[189] The November 9, 1959, issue of *Boxoffice* included, in an otherwise black-and-white issue, a large color photo of Heston driving his white horses in the chariot race and a full-page, color fold-out poster of *Ben-Hur*, "A Momentous Event in Motion Picture History," with a listing on the back of premiere dates and locations for the next six months.[190] The run-up to the premiere gained so much momentum that the RKO Theaters chain took out a large ad in the *New York Times* to congratulate MGM for creating "one of the great entertainment experiences of all time" and asserting that it was a "credit to the entire Motion Picture Industry."[191] RKO theaters even ran one of the two trailers for *Ben-Hur*.[192]

Richard Coe of *The Washington Post* reported on November 13 that the world premiere would be held the next day in Crawfordsville and that the post office would "salute" the event.[193] This was not true. Crawfordsville did have a celebration that weekend, but it was for the "beginning of the 80th year of publication of the famous novel by Lew Wallace."[194] One of the organizers interviewed by the press insisted that it was not the film premiere but the impending Civil War centennial that prompted the ceremonies, but the same article listed a number of high points in the *Ben-Hur* tradition in film and radio.[195] The ceremonies featured the display of Wallace's original manuscript, on loan from the Indiana University Library, insured for $100,000 and under armed guard, at the Lew Wallace Study. They concluded with a gift of twenty-eight copies of the novel translated into different languages presented to the Crawfordsville Library, and a speech by Cecil M. Harden, former Indiana congresswoman and now serving as special assistant for women's affairs to the postmaster general. According to the Indiana papers, the post office "authorized a special envelope." As a side note, the convergence of the Civil War centennial and the release of *Ben-Hur* inspired Jack Pearl's thirteen-page "book-length" magazine feature in *Climax*, "Lew 'Ben-Hur' Wallace: Scapegoat of the Union Army."[196] The last page of the article is devoted to a survey of the *Ben-Hur* tradition.

In the *Wall Street Journal* Vogel assured Loew's shareholders that despite the $15 million price tag plus a similar sum for prints, advertising, and distribution costs,[197] and despite the reality that "few movies have ever pulled in that much revenue," he was "undismayed," basing that on *The Ten Commandments*' $39 million box-office receipts as a minimum, and eyeing *Gone With the Wind*'s $50 million, the sum realized during its original 1939 release and four initial rereleases.[198] Another positive was that unlike many of the contemporary epics, *Ben-Hur* was a studio production, so none of the revenue had to be shared with an independent producer – except for the percentage due Wyler.[199] To increase revenue many exhibitors charged a record $3.50 for a reserved weekend or holiday seat, $1 or more than contemporary premium seats, and in turn MGM charged more than the usual 30 percent rental charge.[200] *Ben-Hur* hard-ticket sales even became the subject of a special feature in the *New York Times*.[201] And in yet another innovative fiscal synergy, American Express, which had just begun issuing credit cards in 1957, announced that they were working out an arrangement that would allow cardholders to purchase *Ben-Hur* tickets on credit.[202]

BEN-HUR IN THE THEATERS

Premieres

The *Wall Street Journal* had already reported in May that Philip Miles' prestigious Forum of the 12 Caesars planned a premiere party.[203] Now *Variety* celebrated the premiere of *Ben-Hur* in its November 18 issue by printing two page-one articles, two more on page three, and another four further in.[204] It also offered a review and a list of sixty-three cast members and their roles. The excitement ranged well beyond the trades. Already in January, 1959, *Life*, with its circulation of 6.4 million, had run a three-page color pictorial of the chariot race, including two shots from above the *spina*, two of Heston at track level, and another of the crowd of extras.[205] The November 16, 1959, issue of *Life* contained Robert Coughlan's sixteen-page article on Lew Wallace and the *Ben-Hur* tradition.[206] "The General's Mighty Chariots" begins with a large-format copy of the Thomas B. Nicholson photograph of Wallace sitting beneath the famous beech tree in Crawfordsville, and lavishes its space on the legendary successes of the Klaw & Erlanger production and the 1925 film before describing the extraordinary career of Lew Wallace. Three weeks later the "Letters to the Editor" helped demonstrate that the tradition was still thriving.[207] One was from Kenyon Nicholson, who wrote that he was six years old when he handed the dry plates to his father to take the famous photograph of Wallace. Another was from Carmel Myers, who included a current photograph of herself at her daughter's wedding. Subsequent magazine articles on *Ben-Hur* in *The Saturday Evening Post* and *Look* would concentrate on Heston's celebrity and his custom-built house above Beverly Hills.[208]

Because advance sales had already reached 100,000, there was no need for additional newspaper publicity for the Loew's State premiere.[209] In attendance at the opening were Wyler, Heston, Harareet, Boyd, and Scott as well as Loew's and MGM executives like Vogel and Siegel and other industry titans including Jack Warner, Spyros Skouras, and Adoph Zukor.[210] Representing the *Ben-Hur* tradition were Ramon Novarro and Mabel Brownell, who had played the role of Esther for Klaw & Erlanger in 1907.[211] A photograph of Heston and Novarro posing together was immediately circulated in newspapers,[212] and Hearst's *News of the Day* prepared a two-minute short-film, "The Night *Ben-Hur* Comes to Broadway," and circulated it to theaters as a news trailer (now a featurette on the DVD). That same day, as Wall Streeters nervously focused on the $15 million in negative costs, Vogel soothed their anxiety by referring to the perennial and frequent successes of the *Ben-Hur* tradition:

> I know of no bigger box office property than "Ben-Hur." And that's not because it's ours. Whether it has been a show, a picture, a circus, or whatever the attraction, I am as positive as whatever is today's date that "Ben-Hur" will top everything for theatrical box office performance.[213]

Tickets for the November 24 black-tie premier at the Egyptian Theater cost $25, $50, and $100. In addition to many of the same *Ben-Hur* principals at a Brown Derby dinner for University of Southern California administrators,[214] *News of the Day* made sure to include Debbie Reynolds, Tony Randall, and Clark Gable in its film coverage, as well as a lingering shot on Messala's chariot. One *Los Angeles Times* columnist added that Ronald Reagan was in attendance, and "Ham on Ryon," made a comment intended for California residents who knew well of Ben-Hur Coffee:

> It runs something like 3 hours and 35 minutes. So, naturally, they have an intermission coffee break. Be funny if they served Hills Bros[215]

The *Times* building must have been buzzing. Columnist Philip Scheuer reported that despite the celebrity gathering, the usual Grauman's forecourt festivities were muted, as was the MGM lion at the beginning of the film, in keeping with the spirit of a "Tale of the Christ."[216] And even Albert Goldberg, *Times* music critic, wrote a few days later of the Los Angeles Philharmonic's rendition of Respighi's *Roman Festivals* that it must be "the noisiest and emptiest piece of claptrap ever written for a symphony orchestra. All it lacked was the chariot race from 'Ben-Hur' on the screen."[217]

The Washington, DC premiere attracted government officials and diplomatic representatives from such distant countries as Ghana and the Philippines as well as Mikhail Menchikov, the ambassador from the Soviet Union.[218] In London the film premiered on December 16, and the following February 18 the Royal Air Force Band performed for a Royal Gala Film Performance attended by the Duke and Duchess of Gloucester.[219] In early September the film premiered in another gala event at Dublin's Ambassador and had its first British showing outside London at Birmingham's Bristol Road.[220] In *Variety's* characteristic prose, "It was an 'all seats sold' affair attended by local big shots." The same issue announced the premiere in Glasgow and "big advanced sales" for the Japanese cities of Sapporo and Nagoya, where three weeks after the box office opened 18,900 tickets had been sold. *News of the Day* covered the gala Tokyo premiere attended by Heston as well as members of the imperial family, including the emperor and empress who were making this their first outing to a public movie theater.[221] The Tokyo venue did not have an empty seat during the first ten weeks of *Ben-Hur*'s engagement.[222] Elsewhere in Asia, Manila's Ideal Theatre, where the film premiered in July, 1960, already had a $250,000 advance sale.

Reviews
Many critics recognized the monumentality of the project and professed their admiration for its accomplishment. *Variety* led with a page-one headline: "Towering B.O. Stature of 'Ben-Hur' Vindicates Joe Vogel's Metro Team."[223] Without naming names, Philip K. Scheuer of the *Los Angeles Times* congratulated "some of the most seasoned minds in Hollywood and their combined know-how."

> MGM has delivered the "Ben-Hur" it promised. It is, whatever the minor pros and cons that will rage over it, magnificent, inspiring, awesome, enthralling and all the other adjectives you have been reading about.[224]

The syndicated Jack Gaver observed the positives for which Zimbalist hired Wyler:

> Spectacle piles upon spectacle in color and via the big-screen Camera 65 process, but there are also genuine warmth and fervor and finely acted intimate scenes that keep the picture as a whole from being classed as merely another super-spec.[225]

Fighting his distaste for the relentless spate of biblical movies in the mid/late 1950s and then singling out *Ben-Hur* as an "unexpected consummation," Bosley Crowther of the *New York Times* conceded that this was "the sturdiest 'Bible movie' ever made."[226] Marjory Adams of the *Boston Globe* went further by recognizing the film's "double appeal – that of faith and divine love on one side, and the attraction of a courageous man fighting adversity and tyranny."[227] Ben Kubasik of *Newsday* described the chariot race as "the most brilliant camera footage ever filmed,"[228] and Scheuer echoed that it "marks an all-time peak in action attained by any camera anywhere." Along these same lines, *Variety* predicted that the chariot race "will probably be preserved in film archives as the finest example of the use of the motion picture camera to record an action sequence."[229]

The flood of exuberantly phrased kudos filled the larger newspaper display ads with bold-faced superlatives like:

MAGNIFICENT ACHIEVEMENT IN MOVIEMAKING
[L.A. MIRROR-NEWS]
A TRUE GIANT OF THE SCREEN . . .
[L.A. HERALD-EXPRESS]
ONE OF THE GREATEST PICTURES OF ALL TIME . . .
[HOLLYWOOD CITIZEN-NEWS]
ONE OF THE BEST, IF NOT THE BEST MOTION PICTURE. I HAVE EVER SEEN.
[LOUELLA PARSONS] [230]

MGM used these and many more like them from newspapers and magazines to fill a six-page company advertisement in *Variety*.[231] The huge ad also included several "religious commendations" from the likes of Norman Vincent Peale ("a superb picture . . . true to the Bible") and Francis Harmon of the National Council of Churches of Christ ("an important, positive contribution of lasting value to millions").

Crowther was one of the few commentators to mention any contemporary political relevance. He wrote that "in the burgeoning of hatred in Ben-Hur one can sense the fierce passion for revenge that must have moved countless tormented people in Poland and Hungary." Wyler would concur with this assessment in interviews for the 1969 rerelease. Crowther also understood that a significant part of the film's success was owed to "old General" Wallace's original story:

> Whatever doubts or misgivings this sideline observer may have had at the prospect of a modern-day film version of the old Gen. Lew Wallace novel, "Ben Hur," were thoroughly dissipated. . . . The reason is very simple and should, from this moment forward, be etched in the consciousness and concept of everyone who aims to make a similar film. It is that the picture's creators have exercised plain integrity – in digging for the novel's basic story and in making it graphic on the screen.

However, in tracing the unique *Ben-Hur* tradition, Crowther almost inadvertently destroyed an important part of it – a rare print of the 1925 film. The last paragraph of his review begins with high praise for the technical achievements of the 1959 version: "Much more could be said in praise of the technical quality of this film, which vastly surpasses the silent version of the same story released back in 1926." When William K. Everson, already an important collector of silent films and a tireless advocate for the long-forgotten medium, read this in the *Times*, his defiant response was to exhibit his unauthorized 16mm print of the synchronized sound version of the 1925/1931 *Ben-Hur* at the Huff Film Society in New York.[232] According to Kevin Brownlow, for whom Everson was a mentor, a competitor notified the FBI, and they seized the print.[233] It required the testimony of Lillian Gish to free Everson from government suspicion, thereby preserving the print of *Ben-Hur* from its possible destruction.[234] Both Brownlow and Everson later maintained in their books on silent cinema that the 1925 *Ben-Hur* was far superior to the remake. Everson in particular wrote:

> By any standards, [the 1925 *Ben-Hur*] is far superior to the abysmal 1959 remake, with its snail's pace and ineptly amateurish miniatures used in the sea battle. Its well staged chariot race, full of brilliantly executed stunts, was certainly the saving grace of the film, but even it lacked the majesty and pomp of the original sequence. (The granting of a dozen Academy Awards to the remake was the final insult!)[235]

Only a few others shared their negative reactions of the film. Most damning was Kubasik, who in saying that the rest of the "tired and sorry spectacle" was "pedestrian and ponderous" and had a "pretentious and unbelievable plot" demonstrated a dislike for the genre, not to mention an unfamiliarity with Josephus and late nineteenth-century religious novels. Paul V. Beckley, by commenting in the *New York Herald Tribune* that the film was "crammed with incident," unknowingly addressed the very word Charlton Lewis in 1880 used in lamenting what the novel lacked.[236] But Beckley, like several others writing otherwise positive reviews, found the film to be excessively gory. He wrote that the film "squirms with energy and is at times so brutal that one feels impelled to warn the squeamish." For him the chariot race was "about as bloody and furious as anything on film," and he thought that the message of spiritual cleansing expressed by the blood and rain running along the ground at the climax of the Crucifixion might be lost in the "physical horror." In fact, the American Humane Association insisted that three seconds of footage showing horses falling "in a tangle of chariot wheels and traces" be removed because they suggested "apparent cruelty."[237] Both Scheuer and Adams struggled with the length of the film and some of its parts, particularly "those agonizing pictures of the lepers." The most self-conflicted seemed to be the reviewer for *The Irish Times*, who although ultimately recommending the film, objected to the length, the music ("a lush bit of Hollywood orientalism"), and the ever-present consciousness that "the primary purpose of the piece is to make money."[238]

Awards and Controversy

During these same first few months, the film was nominated for and received an unprecedented number of peer and critics' awards. On April 4, 1960, it won eleven Academy Awards, a record at the time and not tied until thirty-nine years later. The awards won by *Ben-Hur* were in the categories for Best Picture (Zimbalist), Best Director (Wyler), Best Actor in a Leading Role (Heston), Best Actor in a Supporting Role (Griffith), Best Cinematography (Surtees), Best Art Direction [Set Decoration-Color] (Hornung, Carfagno, Hunt), Best Costume Design [Color] (Haffenden), Best Sound Recording (Milton), Best Film Editing (Winters, Dunning), Best Special Effects (Gillespie, MacDonald, Lory), and Best Dramatic or Comedy Score (Rózsa). The film also won Golden Globes for Best Motion Picture, Director, and Supporting Actor (Boyd), the BAFTA Award for Best Film, and the New York Film Critics Circle Award for Best Film. Rózsa's score was nominated for a Grammy Award.

The NBC broadcast of the Academy ceremonies, hosted by Bob Hope, was viewed in thirty million homes and, through kinescopes and radio, reached an estimated worldwide audience of 250 million persons.[239] They all had the opportunity to hear Charlton Heston speak the unmentionable by giving special thanks to Christopher Fry. This was in response to the controversy over the nomination of Karl Tunberg for the Best Writing [Adapted], which he did not win. This controversy would not concern us except that it burst out into the public arena in late October, 1959, just a few weeks before the New York premiere, and immediately had some effect on the reception of *Ben-Hur*. Critics addressed the issue, but it also served as widely promulgated if unintended publicity for MGM that lasted for a full year. At this point more than fifty years later, it has become a part of the *Ben-Hur* legacy. Also, as we have seen, it was because of the controversy that the relevant correspondence between Wyler, MGM, and the Guild, was preserved, correspondence that was helpful for sorting out the contributions by the many different screenwriters.

We know from an on-set interview in Rome with Philip K. Scheuer of the *Times* that shortly before his death in November, 1958, Zimbalist had begun the campaign to have Fry receive co-credit.[240] The following February 20, Loew's, Inc. made the formal request to the Writers Guild of America, which had sole jurisdiction, to have both Tunberg and Fry credited.[241] When Vidal learned of this, he lodged his own request on March 9, for Guild guidelines stipulated that a writer had to be responsible for at least one third of the script, and, as we have seen, Vidal maintained that at least one third of the script was his work.[242] The dispute was to undergo the regular procedure overseen by the Guild's Credits Arbitration Committee, a panel of three anonymous referees that independently scrutinized the written materials submitted to them. Loew's had submitted two scripts, but these predated most of Fry's changes and could not, of course, reflect the release version of the film, which would not be completed for several more months.

By mid-June the panel members had unanimously decided that Tunberg deserved sole credit.[243] This is when Wyler wrote to the Guild's Executive Director, Michael H. Franklin, to explain that "at least ninety per cent of the added dialogue and rewritten scenes was done during, or just prior to, the time of photography of each scene involved." He also pointed out that Fry contributed to "the writing of many visual and silent scenes of considerable imagination" that would not have been evident from the submitted scripts. Tunberg did not need to argue his own case in public at this point except to tell *Variety* that he had begun work on the script in 1953, worked on it for two years and eight months, and sent additional scenes and dialogue to Zimbalist in Rome.[244] We know independently that he also sent material to Wyler during post-production in California.

Normally a unanimous decision by the Guild's committee could not be appealed, but the WGA made an exception for such a high-profile, complicated case as *Ben-Hur*. Wyler and Siegel lodged a formal protest, but two of the Guild's executives reaffirmed the committee's decision.[245] On Tuesday, October 27, William Wyler lashed out during a speech to the Greater Los Angeles Press Club, and by the next morning the dispute had gone national.[246] The reader will not be surprised to see the second name out of Wyler's mouth, as quoted in the *New York Times*, was that of Lew Wallace:

> Christopher Fry worked eight months on the manuscript, rewriting almost every scene in the picture. Mr. Fry's contribution is enormous, perhaps second only to Gen. Lew Wallace's. His works will be read 100 years from now. Few members of the Screen Writers Guild can make such a claim.

The Guild responded in the press by insisting on the anonymity and fairness of the process, and Edmund Hartmann, current chairman of the Guild, was given equal time at the press club the following week.[247]

A few days later Heston delivered his own insulting remarks. He claimed that the reason that Fry was not receiving screen credit was because he was British and not a member of the Guild:

> Anyone who goes to the film and listens to the speeches will know that not one of them could have been written by a member of the Guild.[248]

In December J. J. Cohn confided in a letter to Wyler, "I am so mad I am about to resign from the human race."[249] More circumspect was the letter Zimbalist's widow wrote to the Guild in early November:

> I think it is inconceivable to anyone who was there working on "Ben-Hur" in Rome to think that Christopher Fry was not one of its principal creators. I know that he was, in Sam's eyes. Mr. Fry's writing was at the heart of something my husband and William Wyler wanted to achieve in this film. Enormous, talented work was done by all who worked on "Ben-Hur." It is sad that one of the most creative is not acknowledged.[250]

In January, 1960, Vidal threw another log onto the fire when he claimed during an interview in Boston that although he and Fry had written the script, the Guild had given exclusive credit for authorship to Tunberg because he had been a former guild president.[251] In fact, Tunberg had been president in 1950/1. Fry himself never entered the public controversy, but at the time the film was opening across the country, the controversy had made its way into individual reviews. W. Ward March, for instance, reviewed the gala premiere in Cleveland, boasted that this was the Ohio premiere, spent the first three paragraphs lavishing compliments on what "could well be the perfect picture" that "may well stand at the celluloid apex so long as the cinema shall last," and then concluded with, "Christopher Fry causes it to speak with authority and authenticity, but is given no credit."[252] A few weeks later Jay Carmody of Washington's *Evening Star*, one of the many members of the press that visited the production in Rome and had a lengthy interview with Fry, called the omission of Fry and Vidal a "cosmic miscalculation."[253] Demonstrating some familiarity with Vidal's statement and Heston's, he blamed the oversight on the "technicality" that neither was a member of the Guild and that therefore Tunberg "gets all of the credit for the adaptation on which he probably did a mere 'some.'"

Of course the countless nationwide reports on April 5, the day after *Ben-Hur* won its eleven Academy Awards, had to account for the Best-Writing [Adaptation] award's being given instead to *Room at the Top*. The short version of a nationally syndicated report, printed on either page one of local newspapers or on the movie listings pages near the newly revised ads for *Ben-Hur* boasting of the eleven Academy Awards, highlighted the glaring anomaly in the third sentence.[254] The longer version said the anomaly was "not a surprise" on account of the controversy involving Wyler, the Guild, and Fry that "colored the voting."[255] Other reports added that "Heston pointedly acknowledged only Fry among the writers in his acceptance speech."[256] Carmody penned a follow-up on April 10, where he said that Heston "proved his worthiness in the courage" of thanking Fry along with Wyler and Siegel.[257] He concluded that at least Heston had set the record straight, but Heston was not finished. Feeling the wrath of the Guild, he wrote them a syndicated letter asserting that he did not need their permission to acknowledge Fry's considerable contribution to *Ben-Hur* and asking if it was their intention "to expunge Mr. Fry's name from the lips of men."[258] In his contemporary diary Heston wrote, "This is rapidly becoming an entertaining controversy."[259]

Tunberg finally responded in a *San Diego Union* interview in June, extending the public battle into its eighth month. He found a friendly ear in James Meade, theater writer for the *San Diego Union*.[260] His opening salvo in "'Ben-Hur' Stirred Big Credit Race" accused Wyler of having a Napoleonic complex, evident in the ubiquitous presence of his name in most of the *Ben-Hur* advertising, and not tolerating solo credit for anyone else. He followed with a sober review of the project's history – new to the audience – from 1953 as a proposal designed to counter the incursions of television, his second draft approved by Zimbalist and Schary, the work with Franklin, the dormant period of turmoil in the studio leading to the presidency of Vogel, and then the production under Wyler from 1957. He explained the Guild's procedures, and after confirming that Fry did not pursue any appeal, he concluded with an accurate and sarcastic anecdote:

> Wyler said Fry's contributions were intangible, scribbled on the backs of envelopes and memo pads, which brought the rejoinder from writer Daniel Taradash, "Why not give director's credit?"

Tunberg concluded by saying, again accurately, that Fry's contributions submitted to the arbitration committee by MGM amounted to no more than about eleven pages of his 200-plus-page script.

Heston responded in August directly to the *San Diego Union*.[261] Here he insisted that although Tunberg did participate briefly in the retake process in Hollywood in the summer of 1959, Wyler rejected his suggestions:

> An examination of my own shooting script for the film, which of course includes all the changes made by Fry, doesn't impel me to question the Guild's finding that Tunberg wrote more of the words in the finished film than Fry did. But it strikes me as unusual, though unquestionably to their right, to judge writing by the pound (or perhaps by the running inch??). Were I a writer, I would rather have written the phrase "To be or not to be . . ." than the whole of, say, *Anthony Adverse*, though the latter is a much longer work. While I don't mean to couple Fry's name with Shakespeare, it does seem that his reputation as perhaps the outstanding poet-dramatist now writing in the language would make his a name most Hollywood writers would be glad to see on the screen beside theirs.

Heston gets the last word for now, but he will be attacked by Vidal in a different controversy three decades later.

CONTINUING SUCCESS

Box office receipts immediately provided a steady revenue stream for MGM. By February, 1960, they passed the $3 million mark from the seventeen domestic roadshow exhibitions alone.[262] This amount included special morning showings provided for students.[263] MGM offered a 99¢ premiere for teens at the Loew's in New York, [264] and *Variety* reported in May, that the children's matinee at the Capri Theater in Kansas City had sold out every Saturday for thirteen weeks.[265] The same theater also feted its 150,000th *Ben-Hur* customer, who confessed that no one in their family of six had been to a movie theater in two years, recalling the flood of rural Protestant patrons to the Klaw & Erlanger production and MGM's pressbook warning about new customers. Another part of the publicity campaign sought out new patrons by featuring Glenn Randall and "The Ben-Hur Horses," who appeared, for instance, on the cover of the October program for the American Royal Horse Show in Kansas

City.[266] Randall provided two teams – each horse was reportedly insured for $100,000 – for each matinee and evening show performing "a variety of tricks which include falling, rearing, and simulating wild fear which urges the horses during the big race." The Pittsburgh Pirates' *1960 World Series Official Souvenir Program* is filled with typical ads from Coca-Cola and local banks and car dealers, but unique among them is the ad for the Warner Theatre, now showing *Ben-Hur*, "breaking records throughout the nation!"[267]

In November, 1960, one year into its run, the film had moved solidly into profitability with MGM reporting more than $40 million in sales.[268] In May, 1961, the Egyptian Theater reported that 829,219 people had seen the film, more than one third of the population of Los Angeles.[269] In Chicago the exclusive engagement at the Michael Todd theater had run for seventy-four weeks and was seen by 1.5 million patrons.[270] In Chicago tickets were available at Sears stores,[271] and a bank in Baltimore gave away one free ticket for every deposit of $25 or more.[272] MGM reported a record quarterly profit of $4.5 million and estimated its 1961 fiscal year profit at $12.5 million.[273]

When reaching the first anniversary of the New York premiere, MGM placed an advertisement in *Life* that listed the 180 American cities and theaters currently showing the film in exclusive engagements, included a clip-out coupon to send to a theater manager for "preferred consideration," and announced that the approaching holiday season would bring the film to hundreds of additional theaters.[274] Finishing up the high-priced exclusive roadshow engagements, MGM was now taking as much as 70 percent of the ticket prices.[275] Six months later *Boxoffice* reported that the film had passed the $50 million mark in the U.S. and Canada in 2250 engagements and that by August bookings would amount to 3500, including some 600 drive-ins.[276] To cite Chicago as a representative example of the success of the regular release at this point, in mid-June, 1962, *Ben-Hur* was playing at sixteen different theaters and drive-ins around the Chicago area.[277] One week later it was playing at thirty.[278] In March, 1963, MGM told the *Los Angeles Times* that *Ben-Hur* was "slated for a multiple run," and later in the week it was advertised at eighteen local theaters as "Academy Award Champion!"[279]

As expected, overseas markets provided enthusiastic audiences, long-running engagements, and even spin-offs. In October, 1960, MGM dispatched Wyler to the premiere in Rome.[280] Italy, of course, was the veritable home of *Ben-Hur*, so much so that the Italian government reportedly sued for a percentage of the profits.[281] In 1962 London's *Publican* still listed *Ben-Hur* at the top of its category in its annual box-office survey.[282] In France *Ben-Hur* was used as the inaugural film at the 1960 Cannes festival in May, although MGM withheld it from the competition because they feared the whims of the jury.[283] Wyler made sure to attend the Paris premiere the following September,[284] and *Le Film Français* would list *Ben-Hur* among the three top box-office draws of 1959, 1960, and 1961 along with *Les Liaisons Dangereuses* and *Guns of Navarone*.[285] The European popularity of *Ben-Hur* was not confined to the native population. A survey published by the U.S. Army and Air Force Motion Picture Service revealed that *Ben-Hur* was the most popular film among American GIs stationed overseas, surpassing even the more militaristic *Guns of Navarone* and *The Alamo*.[286]

It was not finally until December, 1963, four years after the gala premieres, that a different set of ads for more than a dozen theaters announced that the current Christmas season was the "last chance to see this great epic."[287] Even so, while engagements at American theaters and drive-ins were dwindling to a trickle, overseas exhibitions continued from London to New Delhi.[288] By 1967 in Italy alone the film had been seen by eight million spectators who paid nearly $5 million.[289] Until the 1970s it was the all-time top-grosser in Japan.[290] A 1977 rerelease in London attracted a "splendid" box office during a two-week engagement in London.[291]

THE 1969 RERELEASE

In June, 1964, MGM had announced a new *Ben-Hur* domestic roadshow campaign as a cornerstone of its plan to rerelease its most successful films in sequence every seven years, but this did not materialize until 1968 after a $30 million reissue of *Gone With the Wind*.[292] In August of that year, MGM announced that Dan Terrell was preparing an entirely new advertising campaign for a roadshow reissue of *Ben-Hur* the following Easter.[293] In the advertising they again highlighted the pride they had in having created "the world's most honored motion picture," and they used this in print, radio, television ads and in movie trailers. Ticket prices were to cost as much as $5.00 in a market of inflated ticket prices.[294] At the time, the film industry was suffering from a severe recession, losing some $200 million in 1969 alone.[295] Once again, *Ben-Hur* would assist in the rescue.

MGM's decision to rerelease *Ben-Hur* as a roadshow helps demonstrate the rare qualities of the film as a box-office draw. It was one of the few films that had originally earned $30 million, the amount the industry used as a minimum to make a rerelease profitable.[296] And it was one of the few rereleases to be exhibited in the hard-ticket format. When Paramount rereleased *The Ten Commandments*, it did so as a "grind" show and earned only $6 million, far below the total for *Gone With the Wind*. Similarly, rereleases of *West Side Story* and *Around the World in Eighty Days* had brought in only $3 million and $1 million, respectively. In a long feature on this "'Ben-Hur' echo," in February, *Variety* concluded by pointing out that *Ben-Hur* was on the one hand an outmoded genre film but on the other "in a class by itself."

Another unknown factor intriguing industryites is situation of "Ben-Hur" as one film of the Biblical fad of the '50s, albeit the biggest-grossing one. "GWTW" was always a bit unique, was neither part of nor precipitated a Civil War "genre." But "Ben-Hur" was released during the great era of Ancient spectacles – and nobody questions but that this particular genre is now in complete eclipse as far as newly-made pix go. Most observers, however, think that "Ben-Hur" achieved an independent following and reputation which put it in "a class by itself" above and beyond the commercial ups and downs of its genre.[297]

The hard-ticket reissue had huge initial successes in October, 1968, in Tokyo and Osaka, where it pulled in almost $70,000 during its opening week.[298] The American domestic strategy reversed the 1959 schedule by beginning in twenty-six smaller cities leading up to Easter and only later playing New York.[299] Of course at this point theaters did not have to retool as they had in 1959.[300] The American premiere was a gala affair at Miami's Lincoln Theater on February 25, that reportedly evoked a six-minute standing ovation reminiscent of the Broadway premiere of the Klaw & Erlanger production sixty years earlier.[301] Present were Wyler, Heston, Boyd, and Canutt.[302] MGM flew in fifty-seven invited members of the press corps from the twenty-five other cities for two days of activities, including a celebratory press dinner.[303] In interviews with the press, Wyler focused on the parallel between the struggles of the ancient Jews against the Romans and the contemporary Jews against the Arab world.[304] Heston pointed out that his son Fraser was three years old at the time of the initial release and now he was certainly old enough to see the film, like many others of the younger generation. Thinking of that younger demographic, MGM moved the schedule up from June in the hopes that students "might benefit from it in their literature classes."[305] The Chicago, Toronto, Detroit, and Montreal openings took place in the next few days.[306] Some of the performances were benefits. The Washington, DC premiere on April 2 benefitted the March of Dimes, and even Illinois Senator Dirksen allowed himself to be photographed donning a Roman helmet.[307] However, additional festivities for the gala had to be canceled because of the death of former President Eisenhower on March 28.[308]

Public reception was quite good. The opening week in Montreal, for instance, where the 1959 roadshow had run for fifty-two weeks, set a house record, topping the original first week by 48 percent.[309] Similarly in Toronto, where the original release played for seventy-one weeks, the release topped the original first week by 28 percent. The roadshows ran from late February to mid-May, with some VIP Lounge tickets costing as much as $6.00.[310] By early May the film had surpassed the $1 million mark in each of nineteen different cities.[311] Afterwards the film continued to play at local theaters into the early 1970s.[312] Although the reissue never achieved the penetration of the initial release, during one week in

March, 1970, ten neighborhood theaters in Washington, DC, just to cite one example, were playing the film simultaneously.[313]

One critic, John Hartl, described the success as "spotty," that is, good in some cities, not in others.[314] He attributed the reason to MGM's excessive caution in not opening the film in New York until June 26 near the end of its national run as a roadshow.[315] MGM knew that tastes had changed with such young-generation films as *Midnight Cowboy* and *Easy Rider* and that the New York critics would no longer give an old-fashioned studio biblical epic like *Ben-Hur* their strongest endorsement,[316] so Hartl argued that as a result the lack of national publicity – good or bad – from the mainstream critics harmed the reception of the film. Of a different opinion was Hy Gardner, who wrote that the film was so successful in the theaters that spectators would have to wait a long time to see the film on television.[317] As it turned out, just before and even after the television premiere in February, 1971, the film played sporadically, whether in a double feature with *Gone With the Wind* in Portland one month earlier,[318] during the Christmas season in a single-showing benefit performance like that sponsored by the Holy Family Guild of San Diego the following December,[319] or at a Marietta, Georgia, drive-in on Christmas Eve, 1972, spiced with door prizes and live music.[320]

BOX OFFICE

Particularly because *Ben-Hur* had been produced and released during a period of relatively low movie attendance, its success confirmed for MGM and the other studios that blockbuster films were a sound investment.[321] A first-page article in the *Wall Street Journal* in 1960 noted that allocating large sums to an epic-sized religious production provided a method of reducing risk:

> Movie men ... claim that by buying the best possible stories and hiring the biggest stars, they are not only insuring their investments but ushering their product into a derby whose payoff has never been greater. ... Folks aren't going to the movies as often as they used to, but when they do, they go in droves – and they're willing to pay top prices for a real extravaganza.[322]

Accordingly, like the 1925 *Ben-Hur*, the 1959 version was repeatedly cited in reviews and advertisements for subsequent big-budget films, including *Exodus* (1961),[323] *El Cid* (1962),[324] *The Wonderful World of the Brothers Grimm* (1962),[325] *Mutiny on the Bounty* (1962),[326] *Barabbas* (1962),[327] *Four Horsemen of the Apocalypse* (1962),[328] *Lawrence of Arabia* (1963),[329] *Cleopatra* (1963),[330] *How the West Was Won* (1963),[331] *The Fall of the Roman Empire* (1964),[332] and *The Greatest Story Ever Told* (1965),[333] again helping to demonstrate the exemplary status and perennial topicality of *Ben-Hur* dramatic products. In an era of epic blockbusters, *Ben-Hur* was the epic blockbuster that surpassed all of these in earnings. By the time

Variety published its annual list of "All-Time Top Gross Films" in January, 1962, *Ben-Hur* had taken its place among the top three along with *Gone With the Wind* and DeMille's 1956 version of *The Ten Commandments*.[334] *Variety's* box-office tallies were limited to domestic sales only, and $4 million was used as a minimum without any adjustment for inflation or deflation. The 1925 *Ben-Hur* was among them. The reader will not be surprised to learn that of the 246 titles in the list of "All-Time Top Gross Films," there was only one title that belonged to two separate films: *Ben-Hur*.

In May, 1963, *Variety* reported that because of its particular strength overseas, *Ben-Hur* was about to surpass *Gone With the Wind* at $67.2 million.[335] The next reissue of *Gone With the Wind* would restore it to the top of the list, but the 1959 *Ben-Hur* would remain among the top grossers through the general economic inflation of the late 1960s until the dawn of the Spielberg/Lucas era in 1973, being surpassed in domestic sales by only *The Sound of Music* (1965), *Doctor Zhivago* (1965), *The Graduate* (1968), *Airport* (1970), *Love Story* (1970), and *The Godfather* (1972).[336] There is no single figure for its ultimate grosses, but Alex Ben Block and Lucy Autrey Wilson, editors of *George Lucas' Blockbusting*, calculated in 2010 that the film ultimately earned, adjusted for inflation, $754 million, making *Ben-Hur* the ninth biggest grosser of all time, following *Gone With the Wind*, *Star Wars IV*, *The Sound of Music*, *E.T. the Extra-Terrestrial*, *The Ten Commandments*, *Titanic*, *Jaws*, and *Snow White and the Seven Dwarfs*, but above the likes of *Avatar* and *Jurassic Park*.[337] Similarly, Box Office Mojo, adjusting their domestic estimate of $74 million to account for inflated modern ticket prices, estimated $813 million, ranking *Ben-Hur* thirteenth all-time.[338] These totals reflect domestic grosses only. We have already seen in the 1920s, 1930s, and here in the 1960s that *Ben-Hur* was disproportionately successful overseas. The Block and Wilson estimation for the worldwide box office for the 1959 *Ben-Hur* is $1.312 billion.

ARTISTIC AND COMMERCIAL TIE-INS

Books
To help build innovative advertising campaigns and commercial tie-ins ("tie-ups") in February, 1959, MGM invited Oscar Doob, Loew's veteran publicity executive, to come out of retirement and brought Hudgins back from Rome.[339] Bringing in additional experience, Doob in turn hired Harry McWilliams, the former field exploitation chief for Columbia.[340] Paralleling Williamson's strategy in 1902, Doob's special unit immediately sought to precede the film's release with a reprint of Wallace's original novel, including a Deluxe Edition published by Harper & Brothers.[341] In the 1950s, of course, Wallace's work was in the public domain, so Doob

could negotiate agreements with five different publishers to print special editions of the novel in initial press runs of 250,000 copies each.[342] Additional demand for Wallace's novel was coming from public libraries, which noted a resurgence of interest already in the spring.[343]

By July, Doob announced that he had lined up eleven new publications, and, like its musical cousins of the 1890s and early 1900s, Wallace's novel was now applied to several new formats, particularly the mass-paperback format. Dell Books had already negotiated a tie-in agreement in 1957,[344] but now there would be additional paperbacks: a 510-page Collier Books paperback edition ("The stirring tale of the courageous Jew who defied Nero"), a 514-page edition Doubleday's Dolphin Books, a 432-page complete and unabridged Signet title of the New American Library, and a 561-page Cardinal edition of Pocket Books.[345]

Some came value-added. The Bantam paperback, a 282-page "definitive modern abridgement," included a one-page introduction by William Wyler and reached at least its seventh printing. It was subsequently printed in England as a Pan Giant illustrated with six photographs from the film but without the Wyler introduction. In 1960 Heritage Press printed a 486-page edition prefaced by Ben Ray Redman's thirteen-page biographical sketch of Wallace and illustrated by Joe Mugnaini, who signed the 1500 copies sold through The Limited Editions Club. In London Dean's Classics [#36] reissued a 248-page abridged edition first published by Thames in 1955.

The 352-page "modern and readable version, completely rewritten and condensed" by the veteran screen writer, Guy Endore, in the Dell 50¢ Series, appended an "Explanatory Note" that detailed the Ingersoll encounter, surveyed briefly the endurance of *Ben-Hur* in print and on stage and in film, and accounted for the drastic changes he made to the story. Endore focused, for instance, on what he claimed to be a theological non sequitur where Wallace's Wise Men were miraculously led to the Holy Land by god but then left clueless as the location of the Nativity. Also, feeling that Judah's undying hatred for Rome needed further causation, he created a scene in which Judah was condemned to work in a Roman mine (à la *Barabbas* and *Spartacus*). He also found Judah's conversion to be unconvincing (350–1):

> All through the book Ben-Hur has been vowing the destruction of Rome, and yet, suddenly, at the end of the book, Ben-Hur is no longer a Jew and does not feel himself included in the curse on the Jews. Indeed in the last chapter he has even moved to Rome!
> It isn't that he has shown himself very Christ-like at any point. In the scene with Iras who has betrayed him, he does not turn the other cheek: he slaps right back. It is the present author who has revised that scene to make Ben-Hur more Christian, in the sense of more forgiving! (We must remember that Wallace was the man who sent the innocent Mrs. Surratt to the gallows as one of the murderers of Lincoln, and defended that action to the end of his life!)

The 1959 MGM Ben-Hur

In further targeting the younger demographics, Doob lined up a 277-page Frederick Warne & Company edition abridged by I. O. Evans for teenagers, accompanied by Gordon Nicoll's four charcoal sketches and watercolor frontispiece,[346] and a 69-page Grosset & Dunlap edition "abridged and adapted for young readers" by Felix Sutton and illustrated on every page with watercolors, ink drawings, and a print by Louis S. Glanzman. Similarly, Globe Book Company had issued a hardback edition adapted by Glenn Holder in 1954 that included eight photos from the 1925 film, but now it would issue a second edition with photographs from the 1959 film and another in 1969 with the film's reissue.[347] MGM press releases listed as many as eighteen versions of *Ben-Hur* in print. In England Ward Lock & Company published a Children's Classics Edition,[348] and in Italy Fratelli Fabbri published a 150-page Italian version of the novel abridged for juveniles by Andrea Cavalli Dell'Ara with four watercolor illustrations by Signorini, although without acknowledgment to MGM or Loew's. Even *Barron's* highlighted this "brisk demand" for paperback versions of *Ben-Hur* in 1965.[349]

Simon and Schuster's Golden Press signed on to deliver several items in different formats. In 1956 they had issued their "Golden Picture Classic," a juvenile edition of the novel, edited and abridged by Willis Lindquist and abundantly illustrated by Mario Cooper on almost every page. They issued the original 96-page edition in both hardback and paperback. An abbreviated Golden Reading Adventure hardback version had sixty-two pages. Scholastic Book Services reissued this in 1960 with drawings, adapted from the film, by Charles Beck. Appropriately for its intended audience, this edition highlights the chariot race with three of its eleven drawings depicting chariots, by placing two cropped film stills of the chariot race on the paper covers, and leaving only thirteen of its 116 pages for the post-chariot race material. The rear cover blurb concludes, "The trumpet blares. The horses leap forward . . . and two deadly enemies race for life itself."

A different kind of "special hardcover book" resulted from a different type of corporate synergy. Bennett Cerf, co-founder of Random House, sat on the board of Loew's, and so it was Random House that issued the official souvenir booklet for purchase by patrons at theaters and stores alike.[350] The initial order was for two million copies.[351] The front cover of the book is bathed in the golden ochre color used for most of the MGM *Ben-Hur* posters along with Smith's signature title made of monumental stone. The rear cover features a color action shot from the chariot race. The frontispiece looks like an official invitation, with a golden ochre garland surrounding the wording:

METRO-GOLDWYN-MAYER
PRESENTS
A
Momentous Event
in
Motion Pictures
Directed by
WILLIAM WYLER

Attached to the title page is a three-panel fold-out photo of the Antioch Circus during the chariot race, and on the reverse is a Foreword by Vogel paying tribute to Wallace, Zimbalist, Wyler, Tunberg and the four other writers by name, Rózsa, and the thousands of others who helped create the film. There follow two pages describing the *Ben-Hur* tradition from Wallace to Klaw & Erlanger to the 1925 film illustrated with photos of the Capitol statue of Wallace, the raft-scene photo from the stage drama, and the photo of William S. Hart and William Farnum as Messala and Ben-Hur. Four pages present the cast, with sketched portraits by Joe Smith, brief descriptions of their acting careers, and epigrammatic descriptions like those for Esther, "The Beautiful, whose love was stronger than the bonds of slavery," and Messala, "The Roman Warrior, who traded loyalty for power and trust for treachery."[352] One page of various notes on the production in Italy precedes sixteen pages of color photographs of various sizes and arrangements, one page each on Wyler and casting, three describing and illustrating MGM's commitment to the project, one each on the sets, wardrobe and music, and Camera 65. A full page listing the cast and crew backs onto a five-panel fold-out with copies of the six paintings commissioned from Stahl that can be cut along dotted lines and framed. Random House produced the book in several languages as well as in a soft-cover version and a small-format promotional pamphlet version.

Comic Books
There were three major comic-book adaptations accompanying the film. *Classics Illustrated* published their unlicensed graphic version of "Ben-Hur" [#147] in anticipation of the release of the film in November, 1958. Their adaptation begins with a full-page illustration of Herod, "puppet ruler" of Rome, his oriental court enlivened by two pet monkeys eating fruit from a bowl. The story follows the novel. It includes the conversation between Judah and his (unnamed) mother, Judah is the one who loosens the tile, a fair-haired Jesus gives him water in Nazareth, on his return to Antioch Judah immediately seeks out Simonides, and a rope marks the starting line of the chariot race, Messala reaches it first by "prearrangement," and then Judah catches Messala's wheel with his iron-shod axle before "THE RACE WAS WON." The 45-page story is followed by one-page

essays on Lew Wallace, Roman entertainments, and Nero. This version of "Ben-Hur" was translated into several languages and sold abroad, and it would be reissued in the U.S. in 1968, with a different charioteer cover, in anticipation of the 1969 rerelease of the film.

Coordinating with the 1959 release of the film, Dell [#1052] issued a comic-book version celebrating "the heroic struggle of one man who defied the mighty Roman Empire." The rear cover contains a large promo for the film, highlighting the chariot race, and the inner front cover contains additional MGM promotional material. Some of the story follows an older version of the script, e.g. where Judah and Messala throw spears into a random oak beam and Tirzah shouts that the falling tile was not her fault, but the post-race material is limited to just the final two of the thirty-two pages.

National Comics Publications used their DC brand to issue the thirteen-page story, "Superboy Meets Ben-Hur!" in its October, 1961, issue of *Superboy* [#92]. The story, credited to Robert Bernstein,[353] reprises the *Adventure Comics* Superboy story from 1952 but makes significant changes. There is no hot rodder, the discredited professor is now Lana Lang's father, and Professor Lang is being dismissed from the Smallville Museum because he claims a $30,000 bronze Roman statue bust of Ben-Hur in its possession is authentic while the museum director, Dr. Horst, insists that "Ben-Hur never existed! He's only a fictional hero in a novel by Lew Wallace!" In one of the next panels, Superboy, assuming his disguised identity as Clark Kent, is seen reading a copy of "*Ben-Hur* by Lew Wallace" with a *quadriga* on the cover. Superboy flies back to ancient Rome. The long panel depicts Rome as a city by the sea, and then Superboy flies past an arena where "thousands of slaves were thrown to the lions!" In a narration above the next two panels, Superboy describes how, "according to the novel," a tile fell on the governor's head and Ben-Hur was accused of murder and imprisoned. As he flies over the sea, his thought bubble adds that "at this time in history, according to the novel, Ben-Hur was serving as a galley slave aboard a vessel with a lion figurehead on its prow!" With his telescopic vision he finds the galley being attacked by a pirate ship. Superboy pokes multiple holes in the pirate ship's hull to stop the attack, and after the Romans pick the "strange youth" out of the sea, they put him in the galleys just behind Ben-Hur. Superboy is perplexed, however, because the face of this Ben-Hur does not at all resemble the Smallville bust. Using "the special powers the gods gave me," he spells the other slaves by rowing the galley 200 miles by himself "before you can say Julius Caesar!"

He and Ben-Hur escape as Superboy promises the latter that "according to history, you'll use your early talents as a horse-trainer and become a great charioteer!" As in the novel's encounter with Balthasar and Iras, Ben-Hur stops a speeding chariot in the street, and the driver arranges to have Ben-Hur race his team "at the coliseum." The race pits Ben-Hur against a rich Roman named Marcellus, who, like Festus in the previous version, does everything he can to cheat. Again Superboy "invents" popcorn, creates a jet engine, and flies in a new team of four tan horses to help Ben-Hur win the race. The emperor gives him a bronze victory statue filled with gold. All the while, Superboy has remained confused by Ben-Hur's face, but after Marcellus' thugs have hacked and chiseled the statue head to steal the gold, the head now looks like the one Professor Lang purchased. Superboy flies back to Smallville and restores Lang's credibility and position.

DC reissued the story in 1971 [#179], changing some of the coloring, most notably, in rendering the new team of horses in white, not tan. The only story change is the omission of the penultimate two panels, in one of which Superboy explained to his new friend:

> I must leave you, now, Ben-Hur, and return to my world! But remember that your fame will live forever! Some day a man will write a famous book based on your life!

Ben-Hur also appeared as an incidental character in a subsequent Superman story. In 1964 *Action Comics* [#308] issued a story in which a lightning bolt and whirlpool take Superman back through time, where he encounters the Greek mythological heroes Hercules and Jason. Then Ben-Hur in his chariot hastens by them. A lion has frightened his two horses, and the speed and strength of Hercules and then Superman are required to stop the runaway chariot team. Superman is perplexed that Greeks and Romans are in the same place and speaking English, until he realizes he has traveled to a parallel world that is "an exact duplicate of the real Earth, except that certain events and situations are mixed up." That Ben-Hur (with the hyphen) is chosen as the sole Roman representative, rather than Julius Caesar or Mark Antony, both of whom had been featured in the previous year's *Cleopatra*, speaks to the longevity of the impact of the 1959 film in popular culture.

Music

By signing Miklós Rózsa in the summer of 1957, long before the film was cast, MGM and Zimbalist demonstrated how important they thought the musical component would be, and the subsequent praise for and continued presence of the film score has proved them correct. Rózsa had already won two Academy Awards and had been nominated for nine others, but *Ben-Hur* would prove to be his best remembered and most widely recognized achievement. Rózsa's method of creating music themes for love, friendship, hatred, hope, and despair as well as for the Christ recalls the leitmotifs Edgar Stillman Kelley applied to his incidental music for the Klaw & Erlanger production as well as the Roman, Christ, and love themes William Axt and David Mendoza prepared for the 1925 film.

Reputed for its musicals, MGM had helped pioneer the release of soundtrack albums in conjunction with film releases, and they developed their own MGM Records division. *Gigi* had been their prototype in 1958, and *The Billboard*'s chart of the "25 Best Selling LP's" in mid-December, 1958, included *South Pacific* (2), *The Music Man* (4), *Gigi* (7), *My Fair Lady* (10), and *South Pacific* (13) alongside classical and popular albums by Van Cliburn, Mitch Miller, Frank Sinatra, the Kingston Trio, and Johnny Mathis.[354] Six months later *Gigi*, now on the chart for forty-eight straight weeks, was number one, *My Fair Lady* seventh after 165 weeks, *South Pacific* ninth after sixty-two weeks, *The Music Man* thirteenth after sixty-six weeks, and, we take notice, twelfth was Mantovani's *Film Encores, Vol. 1*, now in its eighty-second week, with interpretations of individual themes and songs from such films as *The Wizard of Oz*, *Three Coins in the Fountain*, and *Love Is A Many Splendored Thing*.[355]

Ben-Hur was not a musical, of course, and did not include a song with lyrics, but because MGM marketed *Ben-Hur* as an artistic triumph and because *Ben-Hur* would have one of the longest soundtracks in film history, MGM decided to produce three different recordings of Rózsa's score by the Rome Symphony Orchestra and would begin selling them more than one month before the film was released. The three albums included a two-pocket LP, a single LP of highlights, and a budget LP.[356] This was the year in which stereo LPs were taking hold, so once again a *Ben-Hur* artistic by-product was targeted for new media markets that other literary properties failed to penetrate. The Deluxe Edition [1E1; S-1E1] by MGM Records included the soft-cover version of the 32-page illustrated souvenir booklet from Random House, and it, like the less expensive Lion edition [L-70123; SL-70123] was offered in both monaural and stereo.[357] The single LP, *More Music From Ben-Hur* [MGM E 3900], was released the following year.[358] Separately, Rózsa himself prepared a concert-length "Ben-Hur Suite."[359] The albums were advertised in trade magazines, newspapers, and theater programs. There is an ad for "A magnificent picture! A wonderful record!" even in the program printed especially for the aforementioned Royal Gala Film Performance in London. Heston participated in an additional commercial synergy. Building on his roles as both Ben-Hur and Moses, he recorded readings from "The Five Books of Moses" for a two-LP Vanguard release.[360]

The albums were sold not just in record and music shops but in drugstores, chain stores, and specialty shops.[361] More so than any *Ben-Hur* musical by-product since Paull's march, Rózsa's score had lasting commercial power. Fifty-one weeks on the list of the "50 Best Selling Stereo LP's," the stereo LP recording was still listed thirty-fifth, just above the Rogers and Hammerstein musical *South Pacific* and just below the Broadway cast-version of *The Unsinkable Molly Brown*.[362] Rózsa's score was performed repeatedly or recorded by numerous artists in the 1960s. In 1962 Arthur Fiedler was performing Rózsa's "Parade of the Charioteers" at Boston Pops concerts,[363] and bestselling movie music albums by Mantovani, Percy

Faith, David Rose, Ron Goodwin, and other orchestral conductors and arrangers inevitably included either one of Rózsa's *Ben-Hur* marches or the love theme from *Ben-Hur*.[364] The sheet music reduced for solo piano also sold well for Robbins Music Corporation of New York, and Robbins issued as well "The Christ Theme" for four-part chorus and keyboard accompaniment, the "Love Theme" for string orchestra, and the "Adoration of the Magi" for 4-part chorus, arranged by Harry Robert Wilson. In yet another *Ben-Hur* synergy, the release of the film occasioned London Records' 1960 reissue of Paull's "Ben Hur Chariot Race" performed by The Medallion Concert Band,[365] preceded by the 1956 Willis Music printed edition and followed by the 1961 Century Music printed piano duet.

Merchandise

Still more than half a year prior to the release, Doob made an arrangement with Stone Associates to create and manage merchandising tie-ins.[366] Allan and Martin Stone had risen to prominence in the late 1940s in connection with NBC television's *Howdy Doody*.[367] Heading the licensing agency that sold Howdy Doody records, lariats, beanies, and T-shirts, they had pioneered transmedia merchandising for not only children's television programs but adult television celebrities like Jackie Gleason.[368] In a trade journal Martin Stone shared with readers the benefits and parameters of effective merchandising of a television program and its characters:

> For the client this means ever-increasing sales of the product, for the station this means consistently solid audience ratings as well as a satisfied client closely identified with his program. ... Thru [sic] these tie-ins countless thousands of impressions are made each day upon present and potential viewers thru window and counter displays of the merchandise, point-of-sale material, and newspaper advertising.
>
> ...
>
> Merchandise bearing the names and characters of the show must be of the highest quality. ... Furthermore, the products and related advertising material must take full advantage of the atmosphere and format of the show in question, so as not to foster incongruous tie-ins such as flooded the market during the recent Davy Crockett craze.[369]

For the film industry this kind of commercial application was in its infancy. There was no real precedent for merchandising cinematic characters and properties except for such special-case animated Disney properties as Mickey Mouse and Snow White and perhaps Shirley Temple dolls of the 1930s.[370] Disney had broken new ground in 1954 with its weekly self-promotion broadcast of *Disneyland* and Davy Crocket toy and apparel merchandising, and MGM had experimented with its own self-promotional television program, *MGM Parade* in 1955. But cooperation between the television and film industries was still quite tentative, as we have seen with David Suskind's ploy in 1957, and there was as yet no precedent for licensing a major Hollywood release. The industry was still decades away from the *Star Wars* merchandising revolution of the 1970s. But MGM believed *Ben-Hur* had a unique appeal that would break through long-established barriers between serious Hollywood adult entertainment and juvenile merchandising usually associated with television, so they hired Stone's agency.

Accordingly, in the *Wall Street Journal* Doob claimed they would be "very selective":

> If there's a Ben-Hur necktie, it will have to be a top necktie. If we have a Ben-Hur fabric, it can't be just calico. And if there's a Ben-Hur perfume, we'll naturally want quality Italian perfume.

A petition by an unnamed textile manufacturer to produce "Ben-Hur and Ben-His" towels was "politely but firmly rejected."[371] More in keeping with the prestige of MGM's epic was an arrangement with Ceil Chapman, the New York fashion designer who had developed her reputation by creating gowns and dresses for such contemporary Hollywood notables as Marilyn Monroe and Elizabeth Taylor. She produced a line of "Ben-Hur inspired" dresses previewed before 200 fashion editors at New York's Hotel Pierre in July, 1959,[372] and then colorfully displayed in *Harper's Bazaar* and sold at Saks Fifth Avenue around the time of the film's release in November.[373]

Stone Associates signed more than sixty deals, ranging from Ben-Hur swords and helmets to plaster statuettes and painting sets, usually with a guarantee of 5 percent of the wholesale price to the licensor.[374] Cohen-Hall-Marx Company was hired to license clothing tie-ins like Norwich T-shirts and sweatshirts, Boys Tone and Jewel button-down shirts and Pleetway pajamas made of Ameritex fabric that came with a tag that said "designs and colors inspired by William Wyler's presentation of Metro-Goldwyn-Mayer's *Ben-Hur*,"[375] as well as shorts, blouses, raincoats, pre-teen and teen dresses, and a clip-on tie with adjustable neckband.[376] Pemay, a Manhattan-based distributor of fashion for infants, sent a circular to retailers announcing, "A super-colossal promotion tie-in with one of the most exciting pictures ever made!"[377] Items for sale included boys' and girls' crawler sets, three-piece boys' suits, and girls' toddler dress and skirt-jacket-blouse ensemble. All these items for infants were decorated with either a chariot or a boyish Roman with a crested helmet and spear. In the accessories category there were three colors and styles of women's sandals made by New York's Central Slipper Company,[378] scarves, sun suits, purses, umbrellas, charm bracelets, pins, and rings. Capri Jewelry and, of course, Ben Hur Hair, designed a number of items.[379] Zakim Handprints of Patterson, New Jersey, prepared a collection of Vinyl-Tex wallpapers decorated with chariots, Penco Fabrics printed several patterned drapery fabrics, Schrafft's sold a candy bar, and Koppers sold *Ben-Hur* fine chocolates.[380] Spec-toys, the manufacturer of music and noise makers that had marketed the Davy Crockett Woodland Scouting Signal, now produced the Ben Hur Clarion, a 27-inch horn – "Very Loud!" – with a felt banner and golden tassel.[381] At the premiere at Loew's State in New York, MGM put up a mezzanine display of over 100 merchandise tie-ins decorated with *Ben-Hur* balloons.[382]

Playsets, Toys, Games, and Model Kits
The largest and most comprehensive of the toy sets were the Marx #4701 Series 5000, #4702 Series 2000, and #4696 Official Ben-Hur Playsets. Designed by Frank X. Rice, the larger 1/32-scale set weighed seven pounds and contained an amphitheater complete with an imperial box set off by six Ionic columns, a slave market, a vegetable stall, working catapults, eight colorful plastic *quadrigae*, several tents with poles and spires, and several dozen figures including an emperor and empress, *tubarii*, lions, tigers, horses, gladiators, and soldiers, as well as statue busts on pedestals, braziers, tables, hassocks, lamps, chests, urns, pennants, standards, and more.[383] The entire large set, with a listed retail price of $12.98, included 217 pieces, the smaller at $7.98, had 132 pieces. Printed on several panels of the box top was "SOLD UNDER LICENSE, LOWE'S , INC." At the same time Marx also manufactured and sold a 12-inch metal shield and a 17-inch scabbard lithographed with polychrome images of chariots, emblems, and the name Ben-Hur. The third piece of the set, which sold for $2.89, was a 13-inch plastic sword.

The company sold many of these sets through Sears and other catalog retailers, especially during the Christmas season. The 1960 *Sears Catalogue* advertised them in a two-page color spread that made an additional connection with *Ben-Hur* by saying the ancient gladiators who used the prototypes of the swords and shields fought in Antioch as well as Rome. The visibility of Marx, which by the 1950s had become the largest toy manufacturer in the world,[384] and the importance of the larger two play sets perpetuated a collector-base and subsequent retailing. The large set was featured on the cover of *Plastic Figure & Playset Collector* #14 (August, 1991) and *Playset Magazine* #30 along with the tease, "The Greatest Playset of All Time?"[385] In addition, PlastiMarx, Marx's subsidiary in Mexico, manufactured an alternative set [#2760] in a distinctive gray-swirl and cream, albeit without the Ben-Hur figure.[386] The Ben-Hur set has since been reissued in a recast set [#5105] made in Mexico.

The high visibility of Louis Marx & Company, which had established itself in the 1920s by marketing nearly 100 million low-cost yo-yos, warranted magazine coverage and has afforded us some special insights into the tie-in merchandising process. An in-depth article in *Playset Magazine* traces the project back to such high-profile, early 1950s Ancients as *Quo*

Vadis, The Robe, and *Demetrius and the Gladiators*. At the time Rice had drawn up preliminary designs for an ancient playset in a gladiatorial arena, but the project was not put into production. Similar projects were usually historical, recreating famous infantry battles of the past. Then MGM contacted Marx about *Ben-Hur*, providing them with much more than inspiration. They gave them sketches and photos. In an interview Rice compared the process of making the *Ben-Hur* playset to their usual practice of researching a historical event on their own:

> "[MGM] had preliminary sketches on what they were going to do, photos of what they had done, and it was great information, above what we normally expect." One of the first things MGM did was the chariot race, which took three months to film and provided an exciting centerpiece of the playset. MGM had amazingly good documentation to work from. "They were good enough to supply us with the material, and of course we tried to reproduce them as best we could in the size we were working in and material we were using. It was a very nice working arrangement but again, we didn't have to do a lot of research because they had done it all. We were in reality trying to reproduce what was in that show, rather than trying to imagine an actual event like the Battle of Gettysburg or something." Marx was able to reproduce the movie in miniature. For instance, the chariot, harness designs, criss-crossed railings around the amphitheater, even the iron rings lining the stadium on the playset are identical to props from the movie.... "Replicas, yes. We had their artwork."

As promised at the outset of the merchandising campaign, MGM was taking extraordinary measures to ensure quality products that reflected the cachet of *Ben-Hur*. Rice furthermore specifies that this was rare and innovative:

> These days, licensing begins years before the product comes on the market. But in those days, nobody did anything until the movie had been on the market and became accepted and popular. In the case of Ben-Hur, licensing was months and months before the picture came on the market and that was pretty innovative.

Stone's team presented the company with tickets for a showing before the general release of the film, after which Louis Marx himself remarked, "I've just seen the greatest motion picture of all time!"[387] Rice recalled the company enthusiasm generated by their association with *Ben-Hur*:

> We were approaching it as we normally approach a playset, but Louis got so excited about the concept for it. The fact it was going to be a huge movie, of course, generated his enthusiasm. Then, he wanted us to do this and do that and make it better, and add this, and this and *this* ... We spent a lot of time and money on that project. That really goosed us to do a big job![388]

Stone also signed Acorn Industries, the toy manufacturer headquartered in Plainview, New York. In three separate boxes marked with the large *Ben-Hur* logo they sold a red-crested Roman Helmet [B-200], a Sword and [square] Shield set with a scabbard [B-300], and Roman Armor outfit consisting of a breastplate, cape, and kilt [B-400].[389] Emphasizing authenticity and bypassing the fact that the Romans were the enemy in the film, the top of the box containing the helmet boasted, "THE ONLY OFFICIAL BEN-HUR HELMET. ACCURATE REPLICA OF ROMAN OFFICERS' HEADGEAR. WORN WHEN THE LEGIONS CONQUERED THE ANCIENT WORLD." The *New York Herald Tribune* published a photo of Milt Wynne, a partner and one of the designers, wearing one of the helmets worn in the film while standing next to his son wearing Acorn's child-size imitation.[390]

For the artistically inclined Acorn produced a Paint and Repaint Kit [B-102], a Paint By Imagination Kit [B-101], a "New! Different!" Photo Color Kit [B-201], and 3D Oil Paint Set [300.4] that included a brush, six vials of paint, and a cardboard frame. Acorn sold similar sets for five other storybook properties, but none of them current film releases. Acorn also produced an unconventional board game packaged in a cardboard tube [B-100].[391] Inside was a 3-foot plastic matte that rolled out into a circus marked with six yellow racing lanes, as well as paper chariots. At one end of the circus MGM's *Ben-Hur* logo with racing chariot was prominently displayed across the entire width of the fabric. These were all sold in a Master Display Unit [B-970] decorated with a large photo of a child modeling the armor, shield, and sword as well as a very large rendition of the *Ben-Hur* logo.

In 1955 the Lowell Toy Manufacturing Company of Long Island City had produced a board game associated with the television show *Gunsmoke*.[392] For Stone Associates they now produced the Ben-Hur Chariot Race Board Game.[393] On the standard-size box lid was printed the MGM *Ben-Hur* logo, behind Wagner's featured charioteer on the left and Checa's crashed chariot and *spina* on the right, both in vivid colors. Printed above the logo is: "EXCITING CHARIOT RACE GAME INSPIRED BY MGM'S MIGHTY PRODUCTION." On the lower right is printed: "A Game of Suspense and Skill Played with ROMAN CHARIOTS, Pays off in ROMAN COINS." Inside were a playing board, dice, eight Chariot Speed cards, eighteen Whip cards, and eighteen "gold" coins along with six small plastic chariots. The board had a six-lane circus surrounded on both sides with a 3-D graphic of several thousand spectator seats, roofed colonnades, and VIP sections on each side. The *spina*, set between the six *metae* and two movie-like colossi, is quite detailed. Lowell's owner expressed his hope that this would "replace the hula-hoop fad."[394] A Dutch-language version with a fold-out board depicting an overhead view of the MGM *spina* was sold by Mulder in the Netherlands.

Adams Action Models, a plastic model-kit company founded by Steve Adams earlier in the decade in Hawthorne, California, manufactured a 1/48 scale Ben Hur Racing Chariot [K-450:88]. The kit consisted of two dozen molded, unpainted pieces of a *quadriga* with a driver as well as a gladiator. Although the kit has a 1959 copyright, the colorful box top depicts one of the signature MGM *spina* statues to the far left, and the base decal displays the date "CIRCA A.D. XXXIV," the buyer would not nec-

Figure 14.3 MGM hired successful television exploiteers to build a unique and comprehensive merchandising program that sold over 100 products and grossed an additional $20 million. Counterclockwise: Acorn Oil Paint Set, Adams plastic model kit, Acorn armor set, Robbins sheet music, Golden FunTime Punch-Out Book, Samuel Lowe Coloring Book, Huntley & Palmers cookie tin, Victoria cookie tin, Marx sword and shield, Mulder Chariot Race Game, Lowell Chariot Race Game.

essarily know that this product was licensed by Loew's. An MGM promotional photo, however, verifies that it was.[395]

Activity Books
MGM licensed Golden Press to publish a *Golden Funtime Punch-Out Books* version that consisted of five pages of punch outs. These thin cardboard figures included two *quadrigae*, soldiers, horsemen, Ben-Hur with Esther, two camels, a man with a whip, and what seems to be Balthasar

and Iras in a howdah. Golden Press also licensed Capitol Publishing Company to produce a Golden Playbox, a colorful cardboard box with a charioteer on the front. Inside were eight double-sided cards that children could color and then wipe off along with a box of "magic" crayons. Two of the lined drawings on the cards recreate poses and scenes from the film but not the faces.

Samuel Lowe of Kenosha published a licensed coloring book illustrated by George Pollard. The covers and title page make the connection with the film. The former feature a *quadriga* charging from the large MGM *Ben-Hur* logo and, like many merchandized items, contains the phrase "directed by William Wyler." The latter features a drawing of one of the crouching athletes that decorate the film's *spina*. Below it was a boxed preface that briefly celebrates Wallace, the success of his novel, and the scope of the $15 million "milestone in motion pictures." It concludes:

> To the new "Ben-Hur" motion picture we dedicate this coloring book.
> When you see the movie, be sure to watch closely the wonderful color photography. It will give you ideas on how to color the sketches in these pages.

Almost all of the ninety-five line illustrations represent images from the film, but there is a drawing of Messala and Ben-Hur as boys, and the face of Jesus is depicted. Towards the end there are two pages illustrating Ben-Hur begging Pilate not to execute Jesus and explaining that he has become a man of peace, neither of which appear in the release version of the film but are found in earlier script versions. Similarly, Jesus cures Judah's mother and sister with a wave of the hand during his journey to the cross, not after his death by crucifixion.

International Tie-Ins
Overseas, the Dutch Victoria baking company produced a licensed line of Ben-Hur cookies sold in a large, triangular tin.[396] The embossed silver lid had a depiction of a chariot race reminiscent of Checa's crash, although the conical *metae* are more prominent. The English company, Huntley & Palmers, which had previously put images from television programs on the lids of its cookie tins, turned to cinema and in 1961 sold an oversized tin with images of the *Ben-Hur* chariot race on the lid and all four sides.[397] Separately, four distinct boxes containing 400-piece, fully interlocking jigsaw puzzles display the words "INSPIRED BY THE METRO GOLDWYN MAYER PRESENTATION OF WILLIAM WYLER'S *Ben-Hur*." The MGM *Ben-Hur* logo is also displayed on the box tops, but the manufacturer is not identified except for a small circle that says "British made." The four puzzles are: (1) The Chariot Race; (2) Collecting the Taxes; (3) A Plea for Mercy; (4) Captain of the Guard.[398] The "Plea for Mercy" depicts the arrest of Judah's mother and sister, and the "Captain of the Guard" depicts Gratus' parade through the streets of Jerusalem. Not connected to this set was a licensed

jigsaw puzzle sold in Australia. It depicted the pirates boarding Arrius' galley.[399]

In Spanish-speaking countries, a sixty-page paperback souvenir volume contained a narration of the story that the purchaser filled with the 216 tear-out color photogram stamps of the film. Copyright 1960 by Editorial Bruguera in Barcelona, Buenos Aires, and Bogotá, and distributed in Caracas and elsewhere, the title page affirmed the official authorization by MGM and again cited Wyler as director.

Uncertain Items
It is not clear if some of the other related merchandise were licensed, like the anise-flavored, Ben-Hur hard candy squares manufactured by Wonderle in Scranton, Pennsylvania.[400] In 1962 Remco produced its Big Caesar, a battery-powered Roman galley that used a motor to propel its 29-inch hull along the floor in sequence with the forward-backward-pause movements of its sixteen oars. The Big Caesar, which sold for $8.99 at Sears, came with a horse and chariot along with fifty soldiers and a cardboard Roman fort.[401] Remco also marketed Gallant Gladiator, a smaller, non-motorized Roman galley. Although neither box was marked with MGM, Loew's, or *Ben-Hur* trademarks or logos, the *Wall Street Journal* in May, 1959, reported that Stone had been negotiating for a Roman galley toy.[402] Treasure Books, Inc. of New York published their *Ben Hur Coloring Book* in 1959 without any acknowledgment. In fact, the story told in its sixty-two pages skirts around the MGM film and relies more directly on the novel, although Judah himself brings his mother and sister to Jesus to be cured. Other toys were clearly not licensed, like Mikuni Industry's Mechanical Ben-Hur Trotter [#6410]. This tin wind-up toy, marked "Made in Japan" and sold under the RHI Toys brand, consisted of a single white horse that hopped on his "hind" rabbit-like hooves and pulled a blue chariot with a beige-costumed driver holding a whip.

Ben-Hur vivant
In the country that had long ago sold Ramon Novarro dolls and more recently adopted the expression *arête ton char Ben-Hur* into its vernacular, this new *Ben-Hur* film inspired Alexis and André Gruss and Radio-Télé-Luxembourg to co-produce a live circus adaptation, *Ben-Hur vivant*.[403] Roger Bourgeon wrote the script, and a stereophonic recording featuring Paul-Émile Deiber of the Comédie Française was played through the sound system at the Palais des Sports, where "thundering chariots and roaring real lions gallop around a genuine arena to the delight of the youngsters."[404] Appropriately, the role of Messala was played by a lion tamer. Premiering on December 20, 1961, *Ben-Hur vivant* had considerable success over its four-year run and was taken on tour in France, Belgium, and Spain under the direction of the Grand Cirque de France.[405]

It was revived in 1975/6 by Jean Richard at his Nouvel Hippodrome de Paris.[406] A poster for a Brussels performance of Richard's *Ben-Hur* boasts of 100 artists, gladiators, acrobats, and galley slaves participating in a chariot race and a Roman circus with forty horses, elephants, camels, llamas, and lions.[407] *Ben-Hur vivant* spilled over into other European countries as well. In 1962 and 1963 Sacha Houcke's Ben Hur was the first act on the Blackpool Tower Circus Programme.[408] Houcke belonged to the family that designed the chariot races at the Grand Palais in Paris,[409] and his *jeux équestre romain ben hur* was on the program of the 1962 Swiss National Circus.[410]

In 1963 Bourgeon authored a novel, *Le Fils de Ben Hur*, which continued the story of early Christianity through the great Neronian fire in Rome up to the accession of Vespasian, the savior of Josephus, and described the destruction of Jerusalem and the eruption of Vesuvius through the eyes of Judah's son Philippe.[411] Successful in Europe, the novel was translated into five languages. Not surprisingly, the following year a line of Ben-Hur sunglasses was exported from France and advertised in the *New York Times*.[412] Ben Hur sunglasses were still being advertised and sold by Filene's in Boston and elsewhere in 1971.[413]

The success of what was officially named *Ben-Hur vivant au Grand Cirque de France* spun-off into the French recording industry. Of the musical numbers credited to Bourgeon and composer Maurice Thiriet, four were recorded by such artists and groups as Georges Guétary, Les Hommes (under the direction of Luis Peña), Lucien Lupi, and Franck Pourcel on 45 rpm vinyl records.[414] The four musical numbers were *Chanson de Ben Hur*, *Complainte de L'Opprime*, *Plainte des Legions de Rome*, and *Voice donc*. Separately, André Verchuren and his orchestra recorded *La March de Ben-Hur*, released in both 45 rpm and LP formats.[415] The jacket photographs for the 45 rpm records ranged from drawings of Ben-Hur driving a *quadriga* (Les Hommes; Lupi) to Ben-Hur standing before Calvary (Guétary). The Verchuren jacket photograph recreates the performance, capturing the moment Messala, dressed in black, is falling off his wheel-less chariot as a white-robed, white-booted Ben-Hur looks back at him from his own two-horse chariot.

These occasioned a variety of other recordings. Edmond Taillet and Antoine Cabestron released 45 rpm recordings of *Arrête ton char, Ben-Hur* by André Pascal, Raymond Mamoudy, and Marcel Rossi.[416] Cabestron subtitled his version "cha cha Marseilles." Similarly, Hans Werner and His 40 Violins recorded a cha-cha version of Rózsa's love theme in the 45 rpm format.[417] And the Odéon label reissued Berthe Sylva's recording of *L'Histoire de Ben-Hur*, the song by Louis Poterat and Paul Sterman published in 1929 in association with the French release of the 1925 film.[418]

Three different French narrative recreations of *Ben-Hur* were issued on LPs. Contemporary but not officially associated with the MGM production was a 1959 adaptation by Pierre Chambon on the Festival label of Les Disques de France.[419] The script adapted Wallace's book and included roles for Iras, Amrah, and Malluch, and unlike the other adaptations, an original score, mostly for solo instruments, was commissioned from Étienne Lorin. Here the role of Ben-Hur was played by established theater, film, and television actor Jacques Dacqmine. In 1960 Philips issued a single disk retelling of the story narrated by the Belgian actor, Jean Servais.[420] In telling an abbreviated and simplified version of the MGM adaptation, other established actors like Yves Furet and Jean Rochefort played the roles of Judah and Messala along with speaking roles for only Judah's mother, Tirzah, Esther, Simonides, and Arrius. Snippets of Rózsa's music were used in the background, and, like the earlier radio adaptations and the Chambon album, sound effects like those of a falling tile, soldiers banging at the Hur door, cracking whips, chains, horses' hooves, and crowd noises filled out the realization. The most ambitious of these recorded albums was the *adaptation phonographique* by Lucien Adès for his Le Petit Ménestrel series.[421] Designed for a young audience, this two-disk set came packaged in a twenty-page album containing a French script adapted from the MGM screenplay, photographs of the MGM film, and an arrangement of Rózsa's score, with acknowledgements on several different pages. The story was narrated by Jean Desailly, formerly of the Comédie Français. Playing the role of Ben-Hur was Serge Reggiani, who had starred in Jean Paul Sartre's most recent play.

At the other end of the intellectual spectrum in France, Wyler's reputation as a cinematic artist suffered and earned him "the scorn of intellectuals."[422] As the director associated with the most expensive action sequence ever filmed and a huge money-maker, Wyler mused that "*Cahiers du Cinema* never forgave me. I was completely written off as a serious director by the avant-garde."[423] Even so, Jean Cocteau was said to have had high regard for the film.

Other Impacts
Because the film had long since established and maintained such a high level of public familiarity, homages and parodies remained current as well. The NBC Milton Berle Spectacular featured a musical skit with Berle dressing as Cleopatra, Jack Benny as Ben-Hur, and Laurence Harvey as Spartacus, with cameos by Heston and Kirk Douglas.[424] Broadcast on NBC in March, 1962, the show was repeated in the summer of 1963.[425] In an episode (3.3) of the highly rated *Beverly Hillbillies* broadcast on October 7, 1964 (and repeated July 10, 1965), Jed Clampett buys a movie studio where the head of production plans to make "Spartacus and Ben-Hur Meet Cleopatra and Nero at the Fall of the Roman Empire."[426] In 1970, after the reissue, The Dean Martin Show had Charles Nelson Reilly deliver the line, "Loved Ben, Hated Hur."[427]

Los Angeles remained a hot bed of Ben-Hur activity among diverse segments of the population. During a 1961 football game at the Los Angeles Coliseum, Richard Saukko, wearing one of the outfits Heston had worn in the 1959 film, introduced his white Arabian horse, Traveler [I], as the University of Southern California mascot. The mounted Trojan changed the cumbersome outfit the following year but occasionally wore Heston's helmet again until the year of his retirement in 1988. Also in 1961, students at the California State College in Los Angeles had inaugurated annual Inter-Fraternity Chariot Races.[428] Just like the Pasadena races at the beginning of the century, coverage in the *Los Angeles Times* in 1965 described Ben-Hur as a quasi-historical personage:

> A Greek scholar might have termed it the degeneration of sport. On the other hand, Ben Hur might have been downright fascinated. . . . Tau Kappa Epsilon won after a grueling match with Sigma Nu, but Ben Hur would have disqualified them: who ever heard of a chariot with an aluminum body and rubber-tired wheels?

In 1963 the black community welcomed the opening of the Ben-Hur Supper Club on Western Avenue.[429] Johnny Otis was the headline act, and the club soon feted Tom Bradley, then a newly elected councilman.[430]

In Pasadena that same year Casey Tibbs, rodeo champion turned film actor and stuntman, organized the first annual Rose Bowl Rodeo, advertised as the largest single-day rodeo in the world. One of the scheduled special events was a chariot race that featured some of the horses used in the *Ben-Hur* production.[431] That same week, Dorman's clothing store on La Cienega placed a full-page advertisement in the *Times*, and seven of its eight columns are filled with imagery associated with *Ben-Hur*.[432] A chariot pulled by two well-dressed centaurs races in front of the store, and the store is nestled beneath a colossal stone rendition of the words "BIG SALE" piled high like the *Ben-Hur* stone logo designed by Joe Smith. The copy makes the association not only explicit but adds that the artists insist:

> . . . that we should not come out and have to explain that this mighty sketch is a take-off on the Ben-Hur movie ads. They believe that any reader who cannot instantly tell that for himself would not be bright enough for Dorman's.

Elsewhere in Southern California, Carole Anne Washburn, the Queen of the 72nd Tournament of Roses in 1960, proudly told the press she owned a dapple-gray, gelding thoroughbred named Ben Hur.[433] A hot rod converted from a wooden chariot used in the 1959 MGM film was displayed at the 1967 annual Fresno Autorama Custom Car Show. And Lee's Bars 'N Stools in Anaheim sold a $300 Ben Hur Chariot Bar with two stools made from whiskey barrels.[434]

In the Midwest, Good News Publishers issued a 64-page "One Evening Condensed Book" version of the novel in 1964. The preface narrates a revisionist history, claiming that Wallace was already a devout Christian at the time of the Ingersoll encounter and that he then traveled to Palestine for further study to prepare for writing the book, which can now be viewed as somewhat of a harbinger of the Christian focus that would re-emerge in the 1990s.[435]

In entirely different sectors of the entertainment business, again demonstrating the broad penetration of the *Ben-Hur* phenomenon, Peter Sellers spoofed Francis X. Bushman's role in a *Playboy* pictorial by posing with a topless Iras.[436] Chicago's Capri Cinema advertised its "SeeMoreScope" feature *Goldilocks and The Three Bears* as "the 'Ben Hur' of all nature-camp movies."[437] Another parody came in the inaugural issue of *Sick* in August, 1960, with their review of "Bin Her." They included eight photos from the MGM production along with parodic captions. Photos of Hugh Griffith as the Sheik, for instance, are said to be of Frank Nassar – a reference to the then-president of Egypt – the director of the picture that "took eight years to make, although in the final version, the picture only runs five years." The photo of "Cheston Histon" aiming the spear at Messala is said to be Histon trying to break his contract with his business manager.

As with the Klaw & Erlanger and 1925 MGM productions, the 1959 *Ben-Hur* inspired a minor resurgence in horse and chariot racing after its popularity peaked. The original MGM "Ben Hur Chariots" appeared frequently in the national rodeo and horseshow circuits, for instance, the Phoenix Jaycees 31st Annual Rodeo of Rodeos in March, 1962, and the Flying Horseshoe in Kirkland, Washington, in June, 1963.[438] As late as 1964 eight of the horses used for filming the chariot race were still being harnessed and raced at Tucson's annual La Fiesta de los Vaqueros, and they were still being insured for $100,000 each.[439] The year after the rerelease, the unconventional baseball owner Bill Veeck, who had begun operating Boston's Suffolk Downs, arranged a number of extravaganzas for the opening, culminating in the "Ben Hur Handicap," a chariot race consisting of two trial heats followed by a championship race.[440] Veeck said that he got the idea when he read about the upcoming MGM auction, where he bought four of the *Ben-Hur* chariots for $7600, and borrowed or traded for the one on display at Caesars Palace from his friend Billy Weinberger.[441] This enabled him to precede the racing with a *Ben-Hur*-like parade with local "disc jockeys" dressed in Roman costume and accompanied by Rózsa's march music.

In advertising, Maidenform adapted their long-running "I dreamed –" campaign to *Ben-Hur*. The full-page ad in 1961 issues of *Everywoman's Family Circle, Life,* and *Ladies' Home Journal* depicted a woman driving a chariot while wearing a Roman helmet with a red plume, red epaulets, a red skirt, and her bra. Behind her red cape we see an out-of-focus chariot race between white and brown teams. The signature text reads, "I dreamed I drove them wild in my *maidenform bra*." In July of the

Figure 14.4 The 1959 MGM *Ben-Hur* reached an extraordinarily broad demographic spectrum both in the U.S. and abroad.

same year, *Woman's Day* printed a full-page photo of a brightly painted, home-made, plywood Ben Hur Chariot, "the greatest thing on wheels since Roman days."[442] Readers were urged to write to their Greenwich, Connecticut, post-office box to obtain building instructions.

At this point the *Ben-Hur* tradition had continued so long, the 1959 film inspired nostalgic remembrances of the past. As Ben Hur Farms of Portland, Indiana, was still breeding champions in Midwest and East Coast shows and fairs,[443] Zack Miller's Appaloosa Ben Hur from the 101 Ranch Western Show reappeared in a photographic exhibit at the Idaho State Museum in 1963,[444] and Wallace's chariot race was reprinted in an anthology of eighteen stories about horse racing, Fairfax Downey's *Races to the Swift: Great Stories of the Turf*.[445]

As before, the thrill and concept of chariot racing carried the Ben-Hur name further afield. Racer and boat designer Hal Kelly, whose motto was "You can build a better boat than you can buy," designed an 11ft. 3in. 'C' & 'D' 3-point Cab-over Ben Hur hydroplane and sold the plans through a mail-order catalog.[446] Auto racing was once again compared to chariot racing, as was contemporary Roman traffic.[447] In her syndicated column written in Rome in 1963 under the headline, "Charioteers of Ancient Rome Ride Again," Inez Robb wrote:

> It is often said that all American drivers are cowboys at heart. The tradition and pattern are much more ancient in Italy. All Italian drivers are charioteers by conviction. They drive with the daring of Ben Hur at his peak in the Colosseum. It is exciting to watch if you are observing from the window of a good, sturdy hotel.[448]

A Washington *Evening Star* staff writer joked that a newly manufactured Boeing 747 had an interior large enough for a chariot race.[449] And another columnist even compared the rusty old bolts holding his license plates in place to the menacing serrated blades on Messala's chariot![450]

In the business world, Bob Bennis and Hyman Hurwitz opened a Ford dealership in Sioux Falls, South Dakota, in 1965.[451] They named it "Ben-Hur Ford," using the first three letters of their last names.[452] The dealership reportedly won *Time Magazine*'s "Dealer of the Year" in 1976, and Hurwitz's obituary says that he maintained "a strong tradition of providing 'chariots' to customers across the Midwest."

The 1970s would bring an end to the continuous preponderance of *Ben-Hur* successes and allusions. Some of the most pervasive reasons for this will be discussed in the concluding chapter, but here in connection with chariot racing we can point out that Ringling Brothers announced that they would cease to perform Ben-Hur-style chariot races because their venues were now modern concrete buildings with hard floors.[453] Gone were the days of empty urban and suburban lots where they could erect tents over natural dirt. Perhaps of the greatest symbolic importance was that it was in 1970 that MGM held the historic auction of its huge inventory of costumes and props, including the famed Ruby Slippers as well as the aforementioned *Ben-Hur* chariots and several hundred *Ben-Hur* costumes and props, from Judah's caftan to Messala's black tunic with gold trim to the ill-fated Corinthian charioteer's costume of "green suede with black and gold trim, belt, and helmet."[454] This was one of the major steps the company took in stripping out its film production and distribution units and diversifying into television and its hotel in Las Vegas.[455] Nonetheless, as we shall see in the next chapter, MGM was by no means finished distributing and profiting from its 1959 *Ben-Hur*. And little did anyone think then that MGM might be involved in producing yet another *Ben-Hur* forty-five years later.

NOTES

1 *TFD* 41 (September 20, 1927) 3–4.
2 *LAT* (January 31, 1934) 11.
3 *LAT* (July 14, 1934) 7.
4 *NYT* (September 13, 1936) X4.
5 *LAT* (March 3, 1940) C2.
6 *LAT* (March 5, 1943) 22.
7 *NYHT* (December 28, 1952) D3.
8 *CT* (December 27, 1951) N7.
9 *NYT* (December 8, 1952) 34.
10 *Variety* 195 (August 25, 1954) 1.
11 *NYHT* (July 5, 1953) D3; cf. *NYT* (August 28, 1955) X5.
12 *NYT* (November 4, 1953) 29.
13 *NYHT* (October 8, 1953) 27.
14 *Variety* 195 (August 25, 1954) 1.
15 *CT* (October 9, 1953) A7.
16 *LAT* (January 31, 1954) D1; *TCSM* (June 2, 1954) 4.
17 Heston and Isbouts, *Charlton Heston's Hollywood*, 96–9; *Variety* 203 (August 29, 1956) 7.
18 *NYT* (January 26, 1958) X5.
19 Lev, *Transforming the Screen*, 198.
20 *NYT* (March 9, 1963) 5.
21 *Variety* 208 (October 2, 1957) 16.
22 *Variety* 203 (August 29, 1956) 7; *NYT* (June 28, 1957) 24.
23 Herman, *A Talent for Trouble*, 393.
24 *NYT* (December 8, 1952) 34.
25 Quirk, *Paul Newman: A Life*, 53–4; Herman, *A Talent for Trouble*, 393.
26 *CT* (February 9, 1958) B36.
27 Heston, *An Actor's Life*, 31; Herman, *A Talent for Trouble*, 395.
28 *LAT* (January 17, 1958) 20.
29 *NYHT* (January 10, 1958) 14, *NYT* (January 12, 1958) X7; (January 23, 1958) 23; (January 29, 1958) 70; *Variety* 209 (January 29, 1958) 70.
30 *American Cinematographer* 40 (October, 1959) 625.

31 *LAT* (January 20, 1958) C11. In contrast, MGM omitted the question mark from *Quo Vadis?*
32 *NYT* (March 19, 1958) 34; (April 14, 1958) 20; (May 17, 1958) 12; *LAT* (April 4, 1958) 13; (April 23, 1958) A9; (May 30, 1958) A5.
33 *LAT* (July 9, 1957) A9.
34 Dane, *A Composer's Notes*, 21.
35 *NYT* (December 5, 1954) X9; *Variety* 216 (November 4, 1959) 16.
36 *NYT* (March 2, 1954) B6; Letter from MGM to Mary Dorfman (March 10, 1959), HL.
37 *NYHT* (November 1, 1959) 77, reports that Anderson was too ill to contribute.
38 Script dated September 9, 1954, HL.
39 Script dated June 21, 1955, completed October 14, 1955, authored by Karl Tunberg, University of Missouri-Kansas City.
40 <https://www.youtube.com/watch?v=y_4jGoMfzYM>; and a DVD special feature.
41 Sinyard, *A Wonderful Heart*, 185; Miller, *William Wyler*, 332–4.
42 Herman, *A Talent for Trouble*, 394.
43 Heston, *An Actor's Life*, 57–61.
44 Memo from Jan Lustig (June 21, 1957), HL.
45 Held by The Lilly Library, Indiana University; *Variety* 216 (November 4, 1959) 16.
46 Letter from William Wyler to Christopher Fry (June 19, 1959), HL.
47 Late May: Vidal, *Palimpsest*, 307; Kaplan, *Gore Vidal*, 440–6. June 24: Letter from William Wyler to Michael H. Franklin [SWG] (June 18, 1959), HL.
48 <http://caligula.org/ben-hur.html>
49 Kaplan, *Gore Vidal*, 445.
50 *Chicago Daily Defender* (June 24, 1959) 24.
51 Letter from J. J. Cohn to William Wyler (December 29, 1959), HL
52 *The Guardian* (November 5,1959) 7; Kaplan, *Gore Vidal*, 445.
53 Letter from William Wyler to Christopher Fry (June 19, 1959), HL.
54 Herman, *A Talent for Trouble*, 397–8.
55 *NYT* (January 11, 1959) X7.
56 *BG* (November 15, 1959) A6; *LAT* (June 29, 1958) E1; MGM Pressbook 4.
57 Cunutt and Drake, *Stunt Man*, 1–20.
58 *NYHT* (September 28, 1958) D5.
59 *Variety* 208 (September 11, 1957) 12; Herman, *A Talent for Trouble*, 406–7.
60 Cunutt, *Stunt Man*, viii.
61 Heston, *In the Arena*, 194.
62 Heston, *The Actor's Life*, 60.
63 Herman, *A Talent for Trouble*, 394.
64 Herman, *A Talent for Trouble*, 402.
65 Herman, *A Talent for Trouble*, 403.
66 Herman, *A Talent for Trouble*, 408–9.
67 Herman, *A Talent for Trouble*, 403.
68 Herman, *A Talent for Trouble*, 410.

69 Herman, *A Talent for Trouble*, 404–5; <http://www.thewildeye.co.uk/blog/performers-directors/who-was-remington-olmstead>
70 According to Erkelenz, "*Ben-Hur*: A Tale of the Score," 28, after consultation with Rózsa.
71 Letters from Wyler to the Writers Guild of America (June 17 and 18, 1959), HL.
72 *LAT* (June 29, 1958) E1.
73 "Outlook," broadcast July 13, 1958, on NBC television, UCLA Library.
74 *TCSM* (September 4, 1958) 7.
75 *CT* (July 12, 1958) C8.
76 *LAT* (December 21, 1958) D1.
77 *NYT* (August 10, 1958) X5.
78 *NYT* (June 7, 1958) 11; *BG* (June 7, 1958) 2.
79 Heston, *The Actor's Life*, 44.
80 *The Billboard* 70 (February 3, 1958) 22.
81 E.g. *Cleveland Call and Post* (October 25, 1958) 4C.
82 *Variety* 210 (June 11, 1958) 11; *CT* (September 16, 1958) A6.
83 *CT* (June 30, 1958) B14.
84 *LAT* (June 24, 1958) 16.
85 *LAT* (July 8, 1958) B6.
86 *LAT* (June 29, 1958) E1.
87 *NYT* (June 29, 1958) X5.
88 *Newsday* (July 28, 1958) 1C.
89 *NYHT* (July 18, 1958) 10; *The Sun* (May 25, 1958) FA9.
90 *NYT* (July 18, 1958) 16.
91 *TBS* (July 27, 1958) F9.
92 *LAT* (August 20, 1958) 28.
93 *LAT* (August 12, 1958) C7; cf. Heater, *Fatal Flaws*, 379.
94 *LAT* (September 10, 1958) 22.
95 *TBS* (August 24, 1958) A8.
96 *NYT* (August 10, 1958) X5; *CT* (September 14, 1958) E13.
97 *LAT* (September 15, 1958) 5.
98 *NYHT* (September 28, 1958) D5.
99 *CT* (October 11, 1958) 8.
100 *Variety* 212 (September 24, 1958) 4.
101 *Variety* 212 (September 17, 1958) 3 and 22.
102 *LAT* (October 9, 1958) B11; (October 21, 1958) A9; *CT* (October 12, 1958) G18.
103 *LAT* (November 23, 1958) TW10; *NYHT* (November 23, 1958) SM10.
104 *The Sun* (December 21, 1958) TW14; *LAT* (December 21, 1958) D1; *NYT* (January 11, 1959) X7.
105 *WSJ* (February 27, 1959) 4.
106 *Variety* 214 (March 4, 1959) 7.
107 *Chicago Daily Defender* (May 7, 1959) 21; *Eureka Humboldt [CA] Standard* (December 19, 1959) 32; fold in the possession of the author.
108 *WP* (March 19, 1959) B12; (April 9, 1959) A21.
109 *WP* (April 15, 1959) C6; *LAT* (May 12, 1959) 24; *NYHT* (August 23, 1959) D1.

110 *NYT* (June 28, 1959) BR8.
111 *LAT* (May 29, 1959) B10.
112 *LAT* (July 3, 1959) 16.
113 [Oklahoma City] *Daily Oklahoman* (July 5, 1959) 104; *Variety* 215 (August 5, 1959) 12.
114 *NYT* (May 12, 1959) 47.
115 *NYT* (August 18, 1959) 37.
116 *NYHT* (July 26, 1959) D6.
117 <http://www.tv.com/shows/the-ed-sullivan-show/charlton-heston-xavier-cugat-and-abbe-lane-leon-bibb-120129/>
118 *Boxoffice* 75 (August 10, 1959) 11.
119 *Variety* 215 (August 26, 1959) 7 and 18.
120 *Variety* 216 (September 16, 1959) 5.
121 Cf. *Photoplay Studies* 24 (November, 1959).
122 *BG* (November 1, 1959) 35.
123 MGM Pressbook, 32.
124 *Cinefantastique* 18 (March, 1988) 91, 96, and 100.
125 MGM Pressbook, 30; *Pittsburgh Courier* (July 23, 1960) A17.
126 E.g. *LAT* (September 22, 1959) A1; *WP, Times Herald* (September 6, 1959) H5; *Variety* 215 (August 19, 1959) 2; *NYHT* (October 19, 1959) 13; *CT* (November 1, 1959) F3 and G24.
127 *WP, Times Herald* (November 18, 1959) D8.
128 *BG* (November 1, 1959) A22.
129 *LAT* (November 2, 1959) A11.
130 *BG* (October 11, 1959) A11.
131 *BG* (October 4, 1959) 76.
132 E.g. *Los Angeles Mirror* (November 21, 1959) 3. The eyewitness account by Nosher Powell [Powell, *Nosher*, 215–17] of the stuntman playing the Corinthian being dragged to death cannot be corroborated.
133 *BG* (November 15, 1959) A6 and A43.
134 *TCSM* (October 24, 1959) 11.
135 *CT* (November 5, 1959) B19.
136 *NYHT* (November 15, 1959) D1; *Newsday* (November 18, 1959) 1C; *TCSM* (November 12, 1959) 11.
137 *The Guardian* (November 5, 1959) 7.
138 *The Irish Times* (November 17, 1959) 3.
139 E.g. *Los Angeles Mirror* (November 21, 1959) 3.
140 *American Cinematographer* 40 (October, 1959) 604–5 and 622–5; 41 (February, 1960) 94–5, 112, and 114; 41 (March, 1960) 162–3 and 192.
141 *Newsday* (November 16, 1959) 4C.
142 *NYT* (November 8, 1959) SM26.
143 *Variety* 216 (November 4, 1959) 2.
144 *NYHT* (November 9, 1959) 34.
145 *LAT* (April 4, 1958) 13.
146 *Variety* 210 (May 21, 1958) 22.
147 *LAT* (April 4, 1958) 13.
148 Herman, *A Talent for Trouble*, 413.

149 *LAT* (October 26, 1958) G3.
150 *CT* (August 8, 1958) 17; *Newsday* (August 7, 1958) 3C.
151 Battaglio, *David Suskind*, 33–5.
152 *NYT* (August 14, 1958) 53.
153 *BG* (October 13, 1959) 15.
154 *LAT* (June 12, 1959) A11; *Variety* 215 (July 15, 1959) 28.
155 *Variety* 215 (June 17, 1959) 1–3.
156 *NYT* (July 21, 1959) 25.
157 *BG* (July 29, 1959) 15; (July 26, 1959) A5.
158 *Variety* 214 (March 11, 1959) 22.
159 *Philadelphia Tribune* (July 25, 1959) 10.
160 *Variety* 213 (February 4, 1959) 5; *Variety* 214 (March 25, 1959) 24.
161 *LAT* (July 29, 1959) 19.
162 *NYHT* (August 23, 1959) D1; *TCSM* (July 29, 1959) 5.
163 *LAT* (November 14, 1959) 8.
164 *Variety* 215 (July 22, 1959) 3.
165 *Variety* 214 (April 8, 1959) 4.
166 *Variety* 214 (April 15, 1959) 22; cf. *Variety* 215 (June 10, 1959) 11.
167 *[Chicago] Daily Defender* (June 24, 1959) 24.
168 *Variety* (August 12, 1959) 27.
169 *TCSM* (July 29, 1959) 5.
170 *Variety* 215 (August 26, 1959) 18.
171 *[Chicago] Daily Defender* (June 23, 1959) 17.
172 *LAT* (June 23, 1959) 23.
173 *Variety* 216 (September 2, 1959) 22.
174 *Variety* 216 (September 2, 1959) 73; *Chicago Tribune* (November 22, 1959) 7.12.
175 *Boxoffice* (November 9, 1959) 31.
176 *Variety* 215 (July 8, 1959) 3.
177 *Variety* 215 (July 8, 1959) 3.
178 *Variety* 215 (July 15, 1959) 3.
179 *LAT* (September 18, 1959) A11; *Variety* 216 (September 9, 1959) 7; *Dallas Morning News* (February 14, 1969) 14; *LAT* (September 25, 1959) A11.
180 *Variety* 216 (September 23, 1959) 3.
181 <http://filmscoremonthly.com/notes/ben_hur_info.html>
182 *NYT* (October 7, 1959) 47.
183 *BG* (October 25, 1959) 61; *NYT* (October 7, 1959) 47.
184 *Variety* 216 (November 4, 1959) 5; *Variety* 216 (November 18, 1959) 6.
185 *NYT* (October 11, 1959) X8.
186 *NYHT* (October 19, 1959) 13.
187 *NYHT* (October 31, 1959) 6.
188 *LAT* (October 13, 1959) 25.
189 *NYT* (October 16, 1959) 27.
190 *Boxoffice* (November 9, 1959) 11–18.
191 *NYT* (November 16, 1959) 40.
192 *Variety* 216 (November 18, 1959) 86.
193 *WP* (November 13, 1959) D6.

194 *Valparaiso Vidette Messenger* (November 12, 1959) 10.
195 *Tipton [IN] Tribune* (November 14, 1959) 4.
196 *Climax* 6 (August, 1960) 54–66.
197 *NYHT* (December 6, 1959) D4; cf. *NYHT* (December 6, 1959) D4.
198 *WSJ* (May 18,1959) 1.
199 *WSJ* (September 3, 1959) 19.
200 *NYT* (November 18, 1959) 46.
201 *NYT* (July 21, 1959) 25.
202 *WSJ* (May 18, 1959) 1.
203 *WSJ* (May 18, 1959) 1.
204 *Variety* 216 (November 18, 1959) 1.
205 *Life* 46 (January 19, 1959) 73.
206 *Life* 47 (November 16, 1959) 118–34.
207 *Life* 47 (December 7, 1959) 20 and 23.
208 *The Saturday Evening Post* 233 (August 20, 1960) 20-1 and 40-3; *Look* (May 24, 1960) 56H-L.
209 *NYT* (November 18, 1959) 47; *WP* (November 18, 1959) C9; *Variety* 216 (October 7, 1959) 22.
210 *NYT* (November 19, 1959) 50.
211 *NYT* (November 21, 1959) 26.
212 E.g. *Lebanon [PA] Daily News* (November 20, 1959) 5.
213 *Variety* 216 (November 18, 1959) 1.
214 *LAT* (November 25, 1959) A1; (November 26, 1959) A3.
215 *LAT* (November 25, 1959) B5.
216 *LAT* (November 22, 1959) E1; (November 25, 1959) 2.
217 *LAT* (November 28, 1959) 13.
218 *News of the Day* "'VIP' Opening – Capital Welcome for *Ben-Hur*," UCLA Library.
219 Program in the possession of the author.
220 *Boxoffice* (November 9, 1959) 11–18; *Variety* 220 (September 7, 1960) 13.
221 *News of the Day* "Japan's Emperor Goes to the Movies," UCLA Library.
222 *Variety* 219 (July 6, 1960) 17.
223 *Variety* 216 (November 18, 1959) 1.
224 *LAT* (November 25, 1959) 2.
225 *LAT* (November 20, 1959) B7; *CT* (November 20, 1959) B20.
226 *NYT* (November 22, 1959) X1.
227 *BG* (November 24, 1959) 26.
228 *Newsday* (November 19, 1959) 1C.
229 *Variety* 216 (November 18, 1959) 6.
230 *LAT* (November 30, 1959) C11.
231 *Variety* 217 (December 23, 1959) 10–16.
232 Brownlow, *The Parade's Gone By...*, 411.
233 *The Independent* (April 16, 1996) 12; cf. <http://looking-for-mabel.webs.com/extragirlreview.htm>
234 *Seattle Daily Times* (November 11, 1973) 101.
235 Everson, *American Silent Film*, 293.
236 *NYHT* (November 19, 1959) 17.

237 *TCSM* (January 6, 1960) 7.
238 *The Irish Times* (September 12, 1960) 8.
239 *Boxoffice* 76 (November 9, 1959) 7; <http://tvbythenumbers.zap2it.com/2009/02/17/academy-awards-show-ratings/12818>
240 *LAT* (October 9, 1958) B11.
241 Correspondence between Wyler and Michael H. Franklin (June 18–November 23, 1959), HL.
242 Cf. *NYT* (October 29, 1959) 38.
243 Cf. *Variety* 216 (November 4, 1959) 16.
244 Ibid., 16; *LAT* (October 5, 1955) 29.
245 *NYT* (October 7, 1959) 47.
246 *NYT* (October 29, 1959) 38; *NYHT* (November 1, 1959) 77.
247 *LAT* (November 2, 1959) C11.
248 *BG* (November 5, 1959) 63.
249 Letter from J. J. Cohn to William Wyler, December 29, 1959, HL.
250 Letter from Mary Zimbalist to the Screen Writers Guild, November 2, 1959, HL.
251 *Boston Record American* (January 17, 1960) 17.
252 *Cleveland Plain Dealer* (January 27, 1960) 23.
253 *[Washington, DC] Evening Star* (February 24, 1960) 30.
254 E.g. *Greensboro [NC] Record* (April 5, 1960) 1.
255 E.g. *Seattle Daily Times* (April 5, 1960) 16.
256 E.g. *Springfield [MA] Union* (April 5, 1960) 1.
257 *[Washington, DC] Evening Star* (April 10, 1960) 45.
258 Drafted April 15, 1960, according to Heston, *An Actor's Life*, 92; cf. *Trenton Evening Times* (June 1, 1960) 19.
259 Heston, *An Actor's Life*, 92.
260 *San Diego Union* (June 22, 1960) 11.
261 *San Diego Union* (August 8, 1960) 8.
262 *CT* (February 14, 1960) E11.
263 Cf. Ibid., E11.
264 *Variety* 216 (November 18, 1959) 3.
265 *Variety* 218 (May 25, 1960) 19.
266 Program for the October 14–22, 1960, American Royal Horse Show in Kansas City, 21. Page 49 contains an advertisement for the MGM film at the Durwood Capri Theater in Kansas City.
267 In the possession of the author.
268 *LAT* (November 21, 1960) C14.
269 *LAT* (May 30, 1961) C7.
270 *CT* (April 16, 1961) D12.
271 *CT* (June 30, 1960) A10.
272 *TBS* (March 29, 1960) 36.
273 *TCSM* (September 26, 1961) 4; *Boxoffice* 90 (April 17, 1967) 7.
274 *Life* 49 (November 21, 1960) 88.
275 *Boxoffice* 79 (October 2, 1961) 10.
276 *Boxoffice* 79 (July 3, 1961) 6.
277 *CT* (June 22, 1962) B5.

278 *CT* (June 26, 1962) A4.
279 *LAT* (March 21, 1963) C13; (March 27, 1963) D12.
280 *LAT* (July 30, 1960) A6.
281 *Chicago Daily Defender* (March 28, 1961) 11.
282 *LAT* (December 21, 1962) D9.
283 *NYT* (May 14, 1960) 15.
284 *LAT* (July 30, 1960) A6.
285 *NYT* (January 28, 1962) 87.
286 *Variety* 236 (May 23, 1962) 18.
287 *LAT* (December 12, 1963) C28.
288 E.g. *The Observer* (January 5, 1964) 23; *ToI* (January 31, 1964) 2.
289 *CT* (August 13, 1967) 7.
290 *Variety* 284 (August 25, 1976) 34.
291 *Variety* 286 (March 23, 1977) 46.
292 *Variety* 235 (June 10, 1964) 13; 253 (February 12, 1969) 3; 287 (May 11, 1977) 27.
293 *Variety* 252 (August 28, 1968) 5; 253 (February 12, 1969) 3.
294 *BG* (September 29, 1968) D2.
295 Balio, *Hollywood in the Age of Television*, 259.
296 *Variety* 253 (February 12, 1969) 3 and 17.
297 *Variety* 253 (February 12, 1969) 3 and 17.
298 *Variety* 252 (October 2, 1968) 33.
299 *Variety* 253 (February 12, 1969) 3.
300 *Variety* 254 (February 19, 1969) 4.
301 *Boston Record* (March 6, 1969) 23.
302 *Boston Record American* (February 25, 1969) 32.
303 *Dallas Morning News* (February 27, 1969) 21; *Variety* 254 (February 26, 1969) 19.
304 *Dallas Morning News* (March 3, 1969) 11.
305 *Springfield [MA] Union* (February 28, 1969) 17.
306 *Boxoffice* 94 (February 24, 1969) 11.
307 *[Washington, DC] Evening Star* (March 26, 1969) 2.
308 *[Washington, DC] Evening Star* (April 1, 1969) 27.
309 *Boxoffice* 94 (March 17, 1969) 11.
310 *[Washington, DC] Evening Star* (April 2, 1969) 89.
311 *Boxoffice* 94 (May 5, 1969) 9.
312 E.g. *Boston American Record* (January 15, 1971) 48.
313 *[Washington, DC] Evening Star* (March 26, 1970) 46.
314 *Seattle Daily Times* (May 18, 1969) 109.
315 *Variety* 254 (March 26, 1969) 26.
316 *Boston Record* (January 6, 1970) 10.
317 *Springfield [MA] Union* (December 23, 1969) 17.
318 *[Portland] Oregonian* (January 20, 1971) 35.
319 *San Diego Union* (December 28, 1971) 31; *Dallas Morning News* (April 1, 1972) E3.
320 *Marietta [GA] Journal* (December 21, 1972) 17.
321 *NYT* (December 31, 1961) SM10.
322 *WSJ* (August 3, 1960) 1.

323 *LAT* (January 6, 1961) A11.
324 *WP, Times Herald* (October 10, 1962) C12.
325 *NYT* (August 15, 1962) 45.
326 *NYHT* (January 7, 1962) 16.
327 *BG* (October 21, 1962) A77.
328 *Newsday* (May 31, 1962) 2C.
329 *Variety* 232 (October 2, 1963) 24.
330 *WSJ* (July 26, 1962) 2.
331 *WP, Times Herald* (March 29, 1963) B10.
332 *[Norfolk] New Journal and Guide* (August 15, 1964) 21.
333 *Newsday* (November 16, 1959) 4C.
334 *Variety* 225 (January 10, 1962) 13 and 59.
335 *Variety* 231 (May 29, 1963) 3.
336 *Variety* 269 (January 3, 1973) 30.
337 Block and Wilson, *George Lucas' Blockbusting*, xvi, 323–4.
338 <http://www.boxofficemojo.com/alltime/adjusted.htm>
339 *Variety* 213 (February 11, 1959) 5; (February 18, 1959) 3; *Variety* 214 (April 15, 1959) 7.
340 *Variety* 214 (April 15, 1959) 17.
341 *Variety* 215 (July 8, 1959) 23.
342 *Variety* 214 (April 8, 1959) 4; *NYT* (July 21, 1959) 25; *NYHT* (August 23, 1959) D1.
343 *Variety* 215 (July 8, 1959) 3.
344 *Variety* 205 (January 23, 1957) 61.
345 *CT* (November 29, 1959) D6.
346 *The Guardian* (October 16, 1959) 10.
347 *WSJ* (May 18, 1959) 1.
348 MGM Press release (no date), UVA.
349 *Barron's* (May 3, 1965) 11.
350 *The Story of the Making of Ben-Hur: A Tale of the Christ, from Metro-Goldwyn-Mayer* (New York: Random House, 1959).
351 *Variety* 214 (April 8, 1959) 4.
352 Cf. *NYT* (November 15, 1959) X5.
353 <http://dcindexes.com/features/database.php?site=dc&pagetype=story&id=19736>
354 *The Billboard* 70 (December 15, 1958) 70.
355 *The Billboard* 71 (June 1, 1959) 26.
356 *The Billboard* 71 (April 20, 1959) 9.
357 *The Billboard* 71 (November 16, 1959) 33.
358 *Billboard Music Week* 1 (January 30, 1961) 62.
359 *The Billboard* 71 (July 20, 1959) 16.
360 VRS-9060/1; VSD 2049/50; *NYT* (November 15, 1959) 140.
361 MGM Pressbook, 23.
362 *Billboard Music Week* 1 (May 15, 1961) 28; cf. *Variety* 217 (February 10, 1960) 55.
363 *BG* (May 13, 1962) 93.
364 London Records PS 516; Columbia DS 318; MGM E3894; E.M.I. TWO 318.

365 London HA-R-2274; <http://www.bsnpubs.com/london/londonamerican/6londonam6000.html>
366 *Variety* 214 (April 8, 1959) 4.
367 *The Billboard* 61 (September 3, 1949) 15.
368 *The Billboard* 67 (March 12, 1955) 3.
369 *The Billboard* 67 (September 17, 1955) 20.
370 Marich, *Marketing to Moviegoers*, 128–9.
371 *WSJ* (May 18, 1959) 1; *NYHT* (August 23, 1959) A9.
372 *Philadelphia Tribune* (October 17, 1959) 10.
373 *Variety* 215 (July 15, 1959) 3; *Harper's Bazaar* (December, 1959) 152–3.
374 *Barron's* 39 (October 5, 1959) 5; *NYHT* (August 23, 1959) D1; *Variety* 215 (August 26, 1959) 7.
375 MGM Photo LM 467801, 46799, 46839.
376 MGM Photo LM 46754, 468755, 46887, 46758; MGM Pressbook, 24.
377 MGM Photo LM 46877; <http://www.ic.gc.ca/app/opic-cipo/trdmrks/srch/vwTrdmrk.do?lang=eng&fileNumber=293627>
378 MGM Photo LM 46761; Pressbook, 24.
379 MGM Pressbook, 24.
380 *Variety* 215 (August 26, 1959) 18; MGM Photo LM 46880 and 46782.
381 MGM Photo LM46876.
382 *Variety* 216 (November 18, 1959) 1 and 86; cf. "Costliest Film Makes Screen History," *News of the Day*, UCLA Library; MGM Photo LM 46757.
383 <http://www.playsetmagazine.com/frank_rice.html>
384 Moen, *Toys & Prices 2011*[18], 445.
385 <http://www.collectiblesonlinemarketplace.com/marx-ben-hur.html>
386 *Playset Magazine* 43 (January/February, 2009) 12.
387 *Playset Magazine* 30 (November/December, 2006) 14–27.
388 Ibid., 16.
389 *Toys and Novelties* (January, 1960) 74–5.
390 *NYHT* (August 23, 1959) A9.
391 In the possession of the author.
392 <https://books.google.com/books?isbn=0896892204>
393 In the possession of the author.
394 *BG* (September 27, 1959) 57.
395 MGM Photo LM 46764.
396 MGM Photo LM 45918; *BG* (September 27, 1959) 57.
397 <http://www.huntleyandpalmers.org.uk/ixbin/hixclient.exe?a=query&p=huntley&f=generic_objectrecord_postsearch.htm&_IXFIRST_=1075&_IXMAXHITS_=1&m=quick_sform&tc1=i&partner=huntley&tc2=e&s=3sMI2GZkofi>
398 In the possession of the author; cf. eBay # 120037561759, ended October 10, 2006.
399 In the possession of the author; cf. eBay #220307952096, ended November 13, 2008.
400 <https://mbasic.facebook.com/notes/sweets-n-treats-fenwickgiftscom/sweets-n-treats-presents-ben-hur-candies/267146313305687>
401 *Playset Magazine* 30 (November/December, 2006) 11–13.

402 *WSJ* (May 18, 1959) 1.
403 Landes, *Le cirque et les courses de chars Rome – Byzance*, 11 and 190; Jacques Pessis, *Les Aventuriers de la Radio* (Paris: Flammarion, 1998) 261–4.
404 *The Guardian* (December 18, 1961) 5.
405 Adrian, *Cirque au cinema*, 86.
406 <http://www.circopedia.org/Jean_Richard; cf. http://www.gettyimages.com/detail/news-photo/circus-jean-richard-paris-17-novembre-1975-au-nouvel-news-photo/162756916>
407 In the possession of the author.
408 In the possession of the author.
409 <http://www.imdb.com/name/nm0396345>
410 <http://circus-collection.blogspot.com/2012/03/cirque-knie-1962.html>
411 Bourgeon, *Le Fils de Ben Hur*.
412 *NYT* (June 28, 1964) 25.
413 *Daily Illinois State Journal* (February 7, 1971) 14.
414 Pathe Marconi EG 577M, 460 V525M, EGF 558M, EGF 568.
415 Festival FLD 286; FY 45 2259S.
416 Pathe Marconi EGF 550M; Versailles 90S340.
417 Vega V 45P207.
418 Odéon SOE 3579S.
419 Festival FLD 189S.
420 Philips 77.513
421 ALB 403/4.
422 Williams, *Cocteau*, 22.
423 Herman, *A Talent for Trouble*, 394.
424 <http://www.imdb.com/title/tt0648545; http://www.gettyimages.com/detail/news-photo/pictured-jack-benny-as-ben-hur-kirk-douglas-as-spartacus-news-photo/141300541>
425 *TBS* (August 11, 1963) F7.
426 *CT* (July 10, 1965) C12.
427 *Springfield [MA] Union* (January 29, 1970) 18.
428 *LAT* (December 9, 1965) 3.
429 *Los Angeles Sentinel* (May 16, 1963) A19.
430 *Los Angeles Sentinel* (May 23, 1963) A10.
431 *LAT* (January 17, 1965) WS15.
432 *LAT* (January 5, 1965) 11.
433 *LAT* (December 1, 1960) B1.
434 *LAT* (July 10, 1963) B9.
435 General Lew Wallace, *Ben-Hur* (Westchester, IL: Good News Publishers, 1964).
436 *Playboy* (April, 1964) 112.
437 *CT* (September 21, 1963) A16.
438 *Seattle Daily Times* (May 26, 1963) 39.
439 Programs in the possession of the author.
440 Veeck (with Ed Linn), *Thirty Tons a Day*, 272–7.
441 *BG* (July 8, 1970) 32; (July 11, 1970) 20; *The Sun* (July 8, 1970) C3.
442 *Woman's Day* 24 (July, 1961) 16.

443 *The Arabian Horse* 15 (November, 1963) 19.
444 *Appaloosa News* 17 (June, 1963) 52.
445 Downey, *Races to the Swift*, 187–204.
446 *Hal Kelly's Tested Plans*. [In the possession of the author.]
447 *BH* (February 22, 1970) 84; (June 28, 1970) 45.
448 *Seattle Daily Times* (July 1, 1963) 10.
449 *[Washington, DC] Evening Star* (January 31, 1970) 6.
450 *Seattle Daily Times* (January 2, 1963) 20.
451 *WSJ* (October 16, 1967) 2.
452 <http://www.millerfh.com/memsol.cgi?user_id=783578>
453 *Augusta [GA] Chronicle* (March 15, 1970) 10.
454 *Boston American Record* (February 26, 1970) 18; *MGM Auction Catalog for Wednesday, June 24* [1970] (The David Weisz Company) 1–2 and 15. [In the possession of the author.]
455 *[Baton Rouge] State Times Advocate* (September 18, 1973) 12.

15 The Next Half-Century: New Formats and New Versions

Mass consumer popular culture during the 1970s expanded in technologically invented directions, creating artistic and commercial synergies that would leave *Ben-Hur* behind. Following upon the youth-oriented, culturally subversive, and more sexually explicit films of the late 1960s, the unprecedented success of a new generation of films like *The Godfather* (1972), *The Exorcist* (1973), *Jaws* (1975) and *Star Wars* (1977), and best-selling novels like *The Godfather* (1969), *Love Story* (1970), *The Exorcist* (1971), and *Jaws* (1974), utterly transformed the entertainment landscape. Within this very selective list, the transmedia overlap of a blockbuster like *Star Wars* established new synergistic standards for sustained profitability, making it the *Ben-Hur*-plus of the later twentieth century. Empowering writers and producers were newly created talent agencies like International Creative Management and Creative Artists Agency that specialized in coordinating the development of blockbuster properties.[1] To promote *The Godfather* and *Jaws*, they aggressively purchased the rights to the original bestsellers before they were even published, so this new formula effectively precluded an aging classic like *Ben-Hur*. The chariot race and the spiritual foundations of Christianity, the two narrative and thematic elements that primarily had made *Ben-Hur* such a success as a novel and film, would find relatively little resonance during the next two decades when an incessant and rapidly developing barrage of newly created high-tech adventure films, action-figure merchandising, and then electronic gaming lured the younger generation in unprecedented numbers and percentages. Left at the gate as a hero of the urban roadshow era, *Ben-Hur* would then be dwarfed by the centrifugal forces that were rapidly installing thousands of multiplex theater screens in neighborhood shopping malls, and then millions of computer screens all over the country and around the world.

Nonetheless, *Ben-Hur* would repeatedly resurface and almost always find a willing audience in many of the new entertainment technologies. In 1975 delivery systems were in the early stages of being revolutionized by the launch of SATCOM 1 and the introduction of Sony's Betamax. Within a few years the public would have a more immediate and greater access to vintage Hollywood films than ever before via network or alternative television stations and purchased or rented videocassettes. *Ben-Hur* remained a special part of this new environment, appearing on network, UHF, and cable television, adapted for vinyl, audio cassette, or audio CD, and released on videocassette and DVD. And from the late 1990s, addressing a newly emerging consumer demographic, *Ben-Hur* would begin to re-emerge yet again as an established product and quality entertainment designed to satisfy the desire for Christian and wholesome family entertainment.

THE 1959 *BEN-HUR*

Network Television

The afterlife of the 1959 MGM film peaked on February 14, 1971, when the film premiered on CBS television. At the time the television industry was paying peak prices to replace regular programming with vintage Hollywood films.[2] Fred Silverman, CBS Programming Vice-President, announced in September, 1970, that the network had agreed to broadcast *Ben-Hur* three times in four years for approximately $3 million,[3] adding that *Ben-Hur*'s network debut would mark "the first time that a motion picture numbered among the top ten all-time cinema box office champions will have been shown on television."[4] Boldly scheduling the broadcast to extend four hours and fifteen minutes, CBS pre-empted its entire Sunday night schedule of very popular family shows like *Lassie* and the Ed Sullivan and Glen Campbell hours.[5] To advertise this memorable television event, in addition to high-profile listings and publicity photos, as much as three weeks in advance CBS supplied pressbook-type features and boldfaced 4-inch printed ads to papers like the *Los Angeles Times* and *Chicago Tribune*.[6]

The premiere was indeed a success. *Variety* reported that the Nielsen ratings were "boffo," drawing a 37.1 rating and 56 share, representing approximately twenty-three million homes. This was the third highest rating ever for a movie broadcast on television, following the 1966 and 1968 broadcasts of *The Birds* and *The Bridge on the River Kwai*.[7] In addition, because the number of television households had increased significantly since those films were broadcast in the late 1960s, *Ben-Hur* was estimated to have been watched by sixty million viewers, setting a record.[8] Subsequently newspapers circulated the number as eighty-six million.[9] Whichever is more accurate, the size of *Ben-Hur*'s television audience would not be surpassed until 1976 (*Gone With the Wind*). It even rated along with such traditionally successful live broadcasts as the Bob Hope Christmas Special, the Academy Awards, and Miss America Pageant.[10]

Because it was also the longest broadcast on network television, it generated enormous commercial revenues by selling sixty network and local commercial minutes.[11]

The excitement and novelty of seeing the Oscar-champion *Ben-Hur* on television were not going to last. The small screen made the crowds "look like ants," and many viewers still owned black-and-white sets.[12] In addition to pointing out that "the chariot race in 'Ben Hur,' to take an extreme case, simply demands a large screen," a syndicated feature from the New York Times Service comparing commercial American television with the British system lamented the frequency of commercial interruptions.[13] In addition, network television in the early 1970s was fiercely competitive and run by much-demeaned "suits," so the next broadcast in February, 1972, not only had to compete against the television premiere of *Cleopatra* (1963) but was also divided into two two-hour segments broadcast on two consecutive Sundays.[14] It ranked only fiftieth with a 24 share.[15] The third network broadcast was on Friday night, April 12, 1974, playing opposite *The Greatest Story Ever Told*,[16] establishing a precedent for televising *Ben-Hur* during Easter season. Although no longer able to play the role of financial savior, *Ben-Hur* was used by CBS in answer to NBC's broadcast of *Gone With the Wind* during sweeps month in May 1977.[17] By now the nativity scenes had been cut and the remaining film edited down to fit a three-hour, fifteen-minute time slot, and it earned only the tenth highest rating for the week.[18]

Britain provided an entirely different type of market. After yet another theatrical release in 1977, the 212-minute version of *Ben-Hur* was first shown in its entirely on ITV in May, 1978.[19] The first three hours were shown in the evening, followed by the regular fifteen-minute news broadcast and then the remainder of the film.[20] ITV purchased the film for a reported $800,000, the largest amount for a British film-to-TV sale at the time.[21] Bob Camplin, General Secretary of the Cinematograph Exhibitors' Association, argued that even that price was too low for a film that still had theatrical legs:

> It's generally unfortunate that people with big films like this content themselves with the relatively small amounts given by the companies for television screenings. There's probably still a market for this material which would prove more remunerative than the sale to television.

In 1980 MGM offered *Ben-Hur* up for auction between ITV and BBC, asking $8.7 million for a package that included *Gone With the Wind*.[22] Despite the high cost, broadcasting these films still cost less than producing the equivalent amount of both dramatic and non-dramatic programming. The next year BBC announced that they had completed the deal for $10.5 million.[23]

Local Television
Syndication was one of the more lucrative alternatives to network broadcasting in the 1970s, and in the wake of NBC's current hit, *Saturday Night Live*, Canada's *Second City Television* (*SCTV*) became a popular syndicated sketch-comedy show. During their first season, in May, 1977, *SCTV* enacted a parody of *Ben-Hur* as the feature of their "Dialing for Dollars" afternoon movie. The sketch ran nearly twenty minutes, including mock commercial interruptions. The parody demonstrates that the audience was expected to be familiar with the film, its plot, and characters, not so much because of its occasional showings on television as its associated 1950s nostalgia. Eugene Levi and Dave Thomas played Roman guards Gluteus and Maximus in the manner of Abbott and Costello, and John Candy played Ben-Hur in the manner of Curly of The Three Stooges.

In the first scene Harold Ramis, as Mazzola, encourages his old friend Judah ("Up Mars, down Eros!") to throw a rock that strikes the governor, and then he arrests him and his mother and sister. As Rózsa's Christ theme plays in the background, the second scene in the desert portrays a figure in checkered pants, whose face we cannot see, holding an icy shaker and then pouring the thirsty, exhausted Judah a martini, then handing him an olive. In a galley the slaves sing Rózsa's rowing theme. The hortator takes them through the test from "cruising speed" to "water-skiing speed" and then "reverse." Rózsa's actual battle music plays as a crude model of a ship is lit on fire and a victory scroll ends in Latin, which the narrator admits he cannot read.

After the intermission, Gluteus and Maximus place wagers, performing an Abbott and Costello routine about "her" and "Hur."

> Maximus: "I'm gonna to do you a favor. I'm gonna put your money on a winner, the Judean, Hur. Hur."
> Gluteus: "You mean the blonde over there with the big, eh?"
> Maximus: "No, no, no. Not her, him."
> Gluteus: "Him?" I thought you said you were wagering on her."
> Maximus: "That's exactly what I said. I'm gonna make us both rich."
> Gluteus: "You're wagering on a woman in the chariot race?"
> Maximus: "Are you listening to me? I didn't say I'm wagering on a woman. I'm wagering on Hur! That's him right over there. What's the matter with you?"
> Gluteus: "If that's a woman, I'll eat my toga."

The chariot race is enacted in front of a rear screen projection of a dirt road. In his dying breath Mazzola tells Judah his mother and sister are "leopards." With Rózsa's Valley of the Lepers music in the background, Judah calls for his mother and sister and discovers they are indeed leopards. To Rózsa's Christ theme, they are all served martinis and transformed.

The show was repeated in 1978, 1979, and 1980, when edited versions of the 1959 *Ben-Hur* were just beginning to be shown by local television stations late at night after prime-time network programs and the local news broadcasts, or in the late afternoon or weekend days.[24] In New York in 1980, WABC used the 4:30 p.m. timeslot to show the edited version of the film on two consecutive days before the local news broadcast.[25] During Easter season in 1980, the independent WTTG in Washington, DC broadcast *Ben-Hur* opposite NBC's *Saturday Night Live*, WJLA-ABC's *Saul and David*, and WJZ-ABC's *Barabbas*.[26] On Easter Sunday ABC broadcast *The Ten Commandments* and NBC the second part of *Jesus of Nazareth*.

This same period experienced the rapid growth of UHF television channels. The lasting effect of the All-Channel Receiver Act of 1961 was that television sets now provided viewers with easier access to the UHF channels from 14–83, and by 1980 increased access and therefore increased advertising revenues allowed for rentals of major Hollywood films. This proliferation of television channels meant that *Ben-Hur* could be aired during prime time opposite network programming. In Boston on the evening of August 10, 1980, for instance, viewers were not confined to network live news coverage of the Democratic National Convention but could tune to higher channels carrying *Bonanza*, Red Sox baseball, and *Ben-Hur*, broadcast on channel 56 (WLVI) for two hours over two consecutive nights.[27] WLVI broadcast the film again for Easter in 1982, 1983, and 1984.[28] The increased availability and competition encouraged local programmers to experiment with different ways of increasing revenues. A local channel in New York City ran the film in five parts for five consecutive weekdays, the late afternoon 90-minute time slot affording them more minutes for commercials and promos than the original running length of the film.[29] One hundred and one years after publication, *Ben-Hur* remained a reliable and even superior property for business investment, now benefitting investors who owned a television station that broadcast a copy of a cinematic adaptation funded by a large production company (MGM) that had in essence purchased the rights to Wallace's novel from one producer (Goldwyn) who had purchased the rights from another producer (Erlanger) who had purchased the rights from Wallace's heir.

Videocassettes and the Sony Betamax Case
By 1982 approximately three million videocassette recorders had been sold, another four million were sold in 1983, and nearly twice that amount in 1984.[30] In mid-1980 MGM had partnered with CBS Records Group, a leader in record manufacturing and distribution, and announced the release of their first thirty-two pre-recorded videocassettes from MGM's library.[31] The 1959 *Ben-Hur*, of course, was among the initial group, along with *The Wizard of Oz* and *Doctor Zhivago*. Because of its length, *Ben-Hur* required a two-cassette boxed set. By May, 1981, *Ben-Hur* had already won an ITA Golden Videocassette Award for sales of over $1 million at list price.[32] In 1987 *Video Review* listed it as one of the top ten all-time action/adventure films,[33] and in the rental market *Ben-Hur* predictably

became a favorite for the Easter season.[34] Demonstrating *Ben-Hur*'s characteristic staying power, *Billboard* for the first week of December, 1988, reported that *Ben-Hur* still ranked sixth among sales behind more contemporary films like *E.T. the Extra-Terrestrial*, *Dirty Dancing*, and *Good Morning, Vietnam*.[35]

There were a number of issuances over the twenty-one years beginning with the MGM/CBS Home Video [M90004] of 1980, which ran for 207 minutes without additional features. MGM/UA announced in *Billboard* in 1988 that it was issuing a remastered version in its Screen Epics series, but this did not appear until 1996.[36] Following small- and large-box issues in 1983 and 1987, the latter labeled as "Videophonic," MGM released the thirty-fifth anniversary edition in 1993/4 in Hi-Fi stereo, Dolby Surround sound, along with the feature *Ben-Hur: The Making of an Epic* narrated by Christopher Plummer [M404752].[37] MGM's seventy-fifth anniversary edition in 1996 came in letterbox format with behind-the-scenes footage, the Danova screen test, and other features [M305688]. After another corporate agreement with Time Warner, in 2001 Warner Brothers Classics issued a 222-minute, Widescreen, Letterboxed version that included only the theatrical trailer and Danova screen test [65506]. There were also a number of foreign-language releases, particularly in 2001.

One of the problems with pre-recorded videos was that widescreen films were usually transferred using the pan-and-scan process that eliminated one third of the visual image. For the extraordinarily wide ratio of *Ben-Hur*, this was particularly inappropriate. In 1988 Turner authorized through MGM/UA Home Video a laserdisc version of the film with digital sound. Advertised as a "Deluxe Letterbox Edition" and with a cover design dominated by Smith's colossal stone logo, the laserdisc edition provided a superior digital video transfer, but it was relatively expensive technology for the home viewer and had limited success. But it did accompany the "Videophonic" MGM/UA pan-and-scan videocassette version of *Ben-Hur* that changed to the letterbox format for the chariot race.[38] It had a similar cover design.

As marketed by Sony beginning in late 1975, the Betamax machine had been designed for consumers to record broadcasts, either to time shift programs or to build home libraries. This new technology revolutionized purchasing and viewing habits, enabling consumers to possess their own copies of classic films and view them at their leisure in the privacy of their own home. A determined consumer could record one of the frequent television broadcasts of *Ben-Hur*. But as we have seen, these were almost always severely edited, and even if the signal transmitted by VHF and, less likely, UHF stations was sufficiently strong, reception in most homes during the pre-cable era was not. Advertisements also reminded consumers that these recordings were superior to television broadcasts because they were "completely uncut and without commercial interruptions."[39]

Film studios from the outset perceived the recording capabilities of this new technology as a threat, so in 1976 Universal and Disney filed suit against Sony in one of the most high-profile intellectual property cases of the late twentieth century.[40] Once again *Ben-Hur* was involved, in several ways. At the federal appellate level, in 1981 the Ninth Circuit court ruled that the use of home video recorders to tape copyrighted television programs violated copyright law.[41] Meanwhile, in 1982 Jack Valenti, President of the Motion Picture Association of America, led a Hollywood lobbying campaign to ask Congress to impose a royalty of as much as $100 for every VCR sold and $1–2 for every blank tape as compensation to the film and television industries.[42] His lead warrior and prime witness was none other than Charlton Heston. A decade earlier, as president of the Screen Actors Guild, Heston had already been aware of attempts at developing recorders and prepared his membership for their inevitability.[43] Now he was addressing the Senate Judiciary Committee on the subject. Under the headline "Chariot for Hire," *The Washington Post*'s media specialist Howie Kurtz wrote the feature accompanied by a photo of Heston driving his chariot in *Ben-Hur*. He described the scene in the Senate hearing room accordingly:

> SCENES FROM a Washington movie:
> The high-ceilinged Senate hearing room is aglow with klieg lights. Every seat is filled, and tourists strain to see over the rows of three-piece lobbyists. The senators are poised behind microphones at the dias. The cameras are rolling.
> At the witness table sits the star of the occasion, and for a change in Washington it is a real star: Charlton Heston, whose roles in "Ben-Hur" and "The Ten Commandments" prepared him well for this assignment. Now he is a front man in the Ben-Hur of Washington lobbying extravaganzas.[44]

Heston's script, however, said nothing about chariots. He lambasted the Japanese companies manufacturing the machines that were "gobbling up films and programs millions of times a week." In addition, Heston was the figurehead for an organized letter-writing campaign.

In Sony Corp of America v. Universal City Studios, Inc., [464 U.S. 417 (1984)], the U.S. Supreme Court reversed the appellate court in a 5–4 decision. Writing the majority opinion, Justice Stevens comments extensively on Kalem Co. v. Harper Brothers [222 U.S. 55 (1911)], much more so than on any previous case. In finding that Sony's Betamax sales did not constitute contributory infringement, he distinguishes between the Copyright Act, which limits the liability for infringement committed by another, with the Patent Act, which has a much broader definition of an infringer. Examining the history of this critical legal intersection, he writes (#32–34):

> In *Kalem*, the Court held that the producer of an unauthorized film dramatization of the copyrighted book Ben Hur was liable for his sale of the motion picture to jobbers, who in turn arranged for the commercial exhibition of the film. Justice

Holmes, writing for the Court, explained "The defendant not only expected but invoked by advertisement the use of its films for dramatic reproduction of the story." . . .

The use for which the item sold in *Kalem* had been "especially" made was, of course, to display the performance that had already been recorded upon it. The producer had personally appropriated the copyright owner's protected work and, as the owner of the tangible medium of expression upon which the protected work was recorded, authorized that use by his sale of the film to jobbers. But that use of the film was not his to authorize: the copyright owner possessed the exclusive right to authorize public performances of his work. . . .

The Betamax can be used to make authorized or unauthorized uses of copyrighted works, but the range of its potential use is much broader than the particular infringing use of the film Ben Hur involved in *Kalem*. *Kalem* does not support respondent's novel theory of liability.

Writing the minority opinion, Justice Blackmun [#34] also addressed the definition of contributory infringement by citing first *Kalem Co. v. Harper Brothers* as precedent for imposing liability for copyright infringement "on persons other than those who actually carry out the infringing activity."

Although Lew Wallace was not named, the shortened title of his novel *Ben-Hur* was, and Wallace, along with Harper, was the copyright owner to which Holmes and Stevens referred. The two opinions did mention other film studios (Fox, Paramount, Disney), but the only other artistic product mentioned is *Mister Rogers Neighborhood*, a public television children's show by design, not the commercial rival of *Ben-Hur: A Tale of the Christ*, albeit watched by several million children each weekday. As a point of fact, Fred Rogers, who owned his own production and its copyright, testified [#44] as a witness that he had "absolutely no objection to home taping for noncommercial use." We can assume that Lew Wallace, given the lack of intellectual property protection in his day, would have taken the opposite position. From a larger perspective, Wallace's legal training and insistence on protecting the copyright of *Ben-Hur: A Tale of the Christ* had helped lay the foundation for the legal precedents established in *Kalem* and continued in *Sony*. Like the *Ben-Hur* decision of 1911, the Sony decision of 1984 had a continuing impact on intellectual property decisions, cited in over 500 subsequent court decisions and over 1700 law review articles.[45] In addition to film and television production and recording technology, it has been applied to software reverse engineers, add-on software developers, internet service and access providers, and internet search engines.

Two Animated Versions on Videocassette
The popularity of videocassettes in the 1980s inspired two independent productions, both of them animated and transferred to video. In 1987 Canadian born artists Jean Mathiesen and Al Guest set up an animation

studio, Emerald City Productions, in Dublin, where they produced a number of animated one-hour specials derived from classic novels and stories. Their 48-minute version of *Ben-Hur* was copyrighted in 1987 in the U.K. by Stylus Music, Ltd., and distributed in 1989 by Celebrity Home Entertainment in their "Just for Kids" series. They follow Wallace's story but make some interesting adjustments. It begins not with the Nativity but with Roman troops knocking Amrah off her feet, causing the crowd around her to complain about the Romans – much like the Roman treatment of a Jerusalem woman near the beginning of the 1925 *Ben-Hur*. Iras and Balthasar are omitted entirely. Nonetheless, the religious component fills the final nine minutes. They also make dialogue adjustments for their target juvenile audience. In the initial quarrel, for instance, instead of "Down Eros, up Mars!" Messala uses Wallace's alternative, "Love is nothing, war is everything!" and "What a thing it is to be a Judean. All men and things, even heaven and earth, change, but a Judean – never!" Wallace had used the word "Jew" here. But preserved is the mystery surrounding Judah's introduction to Simonides in Antioch. Malluch spies on Judah and reports back to Simonides, Sanballat conducts the pre-race wagering, and Judah destroys Messala's chariot wheel with his axle. Judah's horses, however, are white and Messala's black, a carry-over from the two MGM films.

In 1990 *A Race to Glory* was distributed by Creative Communications Center of America based in Irving, Texas, although much of the animation was executed in Taiwan and Manila. On the back of their plastic box they quote the Film Advisory Board commendation, saying that their "beautifully animated tales . . . are some of the best we have ever seen." Adapting the 1959 film were Fernando Uribe and Dan Engler, who concentrated the theme of the story on human forgiveness and friendship. They establish the latter theme at the beginning in a friendly chariot race between the young Judah and Messala just before Messala heads off for Rome. Upon his return they quarrel over the Roman occupation of Judea, so when Messala leads the parade through Jerusalem, Judah calls him a "pagan, Roman fool!" As he says this he slams his fist on the parapet tile, causing it to loosen and fall onto the new governor's head, inciting the crowd. As in the 1959 film, the Nazareth scene shows Jesus mostly from the back and depicts mostly the decurion's reaction to seeing him, but there is an interesting moment when the Romans are blinded by the bright sun behind Jesus's face. Judah has grown so strong at the oar that he rows two at a time and Arrius chooses to arm him for the naval battle on deck, where Judah picks a pirate up over his head and tosses him into the sea. On the raft this version of Judah gladly accepts Arrius' ring, expediting a quick change of scene to Jerusalem, where Messala personally orders the leprous Hur women out of the city. Judah and Messala meet after the former rescues Balthasar from Messala's chariot, but Iras is omitted. As befits the name of the film, Messala challenges Judah and promises to tell him the whereabouts of his mother and sister if he wins. The chariot race focuses frequently on Ilderim and the crowd, and at its conclusion Messala is simply dumped in the mud. Messala still refuses to reveal his secret, but Judah inadvertently comes upon his mother and sister on the road and takes them to be healed by the Messiah, thereby proving that he is the son of god. Messala sees this and begs god's forgiveness, and Judah's. The film ends with a handshake, friends once again. In 1992 the film was distributed in Spanish as *Carrera a la Gloria*, and in 1991 Creative Communications Center issued a 35-page, colored, paperback booklet version of the film.

Cable Television and Turner Classic Movies
The rapidly evolving technology of home delivery systems took another step forward the next year. In June, 1985, Ted Turner, a pioneer in using satellite uplinks to transform his local Atlanta UHF channel 17 into a nationwide superstation, announced that he wanted to expand his programming of old movies, television shows, and cartoons by purchasing the MGM film library.[46] The deal was quite complicated, and because the film library was but one part of Kirk Kerkorian's MGM/UA Entertainment Company, Turner found himself paying $1.5 billion in cash financed by junk bonds.[47] As reported in the *New York Times*, the business world believed he had paid too much and risked his TBS holdings,[48] but Turner quickly sold off United Artists and the MGM film production units, and then responded publicly with a statement that focused entirely on the library:

> Whatever the burdens, Mr. Turner says that he is buying a pot of gold that makes it all worthwhile: the MGM film library, a warehouse of 3,600 old films, including "Gone With the Wind," "Ben Hur," and "The Wizard of Oz" and hundred of old favorites. He says that the film library, the largest in the world, will guarantee the prosperity of his superstation, WTBS, which is Turner Broadcasting's biggest moneymaker.... "How can you go broke buying the Rembrandts of the programming business, when you are a programmer?" Mr. Turner asked.[49]

The next year he announced that the Turner film library featured a Prime One film package that included *Ben-Hur* and other high-profile MGM films to be shown on TNT, his newest cable station.[50] Elsewhere Turner made it clear that he hoped to expand into global networking with films like those three MGM giants.[51] In the UK *Ben-Hur* was shown via BRAVO.[52] Finally, Turner's Turner Classic Movies (TCM) debuted on April 14, 1994, with *Gone With the Wind*. Although the 1959 MGM *Ben-Hur* would appear on his other networks and continue to be shown around the country by individual stations, now it had a permanent home on a national cable channel and thrives there to the present day. The same year as the launch of TCM, Chuck Workman produced a nine-minute film, "100 Years at the Movies," containing clips from 225 films, for the 1994 Academy Award Show. The short-film contained not only four clips from the 1959 version of the *Ben-Hur* chariot race, it also included brief clips from the 1907 and 1925 films, demonstrating visually the unique relationship *Ben-Hur* has with cinematic history. TCM has frequently used the film as a promo for many years since.

An original TCM concept was "31 Days of Oscar." Every year the month leading up to the Academy Awards ceremonies features dozens of Oscar-winning films, so *Ben-Hur* is often aired at least twice, considering how many awards it won. In 2002 TCM decided to attract younger demographics during "31 Days of Oscar," so they produced a kids' version of *Ben-Hur* as a commercial promo to be aired on other networks. The one-minute film begins with second and third graders re-enacting the galley scene with hortator and galley slaves, the Valley of the Lepers, and a chariot race run with rocking horses, all to occasional glimpses of admiring parents.

The 1925 *Ben-Hur*

Although the 1925 *Ben-Hur* had disappeared from the American landscape for decades, growing interest in silent, European, and art films among collectors, academics, and independent theater operators in the early 1970s gradually brought it out into the public as a bit of nostalgic curiosity. In addition, MGM's well-publicized auction became the subject of an ABC television special, "Hollywood; The Dream Factory," broadcast in January, 1972.[53] It opened with a big scene from *Show Boat* and then shows the boat being auctioned off, followed by similar sequences for the *Bounty* and *The Wizard of Oz* ruby slippers, and then to illustrate the early days of the studio, they showed the 1925 chariot race sequence. The next year there was a theatrical showing of the 1925 *Ben-Hur* in Middletown, New York.[54] Not an academic exercise, the ad in the local paper said the film contains "footage of hundreds of Italian extras accidentally drowning" and that "hundreds of Arabian horses were killed as the film-makers strove for realism in the great chariot race." But Redmond's independent Cine-Mond outside Seattle engaged the film for several days in January, 1974,[55] followed by a weekend engagement at Portland's Joy Theatre.[56] The Pleasant Street Theatre in Northampton, Massachusetts, still had an organ and a 72-year old organist for accompaniment.[57] There was a more intensive round of showings in 1978/9, at the Vagabond in Los Angeles and the Regency and Undercroft Coffeehouse in New York,[58] for the fiftieth anniversary of a Springfield, Massachusetts theater,[59] and for the Magic Lantern Society in Bremerton, Washington.[60]

Turner created added value for the *Ben-Hur* tradition by co-sponsoring, with London's Thames Television, a restoration of the 1925 *Ben-Hur* by Kevin Brownlow and David Gill, who incorporated the 2-strip Technicolor elements stored in Prague at the Czech Film Archive.[61] Silent-film specialist Carl Davis had composed a new score, already used during Brownlow's and Gill's 1980 British documentary *Hollywood*, which he now conducted with the London Philharmonic Orchestra at the premiere public performance of the restored film in November, 1987, at the London Palladium for the annual London Film Festival.[62] The following January it was presented by the Academy of Motion Picture Arts and Sciences in Los Angeles and the U.S. Film Festival in Park City, Utah,[63] and in July, Brownlow, Gill, and Davis brought the film to the Boston Museum of Fine Arts and the summer festival at SUNY at Purchase where they gave an accompanying lecture, "Silents Please."[64] The film began to appear on local American UHF channels in March, 1988,[65] and Turner created special programming on TNT for Easter, 1989, by scheduling the film in different timeslots on different days, a concept they repeated for Christmas, 1990.[66] In 1988 Turner also released a videocassette of the restored version with a Hi-Fi stereo recording of Davis's soundtrack [M301474].[67] Now fully restored and revived, the 1925 *Ben-Hur* has frequently been presented on TCM, usually on "Silent Sunday Nights," and has been packaged with its 1959 MGM sibling in several DVDs.

DVDs with Commentaries

By the end of the millennium the rights to *Ben-Hur* had been transferred to Time Warner,[68] and the American Film Institute had included the 1959 film among the top 100 films of all time,[69] but forty years of wear and chemical degradation had left it in need of restoration.[70] It was a gradual process that required technological expertise and considerable expenditures of time and money, but many films were in the process of being transferred to the DVD format for the home market. Warner Home Video announced the release of the first DVD version of *Ben-Hur* for March 13, 2001, less than two weeks before the Oscar telecast that would declare *Gladiator*, a new-styled, non-biblical Ancient that earned nearly $500 million, as the winner of the Academy Award for Best Picture.[71] With the extra layers afforded by the DVD format, this edition included commentary by Charlton Heston, still photos, several screen tests, and Rózsa's original overture and intermission in a Dolby remix, but the 2.76:1 aspect ratio of the original film was reduced to 2.5:1.[72] The commentary by Heston is only sporadic but at least dispelled the three rumors attached to the film, that he wore a wristwatch, that there was a red Ferrari in the circus background, and that someone was killed during production. These urban legends are indeed fiction but do serve to demonstrate the continuing survival of the *Ben-Hur* phenomenon within the non-commercial elements of popular culture. In 2003 Warner also released this version in a 3-disc box along with *Casablanca* and *Gone With the Wind*.

The engineers who prepared the Warner Home Video DVD release in

September, 2005, worked from the original 65mm negative to recreate the 2.76:1 image.[73] While the 1987 videocassette that offered the chariot race in letterbox format had to explain on the back of the box that the "black bars" at the top and the bottom of the screen were normal, and while the reviewer in *America Cinematographer* lamented that his 35-inch TV was not large enough to display the detail of the 2001 DVD transfer,[74] this 2005 issue came into a market scattered with wide-format televisions. Even so, critic Dave Kehr pointed out:

> The new "Ben-Hur" DVD is almost too good for its own good. High definition or not, digital video is simply not good enough to register all the detail and depth of field of a 65-millimeter image. The crowd scenes that once revealed hundreds of individual faces are now a blur, and shots that once seemed to stretch infinitely into the distance, as when the Roman legions arrive in Jerusalem, now look puny. A little imagination is needed to augment the pixel count.[75]

This Four-Disc Collector's Edition included a disc containing the Thames Television restoration of the 1925 *Ben-Hur*, and another with both *Ben-Hur: The Making of an Epic* and a new documentary, *Ben-Hur: The Epic That Changed Cinema*, as well as stills, *News of the Day* newsreels from the New York, Los Angeles, Washington, and Tokyo premieres plus copies of the Academy Awards presentations, theatrical trailers from 1959 and 1969, and a running commentary by T. Gene Hatcher. Tucked into a fold inside the box was a small-format, paperback version of the 32-page souvenir booklet.

The first third of the 1994 documentary, *Ben-Hur: The Making of an Epic*, written by Mary Adair Preston and directed by Scott Benson, aims at intriguing viewers with Rudy Behlmers' anecdotes about the Ingersoll encounter, the Klaw & Erlanger production, and the Kalem and 1925 films, illustrated by many rare photos and film clips but dependent upon the traditional inaccuracies, including Hart's claim that one night he won the Klaw & Erlanger chariot race. The remaining two thirds contain filmed comments by Wyler, Yakima and Joe Canutt, J. J. Cohn, Richard Edlund, and others, illustrated by a number of rarely seen clips of the production, like those of building the block wall of the circus and practice chariot racing sessions. The Canutts give a detailed account of the sequence where Ben-Hur, i.e. Joe Canutt, flips over the chariot rail. An interview with Gore Vidal gives him the opportunity to assume his characteristic cynical devilishness, saying Heston was "formed out of solid balsawood" and Tunberg's script was a "piece of junk." More significantly, he claimed that the initial reunion between Messala and Ben-Hur was not gelling, so he rewrote it as "a love scene gone wrong." When he privately suggested to Wyler that he tell Boyd to play the scene as "a lover's quarrel," Wyler hesitated ("Gore, this is *BEN-HUR*! You can't do that to *Ben-Hur*.") but then agreed, assuming that they would not tell Heston.

Figure 15.1 The 1959 *Ben-Hur* remained in release until the early 1970s, when it played on network and local television stations, and then was seamlessly transferred to video and finally DVDs with special features, fully restored from the original 65mm negative, and in elaborate packaging.

Vidal had published this claim as early as 1976 (two years before Heston's diaries were published) in a long essay where he ignores utterly the critical narrative importance of the tile incident, Judah's arrest, and disappearance of Judah's mother and sister:

> The plot of "Ben-Hur" is, basically, absurd and any attempt to make sense of it would destroy the story's awful integrity. But for a film to be watchable the characters must make some kind of psychological sense. We were stuck with the following: the Jew Ben-Hur and the Roman Messala were friends in childhood. Then they were separated. Now the adult Messala returns to Jerusalem; meets Ben-Hur; asks him to help with the Romanization of Judea. Ben-Hur refuses; there is a quarrel; they part and vengeance is sworn. This one scene is the sole motor that must propel a very long story until Jesus Christ suddenly and pointlessly drifts onto the scene, automatically untying some of the cruder knots in the plot. Wyler and I agreed that single political quarrel would not turn into a lifelong vendetta.[76]

By inaccurately problematizing the plot in this way, Vidal slights not only Tunberg, Berhman, and Anderson but Wallace, too. He downplays the tile incident, the arrests, and the scene at Nazareth, which, although it lies geographically between Jerusalem and the sea, Wallace in the novel admits was "aside from any great highway." But it is hardly "pointless," for it establishes a relationship between the condemned Judah and Jesus, which is then paralleled with Arrius, not to mention that the story already includes Jesus in the Nativity scene at the beginning of the novel. He goes on to write that the Screen Writers Guild "mysteriously awarded the credit to the Contract Writer whose script was separated from ours by at least two other discarded scripts," as if Tunberg's repeatedly revised script bore little or no resemblance to the final version. The reader already knows that the early scenes in the 1959 shooting script were very much the same as the two previous scripts and that much of the dialogue in the initial scenes contains Tunberg's lines.

Vidal did much to improve the gift motif, having Messala give Tirzah a brooch "for a woman" and Judah give Messala the foreshadowing white Arab, but these hardly belong to an unrequited homoerotic love scenario. If there is an intimate relationship underlying the initial meeting between Judah and Messala, Tunberg had already filed this on June 21, 1955:

> MESSALA
> The only sanity in an insane world is the loyalty of friends.
> *(handing a goblet to Ben Hur)*
> Let us vow to be true to each other.
> BEN HUR
> With all my heart.

It was Vidal who seems to have written Messala's delicious reference to "unrequited love" in the scene, but it is beyond subtlety to believe that a line referring to the Roman emperor's political agenda and a Judean anti-Roman independence movement was motivated by a simmering lovers' quarrel:

> BEN HUR
> You want my advice?
> MESSALA
> Yes I do.

> BEN HUR
> Withdraw your legions. Give us our freedom.
> MESSALA
> Unfortunately, the Emperor is devoted to his Empire. He's particularly fond of Judea.
> BEN HUR
> Judea is not fond of the Emperor.
> MESSALA
> Oh, is there anything so sad as unrequited love?[77]

Vidal's account has no corroborating testimony. Boyd died in 1977 without public comment, and even Vidal admits that afterwards Wyler repeatedly denied the story before his death in 1981.[78] Heston, whom Vidal grew to despise for his prominent political stances and cinematic heroism, cited his diary entry as proof that Vidal's rewrite was rejected by Wyler. As for Tunberg's script, in the DVD Ralph Winters, one of the film's editors, does say that Wyler had marked sections of the script "terrible, awful, rewrite," but Catherine Wyler counters by saying that her father "agonized over every screenplay he worked on." Damaging his own credibility, Vidal in 1996 claimed that "I had, in my usual swift way, written what proved to be two thirds of the script."[79] He changes other details in all four of his accounts. From a historiographical perspective, Vidal is simply an unreliable source, a grave disappointment because of the artistry that he did bring to the script but discounted because of his characteristic penchant for provocative anecdotal ridicule. From the perspective of this book, Vidal has to be categorized along with Mahan, Hart, and Bushman as yet another celebrity who publicized provocative but unverifiable accounts that have become widely embraced anecdotes of *Ben-Hur* lore.

Gary Leva's 2005 documentary, *Ben-Hur: The Epic That Changed Cinema*, records evaluations of the film by subsequent filmmakers and the impact it had on them. Irvin Kershner, director of *The Empire Strikes Back*, says that "*Ben-Hur* has a special place in the minds of many, many filmmakers," and Robert Dalva, Oscar-nominated editor, says that "All of us as filmmakers have stolen from it. . . . Somehow it's become implanted in our brain." These statements, imprecise as they may seem, speak for all the *Ben-Hur*s in this book. The process of incorporating, processing, and employing them may be unidentifiable, but the original stimulus and ultimate product are not. As proof, George Lucas here says that he "relied on *Ben-Hur*" as he tried to instill in his action sequences the excitement he experienced when first viewing the 1959 film. Ernest Dickerson, cinematographer for *Malcolm X*, recalls "the visceral feeling of being in the galley hull when the guys were rowing" and the blood in the Crucifixion scene, especially in 65mm and color in an era in which the public was so used to black-and-white television screens.

Addressing both the scope and the intimacy of the film, Ridley Scott and

Arthur Max admit that when they were preparing *Gladiator* they referred to *Ben-Hur* as "a master course in production design." Scott adds that he feels frustrated that his arena in *Gladiator* was too small compared to the scale of the circus in *Ben-Hur*. Arnon Milchan, producer of *Once Upon a Time in America*, takes us one step further by asserting that "the size and scope enhances the intimacy of the story." Anthony Pratt, production designer for many large films from *Zardoz* to *The Phantom of the Opera*, compares *Ben-Hur* to *Spartacus* and *Star Wars* in the theme in which a man of "charismatic personality" foments "some sort of rebellion against a tyrannous rule," and then Bruce Crawford summarizes by saying that "You believe those characters exist. That's what makes it intimate." Sharen Davis, costume designer for *Dreamgirls*, also connects the color, form, aging, layering, and texturing of the costumes with creating the believability and realism of the characters, particularly the demure Esther, who looks "sexy, subtle, but real."

In describing the "sophisticated film language" of *Ben-Hur*, Janusz Kaminski, cinematographer for most of Steven Spielberg's films, discusses Surtees' subtle use of lighting to create "extremely evolved images," bathing the evil Romans in bright light during the wagering scene and dimly lighting the admirable Judah, Esther, and his family in scenes of intimacy and pathos, leaving the story to dictate or the audience to decide good versus evil. Don Davis, who scored the *Matrix* trilogy, praises Rózsa's score, particularly in the music accompanying the galley-slave test and the bold decision not to score the chariot race. He states that Rózsa pioneered modern film scoring for the John Williams generation. Joel Cox, editor for most of Clint Eastwood's films, and Dalva identify the intercuts of chariots, wheels, horses, and actors as a turning point in the history of film editing, not only leading to the car chase in *Bullitt* (1968) but, with its unprecedented number of cuts, "[teaching] people how to see action better." All of these statements are accurately illustrated with moments from the film to enlighten the viewer.

Near the end of the documentary, Lucas specifies the pod race in *The Phantom Menace* (1999) as his intentional homage to the 1959 MGM chariot race:

> I decided that I would create a modern version of that race, which was, instead of horses and chariots, it would be speeders hooked behind giant floaters.

His editor Ben Burtt illustrates the visual parallels between each film's lap counters, vehicle sideswipes, and the spilled pod rolling along the track. Arnon Milchin finishes with a generalization about large-concept films of the next generation:

> I think *Ben-Hur* in a subconscious way inspired all of us when we went to big adventure. You say, "O my god, how are we going to pull off so many details with so many hurdles and still tell an intimate story. And then you go to *Ben-Hur* and say that somebody managed to do it, so it can be done.

In 2011 Warner Home Video released a Fiftieth Anniversary Blu-ray edition in a large-format box with an embossed cover and a printed slipcase. This "Limited Edition" of 125,000 numbered copies included all the above special video features and extras, as well as the 1925 film, and added a third documentary, *Charlton Heston & Ben-Hur: A Personal Journey*, narrated mostly by Fraser Heston but including filmed statements by other members of his and Wyler's family. Fraser Heston, Charlton's son, had played the infant Moses in 1956 and was frequently photographed on the Cinecittà set during the 1958 *Ben-Hur* production in Rome. The film itself is restored frame by frame from the original 65mm negative and remastered in 1080p high definition. The box also includes *On the Set of Ben-Hur*, a 128-page hardcover replica of Heston's diary from January 15, 1958, when he was awaiting the casting decision, to April 5, 1960, the day after the Academy Awards presentation. Three pages include ticket-stub replicas and family photos. Another bonus was a 68-page hardback souvenir booklet with full-page stills and production photos along with facsimiles of several pages from the MGM pressbook. The same year Warner also issued a less expensive version of the film without the box and books, and in 2013 they released a double-feature version with *The Ten Commandments*.

Film Music Live and Recorded
Beginning in 1988, Carl Davis occasionally conducted a concert version of his score for the 1925 *Ben-Hur*.[80] In February, 1989, he conducted the Liverpool Philharmonic Orchestra for two screenings of the film,[81] and that same year a recording with the same orchestra appeared in CD format under the Threefold Music and Silva Screen labels. Some years later, in 1996, Gillian Anderson reconstructed and orchestrated a copy of the Axt-Mendoza piano score and performed it live with a viewing of the film at Washington's National Gallery.[82] Thomas May in *The Washington Post* admired "the beguiling – if incessantly recurring – love theme, silkenly orchestrated, between Ben-Hur and Esther." He also identified the awakening experienced by so many contemporary viewers previously unfamiliar with silent-film exhibitions accompanied by a live orchestra:

> Anderson led the musicians with an almost uncanny sense of timing and infinitely subtle shadings of rubato to match the sequences of images. Thanks to the music, the impression of delayed reactions between intertitles and images one often gets from a silent film was replaced with a generally seamless experience.

She conducted a repeat performance with the San Diego Symphony in February, 2007 and again in July, 2011.

Meanwhile, Miklos Rózsa's score was being sold in all available recorded media. In 1991, for instance, Sony Music Special Products reissued the two discs of music recorded by the MGM Studio Orchestra, Frankenland State

Symphony Orchestra, and Symphony Orchestra of Rome [A2K 47020]. In 1995 Turner Entertainment Company, Turner Classic Movies, and Rhino Records made an arrangement to release classic movie soundtracks as CD reissues and digital audio through iTunes.[83] Of course this included their comprehensive reissue of Rózsa's soundtrack for *Ben-Hur*, and this 2-CD issue was elaborately packaged, as the public expected from a featured *Ben-Hur* release [R2 72197]. The hardcover book-like folder held the two CDs in white plastic forms arranged vertically on one side, and filling the extended vertical on the other side was a reproduction of Michelangelo's "Creation of Adam," which had been used as well as the background for the titles of the 1959 film.[84] This housed a 48-page, 5in. × 10in. booklet filled with color, black-and-white, sepia, and transparent stills from the film and photos from the production, carefully arranged around producer Marilee Bradford's extensive, detailed introduction to the novel and MGM films. The second half includes an equally detailed text by Tony Thomas describing the development of Rózsa's score, a list of the musicians who performed during the 1959 recording sessions, and a detailed recounting of the story coordinated with the accompanying musical score. The eighty-eight tracks on the CDs are remastered from the original music production elements, with extended versions of the selections that were edited for the film as well as out-takes and an alternate track of the "Star of Bethlehem," each identified by the recording date. The discs also include alternates like the "Valley of the Dead" played one octave higher, and unused fragments, like the three different versions of "Arrius' Party," where the musicians individually stop playing when Arrius signals them before making his announcement.

The Rhino collection was included in the *Complete Soundtrack Collection from Film Score Monthly* [15.1], a five-disc set in a standard plastic case. The additional three discs include many more alternates, long and short versions, and bonus tracks from the Rózsa materials archived at Syracuse University and also lists of recording dates and exact cue titles.[85] The 26-page pamphlet has informative text about Rózsa and the score, and it recommends accessing more detailed information on their website (www.filmscoremonthly.com/notes), which provides a description of every track in twenty-three pages of Supplemental Liner Notes. The pamphlet also includes facsimiles of all the previously issued *Ben-Hur* vinyl album covers.

The impressive scope of Rózsa's Academy Award-winning score for the 1959 *Ben-Hur* at first earned more accolades and superlatives than scholarly attention. In the 1960s, before film studies developed into a rigorous discipline, film music only rarely warranted contextual, let alone musicological analysis. Helping to establish the trend, Mark Koldys published the first full-length article devoted to the score in 1974,[86] followed by Derek Elley's two-part interview with Rózsa published in *Films and*

Filming in 1977.[87] A longer piece in 1989 by Steven D. Wescott, employed research from the archival material at the George Arents Research Library in Syracuse, New York.[88] Examining the use of the leitmotif in the score, Wescott differentiates the "Roman music" from the "Judean music," particularly as they color the "Ben-Hur" theme and the "Messala motive." He also identifies what he calls the "family of basic themes," e.g. the Christ theme, friendship theme, and the like, concluding that Rózsa had a "clear vision of the programmatic potential inherent in the interweaving of complex dramatic and musical ideas." Wescott made clear that his work was preliminary and called for a "cue-by-cue" examination. Ralph Erkelenz answered that challenge in a series of five essays published by the *Pro Musica Sana*, a publication of the Miklós Rózsa Society, from 2005 to 2009. He offers facsimiles of the score, timings, quotations from the script in over 150 pages of analysis. Employing additional materials from the Library of Congress, the Rózsa Society's cassette recordings, and the Aldebaran 3-CD pirated edition of the original musical tracks, he traces each cue from conception to revisions to recording sessions to editing to film release along with the relevant script edits. Among many matters he discusses "planned overlap," by which Rózsa prepared for film and soundtrack edits by recording *fermata* chords at the end of tracks to accommodate the "seams" between scenes. These matched sound cuts accommodated, for instance, the blends between the shofar and opening credits, and the end of the Nazareth sequence and the beginning of the galley sequence.

Recently, in addition to the Film Score Monthly 5-CD collection, there have been several academic works. Juliane Bally's 2012 German monograph by design examines Rózsa's classical music that formed the basis of his film music leading to *Ben-Hur*,[89] and Roger Hickman's 2011 book surveys Rózsa's musical background, his technique of film scoring, and the filmic context of the *Ben-Hur* score followed by a musicological analysis.[90] Hickman concludes that Rózsa's score, a pinnacle of his career, is one of the finest examples of the mature neo-Romantic style. In a chapter in his 2015 book *Epic Sound*, Stephen C. Meyer further explores Rózsa's use of the leitmotif.[91]

NEW DRAMATIC ADAPTATIONS FOR THE NEW MILLENNIUM

Audio

In the late 1970s or early 1980s, Aim Records of New York targeted children with their Playhouse Presentation series of LP vinyl recordings. These were narrated adaptations of such children's stories as *Alice in Wonderland*, *Red Riding Hood*, and *Chicken Little*. Unique in their portfolio was their adaptation of a complex adult novel like *Ben-Hur*.

The simple production conveyed by only a female narrator and a solo pianist playing variations of the Civil War spiritual, "Michael Row the Boat Ashore." A brief introduction contains some odd comments about ancient chariot races, asserting that races were held in the Colosseum, where contestants carried weapons to push each other onto the track to be trampled. It also says that Ben [sic] was racing for his freedom, but the ensuing narrative says nothing about this. In fact, the narration follows some sections of Wallace's novel very closely and even verbatim, e.g. "There is richer entertainment in the street."

The narration unpredictably varies between using the novel's language and reducing the story to childlike simplicity. At the outset of the galley scene, the listener is told that the motor had not been invented, so ships relied on wind power, and that when it died down, they used manpower supplied by men chained to "huge oars sticking out of holes in the side. There were no windows and no fresh air. ... The dark bottom hold of the ship was extremely hot and smelly. A Roman guard stood over them with a big whip." The story is uniquely proportioned. The spiritual and Christian elements are eliminated entirely, and just the quarrel, tile incident, and arrest continue on into the second side of the album. Ben-Hur stops Messala's charging chariot, but neither Balthasar nor Iras are included in the scene. This leads directly to the chariot race, for which Ben-Hur "selects four Arab horses and a fine chariot." As in the novel, Messala whips Ben-Hur's horses, but then he "drives so close" to Ben-Hur's chariot that their wheels lock and Messala is thrown. Again in just three sentences Judah finds his mother and sister, frees them from prison, "and they live in health and happiness for evermore."

In 1996/7, around the same time the David C. Cook Bible-in-Life series inaugurated its weekly "PIX" small-format graphic readers with the first installment of a serialized *Ben-Hur*, Focus on the Family began producing radio plays for broadcast and purchase in cassette and then CD formats published by the Christian publishing house, Tyndale Inc. This is also when Tyndale reissued the Garfield edition in its Focus on the Family Great Stories series. In accordance with its Christian mission, *Ben-Hur* (2000) was an ideal choice, but despite the organization's strong advocacy the drama does not include the subtitle "A Tale of the Christ." Instead it advertises *Ben-Hur* as "An Epic Tale of Revenge and Redemption." The script by Dirk Maggs unfolds accordingly, emphasizing two of the themes that Wallace paired in his novel. He builds the tale of revenge primarily by magnifying Messala's insensitive pride through wicked humor. In the quarrel he advises Judah that his savior will not be "the Messiah, but Messala." He warns Malluch after the pre-race wagering scene, "Be sure you can pay the debt or I will drink my victory wine from your empty skull," and then leads a chorus of laughter from all the Romans present. For emphasis, Iras admires these qualities: "He has such a cruel beauty. He mocks the fates that other people cower from. He plays to win."

As in the novel, Balthasar delivers the spiritual message that Judah, Simonides, and Ilderim refuse to accept until the final revelation at Golgotha:

> Balthasar: "The seed planted at his birth has grown into a tree, and that tree will put forth an eternity of seeds."
> Ben-Hur: "At this moment he should be seated in the temple being anointed king of the Jews. Instead he's hanging on that cross with the words scrolled as an insult at his head."
> Balthasar: "Why do you think the people turned against Jesus and demanded his death? He came to the temple and did not overthrow the Sanhedrin. He came to the Gate Beautiful and did not overthrow the throne of David. He came to Pontius Pilate and did not condemn Rome. You were all looking for god to send an answer to your prayer for deliverance. Well, god sent the answer, and none of you seem to understand it. Look at the man hanging on that cross. He is that answer, and so is the manner of his death."

When Jesus says, "Father forgive them, for they know not what they do," Simonides remarks that he wishes he had had that spirit of forgiveness on the rack at Antioch. Judah responds, "Only god can forgive on such a scale. . . . Truly, this man is the son of god."

As in the novel, Maggs continues to employ Messala's menacing presence after the chariot race, but in making the transfer from novel to radio drama, he has Messala actually confront Judah, providing not only added emotional conflict but a reaffirmation of the spiritual message that dominates the final half hour of the two-hour drama. Here Judah learns that the army he has mustered for Jesus has disbanded not because of Christ's message of peace but because Messala has bribed them. Messala laughs, then coughs. The dying Messala asks for death by Judah's sword, but Judah's desire for vengeance is still in command: "Let your existence be a living death, as you have made mine." Messala's last lines are to Iras: "Iras, when you poison me, do it with hemlock mixed in wine. When his god judges me, I'll need something to dull the pain."

Technological advancements created the "motion-picture quality sound design" Focus on the Family applied to all its Radio Theater productions. The layers of recorded and sampled sounds and actors' voices create a verisimilar depth that the earlier radio play adaptations of *Ben-Hur* lacked. On the galley we hear a variegated background of splashing water, creaking and thumping wood, rattling iron, groaning slaves, and shouting soldiers. When Judah and Arrius go overboard, our ears are inundated with underwater sounds. The chariot race, lacking the visuals of the two MGM films, thunders along with the layer tracks of the sounds of hooves, wheels, axles, whips, crashes, shouts, crowd noise, and challenges and trash talk by the principals.

Musicals

In 1986 Hugh Martin and Timothy Gray copyrighted their two-act *The Adventures of Ben-Hur: A Musical Spectacle*, and in 1989 Thomas M. Disch wrote his adaptation of *Ben-Hur* for R. Jeffrey Cohen and the RAPP Arts Center in New York's Lower East Side.[92] This innovative play includes both Judah Ben-Hur as well as Lew Wallace and Mary Surratt as characters, replacing the usual huge scope attached to *Ben-Hur* with the stark opposition of creator and creation, judge and judged. These were isolated and minor contributions, but the same Christian advocacy that propelled the Focus in the Family project inspired a new round of large-concept staged musicals of the next few years. In 1999 Florida residents Robert Reeder and Joe Owen along with Major League Baseball pitcher Orel Hershiser formed the Global Impact Concepts to produce *Ben-Hur The Musical*.[93] In keeping with the traditional scope of *Ben-Hur* by-products, they planned a spectacular $8.5 million production and contracted with Joseph Hurt Studios in Georgia to construct eight animatronic white and black Arabs capable of galloping at 30 mph.[94] Like those used for *The County Fair* a century earlier but without the problem of spooking the electromechanical equines, these horses would run directly at the audience, promising to "leave the front-row patrons gasping." Of the twenty-eight scenes, the cross-section galley set revealed both slave-filled hold and deck, and the sea battle climaxed with a 40ft. × 12ft. "wall of fire."[95] Composers Paul Johnson and Ronald Owen with lyricist Chip Hand composed eighteen songs for a cast of forty,[96] and the producers spent $1.2 million on an 87-channel surround sound system to put the auditorium's acoustics on par with the technological advancements expected by contemporary audiences.

GIC ordered logoed T-shirts, baseball caps, umbrellas, shot glasses, mugs, and other souvenirs for the mid-November premiere, when they gave each patron a 5-inch tote bag decorated with their chariot logo (a modified Wagner-type), topped by red woven handles, and filled with Florida salt water taffy. The printing on the reverse of a painted souvenir plate cited Psalm 20:7 and the notice:

> This classic story reminds us all that love and forgiveness are powerful forces of healing in this world and the gift of love God gave us so long ago is still at work among men.

The plan was to run the play for several years in Orlando at the Orlando-Orange County Convention Center, which alone attracted two million of Orlando's annual forty-plus million visitors, and then take it on an extended world tour.[97] Reeder told the press that he offered them "something really different. *Ben-Hur* is a quality alternative, a stunning stage event that you can feel good about attending with your entire family."[98] However, pre-opening ticket sales amounted to only 15,000, and the hoped for corporate sponsorships never materialized. The local business community reported that Orlando visitor attendance was the lowest in seventeen years.[99] As a testimony to the concepts underlying the Christian movement at the turn of the millennium, Reeder called upon the religious community to support their project as an exemplar of wholesome, commercial entertainment:

> We came to Orlando to bring a new dimension to God honoring entertainment, and we have done that. *Ben-Hur* is an amazing work that clearly depicts the work of Christ and communicates forgiveness and restoration powerfully.
>
> It is one of the most powerful evangelical tools this city, or perhaps the entire entertainment world has ever had. We now need God's people to come out in force and support this effort. All of us as Christians have been complaining about the state of entertainment in this country, here is an opportunity to support something that is God honoring and first rate entertainment at the same time. If we don't have the support of our own, our future plans to take Ben-Hur around the country, or the world on tour are in serious jeopardy. We may not be able to stay open at all.

By mid-January, 2000, *Ben-Hur The Musical* was bleeding cash. On some evenings patrons filled only 300 of the 2600 seats in the Linda W. Chapin Auditorium, so Global Impact Concepts shut down the production and declared bankruptcy. The reader is correct in assuming that this was the only major failure in the history of the *Ben-Hur* tradition. Not more than two years later, however, there would be a replacement.

Judah Ben-Hur was the musical creation of the mother-son team of Ellen and David Sanborn. Another multi-million dollar production, the show opened and played fifty-six performances at the University of Singapore's Cultural Centre Theatre in 2002. Under the auspices of Tampa Bay's Youth With a Mission, *Judah Ben-Hur* was performed in 2013 by a company of twenty-four at churches, schools, and community venues in Hawaii and the Philippines "to bring the Gospel in the form of a full-scale theatrical production.... We have seen the evangelistic effectiveness of godly performance," as it says on their website.[100] Although now reduced to a theatrical concert version performed by the Sanborns and four additional actors, the show maintains a website and was still booking Florida church engagements in early 2014 in Brooksville, Port Richey, and Lakeland.[101] Of the two dozen songs, "I Remember You," an Act I love-duet song by Judah and Esther, is available as a music video,[102] and their original cast CD is advertised online.

Wayne R. Scott has been a pioneer in the Christian theater movement on the West Coast. He had begun his work on *Ben-Hur* as a student at the International School of Theology in 1990, where his master's thesis was *Ben-Hur: An Evangelistic Musical Stage Production of the Classical Novel*.[103] He premiered the work in 1992 at San Bernadino's huge Arrowhead Bowl amphitheater, where he says it was witnessed by as many as 10,000 people.[104] In April, 2004, he introduced it during Easter season as one of the first productions at his own LifeHouse Theater in Redlands, California.[105] Like *Judah Ben-Hur*, this production is still being updated and revived. For a recent performance in March/April, 2014, again for Easter, the writer expressed familiar concepts in a press release:

> It is a redemptive and inspiring theatrical experience. It is a challenging production to mount, but ultimately has an emotional impact that really resonates with audiences, leaving them feeling encouraged and joyful when leaving the theater.

Films

Now that a generation had passed since the first run and rerelease of *Ben-Hur*, its secondary distribution on network and local television channels, and its transfer to videocassettes, it was time for yet another film adaptation of the novel. The first of this new era was a direct-to-video/DVD 78-minute animated version produced in 2003 by a consortium headed by Goodtimes Entertainment. Fraser Heston carried on his father's legacy by serving as an executive producer. In one of his last roles, his father voiced the character of Judah Ben-Hur and served as narrator. The film opens and closes with Heston sitting in an easy chair and talking to the camera. The production was, once again, quite ambitious. Hong Kong's Colorland Animation created moving images for some 1250 scenes in Rome, the Eastern desert and cities, and the sea, and drew 237 characters. In producing the all-important chariot race, director and editor Bill Kowalchuk blended new digital 3D technologies with traditional two-dimensional animation. Elsewhere there are some cartoon-like moments, most notably when Ilderim asks Judah to ride his chariot and Judah demonstrates his skill by standing on their backs like a rodeo or circus performer, then pulling them up to a sudden stop right in front of Ilderim.

Furthering the current trend in emphasizing the Christian elements of *Ben-Hur*, the scope of the Nativity scenes are expanded to incorporate such New Testament elements as the slaughter of the innocents and the flight to Egypt. As in the novel, the night of the Nativity an angel announces to the shepherds, "I bring tidings of joy for all people. Unto you this day, a child is born, a savior who is Christ our lord." When in the interview with Arrius Judah reaffirms that "My faith in God has kept me alive," Arrius asks, "Would you give up this faith even if it meant your freedom?" Judah responds, "God is my freedom." Near the end, when Jesus says "It is done," lightning strikes, Judah tells Esther to keep praying, and a magical light swirls around the cross, then envelops Judah's mother and sister, and miraculously cures them. After this Heston narrates as Jesus rises from the tomb, appears before his disciples, teaches them the true meaning of the scriptures, blesses them, and, forty days later, ascends to heaven amid the voices of angels.

They maintain Judah's characterization as a would-be anti-Roman warrior relatively unconcerned with Balthasar's theological instruction. Judah does not understand when Balthasar says, "His kingdom is on the earth, but not of it, not of men, but of men's souls. He is the king of our hearts, of love and forgiveness." In contrast, they make Messala into a most effective object of redemption and forgiveness, much as in *A Race to Glory*. At the outset he and young Judah reminisce about racing each other. Messala taunts him with, "I always won," but Judah retorts, "You always cheated!" At the end of the tile incident, Messala immediately orders the Hur women to be taken away, Judah to be sent to the galleys, and the house closed: "Let this be a lesson to all Hebrews who challenge the Roman Empire!" When Judah returns to the East he asks Messala about his family. Messala laughs and asks, "Where is your god now, Judah. Even he couldn't save them." In the chariot race Messala whips Judah's horses, as in the novel, and comes after Judah's chariot with "spiked" wheel hubs, as in the 1959 film. The cause of his chariot crash is not clear, but after Judah wins the race and runs back to learn Messala's condition, Messala says accusingly, "You did this to me!" However, he reappears at the time of the Crucifixion, when he volunteers to join Judah's anti-Roman army and pleads with Judah, "Can you ever forgive me?"

The 2005 DVD release of the 1959 MGM *Ben-Hur* includes a rare, filmed interview with William Wyler. He repeats the anecdote that just as he had been one of the many assistant directors shooting the chariot race scene in Culver City in 1925 and was now directing the 1959 *Ben-Hur*, he expected that one of his crew would direct the "next *Ben-Hur*." As it turned out, his son David co-produced the next filmed *Ben-Hur*, the 2010 television miniseries. In a pre-release interview, he reminisced about his year in Rome at the age of five, watching the chariot race and being frightened by the leper make-up on his aunt, Cathy O'Donnell who played the role of Tirzah.[106]

Screenwriter Alan Sharp did not believe in continuity. At least publicly he said he had no particular liking for the 1959 film or the novel and that he generally thought of the writing of television screenplays as a functionary job:[107]

> Screenplays are not books, a highly personal way of writing. The executives tell you what they want and you get on with it. My only mistake was reading the original book. . . . I had to give up. I decided to rattle on, invent a few characters and make it plausible and realistic, with a modern gloss. I take the Polish plumber approach.

His screenplay accordingly includes many scenes not in the novel and omits a few of its most iconic. The film skips the Nativity completely and begins, like its animated predecessor, with a childhood cart race between Judah (Joseph Morgan) and Octavius Messala (Stephen Campbell Moore). Judah gets engaged to Esther immediately after her arrival in Jerusalem. Judah and Messala have one of their conversations in a Roman bath. It is Pontius Pilate, not Gratus, who is hit with the tile, and Messala, neither Tunberg's tribune nor Wallace's attaché, is a bungling garrison commander who failed to prevent the "attack" on Pilate and is therefore banished to the far reaches of the empire. Simonides is not tortured per se but temporarily crucified. On the way to the galleys, Jesus does not give Judah a drink but says, "Forgive them, for they know not what they do." The galley exteriors are all the product of CGI, so we do not see any fighting on the deck of Arrius' galley. Instead, during the battle, Judah, now called Number 40, remains in the flooding hold and, failing to unchain a fellow slave who does not want to drown in his Roman chains, euthanizes him. Despite Wyler's comment on the "Making of" DVD that "the story no longer takes place in Rome," many subsequent scenes are set at the court of Tiberius at Capri. There Arrius petitions to adopt Judah (as Sextus Arrius) and introduces his "catamite" to the emperor. For his imperial pleasure Tiberius insists on watching young Arrius fight a Thracian gladiator. Unlike the Thord episode in the novel, this gladiator knocks Judah to the floor, but rather than obey Tiberius' thumbs-down command, the Thracian throws his spear at Tiberius. He misses, so then Judah stabs his weaponless opponent in the chest. Judah and Arrius have scenes of true affection, and the first half of the miniseries concludes when Arrius commits suicide by opening his veins in a bloodied outdoor pool, after which Judah swears vengeance by the urn of Arrius' ashes. Perhaps independently, the initial reunion between Judah and Messala is developed as in the 1925 film in that Messala seems ominous at first but then is clearly happy to see Judah after an interval of five years.

Sharp's newly invented characters include Senator Marcellus Agrippa, the adoptive father of the bastard Messala. A strong character played by James Faulkner, he shares with Tiberius his favorite whore Athene in order to persuade him to name his son the next governor of Judea, a mere stepping stone on the way to the imperial throne. Athene serves several functions. She sleeps with Tiberius to win Marcellus' favor, she sleeps with Messala to learn about Judah, and Judah loses his virginity to her in Capri, and then in Jerusalem she serves as an Iras-like foil to Esther. Several references are made to her skill at delivering poisons, not unlike Robert Graves' Livia in *I, Claudius*. David, not Esther's betrothed in the 1959 script but a secretive Zealot, manages the Hur business and kills a Roman soldier to foment the riot that caused the demise of the House of Hur. During Judah's absence he houses Esther and Simonides and tries to convince the former to marry him. He lies to her by saying that Judah had made a deal with Messala to have Simonides crucified in exchange for his own life. Angry, and no longer Wallace's demure Esther, she spits on Judah's face when he returns to Jerusalem. Messala has a Roman rival, Gaius Antonius, who replaced Messala as garrison commander after the street riots. It is he who is scheduled to drive Tiberius' team of black horses in the annual Passover chariot race, but Athene at the behest of Marcellus poisons Gaius to set up the race to the death between Judah and Messala. The money Messala wagers is not his own but his adoptive father's.

Consequently, the chariot race is a stripped down affair on a dirt track that is unintentionally like the practice track at Daphne described by Wallace. Messala does not have a "Greek" or "spiked" chariot, but in order to create the requisite crashes – Andrew Marton confessed that the width of the four horses abreast made hooking the chariot wheels together problematic – the designers extended the axles on the chariots by nearly one foot in each direction. In the last lap Messala tries to stab Judah with a spear-like weapon, and it is this that causes his crash, after which, a bit stunned, he says, "Did I win?" The relative simplicity of the race was a conscious decision on the part of the film-makers, who confess in the DVD that taking on the 1959 version would be futile.

In the last few minutes of the film, Sharp turns to the Christian concept of forgiveness to tie all his loose ends together. On his deathbed, Messala calls for Judah and admits that he has had nothing but remorse since the fateful day. Judah is in the streets, picking up the cross for Jesus on the way to Cavalry and once again hearing him say, "Forgive them, for they know not what they do." So, Judah does visit and forgive Messala, Athene poisons Marcellus, in the morning Judah's mother (Ruth) and sister wake up cured, and Judah and Esther kiss in the open doorway of the House of Hur.

The film aired on the ABC network during Easter, 2010. By that time the Christian zeal for popular entertainment had subdivided into different categories, and network audiences were already in a steady rate of decline. Also, the secular action features of the story, namely the chariot race and galley scenes, came with such high expectations that anything less than the spectacularly expensive scenes in the 1925 and 1959 films or the more cost-effective animated films would be unsatisfactory. As a result, the 2010 *Ben-Hur* had little impact on the entertainment landscape. Nonetheless, it aired on Canadian, Italian, Swedish, German, and French television in 2010/11, and it was repeated on the Ovation cable network during the Easter season in both 2013 and 2015.

Dramatic Spectaculars

As we have seen, both MGM films had long and very profitable releases in the European capitals. Robert Hossein, a French actor/director in the 1950s, found watching both the 1925 and 1959 films so memorable that when he had reached his seventies five decades later he produced *Ben-Hur Plus grand que la legend* in 2006. Much larger in concept than even the Klaw & Erlanger drama, and encouraged by such recent cinematic blockbusters as *Gladiator* and *Troy*, Hossein mounted a dramatic spectacular in the largest outdoor venue in France, the Stade de France in St. Denis, just north of Paris and at the time the almost hallowed site of France's

1998 World Cup championship.[108] He covered the stadium surface with packed sand, thereby transferring it into a genuine "arena." In addition to the usual speaking roles, he cast several hundred extras to represent Roman soldiers, gladiators, slaves, and pirates who served as stagehands when, for instance, dressed as slaves, they set up the Roman galley in the center of the stadium. Indeed, much of the artistry was invested in setting up and dismantling the monumental sets. Accompanied by a recorded orchestral score, over forty men, for instance, pushed four large rolling set pieces from the corners of the stadium, joined them together into a galley, climbed on board in unison and sat on the rowing benches, doing so as forty more ran out from the corners of the stadium with lengthy oars in their hands, inserted them into the proper slots in the hull, and then climbed on board next to the others. Similarly, two small processions from opposing corners wheeled out 30-foot obelisks, while a dozen more groups wheeled out the *spina* pieces, all of them coming together in the center of the circus in sync with the erection of the obelisks. Overlooking the proceedings at one end of the stadium was a very tall stage with a long flight of thirty-two steps reminiscent of those Arrius mounted in the 1959 film. The opposite end contained the equally tall House of Hur.

The chariot race was run with six *quadrigae* that had been training for nine months.[109] As in the 1959 film, one charioteer goes over a hump and his chariot tosses him into the air. One by one the chariots break down and leave the arena floor, leaving just Messala's blacks and Ben-Hur's whites. His chariot destroyed, Messala is dragged in the dirt around the entire track. The spectators were involved in the proceedings, making it as much an event as a show. Indeed, the weekday night performance was "dress as a Roman" night. When entering the stadium, all those togaed thousands were given a colored handkerchief and instructed to wave it in favor of their chosen charioteer. Something similar was done for the gladiatorial battle as well. A narrator kept them informed of the plot, and to expand the audience enjoyment, the pirates were all played by women. As the narrator described the naval battle, they and the Roman soldiers would freeze several times under refocused spotlights as the narration dictated. The huge arena befitted the large props and crowds for these action scenes, but by design it also enhanced the intimacy of the sparsely populated scenes, be it Judah's meeting with Jesus at the well or Messala's death scene. For the Crucifixion several dozen lepers huddle into a tight circle, hands raised into the air as lightning flashes and thunder echoes throughout the darkened stadium. As the lights come up, the lepers rejoice to find that they are cured. All run to the edge of the arena and hold up their hands to the crowd.

Hossein had produced similar but smaller works before. *Un homme nommé Jésus* and *Jésus était son nom*, for instance, were presented at the Palais des Sports in 1983 and 1991. This new production cost thirteen million euros and was designed to play only five nights – two weekends and one weekday night in late September. But the stadium has a seating capacity of over 80,000, and tickets cost on average 100 euros. Estimates of attendance were in the 260,000 range, and many of them also bought the souvenir program and other souvenirs.[110] Hossein released a CD of the music, which was comprised of selections from symphonic works and ballet music composed by his father André in the 1980s. And later Hossein also issued a DVD of the performance that captured both the perspective of the stadium spectator and close-ups of the principals, as well as more than one hour of special features about the production.

In 2010 the production traveled to Australia as a test case to see if such large-scale outdoor French spectacles could be exported.[111] They rented out Sydney's ANZ stadium, paid $1 million to destroy, replace, and restore the grass surface, and secured the services of native Russell Crowe as the narrator, particularly appropriate after his Academy Award-winning role in *Gladiator*.[112] The stadium managing director declared that signing Crowe was "a stellar moment in major event theatre worldwide." He continued:

> To have the biggest star in Australia join the biggest theatrical event we've ever seen is a ground-breaking event. Ben Hur is more than a big show, it's a new entertainment genre that's sure to excite Australian audiences.

In disparaging the attempt, *Sydney Morning Herald* reviewer Jason Blake evoked the name of J. C. Williamson, spanning more than a century of Australian *Ben-Hur* dramatizations:

> This isn't the first time Sydney has played host to a *Ben-Hur* spectacular. In 1902, J. C. Williamson staged a massive adaptation of Lew Wallace's novel, *Ben-Hur: A Tale of the Christ*, at Her Majesty's on Pitt Street. The four-hour epic included massed choral numbers and a chariot race (and this was indoors, remember), with teams of horses racing at full gallop on a huge treadmill.
> The reviewer for the *Sydney Mail* hailed it as "a riot of scenic magnificence, a revel of superb mounting and dressing and a triumph of mechanism." In short, everything the French auteur Robert Hossein's *Ben-Hur – The Stadium Spectacular* is not.[113]

Local attendees were reportedly puzzled by the French dialogue and the "American-style" action.

Hossein was not alone. In the new millennium the monumentality and iconic status of *Ben-Hur*, the spectacle of not just live horse racing in a family-friendly venue without the gambling and excessive drinking, but chariot racing, accompanied by stimulating loud music, and a simple but classic drama that involved love and vengeance as well as Jesus, the Crucifixion, and a miracle, presented a package that could play to modern audiences enamored of dynamic theatrical events. And, as the late twentieth and early twenty-first centuries would continue to prove, the expired copyright of *Ben-Hur* made it particularly attractive. In 2008/9

Figure 15.2 *Ben-Hur* has been reformatted during the 1990s and early 2000s in musical and dramatic formats, the latter attracting hundreds of thousands of spectators overseas.

the German-born Franz Abraham created a more international *Ben Hur Live*, and while somewhat lesser in the size than Hossein's in that the venue was an indoor arena, it is an ambitious production that incorporates all the above and has maintained its profile over the past five years. Like most of the recent *Ben-Hur* productions, this one was spearheaded by a man of faith. As a fervent, born-again Catholic, Abraham expressed his desire to gain popular appeal through exciting action but also "high seriousness, ... deep emotions, and a great message of peace":

> I had to get my creative team to [achieve] my spiritual vision of faith that will ride above the spectacle. I had to find actors who believe in Ben Hur's message of peace and the inter-religious and inter-cultural dialogue. Is there a message which could be more relevant today?[114]

Abraham, having given the project some thought for more than a decade, enlisted the headline services of Stewart Copeland, known worldwide as the drummer of The Police, who had just had a reunion tour in 2007/8. Copeland composed the music and served as narrator. Behind the scenes, Abraham joined forces with Mark Fisher, who had designed stage sets for Pink Floyd's "The Wall" and the Beijing Olympics opening and closing ceremonies, to produce fifty scene designs. For sound he called upon the leading German practitioners specializing in high-end audio. In this instance they boasted that this would be the first 360° experience with locatable sound.[115] One of the most innovative visual and narrative features came in the pirate attack on the Roman galley. Lightening the mood, the pirates drive nearly a dozen dune buggies. Following the lead of Mel Gibson's *The Passion of the Christ* (2004), Shaun McKenna's text includes Aramaic and Latin. All in all, the production proved to depend upon such a collective of innovative technicians that the story was taken as a given and everything around it was updated to modernize and enhance it, and make it movable. It was a fitting culmination of nearly 120 years of dramatizing *Ben-Hur*. In the words of Patrick Woodroffe, the lighting designer:

> This is a very unique production because nobody had done anything like it before. It's a sports event, a rock concert, a play, a drama – it's many things, so it took us a while to get it together.
> Mark Fisher and his Stufish colleague Ray Winkler, in conjunction with our director Phil McKinley, came up with this really interesting thing. We established this language that was historically based. We were clearly back in Nazareth and in ancient Rome but with a very contemporary take on it.
> We had to be practical; it had to be that you could change the scenery and still have people in 360° look through it and around it and see where the action was in the arena, so lighting clearly became a very important part of that journey.
> It had to establish mood, dynamics, and excitement as well as spectacle, but also generate focus. So it was quite a practical exercise to highlight two people in the company of 150 and try and work out who was saying what and what the story was about. ... Finding out what the vernacular was from the start and working with the writer, Shaun McKenna, was the key for us. You have to get all that stuff right

to allow the audience to suspend their belief and buy into the scene that you are selling them – and I think we got that.

Ben Hur Live premiered at London's O2 (Millennium Dome) on September 17, 2009, and Copeland along with Abraham's Art Concerts group issued a CD with the former's music. Pointing out that there were more than 100 animals in addition to the race horses, American papers reported that it was "more of a circus of *Ben-Hur* than a play."[116] London critics were not overly enthusiastic, but the production continued on its ambitious tour to Germany. Thereafter it ran into problems. Press releases at first blamed the staging or the battleship not fitting into the arena in Milan, but by January one of the production units filed for bankruptcy.[117] Nonetheless, Abraham's website claims that it drew 40,000 spectators in London and an additional 100,000 in Hamburg, Munich, Stuttgart, and Zürich, and the benhurlive.com website announces a tour of South Korea.

CONTINUING INTO THE FUTURE

Although this chapter has focused on the afterlife of the MGM films, the technological advances that preserved and transferred them and related *Ben-Hur* by-products into new media formats, and the larger productions of the last thirty years, the penetration of the *Ben-Hur* tradition into the popular culture has continued in many other ways since the year 2000. The year 2003 saw the introduction of Microid's "Ben Hur – Blood of Braves" game for PlayStation 2, which not only renders Wallace's famed chariot race as an interactive contest but even expands the venues to include the Circus Maximus, Pompeii, and Olympus among the seventeen choices. The next year, just before the invasion of Fallujah in November, 2004, the Third Battalion of the First United States Marines wrapped themselves and their body armor in makeshift togas and held the "First Annual Ben Hur Thundering Third Chariot Race" with confiscated horses and wagons. Until that year Harold Park, Sydney's premier harness racing track, held an annual "Ben Hur" race and advertised its "elegant Ben Hur Champagne Bar."[118]

In the commercial world, the Ben-Hur Shrine in Austin continues its annual circus, and the Ben Hur lodges in Palatine, Illinois and Kansas City, Kansas, continue meeting and serving their communities, maintaining websites and Facebook pages. In recent decades Ben Hur Moving & Storage, Inc. established itself in New York and then Los Angeles. A stylized image of a racing horse adorns the logo on their website and on each of their moving trucks. Separately, Ben Hur Auto Repair operates on Santa Monica Boulevard in Los Angeles. In 2000 Atlantic Cigar of Miami introduced the Dominican Ben Hur line of cigars in a Cameroon wrapper.[119] Although somewhat before the millennium, pinball aficionados were introduced to a solid-state electronic pinball machine filled with *Ben-Hur* iconography that was manufactured by France's Staal Society in 1977.[120] The website of the Internet Pinball Database offers a number of photographs as well as several promotional flyers for "Le fantastique BEN HUR electronique." Then in 1990, Olympia introduced the first of its seventy-seven pachislo machines. This was the "BENHUR," followed by the "Magical BENHUR" the following year.[121]

In popular literature, in 1981 Karl Tunberg co-authored a sequel to Wallace's novel, *The Quest of Ben Hur*, that continues the story into the reign of Nero.[122] This was just three years after Bonanza Books reissued the Garfield edition. More recently in 2002, excerpts from the original novel appeared in Steven D. Price's *Classic Horse Stories: Twenty Timeless Horse Tales*,[123] and in 2011 Lois Scouten published *Messala: The Return From Ruin: A Sequel to Ben-Hur*.[124] This novel changes the novel's ending by having Messala recover from his injuries, fall out of love with Iras, fall in love with another woman, and explore the benefits of Christianity. In the visual arts, the Manchester Art Gallery opened its Clore Interactive Gallery by featuring a model of Alexander von Wagner's painting in which children could race their own "Ben Hur-style chariot."[125] That was in 2002. In drama that same year, Carlos A. Matas copyrighted *Ben-Hur: The Latter Years – Miriam and Vespasian*, and that same year again in London Tom Morris and Carl Heap put on a version of *Ben-Hur* at the Battersea Arts Centre in which Victorian servants, left alone in the mansion while their masters attend the Drury Lane production of *Ben-Hur*, act out the story themselves, again using audience participation by waving handkerchiefs for their favorite charioteer.[126] The BBC began broadcasting their four-part radio play adaptation of *Ben-Hur* in January, 2008, and they have followed with five additional broadcasts, most recently in November, 2013.[127] And in 2012 the Corcoran Gallery of Art in Washington hosted Jefferson Pinder's "Ben-Hur." The brochure describes the continuing influence of the 1959 film as an artistic framework in which to express contemporary social and political issues:

> *Ben-Hur* is a time based endurance piece by Jefferson Pinder in which he continues his investigation of dynamic movement. Accompanied by DJ Tony Tech, six male performers will engage in a performance that tests their strength and physical stamina. Loosely inspired by the galley scene in the 1959 Hollywood epic Ben-Hur, the piece demands that Pinder's crew row themselves to exhaustion. Although specifically about the historical, social, and political ideas surrounding masculinity and "blackness," Pinder's Ben-Hur also evokes our collective experience of human predicament and struggle.

In more secular adaptations, George Lucas's *The Phantom Menace* is not the only popular film that pays homage or makes an allusion to *Ben-Hur*. In *Billy the Kid* (1989), one of several additional problematic Gore Vidal screenplays, Governor Lew Wallace signs the novel. There were many allusions in the 1990s. In the Coen Brothers' *The Big Lebowski* (1998), behind the parking lot of the bowling alley is a suggestive sign for Ben Hur Auto Service. In Oliver Stone's *Any Given Sunday* (1999), the NFL coach played by Al Pacino has a plasma TV playing the chariot race sequence in *Ben-Hur*. In fact, his quarterback (Jamie Foxx) walks past the TV just as the Corinthian charioteer gets run over and the crowd cheers, commenting, "I get it: gladiators of their times." In Mel Brooks' comedy *Robin Hood: Men in Tights* (1993), hands reach through a prison grating like those in the 1959 *Ben-Hur*, only they are giving the finger to their jailers. Billy Crystal's apartment in *Forget Paris* is filled with basketball memorabilia, but the camera often focuses on a poster for the 1959 *Ben-Hur*. In *Titanic* (1997), the film that would tie *Ben-Hur* in winning eleven Oscars, Jack Dawson (Leonardo DiCaprio) excuses himself from the first-class passengers by saying, "It's time for me to go row with the other slaves." In the comedy *Wrongfully Accused* (1998), the prison bus includes one convict who is rowing an oar à la *Ben-Hur*. We hear the music of the 1959 film in Andy Kaufman's *Man on the Moon* (1999) and an imitation in *Boomerang* (1992). Other allusions are found in *Enchanted* (1998), *20 Dates* (1998), and *Rated X* (2000). In a television commercial in 1995, a Pontiac Sunfire GT was inserted into footage from the 1925 chariot race, noting that it had "150 horses," and six different episodes of The Simpsons made allusions to *Ben-Hur*, three to chariot racing, and one each to lepers and the galley and Nazareth scenes.

More recently in *Frost/Nixon* (2008) Richard Nixon expresses the cost of recording his interview by saying, "I didn't realize we were makin' *Ben-Hur*," and later David Frost's producer tells him to ignore "all that shit about *Ben-Hur*." In *A Single Man* (2009) the little girl in the bank has a pet scorpion named Charlton Heston nestled in a jar called the Colosseum. In *The Green Hornet* (2011) Seth Rogen's character refers to the projecting steel hubs on the wheels of his modified car as "the Ben Hur shit." In *Cloud Atlas* (2012) and *Madagascar: Escape 2 Africa* (2008) the phrase "ramming speed" is applied to moving faster in a vehicle. Clearly the phrase has become a permanent expression in the English language. And in a 2013 advertisement, world-record-holding sprint champion Usain Bolt raced against the chariots of the 1959 race to demonstrate the speed of Xfinity.

Finally, as this book goes to press, the most recent version of *Ben-Hur* is being filmed in Italy. This is MGM's third *Ben-Hur*, and, including the three animated versions, the eighth film adaptation overall. The return of the Ancient genre in the new millennium made this inevitable. After the *Cleopatra* debacle in the early 1960s, Ancients returned in the mid-1990s subsequent to the global success of Sam Raimi's syndicated television series *Hercules: The Legendary Journeys*, followed by the Disney *Hercules* in 1997 and Dreamworks' *Gladiator* in 2000. However, MGM is not at all the same film production studio that it was in 1959. It was only in late 2010 that the company emerged from bankruptcy, maintaining an arrangement with United Artists, and then in 2014 it acquired 55 percent in Lightworkers Media and One Three Media, the production companies operated by Roma Downey and Mark Burnett, producers of the very successful television series, *The Bible*. MGM is only part of a larger corporate consortium, and the senior production team of the film includes several additional members.

At this writing it is premature to attempt any analysis, but it is important to note in terms of continuity that much of the film will be shot at Cinecittá, which, as the reader knows, was built on the site of the 1925 MGM production and hosted the 1959 production. That brings at least part of the *Ben-Hur* phenomenon full circle. To extend that circle a bit further and bring this chapter to a close, we will note a bit of irony involving the *Ben-Hur* property, Lew Wallace's legacy, and the important commercial and legal precedents discussed in this book. The reader knows that in 1911 the U.S. Supreme Court decided that Kalem violated the copyright originally assigned to Lew Wallace and that as a result Kalem had to pay a $25,000 fine and their film adaptation of *Ben-Hur* was legally denied distribution. This was more than a century ago, and for much of the twentieth century, that short, black-and-white, silent version of *Ben-Hur* that helped establish movie copyright precedent was considered mostly lost by the Library of Congress, with rare copies held in only a few film archives, one of which was pirated onto a Niles Film Products Super 8 copy and then transferred to VHS in the 1980s. But now the 1907 *Ben-Hur* is completely in the public domain, and the reader can view it online, free.

NOTES

1. Thomas Schatz, "The New Hollywood," in Graeme Turner, ed., *The Film Cultures Reader*, 193.
2. Schatz, "The New Hollywood," 189.
3. *Variety* 260 (September 2, 1970) 45; *[Baton Rouge] Advocate* (February 7, 1971) 149.
4. *[Baton Rouge] State Times Advocate* (January 6, 1971) 30.
5. *Variety* 262 (February 17, 1971) 37.
6. *Augusta [GA] Chronicle* (January 24, 1971) F4; *BG* (February 14, 1971) TV7; *LAT* (February 12, 1971) E26.
7. *Variety* 262 (February 24, 1971) 31.
8. *WP* (April 9, 1972) TC27; *Variety* 267 (June 21,1972) 34; *Newsday* (February 18, 1871) 42A.
9. *Lexington [KY] Herald* (November 11, 1976) 46.
10. *Variety* 263 (May 26, 1971) 35.
11. *Newsday* (February 18, 1971) 42A.
12. *[Washington, DC] Evening Star* (February 15, 1971) 8.

13 *CPD* (December 28, 1971) 6.
14 *NYT* (February 13, 1972) D19; *Boston Herald* (February 10, 1972) 43.
15 *Variety* 266 (February 23, 1972) 39.
16 *CPD* (April 12, 1974) 106.
17 *[State College PA] Centre Daily Times* (May 21, 1977) 19.
18 *Springfield [MA] Union* (May 27, 1977) 8.
19 *Variety* 285 (January 26, 1977) 59.
20 *The Irish Times* (May 6, 1978) 23.
21 *Screen International* 135 (April 22, 1978) 1; *The Irish Times* (December 24, 1979) V.
22 *The Guardian* (November 22, 1980) 24.
23 *NYT* (February 3, 1981) D4.
24 *Springfield [IL] State Journal-Register* (April 14, 1979) 63.
25 *NYT* (January 14, 1980) C17.
26 *WP* (April 5, 1980) E5.
27 *BG* (August 10, 1980) K22; (April 16, 1981) 39; (April 11, 1982) B20; (April 3, 1983) B18.
28 *BG* (April 16, 1981) 39.
29 *NYT* (July 12, 1981) TG1.
30 *CT* (October 3, 1982) NA9; *TCSM* (January 14, 1985) 20.
31 *LAT* (June 5, 1980) F2.
32 *Variety* 304 (October 7, 1981) 102.
33 *CT* (July 24, 1987) F74.
34 *LAT* (April 17, 1987) G15.
35 *WP* (December 4, 1988) TV6.
36 *Billboard* 100 (July 30, 1988) 51.
37 Michael Arick, "The Sound of Money: In Stereo!" *Sight and Sound* 57 (1987) 42.
38 *Trenton Evening Times* (June 13, 1990) 79.
39 *NYT* (March 29, 1981) WC5.
40 *LAT* (January 31, 1979) E12.
41 *NYT* (October 20, 1981) A1.
42 *WP* (July 7, 1983) D10.
43 Raymond, "The Agony and the Ecstasy," 221 and 236.
44 *WP* (July 4, 1982) B4.
45 Samuelson, "The Generativity of *Sony v. Universal*," 1831.
46 *NYT* (August 2, 1985) D3; (December 23, 1985) D3.
47 *NYT* (August 8, 1985) A1.
48 *WSJ* (August 6, 1985) 3.
49 *NYT* (March 30, 1986) F1.
50 *Broadcasting* 114 (March 14, 1988) 30–1.
51 *Broadcasting* 113 (August 17, 1987) 65–6.
52 *The Stage and Television Today* 5862 (August 19, 1993) 25.
53 *Springfield [MA] Union* (January 10, 1972) 7.
54 *Middletown [NY] Times Herald Record* (August 23, 1973) 91.
55 *Seattle Daily Times* (January 13, 1974) 68; (January 18, 1974) 67.
56 *[Portland] Oregonian* (April 5, 1974) 31.

57 *Boxoffice* 111 (May 2, 1977) NE1, NE4.
58 *LAT* (September 13, 1978) G14; *Variety* 292 (October 4, 1978) 6; *Boxoffice* 114 (October 9, 1978) E1; *NYT* (November 7, 1979) C29.
59 *Springfield [MA] Union* (May 3, 1979) 9;
60 *Seattle Daily Times* (April 19, 1979) 49.
61 *LAT* (January 12, 1988) G6.
62 *The Guardian* (November 28, 1987) 12.
63 *Variety* 329 (January 6, 1988) 25.
64 *Boston Herald* (July 14, 1988) 37; *NYT* (June 10, 1988) C10; *Boston Herald* (July 14, 1988) 37.
65 *Boston Herald* (April 25, 1988) 50.
66 *Marietta [NY] Journal* (March 21,1989) 14
67 *Billboard* 100 (October 8, 1988) 60.
68 *Business Wire* (March 15, 1999) 1.
69 <http://www.afi.com/Docs/100Years/100Movies.pdf>
70 *Toronto Star* (February 11, 2000) 1.
71 *Video Store Magazine* 23 (February 18, 2001) 14.
72 *Variety* 382 (March 5, 2001) 42.
73 *NYT* (September 13, 2005) E5.
74 *America Cinematographer* 80 (May, 2001) 14.
75 *NYT* (September 13, 2005) E5.
76 *[Washington] Evening Star* (November 21, 1976) 122.
77 Sinyard, *A Wonderful Heart*, 185–6; cf. *Lust for Life* (1956).
78 Vidal, *Palimpsest*, 304–7.
79 *LAT* (June 17, 1996) F3.
80 *The Guardian* (June 24, 1988) 37.
81 *The Guardian* (February 16, 1989) 22.
82 *WP* (August 5, 1996) D3.
83 *Billboard* 107 (October 28, 1995) 18 and 20.
84 Sinyard, *A Wonderful Heart*, 182–3.
85 <http://filmscoremonthly.com/notes/ben_hur.html>
86 Koldys, "Miklós Rózsa and 'Ben-Hur,'" 3–20.
87 Elley, "The Film Composer," 20–4.
88 Wecott, "Miklós Rózsa's *Ben-Hur*," 183–207.
89 Bally, *Miklós Rózsa*.
90 Hickman, *Miklós Rózsa's* Ben-Hur.
91 Meyer, *Epic Sound*, 142–64.
92 NYPL; *TBS* (July 20, 1989) 1G.
93 <http://www.bizjournals.com/orlando/stories/1999/06/21/story7.html>
94 *WSJ* (November 2, 1899) B2. <http://www.wsj.com/articles/SB941500054570070414>
95 <http://www.prnewswire.com/news-releases/epic-entertainment-takes-to-the-stage-with-premiere-of-ben-hur-the-musical-76976842.html>
96 <http://articles.orlandosentinel.com/1999-08-29/features/9908230241_1_chariot-races-ben-hur-equity>
97 *Sandusky Register* (November 21, 1999) 26.
98 *WSJ* (November 2, 1999) B2.

99 <http://www.crosswalk.com/culture/music/ben-hur-the-musical-540810.html>
100 <http://ywamtampa.com/wordpress/2013/04/judahbenhur2013>; <http://ywamtampa.com/wordpress/pa-focus>
101 <http://www.judahbenhur.com/index.html>; <https://www.facebook.com/YWAMTampa/posts/587805134633667>
102 <https://www.youtube.com/watch?v=xbre7ZWRSsY>
103 OCLC #47019275
104 <http://www.pe.com/articles/hur-693675-april-theater.html>
105 <http://www.lifehousetheater.com>
106 *[Glascow] Sunday Mail* (July 26, 2009) 4849.
107 *[London] Daily Mail* (September 12, 2009) 34.
108 <http://www.payvand.com/news/05/nov/1126.html>
109 *NYT* (September 12, 2006) E2.
110 <http://www.npr.org/templates/story/story.php?storyId=6129746>
111 <http://www.smh.com.au/entertainment/theatre/hold-your-horses-benhur-going-cheap-20101020-16u6x.html>
112 <http://www.stadia-magazine.com/news.php?NewsID=23744>
113 <http://www.smh.com.au/entertainment/theatre/devoid-of-horsepower-epics-biggest-race-is-for-the-exits-20101024-16ze6.html>
114 <http://www.telegraph.co.uk/culture/theatre/london-shows/6126213/Ben-Hur-Live-the-power-of-a-rock-concert.html>
115 <http://www.tpimagazine.com/production-profiles/368727/ben_hur_live.html>
116 *Altoona Mirror* (September 18, 2009) 28.
117 <http://www.thepolicewiki.org/Police_wiki/index.php?title=Ben_Hur_Live>
118 <http://www.hellmann.com.au/news/story/current/staff.pdf>
119 <http://www.smokeshopmag.com/0600/brand.htm>
120 <http://www.ipdb.org/machine.cgi?id=2855>
121 <http://www.pachislodb.com/manufacturer-10.html>
122 Tunberg and Walford, *The Quest of Ben Hur*.
123 Price, *Classic Horse Stories*.
124 Scouten, *Messala*.
125 <http://www.manchestergalleries.org/html/press/press_details.jsp?id=74>
126 Paul, *Film and the Classical Epic Tradition*, 244–8.
127 <http://www.bbc.co.uk/programmes/b007jr6d>

Bibliography

BOOKS AND ACADEMIC JOURNAL ARTICLES CITED

Excludes Editions of *Ben-Hur*, Catalogs, Directories, Proceedings, Reports, Programs, Souvenir Books, Registries, Collector's Guides, Guide Books, Gazetteers, Local Histories, Newspapers, Magazines, Trade Journals, eBay citations and other webpages, and Television and Radio Broadcasts, that are fully cited in the Notes.

Adrian, Paul. *Cirque au cinema, cinema au cirque* (Paris: P. Adrian, 1984).
Aldrich, George I., and Alexander Forbes. *The Progressive Course in Reading – Fifth Book, Part I* (New York: American Book Company, 1900).
Allan, Scott, and Mary Morton, eds. *Reconsidering Gérôme* (Los Angeles: Getty Publications, 2010).
Allen, Jeanne Thomas. "Copyright and Early Theater, Vaudeville and Film Competition," *Journal of the University Film Association* 31 (1979) 5–11.
Allen, Robert C. *Horrible Prettiness: Burlesque and American Culture* (Chapel Hill: The University of North Carolina Press, 1991).
Altman, Diana. [*Hollywood East: Louis B. Mayer and the Origins of the Studio System* (New York: Carol Publishing Group, 1992).
Atkinson, Louise Warren. *The Story of Paul of Tarsus: A Manual for Teachers* (Chicago: The University of Chicago Press, 1910).
Avery, Elroy McKendree. *A History of Cleveland and Its Environs: The Heart of New Connecticut* [sic] (Chicago: The Lewis Publishing Company, 1918).
Axford, Elizabeth C. *Song Sheets to Software: A Guide to Print Music, Software, and Web Sites for Musicians* (Latham, MD: Scarecrow Press, 2004).
Axt, William. *The Toilers* (New York: Robbins Music, 1926).
Azlant, Edward. "Screenwriting for the Early Silent Film: Forgotten Pioneers, 1897–1911," *Film History* 9 (1997) 228–56.
Bak, Richard. *Detroit Land: A Collection of Movers, Shakers, Lost Souls, and History Makers from Detroit's Past* (Detroit: Wayne State University Press, 2011).
Balio, Tino. *Hollywood in the Age of Television* (Cambridge, MA: Unwin Hyman, 1990).
Bally, Juliane. *Miklós Rózsa: Ausbildung und kammermusikalisches Frühwerk*

als Basis für das filmmusikalische Schaffen am Beispiel Ben Hur (Saarbrucken: PFAU, 2012).

Barbee, David Rankin. "President Lincoln and Doctor Gurley," *The Abraham Lincoln Quarterly* 5 (1948).

Barr, Steven C. *The Almost Complete 78 rpm Record Dating Guide II* (Huntington Beach, CA: Yesterday Once Again, 1992).

Bartlett, G. B. *An Evening of Statuary and Tableaux: A Summer Evening's Entertainment* (Boston: Walter H. Baker & Co., 1888).

Bastiani, Ange. *Arrête ton char Ben-Hur!* (Paris: Gallimard, 1954).

Battaglio, Steven. *David Suskind: A Televised Life* (New York: Macmillan, 2010).

Baxley, Jack, C. W. A. MacCormack, and Lewis Lacy. *Shrine Patrol and Band of Ben Hur Temple Cooperating with MacCormack Productions Co., Presents the Oh Joy Musical Review* (Austin: n.p., 1921).

Beasley, David R. *McKee Rankin and the Heyday of the American Theater* (Waterloo, ON: Wilfrid Laurier University Press, 2002).

Beecher, Henry Ward. *The Life of Jesus Christ* (New York: J. B. Ford, 1871).

Behlmer, Rudy. "'Tumult, Battle and Blaze': Looking Back on the 1920s – and Since – with Gaylord Carter, the Dean of Theater Organists," in Clifford McCarty, ed., *Film Music 1* (New York: Garland Publishing, 1989) 19–59.

Bensel, Richard Franklin. *The Political Economy of American Industrialization, 1877–1900* (Cambridge: Cambridge University Press, 2000).

Berenger, Richard. *The History and Art of Horsemanship* (London: T. Davies, 1771).

Bertholf, Kenneth Jr., and Don Dorflinger. *Blairstown and Its Neighbors* (Charleston, SC: Arcadia Publishing, 2011).

Berwick, Edward. *Lives of Marcus Valerius Messala, and Titus Pomponius Atticus* (London: Longman, Hurst, Rees, Orme, and Brown, 1813).

Bierley, Paul Edmond. *John Philip Sousa: A Descriptive Catalog of His Works* (Urbana: University of Illinois Press, 1973).

—. *The Incredible Band of John Philip Sousa* (Urbana: University of Illinois Press, 2006).

Birdsall, William Wilfred, and Rufus Matthew Jones, eds. *Famous Authors and the Literature of England and America* (Philadelphia: American Book & Bible House, 1897).

Birmingham, Stephen. *"The Rest of Us": The Rise of America's Eastern European Jews* (Syracuse: Syracuse University Press, 1999).

Bissell, Lillian. *Music in Cultural Education* (Hartford, CT: Finlay Brothers Press, 1934).

Blaszczyk, Regina Lee. *Imagining Consumers: Design and Innovation from Wedgwood to Corning* (Baltimore: The Johns Hopkins University Press, 2000).

Block, Alex Ben, and Lucy Autrey Wilson, *George Lucas' Blockbusting* (New York: itBooks, 2010).

Blom, Ivo. "*Quo Vadis?* From Painting to Cinema and Everything in Between," in Leonardo Quaresima and Laura Vichi, eds. *La decima musa. Il cinema e le altre arti* (Udine: Forum, 2001) 281–92.

Blotner, Joseph, and Frederick L. Gwynn, eds. *Faulkner in the University* (Charlottesville: University of Virginia Press, 1977).

Bohn, Thomas W., and Richard L. Stromgren. *Light and Shadows: A History of Motion Pictures*[3] (Palo Alto: Mayfield Publishing Company, 1987).
Boomhower, Ray E. *The Sword and the Pen* (Indianapolis: Indiana Historical Society, 2008).
Boradkar, Prasad. *Designing Things: A Critical Introduction to the Culture of Objects* (Oxford: Berg Publishers, 2010).
Bordwell, David, Janet Staiger, and Kristin Thompson. *The Classical Hollywood Cinema: Film Style & Mode of Production to 1960* (New York: Columbia University Press, 1985).
Bossuet, Jacques-Bénigne. *Politique tirée des propres paroles de L'Escriture sainte* (Paris: Paris Cot, 1709).
Bourgeon, Paul. *Le Fils de Ben Hur* (Paris: Robert Laffont, 1963).
Bowers, Q. David. *Encyclopedia of Automatic Musical Instruments* (New York: Vestal Press, 1972).
Bowser, Eileen. *The Transformation of Cinema, 1907–1915*, Part 2 of Charles Harpole, ed., *History of the American Cinema* (New York: Scribner, 1990).
Boyer, Paul S. "Wallace, Zerelda Gray Sanders," in Edward T. James, ed., *Notable American Women, 1607–1950* (Cambridge, MA: Belknap Press of Harvard University Press, 1971).
Brands, H. W. *American Colossus: The Triumph of Capitalism* (New York: Doubleday, 2010).
Brockman, C. Lance, ed. *Theatre of the Fraternity* (Minneapolis: Frederick R. Weisman Art Museum, 1996).
Brooks, Tim, and Brian A. L. Rust. *The Columbia Master Book Discography: Principal U.S. Matrix Series* (Westport, CT: Greenwood Press, 1999).
Brown, Dee. *The Year of the Century: 1876* (New York: Charles Scribner's Sons, 1966).
Browne, Ray B., and Pat Browne, eds. *The Guide to United States Popular Culture* (Bowling Green: Bowling Green State University Popular Press, 2001).
Brownlow, Kevin. *The Parade's Gone By . . .* (New York: Albert A. Knopf, 1968).
—. "Ben-Hur: The Heroic Fiasco," *Films and Filming* 16 (1970) 26–32 and 58–61.
Buckham, John Wright. *Progressive Religious Thought in America: A Survey of the Enlarging Pilgrim Faith* (Boston: Houghton Mifflin Co., 1919).
Caidhyanathan, Siva. *Copyrights and Copywrongs: The Rise of Intellectual Property and How It Threatens Creativity* (New York: New York University Press, 2001).
Caldwell, Howard. *The Golden Age of Indianapolis Theaters* (Bloomington: Indiana University Press, 2010) 67.
Calkins, Ernest. *Modern Advertising* (New York: Appleton, 1905).
Cameron, Alan. *The Last Pagans of Rome* (Oxford: Oxford University Press, 2010).
Campbell, Alexander. *Popular Lectures and Addresses* (Philadelphia: James Challen & Son, 1863).
Campbell, Thomas. *Declaration and Address of the Christian Association of Washington*, (Washington, PA: Brown & Sample, 1809).
Carnes, Mark C. *Secret Ritual and Manhood in Victorian America* (New Haven: Yale University Press, 1989).

Carter, Paul. *The Spiritual Crisis of the Gilded Age* (DeKalb: Northern Illinois University Press, 1971).
Charles, Elizabeth Runde. *Wanderings Over Bible Lands and Seas* (New York: Robert Carter & Brothers, 1867).
Clark, Clifford E. *Henry Ward Beecher; Spokesman for a Middle-Class America* (Urbana: University of Illinois Press, 1978).
Cleary, David Powers. *Great American Brands; The Success Formulas that Made Them Famous* (New York: Fairchild Publications, 1981).
Clum, Woodworth. *Apache Agent: The Story of John P. Clum* (Boston: Houghton Mifflin Company, 1936).
Cocker, Benjamin Franklin. *Christianity and Greek Philosophy: Or, The Relation Between Spontaneous and Reflective Thought in Greece and the Positive Teaching of Christ and his Apostles* (New York: Harper & Brothers, 1870).
Cohn, David L. *The Good Old Days: A History of American Morals and Manners as Seen Through the Sears, Roebuck Catalogs 1905 to the Present* (New York: Simon & Schuster, 1940).
Cohn, Jan. *Creating America: George Horace Lorimer and* The Saturday Evening Post (Pittsburgh: University of Pittsburgh Press, 1989), 69.
Collins, John J. "Josephus on the Essenes. The Sources of His Information," in Zuleika Rodgers, Margaret Daly-Denton, and Anne Fitzpatrick McKinley, eds., *A Wandering Galilean: Essays in Honour of Seán Freyne* (Leiden: Brill, 2009).
Conybeare, William John, and John Saul Howson. *The Life and Epistles of St. Paul* (New York: Scribner, 1869).
Cooper, Patricia Ann. *Once a Cigar Maker: Men, Women, and Work Culture in American Cigar Factories, 1900–1919* (Urbana: University of Illinois Press, 1987).
Cooper, Jr., William H. *The Great Revivalists in American Religion, 1740–1944: The Careers and Theology of Jonathan Edwards, Charles Finney, Dwight Moody, Billy Sunday, and Aimee Semple McPherson* (Jefferson, NC: McFarland & Co., 2010).
Cox, Jim. *Sold on Radio: Advertisers in the Golden Age of Broadcasting* (Jefferson, NC: McFarland & Company, 2008).
Croly, George. *Tarry Thou Till I Come; or, Salathiel, the Wandering Jew* (New York: Funk & Wagnalls Co., 1901).
Cross, Gary S. *An All-consuming Century: Why Commercialism Won in Modern America* (New York: Columbia University Press, 2000).
Crown, Judith. *No Hands: The Rise and Fall of the Schwinn Bicycle Company, an American Institution* (New York: H. Holt, 1996).
Crowther, Bosley. *The Lion's Share: The Story of an Entertainment Empire* (New York: E. P. Dutton & Company, Inc., 1957).
—. *Hollywood Rajah: The Life and Times of Louis B. Mayer* (New York: Holt, 1960).
Cunutt, Yakima, and Oliver Drake. *Stunt Man: The Autobiography of Yakima Canutt* (Norman: University of Oklahoma Press, 1997).
Damon-Moore, Helen. *Magazines for the Millions: Gender and Commerce in the Ladies' Home Journal and the Saturday Evening Post, 1880–1910* (Albany: State University of New York Press, 1996).

Dane, Jeffrey. *A Composer's Notes: Remembering Miklós Rózsa* (New York: iUniverse, Inc., 2006).

Dans, Peter E. *Christians in the Movies: A Century of Saints and Sinners* (Lanham, MD: Rowman and Littlefield, 2009).

Davenport, Benjamin. *The Fifty Best Books of the Greatest Authors Condensed for Busy People; Sketches of the Entire Contents of the Fifty Most Famous Works in the Whole Range of Literature* (Buffalo: 19th Century Book Concern, 1891).

Davis, Glenmore. "The Most Successful Play Ever Produced," *Green Book* (January 1914) 36–45.

Davis, Ronald L. *William S. Hart: Projecting the American West* (Norman: University of Oklahoma Press, 2003).

Davis, Will A. *The Trial of Jesus* (Columbia City, IN: J. W. Adams, 1889).

De Puy, William Harrison, ed. *The University of Literature* (New York: J. S. Barcus & Co., 1896).

Dixon, William Hepworth. *The Holy Land*[3] (Philadelphia: J. B. Lippincott, 1868).

Dorrien, Gary. *The Making of American Liberal Theology: Imagining Progressive Religion, 1805-1900* (Louisville, KY: Westminster John Knox Press, 2001).

Doss, Erika. *Memorial Mania: Public Feeling in America* (Chicago: University of Chicago Press, 2010).

Douglas, Ann. *The Feminization of American Culture* (New York: Anchor Books, 1977).

Douglas, Lloyd C. *Time to Remember* (Boston: Houghton Mifflin, 1951).

Downey, Fairfax, ed. *Races to the Swift: Great Stories of the Turf* (New York: Doubleday & Company, 1967).

Downey, Glanville. *Ancient Antioch* (Princeton: Princeton University Press, 1963).

Dressler, Louis R., ed. *Favorite Masterpieces, Embracing Famous Songs and Those Who Made Them* (New York: The Standard Musical Association, 1897).

Dunn, Jacob Platt. *Memorial and Genealogical Record of Representative Citizens of Indiana* (Indianapolis: B. F. Bowen & Company, 1912).

—. *Indiana and Indianans: A History of Aboriginal and Territorial Indiana and the Century of Statehood* (Chicago and New York: The American Historical Society, 1919).

Eastman, Fred. *Christ in the Drama* (New York: The MacMillan Company, 1947).

Edwards, Holly, ed. *Noble Dreams, Wicked Pleasures: Orientalism in America, 1870-1930* (Princeton: Princeton University Press, 2000).

Ellenberger, Allen R. *Ramon Novarro: A Biography of the Silent Film Idol, 1899-1968* (Jefferson, NC: McFarland & Company, Inc., 1999).

Elley Derek. "The Film Composer," *Films and Filming* 23 (1977).

Elson, Louis Charles. *The History of American Music* (New York: Macmillan Co., 1904).

Emmet, Boris, and John E. Jeuck. *Catalogues and Counters: A History of Sears, Roebuck and Company* (Chicago: University of Chicago Press, 1950).

Epperson, Bruce D. *Peddling Bicycles to America: The Rise of an Industry* (Jefferson, NC: McFarland & Co., 2010).

Erkelenz, Ralph. "Ben-Hur: A Tale of the Score," *Pro Musica Sana* 5 (2005) 1–29; 5 (2006) 3–36; 6 (2007) 4–39; 7 (2008) 3–32; 7 (2009) 3–49.

Erskine, John. *Leading American Novelists* (New York: H. Holt and Co., 1910).

Escott, Paul D. *"What Shall We Do with the Negro?": Lincoln, White Racism, and Civil War America* (Charlottesville: University of Virginia Press, 2009) 136.

Evans, Madison. *Biographical Sketches of the Pioneer Preachers of Indiana* (Philadelphia: J. Challen & Son, 1862).

Everson, William K. *American Silent Film* (New York: Oxford University Press, 1978).

Eyman, Scott. *Lion of Hollywood: The Life and Legend of Louis B. Mayer* (New York: Simon & Schuster, 2005).

Faucett, Bill F. *George Whitefield Chadwick: A Bio-Bibliography* (Westport, CT: Greenwood Press, 1998).

Fearing, Franklin. "Research, Journals, Etc.," *The Quarterly of Film Radio and Television* 7 (1953).

Fell, John L. "Motive, Mischief, and Melodrama: The State of Film Narrative in 1907," in Fell, ed., *Film Before Griffith* (Berkeley: University of California Press, 1983).

Ferree, Barr, ed. *Yearbook of the Pennsylvania Society* (New York: The Pennsylvania Society, 1905).

Fiedler, Leslie A. *The Inadvertent Epic: From Uncle Tom's Cabin to Roots* (New York: Simon & Schuster, 1979).

Fiske, John. "The Progress From Brute to Man," *North American Review* 241 (1873).

—. *The Destiny of Man* (Boston: Houghton Mifflin and Company, 1884).

—. *American Political Ideas Viewed from the Standpoint of Universal History; Three Lectures Delivered at the Royal Institution of Great Britain in May, 1880* (New York: Harper and Bros., 1885).

Flamini, Roland. *Thalberg: The Last Tycoon and the World of M-G-M* (New York: Crown Publishers, 1993).

Forman, Henry James. *Our Movie Made Children* (New York: The MacMillan Company, 1934).

Foster, Charles. *Stardust and Shadows: Canadians in Early Hollywood* (Toronto: Dundurn Press, 2000).

Foster, Frank Hugh. *The Modern Movement in American Theology; Sketches in the History of American Protestant Thought From the Civil War to the World War* (New York: Fleming H. Revell Co., 1939).

Foulke, William Dudley. *Life of Oliver P. Morton* (Indianapolis: The Bowen-Merrill Co., 1899).

Fox, Richard Wightman. *Jesus in America: Personal Savior, Cultural Hero, National Obsession* (New York: HarperSanFrancisco, 2004).

Fox, Stephen. *The Mirror Makers: A History of American Advertising and its Creators* (New York: William Morrow and Company, Inc., 1984).

Freer, Richard D. *Introduction to Civil Procedure* (New York: Aspen Publishers, 2006).

Fried, Stephen. *Appetite for America: Fred Harvey and the Business of Civilizing the Wild* (New York: Bantam Books, 2010).
Frohlich, Louis D., and Charles Schwartz. *The Law of Motion Pictures* (New York: Baker, Voorhis and Company, 1918).
Frye Northrup. *Fearful Symmetry: A Study of William Blake* (Toronto: University of Toronto Press, 2004).
Gamse, Albert, ed. *World's Favorite Marches* (Carlstadt, NJ: Ashley Publications, 1962).
Getchell, Kevin. *Scapegoat of Shiloh: The Distortion of Lew Wallace's Record by U.S. Grant* (Jefferson, NC: McFarland, 2013).
—. *La Crónica de Nuevo México* (January, 2014).
Gillespie, A. Arnold. "Remembrances of Ben Hur" – Part I," *Classic Images* 161 (1988).
Ginsburg, Jane C. "Creation and Commercial Value: Copyright Protections of Works of Information," *Columbia Law Review* 90 (1990) 1865–1938.
Glancy, H. Mark. "MGM Grosses, 1924–1948: The Eddie Mannix Ledger," *Historical Journal of Film, Radio & Television* 12 (1992) 127–44.
Godkin, E. L. "The New and Old Version," *The Nation* 32 (June 9, 1881) 401–2.
Gomery, Douglas. *The Coming of Sound* (New York: Routledge, 2005).
Goodspeed, Edgar Johnson. *Strange New Gospels* (Chicago: University of Chicago Press, 1931).
Gordon, John Steele. *Empire of Wealth: The Epic History of America* (New York: HarperCollins Publishers, 2004).
Grace, Pamela. *The Religious Film: Christianity and the Hagiopic* (Malden, MA: Wiley-Blackwell, 2009).
Grau, Robert. *The Business Man in the Amusement World: A Volume of Progress in the Field* (New York: Broadway, 1910).
Gray, James. *Business Without Boundary: The Story of General Mills* (Minneapolis: University of Minnesota Press, 1954).
Greeley, Horace. *The American Conflict: A History of the Great Rebellion in the United States of America, 1860–1865* (Hartford: O. D. Case and Company, 1867).
Green, Anne. *Flaubert and the Historical Novel:* (Cambridge: Cambridge University Press, 1982).
Gresham, Perry Epler. *Campbell and the Colleges* (Nashville: The Disciples of Christ Historical Society, 1973).
Groner, Alex. *The History of American Business and Industry* (New York: American Heritage Publishing Co, Inc., 1972).
Grossman, John. *Labeling America* (East Petersburg, PA: Fox Chapel Publishing, 2011).
Gunnison, Binney. *New Dialogues and Plays for Young People, Ages Fifteen to Twenty-Five* (New York: Hinds and Noble, 1900).
Gutjahr, Paul C. "To the Heart of Solid Puritans: Historicizing the Popularity of Ben-Hur," *Mosaic* 26 (1993).
—. *An American Bible: A History of the Good Book in the United States, 1777–1880* (Stanford: Stanford University Press, 1999).
Hanson, Victor Davis. "Lew Wallace and the Ghosts of the Shunpike," in Robert

Cowley, ed., *What Ifs? of American History* (New York: G. P. Putnam, 2003), 67–86.

—. *Ripples of Battle: How Wars of the Past Still Determine How We Fight, How We Live, and How We Think* (New York: Doubleday, 2003).

Harner, Gary W. "The Kalem Company, Travel and On-Location Filming: The Forging of an Identity," *Film History* 10 (1998) 188–207.

Harper, J. Henry. *The House of Harper: A Century of Publishing in Franklin Square* (New York: Harper & Brothers, 1912).

Hart, William S. *My Life East and West* (New York: Benjamin Blom, 1968).

Hassan, Wail S. *Immigrant Narratives: Orientalism and Cultural Translation in Arab American* (New York: Oxford University Press, 2011).

Heater, Claude. *Fatal Flaws of the Most Correct Book on Earth* (Longwood, FL: Xulon Press, 2008).

Henderson, Mary C. *Theater in America: 250 Years of Plays, Players, and Productions* (New York: Harry N. Abrams, 1996).

—. *The City and the Theatre* (New York: Back Stage Books, 2004).

Henry, David. "Ben-Hur: Francis Fredric Theophilus Weeks and Patent No 8615 of 1894," *The New Magic Lantern Journal* 5.1 (1987).

Herman, Jan. *A Talent for Trouble: The Life of Hollywood's Most Acclaimed Director, William Wyler* (New York: G. P. Putnam's Sons, 1996).

Hershberg, James G. *James B. Conant: Harvard to Hiroshima and the Making of the Nuclear Age* (New York: Knopf, 1993).

Heston, Charlton. *The Actor's Life: Journals, 1956–1976* (New York: Dutton, 1978).

—. *In the Arena: An Autobiography* (New York: Boulevard Books, 1997).

Heston, Charlton, and Jean-Pierre Isbouts. *Charlton Heston's Hollywood: 50 Years in American Film* (New York: GT Publishing, 1998).

Hewett, Edgar L. *Lew Wallace and the Ben Hur Room* (Santa Fe: School of American Research, Museum of New Mexico, 1943).

Hickman, Roger. *Miklós Rózsa's* Ben-Hur: *A Film Score Guide* (Lanham, MD: The Scarecrow Press, 2011).

Higham, Charles. *Merchant of Dreams: Louis B. Mayer, M.G.M., and the Secret Hollywood* (New York: Donald I. Fine, Inc., 1993).

Hill, Hamlin, ed. *Mark Twain's Letters to His Publishers, 1867–1894* (Berkeley: University of California Press, 1967).

Hirsch, Foster. *The Boys from Syracuse: The Shuberts' Theatrical Empire* (Carbondale: Southern Illinois University Press, 1998).

History of Montgomery County, Indiana (Indianapolis: A. W. Bowen, 1913).

Hobbes, Thomas (trans.). *The History of the Grecian War, Written by Thucydides* (London: G. & W. Whittaker, 1822).

Hoganson, Kristin L. *Consumer's Imperium: The Global Production of American Domesticity, 1865-1920* (Chapel Hill: The University of North Carolina Press, 2007).

Hoge, Sr., Cecil C. *The First Hundred Years Are the Toughest: What We Can Learn from the Century of Competition Between Sears and Wards* (Berkeley: Ten Speed Press, 1988).

Holston, Kim R. *Movie Roadshows: A History and Filmography of*

Reserved-Seat Limited Showings, 1911–1973 (Jefferson, NC: Macfarland, 2013).
Homestead, Melissa J. *American Women Authors and Literary Property, 1822–1869* (New York: Cambridge University Press, 2005).
Hopper, Hedda. *Under My Hat* (Garden City: Doubleday, 1952).
Horder, William Garrett, ed. *The Poet's Bible*³ (London: Ward, Lock & Bowden, Ltd., 1895).
Hoshour, Samuel K. *Autobiography* (St. Louis: John Burns Publishing, 1884).
Hovet, Jr., Ted. *Realism and Spectacle in* Ben-Hur *(1880–1959)* (Ph.D. diss.: Duke University, 1995) 1–35.
—. "The Case of Kalem's Ben-Hur (1907) and the Transformation of Cinema," *Quarterly Review of Film & Video* 18 (2001) 283–94.
Howe, Kathleen. *Revealing the Holy Land; The Photographic Exploration of Palestine* (Berkeley: University of California Press, 1997).
Howells, William Dean. "Certain Dangerous Tendencies in American Life," *Atlantic Monthly* 42 (1878).
Hughes, Richard T. *Reviving the Ancient Faith: The Story of Churches of Christ in America* (Grand Rapids: Wm. B. Eerdmans Publishing Co., 1996).
Huhtamo, Erkki. *Illusions in Motion: Media Archaeology of the Moving Panorama and Related Spectacles* (Cambridge, MA: The MIT Press, 2013).
Hull, Debra B. *Christian Church Women: Shapers of a Movement* (St. Louis: Chalice Press, 1994).
Humphrey, John H. *Roman Circuses: Arenas for Chariot Racing* (London: B. T. Batsford, 1986).
Humphreys, Kristi Rowan. *Faulkner on Stage* (Ph.D. diss., University of Texas at Dallas, 2009).
Hunt, Herbert, and Floyd C. Kaylor. *Washington, West of the Cascades* (Chicago: S. J. Clarke Publishing Company, 1917).
Hurlbut, Jesse Lyman. *The Story of Chautauqua* (New York: G. P. Putnam's Sons, 1921).
Hutchison, William R. *The Modernist Impulse in American Protestantism* (Durham: Duke University Press, 1992).
—. *Religious Pluralism in America: The Contentious History of a Founding Ideal* (New Haven: Yale University Press, 2003).
Iliff, David Gerard. *The Lost Tribe of Ben-Hur* (Indianapolis: Fall Creek Review, 1994).
Jackson, Gregory S. "A Game Theory of Evangelical Films," *Critical Inquiry* 39 (2013) 451–85.
Jacobs, Lewis. *The Rise of the American Film* (New York: Harcourt, Brace and Company, 1939).
Jacobson, Matthew Frye. *Barbarian Virtues: The United States Encounters Foreign Peoples at Home and Abroad, 1876–1917* (New York: Hill and Wang, 2000).
Jameson, Anna. *Legends of the Madonna, As Represented in the Fine Arts* (London: Longman, Brown, Green, and Longmans, 1852).
Jenkins, W. C. "The 'Signs' of the Times," *The National Magazine* 34 (1911) 153–60.

Jones, Jan L. *Renegades, Showmen, & Angels: A Theatrical History of Fort Worth From 1873–2001* (Fort Worth: TCU Press, 2006).

Jones, Oakah L. "Lew Wallace: Hoosier Governor of Territorial New Mexico, 1878–81," *New Mexico Historical Review* 60 (1985).

Judis, John B. *The Folly of Empire: What George W. Bush Could Learn from Theodore Roosevelt and Woodrow Wilson* (New York: Lisa Drew/Scribner, 2004).

Kaplan, Fred. *Gore Vidal: A Biography* (New York: Doubleday, 1999).

Karst, Fred. "Maxinkuckee Magic," *Outdoor Indiana* (July/August 1992) 14.

Keipert, Heinrich. *Bibel-Atlas nach den neuesten und besten Hülfsquellen* (Berlin: G. W. F. Müller, 1851).

Kelley, Edgar Stillman. *Words and Music of Klaw & Erlanger's Production of Gen. Lew Wallace's Ben-Hur* (New York: Towers & Curran, 1902).

Kelly, R. Gordon. "Historical Fiction," in M. Thomas Inge, ed., *Handbook of American Popular Culture* (New York: Greenwood Press, 1988).

Kemp, Barton. *Worcester II* (Charleston, SC: Arcadia Publishing, 2008).

King, Charles William. *The Gnostics and Their Remains, Ancient and Medieval* (London: Bell and Daldy, 1864).

King, Maurice R. *Edgar Stillman Kelley: American Composer, Teacher, and Author* (Ph.D. diss., The Florida State University, 1970).

Klepper, Robert K. *Silent Films, 1877–1996: A Critical Guide to 646 Movies* (Jefferson, NC: McFarland, 1999).

Knox, Thomas Wallace. *The Boy Travellers in the Far East; Part Fourth, Adventures of Two Youths in a Journey to Egypt and the Holy Land* (New York: Harper & Brothers, 1882/3).

Koldys, Mark. "Miklós Rózsa and 'Ben-Hur,'" *Pro Musica Sana* 3 (1974).

Korda, Michael. *Making the List: A Cultural History of the American Bestseller, 1900–1999* (New York: Barnes & Noble, 2001).

Kotar, S. L., and J. E. Gessler. *The Rise of the American Circus, 1716–1899* (Jefferson, NC: McFarland & Co., 2011).

Kyle, Richard G. *Evangelicalism: An Americanized Christianity* (New Brunswick, NJ: Transaction Publishers, 2006).

LaFeber, Walter. *The New Empire* (Ithaca: Cornell University Press, 1963).

Landes, Christian, ed. *Le cirque et les courses de chars Rome – Byzance* (Lattes: Editions Imago, 1990).

Langhorne, John, and William Langhorne (trans.). *Plutarch's Lives, translated from the original Greek, with notes critical and historical, and a new life of Plutarch* (London: Edward and Charles Dilly, 1770).

Last, Jay T. *The Color Explosion: Nineteenth Century American Lithoraphy* (Santa Ana, CA: Hillcrest Press, 2005).

Latrobe, John H. B. *Reminiscences of West Point from September, 1818 to March 1882* (East Saginaw, MI: Evening News, 1887).

Lawrence, D. H. *Studies in Classic American Literature* (New York: Thomas Seltzer, 1923).

Lawrence, Edward A. *Modern Missions in the East* (New York: Harper & Brothers, 1895).

Leach, William. *Land of Desire: Merchants, Power, and the Rise of a New American Culture* (New York: Vintage Books, 1994).
Lears, T. J. Jackson. *No Place of Grace: Antimodernism and the Transformation of American Culture, 1880–1920* (Chicago: The University of Chicago Press, 1983).
Leavitt, John M. "Renan, and the Supernatural," *The American Quarterly Church Review and Ecclesiastical Register* 20 (January, 1860) 489–507.
Leblanc, Jacques, and Grégoire Poccardi. "Étude de la permanence des tracés urbains et ruraux antiques à Antioche-sur-l'Oronte," *Syria* 76 (1999) 91–126.
Ledoux, Gary. *Nantan: The Life and Times of John P. Clum* (Victoria, BC: Trafford, 2007).
Leider, Emily W. *Dark Lover: The Life and Death of Rudolph Valentino* (New York: Farrar, Strauss and Giroux, 2003).
—. *Myrna Loy: The Only Good Girl in Hollywood* (Berkeley: California University Press, 2011).
Leonard, John William. *The Industries of Detroit: Historical, Descriptive, and Statistical* (Detroit: J. M. Elstner, Publishers, 1887).
Lev, Peter. *Transforming the Screen, 1950–1959* (Berkeley: University of California Press, 2006).
Libourel, Jan M. "Galley Slaves in the Second Punic War," *Classical Philology* 68 (1973) 116–19.
Lietzen, Walter, ed. *Ben Hur Lodge No. 322 A.F. & A.M.: 1890–1990* (Kansas City: The Record Publications, 1989).
Lifson, Amy. "Ben-Hur: The Book That Shook the World," *Humanities* 30 (2009) 14–20.
Lightfoot, Joseph Barber. *Saint Paul's Epistle to the Philippians*[2] (London: Macmillan and Co., 1869).
Lighty, Shaun. *The Fall and Rise of Lew Wallace: Gaining Legitimacy Through Popular Culture* (MA Thesis, Miami University, Oxford, OH, 2005).
Lindvall, Terry. *Sanctuary Cinema: Origins of the Christian Film Industry* (New York: New York University Press, 2007).
Lithicum, Richard, ed. *The Ideal Orator* (Chicago: W. R. Vansant, 1904).
Lippy, Charles H. *Being Religious, American Style; A History of Popular Religiosity in the United States* (Westport, CT: Greenwood Press, 1994).
Loney, Glenn. "The Heyday of the Dramatized Novel," *Educational Theatre Journal* 9 (1957) 194–200.
—. ed. *Musical Theatre in America* (Westport, CT: Greenwood Press, 1984).
Lossing, Benson J. *Pictorial History of the Civil War in the United States of America* (Hartford: T. Belknap, 1868).
Lott, Eric. *Love and Theft: Blackface Minstrelsy and the American Working Class* (New York: Oxford University Press, 1993).
Loughney, Patrick. "From 'Rip Van Winkle' to 'Jesus of Nazareth': Thoughts on the Origins of the American Screenplay," *Film History* 9 (1997) 277–89.
Lovoll, Odd S. *Norwegian Newspapers in America: Connecting Norway and the New Land* (Minneapolis: Minnesota Historical Society Press, 2010).
Mabie, Hamilton W. "The Most Popular Novels in America," *Forum* (December, 1893) 508.

Mackintosh, Iain. *Architecture, Actor and Audience* (London: Routledge, 1993).
MacDougall, Curtis Daniel. *Hoaxes* (New York: The MacMillan Co., 1940).
Mahan, W. D. *Archaeological Writings of the Sanhedrin and Talmuds of the Hews, Taken from the Ancient Parchments and Scrolls at Constantinople and the Vatican at Rome, Being the Record Made by the Enemies of Jesus of Nazareth in His Day. The Most Interesting History Ever Read by Man* (St. Louis: Perrin & Smith, 1884).
Malamud, Margaret. *Ancient Rome and Modern America* (Malden, MA: Wiley-Blackwell, 2009).
Mandel, Neville J. *The Arabs and Zionism Before World War I* (Berkeley: University of California Press, 1976).
Maras, Steven. "In Search of 'Screenplay': Terminological Traces in the Library of Congress Catalog of Copyright Entries: Cumulative Series, 1912–1920," *Film History* 21 (2009) 346–58.
Marich, Robert. *Marketing to Moviegoers: A Handbook of Strategies Used by Major Studios and Independents* (Burlington, MA: Elsevier Focal Press, 2005).
Marsden, George M. *Fundamentalism and American Culture: The Shaping of Twentieth-Century Evangelicalism: 1870–1925* (New York: Oxford University Press, 1980).
Martindale, John Robert. *The Prosopography of the Later Roman Empire* (Cambridge: Cambridge University Press, 1971–92).
Marx, Groucho. *Groucho and Me* (New York: Da Capo Press, 1995).
Marx, Samuel. *Mayer and Thalberg: The Make-Believe Saints* (New York: Random House, 1975).
Mason, Steve, ed. *Flavius Josephus: Translation and Commentary* (Leiden: Brill, 2001).
Matthews, Brander. "American Authors and British Pirates," *New Princeton Review* (September, 1887) 201–13.
Mavor, William (trans.). *Select Lives of Plutarch, Containing the Most Illustrious Characters of Antiquity, Abridged From the Original for the Use of Schools* (Philadelphia: A. Small, 1810).
May, John R., and Michael S. Bird. *Religion in Film* (Knoxville: University of Tennessee Press, 1982).
McArthur, Benjamin. *The Man Who Was Rip Van Winkle* (New Haven: Yale University Press, 2007).
McClelland, Gordon T., and Jay T. Last. *California Orange Box Labels: An Illustrated History* (Beverly Hills CA: Hillcrest Press, 1985).
McGill, Frank N. *Masterpieces of World Literature in Digest Form* (New York: Harper & Row, 1949).
McLintock, John, and James Strong, eds. *Cyclopaedia of Biblical, Theological, and Ecclesiastical Literature* (New York: Harper, 1869–80).
McLoughlin, William G. *The Meaning of Henry Ward Beecher: An Essay on the Shifting Values of Mid-Victorian America, 1840–1870* (New York: Alfred A. Knopf, 1970).
McWilliams, Jr., John P. *The American Epic: Transforming a Genre, 1770–1860* (Cambridge: Cambridge University Press, 1989).

Meggs, Philip B. *A History of Graphic Design*[2] (New York: Van Nostrand Reinhold, 1992).

Melville, Herman. *Battle-Pieces and Aspects of the War: Civil War Poems* (New York: Da Capo Press, 1995) 49.

Mendoza, David, and William Axt. *Music Score for Fred Niblo's Metro-Goldwyn-Mayer Production of Ben-Hur* (New York: Photo Play Music Co., 1925).

Menefee, David W. *The First Female Stars: Women of the Silent Era* (Westport, CT: Praeger, 2004).

Meyer, B. H. "Fraternal Insurance in the United States," in *Business Administration* (Chicago: DeBower Chapline Company, 1909).

Meyer, Stephen C. *Epic Sound: Music in Postwar Hollywood Biblical Films* (Bloomington: Indiana University Press, 2015).

Michelakis, Pantelis, and Maria Wyke, eds. *The Ancient World in Silent Cinema* (Cambridge: Cambridge University Press, 2013).

Middleton, Conyers. *The Life and Letters of Marcus Tullius Cicero* (London: Edward Moxon, 1840).

Miller, Gabriel. *William Wyler: The Life and Films of Hollywood's Most Celebrated Director* (Lexington: University Press of Kentucky, 2013).

Miller, George, and Dorothy Miller. *Picture Postcards in the United States, 1893–1918* (New York: Clarkson N. Potter, Inc., 1976).

Miller, Howard. "The Charioteer and the Christ: *Ben-Hur* in America from the Gilded Age to the Culture Wars," *Indiana Magazine of History* 104 (June, 2008) 153–75.

Miller, Jane Taylor. *The Christmas Story: A Group of Tableaux* (New York: National Board of Young Women's Christian Association, 1915).

Miller, William, ed. *Men in Business: Essays on the Historical Role of the Entrepreneur* (New York: Harper & Row, Publishers, 1952).

Mitchell, Wilmot Brookings, ed. *School and College Speaker* (New York: Henry Holt & Co., 1901).

Moen, Justin. *Toys & Prices 2011*[18] (Iola, WI: F+W Media, 2010).

Monks, Leander John, ed. *Courts and Lawyers of Indiana* (Indianapolis: Federal Publishing Co., 1916).

Montgomery, Elizabeth Ryder. *The Story Behind Great Books* (New York: Robert M. McBride & Company, 1946).

Moore, Frank, ed. *The Rebellion Record: A Diary of American Events, with Documents, Narratives, Illustrative Incidents, Poetry, Etc.* (New York: D. Van Nostrand, 1865).

Morgan, David. *Icons of American Protestantism: The Art of Warner Sallman* (New Haven: Yale University Press, 1996).

—. *Visual Piety; A History and Theory of Popular Religious Images* (Berkeley: University of California Press, 1998).

Morrison, Abraham Cressy. *The Baking Powder Controversy* (New York: The American Baking Powder Association, 1907).

Morrow, Barbara Olenyik. From *Ben-Hur* to *Sister Carrie* (Indianapolis: Guild Press of Indiana, Inc.).

Morsberger, Robert E., and Katharine E. Morsberger. "'Christ and a Horse-Race': *Ben-Hur* on Stage," *Journal of Popular Culture* 8 (1974).

Mortenson, Christopher Ryan. *Lew Wallace and the Civil War: Politics and Generalship* (Ph.D. diss., Texas A&M University, 2007).
Mott, Frank Luther. *Golden Multitudes: The Story of Best Sellers in the United States* (New York: MacMillan, 1947).
Munslow, Alun. *Discourse and Culture: The Creation of America, 1870–1920* (London: Routlege, 1992).
Murphy, Gretchen. *Hemispheric Imaginings: The Monroe Doctrine and Narratives of U.S. Empire* (Durham, NC: Duke University Press, 2005).
Musser, Charles. "Passions and the Passion Play: Theatre, Film and Religion in America, 1880–1900," *Film History* 5 (1993) 419–56.
New Biblical Atlas and Scripture Gazetteer, The (Philadelphia: American Sunday School Union, 1840/55).
Newsom, Jon. *Perspectives on John Philip Sousa* (Washington, DC: Library of Congress, 1984) 73.
Niver, Kemp R. (Bebe Bergsten, ed.), *Klaw & Erlanger Present Famous Plays in Pictures* (Los Angeles: Locare Research Group, 1976).
Noll, Mark A. *A History of Christianity in the United States and Canada* (Grand Rapids, MI: Eerdmans, 1992).
Nord, David Paul "The Evangelical Origins of Mass Media in America, 1815–1835," *Journalism Monographs* 88 (1984).
Norman, Albert Francis (trans.). *Antioch as a Centre of Hellenic Culture as Observed by Libanius* (Liverpool: Liverpool University Press, 2000).
Nye, David E. *Electrifying America: Social Meanings of a New Technology* (Cambridge, MA: MIT Press, 1990).
Oberdeck, Kathryn J. *The Evangelist and the Impresario: Religion, Entertainment and Cultural Politics in America, 1884–1914* (Baltimore: The Johns Hopkins University Press, 1999).
O'Connor, Leo F. *Religion in the American Novel* (Lanham, MD: University Press of America, 1984).
O'Neill, Rose Cecil. *The Story of Rose O'Neill: An Autobiography* (Columbia: University of Missouri Press, 1997).
Palmer, John McAuley, ed. *The Bench and Bar of Illinois: Historical and Reminisicent* (Chicago: The Lewis Publishing Company, 1899).
Pariette, Ralph Albert. *The University of Hard Knocks: The School That Completes Our Education* (Chicago: Parlette-Padget Company, 1914).
Paul, Joanna. *Film and the Classical Epic Tradition* (Oxford: Oxford University Press, 2013).
Pavlik, John Vernon, and Shawn McIntosh. *Converging Media: An Introduction to Mass Communication* (Boston: Pearson, 2004).
Pentz-Harris, Marcia L,. Linda Seger, and R. Barton Palmer. "Screening Male Sentimental Power in *Ben-Hur*," in R. Barton Palmer, ed., *Nineteenth-Century American Fiction on Screen* (Cambridge: Cambridge University Press, 2007), 106–32.
Perez, Nissan. *Focus East: Early Photography in the Near East 1839–1885* (New York, Abrams, 1988).
Pessis, Jacques. *Les Aventuriers de la Radio* (Paris: Flammarion, 1998).
Petaja, Emil. *Photoplay Edition* (San Francisco: SISU Publishers, 1975).

Phy, Allene Stuart, ed. *The Bible and Popular Culture in America* (Philadelphia: Fortress Press and Chicago: Scholars Press, 1985).
Pizzitola, Louis. *Hearst Over Hollywood: Power, Passion, and Propaganda in the Movies* (New York: Columbia University Press, 2002).
Pond, James Burton. *Eccentricities of Genius* (New York: G. W. Dillingham, 1900).
Poole, William Henry. *Anglo-Israel; or, The Saxon Race, Proved to Be the Lost Tribes of Israel* (Toronto: Bengough Bros., 1879).
Pope, Daniel. *The Making of Modern Advertising* (New York: Basic Books, Inc., Publishers, 1983).
Poppiti, Kimberly. "Galloping Horses: Treadmills and Other 'Theatre Appliances' in Hippodramas," *Theatre Design & Technology* 41 (2005) 46–59.
—. *Pure Air and Fire: Horses and Dramatic Representations of the Horse on the American Theatrical Stage* (Ph.D. diss., New York University, 2003) 173
Potter, David M. *People of Plenty: Economic Abundance and the American Character* (Chicago: The University of Chicago Press, 1954).
Powell, Nosher. *Nosher* (London: Blake Publishing, 1999).
Presbrey, Frank. *The History and Development of Advertising* (New York: Doubleday, Doran & Company, Inc., 1929).
Preston, Katherine, and David Mayer, eds. *Playing Out the Empire: Ben-Hur and Other Toga Plays and Films, 1883–1908* (Oxford: Oxford University Press, 1994).
Price, Steven D. *Classic Horse Stories: Twenty Timeless Horse Tales* (Guilford, CT: The Lyons Press, 2002).
Prothero, Stephen. *American Jesus: How the Son of God Became a National Icon* (New York: Farrar, Straus and Giroux, 2003).
Putney, Clifford. *Muscular Christianity: Manhood and Sports in Protestant America, 1880–1920* (Cambridge: Harvard University Press, 2001).
Pythian, J. E. *City of Manchester Art Gallery – Handbook of the Permanent Collection of Paintings* (Manchester: Sherratt & Hughes, 1908).
Quargnolo, Mario, Sergio Raffaelli, and Riccardo Redi, "The Heroic Fiasko: Il "Ben Hur" del 1925," *Immagine* 30 (1995).
Quirk, Lawrence J. *Paul Newman: A Life* (Dallas: Taylor Publishing, 1976).
—. *The Films of Myrna Loy* (Secaucus, NJ: The Citadel Press, 1980).
Rabb, Kate Milner, ed. *A Tour Through Indiana in 1840: The Diary of John Parsons of Petersburg, Virginia* (New York: Robert M. McBride & Co., 1920).
Raimondo-Souto, H. Mario. *Motion Picture Photography: A History, 1891–1960* (Jefferson, NC: McFarland, 2007).
Raymond, Emilie. "The Agony and the Ecstasy: Charlton Heston and the Screen Actors Guild," *The Journal of Policy History* 17 (2005) 217–39.
Redmond, Christopher. *Welcome to America, Mr. Sherlock Holmes: Victorian America Meets Arthur Conan Doyle* (Toronto: Simon & Pierre, 1987).
Register, Woody. *The Kid of Coney Island: Fred Thompson and the Rise of American Amusements* (Oxford: Oxford University Press, 2001).
Renan, Ernest (Charles E. Wilbour, trans.). *The Life of Jesus* [*Vie de Jésus*] (New York: Carleton, 1864).

Rice, Jeff. *Digital Detroit: Rhetoric and Space in the Age of Network* (Carbondale: Southern Illinois University Press, 2012).

Richardson, Lawrence. *A New Topographical Dictionary of Ancient Rome* (Baltimore: The Johns Hopkins University Press, 1992).

Riesman, David. "Psychological Types and National Character," *American Quarterly* 5 (1953) 330.

Riley, Patrick (trans.). *Politics Drawn from the Very Words of Holy Scripture* (Cambridge: Cambridge University Press, 1990).

Riley, Philip J., and Robert A. Welch, eds. *The Wizard of MGM: Memoirs of A. Arnold Gillespie* (Duncan, OK: BearManor Media, 2012).

Rivenberg, Leonard L. "Edgar Stillman Kelley and the American Musical Theatre," in Glenn Loney, ed., *Musical Theatre in America* (Westport, CT: Greenwood Press, 1984).

Robinson, David. *From Peepshow to Palace* (New York: Columbia University Press, 1997).

Roeder, Mark A. *A History of Culver and the Culver Military Academy* (New York: I Universe, Inc., 1993).

Roller, Duane W. *The Building Program of Herod the Great* (Berkeley: University of California Press, 1998).

Root, George Livingston. *The Ancient Arabic Order of the Nobles of the Mystic Shrine for North America* (San Antonio: Alamo Print Co., 1916).

Rutherford, Mildred. *American Authors: A Handbook of American Literature From Early Colonial to Living Writers* (Atlanta: The Franklin Printing and Publishing Co., 1894).

Sampson, Robert D. *John L. O'Sullivan and His Times* (Kent: The Kent State University Press, 2003).

Samuelson, Pamela. "The Generativity of *Sony v. Universal*: The Intellectual Property Legacy of Justice Stevens," *Fordham Law Review* 74 (2006) 1831–76.

Sanford, Charles L. *The Quest for Paradise: Europe and the American Moral Imagination* (Urbana: University of Illinois Press, 1961).

Sankey, Ira David, James McGranahan, and George C. Stebbins. *Christian Endeavor Edition of Sacred Songs* (Boston: United Society of Christian Endeavor, 1897).

Schleifer, Martha Furman, ed. *American Opera and Music for the Stage; Early Twentieth Century* (Boston: G. K. Hall & Co., 1990).

Schneirov, Matthew. *The Dream of a New Social Order: Popular Magazies in America, 1893–1914* (New York: Columbia University Press, 1994).

Schwartz, Joshua. "Gambling in Ancient Jewish Society and in the Graeco-Roman World," in Martin Goodman, ed., *Jews in a Graeco-Roman World* (Oxford: Oxford University Press, 1998) 145–65.

Scodel, Ruth. "The 1925 *Ben-Hur* and the 'Hollywood Question,'" in Michelakis and Wyke, *The Ancient World in the Silent Cinema*.

Scodel, Ruth, and Anja Bettenworth. *Whither Quo Vadis: Sienkiewicz's Novel in Film and Television* (Malden, MA: Wiley-Blackwell, 2009).

Scouten, Lois. *Messala: The Return From Ruin: A Sequel to Ben-Hur* (Toronto: EPS, 2011).

Seager, Richard Hughes. *The World's Parliament of Religions: The East/West Encounter, Chicago, 1893* (Bloomington: Indiana University Press, 1995).

Segrave, Kerry. *Piracy in the Motion Picture Industry* (Jefferson, NC: McFarland, 2003).

Shi, David E. *The Simple Life: Plain Living and High Thinking in American Culture* (New York: Oxford University Press, 1985).

Shuckburgh, Evelyn Shirley. *The Epistles of Horace, Book I*: (Cambridge: Cambridge University Press, 2013).

Sinyard, Neil. *A Wonderful Heart: The Films of William Wyler* (Jefferson, NC: McFarland & Company, 2013).

Sivulka, Juliann. *Stronger Than Dirt: A Cultural History of Advertising Personal Hygiene in America, 1875–1940* (New York: Humanity Books, 2001).

Skeat, Walter F. *Shakespeare's Plutarch* (London: MacMillan and Co., 1875).

Slater, Thomas J. "June Mathis's *Classified*: One Woman's Response to Modernism," *Journal of Film and Video* 50 (1998).

—. "The Vision and the Struggle: June Mathis's Work on *Ben-Hur*," *Post Script* 28 (2008) 64.

Slide, Anthony. *Early American Cinema* (Metuchen: Scarecrow Press, 1994).

—. *American Racist: The Life and Films of Thomas Dixon* (Lexington: The University of Press of Kentucky, 2004).

Smallwood, E. Mary. *The Jews Under Roman Rule: From Pompey to Diocletian* (Leiden: E. J. Brill, 1976).

Smiley, Robin H. "Epics of Christianity," *Firsts: The Book Collector's Magazine* 19 (April 2009) 31–51.

Smith, Henry B. "Renan's Life of Jesus," *The American Presbyterian and Theological Review* 2 (January, 1864) 136–69.

Smith, Henry Nash, ed. *Popular Culture and Industrialism, 1865–1890* (New York: New York University Press, 1967).

—. *Virgin Land: The American West as Symbol and Myth* <http://xroads.virginia.edu/~HYPER/HNS/>

Smith, Pogson. *Zerah: The Believing Jew* (New York: New York Episcopal Press, 1837).

Smith, William. *Dictionary of Greek and Roman Biography and Mythology* (New York: Harper & Brothers, Publishers, 1860).

—. *A Dictionary of the Bible: Comprising its Antiquities, Biography, Geography, and Natural History* (London: John Murray, 1863).

Smith, William (trans.). *Thucydides: The History of the Peloponnesian War* (London: John Watts, 1753).

Soares, André. *Beyond Paradise: The Life of Ramon Novarro* (New York: St. Martin's Press, 2002).

Solomon, Jon. *The Ancient World in the Cinema* (South Brunswick, NJ: A. S. Barnes, 1978).

—. "Lew Wallace and the Dramatization of *Ben-Hur*," in Stephan Heilen, Robert Kirstein, et al., eds., *In Pursuit of* Wissenschaft: *Festschrift für Willam M. Calder, III zum 75. Geburtstag* (Zürich: Georg Olms, 2008).

—. "The Reception of Ancient Greek Music in the Late Nineteenth Century," *International Journal of the Classical Tradition* 17 (2010).

—. "The Music of *Ben-Hur*," *Syllecta Classica* 23 (2012).
—. "*Ben-Hur* and *Gladiator*: Manifest Destiny and the Contradictions of American Empire," in Almut-Barbara Renger and Jon Solomon, eds., *Ancient Worlds in Film and Television: Gender and Politics* (Leiden: Brill, 2013).
—. "The Kalem *Ben-Hur* (1907)," in Pantelis Michelakis and Maria Wyke, eds., *The Ancient World in Silent Cinema* (Cambridge: Cambridge University Press, 2013).
Sousa, John Philip. "The Menace of Mechanical Music," *Appleton's Magazine* (September, 1906).
Spelman, Edward (trans.). *The Roman Antiquities of Dionysius Halicarnassensis* (London: n.p., 1758).
Spiller, Robert Ernest, Robert Ernest, Willard Thorp, and Thomas H. Johnson, et al., eds. *Literary History of the United States* (New York: Macmillan, 1953).
Stallard, Matthew, ed. *Paradise Lost: The Biblically Annotated Edition* (Macon, GA: Mercer University Press, 2011).
Stanton, Elizabeth Cady, Susan B. Anthony, Matilda Joslyn Gage, and Ida Husted Harper. *History of Woman Suffrage* (New York: Fowler & Wells, 1881).
Steinbrink, Jeffrey. "Why the Innocents Went Abroad: Mark Twain and American Tourism in the Late Nineteenth Century," *American Literary Realism, 1870–1910* 16 (1983).
Stocking, Jr., George W. *Race, Culture, and Evolution: Essays in the History of Anthropology* (Chicago: The University of Chicago Press, 1982).
—. *Victorian Anthropology* (New York: The Free Press, 1987).
Storino, Louis. *Chewing Tobacco Tin Tags, 1870–1930* (Atglen, PA: Schiffer Publishing Ltd., 1995).
Stowe, Harriett Beecher. *Footsteps of the Master* (New York: J. B. Ford & Company, 1877).
Strasser, Susan. *Never Done: A History of American Housework* (New York: Pantheon Books, 1982).
—. *Satisfaction Guaranteed; the Making of the American Mass Market* (New York: Pantheon Books, 1989).
Street, Brian V. *The Savage in Literature: Representations of "Primitive" Society in English Fiction, 1858–1920* (London: Routledge & Kegan Paul, 1975).
Strong, Josiah. *Our Country; Its Possible Future and its Present Crisis* (New York: The Baker & Taylor Co., for The American Home Missionary Society, 1885).
Sutton, Allan. *American Record Labels and Companies: An Encyclopedia (1891–1943)* (Denver: Mainspring Press, 2000).
Tarbell, Ida Minerva. *All in the Day's Work: An Autobiography* (Urbana: University of Illinois Press, 2003).
Tebbel, John. *A History of Book Publishing in the United States* (New York: R. R. Bowker, 1975).
Theisen, Lee Scott. "'My God, Did I Set All This in Motion?' General Lew Wallace and *Ben-Hur*," *The Journal of Popular Culture* 18 (1984) 33–41.
Thomas, Bob. *Thalberg: Life and Legend* (Garden City, NJ: Doubleday & Company, Inc., 1969).
Thorold, W. J., ed. *Our Players' Gallery* (New York: n.p., 1901).

Tibbetts, John C. *The American Theatrical Film: Stages in Development* (Bowling Green, OH: Bowling Green State University Press, 1985).
Tibbetts John C., and James M. Welsh. *The Encyclopedia of Novels Into Film* (New York: Facts on File, 2005).
Tilley, Carol. "Superman Says, 'Read!' National Comics and Reading Promotion," *Children's Literature in Education* 44 (2013).
Tinajero, Araceli. *El Lector: A History of the Cigar Factory Reader* (Austin: University of Texas Press, 2010).
Trachtenberg, Alan. *The Incorporation of America; Culture and Society in the Gilded Age* (New York: Hill and Wang, 1982).
Trench, Richard Chevenix. *The Star of the Wise Men: Being a Commentary on the Second Chapter of St. Matthew* (Philadelphia: H. Hooker, 1850).
Tunberg, Karl, and Owen Walford. *The Quest of Ben Hur* (Hammondsworth: Penguin, 1981).
Tupper, Martin Farquhar. *Tupper's Proverbial Philosophy* (Milwaukie: I. A. Hopkins, 1849).
Turner, Frank M. "Christians and Pagans in Victorian Novels," in Catharine Edwards, ed., *Roman Presences: Receptions of Rome in European Culture, 1789-1945* (Cambridge: Cambridge University Press, 1999).
Turner, Graeme, ed. *The Film Cultures Reader* (London: Routledge, 2002).
Tuska, Jon. *Billy the Kid: A Handbook* (Lincoln: University of Nebraska Press, 1983).
Tyler, Lyon Gardiner. *Men of Mark in Virginia: Ideals of American Life* (Washington, DC: Men of Mark Publishing Co., 1897).
Vanderwood, Paul J. *Juan Soldado: Rapist, Murderer, Martyr, Saint* (Durham, NC: Duke University Press, 2004).
Van de Velde, Charles William Meredith. *Map of the Holy Land* (Gotha: Justus Perthes, 1858).
—. *Memoir to Accompany the Map of the Holy Land* (Gotha: Justus Perthes, 1858).
Van Doren, Carl. *The American Novel, 1789–1939* (New York: Macmillan Co., 1940).
Van Dyke, Paul. *Referendum for the Illustrations in the Garfield Edition of General Lew. Wallace's Novel "Ben-Hur"* (New York: Harper & Brothers, 1893).
Van Nostrand, Albert. "Making and Marketing Fiction," *American Quarterly* 8 (1956) 147–54.
Vardac, A. Nicholas. "Filmed Scenery on the Live Stage," *Theater Journal* 58 (December, 2006).
Veeck, Bill, and Ed Linn. *Thirty Tons a Day* (New York: The Viking Press, 1972).
Vidal, Gore. *Palimpsest: A Memoir* (New York: Random House, 1995).
Vidor, King. *A Tree Is a Tree* (New York: Harcourt, Brace and Company, 1953).
Vieira, Mark A. *Irving Thalberg: Boy Wonder to Producer Prince* (Berkeley: University of California Press, 2010).
Vogel, Lester I. *To See a Promised Land: Americans and the Holy Land in the Nineteenth Century* (University Park: The Pennsylvania State University Press, 1993).

Vollmer, Clement. *The American Novel in Germany, 1871–1913* (Philadelphia: International Printing Co., 1918).

Vorenberg, Michael. *Final Freedom: The Civil War, the Abolition of Slavery, and the Thirteenth Amendment* (Cambridge: Cambridge University Press, 2004).

Wade, Wyn Craig. *The Fiery Cross: The Ku Klux Klan in America* (Oxford: Oxford University Press, 1987).

Wallace, Lew. *The Fair God* (Boston: James R. Osgood and Company, 1873).

—. "The Boyhood of Christ," *Harper's New Monthly Magazine* 74 (December, 1886) 3–17.

—. *The First Christmas* (New York: Harper & Bros., 1899).

Wallace, Susan E. "Oriental Splendors – Ben-Hur at the Shrine of the Three Wise Men of the East," *Louisville Courier Journal* (July 15, 1888) 9.

Waller-Zuckerman, Mary Ellen. "'Old Homes, in a City of Perpetual Change': Women's Magazines, 1890–1916," *Business History Review* 63 (1989).

Wallis, Michael. *The Real Wild West: The 101 Ranch and the Creation of the American West* (New York: St. Martin's Press, 1999).

Ware, William. *Letters of Lucius M. Piso, From Palmyra, to His Friend Marcus Curtius, at Rome, Now First Translated and Published* (New York: C. S. Francis, 1837).

—. *Julian; or Scenes in Judea* (New York: C. S. Francis, 1841).

Warfield, Patrick. "The March as Musical Drama and the Spectacle of John Philip Sousa," *Journal of the American Musicological Society* 64 (2011).

Warner, Charles Dudley, Hamilton Wright Mabie, Lucia Isabella Gilbert Runkle, et al., eds. *Library of the World's Best Literature Ancient and Modern* (New York: R. S. Peale and J. A. Hill, 1896/7).

Wecott, Steven D. "Miklós Rózsa's *Ben-Hur*: The Musical-Dramatic Function of the Hollywood *Leitmotiv*," in Clifford McCarty, ed., *Film Music 1* (New York: Garland Publishing, 1989).

Weil, Gordon Lee. *Sears, Roebuck, U.S.A.; the Great American Catalog Store and How it Grew* (Briarcliff Manor, NY: Stein and Day, 1977).

Weiser, Norman S. *The Writer's Radio Theater, 1940–41* (New York: Harper & Brothers, 1941).

Werner, M. R. *Julius Rosenwald: The Life of a Practical Humanitarian* (Harper & Brothers, 1939).

Whiston, William (trans.). *The Works of Flavius Josephus* (Philadelphia: Leary & Getz, 1856); (New York: Leavitt and Allen, 1858); (New York: Oakley, Mason & Co., 1869).

White, Truman C. *Our County and Its People: A Descriptive Work on Erie County, New York* (Boston: The Boston History Company, Publishers, 1898).

Wiebe, Robert H. *The Search for Order, 1877–1920* (New York: Hill and Wang, 1967).

Williams, James S. *Cocteau* (Manchester: Manchester University Press, 2006).

Williams, Linda. *Playing the Race Card: Melodramas of Black and White from Uncle Tom to O.J.* (Princeton: Princeton University Press, 2002).

Wills, Gary. *Lincoln at Gettysburg: The Words that Remade America* (New York: Simon & Schuster, 1992).

Wilson, George H. and Calvin B. Cady, eds. *The Musical Yearbook of the United States* 10 (Chicago: Clayton F. Summy, 1893).

Wiltshire, Susan Ford. "The Classicist President," *Amphora* 5 (2006) 1–3.

Winston, Diane. "Living in the Material World: Salvation Army Lassies and Urban Commercial Culture, 1880-1918," in John M. Giggie and Diane Winston, eds., *Faith in the Market: Religion and the Rise of Urban Commercial Culture* (New Brunswick, NJ: Rutgers University Press, 2002).

Wolf, Raymond A. *West Warwick* (Charleston, SC: Arcadia Publishing, 2011).

Wolff, Michael, ed. *The Collected Essays of Sir Winston Churchill* (London: Library of Imperial History, 1976).

Woman's Who's Who of America, 1914–1915 (New York: The American Commonwealth Company, 1914).

Wood, James Playsted. *Magazines in the United States*[3] (New York: The Ronald Press Company, 1971).

Worthy, James C. *Shaping an American Institution: Robert E. Wood and Sears, Roebuck* (Urbana: University of Illinois Press, 1984).

Wright, Paul. *The New and Complete Life of Our Blessed Lord and Saviour, Jesus Christ* (London: [Printed for] Alexander Hogg, 1795).

Wu, Timothy. "Copyright's Communications Policy," *Michigan Law Review* 103 (November, 2004) 278–366.

Wyke, Maria. *Projecting the Past: Ancient Rome, Cinema, and History* (New York: Routledge, 1997).

Young, William. *Lew Wallace's Ben-Hur, a Play Arranged for the Stage* (New York: Harper & Brothers, 1899).

Zach, Karen Bazzani. *Crawfordsville, Athens of Indiana* (Charleston, SC: Arcadia Publishing, 2003).

Zakim, Michael, and Gary J. Kornblith, eds. *Capitalism Takes Command: The Social Transformation of Nineteenth-Century America* (Chicago: The University of Chicago Press, 2012).

Index

GENERAL INDEX

1880s, 3–6, 13, 32, 115, 141, 163, 189, 196, 200, 203, 206–7, 210–11, 218, 231–2, 250, 255, 269–70, 272–3, 280, 312, 408, 412, 424, 457–8, 523, 675, 686
1890s, 5–6, 22, 37, 116, 138, 145, 156–7, 165, 170, 175, 189, 212, 231, 251, 255, 280, 282, 289, 297, 304, 312, 314, 340, 381, 457, 459, 461, 478–9, 487, 510, 526, 529, 532, 533, 637, 686, 697, 710, 792

abolition, 35, 100n, 195, 198
Academy Awards, 1, 567, 731, 732, 752, 771–2, 782–3, 785, 787, 796, 825–6, 829–31, 833–6, 839, 841–2, 853, 858
adaptation and adaptability, 4, 12, 14, 23, 60, 82, 108, 119, 145, 147, 163–4, 167–9, 173–4, 210, 220–3, 227, 231–2, 234, 236–7, 255, 257–60, 270–1, 278, 280–1, 289–90, 292–3, 292, 303, 313, 317, 323–4, 341–2, 344–5, 352, 360, 362, 366, 370, 384, 386, 394, 415, 418–19, 422, 425, 427, 429–32, 440, 459, 470, 475, 509, 512, 526, 533–5, 541, 545, 548–9, 552, 561–2, 566–7, 571, 575, 579, 589, 595, 622–4, 626, 629–30, 637, 644, 661–3, 665–6, 669–72, 675, 729, 742, 746, 785, 794, 805–7, 828, 843–8, 853, 858–9; see also dramatization
advertising, 12–14, 32, 91, 106, 113–15, 117, 124–5, 137, 140, 141–2, 144, 151, 155, 158, 163, 165–6, 173–4, 177–9, 182, 209–10, 217, 227, 229, 234, 236, 238, 242, 246, 249–55, 286, 294–6, 299–300, 304–5, 320, 348, 351, 353–4, 364, 367–8, 374, 378, 380, 383, 385, 387, 388, 394, 409–10, 415, 420–2, 424–5, 427, 429–32, 435, 437–49, 454, 457–8, 460–1, 465, 468, 470, 473, 475–9, 481–6, 490–1, 496, 500, 502, 511, 516, 521–2, 524–5, 529, 533–4, 536–42, 545–6, 548–9, 563, 566, 579, 598–9, 601, 611, 613–15, 617, 622–3, 628–30, 633–4, 637–44, 661–2, 666, 672–3, 676, 680, 684, 686, 688–90, 692–3, 695–7, 699, 702–4, 708, 728, 734, 767–9, 772, 778, 781, 785, 787–8, 790–1, 797–8, 800, 806, 808–11, 818n, 825, 828–3, 844, 847, 856, 858
agreements and contracts, 13, 32, 105, 133, 141, 144, 149–50, 158, 172, 175, 180, 201, 227–8, 236–7, 239, 241, 245–7, 256–8, 266–7, 285–6, 313, 315–17, 321–2, 333–4, 338, 346, 353–4, 357–9, 364, 369, 382, 396, 410, 413, 509, 523, 543, 552, 561, 563–7, 569, 571–2, 574, 576–7, 596, 598–9, 605, 608, 619, 624, 641, 643, 667, 688, 731, 752–3, 757, 775–6, 791–2, 809, 829, 846
Alamo, 29
allegory, 93–4, 154, 248–9
amateurs, 111, 221, 224–5, 228, 240, 263n, 278, 280, 295, 347, 604, 609, 626, 640, 707
American exceptionalism, 204
American Restoration Movement, 192
Andersonville, 37, 93, 683
anger (theme), 23, 65–6, 77, 323, 537, 540, 593–4, 739, 744–5, 748, 844, 850; see also Quarrel
anthologies, excerpts, and selections, 5, 13, 114, 125–6, 139, 145, 165, 167–8, 171, 173–4, 212, 219, 221–2, 227, 229, 239, 251, 258, 260, 271, 306, 347–8, 353–4, 385, 420, 428, 440, 664, 675, 681, 705, 811, 842, 853, 857
Antioch, 40, 64–5, 75, 77, 86–90, 100, 105, 152, 174, 177, 214n, 222, 281, 292, 323, 326, 329–30, 335, 348–9, 358, 373, 511, 515, 540, 567, 586–7, 589, 592, 600, 618–19, 627, 631, 667, 674, 711, 740, 751, 768, 794, 800, 832, 845
antiquity, 9, 12, 19, 22, 24, 27–9, 49, 57, 59, 61, 65, 67–9, 72, 75, 77–82, 84, 86–9, 91, 94, 96, 103–4, 107–8, 118, 129, 134n, 140, 154, 197–8, 200–4, 206, 211, 214n, 217, 244, 253, 283, 306, 313, 340–1, 344, 372, 412, 414, 420, 427, 430–1, 440, 448, 460, 468–9, 482, 512, 551, 562, 570, 573, 580, 583–4, 593, 601–2, 619, 625, 631, 636, 661, 663, 668, 671, 673, 683, 688, 704–5, 708, 710, 767, 789, 795, 800–2, 811, 835, 844, 855, 858
anti-Roman politics, 31, 58–9, 61–2, 66–7, 73–8, 200, 206, 216n, 223, 323, 326, 334, 537, 540, 587, 589, 733–4, 747, 752, 756, 761, 838, 848–9
Apaches, 43
Arabia, 68, 201
Arabian horses, 170, 480, 484, 514–15, 518, 522, 594, 635, 665, 706–8, 710, 759, 765, 808, 834, 838, 844, 846
Arabic language, 91, 166–7, 522, 596
Arabs and Arabic culture, 74, 167, 203, 247–50, 306, 340, 412, 747, 789–90

Index

Aramaic, 19, 87, 855
archaeology, 87–9, 155, 201–2, 319, 359
art-song, 91, 127, 138, 269–75, 277, 283, 354
Astor Library, 154
Athenaeum Library, 88
Athens and Athenians, 29–30, 69–71, 75, 81, 214n
Atlanta, 222, 224–5, 244–5, 255, 288, 373, 375, 378–80, 389, 408, 477, 486, 528–9, 562, 616–17, 626, 635, 642, 674, 684–5, 833
auctions, 375–6, 477, 518, 553, 809, 811–12, 826, 834
audiences and public responses, 12, 14, 30, 53, 72, 79, 96, 107, 109, 119–20, 122–7, 133, 140, 147, 150–1, 155, 158, 168–72, 180, 191, 197, 202, 221, 223–5, 229, 233, 235, 237, 240–3, 248–9, 252–3, 260, 267, 272, 284, 286–8, 291, 296, 318, 322, 325, 327–30, 332, 334–5, 337–44, 351–7, 360, 363, 366–7, 370–1, 377, 379–80, 382–3, 385–6, 389–90, 392, 416, 420, 432, 437–8, 445, 456, 465, 467, 470, 509–10, 514, 518, 525–9, 532–3, 537, 542, 545, 548, 564, 570, 579, 582, 584, 586–9, 592, 594–600, 603–5, 607, 613, 615–16, 619–20, 622, 625, 628, 632, 635, 644, 661, 673, 675, 701, 729, 733, 760–1, 773–5, 777, 783, 785–7, 793, 798, 807, 824–5, 827, 832, 840, 846, 848, 851–7
auditors, 30, 122, 126, 224, 297, 526
Austin, 3, 304, 306, 383, 411–12, 447, 451, 856
Australia, 203, 296, 305, 357, 359–60, 364–8, 372, 391–2, 397, 400–2, 405, 468, 484, 523, 567, 576, 611, 613, 621, 805, 853; *see also* Sydney
authenticity and accuracy, 17, 63, 107–9, 242, 278, 320, 339–40, 395, 403, 582–3, 600, 602, 628, 644, 667, 698, 772–3, 785, 795, 801–2, 836, 838
authorization, licenses, and permissions, 5–6, 12–13, 17, 32, 37, 60, 64, 66, 84, 116, 130–1, 133, 138–42, 146–9, 167, 174, 218–20, 226–8, 230–1, 234–7, 239–42, 250, 260, 270–2, 278–81, 285, 289, 291, 296–7, 303, 314, 316, 318, 321, 340, 346–7, 377, 389, 414, 423, 425, 440, 452, 513, 518, 524, 536, 538, 543–4, 550, 552, 562, 583, 626, 728, 772, 778, 782, 785, 794, 798–805, 831
Aztecs, 40, 64, 216–17

Baltimore, 34–5, 43, 65, 94, 184, 222, 225, 228, 276, 287–8, 334–5, 337–8, 363, 372–3, 391, 397, 409, 420, 462, 488, 501, 508, 532, 556, 606, 615, 630–1, 635, 640, 662, 674, 679, 690, 704, 710, 787
band organ, 298
Baptists, 108–9, 158, 191–4, 207, 217, 229, 242, 442, 517, 525, 529, 531, 674
baseball, 160, 420, 458, 477, 488, 490, 633, 706–7, 809, 828, 846
basketball, 488, 675, 858
bestsellers, 4, 8, 12–13, 38, 102, 110, 115, 121, 129, 164, 210, 212, 230–1, 384, 483, 513, 534–5, 544, 551, 672–3, 676, 684, 686, 824
Betamax, 825, 828–31
Bethlehem, 47, 52, 59, 63, 68, 72, 84, 86, 114, 145, 177, 207, 219, 229, 259, 319, 333–4, 349, 352, 354, 370, 514, 516, 520, 531, 572, 587–8, 590, 595, 601, 613, 625, 739, 754, 842
bindings, 13, 116, 130, 141, 143, 151, 155–6, 158, 174, 212, 768
Black Hawk War, 20
blockbusters, 1, 4–5, 11, 14, 489, 596, 599, 604, 774, 790–1, 824, 851
Blu-ray, 841
booksellers, 129, 535
Boston, 41, 46, 86, 88–9, 100, 126–7, 134, 144, 152, 164, 168–9, 184, 215, 222–5, 259, 262, 271–2, 275, 279, 286, 296, 307, 311, 314, 317, 331, 337–9, 347, 354–7, 361, 363–4, 369, 372, 388, 390–1, 397, 400, 402, 407, 412, 448, 454, 458, 467, 476, 496, 506, 523, 525, 528, 530, 534, 555, 562, 599, 601, 610, 618, 621, 627, 630, 631, 634–5, 638, 643, 657, 674, 678, 682–3, 691, 704, 706–7, 710, 769, 773, 775–6, 780, 784, 797, 806, 809, 828, 835
box offices, 357, 374, 376, 378, 601, 603, 607, 623, 661, 680, 778–80, 786–8, 790–1, 825
brands and branding, 3, 5, 7, 13–14, 164, 209–10, 298, 409–10, 423, 425, 427–8, 431–2, 438–9, 444–5, 448, 454, 458, 460–1, 464–6, 472, 478, 480–2, 486, 502n, 599, 639–40, 643, 663, 688, 690, 692–3, 695–7, 699, 704, 793, 802, 805, 854
Brazil, 42, 82
Broadway, 1, 229, 256, 261n, 311, 316–17, 321, 346, 385, 387, 394, 443, 473, 486, 566, 599, 617, 630, 636, 643, 701, 775, 779, 789, 797; *see also* Broadway Theatre
Broadway Theatre, 239, 321, 337, 342–4, 346, 352, 354, 357, 359, 363, 372, 384–5, 389, 462, 597, 636, 789
Brooklyn, 126, 158, 171, 195, 222–5, 313, 357, 372, 374, 488, 510, 521, 530, 535–6, 617, 628, 643
bubonic plague, 311, 367
budgets and expenses, 1, 41, 120, 127, 144–5, 159, 173, 209–10, 212, 233, 239, 250–1, 298, 369, 381–2, 389, 393–4, 509, 523, 531, 539, 545, 549, 551, 563–4, 566, 568, 576, 604, 618, 621, 648, 680, 728–31, 766–8, 772, 790, 807, 829, 841, 851
buffalo hunting, 38
burlesque, 387–8
business and commerce, 1, 3–7, 9–10, 12–15, 17, 39, 41, 49, 91–2, 95–6, 102, 105, 110, 112, 116, 123, 127, 130, 140–1, 156, 162, 164–5, 180, 188–9, 197, 202, 206, 208–9, 212, 218, 225–7, 231–2, 234, 251, 253, 255, 257, 261–2, 269, 280–1, 286, 289–90, 294, 297–8, 303–4, 315, 345–6, 348, 353, 359, 367, 373, 377, 381, 385, 387, 392–3, 403, 408–90, 509–10, 519, 544, 551–2, 564, 567, 569–70, 573, 576, 578, 600, 607, 622, 625, 637–43, 645, 661–2, 673, 681, 686–705, 759, 762, 768, 772, 774, 776, 789, 791–805, 809, 811, 824, 826–31, 833–5, 847, 856, 859
Butler Library, 115

Caesarea, 64, 100n, 765
Caesars, 53, 59, 61, 63, 66–7, 75, 125, 211, 326, 470, 590, 627, 635, 667, 739–40, 778, 805, 809
California, 3, 243, 288, 295, 305, 309, 388, 417, 420, 442–4, 462–3, 468, 470–1, 488–9, 495–6, 502–3, 508, 511, 518, 531–2, 568–9, 572, 581, 585, 644, 689, 700–1, 708, 711; *see also* Los Angeles; Pasadena; San Diego; San Francisco

cameras, lenses, and filters, 210, 346–7, 535, 537, 540–1, 570, 572, 579–80, 585, 588–91, 593–5, 597, 606, 620, 633, 640, 644, 650n, 746, 748, 759, 764, 766, 773–4, 780–2, 794, 858
Camera 65, 773, 779, 792
Canada, 117, 129–30, 133, 145, 156–7, 173, 227, 233, 272, 300, 391, 419, 513, 523, 541, 548, 574, 671, 704, 775, 787, 827, 831, 851
Cannes Film Festival, 787
Capri, 739, 756, 850
cards, 166, 210, 345, 419–20, 422, 429–30, 434, 437, 474, 478–9, 482–3, 611–12, 637, 766–7, 769, 802, 804; see also credit cards; lobby cards; postcards
Carthage, 74, 201, 215n, 751–2, 762
cartoons, 435, 539, 551, 628–9, 634, 666, 685, 690, 703, 706, 712
catacombs, 211, 515, 518, 668–9, 683; see also St. Calixto
Catholics, 105, 107, 110–11, 120, 134, 146–7, 150, 182–3, 191, 197, 214, 242, 414, 675, 684, 729, 769, 855
CDs, 825, 841–4, 847, 853, 856
celebrity, 158, 283, 346, 348, 438, 676, 688, 709, 779, 832, 839; see also Wallace, Lew, as celebrity
Chace Act, 133
characterizations, 256, 323, 664, 702, 734–5, 744, 763, 848–9
charioteers, 69, 326, 328, 332, 348, 410, 421–2, 425, 430–5, 439, 443–5, 454, 458, 460, 465, 469, 472, 475–8, 480, 482, 624, 633–4, 679, 696–9, 701–2, 710, 732, 792–3, 800, 807, 845, 849, 850
chariots and chariot racing, 2–3, 5, 7, 13–14, 28, 53–4, 58–60, 65–6, 74, 77, 81–2, 86, 88–90, 93, 103–4, 107, 110, 113, 121–2, 162, 164, 166–78, 189, 199, 206, 210, 215, 219, 223–4, 226, 230–1, 233–4, 240, 243–4, 246, 249, 255, 258, 269, 280–9, 291–2, 304–6, 311, 313–14, 317, 319–21, 326–30, 334–44, 347, 352–6, 358–9, 362–4, 366, 370–1, 374, 378, 380, 386–8, 390, 393, 395, 409–10, 412, 420–45, 449, 454, 457–8, 460–80, 482–3, 490–1, 510–11, 514, 518, 520–2, 528, 530, 534, 536–45, 548, 550–1, 563, 572, 579–80, 583–7, 592–600, 602, 605, 610, 613–21, 626–36, 639–44, 662–3, 665, 668–74, 678, 682–9, 691, 693–7, 700–13, 723, 728, 731–3, 736–7, 742, 745, 752, 754, 756, 759, 761–70, 772–5, 777–82, 787, 793–806, 808–9, 811–12, 824, 826–7, 829–30, 832–4, 836, 840, 844–6, 848–53, 856–8
charities and benefits, 3, 58, 158, 170–1, 184, 189, 219, 225–6, 231, 233, 236, 242, 248, 250–1, 255–6, 258, 275, 285, 287, 413–14, 510, 525, 527, 532, 625, 682, 777, 789–90
Chautauqua, 5, 116, 119, 121–5, 130, 136, 149, 189, 217, 243–5, 271, 276, 367, 451, 511, 528, 532, 534
Chicago, 41, 107–8, 110, 120, 124, 126, 130, 145, 149, 158, 160, 163, 165, 167, 175, 177, 195–6, 203, 225, 230, 242, 256, 259, 271, 276, 279–80, 293, 296, 304–5, 311, 317, 337, 342, 349, 354, 357, 359–61, 364–5, 369, 372, 376, 381, 384, 388, 391, 411, 421, 425, 445, 454, 457–8, 461, 464–6, 470, 473, 486, 513, 515, 518, 520, 523, 529, 535, 546, 562, 596, 599, 601, 617, 631, 635, 642, 662, 674–5, 677–8, 682, 695, 697–8, 701, 704, 706–7, 709–10, 713, 729, 776, 787, 789, 809
children, 24, 84, 93, 119, 171, 177, 201, 203, 212, 223, 225, 332, 373, 382, 429, 435, 437–8, 440, 482, 513, 532, 585, 588–9, 606, 614, 616, 627, 633–4, 661, 664, 674, 704, 710, 735, 738, 786, 793, 798, 804, 831, 843, 857
China, 484, 527, 611, 621–2, 625
Christianity and Christians, 10, 14, 19, 21, 24–6, 39, 46–7, 50, 52, 54, 58–61, 63, 67, 69–70, 79, 83, 93, 103–4, 108–11, 115–17, 123, 158–9, 163–4, 189–93, 196–200, 204–7, 209, 211, 218, 225–6, 228, 245, 251, 258, 317, 319, 321, 356, 370, 380, 382, 388, 393, 409, 414, 530, 533, 547–8, 551, 590, 597, 608, 611, 621, 625–6, 628, 632, 667–8, 674, 704, 710–11, 734, 738, 772, 792, 806, 809, 824–5, 844, 846–8, 851, 857
Christian Science movement, 207
Christmas, 13, 15–16, 106, 110, 115, 119, 121, 126, 130, 140–4, 154–5, 158, 165, 169, 171, 178, 192, 212, 229, 234, 258, 260–1, 359, 378, 383, 386, 423, 447, 510, 525, 583, 596, 625, 630, 638, 674, 691–2, 697, 706, 769, 788, 790, 800, 825, 835; see also Wallace, The First Christmas
Christology, 10, 191, 204
chromolithography see lithography
churchgoers, 189, 379–81
Church of Christ, 25, 192–3
church venues, 120, 124–6, 158, 169, 171, 189, 194, 207, 220–1, 225, 228–9, 231–5, 240–2, 252, 255, 258, 295–6, 355, 367, 379–81, 392, 416, 430, 442, 509–13, 525, 527, 529–34, 547–8, 616–18, 621, 630, 644, 673–4, 678, 682, 684, 772, 847
cigar-factory lectors, 428, 627
Cincinnati, 3, 35–6, 48, 62, 65, 94–5, 146–9, 162, 169, 240–1, 245, 270, 279, 295, 311, 346, 351, 353, 358–9, 372, 375–8, 382, 385–6, 421, 446, 450, 480, 483, 511–12, 523, 530–3
Cinecittà, 679, 729, 731–2, 757, 759, 764, 766, 841, 859
cinema and moving pictures, 1, 7, 9–12, 14, 102, 108, 164, 169, 257, 261, 269, 296–7, 303, 324, 342, 372, 390, 392, 394, 473, 482, 509, 530–5, 537–9, 541–53, 556–62, 566–7, 572, 575–6, 579, 585–6, 588, 590–2, 594, 597–600, 602–25, 629–30, 637, 639, 644–5, 661, 672, 680–2, 684, 689, 729–31, 782, 785, 798, 804, 807, 825, 828, 834, 836, 839, 851
Cinema Arts Library, 572, 647
Cinéma Madeleine, 610–11
cinematographers, 595, 642, 732, 773, 783, 839–40
Cinerama, 774
Cineteca di Bologna, 550
Circus Maximus, 87, 89–90, 218, 567, 575, 578, 583, 600, 632, 683 710, 758, 856
circus venues, 86–90, 152, 174, 177, 196, 218, 222, 291–2, 329–30, 333, 335, 339, 341, 347–9, 358, 372–3, 379, 411, 425, 430–1, 440, 450, 457, 460, 468, 482–4, 490, 515, 522, 541, 567, 575, 578–9, 583–5, 593–4, 600, 606, 616, 618, 632–4, 644, 666–7, 683, 687, 708–10, 736, 758–9,

765–6, 768, 794, 802, 805–6, 835–6, 840, 852, 856
City Island, 486, 636
civic pride, 311, 361, 776, 786
Civil War, 19, 32, 34–5, 38, 103, 112, 120, 210–11, 213n, 346, 410, 482, 489, 675–6, 684, 686, 778, 789, 844
classics, 103, 145, 618–19, 672, 790–2, 829
clergy, 19, 23, 195–8, 241–2, 355, 363, 367–8, 518, 521, 527, 534, 547, 616, 772
Cleveland, 44, 97, 123, 145, 151, 265, 312, 315, 372–3, 378, 388, 392, 395, 403, 420, 444, 464, 478, 480, 498–9, 502, 529, 601, 606, 614, 692, 706–7, 785
collectors, 9, 212, 477, 673, 696, 834, 836
colonialism and empire, 5, 22, 29, 31, 37–9, 61, 63–5, 67, 81, 84, 87–8, 92, 94, 129–30, 147, 164, 198, 173, 201, 203–6, 208, 216n, 283, 296, 409, 573, 629, 664, 670–1, 673, 774, 795, 839, 849
Colonial Theatre, 338, 347, 354–5, 357, 363–4, 599–601, 638, 678
Colosseum, 200–1, 513, 563, 750, 811, 844, 858
colossi, 584–5, 770, 802, 808, 824, 829; *see also* Joseph J. Smith
Columbian Exposition, 160, 203
comics, 666–72, 795–6
commencements and graduations, 15, 168, 189, 510, 526, 675
competition, 303, 373, 390, 425, 427, 438, 455, 461, 485, 490, 607, 633, 634, 689, 705, 720n, 787, 826, 828
computers, 551, 824
Coney Island, 7, 15, 304, 409, 461–2, 535–6, 709
Confederates and Confederacy, 32, 34–7, 567
conquistadors, 31, 40, 64, 94
Constantinople, 86, 92, 95–6, 113, 116, 119–20, 126, 128–9, 131, 160, 486, 627, 685
consumers and consumerism, 3, 5–7, 9, 11, 14, 17, 96, 112, 165, 174–5, 189, 196, 209–12, 250, 261, 287, 289, 297–8, 301, 307, 314, 345, 353, 410, 425, 428, 431, 434, 437–8, 442–3, 445, 454–5, 457–8, 509, 689, 691, 693, 697, 824–5, 829
contests, 305, 387, 419, 443–4, 461, 469, 615, 633, 640, 671, 686–7, 689, 702, 705, 767, 772, 844, 856
controversy, 34, 67, 162, 197, 430, 551, 604, 621, 624–5, 728, 732, 755, 782–6
copies, 7, 13, 15–16, 40, 99, 113, 116–18, 123, 126, 133, 138, 141, 144–5, 150–1, 155–7, 159, 164, 166–7, 169, 173, 175, 177–8, 180, 196–7, 202, 212, 216, 227, 250, 255, 262, 271, 287, 293–4, 301, 316, 349–51, 353, 364, 367, 385, 420, 422, 512, 524, 550, 572, 616, 637, 672, 768–70, 778, 793–4, 829, 836, 841, 859
copyright, 5–8, 10, 12–13, 32, 105, 112, 117, 128–30, 133, 138, 144–6, 150–1, 156–7, 165, 172, 174–5, 178, 180, 186, 212, 219, 221, 226–8, 236, 245–6, 258, 260, 266, 271–2, 279–80, 289, 292–3, 298, 306, 309, 315–17, 321, 346, 349, 351, 353, 385, 390, 409, 414–15, 422–3, 425, 473, 509, 510, 512, 516, 523, 524, 535, 537, 543, 544, 545, 546, 547, 548, 549, 551, 552, 561, 564, 566, 613, 661, 671, 693, 802, 805, 830–2, 846, 853–4, 857, 859; *see also* authorizations, licenses, and permissions; rights
Copyright Act, 172, 227, 300, 830
Corinth, 80, 335, 634, 812, 815n, 858
costumes, 40, 84, 201, 220–1, 224, 227, 233, 235, 237, 240–2, 245, 248–9, 281, 319, 351, 368, 381, 389, 412, 456, 469–70, 525, 536–7, 575, 580, 602, 606, 613–14, 623–4, 628, 709, 759–60, 765, 767, 775, 783, 809, 812, 840
cowboys, 394, 469, 507, 536, 624, 710, 811
crash machine, 325
Crawfordsville, 6, 8, 21–2, 24, 32, 35, 38–9, 41, 43, 55–7, 96, 146, 231–5, 237, 239–42, 246, 251, 256, 306, 314, 317–18, 320, 341, 413, 416–17, 421–2, 437, 448, 455–7, 466, 483, 488, 512, 518, 529–30, 532, 666, 676, 691, 698, 702, 768, 777–8
credit cards, 778
critics and criticisms, 10–11, 84, 89–91, 104, 109–12, 120, 131, 201, 340, 342–3, 360, 369–70, 379, 576, 583, 593, 596, 613, 619–21, 708, 710, 729, 772, 779–80, 782–3, 790, 836, 856
crowds, 62, 122, 126, 200, 221, 243–5, 257, 291, 293, 329–30, 338, 341, 347, 362–3, 373, 376, 381, 391, 409, 461, 464, 468, 470–2, 488, 532, 537, 540–1, 573, 584, 588–9, 596, 599, 604, 606, 608, 613, 625, 663, 665, 668, 680, 705, 748, 772, 826, 852; *see also* spectators
Crucifixion, 52, 55–7, 91–2, 104, 112, 125, 154, 169, 189, 196, 201, 223, 247, 333–4, 467, 521, 564, 585, 587, 594–5, 665, 667–8, 670, 675, 684, 709, 733, 738, 748, 753, 756–7, 761–5, 782, 804, 839, 849, 852–3
Crusades, 30, 513
Culver City, 568, 571, 574, 576, 581, 584, 591, 679, 732, 849
customers, 1, 9, 146, 178, 225, 250, 297, 409, 423, 429, 448, 456, 458, 531, 696, 786, 811
cyclorama, 336, 358, 363
Czech Film Archive, 835

damages, 149, 256, 451, 523, 524, 543, 549, 577
dances and dancers, 108, 235, 247–50, 253, 306, 327, 334, 382, 393, 419, 484, 691, 751, 762
Daphne, 39–40, 55, 58, 75–6, 86, 90, 103, 171, 174, 233, 242, 249, 282, 317, 326–8, 334, 338, 340–1, 347, 350, 354, 385, 397n, 514, 520, 537–8, 595, 674, 851
Darwinism, 203–5, 214
debates, 623, 624, 680
debt, 31, 37–8, 96, 532, 844
declamations, 13, 29, 167–9, 287, 305, 347, 510, 526; *see also* lectures; readings; sermons
dedications, 16, 118–19, 121, 130, 144, 152, 166, 174, 252, 460, 565, 663, 673
Delphi, 88, 154
demographics, 9, 39, 102, 105, 111, 113–14, 119, 124, 175, 177, 188, 255, 295–6, 306, 317, 361, 362, 393, 409, 428, 431, 438, 467, 638, 644, 661, 673, 789, 793, 810, 825, 834
Detroit, 8, 118, 124, 221–2, 224–5, 382, 405, 408, 425–8, 443, 452, 454, 464, 472, 475, 482, 486, 488, 493, 499, 502, 510, 562, 601, 789
dialogue, 198, 221, 243, 246, 256, 280–1, 318, 321–2, 324, 327, 332, 357, 370, 397, 589–90, 619, 664, 666, 668–9, 734, 739, 741–8, 750, 754–7, 763, 784, 832, 838, 853

distribution, 174, 348, 384, 391, 410, 458, 516, 534–5, 542, 545, 551, 561, 569, 608, 613, 621, 644, 728, 772, 775, 778, 805, 812, 828, 832–3, 848, 859
dogs, 3, 140, 484, 633, 635
dramatization, 6, 12–13, 17n, 52, 96, 105, 116, 219, 227–9, 231, 245, 256–8, 312–13, 315–17, 319–20, 332, 346, 389, 523, 533, 542, 546, 548, 550–1, 602, 634, 661–3, 665–6, 773, 830, 853, 855; *see also* adaptation and adaptability
drills, 235, 248–50, 256, 593, 696
Drury Lane, 321, 337, 339, 357, 359, 364, 369–72, 383–4, 403n, 608, 857
duumvir, 82, 99n, 104, 743
DVDs, 779, 813n, 825, 835–7, 839, 848–51, 853

Easter, 13, 142, 369, 529, 607, 664, 788–9, 826, 828–9, 835, 847–8, 851
economic perspectives, 6, 14, 31, 165, 189–90, 208–12, 213n, 217, 227, 252, 255, 345–6, 410, 412, 417, 425, 429–30, 434, 439, 442, 445, 486, 510, 514, 569, 686, 691, 703–4, 766, 791
education, 19–21, 26–9, 84, 103, 122, 124, 168, 193, 212, 225, 232, 278, 318, 380, 415, 509, 511, 583, 609, 614, 625–6, 630–1, 644, 663, 675, 685, 688, 769–70, 772, 776
Egypt, 7, 12, 35, 59, 67–70, 73–6, 80, 84, 98, 109, 121, 125, 128, 152, 201–2, 215, 248, 273–5, 278–80, 306, 329, 331, 412, 460, 517, 601, 604–5, 638, 681, 708, 736, 738, 809, 848
Egyptian Theater, 775, 777, 779, 787
Electric Park, 462
electricity and electronics, 7, 15, 250, 258, 294, 311, 320, 335, 337, 344–5, 354–6, 360, 373, 376–7, 391, 393, 409, 443, 456, 461–4, 472–5, 490, 525, 574, 601, 637, 661, 678, 696, 698, 824, 846, 857
elocution, 168, 170–1, 221, 223–4, 240, 259, 347, 421, 512, 529, 620
endorsements, 5, 13, 32, 127, 147, 160–3, 180, 250, 289, 313, 317, 320–1, 344–5, 356, 421–2, 437–8, 442–3, 616, 622, 626, 637–42, 688, 790
England and Great Britain, 17n, 21, 23, 68, 99, 106, 115–17, 129–31, 138–9, 144–6, 150, 156–7, 169, 173, 182n, 194, 199, 205, 219, 227, 262n, 280, 282, 293, 296, 311, 319, 321, 339, 344, 357–60, 362, 364, 366, 369–72, 389, 391–2, 447, 452, 461, 516, 522–5, 528, 562, 573, 608, 610, 622–4, 626, 633, 635, 637, 666, 679, 683–5, 699, 708–10, 735–6, 755, 772, 780, 784, 792–3, 804, 826, 835; *see also* London
English language, 145, 164, 180, 182n, 197, 214n, 218, 340, 370, 518, 524, 610–11, 674, 765, 769, 796, 858
entertainment, 9, 14, 30, 46, 105, 158, 169–72, 189, 220–1, 224–7, 229, 235–6, 240–2, 247–9, 257–60, 311, 324, 353, 362, 388, 390, 421, 435, 429, 461, 468, 509–11, 518, 524, 531, 533–4, 541, 598–9, 604, 606, 609, 625–6, 629, 632, 643, 664, 674, 681, 705, 709–11, 771–2, 776–7, 785, 795, 799, 809, 824–5, 832–3, 842, 844, 847–8, 851, 853
entr'acte, 248, 389
entrepreneurship, 14, 174, 226, 367, 408–10, 413, 460, 509, 561, 564, 728
ephemera, 9, 15–16, 115, 123, 125, 173, 256, 272, 293, 295–6, 349, 351, 412, 422–4, 427–8, 439, 448–9, 460, 483, 621, 689, 713
epic, 10, 27, 94, 103, 134n, 208, 216n, 307n, 539, 551, 562, 571, 586, 607, 613, 662, 728–9, 731, 733, 760, 767, 774, 778, 788, 790, 799, 829, 836, 839, 843–4, 853, 857
Essenes, 59–60
ethnology and ethnics, 40, 68–9, 84, 189–90, 200–4, 206, 340, 588, 592, 625, 761
ethnomusicology, 340
Europe and Europeans, 3, 19–20, 26, 30, 48, 68, 146, 147, 160, 164, 168, 192, 194, 196–7, 200–4, 211, 219, 257, 270–1, 279, 283, 289, 314, 343, 356, 359–60, 362, 364, 393, 445, 460, 520, 527–8, 542, 573–4, 579, 582, 601, 607–8, 611, 621, 625, 699, 766–7, 788, 806, 834, 851
exclusivity, 231, 236, 239, 241, 246, 299, 316, 321, 419, 429, 546, 548, 561, 566, 598, 603, 607, 613–14, 618, 638, 641, 644, 688, 696, 775–6, 784, 787, 831

excursions, 243, 343, 355, 363, 373–4, 376, 381, 386, 411, 450–1, 456, 489
exploitation, 14, 54, 180, 231, 563, 593, 596–621, 687, 768, 791
extras, 337, 381, 536, 578, 580–1, 584, 600, 606–7, 618, 624, 644, 680, 765–6, 778, 834, 852

Fascists, 567, 574, 607, 621, 625
film studies, 11, 842
film widths, 640, 759, 770, 772, 774–6, 782, 836–9, 841
Flavians, 73
football, 244, 420, 468–71, 488, 633, 707, 808
formats, 3, 272, 292, 300, 353, 509, 629, 664, 769, 771, 774, 778, 792–4, 798, 806, 824–5, 829, 835–7, 841, 844, 854, 856
Fort Donelson, 32, 34
Fort Sumter, 32
Fourth of July, 206, 443, 531
France, 23, 26, 37, 42, 148, 155–6, 164, 166, 182n, 197, 200, 248, 280, 339, 359, 372, 447, 569, 600, 610–11, 625, 639, 643, 671, 684, 697, 704, 712, 787, 805–7, 851–3, 857; *see also* Paris
friendship (theme), 323, 362, 412, 590, 670, 734, 749, 755, 760, 796, 832, 843
frontier, 19–20, 43, 145, 188, 192, 345, 413

Galilee and Galileans, 31, 60, 62–6, 72–4, 78, 80, 128, 163, 202, 331–2, 540, 628, 674, 733, 735, 745, 747
galleys, 6, 35, 49, 53–4, 57, 65–6, 77–80, 82, 104, 171–2, 222, 249, 260, 317, 319, 324–6, 331, 347, 349, 351–2, 385, 389, 416, 418, 422, 449, 493, 511, 513–14, 539, 541, 545, 579–81, 587, 591–2, 595, 602, 606, 614, 618–20, 634, 644, 663, 665–7, 670, 678, 686, 707, 732–3, 737, 742–5, 754–5, 761, 764, 766, 795, 805–6, 827, 834, 839–40, 843–6, 849–52, 855, 857–8; *see also* Sea Battle (episode)
George Eastman House, 210, 515–16, 553n, 682
German language, 12, 26, 84–5, 87, 145–9, 159, 167, 174, 217, 219, 425, 431, 843, 851
Germany and Germans, 89, 145–7, 149, 157, 193, 197, 219, 270, 272, 276, 280, 298, 303, 306, 339, 359, 372, 391, 424–5, 431, 447–8, 451, 477, 562–3,

Index

575, 584, 606, 608–9, 622, 629, 653n, 678, 684, 699, 709, 855–6
Gettysburg, 70, 259, 600, 801
Gilded Age, 10, 26, 95, 189, 208–12
gladiators, 75, 103, 111, 152, 200, 364, 671, 754, 800–2, 805–6, 850–3, 858
Golden Gate Amusement Park, 462
Golgotha, 57, 91–2, 670, 709, 757, 762, 845
Grand Opera House (Cincinnati), 172, 253, 287, 351, 375, 379, 385–6, 529
graphics, 410, 422, 439
Greece and Greeks, 12, 19, 22–4, 26, 28–30, 61, 67–70, 73, 75, 81, 84, 86, 88–91, 98–100, 103–4, 128, 159, 177, 194, 198–9, 201–3, 205, 250, 253, 258, 279, 305, 326–7, 340, 398, 572, 593–4, 665, 701, 737, 741, 796, 851

halftones, 151, 305, 347, 378, 425, 429, 438, 442–3, 458, 482, 489; *see also* illustrations and sketches
Hebrew culture, language, and religion, 19, 24, 54, 61, 69, 71, 79, 90–1, 121
Hebrews, 35, 61, 66, 69, 71, 340, 849
Henry Ford Museum, 466–7
Her Majesty's Theatre (Sidney), 311, 364–8
heroism, 20, 22–23, 30, 39, 41, 54, 62, 83, 93, 107, 110–11, 160, 189, 199–200, 211, 216n, 273, 338, 370, 410–11, 456–7, 462, 469, 488–9, 567, 573, 578, 587, 600, 632, 639, 644, 665, 705, 710, 750, 756, 762, 795–6, 824, 839
Herrick Library, 572, 624, 755
Hinduism, 67, 69, 98n, 202, 272
hippodromes, 86, 88–9, 100n, 468, 616, 627, 710, 806
Hollywood, 12, 276, 312, 488, 567–8, 571, 573, 577–8, 581–6, 593, 596, 605, 613, 623, 625, 628–9, 634, 662, 679, 681–2, 689–90, 713, 728, 730–1, 759, 762–3, 773–6, 780–2, 786, 799, 808, 825, 828, 830, 834–5, 857
Holy Land, 19, 48–9, 72, 74, 79, 84–6, 97n, 98n, 152, 201–2, 242, 245, 431, 437, 520, 614, 792
homages, 73, 416, 485, 807, 840, 857
horses, 3, 23, 56, 74, 81, 87–8, 122, 140, 152, 170, 173, 230, 234, 264n, 283–4,

286, 291, 305, 311, 319–21, 328, 330, 334–5, 337–9, 341, 356, 359, 362–4, 368–9, 381, 388, 390, 394, 409, 420–2, 425, 430, 432, 434–5, 439, 460–2, 464–5, 468, 471–3, 477–8, 480, 482, 48–5, 579–80, 585, 587, 592–4, 597–8, 605, 614, 624, 628–9, 632–3, 636, 643, 668–70, 678–9, 684–5, 689, 700–2, 705–10, 712, 742, 752, 754, 759–62, 764–7, 773, 777, 782, 786–7, 793, 795–6, 800, 803, 805–11, 818n, 832, 834, 840, 844, 846, 849–51, 853, 856–8; *see also* Arabian horses; Ben Hur Horses; chariots and chariot racing; thoroughbreds
Hotel Normandie, 7, 472–4, 637, 678
hot rods, 670–1, 808
humor, jokes, puns, 252–3, 450–1, 598, 610, 631, 634, 682, 706, 711–13, 739, 752, 766–7, 811, 844; *see also* cartoons
Hungary, 781
hyphen, xii, 71, 177, 236, 282, 322, 352, 408, 427, 442, 444, 446, 485, 638, 675, 693, 698, 732, 771, 774, 796

Illinois, 96, 124, 128, 144, 229, 240, 308, 337, 357, 359–60, 365, 408, 412, 422, 439–40, 455–6, 458, 480, 486, 510, 533, 541, 546, 615, 678, 699, 708, 789, 856; *see also* Chicago
illustrations and sketches, 20, 48, 142, 152–5, 166, 212, 249–50, 263n, 306, 347, 349, 352, 358, 365, 421, 429, 437, 442, 460, 513, 520–1, 583, 672–3, 695, 706, 768, 770, 792–4, 797, 801, 804, 808, 836; *see also* halftones; imagery
imagery, 2–3, 5, 14, 58, 61, 98, 143–4, 200, 202–3, 205, 209–10, 228, 230, 249, 277, 281, 288, 305, 342, 353, 388, 409–10, 421, 427, 429, 432, 437–9, 442, 445, 448, 460, 466, 470–1, 478–9, 482, 486, 489–90, 509, 513–14, 516, 520–1, 527, 541, 553, 559, 581, 611, 629, 632–3, 639, 641, 667, 683, 686, 690, 696, 702–3, 705–6, 709, 743, 772, 797, 800, 804, 808, 840, 856
imitation, 70–1, 96, 128, 163, 210, 279, 281, 299, 322, 340, 409, 544, 632, 802, 858

immigrants, 149, 188, 209, 305, 412, 425
India, 68, 157–8, 166, 278, 282–3, 296, 444, 484, 520, 523, 572, 611, 613, 679, 788
Indiana, 6, 19, 23, 25–6, 30, 32, 42–4, 54–5, 57, 94, 101, 118, 120, 124–5, 146, 150–7, 162, 183–4, 191, 193, 219, 228–9, 232, 235, 239–40, 247, 264–5, 279–80, 304, 315, 320, 339, 345, 361, 389, 400, 405, 411, 413, 416–17, 419, 448, 455–6, 467, 483, 485–6, 491–2, 500, 507, 525–6, 530, 546, 553, 638, 675–6, 699, 708, 777–8, 811; *see also* Indianapolis
Indianapolis, 20, 25, 27, 31, 46, 50–1, 56, 72, 111, 117, 120, 123, 126, 140, 160, 192–3, 195, 222, 226–7, 232–3, 263–4, 280, 304, 372, 378, 380, 390, 404, 406–7, 413, 417, 422, 440, 455–6, 458–9, 461, 466, 477–8, 485–6, 488, 491–3, 500, 505, 507, 552, 560, 647, 704–5
industry, 9, 14, 102, 126, 188, 204, 209, 211, 287, 297, 303, 307, 313, 316–17, 345, 408, 410, 412–13, 424–5, 427, 432, 440, 454, 464, 466, 476, 486, 509, 536, 539, 543, 546, 549–52, 561, 564, 567–9, 577, 579–80, 598, 603, 607, 611, 616–17, 621–4, 643–4, 661, 673, 682, 686, 697–8, 700, 728, 730, 766, 774, 776–7, 779, 788–9, 798–9, 801, 805–6, 825, 830
inflation, 9, 788, 791
initiation, 261, 381, 411, 415, 418, 525
injunctions, 239, 313, 388, 512, 524, 543, 546–7, 562–3
innovation, 14, 41, 79, 141, 199, 243, 249–50, 320, 335, 343, 357, 383, 385, 410, 429, 435–6, 466, 478, 533, 539, 585, 589, 597, 604, 606, 629, 693, 750, 756, 771, 778, 791, 801, 846, 855
insurance, 3, 104, 314, 368, 408, 412–13, 417, 422–3, 571, 643, 661, 712, 776–7, 787, 790, 809
intellectual property, 5, 280, 303, 544, 830–1
internationality, 1, 5, 13, 37, 121–2, 129, 133, 138, 146, 156, 159, 206, 208, 226, 317, 340, 342, 358–60, 382, 523, 569, 582, 608, 624, 635, 661, 691, 708, 775–6, 804–5, 855

interviews, 22, 46, 120, 219, 221, 228, 240, 242, 267, 314, 317–18, 325, 331, 338, 356, 362, 416, 552, 564, 575, 579, 598–9, 601, 608, 663, 710, 766, 772–3, 777, 781, 783–5, 789, 801, 836, 842–3, 848–9, 858
invention, 39–40, 53, 58, 69–70, 103, 105, 107, 110, 160, 209–10, 237, 269, 287–8, 298, 303, 314, 332, 344–5, 352, 410, 456, 478, 533, 588, 599, 623, 666, 669, 671, 742, 754, 796, 824, 844, 849–50
Israel and Israelis, 66, 70, 72, 84, 108, 201, 332, 414, 492, 664, 685, 767
Italy and Italians, 42, 82, 147–8, 157, 164, 305, 317, 359, 546, 562–3, 567–75, 577–83, 591–2, 599, 601–2, 621–2, 625, 644, 679–80, 729–32, 753, 759, 765–8, 787–8, 793–4, 799, 811, 834, 851, 858

Japan, 233, 483, 520, 712, 780, 788, 805, 830; see also Tokyo
Jebel es Zubleh, 84–5, 201
Jerusalem, 30, 47, 49, 53, 63–5, 67, 72–3, 76, 79, 82, 84, 86, 94, 105, 165, 198, 202, 249, 282, 322–3, 326, 330, 334, 431, 467, 514–17, 520, 537, 540, 573, 588–9, 592, 595–6, 600, 602, 663, 669, 685, 735, 742, 745–6, 748, 751, 754, 757–8, 765, 804, 806, 832, 836, 838, 849–50
Jews, 7, 23, 47–9, 53–4, 57–73, 75–6, 79–80, 92–4, 109, 128, 131–60, 163, 170, 172, 189, 198, 202, 207, 212n, 214n, 224, 243, 323, 329–31, 341, 356, 370, 409, 511, 579, 582, 588, 590, 593–4, 625, 628, 668–70, 676, 685, 713, 734, 737, 741, 745–7, 749, 755–7, 760, 772, 789, 792, 832, 838, 845
Joppa Gate, 203, 230, 242, 246, 249, 514–15, 520, 573, 578, 600, 739
Judaism, 19, 49, 54, 57, 59, 61, 72, 96, 274
Judea, 24, 47, 57, 62, 64–6, 73, 75–6, 79–80, 82, 84, 91, 93, 103, 107, 131, 198, 206, 259, 333, 358, 514, 520, 588, 663, 667, 669, 742, 744–7, 750–1, 757–8, 762, 827, 832, 838–9, 843, 850

Kansas and Kansas City, 3, 125, 196, 378–9, 408–11, 439, 445, 448, 462, 480, 485, 523, 529, 532, 557n, 705, 786, 818n, 856
Kentucky, 129, 192–3, 230, 244, 312, 315, 414, 419, 453–4, 484, 528, 530, 632, 705, 707
Kentucky Derby, 632, 705
Kewpies, 435–6
kindergarten, 171, 225
Kinetoscope, 210, 534, 542

Lake McDonald, 411, 451
Lake Maxinkuckee, 55
Latin, 19, 21–2, 26–7, 29, 32, 69, 82, 86, 91, 99n, 103–4, 214n, 705, 827, 855
law, lawsuits, and legal proceedings, 5, 7, 12–13, 31–2, 34–5, 41, 48, 60, 65, 67, 71, 73, 94, 117, 129–30, 133, 150, 172, 210, 227, 241, 246, 271, 317, 367, 374, 382, 419, 427, 472, 510, 523–4, 535, 543–6, 547–8, 550–2, 563, 566, 577, 589, 613, 625, 676–7, 701, 741, 767, 774, 785, 830; see also injunctions; legality
lectures, 5–6, 9, 26, 38, 41, 46, 76, 115, 120–7, 138, 140, 157–9, 165, 195, 212, 217, 227, 229, 236, 244, 250, 258, 285, 340, 367–8, 420–1, 430, 462, 509–13, 518–19, 521–33, 535, 546, 548, 589, 616, 674, 688, 769, 835; see also declamations; readings; sermons
legal expenses, 509, 523, 545
legality, 5–7, 9, 12–13, 20, 60, 77, 105, 117, 127–33, 138, 142, 148, 160, 227–8, 235, 237, 239, 241–2, 247, 258, 271, 285–7, 299, 301–3, 312–13, 315–16, 321, 352, 358, 367, 372, 409, 419, 423–4, 427, 447, 451, 472–3, 476, 480, 482, 509, 518, 523–5, 530, 535, 543–5, 547–52, 561–5, 571, 605–6, 619, 624, 643, 679, 682, 699, 701, 707, 755, 830–1, 859
legions, 23, 31, 62–3, 65–6, 78, 107, 331, 585, 587–8, 595–6, 674, 733, 739, 745, 802, 806, 836, 839
legitimate literature and theaters, 102, 103, 558n, 596, 598, 603–5, 607, 610, 644, 680
leisure, 57, 77, 113, 165, 174, 210, 298, 408, 410, 686, 705, 707–11, 739, 829
leitmotifs, 325, 332, 339, 591, 796, 843
lepers and leprosy, 7, 54, 59, 65–6, 73, 79, 83, 93, 104, 169, 171–2, 190, 223, 229, 243, 249, 319, 331–2, 358, 511, 515, 517, 520, 528, 595, 620, 625, 665–7, 733, 736, 746–7, 761, 782, 827, 832, 834, 849, 852, 858
letterbox format, 829, 836
letterhead, 116, 122, 180, 294–5, 416, 425, 428, 430, 439, 458, 469, 478
lettering, 343, 348, 374, 427–8, 443, 451, 461, 475, 477, 486, 596, 618, 633, 685, 811
letters and correspondence, 5, 10, 13, 22, 35, 37, 46, 48–9, 54–5, 57, 70, 77, 80, 82, 91–2, 94–6, 106, 112–13, 115–16, 118–23, 126–9, 133, 135n, 140–1, 146–9, 151–3, 156–7, 159–60, 162–3, 170, 172–4, 178, 180, 198, 218–19, 226–8, 235–6, 239, 241–2, 256–8, 278–80, 286, 289, 291, 313, 315, 352, 395n, 410–11, 437, 454, 523, 544, 562, 567, 575, 578–80, 600, 616, 631, 640, 706, 753–4, 756, 767, 789, 783–5, 830
Lew Wallace Study, 676, 777
libraries, 15, 48, 86, 88, 167–8, 211, 293, 618, 626, 684, 711, 733, 753, 755, 769, 772, 777–8, 792, 828–9, 833, 843
Library of Congress, 40, 48–9, 53–4, 57, 67, 88, 189, 215n, 221–2, 228, 262n, 306, 452, 490n, 523, 550, 859
lights and lighting, 7, 210, 223, 235, 237, 249–50, 259, 314, 322, 325, 329–30, 332, 341, 346, 355, 358, 370, 463, 472–3, 475, 490, 572–3, 581, 589, 591, 595, 605, 608, 661, 670, 683, 698, 770, 773, 830, 840, 848, 852, 855–6; see also Seekers After "the Light" from "Ben-Hur"
Lilly Library, 183n, 219, 278–80, 304, 405, 536, 553n
Lincoln County war, 43, 92, 94
literacy, 112, 180, 210, 272
literary property, 1, 5–6, 14, 226, 231, 313, 509, 568, 672, 680
literature, 1, 4–7, 9–14, 19, 25, 27, 29–31, 41, 52, 81, 84, 94, 102–3, 110–11, 113, 115, 117–19, 121, 124–5, 127, 140, 146, 150, 163–4, 169, 188–9, 191, 193–4, 199, 201–3, 212, 218, 226–7, 230–1, 251, 313, 315, 318, 345–6, 356, 366, 393, 409, 423, 454, 456, 509, 511, 523, 526–7, 531, 534–5, 543, 564, 568, 624, 627, 637, 661, 666, 672, 680, 685, 789, 857
lithography, 210, 288–90, 293–4,

386, 425, 427, 430, 432, 461, 478, 482, 485, 490n, 699, 770, 800
lobby cards, 611, 618, 769
local productions, venues, and reception, 3, 6, 15, 20, 27, 55, 118, 120, 124, 158, 160, 167, 170–2, 192–3, 207, 221, 224–6, 232, 234, 237, 240, 248, 250–2, 255, 276, 330, 343, 355, 360, 373–4, 376, 382–7, 408–9, 415–16, 420, 424, 430–1, 438–40, 443–5, 448–9, 452, 455–6, 461, 467, 469–70, 473, 475, 480, 486, 488, 525–6, 528, 532, 539, 542, 546–8, 585, 599, 601–2, 604–5, 608, 614–16, 618–20, 624, 629–33, 636, 640–5, 678, 684, 686, 691, 699, 701–2, 704, 708, 766, 769, 772, 775–7, 780, 785, 787, 789, 809, 826–8, 833–5, 837, 847–8, 853
Loew's theaters, 608, 614–17, 774–5, 777, 779, 786, 800
Logansport, 229, 232, 319, 486, 529, 699, 702
logo, 3, 6, 91, 255, 418, 427, 439, 442–4, 459–60, 465, 476, 478, 482, 629, 686–9, 693–4, 696–7, 699–700, 770, 772, 801–2, 804–5, 808, 829, 846, 856
London, 1, 23, 131–2, 134n, 144, 164, 181n, 207, 279–81, 303, 311, 317, 321, 334, 337, 339, 342, 344, 354, 357–60, 364, 366, 369–72, 379, 383–5, 403n, 480, 550, 608, 610–12, 619, 625, 630, 635, 680, 682, 709, 712, 730, 769, 772–3, 775, 780, 787–8, 792, 797, 834–5, 856–7
Los Angeles, 169, 275, 288–9, 295–6, 317, 417, 420, 440–4, 456, 462, 464, 468–9, 510–11, 529, 547, 549, 551, 568–71, 581, 583, 585, 601–5, 614, 623, 627–30, 632–3, 635–7, 640, 674, 677–8, 681–2, 686, 688–90, 695, 697–702, 706, 709–11, 729, 762, 767–8, 776, 779–80, 784, 787, 808, 825, 834–6, 856
Louisville, 141, 230, 251, 255, 262n, 373, 375, 378, 448–9, 486, 704
LPs, 728, 797–8, 806, 843
Lyceum circuit, 157, 222, 259, 378, 383, 387, 511
lyrics, 91, 127, 138, 266n, 269–82, 291, 299, 322, 327, 329, 386, 397n, 414, 734, 797

machinery and mechanisms, 3–4, 7, 86, 155, 188, 209–10, 241, 269, 278, 297–8, 300, 303, 311, 313–14, 320–1, 325, 335, 337–8, 343, 345, 355–6, 363, 366, 368–9, 372–4, 392, 398n, 422, 427, 456–7, 461–2, 471–2, 482, 533, 543, 606, 642, 678, 685, 698, 702, 709, 805, 829–30, 846, 853, 857; see also inventions
magazine revolution, 431
magazines, 1, 13, 15, 19, 38, 48, 95, 97n, 106, 111, 119, 140, 145, 149–50, 152, 166, 173, 196, 198, 210, 212, 272, 276, 294, 321, 340, 342, 347–8, 353, 358, 385, 410, 423, 431–9, 457–8, 460, 467, 470, 472–3, 480, 482–3, 510, 512, 550, 641–3, 661, 671, 693, 702–3, 765, 778–9, 781, 797, 800, 811
Magi, 47, 50, 54, 68, 128, 322, 340, 517, 520, 798
male gaze, 224, 468, 485
managers and management, 73, 76, 123, 218, 224, 226, 231, 237, 239, 244–6, 250, 256–7, 262n, 285–6, 303, 312–13, 315, 320, 335, 340, 343, 357, 361, 364, 369, 373, 376, 378–9, 382, 384, 387, 409, 442, 462, 470, 475, 516, 530, 533–6, 543, 546–7, 561, 565, 578, 581, 598, 607, 611, 615–18, 625, 630–1, 645, 679, 707, 730, 748, 757, 766, 769, 771–2, 774–6, 787, 809, 824, 850
Manchester, 162, 391, 621, 709, 711, 857
manifest destiny, 203–6
Manila, 287, 780, 832
manufacturing, 3, 8–9, 12–14, 162, 250–2, 294, 307n, 409, 422, 424–6, 428–9, 439–40, 445–8, 454, 457–9, 461, 464–5, 480, 482–3, 509, 532, 535, 543, 549, 631, 637, 640, 643, 666, 686, 688, 692–99, 728, 799–802, 804–5, 811, 828, 857
manuscripts, 37–9, 43, 48, 52, 82, 92, 97n, 102–5, 110, 128, 142, 156, 188, 198, 269, 279, 315–16, 318, 347, 349, 358, 379, 405n, 521, 622, 663, 688, 777, 784
marches, 7, 138, 209, 259, 269, 283, 285–6, 288–306, 314, 317, 330, 341, 410, 422, 424, 460, 527, 530, 587, 589, 629, 631, 637, 661, 677–8, 732, 797, 806, 809
markets and marketing, 3, 5, 7, 12–15, 31, 39, 104–6, 115–17, 130–1, 133, 138, 141–2, 147–9, 151, 155–6, 163, 167, 174–5, 180, 188, 203, 208–9, 212, 226–7,

231, 269, 272, 288–9, 294, 297–301, 303–4, 314, 343, 351, 359, 375, 381–2, 416, 429, 432, 438, 440, 446–8, 458, 461, 467, 510, 562, 611, 624–5, 637, 640, 661–2, 673, 689, 693, 728, 770–1, 776, 787–8, 797–8, 800–1, 805, 826, 828–9, 833, 836
martyrdom, 200, 218, 331
Maryland, 26, 35, 100n, 193, 226, 363, 452, 684, 711
masons, 410–11
Memphis, 273–5, 280
Memphis, TN, 34, 65, 94, 378–9, 381–2
merchandising, xii, 1, 9, 14, 165–6, 728, 798–805, 824
merchants, 12, 41, 79, 93, 252, 386, 465
Messiah, 53–4, 63, 74, 131, 134, 144, 163, 184, 274, 355, 587, 590, 628, 733, 745, 756, 833, 844
metal disks see tune sheets
Methodists, 123, 125, 148–9, 169, 191, 209, 213n, 232–3, 240, 242, 245, 263n, 296, 430, 510, 512, 531, 534, 616–17
Mexico and Mexican, 24, 31–2, 37–9, 41–3, 62, 68, 92, 94, 120, 158, 204, 206, 411, 483, 486–8, 562, 579, 602, 627, 675, 697, 775, 800
middle class, 26, 189, 213n, 432
military, 20, 22, 24, 28, 30–2, 37–8, 43, 57, 61–2, 67, 73, 76–9, 82, 93–5, 100, 103, 105, 113, 122, 124, 170, 185, 200, 207–8, 235, 258–9, 287, 292, 295, 324, 484, 540, 551, 569, 584, 590, 593, 683, 692, 737, 745
millionaires, 159, 211, 470
Milwaukee, 3, 125–6, 163, 167, 170, 225, 230, 248–9, 256, 337, 378, 406n, 529, 686, 692–4
mines and mining, 7, 9, 21, 37, 120, 408, 476–7, 489–90, 591, 634, 686, 699–701
Minneapolis, 149, 169, 373, 375, 378, 429–31, 454, 458, 523, 532–3, 617, 702, 768
Minnesota, 7, 127, 140, 168, 240, 295, 429–30, 450, 498, 531, 702; see also Minneapolis
Misenum, 79–80, 152–3, 230, 249, 333, 751
Mississippi, 34, 381, 450, 606
Mississippi River, 7, 450
models
  exemplars, 3, 22, 26, 32, 38, 48, 61, 66–7, 70–2, 75–7, 94, 197–8, 219, 230, 232, 303, 389, 412–13, 468–9, 475, 661, 669, 695, 700–1, 731, 747, 774

models (*cont.*)
  humans, 524–6, 528, 711, 802
  miniatures, 314, 591, 614, 633–4, 693, 732, 802–3, 827, 857; *see also* brands and branding
Mohonk Mountain House, 258
Monocacy, 37, 95, 675
Monroe Doctrine, 204
Morgan Library, 152, 186n
Morrill Act, 210
Motion Picture Production Code, 729
municipalities, 3, 5, 100n, 188, 241, 255, 257, 381, 486–9
muscularity, 199, 484
music, 7, 36, 73, 90, 140, 166, 168–9, 212, 219, 222, 226, 228–9, 239, 248, 259, 269–307, 312, 319, 321, 323–8, 331–2, 339–40, 344–5, 347–9, 353–8, 360, 369, 380, 389, 397n, 399n, 411, 419–23, 454, 460, 466–7, 510, 527, 530–1, 533, 550–1, 562, 570, 572, 585, 600, 614, 619, 623, 628–32, 642, 661, 663–6, 674, 677–9, 684, 688–9, 708, 732, 734, 744, 771–2, 776, 779–80, 782, 790, 792, 794, 796–8, 800, 803, 806–7, 809, 827, 840–3, 846–8, 853–6, 858
musicals and musicales, 357–8, 362, 531, 632, 674, 708, 791, 796–7, 806–7, 842, 846–8, 854
music boxes *see* tune sheets
music videos, 847
mythology, 47, 69, 75, 81, 87, 102, 111, 155, 197, 199, 253, 460, 466, 701, 749, 796

narration, 84, 119, 190–1, 199, 216n, 223, 512, 527, 616, 628, 630, 663–6, 668, 670, 739, 795, 805, 807–9, 827, 829, 841, 843–4, 848, 852–3, 855
narrative, 7–8, 15, 39–40, 47, 52–9, 62, 65, 84, 87, 102–3, 108–9, 117, 119, 189–90, 198–200, 208, 213n, 214n, 216n, 217n, 223, 246–7, 249, 273, 334, 381, 521, 551, 567–8, 586–7, 589–90, 592, 594, 619, 664, 667, 671, 733, 747, 751, 763, 773, 806, 824, 837, 855
nationality and national scope, 1, 3, 15, 32, 120, 131, 150, 160, 171, 177, 195–6, 208–10, 251, 255, 299, 339–40, 342, 361, 368, 392, 408, 413–14, 416, 433, 438–9, 460, 470, 472, 547, 571, 607, 641, 661, 676, 681, 693, 702, 711, 728, 769–70, 773, 776, 781, 784–5, 787, 790, 809, 833
navy, 7, 78, 80, 104, 334, 341, 525, 579, 581, 665, 670, 692, 733, 748, 761, 773, 832, 852
Nazareth, 49, 58, 63, 64, 83, 108, 117, 190, 325, 331–2, 349, 522, 591, 628, 663, 733, 737, 739, 743, 747, 761, 763–5, 794, 828, 832, 838, 843, 855, 858
Nazis, 664, 683
nebel, 90–1, 270, 278–9, 323
Nebraska, 124, 169, 417, 532
negotiation, 6, 12, 30, 37, 140, 147, 150, 151, 156, 175, 212, 237, 246, 256, 285–6, 315, 332, 356, 359, 372, 409, 470, 552, 562–3, 565, 569, 572, 574, 598, 641, 731, 759, 764, 774, 791–2, 805
networks, 1, 11, 32, 79, 193–4, 314, 349, 358, 373, 422, 437, 456, 629, 631, 661–2, 666, 690, 825–8, 833–4, 837, 848, 851
Nevada, 7, 444, 476–7, 510, 634, 701
New England, 41, 111, 127, 195, 219, 272, 275–6, 279, 356, 373–4, 529, 616, 697
New Mexico, 43, 92, 55–6, 82, 92, 96, 102, 105, 113, 115, 120–1, 162, 169, 204, 444, 466, 476–7, 488, 529, 622, 666, 676; *see also* Santa Fe
New Testament, 12, 27, 47, 58, 63, 68, 73, 75, 83–4, 104, 108, 164, 191–7, 199, 213–14n, 226, 349, 381, 415, 513, 582, 619, 848; *see also* Luke; Matthew
Newton Bill, 550
New York, 7, 21, 23, 37, 41, 43n, 48, 103, 105–6, 116–17, 120–2, 125–6, 141, 151–2, 157–9, 162, 168, 169, 171, 175, 218–19, 222, 239, 243–4, 246, 250, 257–9, 278–9, 287, 292–6, 301, 304–6, 311, 314–15, 317–21, 334, 337, 339, 341–3, 345, 348–9, 351, 354, 356–7, 359, 361–2, 364, 366–7, 372–6, 380, 383–7, 389–94, 409, 413, 420, 428, 439, 443–4, 448, 451, 452, 462, 464, 468–9, 472–3, 482, 484, 486, 488, 514, 518, 522–5, 528, 532, 537, 541, 544, 550–1, 561–5, 574, 577–80, 584, 586, 596–9, 601–2, 604, 610, 614–15, 617–18, 620, 622, 629–32, 634–8, 642–3, 673–4, 677–80, 695, 697–8, 701, 706–11, 733, 753, 768–9, 772–4, 776–7, 782–3, 786–7, 789–90, 798–801, 805, 828, 834, 836, 843, 846, 856
New Zealand, 367–8, 391–2, 523, 673
Nielsen ratings, 825
Nile River, 12, 70, 97n, 246, 248, 273–4, 278–80, 480
nineteenth century, 1, 6, 8, 14–15, 19, 22, 28, 60, 68, 87, 89, 110, 115, 149, 153, 167, 171, 188–9, 191–2, 194, 197, 200, 204, 206, 208, 211, 217, 227, 251, 269, 283, 288, 305, 313, 409, 412, 442, 475, 551, 675, 701, 734, 782
Nobel Prize for Literature, 9
nostalgia, 141, 275, 345, 614, 636–7, 677–8, 680, 692, 696, 705–6, 710, 724n, 811, 827, 834
novels, 2, 6–7, 9–10, 12, 19–20, 30–1, 40, 54, 65, 109–10, 115–17, 129–31, 134n, 146, 156, 163–5, 168, 180, 188, 198–9, 210, 203, 207–8, 231, 270, 283, 341, 428, 512, 534–5, 550–1, 594, 626–8, 661, 671, 673–5, 782, 824, 832
novice theatregoers, 380
Numidia, 762
nylons, 662, 697

Oakland, 158, 229, 295, 299, 486
Oberammergau, 241, 342, 513
Ocean Park, 7, 409, 443, 462–4, 472, 535, 709
Ohio, 34–5, 62, 112, 146, 171–2, 239–41, 247, 253, 339, 373, 413, 416, 422, 439, 449–50, 454, 456, 464–5, 477, 483, 488, 493n, 510–12, 518, 529, 532, 534, 614, 616, 620, 666, 688, 785; *see also* Cincinnati
Ohio River, 7, 15, 408, 450
Old Testament, 54, 59–60, 71–3, 83, 194, 411, 513, 593, 608, 610
Olympia and Olympic Games, 24, 81, 88–9
opera, 164, 219, 345, 362, 366, 392, 613, 679, 767
opera houses, 124–5, 172, 222, 225–7, 240–1, 250, 253, 257, 287, 338, 351, 354–5, 356, 362, 373, 375, 379, 385–7, 390–1, 393, 475, 504n, 529, 532, 548, 607
orientalism, 12, 20, 73, 74, 117, 141, 154, 181, 201–3, 205, 224–5, 230, 236, 240, 242, 272, 275, 328, 408, 412, 460, 466, 509, 520, 592, 639, 642, 662, 782, 794
Orlando, 846
Ottoman Empire, 5, 92, 147
outlaws, 200, 747

Index

Pacific Southwest Exhibition, 422
packaging, 5, 144, 149, 198, 210, 217n, 299, 305–6, 427, 442–4, 446–7, 454, 563, 638, 691–2, 799, 802, 807, 826, 833, 835, 837, 842
pagans and paganism, 39, 54, 74, 79, 90, 249, 327, 356, 393, 588, 740, 832
pageants, 229–31, 255, 258, 261, 297, 470, 597–8, 633, 661, 691, 707–11, 825
Palestine, 167, 202, 215, 466, 569–70, 685, 809
Palmer's Theatre, 219, 235, 237–9, 251, 261n, 265n
Panama-Pacific Exposition, 259, 391
Pan-American Exposition, 466–7
Panic of 1873, 189, 209
pantomime, 229, 231, 236, 239, 246–8, 250, 252, 256–7, 261, 297, 322, 327, 397, 523, 544, 548, 619–20; *see also* Ben-Hur, in Tableaux and Pantomime
parades and floats, 209, 230–1, 249, 263n, 411, 421–2, 469, 492n, 627, 634, 661, 675–6, 687, 689, 691, 707, 709, 732, 763–4, 773, 797, 804, 809, 832
Paris, 173, 182n, 202, 278, 287, 339, 344, 359, 362, 368, 372, 388, 541–2, 581, 610–13, 618, 621, 633, 643, 671, 684, 688, 697, 787–8, 806, 851–2
parlors, 138, 255, 269–338, 347
parodies, 387–9, 629, 631–2, 634, 804, 807, 809, 827
Pasadena, 7, 409, 420–1, 468–71, 474, 586, 689, 707, 808
passion play, 462, 531
patents, 162, 209–10, 237, 297, 300–1, 303, 311, 314, 334–5, 398n, 410, 422, 427, 439, 477, 505n, 524, 549, 690, 693, 695–6, 720–3n, 830
patriotism, 23, 47, 66, 206–7, 258, 287, 531, 462, 740
patronage, 26, 75, 103, 200, 217n, 312
Pennsylvania, 26, 170–1, 192, 230, 252–3, 257, 263n, 266n, 293, 308n, 363, 383, 412, 450, 480, 488, 510, 525, 528–9, 531, 642, 805; *see also* Philadelphia
percentages, 1, 6, 41, 105, 130, 150, 156, 157, 172, 174, 209, 236, 256, 286, 315, 389, 457, 534, 564, 576, 599, 607, 689, 729, 731, 769, 778, 785, 787, 789, 799, 824; *see also* profits; revenues

petroleum and gasoline, 408, 452, 454, 457, 464, 477, 490, 551, 699–701, 703
Pharisees, 59, 61, 203
Philadelphia, 23, 25, 43n, 49, 85, 162, 171, 209, 221–2, 224, 245, 255, 278, 283, 286, 299–300, 309n, 354, 355–7, 362, 372, 384, 387, 390–1, 458, 468, 488, 513–14, 529, 562, 599, 601, 773, 775
philanthropy, 93, 211, 410, 419, 668
phonographs and players, 210, 294, 297, 299, 301–3, 410, 533, 698, 807
photographers, 202, 253, 255, 346–7, 352
photographs, 7, 13, 56, 151, 162, 166, 177, 178, 202, 212, 215n, 249, 255, 271, 297, 312, 318, 322, 326, 342, 346–53, 361, 369, 374, 385–7, 402n, 421–2, 431, 450–1, 455, 457, 463, 470–3, 484, 488, 509, 512–13, 518, 520, 524, 543, 546, 549, 552, 581, 584, 591, 594, 596–7, 602, 606, 618, 626, 635, 639–40, 662, 675, 684, 688–9, 695, 702, 709, 767, 769, 778–9, 789, 792–4, 806–7, 811, 841, 857
piano and organ rolls, 298–9, 302, 423, 678
pigs, 3, 140, 484
pinball, 698, 856–7
piracy, 80, 301, 303, 550, 546–7, 591, 843, 859
pirates, 21, 39, 78–80, 82, 95, 99n, 103, 325, 338, 385, 619, 667, 670, 795, 805, 832, 852, 855
plagiarism, 127–9
plagues, 69, 311, 325, 367–8
plays, 7, 9–10, 12,14, 17n, 38–9, 57, 66, 94, 138, 150, 164, 166, 218, 241, 245, 259, 312–13, 317–34, 337, 341–81, 383–94, 423, 462, 513, 531–2, 534–5, 542–4, 550, 552, 561–6, 569, 571–2, 589–91, 597–600, 602–3, 605, 607, 610, 614, 616, 628, 630, 636, 644, 662, 664–6, 669, 672, 676, 678–9, 685, 701, 807, 844–6, 855–7
Playstation 2, 856
poetry, 27, 50, 72, 81, 91, 103, 208, 211, 232, 270, 272, 280, 283, 307, 423, 592
politics, 22, 30–2, 40, 52–3, 57–8, 61–8, 72–3, 76, 78, 82, 92–3, 107, 119–20, 122, 128, 158, 160–2, 165, 190, 194, 203–8, 213n, 220, 255, 388, 414, 416–18, 511, 567–8, 581–2, 588, 590,

595, 610, 625, 633, 675, 685, 737, 739, 740–52, 760, 781, 838–9, 857; *see also* anti-Roman politics
Pompeii, 80, 583, 856; *see also* *Last Days of Pompeii, The*
popularity, 6, 11, 14, 54, 83, 102, 107, 110, 115–17, 121, 131, 140, 147, 171, 188, 202, 239, 255, 269, 281, 283, 294–7, 304–5, 355, 362, 370–1, 384–5, 387, 393, 427, 457, 489, 509, 532, 552, 565, 569, 596, 604, 617, 622, 626–7, 674–5, 678, 685, 788, 809, 831
popular arts, 5–7, 9, 11–14, 17, 26, 96, 107, 109, 115, 129, 196, 281, 289, 359, 410, 423, 438, 460, 489, 543, 661
popular culture, 11, 12, 14, 17, 60, 71, 96, 123, 160, 188, 203, 210, 283, 314, 346, 381, 489–90, 510, 513, 550, 635, 662–3, 686, 701, 707, 711, 731, 796, 824, 835, 856
popular literature, 1, 5–7, 9–10, 20, 25, 39–40, 50, 52, 102, 105, 110, 122, 130, 163–5, 200–3, 211–12, 226, 341, 384, 455, 489, 564, 627, 671, 729, 857
popular music, 269, 276, 294, 296, 303, 305–7
postcards, 8, 15, 42, 55, 162, 178–9, 420–2, 427, 431, 439, 451, 455, 461–4, 467, 473, 475, 478, 483–4, 486, 488, 611, 641, 688–9, 699, 702, 768
Presbyterians, 21, 158, 193, 195, 197, 207, 241–2, 258, 510, 531–3
prices, 115–17, 119, 142, 155–6, 165, 173, 177–8, 180, 225, 294, 296, 303, 315, 348, 351, 357, 360–1, 363, 376, 386, 390, 401n, 425, 429–31, 448, 464, 469, 477, 532, 542, 552, 563, 565, 569, 572, 598, 604, 607, 611, 613–15, 645, 691, 698, 787–8, 790–1, 799–800, 825–6, 828
profits and profitability, 1, 5, 9, 38, 41, 54, 96, 102, 105, 113, 115, 125, 140–1, 144, 148, 156–7, 159, 163, 165, 167, 173, 175, 212, 220, 226, 231, 251, 257, 285, 311, 313, 318, 346, 353, 355, 357, 362, 373, 383–4, 391, 393, 484, 509–10, 532, 550–1, 563–4, 598, 618, 623–4, 637, 640, 646n, 690, 728–9, 731, 768, 787–8, 812, 822, 824, 851; *see also* revenues

programming (lecture, musical, and theatrical), 121–2, 157–8, 169, 172, 220, 229, 233, 240–2, 247, 249, 259, 286–8, 295, 329, 351, 510, 530–1, 542, 546–7, 550, 607, 618, 679, 806; *see also* radio programs and programming; television programs and programming
programs (printed), 13, 125–6, 166, 219, 222, 229, 236–9, 246–54, 258–9, 266n, 272, 283–5, 321–2, 334–5, 337, 349, 351, 356, 365, 385–8, 396n, 420, 423, 440, 467, 485, 513, 607, 611, 637, 688, 786–7, 797, 853
programs and campaigns (advertising), 410, 427, 430–1, 439, 442, 476, 768, 775, 798–9, 803; *see also* advertising
propaganda, 392, 604, 621, 626
property (artistic and literary), 1, 3, 5–6, 12, 14, 20, 96, 102, 105, 117, 121, 131–2, 141, 147, 165, 180, 188, 212, 218–19, 226, 230–1, 239, 255, 313, 315–17, 346, 372, 393, 409, 440, 509, 512, 523, 527, 543, 545, 552, 561, 564–6, 568–9, 573, 575–6, 597, 616, 622, 637, 645, 661, 672, 680, 728, 730, 767, 774, 779, 828, 859
property (intellectual), 5, 280, 303, 544, 830–1
propriety, 83, 95, 107–8, 112, 142, 151, 325, 342–3, 345, 374, 691
Protestants, 105, 107, 190, 193, 195–7, 216n, 242, 786
psychology, 252, 253, 438, 490, 838
publicity and promotion, 11, 102, 105, 113, 115, 117–18, 120–1, 146, 151, 154, 166, 177, 221, 224, 226, 228, 240, 242, 244, 247, 250, 256–7, 312, 317, 319–22, 335, 343, 346, 354–6, 358, 363, 373–4, 376, 378, 382, 385, 388–9, 391–2, 415, 422, 432, 440, 462, 511, 512, 525, 536, 545, 547, 551, 565–6, 568, 570–1, 574, 577–8, 581, 583–4, 596, 599, 600, 601, 605, 606, 611, 618, 623, 630, 632, 633, 636, 638, 640, 662, 671, 673, 676, 681, 682, 703, 707–8, 729, 731, 759, 766–74, 769, 772, 775–6, 779, 783, 786, 790–1, 793–5, 798–9, 825, 848, 856–7
Puritans, 219, 270, 380

puzzles, 482, 637, 685, 728, 804–5

quality, 113, 131, 144, 148, 154, 188, 253, 273, 275, 289, 341, 356, 380, 409–10, 423, 425, 430–1, 434, 437–9, 442, 448, 458, 460, 465, 483, 581, 611, 693, 696, 745, 755, 762, 783, 798–9, 801, 825, 845–6

radio, 4, 297, 307, 409, 438, 550–1, 616, 629–32, 634, 658n, 661, 662–6, 668–9, 672, 675, 677, 685, 688–90, 712–13, 772, 777, 783, 788, 805, 807, 844–5, 857
radio programs and programming, 629–32, 662–3, 685, 688–90
readers and readership, 3, 6, 9, 30, 40, 50, 53, 58, 71, 83, 86, 90, 93, 103–4, 107, 109–12, 116–20, 126, 131, 142, 147, 154, 157, 163, 171, 188, 190–1, 194, 196–7, 201–3, 208, 211–12, 223, 242, 278, 296, 320, 347, 364, 368, 431–2, 438, 458, 460, 480, 511, 523, 530, 533, 543, 604, 615, 627–8, 673, 680, 682, 685, 690, 702, 711, 773, 793, 808, 844
readings and recitations, 21, 41, 115, 121–3, 125, 158, 167, 169–72, 207, 212, 218–22, 226, 228–30, 234, 238–40, 242, 251, 255, 258, 260, 262, 269, 272, 287, 289, 297, 305, 381, 420–1, 510–11, 519–21, 523, 526, 533, 548, 609, 626, 630, 674, 797; *see also* declamations; lectures; sermons
rebellion, 39, 59, 61, 62, 63, 65, 76, 93, 104, 198, 204, 206, 737, 741, 745, 747, 840
receipts, 5–6, 233, 267n, 315, 343, 346, 355, 358, 361, 362, 371–2, 374, 377, 383, 389, 391, 443, 532, 577, 601, 603–4, 607–8, 618, 661, 680, 778, 786
reception, 9, 111, 147, 150, 169, 189, 201, 212, 596, 610, 629, 783, 789, 790
recordings, 7, 288, 297–303, 305–6, 309n, 321, 454, 637, 678, 772, 777, 783, 797, 805–6, 829–31, 835, 841–3
reissues and rereleases, 11, 134n, 144, 160, 163, 180, 251, 292, 306, 618–19, 621, 624, 626, 691, 780, 786, 788, 792–793, 795–6, 798, 800, 806–7, 809, 841–2, 844, 848, 857

religion, 13, 20, 25, 39–40, 46–7, 51–4, 61–2, 68–9, 73, 79, 102–3, 108–11, 116, 118, 126, 131–3, 134n, 163–4, 177, 190–1, 193–4, 197, 203, 211, 213n, 232, 257, 259, 274, 314, 317, 320, 322, 341–6, 356, 358, 366, 370–1, 374, 379–82, 384, 387, 389–90, 414, 509, 513, 518, 520–1, 532, 540, 546–7, 588, 598, 616, 623–5, 663–4, 668, 673, 675, 680, 729, 744, 769, 772, 781–2, 790, 827, 832, 847, 855; *see also* theology
Religious Motion Picture Foundation, 616
remodeling, 337, 360, 775
Republicans, 41–2, 48, 50, 124, 232, 554, 675, 702
retail sales and retailers, 3, 9, 12–14, 102, 105, 115–16, 156, 175, 189, 209, 211, 250, 252, 254–5, 288, 296, 303, 351, 387, 408, 424–5, 429–30, 437, 440, 446, 458, 478, 480, 691–2, 696, 699, 799–801
revelation, 10, 25, 52, 189–90, 204, 332, 334, 358, 620, 845
revenues, 38, 369, 431, 471, 473, 607, 624, 731, 778, 786, 826, 828
reverence, 6–7, 47, 50, 83–4, 90, 104, 107, 109–13, 131, 133, 170, 190, 199, 218, 241–2, 249, 251, 322, 354, 356, 358, 371, 380, 382, 390, 414, 564–6, 582, 586, 599, 602, 621, 645, 763
Revised Statutes, 246, 548
rights (literary, dramatic, cinematic), 6, 7, 131, 156, 175, 227–9, 239, 245–6, 251, 312, 316, 321, 357, 367, 392, 409, 518, 523–5, 543, 561–6, 569, 571, 574, 613, 624, 637, 646n, 680, 774, 824, 835; *see also* authorizations, licenses, and permissions; copyright
River View Park, 462
roadshows, 351, 385, 572, 585, 596, 599, 603, 605, 607, 614, 616, 619, 624, 641, 645, 672, 680, 769, 776–7, 786–90, 824
rodeo, 634, 707, 808–9, 848
roller coasters, 7, 210, 409, 461–4, 490
Rome and Roman, 6–7, 12, 19, 22–4, 28–9, 31, 35, 38–9, 49, 53–4, 57–9, 61–7, 70, 73–84, 86–91, 93–5, 97, 99–100n, 103, 107, 118–19, 129, 131, 134, 152, 154–5, 164, 168, 170, 182, 198–204, 206–8, 211–16, 218, 223, 243, 248–50, 253, 270, 282–3,

287, 291, 299, 305–6, 313, 317, 322–4, 326, 328–34, 341, 348–9, 352–3, 372, 388, 409, 414, 416, 418, 420–2, 425, 434, 443, 448–9, 460, 465, 468–71, 473–5, 482, 493, 510–11, 514–15, 517, 522, 537, 539–41, 543, 545, 551, 553, 571–5, 578, 581, 583–4, 587–96, 600, 602, 606–7, 614, 619, 622, 624–5, 628–9, 638, 644, 663, 665–71, 673, 678, 681, 683, 689, 697, 699, 703–6, 708–10, 729–42, 744–8, 750–9, 761–8, 773, 775, 780, 783–5, 787, 789–92, 794–7, 799–802, 805–7, 809, 811, 827, 832, 836, 838–45, 848–50, 852, 855; see also anti-Roman politics
Rose Bowl, 471, 808
royalties, 6, 11, 13, 41, 96, 105, 117, 121, 130, 133, 138, 147–8, 150, 156–7, 165, 167, 172, 174, 182n, 228, 236, 256, 285, 286, 296, 315–16, 343, 345, 346, 371, 385, 389, 393, 413–14, 543, 564, 610, 729, 830
rumors, 117, 154, 234, 330, 369, 384, 561, 563–4, 569–71, 573–5, 577, 676, 681, 835
rural communities, 6, 8, 174–5, 188–9, 232, 240, 255, 355, 380–2, 456, 485, 532, 598, 616, 786

Sadducees, 59–60, 760
safety bicycle, 210, 304, 314, 457–8
St. Calixto, 211, 518; see also catacombs
St. Louis, 3, 124, 149, 222, 231, 240, 272, 311, 351, 360–3, 372, 378, 384, 387, 389, 391, 393, 420, 444, 447, 450, 465, 476, 480, 485–6, 542, 643
St. Petersburg, 339, 359, 372
sales, 2, 5–6, 11, 13, 32, 37, 90, 92, 96, 102, 104, 106, 110, 112, 115–19, 121, 123, 126, 130–1, 138, 141–2, 147–9, 151, 156, 159, 167, 173, 175, 178, 188–9, 209, 212, 227–8, 236, 244, 249–51, 253, 255, 256, 271, 285, 293–4, 296, 297, 305, 315, 348, 351, 353, 355, 367, 369, 371, 374, 376–9, 385–7, 392, 410, 422, 425, 427, 439, 443–4, 446, 448, 455, 457, 461, 467, 510, 525, 545, 551, 553, 564, 570, 607, 618, 624, 636, 642, 681, 686, 690, 692, 711, 772, 774–6, 788–80, 787, 791, 798–9, 826, 828–31, 846–7

salvation, 193–5, 206, 210, 216n
San Diego, 444–5, 541–2, 606, 688, 711–12, 719, 777, 785–6, 790, 841
San Francisco, 7, 229, 241, 259, 287–8, 296, 311, 317, 339, 351, 361, 382–3, 388, 391, 458, 486, 492n, 523, 529, 531, 601, 632, 679, 689, 708, 772
Santa Eulalia, 37
Santa Fe, 42–3, 55, 56, 59, 91, 112, 162, 169, 413, 466, 470, 488, 529, 627, 676
Satellites of Mercury, 230
scenery, 202, 233–5, 239, 241–2, 245, 250, 256, 281, 334, 337, 356, 368, 382–4, 389, 536, 575, 644, 855
schools and colleges, 13, 20–1, 24, 26, 31–2, 103, 110–12, 124, 128, 145, 149, 162, 168–9, 182n, 189, 193, 195, 210–11, 224–5, 240–3, 255, 259–60, 295, 387, 418–19, 421, 440, 443, 470–1, 486, 509, 511, 525, 528, 532, 585, 616, 618, 626, 630, 635, 665, 669, 673–5, 683–4, 691, 702, 708, 769–70, 772, 777, 808, 847; see also Sunday School
Scottish Rite temples, 250
scripts and screenplays, 6, 315–16, 318–19, 321, 323, 326, 535–6, 550, 576, 583, 663–6, 668–9, 730, 732–57, 759–63, 765–6, 768, 783–6, 795, 804–5, 807, 830, 836, 838–9, 843–4, 849, 857–9
seats and seating capacity, 86, 89–90, 123, 125, 158, 225, 235, 244, 248, 267n, 335, 354–5, 357, 360–1, 369, 371, 373–9, 390–1, 469, 475, 584, 593, 600, 617, 708, 771, 775–6, 778, 780, 802, 847, 853
Second Circuit Court, 524
Second Great Awakening, 192
Senate (Roman), 75, 83, 95, 596, 850; see also U. S. Senate
sermons, 51, 83, 169, 195–6, 208, 258, 367–8, 414, 416, 510, 516, 547, 617, 675; see also declamations; lectures; readings
Shanghai, 611, 621–2, 625, 644, 699
Shiloh, 34, 38, 41, 50, 92–5, 100–1, 103, 113, 120, 158, 677
slaves and slavery, 21, 30, 35, 69, 80, 171, 279, 282, 306, 324–6, 328, 331, 349, 388, 449, 511, 514, 540, 580, 587, 589, 591, 620, 663, 667–8, 683, 686, 707, 743–4, 746–7, 750–1, 754, 764–5, 794–5, 800, 806,

827, 834, 840, 845–6, 850, 852, 858
slogans, 425, 430–1, 434, 437–8, 442, 465, 688
smaller localities and venues, 383, 390
Social Darwinism, 203–8
Social Gospel Movement, 199, 205
songs, 72, 138, 207, 239, 243, 269, 271–9, 282–3, 305–7, 327, 420, 460, 527, 530–1, 534, 797, 846–7; see also art-song
souvenirs, 142, 166, 385, 420, 422–3, 506, 640, 644, 689, 787, 793, 797, 805, 836, 841, 846, 853
Soviet Union, 780
Spain, 21, 31, 37, 54, 206, 296, 610–11, 688, 759, 775
Spanish-American War, 206, 287–8
Spanish language, 40, 166, 270, 301, 805, 833
special features, 778, 813n, 840, 853
spectacles and spectaculars, 3, 201, 203, 218–20, 236–7, 241, 246–8, 252–3, 287, 311, 313, 320–1, 341–2, 345, 358, 363, 366, 380–1, 390, 392, 462, 470, 472, 527, 536, 545–6, 552, 597, 606, 614, 619–20, 631, 638–9, 644–5, 682, 729, 762, 772, 779–80, 847, 848
spectators, 4, 6–7, 9, 28–9, 224, 244–5, 329–30, 335, 389, 409, 455, 468, 471, 474, 482, 527, 568, 584, 593–4, 610, 634, 668, 770, 773, 788, 790, 802, 852–4, 856; see also crowds
speculators, 356, 377, 379
spina, 86–7, 100n, 335, 348, 431, 472, 584–5, 668, 670, 759, 770, 778, 802, 804, 852
sports, 218, 631, 705–7, 772, 805, 852, 855; see also Ben Hur sports teams
Stade de France, 851–2
stadia, 3, 80, 86–9, 100n, 328, 394, 425, 471, 711, 763, 801, 852–3
stages, 4, 10, 13–14, 41, 60, 104, 108, 200, 202, 219–1, 223, 225, 239–41, 256–8, 260–1, 264, 281, 284, 287, 297, 311–15, 320–5, 327–35, 337–9, 341–8, 350–4, 356–60, 362, 364, 367, 370, 373, 375–6, 380, 382, 384–6, 388, 392, 394, 398, 460–1, 473, 484, 533–6, 543, 545, 564–6, 572–3, 585, 589, 591–3, 597–601, 604–7, 611, 613–14, 616, 620, 628–9, 632, 636, 644, 676, 682, 686, 708,

stages (cont.)
  730, 766–7, 770, 792, 794, 846–7, 852, 855
Statuary Hall, 417, 768
stereopticon and (magic) lantern slides, 6, 138, 207, 212, 236, 250, 272, 367–8, 420–1, 430, 462, 509–35, 557, 616, 661, 666, 678
Stone-Campbell Movement, 190–4, 505
students, 104, 120, 145, 168–9, 189, 193, 295, 306, 381, 532, 616, 626, 631, 633, 674, 769, 773, 786, 789, 808
suburbs, 355, 367, 374, 431, 688, 701, 811
success, 1, 5–7, 9–14, 19–20, 26, 32, 38, 40, 47–8, 86, 90–1, 96, 102, 104–5, 110, 113, 115, 116, 123, 125, 127, 140–1, 146, 148–9, 156–7, 160, 163–4, 169, 188–9, 198–9, 202–3, 208, 211–12, 225, 231, 233–5, 243, 251, 281, 283, 286, 289–90, 292, 294, 297, 312, 314, 317, 320, 342–3, 357, 361, 363, 366–7, 370–2, 376, 380, 382, 409–10, 412, 419, 423–4, 438, 475, 512, 527, 530, 532, 543, 552, 562, 564, 570, 575, 577, 603–4, 608, 613, 616, 623–4, 627, 636–8, 644–5, 672, 679, 699, 709, 728, 730, 731–2, 760, 770, 773–4, 778–9, 781, 786–91, 804–6, 811, 824–5, 829, 858–9
suffrage, 25, 192,195, 213n, 240
Sundays, 25, 125, 163, 191–2, 240, 295, 358, 360, 367–8, 375–6, 378, 384, 412, 425, 430, 440, 442, 454, 529, 551, 585, 595–6, 610, 616–17, 625, 630, 631, 664, 667, 710, 732, 760, 765, 776, 825–6, 828, 835
Sunday School, 110, 149, 189, 229, 260, 295, 525, 674
Sydney, 296, 305–6, 311, 339, 359, 363–8, 385, 400n, 468, 529, 611, 853, 856
synergies, 5, 7, 11–13, 20, 166, 180, 226–7, 231, 234, 249–55, 300, 304, 314, 348, 373, 384–7, 420–2, 430, 460, 475, 527, 531, 533, 542, 551, 569, 611, 637–43, 661, 728, 774, 778, 793, 797–8, 824
Syria, 62, 64–5, 74–6, 80, 84, 86, 166, 274, 628

tableaux, 6, 170, 219–24, 227–61, 287, 289, 297, 314, 321, 347, 350, 352, 353, 370, 420, 448, 510, 523, 709; see also Ben-Hur, in Tableaux and Pantomime

Tarzana, 489
taste, 25, 30, 96, 107–9, 113, 144, 167, 170, 270–1, 355, 429, 602, 644, 780, 790
technicians, 577, 585, 642, 644, 855
Technicolor, 578, 587–8, 595–6, 602, 613, 619, 624, 644, 680–1, 729, 751, 777, 834–5
technologies, 3, 140, 209, 252, 297, 305, 454, 456, 509, 510, 533–4, 544, 551, 616–18, 661–3, 679, 728, 824–5, 829–31, 833, 835, 845–6, 848, 856
tedium, 32, 104, 109, 126–7, 221, 228, 370
television, 1, 4, 11, 164, 297, 409, 438, 551, 662, 681, 682, 695, 729, 765, 772, 774, 786, 788, 790, 798–9, 802–4, 807, 812, 825–31, 833–7, 839, 848–51, 858–9
television programs and programming, 690, 798, 804, 825–30, 833, 835
temperance, 25, 225, 513
Texas, 3, 7, 30–1, 229, 295, 304, 383, 411, 444, 451, 453, 455, 457, 488–9, 711, 777, 832
theater arts, 9, 219–21, 225, 230, 237, 251, 257, 311–13, 315, 317, 319, 339, 342–5, 348, 361–4, 366, 368, 370, 374, 381, 385, 392–3, 456, 511, 525, 528, 534, 548, 561–6, 580, 598, 601, 607, 614, 632, 637, 640, 662, 779, 847–8, 853
themes, 10, 38–9, 103, 113, 118, 284, 289, 292, 298, 322, 324–6, 331, 339, 347, 371, 414, 439, 464, 602, 631, 669, 689–90, 702, 769, 796, 832, 840–1, 843–4
theology, 12, 61, 69, 190–2, 194, 196, 206, 272, 333, 625; see also religion
thoroughbreds, 338, 381, 632, 635–6, 707, 808
Tiberias, 80
tickets and admissions, 35, 52, 110, 125, 225, 244, 248–50, 257, 311, 343, 355–7, 361–3, 371, 373–9, 382–3, 385, 387, 390–2, 456, 461, 467, 469, 532–3, 572, 598, 603–4, 606–7, 610, 615–16, 680, 707, 711, 774, 776, 777–80, 787–9, 791, 801, 841, 846–7, 853
tie-ins, 1, 12, 253, 387, 409, 482, 569, 598, 639, 641, 728, 766, 787–805
Tijuana, 486–7, 636
Titanic, 258, 448
toga plays, 10
Tokyo, 775, 780, 789, 836
Tom shows, 12

touring, 5–6, 41, 46, 120, 123–7, 138, 157, 159, 203, 227, 235, 240, 345, 359–62, 367, 375, 378, 382–4, 392–3, 484, 511, 603, 662, 708, 711, 767, 805, 846–7, 856
Tournament of Roses, 420, 468–70, 689, 808
tours, 5, 123, 157, 159, 392, 393
trademarks, 5, 13, 209–10, 251, 280, 408, 423, 427, 429, 431, 439–40, 443, 445, 458–61, 478, 698, 805
trains and railroads, 3, 34, 50, 66, 97, 124, 127, 163, 210, 243, 245, 312, 338, 355–6, 361, 363, 373–5, 378–9, 381, 386, 392, 401, 408, 455–7, 470, 490, 551, 584, 597, 678, 703–4, 759
translation, 12, 22–3, 28, 30, 48, 60–1, 71, 80–1, 89–90, 99, 105, 129, 134, 138, 146–9, 164, 166–7, 182, 197, 227, 314, 344, 543, 569, 575, 583, 611, 688, 778, 795, 806
treadmills, 166, 314, 335–6, 338, 358, 363, 385, 597, 620, 632, 678, 686, 708, 853
triumph, 60–1, 78–9, 82, 87, 155, 168, 189, 172, 211, 240, 249, 317, 330, 332, 434, 438, 458, 539, 541–2, 585, 587, 597, 613–14, 627–8, 668, 750–1, 756, 761, 765; see also victory
trolleys, 3, 457
tune sheets, 297–8, 302
Turkey, 5, 115, 117, 120–2, 124–7, 157–9, 245, 523

universalism, 40, 69–70, 203–6, 527
University of Iowa Libraries, 245
University of Virginia Library, 272

Vaudeville, 295, 387–8, 392, 451, 530, 534, 614–16, 618, 622, 629
vengeance, 53, 60, 87, 93, 95, 154, 196, 210, 324, 329, 331, 333, 339, 572, 591, 608, 664, 669–70, 736, 742, 746, 769, 838, 845, 850, 853
venues, 86, 88–9, 100, 124, 158, 171, 212, 225, 241, 243, 247, 251, 255, 269, 287–8, 298, 311, 316, 337, 357, 360, 372, 375, 383, 390, 456, 462, 468, 528, 544, 548, 633, 775–7, 780, 811, 847, 851, 853, 855–6
victory, 31–2, 34, 41, 62, 65, 78, 82, 90, 104, 122, 170, 172, 177, 224, 232, 258, 285, 287, 291, 326, 330, 335, 339, 362, 409, 430, 434–5,

Index

437, 439, 455, 458, 465, 468–70, 484, 547, 549, 587, 593–4, 602, 629, 644, 663, 668–71, 682–3, 689, 691, 703–4, 706–8, 720n, 743, 755, 764–5, 772, 782–3, 794, 796, 808, 811, 827–8, 834, 836, 844, 849; see also triumph
video games, 551, 856
video recording, 550, 825, 828–33, 835–7, 841, 848
villainy, 7, 60, 73–4, 195, 199–201, 213n, 352, 370, 580, 608–9, 738, 745, 840
Virginia, 226, 288, 363, 381, 489, 532, 617, 699
visibility, 7, 175, 195, 213n, 373, 385, 423, 431, 443, 635, 690, 695, 728, 800

Wabash River, 21
WAMPAS Frolic, 632
Washington (state), 7, 444–5, 456, 476, 528, 690, 809, 834
Washington, DC, 37, 40, 48, 86, 88–9, 95, 147, 152, 207, 220, 222, 224–5, 227–8, 233, 256, 258–60, 372, 288, 295, 304, 362–3, 391, 417–18, 445, 518, 527, 529–30, 532, 601, 607, 617, 620, 633, 675, 684, 691, 775, 780, 789–90, 828, 830, 836, 841, 857
websites, 3, 192, 261, 303, 423, 457, 476, 692–3, 698, 709, 842, 847, 856–7
wheelchair, 107–8, 668, 710
White House, 41, 94, 153, 206, 675
Wichita Forum, 475

widescreen format, 729, 774–5, 829
women, 10, 23, 49, 108, 158, 170, 177, 192, 213n, 219–20, 233, 248–9, 260–1, 266n, 276–7, 306, 388, 411, 414–15, 417–18, 437, 451, 457, 468, 510, 529, 573, 582, 600, 639–40, 663, 692, 710, 765, 772, 778, 852
World War I, 391, 465
World War II, 3, 412, 662, 664, 683, 692, 694
World Year, 24
World's Fairs, 162, 384, 387, 391, 420, 447, 679
World's Parliament of Religions, 203

Zealots, 60, 62–4, 67–8, 745, 850

BEN-HUR INDEX

Amrah, 57, 64, 66, 108, 222, 229, 233, 262, 282, 319, 321, 324, 326, 331–2, 360, 511, 515–17, 520, 540, 589–90, 666–7, 733, 746, 807, 832
Arrius, Quintus, 57–8, 66, 77–80, 82, 95, 99, 153, 155, 206, 210, 222, 243, 259–60, 321, 324–6, 331, 333–4, 341, 347, 349, 385, 398, 415–16, 449, 511, 514–17, 537, 539–41, 586–7, 614, 663, 665, 668, 671, 732–3, 736–7, 743–5, 747, 750–2, 754–6, 758, 761–5, 767, 805, 807, 832, 838, 842, 845, 848, 850, 852
Athene, 850–1

Balthasar, 7, 35, 39, 54, 56, 58–9, 64, 67–70, 74, 98, 125, 128, 142, 190, 222, 234, 274, 282, 321–2, 326, 328–9, 331, 333, 349, 351–2, 386, 415, 516–18, 521, 540, 572, 587, 595, 666, 669–70, 732–3, 736–8, 746–8, 752, 754, 756, 762, 795, 803–4, 832–3, 844–5, 848–9
beech tree, 38, 55–6, 413, 421–2, 518, 778–9
Belasco & Robson Ben Hur Company, 391
Ben-Hur (1899), 1, 3, 6, 10, 13, 15, 115, 166, 173, 231, 244, 255–7, 269, 279–81, 286–7, 289, 296–7, 305, 311–94, 410, 420, 423–4, 439, 447, 456, 461–2, 469, 473, 475–6, 483, 488, 510, 532–34, 536, 542–3, 545–7, 552, 563–4, 566, 569, 573, 579, 592–3, 596–602, 608,

610, 614, 620, 630, 632, 636, 644, 661–2, 669, 672, 676, 678–9, 685, 693, 738, 759–60, 771, 775, 779, 786, 789, 794, 796, 809, 836, 851; see also Klaw & Erlanger
Ben-Hur (1907), 7, 10, 13, 127, 172–3, 228, 250, 303, 419, 462, 473, 509, 525, 534–52, 557–8, 561–2, 568, 571, 590–1, 594, 661, 677, 767, 773, 830–1, 834, 836, 859
Ben-Hur (1925), 1, 10, 13, 106, 108, 147, 223, 261, 292, 306, 323, 340, 394, 483, 486, 488, 550, 561–661, 667, 669, 674, 679–82, 691, 699, 703, 729, 739, 746, 750–1, 759, 763, 767, 769, 773, 775, 779, 781–2, 790–1, 793–4, 796, 806, 809, 832, 834–6, 841, 849–51, 858–9
synchronized sound version, 562, 599, 617–21, 624, 679, 728, 782
Ben-Hur (1931), 630–1, 662
Ben-Hur (1937), 662–3
Ben-Hur (1940), 664–5
Ben-Hur (1959), 1, 3, 9, 11, 14, 108, 164, 293, 296, 311, 338, 372, 551, 584, 592, 597, 607, 624, 644, 662, 681, 686, 690, 692–3, 695, 700, 704, 713, 728–812, 825–30, 832–42, 849–52, 857–9
Ben-Hur (2002), 857
Ben-Hur (2003), 831–2
Ben-Hur (2008), 857
Ben-Hur (2010), 849–51
Ben-Hur (2012), 857
Ben-Hur (2016), 1, 4–5, 812, 858–9

Ben-Hur - Blood of Braves, 856
Ben-Hur agency, 458
Ben-Hur: An Evangelistic Musical Stage Production of the Classical Novel, 847–8
Ben-Hur as a historical person, 469, 671, 683, 710, 808
Ben-Hur: A Tale of the Christ, Tale of the Christ (1880), 1–2, 5, 8–11, 13–17, 19, 21–2, 24–5, 27–8, 30–2, 35, 38–41, 46, 50, 54, 57–9, 62, 77, 79, 82, 85, 91–4, 97–8n, 102, 108, 110, 112–13, 115, 118, 120, 123, 125–30, 133, 138, 140–1, 144–5, 150–1, 156–9, 162–5, 167–8, 171–4, 180, 188–90, 192, 196–7, 199, 203, 206–12, 224, 226–7, 230–1, 235, 241–2, 245, 251, 256, 260, 269–70, 275, 280–1, 287, 305, 312, 332, 345, 351, 379, 408–9, 412, 414–15, 421, 423, 425, 428, 437, 455, 466, 483–4, 489, 509–10, 512, 516, 528–9, 535, 608, 627–8, 637–8, 644, 663, 666, 673–5, 686, 760, 769, 831, 853
Boys' Ben-Hur, The, 422, 627, 634
Garfield edition, 5, 13, 113–14, 151–9, 173–4, 177, 180, 202, 215, 251–2, 305, 350–1, 386, 434, 460, 482, 600, 673, 844, 857
Player's Edition, The, 166, 174, 321, 351–3, 351–3, 365, 385–6, 391
Wallace Memorial Edition, 6, 172–4, 177–80
Ben Hur apartments, 7, 413, 486, 490, 507, 702

Ben-Hur Athletic Association, 488
Ben-Hur auto repair, 642, 856
Ben-Hur Auto Service, 858
Ben-Hur automobiles, 3, 164, 408, 410, 435, 455, 464–6, 635, 637, 703–4, 710
Ben-Hur Avenue, 465, 488
Ben-Hur Bakelite, 3, 15, 698
Ben-Hur Baking Powder, 440–2, 489
Ben-Hur Bazaar, 485
Ben-Hur Beer, 445, 490
Ben-Hur Bicycles, 3, 164, 280, 304, 314, 408, 410, 457–61, 464, 478, 490, 696, 704
Ben-Hur Bitters, 445, 496
Ben-Hur Blouse Company, 643, 697, 799
Ben-Hur board games, 482, 490, 728
Ben-Hur boats, 7, 15, 21, 222, 274, 329, 353, 366, 411, 420, 449–56, 483, 489–91, 498, 568, 580, 592, 611, 683, 689, 704, 710, 811
Ben-Hur Bottling Company, 698
Ben-Hur bridges, 3, 488–9
Ben Hur buggy blankets, 448
Ben Hur bulls, 3, 484
Ben Hur Café, 486–8
Ben-Hur Calendar, 348, 423
Ben Hur Camp, 488
Ben-Hur Cantata, 7, 280–3, 734
Ben Hur Case, The, 543, 546, 549
Ben Hur catsup, 444, 698
Ben Hur Champagne Bar, 856
Ben Hur chewing tobacco, 3, 427–8
Ben Hur China, 3, 688
Ben-Hur Cigars, 1, 3, 4, 8, 15, 140, 255, 408, 424–8, 442, 475, 493, 699, 856
Ben Hur Circle, 412, 691
Ben Hur clocks, 3, 422, 480–1, 643
Ben Hur Clothing Company, 643, 697
Ben-Hur Clubs, 343, 355
Ben Hur Coal Company, 476
Ben-Hur Coffee, Teas, & Spices (and Extracts), 3, 7, 424, 440–5, 454, 456, 489, 640–2, 662, 666, 686–90, 779
Ben Hur Company of Albuquerque, 388
Ben Hur composition books, 483, 490
Ben Hur Construction Company, 3, 393, 409, 424, 475–6, 643
Ben Hur Day, 387, 420, 467
Ben Hur Divide Mining Company, 476
Ben Hur dogs, 3, 140, 484, 633, 635
Ben-Hur Dough Boys, 434–7, 439–40

Ben Hur Drive, 488
Ben Hur Drive-in, 702
Ben Hur Estates, 701–2
Ben-Hur Extracts *see* Ben-Hur Coffee
Ben Hur farms, 486, 708, 811
Ben Hur fences, 478–80, 698
Ben-Hur Fishing Club, 478
Ben-Hur Flour, 1, 3, 7–8, 15, 32, 139–40, 152, 255, 386, 408, 424, 428–40, 442, 444, 495, 531, 661
Ben Hur fly reels, 477–8
Ben-Hur Ford, 811
Ben-Hur Freezers, 3, 662, 666, 693–4
Ben Hur Genuine Black Band Splint, 477
Ben Hur gladiola, 485
Ben Hur goats, 484
Ben Hur Gold Mining Company, 476
Ben Hur groceries, 485, 702
Ben Hur Hair products, 662, 686, 695–6
Ben-Hur halls, 255, 392, 486, 490, 509, 532, 548, 691
Ben Hur hardware, 408, 461, 477–8, 480, 490, 696–7
Ben-Hur Harnesses, 3–4, 478
Ben Hur Highway, 488
Ben Hur Horse Feed, 439
Ben-Hur Horse & Mule Feed, 439
Ben Hur Horses, The, 786
Ben Hur hotels and motels, 485–7, 490, 636, 702
Ben-Hur, in Tableaux and Pantomime, 1, 6, 108, 138, 157–8, 166, 171, 218, 231–58, 269, 286, 289, 296, 314–16, 347, 387, 424, 520, 523, 524, 526, 661
Ben Hur Lane, 488
Ben Hur lap robe, 448
Ben Hur Leasing Company, 476
Ben Hur Life Association, 419
Ben Hur Live, 854–6
Ben-Hur lodges, 3, 411–12, 417, 525, 691, 856
Ben Hur manufacturing, 3, 448, 483, 666, 686, 692–4
Ben Hur marches, 304–6, 460, 629; *see also* Paull
"Ben-Hur Marsch," 306, 629
Ben-Hur Marine Guards, 422
Ben-Hur Match Company, 467
Ben-Hur Metal Polish Company, 466
Ben-Hur Mining Company, 476
Ben Hur Motor Company, 454, 464
Ben Hur Moving & Storage, 856
Ben-Hur name, 3, 5, 71, 255, 280, 385, 410–11, 423, 443, 477, 484, 490, 681, 687, 690–1, 697, 701, 811
Ben Hur narcissus, 711
Ben Hur oil companies, 699, 477

Ben Hur Oranges, 3–4, 444, 490
"Ben-Hur Overture," 305
"Ben Hur Patrol," 306
Ben Hur Perfume, 3, 15, 446–7, 489, 638–41, 643, 691–2, 799
Ben-Hur petroleum companies, 408, 477, 490, 699–701
Ben-Hur phenomenon and tradition, 2, 3, 5–6, 9, 11, 15, 83, 91, 111, 113, 116, 133, 138, 140, 175, 180, 188, 212, 224, 225, 226, 231, 234, 239, 251, 255, 271–2, 280, 287–8, 296–8, 300, 305, 307, 311, 314, 345, 361, 368, 372–3, 379, 388, 408–9, 424, 454–5, 462, 467, 532–3, 535, 550, 564, 566–9, 596, 602, 606, 610, 614, 618, 626, 629–30, 636–7, 642, 668, 676, 686, 690, 696, 773, 777–9, 781, 794, 809, 811, 834–5, 847, 856, 859
Ben Hur pigs, 3, 140, 484
Ben Hur pinball, 698, 856–7
Ben-Hur pirates, 546–7
Ben-Hur Plus grand que la legend, 851–4
Ben Hur Ponies, 629
Ben-Hur Products, Inc., 698–9
Ben Hur Purse, 448
Ben Hur python, 484
"Ben Hur Quickstep," 304
Ben Hur Racer, 462–4, 467–8, 472
Ben Hur Racing Coaster Company, 464
Ben Hur razors, 447–8, 489, 641, 699
"Ben Hur's Ride," 304
Ben Hur Road, 488
Ben-Hur roller coasters, 461–4; *see also* Ben Hur Racer
Ben-Hur Route, 456
Ben Hur Rubber & Tire Company, 466
Ben-Hur Rye, 445
Ben Hur Sachets, 446
Ben Hur salmon, 444–5, 489, 687, 698
Ben Hur Savings & Loan, 701
Ben-Hur Scrap, 428
Ben-Hur serenades, 276–8, 307n
Ben Hur sewing machines, 3–4, 478
Ben Hur sheep, 484
Ben Hur shoes, 448–9, 697
Ben Hur Shoe Polish, 3–4, 448, 489
Ben-Hur Shrines and Shriners, 3, 140, 162, 250, 304, 306, 410–12, 419, 456, 491n, 498n, 632, 691, 708, 856
Ben Hur Sigarenfabrieken, 699
Ben-Hur slot machine, 482
Ben-Hur Soap, 441, 445, 489, 640, 662, 691
Ben-Hur - Souvenir Album, 321–2, 335, 348–51, 353

Index

Ben Hur Specials, 456, 466
Ben-Hur Spices *see* Ben-Hur Coffee
Ben Hur Sports Shop, 702
Ben Hur sports teams, 477, 487–8, 490
Ben Hur Stables, 632, 636, 679, 707
Ben Hur Steel Racing Car, 467
Ben-Hur sterling, 483
Ben Hur Street, 488
Ben-Hur Suite, 797
Ben Hur Suits, 253
Ben-Hur Sulky Wheels, 458
Ben-Hur Supper Club, 808
Ben-Hur tableaux, 221, 226–9, 231, 235–6, 241, 243–4, 250, 272, 287, 292, 353, 420; *see also Ben-Hur, in Tableaux and Pantomime*
Ben-Hur Talcum Powder, 599, 638, 691
Ben-Hur Tea, 442, 642; *see also* Ben-Hur Coffee
Ben-Hur Team Harness, 478
Ben Hur Temple, 3, 411–12
Ben-Hur: The Latter Years – Miriam and Vespasian, 857
Ben-Hur: The Making of an Epic, 829, 836
Ben-Hur The Musical, 846–7
Ben Hur Thundering Third Chariot Race, 856
Ben Hur tobacco, 408, 427–8, 489, 637
Ben Hur Tomatoes, 3, 444, 489
Ben Hur Tomato Catsup, 444, 698
Ben Hur tools, 3, 490, 696
Ben Hur Trailer, 3, 662, 692–4, 721
Ben-Hur Transfer, 704
Ben-Hur Union, 412, 491n
Ben-Hur vivant, 805–7
"Ben Hur Waltzes," 277, 305
Ben Hur watches, 3, 387, 480–2, 490, 642, 697
Ben-Hur Weathered Oak Wall Clock, 428
Ben Hur whiskey, 3–4, 445, 489

"Charioteer, The," 304–5
"Chariot Race or Ben Hur March, The," 288–303; *see also* Paull
"Chariot Race, The," 283–8; *see also* Sousa

Devadasi, 326, 328
Drusus, 259, 321, 328, 330, 349, 353, 671, 734, 736, 742, 744

editions, 2, 5–6, 11, 13, 84, 113–20, 124, 130–3, 135n, 137n, 138, 140–59, 166–8, 172–80, 182n, 186n, 202, 212, 227, 235, 246, 251, 280, 292–3, 295–6, 305–6, 321, 350–4, 365, 367, 385–6, 391, 420–1, 425, 434, 460, 482, 611, 618, 626–7, 637, 672–3, 677, 728, 768, 772, 791–3, 797–8, 829, 835–6, 841, 843–4, 857
"Egyptian Song: From 'Ben-Hur,'" 279
Esther, 7, 21, 35, 39, 53, 58, 66, 73–4, 99n, 108–9, 163, 184n, 191, 212, 222–3, 233–4, 246, 259, 274, 282, 318, 320–1, 326, 328–33, 344, 348–9, 352–3, 402n, 457, 511, 515–17, 521, 563, 572, 586–7, 589, 592–3, 595–7, 615, 663, 665–6, 668, 670, 709, 732–3, 735–9, 745–8, 750, 752, 754, 761, 765, 767, 779, 794, 803, 807, 840–1, 847–51
"Evening With Ben-Hur, An," 6, 220–9, 258, 529

Flavia, 751, 762, 767

Gaspar, 68–9, 98, 103, 128, 142, 194, 322, 333, 572, 739, 748, 754
Gratus, Valerius, 39, 49, 57, 64–6, 74, 77–8, 81, 95, 152, 323, 352, 416, 589–90, 736–7, 742, 744–5, 758, 804, 849

"Histoire de Ben-Hur, L'," 277, 806
House of Hur, 22, 57–8, 60, 71, 102, 259, 349, 511, 537, 539, 586, 588–9, 745, 747, 752, 754, 759, 761, 765, 850–2
"How I Came to Write *Ben-Hur*," 46–50, 52–6, 63–4, 68, 71–3, 77–9, 88, 97n, 157–8, 165, 190, 229, 317, 434, 467, 576

Ilderim, 39, 56, 58, 64–5, 74, 86, 89, 128, 177, 222, 258, 281–2, 321, 326, 328, 332, 343, 347, 349–50, 511, 514, 517, 540, 572, 587, 592, 638, 671, 732–3, 742, 745–7, 752–3, 756, 758, 762, 764, 809, 833, 845, 848
Iras [and Iris], 7, 39, 58–9, 66, 73–4, 76, 93, 108–9, 125, 152, 168, 197, 208, 214, 222–3, 234, 239, 243, 246, 247–9, 258–9, 266, 272–4, 279, 281–2, 319, 321, 328–31, 333–4, 339, 348–9, 351–3, 393, 511, 514–15, 517–18, 521, 528, 540, 572–3, 586, 592–3, 601–2, 611, 638–9, 663–4, 670, 681, 736, 738, 748, 752, 754, 762, 792, 795, 804, 807, 809, 832, 844–5, 850, 857
Ithamar, 71–2, 78, 82, 321, 324, 326, 734

Judah Ben-Hur (2002), 847–8
Judas Ben-Hur, 10

"Kapila," 272–3

"Lament, The," 272–6, 279–80, 329, 393–4
Little Ben-Hur, 425

Madonna and Mary, 59, 63, 68, 79, 98n, 125, 134n, 178, 246, 261, 342, 514, 516, 522, 582, 588–9, 596, 663, 768
Marcellus, 796
Marcellus Agrippa, 850–1
Melchior, 68–70, 98n, 128, 142, 272, 322, 333, 516, 572
Messala [Messalla], 7, 24, 28, 39, 49, 53–4, 57–60, 64–7, 74–8, 81–2, 86–90, 93, 99, 103, 107, 110, 154, 170–1, 177, 206, 208, 210, 222, 227, 233, 243–4, 249, 259–60, 263, 270, 273, 281–2, 284, 287, 291, 319, 321, 323–4, 326–31, 333–5, 337–9, 344, 349, 352, 360, 382, 388, 416, 510–11, 515, 517, 521–2, 536–41, 572–3, 579–80, 585–6, 589–90, 592–4, 600, 619, 625, 629–31, 633–5, 662–71, 673, 681, 704, 706, 709, 731–7, 739–42, 744–50, 752, 754, 756–8, 760–1, 764–5, 779, 794–5, 804–7, 809, 811–12, 832–3, 836, 838–9, 843–5, 849–52, 857
mother of Ben-Hur, 7, 22–3, 49, 53–4, 57–9, 61–62, 65–6, 70–1, 83, 93, 108, 165, 171, 177, 190, 207, 213n, 219, 222–3, 237, 243, 249, 258, 260, 262n, 270, 281–2 [Jerusha], 321, 323–5, 329, 331–2, 334, 349, 352–3, 360, 384, 391, 415–16, 511, 514–17, 519–20, 528, 540, 572, 586–7, 589–92, 594–6, 600, 614–15, 638, 663–7, 670, 733, 736–8, 740 [Miriam], 741–2, 747–8, 751–3, 758, 764–5, 794, 804–5, 807, 827, 833, 837, 844, 848, 851 [Ruth]

Nativity, 7, 24, 52–4, 58, 62, 64, 68, 104, 520, 582, 586–8, 594, 667, 674, 733, 763, 771, 792, 826, 832, 838, 848–9
Nazarene, 109, 223, 234, 281, 331–2, 334, 353, 413, 415

Orchard of Palms, 210, 243, 249, 281, 326, 334, 347, 514, 540, 587, 592, 752

Passion of Christ, the, 47, 50, 53, 59, 105, 241, 342, 513, 561, 595

Pontiac Sunfire commercial, 858
Prince Ben Hur, Mental Genius, 631

Quarrel (episode), 49, 57–8, 65, 77, 233, 249, 270, 281, 323, 328, 352, 589–90, 593, 595, 663–4, 667, 669, 732–5, 739, 749, 754, 760, 761, 764, 832, 836, 838–9, 844

Rabbi Samuel, 63, 128, 246, 356
Race to Glory, A, 832–3, 849
Raft (episode), 349, 602, 670, 733, 744, 762, 764, 794, 832
Referendum for the Illustrations in the Garfield Edition of General Lew Wallace's Novel "Ben-Hur," 155

Schenectady program, 252–3, 448
Sea Battle (episode), 53, 113, 389, 511, 514–15, 579–80, 586–7, 596–7, 617–18, 644, 682, 782, 846; *see also* galleys
Seekers After "The Light" From "Ben-Hur," 13, 106, 138–9, 141–2, 227, 235, 271, 423, 672
Simonides, 21, 35, 39, 53, 56, 58–60, 64–5, 73–4, 89, 103, 108, 210, 222, 227, 233–4, 242, 246, 249, 259–60, 319, 321, 323, 326, 328–31, 333–4, 341, 343, 347, 349, 352–3, 360, 369, 378, 383, 386, 399–400, 402, 416, 421, 511, 514–15, 517, 521, 572, 586–7, 589, 591–2, 627, 630, 665, 668, 678, 709, 732–3, 736–8, 742–3, 745–7, 751–2, 754, 761, 794, 807, 832, 845, 850
Smoke's Ben Hur Soda Grill, 486
Society of Ben Hur, 412
Star of David, 761

Taylor Ben Hur Coal Company, 476
Theus, 69
Thord, 39, 78, 90, 223, 249, 281–2, 333, 364, 595, 734, 850
"Three Dances from Ben Hur," 306
Tile incident (episode), 22–3, 49, 54, 57–8, 65, 77, 94, 104, 107, 219, 222, 230, 243, 323, 514–15, 538–40, 589–90, 595, 663–4, 670, 709, 733–4, 745, 756, 761, 764, 794–5, 807, 832, 837–8, 844, 849, 851
Tirzah, 39, 56–7, 64, 66, 72–3, 90–1, 108, 196, 207, 222–3, 233, 243, 247, 249, 259, 266, 270, 272, 276, 278–82, 304, 321, 323–5, 331, 349, 386, 411, 416, 511, 514–17, 586, 589, 614, 663, 666, 678, 732, 734, 740, 745–6, 748, 750, 752, 754, 757, 795, 807, 838, 849
"Tirzah's Serenade," 276–7
Tower of Antonia, 152, 331, 416, 515, 520, 739, 741, 748, 754, 758–9, 761, 764
Tribe of Ben-Hur, 3, 6–7, 138, 226, 232, 255, 261, 265, 306, 314, 320–1, 381, 387, 408, 412–24, 462, 467, 483, 488, 491–3, 518, 525, 528, 530–2, 542, 627, 686, 691
"Tribe of Ben-Hur March," 306

UHF stations, 825, 828–9, 833, 835

Via Dolorosa, 596, 746, 757, 764, 773

"Wake not, but hear me, Love," 72, 266n, 269–74, 276–8, 280, 512, 530, 734
Wise Men, 7, 27, 46–7, 52, 57, 63, 67–70, 84, 98, 104, 128, 141–2, 165, 177–8, 201, 203, 211, 222, 229–30, 233, 235, 242, 249, 322, 326, 334, 347, 352, 354, 427, 477, 514–15, 518, 572, 574, 587, 595, 709, 733, 739, 792

Xfinity commercial, 858

PERSONAL NAMES, COMPANIES, INSTITUTIONS, SOCIETIES, AND UNIONS INDEX

ABC, 690, 828, 834, 851
Abraham, Franz, 855–6
Academy of Motion Picture Arts and Sciences, 835
Achilles, 28
Acorn Industries, 801–3
Ademollo, Carlo, 490n
Adès, Lucien, 807
A. Hoen Lithograph Company, 288, 292
Aiken, George, 12
Ajax, 253
Albert, Ernest, 334, 399n
Alden, Henry, 106, 119, 150–1
Alden, Herbert, 626
Aldrich, George, 13, 114, 145
Aldrich, Thomas Bailey, 126–7, 275
Alexander the Great, 28, 78
Alger, Horatio, 216n
Alison, George, 360
Allen, J. W., 259
Allen, L. L., 464
Allen, W. W., 219, 313
Alma-Tadema, Lawrence, 587
American Colotype Company, 349
American Express, 778
American Film Institute, 835
American Humane Association, 782
American Palestine Exploration Society, 202
American Printing-House for the Blind, 144, 181
American Tract Society, 197
Amosophic Society, 29
Amyot, Jacques, 23
Anacreon, 103
Ananus *see* Hannas
Anderson, Gillian, 841
Anderson, Maxwell, 733, 746–8, 813n, 838
Anderson, W. L., 250
Antony, Mark, 73, 75–6, 394, 796
Apollo, 154, 249, 327, 347, 350, 385, 397n, 592, 701
Apthorp, William P., 356
Arcaro, Eddie, 706
Armándola, Jose [Wilhelm August Lautenschläger], 306, 629
Armstrong, Louis Oliver, 512–13
Aronson, Alexander, 581
Ashley, Glenn W., 304
Astor, Mary, 689
Astor, Vincent, 566
Atlantic Cigar, 856
Augustus, 62, 73, 75–6, 78, 414, 739
Autier, Joseph, 182n
Avery, Sewell, 168
Axt, William, 599, 614, 629–30, 657, 796, 841

Babgy, B. P., 464
Bainforth & Havlin, 376–7
Balkin, Harry H., 689
Ball, Lucille, 838
Ballentine Beer, 703
Ballets Africans, Les, 767
Bally, Juliane, 843
Balzar, Fred B., 634
Bara, Theda, 394, 573
Barden, Lura, 526
Barkley, Thomas J., 440–1
Barnard, Charles, 313
Barnum, P.T., 157, 337, 468, 679, 709
Barrett, Albert A., 454

Index

Barrett, Lawrence, 98n, 116, 218, 317
Barrett, Wilson, 163, 219, 528
Barrymore, John, 584
Barrymore, Lionel, 584, 710
Bartlett, Elisha P., 451
Baum, L. Frank, 12, 676
Baworowski, Antonio C., 146, 148
Baz, Ben-Hur, 483
BBC, 826, 857
Beach, Rex, 562
Beal, John, 666
Beale, Joseph Boggs, 513, 515–16, 518, 678
Beatty, Clyde, 666
Beaumont, William L., 628
Beckley, Paul V., 782
Bede, 67–8, 98
Beecher, Henry Ward, 51, 194–5, 198–9
Beecher, Lyman, 195
Beecher, Willis, 121
Behlmer, Rudy, 568, 836
Behr, Siegfried, 643, 693, 695
Behrman, S. N., 733, 747–53
Beissenherz, Henry D., 280
Bell & Howell, 585, 640
Bell, E. Hamilton, 319
Bell, Frank, 476
Bell Syndicate, 667
Belmont, Joe, 299–301, 527
Belmont Park, 706–7
Benecke, Ernest, 202
Bennett, Enid, 580, 611, 621
Bennis, Bob, 811
Benny, Jack, 807
Benson, Scott, 836
Berenger, Robert, 88
Berg, Albert W., 219
Berhman, S. N., 733, 748–53
Berle, Milton, 807
Berliner, Emile, 210
Bernard, Oliver P., 334
Bernstein, Robert, 793
Bert, Mabel, 360, 384, 391
Berti, Marina, 767
Bien, Hermann Milton, 163
Bierley, Paul, 283, 292
Billy the Kid, 43, 56, 92, 94, 200, 215, 675, 676, 857
Bingham, John, 37
Biograph Company, 535, 543, 561
Bissell, Lillian, 276
Blackmun, Justice Harry, 831
Blake, Robert Wilkin, 711
Blake, William, 72
Blakely, David, 285–6
Boas, Franz, 203
Bok, Edward, 432
Bolt, Usain, 858
Bonsall, Mary, 245
Booth, Edwin, 218, 317, 636
Bossuet, Jacques-Bénigne, 51, 194
Bourgeon, Paul, 805–6
Bowes, Major Edward, 571–4, 630, 658n

Boyd, Steven, 732, 768, 772, 779, 783, 789, 836, 839
Boy Scouts of America, 180, 585, 772
Brabin, Charles, 573–7, 606
Bradford, Ellen Knight, 6, 13, 171, 220–8, 230, 232–7, 239–40, 247–8, 250–1, 255, 258, 260, 289, 314
Bradford, Marilee, 842
Bradley, Charles H., 129
Bradley, David, 693
Bradley, Tom, 808
Brando, Marlon, 731
Brauer, Ruford, 219
Breckenridge, Ellis John, 163
Briggs, C. W., 513, 515–16, 518–19
Bronson, Betty, 582, 596, 617
Brooks, Eldridge S., 163
Brooks, Joseph, 314–15, 318, 320, 349, 352, 358–9, 364, 369, 371–2, 388, 393–4
Brooks, Mel, 858
Brown, W. N., 476
Browne, Ray and Pat, 311
Brownell, Mabel, 779
Brownlow, Kevin, 567–8, 573, 575, 585, 644, 782, 834–5
Brutus, 24, 75–6, 200
Buhler, Richard, 385, 390
Bulova, 481, 697
Bulwer-Lytton, Edward, 167, 198, 218, 283
Burgess, Neil, 313, 334, 397n
Burnett, Mark, 859
Burtt, Ben, 840
Bushman, Francis X., 567–8, 573, 579–80, 585, 597, 600, 602, 630, 640, 661–2, 681, 701, 703, 713, 767, 809, 839
Bushnell, Horace, 196
Byron, Joseph, 312, 346–53, 369, 386

Cabanne, Christy, 577, 588, 682
Caesar, Julius, 28, 76, 78–9, 99n, 628, 704, 795–6; see also *Julius Caesar*
Caiaphas, 65
Caille Brothers, 482
Caldwell, H. H., 586, 593–4
Calkins, Earnest, 438
Cameron, Edgar, 422, 490
Cameron, Walter, 677, 679
Camillus, 29
Campanari, Leandro, 279, 283
Campbell, Alexander and Thomas, 192–4
Campbell, Glen, 825
Campbell Soup, 435–6
Camplin, Bob, 826
Canby, General Edward, 24
Candy, John, 827
Canutt, Joe, 773, 836
Canutt, Yakima, 393, 731–3, 742, 759–60, 763, 765, 768, 789, 836
Carfagno, Edward, 783
Carlin, Phillips, 631

Carmody, Jay, 785
Carnegie, Andrew, 211
Carpenter, Richard J., 304
Carter, Paul, 10, 92, 95
Catholic Legion of Decency, 729
Cauble, Aurelia J., 419
CBS, 666, 681, 720n, 769, 825–6, 828–9
Central Cycle Manufacturing Company, 304, 458–9
Cerf, Bennett, 793
Chadwick, G. W., 127, 274–6, 283, 339, 393
Chaffee & Selchow, 482
Chalmers, Thomas, 51, 194
Chambon, Pierre, 807
Chandler, Jeff, 666
Chandler, Raymond, 677
Chaplin, Charlie, 483, 619, 684
Chaplin, Sidney, 563
Chapman, Ceil, 799
Charles, Elizabeth Rundle, 74
Chastain, Ben-Hur, 484
Checa, Ulpiano, 173, 176–8, 289–90, 294, 305–6, 348, 409, 429, 444, 460, 470, 475, 477, 483, 489–90, 518, 626, 700, 802, 804
Chevrolet, Louis, 466
Christ, 1, 5, 7, 10, 13, 15, 19, 25, 32, 38–9, 46–7, 49–54, 58–9, 62–4, 66, 70, 72, 74, 78–9, 83, 93, 102–10, 115, 117, 119, 125, 138–42, 145, 148–51, 154, 157–8, 163, 166, 168, 171, 177, 188, 190–200, 203, 205–9, 217, 223, 227–8, 230, 234, 236, 241–2, 250–1, 257, 260, 281, 314, 316, 325, 332, 334, 339, 342, 347, 349, 355, 358, 362, 372, 509, 511, 514–15, 517–19, 521–2, 527, 529, 533–4, 542, 551, 564, 570, 586, 594–5, 602, 625, 630, 644, 666–7, 670, 674, 686, 733–4, 746, 757, 763, 773, 792, 796, 798, 827, 838, 843, 845, 847–8; see also God; Jesus
Churchill, Winston, 673, 714
Cicero, 77–8, 200, 414
Clark & Cox, 13, 230, 233, 236, 239, 246–7, 249, 251, 255, 258, 260, 264, 266, 267, 269, 310, 523
Clark, J. O. A., 163
Clark, Walter C., 233, 239, 244, 245–7, 249–51, 255, 256–8, 316–17, 523–4
Classical Cinematograph Corporation, 566, 569, 574, 577, 645n
Cleanthes, 69, 98n, 103, 284, 672
Clemens, Samuel [Mark Twain], 19, 156–7, 202, 667
Cleopatra, 73, 75–6, 680, 711, 807; see also *Cleopatra*

Cleveland, Grover, 163, 237
Clum, John Philip, 518, 529–32
Coad, Joyce, 630
Coca-Cola, 209, 408, 768–9, 787
Cocteau, Jean, 807
Cody, Buffalo Bill, 200
Cody, John H., 304, 460
Coff E. Bean, 443
Cohn, Jan, 438
Cohn, J. J., 753, 756, 784, 836
Colby, C. L., 170
Colgate, 209, 445, 691
Collins, Arthur, 357–9, 364, 368–71, 392
Colman, Ronald, 666
Columbia, 293, 301, 303, 630–1, 662, 704, 720n, 791
Commager, Henry Steele, 673
Constantine, 63
Coogan, Jackie, 577
Cook, David C., 844
Cooke, Edward G., 373, 380, 383, 534
Cooper, Drury W., 544–5
Cooper, James Fennimore, 145, 208
Cooper, Mario, 793
Corrigan, Emmett, 343, 394, 398n, 400n
Coughlan, Robert, 778
Cowley, Malcolm, 637
Cox, David W., 13, 232–3, 235–7, 239–43, 246–7, 251, 256, 260, 523; see also Clark & Cox
Cox, Jacob, 25
Cox, Joel, 840
Cox, Leonard E. L., 631
Crane, Steven, 19
Crawford, Bruce, 840
Crowe, Russell, 853
Crowther, Bosley, 573–4, 580, 780–1
Crystal, Billy, 858
Cummins, James, 672
Currie, Finley, 732
Currier, Frank, 398n, 602, 614
Curtis, Cyrus Hermann, 431
Custer, George, 200, 631
Cyrenius [Quirinius], 62–3, 66, 76–7, 98, 323

Dacqmine, Jacques, 807
Daggett, Charles D., 468–9
Daisy Miller, 201
Dalva, Robert, 839–40
Danova, Cesare, 739, 829
Davies, Marion, 584
Davis, Carl, 835, 841
Davis, Don, 840
Davis, Glenmore, 9
Davis, Sharen, 840
Davis, Will, 169
Deiber, Paul Émile, 805
Della Corte, Matteo, 583
Dell'Ara, Andrea Cavalli, 793
DeMille, Cecil B., 342, 573, 591, 599, 622–3, 625, 677, 680–1, 729, 731, 791
Demosthenes, 32, 78, 94

Desailly, Jean, 807
de Tocqueville, Alexis, 204
Deutsche Verlags-Anstalt, 146, 149, 181
Diaz, Porfirio, 411
Dickens, Charles, 141, 167, 513, 667
Dickerson, Ernest, 839
Dietz, Howard, 618–19
Dillingham, Charles B., 562, 565–6, 603, 615
Dionysius of Halicarnassus, 89–90
Disch, Thomas, M., 846
Disney, 798, 830–1, 858
Dixon, Thomas, 10, 646n
Dixon, William Hepworth, 48, 72, 74, 84, 98n
Dodson, J. E., 369, 383, 402n, 678
Doob, Oscar, 791–3, 798–9
Doré, Gustav, 512–13
Doren, Carl Van, 7
Dotterer, A. F., 202
Douglas, Kirk, 807
Douglas, Lloyd C., 180, 673, 729
Downey, Roma, 859
Doyle, Arthur Conan, 164
Drummond, Henry, 144
Du Camp, Maxime, 202
Duke, James, 209
Duneka, Frederick A., 186n, 544
Dunn, James, 766
Dutch, Dana E., 669
Dwight, Harold, 432, 438
Dyer, Frank L., 545

Earle, Ferdinand, 589, 601
Eason, B. Reeves, 585, 593–4, 621, 680, 682, 759
Eastman, Fred, 10
eBay, 15, 518, 699
Eddy, Mary Baker, 207
Edington, Harry, 578, 625, 682
Edison, 210, 295, 297, 299, 301–3, 533, 535, 545, 549, 573
Edison, Thomas, 210, 297, 303, 545
Edwards, J. Gordon, 563, 574
Edwards, Osman, 372
Eisenhower, Dwight D., 789
Elgin, 481, 697
Elley, Derek, 842–3
Ellington, Elphie A., 664
Ellsler, Effie, 312
Emerson, Ralph Waldo, 19, 211
Emmerling, Walter, 690
Endore, Guy, 790
Engels, Frank, 339
Engler, Dan, 832
Enright, George W., 335
Eph Joel, 234, 251, 448
Erkelenz, Ralph, 843
Erlanger, Abraham, 6, 166, 229, 310–15, 340, 344–5, 352, 364, 369, 380, 393–4, 562–7, 569–72, 574, 576–7, 591, 593, 596, 599–604, 613, 615, 622, 624, 644–5, 729, 731, 828; see also Klaw & Erlanger
Erlanger, Mitchell L., 313
Erskine, John, 9, 622
Erté, 108, 592, 593
Ethier, Aphonz, 382–3, 394
Evans, General H. Clay, 88
Evelyn, N., 484
Everson, William K., 781–2

Fabricius, 737, 751
Facebook, 3, 411–12, 856
Facer, Thomas, 282
Fairbank, John Wilder, 527–30, 532, 555
Fairbanks, Douglas, 563, 584, 605
Famous Players-Lasky, 571, 582, 607
Farnum, William, 166, 338, 344, 351–4, 362–3, 374, 379–80, 382, 384, 389, 394, 483, 562, 628, 662, 678, 794
Faulkner, James, 850
Faulkner, William, 381
Fiedler, Arthur, 797
Fiedler, Leslie, 10
Field, Henry, 202
Field, Marshall, 211
Finney, Charles G., 194
Fisher, Bud, 628–9
Fisher, Grace Dothea, 229
Fisher, Mark, 855–6
Fiske, John, 204–5
Fiske, Minnie Maddern, 357
Fitch, Tom, 511
Flaubert, Gustave, 201
Fleming, Rev. S. J., 243
Flowers, Charles Montaville, 421, 511-13, 684
F. M., 142, 235, 181n, 672
Focus on the Family, 844–5
Ford Motor Company, 465, 472, 475, 634, 702, 704, 811
Forman, Henry James, 627
Forbstein, Leo, 614
Forrest, Edwin, 200
Fort Pitt Brewing, 445
Foster, Frank Hugh, 196
Foster, Gertrude, 243
Fox see Twentieth-Century Fox
Fox, William, 394
Foxx, Jamie, 858
Franklin, Benjamin, 701
Franklin, Jesse, 416
Franklin, Michael H., 783, 786
Franklin, Sidney, 731, 733
Franz, Robert, 270
Fraser, Alexander, 462, 464
Fraunfelter China Company, 688
Frazer, Robert, 239
Frazier, Robert, 394
Frederick Warne & Company, 130–3, 144–5, 150, 793
Freeman, H. A., 291, 299, 386
Freeman, Walter W., 561
Frohman, Charles, 312–13, 354, 357, 364

Index

Frohman, Daniel, 319, 343, 346
Fry, Christopher, 732–3, 742, 753, 755–7, 760–1, 764, 768, 773, 783–6
Furet, Yves, 807

Gable, Clark, 584, 779
Gallup, George, 672
Garbo, Greta, 582
Gardiner, James L., 674
Garfield, James A., 5, 92, 111–15, 128, 151–2, 251–2, 285, 600, 673
Garneau, Mimi, 708
Garson, Greer, 676
Gauntier, Gene, 10, 535–7, 540, 548
Gaynor, Janet, 689
General Mills, 439, 495
George, Grace, 318, 320
George, Lloyd, 610
George W. Bond & Company, 421, 518
George Worthington Company, 478
Gerard, David, 306, 413–19, 491–2, 531
Gerber, David, 544–5
Gérôme, Jean-Léon, 100n, 203, 215n
Gibbon, Edward, 29, 62–4, 67, 72, 75, 90, 199, 673
Gibbons, Cedric, 583
Gibson Brothers, 253
Gibson, Mel, 855
Gilbert and Sullivan, 369
Gilbert, John, 584
Gilbert, William, 675
Gilder, Richard Watson, 113
Gilder, Jeannette L., 313
Gill, Basil, 394
Gillespie, A. Arnold, 580, 783
Gillette, William, 313, 315
Gillington, May Clarissa [Byron], 281–3
Gilmore, Patrick, 288
Gilpin, William, 204
Girard, Harry, 279
Gish, Lillian, 582, 584, 782
Glanzman, Louis S., 793
God, 35, 46, 50–4, 60–1, 66, 69–70, 79, 98n, 111, 142, 150–1, 190, 194, 197–9, 207, 278, 324, 326, 415, 515, 520, 588, 638, 664, 666, 670, 735–7, 739–42, 744, 752–3, 755–6, 762, 764, 792, 833, 845–9; see also Christ; Jesus
Godsol, Frank Joseph, 569, 571, 574, 644
Goelet, Robert W., 566
Goldwyn Pictures, 6, 551, 567, 569, 570–4, 577, 730, 774
Goldwyn, Samuel, 567, 569, 584, 828
Goodrich, Samuel, 20–1
Goodtimes Entertainment, 848
Granger, Stewart, 731

Grant, Ulysses S., 34–5, 37–8, 92–5, 113, 675
Grauman, Sid, 584, 604–5, 614, 633, 779
Graves, J. A., 627
Graves, Robert, 844
Gray, Thomas, 276
Gray, Timothy, 846
Greci, José, 768
Greeley, Horace, 103
Greene, John Bulkley, 202
Green Giant, 687, 702
Gregory, Frank W,. 56
Grey, Griffith, 607
Griffith, D. W., 562–4, 570, 574, 591, 599
Griffith, Hugh, 732, 752, 783, 809
Griffith, J. C., 377
Griggs, John W., 548
Griswold, Morley, 634
Gros, Ernest, 334, 399
Grosset & Dunlap, 2, 165, 173, 178, 180, 618, 626, 672, 793
Grothkopf, Chad, 667–8
Gruen Watch Company, 480, 482, 642–3
Gruss, André, 805
Guazzoni, Enrico, 579
Guest, Al, 831–2
Gunnison, Binney, 168
Gurley-Kane, Evelyn, 207, 258–61, 391, 511, 684
Gurlitz, Augustus T., 523
Gutjahr, Paul, 10, 198, 214n, 217n

Hagen, Claude, 10, 166, 335, 337–8, 369–70, 385, 393, 398n, 461–2
Haggard, H. Rider, 203
Haley, Alex, 10
Hall, F. A., 304
Hall, Robert, 51, 194
Hall, Thurston, 394, 678
Halleck, General Henry, 34–5, 120
Hamilton, Sir Ian, 622
Hammer, [Johannes] Bonaventure, 146, 148–9, 182n, 425
Hand, Chip, 846
Hannas, 64–5
Hanson, Victor Davis, 92–4
Harareet, Haya, 732, 767, 772, 779
Harden, Cecil M., 778
Harmon, Francis, 781
Harper & Bros., 1, 5–7, 11, 13, 15, 32–4, 38, 46, 82, 91–2, 102–3, 105–6, 110, 112–21, 123, 128–30, 138–52, 154–60, 163, 165–7, 172–6, 178, 180, 188, 197–8, 201–2, 212, 219, 221, 226–30, 235–9, 241, 245–6, 250–1, 256, 258, 270–2, 275, 278–80, 285, 295, 303, 305, 313–16, 321, 329, 345, 352–3, 365, 379, 385–6, 391, 409, 413–14, 421–3, 431–2, 434–5, 437, 467, 470, 509–10, 513, 523–4, 530, 533–6, 543–5, 548, 551, 561–6, 570, 613, 626–7, 673, 791, 830–1
Harris, Hannah, 283
Harrison, Benjamin, 222, 232–4, 638, 675
Harrison, William Henry, 19
Hart, William S., 319, 338, 341, 344, 352, 354, 394, 536, 573, 678, 794, 836, 839
Hartl, John, 790
Hartmann, Edmund, 784
Harvard University, 70, 103, 270, 384, 449, 454, 733, 753, 773
Harvey, Col. George B., 173–5
Hawkins, Elizabeth [Waller], 24
Hawkins, Jack, 732, 772–3
Hawthorne, Nathaniel, 28, 145, 527
Hayes, Rutherford B., 41–2, 113, 151
Hayne, Paul H., 46
Hays, Will, 605, 616
Heap, Carl, 857
Hearst, William Randolph, 159, 574
Heater, Claude, 767
Hecht-Hill-Lancaster, 731
Heichen, Paul, 146–7
Helling, William, 457
Henigson, Henry, 748, 757, 759
Henty, G. A., 203
Hercules, 484, 796
Herod, 24, 47, 53, 58, 62, 64, 73, 75–6, 79, 81–2, 194, 221–2, 233, 242, 249, 261, 514–15, 517, 674, 794
Hershiser, Orel, 846
Hess, Erwin L., 666–7
Heston, Charlton, 713, 731, 753, 759–62, 765–9, 772–3, 777–80, 783–6, 789, 797, 807–9, 830, 835–7, 839, 841, 848, 858
Heston, Fraser, 789, 841, 848
Hewett, Edgar L., 162
Hichens, Robert, 12
Hickman, Roger, 843
Hickok, Wild Bill, 200
Higginson, Thomas Wentworth, 244
Higham, Charles, 568
High Rollers Extravaganza Company, 388
Hilliker, Katherine, 586, 593–4
Hippolytus, 81
Hirtenstein, Max, 643, 693
Hobbes, Thomas, 30, 44n
Hoffman, Chas, 305
Holder, Glenn, 793
Holding, Carlisle B., 163
Holland, 391, cf. 439
Hollinger, Beth, 767
Holloway, W. R., 95
Holman, Theodore, 534
Holmes, Burton, 533

Holmes, Dwight, 674
Holmes, Oliver Wendell, Jr., 127, 548–9, 830–1
Holmes, Oliver Wendell, Sr., 7, 126–7
Holmes, Sherlock, 313, 535
Homer, 27–8, 81, 103, 134n, 216n, 622
Hooker, Isabella Beecher, 195
Hope, Bob, 682, 685, 711, 783, 825
Hopper, Hedda, 681, 689, 708, 729–31, 766–8
Horace, 29, 75–6
Hoshour, Samuel K., 26–7, 31, 47, 146, 165, 191, 193–4
Hossein, Robert, 851–3
Houcke, Sacha, 806
Hough, Charles M., 562–3
Houghton, Henry O., 126
Houghton Mifflin, 112, 140–1, 174, 238, 251, 562
Houghton, Osgood, and Company, 112
Howe, Herbert, 577
Howells, William Dean, 126–7, 156, 201, 211
Hoyns, Henry, 175, 178
HUAC, 740
Hudgins, Morgan, 767, 791
Hudson, Rock, 731
Huff Film Society, 782
Hughes, Rupert, 276
Hume, Willis, F., 518, 520
Huntley & Palmers, 803–4
Huntley, Chet, 765
Hurlbut, Jesse Lyman, 122
Hurwitz, Hyman, 811
Hyde, Marguerite, 533

Ingersoll, Robert, 46–7, 50–4, 57–9, 83, 92, 97n, 111, 117, 190, 195, 245, 362, 374, 401n, 455, 567, 600, 792, 809, 836
Ingraham, Joseph Holt, 103, 110, 131, 134n, 198
Ingram, Rex, 563, 569
Ishmael, 6–5

Jackson, Horace, 583, 622
Jackson, Thomas P., 427
Jaffe, Sam, 732
James, George Payne Rainsford, 30
James, Henry, 19, 115, 201, 207
James, Jesse, 200
James Nisbet & Company, 144
Jefferson, Joseph, 312
Jefferson, Thomas, 197
Jergens, 3, 446, 638–41, 643, 691–2
Jesus, 10, 12, 47, 49–50, 52–3, 58–9, 63–5, 72, 83–4, 93, 95, 98, 105, 108–11, 117, 149–50, 163–4, 185, 190–9, 207, 213–15, 236, 257, 314, 325, 332, 334, 342, 349, 414, 514–15, 517–18, 520–1, 528, 559, 591, 595–6, 614,
628, 663, 667, 674, 737, 746–8, 756, 763–4, 767, 794, 804–5, 828, 832, 838, 845, 848, 850–3
Joannes Brothers, 443–4, 686, 688, 690; see also Christ; God
Joannes-Spane Company, 442
John Holland Pens, 13, 161–2, 345
John J. Schulten & Company, 448
John of Hildesheim, 68
Johnson, Andrew, 37
Johnson, Orrin, 383, 394, 678
Johnson, Paul, 846
Johnson, William [Billy], 412
Johnson, William Martin, 152–5, 305, 431, 673
Johnston, Annie Fellows, 163
Jolson, Al, 632
Jones, Minnie, 171, 224
Jones, Thomas J., 529–30
Josephus, 48–9, 59–80, 90, 99n, 107, 203, 214n, 582, 782, 806
Josselyn, William H., 530, 532
Judas of Galilee, 60, 62–7, 72–3, 128, 747

Kaiser Wilhelm, 614
Kalem see Ben-Hur (1907)
Kaminski, Janusz, 840
Kaplan, Dave and Bessie, 485
Kayser Ellison & Company, Ltd., 699
Keel, A. Chester, 579
Keipert, Heinrich, 84
Kelleher, Helen, 229
Kelley, Edgar Stillman, 166, 312, 319–32, 339–41, 344–5, 347, 349, 352–4, 356–7, 362, 365, 374, 376, 399n, 570, 591, 623, 678–9, 796
Kelly, Hal, 15, 811
Kelly, William J., 394
Kelly, W. S., 534
Kemp, Victor, 279
Keon, Miles Gerald, 163
Kerkorian, Kirk, 833
Kerr, Rev. W. H., 518
Kershner, Irvin, 839
King Edward VII, 311, 371
King Edward VIII, 711
King George V, 371, 610
King James Bible, 71, 90. 196
King, Jennie, 276
Kingsley, Charles, 152, 199
Kingsley, F.M., 164
Kiralfy Brothers, 218–19, 237
Kirkus, Virginia, 627
Klaw & Erlanger, 3, 6–7, 10, 13, 15, 32, 115, 151, 166, 172–3, 226, 231, 237, 244, 255–8, 269, 279–81, 286–7, 289, 296–7, 305, 311–22, 333–4, 336–8, 342–8, 350, 354–6, 358–9, 361–4, 368–98, 410, 420, 423–4, 439, 447, 456, 461–2, 469,
473, 475–6, 483, 488, 510–11, 518, 525, 530, 532–4, 536, 542–3, 545–7, 552, 561–4, 566, 569, 573, 579, 592–3, 596–602, 608, 610, 614, 620, 630, 632, 636, 644, 661–2, 669, 672, 676, 678–9, 685, 693, 738, 759–60, 771, 775, 779, 786, 789, 794, 796, 809, 836, 851
Klaw, Marc, 6, 312, 359, 394, 562–5, 678; see also Klaw & Erlanger
Kleine, George, 513, 515–16, 520–1, 533, 535, 543–4, 553n, 562
Klepper, Robert, 10
Knight, Henry Gally, 74
Knight, Horatio Gates, 220
Knights of Pythias, 411–12, 414, 491, 530
Koldys, Mark, 842
Kowalchuk, Bill, 848
Kroeger, Ernest Richard, 271–4, 276, 283
Kroll, Julius, 769
Krout, Mary Hannah, 20
Kunkel Bros., 272
Kurtz, Howie, 830

Lacombe, Judge Emile, 512, 524, 544
Laemmle, Jr, Carl, 729
Lain, Clara R., 454, 689
Lamarr, Hedy, 681
Lampman, Ben Hur, 483
Lamson, Gardner S., 275–6
Lancaster, Burt, 731
Lane, Henry Smith, 32
Lane, Joanna Elston, 32, 48
Langhorne and Langhorne, 22–3
Larkin, John, 545, 563
Lawrence, D. H., 9
Lawrence, Eugene, 120, 140
Lawrence, Jerome, 666
Leach, William, 12–13
Lederer, George, 357, 599–600
Leeds & Catlin, 301–3
Lee, Henry, 319, 353
Lee, Robert E., 666
Lehman, Herbert, 673
Lehr, Abraham, 571
Leva, Gary, 839
Lewis, Charlton T., 82, 103–4, 188, 782
Lewis, John Frederick, 203
Lichty, George, 690
Lincoln, Abraham, 34–5, 37, 48, 70, 258, 675, 683, 701, 792
Lincoln, Charles P., 527, 529
Lincoln, Harry J., 294
Linderfelt, Klas, 167
Lindquist, Willis, 793
Lindsley, Charles Frederick, 630
Linick, Leroy, 733
Linthicum, Richard, 168
Lipke, Katherine, 604
Lippy, Charles, 191
Litt, Jacob, 320–1
Livy, 99n, 200

Index

Lloyd, Harold, 584
Lockwood, George R., 141, 423
Loew, Marcus, 563, 565, 567, 569, 574–7, 579–80, 596–7, 603, 608, 644
Loew's Incorporated, 608, 623, 730, 768–9, 778–9, 783, 791, 793, 803, 805
Loftus-Hubbard, 429–31, 435, 531
Longfellow, Henry Wadsworth, 150, 275
Long, Samuel, 535
Louis Marx & Company, 800–1
Lowe, Samuel, 803–4
Lowell, James Russell, 126, 133
Lowell Toy Manufacturing Company, 802
Loy, Myrna, 582, 584
Luburg Manufacturing, 458
Lucas, Albert, 367, 529
Lucas, George, 791, 839–40, 857
Lucas, Harry K., 547
Ludlam, Henry, 243
Luffer, Emil W., 477
Luke, 62, 65, 68, 71, 76, 98n, 108, 332, 674
Lustig, Jan, 733, 746
Lyceum Bio-Scenograph Company, 546–7
Lyon, Annie M., 276
Lyons, Esther, 313
Lyons, Gretchen, 320

McAllister Company, 513–16, 520–1, 531, 553n
McAvoy, May, 597, 601, 617, 620, 639, 643–4
McCall, Maude Burt, 171
McCarthy, Joseph Jefferson, 598–601, 606–7, 641, 682
McCarthy, Senator Joseph, 740
McCormick & Company, 690
McCormick, Dr. Leo J., 769, 772
McCosh, Zara, 239
MacDonald, Ramsay, 610
McDonald, Senator Joseph Ewing, 24
McDowell, Claire, 600
MacDowell, Edward, 276, 319
McGill, Frank N., 673
McIntosh Company, 513–15, 520–1, 529
McKee, Irving, 9, 41, 56, 91–2, 98n, 100n, 105, 116, 262n, 319–20, 391–2, 399n, 468, 676
McKenna, Shaun, 855–6
McKinley, Phil, 855
McKinley, William, 163, 206, 467
McLemore, Henry, 706, 710–11
McNutt, Rev. George Lorin, 525–7
McWilliams, Harry, 791
McWilliams, John P., 208
Maggs, Dirk, 844–5
Mahan, William D., 127–9, 133, 839
Maier-Krieg, Eugene, 584

Mannix, Eddie, 624, 759
Manners, Marian, 640
Marangella, Lou, 578, 581
Marbury, Elisabeth, 313–15
Marcello, Carlo Raffaele, 671
Marchand, Gertrude, 224
Marion, Frank J., 535–7, 552
Martin, Harry G., 276
Martin, Hugh, 846
Marton, Andrew, 732–3, 759, 763, 851
Marx, Chancellor Wilhelm, 608
Marx, Groucho, 314
Marx, Louis, 800–1
Marx, Samuel, 567, 580
Marx toys see Louis Marx & Company
Marx, Wilhelm, 608
Mary Magdalene, 595
Matagorda, 453, 455, 486
Matas, Carlos A., 857
Mathiesen, Jean, 831–2
Mathis, June, 567, 571–9, 589–90, 644, 733–4, 751, 797
Matteotti, Giacomo, 581
Matthew, 47, 62–3, 68–9, 73, 83, 93, 332, 415–16
Matthews, William Smyth Babcock, 279
Mature, Victor, 681
Max, Arthur, 839–40
Mayer, David, 10
Mayer, Louis B., 567, 574–6, 578–81, 583, 596, 607, 613, 621–2, 644, 682, 730–1
Mazoyer, Phillippe, 611, 653n
Meade, James, 785
Meagher, Edward, 511
Mears, Ben, 378, 630
Mellarde, Pierre, 280
Melville, Herman, 34, 208
Melville, Prof. W. B., 253
Menchikov, Mikhail, 780
Mendoza, David, 599, 614, 629–30, 796, 841
Mercer, Virginia Saffel, 171–2
Meredyth, Bess, 10, 577, 590, 592, 595, 733
Merrifield, C. E., 280, 304
Merrill, Selah, 202
Mersand, Joseph, 769, 772
Messalina, 76
Messick, Fredrick, 304
Metro-Goldwyn-Mayer [MGM], 1, 3–4, 10, 13–14, 106, 147, 164, 178, 180, 261, 269, 292–3, 296, 306, 311, 313, 323, 340, 372, 394, 422, 480, 482–3, 486, 488, 535, 549–51, 561, 566–8, 574–81, 583–5, 589, 595–6, 598–600, 603–9, 611–16, 618, 621, 623–4, 626, 629–30, 632–4, 640–2, 644, 661–2, 669, 672, 676, 679–82, 685–6, 690, 692–3, 699–700, 703–4, 707–8, 710, 728–33, 746, 753, 755–7, 759, 762–81, 783, 786–91, 793–812,
813n, 825–6, 828–9, 832–5, 840–2, 845, 849, 851, 856, 858–9
Metro Pictures, 569, 571, 574
Metropolitan Opera, 287, 536
Meyer Bros. & Co., 348
Meyer, Stephen C., 843
MGM/UA, 829, 833
Michel, P. B., 470
Mickey Mouse, 489, 798
Microid, 856
Milchin, Arnon, 840
Miller, Albert S., 236–37, 246, 264n
Miller, Elizabeth, 164
Miller, Jane Taylor, 260
Miller, Lewis, 123
Miller, Lucy Key, 710
Miller, Marvin, 666
Miller, Mitch, 797
Miller, Zack, 485, 487, 811
Milne, Saidee Vere, 258
Milton Bradley, 637
Milton, John, 29, 152
Miriam, 39, 57, 64, 71–2, 734, 740–1, 746–7, 752, 757, 767, 787
Mitchell, Margaret, 10
Mitchell, Wilmot Brookings, 168
Mix, Tom, 632
M. L. Brandt Cutlery, 448
Moebs Cigars, 408, 424–8, 493n
Monarch Bicycle Company, 457
Monk, 338, 379, 390
Monta, Rudi, 755
Montezuma, 39, 54, 231
Montgomery County (IN), 99n, 232, 413, 419
Montgomery Ward, 168, 175, 178, 299, 301, 303, 533, 692
Moody, Dwight L., 194
Moore, Stephen Campbell, 849
Mott, Frank Luther, 164, 672
Morgan, Edward, 319, 343, 351–2, 369, 393–4
Morgan, Joseph, 849
Morris, Tom, 857
Morsberger, Robert and Katherine, 9, 31, 37–9, 395n
Morse, Edward H., 305–6
Morse, Helen McGregor, 219–20
Morse, Salmi, 241
Mortimer, Win, 670
Morton, Oliver P., 26, 32, 35
Moses, 35, 63, 66, 71–2, 551, 663, 731, 749, 769, 797, 841
Moses, Thomas Gibbs, 250
Motion Picture Patents Company, 545, 549
Mott, Luther, 164, 672
Mowbray, Henry Siddons, 152, 434
Mugnaini, Joe, 792
Müller, Karl Otfried, 87
Munro, D. B., 340
Murkland, P. A., 175, 177–8
Muskogee, 387, 420
Mussey, Reuben D., 228

Mussolini, Benito, 568, 581, 625, 679, 683
Myers, Carmel, 573, 584, 602, 629, 638–41, 661, 681–2, 767, 779
Myers, Zion, 629

Nahar, Ednorah, 169, 171
Napoleon, 288, 312–13, 457, 513, 631, 785
Napoleon, Louis, 204
National Screen Service, 769
NBC, 631, 666, 682, 689, 765–7, 772, 783, 798, 807, 826–8
Neilan, Marshall, 563, 570, 575
Nero, 61, 63, 78, 163, 200, 218, 635, 668, 792, 795, 806–7, 857
New Haven Clock Company, 481–2
New Lindell Mills, 139, 428
Newman, Paul, 731
Niblo, Fred, 571, 575–84, 591–2, 596–601, 606, 611, 613–14, 618, 621–2, 644, 648–9, 681
Nicholson, Kenyon, 779
Nicholson, Meredith, 677
Nicholson, Thomas B., 56, 318, 778
Nielsen, Leslie, 739
Nixon & Zimmerman, 354, 357, 362
Noll, Mark, 191
North, Thomas, 23
Nosler, Lloyd, 586, 596, 681
Novarro, Ramon, 486, 567, 577, 579–80, 585, 592, 597, 600–4, 611, 614–15, 620–1, 624, 628, 633, 635, 639, 643–4, 661–2, 681, 703, 729, 731, 767, 779, 805

Odd Fellows, 412, 529
O'Donnell, Cathy, 732, 766, 849
Olcott, Sidney, 535–9, 548, 552
Olmsted, Remington, 764
Olney, Jesse, 21
Olympia brand, 298, 857
Osgood and Company, 39
Osgood, Charles Laurie, 269–72, 275
Ossian, 28
O'Sullivan, John L., 204, 216n
Oswald, Julius A., 422
Owen, Bernard C., 306
Owen, Joe, 846
Owen, Ronald, 846

Page Fence, 479–80
Pain's Fireworks Company, 219, 536–7
Paling, W. H., 305–6, 310n
Palmer, Joe H., 706
Palmolive-Peet, 445
Panavision, 773–4
Pantages, Alexander, 613, 616
Paramount, 563, 579, 608, 730, 788, 831
Pariette, Ralph Albert, 172
Parker, Horatio, 339, 389

Parker, Lottie Blair, 564
Parsons, Charles, 154
Parsons, Louella, 781
Parufamet, 608–9, 611–12, 629
Pastor, Bob, 486
Patrick, Johnny, 632
Patten, Jefferson, 313
Paull, Edward Taylor, 7, 138, 255, 269, 279–80, 288–306, 314, 386, 410, 420, 424, 460, 510–11, 527, 530, 631, 637, 661, 677–8, 797–8
Payne, Wilfred, 382
Peale, Norman Vincent, 781
Pearl, Jack, 778
Peet Bros., 445
Pepper, Harry, 278
Percy, Lord Eustace, 625
Pericles, 70, 78
Perry Mason Company, 467–8
Petermann, Augustus, 85
Peters, W. I., 304
Pettit, Henry, 278–9
Pickford, Mary, 563, 584, 605
Pilate, Pontius, 39, 59, 61, 62, 65, 66, 74, 78, 104, 198, 331, 595, 667, 737, 745, 747–8, 751–2, 756–7, 762, 764, 804, 845, 849–50
Pindar, 28, 81
Pinder, Jefferson, 857
Platzer, Frank, 334
Pliny, 80, 89, 99
Plummer, Christopher, 829
Plutarch, 22–4, 28–9, 43, 73, 75, 77–9, 94, 99n, 200
Poe, Edgar Allen, 19, 28
Poland, 164, 166–7, 625, 781
Pompey, 78–9, 99n
Pond, Major James B., 157–9, 239, 285, 313, 528
Pope, Alexander, 28, 134n
Pope Leo XIII, 148, 383
Poppaea, 61, 63
Portalupi, Piero, 773
Porter, Edwin S., 533
Porter, Jane, 21
Potter, Dr. William H., 339
Powell, John Wesley, 203
Powell, Mrs. Henry A., 171
Pratt, Anthony, 840
Prescott, William H., 24, 39–40
Preston, Mary Adair, 836
Preston, Nannie, 516
Proctor & Gamble, 209
Pryor, Arthur, 300–1
Pyle, Ernie, 683
Pyrrhus, 22–3, 77, 94–5

Quarles, Rev. James A., 128
Queen Alexandra, 371
Queen Mary, 705
Querrie, John C., 304
Quintilian, 99n

R. J. Lakin & Company, 709
Raboch, Al, 577, 588
Railton, George Scott, 207
Randall, Glenn, 759, 761, 765, 767, 779, 786–7

Random House, 793–4, 797
Raphael, 582
Reagan, Ronald, 779
Redondo Beach, 243
Reeder, Robert, 846–7
Reggiani, Serge, 807
Regina, 297–8
Reid, David F., 465
Reilly, Charles Nelson, 807
Reinhardt, Max, 563
Reinisch, Josef J., 219, 313
Renan, Ernest, 111, 197, 214n
Reo Motors, Inc, 703
Reynolds, Debbie, 779
Rhino Records, 842
Rhomberg Distilling Company, 445
Rice, Elwood E., 472–5
Rice, Frank X., 800–1
Rice, Josephine Bonaparte, 533
Richard, Jean, 806
Richards, Carol, 734
Rider, Captain J. A., 527–8, 532
Riley Brothers, 6, 13, 138, 236, 250, 510, 512, 516–17, 519–25, 527–8, 531, 544, 553n
Riley, James Whitcomb, 146
Ringling Brothers, 468, 485, 709, 811
Ripley, Bob, 666
Ripley, George, 102–4, 110, 134n, 188, 198
Roach, Hal, 604
Robinson, Charles, 388
Robinson, John, 450
Robinson, William, 768–9
Rochefort, Jean, 807
Rockefeller, John D., 158, 211
Rockwood, George, 348
Rogers, Fred, 831
Rogers Peet Company, 634
Rogers, Randolph, 162
Rogers, Rev. A. D., 527–30, 532
Rogers, Roy, 767
Roosevelt, Franklin, 673, 675, 679
Roosevelt, Theodore, 383
Rose, David, 666, 798
Rose, Frank Oakes, 219, 536–7
Rose, Henry R., 532
Rose Publishing, 144–5
Rosenquist, Lewis, 673
Ross Verlag, 611–12
Routledge, 132–3
Royal Milling Company, 430–2, 434–5, 437–8, 440, 495n
Rózsa, Miklós, 296, 732, 744, 771, 776–7, 783, 794, 796–8, 806–7, 809, 827, 835, 840–3
Rudisill Concert Company, 258
Ruiz, Wulfano and Umberto, 486
Rural Free Delivery, 175, 616
Ruth, Babe, 706
Ryan, T. R., 334

St. John, Betta, 734
S & H Green Stamps, 429

Saks, 695, 697, 799
Sallman, Warner, 198
Salvadori, Enrico, 148
Salvation Army, 207
Salvini, Alexander, 218, 313, 512
Saltzman, Auguste, 202
Sampson Low, 116, 130
Sanborn, Ellen and David, 847
Sanders, George, 681
Sandow, 344, 484
Sanford, Charles L., 207–8
Santa Claus, 773
Satchwill, Dudley T., 305
Saull, Edward H., 305–6
Sawyer, Frank E., 278
Schallert, Edwin, 601–2, 604–5, 608, 617, 621, 623, 645, 681, 709, 729
Schary, Dore, 729–30, 786
Schenck, Joseph, 576
Schenck, Nicholas, 576
Scheuer, Philip K., 709, 779–83
Scipio, 80
Schrotter, Gustav, 669
Schurman, Jacob Gould, 608
Scott, Martha, 766–7, 773
Scott, Ridley, 839–40
Scott, Sir Walter, 27, 73
Scott, Wayne R., 847–8
Screen Actors Guild, 830
Screen Writers Guild, 732–3, 756, 783–6, 838
Scudder, Horace, 111–12
Sears, 1, 6, 11, 13, 173–80, 209, 212, 216n, 299, 301, 303, 420, 467, 483, 552, 626, 628, 693, 787, 800, 805
Sears, Edmund H., 628
Seavey, Lafayette W., 237, 239, 250
Seibert, Henry W. [H. W. S.], 149
Sejanus, 59, 74, 78, 82, 93, 95, 331, 736
Selig, 321, 396, 535, 562
Sellers, Peter, 809
Sells Brothers Circus, 339, 468
Selznick, David O., 564, 680
Seneca, 81, 99n
Serling, Rod, 774
Shakespeare, William, 27, 29, 38, 73, 75, 218, 614, 628, 630, 786
Sharp, Alan, 849–51
Sharp, Sidney, 342
Shaw, George Bernard, 680
Shaw, Mary, 319, 360
Sheldon, Charles, 8, 12–13, 164–5, 199, 212, 513
Sheldon, Edward, 12
Sherwood, Robert E., 619
Shubert, J. J. and Lee, 572, 590
Shumate Razor Company, 447–8
Sidel, Adolph, 580
Siegel, Samuel, 259
Siegel, Sol, 730, 768, 775, 779, 784–5

Sienkiewicz, Henryk, 9, 148, 164–5, 317
Silverman, Fred, 825
Simonides of Cos, 99n
Sindlinger & Company, 769
Sitting Bull, 200
Skelton, Red, 709, 729
Skouras, Spyros, 779
Smith, Benjamin E., 145
Smith, Bruce, 334
Smith, Fannie, 170
Smith, Frederick James, 570–1
Smith, Joseph J., 770, 793–4, 808, 829
Smith, Red, 706
Smith, Rev. William, 30
Smith, Sir William, 75, 81–2, 86–7, 89–91, 155, 593
Smith, Walter, 631
Sniffen, R. P., 175, 180
Snyder, Earl P., 701
Snyder, Frank L., 413, 416
Snyder, J. C., 422, 627
Soares, André, 567
Socrates, 69
Solingen-Merscheid Company, 641, 699
Sony, 550, 825, 828–31, 841–2
Soper, Henry M., 167
Sophocles, 81
Sousa, John Philip, 255, 269, 283–89, 291–3, 300–1, 314, 424, 440, 510
Sparling, Herbert, 279
Spartacus, 200, 807
S.P.C.A., 585
Spencer, Herbert, 204–5
Splane, John R., 443
Spofford, Ainsworth Rand, 48, 88, 221
S. R. James, 252
Stagg, Amos Alonzo, 244
Stahl, Ben, 768–9, 770, 794
Stange, Stanislaus, 164
Stanton, Edwin, 37, 94
Starr, Belle, 200
Stauffer, Aubrey, 305
Stearns, Marion, 223–4
Stevens, Justice John Paul, 830–1
Stone, Allan and Martin, 798–9, 801–2, 805
Stone, Oliver, 858
Stowe, Harriet Beecher, 12, 19, 165, 195, 198, 607
Stowe, William P., 148
Strauss, David Friedrich, 197
Strauss, Richard, 356
Strickland, Howard, 772
Stroheim, Eric von, 571, 574, 576
Strong, James, 202
Strong, Josiah, 205
Struss, Karl, 595
Stuart Female Seminary, 451
Suetonius, 200
Sullivan, Ed, 624, 681, 769, 825
Sultan Abdul Hamid II, 92, 120, 122, 147, 159
Sumner, William Graham, 204

Sunday, Billy, 390
Surratt, Mary, 37, 94, 792, 846
Surtees, Robert, 732, 773, 783, 840
Suskind, David, 774, 799
Sutton, Felix, 793
Swing, David, 195–6, 381
Switzer, George Washington, 232–3
Sylva, Berthe, 806
Syracuse University, 842–3

Taber, I. W., 145
Taber, Robert, 369
Tacitus, 63, 75, 99n, 200
Talbot, Lida Hood, 171, 230, 240, 242
Talbot, Lyle, 709
Talbot, William H., 477
Tallandier, Jules, 611
Tarkington, Booth, 41, 146
Tarzan, 409
Taylor, Robert, 731
Taylor, Zachary, 32, 94
Teal, Ben, 335, 343, 349, 352, 369, 374, 376, 393–4
Tearle, Conway, 366, 394
Temple, Harry, 250, 536
Temple, Jeannette, 675
Temple, Shirley, 798
Terrell, Dan, 788
Thalberg, Irving, 566–7, 574–9, 581, 583–4, 586, 591, 596, 644–6, 648–51, 681, 729
Thames Television, 834–6
Theatrical Syndicate, 313–14, 354, 357, 364
Thiriet, Maurice, 806
Thomas, F. W., 12
Thomas J. Barkley Company, 440–3
Thomas, Tony, 842
Thompson, Clara Louise, 240
Thompson, L. N., 210
Thompson, Maurice, 42–3
Thomson, Rev. William M., 202
Thoreau, Henry David, 19
Thorpe, Richard, 761
Thucydides, 29–30, 49, 70–1
Tiberius, 65, 78, 108, 628, 739, 751, 756, 762, 764, 850
Ticknor, Benjamin H., 112, 126
Time Warner, 829, 835
Tissot, James, 582
TNT, 833, 835
Tom, 338–9
Toogood, Margaret, 35
Towle, Charles F., 361, 377–8, 393–4
Townsend, Edward W., 549
Trachtenberg, Alan, 9
Tracy, Rev. Dr. N. W., 529, 533
Trigger, 767
Truman, Harry, 685
Tucker, Julia, 229
Tucker, Louis, 628
Tunberg, Karl, 730, 732–56, 760, 762–5, 768, 783–6, 794, 836, 838–9, 849, 857
Turner, Ted, 833

Turner Broadcasting, 833–5, 842
Turnure, Arthur B., 151
Twentieth-Century Fox, 573, 632, 729, 731, 831

Ühlein, Herman, 692–3
Ultra Company, 563
Union Literary Society, 27
Unione Cinematografica Italiana, 572
United Artists, 563, 576, 641, 775, 833, 859
Universal, 550–1, 573, 584, 617, 623, 708, 729, 731, 830–1
Union Army, 3, 31, 34–5, 92, 113, 120, 158, 270, 675, 677, 778; see also U. S. Army
University of Notre Dame, 120, 124, 189
University of Southern California, 572, 777, 779, 808
Uribe, Fernando, 832
Urich, George, 700
USA Life One Insurance, 423
U. S. Army, 19, 147, 624, 662, 683–4, 692, 788; see also Union Army
U. S. Constitution, 206, 546
U. S. Copyright Office, 221; see also copyright
U. S. Marine Band, 259–60, 285, 295
U. S. Marines, 856
U. S. Senate, 24–5, 32, 34, 128, 160, 162, 222, 258–9, 740, 789, 830
U. S. Supreme Court, 7, 105, 298, 303, 419, 536, 538, 544, 548–50, 552, 561, 563, 701, 830, 859
U. S. War Department, 34, 498

Valenti, Jack, 830
Valentino, Rudolph, 567, 569, 571
Van Camp, 461, 478, 696–7, 704
Vanderbilt, Cornelius, 211
Van Dyke, Paul, 155
Vardac, Nicholas, 682
Vaughn, Kate Brew, 686–7
Veeck, Bill, 809
Vespasian, 80, 99n, 806, 857
Victor Animatograph Company, 520
Victor Talking Machine Company, 300–1, 303, 309n, 310
Victoria baking company, 803–4
Victorio, 92, 94
Vidal, Gore, 732–3, 742, 753–6, 760–2, 783–6, 836–9, 857
Vidor, King, 545, 599
Viele, Egbert, 158
Vincent Brothers, 428
Vincent, George, 245
Vincent, H. H., 364, 366–7
Vincent, John Heyl, 123, 243
Viopticon, 520

Vitaphone, 604, 618
Voellmy, Emil, 482–3
Vogel, Joseph R., 730–1, 766, 769, 775, 778–80, 786, 794
Voris, Samuel, 413

Wabash College, 21, 24, 241, 702
Wachner, Sophie, 570
Wagner, Alexander von, 162, 209, 288–90, 294, 304–5, 348, 387, 409, 422, 425, 427, 430–2, 434, 440, 442–5, 448–9, 458–60, 475, 477–8, 482, 490n, 512, 518, 687–9, 698, 700–2, 709, 802, 846, 857
Wagner, Richard, 209, 339, 356–8
Wagner, Ruth Ellen, 675
Wainwright, Lucius M., 458, 460
Wallace, Agnes (Steiner), 49, 70, 97
Wallace, Andrew, 19
Wallace, David, 19, 22, 24–32, 39, 67, 70, 158, 191–2, 195
Wallace, Esther Test, 21, 53, 73, 99, 191
Wallace, Henry, 6–7, 19, 32, 37, 56, 96, 117, 120, 162, 172–4, 186n, 296, 315–16, 318, 345, 353, 389, 455, 535–7, 543–6, 552, 561, 564–6, 597, 622
Wallace, Lew
  An Autobiography, 20–1, 24–5, 28–30, 32, 34, 38–9, 46–8, 56–7, 70, 73, 92, 116, 141, 172, 190–3, 201, 423
  as administrator, 6, 10, 41–3, 212, 232, 675
  as businessman, 3, 5–6, 10, 13–15, 121, 123, 150, 212, 232, 675
  as celebrity, 6, 20, 25, 34, 102, 109, 115, 120–1, 123–9, 140, 160–3, 165, 212, 232, 345, 413, 415, 438, 457, 676
  as governor, 42–3, 55–6, 82–3, 92, 94, 103, 105, 113, 115, 120, 123, 529, 627, 666, 676, 850
  as lawyer, 10, 21–2, 32, 37–8, 41–3, 96, 119–20, 159, 416, 677, 684
  as politician, 32, 103, 105, 119–20, 160–2, 165
  as soldier, 20, 31–8
  as visual artist, 20, 25–6, 37–8, 41, 192, 416
  authorial control, 12, 20, 123, 148, 157, 165, 173, 231, 236, 245, 258, 286, 313, 316, 353, 359, 409, 561, 568, 572, 574–5, 580, 730
  Ben-Hur, in Tableaux and Pantomime, 6, 138, 157, 231–42
  Boyhood of Christ, The, 5, 13, 106, 135, 138–42, 148–51, 157–8, 166, 190–1, 227, 234
  Chariot Race, The 5, 13, 139, 385
  Commodus, 38–9, 41, 57, 149–50, 160, 166, 183, 216, 218, 227, 317
  death of, 6, 15
  education, 19–22, 26–8, 30–1
  Fair God, The, 13, 24, 31, 38–41, 45, 48, 53–4, 56–7, 64, 69, 94, 97, 105, 110, 112, 120, 140–1, 158, 174, 204, 216–17, 231, 238, 251, 270, 562, 622
  First Christmas, The, 5, 13, 27, 46–7, 50–1, 106, 139, 165–6, 191, 194, 531
  "intimate friend" of, 46, 129, 232
  Light Infantry Tactics, 37, 94
  Man-at-Arms, The, 30, 40
  Marmion, 27
  mother of, 20–2, 25, 27, 44n, 47, 73, 99n, 191–2
  Prince of India, 13, 115, 129, 133, 148, 156–8, 160, 166, 173, 256, 286, 315, 388–9, 394, 413, 562, 564, 622
  reputation, 95–6, 102, 113, 116–18, 122, 128, 140, 159, 161, 189
  research, 24, 39, 40, 48–9, 53–4, 57, 63, 67–8, 81, 84, 86–90, 96, 189–90, 203, 214n
  self-mythologizing, 25, 47
  "Stolen Stars, The", 35, 270
Wallace, Lewis, Jr., 563, 565
Wallace, Susan, 20, 32, 35, 38, 42, 46–8, 56–7, 91–2, 106, 112–13, 116, 118–19, 121–2, 125–7, 129–30, 134–7, 141–2, 144, 146, 157, 172, 180–3, 186, 262, 345, 385, 405, 437–8, 504, 543, 564, 663, 676
Wallace, William, 21, 23, 26–7, 29, 31
Wallace, Zerelda Sanders, 25, 99n, 191–3, 195, 240, 676
Walsh, George, 483, 567, 573, 577, 579
Wanamaker, John, 175, 209, 211
Wanamaker's, 638, 697
Ward, Judge Henry G., 545–6, 548–9
Wards see Montgomery Ward
Ware, William, 91, 198, 214n
Warfield, David, 603
Warner Brothers, 680, 709, 829
Warner, Charles Dudley, 145
Warner, H. B., 342
Warner Home Video, 835–6, 841
Warner, Jack, 779
Warner, William J., 462
Washburn, Carole Anne, 808
Washington, George, 457, 470
Watson, Neal, 233

Wayne County Seminary, 26, 193
Weeks, Edward, 672
Weeks, Frank F., 516, 524–5
Weidersein, Grace, 435–6
Wellman, Harold E., 773
Wellman, Rev.. E. Homer, 521, 523, 529
Wells, Thomas B., 563
Wescott, Steven D., 843
West, James E., 180
West Point, 19, 24, 26, 29, 37, 94
Westclox, 480–1, 643
W. F. Mangels Company, 461
When Clothing Store, 227
Whiston, William, 60–1, 80, 90
Whitaker, Justice Edward G., 563, 565
White, Albert, 376
White, Jules, 629
Whiteside, Walker, 318–20, 760
Whitman, Walt, 208, 211
Wiggins, "Mac", 469–70
Wilber, M. D., 524
Wilde, Walter B., 455
Wilfrey, Rev. Earl, 530–1
William H. Labb Company, 462

Williams, Brown, and Earle, 514, 516
Williamson, J. C., 357, 364–8, 385, 392, 791, 853
Wilson, Ben, 707
Wilson, Carey, 577, 590, 592, 595, 601, 622, 681, 733
Wilson, Earl, 773
Wilson, Harold, 684
Wilson, Harry Robert, 798
Wilson, Lucy Autrey, 791
Wilson, Woodrow, 207, 258, 418
Wingate, John, 320–1, 340–1, 397n
Wirz, Henry, 37, 57
Wissler, A. J., 55
Wm. Tegge & Company, 427
Women's Christian Temperance Union, 25, 225
Woodhull, Victoria, 195
Woodruff, Henry, 383–4, 394
Workman, Chuck, 833–4
Wrangham, Francis, 23–4
Wright, Rosamunde Rae, 585
Writers Guild of America, 733, 782, 809
Wurlitzer, 298
Wyatt, Benjamin, 369

Wyler, Catherine, 839
Wyler, Robert, 733
Wyler, William, 584, 731–3, 741–2, 753, 755–7, 760–8, 773–4, 777–81, 783–7, 789, 792, 794, 799, 804–5, 807, 836, 838–9, 841, 849–50

Xander, Henry, 285, 288

Y.M.C.A, 125, 157, 170, 199, 421, 461, 488, 511, 528–9, 532, 708
Young, William, 166, 312, 317–19, 321–4, 326–9, 331–4, 341, 346–7, 349, 352, 356, 358, 374, 376, 397n, 399n, 545, 565, 571–2, 575, 589–90, 669, 733
Y.W.C.A., 158, 229, 260

Zeno, 69
Ziegfeld, Florenz, 340, 562, 565–6, 603, 615
Zimbalist, Sam, 730–2, 761, 763, 768, 774, 780, 783–4, 786, 794, 796
Zimmerman, August, 149

NON-*BEN-HUR* TITLES INDEX

20 Dates, 858
20,000 Leagues Under the Sea, 231, 535

Action Comics, 796
Adnah: A Tale of the Time of Christ, 163
Airport, 791
Alamo, The, 788
Alice's Adventures in Wonderland, 9, 231, 409, 489, 843
Anthony Adverse, 673
Any Given Sunday, 858
Around the World in Eighty Days, 788
Avatar, 791

Barabbas, 790, 792, 828
Ben-Beor: A Story of the Anti-Messiah, 163
Ben Ezra; Or, The Midnight Cry, 628
Beverly Hillbillies, 807
Bible, 10, 12, 22, 48, 63, 71, 74, 91, 98, 100, 121, 131, 134, 142, 154, 175, 192–4, 196, 198, 201, 206, 214–17, 252, 281, 342, 367, 380, 414–16, 421, 423, 462, 513, 520–1, 534, 567, 573, 582, 587, 602, 625–6, 638, 661, 672, 681, 685, 733, 780–1, 789–90, 835, 844, 859; *see also* New Testament; Old Testament
Bible, The, 859

Big Fisherman, The, 673
Big Lebowski, The, 858
Big Parade, The, 581, 596, 599–601, 603–5, 607–8, 613, 615, 618–19, 621–4, 637, 645, 680–1, 729
Big Sleep, The, 677
Birth of a Nation, The, 562, 596, 599, 618–19, 623, 637, 646
Boomerang, 858
Broadway Bill, 680

Caesar and Cleopatra, 680
Casablanca, 835
Cecil and Sally, 632
Centennial, 209, 278
Chain, The, 674
Charioteer, The, 674
Cimarron, 621, 675
Classics Illustrated, 669, 794–5
Cleopatra (1917), 394
Cleopatra (1963), 731, 790, 796, 826, 858
Cloud Atlas, 858
County Fair, The, 313, 334, 846

"Daisy Bell", 460
Dames, 394
Demetrius and the Gladiators, 801
Dion and the Sibyls, 163
Doctor Zhivago, 791, 828

Easy Rider, 790
El Cid, 790
Enchanted, 858

Esther: A Sequel to Ben Hur, 163
E.T. the Extra-Terrestrial, 791, 829
Exodus, 790

Fabiola, 200, 680
Fall of the Roman Empire, The, 790
Family Christian Almanac, 197, 200
Famous Authors Illustrated, 669
Famous Paintings of the World, 160
Festival at Meron, 674
Flash Comics, 667
Footsteps of the Master, 199
Forget Paris, 858
Four Horsemen of the Apocalypse, 569, 571, 573–5, 610, 790
Free-Soil Banner, 32
Frost/Nixon, 858

Garden of Allah, The, 12, 392
Gentleman's Agreement, 674
Gladiator, 200, 835, 840, 851, 853, 858
Godfather, The, 791, 824
Gone With the Wind, 1, 10, 564, 624, 672–3, 679–80, 777–8, 788, 790–1, 825–6, 833, 835
Goodbye To the Past, 673–4
Graduate, The, 791
Greed, 574, 576

Green Hornet, The, 858
Guns of Navarone, The, 788

Hallmark Playhouse, 666
Harper's Monthly, 5
Harper's New Monthly Magazine, 38, 119, 140, 149–50
Harper's Weekly, 33, 34, 46, 106, 120, 140, 156, 230, 270, 314, 385, 391, 432, 434–5, 467, 470
Harry Potter, 1
Her Ben: A Tale of Royal Resolves, 163
Hercules (1997), 858
Hercules: The Legendary Journeys, 858
Herdsman, The, 674
High Calling, The, 674
How the West Was Won, 790
Hunchback of Notre Dame, The, 680, 729
Hunger Games, The, 1

I, Claudius, 850
Iliad, 28, 81, 134, 622
In His Steps, 8, 12–13, 105, 164–5, 199, 212, 513, 528, 531, 534, 672
In the Years of Our Lord, 674
Intolerance, 562, 578, 591, 623
It's a Wonderful World, 394
Ivanhoe, 73, 118, 167, 251, 626, 729

Jaws, 791, 824
Jazz Singer, The, 617, 728
Jesus of Nazareth, 828
Joel: A Boy of Galilee, 163
Julius Caesar, 628, 630
Jurassic Park, 791

Last Days of Pompeii, The, 9–10, 80, 167, 198, 215n, 219, 231, 283, 546, 622
Lawrence of Arabia, 790
Liaisons Dangereuses, Les, 788
Life of Moses, The, 551
Little Lord Fauntleroy, 10, 17n
Lord of the Rings, 1
Love Story, 791

Madagascar: Escape 2 Africa, 858
Man on the Moon, 858
Messala The Return From Ruin: A Sequel to Ben-Hur, 857
Messalina, 579
Midnight Cowboy, 790
Mutiny on the Bounty, 790
My Favorite Story, 665–6

Our English Cousin, 38

Peter Pan, 9, 281, 409, 502, 582, 630, 707, 724n
Passion of the Christ, The, 855
Popular Comics, 666
Printers' Ink, 438, 458, 473
Private Life of Helen of Troy, The, 622
Progressive Course in Reading, 13, 114, 145

Quest of Ben Hur, The, 857
Quo Vadis?, 9–10, 105, 148, 164, 184, 259, 317, 388–9, 534, 551, 569, 599, 623, 651, 653, 680, 681, 710, 729–30, 765, 813n

Raintree County, 774
Rated X, 858
Richelieu, 218
Rip Van Winkle, 312, 513
Robber: A Tale of the Time of the Herods, The, 674
Robe, The, 673, 680, 729, 734, 801
Robin Hood: Men in Tights, 858
Roots, 10

Samedi, Le, 671–2
Samson and Delilah, 681
Saturday Evening Post, The, 431–2, 434–5, 437–8, 779
Saturday Night Live, 827–8
Saul and David, 828
Scarlet Letter, The, 145, 167, 527
Second City Television, 827

Sign of the Cross, 10, 163, 219, 528, 680, 729
Simpsons, The, 858
Single Man, A, 858
Sleeping Beauty and the Beast, The, 358–9
Son of Issachar, A, 163
Son of the Prefect: A Story of the Reign of Tiberius, The, 628
Sound of Music, The, 791
South Pacific, 797
Spartacus, 731, 776, 792, 804, 840
Star Wars, 1, 11, 791, 799, 824, 840
Star Wars Episode I: The Phantom Menace, 840, 857
Strange Lady in Town, 676
Superboy, 670–1, 795–6

Ten Commandments, The, 573, 579, 599, 617, 623, 637, 713, 730, 731, 760, 767, 777–8, 791, 828, 830, 841
Texas Carnival, 709
Titanic, 791, 858
Trilby, 10
Tros of Samothrace, 673
Troy, 851

Uncle Tom's Cabin, 6–8, 10, 12, 116, 156, 167, 198, 212, 231, 314, 513, 535, 547, 599
Unknown Disciple, The, 674

Way Down East, 564, 599, 637
When He Came to Himself, 628
Wizard of Oz, The, 1, 9, 362, 409, 489, 622, 676, 797, 828, 833–4
Wonderful World of the Brothers Grimm, The, 790
Wrongfully Accused, 858

Year One, The, 313, 334
Youth's Companion, 46, 47, 431, 434, 467, 634

Zatthu: A Tale of Ancient Galilee, 628
Zenobia, 198, 214n